ABOUT THE AUTHOR

J. Gordon Melton is the director of the Institute for the Study of American Religion in Santa Barbara, California, one of America's leading religious studies centers. He is the author of more than 40 reference and scholarly books in the field. Melton is also the president of the American chapter of the Transylvanian Society of Dracula, a network of scholars and others who have an interest in Dracula and vampire studies. Through the 1990s he developed a real interest in making factual material about Dracula and vampires available to the growing audience of vampire fans.

His life-long interest in vampires, reaching back to his teen years, led to his spending his leisure time with vampire novels and movies and eventually to his authoring a set of books exploring the worlds of the Undead in the 1990s, including *The Vampire Gallery: A Who's Who of the Undead* and *VideoHound's Vampires on Video*. He has also been featured on a number of shows on vampires on the History Channel, A & E, and The Learning Channel. In 1997, he joined with two of his colleagues in organizing *Dracula '97*, the centennial celebration of the publication of Dracula held in Los Angeles.

Also from Visible Ink Press

Please visit us at www.visibleinkpress.com.

THE VAMPIRE BOOK

THE ENCYCLOPEDIA OF THE UNDEAD

The Vampire Book
BOOK
The Encyclopedia of the Undead

Visible Ink Press®
43311 Joy Rd., #414
Canton, MI 48187-2075

Visible Ink Press is a registered trademark of Visible Ink Press LLC.

Most Visible Ink Press books are available at special quantity discounts when purchased in bulk by corporations, organizations, or groups. Customized printings, special imprints, messages, and excerpts can be produced to meet your needs. For more information, contact Special Markets Director, Visible Ink Press, www.visibleinkpress.com, or 734-667-3211.

Managing Editor: Kevin S. Hile
Art Director: Mary Claire Krzewinski
Typesetting: Marco Di Vita
Proofreaders: Sharon Gunton and Sharon Malinowski

ISBN 978-1-57859-281-4
Cover images: Shutterstock.

Library of Congress Cataloguing-in-Publication Data
Melton, J. Gordon.
    The vampire book : the encyclopedia of the undead / by J. Gordon Melton. — 3rd ed.
        p. cm.
    Includes bibliographical references and index.
    ISBN 978-1-57859-281-4 (alk. paper)
    1. Vampires—Encyclopedias. I. Title.
BF1556.M46 2011
398'.45—dc22   2010024263

Printed in the United States of America

10 9 8 7 6 5 4 3 2 1

THE VAMPIRE BOOK

THE ENCYCLOPEDIA OF THE UNDEAD

THIRD EDITION

J. GORDON MELTON, PhD

VISIBLE
INK
PRESS

Detroit

Contents

A ....[1]

Ackerman, Forrest James • Aconite • The Addams Family • Africa, Vampires in • African American Vampires • Allatius, Leo • Alnwick Castle, The Vampire of • Aluka • America, Vampires in • Anemia • Angel • Animals • Appearance of a Vampire • Armand • Armenia, Vampires in • Ashley, Amanda • Atlanta Vampire Alliance • Australia, Vampires in

B ....[31]

Babylon and Assyria, Vampires in Ancient • Baker, Roy Ward • Balderston, John L. • Baltic States, Vampires in the • Bangs, Nina • Banks, L. A. • Bara, Theda • Baron Blood • Bathory, Elizabeth • Batman • Bats, Vampire • Bava, Mario • Belanger, Michelle • Bergstrom, Elaine • Berwick, The Vampire of • Bibliography, Vampire • Bistritz • Blacula • Blade the Vampire Slayer • Blood • Bloodrayne • Borgo Pass • Borland, Caroll • Bouchard, Angélique • Boucicault, Dion • The Bram Stoker Society • *Bram Stoker's Dracula* • Brides, Vampire • Brite, Poppy Z. •

Browning, Tod • Bruja • Bruxa • *Buffy the Vampire Slayer* (movie) • *Buffy the Vampire Slayer* (television series) • Bulgaria, Vampires in • Bullet • Bunnicula • Burton, Richard Francis • Byron, Lord George Gordon

C ....[99]

Calmet, Dom Augustin • The Camarilla: A Vampire Fan Association • Carfax • Carmilla • Carradine, John • Carter, Margaret Louise • Cast, P. C. & Kristin • Castle Dracula • Chaney, Alonso "Lon" • Chaos! Comics • Characteristics of Vampires • Charnas, Suzy McKee • Chase, Cornelia • Chetwynd-Hayes, Ronald Henry Glynn • China, Vampires in • Christianity and Vampires • Chupacabras • Coffins • Coleridge, Samuel Taylor • Collins, Barnabas • Collins, Nancy A. • Collinsport Players • Comic Books, The Vampire in • Cooke, Thomas Potter • Coppola, Francis Ford • Corman, Roger William • Count Dracula • Count von Count • Crime, Vampiric • Croglin Grange, The Vampire of • Crucifix • Cruise, Tom • Cullen, Edward • Cult of the Vampire • Cuntius, Johannes • Curtis, Dan • Cushing, Peter • Czech Republic and Slovakia, Vampires in the

X, Y, Z ..[825]

Photo and Illustration Credits

Photos and illustrations used in this book were reprinted with permission from the following sources.

Forrest Ackerman: 2

American International Pictures: 8

Bram Stoker Society: 400

Margaret Carter: 108

Chaos! Comics: 117, 145, 375

Concorde Films: 246

Candy Cosner: 189

Count Dracula Fan Club: 194

Dan Curtis Productions: 166, 176, 177, 181, 268, 496, 668

David del Valle Archive: 9, 21, 23, 48, 61, 64, 72, 75, 77, 80, 82, 107, 119, 120, 163, 197, 206, 209, 210, 211, 218, 225, 238, 249, 265, 289, 314, 324, 354, 357, 359, 377, 378, 413, 418, 422, 431, 436, 437, 438, 450, 451, 459, 476, 482, 488, 506, 513, 564, 590, 617, 618, 621, 627, 661, 681, 708, 732, 759, 760, 783, 801, 803, 804, 817, 820, 821, 829

Eclipse Enterprises: 143

P.N. Elrod: 236

Hammer Films: 44, 326, 338, 417, 666

Del Howison: 174

iStock: 337

Steven Lungley: 303

Malibu Comics: 440

J. Gordon Melton Collection: 18, 60, 62, 79, 84, 111, 113, 151, 152, 162, 199, 216, 229, 251, 255, 257, 262, 298, 332, 340, 376, 383, 394, 423, 432, 433, 452, 516, 528, 539, 582, 583, 585, 587, 619, 630, 637, 671, 672, 684, 695, 702, 703, 714, 720, 739, 755, 777, 780, 781, 786, 791, 823, 827

Elizabeth Miller: 464

Palladium Books, Inc.: 272, 276
Public domain: 285, 386, 415, 659, 793
Realm of the Vampire: 756
Recycled Paper Greetings: 355, 517
Santa Barbara Centre for Humanistic Studies: 361, 794
Leslie Shepard: 636
David J. Skal: 639
Wendy Snow-Lang: 518
Jeff Thompson: 141, 142, 592
Vampire International Network: 752
Vampire Studies Chicago (Martin V. Riccardo): 56, 295, 454, 500, 572, 574, 814
White Wolf Game Studio: 274, 767
Jeanne Youngson Collection: 42, 219, 222, 669, 670

FOREWORD TO THIRD EDITION

Martin V. Riccardo

In the Bible's book of Leviticus, chapter 17, verse 14, it is written: "You shall not eat the blood of any flesh at all, because the life of the flesh is in the blood, and whosoever eateth it shall be cut off." That is the pitiable state of the vampire: to be cut off, cut off from the living and cut off from the dead. He or she is forced to live in a half-world, a lonely isolated existence of darkness and horror, driven solely by a fierce, uncontrollable lust for blood. Like the amphibian who can live both in the water and on land, the vampire can freely cross the border between the graveyard and the realm of living beings, yet the vampire is a prisoner agonizingly torn between the two worlds, a creature trapped in the depths of evil. The vampire is the outcast, the outlaw, the dangerous outsider who flagrantly violates all of society's norms. Vampires are the tragic rebels of the night who rage against the finality of death only to find that they must take life in order to prolong their own semblance of it. This powerful portrait of vampires is just a part of what makes them such compelling figures to mere mortals.

Our modern conception of a vampire began as a terrifying superstition that was once rampant in Eastern Europe for hundreds of years. The people of that region truly believed that these revenants could come back from the grave to drain the life out of the living. Over the centuries this strange belief has evolved into a dark romantic fantasy in fiction, film, and other media. The vampire has now become an expression of the dark side of human nature. They can represent mystery, danger, darkness, aggression, death, and all kinds of forbidden desires. In many ways the vampire is the grand archetype of all the dark, repressed urges in the human heart.

While they have a long history in our collective imagination, vampires have bounded into the twenty-first century with a passion. For the first time an actor playing the role of a real vampire in a film (Willem Dafoe for his performance in the 2000 movie *Shadow of the Vampire*) was nominated for an academy award,. It is now common to find book stores stocked with multiple rows of vampire novels on display. It is not unusual to see major motion pictures featuring vampires being released every month. As this edition of *The Vampire Book* hits the bookshelves, we are riding the largest wave of vampire interest that there has ever been. The current surge of popularity is primarily due to the wildly successful *Twilight* novels by Stephenie Meyer and the movies based on them. This love story between the vampire Edward and the all-too-human Bella has touched an emotional cord for millions of devoted fans around the world. At the same time, popular television series have also capitalized on the romantic aspects of the unearthly vampire with shows such as *The Vampire Diaries* (based on the novels by L.J. Smith) and *True Blood* (based on the novels by Charlaine Harris).

Young people are usually the driving force behind popular culture. The flourishing success of the vampire romance novel indicates that many young women have acquired an addictive thirst for this genre. Since vampires have become an all-purpose fantasy outlet, they also have an appeal to young men who may enjoy video games and comic books (graphic novels). This is reflected in the successful action-adventure horror movies featuring vampires, such as the *Underworld* and *Blade* films, as well as the frightening *30 Days of Night*. In a similar vein, the fast-paced film *Van Helsing*, released in 2004, earned a worldwide gross of over 300 million dollars. Even that was eclipsed by the earnings of each of the *Twilight* films.

Ancient as they are, vampires in recent years have proven not only to be resilient but also ever-changing. Stephenie Meyer has her vampires displaying eyes with colors that change like mood rings, and skin that glitters in the sunlight like diamonds. While these traits are quite specific to her novels, there are other characteristics of the vampire that have recently become more universal. The ability of vampires to move at superhuman speed is not only prominent in the *Twilight* series, but is commonly shown in current screen portrayals of the undead, including shows like *True Blood* and *The Vampire Diaries*. This can be considered a relatively new addition to the vampire's array of powers. It was alluded to in Bram Stoker's novel *Dracula* when he used the phrase, "The dead travel fast." It was apparent in the 1922 silent film *Nosferatu* when Count Orlock moves at high speed to transport his coffins from his castle to a coach. This power of moving faster than mortals can grasp was then fully developed in the 1990 film *Nightlife* with Ben Cross. However, it wasn't until we entered the new millennium that vampires routinely exhibited this skill. This is just one example that clearly reveals how the vampire mythos is continuously expanding and evolving.

This new edition of *The Vampire Book* not only provides the most comprehensive and exhaustive exposition of everything relating to vampires, but it also has kept pace with the latest developments in the ever-expanding world of the bloodthirsty undead. In my opinion the author, my friend J. Gordon Melton, is the one person on the planet who has a truly encyclopedic knowledge on the subject of vampires. Even Dracula himself could learn a lot about vampires from Gordon. For our sakes he has spent many long hours watching movies and reading novels, some of dubious quality, in order to unearth the many buried treasures of the vampire world. He has maintained an undying devotion to the undead that has stood the test of time. This volume is a testament to his remarkably extensive research. Here you will find amazing information that will increase your knowledge and stir your imagination. With luck, *The Vampire Book* might even enhance your nightmares.

INTRODUCTION

J. Gordon Melton

This third edition of *The Vampire Book* emerges as vampires have enjoyed an amazing twenty years of popularity in North America and Europe. Interest had almost died out in the mid 1980s—no new vampire novels were being published and no new vampire flicks followed up on the previous decade, which had climaxed with Frank Langella's *Dracula* and George Hamilton's *Love at First Bite*. By the end of the decade, however, a new wave of interest had begun to manifest itself. Some would date this new interest from the second of the Anne Rice vampire novels, *The Vampire Lestat*, which appeared in 1985. In any case, by the end of the decade, everywhere one looked—books, comics, movies, trading cards, games—vampires had come back to life.

During the early 1990s, we thought that the boom was being fueled by the approach of the year 1997, the centennial of the publication of Bram Stoker's *Dracula*. Certainly the number of new Dracula publications lent credence to the idea. But at the same time, Rice's novels were topping the charts, and Laurell Hamilton's novels began to be noticed, too. No one picked up on the vampire's quiet penetration of the romance novel genre nor understood that the vampire role-playing game was not just a fad. The centennial was celebrated widely, and then, instead of the expected let down, a new television show about a young vampire slayer appeared as a mid-season entry on the WB Network's prime-time lineup. *Buffy the Vampire Slayer* was the first successful show on the relatively new network and led the way in its courting of a young adult-teen market. The show became a phenomenon that soon attracted older vampire enthusiasts and then a range of people not previously attracted to horror entertainment. Within a few years it would become the darling of the recently appointed professors of television arts in colleges throughout the English-speaking world.

Buffy the Vampire Slayer would run for seven seasons, and its spinoff show, *Angel*, for five. It would become for the world of *Dracula* and vampires what *Star Trek* had become for science fiction. It would command so much scholarly comment that by the end of the decade almost half of all that had ever been written about vampires of a scholarly nature had come from those academics studying *Buffy* and *Angel*. More than a hundred novels featuring the characters from Buffy were written, and the *Buffy the Vampire Slayer* comic book from Dark Horse became the second longest running vampire comic in the English-speaking world. Dropped after the show ended in expectation of a decline in fan interest, it would be revived when creator Joss Whedon decided to continue the story of his characters in comic book form (which he also did with the characters from *Angel*).

Meanwhile, romance publishers could not deny the popularity of the vampire, which developed an ever-growing presence among the audience of female readers who made romance novels fifty percent of paperback book sales. And among romance writers a new trend became evident. Rice had continued the storyline and characters from her first two books into a saga stretching through a dozen titles, and she was joined by Chelsea Quinn Yarbro, who had annually brought out one or more new volumes detailing further adventures of her main vampire character, St. Germain, and Fred Saberhagen, who would eventually produce ten novels of the further adventures of his heroic Dracula. The new generation of vampire romance novelists started turning out series of novels that followed groups of related characters through three or six or as many as a dozen or more (L. A. Banks, Christine Feehan, Sherrilyn Kenyon) installments.

The void created by the ending of the *Buffy the Vampire Slayer* television show was being filled by authors writing for high school and junior high school youth (called the young adult market in the publishing world). Lisa Jane "L. J." Smith had a very successful young adult series, "The Vampire Diaries," back in the 1990s, but now a set of new writers were appearing—most notably a young Mormon housewife named Stephenie Meyer. Meyer would write what became the next blockbuster series about a young woman coming of age and her vampire lover. The *Twilight* saga would stretch through four hefty volumes that not only would create the next generation of young vampire enthusiasts but also challenge the dominance of the Harry Potter books, a non-vampire set of novels by J. K. Rowling that had taken the young adult (and even younger) world by storm.

By the end of the decade, with the *Twilight* saga breaking records not just in the vampire world but the whole realm of popular culture, vampires could seemingly be found everywhere. They were especially entrenched, however, in some very specific places. Even as Buffy was making her impact on American television, in far off Japan the vampire was making its presence felt on the small screen with a number of series being offered for children and youth, more than half being animated (or animé) series (*Hellsing*, *Karin*, *Trinity Blood*, *Black Blood Brothers*, to name a few). The emergence on television of more than a dozen of these series heralded their future arrival in the West in both manga comic book and DVD format.

Along with the many television vamps and the vampire DVDs (many direct-to-DVD movies), the vampire also continued its startling presence in comic books. A list of comic book vampires made by Massimo Introvigne, Robert Eighteen-Bisang, and myself (http://www.cesnur.org/2008/vampire_comics.htm) contains some 10,000 separate comic book issues with vampire stories released by the year 2000. That list notes the rising presence of vampires through the 1990s, and as the second decade of the new century begins, we now know that the vampire continues as the second most popular comic book character (behind the superhero).

Romance books currently account for fifty percent of all new paperback book sales annually in the United States. In spite of the resistance of many editors who personally dislike vampire novels, every romance publishing house now has its stable of authors who specialize in and are almost solely known for writing vampire novels. Many of these writers began their careers with the POD (publish on demand) houses, where vampire

THE VAMPIRE BOOK: THE ENCYCLOPEDIA OF THE UNDEAD

romance novels formed a separate category soon after the different companies were founded in the 1990s. POD novels still constitute a sizeable portion of new vampire novels published annually.

The radical increase in the vampire's presence in popular culture in the last decade has been dominated by *Buffy* and *Twilight*. These two phenomena point to a continuing truth about interest in vampires. Overwhelmingly, people who are vampire fans in later life began their attachment to vampires as teenagers. They go through a period of enthusiasm as only teens can have and then settle down to a lifetime of being entertained by the vampire and using their favorite fanged monster as an entity to assist them in thinking about real life issues such as the nature of sexuality, exerting personal power in social situations, and the possibilities of life after death. The vampire invites exploration of the "dark side," which should not to be confused with one's evil side but includes, rather, those aspects of the personality that are suppressed by one's culture or by one's personal situation.

The vampire has always found a most favorable hearing among people who think of themselves as socially on the edge—alienated, not acceptable, different, confined, eccentric. That being said, it is to be noted that vampire fans are neither psychologically pathological nor members of a socially oppressed social class. Rather, they are people who are socially a little bit different, often in quite invisible ways, often just in their own minds. Many are not so different themselves as they are strongly empathetic to those who are different. They find the mainstream of popular culture (from fashion to sports) boring and choose their friends, like Buffy and Bella did, from among those put down and even laughed at by their classmates—the nerds, the drama crowd, the idealistic, the sexually estranged, the poets and visionaries. The life-long vampire enthusiasts usually grow out of their adolescent differences (or discover a socially accepted form of it) but they retain the memory of their growing-up years and have great tolerance of those who got stuck there.

Thus, *The Vampire Book* is a product of a lifetime of love of all things vampiric by someone who has always been a collector and who now resides in a house surrounded by books, pictures, toys, trading cards, videos, and a variety of objects with the image of a vampire or a vampire hunter. It is an attempt to bring order to a personal life, as well as to a larger world of interest in the vampire. As attention to vampires exploded in the 1970s, it grew so fast that misinformation was everywhere. The first edition was written with the idea of cutting through that misinformation. That task largely accomplished, this edition concentrates on exploring the many new realms into which the vampire has made his/her presence felt.

The last edition came out in 1998, just as we realized that *Buffy* was going to be a hit. Now, sitting at the close of the first decade of the new century, this new edition can explore the *Buffy* phenomenon and its immense fallout fully. New entries discuss the vampire on television, the *Twilight* saga, romance novels, and vampire-related paraphernalia. There are a number of new entries on the authors of the more popular vampire novels—from horror writer Steve Niles to romance queens like Charlaine Harris and Sherrilyn Kenyon. There are entries on the most popular vampire movies of the last decade that took their place as top-grossing products of Hollywood—*Blade, Underworld, Van Helsing,* and the *Twilight* films. Of course, I have tried to update all the older entries and dropped a few entries on topics that seem less pertinent today.

THE VAMPIRE BOOK: THE ENCYCLOPEDIA OF THE UNDEAD

I call attention to the arrival on the scene of that group of people generally called real vampires: individuals who self-identify as vampires. The last decade has seen the emergence of a visible vampire community, if one with a very low profile. Those of us who study the vampire always get a round of calls each October from journalists wishing to interview such self-identified vampires, though a spectrum of members of the community have now offered themselves as spokespersons and can be easily found on the Internet. In 1998 the real vampire community was just becoming visible in the old Gothic rock music clubs and was best known for the few among them who actually drank small quantities of blood. Through the last decade, that community has become more visible, and the psychic vampires among them asserted themselves as the larger, more prominent element of the community. That community is now distinguished by some articulate leadership, such as Michelle Belanger, that has created structures for interacting with the public, such as the Atlanta Vampire Alliance (http://www.atlantavampirealliance.com/). The community has become the subject of several scholarly studies, most notably Joseph Laycock's *Vampires Today: The Truth about Modern Vampirism* (2009).

Increasingly, keeping up with the growing vampire world is beyond the ability of any one person. Thus, I am especially grateful to those who have contributed most to keeping me informed and in sharing their knowledge with the readers of this volume through me (especially those who have written for this volume). To Marty Riccardo, Robert Eighteen-Bisang, Massimo Introvigne, Lee Scott, Angela Aleiss, Marco Frenschkowski, Jeff Thompson, Elizabeth Miller, and Brad Middleton, I close by offering my special thanks. I truly value you friendship and could not have done this book without you.

ACKNOWLEDGEMENTS

The older I get, the more I recognize and am grateful for the community of scholars who form a context of discourse and assistance for fellow scholars in their attempt to push forward the dialogue on any given topic. In that regard, I know better than anyone that this book could not have been completed without the assistance of many people—some of whom I have never met or met only superficially, but whose work forms the environment out of which this volume has emerged. In the last few years, for example, I have become especially aware of the several hundred scholars who have contributed to scholarship on *Buffy the Vampire Slayer* and the related work of Joss Whedon, one of the growing edges of vampire scholarship. Originally brought together as an Internet community around *Slayage: The Online International Journal of Buffy Studies* by David Lavery and Rhonda Wilcox, they have most recently been organized into the Whedon Studies Association. The *Buffy* phenomenon, and even more recently, the *Twilight* phenomenon, has greatly enlarged the number of scholars talking about vampires.

I am especially aware of those colleagues with whom I am in regular contact about subjects vampiric—new literature, recent news, the latest comic books, obscure studies—and who have become the most active people in keeping my knowledge growing and active. That small circle would include Marty Riccardo (who graciously has written the preface for this volume), fellow collectors and friends Massimo Introvigne and Robert Eighteen-Bisang, premiere Dracula scholar Elizabeth Miller, and my go-to person for vampire trading cards—Lee Scott. A variety of people in the vampire community either sent me information and/or made valuable comments over the last decade, many now detached from their source, but in some form found their way into this new edition.

In the immediate work of preparing this revised text, I am especially grateful for the several people who wrote new entries for me. UCLA instructor and cinema expert Angela Aleiss wrote a set of new entries, primarily related to the *Twilight* phenomenon, and helped me with important comments on a number of additional older entries on vampire films. She also contributed entries on the *Hour of the Wolf, London after Midnight,* and *Near Dark.*

In the 1990s, I came to know Maro Frenschkowski, a German scholar of the history of religion and Protestant theology, a teacher of New Testament studies, and an expert on ancient Christianity and new religions movements. Only later did I discover that he was a lifelong devotee of weird fiction (he is currently working on a complete multivolume annotated edition of the work of H. P. Lovecraft). From his vast knowledge of the vampire from a European perspective, Dr. Frenschkowski not only contributed the entry on Germany, but gave me a set of extensive comments on the second edition of *The Vampire Book*, which have been integrated into the A–Z text.

Throughout the whole process of originally doing *The Vampire Book* right up to the present, Jeff Thompson has been there. Jeff, a professor of English at Tennessee State University, is a devoted follower of *Dark Shadows*, and I have continually found my way to his encyclopedic knowledge of the continuing community of DS fans to check facts and keep up with trends. He started out by writing a master's thesis on writer Daniel Ross and has most recently written two fine studies on *Dark Shadows* and its creator, Dan Curtis.

Several people contributed single entries on particular areas of expertise, most notably Brad Middleton, the creator of "Vampyres Only," one of the oldest Internet vampire sites (http://www.vampyres.com), who authored the television entry, and Uwe Sommerlad who made extensive comments on the entry on Peter Cushing. Continued in updated form from earlier editions are entries contributed by Susan R. Kagan (Music), Isotta Poggi (Italy), and Margaret Shanahan (Psychology). Michelel Belanger made valuable comments on the entries reporting on the contemporary community of self-identified vampires.

In the new century, I still value what is now a 20-plus year relationship with Metro Entertainment, the comic book shop in Santa Barbra, California, which keeps me aware of the new vampire comics, graphic novels, and related materials. They have been proactive in letting me know what was available and obtaining copies for me.

I am, of course, indebted to Roger Janecke, who heads Visible Ink Press, for his continued faith in and promotion of *The Vampire Book*, and Kevin Hile for his editorial work on this new edition.

THE VAMPIRE BOOK: THE ENCYCLOPEDIA OF THE UNDEAD

Vampires: A Chronology

Prehistory	Vampires emerge as part of the mythology of most of the world's peoples.
1047	First appearance of the word "upir" (an early form of the word later to become "vampire") in a document referring to a Russian prince as "Upir Lichy", or wicked vampire.

1100s

1190	Walter Map's "De Nagis Curialium" includes accounts of vampire like beings in England.
1196	William of Newburgh's "Chronicles" records several stories of vampire like revenants in England.

1400s

1428–1429	Vlad Tepes, the son of Vlad Dracul, is born.
1463	Vlad Tepes becomes Prince of Wallachia and moves to Tirgoviste.
1442	The Turks imprison Vlad Tepes and his father.
1443	The Turks take Vlad Tepes hostage.
1447	Vlad Dracul is beheaded.
1448	Vlad briefly attains the Wallachian throne. Dethroned, he goes to Moldavia and befriends Prince Stefan.
1451	Vlad and Stephan flee to Transylvania.
1455	Constantinople falls.
1456	John Hunyadi assists Vlad Tepes to attain Wallachian throne. Vladislav Dan is executed.
1458	Matthias Corvinu succeeds John Hunyadi as King of Hungary.

1459	Easter massacre of boyers and rebuilding of Dracula's castle. Bucharest is established as the second governmental center.
1460	Attack upon Brasov, Romania
1461	Successful campaign against Turkish settlements along the Danube; summer retreat to Tirgoviste.
1462	Following the battle at Dracula's castle, Vlad flees to Transylvania. Vlad begins 13 years of imprisonment.
1475	Summer wars in Serbia against Turks take place. November 1475: Vlad resumes throne of Wallachia.
1476–1477	Vlad is assassinated.

1500s

1560	Elizabeth Bathory is born.

1600s

1610	Bathory is arrested for killing several hundred people and bathing in their blood. Tried and convicted, she is sentenced to life imprisonment, being bricked into a room in her castle.
1614	Elizabeth Bathory dies.
1610	Leo Allatius finishes writing the first modern treatment of vampires, "De Graecorum hodie quirundam opinationabus."
1657	Fr. Françoise Richard's "Relation de ce qui s'est passé a Sant-Erini Isle de l'Archipel" links vampirism and witchcraft.
1672	A wave of vampire hysteria sweeps through Istra.
1679	A German vampire text, "De Masticatione Mortuorum," by Phillip Rohr, is written.

1700s

1710	Vampire hysteria sweeps through East Prussia.
1725	Vampire hysteria returns to East Prussia.
1725–1730	Vampire hysteria lingers in Hungary.
1725–1732	The wave of vampire hysteria in Austrian Serbia produces the famous cases of Peter Plogojowitz and Arnold Paul (Paole).
1734	The word "vampyre" enters the English language in translations of German accounts of European waves of vampire hysteria.
1744	Cardinal Giuseppe Davanzati publishes his treatise "Dissertazione sopre I Vampiri."
1746	Dom Augustin Calmet publishes his treatise on vampires, "Dissertations sur les Apparitions des Anges des Demons et des Espits, et sur les revenants, et Vampires de Hundrie, de Boheme, de Moravic, et de Silesie."

1748	The first modern vampire poem, "Der Vampir," is published by Heinrich August Ossenfelder.
1750	Another wave of vampire hysteria occurs in East Prussia.
1756	Vampire hysteria peaks in Wallachia.
1772	Vampire hysteria occurs in Russia.
1797	Goethe's "Bride of Corinth" (a poem concerning a vampire) is published.
1798–1800	Samuel Taylor Coleridge writes "Christabel," now considered to be the first vampire poem in English.

1800s

1800	"I Vampiri," an opera by Silvestro de Palma, opens in Milan, Italy.
1801	"Thalaba" by Robert Southey is the first poem to mention a vampire in English.
1810	Reports of sheep being killed by having their jugular veins cut and their blood drained circulated through northern England. "The Vampyre," an early vampire poem, by John Stagg is published.
1813	Lord Byron's poem "The Giaour" includes the hero's encounter with a vampire.
1819	John Polidori's "The Vampyre," the first vampire story in English, is published in the April issue of "New Monthly Magazine." John Keats composes "The Lamia," a poem built on ancient Greek legends.
1820	"Lord Ruthwen; ou, Les Vampires" by Cyprien Berard is published anonymously in Paris. June 13, 1820: "Le Vampire," the play by Charles Nodier, opens at the Theatre de la Porte Saint-Martin in Paris. August, 1820: "The Vampire; or, The Bride of the Isles," a translation of Nodier's play by James R. Planche, opens in London. March 1829: Heinrich Marschner's opera "Der Vampyr," based on Nodier's story, opens in Liepzig, Germany.
1841	Alexey Tolstoy publishes his short story "Upyr," while living in Paris. It is the first modern vampire story by a Russian.
1847	Bram Stoker is born. "Varney the Vampire" begins lengthy serialization.
1851	Alexandre Dumas's last dramatic work, "Le Vampire," opens in Paris.
1854	The case of vampirism in the Ray family of Jewell, Connecticut, is published in local newspapers.
1872	"Carmilla" is written by Sheridan Le Fanu. In Italy, Vincenzo Verzeni is convicted of murdering two people and drinking their blood.
1874	Reports from Ceven, Ireland, tell of sheep having their throats cut and their blood drained.
1888	Emily Gerard's "Land beyond the Forest" is published. It will become a major source of information about Transylvania for Bram Stoker's "Dracula."
1894	H. G. Wells's short story "The Flowering of the Strange Orchid" is a precursor to science fiction vampire stories.

1897   *Dracula* by Bram Stoker is published in England. *The Vampire* by Rudyard Kipling becomes the inspiration for the creation of the vamp as a stereotypical character on stage and screen.

1900s

1912   "The Secrets of House No. 5," possibly the first vampire movie, is produced in Great Britain.

1913   "Dracula's Guest" by Bram Stoker is published.

1922   "Nosferatu," a German-made silent film produced by Prana Films, is the first attempt to film *Dracula*.

1924   Hamilton Dean's stage version of "Dracula" opens in Derby, England. Fritz Harmann of Hanover, Germany, is arrested, tried and convicted of killing more than 20 people in a vampiric crime spree. Sherlock Holmes has his only encounter with a vampire in "The Case of the Sussex Vampire."

1927   February 14: Stage version of *Dracula* debuts at the Little Theatre in London. October 1927: An American version of *Dracula*, starring Bela Lugosi, opens at Fulton Theatre in New York City. Tod Browning directs Lon Chaney in "London after Midnight," the first full-length feature film. The last known copy of the film was destroyed in a 1967 fire.

1928   The first edition of Montague Summers's influential work *The Vampire: His Kith and Kin* appears in England.

1929   Montague Summers's second vampire book, *The Vampire in Europe*, is published.

1931   January 1931: Spanish film version of "Dracula" is previewed. February: American film version of "Dracula" with Bela Lugosi premiers at the Roxy Theatre in New York City; Peter Kurten of Düsseldorf, Germany, is executed after being found guilty of murdering a number of people in a vampiric killing spree.

1932   The highly acclaimed movie *Vampyr*, directed by Carl Theodor Dreyer, is released.

1936   *Dracula's Daughter* is released by Universal Pictures.

1942   A. E. Van Vought's "Asylum" is the first story about an alien vampire.

1943   *Son of Dracula* (Universal Pictures) stars Lon Chaney, Jr., as Dracula.

1944   John Carradine plays Dracula for the first time in *Horror of Dracula*.

1953   *Drakula Istanbula*, a Turkish film adaptation of *Dracula*, is released. *Eerie* No. 8 includes the first comic book adaptation of *Dracula*.

1954   The Comics Code banishes vampires from comic books. *I Am Legend* by Richard Matheson presents vampirism as a disease that alters the body.

1956   John Carradine plays Dracula in the first television adaptation of the play for *Matinee Theatre*. *Kyuketsuki Ga*, the first Japanese vampire film, is released.

1957   The first Italian vampire movie, *I Vampiri*, is released. American producer Roger Corman makes the first science fiction vampire movie, *Not of This Earth*. *El Vampiro*, with German Robles, is the first of a new wave of Mexican vampire films.

1958   Hammer Films in Great Britain initiates a new wave of interest in vampires with the first of its "Dracula" films, released in the United States as the *Horror of Dracula*. The first issue of *Famous Monsters of Filmland* signals a new interest in horror films in the Untied States.

1959   *Plan 9 from Outer Space* is Bela Lugosi's last film.

1961   *The Bad Flower* is the first Korean film adaptation of *Dracula*.

1962   The Count Dracula Society is founded in the United States by Donald Reed.

1964   *Parque de Juelos* (*Park of Games*) is the first Spanish-made vampire movie. *The Munsters* and *The Addams Family*, two comedies with vampire characters, open in the fall television season.

1965   Jeanne Youngson founds The Count Dracula Fan Club. *The Munsters*, based on the television show of the same name, is the first comic book series featuring a vampire character.

1966   *Dark Shadows* debuts on television.

1967   April 1967: In episode 210 of *Dark Shadows*, vampire Barnabas Collins makes his first appearance.

1969   First issue of *Vampirella*, the longest running vampire comic book to date, is released. Denholm Elliot plays the title role in a BBC television production of *Does Dracula Really Suck?* (aka *Dracula and the Boys*) is released as the first gay vampire movie.

1970   Christopher Lee stars in *El Conde Dracula*, the Spanish film adaptation of *Dracula*. Sean Manchester founds The Vampire Research Society.

1971   Marvel Comics releases the first copy of a post-Comics Code vampire comic book, *The Tomb of Dracula*. Morbius, the Living Vampire, is the first new vampire character introduced after the revision of the Comics code allowed vampires to reappear in comic books.

1972   *The Night Stalker*, starring Darrin McGavin, becomes the most watched television movie of its time. *Vampire Kung-Fu* is released in Hong Kong as the first of a string of vampire martial arts films. *In Search of Dracula* by Raymond T. McNally and Radu Florescu introduces Vlad the Impaler, the historical Dracula, to the world of contemporary vampire fans. *A Dream of Dracula* by Leonard Wolf complements McNally and Florescu's effort in calling attention to vampire lore. *True Vampires of History* by Donald Glut is the first attempt to assemble the stories of all the historical vampire figures. Stephan Kaplan founds The Vampire Research Centre. Count von Count makes his first appearance on Sesame Street, the children's television show.

1973 Dan Curtis Productions' version of *Dracula* (1973) stars Jack Palance in a made-for-television movie. Nancy Garden's *Vampires* launches a wave of juvenile literature for children and youth.

1975 Fred Saberhagen proposes viewing Dracula as a hero rather than as a villain in *The Dracula Tape*. *The World of Dark Shadows* is founded as the first *Dark Shadows* fanzine.

1976 *Interview with the Vampire* by Anne Rice is published. Stephen King is nominated for the World Fantasy Award for his vampire novel *'Salem's Lot*. Shadowcon, the first national *Dark Shadows* convention, is organized by *Dark Shadows* fans.

1977 A new dramatic version of *Dracula* opens on Broadway, starring Frank Langella. Louis Jordan stars in the title role in *Count Dracula*, a three-hour version of Bram Stoker's book on BBC television. Martin V. Riccardo founds the Vampire Studies Society.

1978 Chelsea Quinn Yarbro's book *Hotel Transylvania* joins the volumes of Fred Saberhagen and Anne Rice as the third major effort to begin a reappraisal of the vampire myth during the decade. Eric Held and Dorothy Nixon found the Vampire Information Exchange.

1979 Based on the success of the new Broadway production, Universal Pictures remakes *Dracula* (1979), starring Frank Langella. The band Bauhaus's recording of "Bela Lugosi's Dead" becomes the first hit of the new gothic rock music movement. *Shadowgram* is founded as a *Dark Shadows* fanzine.

1980 The Bram Stoker Society is founded in Dublin, Ireland. Richard Chase, the so-called Dracula Killer of Sacramento, California, commits suicide in prison. The World Federation of Dark Shadows Clubs (now Dark Shadows Official Fan Club) is founded.

1983 In the December issue of *Dr. Strange*, Marvel Comics' ace occultist kills all of the vampires in the world, thus banishing them from Marvel Comics for the next six years. The *Dark Shadows* Festival is founded to host an annual convention.

1985 *The Vampire Lestat* by Anne Rice reaches the bestseller list. After a decade away from the vampire genre, Rice will subsequently publish a series of bestselling titles know collectively as the "Vampire Chronicles."

1987 Two movies aimed at a youthful audience, *Lost Boys* and *Near Dark*, herald the coming revival of interest in vampires in the West.

1989 The overthrow of Romanian dictator Nikolai Ceaucescu opens Transylvania to Dracula enthusiasts. Nancy Collins wins a Bram Stoker Award for her vampire novel *Sunglasses after Dark*.

1991 *Vampire: The Masquerade*, the most successful of the vampire role-playing games, is released by White Wolf.

1992 *Bram Stoker's Dracula*, directed by Francis Ford Coppola, opens. Andrei Chikatilo of Rostov, Russia, is sentenced to death after killing and vampirizing some 55 people.

1994 The film version of Anne Rice's *Interview with the Vampire* opens with Tom Cruise as the Vampire Lestat and Brad Pitt as Louis. It becomes the largest grossing vampire movie of the twentieth century. Michelle Belanger founds the International Vampire Society, which later evolves into House Kheperu.

1995 Major vampire movie releases include: *The Vampire in Brooklyn, Dracula: Dead and Loving It., Nadja,* and *The Addiction*

1996 Rod Ferrell and his "vampire clan" murder two people in Florida. The killings have the larger effect of separating the vampire game-playing community and the community of self-identified real vampires. *The Lunatic Café* and *Bloody Bones,* books four and five in Laurel Hamilton's increasingly successful novels about vampire hunter Anita Blake, signal the author's challenge to Anne Rice's dominant role in vampire-related fiction. His books would be serialized as comic books in 2007; January 1996: *From Dusk Till Dawn,* written by Quentin Tarantino and starring George Clooney, opens nationwide.

1997 March 10, 1997: The first episode of *Buffy the Vampire Slayer* airs on the WB cable channel, originally a mid-season replacement for a cancelled show. The show energizes a new generation of post-Anne Rice vampire fans. August 14–17, 1997: Dracula '97, which convened in Los Angeles, California, is the largest of a set of gathering to celebrate the centennial of the publication of *Dracula.*

1998 The first of three movies based on the Marvel Comics character Blade the Vampire Slayer is released. Each of the three would join the list of the ten top-grossing vampire movies of all time. October 5, 1998: The first episode of *Angel,* the spinoff of the *Buffy the Vampire Slayer,* airs. Anne Rice returns to the Roman Catholic Church and begins the transition from writing vampire novels to writing Christian-oriented fiction.

2000s

2000 The Count Dracula Fan Club changes its name to Vampire Empire. Anne Rice dissolves the Lestat Fan Club.

2001 *Dead until Dark,* by Charlaine Harris, appears. It is the first of the set of novels featuring waitress Sookie Stackhouse and her vampire boyfriend, Bill Compton. It is later adapted as the popular television series *True Blood.*

2002 *30 Days of Night,* a three-issue comic book mini-series that is later made into a movie, launches the careers of writer Steve Niles and artist Ben Templesmith.

2003 *Blood Canticle,* the last of Anne Rice's vampire novels, is released. *Underworld,* the first of three movies focused on a vampire–werewolf feud, is released. All three movies join list of ten top-grossing vampire movies. The movie version of *The League of Extraordinary Gentlemen,* based on comic book, includes Mina Murray (from *Dracula*) who has now been transformed into a vampire.

2004   The role-playing game *Vampire: The Masquerade* is superseded by *Vampire: The Requiem. Van Helsing,* staring Hugh Jackman, jumps to the head of the list of top-grossing vampire movies, where it remains until replaced by *I Am Legend* in 2007. Anne Rice moves from New Orleans to California.

2005   The Atlanta (Georgia) Vampire Alliance is founded as an organization for real self-identified vampires. Stephenie Meyer publishes *Twilight,* the fist volume of her young adult novels. The series become a phenomenon among teenage girls and catalyzes the formation of a new generation of vampire fans.

2006   Voices of the Vampire Community (VVC) is formed as a loose association of groups of self-identified vampires.

2007   TWILIGHT is a structure in which individuals involved in vampirism can engage people who have a serious and/or academic interest in what exists today as vampirism in Western society. The third adaptation of Richard Matheson's *I Am Legend,* starring Will Smith, becomes the top-grossing horror movie of the year and the top-grossing vampire movie of all time. The first meeting of the revived Anne Rice Lestat Fan Club, authorized by Rice to help post-Katrina New Orleans, meets over Halloween. *The Lair,* a gay-oriented vampire series, airs its first season on cable television.

2008   November 21, 2008: *Twilight* opens and quickly replaces *I Am Legend* as the top-grossing vampire movie of all time.: *Twilight: New Moon* opens to a larger first weekend box office and is projected to surpass *Twilight.*

2009   *The Vampire Diaries,* based on the 1990s young adult novels of Lisa Jane Smith, is launched as a successful television series on the CW network.

2010   *Twilight: Eclipse* debuts, setting record sales at the box office.

PREFACE: "WHAT IS A VAMPIRE?"

J. Gordon Melton

While having spent the greater part of my adult life studying the many different religious groups in North America and devoting my career to research and writing about religious groups, I have also had a fascination with the vampire since my teen years. During high school, I initially discovered science fiction and then horror fiction. In sampling horror novels, I soon found that I enjoyed vampire novels by far the most. Thus, for the past 40 years, a measureable percentage of my recreation has been spent on reading vampire books and watching vampire movies.

Reading vampire novels led quite logically to the perusal of the few available nonfiction books on vampires, especially those dealing with vampire folklore and accounts of reportedly "real" vampires. Raymond T. NcNally (1931–2002) and Radu Florescu's (1925–) *In Search of Dracula* had a profound effect on the image of the vampire in the 1970s. The authors claimed that the character Dracula in Bram Stoker's novel was actually based on Vlad Tepes, a fifteenth century warlord and prince of Wallachia, a region in Romania. However, to attempt a survey of nonfiction vampire literature in any fashion is to step into a morass as deep and murky as any pictured in a gothic novel. The field of vampirology has been dominated by the pioneering work of Dudley Wright and the volumes of Montague Summers. While their frequently reprinted works provided a starting point for consideration of the vampire and made available previously hard-to-obtain texts, they also introduced a number of errors into the popular literature. Many subsequent writers on the subject relied upon them and repeated errors in book after book. (Since the first edition of this encyclopedia, the attempt to correct errors in the literature has been greatly assisted by Elizabeth Miller's important and valuable study, *Dracula: Sense and Nonsense* [2000], which has probed the Dracula literature and pointed out numerous errors that had continued to appear through the late twentieth century.)

The over-reliance on Wright and Summers, the scholarly marginalization of vampire beliefs, and the enthusiasm of vampire fans for cheap novels and genre movies created a climate that did not favor the correction of common errors in vampire literature.

Only with the development of a new and growing interest in vampires over the last three decades have questions of the origins of vampire lore and the historical nature and role of belief in vampires once again taken their place in scholarly agendas.

The Vampire Book: The Encyclopedia of the Undead was conceived as a compendium of vampires, vampirism, and vampire lore in modern popular culture. The literature is vast, and not since Summers has an attempt been made to summarize all of the writing on vampires. To accomplish that task, I relied on my personal collection, which includes more than 5,000 titles on vampires (primarily vampire novels and short story anthologies) as well as an extensive collection of vampire comic books. In addition, the Davidson Library at the University of California—Santa Barbara house hundreds of additional resources (in particular books and journals on folklore, psychology, and literary and film criticism) that contain chapters and articles on vampires. Recent books on ethnic folklore have provided a particularly rich and largely untapped resource. These materials became the starting point for this volume. During the course of revising this book, I have met with numerous people involved at various levels with vampire organizations and publications of vampire fanzines. Martin Riccardo of Vampire Studies in Chicago has been particularly helpful over the years in calling my attention to the location of needed material as have fellow collectors Robert Eighteen-Bisang, Massimo Introvigne, and Melinda Hayes.

While assembling *The Vampire Book,* I assumed a decidedly contemporary perspective. Along with my coverage of vampire folklore and literature, I turned to contemporary organizations, movies, television shows, websites, and fanzines as topics of consideration. Today's heightened interest in vampires and the ideas currently dominating fiction and nonfiction oriented me whenever I got lost in the mass of data. Thus, beginning with a popular idea about the nature of vampires, I could then check the idea against Bram Stoker's *Dracula* and work my way through the literature, tracing its origins and assessing its relationship to vampire folklore and history as a whole. Not the least of the important and perennial questions to which this process forced me to return was the simple, definitional one, "What is a vampire?"

The common dictionary definition of a vampire serves as a starting point for inquiry. A vampire is a reanimated corpse that rises from the grave to suck the blood of living people and thus retain a semblance of life. That description certainly fits Dracula, the most famous vampire, but is only a starting point and quickly proves inadequate in approaching the realm of vampire folklore. By no means do all vampires conform to that definition.

For example, while the subject of vampires almost always leads to a discussion of death, all vampires are not resuscitated corpses. Numerous vampires are disembodied demonic spirits. In this vein are the numerous vampires and vampire-like demons of Indian mythology and the *lamiai* of Greece. Vampires can also appear as the disembodied spirit of a dead person who retains a substantial existence; like many reported ghosts, these vampires can be mistaken for a fully embodied living corpse. Likewise, in the modern secular literary context, vampires sometimes emerge as a different species of intelligent life (possibly from outer space or the product of genetic mutation) or to otherwise normal human beings who have an unusual habit (such as blood-drinking) or an odd power (such as the ability to drain people emotionally). Vampire animals, from the traditional bat to the delightful children's characters Bunnicula and Count von Count, are by no means absent from the literature. These vampires exist in a number of forms, although by far the majority of them are the risen dead.

As commonly understood, the characteristics shared by all of these vampire entities is their need for blood, which they take from living human beings and animals. A multitude of creatures from the world's mythology have been labeled vampires in the popular literature simply because periodic bloodsucking was among their many attributes. When the entire spectrum of vampires is considered, however, that seemingly common definition falls by the wayside, or, at the very least, must be considered only supplemental to the overall nature of some vampires. Some vampires do not take blood; rather they steal what is considered the life force from their victims. A person attacked by a traditional vampire suffers the loss of blood, which causes a variety of symptoms: fatigue, loss of color in the face, listlessness, depleted motivation, and weakness. In this aspect, it is similar to unchecked tuberculosis, a wasting disease.

Nineteenth-century romantic authors and occultists suggested that real vampirism involved the loss of psychic energy to the vampire and wrote of vampiric relationships that had little to do with the exchange of blood. Dracula himself quoted the Bible in noting that "the blood is the life." Thus, it is not necessarily the blood itself that the vampire seeks but the psychic energy or "life force" believed to be carried by it. The metaphor of psychic vampirism can easily be extended to cover various relationships in which one party steals essential life elements from the other, such as when rulers sap the strength of the people they dominate.

On the other extreme, some modern "vampires" are simply blood drinkers. They do not attack and drain their victims, but obtain blood in a variety of legal manners (such as locating a willing donor or a source at a blood bank). In such cases, the consumption of the blood has little to do with any ongoing relationship to the source of the blood. It, like food, is merely consumed. Oftentimes, modern vampires even report getting a psychological or sexual high from drinking blood.

Once it is settled that the word "vampire" covers a wide variety of creatures, a second problem arises. As a whole, the vampires themselves are unavailable for direct examination. With a few minor exceptions, the subject of this volume is not vampires *per se*, but the human belief about vampires and vampirism. That being the case, some methodology was needed for considering human belief in entities that objectively do not exist—indeed, for understanding my own fascination with a fictional archetype. Not a new problem, the vast literature on vampirism favors one or two basic approaches. The first offers explanations in a social context. That is to say, the existence of vampires provides people with an explanation for otherwise inexplicable events (which in the modern West we tend to explain in scientific terms). The second approach is psychological and explains the vampire as existing in the inner psychic landscape of the individual. The two approaches are not necessarily mutually exclusive.

The worldwide distribution of creatures that can properly be termed "vampires" or have vampire-like characteristics suggests an approach that allows some semblance of order to emerge from the chaos of data. I began with the obvious. The very different vampire-like creatures around the world function quite differently in their distinct cultures and environments. Thus, the *camazotz* of Central America shares several characteristics with the vampire of eastern Europe, but each plays a distinct role in its own culture's mythology and is encountered in different situations. While a host of statues and pictures of the *camazotz* survived in Central America, no eastern European peasant would think of creating such a memorial to the vampire. In each culture, the "vampire" takes on unique characteristics because of this, each being considered within its indigenous context.

Despite these cultural differences, there are common vampire types that seem to bridge cultural boundaries. For example, the *lamiai*, which is among the older of the Greek vampire creatures, seems to have arisen in response to the variety of problems surrounding childbirth. The *lamiai* attacked babies and very young children. Thus, otherwise unexplained deaths of a child or a mother giving birth could be attributed to vampires. This is similar to the function of of the Indonesian *langsuyar* and the Jewish Lilith.

In like measure, vastly different cultures possessed a vampire who primarily attacked young women. Such vampires, which appeared repeatedly in the folklore of eastern Europe, served a vital role in the process of social control. The stories of these young, handsome male vampires warned maidens in their early post-pubescent years not to stray from the counsel of their elders and priests and to avoid glamorous strangers who would only lead them to disaster.

Another large group of vampires grew out of encounters with death, especially the sudden unexpected death of a loved one due to suicide, accident, or an unknown illness. People dying unexpectedly left relatives and friends behind with unfinished agendas with the deceased. Strong emotional ties and uncorrected wrongs felt by the recently deceased caused them to leave their resting place and attack family members, lovers, and neighbors against whom they might have had a grievance. If unable to reach a human target, they turned to the victim's food supply (i.e., livestock). Stories of attacks by those recently deceased adult vampires on their relatives and neighbors or their livestock directly underlie the emergence of the modern literary and cinematic vampire.

Thus, as the entries on different vampires and vampirelike creatures were written for this book, some attempt was made to supply background on the particular culture and larger mythological context in which the vampire entity operated. Such an approach led to the inclusion of what, strictly speaking, were non-vampire entities; these creatures were included because they filled the role in their culture that were taken by vampires in other cultures. For example, most African peoples did not have a vampire creature in their mythology, but many of the characteristics and abilities commonly associated with vampire beings in Asia or Europe are attributed to the African witch.

Leaving folktales behind, the literary vampire of the nineteenth century transformed the ethnic vampire into a cosmopolitan citizen of the modern imagination. The literary vampire interacted in new ways with human society. While the early literary vampires pictured by such writers as Goethe, Coleridge, Shelly, Polidori, Byron, and Nodier were basically parasites, possessing few traits to endear them to the people they encountered, nevertheless they performed a vital function by assisting the personification of thet darker side possessed by human beings. The romantic poets of the nineteenth century assigned themselves the task of exploring the dark side of the human consciousness.

In the movement to the stage and screen, the vampire was further transformed. The demonic vampire gained some degree of human feelings, and even as a villain possessed some admirable traits that brought the likes of actor Bela Lugosi a large and loyal following. Lugosi brought before the public an erotic vampire that embodied the release of the sexual urges that were so suppressed by Victorian society. In the original stage and screen presentations of Dracula, the vampire's bite substituted for the sexual activity that could not be more directly portrayed. This inherent sexuality of the vampire's attack upon its victims became more literally portrayed in the 1960s—on the one hand through new adult-oriented pornographic vampire movies and on the other in a series of novels and movies that centered upon a sensual and seductive vampire. Fran Langella's portrayal *Dracula* (1979) and Gary Oldman's in *Bram Stoker's Dracula* (1992) were outstanding examples of this latter type of seductive vampire.

The vampire's amazing adaptability accounts for much of its popularity. It served numerous vital functions for different people during previous centuries. For enthusiasts, today's vampire symbolizes important elements of their lives that they feel are being culturally suppressed. The most obvious role thrust upon the contemporary vampire has been that of cultural rebel, a symbolic leader advocating outrageous alternative patterns of living in a world demanding conformity. An extreme example of this new vampire is the vegetarian vampire, such as Bunnicula and Count Duckula, that introduces the vampire to children and has emerged as an effective tool in teaching children tolerance of other children who are noticeably different.

A psychological approach to the vampire supplements an understanding of its social function. Twentieth-century psychotherapists discovered that modern, post-Dracula vampires and vampiric relationships actively distorted their patients' lives. Out of the experiences reported to them, particularly the classic nightmare, many psychologists called attention to the role of specific, common psychological events in the creation and continual reinforcement of vampire beliefs. Margaret Shanahan, who wrote the entry on psychological perspectives for this volume, noted the role of the vampire as a symbol of the widespread experience of of inner emptiness she and her colleagues find in their clients. Such inner emptiness leads to a longing for emotional nutrients, which can lead to an exaggerated desire for food or to an envy for those perceived to possess an abundance of nutrients (rich in the life force) and a desire to steal that energy. In its most extreme form, such fixations can lead to various forms of blood consumption and even homicidal acts.

Such psychological approaches also explain some popular social pathologies, especially the common practice of scapegoating. Groups can be assigned characteristics of a vampire and treated accordingly with rhetoric that condemns them to the realms outside of social communion. If not controlled, such rhetoric can lead to modern forms of staking and decapitation.

Throughout the twentieth century, various groups have been singled out and labeled as "vampires." Women became "vamps," and bosses became bloodsuckers. Self-declared victims have branded a wide variety of social groups, rightly or wrongly, as their vampire oppressors.

These two approaches to the vampire—which emerge at various appropriate points through the text of this book—seem to account for most of the phenomena of vampirism that I have encountered. Further, they suggest that the vampire (or its structural equivalent) is a universal figure in human culture, which emerged independently at many points in different societies. There is little evidence to suggest that the vampire emerged in one time and place and then diffused around the world from a primal source.

Ackerman, Forrest James (1916–2008)

Forrest James Ackerman, (generally referred to simply as "Forrest J Ackerman" with no period after the middle initial) **science fiction** and horror fiction writer and editor, was born on November 24, 1916, in Los Angeles, the son of Carroll Cridland Wyman and William Schilling Ackerman. After attending the University of California at Berkeley for a year (1934–35), Ackerman held a variety of jobs and spent three years in the U.S. Army before founding the Ackerman Science Fiction Agency in 1947. By that time, he had been a science fiction fan for many years and in 1932 had been a co-founder of *The Time Travelers*, the first science fiction fanzine. He was a charter member of the Los Angeles chapter of the Science Fiction League, an early fan club, and attended the first science fiction fan convention in 1939.

Since that time he spent his life promoting the science fiction and horror genres in both print and film media. That lifetime of work earned him a special place in the world of science fiction as a behind-the-scenes mover and shaker in the development of the field. Besides writing numerous fiction and nonfiction articles, Ackerman worked as the literary agent for a number of science fiction writers. Along the way he amassed an impressive collection of genre literature and artifacts that were housed at his Hollywood home, lovingly dubbed the Ackermansion. Among his prized artifacts were a **Dracula** ring worn by **Bela Lugosi** as Count Dracula; Bela Lugosi's robe worn in the movie *The Raven*; a cape made for Bela Lugosi in 1932 and subsequently worn by him in his stage portrayal of Dracula (the cape was finally worn in Lugosi's last movie, *Plan 9 from Outer Space*). He also had a first edition of the novel *Dracula*, signed by **Bram Stoker** and with an inscription by Bela Lugosi to Ackerman.

Ackerman is most remembered by the general public as the editor of and main writer for *Famous Monsters of Filmland*, an important fan magazine that emerged in 1958

Forrest Ackerman (right), with Vincent Price reading the magazine he founded and wrote for: *Famous Monsters of Filmland.*

as monster movies were becoming recognized as a separate genre of film with its own peculiar audience. During the 20 years of its existence, the magazine filled a void for the growing legion of horror and monster movie fans. Up to this time, there were no vampire fan clubs or periodicals. Ackerman sold the idea of *Famous Monsters* to publisher James Warren. The first issue was released as a one-time publication, but the response was far beyond what either had imagined. It soon became a periodical. In the first article of the premier issue, "Monsters Are Good for You," Dr. Acula (one of Ackerman's pseudonyms) suggested, "A vampire a day keeps the doctor away." Ackerman made broad contributions to the larger science fiction and horror field while furthering the development of the vampire in popular culture. He regularly featured vampire movies and personalities—though they shared space with other monsters—on the pages of *Famous Monsters*. He edited and authored a number of books including an important vampire title, *London After Midnight Revisited* (1981), a volume about the famous original vampire feature directed by **Tod Browning**. More recently, he put together several retrospective volumes on *Famous Monsters of Filmland*. He appeared in some 210 genre movies, mostly in cameo parts, including two vampire films, *Queen of Blood* (1966) and *Dracula vs. Frankenstein* (1971).

Possibly his most significant contribution to the vampire field was the creation of **Vampirella**. Ackerman partly developed the idea of Vampirella, a sexy young vampire from outer space, from the movie character Barbarella, who was created by **Roger Vadim** and portrayed by Jane Fonda (Vadim's wife at the time). The first issue of the *Vampirella* **comic book** appeared in 1969 and went on to become the most successful vampire comic book ever. It ran for 112 issues and, revived in the 1990s by Harris Comics, again became a top seller.

In 1953 he was given the first Hugo Award as science fiction's number one fan personality. He was awarded the Ann Radcliffe Award from the **The Dracula Society** in 1963 and again in 1966. In 1997, Ackerman's lifetime of service to fandom was recognized with a special award at the **Dracula '97: A Centennial Celebration** in Los Angeles. Ackerman spent much of the last years of his long life attending various fan conventions where he spoke of his many adventures in fandom, listened to numerous reviews of his work, and received adulations for his promotion of science fiction and horror. In 2008, word of failing health circulated on the Internet, and he passed away from congestive heath failure in Los Angeles on December 4, 2008. In April 2009, a massive auction of his collection, including the Dracula related items, was held as part of the annual auction of Hollywood memorabilia by Profiles in History.

Sources:

Ackerman, Forrest J. *Famous Monsters of Filmland*. Pittsburgh, PA: Imagine, Inc., 1986.
———. *Forrest J Ackerman's World of Science Fiction*. London: Stoddart, 1997.
———, and Philip J. Riley, eds. *London After Midnight Revisited*. Metropolis Books, 1981.
Stine, Jean Marie, and Forest J Ackerman. *I, Vampire*. Greenwich, CT: Longmeadow Press, 1995.

 Aconite

A conite (*aconitum napellus*) is another name for wolfsbane or monkshood. This poisonous plant was believed by the ancient Greeks to have arisen in the mouths of Cerberus (a three-headed dog that guards the entrance to Hades) while under the influence of Hecate, the goddess of magic and the underworld. It later was noted as one of the ingredients of the ointment that witches put on their body in order to fly off to their sabbats. In **Dracula** (**Spanish, 1931**), aconite was substituted for **garlic** as the primary plant used to repel the vampire.

Sources:

Emboden, William A. *Bizarre Plants: Magical, Monstrous, Mythical*. New York: Macmillan Publishing, 1974. 214 pp.

The Addams Family

Originating as a cartoon series that first appeared in the *New Yorker* magazine, *The Addams Family* became one of the more notable sets of comic characters in American popular culture. The cartoons were originally the product of Charles S. Addams (1912–1988), whose work had become a regular feature of the *New Yorker* in the 1930s. His work was anthologized in a series of books beginning with *Drawn and Quartered* in

1942. *The Addams Family* was but one aspect of Addams's world which included a wide variety of the bizarre and monstrous that he tended to portray in everyday settings.

The Addams Family cartoons were transformed into a situation comedy **television** series for the fall 1964 season. Since Addams had never assigned names to the members of the cartoon family, they had to be created. Carolyn Jones was selected to play Morticia Addams, the family matriarch with the long black hair and a revealing, skin-tight black dress. She continued the image of the **vamp** made popular earlier in the century and utilized by horror film hostesses **Vampira** and **Elvira**. John Astin portrayed her husband, Gomez, a lawyer. Their children were named Pugsley and Wednesday (Ken Weatherwax and Lisa Loring). Uncle Fester (Jackie Coogan), Grandmama (Blossom Rock), and the butler, Lurch (Ted Cassidy) rounded out the home's residents. The dynamics of the show, true to Charles Addams's world, rested on the family's turning the bizarre into the norm, and then interacting with the members of normal society.

The Addams Family first aired on ABC on September 18, 1964, and lasted for two seasons. It went up against a similar series on CBS, **The Munsters**, which also began in 1964 and ran for two years. *The Addams Family* was revived in 1973 as an animated children's show produced by the Hanna-Barbera Studios and aired on Saturday mornings. Hanna-Barbera also produced a **comic book** version of *The Addams Family*, which first appeared in October 1974, but only three issues were published before the series folded. *Halloween with the Addams Family* (first aired on October 30, 1977), a full-length feature film with the original cast, was another unsuccessful attempt to revive interest in *The Addams Family* during the 1970s.

Little was heard from the family through the 1980s, but in 1991, Angelica Huston and Raul Julia were selected to star in the full-length movie of *The Addams Family*, produced by Paramount Pictures. The highly successful movie, in turn, inspired two board **games,** The Addams Family Reunion Game and The Addams Family Find Uncle Fester Game, an Addams Family pinball game, a home computer game, and two separate **juvenile** novelizations aimed at different age groups. In 1992, a new *The Addams Family* cartoon series, also produced by Paramount, starred the voices of Nanci Linari and John Astin as Morticia and Gomez, respectively. At the end of 1993, a sequel to the 1991 movie, *Addams Family Values*, was released; it again starred Angelica Huston and Raul Julia. DVDs and the Internet have given *The Addams Family* new life and several Internet based fan clubs continue into the new century.

Sources:

The Addams Family—The Official Poster Book. New York: Starlog Communications International, 1992.

Anchors, William E., Jr. "The Addams Family." *Epi-log* 37 (December 1993): 44–51, 64.

Calmenson, Stephanie. *The Addams Family.* New York: Scholastic, Inc., 1991. 72 pp. A novelization of the 1991 movie for children.

Cox, Stephen. *The Addams Chronicles: An Altogether Ooky Look at the Addams Family.* Nashville, TN: Cumberland House Publishing, 1998.

Faucher, Elizabeth. *The Addams Family.* New York: Scholastic, Inc., 1991. 141 pp. A novelization of the 1991 movie for teens.

Ferrante, Anthony C. "The Campaign for *Addams Family Values.*" *Fangoria* 129 (December 1993): 46–52.

Jones, Stephen. *The Illustrated Vampire Movie Guide.* London: Titan Books, 1993. 144 pp.

The Official Addams Family Magazine. New York: Starlog Communications International, 1991.
Van Hise, James. *Addams Family Revealed: An Unauthorized Look at America's Spookiest Family.*
  Las Vegas, NV: Pioneer Books, 1991. 157 pp.

Africa, Vampires in

The peoples of Africa have not been known, in spite of their elaborate mythology, to hold a prominent belief in vampires. **Montague Summers**, in his 1920s survey of vampirism around the world, could find only two examples: the *asasabonsam* and the *obayifo*. Since Summers, very little work has been done to explore vampirism in African beliefs.

The *obayifo*, unknown to Summers, was actually the Ashanti name for a West African vampire that reappeared under similar names in the mythology of most of the neighboring tribes. For example, among the Dahomeans, the vampire was known as the *asiman*. The *obayifo* was a witch living incognito in the community. The process of becoming a witch was an acquired trait—there was no genetic link. Hence, there was no way to tell who might be a witch. Secretly, the witch was able to leave its body and travel at night as a glowing ball of light. The witches attacked people—especially children—and sucked their **blood**. They also had the ability to suck the juice from fruits and vegetables.

The *asasabonsam* was a vampirelike monster species found in the folklore of the Ashanti people of Ghana in western Africa. In the brief description provided by R. Sutherland Rattray, the *asasabonsam* was humanoid in appearance and had a set of iron teeth. It lived deep in the forest and was rarely encountered. It sat on treetops and allowed its legs to dangle downward, using its hook-shaped feet to capture unwary passersby.

Working among the tribes of the Niger River delta area, Arthur Glyn Leonard found a belief that witches left their homes at night to hold meetings with demons and to plot the death of neighbors. Death was accomplished by "gradually sucking the blood of the **victim** through some supernatural and invisible means, the effects of which on the victim is imperceptible to others." Among the Ibo, it was believed that the blood-sucking process was done so skillfully that the victim felt the pain but was unable to perceive the physical cause of it, even though it would eventually prove fatal. Leonard believed that **witchcraft** was, in reality, a very sophisticated system of poisoning (as was a certain amount of sorcery in medieval Europe).

P. Amaury Talbot, working among the tribes in Nigeria, found witchcraft a pervasive influence, and that the most terrible power attributed to witches was the "sucking out the heart" of the victims without them knowing what was happening to them. The witch could sit on the roof at night and by magical powers accomplish the sucking. A person dying of tuberculosis was often thought to be the victim of such witchcraft.

Among the Yakö people of Nigeria, Daryll Forde discovered that disembodied witches were believed to attack people while they slept at night. They could suck their blood, and ulcers were believed to be a sign of their attack. They could also operate like an **incubus/succubus** and suffocate people by lying on top of them.

The question of witchcraft was evoked by anyone who suffered a hurtful condition, and anyone accused was severely dealt with by various trials by ordeal. Generally women who were barren or post-menopausal were primary subjects for accusations. It was not uncommon to sentence a convicted witch to death by **fire**.

Melville Herskovits and his wife Frances Herskovits were able to trace a witch/vampire, whose existence was acknowledged by most West African tribes, to similar vampire figures found in the Caribbean, the **loogaroo** of Haiti, the *asema* of Surinam, and the **sukuyan** of Trinidad. These three vampires are virtually identical, though found in colonies of the French, Dutch, and English. The vampire beliefs seem an obvious example of a common view carried from Africa by the slaves, which then persisted through the decades of slavery into the present.

More recently, John L. Vellutini, editor of the ***Journal of Vampirology***, took up the challenge of exploring the whole question of vampirism in Africa. The results of his discoveries have been summarized in two lengthy articles. Like researchers before him, Vellutini found scarce literal vampirism in Africa. However, he argued that beneath the surface of African beliefs about witchcraft, much material analogous to the eastern European or **Slavic vampire** could be found. Witches were seen as powerful figures in African culture with numerous powers, including the ability to transform into a variety of **animal** shapes. Using their powers, they indulged themselves in acts of cannibalism, necrophagy (i.e., feeding on corpses), and vampirism. These actions usually constituted acts of **psychic vampirism** rather than physical malevolence. For example, Thomas Winterbottom, working in Sierre Leone in the 1960s, noted:

A person killed by witchcraft is supposed to die from the effects of a poison secretly administered or infused into his system by the witch; or the latter is supposed to assume the shape of some animal, as a cat, or a rat, which, during the night, sucks the blood from a small and imperceptible wound, by which a lingering illness and death are produced.

With similar results, the *obayifo,* an Ashanti witch, sucked the blood of children as it flew about in its spirit body at night. Among the Ga people, M. J. Field found that witches gathered around a *baisea,* a type of pot, which contained the blood of their victims—though anyone looking into it would see only **water**. In fact, the liquid was believed to hold the vitality they had taken from their victims.

When a person was accused of witchcraft, he or she was put through an ordeal to determine guilt, and if found guilty, executed. The methods adopted by some tribes bore a strange resemblance to the methods applied to suspected vampires in eastern Europe. For example, one tribe began the execution by pulling the tongue out and pinning it to the chin with a thorn (thus preventing any final curses being given to the executioners). The witch was then killed by being impaled on a sharpened **stake**. On occasion, the head was severed from the body and the body burnt or left in the woods for predators.

Even more closely tied to the practices of European witchcraft were the efforts taken to ascertain if a deceased person was a witch. The corpse of the accused witch would be taken from the ground and examined for signs of blood in the burial plot, incorruption, and abnormal swelling of the corpse. The grave of a true witch would be found to have a hole in the dirt that led from the body to the surface that the witch could use to exit the ground in the form of a **bat**, rat, or other small animal. It was believed that the witch could continue to operate after his/her death, and that the body would remain as at the time of death. By **destroying** the body, the spirit was unable to continue its witchcraft activity.

Witches also had the power to raise the dead and to capture a departed spirit, which they turned into a ghost capable of annoying the kinsmen of the departed person. There was also widespread belief throughout West Africa in the *isithfuntela* (known by different names among different peoples), the disinterred body of a person enslaved by a witch to do the witch's bidding. The witch reportedly cuts out the tongue and drives a peg into the brain of the creature so that it becomes zombie-like. The *isithfuntela* similarly attacked people by hypnotizing them and then driving a nail in their heads.

Vellutini concluded that Africans shared the belief with Europeans in the existence of a class of persons who could defy death and exert a malignant influence from the grave. Like the European vampires, African vampires were often people who died in defiance of the community mores or from **suicide**. Unlike the literary vampire, the African vampires were simply common people like the vampires of eastern Europe.

Vellutini speculated that African beliefs in witches and witchcraft might have spread to the rest of the world, although anthropologists and ethnologists did not encounter these beliefs firsthand until the nineteenth century. While certainly possible, further research and comparison with evidence for alternative theories, such as that proposed by **Devendra P. Varma** for the Asian **origin** of vampire beliefs, must be completed before a consensus can be reached.

Sources:

Forde, Daryll. *Yako Studies*. London: Oxford University Press, 1964. 288 pp.

Leonard, Arthur Glyn. *The Lower Niger and Its Tribes*. London: Macmillan and Co., 1906.

Rattray, R. Sutherland. *Ashanti Proverbs*. Oxford: Claredon Press, 1916. 190 pp.

Summers, Montague. *The Vampire: His Kith and Kin*. London: Routledge, Kegan Paul, Trench, Trubner, & Co., 1928. 356 pp. Rept. New Hyde Park, NY: University Books,1960. 356 pp.

Talbot, P. Amaury. *In the Shadow of the Bush*. London: William Heinemann, 1912. 500 pp.

Vellutini, John L. "The African Origins of Vampirism," *Journal of Vampirology* 5, 2 (1988): 2–16.

———. "The Vampire in Africa," *Journal of Vampirology* 5, 3 (1988): 2–14.

White, Luise. *Speaking with Vampires: Rumor and History in Colonial Africa*. Berkeley, CA: University of California Press, 2000.

African American Vampires

Vampire beliefs have not been prominent among African Americans, though a few have been reported. These few were seemingly derived from the mythologies of **Africa**, which believed in both vampires and witches who acted like vampires, and were brought to the United States either directly or by way of Haiti or the other French islands in the Caribbean. Folklorists working among African Americans in the southern United States in the late nineteenth and early twentieth centuries found a number of accounts of vampires. Some were more traditional bloodsuckers. One account from Tennessee told of an old woman whose health seemed to constantly improve while the children's health declined because she sucked their **blood** while they slept: "de chillun dies, an' she keeps on a-livin'." The most definable vampire figure reported among African Americans was the *fifollet*, or the *feu-follet*, known to the residents of Louisiana. The *fifollet*, the traditional will-o'-the-wisp (light seen at night over the swamp areas), derived from the French **incubus/succubus** figure, was the soul of a dead person that had been

Teresa Graves, who starred in the movie *Old Dracula,* **was one of the first African Americans to be featured in a vampire film.**

sent back to Earth by God to do penance, but instead attacked people. Most of the attacks were mere mischief, but on occasion, the *fifollet* became a vampire that sucked the blood of people, especially children. Some believed that the *fifollet* was the soul of a child who had died before baptism.

Modern African American Vampires: Vampires have made only infrequent appearances in African American folklore, and, similarly, African Americans have been largely absent from vampire movies and novels through the twentieth century. The few black vampire movies emerged in the era of blaxploitation movies in the early and mid-1970s. Only one African American vampire character, Prince Mamuwalde (better known as Blacula), attained any fame beyond the fans of vampire movies. The Prince, portrayed by Shakespearean actor **William Marshall**, appeared in two movies, *Blacula* (1972) and *Scream Blacula Scream* (1973). Released the same year as *Blacula* was *Alabama's Ghost* (1972), a blaxploitation movie in which a vampire rock group battles a ghost. Another lesser-known African American vampire movie is the 1973 *Ganja and Hess* (released in video under a variety of names including *Blood Couple, Double Possession, Black Evil,* and *Black Vampire*). Like *Blacula,* the movie was set in New York. It concerned Dr. Hess Green (played by Duane Jones), who becomes a vampire after being stabbed with an ancient African dagger by his assistant. The vampire never became a prominent role for black actors, however, and with a few notable instances—Teresa Graves in *Old Dracula* (also known as **Vampira**) and Grace Jones in *Vamp*—few have appeared in leading roles.

Meanwhile, in the 1970s, **Marv Wolfman**, who created the very successful vampire comic series, *Tomb of Dracula*, included the African American **Blade the Vampire Slayer** among the major characters. Through the several attempts to revive the series, Blade emerged as the single most popular of Wolfman's characters and eventually in the mid-1990s got his own Marvel **comic book** series. As Blade emerged to prominence, the character was altered to more closely conform to the superhero for which Marvel was best known, and his half-vampire nature emphasized. Beginning in 1997 this new Blade, became the subject of three very successful movies starring Wesley Snipes. In the wake of Blade's success, as the DVD market and independent movie industry expanded, a set of new African American vampire movies, most going straight to DVD, appeared. These latter include *Cryptz* (2002), *Vegas Vampires* (2004), *Vampiyaz* (2004), *Vampz* (2004), *Vampire Assassin* (2005), *Bloodz Vs Wolvez* (2006), and *Dead Heist* (2007).

Like the new set of vampire movies, some vampire novels were included among the growing number of books written especially for an African American audience. Only a few of these, most notably Jewelle Gomez's *The Gilda Stories* (1991), gained a larger audience. Then in 2003, Leslie E. Banks, writing under her pseudonym **L. A. Banks**, issued *Minion*, the first of what became her Vampire Huntress books. The series, built around a young African American **vampire hunter** named Damali, found an audience among readers of romance novels, and by 2009, a dozen titles had appeared. Banks emerged as the most successful African American vampire author to date.

Sources:

Brandon, Elizabeth. "Superstitions in Vermillion Parish." In Mody C. Boatright, Wilson M. Hudson, and Allen Maxwell, eds. *The Golden Log.* Dallas: Southern Methodist University, 1962, 108–18.

Gross, Edward, and Marc Shapiro. *The Vampire Interview Book: Conversations with the Undead.* East Meadow, NY: Image Publishing, 1991. 134 pp.

Lavergne, Remi. *A Phonetic Transcription of the Creole Negro's Medical Treatments, Superstitions, and Folklore in the Parish of Pointe Coupée.* New Orleans, LA: Master of Arts thesis, Louisiana State University, 1930.

Murphy, Michael J. *The Celluloid Vampires: A History and Filmography, 1897–1779.* Ann Arbor, MI: Pierian Press, 1979. 351 pp.

Puckett, Newbell Niles. *Folk Beliefs of the Southern Negro.* Chapel Hill, NC: University of North Carolina Press, 1926. Rept. New York: Negro Universities Press, 1968.

Rovin, Jeff. *The Encyclopedia of Super Villains.* New York: Facts on File, 1987. 416 pp.

African American actress and singer Grace Jones starred in *Vamps.*

Alien Vampires   *see:* Science Fiction and the Vampire

Allatius, Leo (1586–1669)

Seventeenth-century Greek theologian, scholar, and keeper of the Vatican library, Leo Allatius (also known as Leone Allacci) was also a vampirologist and possibly the first modern author to write a lengthy part of a book on vampires. Allatius was born in 1586 on the Greek island of Chios. In 1600 he moved to **Rome** to attend the Greek College there. It is not known whether his mother was a catholic Christian (his father was orthodox), or whether he converted to the Roman Church. Allatius was deeply convinced of the inner spiritual unity of the Greek and the Roman Church and later worked incessantly for a reunion of the churches. After completing his studies, he returned to Chios as the assistant to the Roman Catholic Bishop Marco Giustiniani. He later moved back to **Italy** to study medicine and rhetoric, and worked for many years at the Vatican library, where he organized, among other things, the transport of the Palatine Library to Rome.

In 1645 he completed *De Graecorum hodie quorundam opinationibus*, in which he discussed many of the beliefs common to the people of **Greece**, making Allatius an early example of modern folklore studies. Allatius covered the Greek vampire traditions in great detail. He described the *vrykolakas*, the undecomposed corpse that has been taken over by a demon, and noted the regulations of the Greek Church for the discernment and disposal of a *vrykolakas*. He then noted his own belief in the existence of vampires, which had occasionally been reported on Chios.

While Allatius personally accepted the reality of vampires, and his book helped to popularize the connection between Greece and vampires, he did not dwell upon the subject throughout his life. He continued to work at the Vatican library, and in 1661, was honored by being appointed its custodian. Allatius died in Rome on January 19, 1669.

Sources:

Hartnup, Karen. *On the Beliefs of the Greeks: Leo Allatios and Popular Orthodoxy*. Leiden: Brill, 2004. 370 pp.

Summers, Montague. *The Vampire: His Kith and Kin*. London: Routledge, Kegan Paul, Trench, Trubner, & Co., 1928. 356 pp. Rept. New Hyde Park, NY: University Books, 1960. 356 pp.

Alnwick Castle, The Vampire of

Among the famous case reports of real vampires were those of **William of Newburgh,** who, in the twelfth century, collected a variety of accounts of vampires in England. One incident that occurred in his lifetime concerned a man who served the Lord of Alnwick Castle. The man, who was himself known for his wicked ways, was further plagued by an unfaithful wife. Having hidden on the roof above his bed to see her actions for himself, he fell to the ground and died the next day.

Following his burial, the man was seen wandering through the town. People became afraid of encountering him and locked themselves in their houses after dark each day. During this time an epidemic of an unnamed disease broke out and a number of people died. The sickness was blamed on the "vampire." Finally, on Palm Sunday, the local priest assembled a group of the more devout residents and some of the leading citizens who proceeded to the cemetery. They uncovered the body, which appeared gorged with **blood** that gushed forth when it was struck with a spade. Having decided that the body had fed off the blood of its many **victims,** it was dragged out of town and burned. Soon thereafter, the epidemic ended, and the town returned to normal.

Sources:

Glut, Donald G. *True Vampires of History*. New York: H.C. Publishers, 1971. Rept. Rockville, MD: Sense of Wonder, 2004.

Alqul *see:* Ghouls

Alternate Shadows *see:* Dark Shadows Fandom

Aluka

Aluka is the word for a leech (*Haemopsis sanguisuga*) in ancient Hebrew. The word appeared in the Jewish Bible in Proverbs 30:15, where it was variously translated as

leech or horseleech. The word was derived from an Arabic word (*alukah*), meaning "to hang to." In Syria and Israel, there were several species of leeches, one of which would attach itself to the neck of horses as they drank from streams. Others dwelt in more stagnant **waters** and would cling to the legs of any who wandered their way. They were known for their tenacity in adhering to the skin, and often could only be detached by killing them.

Some have suggested that the cryptic expression in Proverbs, "The leech (*aluka*) has two daughters, Give, Give," in fact, referred not to the common leech but to a mythological vampire figure, a Syrian/Hebrew derivation of the Arabic **ghoul**, which sucked **blood** and dined on the flesh of the dead. During the nineteenth century, such an interpretation was offered by several Bible scholars, however, it was always a minority interpretation and is no longer regarded as a viable option by contemporary scholars.

Sources:

Gehman, Henry Snyder. *The New Westminster Dictionary of the Bible.* Philadelphia: Westminster Press, 1970. 1027 pp.

America, Vampires in

European settlers who came to America brought their belief in vampires with them, though most English colonists arrived before the vampire became part of the popular culture of Great Britain. Certainly, Polish settlers from the northern Kashab area of **Poland** brought and kept alive vampire beliefs in their Canadian settlements. Amid the vast mythology of the many Native American tribes there have been few vampires reported, and even passing references to American Indians are rare in vampire literature. Similarly, there have been few reports from the **African American** community, though remnants of **African** vampire mythologies have appeared in the South.

Vampirism in New England: While reports of vampires in the United States have been infrequent, there were stories scattered throughout the nineteenth century of what appear, at least on cursory examination, to document a belief in vampires and action taken against them by settlers in a rather confined area in New England. The first such incident reportedly occurred during the American Revolution. A man named Stukeley, who had 14 children, began to experience the death of his brood one by one. After six had died, one of the deceased, his daughter Sarah, began to appear in dreams to his wife. The bodies were exhumed and all but that of Sarah had decomposed. Her body was remarkably preserved. From each body, they cut out the heart, which they burned before reburying the bodies. The first account of this story was not published until 1888, a century after it supposedly occurred. No contemporary accounts of this story exist.

A similar early case was reported in 1854, much closer to the time of its occurrence. It concerned the Ray family of Jewett City, Connecticut. Besides the father and mother, there were five children. Between 1845 and 1854, the father and two sons died of consumption, and a third son had taken ill. (Throughout the nineteenth century, consumption, i.e., tuberculosis, was a deadly disease with no known cause or cure. It thus became the subject of much occult speculation.) The family, believing that their deceased relatives were the cause of the problem, exhumed the bodies and burned them. How prevalent this belief was is not known, but there certainly existed a community of belief that passed from generation to generation. Henry David Thoreau recorded in his journal on September 16, 1859, "I have just read of a family in Vermont who, several of its members having died of consumption, just burned the lungs, heart, and liver of the last deceased in order to prevent any more from having it." Another story was published in a Vermont paper in 1890. It concerned the Corwin family, who lived in Woodstock, Vermont. Six months after one of the Corwins had died of consumption, a brother took sick. The family disinterred the body of the first brother and burned the heart. Unfortunately, there is no contemporary account of this incident, only a newspaper story published 60 years after the reported occurrence.

Among the widely retold accounts was that of the family of Mary E. Brown of Exeter, Rhode Island. Mary died of tuberculosis in December 1883. Six months later, her oldest daughter also died. In 1888, her son Edwin and his sister Mercy contracted the disease. Mercy died in January 1892. Edwin, though ill, clung to life. Two months later, the family, deciding that a vampire was involved, exhumed the bodies of all their dead relatives. The mother and oldest daughter were mere skeletons, but Mercy's body appeared to be healthy and full of **blood,** and the body was turned sideways in the **coffin.** They concluded that Mercy was a vampire, and therefore, her heart was cut out and burned before the body was reburied. The ashes were dissolved in medicine and given to Edwin. It did not help, however, and he died soon afterward. Mercy's body remains buried in the cemetery behind the Chestnut Hill Baptist Church in Exeter, and some local residents still think of her as the town's vampire.

George R. Stetson, the first scholar to examine the stories, noted, "In New England the vampire superstition is unknown by its proper name. It is there believed that consumption is not a physical but a spiritual disease, obsession, or visitation; that as long as the body of a dead consumptive relative has blood in its heart it is proof that an occult influence steals from it for death and is at work draining the blood of the living into the heart of the dead and causing its rapid decline." John L. Vellutini, editor of the *Journal of Vampirology*, has done the most complete examination of the accounts and has made a number of pertinent observations on these cases. Like Stetson, he found that "vampirism" was not used in the earlier accounts to describe the actions against the corpses. The subject of vampirism was seemingly added into the accounts by later writers, especially journalists and local historians. Thus, by the time of the Mercy Brown case in 1892, vampirism was being used as a label to describe such incidents.

Psychic Vampirism in New England: As early as 1871, pioneer anthropologist Edward B. Tyler, in his work *Primitive Culture*, proposed a definition of vampirism, possibly with the New England cases in mind. Tyler wrote, "Vampires are not mere creations of groundless fancy, but causes conceived in spiritual form to account for specific facts of wasting disease." In this interpretation, vampirism occurred when "the soul of a dead man goes out from its buried corpse and sucks the blood of living men. The **victim** becomes thin, languid, bloodless, and, falling into rapid decline, dies." He further noted, "The corpse thus supplied by its returning soul with blood, is imagined to remain unnaturally fresh and supple and ruddy." Tyler's definition of vampirism was close to what had become known as **psychic vampirism.** It was almost identical to the definition proposed by the French psychical researcher **Z. J. Piérart** during the 1860s that was popular in occult circles for the rest of the 1800s. It differed radically from the idea of the

eastern European vampire, which was believed to be a revived corpse that attacked living people from whom it sucked the blood.

The belief, discovered by Stetson, underlying the practice of removing and burning the heart of a deceased tubercular patient could properly be described as a form of psychic vampirism. Vellutini also observed that no belief in vampires (that is, the resuscitated corpse of eastern European vampire lore) was ever present in the belief system of New England.

The practice of attacking the corpses of dead tubercular patients disappeared in the early twentieth century, due, no doubt, to the discovery of the cause and then the cure of tuberculosis. Periodically, accounts of the New England cases were rediscovered and published. As recently as 1993, Paul S. Sledzik of the National Museum of Health and Medicine reported on his examination of a cemetery near Griswold, Connecticut, of corpses that showed signs of tuberculosis, which had been mutilated in the nineteenth century.

Sources:

"Early New Englanders Ritually 'Killed' Corpses, Experts Say." *New York Times* (October 31, 1993): 1.

Stetson, George R. "The Animistic Vampire in New England." *The American Anthropologist* 9, 1 (January 1896): 1–13.

Tyler, Edward B. *Primitive Culture*. 2 vols. 1871. 4th ed. London: John Murray, 1903.

Vellutini, John L. "The Myth of the New England Vampire." *Journal of Vampirology* 7, 1 (1990): 2–21.

Anarchs *see: Vampire: The Eternal Struggle*

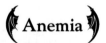

Anemia

Anemia is a disease of the **blood** that has come, in some quarters, to be associated with vampirism. Anemia is caused by a reduction of either red blood cells or hemoglobin (the oxygen-carrying pigment of the cells) relative to the other ingredients in the blood. The symptoms include a pale complexion, fatigue, and in its more extreme instances, fainting spells. All are symptoms usually associated with a vampire attack. In **Bram Stoker**'s novel, *Dracula* **(1897)**, during the early stages of **Lucy Westenra**'s illness, Dr. **John Seward** hypothesized that possibly she was suffering from anemia. He later concluded that she was not suffering from the loss of red blood cells, but from the loss of whole blood. Dr. **Abraham Van Helsing** agreed with his friend, "I have made careful examination, but there is no functional cause. With you I agree that there has been much blood lost; it has been, but is not. But the conditions of her are in no way anemic." (Chapter 9) Thus, the association of anemia and vampirism was dismissed.

Angel

The successful 1997 **television** series, *Buffy the Vampire Slayer*, introduced several new vampire characters as objects of the Slayer's deadly intentions. However, one of the vampires proved distinctive, Angel or Angelus (David Boreanaz). He was young and handsome. He appeared to be only a few years older than vampire slayer **Buffy**

Summers (Sarah Michelle Geller), but in fact was some 240 years old. After an intense but doomed attempt to have a relationship with Buffy, he left for Los Angeles and for five years was head of his own detective agency, searching for redemption.

Angel was born as Liam in 1727, in Galway, **Ireland**, the son of a cloth merchant. Living a life in the taverns, he eventually met a woman named Darla (Julie Benz) who turned out to be a vampire. She sired him and as a vampire he took the name Angelus, a reference to his reputation as a vicious monster with an angelic face. He spent the first decades as a vampire in Europe. He killed freely, like other vampires, lacking any conscience. Early victims included his own family and neighbors. His search for further **victims** eventually led him to eastern Europe. In 1898, Angelus slew the favorite daughter of a tribe of Romanian **Gypsies**. In retaliation, the Kalderash clan cursed him by restoring his human soul, thus afflicting him with a conscience and condemning him to an eternity of remorse for the many people he had killed as Angelus. From that time forward, in spite of the **blood** lust, he found himself unable to feed on a human being. He changed his name from Angelus to Angel, and shortly thereafter, he moved to **America**. He lived alone and shunned the company of other vampires.

Angel found his way to the California town of Sunnydale in the mid-1990s, where he renewed his acquaintance with some old friends, Darla and The Master. He refused the offer of The Master to return to the fold. In the meantime Angel took a liking to Buffy and made himself her self-appointed guardian, warning and protecting her. One evening, as three vampires sent by the Master attacked Buffy, Angel helped defeat them. His intervention warned her of the Master's initial attempt to establish himself in Sunnydale, taking advantage of a particular moment each century, the Harvest. Later, he again came to her aid and was injured. Buffy found herself falling in love with him, as she cared for his wounds.

Angel soon had to confront two new vampires who arrived in Sunnydale to fill the vacuum caused by the death of the Master: Drusilla, whom he had driven mad and sired; and **Spike** (James Marsters), whom Drusilla (Juliet Landau) had sired.

While Buffy was concentrating on Spike and Drusilla, Angel placed his ability to feel human emotion in jeopardy when he and Buffy shared an intimate moment. The result was disastrous; Angel lost his soul (conscience) and reverted to his previous persona of Angelus. As the second season ended, Buffy now realized that she had to destroy the evil vampire with whom she had fallen in love, stabs him with a sword, and sends him to the hell realms.

He returned the next season after what had been a century in hell-time and spent much of the season readjusting to life as Angel again. He recovered and won everyone's trust in time to fight the last battle on Buffy's graduation day. But knowing that his relationship with Buffy was doomed, he withdrew from Sunnydale (and the *Buffy the Vampire Slayer* show and moved to Los Angeles.

Angel's further adventures would continue on his own show, called simply *Angel*, which finds him in Los Angeles fighting evil, including his fellow vampires, but trying to find some means of ridding himself of his load of guilt, balancing the ledger of his life that now weighed against him with the many people he has killed, and looking for some possible future redemption. Meanwhile, as he moves through the city, he runs into **Cordelia Chase**, one of Buffy's classmates who had joined her circle of vampire fighters,

but who was in Los Angeles unsuccessfully pursuing an acting/modeling career and broke. She talks her way into a job by convincing Angel to form a detective agency to give a business-like structure to his activities, as well as provide an income.

They are initially joined at Angel Investigations by Doyle, a half-demon with the ability to have visions of people in distress and in need of their services. Doyle also supplies a connection to "The powers that be," an ancient being who operated from a different dimension, and who, as far as they have the ability (which is strictly limited), guides humanity in goodness. When Doyle is killed, he passes his powers to Cordelia. Angel Investigations is subsequently joined by former watcher Wesley Wyndam-Pryce (Alexis Denisof), now describing himself as a "rogue demon hunter," and the street-wise demon fighter, Charles Gunn (J. August Richards). They are also assisted by demon and karaoke bar-owner Lorne (Andy Hallett), whose major ability is sensing the futures of people when they sing for him.

Emerging as the major enemy opposing Angel Investigations is the large law firm of Wolfram & Hart, a powerful international law firm, that is actually a front organization for a demonic cabal known as the Wolf, Ram, and Hart, who now appear as the firm's Senior Partners. Among the first actions against Angel is sending the rogue vampire slayer, over whom Wesley had watched, Faith (Eliza Dushku) to kill Angel. She is defeated and under Angel's influence begins her own redemptive process. Along the way, the team enters into another dimension where they encounter psychically wounded Fred, who eventually joins their team adding her genius level intellect.

Angel's life takes a new direction when Darla resurfaces, pregnant with what proves to be their son Connor. Soon after his birth, however, Connor is stolen by Angel's old enemy Holtz who takes Connor into the hell dimension where he is raised to think that Angel is completely evil. When they return, with Connor now a young man, Holtz commits suicide in such a way it appears Angel has murdered him. Angel has now to attempt a reconciliation with his estranged son, deal with a possessed Cordelia who has lost her memory, and a powerful Beast creature who seems beyond him and his team. In order to kill the latter, he has to relinquish his soul for a time and revert to his Angelus persona.

To deal with Connor, he makes a deal with Wolfram & Hart to take over their offices in Los Angeles. In return Connor's memories are erased and he is placed with a normal family. Cordelia was finally freed from the evil entity Jasmine who had possessed her, but immediately fell into a coma. She revived only for a short time before dying, though she later reappeared as a spirit entity. After the final battle in Sunnydale that left only a crater where the city had one existed, Spike survived as a spirit who popped up at Wolfram & Hart to join the fight against evil. He finally gets his body back. Once he and Angel resolve their jealousies over Buffy, they become staunch allies.

In the end, Angel comes to see that he cannot stop the forces of evil represented by Wolfram & Hart, but he can have a temporary victory by severing the Senior Partners' hold on Earth. He and his remaining team assassinate the members of the Circle of the Black Thorn, the group through which the Senior Partners work on Earth. In the process Wesley is killed and Gunn is wounded but manages to make it to the spot behind the Hyperion Hotel in Los Angeles. He joins Angel, Spike, and Illyria (a demon who has taken over Fred's body), for the final battle with the forces the Senior Partners have aligned for their destruction. As the final episode ends they move forward with the words, "Let's go to work."

Angel—The Comic Book: In 1999, Dark Horse Comics, which had the license for the *Buffy the Vampire Slayer* comics, began publishing an *Angel* comic book. Two series appeared before it was discontinued in 2002. Then in 2005, IDW picked up the license and began issuing *Angel* comics as a set of successive miniseries. Then in 2007, creator Joss Whedon authorized a continuation of the story from the *Angel* television show. The story was developed by writer Brian Lynch working with Whedon.

In *Angel: After the Fall,* the battle with the Senior Partners results in the movement of the city of Los Angeles into a hell dimension. In an attempt to deprive him of his strength and immortality when he needed it most, the Senior Partners have also turned Angel into a human, forcing Angel and Wesley to rely on mystical enchantments to provide Angel with at least a measure of his old abilities. He begins to reassemble his team, including Illyria. Lorne helps recruit new friends. In the process, Connor is killed. They defeat the demons that infest Los Angeles, but the city is still the target of the Senior Partners. Angel finally devises a scheme. Knowing that they need him alive, he allows Gunn to kill him. Time began again, they are returned to the spot behind the hotel ready to fight and defeat the forces sent by Wolfram & Hart. Everyone, including Connor, retained their memory of what has occurred and Angel became a hero.

Angel as Cult Phenomenon: Though never as popular as *Buffy the Vampire Slayer,* *Angel* and its characters attained a following of their own, especially in the year after the end of the *Buffy* episodes, when *Angel* continued. Among the most important items indicative of the show's permeation of the popular culture, along with the comic books, were a set of young adult novels some of which, like the *Buffy* novels, were translated into several languages, including German and French. There were also a number of action figures and **trading card** sets. Along with *Buffy, Angel* attracted the attention of the scholarly community as part of the larger Whedonverses. Consideration of the show manifested in a number of academic papers delivered at the various Whedonverses conferences, and at least two books. Spike, who came to rival Angel as the most popular vampire character, bolstered the crossover attention between the two television series. Most of the comic books featuring Spike have been part of the *Angel* comics from IDW.

Angel was portrayed by David Boreanaz. The part was his first big break, though he had earlier had a bit part in one vampire movie, *Macabre Pair of Shorts* (1996). He followed eight years of work on first *Buffy the Vampire Slayer* and then *Angel* with several movies, before starring in the very successful ongoing series, *Bones,* beginning in 2005. He has been the subject of an annual wall calendar since 1999.

Sources:

Abbott, Stacey, ed. *Reading Angel: The TV Spin-off with a Soul.* London: I. B. Tauris, 2005. 265 pp.

Golden, Christopher, and Nancy Holder. *Buffy the Vampire Slayer: The Watcher's Guide.* New York: Pocket Books, 1998. 298 pp.

Holder, Nancy, with Jeff Mariotte and Maryelizabeth Hart. *Angel: The Casefiles. Vol. 1.* New York: Simon Pulse, 2002. 405 pp.

Ruditis, Paul. *Buffy the Vampire Slayer: The Watcher's Guide. Volume 3.* New York: Simon Spotlight, 2004. 359 pp.

Stafford, Nikki. *Once Bitten: An Unofficial Guide to the World of Angel.* Toronto: ECW Press, 2004. 438 pp.

Topping, Keith. *Hollywood Vampire: A Revised and Updated Unofficial and Unauthorized Guide to Angel.* London: Virgin, 2001. 280 pp.

Yeffeth, Glenn, ed. *Five Seasons of Angel: Science Fiction and Fantasy Writers Discuss Their Favorite Vampire*. Dallas, TX: Benbella Books, 2004. 216 pp.

Angélique *see:* Bouchard, Angélique

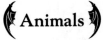

Animals

The vampire's relationship to the animal kingdom is manifested in its ability to achieve **transformation** into various animal shapes; its command over the animal kingdom, especially the rat, the owl, the **bat**, the moth, the fox, and the wolf; and to a lesser extent its prey upon animals for food. Also, on rare occasions, animal vampires have been reported.

Animals in Vampire Folklore: In the older folklore, the vampire's command of animals or the ability to transform into animals was a minimal element at best. However, the vampire was often associated with other creatures, such as **werewolves**, who were defined by their ability to transform themselves. Among the vampires who did change into animals were the *chiang-shih* vampires of **China**, who could transform into wolves.

More importantly, the vampire, especially in western Europe, saw the animal world as a food supply and would often attack a village's cattle herd and suck the animals' **blood**. Sudden, unexpected, and unexplained deaths of cattle would often be attributed to vampires. For example, Agnes Murgoci noted that one of the first tests in determining if a recently deceased man had become a vampire would be the sudden death of his livestock. Sir James Frazer observed that in **Bulgaria**, where the cattle suffered from frequent vampire attacks, people treated such attacks by having their herds pass between two bonfires constructed at a nearby crossroads known to be frequented by wolves. Afterward, the coals from the bonfires were used to relight the fires in the village. In **Japan**, the vampire kappa lived at the water's edge and would attack cows and horses and try to drag them into the **water**.

A few animals, particularly cats and horses, were also believed to have a special relationship to vampires. It was thought in many Eastern European countries that if one allowed an animal such as a cat to jump over the corpse of a dead person prior to burial, the person would return as a vampire. (This belief emphasized the necessity of the deceased's loved ones to properly mourn, prepare, and care for the body.) The horse, on the other hand, was frequently used to locate a vampire. Brought to the graveyard, the horse would be led around various graves in the belief that it would hesitate and refuse to cross over the body of a vampire.

Dracula's Animals: Dracula's command of the animal kingdom appeared quite early in **Bram Stoker's** novel. In the first chapter of *Dracula* (1897), even before **Jonathan Harker** arrived at **Castle Dracula**, the carriage he was traveling in was suddenly surrounded by an intimidating ring of wolves. Just as suddenly, the driver (later shown to be Dracula in disguise) dismissed the wolves with a wave of his arm. After he arrived at the castle and began to familiarize himself with the Count, Harker noticed the howling of the wolves. Dracula then spoke one of his most memorable lines: "Listen to them—the children of the night. What **music** they make." Later, in **London**, while

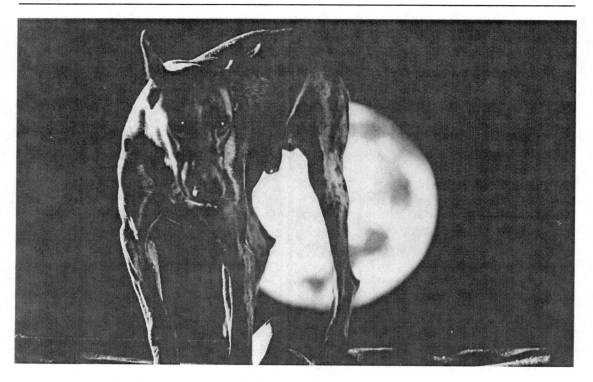

Vampires can turn into animals, or animals can even be vampires, as was the case in the film *Dracula's Dog*.

Dracula was continuing his attack upon **Lucy Westenra**, he called Bersicker, a wolf from the local zoo, to his aid. Bersicker assisted Dracula by breaking the window at the Westenra home to give Dracula a means of entrance.

Abraham Van Helsing warned the men who would finally track Dracula and kill him that Dracula could not only alter the **weather**, but that he also could "command the meaner things; the rat, and the owl, and the bat—the moth, and the fox, and the wolf." The men discovered the truth of his words for themselves when they broke into Dracula's residence, **Carfax**, and were suddenly set upon by thousands of rats.

Transformation: Stoker first hinted at Dracula's ability to transform himself into animal form when the imprisoned Harker looked out of his window to see Dracula crawling down the castle wall. "What manner of man is this, or what manner of creature is it in the semblance of man?" Harker wondered (chapter 3). Dracula traveled to England aboard a ship, the *Demeter*, which he caused to be wrecked upon the shore at **Whitby**. Dracula escaped the wreckage in the form of a dog. Through the rest of the novel Dracula made few appearances, however, he constantly hovered in the background in the form of a bat. Observed outside of **R. N. Renfield**'s window at the asylum, **Dr. John Seward** noted the strange behavior of a large bat. "Bats usually wheel and flit about, but this one seemed to go straight on, as if it knew where it was bound for or had some intention of its own" (chapter 11).

Stoker's characters were, of course, familiar with the vampire bats of Central and **South America** and understood the vampire's close association with the bat. At one point Seward examined one of the children bitten by Lucy who had been admitted to a hospital. The doctor attending the boy hypothesized that the wounds on his neck were caused by a bat. "'Out of so many harmless ones,' he said, 'there may be some wild specimen from the south of a more malignant species. Some sailor may have brought one home, and it managed to escape; or even from some Zoological Gardens a young one may have got loose, or one be bred there from a vampire'" (chapter 15).

Animals and the Contemporary Vampire Myth: While there has been, as a whole, less attention paid to animals in the *Dracula* movies and stage plays, the command of animals is an essential element in the alteration of the plot in the first of the Dracula movies, *Nosferatu, Eine Symphonie des Grauens.* Building upon Dracula's command of the rats that so bedeviled Van Helsing and the men as they entered Carfax, **Graf Orlock**, the Dracula character in *Nosferatu* commanded plague-bearing rats. He arrived at Bremen with the rats, and the pestilence that accompanied them was a sign of the vampire's presence. The death of the vampire brought an end to the plague.

The vampire's ability to transform into different forms, especially that of a bat, has remained an essential element to most modern vampire movies and novels. The improvement of special effects in movies has allowed for more lifelike transformations to be depicted. Special effects in the recent **Bram Stoker's Dracula** were among the movie's more impressive features. There has been a noticeable trend, however, to strip the vampire of its less believable qualities. Both **Anne Rice** and **Chelsea Quinn Yarbro**, for example, have denied their vampires the ability to transform themselves out of human shape, though they retain other supernatural abilities.

During the last generation, as the vampire became the hero or at least the sympathetic figure with whom the reader identified, the question of the vampire feeding off of humans rose to the fore. If a vampire renounces the taking of blood from human **victims**, there are few nutritional options remaining: purchasing blood from various sources, finding willing donors, artificial blood substitutes, or animals. Animals were the most frequently chosen objects, and novels frequently include reflections on the adequacy of animal blood. In Rice's **Interview with the Vampire**, Louis was unable to bring himself to attack a human for the first four years of his vampiric existence and lived off the blood of rats and other animals.

Animal Vampires: On occasion, quite apart from stories of vampires changing into animal forms, stories of vampire animals have surfaced. As early as 1810, stories came from the borderland between England and Scotland of sheep, sometimes as many as 10 a night, having their jugular vein cut and their blood drained. The best known incident of a similar occurrence, reported by Charles Fort, concerned a rash of sheep killings near Caven, **Ireland**, in 1874. Some 42 instances of sheep having their throats cut and blood drained (but no flesh consumed) had been noted. Near the dead sheep, footprints of a dog-like animal were found. Finally a dog, seemingly the offending animal, was shot. At that point the affair should have ended. However, the sheep kept dying and more dogs were shot. Then reports began to come in from Limerick, more than 100 miles away. Accounts ended in both communities without any final resolution. In 1905, a similar spat of sheep killings occurred in England near Badminton in Glouces-

ter. Such incidents have become part of the UFO lore of the last generation in North America. Another famous event involving possible animal vampires was the cutting of the throat of Snippy the horse in Colorado in September 1967.

Several novels have featured animal vampires, the most famous being Ken Johnson's *Hounds of Dracula* (1977) (also released as *Dracula's Dog*), that was made into the movie, *Zoltan: Hound of Dracula*. As a whole, however, animals, overwhelmingly dogs, such as were seen in the 2007 movie *I Am Legend*, have played secondary and supportive roles in vampire novels and movies. Youthful vampire readers may be familiar with the vampire rabbit **Bunnicula**, the subject of a host of books by James Howe, and the vampire duck, **Count Duckula**, star of an animated **television** series and a Marvel **comic book**. Both Bunnicula and Count Duckula were vegetarians.

The popularity of the vampire in the popular culture has led to attempts to identify animals which, like vampire bats, leeches, and mosquitoes, have vampirelike characteristics. The lists include numerous insects who live partly on blood. Thus, the discovery of a new blood-sucking fish in the Amazon in 2005 made headlines. The new fish is closely related to the candiru, a previously known parasitic, blood-sucking species of catfish that burrows into the gills of other fish and after attaching itself with spines, sucks its blood. The most famous new species with vampirelike qualities is the illusive **chupacabra**, that has been frequently reported since the 1990s but whose existence is still very much in doubt.

Sources:

Fort, Charles. *Lo!*. London: V. Gollancz, 1931. 351 pp. Rept. New York: Ace Books, 1931, 1941.

Johnson, Ken. *Hounds of Dracula*. New York: New American Library, 1977. Reprinted as *Zoltan: Hound of Dracula*. London: Everest Books, 1977. Reprinted as *Dracula's Dog*. New York: New American Library, 1977.

Keel, John A. *Strange Creatures from Time and Space*. Greenwich, CT: Fawcett Publications, 1970.

Schutt, Bill. *Dark Banquet: Blood and the Curious Lives of Blood-Feeding Creatures*. New York: Harmony Books, 2008.

Anne Rice's Vampire Lestat Fan Club *see* Vampire Fandom: United States

Appearance of a Vampire

Any discussion of the appearance of the vampire must take into account the several vampire types. The contemporary vampire of the 1980s and 1990s has shown a distinct trend toward a normal appearance that allows them to completely fit in with human society and move about undetected. Such modern vampires have almost no distinguishing **characteristics** with the exception of **fangs** (extended canine teeth), which may be retractable and show only when the vampire is feeding. As such, the contemporary vampire harks back to the vampire characters of the pre-**Dracula** literary vampires. There was little in the appearance of Geraldine, **Lord Ruthven**, *Varney the Vampyre*, or **Carmilla** to distinguish them from their contemporaries (though Varney had prominent fangs).

During the last generation, vampire novelists have occasionally sought some way to make the vampire's appearance distinctive while keeping them able to blend into society. **Anne Rice** describes the vampires skin as pale and reflective though possibly the

Bela Lugosi (seen here in *Mark of the Vampire*) is most responsible for developing the stereotypical appearance of a vampire.

most notable alteration are the fingernails that look like they were made of glass. **Stephenie Meyer**, in her *Twilight* series, posits vampires who have a heightened even supernatural beauty. While Rice's vampires are beautiful, because of the tendency of older vampires to turn humans whom they find attractive and with whom they have fallen in love, Meyer suggests that becoming a vampire enhances the level of beauty in the person who is turned. Their skin becomes flawless and takes on a texture and feel resembling marble. If exposed to **sunlight**; it will sparkle.

In the television series ***Buffy the Vampire Slayer*** and its spinoff *Angel*, the vampires usually appeared just as they had in real life. Only when aroused, angry, or about to feed do they take on a distinctive appearance. As was the case in the 1990s television series ***Forever Knight***, the vampires in *Buffy* for a brief time change dramatically and horrifically. They are said to put on their "game face." The eyes change color, the face distorts, and the fangs come out of hiding. They are obviously something different.

In spite of the changes introduced by *Forever Knight, Buffy the Vampire Slayer,* and the writings of Anne Rice and Stephenie Meyer, the contemporary vampire is still largely based on the dominant figure of Dracula as developed for the stage by **Hamilton Deane** and especially as portrayed by **Bela Lugosi**. Hamilton Deane must be credited with the domestication of Dracula and making him an acceptable attendee at the evening activities of Victorian British society. Deane's Dracula donned evening clothes and an **opera** cape with a high collar.

Bela Lugosi in the movie **Dracula (1931)** confirmed Deane's image of the vampire in popular culture and added to it. He gave Dracula an eastern European accent and a swept-back, slicked-down hairdo with a prominent widow's peak. In the **Horror of Dracula** (1968), **Christopher Lee** added the final prominent feature to Dracula's appearance, the fangs. Prior to Lee the vampire had no fangs, at least no visible ones. Lee, the first prominent vampire in Technicolor, also gave Dracula a set of red eyes, which to a lesser extent has become a standard (though by no means unanimous) aspect of the vampire's appearance, especially in motion pictures. Since Lee, the image of the vampire in popular culture has been set. The fangs, the cape, and to a lesser extent, the evening clothes, the red eyes, and the widow's peak now quickly convey the idea that a person is a vampire. The use of these definitive signs of a vampire's appearance is most evident on greeting cards and the artwork on the cover of vampire novels and **comic books**.

This modern image of the vampire, with the exception of the extended canine teeth, varies considerably from both that of Dracula, as presented in the original novel of **Bram Stoker**, and the vampire of folklore. The latter, at least in its eastern European incarnation, was a corpse, but a corpse notable for several uncorpselike characteristics. Its body might be bloated and extended so that the skin was tight like a drum. It would have extended **fingernails** that had grown since its burial. It would be dressed in burial clothes. It would stink of death. The ends of its appendages might show signs of having been eaten away. In appearance the folkloric vampire was horrible, not so much because it was monstrous, but because of its disgusting semi-decayed nature.

Between the folklore vampire and the contemporary vampire of popular culture lies the Dracula of Bram Stoker's novel. He was described in some detail in the second chapter of the book—he was dressed in black clothes; his hair was profuse and his eyebrows massive and bushy; he had a heavy moustache; his skin was pale; he had hair in the palm of his hand and long extended fingernails. Most noticeable were the brilliant extended canines that protruded over his lower lips when the mouth was closed. His eyes were blue, though they flashed red when he was angry or upset. He was of mature years, though he got younger as the novel proceeded. **John Carradine**'s stage productions of *Dracula* in the 1950s were probably closest to Dracula as he appeared in the novel.

Armand

Armand is a 400-year-old, teenaged-looking vampire and major character in "The Vampire Chronicles" of **Anne Rice**. He is introduced in *Interview with the Vam-*

pire where in the years immediately prior to the French revolution he headed a group of vampires who performed at the Theater of the Vampires in Paris. He first appeared on the streets of Paris after learning of the presence of fellow vampires Louis and Claudia in the city. He broke up a fight between Louis and one of the other vampires, whom he had sent to present the two with an invitation to the theater. After the performance the following evening, he and Louis, who were strongly attracted to each other, had a conversation concerning God and the meaning of existence, during which Louis was forced to confront the meaninglessness of life.

Louis also had to deal with Claudia's jealously over his obvious infatuation with Armand and her own dilemma of being trapped in the body of a child. His acknowledgment of his feelings for Armand freed him to create a companion for Claudia, in the older woman Madeleine, a dollmaker. Armand's feelings for him saved Louis's life when he, Madeleine, and Claudia were taken captive by the Parisian vampires who executed Claudia and Madeleine. The vampires had confined Louis in a **coffin**, but Armand released him. In return for the favor, an angry Louis warned Armand that he was about to vent his anger. Thus Armand escaped when Louis burned the theater, killing the vampires caught in its confines.

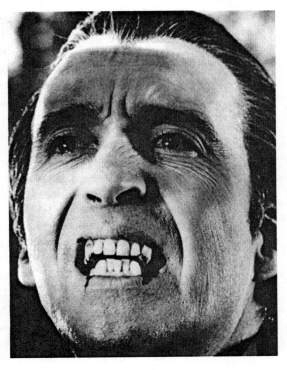

Christopher Lee, shown here in *Taste the Blood of Dracula,* was responsible for popularizing the idea that vampires have fangs.

In the second volume of the Chronicles, *The Vampire Lestat,* Armand's background is laid out. He was born in Southern **Russia** but as a child his family was taken prisoner by Tartars and sold into slavery in Constantinople. He was bought by a vampire named Marius and taken to Venice. Marius used him as a model for a painting, *The Temptation of Amedeo.* Armand was only 17 years old when Marius made him a vampire. Through the centuries he retained his youthful appearance with auburn hair, brown eyes, and a beautiful face. When Marius's home was invaded by a group of Satanists, Armand was inducted into their coven and went on to become an accomplished Satanist leader. He moved out across Europe gathering potential Satanists into new covens. Eventually he settled in Paris as the head of a coven. Over the years he had fed regularly, and perfected a technique of drawing people with a death wish to him, but kept several matters to himself. He never made another vampire. He also had lost (or never possessed) any belief in God or **Satan**.

He had been in Paris a century when **Lestat** arrived, and as a new vampire encountered Armand and his coven. Attempts to bring Lestat into the coven resulted in its being destroyed and most of their number being killed. Eventually, Lestat bought and gave them the theater, hence when they discovered that Claudia had attempted to kill Lestat, they were particularly incensed.

After Louis burned the theater, he and Armand traveled the world together. They lived together in New York City for many years, only returning to **New Orleans** in the mid-1970s. A short time later, they went their separate ways.

After Louis gave the interview that became the book, *Interview with the Vampire*, Daniel Molloy, the interviewer, came to New Orleans looking for Lestat but found Armand instead. He developed a relationship with Armand, but was frustrated as Armand would come and go at will leaving Daniel begging Armand to give him the Dark Gift (**transformation** into a vampire). Through Daniel, Armand learned about the twentieth century, and finally decided to leave his old ways behind. He became obsessed with new technological gadgets from food blenders to television. He quickly made a fortune and built a fantasy shopping entertainment complex near Miami called the Night Island.

While he refused to make Daniel a vampire, Armand did give Daniel an amulet that contained a vial of his **blood**. If ever he was in danger from other vampires, he was to break the vial and drink it. They would feel Armand's power and stay away from him. However, Armand's continued refusal to make him a vampire was a constant source of conflict. Daniel left and allowed his life to degenerate. Finally, in 1985, Armand reconnected with his disparate young lover.

In 1985 there was crisis in the vampire community. Around the world, vampires were being killed. It was the work of Akasha, the awakened primal vampire, but Armand was not yet aware of her activity. Through his clairvoyance, Daniel perceived Akasha as the name of the new evil. In the face of the threatening situation, Armand broke down and made Daniel a vampire, the only time he had transformed anyone.

After the final confrontation with Akasha, the surviving vampires gathered at Night Island to recoup, but then go their separate ways. Several years later Armand went to New Orleans to meet Lestat, about whom he had developed some concern. He met his old friend as Lestat was about to embark on his adventure into heaven and hell. He was still around when Lestat returned. Lestat again destroyed Armand's worldview with his story of the great beyond. The religious feelings that welled-up inside him led him to commit **suicide** by exposure to the sun. Several other vampires imitated his action.

In the vampire world dying is often not the end, and such was the case with Armand. In Rice's later book, *The Vampire Armand*, we learn that his suicide attempt was a failure, though he was badly burned in the process. He is eventually rescued by two children, Benji and Sybelle, whom he came to love and with whom he resided. To his chagrin, Marius turned the pair into vampires, blunting Armand's hope that they have a full normal life.

Sources:

Ramsland, Katherine. *The Vampire Companion: The Official Guide to Anne Rice's The Vampire Chronicles.* New York: Ballantine Books, 1993. 507 pp.

Rice, Anne. *Interview with the Vampire.* New York: Alfred A. Knopf, 1976. 372 pp. Rept. New York: Ballantine, 1979. 346 pp.

———. *Memnoch the Devil.* New York: Alfred A. Knopf, 1994. 354 pp. Rept. New York: Ballantine Books, 1995. 434 pp.

———. *The Queen of the Damned.* New York: Alfred A. Knopf, 1988. 448 pp. Rept. New York: Ballantine Books, 1989. 491 pp.

———. *The Vampire Armand.* New York: Alfred A. Knopf, 1989. 388 pp.

————. *The Vampire Lestat.* New York: Alfred A. Knopf, 1985. 481 pp. Rept. New York: Ballantine Books, 1986. 550 pp.

Armenia, Vampires in

Armenia is an ancient land situated between Turkey and **Russia**. It was the first land to make **Christianity** its state religion. The Armenian church is similar to the Eastern Orthodox churches, but did not follow the development of Orthodox theology through the fifth to seventh centuries. Late in the nineteenth century, Armenia was the location of a number of massacres by occupying Turkish soldiers. Throughout most of the twentieth century it was a part of the Soviet Union until that country broke up in the early 1990s.

Little has been written about vampirism in Armenia. Its place in vampire history is due to an account in an 1854 text by Baron August von Haxthausen that was mentioned by **Montague Summers**. Von Haxthausen visited Mount Ararat in the Caucasians. According to local legend there was a vampire, *Dakhanavar*, who protected the valleys in the area from intruders. He attacked travelers in the night and sucked the **blood** from people's feet. He was outwitted by two men who heard of the vampire's habits and slept with their feet under the other's head. The vampire, frustrated by encountering a creature that seemed to have two heads and no feet, ran away and was never heard of again.

Sources:

Summers, Montague. *The Vampire in Europe.* London: Routledge, Kegan Paul, Trench, Trubner & Co., 1929. 329 pp. Rept. New Hyde Park, NY: University Press, 1961. 329 pp.

von Haxthausen, August. *Transcaucasia.* London: Chapman and Hall, 1854. 448 pp.

Asasabonsam *see:* Africa, Vampires in

Asema *see:* South America, Vampires in

Ashley, Amanda

Amanda Ashley is the pseudonym of writer Madeline Baker. Baker was born, raised, married and still resides in southern California. Her first books were Western historical romances written under her real name. At one point, her editor asked if she would like to try her hand at a paranormal story. She produced a short story, "Masquerade" for an anthology, *The Topaz Man Favorites, Secrets of the Heart.* She found she liked vampires, so she chose a pseudonym and got to work. Having read a few vampire books, she came to see the potential of vampires as great heroes with an element of danger built in. In different novels she experimented with a variety of types from the pure hero to the conflicted vampire still struggling to be human. At one point she even played with Elvis Presley as a vampire. Their heroic quality is best seen in their willingness to give up even their immortality for the one woman who can perceive the humanity that resides within their monstrous exterior.

Ashley/Baker was among the pioneers of the contemporary vampire romance novels, though she followed a generation of romance vampire novelists such as Lori Herter,

Florence Stevenson, and the prolific **Daniel Ross**. Of almost a dozen vampire romance titles that appeared in 1995, her book, *Embrace the Night*, and a title by **Linda Lael Miller** rose from the stack. Ashley and Miller began to redefine the field and open the way that numerous later authors tred.

In her first novel, Ashley introduced Gabriel, who through his hundreds of years of existence had yet to solve the problem of loving mortals who aged and died on him and the subsequent loneliness. The novel begins with his love of Sara whom he meets as a child in 1881 and then moves a hundred years into the future when he meets a new Sarah to whom he is drawn . The magnetic Gabriel would become the model for a number of vampires that appeared after him.

Much to the delight of her readers, she would frequently revisit the theme of the lonely vampire searching for eternal love in the present but always haunted by his knowledge that while his life goes on, the best of love will die. Her vampires began as rather traditional, especially in their need for darkness during the daylight hours, but as she wrote more and more she varied the rules. Vincent Cordova, the vampire of *Night's Touch*, fathers two children (twins). They are human even though their mother is the daughter of a vampire couple. Other vampires have become daywalkers and some see their reflections in **mirrors.** Ashley has survived the ups and downs of the vampire book market, and even with more than a dozen vampire titles on the shelves, she has no plans to stop—with several new titles in the pipeline. She began her career with the Love Spell imprint of Dorchester Publishing, switching to Zebra Books at the much larger Kensington Publishing Corporation in 2004. All of her vampire titles remain in print (as of 2009).

Sources:

Ashley, Amanda (pseudonym of Madeline Baker). *After Sundown*. New York: Zebra Books/Kensington Publishing, 2004. 384 pp.

———. *A Darker Dream*. New York: Love Spell, 1997. 392 pp.

———. *Dead Perfect*. New York: Zebra Books/Kensington Publishing, 2008. 384 pp.

———. *Dead Sexy*. Zebra Books: New York, 2007. 362 pp.

———. *Deeper Than the Night*. New York: Love Spell, 1996. 391 pp.

———. *Desire After Dark*. New York: Zebra Books,/Kensington Publishing, 2006.

———. *Embrace the Night*. New York: Love Spell, 1995. 441 pp.

———. *Midnight Embrace*. New York: Love Spell, 2002. 378 pp.

———. *Night's Kiss*. New York: Zebra Books/Kensington Publishing, 2005. 345 pp.

———. *Night's Master*. New York: Zebra Books/Kensington Publishing, 2008. 377 pp.

———. *Night's Pleasure*. New York: Zebra Books/Kensington Publishing, 2009. 384 pp.

———. *Night's Touch*. New York: Zebra Books/Kensington Publishing, 2007. 380 pp.

———. *Shades of Gray*. New York: Love Spell, 1998. 390 pp.

———. *Sunlight/Moonlight*. New York: Love Spell, 1997. 394 pp.

———. *A Whisper of Eternity*. New York: Zebra Books,/Kensington Publishing, 2004. 352 pp.

Ashley, Amanda, Christine Feehan, and Ronda Thompson. *After Twilight*. New York: Lobe Spell, 2001. 395 pp.

Ashley, Amanda. et al. *Midnight Pleasures*. New York: St. Martin's Paperbacks, 2003. 374 pp.

Blake, Jennifer, Madeline Baker, et al. *Topaz Man Favorites: Secrets of the Heart: Five Irresistible Love Stories*. New York: Topaz, 1994. 381 pp.

Sherida, Barbara. "Interview with Amanda Ashley." Posted at http://paranormalromance.org/AmandaAshley.htm. Accessed on April 10, 2010.

Asiman *see:* Africa, Vampires in

Aspen *see:* Stake

Assamite Vampire Clan *see: Vampire: The Eternal Struggle*

Assyria, Vampires in *see:* Babylon and Assyria, Vampires in Ancient

Aswang *see:* Philippines, Vampires in the

Atlanta Vampire Alliance & Suscitatio Enterprises, LLC

The Atlanta Vampire Alliance is a vampire organization founded in 2005 in Atlanta, Georgia. It describes itself as an alliance of like-minded individuals, including both sanguinarian (those who drink **blood**), and **psychic** (or energy) vampires who work for the progress and education of both the greater and local vampire community. It offers self-identified vampires a respectful environment and promotes serious dialog and continuing education. The organization consults with a wide range of interested outsiders, including members of the media, law enforcement, clergy, and the academic world.

Members of the organization have tried to correct stereotypical images of self-identified vampires and in 2006 in conjunction with their research company Suscitatio Enterprises, LLC, launched a massive two-part survey of the vampire community. This 988 question survey, known as the Vampirism and Energy Work Research Study, was distributed worldwide to people who identified themselves as vampires both on the Internet and offline. Between 2006 and 2009, more than 950 vampires from over 40 countries completed the surveys. The results detailed the reality of vampire existence and what appeared to be a rather mundane community of people who otherwise blended into their larger environment, society, and culture. However, the unusual characteristics revealed by the study include individual vampire activities, higher than normal prevalence rates of certain medical conditions, and a diversity of religious beliefs and practices. The research study results are posted at http://www.suscitatio.com/.

The organization contends that vampirism itself is neither a religion nor a faith-based collective. Members represent a variety of diverse spiritual beliefs or paths across the religious spectrum (although a high percentage follow paths representative of Western Esotericism). The organization also hosts frequent gatherings in the Atlanta area as well as co-sponsors larger conferences of vampires that include such well-known speakers as **Michelle Belanger,** Pam Keesey, and members of the law-enforcement community. The Alliance also participates in the Voices of the Vampire community.

Sources:

Atlanta Vampire Alliance. Posted at http://www.atlantavampirealliance.com/. Accessed on April 10, 2010.

Belanger, Michelle A. *Vampires in Their Own Words: An Anthology of Vampire Voices*. York Beach, ME: Weiser Books, 2007.

Falk, David, and Kiara Falk. "'Predatory Spirituality:' Vampire Religion In America?" *Sacred Tribes Journal* 3, 2 (2008): 102–131. Posted at http://www.sacredtribesjournal.org/index.php?option=com_content&task=view&id=83&Itemid=68. Accessed on April 10, 2010.

Laycock, Joseph. *Vampires Today: The Truth about Modern Vampirism*. Westport, CT: Praeger, 2009. 200 pp.

Nocturnum, Corvis. *Allure of the Vampire: Our Sexual Attraction to the Undead*. Dark Moon Press, 2009. 284 pp.

Steiger, Brad. *Real Vampires, Night Stalkers, and Creatures from the Darkside*. Visible Ink Press, 2009. 287 pp.

Suscitatio Enterprises, LLC. Posted at http://www.suscitatio.com/. Accessed on April 10, 2010.

Williams, DJ. "Contemporary Vampires and (Blood-Red) Leisure: Should We Be Afraid of the Dark?" *Leisure/Loisir* 32, 2 (2008): 513–539.

❨ Australia, Vampires in ❩

Vampires do not play a large part in the folklore of Australia. However, in Aboriginal cultures, there existed the *yara-ma-yha-who*, a vampirelike being. It was described as a little red man, approximately four feet tall, with an exceptionally large head and mouth. It had no teeth and simply swallowed its food whole. Its most distinguishing features, however, were its hands and feet. The tips of the fingers and toes were shaped like the suckers of an octopus.

The *yara-ma-yha-who* lived in the tops of wild fig trees. It did not hunt for food, but waited until unsuspecting **victims** sought shelter in the tree and then dropped on them. The story of the *yara-ma-yha-who* was told to young children who might wander from the tribe, and naughty children were warned that it might come and take them away.

When a person camped under a fig tree, a *yara-ma-yha-who* might jump down and place its hands and feet on the body. It would then drain the **blood** from the victim to the point that the person was left weak and helpless, but rarely enough, at least initially, to cause the victim to die. The creature would later return and consume its meal. It then drank **water** and took a nap. When it awoke, the undigested portion of its meal would be regurgitated. According to the story, the person regurgitated was still alive, and children were advised to offer no resistance should it be their misfortune to meet a *yara-ma-yha-who*. Their chances of survival were better if they let the creature swallow them.

People might be captured on several occasions. Each time, they would grow a little shorter until they were the same size as the *yara-ma-yha-who*. Their skin would first become very smooth and then they would begin to grow hair all over their body. Gradually they were changed into one of the mythical little furry creatures of the forest.

Australian Pop Culture: Quite separate from Aboriginal folklore, the British settlers brought the vampire to Australia in the later nineteenth century. Among the first reprints of *Dracula* (occurring almost simultaneously with the first edition) was the Colonial edition released by Hutchinson that circulated outside England in what were then colonies, including Australia. As Australia developed its own distinctive popular culture, the vampire was present in, for example, the 1950s novellas of Michael Waugh and the 1970s vampire **comic books** of Gerald R. Carr. Outside the country, most note has been taken of several Australian vampire movies, which would include *Barry MacKenzie Holds His Own* (1974), *Thirst* (1979), *Outback Vampires* (1987), *Pandemonium* (1988), *Bloodlust* (1992), *Island of the Vampire Birds* (1999), *Bloodspit* (2002), and *Reign in Darkness* (2002).

Sources:

Ryan, John. *Panel by Panel: An Illustrated History of Australian Comics*. North Melbourne: Cassell Australia, 1979.

Smith, W. Ramsey. *Myths and Legends of the Australian Aboriginals*. New York: Farrar & Rinehart. 356 pp.

Waugh, Michael. *Back from the Dead*. Sydney, Aust.: Cleveland, 1955.

———. *Fangs of the Vampire*. Sydney, Aust.: Cleveland, 1954.

Babylon and Assyria, Vampires in Ancient

During the nineteenth century, the writings of ancient Mesopotamia (the lands between the Tigris and Euphrates River Valleys, present-day Iraq) were discovered and translated. They indicated the development of an elaborate mythology and a universe inhabited by a legion of deities of greater and lesser rank. From this vast pantheon, the closest equivalent of the true vampire in ancient Mesopotamian mythology were the seven evil spirits described in a poem quoted by R. Campbell Thompson that begins with the line, "Seven are they! Seven are they!":

> Spirits that minish the heaven and earth, That minish the land, Spirits that minish the land, Of giant strength, Of giant strength and giant tread, Demons (like raging bulls, great ghosts), Ghosts that break through all houses, Demons that have no shame, Seven are they! Knowing no care, they grind the land like corn; Knowing no mercy they rage against mankind, They spill their **blood** like rain, Devouring their flesh (and) sucking their veins.

> They are demons full of violence, ceaselessly devouring blood.

Montague Summers suggested that vampires had a prominent place in Mesopotamian mythology, beyond that suggested by the belief in the seven spirits. In particular he spoke of the *ekimmu*, the spirit of an unburied person. He based his case on an exploration of the literature concerning the Netherworld, the abode of the dead. The Netherworld was portrayed as a somewhat gloomy place. However, an individual's life there could be considerably improved if at the end of their earthly existence they received a proper, if simple, burial that included the affectionate care of the corpse. At the end of tablet 12 of the famous *Gilgamesh* (or *Gilgamish*) *Epic*, there was an accounting of the various degrees of comfort of the dead. It closed with several couplets concerning the state of the person who died alone and unburied, which Summers quoted as:

The man whose corpse lieth in the desert—Thou and I have often seen such an one—His spirit resteth not in the earth; The spirit hath none to care for it—Thou and I have often seen such an one The dregs of the vessel—the leaving of the feast, And that which is cast into the street are his food.

The key line in this passage was "His spirit resteth not in the earth," which Summers took to mean that the spirits of those who died alone (i.e., the *ekimmu*) could not even enter the Netherworld and thus were condemned to roam the earth. He then connected this passage with other passages concerning the exorcism of ghosts, and quoted at length various texts that enumerated the various ghosts that had been seen. However, the ghosts were of a wide variety, as one text stated:

The evil spirit, the evil demon, the evil ghost, the evil devil, From the earth have come forth; From the underworld into the land of the living they have come forth; In heaven they are unknown On earth they are not understood They neither stand nor sit, Not eat nor drink.

It appeared that Summers confused the issue of revenants and the return of the dead who could become vampires with ghosts of the deceased who might simply haunt the land. The ghosts were plainly noncorporeal—they neither ate nor drank, whereas the dead in the underworld had a form of corporeal existence and enjoyed some meager pleasures. The source of this misunderstanding was an inadequate translation of the last parts of the *Gilgamish Epic*. The line "The spirit resteth not in the earth," was originally translated in such a way as to leave open the possibility of the dead wandering in the world of human habitation. However, more recent translations and a survey of the context of the last couplets of the *Gilgamish Epic* made it clear that the dead who died in the desert uncared for (the *ekimmu*) roamed restlessly not on earth but through the Netherworld. David Ferry's translation, for example, rendered the passage thusly:

And he whose corpse was thrown away unburied? He wanders without rest through the world down there

The One who goes to the Netherworld without leaving behind anyone to mourn for him?

Garbage is what he eats in the Netherworld. No dog would eat the food he has to eat.

Thus while the idea of vampires did exist in Mesopotamia, it was not as prominent as Summers would indicate. Summers should not be overly chastised for his error, however, because even eminent scholar E. A. Wallis Budge made a similar mistake in his brief comments on tablet 12 in 1920:

The last lines of the tablet seem to say that the spirit of the unburied man reposeth both in the earth, and that the spirit of the friendless man wandereth about the street eating the remains of food which are cast out of the cooking pots.

However, neither Budge nor E. Campbell Thompson, whom Summers quoted from directly, made the error of pushing these several texts in the direction of a vampirish interpretation.

Sources:

Ferry, David. *Gilgamesh: A New Rendering in English Verse.* New York: Farrar, Straus, and Giroux, 1992. 99 pp.

George, Andrew R., *The Babylonian Gilgamesh Epic. Introduction, Critical Edition and Cuneiform Texts.* 2 vols. Oxford: Oxford University Press, 2003.

Spence, Lewis. *Myths and Legends of Babylonia and Assyria.* London: G. G. Harrap, 1928. 411 pp.

Summers, Montague. *The Vampire: His Kith and Kin.* London: Routledge, Kegan Paul, Trench, Trubner, & Co., 1928. 356 pp. Rept. New Hyde Park, NY: University Books, 1960. 356 pp.

Thompson, E. Campbell. *The Devils and Evil Spirits of Babylonia.* 2 vols. London: Luzac, 1903–04.

———. *Semitic Magic: Its Origin and Development.* London: Luzac, 1908. 286 pp.

Baker, Roy Ward (1916–)

Roy Ward Baker, a director of vampire movies for **Hammer Films** in the 1970s, was born in London In 1934, he joined Gainsborough Studios as an assistant director. He worked at Gainsborough through the decade, but left in 1940 to become an officer in the British army. While in the service, he directed films for the Army Kinematograph Service. After the war he returned to directing for various studios including 20th Century Fox, where he directed four films in the early 1950s.

In the late 1960s, Baker began to work for Hammer Films, where he directed *The Anniversary, Quatermass and the Pit* (1969), one of the studio's very successful Quatermass series. In 1971, he was assigned the first of several vampire movies that Hammer Films became so well-known for during the 1960s. *The Vampire Lovers* (1970) was the first of the Hammer productions based on **Sheridan Le Fanu**'s story of a female vampire, **"Carmilla"**. Starring **Ingrid Pitt**, it was one of the best of the Hammer productions. Baker was then immediately put to work on the next **Christopher Lee** Dracula movie, *The Scars of Dracula* (1970). It was an original story involving a young man who wandered into **Castle Dracula** only to meet disaster. The man was avenged by his girlfriend and brother, and **Dracula** was finally killed by a bolt of lightning. The film was a commercial success in both England and America and Baker continued to work on other Hammer horror movies such as *Dr. Jekyll and Sister Hyde* (1971).

Baker's last vampire film for Hammer came at a crucial point in the studio's life. The company was in financial trouble and gambled on a project in cooperation with Shaw Brothers, a film company in Hong Kong. The project was a movie that mixed the vampire horror genre with the martial arts movie. Baker was chosen to direct the film variously known as *The Legend of the Seven Golden Vampires* and *The Seven Brothers Meet Dracula*. In the story **Abraham Van Helsing** (played by **Peter Cushing**) traveled to China in search of the elusive Dracula. The crusade to destroy Dracula and his new Chinese vampire allies frequently turned into a martial arts demonstration. Even the combination of Cushing's serious performance and Baker's mature direction could not rescue the unbelievable plot. Rather than saving Hammer, the film helped seal its fate. Warner Bros. refused to release the film to its potential major market in America, and Hammer went into bankruptcy in 1975.

In his post-Hammer period, Baker was called on to direct at least one other vampire/horror movie, *The Monster Club* (1981). The movie, which starred an aging **John**

Carradine as author **Ronald Chetwynd-Hayes,** featured several episodes based on Chetwynd-Hayes's short stories, including one vampire tale. Veteran actor Vincent Price helped Carradine introduce the film's distinct episodes and provided a transition between each. Price played Eramus, one of the few times he played a vampire.

Since retiring in the early 1990s, Baker published his memoirs and has appeared in a number of documentaries discussing his Hammer years, including *The Vampire Interviews* (1994), *100 Years of Horror* (1996), *Inside the Fear Factory* (2003), and most recently *Hammer Horror: A Fan's Guide* (2008).

Sources:

Baker, Roy Ward. *Director's Cut: A Memoir of 60 Years in Film and Television.* London: Reynolds and Hearn, 2000.

Flynn, John L. *Cinematic Vampires.* Jefferson, NC: McFarland and Company, 1992. 320 pp.

Smith, John M., and Tim Caldwell. *The World Encyclopedia of Film.* New York: Galahad Books, 1972. 444 pp.

❨ Balderston, John L(loyd) (1889–1954) ❩

John L. Balderston was the playwright of the American version of *Dracula: The Vampire Play in Three Acts.* He was born on October 22, 1889, in Philadelphia, the son of Mary Alsop and Lloyd Balderston. He attended Columbia University and began a career in journalism in 1911 as the New York correspondent of the *Philadelphia Record.* In 1915, he moved to England and worked as editor for *The Outlook*; from 1923 to 1931 he was the chief London correspondent of the *New York World.*

Balderston authored his first play, *The Genius of the Marne,* in 1919. He followed with *Morality Play for the Leisured Class* (1920), *Tongo* (1924), and *Berkeley Square* (1926). Balderston was still in England in 1927 when producer Horace Liveright attempted to purchase the American dramatic rights to **Dracula** from **Bram Stoker's** widow. Florence Stoker did not like Liveright, who turned to Balderston to assist him in the negotiations. Balderston had become known to Liveright after his play, *Berkeley Square,* a ghost story, became a hit both in London and New York. Balderston secured the rights from Mrs. Stoker, and Liveright then hired him to modernize the stage version of *Dracula* by **Hamilton Deane** that had been playing in England.

Balderston's version of the play was very different from earlier ones. His major changes included combining the characters of **Lucy Westenra** and **Mina Murray** into a single character, Lucy Seward, who became the daughter of the now mature **John Seward.** Originally Seward had been Lucy's young suitor. Lucy's other suitors, **Quincey P. Morris** and **Arthur Holmwood,** completely disappeared from the play.

Published by Samuel French, Balderston's version has become the most influential of the several dramatic versions of the novel. It opened on Broadway on October 5, 1927 and, after 241 performances, went on the road to Los Angeles and San Francisco. It spawned both a midwestern and East Coast touring company. It has subsequently been the version most frequently used when the play has been revived through the years. Its most important revival began in 1977 when it opened for a new run on Broadway. Balderston's version also became the basis of two film versions of *Dracula*—the 1931 version with **Bela Lugosi** and the 1979 version with **Frank Langella.** Langella, it should be noted, starred in the 1977 stage revival.

Balderston went on to work on two more plays: *Red Planet* (1932, with J. E. Hoare), and *Frankenstein* (1932, with Peggy Webling). He also translated the Hungarian play *Farewell Performance* (1935) into English. He retired to Beverly Hills, California, where he died on March 8, 1954.

Balderston's papers are on deposit at the Billy Rose Theatre Division of the New York Public Library for the Performing Arts.

Sources:

Glut, Donald F. *The Dracula Book.* Metuchen, NJ: Scarecrow Press, 1975. 388 pp.

Skal, David J., ed. *Dracula: The Ultimate, Illustrated Edition of the World-Famous Vampire Play.* New York: St. Martin's Press, 1993. 153 pp.

———. *Hollywood Gothic: The Tangled Web of Dracula from Novel to Stage to Screen.* New York: W. W. Norton & Company, 1990. 242 pp.

Who Was Who in the Theatre: 1912–1976. London: Pitman, 1972. Rept. Detroit, MI: Gale Research Inc., 1972.

❦ Baltic States, Vampires in the ❦

The Baltic States of Estonia, Latvia, and Lithuania are three small countries located on the southeastern shore of the Baltic Sea. They share a common religion, Western Christianity (with the Estonians in the Lutheran fold, Lithuanians being Roman Catholics, and Latvians split between them), and have a long history of withstanding the encroachments of their neighbors to the south (Poland) and east (Russia). They are not united ethnically, and are not Slavs. The Estonians were closely related to the Finns. The Latvians descended from the Letts, an ancient Baltic tribe. The Lithuanians derived from the ancient Balts, a tribe that moved into the Niemen River valley from the West. Lithuanian is the oldest of the Baltic languages.

Both Estonia and Latvia were brought into the Roman Catholic fold in the thirteenth century by the Germanic Knights. In the fourteenth century, Lithuania grew into a large kingdom that included Byelorussia and parts of the Ukraine and Russia. During the next centuries, however, it faded in power. All of the Baltic States existed as independent nations between World Wars I and II. They were annexed by Russia during World War II and remained a part of the U.S.S.R. until the disintegration of the Soviet Union in the early 1990s. Historically, the Baltic States have not shown a vital vampiric tradition, although they shared a belief in revenants with their Polish and Russian neighbors.

Twentieth-century Vampires: In this century, the story of one case of vampirism in Lithuania has been frequently repeated since its inclusion by **Montague Summers** in his book *The Vampire in Europe.* The case referred to events in the life of Captain Pokrovsky. In a village near his family estate, Captain Pokrovsky learned of a man who had recently remarried and was growing pale and listless. He reported that the villagers believed him under attack by a vampire. Pokrovsky sent a physician to examine the man. The doctor discovered a loss of **blood** and a small puncture wound on the neck.

There was no other wound that could account for the blood loss. Various efforts did not prevent the wound on his neck from growing larger, and the man eventually died. Following his death, his wife felt compelled for her own safety to leave the community lest she be attacked by the villagers as the vampire who killed her husband.

Sources:

Summers, Montague. *The Vampire in Europe*. London: Routledge, Kegan Paul, Trench, Trubner, & Co., 1929. 329 pp. Rept. New Hyde Park, NY: University Books, 1961. 329 pp.

Bangs, Nina

Romance writer Nina Bangs is the author of multiple series of vampire novels. Bangs was born in San Antonio, Texas, but largely grew up in New Jersey. She attended Rutgers University and, after graduation with a degree in English, became an elementary school teacher. Only after she had spent some years teaching, and reading romance novels in her leisure time, did she try her hand at writing. She was between jobs, with time on her hands when she penned her first book. She had written five book-length manuscripts before selling one of them, *An Original Sin* (1999), to Dorchester Publishing at the end of the 1990s.

After turning a half dozen romance novels, Bang turned her attention to the first vampire series, which came to be called the "Mackenzie Vampires" series. The first volume appeared early in 2004. Each of the four novels pits a female protagonist against one of the Mackenzies, a Scottish vampire line whose unattached males tend to be young, handsome alpha males ready for love and adventure. The first novel finds Blythe, an employee of Ecstasy, Inc. (a company that assists clientele in obtaining happiness), dealing with the seductive Darach Mackenzie, a five-hundred-year-old vampire. Subsequent volumes focus on other couples—human female and vampire male—but bring back characters from the earlier stories.

Just as the second volume of the Mackenzie vampire saga was to appear, the first volume of the "Castle of Dark Dreams" trilogy introduced readers to three vampires— Eric, Brynn, and Conall McNair. They inhabit a castle that is also an adult theme park where adventurous women can assume fantasy roles in which eroticism is a commanding factor. Each of the three volumes introduced one of the brothers and the woman who challenged him.

In 2008, Bangs initiated a new "Gods of the Night" series, which did not involve vampires as major players, but included vampires as part of the supernatural environment in which all the action takes place. Thus, while Bangs is not bound to vampires, the **good guy vampires** she has created have assumed an important and continuing role in pushing her career forward. She has become a member of the small cadre of romance authors best known for their vampire characters.

Sources:

Bangs, Nina. *Master of Ecstasy*. MacKenzie Vampires, Book 1. New York: Love Spell, 2004. 358 pp.
———. *Night Bites*. MacKenzie Vampires, Book 2. New York: Love Spell, 2005. 339 pp.
———. *One Bite Stand*. MacKenzie Vampires, Book 4. Leisure Books: New York, 2008. 321 pp.
———. *A Taste of Darkness*. MacKenzie Vampires, Book 3. New York: Leisure Books, 2006. 337 pp.

————. *Wicked Fantasy*. The Castle of Dark Dreams Trilogy, Book 3. Berkley: New York, 2007. 320 pp.

————. *Wicked Nights*. The Castle of Dark Dreams Trilogy, Book 1. New York: Berkley, 2005. 309 pp.

————. *Wicked Pleasure*. The Castle of Dark Dreams Trilogy, Book 2. Berkley: New York, 2007. 320 pp.

Gentle, Dee. "Interview with Nina Bangs." Posted at http://paranormalromance.org/Nina-Bangs07.htm. Accessed on June 15, 2009.

Banks, L. A. (1959–)

L. A. Banks, a pen-name for Leslie Esdaile-Banks is the writer of the popular "Vampire Huntress Legend" series of romance novels, the first volume of which appeared in 2003. She has emerged through the first decade of the twenty-first century as one of the most successful and prominent African-American authors. Banks is a graduate of the University of Pennsylvania and subsequently received her master's degree from Temple University. A product of Philadelphia, she has made it her home as an adult.

Banks introduced her main character, Damali Richards, a strong female slayer—termed a Neteru—a Balance Swaying Force of Light, in *Minion*. In her normal persona, Richards is a spoken word performer who works with a band. The band's musicians—Marlene, Shabazz, Big Mike, Rider, Jose, J.L., and Dan live together and hunt vampires after their gigs.

In *Minion*, local gang members have come under attack and those who fell victim have been found mutilated to a point beyond recognition. The perpetrator is discovered to be Fallon Nuit, a power vampire, who is the ongoing villain in the series. Enter Richards and her cohorts, and her former lover, Carlos Rivera, who is now a youthful vampire growing stronger night by night, and who will push the plot forward as he runs between Richards and Nuit.

As the story develops, Banks introduces a number of variations on the vampire myth. The vampires believe, for instance, that if they could impregnate Richards as she enters into adulthood (i.e. her twenty-first birthday), the child would be a daywalker, a vampire freed from their nocturnal limitations with the power to create further day-walkers. When vampires feed, they hide the bite marks to conceal their presence from humans. Vampires emanate from the sixth level of hell. They are ruled by a Vampire Council with one Council Level vampire master for each of the five inhabited continents. It is from this powerful realm all evil comes; thus a huntress is needed to balance the situation for the embattled human race.

Beginning with an idea out of ***Buffy the Vampire Slayer***, in Banks's world there is a vampire huntress born every millennium, surrounded by a group of associates who protect her backside, and a vampire lover in search of his soul. But Banks set the idea in a hip-hop urban African-American setting and developed it with her own unique slant. The huntress, for example, is special, in part, because she is born to live through the change of the millennium, and as such she has a different alignment of the planets in her horoscope. As she grows, her powers slowly emerge. She will develop her full powers on her twenty-first birthday, but begins vampire hunting before that time. Eventually, the

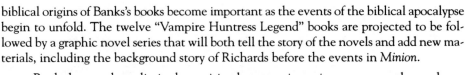

biblical origins of Banks's books become important as the events of the biblical apocalypse begin to unfold. The twelve "Vampire Huntress Legend" books are projected to be followed by a graphic novel series that will both tell the story of the novels and add new materials, including the background story of Richards before the events in *Minion*.

Banks has not been limited to writing her vampire series, now more than a dozen titles strong, but has produced twenty-five additional novels in a variety of genres written under several pennames. She maintains an Internet site at http://www.vampire-huntress.com/.

Sources:

Banks, L. A. *The Awakening : A Vampire Huntress Legend*. Strange Fruit, 2004. 304 pp.

———. *The Bitten: A Vampire Huntress Legend*. New York: St. Martin's Griffin, 2005. 454 pp.

———. *The Cursed: A Vampire Huntress Legend*. New York: St. Martin's Griffin, 2007. 491 pp.

———. *The Darkness: A Vampire Huntress Legend*. New York: St. Martin's Griffin, 2008. 512 pp.

———. *The Damned: A Vampire Huntress Legend*. New York: St. Martin's Griffin, 2006. 496 pp.

———. *The Forbidden: A Vampire Huntress Legend*. New York: St. Martin's Griffin, 2005. 457 pp.

———. *The Forsaken: A Vampire Huntress Legend*. New York: St. Martin's Griffin, 2006. 432 pp.

———. *The Hunted: A Vampire Huntress Legend*. New York: St. Martin's Griffin, 2004. 512 pp.

———. *Minion: A Vampire Huntress Legend*. New York: St. Martin's Press, 2003. 288 pp.

———. *The Shadows: A Vampire Huntress Legend*. New York: St. Martin's Griffin, 2008. 368 pp.

———. *The Thirteenth: A Vampire Huntress Legend*. New York: St. Martin's Griffin, 2009. 304 pp.

———. *The Wicked: A Vampire Huntress Legend*. New York: St. Martin's Griffin, 2007. 448 pp.

———, Donna Hill, Monica Jackson, J. M. Jeffries, and Janice Sims. *Creepin': Payback Is a Bitch/The Heat Of The Night/Vamped/Balancing The Scales/Avenging Angel*. Harlequin: New York, 2007. 400 pp.

Fary, Lisa. "Interview: LA Banks." Pinkraygun.com. Posted at http://www.pinkraygun.com/2009/02/18/interview-la-banks/. Accessed on July 1, 2009.

Baobban Sith *see:* Ireland, Vampires in

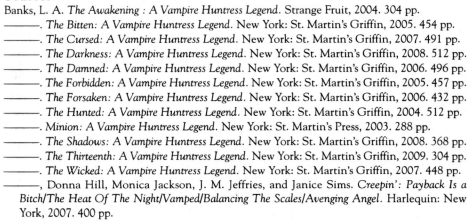

Bara, Theda (1889–1955)

Theda Bara is best known as the silent movie star who brought the character of **the vamp**—the woman who used her allure to attach herself to a man and seduce and destroy him—to the silver screen. Bara was born Theodosia Goodman in Cincinnati, Ohio. Her father was an immigrant from Eastern Europe and her mother a wigmaker of French/German descent. She grew up in the prosperous Jewish community in the Avondale section of the city. She was drawn to acting at an early age and was a member of the drama club in high school. After two years at the University of Cincinnati, she dropped out, moved to New York, and became a stage actress.

In 1914, with her career stagnant, she met movie director Frank Powell. Through him, she obtained her first part as an extra in a now lost film, *The Stain*. But by the end of the year she had been cast as the villainess in the Fox Company's new film, *A Fool There Was*. It was shot at the Fox Studio in Ft. Lee, New Jersey, while Theda lived in New York. The play from which the film had been adapted was inspired by a Rudyard Kipling poem, "The Vampire," and was written by Porter Emerson Browne. It opened in New York in

1909 to critical and popular acclaim. The film version made Goodman, reborn as Theda Bara, a star. She played the vampire who destroyed the life of an American diplomat. William Fox may have decided to bank his future on the film because of the success of another recent film with a similar theme, *The Vampire*, released by the Kalem Film Company.

The uniqueness of *A Fool There Was* rested not so much with its originality as with the publicity program created by Fox. To sell the film with the unknown star, a fictional biography of Theda Bara was created and presented at a press conference in January 1915. She was described as an Arabian actress and came before the reporters in a fur-bedecked coat. After the press conference, a young Louella Parsons was granted a brief few minutes with Theda, who confessed to the charade. Parsons sucked up the exclusive, a leak planned all along by Fox's publicity men. The day after the newspapers published the press account, Parsons released her exclusive, and the planned leak turned Theda into one of the most talked-about women in the country. The movie had not yet opened.

A Fool There Was became one of the highest-grossing films of 1915. It was introduced by a live actor who read Kipling's poem. The critics praised Theda as a great actress and commended the film for not giving in to demands for a happy ending. Fox searched for other films for his new star, and assigned Bara to a role in her second movie, *The Kreutzer Sonata*. She again played a wicked woman who stole the husband of another woman. She did not get away with it this time, however, and the wife eventually killed her. Her third film, *The Clemenceau Case* could also be classified as a vamp movie and was enormously successful. Theda was being praised by critics, drawing large audiences, and becoming the target of moral critics who were calling for the banning of her films.

During the filming of Theda's fourth movie, *The Devil's Daughter*, the nickname she had picked up around the set, "Vamp," was mentioned to a reporter. He used it, and it became the common way to describe Theda and the roles in which she was being cast. As she played the part to reporters at press conferences, the publicity scripts became more involved and eventually suggested she was a reincarnation of some famous wicked ladies such as Lucretia Borgia or **Elizabeth Bathory**.

While Theda received good reviews for her next film, *The Two Orphans*, in which she played a heroine, it was a flop at the box office due in large part to Fox pulling the publicity budget. Fox wanted her to return to the vamping. The next film was a gangster movie with the made-for-Theda title *Sin*. The Fox publicity camp went to work calling the nation to "Sin with Theda Bara." *Sin* was a great success in spite of being banned in several states.

Over the next several years Theda starred in a host of films (without dialogue to worry about, the production time on films was relatively short), and while she played a variety of roles, she continually returned to the vamp role her audiences yearned for. Her star status earned her leads in more impressive films such as *Carmen*, *Camille*, and *Cleopatra*. Theda's vamp image permeated the popular culture and inspired a number of songs (mostly comedies) such as "The Vamp," "I'm a Jazz Vampire," "Since Sarah Saw Theda Bara," and "Sally Green, the Village Vamp," as well as a new dance, The Vampire Walk. However, by 1919, from the heights of stardom, her career began to wane. Theda was assigned to a series of bad films and her drawing power dropped seriously. In attempting to change her image, she starred as an Irish lass in *Kathleen Mavourneen*, which received good reviews but turned into a disaster. It was rejected by the Irish be-

cause it portrayed the poverty in the old country and because Theda, a Jew, starred as an Irish girl. Angry theater patrons set off stink bombs and riots.

Theda left Fox in 1920 and found herself at age 35 a largely unmarketable commodity. While she made several movies during the 1920s, her career was obviously over, and after *Madame Mystery* in 1926, she never returned to the movies (although she did appear on the stage occasionally). She lived a long life in her Beverly Hills home, remembered to her death as the original vamp. She died in Hollywood in 1955.

Sources:

Genini, Ronald. *Theda Bara: A Biography of the Silent Screen Vamp, with a Filmography.* Jeffersonville, NC: McFarland & Company, 2001. 168 pp.

Golden, Eva. *Vamp: The Rise and Fall of Theda Bara.* Vestal, NY: Emprise Publishing, 1996. 273 pp.

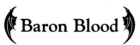

Baron Blood

The vampire Baron Blood was one of a host of super villains created by Marvel Comics as worthy adversaries of its very successful superheroes. He first appeared in *The Invaders* (No. 7) in 1976, a time when Marvel was well into its creation of what came to be known as the alternative "Marvel Universe" (a world where all of their comic superheroes could exist and interact). Baron Blood was born late in the nineteenth century as John Falsworth, the younger son of Lord William Falsworth, a British nobleman. Shortly after the turn of the century, when his brother inherited control of the family fortune, the younger Falsworth went to Romania to search for **Dracula**. He planned to gain control of Dracula and become a powerful person, but he underestimated the Count's powers and was instead turned into a vampire. Falsworth returned to England as Dracula's servant and agent to create havoc in England. He became Dracula's instrument of revenge for the defeat described in **Bram Stoker**'s novel.

Falsworth became a German agent during World War I, which is when he first assumed his identity as Baron Blood. After the war, he disappeared until he reemerged as a Hitler supporter in World War II. He returned to England, posing as his own grandson, and took up residence at Falsworth Manor. He attacked his own family, but was defeated by the Invaders, the super-team that had been assembled to defeat the Third Reich. He was killed by a stalactite threaded through with silver. He was then entombed in a chapel with a **stake** in his heart and his casket surrounded by **garlic**.

Baron Blood did not reappear until 1981, when Captain America, one of the original Invaders, was summoned to England. The now aged Lord Falsworth believed that Baron Blood was the cause of a rash of what had been defined as slasher murders. Captain America then discovered that Baron Blood was not in his tomb. He had been resurrected some years before by a Dr. Charles Cromwell, who had been sent to Blood's tomb by Dracula. After awakening, Blood killed Cromwell and assumed his identity. He lived quietly for many years taking **blood** from his patients. Captain America tracked him down, killed him, then decapitated him and burned his body.

Captain America had finally disposed of Baron Blood, but he was too worthy a villain to leave in the ashes. He initially reappeared in the form of Victor Strange, brother of Marvel's sorcerer hero Dr. Stephen Strange. Victor had died and was frozen cryogenically. When Dr. Strange tried to revive him with magical spells, one of the spells worked but turned Victor into a vampire. Therefore, when the cryogenic machine was turned off in 1989, Victor awoke as a vampire. He donned a costume similar to Baron Blood's, and was named Baron Blood by Marie Laveau, the voodoo priestess whom Strange was fighting at the time of Victor's resurrection. Baron Blood settled in Greenwich Village and, like the vampire **Morbius** (another Marvel vampire), satisfied his craving for blood by attacking criminals. He reappeared occasionally in Dr. Strange episodes until August 1993, when he committed **suicide** by plunging a knife into his midsection. Dr. Strange buried the Baron, but there was no reason to believe that Baron Blood had finally been destroyed.

Baron Blood had a second reincarnation in 1999 in the person of Kenneth Creichton, a relative of the original Baron Blood. Suffering from anemia, he is approached by Baroness Blood and finally accepts her offer to be changed into a vampire. Thus he becomes the new Baron Blood. Meanwhile, the Baroness discovers the Holy Grail. The baron is present at Glastonbury when, in the presence of the group of vampires, she drinks from the Grail, thus attaining the power to walk about in the daylight. She refuses to share the power with the others and destroys the Grail. As the sun rises, Baron Blood is among those who disintegrate in its rays.

In 2007, Baron Blood was resurrected yet again in the story line of the third series of comics devoted to Blade the Vampire Hunter in which Blade's father becomes a vampire in order to survive a terminal disease. He has lost his soul and in the process of seeking its restoration encounters a prophecy. This prophecy, when fulfilled —as it is at the end of the series (N.12)—causes the reemergence of a number of vampires. All of these vampires, including the infamous Baron Blood, remain alive (2009) and walking the earth.

Sources:

Abnett, Don, et al. "Blood Lines." *Knights of Pendragon* (UK) 9, 10 (April, May 1993).
Blade. Nos. 1–12. New York: Marvel Comics, 2006–07.
Captain America. Nos. 253–354. New York: Marvel Comics, 1981.
David, Alan. "Baron Blood." *Official Handbook of the Marvel Universe* 2, 16 (June 1987).
Dr. Strange: Sorcerer Supreme. Nos. 10, 14, 16, 29, 56. New York: Marvel Comics, 1989–93.
The Invaders. Nos. 7–9. New York: Marvel Comics, 1976.
Rovin, Jeff. *The Encyclopedia of Super Villains.* New York: Facts on File, 1987.

Bathory, Elizabeth (1560–1614)

Elizabeth Bathory, a Slovakian countess who was said to have tortured and murdered numerous young women, became known as one of the "true" vampires in history. Bathory was born in 1560, the daughter of George and Anna Bathory. Though frequently cited as Hungarian, due in large part to the shifting borders of the Hungarian Empire, she actually lived most of her life in what is now the Slovak Republic. Her adult life was spent largely at Castle Cachtrice, near the town of Vishine, northeast of present-day Bratslava, where Austria, Hungary, and the Slovak Republic come together. (The castle was mistakenly cited by **Raymond T. McNally** as being in **Transylvania**.) Bathory grew up in an era when much of Hungary had been overrun by the Turkish forces of the Ottoman Empire and was a battleground between Turkish and Austrian (Hapsburg) armies. The area was also split by religious differences. Her family sided with the new wave of Protes-

Elizabeth Bathory, who was known as the "female Dracula."

tantism that had attempted to reform the traditional Roman Catholicism. She was raised on the Bathory family estate at Ecsed in Transylvania. As a child she was subject to seizures accompanied by intense rage and uncontrollable behavior. In 1571, her cousin Stephen became Prince of Transylvania and, later in the decade, additionally assumed the throne of Poland. He was one of the most effective rulers of his day, though his plans for uniting Europe against the Turks were somewhat foiled by having to turn his attention toward fighting Russia, whose **Czar Ivan the Terrible** desired Stephen's territory.

In 1574, Elizabeth became pregnant as a result of a brief affair with a peasant man. When her condition became evident, she was sequestered until the baby arrived because she was engaged to marry Count Ferenc Nadasdy. The marriage took place in May 1575. Count Nadasdy was a soldier and frequently away from home for long periods. Meanwhile, Elizabeth assumed the duties of managing the affairs at Castle Sarvar, the Nadasdy family estate. It was here that her career of evil supposedly really began—with the disciplining of the large household staff, particularly the young girls.

According to the story that would be repeated many times, Elizabeth's level of cruelty was noteworthy even in light of the relatively high level of cruel and arbitrary behavior directed by those in power toward those who were servants. It was said that she went out of her way to find excuses to inflict punishments and delighted in the torture and death of her **victims** far beyond what her contemporaries could accept. She would stick pins in various sensitive body parts, such as under the **fingernails**. In the winter she would execute victims by having them stripped, led out into the snow, and doused with **water** until they were frozen.

Elizabeth's husband was also accused of joining in on some of the sadistic behavior and actually teaching his wife some new varieties of punishment. For example, he is credited with showing her a summertime version of her freezing exercise—he had a woman stripped, covered with honey, then left outside to be bitten by numerous insects. Following his death in 1604, Elizabeth moved to Vienna, and also began to spend time at her estate at Beckov and at a manor house at Cachtice, both located in the present-day country of Slovakia. These were the scenes of the most famous and vicious acts associated with Elizabeth.

In these years, Elizabeth's main confidant was a woman named Anna Darvulia, about whom little is known. When Darvulia's health failed in 1609, Elizabeth turned to Erzsi Majorova, the widow of a local tenant farmer. Majorova is credited with Elizabeth's eventual downfall by encouraging her to include a few women of noble birth among her victims. Because she was having trouble procuring more young servant girls as rumors of her activities spread through the countryside, Elizabeth followed Majorova's advice.

At some point in 1609, Elizabeth was accused of killing a a young noble woman and attempting to cover it by claiming her death to be a **suicide**.

As early as the summer of 1610, an initial inquiry had begun into Elizabeth's affairs. Underlying the inquiry, quite apart from the steadily increasing number of victims, were political concerns. The crown hoped to confiscate Elizabeth's large landholdings and escape payment of an extensive loan received from her husband. With these things in mind, Elizabeth was arrested on December 29, 1610.

Elizabeth was placed on trial a few days later. It was conducted by Count Thurzo as an agent of the king. As noted, the trial (rightly characterized as a show trial by Bathory's biographer Raymond T. McNally) was initiated to not only obtain a conviction, but to also confiscate her lands. A week after the first trial, a second trial was convened on January 7, 1611. At this trial, a register found in Elizabeth's living quarters was introduced as evidence. It noted the names of 650 victims, all recorded in her handwriting.

The trials included testimonies of both those who witnessed deaths and some who had survived. The latter recounted how they had been pierced, pinched, beaten, and burned, and they identified Elizabeth as their torturer. In the end, the court received evidence of recovered skeletons and cadaver parts, the reports of the witnesses, and a letter from the Hungarian King Mathias II (r. 1608–1619) indicating that he knew of at least three hundred victims. They convicted the countess and her co-conspirators of only eighty counts of murder, still a hefty number. Her accomplices were sentenced to be executed, the manner determined by their roles in the tortures. Elizabeth was sentenced to life imprisonment in solitary confinement. She was placed in a room in her castle at Cachtice without windows or doors and only a small opening for food and a few slits for air. There she remained for the next three years until her death on August 21, 1614. She was buried in the Bathory land at Ecsed.

At least two basic questions have arisen out of Elizabeth's trial and conviction. The first regards the actual extent of her crimes. She claimed innocence on all counts, a view largely supported by Laszlo Nagy. Writing in the early 1980s, he suggested that she was the victim of a pro-Hapsburg, anti-Protestant conspiracy. However, Nagy is in the minority. Most researchers have suggested that she killed at least fifty to sixty victims, with some accepting the higher numbers of three hundred, six hundred, or 650. Contemporary forensic psychologist Katherine Ramland concluded, "Even disregarding tales gained through torture, the evidence from the many missing girls, testimony from damaged survivors, and the discovery of human remains all serve to underscore the charge of extreme torture and serial murder."

Elizabeth as Vampire: But, above and beyond Elizabeth's reputation as a sadistic killer with at least eighty victims, she has also been accused of being both a **werewolf and a vampire**. During her trials, testimony was presented that on occasion, she bit the flesh of the girls while torturing them. These accusations became the basis of her connection with werewolfism. The connection between Elizabeth and vampirism is somewhat more tenuous. Of course, it was a popular belief in Slavic lands that people who were werewolves in life became vampires in death, but that was not the accusation leveled at Elizabeth. Rather, she was accused of draining the **blood** of her victims and bathing in it to retain her youthful beauty: she was by all accounts a most attractive woman.

No testimony to this activity was offered at her trial, and in fact, there was no contemporary testimony that she engaged in such a practice. Following her death, the

Ingrid Pitt played Elizabeth Bathory in the film *Countess Dracula*.

records of the trials were sealed because the revelations of her activities were quite scandalous for the Hungarian ruling community. King Matthias forbade the mention of her name in polite society. It was not until one hundred years later that a Jesuit priest, Laszlo Turoczy, located copies of some of the original trial documents and gathered stories circulating among the people of Cachtice, the site of Elizabeth's castle. Turoczy included an account of her life in a book he wrote on Hungarian history. His book initially suggested the possibility that she bathed in blood. Published in the 1720s, it appeared during the wave of vampirism in Eastern Europe that excited the interest of the continent. Later writers would pick up and embellish the story. Two stories illustrate the legends that had gathered around Elizabeth in the absence of the court records of her life and the attempts to remove any mention of her from Hungarian history:

> It was said that one day, the aging countess was having her hair combed by a young servant girl. The girl accidently pulled her hair, and Elizabeth turned and slapped the servant. Blood was drawn, and some of it spurted onto Elizabeth's hands. As she rubbed it on her hands, they seemed to take on the girl's youthful appearance. It was from this incident that Elizabeth developed her reputation for desiring the blood of young virgins.

The second story involves Elizabeth's behavior after her husband's death, when it was said she associated herself with younger men. On one occasion when she was with one of those men, she saw an old woman. She remarked, "What would you do if you had to kiss that old hag?" He responded with expected words of distaste. The old woman, however, on hearing the exchange, accused Elizabeth of excessive vanity and noted that such an aged appearance was inescapable, even for the countess. Several historians have tied the death of Bathory's husband and this story into the hypothesized concern with her own aging, and thus, the bathing in blood.

Elizabeth has not been accused of being a traditional blood-drinking or blood-sucking vampire, though her attempts to take and use the blood to make herself more youthful would certainly qualify her as at least a vampire by metaphor. Previously a little known historical figure, she was rediscovered when interest in vampires rose sharply in the 1970s; since that time she has repeatedly been tied to vampirism in popular culture. Noticeable interest in Elizabeth was evident in the publication of a series of books in the early 1970s beginning with Valentine Penrose's *Erzsebet Bathory, La Comtesse Sanglante*, a 1962 French volume whose English translation, *The Bloody Countess*, was published in 1970. Bathory was also mentioned in later books; **Donald Glut's** *True Vampires of History* (1971) and Gabriel Ronay's *The Truth about Dracula* (1972). Penrose's book inspired the first of the Bathory films; the movie in turn, inspired a novel based on its screenplay, *Countess Dracula* by **Michael Parry**. The celebration of the mythical countess in the 1970s motivated Dracula scholar Raymond McNally (1931–2002) to produce by far the most authoritative book on Elizabeth to date—*Dracula was a Woman: In Search of the Blood Countess of Transylvania*—which appeared in 1984. Based on a new search through the original court documents, and a broad understanding of Eastern European history and folklore, McNally thoroughly demythologized the legend and explained many of the problems that had baffled previous researchers.

Bathory on Film: The first movie inspired by the stories connecting Bathory to vampires was the now largely forgotten *I Vampiri* (released in the United States as *The Devil's Commandment*), notable today because of the work of future director **Mario Bava** as the film's cameraman. A decade later, as part of its vampire cycle, **Hammer Films** released what is possibly the best of the several movies based on Elizabeth's life, *Countess Dracula* (1970). **Ingrid Pitt** starred in the title role. The film was built around the mythical blood baths and portrayed her as going increasingly crazy as she continued her murderous career. *Daughters of Darkness* (1971), one of the most artistic of all vampire films, brought the countess into the twentieth century in a tale with strong **lesbian** overtones. In the movie, Elizabeth and her companion Iona check into an almost empty hotel where they meet a newlywed couple. When it is revealed that the husband has a violent streak, the stage is set for Elizabeth and Iona to move in and "help" the new bride. A series of vampiric encounters ensues, and in the end, the wife (the newest vampire) emerges as the only survivor. Jesus Franco's 1973 erotic film with Bathory, *Las avaleuses*, is remembered more for its challenge to censorship standards of the day and appeared in a variety of cuts under almost a dozen different names such as the *Bare Breasted Countess*, *Female Vampire*, *Jacula*, *La comtesse noire*, and *The Loves of Irina*.

Elizabeth, (or a character modeled on her) also appeared in *Legend of Blood Castle* (1972), *Curse of the Devil* (1973), *Immoral Tales* (1974), and *Mama Dracula* (1979), all films of lesser note. In 1981, a full-length animated version of Elizabeth's story was released in Czechoslovakia. More recent films featuring the Countess include *Thirst* (1980),*The Mysterious Death of Nina Chereau* (1987), *Vampire Ecstasy* (1999), *Mistress of Seduction* (2000), *Metamorphosis* (2004), *Tomb of the Werewolf* (2004), *Night Fangs* (2005), *Stay Alive* (2006), *Demons Claw* (2006), *Blood Countess* (2008), *Blood Scarab* (2008), and *Bathory* (2008). In addition, filmmaker **Don Glut** has recently completed a film trilogy in which a contemporary Bathory (now assuming the title Countess Dracula as the widow of the infamous Transylvanian count) who goes in search of a formula that will allow her to walk in the daylight without harm: *The Erotic Rites of Countess Dracula* (2003), *Countess Dracula's Orgy of Blood* (2004), and *Blood Scarab* (2008).

Bathory and Dracula: Bram Stoker, the author of **Dracula** (1897), possibly read of Elizabeth in *The Book of Werewolves* by Sabine Baring-Gould (1865) where the first lengthy English-language account of Elizabeth's life appeared. In his book on Bathory Raymond McNally suggests that the description of Elizabeth might have influenced Stoker to shift the site of his novel from Austria (Styria), where he initially seemed to have set it, to Transylvania. In like measure, McNally noted that Dracula became younger and younger as the novel proceeded, an obvious allusion to the stories of Elizabeth bathing in blood to retain her youth. He made a strong case that the legends about her "played a major role in the creation of the character of Count Dracula in the midst of Bram Stoker." In her survey of problems in Dracula research, however, Elizabeth Miller calls McNally's suggestion into question. She argues that the real connection between Bathory and *Dracula* do not go back to Baring-Gould, or Stoker, but rather are of more recent origin, namely Donald Glut's *True Vampires of History* (1971) and Gabriel Ronay's *The Dracula Myth* (1972). Miller bases her case primarily on her study of Stoker's notes for *Dracula* in which there is no mention of Bathory anywhere. More recently, in the annotated edition of the notes, she added that "there is no proof that her story influenced the creation of Dracula." (Eighteen-Bisang & Miller 2008).

Sources:

Baring-Gould, Sabine. *The Book of Werewolves*. London: Smith, Elder, 1865. Rept. New York: Causeway Books, 1973.

Bathory, Gia. *The Trouble with the Pears: An Intimate Portrait of Erzsebet Bathory*. Bloomington, IN: AuthorHouse, 2006.

Eighteen-Bisang, Robert, and Elizabeth Miller. *Bram Stoker's Notes for Dracula: A Facsimile Edition*. Jeffersonville, NC: McFarland & Company, 2008.

Glut, Donald F. *True Vampires of History*. New York: HC Publishers, 1971.

McNally, Raymond T. *Dracula Was a Woman: In Search of the Blood Countess of Transylvania*. New York: McGraw-Hill, 1983. Rept. London: Robert Hale, 1984. Rept. London: Hamlyn, 1984.

Miller, Elizabeth. *Dracula: Sense and Nonsense*. UK; Desert Island Books, 2000.

Mordeaux, A. *Bathory: Memoir of a Countess*. Charleston, SC: Book Surge, 2000.

Nagy, László;. *A rossz hirü Báthoryak*. Budapest: Kossuth Könyvkiadó, 1984.

Parry, Michel. *Countess Dracula*. London: Sphere Books, 1971. Rept. New York: Beagle Books, 1971.

Penrose, Valentine. *Erzsebet Bathory, La Comtesse Sanglante*. Paris: Mercure du Paris, 1962. English translation as: *The Bloody Countess*. London: Calder & Boyars, 1970. Rept.: London: Creation Books, 1996. 157 pp.

Ramsland, Katherine. "Lady of Blood: Countess Bathory." Tru TV Crime Library. Posted at http://www.trutv.com/library/crime/serial_killers/predators/bathory/countess_1.html. Accessed May 15, 2009.

Ronay, Gabriel. *The Truth about Dracula.* London: Gallancz, 1972. Rept. New York: Stein and Day, 1972.

Thorne, Tony. *Countess Dracula: The Life and Times of Elisabeth Bathory, the Blood Countess.* London: Bloomsbury, 1997. 274 pp.

Bathory Palace *see:* Vampire Fandom: United States

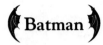

Batman

Like Superman, Batman is one of the most popular late twentieth-century superheroes. Batman (a DC Comics character) created a popularized image of the bat, the development of which to some extent must be credited to **Dracula**, the 1897 book by **Bram Stoker**, and its translation in the 1920s and 1930s to the stage and motion picture screen. However, Batman was not a vampire—he was a human hero with human resources, and his enemies, while often very strange, were usually human as well.

Batman first appeared in *Detective Comics* No. 27 in 1939. Dr. Thomas Wayne and his wife were killed in a mugging. In his grief, their son Bruce Wayne grew up with the idea of becoming a policeman. He studied criminology and developed his body to an amazing degree. As a young adult, he changed his plans and decided to become a vigilante. He settled on the Batman costume after two events—first a bat flew in the window as he was trying to find a uniform to put fear into the hearts of his criminal enemies. Later, the independently wealthy Wayne fell through the floor of his mansion and discovered a bat-infested cave—the perfect headquarters for Batman.

The clear association of Batman with **Dracula** must have been in the mind of his creators, because a scant four months after his initial appearance, he encountered a vampire in a two-part story in issues No. 31 and No. 32 of *Detective Comics* in September and October 1939. A vampire tried to take control of Bruce Wayne's girlfriend, unaware that Wayne was Batman. Batman tracked the Monk, as the vampire was known, to his home in Hungary, which was also the home of his allies, the **werewolves**. Batman eventually found the vampire and his vampire bride asleep and killed them with a silver **bullet** fired into the **coffins**.

The full development of Batman as a definitive comic book hero in the years after World War II occurred as the debate over the effect of comic books on children proceeded. After DC Comics subscribed to the Comics Code in 1954, there was little opportunity (or reason) for Batman and his new sidekick Robin the Boy Wonder to encounter vampires and the supernatural. However, as Batman's popularity—and subsequently the number of comic books carrying his stories—increased, new villains were continually generated. Thus it was inevitable, after the lifting of the ban on vampires by the revised Comics Code in 1971, that Batman would come face-to-face with another bloodthirsty enemy.

Batman's next encounter with a vampire, Gustav Decobra, occurred in the January 1976 *Detective Comics* (No. 455). Stranded by car trouble, Bruce Wayne and his butler Alfred entered a seemingly deserted house only to find a coffin in the center of the living room. As they searched the house, the vampire emerged from the coffin. After Wayne saw the vampire, he changed into Batman. In the ensuing fight, Batman rammed

A terrifying example of a film version of a vampire bat from the movie *Blood and Roses*.

a **stake** into the vampire's chest. However, this did no good because Decobra had cleverly hidden his heart elsewhere. Batman then retreated from this first battle. By the time of their next confrontation, he figured out that Decobra had hidden his heart in a grandfather clock at the house. When Batman impaled the heart with an arrow, Decobra died.

Several years prior to this encounter with Decobra, Batman had begun an ongoing relationship with Kirk Langstrom. Langstrom developed a serum to turn himself into **Man-Bat**. Though not originally a **vampire bat**, Man-Bat would eventually encounter vampires and bring Batman into the realm with him. Both Man-Bat's and Batman's encounter with vampires were orchestrated by writer Gerry Conway, the first writer for Marvel's *The Tomb of Dracula*, and artist Gene Colan, who had worked through the 1970s on *The Tomb of Dracula*. Both were working for DC during the early 1980s.

In 1982, immediately after the conclusion of the first episode with Man-Bat, where he was cured of the condition that had turned him into a bat, Batman (now in the hands of writer Conway and artist Colan) squared off against vampires again. An unsuspecting Robin was captured by his girlfriend, Dala, who turned out to be a vampire. He attempted to escape, but in the process he was confronted by Dala's colleague, the resurrected Monk. Robin was bitten and then allowed to escape. Because the only way to save Robin was with a serum made from the vampire's **blood**, Batman went after the vampires. Unsuccessful in his first encounter, Batman was bitten and also became a vampire. He then set up a second confrontation that was successful and he was able to obtain the necessary ingredients to return himself and Robin to normalcy.

Except for his ongoing relationship with Man-Bat, Batman did not confront a vampire again until 1991. The new story was published in a comic book monograph rather than either of the Batman comic book serials. It concerned Batman's adventures in what was described in the introduction as an "alternative future" and a Batman who was "an altogether different Batman than we're used to." In *Batman and Dracula: Red Rain*, Gotham City was under attack by a group of vampires led by Dracula. Batman (without Robin) was drawn into the fray. In his effort to find what was believed to be a serial killer, he met Tanya, a "good" vampire who had previously organized opposition to Dracula. She had developed a methadone-like artificial substitute that quenched the vampire's need for blood. After they united to fight Dracula, Batman was wounded in battle and became a vampire. In his closing lines he repeated Tanya's phrase, "Vampires are real … but not all of them are evil." In the sequel, *Batman Bloodstorm*, Batman finally defeated Dracula and the vampires, and in his closing report to Commissioner Gordon, indicated the means for disposing of the last vampire, Batman himself. Commissioner Gordon and Alfred, Bruce Wayne's faithful butler, kill Batman by staking him.

That Batman is staked but not decapitated allows him to return in the third volume of the Red Rain series, *Crimson Mist* (1998). Alfred removes the **stake** hoping that Batman will revive to handle a crime wave striking Gotham. He succeeds in killing and drinking from a number of his old enemies, but finally two of them, Killer croc and Two-Face, make common cause with Commissioner Gordon and Alfred. They agree that the human Batman would not handle the situation in the same manner as the vampire Batman. They agree to lure Batman to the Batcave where they plan to set off explosions that will collapse the roof and expose Batman to the Sun. Once the five are in the Batcave, a fight ensues. Alfred, Killer Croc and Two Face are killed, and subsequently Commissioner Gordon springs the trap. Gordon is killed as the roof collapses on him, and as the story ends, Batman walks into the sunlight, presumably to die the final death.

In 2007, DC released the "Batman and Dracula" trilogy in a collected edition under the title *Tales of the Multiverse: Batman-Vampire*. The story line appears to have had some influence on the 2005 feature film, *Batman vs. Dracula: The Animated Movie*. Meanwhile, the unvampirized Batman continued his adventures in *Batman* and *Detective Comics* and a variety of spin-off titles, where he occasionally confronts a vampire. In the vast Batman literature, there have also been a very few appearances of a vampire Batman.

Sources:

Batman. Nos. 348–51. New York: DC Comics, 1982.

Detective Comics. No. 455. New York: DC Comics, 1982.

The Greatest Batman Stories Ever Told. New York: DC Comics, 1988.

Moench, Doug, et al. *Batman & Dracula: Red Rain*. New York: DC Comics, 1991.

———. *Batman Bloodstorm*. New York: DC Comics, 1994.

———. *Batman: Crimson Mist*. New York: DC Comics, 1998.

Rovin, Jeff. *The Encyclopedia of Superheroes*. New York: Facts on File, 1986.

🌙 Bats, Vampire 🌙

Vampire bats, three species of which exist in Mexico and Central and South America, have become an integral part of the modern myth of vampires, and bat symbolism is inseparable from current iconography of the contemporary vampire. Europeans discovered and first described vampire bats in the sixteenth century. Modern biologists who specialize in the study of bats recognize as vampires only three species of the mammalian family Phyllostomatidae, subfamily Desmodontinae. The most common is *Desmodus rotundus*. Rarer are *Diaemus youngi* and *Diphylla ecaudata*.

The Nature of Vampire Bats: Bats are the only mammals that can fly. There are almost one thousand species, nearly one-fourth of all the mammalian species now on earth. The largest have a wingspan of several feet. Much of their time is spent sleeping while hanging upside down, a position from which they can drop into space and easily begin flying.

Vampire bats are characteristically distinguished from other bats by their feeding habits. Whereas most species of bats feed off fruits and other plants and/or insects, the vampires live exclusively off the **blood** of various vertebrates. *Diaemus* and *Diphylla* will feed on birds, but *Desmodus*, the common vampire bat, feeds exclusively on other mammals. Their teeth include razor-sharp incisors with which they cut into their prey. Rather than suck the blood, however, they allow it to flow and lap it up with their tongue, somewhat like a cat drinking milk. They also seem to have an anticoagulant substance in their saliva that helps keep the blood of their **victims** flowing during feeding. They are quite agile and mobile and can walk, run, and hop, unlike some species. They have a good sense of smell and large eyes that provide clear **vision**. The average adult vampire bat nightly consumes some fifteen milliliters of blood—approximately forty percent of their prefeeding weight. After feeding, the stomach and intestinal area appear bloated, and some of the feast will have to be digested before the bat can return home.

In real life, the vampire bat has emerged as a problem among South American farmers as a carrier of rabies, which it transmits to the cattle it feeds on. Vast eradication programs have been developed but with mixed results.

Two sixteenth-century Europeans, Dr. Oliedo y Valdez (1526) and M. Giroalme Benzoni, (1565) were the first to bring word of the vampire bat to their homelands. Benzoni, in his *History of the New World*, notes:

> There are many beasts which bite people during the night; they are found all along this coast to the Gulf of Paria and in other areas, but in no other part are they as pestiferous as in this province Nuevo Cartago, today Costa Rica; they have gotten to me at several places along this coast and especially at Nombre de Dios, where while I was sleeping they bit the toes of my feet so delicately that I felt nothing, and in the morning I found the sheets and mattresses with so much blood that it seemed that I had suffered some great injury. (Turner, 2)

A reoccurrence of this rare event (as vampire bats do not normally like human blood) was noted several centuries later by Charles Waterton, author of *Wanderings in*

South America, who awakened one morning after sleeping on a hammock to find his friend complaining that vampire bats had attacked him. Waterton looked into the matter:

> On examining his foot, I found the vampire had tapped his great toe: there was a wound somewhat less than that made by a leech; the blood was still oozing from it. Whilst examining it, I think I put him in a worse mood by remarking that an European surgeon would not have been so generous as to have blooded him without making a charge. (Robertson, 71)

Waterton had a much friendlier attitude toward the vampires:

> I had often wished to have been once sucked by the vampire.... There can be no pain in the operation, for the patient is always asleep when the vampire is sucking him; and for the loss of a few ounces of blood, that would be a trifle in the long run. Many a night have I slept with my foot out of the hammock to tempt this winged surgeon, expecting he would be there; but it was all in vain.

On his journey around the world in the 1880s, Charles Darwin observed the vampire bat feeding and wrote the first brief "scientific" account, which was published in 1890.

The Bat in South American Folklore: Bats in general, and the vampire bat in particular, have not gone unnoticed by the peoples of South America, who have integrated them into their mythology. E. W. Roth, an ethnologist who studied the people of Guyana (Guinea), had informally designated one of their plants "bat's bane" because its juice, when rubbed on the toes, would kill an attacking bat. The native folklore contains several tales of such bats. **Camazotz** was a significant deity among the ancient Maya of Guatemala. A god of the caves, he was seen as dwelling in the Bathouse in the Underworld, and he played a key part in the story told in the Maya's sacred book, *Popul Vuh*.

The Bat in Western Folklore: Although the bat was not tied to the vampire myth until the nineteenth century, it has appeared repeatedly since the days of Aesop and his fables. Early observers of bats commented on the likeness in features with human beings. They also observed bats suckling their young from a pair of breast nipples. Because bats are creatures of the night, in many cultures, they came to be associated, as did the owls, with the unknown, the supernatural, and more sinister aspects of life. In Greek mythology, bats were sacred to Proserpina, the wife of Pluto, god of the underworld. In the Middle Ages, bats came to be associated with the Christian devil. They were often believed to be signs of—and even agents of—death.

Bats did have some positive associations. Among the Gypsies, for example, they were seen as bearers of good luck. Gypsies prepared small bags of dried bat parts for children to wear around their necks. In Macedonia, bat bones were kept as good luck objects. Possibly the most positive use of the bat has been in heraldry. Several families in both continental Europe and the British Isles have a bat on the family heraldic crest. The Wakefield family crest, for example, is topped by a bat with wings outspread and also has three owls, another night creature, on the shield.

The Spanish conquistadors interpreted the new variety of bats, the blood-drinking ones that they found in Mexico and South America, in light of both the prior image of bats in Western folklore and their traditional beliefs about "human" vampires. For

example, they not only called them vampire bats but also described them as "blood-sucking" creatures rather than "blood-lapping" ones. Over the next centuries the association of bats and vampires gradually grew stronger. William Blake utilized a vampire bat in the artwork for his epic poem *Jerusalem* to symbolize the Spectre, the annihilating and constricting energies in the human psyche. Bats also appear in Francisco Goya's *Los Caprichos* (1796–98), where they hover above the figure of Reason in "The Sleep of Reason Produces Monsters" and behind the babies in "There Is Plenty to Suck." Although bats and vampires were often connected by the mid-nineteenth-century (for example, they appear on the cover page of ***Varney the Vampyre***), it was not until ***Dracula*** (1897) that they became inextricably associated. In *Dracula,* the bat is one of the creatures of the night that **Dracula** rules and into which he can transform. The bat appears early in the story and hovers outside the window of **Jonathan Harker**'s room at **Castle Dracula**. Later, Harker observes Dracula assuming batlike **characteristics** as he crawls down the outside wall of the castle. Once the action transfers to England, Dracula's presence is more often signaled by the bat than by his human form. Dracula's appearances in bat form are always at night, and the association of the vampire with the bat contributed substantively to the twentieth-century understanding of the vampire as an exclusively nocturnal being.

With the popularization of vampires in the post-World War II West, the bat became one of the most common images in horror movies and during Halloween. Naturalists who study bats have carried on a "public relations" program for them because they believe bats have a bad image as a result of their popular association with Dracula. Bats have taken center stage in several vampire films including *Bats* (1999), *Fangs* (2001) *Vampire Bats* (2005), and *Bats: Human Harvest* (2007).

Sources:

Allen, Glover Morrill. *Bats*. New York: Dover Publications, 1939, pp. 1–25.

Brown, David E. *Vampiro: Vampire Bat in Fact & Fantasy*. Salt Lake City, UT: University of Utah Press, 1999.

Darwin, Charles. *Journal of Researches into the Natural History and Geology of the Countries Visited During the Voyage of H. M. S. Beagle Round the World*. London: John Murray, 1879, p. 22.

Hill, John E., and James D. Smith. *Bats: A Natural History*. London: British Museum, 1984, pp. 158–64.

Robertson, James. *The Complete Bat*. London: Chatto & Windus, 1990, pp. 62–72.

Schutt, Bill. *Dark Banquet: Blood and the Curious Lives of Blood-Feeding Creatures*. New York: Harmony Books, 2008.

Turner, Dennis C. *The Vampire Bat: A Field Study in Behavior and Ecology*. Baltimore, MD: Johns Hopkins University Press, 1975, pp. 1–7.

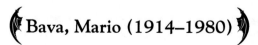 Bava, Mario (1914–1980)

Mario Bava was the horror film director responsible for several of the most memorable vampire films of the 1960s. He was born on July 31, 1914, in San Remo, Italy, the son of Eugenio Bava, a pioneer Italian cameraman. Bava followed his father's occupation and entered the film industry in the 1930s as World War II began. He worked as a cameraman for two decades before he became a director. The disruption of the industry through the 1940s limited the number of features he worked on; but beginning in 1950, he worked on one or more films almost every year. His first directing work was in 1956 when Riccardo Freda quit his directing position in the middle of filming *I Vampiri*, one of several movies inspired by the **Elizabeth Bathory** legend. Bava was asked to finish the film, and his directing career was born.

In 1960, Bava directed *La Maschera del Demonio*, now an important and classic vampire film. Among other things, the film lifted its female lead, **Barbara Steele**, to stardom, at least among horror movie fans. The story concerned a seventeenth-century witch, Princess Asa, who was killed by having a spiked mask (hence the name of the movie) driven onto her face. She was revived by a drop of **blood** that fell on her tomb simultaneously with the arrival of a present-day double named Katia (also portrayed by Steele). Princess Asa, aided by Dominici, a vampire, attempted to find a new life by taking over the body of Katia.

La Maschera del Demonia (released in the United States as *Black Sunday* and in Great Britain as *Revenge of the Vampire*) was a black-and-white feature, but it set the stage for Bava's color productions later in the decade. While Bava often made his films on a low budget, he became known for his ability to take inexpensive sets and, through the utilization of light, convey the **gothic** atmosphere of the supernatural world. Bava believed in the worlds of the real and the unreal, the natural and the supernatural, and felt that he lived his life at the border between the two. In that borderland horror arose and intruded upon normal reality, and Bava assumed that each person was more or less aware of the presence of that borderland in their own life. In his films, the psychological state of his characters was more important than the plot, which led many viewers to complain about the slow movement and lack of action in Bava productions. Although his plots moved slowly at times, Bava had no problem showing explicit violence on the screen. *La Maschera del Demonio* was banned in England for many years and faced problems with censors in both Canada and Mexico. Several of its scenes were edited before release in the United States.

Before the 1960s were over, Bava made four more movies that featured vampirism. After *Black Sunday*, Bava returned to the vampire theme in 1961 with *Ercole al Centro della Terra* (released in the United States as *Hercules in the Haunted World*). Bava brought in **Christopher Lee** from England to play Lico the vampire, Hercules's opponent. He then returned to Russian literature for inspiration. (*Black Sunday* was based on a story by Nicolas Gogol). *I tre Volti della Paura* (released in the United States as *Black Sabbath*, in an attempt to associate it with the very successful *Black Sunday*) consisted of three short stories brought together to create a full-length feature. The third story (in the American version) was a rather faithful adaptation of Alexey Tolstoy's *The Wurdalak*, and was notable for the only appearance of horror superstar Boris Karloff as a vampire. He played a peasant who returned to his home to attack his family.

Sei Donne per l'Assassino (released in the United States as *Blood and Black Lace*) was the bloodiest of Bava's vampire movies. He took a mystery story and rewrote it as a vampire tale. In the movie, the vampire was shown as a serial killer who attacked models at a beauty salon. When found, each **victim** was half-naked, disfigured, and drained of **blood**. Blood abounded on the screen, and Bava dwelt on the gore as a means of drawing the audience into the mind of the killer.

In 1965, Bava made his last vampire movie, *Terrore nello Spazio* (released in the United States as the *Planet of the Vampires*), which turned out to be one of the pioneer-

ing **science fiction** vampire motion pictures. In the film, a space crew lands on another planet and encounters vampires. The vampires take over the ship and, as the movie ends, are preparing to invade Earth.

Bava continued to make movies regularly through the mid-1970s. He spent part of that time in the United States making some of the early "splatter" movies. His *Blood and Black Lace* served as somewhat of a transition film into this emerging horror genre. He directed his last movie, *La Venere dell'ille,* in 1979, the year before his death.

While Bava made more than twenty movies, his vampire movies were his most memorable. Although the vampire movies were only a small percentage of his total output, his name belongs on the short list of directors who made the most vampire movies during their careers.

Sources:

Flynn, John L. *Cinematic Vampires.* Jefferson, NC: McFarland & Company, 1992.

Guariento, Steve. "Bava Fever!" *Samhain* Part 1, 37 (March/April 1993): 22–26; Part 2, 38 (May/June 1993): 23–26; Part 3, 40 (September/October 1993): 22–26.

Howarth, Tony. *The Haunted World of Mario Bava.* Godalming, Surrey, UK: FAB Press, 2003.

Lucas, Tim. *Mario Bava: All the Colors of the Dark.* Cincinnati, OH: Video Watchdog, 2007.

Parish, James Robert. *Film Directors Guide: Western Europe.* Metuchen, NJ: Scarecrow Press, 1976.

Quinlan, David. *The Illustrated Guide to Film Directors.* Totowa, NJ: Barnes & Noble Books, 1984.

Thompson, David. *A Biographical Dictionary of Film.* New York: William Morrow and Company, 1976.

Ursini, James, and Alain Silver. *The Vampire Film.* South Brunswick, NJ: A. S. Barns and Company, 1975.

Belanger, Michelle

Through the first decade of the twentieth century, Michelle Belanger has emerged as the single most prominent spokesperson for the self-identified vampire community. She was born and raised in Ohio. According to her own account, she was born with a heart defect which, while significantly repaired with some early surgery, left her low in vital energy. She learned before she knew what she was doing to take energy from those she came in contact with, and thus markedly improved her own vitality. As a teenager, she learned to take such energy while she gave people backrubs. She experienced a watershed event when her grandmother cut her off from her friends. She stopped giving many backrubs and grew ill. Over her early adult years, as her condition failed to respond to medical care, she finally figured out her vampire nature.

Belanger welcomed the emergence of the vampire community of the 1980s. While mostly built by people interested in vampire novels and movies, a variety of people showed a more serious interest, and she became aware that several groups had appeared that provided an initial home for real vampires. In the 1980s she also began her study of various systems based on psychic energy such as Reiki and Qigong.

In the early 1990s she attended John Carroll University in Cleveland, Ohio. While there she founded a magazine, *Shadowdance.* She also became involved in the role-playing game, **Vampire: The Masquerade**, and began to write the early version of what became her 2004 publication on working with magical and psychical energies,

The Psychic Vampire Codex. Shadowdance provided a point of contact for people to write to her about their vampire experiences. By 1994, she saw a need to provide a forum for this small group of people and she founded the International Vampire Society. In September 1995 she began publishing the society's magazine, *The Midnight Sun*. Her public role set her up for contact with Father Sebastian, who had developed similar interests and had begun to organize vampires in the New York City area. The two came into contact in 1998. He encouraged her to make her presence felt on the Internet. She saw the first edition of his vampire ethics code, the Black Veil, which he had adapted from *Vampire: The Masquerade*. The two worked together for several years; In 2000 she rewrote the Black Veil into a more acceptable version, which she expanded from seven to thirteen codes of ethics. Her version now circulates as the "13 Rules of the Community." She also allowed Sebastian to publish a version of the *Codex*. During the years in contact with Father Sebastian, the International Vampire Society evolved into the House Kheperu. The occult-oriented groups began to explore past lives and came to feel that they were once together in ancient Egypt. The group associated for a while in the 1990s with The Sanguinarium, a network of vampires and groups founded by Father Sebastian. In more recent years, Belanger and Sebastian have gone in separate directions.

Through the first decade of the twentieth century, Belanger has become well-known as a self-identified vampire willing to speak to the media. She has published a series of books and numerous articles. The most recent, *Vampires in Their Own Words: An Anthology of Vampire Voices*, attempts to provide a spectrum of self-identified vampires to speak about their life.

Belanger continues to reside in her home state.

Sources:

Belanger, Michelle A. *Psychic Vampire Codex: Manual of Magick & Energy Work.* York Beach, ME: Weiser Books, 2004. 284 pp.

———. *Scared Hunger.* Lulu.com, 2005. 142 pp.

———. *The Vampire Ritual Book.* CreateSpace, 2007. 160 pp.

———. *Vampires in Their Own Words: An Anthology of Vampire Voices.* York Beach, ME: Weiser Books, 2007. 288 pp.

———. *Walking the Twilight Path: A Gothic Book of the Dead.* St. Paul. MN: Llewellyn Publications, October 1, 2008. 336 pp.

Laycock, Joseph. *Vampires Today: The Truth about Modern Vampirism.* Westport. CT: Praeger, 2009. 200 pp.

Bergstrom, Elaine (1946–)

Elaine Bergstrom, a science fiction/horror fiction writer who has written five vampire books, was born in 1946 in Cleveland, Ohio. Bergstrom burst into the vampire scene in 1989 with the publication of *Shattered Glass*, a novel that introduced a new vampire, Stephen Austra, and his vampire family. They were an old and powerful family who quietly existed as glass workers, specifically the special leaded glass that went into the old cathedrals of Europe and their modern imitations. *Shattered Glass* brought Austra to the United States where he met artist Helen Wells, who he turned into a vampire like him-

Novelist Elaine Bergstrom.

self. She became a continuing part of his story. The initial conflict concerned Austra's renegade brother who forced the "good" Stephen into a final showdown. Included in the novel was one of the more horrorific chapters in vampire literature—Austra's brother surprised the two lovers in bed in a hotel room and proceeded to vampirize them in a slow torturous act.

The Austra family story was resumed in the subsequent novels, *Blood Alone* (1990), *Blood Rites* (1991), and Nocturne (2003), and Elizabeth Austra meets the supernatural-seeking reporter Carl Kolchak in a short story included in the anthology *Kolchak: The Night Stalker Chronicles* (2005). Bergstrom's fourth vampire novel, *Daughter of the Night* (1992), was based on the life of **Elizabeth Bathory** and was especially inspired by its treatment in **Raymond T. McNally**'s biographical study, *Dracula Was a Woman*. Additional titles from this very productive author have included *Tapestry of Dark Souls*, (1993), a novel built around the characters of TSR, Inc.'s *Ravencroft*, one of the vampire-oriented, role-playing **games**, and an exploration of the further adventures of *Mina*, the character attacked by **Dracula** in the original **Bram Stoker** novel, and its sequel, *Blood to Blood: The Dracula Story Continues* (2000).

Sources:

Bergstrom, Elaine. *Blood Alone*. New York: Jove Books, 1990.
———. *Blood to Blood: The Dracula Story Continues*. New York: Ace, 2000.
———. *Blood Rites*. New York: Jove Books, 1991.
———. *Daughter of the Night*. New York: Jove Books, 1992.
——— (as Marie Kiraly). *Mina: The Dracula Story Continues*. New York: Berkley Books, 1994.
———. *Nocturne*. New York: Ace Books, 2003.
———. *Shattered Glass*. New York: Jove Books, 1989.
———. *Tapestry of Dark Souls*. Geneva, WI: TSR, Inc., 1993.

Berwick, The Vampire of

Among the incidents of vampirism reported by **William of Newburgh** in his *Chronicles*, completed in 1196 C.E., was the case of the Berwick vampire. The subject of the account was a rather wealthy man who lived in the twelfth century in the town of Berwick in the northern part of England near the Scottish border. After his death, the townspeople reported seeing his body roaming through the streets at night keeping the dogs howling far into the evening. Fearful that a plague (associated with such revenants in popular lore) might attack the population, the townspeople decided to dismember the body and burn it. That action having been accomplished, the body no longer appeared in town; however, a disease did sweep through the town causing many deaths that were attributed to the after-effects of the vampire's presence.

Sources:

Frenschkowski, Marco. "Vampire in Mythologie und Folklore." In Thomas Le Blanc, Clemens Ruthner, and Bettina Twsrsnick, eds. *Draculas Wiederkehr. Tagungsband 1997.* Wetzlar: Phantastische Bibliothek, 2003, pp. 28–58.

Glut, Donald G. *True Vampires of History.* New York: H C Publishers, 1971. 132 pp.

Bhuta *see:* India, Vampires in

Bibliography, Vampire

In addition to the information about vampires that can be extracted from horror bibliographies such as Edward F. Blieler's classic *The Guide to Supernatural Fiction* (1983) and Don D'Ammassa's *Encyclopedia of Fantasy and Horror Fiction* (2006), a small group of dedicated collectors and researchers have compiled vampire bibliographies. These works contain important information about the scope and development of the genre. **Donald Glut**'s *The Dracula Book* (1975) revolves around **Dracula** but has bits and pieces of information on other vampires. The first attempt to compile a comprehensive bibliography of English-language vampire fiction, nonfiction and other media appeared in 1983. **Martin V. Riccardo**'s *Vampires Unearthed* became the basis of all future vampire bibliographies.

The literary vampire has received the lion's share of attention. In the mid-1970s, **Margaret L. Carter** began to compile a bibliography of English-language vampire fiction. Her work includes a series of publications that combine her interests in bibliographic and literary criticism. Her early works, *Shadow of a Shade: A Survey of Vampirism in Literature* (1975), *Specter or Delusion? The Supernatural in Gothic Fiction* (1987), and *Dracula: The Vampire and the Critics* (1988), culminated in *The Vampire in Literature: A Critical Bibliography* (1989). Carter has produced annual supplements (which are now being issued in electronic form) to accommodate new vampire fiction and to add references to items missed in the 1989 work. Her work is especially notable for her attention to the vampire in short fiction. Carter has also compiled anthologies of vampire fiction, written vampire short stories, and edited a magazine of vampire fiction.

The new popularity of vampire fiction was demonstrated by an excellent annotated bibliography of vampire literature by Greg Cox. *The Transylvanian Library: A Consumer's Guide to Vampire Fiction* (1993) provides a light, but useful romp through the world of the literary vampire—from **John Polidori**'s "The Vampyre" to the novels and stories of 1988. Cox was an assistant editor for TOR Books, which has published a number of vampire novels including the works of **Brian Lumley** and **Chelsea Quinn Yarbro**. Of a more serious nature is Brian Frost's *The Monster with a Thousand Faces* (1989), which also covers vampire fiction through the nineteenth and twentieth centuries and is notable for its discussion of many obscure works.

The work on vampire literature has been further expanded by bibliographical work on **Bram Stoker**, with notable publications by Richard Dalby and William Hughes.

Through the 1990s, Robert Eighteen-Bisang, who owns Transylvania Press in White Rock, British Columbia, has been gathering what has become the largest and most comprehensive collection of vampire literature ever assembled. His collection is the basis of a massive bibliography of vampire fiction and nonfiction titles which he has been working on for the last two decades.

In collaboration with J. Gordon Melton (who owns a similar overlapping collection) Eighteen-Bisang is compiling a set of specialized bibliographical volumes. They published an initial survey of the editions of **Dracula** in 1998. Continuing bibliographical work into the twenty-first century has been complicated by the explosion of titles, many of which have been produced with little fanfare through publish-on-demand companies and the accompanying development of the electronic publishing industry. During the decade 2000–2009, more new vampire titles were published than in the three previous decades combined.

While most of the bibliographical work was being done in North America, at least one important effort occurred in Europe. Author and anthologist Jacques Finnè produced the *Bibliographie de Dracula* in 1986. This book-length annotated work is built upon Riccardo's earlier effort, but is important for its inclusion of non-English titles. Finnè has been supplemented most recently by Clemens Ruthner, "Vampirismus—Forschungsbibliographie" (2003) (posted at http://elib.at/index.php/Vampirismus_-_Forschungsbibliographie_-_Clemens_Ruthner_-_2003).

Comic books, which are given a short chapter by **Riccardo,** have become an increasingly important home to the vampire. J. Gordon Melton compiled an initial bibliography which was published in 1994 as *The Vampire in the Comic Book*. A far more exhaustive bibliography was compiled by Massimo Introvigne (who owns the most extensive collection in existence), Melton, and Eighteen-Bisang. Their list of more than eleven thousand twentieth-century vampire comics was posted on line in 2007. It can be accessed at http://www.cesnur.org/2008/vampire_comics.htm.

Vampire movies form a discrete niche in modern culture. While many of the most important movies are adaptations of novels such as Dracula, **Interview with the Vampire** and *Let the Right One In*, there are many original titles. Donald Reed published the first vampire movie guide in 1965. It has been followed by specialized movie bibliographies on Dracula or **Hammer Films** and comprehensive illustrated guides such as Steve Jones's *The Illustrated Vampire Movie Guide* (1993) and J. Gordon Melton's *Videohound's Vampires on Video* (1997).

Sources:

Altner, Patricia. *Vampire Readings: An Annotated Bibliography*. Lanham, MD: Scarecrow Press, 1998. 161 pp.

Bleiler, Everett F. *The Guide to Supernatural Fiction*. Kent, OH: Kent State University Press, 1983.

Carter, Margaret L. *Dracula: The Vampire and the Critics*. Ann Arbor, MI: UMI Research Press, 1988. 274 pp.

———. *Shadow of a Shade: A Survey of Vampirism in Literature*. New York: Gordon Press, 1975. 176 pp.

———. *Specter or Delusion? The Supernatural in Gothic Fiction*. Ann Arbor, MI: UMI Research Press, 1987. 131 pp. A revision of Ph.D. dissertation at the University of California-Irvine.

———. *The Vampire in Literature: A Critical Bibliography*. Ann Arbor, MI: UMI Research Press, 1989. 135 pp.

Cox, Greg. *The Transylvanian Library: A Consumer's Guide to Vampire Fiction*. San Bernadino, CA: Borgo Press, 1993. 264 pp.

Dalby, Richard. *Bram Stoker: A Bibliography of First Editions, Illustrated*. London: Dracula Press, 1983. 81 pp.

D'Ammasssa, Don. *Encyclopedia of Fantasy and Horror Fiction*. New York: Checkmark Books, 2009. 488 pp.

Eighteen-Bisang, Robert, and J. Gordon Melton. *Dracula: A Century of Editions, Adaptations and Translations. Part One: English Language Editions*. Santa Barbara, CA: Transylvanian Society of Dracula, 1998. 41 pp.

Finné, Jacques. *Bibliographie de Dracula*. Lausanne, Switzerland: L'Age d'Homme, 1986.

Frost, Brian. *Monster with a Thousand Faces*. Bowling Green, OH: Bowling Green State University Press, 1989. 215 pp.

Glut, Donald F. *The Dracula Book*. Metuchen, NJ: Scarecrow Press, 1975. 388 pp

Harvey, Robert J. *Dark Visions: A Price Guide to Collectible Vampire Literature*. Fort Worth TX: The Author, 1995. 146 pp.

Hughes, William, *Bram Stoker: A Bibliography*. Brisbane, Aust.: University of Queensland Press, 1997.

———, and Richard Dalby. *Bram Stoker: A Bibliography*. Westcliff-on-Sea, Essex, UK: Desert Island Books, 2004. 184 pp.

Introvigne, Massimo, J, GordonMelron, and Robert Eighteenteen-Bisang. "English-Language Vampire Comics, 1935–2000—A list and a catalogue of the holdings of CESPOC Library" (Center for Studies on Popular Culture, Torino, Italy). Posted at http://www.cesnur.org/2008/vampire_comics.htm.

Melton, J. Gordon. *Chronicling the Vampire: A Collector's Guide to the Vampire Writings of Anne Rice*. Santa Barbara, CA: Transylvanian Society of Dracula, 1998. 32 pp.

———. *The Official Vampirella Collector's Checklist, 1969–1998*. Santa Barbara, CA: Transylvanian Society of Dracula, 1999. 30 pp.

———. *The Vampire in the Comic Book*. New York: Count Dracula Fan Club, 1993. 32 pp. rev. ed. with Lee Scott. New York: Dracula Press, 1994. 76 pp.

Riccardo, Martin V. *Vampires Unearthed: The Complete Multi-Media Vampire and Dracula Bibliography*. New York: Garland Publishing, 1983. 135 pp.

Bistritz

istritz (or Bistrita) is a town of some 35,000 inhabitants located in northeastern **Transylvania** in present-day **Romania**. It entered into the world of vampires as the first location visited by **Jonathan Harker,** in **Bram Stoker**'s novel, *Dracula*. It is only 50 miles from **Borgo Pass** where Harker was met by the carriage that took him to **Castle Dracula**. Bistritz was an old German settlement and the tower of the German Church found there is still the highest in all of Romania. Harker's account mentions a series of fires between 1836 and 1850 that destroyed much of the old town. In Stoker's day, the town had approximately 12,000 residents.

While there Harker stayed at the Golden Krone (Crown) Hotel. Unlike the very real Bistritz, the Golden Krone is a complete fiction, or at least it was. In 1974, in order to take advantage of the tourists interested in **Dracula**, a Golden Krone Hotel was opened, and the meal Harker ate while at the hotel was placed on the menu. Robber steak con-

Author J. Gordon Melton in front of a restaurant at the Golden Krone Hotel in Bistritz. The sign discusses Jonathan Harker's stop at the same restaurant in *Dracula*

sisted of bits of bacon, onion, and beef roasted on an open fire together with red pepper on a stick. It was served with Mediasch **wine**. Today a tourist at the Golden Krone can also dine on "Elixir Dracula," (a red liquor made from plums), stuffed cabbage Birgau, Dracula cakes, and Dracula red **wine**. The hotel also sells a line of Dracula **paraphernalia** and souvenirs.

Sources:

McKenzie, Andrew. *Dracula Country*. London: Arthur Barker, 1977. 176pp.

Bite Me in the Coffin Not in the Closet Fan Club *see:* Vampire Fandom: United States

Blacula

In the late 1960s the movie industry began to generate a series of movies specifically directed toward the African-American community. While the vampire was essentially a European folk character, and there have been only a few references to vampires in Africa or in African-American lore, it was inevitable that "blaxploitation" producers would consider the possibilities of a Black vampire motion picture. In 1972 the first of the two most important **African-American vampire** movies, *Blacula*, starring **William Marshall**, appeared.

Blacula told the story of Prince Mamuwalde, an African leader in 1780 who was trying to find a way to stop the slave trade that haunted Africa's west coast. He sought out Count **Dracula** (Charles Macaulay) to obtain his assistance in the endeavor. Dracula merely laughed at the Prince, who with his wife Luva, started to leave. Before they could get away, however, they were attacked by Dracula and his vampire cohorts. Mamuwalde was vampirized and sealed in a tomb. Luva was left to die of starvation, unable to help her husband as Dracula cursed Mamuwalde to become Blacula, his African counterpart.

The story then switches to 1965 when some Americans purchase the furnishings of **Castle Dracula** and ship them to Los Angeles, unaware that the ornate **coffin** they have obtained houses Blacula's body. Blacula is awakened and discovers a new love, Tina, the exact image of his Luva. As the plot progresses, she falls victim to a shooting incident, and he turns her into a vampire to save her. But then she is staked to death, and in his grief Blacula commits **suicide** by walking into the **sunlight**.

Blacula was revived by the magic of voodoo a year later in a sequel, *Scream Blacula Scream*. In collusion with the voodoo priestess Lisa, he searches for a way to rid himself of his vampirism, but is thwarted by the police. In a novel, but entirely appropriate, twist of the storyline, he is killed by a pin stuck through the heart of a voodoo doll.

Because of the large audience of vampire movie enthusiasts, the *Blacula* movies have had a heightened popularity and join the list of those few blaxploitation films which found a broad audience beyond the African-American community. *Blacula* was awarded the Ann Radcliffe Award by the The Count Dracula Society.

Sources:

Flynn, John L. *Cinematic Vampires*. Jefferson, NC: McFarland and Company, 1992. 320 pp.

Gross, Edward, and Marc Shapiro. *The Vampire Interview Book: Conversations with the Undead*. East Meadow, NY: Image Publishing, 1991. 134 pp.

Blade the Vampire Slayer

Shakespearean actor William Marshall in his most famous role as Blacula.

In April 1971, following the change in the Comics Code that allowed vampires to return to **comic books**, Marvel Comics introduced its new vampire comic book, **The Tomb of Dracula**. It brought the story of **Dracula** into the 1970s and brought together descendants of the characters in **Bram Stoker**'s novel to fight the revived vampire. During the course of the long running series, Marvel also introduced several new characters. Among the most enduring was Blade the Vampire Slayer. Blade, an African American, further reflected the social changes in post-World War II America. These changes had also been noted by readers in the appearance of a woman, Rachel Van Helsing, as a strong weapon-carrying vampire slayer who assumed the role once held by her grandfather, **Abraham Van Helsing**.

Blade was a warrior equipped with a set of teakwood knives. He initially appeared in the July 1973 (No. 10) issue of *The Tomb of Dracula* on the London docks, where he proceeds to kill several vampire members of Dracula's Legion. Their deaths lead to Blade meeting Quincy Harker and Rachel Van Helsing. After introductions, the action takes Blade to the ship *Michelle* over which Dracula has assumed control. Their initial confrontation ends in a draw, but Dracula escapes and the ship is destroyed by an explosion. Blade returned two issues later to help Harker and Frank Drake (a modern descendent of Dracula) find Harker's daughter Edith who had been kidnapped by Dracula.

The story of Blade's early involvement with vampires was finally told in the October 1973 (No. 13) issue. At the time of his birth, his mother was visited by a physician, Deacon Frost, who turned out to be a vampire. Frost killed his mother, and Blade dedicated his life to looking for him. That search grew into an enmity against all vampires and led him to the recently revived Dracula. He had worked primarily in **America**, and thus had never met Harker, Van Helsing, or Drake, but had heard about their activities.

Wesley Snipes played Blade the Vampire Slayer in the movie adaptations of the successful Marvel comic books.

Blade frequently reappeared through the seventy issues of *The Tomb of Dracula*. He also made a guest appearance in the Fall 1976 issue (No. 8) of *Marvel Preview*. The battle between Blade and Dracula seems to reach a conclusion when Blade sticks one of his knives into Dracula, who apparently dies. However, others steal the body, the knife is removed, and Dracula is revived. Later, Dracula seems to win when he bites Blade. But it turns out that because of the unusual circumstances involving the vampire present at the time of Blade's birth, Blade is immune to the vampire state.

In the June 1976 issue (No. 48), Blade teams with another new character introduced into *The Tomb of Dracula*, Hannibal King. He, too, had an encounter with Deacon Frost, the vampire that killed Blade's mother. In the February 1977 issue (No. 53) the two finally track Frost down and destroy him.

Vampires were banished from Marvel Comics in 1983, and very few characters from *The Tomb of Dracula* appeared during the next six years. Blade practically disappeared, but quickly made his presence felt after the reintroduction of vampires into the Marvel Universe in issues 10 and 14 of *Dr. Strange: Sorcerer Supreme* (November 1989, February 1990). Blade next appeared in the revival by Epic Comics (a subsidiary of Marvel) of *The Tomb of Dracula* (1991–1992), which resumed the story from the end of the first series without reference to the banishment of vampires and the destruction of Dracula in 1983.

In 1992 Marvel united its older occult-oriented characters and created some new ones when it created a new realm on the edge of the Marvel Universe that would be the arena of the **Midnight Sons**. In this new storyline, vampires had been banished from the world in 1983 by a magical formula of Marvel's master of the occult arts, Dr. Strange. His magical operation created the Montesi effect. That effect was being weakened and allowed a new assault upon the world by the forces of supernatural evil. These forces were led by Lilith (the ancient Hebrew demoness, not Dracula's daughter).

The new evil forced the return of the old vampire fighters, including Blade, who received a new image more akin to Marvel's other superheroes and had his weapons system upgraded. The fresh storyline was created simultaneously in five different comic book titles under the collective heading **Midnight Sons**. Blade and his old acquaintances Frank Drake and Hannibal King unite as a private investigation organization, *The Nightstalkers*. The adventures of *The Nightstalkers* lasted until early in 1994 when both Drake and King were killed in the war with the supernatural forces of evil. Blade survived to continue the fight in his own new comic book series *Blade, the Vampire-Hunter* which ran for ten additional issues (1994–1995).

For several years, Blade was not heard from, and then in 1997 a new *Blade* series was launched with a preview issue (reprinting a story from *The Tomb of Dracula*) released in anticipation of the series which began in March 1998 and the movie, *Blade*, with Wesley Snipes in the title role, which appeared later in the year. The movie, in which Blade emerged as a day-walking half-vampire superhero, gave the evolving character an audience unavailable to the average comic book character, and the initial movie became one of the top five all-time grossing vampire movies. The initial story pitted Blade against his old nemesis **Deacon Frost** and a global vampire community whose clans (called houses) are organized under a council. It prompted two sequels, in the first of which Blade fights a breed of new super vampires and in the second, a revived Dracula. A underlying theme throughout the series is the vampire's search for Blade's ability to move about in the daylight without disintegrating into ash.

The success of the blade movies led to a television series that began airing in 2006 on Spike TV. *Blade: The Series* starred Kirk "Sticky Fingers" Jones as Blade and was based in Blade's birthplace, Detroit. He found himself up against Marcus Van Sciver (Neil Jackson), a powerful vampire with the House of Chthon. Unfortunately, it failed to find an audience and was cancelled before the first season was aired.

Sources:

Blade. No. 1–12. New York: Marvel Comics, 2006–07.

Blade the Vampire Hunter. No. 1–10. New York: Marvel Comics. 1999–2000.

Blade 2 Movie Adaptation. New York: Marvel, 2002. 48 pp.

Dorff, Stephen. *Blade*. New York: HarperPaperbacks, 1998. 343 pp.

The Nightstalkers. Nos. 1–18. New York: Marvel Comics, 1992–94.

Rhodes, Natasha. *Blade: Trinity*. UK: Black Flame, 2004. 416 pp.

The Tomb of Dracula. 4 vols. New York: Epic Comics, 1991.

The Tomb of Dracula. 70 vols. New York: Marvel Comics, 1971–79.

Blautsauger *see:* Germany, Vampires in

Blood

Nothing has so defined the vampire as its relationship to blood. The vampire was essentially a bloodsucker, a creature who lived off of the blood of humans. Quite early in his visit to **Castle Dracula, Jonathan Harker** was lectured by his host on the general importance of blood. He noted that the Szekelys, "we of the Dracula blood," helped to throw off the despised Hungarian yoke. He further noted, in a line which soon would take on a double meaning, "Blood is too precious a thing in these days of dishonorable peace …" (chapter 3). As Harker tried to understand his desperate situation, he noted that **Dracula** had bad breath with "a bitter offensiveness, as one smells in blood." He discovered the secret when he found Dracula asleep with his mouth redder than ever and "on the lips were gouts of fresh blood, which trickled from the corners of the mouth and ran over the chin and neck…. It seemed as if the whole awful creature were simply gorged with blood; he lay like a filthy leech, exhausted with his repletion." Harker lamented his role in freeing Dracula on **London**.

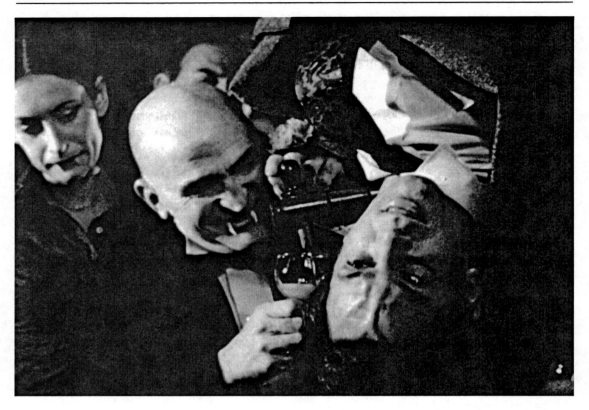

The quest for blood is the common trait that all vampires share. Here, a vampire drains an unwilling victim's blood in the film *Vault of Horror*.

The Significance of Blood: Since ancient times, humans have seen the connection between blood and life. Women made the connection between birth and their menstrual flow. Hunters observed the relationship between the spilling of blood and the subsequent loss of consciousness, the ceasing of breath, and eventual death of the animals they sought. And if an animal died of some cause with no outward wound, when cut, the blood often did not flow. Blood was identified with life, and thinkers through the ages produced endless speculations about that connection. People assigned various sacred and magical qualities to blood and used it in a variety of rituals. People drank it, rubbed it on their bodies, and manipulated it in ceremonies.

Some believed that by drinking the blood of a victim the conqueror absorbed the additional strength of the conquered. By drinking the blood of an animal one took on its qualities. As late as the seventeenth century, the women of the Yorkshire area of England were reported to believe that by drinking the blood of their enemies they could increase their fecundity.

Among blood's more noticeable qualities was its red color as it flowed out of the body, and as a result redness came to be seen as an essential characteristic of blood, the vehicle of its power. Red objects were often endowed with the same potency as blood. In particular, red **wine** was identified with blood, and in ancient Greece, for example, red wine was drunk by the devotees of the god Dionysus in a symbolic ritual drinking of his blood.

Blood was (and continues to be) seen as somehow related to the qualities possessed by an individual, and beliefs carried references to admirable people as having "good" blood or evil persons as possessing "bad" blood. The blood of the mother was passed to the child, and with it the virtues and defects of the parents were passed to any offspring. Thus blood, in a somewhat literal sense, carried the essential characteristics of the larger collectives—families, clans, national/ethnic groups, even whole races. Such beliefs underlie the modern myth that permitted the Nazi purge of Jews and other supposed lesser races and the practices in American blood banks until recent decades to separate "Negro" blood from that of "white" people.

To a lesser extent, blood was identified with other body fluids, most notably semen. In the process of creating a baby, men do not supply blood, only their seed. Thus it was through the semen that male characteristics were passed to the child. In the mythology of race, each of the body fluids—semen, the blood that flowed when the hymen was broken, and menstrual blood—were associated together as part of sexual life and ascribed magical properties. This association was quite explicit in the sexual teaching of modern ritual magic.

Blood in the Biblical Tradition: The ancient Jewish leaders made the same identification of blood and life. In the biblical book of Genesis, God tells Noah:

> But you must not eat the flesh with the life, which is the blood, still in it. And further, for your life-blood I will demand satisfaction; from every animal will I require it, and from a man also will require satisfaction for the death of his fellow-man.

> He that shed the blood of a man, for that man his blood shall be shed; for in the image of God has God made man.

Israel instituted a system of blood sacrifice in which animal blood was shed as an offering to God for the sins of the people. The book of Leviticus included detailed rules for such offerings with special attention given to the proper priestly actions to be taken with the blood. The very first chapter stated the simple rules for offering a bull. It was to be slaughtered before the Tent of the Presence, and the priest was to present the blood and then fling it against the altar. The mysterious sacredness of the blood was emphasized in that God reserved it to himself. The remaining blood was spilled before the altar, and strictures were announced against the people eating the blood. "Every person who eats the blood shall be cut off from his father's kin" (Lev 7:27).

Special rules were also established for women concerning their menstrual flow and the flow of blood that accompanied childbirth. Both made a woman ritually impure, and purification rituals had to be performed before she could again enter a sanctuary. In like measure, the discharge of semen caused a man to be ritually impure.

The most stringent rules concerning blood were in that section of Leviticus called the Holiness Code, a special set of rules stressing the role of the people, as opposed to the priest, in being holy before God. Very early in the code, the people are told:

> If any Israelite or alien settled in Israel eats blood, I will see my face against the eater; and cut him off from his people, because the life of a creature is the blood, and I appoint it to make expiation on the altar for yourselves; for

the blood is the life that makes expiation. Therefore I have told the Israelites that neither you, nor any alien settled among you, shall eat blood.

Indeed, "For the blood is the life" has been the most quoted Biblical phrase in the vampire literature.

Christianity took Jewish belief and practice to its extreme and logical conclusion. Following his death and (as Christians believe) his resurrection, Jesus, its founder, was worshiped as an incarnation of God who died at the hands of Roman executioners. Christians depicted his death as a human sacrifice, analogous, yet far more powerful, than the Jewish animal sacrifices. As the accounts of his last days relate Jesus instituted the Lord's Supper during which he took a cup of wine and told his disciples, "Drink from it, all of you. For this is my blood, the blood of the covenant, shed for many for the forgiveness of sins" (Matthew 26:27). Following his sentencing of Jesus, the Roman governor Pilate washed his hands and told the crowd who had demanded Jesus's death, "My hands are clean of this man's blood." The crowd replied, "His blood be upon us, and on our children" (Matthew 27:24–26). As he hung on the cross, a soldier pierced his side with a lance, and his blood flowed from the wound.

Early Christian thought on the significance of Christ's death was clearly presented in the Apocalypse (The Book of Revelation) in which John spoke of Jesus as the one who "freed us from our sins with his life's blood" (Revelation 1:5). He admonished those suffering persecution by picturing their glory in heaven as the martyrs for the faith. They wore a white robe which had been washed in the blood of the Lamb.

In Christian lands, to the common wisdom concerning life and blood, theological reflection added a special importance to blood. The blood of Christ, in the form of the red **wine** of the Eucharist, became the most sacred of objects. So holy had the wine become that during the Middle Ages a great controversy arose over allowing the laity to have the cup. Because of possible carelessness with the wine, the Roman Catholic Church denied the cup, a practice which added more fuel to the fire of the Protestant Reformation of the sixteenth century.

In the light of the special sacredness of Christ's blood, the vampire, at least in its European appearances, took on added significance. The vampire drank blood in direct defiance of the biblical command. It defiled the holy and stole that which was reserved for God alone.

The Vampire and Hematology: The vampire myth arose, of course, prior to modern medicine. It has been of some interest that ***Dracula*** was written just as modern medicine was emerging, and **Bram Stoker** mixed traditional lore about blood with the new medicine. **Lucy Westenra,** even as she anticipated her marriage to **Arthur Holmwood,** lay hovering near death. Reacting quickly, **Abraham Van Helsing** gathered Holmwood and Lucy's two other suitors, **Quincey P. Morris** and **Dr. John Seward,** to apply a wholly unique scientific remedy to the vampire's attack. He had diagnosed a loss of blood, and now Van Helsing ordered a transfusion, at the time a new medical option. He and each of Lucy's suitors in turn gave her their blood. Following her death, Holmwood, in his grief and disappointment, made the observation that in the giving of blood he had in fact married Lucy and that in the sight of God they were husband and wife. Van Helsing, assuming his scientific role, countered his idea by suggesting that such an observation would make Lucy a polyandrist and the previously married Van Helsing a bigamist.

The idea of using a transfusion to counter the vampire introduced a new concern into the developing myth of the vampire through the twentieth century, especially as the supernatural elements of the myth were being discarded. If vampirism was not a supernatural state, and rather was caused ultimately by a moral or theological flaw of the original vampires, then possibly the blood thirst was the symptom of a diseased condition, caused by a germ or a chemical disorder of the blood, either of which might be passed by the vampire's bite. In the mid-1960s there was brief, yet serious, medical speculation that vampirism was the result of misdiagnosed **porphyria**, a disease that causes its **victims** to be sensitive to **sunlight** and which could be cured or helped.

Anemia is a disease of the blood that was initially associated with vampirism. Anemia is caused by a reduction of either red blood cells or hemoglobin (the oxygen-carrying pigment of the cells) relative to the other ingredients in the blood. The symptoms include a pale complexion, fatigue, and in its more extreme instances, fainting spells. All are symptoms usually associated with a vampire attack. In Bram Stoker's novel, *Dracula*, during the early stages of Lucy Westenra's illness, Dr. John Seward hypothesized that possibly she was suffering from anemia. He later concluded that she was not suffering from the loss of red blood cells, but from the loss of whole blood. Dr. Abraham Van Helsing agreed with his friend: "I have made careful examination, but there is no functional cause. With you I agree that there has been much blood lost; it has been, but is not. But the conditions of her are in no way anaemic" (chapter 9). While Stoker dismissed any association of anemia and vampirism, over the succeeding decades, attempts to posit anemia as the underlying explanation of vampirism occasionally emerged.

The Literary Tradition: Increasingly through the century, as knowledge of the minute details concerning the function and makeup of human blood were explored by research specialists, novelists and screenwriters toyed with the idea of vampirism as a disease. During the last years of the **pulp fiction** era, writers such as Robert Bloch, George Whitley, David H. Keller, and William Tenn suggested the diseased **origin** of vampirism in a series of short stories. For example, in William Tenn's 1956 short story "She Only Goes Out at Night," Tom Judd, the son of a village doctor, falls in love with a strange woman. Tom's father coincidentally discovers an epidemic in town whose victims are all anemic. The woman, who has just moved to town, is a Romanian by descent and only comes out at night. Putting the sudden wave of anemia together with the behavior patterns of the woman, the wise old doctor suggests she is a vampire. As he explains it, the vampire condition is passed from parent to child, though usually only one child in each generation develops it. His son still wants to marry the woman. He responds with a medical observation, "Vampirism may have been an incurable disease in the fifteenth century, but I am sure it can be handled in the twentieth." Her symptoms suggests she has an allergy to the sun, for which he prescribes sunglasses and hormone injections. He then deals with her blood thirst by supplying her with dehydrated crystalline blood which she mixes with **water** and drinks once a day. The vampire and Tom live happily ever after.

Vampirism as disease came powerfully to the fore in the late 1960s **television** series *Dark Shadows*. Dr. Julia Hoffman was introduced into the show to treat the problems of Maggie Evans, one of the show's main characters. A short time after her initial appearance, she meets **Barnabas Collins** and discovers that he is a vampire. Rather than seek to destroy him, however, she devises a plan to assist him in a cure of his vampiric

condition. Collins soon grows impatient and demands that the process be speeded up. His body does not react favorably to the increased dosages of Hoffman's medicines, and he reverts to his true age—two hundred years old. He is able to revive his youth by biting a young woman, and he then turns on Hoffman. Hoffman is able to thwart his efforts by threatening him with her research book, which contains all the details of her treatments and reveals Collins's true nature. Before Collins can locate the book, he and the storyline are transported into the past, to 1795.

Shortly after his return to the present (1968), Collins is in a car accident. Hospitalized, he receives a transfusion that temporarily cures him. He is a human and, for the first time in two hundred years, is able to walk in the sunlight. He is, however, returned to his vampiric state by the bite of his former love, **Angelique Bouchard**, who has died and returned as a vampire.

A character similar to Hoffman also appeared in the recent television series, *Forever Knight*. Nicolas Knight, the show's vampire, is a policeman on the Toronto police force. His friend and confidante is Dr. Natalie Lambert, a forensic pathologist. Throughout the series, she seeks a means to transform Knight into a human, but with negative results. In the decades since World War II, novelists have also explored the idea that a diseased condition produced vampirism. Simon Raven's *Doctors Wear Scarlet* (1960), for example, described vampirism as a form of "sado-sexual perversion." The story sent the hero, Richard Fountain, to Greece to escape an oppressive personal situation in England. In Greece he meets a beautiful vampiress who slowly drains his blood. He is rescued before he is killed and returns safe to his British home.

Jan Jennings's *Vampyr* (1981) brings a research scientist into a relationship with Valan Anderwalt, a vampiress. The scientist, in love with Valan, tries to find the causes of her state. He traces vampirism to ancient **China** and finds it to be a contagious physical condition which had been brought to **America** by the early Dutch colonists. Unfortunately, he is not able to make any progress in curing her.

That same year Whitley Strieber introduced an interesting triangle relationship in *The Hunger*. Miriam Blaylock is an immortal alien vampire. She is on earth and can transform humans into vampires. Such human vampires, however, are not immortal and begin to age and disintegrate after several centuries pass. Not wishing to lose another companion, Blaylock seeks out the services of an expert in longevity, Sarah Roberts, in the hopes that she will be able to save John, her present male companion. Unfortunately, no solution presents itself before John succumbs to his deteriorating condition. Most recently, Dan Simmons sent his leading character, Kate Neuman, a hematologist, into post-revolutionary **Romania** in *Children of the Night*. The book begins with her using her knowledge of rare blood diseases to treat people in Bucharest. While there, she falls in love with a seven-month-old boy, Joshua, presumably an orphan. He is unique in that he requires biweekly transfusions to stay alive. He also has unusual blood which, she comes to believe, holds the clue to cures for AIDS, cancer, and other blood diseases. She arranges his adoption and brings him home with her to Colorado. Soon after, the boy is kidnapped and returned to Romania. In the exciting climax of the story, she is forced to return to Romania and face the boy's father, **Vlad the Impaler**, the real Dracula. Because Dracula was dying, his son, Joshua, was to become the leader of the family in his place.

Conclusion: The traditional beliefs that surrounded blood, the medical exploration of its properties, and the analogies it harbored to life itself, facilitated the adaptability of the vampire myth to a seemingly endless number of situations. Such adaptability has provided an understanding of why the vampire myth has stayed alive and has so many devotees to this day. Scientific considerations of the vital function played by blood in the human body have, if anything, given it an even more mystical place in human life and promoted the belief in its sacredness in this post-secular society.

Since the early 1990s, blood and related body fluids have been very much in the news around such subjects as AIDS, the analysis of blood in criminal investigations, and genetic research around DNA. Interestingly, little has been done by vampire writers to exploit these burgeoning fields in the equally expanding field of vampire fiction.

Sources:

Cox, Greg. *The Transylvanian Library: A Consumer's Guide to Vampire Fiction*. San Bernadino, CA: Borgo Press, 1993.

Scott, Kathryn Leigh, ed. *The Dark Shadows Companion: 25th Anniversary Collection*. Los Angeles: Pomegranate Press, 1990.

Simmons, Dan. *Children of the Night*. New York: G. P. Putnam's Sons, 1992.

Strieber, Whitley. *The Hunger*. New York: William Morrow, 1981.

Teem, William. "She Only Goes Out at Night." *Fantastic Universe* 6, 3 (October 1956). Reprinted in *Weird Vampire Tales*. Ed. by Robert Weinberg, Stefan R. Dziemianowicz, and Martin H. Greenberg. New York: Gramercy Press, 1992.

Blood Drinking *see:* Crime, Vampiric

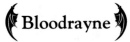

Bloodrayne

Bloodrayne is a female **dhampir** (a child who has one vampire and one human parent, and who has special powers allowing her to become an effective vampire hunter), who initially appeared in a 2002 video game. In the game, she is introduced as an independent, but effective, vampire slayer, which brings her to the attention of the Brimstone Society, an organization dedicated to ridding the world of vampires. They overcome their reluctance to hire anyone with any vampire blood in them, and eventually Bloodrayne, or Rayne as she is informally called, becomes their agent. In her initial gaming adventure, she goes against the Gegengheist Gruppe (or Counter-Ghost Group), an organization attempting to bring Hitler into Germany's leadership through the use of occult artifacts, including an item that belonged to the Devil.

The initial game was popular enough to lead to a sequel, a ongoing set of comic books, and two movies. The comic books were produced by Digital Webbing. The first of the series appeared in 2004, picking up the story line from the comics and placing Bloodrayne in the 1930s fighting both vampires and Nazis. The initial story has her thwarting a plot to smuggle a Vampire King on board the Hindenberg airship as it is ready to leave for the United States. Bloodrayne quickly found a comic reading audience and several miniseries and oneshots followed annually. They became known for the excellent artwork, the print quality, and the many variant covers of each issue, a practice previously found in the ***Vampirella*** comics from Harris Publications and the many titles from Chaos! Comics.

The first *Bloodrayne* movie (2005) takes the slayer to eighteenth-century **Romania** where we learn that her career is launched when her vampire father Kagan kills Rayne's mother. Rayne (played by Laura Bailey) has grown up, however, and is now hunting her father. A fortune teller informs her of a talisman called simply "the eye," which Kagan is also seeking. Meanwhile, both Kagan and members of the Brimstone headquartered in a Romanian castle are searching for her, though for very opposite reasons. Rayne heads for the monastery where "the eye" is hidden and the convergence of her seekers at that place sets the stage for a final confrontation.

The relatively low-budget first movie found its way into the circle of top-grossing vampire movies, allowing Rayne to make a second appearance in *BloodRayne 2: Deliverance* (2007). Rayne (now portrayed by Natassia Malthe) finds herself in the nineteenth-century American West where she encounters the infamous outlaw gunslinger-turned-vampire, Billy the Kid, who has established his home in the town of Deliverance during the 1880s. Billy has taken the townspeople's children hostage as his means of control and Bloodrayne must ally herself with sheriff-turned-vampire-hunter Pat Garrett to defeat vampire Billy and save the youngsters.

Sources:

Bloodrayne. http://www.bloodrayne.com/loband/index.html.
BloodRayne: Dark Soul. Echo 3, 2005.
BloodRayne: Lycan Rex. Digital Webbing, 2005.
Bloodrayne: Plague of Dreams. Digital Webbing, 2006.
Bloodrayne: Raw. Digital Webbing, 2005.
Blood Rayne: Raw II. Digital Webbing, 2007.
Bloodrayne: Red Blood Run. Nos. 1-3. Digital Webring, 2007.
BloodRayne: Seeds of Sin. Digital Webbing, 2005.
Bloodrayne: Skies Afire. Digital Webbing, 2004.
Blood Rayne: Tibetan Heights. Digital Webbing, 2007.
Bloodrayne: Tokyo Rogue. Nos. 1-3. Digital Webbing, 2009.
Bloodrayne: Twin Blades. Digital Webbing, 2006.

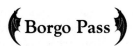

Borgo Pass

A mountain pass in **Transylvania** (at the time a part of **Hungary** and now located in **Romania**) made famous in the opening chapter of **Bram Stoker's** *Dracula*, Borgo Pass (or Tihuţa Pass in Romanian) is an oft-trod passageway through the Carpathian Mountains in Eastern Europe. *Dracula* opens with the journey of **Jonathan Harker** to **Castle Dracula**. Arriving at the city of **Bistritz**, he receives a letter from Count Dracula directing him to the Borgo Pass (which begins near the town of Tihucza). The next day he takes the coach from Bistritz to Bukovina and is let out at the Pass. Here he is met by a coach with a mysterious driver (later revealed to be Count Dracula himself) and taken to Castle Dracula. The scene at Borgo Pass has been most effectively used over the years in the various Dracula movies to build an initial atmosphere of foreboding.

In spite of its remote location, the **Transylvanian Society of Dracula** in Romania regularly calls its members to meetings in the Borgo Pass, especially at Halloween at the Castle Dracula Hotel.

Sources:
The Annotated Dracula. Edited by Leonard Wolf. New York: Ballantine Books, 1975. 362 pp.

Borland, Caroll (1914–1994)

Caroll Borland, the female star of the film *Mark of a Vampire* (1935), graced audiences with her presence opposite costar **Bela Lugosi**. Born in Fresno, California, Borland developed a love for acting in her early teens. In 1929 she saw Lugosi perform in the stage production of **Dracula** in Oakland, California, and became infatuated with him. She wrote a short novella as a sequel to *Dracula* called *Countess Dracula* which concerns two couples who find their way to **Castle Dracula**. According to the script, they meet the Count, who tells them of the death of his "sisters" and hence his solitary existence. Borland subsequently contacted **Lugosi**, who invited her to join him for breakfast at his hotel. She later did a reading of her story for him.

While Lugosi was in Hollywood making *Dracula*, Borland was finishing high school and winning the California Young Shakespearean Actress Award. Her prize included a scholarship to the University of California. She did not remain long in school. Lugosi invited her to take the part of **Lucy** in a revival of the *Dracula* play, which was produced following the success of the movie. The tour, while brief, established their relationship, and in 1934 she auditioned for the part of Luna in *Mark of a Vampire*. Lugosi assisted her in landing the part (which included an under-the-table bribe). The part included only one line of dialogue, but the image created of the female vampire became one of the most memorable among 1930s films, and is sometimes cited as the direct inspiration of Morticia Addams (of **TheAddams Family**), and later of **Vampira** and **Elvira**.

Borland suffered for her role in *Mark of a Vampire*. Rumors circulated that she could not handle dialogue and hence she was offered only bit parts in the years to follow. She married, left acting, and became a teacher. Her novel was finally published shortly after her death in 1994.

Sources:
Borland, Caroll. *Countess Dracula.* Absecon, NJ: MagicImage Filmbooks, 1994. 143 pp.

Bouchard, Angélique

Angélique Bouchard (Lara Parker), the other vampire who appeared on the **Dark Shadows** television series, was introduced during the episodes that told the story of **Barnabas Collins's origin** in the 1790s. Barnabas had been engaged to marry a woman named Josette du Prés. Angélique, a witch, decided that she wanted him enough to interfere with the wedding by casting a spell on Josette that would cause her to fall in love with Jeremiah Collins, Barnabas's uncle. Angélique's actions did not win Barnabas to her, but it did lead to his killing his uncle in a duel. Angry and frustrated, Angélique unleashed a curse on Barnabas. Shortly thereafter a bat attacked him and he emerged from the encounter as a vampire. Angélique was the first person seen by the new vampire and her magical skill could not prevent her from becoming his initial **victim**.

Lara Parker as Angelique Bouchard in the original
Dark Shadows.

Barnabas's vampirism would soon lead to his confinement in the Collins family crypt in New England for two centuries. He was released in the late 1960s and in 1969, Angélique again entered Barnabas's life as Cassandra Collins, the wife of Roger Collins. At this point, Barnabas had been temporarily cured of his vampirism. His brief return to mortality was interrupted by the arrival of Nicolas Blair, who claimed to be Cassandra's brother. His first encounter with Blair, a warlock, led to a new attack by a **bat**. As a result Barnabas did not become a vampire, but did fall under Blair's power. Cassandra was killed; however, Blair raised her as a vampire. Like Barnabas, Angélique was a nocturnal creature with prominent **fangs**, who could be killed by **fire**, daylight, and a heartfelt **stake**. She eventually became the instrument of Barnabas's return to the vampiric life. After she bit him, he again became a vampire at the cost of temporarily transferring his allegiance away from Blair to her. Angélique's life as a vampire soon ended, but death is always a temporary matter for the magical creature.

Angélique was resurrected in 1998 in a novel written by Lara Parker, the actress who played her in the original series. The book traces Angélique's early life on Martinique in more depth than allowed by the series and covers early events in her life that turned her first to witchcraft and evil, and the attempts she made to escape her fate. The plot covers in depth the background to events mentioned in the TV show. In the novel, Parker describes the circumstances leading to the meeting between Angélique and Barnabas Collins, a soldier with whom she falls in love. As he heads off to war, he promises to wed her upon his return. Instead, he becomes engaged to her friend Josette. And Barnabas learns the consequences of spurning a witch.

This first novel received enough positive attention as to allow Parker to write other "Dark Shadows" titles, though they did feature Angélique.

Sources:

Parker, Lara, *Dark Shadows: Angélique's Descent.* New York: HarperEntertainment, 1998. 256 pp.
Scott, Kathryn Leigh, ed. *The Dark Shadows Companion: 25th Anniversary Collection.* Los Angeles: Pomegranate Press, 1990. 208 pp.

❦ Boucicault, Dion (1820–1890) ❦

Dion Boucicault was perhaps the most commercially successful playwright of the Victorian Era; his plays on the vampire theme were an important landmark in the spread of the vampire in the popular consciousness in mid-nineteenth-century England. Born Dionysus Larder Boursiquot in Dublin, he left school at an early age to join an

English **drama** company with whom he acted under the stage name Lee Moreton. He also began to write his own plays and gradually gave up acting for playwriting. In 1844 he began a four-year period in France studying the French stage and absorbing popular plots. He was in Paris in December 1851 to see his second version of *The Vampire* and after his return to England he quickly composed a vampire play for the popular actor Charles Keane (1811–68). Boucicault also had the use of the new Princess Theatre which had a full set of innovative technical resources.

Keane refused the part (as he was already engaged in another production) and Boucicault assumed the role himself. Keane's young ward Agnes Robertson did accept the female lead, and during the process of rehearsing Boucicault fell in love. In the next few years he would write plays not only for Keane but for Robertson. *The Vampire* earned Boucicault good reviews for his acting, but Robertson's review fell far short of expectations, and the play was not a commercial success. *The Vampire, A Phantasm in Three Dramas*, which opened in June 1852 at the Princess, was set in Wales. Its three acts followed a set of characters through their descendants, each act set one hundred years after the previous one. The heroine learns of her danger through a dream sequence in which the portraits of her ancestors come to life to warn her. The vampire is seen as seeking the love and **blood** of a virgin which, if found, will give him new life for another century.

In 1853, Boucicault and Robertson moved to the United States where they would stay until the outbreak of war. While here he rewrote *The Vampire* and came out with a new play, *The Phantom*, a much simplified and more realistic drama. He did not, for example, keep the scene in which the portraits came to life. *The Phantom* opened in Philadelphia in 1856 and in New York the following year. It became a standard part of his repertoire and he continued to develop it. Along the way, he even moved the setting from Wales to Scotland (à la Charles Nordier) and his own vampire character, Alan Raby, became Sir Alan Ruthven. The new play opened in **London** in 1861 and appears to have been much more successful than his first.

Boucicault himself seems to have had an understanding that in plays like *The Phantom* he was playing to a popular audience, not producing great drama or art. In reference to this, he is noted as having observed, "I can spin out these rough-and-tumble dramas as a hen lays eggs. It is a degrading occupation, but more money has been made out of Guano than out of poetry." Boucicault moved back to America in 1870 and stayed there until his death in 1890.

Sources:

Fawkes, Richard. *Dion Boucicault; A Biography*. London: Quartet, 1979. 292 pp.

Stuart, Roxana. *Stage Blood: Vampires of the 19th Century*. Bowling Green, OH: Bowling Green State University Popular Press, 1994. 377 pp.

Walsh, Townsend. *The Career of Dion Boucicault*. New York: Benjamin Blom, 1967. 224 pp.

The Bram Stoker Club *see:* The Bram Stoker Society

❰ The Bram Stoker Society ❱

The Bram Stoker Society was founded in 1980 to encourage the study and appreciation of the work of **Bram Stoker**, the author of **Dracula**. The society has devel-

oped a program to promote the appreciation of Stoker's work, especially as it relates to his life in Ireland, his birthplace. The society encourages research into the Irish associations of the Stoker family, promotes tourism connected with Stoker and other Irish **gothic** novelists (such as **Sheridan Le Fanu**), and campaigns for plaques to be placed on the Irish sites associated with the Stoker family. In 1983, partially in response to the society's efforts, a plaque was placed at No. 30 Kildare Street in Dublin, where Stoker resided in 1871. Stoker's granddaughter Ann Stoker, and his grandnephew Ivan Stoker-Dixon, attended the unveiling of the plaque, sponsored by the Irish Tourist Board.

In September 1986, the society suspended its independent existence and reorganized as The Bram Stoker Club of the Philosophical Society in Trinity College, Dublin. Stoker was at one time president of the Philosophical Society. On the occasion of the inauguration of the society, the Bram Stoker Archives were opened. The archives consisted of **Leslie Shepard**'s collection of Bram Stoker materials (first editions, autographs, and other memorabilia) on display in the Graduate Memorial Building. The exhibition was intended to be on permanent public display, but the issue of lack of proper security for the collection led Shepard to withdraw the materials from the room in May 1989.

In the wake of the disruption caused by the withdrawal of the collection, the society reorganized separately from the club and the college. The club has continued in existence as an approved independent body in Trinity College, and is affiliated with the Bram Stoker Society in Dublin. It currently sponsors the Bram Stoker International Summer School for a weekend each June (since 1991), held in Clontarf, Dublin, near Stoker's birthplace. It publishes a newsletter and an annual journal. It has pressed for the establishment of a permanent Bram Stoker museum in Dublin, a goal yet to be realized. Until his death in 2004, Les Shepard was the primary driving force in the society. The society may be contacted through Brian J. Showers (gothicdublin@gmail.com) or Albert Power (gothicalbert@eircom.net). It maintains an Internet presence at http://www.brianjshowers.com/stokersociety.html.

Sources:

Shepard, Leslie. *Bram Stoker: Irish Theatre Manager and Author.* Dublin: Impact Publications, 1994. 20 pp.

———, and Albert Power, eds. *Dracula: Celebrating 100 Years.* Dublin: Mentor Press, 1997. 192 pp.

Bram Stoker's Dracula

The most recent of the many attempts to bring the novel **Dracula**, by **Bram Stoker**, to the motion picture screen appeared in 1992 from Columbia Pictures. Directed by one of Hollywood's top directors, **Francis Ford Coppola**, it opened on Friday, November 13, and became the largest non-summer movie opening of all time.

Coppola had a goal of making a more accurate version of Stoker's original novel, and his version relied more closely on the storyline of the book than any previous *Dracula* movie. The story opened with **Jonathan Harker** (played by Keanu Reeves) leaving his fiance, **Mina Murray** (Winona Ryder), to travel to **Castle Dracula** in **Transylvania**. His first encounters with Dracula (**Gary Oldman**) reflected the major incidents recorded in the book, though Dracula's colorful appearance could hardly have been more different from his description in the novel. Their encounter as Harker was shaving produced one of the film's most memorable moments. Harker had cut himself, and Dracula took the razor from Harker and licked it to taste the drops of **blood**. Harker was attacked by the three female **vampire brides**, residents of the castle, and was only able to escape after Dracula left for England.

In England, the three suitors of **Lucy Westenra** (Sadie Frost)—**Quincey P. Morris** (Bill Campbell), **Arthur Holmwood** (Cary Elwes), and Dr. **John Seward** (Richard E. Grant)—rose to the occasion as Dracula launched his attack on her. Unable at first to determine the cause of her problems, Seward called in Dr. **Abraham Van Helsing** (Anthony Hopkins). Van Helsing organized the opposition that finally defeated Dracula after tracking him back to his castle.

While Coppola's version of *Dracula* is by far the most faithful to the book, it deviated at several important points. For example, as a prelude to the movie, Coppola briefly told the story of **Vlad the Impaler**, the fifteenth-century Romanian ruler who served as a historical reference for the Dracula character. This prelude indicated the influence of the books by **Raymond T. McNally** and **Radu Florescu**, creating fans for Vlad, the historical Dracula. In introducing the theme of Vlad the Impaler, Coppola

Winona Ryder as Mina Murray and Gary Oldman as Dracula in *Bram Stoker's Dracula*.

borrowed an idea from the **Dan Curtis/**Jack Palance **version of** *Dracula* (1973). Curtis used Vlad's story to provide the rationale for Dracula's attack upon the specific women he chose as targets in England. In *Dracula* (1974), Palance saw a picture of Lucy, Harker's fiance, who was the mirror image of his lost love of the fifteenth century. He traveled to England in order to recapture the love of his pre-vampire life. In *Bram Stoker's Dracula*, Winona Ryder played not only Mina Murray, but Elizabeth, Dracula's original love. To continue the storyline, Coppola allowed Dracula to walk around London freely in the daytime (as Dracula seemed able to do in the novel), but he now used his time in the city to establish a liaison with Mina and, with his suave continental manners, win her love. In the final scene, Mina went to the dying Dracula and through her love facilitated his redemption as he died.

Vlad's reaction to the death of Elizabeth (or Elisabeta), who committed **suicide** and hence could not go to heaven in Eastern Orthodox theology, provided Coppola with an explanation of the **origin** of Dracula's vampirism. Since she could not go to heaven, Dracula blasphemed God and symbolically attacked the cross with his sword. Blood flowed from the impaled cross, Dracula drank, and presumably as a result was transformed into a vampire.

Coppola also enlarged upon the account of **R. N. Renfield**, another character in the original novel who was introduced as a resident of the insane asylum managed by

John Seward, with no explanation as to the reason for his being there. His mental condition was explained by Coppola as a result of having traveled to **Castle Dracula**; Renfield became insane because of his encounters with the residents. This earlier connection with Dracula also explained why he, but none of the other inmates of the asylum, reacted to Dracula's arrival and activities in London.

Bram Stoker's Dracula was accompanied by a massive advertising campaign which included more than one hundred separate pieces of **paraphernalia** and souvenir items, including a novelization of the script, a four-issue **comic book** series, two sets of **trading cards**, jewelry, T-shirts, posters, a board game, and several home computer **games**. The TNT cable television network sponsored a sweepstakes the week of the movie's opening that offered the winner a trip to London, "one of Dracula's favorite cities!" While it opened to mixed reviews (an occupational hazard with any horror genre film), the Coppola movie shows every sign of taking its place as one of the most memorable *Dracula* adaptations of all time. It opened in Bucharest, **Romania**, in July 1993, at which time a special drink, dubbed "Dracula's Spirits" and made of vodka and red fruit juice, was issued by a Romanian distillery. In spite of the mixed reviews, the movie surprised media observers by becoming the largest box office opening ever experienced by Columbia and the largest ever for a non-summer opening. It played on almost 2,500 screens around the country and grossed more than $32 million.

Sources:

Biowrowski, Steve. "Coppola's Dracula." *Cinefantastique* 23, 4 (December 1992): 24–26, 31, 35, 39, 43, 47, 51, 55. One of a set of articles on the Coppola film in this issue of *Cinefantastique*.

Coppola, Francis Ford, and James V. Hart. *Bram Stoker's Dracula: The Film and the Legend*. New York: Newmarket Press, 1992. 172 pp. Rept. London: Pan Books, 1992. 172 pp.

Coppola, Francis Ford, and Eiko Ishioka. *Coppola and Eiko on Bram Stoker's Dracula*. San Francisco: Collins Publishers, 1992. 96 pp.

Holte, James Craig. *Dracula in the Dark: The Dracula Film Adaptations*. Westport, CT: Greenwood Press, 1997. 161 pp.

Rohrer, Trish Deitch. "Coppola's Bloody Valentine." *Entertainment Weekly* No. 145 (November 20, 1992): 22–31.

Saberhagen, Fred, and James V. Hart. *Bram Stoker's Dracula*. New York: New American Library, 1992. 301 pp.

Steranko, Jim. "Bram Stoker's Dracula." *Preview* 2, 49 (November/February 1993): 18–39, 59.

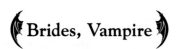

Brides, Vampire

Vampire brides is a popular term that refers to the harem-like arrangement that is believed to exist between the vampire (a male) and his **victims** (a group of young women). The idea derived entirely from **Bram Stoker**'s novel *Dracula*. During the opening chapters the title character lived in his remote castle home with three young **women**. They were described by a number of names including "young women," "weird sisters," and "ghostly women." At the end of the novel, **Abraham Van Helsing** entered **Castle Dracula** to kill the women, whom he simply called "sisters." The idea of calling them "brides" possibly derived from the incident in the novel when, following the death of **Lucy Westenra**, Lucy's fiance **Arthur Holmwood** suggested that the sharing of **blood** created a husband-wife relationship between himself and his now dead wife-to-be. How-

ever, the idea also received its substance from various movies which pictured a male vampire in a continuing relationship with several female vampires. Commonly in vampire novels and movies, vampires attack a person of the opposite sex. Most vampires were male and most of their victims, with whom they developed a close relationship, were women. This relationship has often been developed, by implication if not actual reference, in a manner similar to the popular image of the Middle Eastern harem. Frequently, the women were clothed in frilly bed clothes while the man was in formal dress. This image of the vampire brides was present in the two **Count Yorga** films and in **John Carradine**'s *The Vampire Hookers* (1979).

The "brides of Dracula" as portrayed in Francis Ford Coppola's *Bram Stoker's Dracula*. Keanu Reeves (center) played Jonathan Harker in the film.

The idea of the vampire brides emphasized the sexual nature of the vampire's relationship to his victims. The vampire attacked (raped) his victims and then tied them to him in a slavelike relationship in which love played little or no part. In *Dracula*, the three women accused him of never having loved and of loving no one in the present.

As part of the 1990s wave of interest in all things related to Dracula, it seemed inevitable that the stories of the brides would be explored by novelists. The first was **Elaine Bergstrom** in her Dracula sequel, *Mina* and at the end of the 1990s, **Chelsea Quinn Yarbro** published two volumes of a projected trilogy telling their story. In his alternate history novels (*Anno Dracula, The Bloody Red Baron*, and *Judgment of Tears*) in which Dracula takes over England, Kim Newman turns Dracula into a polygamist who not only has Queen Elizabeth as a spouse/prisoner, but a half dozen others: some real historical figures (such as Barbara of Celje, c. 1395-1441), some female characters from other fictional works (Sadie Thompson, Princess Asa).

In the movies, especially the various adaptations of Dracula, the brides have been minor characters, though they are involved in a famous attack/seduction scene with **Jonathan Harker** (Keanu Reeves) in **Francis Ford Coppola**'s *Bram Stoker's Dracula*. They have their most expansive participation in *Van Helsing*, where Marishka (Josie Maran), Aleera (Elena Anaya), and Verona (Silvia Colloca) assume a place in the battles between the movie's title character and Dracula.

Sources:

Kiraly, Marie (pseudonym of Elaine Bergstrom). *Mina*. New York: Berkley Books, 1994. 352pp.

Newman, Kim. *Anno-Dracula*. London: Simon and Schuster, 1992. 359 pp.

———. *The Bloody Red Baron*. New York: Carroll & Graf, 1995. 358 pp.

———. *Judgment of Tears: Anno Dracula 1959*. New York: Carroll & Graf, 1998. 291 pp.

Yarbro, Chelsea Quinn. *The Angry Angel*. New York: Avon Books, 1998. 359 pp.

———. *Soul of an Angel*. New York: Avon, 1999. 378 pp.

Brite, Poppy Z. (1967–)

Novelist Poppy Z. Brite emerged in the 1990s as the literary representative of the **gothic** punk culture, usually thought of as centering on goth music and the night-clubs where it flourishes. She also highlighted the vampiric element of that subculture through her first novel, *Lost Souls* (1992), which was nominated for Best First Novel of 1992 by the Horror Writers of America and for The Lambda Literary Award.

Brite was born and raised in **New Orleans**, where she returned after attending college at the University of North Carolina. While establishing herself as an author she held a number of odd jobs, including a stint as an exotic dancer, and still occasionally models. Her first stories appeared in the now-defunct magazine, *The Horror Show* between 1985 and 1990.

Lost Souls traces the modern adventures of a small group of vampires headed by Zillah, a 100-year-old vampire who, as the result of a one-night stand with a vampire, became the father of Nothing. As the alienated Nothing grew into adolescence, he left the parents who adopted and raised him and headed out to find his roots. He eventually encountered the ageless Zillah, learned the story of his **origin**, and returned to the French Quarter and the room where he was conceived. Brite followed her initial success with equally fine (if nonvampiric) novels: *Swamp Foetus*, *Drawing Blood*, and *Exquisite Corpse*, and a biography of rock musician and actress Courtney Love-Cobain.

Brite returned to vampires in two anthologies, hailed as among the finest collections of contemporary vampire stories: *Love in Vein* (1994) and *Love in Vein II* (1996), but has done very little in the genre since.

Sources:

Brite, P. Z. *Lost Souls*. New York: Asylum/Delacorte, 1992. 359 pp. Rept. New York: Dell, 1992. 355 pp.

———, ed. *Love in Vein*. New York: HarperPrism, 1994. 405 pp.

———. *Love in Vein II*. New York: HarperCollins, 1996.

"Interview: Poppy Z. Brite." *Journal of the Dark* 6 (Spring 1996): 7–8.

Browning, Tod (1882–1962)

Tod Browning, a career director of horror films who brought both **Lon Chaney Jr.** and **Bela Lugosi** to the screen in their first vampire roles, is best remembered today for his work on a single film, ***Dracula* (1931)**. He was born July 12, 1882, and raised in Louisville, Kentucky, but at the age of sixteen ran away from home and joined a carnival. For years he made his living by assuming various "horror" persona. His carnival performances led to his career as an actor. He appeared in his first film in 1913 and was soon working behind the camera. He assisted in directing for a couple of years and in 1917 directed his first movies, *Jim Bludso* and *Peggy, the Will o' the Wisp*. In 1919 he met Lon Chaney, who had a part in *The Wicked Darling*. They went their separate ways through the early 1920s, but were reunited at MGM in 1925 and for the next five years had one of the most fruitful collaborations Hollywood has known. Browning appreciated Chaney's ability to distort his face and apply makeup, and he developed scripts especially for the actor. Together they made *The Unholy Three* (1925), *The Blackbird* (1926), *The Road to Mandalay* (1926), *The Unknown* (1927), **London after Midnight** (1927), *West of Zanzibar* (1928), *The Big City* (1928), and *Where East Is East* (1929).

In 1927 Browning directed *London after Midnight,* the first vampire feature film, in which Chaney played both the vampire and the detective who pursued him. The film was memorable because of the extraordinary distorting makeup Chaney developed which, although highly effective, gave him great discomfort. The movie was based upon a novel, *The Hypnotist,* written by Browning, and then became the basis of a novelization by Marie Coolidge-Rask published in 1928 with stills from the movie. In Browning's plot, the vampire turned out to be an identity assumed by the detective to trap a criminal.

In 1930, as **Universal Pictures** was making its transition to talking movies, the company hired Browning to film *Dracula.* Browning immediately thought of Chaney for the starring role and approached him about the part. Unfortunately, before he could respond, Chaney died. Eventually, after a highly publicized search for an actor to play the title role, Bela Lugosi was selected.

Director Tod Browning, who became famous for directing the classic 1931 version of *Dracula.*

Browning has been seen by most film critics as a mediocre and unimaginative director, especially criticized for his largely stationary camera. He was now set to do what would become his most memorable film, an adaptation of the **Hamilton Deane** play as revised by **John L. Balderston**. Browning is best remembered for adding the opening scenes that occur in **Castle Dracula** during which Lugosi speaks his most memorable lines. The scene with Dracula standing on the stairs with a giant spider web behind him to welcome **R. N. Renfield** (in this version it is he, not **Jonathan Harker**, who goes to **Transylvania**) has been among the most reproduced images in movie history. These opening scenes lifted the movie from being merely a filmed stage play, the impression it gave once the action shifted to **London**.

Browning's *Dracula* must be seen in the context of its time. For all practical purposes it was the first *Dracula* movie. Few people had seen the banned *Nosferatu* or the other even lesser-known European attempts at adaptation. It was also one of the first horror movies with sound. Given the level to which movies had progressed, the low expectations for the film's success, and the financial hardship then being experienced by Universal, the production values of *Dracula* are understandable. Still, even today the opening scenes are effective, though post-**Hammer Films** audiences have been quick to note the sanitized presentation of a Dracula without visible **fangs** who never bites his **victims** in front of the audience. Nonetheless, one cannot deny the audience response to the movie; Universal credited it with keeping the company from bankruptcy.

THE VAMPIRE BOOK: THE ENCYCLOPEDIA OF THE UNDEAD

Tod Browning (left, with knee bent) directs the cast of *Dracula*, including Bela Lugosi (second from the left).

Browning would go on to make several more films in the 1930s. His next film, *Freaks*, became one of the most controversial movies of the era. A pet project, the movie harked back to his carnival days and pictured the lives of various people who were born with bodies that pushed them outside of acceptable society. It was banned in twenty-eight countries and was a commercial flop in the United States. He returned to the vampire theme in 1935 with *Mark of the Vampire*, a talkie remake of *London after Midnight*. Browning retired in 1939 following his work on *The Devil Dolls*, and lived quietly until his death on October 6, 1962.

Sources:

Coolidge-Rask, Marie. *London after Midnight*. New York: Grosset & Dunlap, 1928. 261 pp.

Everson, William K. *Classics of the Horror Film*. New York: Citadel Press, 1990. 247 pp.

Glut, Donald G. *The Dracula Book*. Metuchen, NJ: Scarecrow Press, 1975. 388 pp.

Herzogwenrath, Bernd. *The Cinema of Tod Browning: Essays of the Macabre and Grotesque*. Jeffersonville, NC: McFarland & Company, 2008. 249 pp.

———. *The Films of Tod Browning*. London: Black Dog Publishing, 2006. 238 pp.

Holte, James Craig. *Dracula in the Dark: The Dracula Film Adaptations*. Westport, CT: Greenwood Press, 1997. 161 pp.

Quinlan, David. *The Illustrated Guide to Film Directors*. Totowa, NJ: Barnes & Noble Books, 1984. 335 pp.

Skal, David. *Dark Carnival: The Secret World of Tod Browning, Hollywood's Master of the Macabre*. New York: Doubleday and Company, 1995. 359 pp.

Thompson, David. *A Biographical Dictionary of Film*. New York: William Morrow and Company, 1976. 629 pp.

Bruja

*B*ruja is the Spanish name for a witch. A *bruja* was very much like the *strega* of Italy and **bruxa** of neighboring Portugal. The term was found throughout Latin America where it was used simultaneously with local names for witches and for witch/vampires, such as the *tlahuelpuchi*, the blood-sucking witch of Mexico. In both Spain and the Americas, the *bruja* was a living person, usually a woman, who was able to transform herself into various kinds of animals and attack infants.

Sources:

Nutini, Hugo G., and John M. Roberts. *Bloodsucking Witchcraft: An Epistomological Study of Anthropomorphic Supernaturalism in Rural Thaxcala*. Tucson: University of Arizona Press, 1993. 476 pp.

Bruxa

The *bruxa* (female) or *bruxo* (male) was the witch figure of Portugal, similar in many ways to the **bruja** of Spain and Mexico. The *bruxa* was a pre-Christian figure that became prominent in the Middle Ages. At that time, the Inquisition focused attention upon pagan beliefs and demonized them as malevolent activities of **Satan**. In rural Portugal, belief in **witchcraft** survived into the twentieth century and the government periodically has taken measures to destroy its continuing influence.

The *bruxa* (who was generally described as a woman) entered the lists of vampire entities due to her bloodsucking attacks upon infants. She also assumed the form of various animals, most often a duck, rat, goose, dove, or ant. Her power was largely confined to the hours from midnight to two o'clock in the morning. The witches in a region gathered at the crossroads on Tuesdays and Fridays, and these days assumed negative connotations in Portuguese folklore. At their gatherings, the witches were believed to worship Satan, from whom they gained various evil powers, such as the evil eye.

Protection from a **bruxa** was supplied by a wide variety of magical amulets. Children were also protected by the use of iron and steel. A steel nail on the ground or a pair of scissors under their pillow would keep the witches away. There was also a belief in the spoken word, and the folklore was rich in examples of various incantations against witches. **Garlic** would be sewn into the clothes of children to protect them from being carried away by witches.

After an attack, attempts would be made to identify the malevolent witch. The mother of the deceased child could boil the child's clothes while jabbing them with a sharp instrument. The witch would supposedly feel the jabs on her own body and would be compelled to come and ask for mercy. Or the mother might take a broom and sweep the house backwards, from the door inward, while repeating an incantation to make the witch manifest. The broom, a symbol of witchcraft, was used to cause witches to relax. As recently as 1932, author Rodney Gallop reported the case of an infant in the town of Santa Leocadia de Baiao who had died of suffocation. The parents were sure that it had been "sucked by witches." The grandmother reported seeing the witch fly away disguised as a black sparrow.

Because of her ability to transform into animal forms, the *bruxa* was often associated with the **lobishomen**, the name by which **werewolves** were known in Portugal. The lobishomen was also known to change form on Tuesdays and Fridays, the same days the witches gathered.

Sources:
Gallop, Rodney. *Portugal: A Book of Folk-Ways*. Cambridge: Cambridge University Press, 1936. 291 pp.

Buffy   *see:* Summers, Buffy

Buffy the Vampire Slayer (Movie)

The popularity of the **Buffy the Vampire Slayer** television series often obscures the modestly successful 1992 movie that began the whole phenomenon and essentially

In the film version of *Buffy the Vampire Slayer,* Kirsty Swanson plays Buffy, who has to contend with the vampire king Lothos (Rutger Hauer).

launched the career of Joss Whedon. Although *Buffy the Vampire Slayer* was based on his original screenplay, Whedon has complained that the end product bore but faint resemblance to his original work.

The storyline of the movie centers upon **Buffy Summers** (Kristy Swanson), a cheerleader at Hemery High School in Los Angeles in the early 1990s. As she went about her vapid existence in which the next trip to the mall or the school dance were her only concerns, she met a strange man named Merrick (Donald Sutherland) who informed her that she was the Chosen One. Once each generation, there is a Chosen One who will stand alone against the vampires and the forces and entities of the evil supernatural world. That person is called the Slayer. As can be imagined, this news was, to say the least, most disturbing to the young teenager.

Buffy initially rejected the idea, but the naturally athletic cheerleader also found herself drawn to Merrick, the man destined to be her trainer. She had had strange dreams in which she faced enigmatic creatures in historical settings. Merrick claimed that her dreams were, in fact, her memories of real events from previous lives. He also claimed that he was also present when they occurred.

Once he secured Buffy's attention, Merrick elaborated on her role as one of the Order of Slayers. Each woman who was a Slayer had a birthmark on her left shoulder. Each would be reincarnated over and over again and spend each new lifetime stopping the spread of vampirism. History aside, Buffy had a more immediate crisis. Lothos (Rutger Hauer), a one thousand two hundred-year-old vampire king, had come to Los Angeles, and Merrick took Buffy to the local cemetery to observe the emergence of some of Lothos's first **victims** from their graves. Her encounter with the new vampires convinced Buffy of the truth of all Merrick had told her.

While trying to lead an outwardly normal life, Buffy spent her afternoons perfecting her fighting skills which she demonstrated each evening by dispatching Lothos's minions with a **stake**. Her activity soon caught the attention of Lothos, who in his anger killed Merrick. He also concluded that Buffy was the new Slayer. Because she stood between him and his destiny she had to be slain. He gathered his group of new followers for an attack upon the upcoming school dance in the gym. At the dance, Buffy squared-off against Lothos, although it took all of her martial arts skills. During the fight, she made a stake from a broken chair and drove it home with a well-placed kick. Lothos died with the now immortal word, "Oops!" With Lothos out of the way, it appeared that Buffy could finish high school and resume her vampire slaying as an adult. But such was not to be the case. As would be made known in 1997 in the new *Buffy the Vampire Slayer* television series, she had burned down the very gym in which Lothos had died in order to destroy more of his minions. She was then transferred to a suburban high school in the community of Sunnydale.

The Buffy movie was released to mixed reviews and a largely negative reaction from vampire fans. It clicked neither as a horror movie nor as a comedy. However, it did reasonably well at the box office, emerging over the years as one of the twenty-five highest grossing vampire movies, ahead of such honored classics as *The Hunger* and *Near Dark*, and a soundtrack CD followed.

In 1999, the movie would be adapted as a comic book/graphic novel, *Buffy the Vampire Slayer: The Origin*, with the storyline slightly altered to make it fit into the plot of the first season of the television series. There are several discrepancies between the movie version of the story and the television version. In the movie, Buffy comes from a well-to-do family and she is a stereotypical shallow valley girl. Buffy is a senior in the movie but will begin the television series as a sophomore. The movie vampires do not turn to dust when staked, nor do they show the facial change so notable of the series vampires. Both slayers and their watchers are repeatedly reincarnated and the former identified by a mole on their shoulder.

Sources:

Golden, Christopher, Dan Brereton, and Joe Bennett. *Buffy the Vampire Slayer: The Origin*. No. 1–3. Milwaukie, OR: Dark Horse Comics, 1999.

Hemery High School Yearbook 1992. Los Angeles: Twentieth Century Fox, 1992. 28 pp.

❮ *Buffy the Vampire Slayer* (Television Series) ❯

The original **Buffy the Vampire Slayer** movie appeared in 1992 to mixed reviews. Its creator Joss Whedon (born Joseph Hill Whedon, 1964) considered it a significantly

The cast of the television series *Buffy the Vampire Slayer,* starring Sarah Michelle Geller (center) as Buffy.

altered representation of his original screenplay but also a stage of development of the Buffy character he wanted. He has noted that he traces his interest in the character of Buffy as an attempt to reimagine a horror stereotype, the image of a naïve but beautiful young woman wandering into a dark alley only to be dispatched by some monster. He looked for a movie in which the girl goes into the alley and turns the tables on the monster using her own remarkable strength and powers.

During the years following the movie, Whedon expanded his knowledge of the vampire genre as it had appeared on both television and in the movies and thought more about the nature of horror. The darker world inhabited by the television Buffy manifested from the very first episode, in which Whedon now set his characters in a world reminiscent of the Chtulu mythos of H. P. Lovecraft. Whedon concentrates on the immediate battle between good and evil, between the "powers that be" and the forces of supernatural evil that once overran planet earth. These forces have been pushed back into the nether reaches, but are constantly trying to return through the Hellmouth, which Weadon locates in Sunnydale, a small California city that bears a remarkable resemblance to Santa Barbara. (An original Hellmouth is found in the sleepy town of Caicais, Portugal, and so designated because of an unusual rock formation that an angry sea had carved out of the rocky shoreline.) Whedon's world is inhabited by a spectrum of demonic characters, most importantly the vampires. To keep the vampires in check, the cosmos regularly spits up a slayer, a young female with some extraordinary abilities.

There is but a single slayer at any given moment, but as soon as a slayer is killed, a new one arises to take her place. There are several slayers in training at any time. At the end of Season One, Buffy dies for a few minutes only to be revived. Her death, however, calls up the next slayer, first Kendra Young (Bianca Lawson) and then Faith Lehane (Eliza Dushku), and for the remainder of the series two slayers exist simultaneously.

Whedon conceived of vampires as deceased humans reanimated by invading demonic spirits. When killed, they immediately disintegrate into dust (very much as **Dracula** in **Hammer's** *The Horror of Dracula*), a convenient revision of the vampire myth which keeps the authorities uninvolved since the Slayer does not leave a pile of corpses behind no matter how many vampires she eliminates. Vampires have the memory of the person whose body they inhabit, but no soul, hence no conscience. Most vampires in Buffy, lacking a soul, are evil and fit only for quick dispatch, and most episodes began with the Slayer doing just that. Angel, the vampire who falls in love with Buffy, is cursed with a soul/conscience that continually wars with his vampiric urges, thus creating his special hell.

In creating Angel, Whedon adapted his unique idea of the vampire to the new conflicted vampire explored by **Dan Curtis** in *Dark Shadows* and **Anne Rice** in her novels, and the good-guy vampire developed in the comic book *Vampirella* and the novels of **Chelsea Quinn Yarbro** and **Fred Saberhagen**. Just as the original Buffy movie was released, a good-guy vampire appeared on television in the person of Nick Knight, the vampire detective in *Forever Night*. When emotionally upset or about to feed, the vampires of *Forever Knight* put on what became known as a "game face," a horrific appearance not unlike that of a klingon on *Star Trek*. Finally, from the Hong Kong vampire movies, Whedon introduced the martial arts as a major weapon in the Slayer's arsenal.

In spite of Whedon's maturing vision, the television series attempted to provide some continuity with the movie. After the events at her Los Angeles high school, **Buffy Summers** and her mother hoped to finally resume a normal life, but through the show's early episodes Buffy comes to understand that normality and peace were not central to her existence.

She was bothered by dreams and, more importantly, has the burden of understanding the significance of the wave of deaths and disappearances among her new classmates. One body had even dropped out of a locker in the gym. The librarian, **Rupert Giles**, offered her a book on vampires.

Very early in her career at Sunnydale, Buffy found a support group among a small group of students who come to believe in the existence of vampires and appreciate Buffy's distinctive position in life. Willow Rosenberg (Alyson Hannigan) is a shy computer nerd, pretty, but rather inept socially. **Xander Harris** (Nicholas Brendon) is a young teen who is too unhip to be popular. **Cornelia Chase** (Charisma Carpenter), one of the most popular (and shallow) girls in school, was rewarded for her attempts to introduce Buffy into the circle of the school's elite by being drawn into the Slayer's supernatural world. The group was held together by the wise Giles, Buffy's Watcher, whose library also became their headquarters. Giles relied on Willow to extend his knowledge through her knowledgable use of the **Internet**.

Only reluctantly did Buffy reconcile herself to her Chosenness. Her immediate task was to handle the Master, a powerful ancient vampire king who had planned to renter the world of humans from which he had been banished. Each century there is an evening, called the Harvest, when he can select another vampire, a vessel, and send him out into the world. On the evening in question, his vessel Luke took over The Bronze, a teen club, and began to feed. The Master felt the **strength** received from each feeding, as if he had been feeding himself. Unfortunately for the Master, before he could gain the strength to break free, Buffy arrived and killed Luke.

The key person in her last-minute rescue of her classmates was a young man who warned her about the Harvest. Although he appeared to be a young man only a few years older than Buffy, he turned out to be a two hundred and forty-year-old vampire named **Angel** (David Boreanaz). Once a vicious killer, he encountered some **Gypsies** who punished him by restoring his soul, or conscience, with a magical curse. With his soul restored, Angel found that he could no longer kill.

Although Buffy stopped the Master, it was only temporary. He would be back and it would be Angel who again intervened and told of a prophecy indicating that on the following evening Buffy would have to fight the Master and she would lose. The next evening, at the school dance, Buffy and the Master did fight, and Buffy did lose. However, she was rescued and revived by her friends and ended the initial season by destroying the Master permanently.

Seasons Two and Three saw Buffy and her colleagues through the last two years of high school, during which time they slew countless vampires and a few supernatural baddies of a non-vampiric nature, mostly demons of one sort or the other. Buffy's love life with her vampire boyfriend Angle blossomed, but had a disastrous ending when during their intimate time together, Angel had a moment of joy and reverted to his vampire nature. Buffy had to impale him with a sword.

She also had her first encounters with **Spike** (James Marsters) and his slightly crazy girlfriend Drusilla, in what would become a rocky relationship. Willow's heart would be broken when Xander became involved with someone, but she would recover with the help of Oz, the loveable werewolf. Buffy's rivalry with the other slayer Faith would lead Faith into an alliance with Sunnydale's mayor, who turned out to be a demon, and would culminate at their high school graduation. When the vampire was able to come out in the daytime momentarily, Buffy and her friends had to organize the student body to fight for their future. The mayor would be killed when he chased Buffy into the school which had been loaded with explosives. Recalling the fire at her first outing, Buffy ended her high school career by destroying Sunnydale High.

Angel who has returned from the hell Buffy had sent him to, recovered to join the graduation battle, but immediately afterwards, left for Los Angeles and his new series built around his quest for redemption. Cornelia would soon also find her way to Angel's door, leaving Giles, Willow, and Xander to carry on in Sunnydale. Willow and Buffy would attend college, at the University of California at Sunnydale, while Xander tried his hand at a construction job. With the school library destroyed, their new headquarters would become a local magic shop now run by Giles. Buffy got a new love life in the person of Riley Finn, a soldier with a unit called the "Initiative," which specializes in fighting the supernatural invaders with the latest technology. Among their victims is Spike, who has a chip placed in him preventing him from doing any harm to humans. Eventually Oz would leave to try to find a cure for his lycanthropy, and Willow would discover that she is a lesbian. Unlike Riley, whom the fans generally disliked, they fell in love with Willow's girlfriend, Tara Maclay. Xander would eventually fall for Anya, a demon who gave up her powers to be with him.

Buffy's family would be enlarged at the beginning of Season Five with the addition of a sister, Dawn, who arrives out of nowhere, complete with a set of memories involving the main characters, who weave her into the action as if she had always been present. Buffy eventually discovers that Dawn is a mystical object known as the Key, transformed into human form and sent to the Slayer for protection. When the villainous Glory (Clare Kramer) uses Dawn to break down the barriers separating the dimensions, Buffy sacrifices her own life to save the world as we know it.

Buffy's death sets the scene for Willow to emerge as a witch whose magic is real and powerful. It is powerful enough to bring Buffy back from the grave, and send her on a quest for power that becomes addictive and almost costs her the relationship with Tara. In her attempt to readjust from being pulled back from her brief visit to a heaven-like realm, Buffy begins an intense relationship with the vampire Spike, who falls for Buffy only to find her still in love with Angel.

Willow is recovering from her addiction to magic only to have Tara taken from her by a stray bullet intended for Buffy. In her grief, she tracks down Warren Mears, who fired the bullets and she uses her magic powers to skin him alive. She then transforms into her opposite, popularly called Dark Willow, but recovers to engage in the final battle that pits Buffy against the First Evil, a being that has manifested from all the evil in existence. The First makes itself known through its agent-sidekick Caleb, a serial killer who appears as a priest. The First is an incorporeal entity who able to come to earth because of the instability introduced into the cosmos when Buffy is raised from the dead. He sets about to destroy the slayers-in-waiting and the Watchers Council that oversees them. The surviving slayers come to Sunnydale, where a final battle is in the making at the Hellmouth.

In the final episode, Buffy, Spike, the rehabilitated Faith, and all the would-be slayers fight against the horde of vampires who are storming into the human realm. In the battle Anya dies and Spike shows his love for Buffy by sacrificing himself. The amulet he wears, which channels the sun's light, turns the tide of the battle. Sunnydale is destroyed, but humanity is saved.

Whedon uses the last episode to punctuate the feminist message he has been projecting through the series: Every woman is a potential slayer, they just have to step forward and claim their status. In the final episode, Willow uses her magic powers to turn all of the potential slayers into actual slayers. Henceforth, there will be more than one slayer.

On Television: The first episode of *Buffy the Vampire Slayer* aired on March 10, 1997, on the WB network, and is credited with saving the young network and setting it on a firm footing with its youthful audience. The first five seasons remained on the WB, but the last two were run on the UPN Network. The show then ran in syndication on the FX cable network. In England the show ran on Sky1 and BBC2. On both networks, it was run in two versions. In the afternoon, presumably when a younger audience was watching, it was run in a sanitized version, with violence and sex deleted. The original version was run in the evenings during prime time. The series was also translated for viewing in France, Germany, Italy and Russia, and other countries.

Aftermath: *Buffy the Vampire Slayer* remained on the air for seven seasons (1997–2003) while the spin-off *Angel* ran for five (1999–2004). *Angel* became the first story line developed from the original series. Besides Cornelia, several Buffy characters found their way to Los Angeles to become regulars on the show, including Faith and the vampires Harmony Kendall (Mercedes McNab), Darla (Julie Benz) and after the last battle in Sunnydale, Spike.

In 2007, Season Eight of Buffy would appear in a most unusual format, the comic book. An original "Buffy the Vampire Slayer" comic series had appeared from Dark Horse comics with sixty-three issues between 1990 and 2003. A variety of miniseries were subsequently published. But in 2007, Dark Horse began a second series that was partially written by Joss Whedon and sanctioned as an official continuation of the story after the end of the television series. It is popularly termed "the eighth season". As of the summer of 2009, twenty-six issues of a projected forty issues have appeared.

As the eighth season has unfolded, Buffy has robbed a Swiss bank to obtain the funds to set up a technologically sophisticated central command for those slayers aligned

to her (about 500 of the 1,800 in existence). Also at Buffy's command is a large number of psychics and witches. To help protect the famous slayer, two decoy slayers have been deployed. From headquarters in a Scottish castle, Buffy and Xander have organized the slayers into ten squads. Giles heads one in England, while Robing the principal of Sunnydale High School at the time when the town was destroyed, leads one in Cleveland, Ohio. Two other slayers, Vi and Rona, who appeared in the seventh season, are operating in New York and Chicago.

The United States government, already aware of the existence of a variety of demonic beings, did not ignore the destruction of Sunnydale. They now look upon Buffy and her allies as a dangerous "terrorist" group that must be handled in the same manner as vampires and demons. They have recruited Amy Madison (a witch from the original series) and the still skinless Warren Mears. And, in case the government's coming after her is not enough, Buffy must stave off the ambitions of a British socialite-turned-slayer named Lady Genevieve Savidge, who wishes to take Buffy's place at the head of the slayer organization. And among the vampires, a savvy group from Japan are working on a way to reverse Willow's global activation of the Potential Slayers. Behind all these forces targeting Buffy is an enigmatic character named Twilight. He heads a secret organization not unlike the original Initiative that views Buffy and the slayers as the enemy of humanity, as harmful as the vampires and demons. He aims to end the age of magic, both good and evil.

Buffy culture: Buffy the Vampire Slayer became a "cult" phenomenon that spun off numerous items beginning with a series of books, some novelized versions of the different episodes and others as entirely new stories. The comic books, action figures, and some twenty sets of trading cards soon followed. Pictures of the primary cast members and the show's logo could be found on items from watches to lunch boxes, with T-shirts being among the most popular.

The show grew with an expansion of the Internet, and fan activity made full use of it. Internet networks led to organization of the first fan gatherings, and many of the cast members showed up for an annual gathering in Los Angeles. Fan fiction also became quite popular until suppressed for a host of copyright and trademark considerations.

A most fascinating phenomenon was found within the scholarly community, where an appreciation of Buffy, then Angel, and then the work of Joss Whedon evolved. Interest developed initially among professors of cinema and television, but soon spread to scholars of literature, sociology, philosophy, and religious studies. An initial conference was held at the University of East Anglia in Norwich, England in October 2002 under the title "Blood, Text and Fears: Reading around Buffy the Vampire Slayer." The conference brought together a hundred scholars from across Europe and North America and as far away as Australia. Recognizing the emerging field of "Buffyology," two American scholars, Rhonda Wilcox and David Laverty, put together Slayage—an online scholarly journal, a network of scholars, and beginning in 2004, biennial conferences. Almost four hundred scholars showed up for the 2004 conference in Nashville, Tennessee. The next conference is projected for St. Augustine Florida in the summer of 2010.

The scholarly attention to Buffy and what is now termed the "Whedonverses," has had a dramatic effect on the production of academic work on vampires. More than half of all the published scholarly articles on vampires have had *Buffy the Vampire Slayer* and/or

Angel as their subject. Slayage also gives the Mt. Pointy awards for the best writing on the Whedonverses, the award being named for the stake that the slayer Kendra gave to Buffy.

Sources:

Beatrice, Allyson. *Will the Vampire People Please Leave the Lobby? True Adventures in Cult Fandom*. Naperville, IL: Sourcebooks, Inc., 2007. 272 pp.

Golden, Christopher, and Nancy Holder. *Buffy the Vampire Slayer: The Watcher's Guide*. New York: Pocket Books, 1998. 298 pp.

Golden, Christopher, Stephen R. Bissette, and Thomas E. Sniegoski. *Buffy the Vampire Slayer: The Monster Book*. New York: Pocket Books, 2000. 370 pp.

Holder, Nancy, with Jeff Mariotte and Maryelizabeth Hart. *Buffy the Vampire Slayer: The Watcher's Guide. Volume 2*. New York: Pocket Books, 2000. 472 pp.

Koontz, K. Dale. *Faith and Choice in the Works of Joss Whedon*. Jeffersonville, NC: McFarland & Company, 2008. 231 pp.

Ruditis, Paul. *Buffy the Vampire Slayer: The Watcher's Guide*. Volume 3. New York: Simon Spotlight, 2004. 359 pp.

South, James, ed. *Buffy the Vampire Slayer and Philosophy*. LaSalle, IL: Open Court, 2003. 335 pp.

Stafford, Nikki. *Bite Me! The Unofficial Guide to Buffy the Vampire Slayer*. Toronto: ECW Press, 2007. 397 pp.

Topping, Keith. *The Complete Slayer: An Unofficial and Unauthorised Guide to Every Episode of Buffy the Vampire Slayer*. London: Virgin, 2004. 704 pp.

Wilcox, Rhonda V. *Why Buffy Matters: The Art of Buffy the Vampire Slayer*. I. B. Tauris & Company, 2005. 246 pp.

———, and David Lavery, eds. *Fighting the Forces: What's at Stake in Buffy the Vampire Slayer*. Lanham, MD: Rowman & Littlefield Publishers, 2002. 290 pp.

Yeffeth, Glenn. *Seven Seasons of Buffy: Science Fiction and Fantasy Writers Discuss Their Favorite Television Show*. Dallas, TX: Benbella Books, 2003. 205 pp.

———, ed. *Five Seasons of Angel: Science Fiction and Fantasy Writers Discuss Their Favorite Vampire*. Dallas, TX: Benbella Books, 2004. 216 pp.

Bulgaria, Vampires in

Bulgaria is one of the oldest areas of Slavic settlement. It is located south of Romania and sandwiched between the Black Sea and Macedonia. In the seventh century C.E., the Bulgar tribes arrived in the area of modern Bulgaria and established a military aristocracy over the Slavic tribes of the region. The Bulgars were only a small percentage of the population, and they eventually adopted the Slavic language.

Christianity arrived with force among the Bulgarians in the ninth century when Pope Nicholas I (r. 858–867) claimed jurisdiction over the lands of the former Roman province of Illyricum. He sent missionaries into Bulgaria and brought it under Roman hegemony. The Bulgarian ruler, Boris-Michael, was baptized in 865, and the country officially accepted Christianity. The pope sent two bishops but would not send an archbishop or appoint a patriarch, causing Boris to switch his allegiance to the eastern church in Constantinople. A Slavic liturgy was introduced to the church and has remained its rite to the present.

Among the many side effects of Byzantine influence in Bulgaria was the growth of a new rival religious group, the Bogomils. The Bogomils grew directly out of an older group, the Paulicians, whose roots went back to the dualistic Maniceans. The Paulicians had been moved into Bulgaria from Asia Minor in order to prevent their alignment with the Muslim Arabs. The Bogomils believed that the world had been created by the rejected son of God, Satanael. While the earthly bodies of humans were created by Satanael, the soul came from God. It was seen by the church as a rebirth of the old gnostic heresy. Jan L. Perkowski has argued at length that it was in the conflict of Bogomil ideas, surviving Paganism, and emerging Christianity that the mature idea of the Slavic vampire developed and evolved. However, his argument was not entirely convincing in that vampires developed in quite similar ways in countries without any Bogomilism. When the Christian Church split in 1054, the Bulgarians adhered to the orthodoxy of Constantinople.

The Bulgarians gained their independence at the end of the twelfth century, but were overrun by the Ottomans in 1396. They remained under Ottoman rule until 1878, when Turkish control was restricted by the Congress of Berlin, but they did not become independent until 1908.

The Bulgarian Vampire: The Bulgarian words for the vampire, a variety of the **Slavic vampire,** derived from the original Slavic opyrb/opirb. Its modern form appears variously as *vipir, vepir,* or *vapir*), or even more commonly as *vampir,* a borrowing from Russian. The modern idea of the vampire in Bulgaria evolved over several centuries. Most commonly, the Bulgarian vampire was associated with problems of death and burial, and the emergence of vampires was embedded in the very elaborate myth and ritual surrounding death. At the heart of the myth was a belief that the spirits of the dead went on a journey immediately after death. Guided by their guardian angel, they traveled to all of the places they had visited during their earthly life. At the completion of their journey, which occurred in the forty days after their death, the spirit then journeyed to the next life. However, if the burial routine was done improperly, the dead might find their passage to the next world blocked. Generally, in Bulgaria, the family was responsible for preparing the body for burial. There were a number of ways in which the family could err or become negligent in their preparation. Also, the body had to be guarded against a dog or cat jumping over it or a shadow falling on it prior to burial. The body had to be properly washed. Even with proper burial, a person who died a violent death might return as a vampire.

As in other Slavic countries, certain people were likely candidates to become vampires. Those who died while under excommunication from the church might become a vampire. Drunkards, thieves, murderers, and witches were also to be watched. Bulgaria was a source of tales of vampires who had returned to life, taken up residence in a town where they were not known, and lived for many years as if alive. They even married and fathered children. Such people were detected after many years because of some unusual event that occurred. Apart from their nightly journeys in search of **blood,** the vampire would appear normal, even eating a normal diet.

Among the Gagauz people—Bulgarians who speak their own language, Gagauzi—the vampire was called *obur,* possibly a borrowing from the Turkish word for glutton. As with other vampires among the southern **Slavs,** the *obur* was noted as a gluttonous blood drinker. As part of the efforts to get rid of it, it would be enticed by the offerings of rich food or excrement. The *obur* was also loud, capable of creating noises like firecrackers, and could move objects like a poltergeist.

James Frazer noted the existence of a particular Bulgarian vampire, the *ustrel*. The *ustrel* was described as the spirit of a child who had been born on a Saturday but who died before receiving baptism. On the ninth day after its burial, a *ustrel* was believed to work its way out of its grave and attack cattle or sheep by draining their blood. After feasting all night, it returned to its grave before dawn. After some ten days of feeding, the *ustrel* was believed to be strong enough that it did not need to return to its grave. It found a place to rest during the day either between the horns of a calf or ram or between the hind legs of a milch-cow. It was able to pick out a large herd and begin to work its way through it, the fattest animals first. The animals it attacked—as many as five a night—would die the same night. If a dead animal was cut open, the signs of the wound that the vampire made would be evident.

As might be suspected, the unexplained death of cows and sheep was the primary sign that a vampire was present in the community. If a *ustrel* was believed to be present, the owner of the herd could hire a *vampirdzhija*, or **vampire hunter**, a special person who had the ability to see vampires, so that all doubt as to its presence was put aside. Once it was detected, the village would go through a particular ritual known throughout Europe as the lighting of a needfire. Beginning on a Saturday morning, all the fires in the village were put out. The cattle and sheep were gathered in an open space. They were then marched to a nearby crossroads where two bonfires had been constructed. The bonfires were lit by a new **fire** created by rubbing sticks together. The herds were guided between the fires. Those who performed this ritual believed that the vampire dropped from the animal on whose body it had made its home and remained at the crossroads where wolves devoured it. Before the bonfires burned out, someone took the flame into the village and used it to rekindle all the household fires.

Other vampires, those that originated from the corpse of an improperly buried person or a person who died a violent death, were handled with the traditional **stake**. There were also reports from Bulgaria of a unique method of dealing with the vampire: bottling. This practice required a specialist, the *djadadjii*, who had mastered the art. The *djadadjii*'s major asset was an icon, a holy picture of Jesus, Mary, or one of the Christian saints. The vampire hunter took his icon and waited where the suspected vampire was likely to appear. Once he saw the vampire, he chased it, icon in hand. The vampire was driven toward a bottle that had been stuffed with its favorite food. Once the vampire entered the bottle, it was corked and then thrown into the fire.

The folklore of the vampire has suffered in recent decades. The government manifested great hostility toward all it considered superstitious beliefs, which included both vampires and the church. As the church was suppressed, so was the unity of village life that provided a place for tales of vampires to exist.

Sources:

Abbott, G. F. *Macedonian Folklore*. Chicago: Argonaut, Inc., Publishers, 1986.

Blum, Richard, and Eva Blum. *The Dangerous Hour: The Lore of Crisis and Mystery in Rural Greece*. London: Chatto & Windus, 1970. 410 pp.

Brautigam, Rob. "Vampires in Bulgaria." *International Vampire* 1, 2 (Winter 91): 16–17.

Frazer, James G. *The Golden Bough*. Vol. 10. *Balder the Beautiful: The Fire-Festivals of Europe and the Doctrine of the External Soul*. London: Macmillan and Co., 1930. 346 pp.

Georgieva, Ivanichka. *Bulgarian Mythology*. Sofia: Svyet, 1985.

Nicoloff, Assen. *Bulgarian Folklore.* Cleveland, OH: The Author, 1975. 133 pp.

———. *Bulgarian Folktales.* Cleveland, OH: The Author, 1979. 296 pp.

Perkowski, Jan L. *The Darkling: A Treatise on Slavic Vampirism.* Columbus, OH: Slavica Publishers, 1989. 174 pp.

St. Clair, Stanislas Graham Bower, and Charles A. Brophy. *Twelve Years Study of the Eastern Question in Bulgaria.* London: Chapman & Hall, 1877. 319 pp.

Summers, Montague. *The Vampire in Europe.* 1929. New Hyde Park, NY: University Books, 1961. 329 pp.

Bullet

According to **Abraham Van Helsing**, the vampire expert in the novel *Dracula*, a "sacred bullet" fired into a **coffin** containing a vampire will kill it. It was not an option that was pursued during the course of *Dracula*. Generally, however, a bullet, in this case a silver bullet, was the traditional means of killing **werewolves,** and guns have been thought to have little or no effect on vampires. **Stoker** derived this insight directly from Emily Gerard's article, "Transylvanian Superstitions" later incorporated in her book,*The Land beyond the Forest,* his major source for information on **Transylvania.** Gerard reported that a bullet fired into the coffin was a means of killing vampires among the Transylvanian peasantry.

The idea was used in twentieth-century novels and movies, which frequently pictured the vampire's fate when confronted with modern weaponry. In those cases, however, if the vampire was hurt by the attack, the harm was very temporary, and the vampire quickly recovered to wreak vengeance upon those secularists who would put their faith in modern mechanical artifacts.

Relative to vampire movies, attacking vampires with bullets can be divided into three categories: incidents in which a bullet is fired into a vampire's body, usually with no effect; a bullet fired into the head with the idea of causing significant destruction to the brain; and fire from automatic weapons, which have the effect of cutting through the body (much as a large sword) destroying body parts and severing the spine. Occasionally, guns may be used to deliver silver or wood into a vampire.

Sources:

Gerard, Emily. *The Land beyond the Forest.* 2 vols. New York: Harper and Brothers, 1888.

———. "Transylvanian Superstitions." *The Nineteenth-Century* 18 (1885): 135–50. Rept. in Peter Haining, ed. *The Dracula Scrapbook.* New York: Bramwell House, 1975.

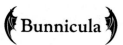 Bunnicula

This vampire, a favorite of children, does not wear a tuxedo and cape and his hair does not sweep back in a widow's peak. He also does not need to shape-shift into an **animal** form, because he already is a rabbit. He does not partake of **blood**, but rather a series of adventures, all of which are chronicled by James and Deborah Howe, who have coauthored several books featuring the character Bunnicula.

According to the premier story, *Bunnicula* (1979), Bunnicula made his first appearance in a theater during a **Dracula** movie. He was found by Pete and Toby Monroe, who

made him their pet, and named him Bunnicula after the movie. He joined the Monroe's other two pets, Chester the cat and Harold the dog. Even though he does not suck blood, Bunnicula attacks objects such as carrots and tomatoes and sucks the juice out of them, leaving only a husk behind. He sleeps all day and has two **fangs**, just like Count **Orlock**.

One evening soon after his arrival, Bunnicula awoke from his daytime **sleep** and, during the night, headed for the kitchen. Chester spotted him raiding the refrigerator. He left behind the white husk of a tomato from which he had sucked the life (color) and juice. While Mrs. Monroe was baffled, Chester, who spent his spare time reading books, figured out that Bunnicula was a vampire. Chester also knew how to deal with the situation. He placed **garlic** on the floor in such a way as to keep the rabbit out of the kitchen. It was Harold who recognized that Chester was starving Bunnicula and doing so for no reason. Harold believed the rabbit was not doing anyone any harm and Chester should not act in a hostile manner toward him. While convincing Chester of the righteousness of his argument, he smuggled the thirsty Bunnicula into the kitchen. Eventually Chester, Harold, and Bunnicula would become friends and share a number of adventures.

By the 1990s, Bunnicula had become a well-recognized character in English-language children's literature, completely accepted by teachers and parents in spite of the vampire element. Author James Howe turned out a host of stories and a variety of activity books provided entertainment and education for Bunnicula's youthful fans. Additionally, the earlier books remained in print in new editions.

Sources:

Howe, Deborah and James Howe. *Bunnicula*. New York: Atheneum Publishers, 1979. Rept. New York: Avon, 1980. 98 pp.

Howe, James. *The Celery Stalks at Midnight*. New York: Macmillan Company, 1983. 144 pp.

———. *Nighty-Nightmare*. New York: Macmillan Company, 1987. 121 pp.

———. *The Fright Before Christmas*. New York: William Morrow and Company, 1988. 48 pp.

———. *Scared Silly: A Halloween Treat*. New York: Morrow, 1989. 40 pp.

———. *Hot Fudge*. New York: William Morrow and Company, 1990. 48 pp.

———. *Creepy-Crawly Birthday*. New York: William Morrow and Company, 1991. 48 pp.

———. *Bunnicula Fun Book*. New York: Morrow Junior Books, 1993. 164 pp.

———. *Rabbit-Cadabra*. New York: Morrow, 1993. 48 pp.

———. *Bunnicula Escapes*. New York: Tupelo Books, 1994. 12 pp.

———. *Bunnicula Strikes Again*. New York: Aladdin Library, 2001. 128 pp.

———. *Howie Monroe and the Doghouse of Doom*. Series: Tales from the House of Bunnicula. New York: Athenaeum, 2003. 96 pp. hb. Illus. Bret Helquist.

———. *The Vampire Bunny (Bunnicula and Friends)*. New York: Athenaeum, 2004. 48 pp.

———. *Bunnicula Meets Edgar Allen Crow*. New York: Ginee Seo Books, 2006. 138 pp.

Burma, Vampires in *see:* Myanmar, Vampires in

Burton, Richard Francis (1821–1890)

Richard Francis Burton, the writer and explorer who first opened the world of Asian vampires to the West, was born March 19, 1821, in Hertfordshire, England. He never participated in the school system as his parents were constantly on the move. Instead, he was educated by tutors at different locations around the world. He became fluent in half a dozen languages as a youth and mastered new ones at a regular pace throughout his adult years.

In 1842 he became a cadet in the Indian army and began his adult career, which, like his childhood, was one of wandering. While in India he learned several of the Indian languages and gathered a number of manuscripts of Indian works. Following his return to England in 1849, he published his first books, early studies of Indian languages, and a series of papers for the Asiatic Society. However, by this time he had his eye on what was to become his most famous venture, a pilgrimage to Mecca. Disguising himself as a Muslim he joined the Hajj in Egypt and made his way to the shrine forbidden to all non-Muslims. His three-volume account, *A Pilgrimage to El-Medinah and Meccah*, appeared in 1855.

He returned to India, which he used as a launching point for his explorations of Africa. In 1858 he penetrated the then unexplored territories of Central Africa and discovered one of the sources of the Nile. He followed this with a trip across America to Utah and wrote a book on the Mormons. He also served as a consul in West Africa and South America. He first visited Damascus in 1869.

In the early 1860s Burton lost many of the manuscripts that he had gathered through the years in a fire at the warehouse where they were stored. One of the manuscripts that survived, however, was a collection of tales of King Vikram, a historical figure in India who had become a mythological giant, much as King Arthur had in British history. The particular set of stories translated and published by Burton were the Indian equivalent to the more famous *Arabian Nights* tales. They were of further interest, however, in that the storyteller was a vampire, in the mythology of **India**, the **vetala**, or *betail*.

According to the story, King Vikram had been tricked by a yogi to come to the local cremation grounds and then further tricked to travel to a certain location and bring back a body he would find. When Vikram found the body, it turned out to be the vampire.

When Vikram reached the cremation ground, his final audience with the yogi revealed a much about the Indian attitude toward the afterlife and included a confrontation with several vampire figures. There was, for example, a **Kali** temple, with Kali in her most vampiric setting, described in some detail. *Vikram and the Vampire* was first published in 1870.

In 1872 Burton became consul in Trieste, Italy and lived there for the rest of his life. He published two more outstanding books, *The Book of the Sword*, a comprehensive history of the weapon, and fifteen volumes of *The Book of a Thousand Nights and a Night*. The latter became, and has remained, Burton's most popular book. Its immediate sales provided him with enough money in royalties for a more than comfortable retirement.

After his death at Trieste, on October 20, 1890, Burton's wife burned a number of his writings, including his private diary and his commentary on *The Perfumed Garden*, a Persian sex manual. (He had earlier published an edition of the renowned Indian sex manual the *Kama Sutra*.) As his literary executor, she took complete control of his writings, regulated their publication, and tried to suppress knowledge of those aspects of Burton's romantic life which might have brought offense to Victorian society. In 1897 she oversaw the publication of a new edition of *Vikram and the Vampire*, for which she wrote the preface.

Sources:

Burton, Isabel. *The Life of Sir Richard Burton.* 1893. 2nd ed.: 2 vols. London: W. W. Wilkins, 1898.
Burton, Richard F. *Vikram and the Vampire.* 1870. Rept. London: Tylston and Edwards, 1897. 243
    pp. Rept. New York: Dover Publications 1969. 243 pp.
Godsall, Jon R. *The Tangled Web: A Life of Sir Richard Burton.* Leicester: Troubador, 2008.

Byron, Lord George Gordon (1788–1824)

Lord George Gordon Byron, purported author of the first modern vampire story in English, was born in 1788 in London, the son of Catherine Gordon and John Byron. After his father spent the fortune brought to the marriage by Catherine, she took Byron to Aberdeen, Scotland in 1790, where he had a poor but somewhat normal childhood, disturbed only by a lame foot. His father died in 1791. Due to the untimely death of a cousin in 1794, he became the family heir, and when his great-uncle died in 1798, he became Lord Byron. Soon thereafter, he and his mother moved to the family estate in Nottinghamshire. In 1801 he entered Harrow School, and four years later went on to Trinity College at Cambridge University.

While at Cambridge Byron privately published his first poetry collection, *Fugitive Pieces* (1806). The next year another collection was published as *Hours of Idleness* (1807). He received his master's degree in 1808 and the following year took his seat in the House of Lords. He spent much of 1809 and 1810 traveling and writing Cantos I and II of *Childe Harolde.* Its publication in 1812 brought him immediate fame. He also began his brief liaison with Lady Caroline Lamb.

The following year he broke off the relationship with Lamb and began his affair with his half-sister Augusta Leigh. At about the same time he was also initially exploring the subject of vampirism in his poem "The Giaour," completed and published in 1813. In the midst of the battles described in the poem, the Muslim antagonist speaks a lengthy curse against the title character, the *giaour* (an infidel, one outside the faith). Upon death, the infidel's spirit would surely be punished. However, the Muslim declared that there would be more:

> But first, on earth as Vampire sent, Thy corpse shall from its tomb be rent:
> Then ghastly haunt thy native place, And suck the **blood** of all thy race;
> There from thy daughter, sister, wife, At midnight drain the stream of life;
> Yet loathe the banquet which perforce Must feed thy livid living corpse.
> Thy **victims** are they yet expire Shall know the demon for their sire, As
> cursing thee, thou cursing them, Thy flowers are withered on the stem.

In "The Giaour" Byron demonstrated his familiarity with the Greek *vrykolakas*, a corpse that was animated by a devilish spirit and returned to its own family to make them its first victims. While the Greek vampire in "The Giaour" would be the only overt mention of the vampire in Byron's vast literary output, it merely set the stage for the more famous "vampiric" incident in Byron's life. Meanwhile, in January 1814, Byron married Annabelle Milbanke. Their daughter was born in December. Early in 1816, the couple separated after she and British society became aware of Byron's various sexual encounters. When both turned on him, he decided to leave the country (for good as it turned out).

In the spring of 1816, Byron left for the Continent. Accompanying him was a young physician/writer, **John Polidori**, who among other services supplied Byron with a spectrum of mood-altering and hallucinogenic drugs. By the end of May, they had arrived in Geneva and early in June rented the Villa Diodati, overlooking the Lake of Geneva. Joining him were Percy Shelley, Mary Godwin, and Godwin's stepsister, Claire Clairmont, another of Byron's mistresses. On June 15, weather having forced them inside, Byron suggested that each person write and share a ghost story with the small group. Two evenings later the stories began. The most serious product of this adventure was, of course, *Frankenstein*, Godwin's story expanded into a full novel.

Byron's contribution to the ghostly evening was soon abandoned and never developed. It concerned two friends who, like himself and Polidori, left England to travel on the Continent, in the story's case, to Greece. While there, one of the friends died, but before his death obtained from the other a promise to keep secret the matter of his death. The second man returned to England only to discover that his former companion had beaten him back home and had begun an affair with the second man's sister. Polidori kept notes on Byron's story, which Byron had jotted down in his notebook. (Two novels, both later made into movies, *Gothic*, directed by Ken Russell, and *Haunted Summer*, offered an account of Byron and his associates during these weeks in Switzerland.) Byron and Polidori parted company several months later. Polidori left for England and Byron continued his writing and the romantic adventures that were to fill his remaining years. The ghost story seemed a matter of no consequence. Then in May 1819, he saw an item concerning a tale, "The Vampyre," supposedly written by him and published in the *New Monthly Magazine* in England. He immediately wrote a letter denying his authorship and asking a retraction. As the story unfolded, Byron discovered that Polidori had written a short story from his notes on the tale told by Byron in 1816 in Switzerland. Polidori's story was the first piece of prose fiction to treat a literal vampire, and the publisher of the *New Monthly Magazine* took it upon himself, based upon Polidori's account of the story's origin, to put Byron's name on it. In the light of a not unexpected response, he quickly published it in a separate booklet over Byron's name, and had it translated into French and German. Both Polidori and Byron made attempts to correct the error, and before the year was out Byron had the "Fragment of a Story" published as part of his attempt to distance himself from the finished story. The problem he encountered in denying his authorship was amply demonstrated in 1830 by the inclusion of "The Vampyre" in the French edition of his collected works. Byron must have been further irritated by Polidori's choice of a name for the vampire character in the story, **Lord Ruthven**, the same name given to the Byron-figure in Lady Caroline Lamb's fictionalized account of their liaison, *Glenarvon* (1816).

Once the Polidori incident was behind him, Byron never returned to the vampire in any of his writings. Twentieth-century critics, however, have seen vampirism as a prominent metaphor in the romantic treatment of human relations, especially destructive ones. Vampires are characters who suck the life force from those they love, and the romantic authors of the early nineteenth century, such as Byron, utilized psychic vampirism despitenever labeling such characters as vampires.

For example, critic James B. Twitchell saw the psychic vampire theme as an integral aspect of Byron's dramatic poem *Manfred*, the first acts of which were written in the summer of 1816 at the Villa Diodati. Illustrative of this "vampirism" was a scene in the first act in which the person who had just stopped Manfred from **suicide** offered him a glass of **wine**. Manfred refused comparing the wine to blood—both his blood and that of his half sister with whom he had an affair. Here Twitchell saw a return to the Greek vampires who first drank/attacked the blood/life of those closest to them. Manfred was an early manifestation of "l'homme fatal," the man who acts upon those around him as if he were a vampire.

During a severe illness in April 1824, Byron underwent a series of bleedings that, ironically, probably caused his death. He died April 19, 1824. His body was returned to England for burial. In the mid 1990s, novelist Tom Holland issued an entertaining book based on the premise that Byron did not die, but lives on as a vampire.

Sources:

Bone, Drummond. *The Cambridge Companion to Byron.* Cambridge, UK: Cambridge University Press, 2005. 360 pp.

Byron, Lord. *The Complete Poetic Works of Byron.* Boston: Houghton Mifflin Company, 1933. 1,055 pp.

Dangerfield, Elma. *Byron and the Romantics in Switzerland, 1816.* London: Ascent Books, 1978. 93 pp.

Edwards, Anne. *Haunted Summer.* New York: Coward, McCann & Geoghegan, 1973. 278 pp.

Eisler, Benita. *Byron: Child of Passion, Fool of Fame.* New York: Vintage, 2000. 880 pp.

Holland, Tom. *The Vampyre: Being the True Pilgrimage of George Gordon, Sixth Lord Byron.* London: Little Brown and Company, 1995. 339 pp.

Senf, Carol. *The Vampire in Nineteenth-Century English Literature.* Bowling Green, OH: Popular Press, 1988. 204 pp.

Twitchell, James B. *The Living Dead: A Study of the Vampire in Romantic Literature.* Durham, NC: Duke University Press, 1981. 219 pp.

Volk, Stephen. *Gothic.* London: Grafton, 1987. 222 pp. Novelization of Ken Russell film.

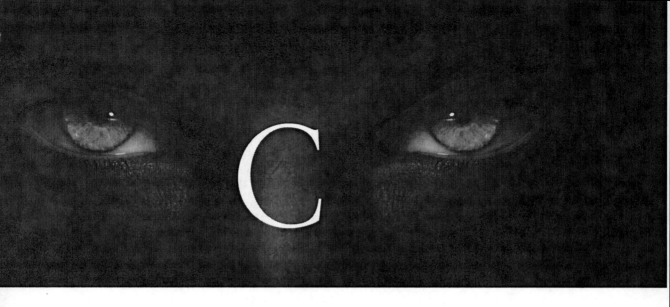

Caine *see* Vampire: The Eternal Struggle

Callicantzaros *see:* Greece, Vampires in

❨ Calmet, Dom Augustin (1672–1757) ❩

Dom Augustin Calmet, a French Roman Catholic biblical scholar and the most famous vampirologist of the early eighteenth century, was born February 26, 1672, at Mesnil-la-Horgne, Lorraine, **France**. He studied at the Benedictine monastery at Breuil, and entered the order in 1688. He was ordained to the priesthood in 1696. He taught philosophy and theology at the Abbey at Moyen-Moutier and during the early years of his career worked on a massive twenty-three-volume commentary of the Bible which appeared between 1707 and 1716. His biblical writings established him as one of the church's leading scholars, and he spent many years trying to popularize the work of biblical exegesis in the church. He was offered a bishopric by Pope Benedict XIII, but Calmet turned it down. However, in spite of his learned accomplishments, Calmet is most remembered today for his single 1746 work on vampires, *Dissertations sur les Apparitions des Anges des Démons et des Espits, et sur les revenants, et Vampires de Hingrie, de Boheme, de Moravie, et de Silésie.*

Like the work of his Italian colleague, **Giuseppe Davanzati**, Calmet's study of vampirism was started by the waves of vampire reports from **Germany** and Eastern Europe. Vampirism, for all practical purposes, did not exist in France, and was largely unknown to the scholarly community there until the early eighteenth century. Calmet was impressed with the detail and corroborative testimonies of incidents of vampirism coming out of Eastern Europe and believed that it was unreasonable to simply dismiss them. In addition, as a theologian, he recognized that the existence and actions of such bloodsucking revenants could have an important bearing on various theological conclusions

concerning the nature of the afterlife. Calmet felt it necessary to establish the veracity of such reports and to understand the phenomena in light of the church's view of the world. Calmet finished his work a short time after the Sorbonne roundly condemned the reports and especially the desecration of the bodies of the people believed to be vampires.

Calmet defined vampires as people who had been dead and buried and who then returned from their graves to disturb the living by sucking their **blood** and even causing death. The only remedy for vampirism was to dig up the body of the reported vampire and either sever its head and drive a **stake** through the chest or burn the body. Using that definition, Calmet collected as many of the accounts of vampirism as possible from official reports, newspapers, eyewitness reports, travelogues, and critical pieces from his learned colleagues. The majority of space in his published volume was taken up with the anthology of all his collected data.

Calmet then offered his reflections upon the reports. He condemned the hysteria that had followed several of the reported incidents of vampirism and seconded the Sorbonne's condemnation of the mutilation of exhumed bodies. He also considered all of the **explanations** that had been offered for the phenomena, including regional folklore, normal but little known body changes after death, and premature burial. He focused a critical eye upon the reports and pointed out problems and internal inconsistencies.

In the end, however, Calmet was unable to conclude that the reports supported the various natural explanations that had been offered, though he was unwilling to propose an alternative. He left the whole matter open, but seemed to favor the existence of vampires by noting that "it seems impossible not to subscribe to the belief which prevails in these countries that these apparitions do actually come forth from the graves and that they are able to produce the terrible effects which are so widely and so positively attributed to them." He thus touched off the heated debate, which was to ensue during the 1750s. As contemporary scholar Massimo Introvigne has noted, in his first edition Calmet had posed five possible explanations of the stories he had considered. Three he dismissed, leaving him with the possibility that vampires were the result of the devil's activity or mere superstition. While leaning toward superstition, he did not reach a firm conclusion. However, in his third and last edition, he did conclude that such creatures as vampires could return from the grave.

Calmet's book became a bestseller. It went through two French editions in 1746 and 1749, and then the third edition in 1751 appeared under a new title *Traité sur les Appartions des esprits et su les vampires ou les Revenans de Hongrie, de Moravie, etc*. It appeared in a German edition in 1752 and an English edition in 1759 (reprinted in 1850 as *The Phantom World*). Relying primarily on the first edition, Calmet was immediately attacked by colleagues for taking the vampire stories seriously. While he tried to apply such critical methods as he had available to him, he only lightly questioned the legitimacy of the reports of vampiric manifestations. In 1751, he did question the reports in reaching his more skeptical conclusion.

As the controversy swelled following publication of his book, a skeptical Empress Maria Theresa stepped in. A new outbreak of vampirism had been reported in Silesia. She dispatched her personal physician to examine the case. He wrote a report denouncing the incident as supernatural quackery and condemned the mutilation of the bodies. In response, in 1755 and 1756, Maria Theresa issued laws to stop the spread of the vampire hysteria, including removing the matter of dealing with such reports from the hands of the clergy and placing it instead under civil authority. Maria Theresa's edicts came just before Calmet's death on October 25, 1757.

In the generation after his death, Calmet was treated harshly by French intellectuals, both inside and outside the church. Later in the century, Diderot condemned him. Possibly the final word on Calmet came from Voltaire, who sarcastically ridiculed him in his *Philosophical Dictionary.* Though Calmet was favorably cited by **Montague Summers,** who used him as a major source for his study of vampires, his importance lies in his reprinting and preserving some of the now obscure texts of the vampire wave of eighteenth-century Europe.

Sources:

Calmet, Dom Augustin. *Dissertations sur les Apparitions des Anges des Démons et des Espits, et sur les revenants, et Vampires de Hingrie, de Boheme, de Moravie, et de Silésie.* Paris, 1746. English translation as *The Phantom World.* 2 vols. London: Richard Bentley, 1850.

————. *Traité sur les Apparitions des esprits et sur les vampires ou les Revenans de Hongrie, de Moravie, etc.* 2 vols. Paris: Debure, 1751.

Frayling, Christopher. *Vampyres: From Lord Byron to Count Dracula.* London: Faber and Faber, 1991. 429 pp.

Introvigne, Massimo. *La strippe di Dracula: Indagine sul vampirismo dall'antichita ai nostri giorni.* Milan: Arnoldo Mondadori Editore, 1997. 474 pp.

Martin, Philippe, ed. *Dom Augustin Calmet: un itinéraire intellectual.* Paris: Riveneuve, 2008.

Summers, Montague. *The Vampire: His Kith and Kin.* London: Routledge, Kegan Paul, Trench, Trubner & Co., 1928. 356 pp. Rept. New York: University Books, 1960. 356 pp.

❦ The Camarilla: A Vampire Fan Association ❧

The Camarilla: A Vampire Fan Association is a **gothic** vampire fan club founded in the early 1990s by players of ***Vampire: The Masquerade,*** the most popular of the vampire-oriented role-playing (or storytelling) **games**. In the game, the players assume the role of a vampire who is a member of a vampire society called the Camarilla. In the myth, vampires created the Camarilla after the Inquisition in an effort to keep their race from being totally annihilated. They organized the Camarilla into **clans**, each of which was distinguished by a peculiar aesthetic/intellectual approach to the vampiric condition, or by a certain ethnic **origin**.

The Camarilla: A Vampire Fan Association focuses on the vampire as a tragic and romantic figure and tends to avoid its violent aspects. Members of the club join a clan and create a vampire persona which is lived out in club activities, such as gaming sessions. The club emphasizes member participation and encourages new members to become active in a local chapter or even begin one themselves. Chapters are often involved in raising money for local charities or hosting **blood** drives, etc. Community service is emphasized as much as role-playing.

In the Camarilla local chapters in close proximity may be grouped into domains and all chapters and domains in a geographical area are organized into regions. In the

United States there are eight regions. At each level a coordinator and storyteller is elected as the primary officers. Regions are further grouped into nations, each of which has a national coordinator and national storyteller who oversee club activities in their country. National officers report to the global office. In the United States, the national coordinator and national storyteller are elected by the regional officers.

Overall oversight of the Camarilla is in the hands of the global officers, who are appointed in consultation with the affiliated nations. The primary officers are the Camarilla's Club Director and the Master Storyteller. At the national and international level, contact and coordination of regional and national events are done through the online website, through which individuals may become members. Individual members receive the monthly newsletter (posted online) and the journal *Epitaph*. The Camarilla is best contacted through its webpage, http://camarilla.white-wolf.com/.

Most recently, German scholar Marco Frenschkowski ("Vampire in Mythologie und Folklore," in Thaomas Le Blanc, Clamens Ruthner, and Bettina Twsrsnick, eds., *Draculas Wiederkehr. Tagungsband 1997*, Wetzlar: Phantastische Bibliothek 2003, pp. 28–58) offered a detailed deconstruction of the story. Taking as a starting point the observation that the narrator of the story "Laura" needs to visit the physician Dr. Hesselius many years later, interpreting "Carmilla" as a symbolic figure in the imagination of suppressed lesbian Laura. Frenschkowski also gives attention to the many intertextual references in "A Glass Darkly" of which "Carmilla" is just a part.

Sources:

Rein-Hagen, Mark. *Vampire: The Masquerade*. Stone Mountain, GA: White Wolf, 1991. 263 pp.

Wright, Jana. *The Tome of the Kindred*. Seattle, WA: The Camarilla, 1993. 44 pp.

Camazotz *see:* Mexico, Vampires, in

Cappadocian Vampire Clan *see:* Vampire: The Eternal Struggle

Carfax

In **Bram Stoker**'s novel ***Dracula,*** **(1897)** Carfax was a residence purchased by **Dracula** prior to his leaving his castle. The purpose of **Jonathan Harker**'s visit to **Transylvania** at the beginning of the novel was to complete the transaction by which Dracula secured a somewhat secluded home for himself relatively close to **London**. (Other firms were employed to secure his London residences and carry out various business transactions. Thus, neither Harker nor any other single person would know more than a small portion of what Dracula was attempting to accomplish.) Carfax was a fictional estate of some 20 acres located by Stoker in Purfleet. While modern London has almost reached out to Purfleet, in the 1890s Purfleet was a secluded village some ten miles from the edge of London's East End, on the northern side of the River Thames in Essex. Stoker described the estate as being surrounded by a high wall built of stone. It had been abandoned for some years and was in a state of decay. He continued, "There are many trees on it, which makes it in places gloomy, and there is a deep, dark-looking pond or small lake, evidently fed by some springs." It was located adjacent to an old church on one side and a lunatic asylum (the one run by **Dr. John Seward**) on the other.

Dracula's boxes of **native soil** were shipped from **Whitby,** where Dracula landed in England, to London. From there they were transported to Carfax. Carfax served as Dracula's "headquarters" from which he launched his attacks upon **Lucy Westenra, Mina Murray,** and **R. N. Renfield,** the resident of the asylum next door. Later Dr. **Abraham Van Helsing** and the cadre of men dedicated to **destroying** Dracula entered Carfax and sanitized the boxes of earth with a **eucharistic wafer** thus rendering them useless.

In the rewritten script for **Universal Pictures'** *Dracula* **(1931)** movie with **Bela Lugosi,** Carfax and the church next door were combined and called Carfax Abbey. That change seems to have been the idea of screenwriter Louis Bloomfield, who had been hired to rework the **John L. Balderston** version of the **Hamilton Deane** play, the basis of the movie's script. Carfax "Abbey" initially appeared in the preliminary "First Treatment" submitted by Bloomfield to Carl Laemmle, Jr., at Universal, on August 7, 1930. That document was then rewritten by Bloomfield and Dudley Murphy, the first screenwriter assigned to the movie. Their work was finally revised by Garrett Fort. Bloomfield and Universal parted company, and his work was not acknowledged in the final credits for the film. However, the idea of Carfax Abbey continued through both the Murphy and Fort revisions into the final movie. From the movie, it passed into the popular culture and reappeared in later movies which relied more on Universal's production than any rereading of the book.

Carfax, like Seward's asylum, was pure fiction. As **Leonard Wolf** noted, there was a Carfax Road and a Carfax Square in London, but neither were near Purfleet. **Raymond T. McNally** and **Radu Florescu** seem to have confused Carfax estate and the later idea of Carfax Abbey and searched for a possible reference to the latter in Purfleet. Based on information supplied by Alan Davidson, they accepted the idea that Lesnes Abbey, originally founded in 1178 C.E., but on the opposite side of the Thames River from Purfleet, might have inspired Stoker's Carfax. The Abbot's House, part of the Lesnes complex later used as a manor house, still existed in the 1890s. However, if Lesnes Abbey (on the south side of the Thames) was the historical reference to Carfax, then there would be no reason for Dracula (as a **bat**) to fly south across the Thames (as he did in chapter 23).

Sources:

Riley, Philip J. *Dracula (The Original 1931 Shooting Script)*. Atlantic City, NJ: MagicImage Film-books, 1990.

Stoker, Bram. *The Annotated Dracula*. Edited by Leonard Wolf. New York: Ballantine Books, 1975. 362 pp.

———. *The Essential Dracula*. Edited by Raymond McNally and Radu Florescu. New York: Mayflower, 1979. 320 pp.

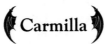 Carmilla

Carmilla is the title character in the vampire novelette by British writer **Sheridan Le Fanu.** "Carmilla" was originally published as a short story in a story collection entitled *In a Glass Darkly* in 1872. The story took place in rural Styria, where Laura, the heroine and narrator, lived. Her father, a retired Austrian civil servant, had been able to purchase an abandoned castle cheaply. Carmilla first appeared in the opening scene of the story as she entered the six-year-old Laura's bed. Laura fell asleep in her arms but suddenly

awakened with a sensation of two needles entering her breast. She cried out, and the person Laura described only as "the lady" slipped out of bed onto the floor and disappeared, possibly under the bed. Her nurse and the housekeeper came into the room in response to her cries, but found no one and no marks on her chest. Carmilla reappeared when Laura was 19 years old. The carriage in which Carmilla was traveling had a wreck in sight of the castle. Carmilla's mother, seemingly in a hurry to reach her destination, left Carmilla at the castle to recover from the accident. When Laura finally met their new guest, she immediately recognized Carmilla as the same person who had visited her 12 years previously, and thus the vampire was loosed again to prey on Laura. Gradually her identity was uncovered. She began to visit Laura in the form of a cat and a female phantom. Laura also noticed that she looked exactly like the 1698 portrait of Countess Mircalla Karnstein. Through her mother, Laura was a descendent of the Karnsteins.

At this point, an old friend of the family, General Spielsdorf, arrived at the castle to relate the account of his daughter's death. She had been wasting away; her condition had no known natural causes. A physician deduced she was the **victim** of a vampire. The skeptical general waited hidden in his daughter's room and actually caught the vampire, a young woman he knew by the name of Millarca, in the act. He tried to kill her with his sword, but she easily escaped.

As he finished his account, Carmilla entered. He recognized her as Millarca, but she escaped them before they could deal with her. They all then tracked her to the Karnstein castle some three miles away where they found her resting in her grave. Her body was lifelike, and a faint heartbeat detected. The casket floated in fresh **blood**. They drove a **stake** through her heart in reaction to which Carmilla let out a "piercing shriek." They finished their gruesome task by severing her head, burning the body, and scattering the ashes.

One can see in Le Fanu's tale, which would later be read by **Bram Stoker,** the progress of the developing vampire myth to that point. People became vampires after committing **suicide** or following their death if they had been bitten by a vampire during their life. The latter was the cause in Carmilla's case. Le Fanu understood the vampire to be a dead person returned, not a demonic spirit. The returned vampire had a tendency to attack family and loved ones, in this case, a descendent, and was somewhat geographically confined to the area near their grave. And while somewhat pale in complexion, the vampire was quite capable of fitting into society without undue notice. The vampire had two needle-like teeth (**fangs**), but these were not visible at most times. Bites generally occurred on the neck or chest.

Carmilla had nocturnal habits, but was not totally confined to the darkness. She had superhuman **strength** and was able to undergo a **transformation** into various shapes, especially those of **animals**. Her favorite shape was that of a cat, rather than either a wolf or a **bat**. She slept in a **coffin**, which she could leave without disturbing any dirt covering the grave.

As would be true in ***Dracula*, (1897)** the mere bite of the vampire neither turned victims into vampires nor killed them. The vampire fed off the victim over a period of time while the victim slowly withered away. The victim thus fulfilled both the vampire's daily need for blood and its fascination for a particular person whom it chose as its victim.

As many have noted in discussing Carmilla, her fascination with Laura and the general's daughter, an attachment "resembling the passion of love," has more than pass-

ing **lesbian** overtones. In horror stories, in general, authors have been able to treat sexual themes in ways that would not have been available to them otherwise. Early in the story, for example, Carmilla began her attack upon Laura by placing her "pretty arms" around her neck, and with her cheek touching Laura's lips, speaking soft seductive words. While earlier writers had written about the vampirelike *lamiai* and other female vampires who attacked their male lovers, "Carmilla" introduced the female revenant vampire to **gothic** literature.

One unique element of vampire lore in "Carmilla" that was not used by later writers was Le Fanu's suggestion that the vampire was limited to choosing a **name** that was anagrammatically related to its real name. Both Carmilla and Millarca were derived from Mircalla.

"Carmilla" would directly influence Stoker's presentation of the vampire, especially his treatment of the female vampires who attack **Jonathan Harker** early in *Dracula*. The influence of "Carmilla" was even more visible in "Dracula's Guest", the deleted chapter of *Dracula* later published as a short story.

Through the twentieth century, "Carmilla" has had a vital existence on the motion picture screen. The story served loosely as inspiration for *Vampyr*, **Carl Theodor Dreyer**'s 1931 classic, though "Dracula's Guest" provided the base for **Universal Pictures'** first post–*Dracula* movie with a female vampire, *Dracula's Daughter* (1936). However, with the expanded exploration of the vampire theme in the movies after World War II, "Carmilla" would be rediscovered. The first movie based directly on "Carmilla" was the 1961 French *Et Mourir de Plaisir* (also called *Blood and Roses*) directed by **Roger Vadim** and starring his wife, Annette Vadim. It was followed in 1962 by *La Maldicion of the Karnsteins* (also known as *Terror in the Crypt*). Then at the beginning of the 1970s, in the wake of its other successful vampire movies, **Hammer Films** would turn to Carmilla and her family for three movies: *Lust for a Vampire* (1970), *The Vampire Lovers* (1970)—possibly the most faithful attempt to tell the Le Fanu story—and *Twins of Evil* (1971). The Hammer movies inspired other attempts to bring "Carmilla" to the screen, the first being three Spanish productions. *La Hija de Dracula* (*The Daughter of Dracula*) was released in 1972. *La Comtesse aux Seiens Nux* (1973) was released under a variety of titles, including a 1981 highly edited version, *Erotikill*. *La Novia Ensangretada* (1974) was released in the United States as *Till Death Do Us Part* and *The Blood Spattered Bride*. Over the last 20 years, "Carmilla"-inspired movies have included *The Evil of Dracula* (1975), *Valerie* (1991), and *Vampires vs. Zombies* also released as *Carmilla the Lesbian Vampire*, (2004). **Television** adaptations were made in England in 1966, **Spain** in 1987, and the United States as part of a short-lived series, Nightmare Classics, in 1989.

"Carmilla" was brought to the world of **comic books** in 1968 by Warren Publishing Company's *Creepy* No. 19, one of the comic magazines that operated outside of the Comics Code, which forbade the picturing of vampires in comic books. In the 1970s, Malibu Comics released a six-part adult version of *Carmilla*. In 1972, the story was included on a record album, *Carmilla: A Vampire Tale*, released under the Vanguard label by the Etc. Company.

Sources:

Glut, Donald F. *The Dracula Book*. Metuchen, NJ: Scarecrow Press, 1975. 388 pp.
Le Fanu, Sheridan. *In a Glass Darkly*. London: P. Davies, 1929.

————. *Carmilla*. Rockville, MD: Wildside Press/Prime Classics Library, 2000. Cramilla is currently available in a variety of print editions, and its text is also accessible at several Internet sites.

❮ Carradine, John (1905–1988) ❯

Born Richmond Reed Carradine on February 5, 1905, in New York City, John Carradine first appeared as **Dracula** in the 1944 movie *House of Frankenstein*, and frequently recreated the part throughout the rest of his career. Carradine grew up in a educated family. His mother was a surgeon and his father a lawyer who also worked at times as a poet, artist, and Associated Press correspondent in London. Carradine originally planned to become a sculptor and to that end attended the Graphic Art School in Philadelphia. However, inspired by the Shakespearean actor Robert Mitchell, he began to train for the stage.

In 1925 he set out on his own, making a living as a sketch artist. In **New Orleans** that year he made his stage debut in *Camille* and then joined a touring Shakespearean company. In 1927 he moved to Hollywood and worked as an actor, in Shakespearean plays when possible. In 1930 he appeared for the first time in a movie, *Tol'able David*, using the name Peter Richmond. He appeared in his first horror movie, which was also his first motion picture for **Universal Pictures**, in 1933's *The Invisible Man*. In 1935 he signed a long-term contract with 20th Century Fox and changed his stage name to John Carradine. That same year he married Ardanelle Cosner.

Through the 1930s he appeared in a number of notable movies including *The Prisoner of Shark Island* (1936) and *Stagecoach* (1939), but he is possibly most remembered for his portrayal of the drunk minister in *The Grapes of Wrath* (1939). In the 1940s he appeared in the "B" horror movies that had become a staple of Universal Studios's schedule. Then in 1944 he accepted the role of Dracula in *House of Frankenstein*, which he agreed to do if he could take his portrayal from **Bram Stoker's** novel rather than the then more famous portrayal of **Bela Lugosi**. Carradine's performance somewhat saved the movie and its highly contrived plot and established him as one of the most popular interpreters of the Count.

Meanwhile, Carradine had formed a drama company and laid plans for a career as a Shakespearean actor. His work was greeted with rave reviews, but his plans were blocked by his first wife (whom he had divorced in 1944), who had him thrown in jail for "alimony contempt." With his new wife, Sonia Sorel, he returned to Hollywood and accepted the offer to assume his vampiric role in *House of Dracula*. Carradine's most famous scene was Dracula's attack upon the heroine as she played "Moonlight Sonata" on the piano. About to claim his **victim**, he was repulsed by the **crucifix** hanging around her neck.

Carradine returned to the Dracula role in the 1950s on the stage. He moved even farther from the Lugosi presentation of Dracula, and referred directly to the text of the novel in creating his own makeup, which included white hair and a white mustache. He kept both the **opera** cape and the evening clothes. Memorable in his performance was a humorous line he added to the script at the end, "If I'm alive, what am I doing here? On the other hand, if I'm dead, why do I have to wee-wee?" In 1957 Carradine became possibly the first **television** Dracula in a program for NBC's live "Matinee Theatre." In

1957, following a divorce two years earlier, Carradine married Doris Rich.

From the 1960s until his death in the 1988, Carradine appeared in numerous "B" films, including a variety of vampire movies. The first of the new vampire movies was *Billy the Kid vs. Dracula*, an unfortunate marriage of the vampire and western genres. In 1967 Carradine traveled to **Mexico** for *Las Vampiros* (*The Vampires*), a film in which he had little creative input. The only English-speaking person on the set, he learned enough Spanish to deliver the famous line he had added to the play. He followed *Las Vampiros* with *The Blood of Dracula's Coffin* (1968), the first of several movies he made under the direction of Al Abramson. The next came almost immediately, *Dracula vs. Frankenstein* (also known as *The Blood of Frankenstein*, 1969). Through the 1970s he appeared in *Vampire Men of the Lost Planet* (1970), *Horror of the Blood Monsters* (1971), *House of Dracula's Daughter* (1973), *Mary Mary Bloody Mary* (1975), *Nocturna* (1978), and *The Vampire Hookers* (1979). His final appearances in vampire movies were in *Doctor Dracula* (1980) and *The Monster Club* (1981). In most of these movies, though by no means all, Carradine played the part of the vampire.

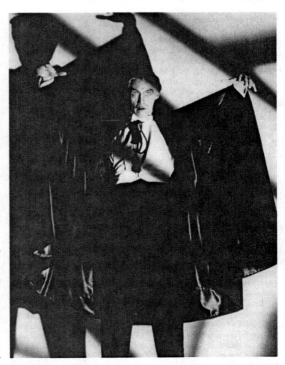

John Carradine as Dracula in *House of Frankenstein*.

Carradine married Emily Cisneros in 1975, four years after the death of his third wife. He continued to make movies through the 1980s and won an award at the Sitges Film Festival in 1983 as best male actor for his work in *House of Long Shadows* (1983). He died November 27, 1988, in Milan, Italy, after climbing the 328 steps of the Duomo, the famous cathedral. He collapsed and was taken to the hospital where he died of heart and kidney failure.

Known for his deep, distinctive, classically trained baritone voice, Carradine appeared in an unknown number of films (some estimates go as high as 500). In spite of the negative reaction to his later portrayals of Dracula (and other vampires), he is remembered from his early films and stage work as one of the most important people to take up these roles. Except for **Christopher Lee,** he played Dracula more than any other actor, and appeared in a starring role in more vampire movies than any actor before or since.

Sources:

The Annual Obituary, 1988. Edited by Patricia Burgess. Chicago: St. James Press, 1989.

Carradine, John. "Introduction." *House of Dracula (The Original Shooting Script).* Edited by Philip Riley. Absecon, NJ: MagicImage Filmbooks, 1993.

Glut, Donald. *The Dracula Book.* Metuchen, NJ: Scarecrow Press, 1975. 388 pp.

The International Dictionary of Films and Filmmakers: Volume II, Actors and Actresses. Edited by James Vinson. Chicago: St. James Press, 1985.

Weaver, Tom. *John Carradine: The Films.* Jeffersonville, NC: McFarland & Company, 2008. 408 pp.

Carter, Margaret Louise (1948–)

Margaret Louise Carter, bibliographer, author, and editor, was born in Norfolk, Virginia. She had developed an interest in vampires after reading **Dracula (1897)** at the age of 13. In 1970, while in college, she compiled an anthology of vampire stories, *Curse of the Undead*. That same year she wrote the preface to a reprint of **Varney the Vampyre** edited by **D. P. Varma**. Two years later she edited a second collection of short stories, *Demon Lovers and Strange Seductions*.

In 1975 she began the work that has to date brought her the greatest degree of fame in the vampire world. *Shadow of a Shade: A Survey of Vampirism in Literature*, which won **The Dracula Society** award in 1976, was the first of four books on vampire and **gothic** horror **bibliography** and literary fiction. It was followed by *Specter or Delusion? The Supernatural in Gothic Fiction* (1987), *Dracula: The Vampire and the Critics* (1988), and her monumental *The Vampire in Literature: A Critical Bibliography* (1989), which included a comprehensive listing of English-language vampire fiction. Each item in the bibliography was annotated with a set of codes indicating the nature of the vampire and/or vampirism to be found in the work. It appeared amidst an unprecedented growth in interest in the literary vampire. Carter has annually issued a supplement that cites all of the year's new fiction as well as any past items she missed in the original bibliography. In recent years, the annual supplements have been issued in electronic form on her website. In this work she has placed future writers on vampires in her debt.

Writer and bibliographer Margaret Carter.

Most recently, she has contributed to nonfiction writing with her study of *Different Blood: The Vampire As Alien*, in which she explores the continuing relevance of the vampire as other against the popular sympathetic vampire one often finds in romantic fiction.

Carter is also a writer of vampire fiction. Her first vampire short story, "A Call in the Blood," appeared in 1987. She has continued as a productive author to the present, with her most recent titles including *Sealed in Blood* (2003), *Child of Twilight* (2003), and *Crimsom Dreams* (2004). For over a decade she edited *The Vampire's Crypt*, a journal featuring vampire-oriented short fiction (1991–2002).

Carter is also an active participant and officer in **The Lord Ruthven Assembly**. She continues to promote young authors through her Internet site, Carter's Crypt (http://www.margaretlcarter.com/).

Sources:

Carter, Margaret L. *Crimson Dreams*. Amber Quill Press, 2004. 190 pp.

———. *Curse of the Undead*. Greenwich, CT: Fawcett, 1970. 223 pp.

————. *Demon Lovers and Strange Seductions.* Greenwich, CT: Fawcett, 1972. 207 pp.

————. *Different Blood: The Vampire As Alien.* Amber Quill Press, 2004. 168 pp.

————. *Dracula: The Vampire and the Critics.* Ann Arbor, MI: UMI Research Press, 1988. 274 pp.

————. *Sealed in Blood.* Amber Quill Press, 2003. 198 pp.

————. *Shadow of a Shade: A Survey of Vampirism in Literature.* New York: Gordon Press, 1975. 176 pp.

————. *Specter or Delusion? The Supernatural in Gothic Fiction.* Ann Arbor, MI: UMI Research Press, 1987. 131 pp.

————. *The Vampire in Literature: A Critical Bibliography.* Ann Arbor, MI: UMI Research Press, 1989. 135 pp.

Cast, P. C. and Kristin

P. C. and Kristin Cast are the co-authors of a popular young adult "House of Night" vampire series, launched in 2007. P. C. Cast, Kristin's mother, was born in Watseka, Illinois. After high school she joined the Air Force and after her service pursued a college degree with a literature major and a minor in secondary education. She resides in Oklahoma and since 1993 has taught English at South Intermediate High School in Broken Arrow. Her first book, *Goddess of the Sea*, appeared in 2003. Meanwhile, in the 1980s, she married and had a daughter. Kristin grew up in Oklahoma and after high school attended Tulsa University. In 2005, P. C.'s book agent suggested that she try to do a young adult vampire novel. As Kristin was showing a bent for writing, it seemed natural to work together on the new venture.

The "House of Night" series introduces 16-year-old Zoey Redbird, who lives at a time when vampires are out in the open and tolerated by humans, at least most of them. As children grow up, the vampires will mark some as special and they will be transferred from their normal situation to the House of Night school where they will continue their education and be groomed as future "vampyres." Should their body reject the transformation, they will die.

Zoey is part white-part Native American (with a Cherokee grandmother). She is a typical angst-filled teenager. She has been marked by no less a personage than the goddess Nyx (a reflection of the pantheon Casts's earlier books had featured) and an indication that she has strong inherent powers. She seems to fit right in at the new school. She has friends and several boys who wish to be her special one, including the hottest of the lot. She has an antagonist, Aphrodite, who seems the jealous type, among her other faults, and if Aphrodite fades, Neferet stands ready to cause trouble. The various cliques at the school set the possibilities of a host of stories. The vampires in the several books of the "House of Night" series are basically good guy vampires, and **St. Germain** (**Chelsea Quinn Yarbro's** main character) and **Angel** and **Spike** from *Buffy the Vampire Slayer* inform the Casts's vampyres. However, their real distinctiveness comes from their mining the world of Western Paganism. They exist in a culture that is matriarchal. Also, their vampirism is more a biological condition than a supernatural transformation. In addition, the vampire mythos is based on biology. In some teenagers, hormones trigger a reaction in the DNA; their bodies begin a physiological process that transforms them either into a vampyre or a corpse. Their special powers are all earth-

based abilities, such as controlling the element of air, or having a special connection to horses. Casts's vampires are also not immortal, just very long lived.

Casts's vampires, as might be supposed from their all attending the same school, have a very communal existence. Early in one, the reader is introduced to a coven, the Dark Daughters, headed by Zoey's rival Aphrodite. When she abuses her powers, Aphrodite loses her position as high priestess in training and Zoey become the new leader.

As of 2009, Kristin Cast is finishing college and the "House of Night" series continues, with five volumes out and additional titles in the pipeline. Updates are always available from the Casts's Websites at http://www.houseofnightseries.com/ and http://www.pccast.net/.

Sources:

Cast, P. C., and Kristin Cast. *Betrayed*. House of Night, Book 2. St. Martin's Griffin, 2007. 320 pp.

———. *Chosen*. House of Night, Book 3. St. Martin's Griffin, 2008. 320 pp.

———. *Hunted*. House of Night, Book 5. St. Martin's Griffin, 2009. 323 pp.

———. *Marked*. House of Night, Book 1. St. Martin's Griffin, 2007. 306 pp.

———. *Untamed*. House of Night, Book 4. St. Martin's Griffin, 2008. 352 pp.

"P.C. Cast & Kristin Cast Interview & Bibliography." Love Vampires. Posted at http://www.love-vampires.com/pccast.html. Accessed on April 5, 2010.

❨ Castle Dracula ❩

The first section of **Bram Stoker**'s novel *Dracula* (1897) concerns **Jonathan Harker**'s trip to Castle Dracula and his adventures after he arrives. During the last generation, as it was discovered that Stoker's character **Dracula** was based, in part, upon a real person, **Vlad the Impaler,** the question was posed, "Could Castle Dracula be a real place?" The search for Dracula's castle began. This search took on two aspects: the search for the castle that was the home for Vlad the Impaler and the search for the castle that Bram Stoker actually used as a model for the castle described in his novel.

As described in the novel, the castle was near **Borgo Pass**. It was reached from Pasul Tihuts, a point near the summit of the crossing, on a road leading south along a mountainous road into the high mountains where the castle was located. Harker's journey from the pass to the castle was at night, and he reached it by horse-drawn coach with enough of the evening left to have dinner and his first visit with Dracula before dawn. Upon his arrival, he noticed a large courtyard. He was dropped in front of an old large door placed at an opening in a stone wall. Even in the dim light of the evening, the wall showed signs of age and weathering. In the light of day, he discovered that the castle sat on a great rock overlooking the surrounding forest which was sliced by several river gorges.

The castle was built so as to be nearly impregnable to attack. The large windows were placed above the level where arrows and other projectiles (at least those of pre-modern warfare) could reach. To the west was a large valley and a mountain range.

Entering the castle he saw a large winding staircase and a long corridor. At the end of the corridor, he entered a room where supper awaited him. The rooms in which Harker was to spend most of his time joined an octagonal room that stood between the

Castle Dracula, Curtea de Arges, Romania.

room in which he ate and his bedroom. His bedroom overlooked the court where he had originally stepped off the coach. The door to the room opposite his bedroom was locked, but another opened to the library, which was full of materials from England.

He explored one forbidden wing of the castle in the southwest corner at a lower level. Here he found comfortable furniture, but it lay covered in the **dust** of abandonment. The windows were filled with diamond-shaped panes of colored glass. Here he would encounter the three vampire **brides** who resided at the castle with Dracula.

Harker climbed out a window on the south wall to make his way to the window on the east side of the castle, below his bedroom, into which he had seen Dracula go. In the first room he entered, he found a pile of gold, also covered with dust. He followed a staircase downward to a tunnel, and meandering through the tunnel he came upon the chapel that had been used as a burial place. Here he discovered the boxes of **native soil** ready to be sent to England, in one of which Dracula lay in his **sleep**-like state. The three **women** slept in the chapel. There was one large tomb, not noticed by Harker but later sanitized by **Abraham Van Helsing**, labeled with the single word DRACULA.

The Search for Castle Dracula: In recent decades, as the fact that the title character in Stoker's novel was based on a real person, Vlad the Impaler, a ruler in what

today is **Romania**, people suspected that there was possibly a real Castle Dracula. Given the accuracy of Stoker's novel in describing many aspects of the **Transylvanian** landscape, the first place to look for a real Castle Dracula would seem to be near Borgo Pass. And in fact there were two different castles near both **Bistritz** (also spelled Bistrita) and the Borgo Pass road. The first was built in the thirteenth century some five kilometers north of the city at Dealu Cetatii. It fell into disuse and was in a dilapidated state by the early fifteenth century at which time the townspeople took the stones and reused them in refortifying Bistritz proper.

Castle Bistrita was built in the 1440s by John Hunyadi (d. 1456), a contemporary of Vlad the Impaler. Hunyadi was the "governor" of **Hungary** whose territory covered much of Transylvania. The two, whose lands adjoined each other, were in frequent competition and on occasion were allied. Hunyadi died in the siege of Belgrade, though the Christian forces won the battle and turned back the Turkish attempt to take the city. While it may be that Vlad the Impaler resided at Castle Bistrita for a brief period during the last years of Hunyadi's life, it could in no sense be called Castle Dracula. Today no remains of Castle Bistrita exist. It was destroyed at the end of the fifteenth century by the largely German population of the area in an act of defiance against their former Hungarian rulers.

Hunyadi had a second and more important castle located at Hundoara some 100 miles southwest of Borgo Pass. This impressive thirteenth-century structure still exists and has been restored and opened to the public. **Vlad Dracul** was believed to have visited this castle on at least one occasion during his early years. In 1452, while loosely allied with Hunyadi, Dracula was greeted somewhat as a friend. A decade later, however, he returned as a prisoner of Hunyadi's son Matthias Corvinus and began 12 years of imprisonment at Pest and **Visegrád**. Despite Vlad's presence at the castle at Hundoara, it was not Castle Dracula.

Dracula was actually the prince (ruler) of Wallachia. His territory was south of Transylvania, immediately on the other side of the Carpathian Mountains. In the mountains, overlooking the Dambovita River, near the town of Campulung, and protecting Bran Pass (the road through the Bucegi Mountains), is Castle Bran. It was originally built in the thirteenth century by the knights of the Teutonic Order. In the fourteenth century, the Teutonic Order having been expelled, the castle was taken over by the German merchants of Brasov who used it as their defense post and customs station. Brasov was located in the Transalpine area, which included the Carpathian Mountains and that area immediately to the north and south of the mountains. Though the Transalpine area was officially part of Hungarian territory, the Prince of Wallachia served as military overseer of the area in return for certain Transylvania duchies. Most of the time, neither Hungary nor Wallachia actually controlled the castle, which was in the hands of the very independent German merchants.

Castle Bran has often been touted, especially by the Romanian tourist authorities, as the real Castle Dracula. During its years under the control of the German leadership in Brasov, it is possible that Vlad Dracula visited it on occasion in the early 1450s. He was officially the Voivode of the Transalpine area. Historians **Radu Florescu** and **Raymond T. McNally** noted that it possessed the atmosphere that Stoker was attempting to evoke in his descriptions of Castle Dracula. "The analogies between Stoker's mythi-

Author J. Gordon Melton stands inside Castle Dracula, Curtea de Arges, Romania.

cal Castle Dracula and the real Castle Bran are simply too close to be coincidental." It had an inner courtyard and a secret underground passageway. A steep winding staircase could take a resident to a secret escape route deep inside the mountain. Though Florescu and McNally may have somewhat overstated their case, Dracula may have drawn, in part, from his knowledge of Castle Bran when he built his own mountain retreat.

The Real Castle Dracula?: The only castle that might be considered the actual Castle Dracula (remembering that no castle other than the one in Stoker's imagination ever had that name) was the castle built and inhabited by Vlad the Impaler during his years as Prince of Wallachia. This castle overlooks the River Arges near the town of Poenari, in the foothills of the Transylvanian Alps. It is located approximately 20 miles north of Curtea de Arges, the original capital of Wallachia, and was for many years the center of the Romanian Orthodox Church. When Vlad assumed the throne in 1456, there were two fortresses about a mile from each other on opposite sides of the river. Castle Poenari, the castle on the left side of the river, seems to have been built on the site of an even older fortress on the Arges River when this land was the center of the country called Dacia. Abandoned, it was rebuilt in the thirteenth century by Romanians attempting to block the incursions by Hungarian and/or Teutonic soldiers from the north. In 1455 it was in disrepair from recent battles with various invading armies, but was still habitable.

On the right side of the river was the Castle of the Arges. It was built a century before Vlad's time, although some historians have argued that even earlier it was a Teutonic outpost tied to the castle at Fagaras, just across the mountains to the north. McNally and Florescu have argued that it was not Teutonic, but built by the early Wallachian rulers and modeled on Byzantine patterns.

At the end of the fourteenth century, Tartars invaded the area. The remnant of the Wallachian forces (and many of the country's elite) eventually took refuge in the Castle of the Arges. The Tartars lay seize to the castle and finding almost no opposition soon captured it. However, its inhabitants escaped through the secret passageway under the castle. As a consolation prize, the Tartars largely destroyed the castle.

Of the two castles that Dracula found, the Castle of the Arges was in the more strategic position, possibly the major reason for his choice to rebuild it instead of settling at Poenari. It was located on a precipice overlooking the River Arges at the point where the valley of the Arges narrows and the foothills of the Carpathians turn into mountains.

The rebuilding process has become one of the more famous stories of Vlad, one of the earlier incidents confirming his nickname, "The Impaler." He had discovered that the boyars, the elite families of Wallachia, had been responsible for the death of his father and the torture and murder of his older brother. He decided to gain his revenge and get his castle built at the same time. During the Easter celebration following his taking up residence in his capital at **Tirgoviste**, he arrested all of the boyars (men, women, and children). Still dressed in their finest Easter clothes, they were forced to march to Poenari and rebuild the castle. The material from Poenari was carried across the river to construct the new residence overlooking the Arges. The boyars were forced to work until the clothes fell off their backs ... and then had to continue naked.

Vlad's Castle was quite small when compared to either Castle Bran or Hundoara. It was only some 100 feet by 120 feet. It rested on a precipice that looked out over the River Arges. To the north were the mountains dividing Transylvania and Wallachia, and to the south a commanding view of the countryside. There were three towers and walls thick enough to resist Turkish cannon fire. It seems to have been made to house about 200 people. According to legend, a secret staircase led into the mountain to a tunnel, which in turn, led to a grotto that opened on the bank of the river below the castle, though no evidence of the secret passage has been uncovered.

The Turks attacked and captured the castle in 1462. Vlad escaped north through the mountains, but his castle was severely damaged by the invaders. It was used by some of his successors as a mountain retreat. However, it was gradually abandoned and left to the ravages of time and **weather**. Built originally as a defensive position, it was too far outside the commercial routes that dominated the life of the region.

As late as 1912 the towers of the castle still stood. However, on January 13, 1913, an earthquake hit the area. It toppled the main tower into the river. A second earthquake in 1940 further damaged the castle. Then in the 1970s the Romanian government, responding to increased tourist interest in locations associated with Dracula, carried out a partial reconstruction and built a walkway up the mountainside to the cas-

tle's entrance. Today the mountain upon which Castle Dracula rests can be reached by car about an hour's drive north of the city of Pitesti. The walk up the mountain to the entrance takes approximately 45 minutes.

The Problem of Castle Dracula: The search for Castle Dracula highlighted the problem of reconciling Stoker's fictional Dracula with historical reality, a problem created by readers' excursions into Stoker's fictional world and made possible by Stoker's attempts to create as realistic a setting as possible. His book was set in Transylvania. Vlad the Impaler was a prince of Wallachia. While born in Transylvania, he resided all of his adult life in Wallachia, except for a period of imprisonment in Hungary. The geography of the novel and of Vlad's life are impossible to reconcile, a fact clearly demonstrated in **Francis Ford Coppola**'s movie *Bram Stoker's Dracula* and its almost comical attempts to place Dracula at the Castle on the Arges and near Borgo Pass at the same time.

There was no actual structure ever called Castle Dracula, only a small castle built by Vlad the Impaler. Though Vlad the Impaler's small castle had its place of importance in Romanian history, it was not known by Stoker and did not serve as a model for his Castle Dracula. It is probable that no castle in Eastern Europe served as the model for Castle Dracula, and the search must be directed closer to home. Thus some suggested that a castle at Cruden Bay, Scotland, where Stoker stayed while writing Dracula, was the model. However, from Stoker's manuscripts it is now known that the section of the novel on the castle was written before he traveled to Cruden Bay and that that section of the book remained essentially unchanged through publication. It would appear that Stoker's castle was a matter of pure imagination, a castle constructed from images of the romantic castles of European fairy tales and folklore.

Sources:

Ambrogio, Anthony. "Dracula Schmacula! Misinformation Never Dies." *Video Watchdog* No. 19 (September/October 1993): 32–47.

Florescu, Radu, and Raymond T. McNally. *Dracula: A Biography of Vlad the Impaler, 1431–1476.* New York: Hawthorn Books, 1973. 239 pp. This volume contains pictures of the several castles associated with Vlad the Impaler.

McNally, Raymond T., and Radu Florescu. *In Search of Dracula.* Greenwich, CT: New York Graphic Society, 1972. 223 pp. Rept. New York: Warner Books, 1973. 247 pp.

Moisescu, Nicolae. *Curtea de Arges.* Bucharest, Romania: CORESI, 1993. 76 pp.

Chaney, Alonso "Lon" (1893–1930)

Alonso "Lon" Chaney, the actor known for his numerous extraordinary characterizations in over 100 silent movies during the first decades of the twentieth century, was the first actor to play a vampire in an American feature-length movie. He was born on April 1, 1893. Both of Chaney's parents were deaf, and during most of his early life his mother was bedridden. Chaney developed his skill as a silent movie actor by communicating to his mother through mimicry and gesture every day. He was still a boy when, in 1901, he began his acting career on the stage. He played a variety of roles and became fascinated with makeup and its interaction with characterization.

Chaney's first film role was in 1913 in *Poor Jake's Demise*. Then **Universal Pictures** signed him to an exclusive contract (for $5.00 a day), and through the rest of the decade he assumed roles in over 100 films. He was first promoted as a star in 1919 when he played a fake cripple in *The Miracle Man*. He went on to his greatest successes as Quasimoto in *The Hunchback of Notre Dame* (1923) and in the title role of *The Phantom of the Opera* (1925).

Chaney worked on occasion with director **Tod Browning.** Their first collaboration was in 1921 in *Outside the Law*. Browning's alcoholism prevented their steady association. It was Chaney's second encounter with alcoholism; earlier he had divorced his wife and taken custody of their son because of her addiction to the bottle. In 1925 Chaney signed a long-term contract with MGM. Soon afterward he again teamed with Browning to do *The Unholy Three*. He would return to Universal only once, for *The Hunchback of Notre Dame*.

In 1927 Browning and Chaney teamed for the last time in **London After Midnight**. Chaney played a double part as a vampire and a police inspector from Scotland Yard. As the police sleuth, Chaney initiated a scheme to uncover a murder. He assumed the role of a vampire in order to force the real murderer to reveal himself. Once that occurred, Chaney took off the elaborate makeup and revealed himself as the inspector.

Although *London After Midnight* turned out to be his only vampire role, this was almost not the case. In 1930 he made the transition to sound in a new version of *The Unholy Three*, directed by Jack Conway. Meanwhile Browning had moved back to Universal, which had finally attained the film rights to **Dracula**. The studio announced the reunion of Browning and Chaney for the film. Unfortunately, Chaney had developed cancer, and before he could even be signed for the part he died on August 26, 1930. In 1957 his life was brought to the screen in *Man of a Thousand Faces* with James Cagney in the title role.

Sources:

Blake, Michael F. *The Films of Lon Chaney*. Lanham, MD: Madison Books, 2001. 304 pp.

————. *A Thousand Faces: Lon Chaney's Unique Artistry in Motion Pictures*. Lanham, MD: Vestal Press, 1995. 398 pp.

Flynn, John L. *Cinematic Vampires*. Jefferson, NC: McFarland Company, 1992. 320 pp.

Chaos! Comics

Chaos! Comics originated from the fertile imagination of writer/publisher Brian Pulido. He launched his career with *Evil Ernie*, published by Eternity Comics (an imprint of Malibu Comics). Although a relatively successful title, Malibu dropped *Evil Ernie*. Left in the lurch, and lacking any publishing experience, in November 1992 Pulido founded Chaos! Comics along with illustrator Steven Hughes and wife Francisca Pulido. The new *Evil Ernie: The Resurrection*, appeared in June of the following year.

Chaos! Comics quickly gained a reputation among the independent comic publishers for the quality of its publication. Pulido attempted to bring together quality horror fiction writing and state-of-the-art artwork and reproduction, with high-quality packaging. He followed *Evil Ernie* with a series of equally appealing characters, each of whom soon after their appearance became the subject of their own comic book title, beginning with Lady Death, and then the two new vampire creatures, Purgatori and Chastity.

Issue No.1 of *Lady Death* debuted in 1994 within months of the appearance of two other prominent new series featuring female characters, *Shi* and *Vengeance of Vampirella*. The three titles together launched a new phenomenon, the "Bad Girl" comic, now commanding an impressive share of the comic book market. Bad Girls were females who possessed all of the femininity for which any young male could hope while holding their own against forces that would challenge any superhero. Lady Death went on to become the top-selling female graphic art character in **America**. Chaos! was nominated by Diamond Comic Distribution as New Publisher of the Year in 1994 and won the Comic Buyers Guide Award for Customer Service in 1996. It secured its place in the comic world with its many innovations including the "commemorative" edition, the velvet cover, the leather cover, the **"coffin"**-shaped cover, the canvas cover, glow-in-the-dark chromium **trading cards**, and clear chromium cards.

Chaos! entered the vampire realm with the introduction of Purgatori, the demonic vampire, who made her first appearance in the March 1995 issue of *Lady Death*. According to her myth, Purgatori originated in ancient Egypt as a young slave named Sakkara. One day, the queen of Egypt, a **lesbian**, adopted her as a favorite in her harem. However, at the same time the queen was contemplating marriage with the ruler of a neighboring land who possessed the army she needed to stifle the unrest in her own land. The future bridegroom demanded that the queen kill all of her lovers. Only Sakkara managed to survive the slaughter.

Cover art from Chaos! Comics' **Chastity**.

She escaped and found her way to a vampire whom she had been told would give her immortality. She shared **blood** with Kath, the vampire, who sensed the blood of fallen angels flowing in her. He knew that she would be unique as a vampire creature, and she in fact emerged as the vampire creature Purgatori. A purely supernatural being, she had reddish skin, two horns, prominent **fangs**, and a set of batlike wings.

Enraged at her betrayal by the queen, she appeared at the queen's wedding and wreaked havoc on the wedding party, in the process turning several of the distinguished guests into vampires. The new vampires would become her mortal enemies. At a later date, she summoned Lucifer and asked him to take her. As he drew her near her, she brazenly stuck her fangs in him and tasted his blood. Outraged at her impudent behavior, he banished her to Necropolis (the city of the dead) where she sought Lady Death with whom to share some blood. Lady Death wanted nothing to do with Purgatori's schemes and banished the upstart to earth in the present to wander as a lowly bloodsucker.

Purgatori would soon be joined by young Chastity Marks in 1996 who would make her mark facing off against Evil Ernie. Chastity, a teenager who became a vampire in

London while working as a roadie for a punk rock band, would go on to become Ernie's enemy in his post-apocalyptic world.

The last series featuring Purgatori and Chastity appeared from Chaos! in 2002. That year, Chaos! Comics ran into severe financial problems and was forced to declare bankruptcy. Its vampire titles were sold to Tales of Wonder, who licensed them to Devil's Due Publishing. Devil's Due brought out only one series with a Chaos! vampire character, a last series featuring Purgatori (2005), but cancelled it when sales were low.

Sources:

Evil Ernie: Straight to Hell. Nos. 1–5. Phoenix, AZ: Chaos! Comics, 1995–96.
Lady Death. Nos. 1–4. Phoenix, AZ: Chaos! Comics, 1995.
Purgatori. Phoenix, AZ: Chaos! Comics, 1995.
Purgatori: Dracula Gambit. Phoenix, AZ: Chaos! Comics, 1996.
Purgatori: The Vampires Myth. Nos. 1–3. Phoenix, AZ: Chaos! Comics, 1996.

❲ Characteristics of Vampires ❳

Throughout history, vampires have been known by their defining characteristics. Vampires were known to be dead humans who returned from the grave and attacked and sucked the **blood** of the living as a means of sustaining themselves. The idea of the vampire came to the attention of both the scholarly community and the public in the West because of reports of such creatures in Eastern Europe in the seventeenth and eighteenth centuries. The vampire was seen as a prominent character in the folklore of people from **Greece** and Turkey in the south to **Germany** and **Russia** in the north. The descriptions of vampires in these countries set the image of vampires for the debates about their existence in the eighteenth century. The descriptions of the vampire from Greece and among the **southern Slavs** became the basis of the development of the literary vampire of the nineteenth century. **Bram Stoker**, the author of ***Dracula* (1897)**, drew heavily upon earlier vampire stories and the accounts of vampires in **Transylvania** and **Romania.** By the end of the nineteenth century and through the twentieth century, using a definition of the vampire drawn from European folklore and mythology, ethnographers and anthropologists began to recognize the existence of analogous beings in the folklore and mythology of other cultures around the world. While these entities from Asian, African, and other cultures rarely conformed entirely to the Eastern European vampire, they shared significant characteristics and could rightly be termed vampires or at least vampirelike entities.

The Modern Vampire: The vampire has become an easily recognizable character in Western popular culture. As defined by recent novels and motion pictures and as pictured in **comic books** and on greeting cards, vampires have several key attributes. Vampires are like "normal" human beings in most respects and are thus able to live more or less comfortably in modern society. They are different, however, in that they possess a pair of **fangs**, tend to dress in formal wear with an **opera** cape, have a pale complexion, sleep in **coffins**, are associated with **bats**, and only come out at night. Their fangs are used to bite people on the neck and suck blood, the substance from which they are nourished. Fangs have become the single most recognizable feature of a male or female vampire, immediately identifying the vampire character to an audience and signaling immediate danger to the prospective **victim.**

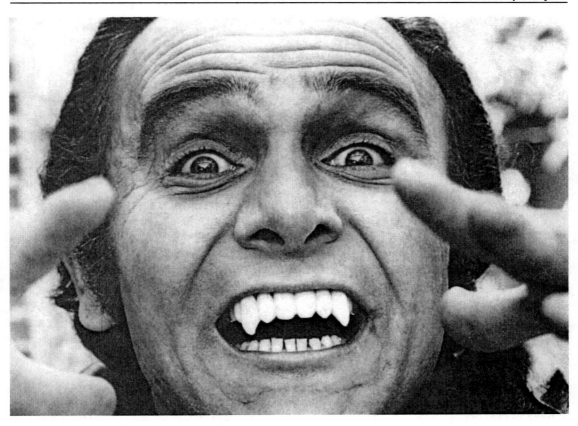

Prominent fangs are a common characteristic of vampires, as shown here in a scene from the film *Grave of the Vampire*.

In addition, vampires are basically creatures of the night, and during the day they enter a coma-like vampire **sleep**. They have red eyes and are cold to the touch. They may not be able to enter a room until invited. In addition, vampires possess some unusual "supernatural" attributes. They have great **strength**, they can **fly** (or at least levitate), they possess a level of **hypnotic power** (thus forcing the compliance of victims or causing the forgetfulness of the vampire's presence), they have acute night **vision**, and they can undergo a **transformation** into a variety of **animals** (usually a bat or possibly a wolf). Vampires avoid **garlic, sunlight**, sacred symbols such as the cross (the **crucifix**) and holy **water**, and they may need to sleep on their **native soil**. They may be killed by a wooden **stake** thrust in their heart, or by **fire**. While the stereotype has been challenged in recent decades, a disproportionate number of vampires were drawn from European nobility. They were suave and cultured and readily welcomed into almost any social context. The most recognizable vampire is, of course, **Dracula**. He was preceded by **Lord Ruthven** and Countess **Carmilla** Karnstein. More recently **Barnabas Collins**, of an aristocratic American family, and **Lestat de Lioncourt**, born of the French lesser nobility, have reinforced popular images of the vampire.

Bela Lugosi, shown here in the 1931 film *Dracula,* popularized the aristocratic characteristics now common to vampires.

Folkloric Vampires: The vampire was not always so described. Folkloric vampires appeared in numerous forms as demonic creatures. The Malaysian *penanggalan,* for example, was pictured as a severed head with entrails dangling down. The Indian goddess **Kali** had a hideous form and was often shown dancing on corpses with fangs protruding from her bloodied lips. However, most commonly the vampire appeared as the corpse of a person recently deceased. It could be recognized by its dress in burial clothes and could be identified by someone who had known them in life and understood that they were deceased and should not be walking around the town. As often as not, the vampire would never be seen, but its presence would be detected by the effects of its action, usually the wasting away and dying of people from unknown causes or the unusual and unexpected deaths of livestock.

Vampires, if seen, generally appeared to the people closest to them. In some cases, especially among the **Gypsies** and southern Slavs, they would return to engage in sexual relations with a former spouse or lover; in most other cases, they would launch a personal attack on family members, friends, or local livestock. Often the vampire would assume a new existence, something that approached normal life. In **Malaysia**, for example, the *langsuyar* assumed the role of a wife and could bear and raise children. She would usually be detected by some chance event during the course of her life. In Eastern Europe, primarily male vampires were reported to have ventured far from home, where they were not known, and continued their life as before their death, even to the point of marrying and fathering children.

The vampire of folklore had some supernatural attributes above and beyond the mobility one generally does not expect of the dead. It could change form and appear as a host of different animals, from a wolf to a moth. Interestingly, the bat was rarely reported as a vampiric form. Some people reported vampires with flying ability, especially in Oriental cultures, but flying or levitation was not prominent among Eastern European vampires.

The original vampires, those described in the folklore and mythology of the world's people, exist as an evil entity within a complex understanding of the world by a particular ethnic group. Thus they would assume characteristics drawn from that group's culture and fitting that group's particular need. Given the variety of vampirelike creatures, both demons and revenants, reported from cultures around the world, almost any characteristic reported of a vampire would be true of one or more such entities.

The Literary Vampire: At the beginning of the nineteenth century, the vampire became the focus of a set of writers, primarily in **France** and the **United Kingdom**. In their hands, the folkloric vampire, almost exclusively in its Eastern and Southern Eu-

ropean form, was transformed into a **gothic** villain. While retaining many of the characteristics from the reports of vampires that had filtered into Western Europe in the previous century, writers were quite selective in their choice of acceptable attributes. In the process of creating a literary character, they also added attributes that had no correlation in the folklore literature. Lord Ruthven, the character of the original vampire story written by **John Polidori**, was of noble birth.

Charnas, Suzy McKee (1939–)

Suzy McKee Charnas, author of *The Vampire Tapestry*, was born in New York City and attended Bernard College, where she received her bachelor's degree, and New York University, where she received her master's degree, in 1961 and 1965 respectively. Following college she spent two years in Nigeria with the Peace Corps, and after graduate school served as a junior high school teacher. She became a full-time writer in 1969. Her first novel, *Walk to the End of the World*, appeared in 1974. It was part of a projected trilogy that took over a decade to complete (during which time other novels were published). While the second volume of this futuristic feminist epic, *Motherlines* appeared relatively quickly (1978), the last volume, *The Furies*, was not completed until the mid-1990s. The series is about the anger of **women** and the justice of the reward they receive when men are vanquished.

During the course of her writing, Charnas first probed the vampire in her 1980 volume, *The Vampire Tapestry*. The novel, generally judged one of the better vampire novels of the century, tells the story of the vampire, described as a separate species who has lived at the edge of human society for millennia, and of one particular vampire, Edward Weyland, who appeared in the 1970s as a college professor of anthropology whose life is centered around a dream laboratory. His job not only gives him an excuse to be nocturnal, but also supplies him with the necessary supply of food. His problems begin with the discovery of what he is by a young female employee of the college. Besides being reprinted a number of times, excerpts of the text were adapted as a play and produced in San Francisco in 1980 under the title *Vampire Dreams*. Charnas returned to the vampire theme in the 1990s with *The Ruby Tear* written under her pseudonym Rebecca Brand. The story concerns the ongoing battle between a vampire, Baron von Cragga, and the Griffin family, whose current male representative Nicolas Griffin has written a play describing the tear-shaped jewel he owns. Von Cragga wants the jewel and the play becomes the catalyst for his final efforts to recover it.

Charnas did not abandon vampires in the new century. Her first offering was a short story, "Unicorn Tapestry," in an anthology of her fiction, *Music of the Night*, issued as an electronic book in 2001. Then in 2004, she delivered the further adventures of Edward Weyland as part of another anthology, Stagestruck Vampires, which includes three short stories with her vampire hero. In one story, co-authored with **Chelsea Quinn Yarbro**, Weyland meets up with the Comte de **Saint Germain**. Charnas maintains an Internet site at http://www.suzymckeecharnas.com/.

Sources:
Charnas, Suzy McKee. *Music of the Night*. Electric Story, 2001.

———— (as Rebecca Brand). *The Ruby Tear.* New York: TOR, 1997. 247 pp.

————. *Stagestruck Vampires.* San Francisco: Tachyon Publications, 2004. 256 pp.

————. *The Vampire Tapestry.* New York: Simon and Schuster, 1980. Rept. Albuquerque, NM: Living Branch Press, 1993. 285 pp.

❰ Chase, Cordelia ❱

Cordelia Chase is a companion of **Buffy Summers** and later of the vampire **Angel** on the ***Buffy the Vampire Slayer* television series** and then its spinoff *Angel.* A character created by Joss Whedon, she initially appeared in the first season of *Buffy the Vampire Slayer,* with the plot featuring her initially in the eleventh episode, "Out of Mind, Out of Sight," when she is running in the Sunnydale High School May Queen contest. By this time she has been introduced as the beautiful daughter of well-to-do parents and the head of a group of the most popular girls on campus, informally called the Cordettes. Needless to say, she represents the glamorous high-status females who have no trouble attracting multiple dating partners.

Cordelia was initially interested in recruiting the attractive Buffy into her clique of cool people, but began to avoid her after seeing her association with "losers" such as **Willow Rosenberg** and **Xander Harris.** Buffy, attacking Cordelia with a **stake** (while searching for a vampire behind the local teen hangout spot, the Bronze) did little to cement an initial positive relationship.

Cordelia's relationship to Buffy changed when she and the Cordettes find themselves under attack from an invisible entity. She came to Buffy and asked for help. Buffy was able to track the problem to Marcie Ross, who had been treated as if she were invisible during her high school years and as a result became literally invisible. Buffy's stopping Marcie begins a new relationship with Cordelia, which is really reoriented when a short time later she sees Buffy kill the vampire known as the Master. Cordelia is now fully aware of the supernatural realities invading the high school from the Hellmouth below.

During the second season, Cordelia hangs out increasingly with Buffy and her vampire/demon-fighting group. About halfway through the season, she finds herself arguing vehemently with Xander, whom she has previously held in contempt, only to end the argument in his arms kissing him passionately. Though seeming to have little in common, they begin dating. Publicly dating Xander further changes her, leads to a split with the Cordettes, and revises her opinion of uncool boys. She dates Xander into season three, but eventually breaks up with him. Shortly thereafter her status is deflated when tax problems cause her family to lose everything. Though they are no longer dating, Xander quietly pays for a dress so Cordelia can attend the senior prom.

Cordelia helps Buffy fight the mayor at the graduation ceremony, but then leaves for Los Angeles where she hopes to have a career in acting. She works at Angel Investigations, Angel's private detective agency, while awaiting a break that would never come. Actually, she is the one who convinces Angel, Buffy's former vampire boyfriend, to found the agency as a vehicle for his efforts to do good. When Angel's associate Doyle dies, he passes to Cordelia his ability to have visions of people in need of Angel's help. Though painful when they occur, she comes to see the visions as her reason to be alive. After a particularly painful vision on her twenty-first birthday, she accepts an offer to become a half-demon, which allows her to have the visions without pain and deterioration of her brain.

Her new status allows Cordelia to be deceived, and after three months she is fed half-truths about Angel that lead to their alienation. She also takes up with Conner, Angel's alienated son and becomes possessed by the entity Jasmine, during which time she has sex with Connor and becomes pregnant. Connor and Cordelia finally perform a ritual to force Jasmine out, but as a result Cordelia falls into a coma.

Cordelia awoke to find Angel in charge of the Los Angeles office of Wolfram & Hart, the legal firm that both represented and controlled the dark forces against which Buffy, Angel, and their cohorts fought. She believed Angel had made a bad decision, but finally informed him that her return was only temporary and she kissed him goodbye. Angel then received word that Cordelia had died in the hospital. After her final death, Cordelia would reappear in spirit form on several occasions, once in the final episode of the *Angel* series, and later in the *Angel* and *Buffy the Vampire Slayer* **comic books**.

Noting the significant transformation of the Cordelia Chase character, film and literature scholar Jes Battis observed that Cordelia began as a "self-centered, acerbic, and popularity-obsessed teenager" but ends as an elevated being, whose last favor to Angel is to remind him that he is quite capable of doing his work without "the nefarious resources of Wolfram and Hart." She reminded those around Angel that they were family, and she pushes them beyond their alleged limitations.

Cordelia Chase was portrayed by Charisma Carpenter (1970–). She had appeared in several television series prior to becoming part of the Buffy cast and has continued her television and movie career since Angel concluded, including several episodes of CSI.

Sources:

Battis, Jes. *Blood Relations: Chosen Families In Buffy The Vampire Slayer and Angel*. Jeffersonville, NC: McFarland & Company, 2005. 190 pp.

Holder, Nancy, with Jeff Mariotte and Maryelizabeth Hart. *Angel: The Casefiles*. Vol. 1. New York: Pocket Books, 2002. 505 pp.

———. *Buffy the Vampire Slayer: The Watcher's Guide*. Volume 2. New York: Pocket Books, 2000. 472 pp.

Chedipe *see:* India, Vampires in

Cheeky Devil Vampire Research *see:* Vampire Fandom: United States

Chetwynd-Hayes, Ronald Henry Glynn (1919–2001)

Ronald Henry Glynn Chetwynd-Hayes, horror short story writer and anthologist, was born in Middlesex, England, the son of Rose May Cooper and Henry Chetwynd-Hayes. He grew up in England and following his service in the British Army during World War II began a career in sales. His first novel, *The Man from the Bomb*, appeared in 1959. During the 1970s he emerged as a popular writer and anthologist of horror stories. His first vampire story, "Great Grandad Walks Again," appeared in 1973 in *Cold Terror*, a collection of his short stories.

Through the 1970s he edited more than twenty volumes of horror, ghost, and monster stories, as well as several collections of his own works; he was equally productive through the 1980s. Most notable among his titles was *The Monster Club* (1975), later made into a 1980 movie starring **John Carradine** and Vincent Price (who played the author). In 1980 he authored a vampire novel, *The Partaker*, and later edited two anthologies of vampire stories, *Dracula's Children* (1987) and *The House of Dracula* (1988). In 1988 Chetwynd-Hayes received the Bram Stoker Award for his achievements from the Horror Writers of America.

Sources:

Chetwynd-Hayes, Ronald, ed. *Dracula's Children*. London: William Kimber, 1987. 208 pp.

———. *The House of Dracula*. London: William Kimber, 1988. 206 pp.

———. *The Monster Club*. London: New English Library, 1975. 192 pp.

———. *The Partaker*. London: William Kimber, 1980. 224 pp.

———. *The Vampire Stories of R. Chetwynd-Hayes*. Edited by Stephen Jones. Minneapolis: Fedogan & Bremer, 1997. 251 pp.

Chiang-shih *see:* China, Vampires in

Children's Vampiric Literature *see:* Juvenile Literature

China, Vampires in

When Western scholars began to gather the folklore of China in the nineteenth century, they very quickly encountered tales of the *chiang-shih* (also spelled *kiang shi*), the Chinese vampire, generally translated into English as "blood-sucking ghost." Belief in vampires partially derived from a Chinese belief in two souls. Each person had a superior or rational soul and an inferior or irrational soul. The former had the form of the body and upon separation could appear as its exact double. The superior soul could leave the sleeping body and wander about the countryside. For a short period it could possess the body of another and speak through it. If accidents befell the wandering soul, it would have negative repercussions on the body. On occasion the superior soul appeared in an **animal** form.

The inferior soul, called the *p'ai*, or *p'o*, was the soul that inhabited the body of a fetus during pregnancy and often lingered in the body of a deceased person, leading to its unnatural preservation. When the *p'ai* left, the body disintegrated. The *p'ai*, if strong, preserved and inhabited the body for a long period and could use the body for its own ends. The body animated by the *p'ai* was called a *chiang-shih*, or vampire. The *chiang-shih* appeared normal and was not recognized as a vampire until some action gave it away. However, at other times it took on a hideous aspect and assumed a green phosphorescent glow. In this form the *chiang-shih* developed serrated teeth and long talons.

The Origin and Destruction of the Chiang-shih: The *chiang-shih* seems to have originated as a means of explaining problems associated with death. The *chiang-shih* arose following a violent death due to **suicide**, hanging, drowning, or smothering. It could also appear in a person who had died suddenly, or as a result of improper burial procedures. The dead were thought to become angry and restless if their burial was post-

poned for a long time after their death. Also animals, especially cats, were kept away from the unburied corpse, to prevent them from jumping over it, lest they become vampires themselves.

The *chiang-shih* lacked some of the powers of the Slavic vampire. It could not, for example, dematerialize, hence it was unable to rise from the grave, being inhibited both by **coffins** and the soil. Thus their **transformation** had to take place prior to burial, an added incentive to a quick burial of the dead. The Chinese vampires were nocturnal creatures and limited in their activity to the night hours. The *chiang-shih* had trouble crossing running **water**. The *chiang-shihs* were very strong and vicious. Reports detailed their attacks upon living people, where they ripped off the head or limbs of their **victims**. This homicidal viciousness was their most often reported trait. They usually had to surprise their victims because they had no particular powers to lure or entrance them. Besides their homicidal nature, the *chiang-shih* might also demonstrate a strong sexual drive that led it to attack and rape women. Over a period of time, the vampires gained **strength** and began to transform to a mobile state. They would forsake the coffin habitat, master the art of **flying**, and develop a covering of long white hair. They might also change into wolves.

In general, the vampire began its existence as an unburied corpse. However, on occasion there were reports of unburied body segments, especially the head, being reanimated and having an existence as a vampire. Also, reports have survived of the ever-present Chinese dragon appearing as a vampire.

People knew of several means of **protection** from a vampire. **Garlic**, an almost universal medicinal herb, kept vampires away. Salt was believed to have a corrosive effect on the vampire's skin. Vampires were offended by loud noises, and thunder would occasionally kill one. Brooms were handy weapons with which a brave soul could literally sweep the vampire back to its resting spot. Iron filings, rice, and red peas created barriers to the entry of the vampire and would often be placed around a vacant coffin to keep a vampire from taking it as a resting place.

If the vampire reached its transformative stage as the flying hairy creature, only thunder or a **bullet** could bring it down. In the end, the ultimate solution was cremation, the purifying **fire** being something of a universal tool of humankind.

The *Chiang-shih* in Literature: The *chiang-shih* was the subject of numerous stories and folktales. In the seventeenth century, the vampire became the subject for one of China's most famous short story writers, Pu Songling (1640–1715), author of the 16-volume *Liao Choi*. His story "The Resuscitated Corpse," for example, concerned four merchants who stopped at an inn. They were housed for the night in the barn, where, as it happened, the body of the innkeeper's daughter-in-law lay awaiting burial. One of the four could not sleep and stayed up reading. The corpse, now bearing **fangs,** approached the three sleeping men and bit each one. The other man watched frozen in fright. He finally came to his senses and, grabbing his clothes, fled with the vampire hot on his trail. As she caught up to him, he stood under a willow tree. She charged with great speed and ferocity, but at the last second the man dodged, and she hit the tree with full force, her long **fingernails** imbedded in the tree. The man fainted from fright and exhaustion. The next day the innkeeper's staff found the three dead merchants and the body of his daughter-in-law lying in her place but covered with **blood**. She was as fresh as the day she died, as she still had her *p'ai*, her inferior soul. The innkeeper confessed that she had died six months earlier, but he was waiting for an astrologically auspicious day for her burial. (There is a vague possibility that Pu Songling was influenced by European sources via **Russia**, as the vampire is a relative late-comer in Chinese ghostly tales. A variety of his stories have been made into English and a complete edition into German was made by Gottfried Rösel and published in five large volumes 1987–1992.)

Hungry Ghosts: The modern idea of the vampire in Chinese culture is also tied to the notion of the hungry ghost. The idea has roots in both Buddhism and Taoism, which posit that neglect of one's ancestors can lead to the emergence of hungry ghosts. The Buddhist Avatamsaka or Flower Garland Sutra, for example, suggests that evil deeds can cause a soul to be born in one of six possible realms. Serious evil deeds such as killing, stealing, or sexual misconduct will cause a soul to be born as a hungry ghost, while desire, greed, and ignorance effect such rebirth as they are motives for people to perform evil deeds. Many legends speak of a greedy woman who refused to share food becoming a hungry ghost in the next life.

Each summer, the Chinese celebrate Ullam-bana, the festival of Hungry Ghosts, on the fifteenth day of the seventh month in the Chinese lunar calendar (usually in August). The fifteenth day of a lunar month is the full moon. The Chinese believe that during the seventh month, the gates of hell are opened up and hungry ghosts are free to roam the earth seeking food and making mischief. These ghosts are the forgotten, people whose living descendents no long offer homage. They have long thin necks and large empty bellies. At this time, people will burn specially printed currency popularly called "hell money" which the ghosts can spend in hell to make a more comfortable life for themselves.

People will acknowledge the wandering ghosts at this time to prevent them from making mischief and/or bring bad luck. This acknowledgement will take the form of a feast on Ullam-bana in which food is offered to the ghosts.

Modern Vampires in China: The Chinese vampire was given a new lease on life by the post–World War II development of the film industry in Hong Kong and to a lesser extent in Taiwan. Actually, at least three vampire movies had been made in Hong Kong in the 1930s, prior to World War II—*Midnight Vampire*, *Three Thousand Year Old Vampire*, and *Vampires of the Haunted Mansion*. Several more would appear in the 1950s, such as *Vengeance of the Vampire* (1959), however, the late twentieth-century explosion of vampire movies really begins with two Hong Kong-based firms, Catay-Keris and the Shaw Brothers, which began making vampire films in **Malaysia** using Malaysian themes in the 1950s, but were rather late in developing Chinese vampire movies. Among the first Chinese vampire movies was *Xi Xuefu* (*Vampire Woman*) produced by Zhong Lian in 1962. Like many first ventures into vampirism, it was ultimately a case of mistaken attribution. The story concerned a woman who, after she was found sucking the blood out of her baby, was accused of vampirism and was executed by burning. Later it was discovered that the baby had been poisoned, and she was only trying to save it.

The vampire theme in Chinese movies was really launched a decade later with the first of the vampire-martial arts movies, *Vampire Kung-fu* (1972). Then two years later a combined Shaw Brothers-**Hammer Films** production, variously titled *The Legend of the Seven Golden Vampires* and *The Seven Brothers Meet Dracula*, became one of the great disasters in horror film history. *The Legend of the Seven Golden Vampires*, directed by **Roy**

THE VAMPIRE BOOK: THE ENCYCLOPEDIA OF THE UNDEAD

Ward Baker and starring **Peter Cushing**, transferred the **Dracula** story to China where **Abraham Van Helsing** was called to protect a village from a band of vampires who had learned martial arts skills. The film was so bad that its American distributor refused to handle it. In the 1980s, the Hong Kong filmmakers rediscovered the vampire horror genre. Among the best known movies was the "Mr. Vampire" comedy series that was started in 1985 by Golden Harvest and Paragon Films. Drawing on several aspects of Chinese folklore, the films featured what have come to be known as the hopping vampires—loose-robed vampires that hopped to move around—a character developed from a character in Chinese mythology, the blood-sucking ghost. The first film was so popular it spawned four sequels, a **television** series in **Japan**, and a rival production, *Kung-fu Vampire Buster* (1985). A second very successful movie was *Haunted Cop Shop* (1984) concerning vampires who took over a meat-packing plant and were opposed by a Monster Police Squad. A sequel appeared in 1986. Other notable Hong Kong films included: *Pao Dan Fei Che (The Trail,* 1983), *Curse of the Wicked Wife* (1984), *Blue Lamp in a Winter Night* (1985), *Dragon Against Vampire* (1985), *The Close Encounter of the Vampire* (1985), *Love Me Vampire* (1986), *Vampire's Breakfast* (1986), *Vampires Live Again* (1987), *Toothless Vampires* (1987), *Hello Dracula* (1986), *Vampires Strike Back* (1988), *Spooky Family* (1989), *Crazy Safari* (1990), *First Vampire in China* (1990), *Spooky Family II* (1991), and *Robo Vampire* (1993). As might be perceived by the titles, many of these movies were comedies, a few unintentionally so. Taiwanese films of the same era included *The Vampire Shows His Teeth* I, II, and III (1984–86), *New Mr. Vampire* (1985), *Elusive Song of the Vampire* (1987), and *Spirit vs. Zombie* (1989).

With the hopping or jumping vampires, a different mythology about dealing with vampires evolved. They could be subdued with magical talismans, usually wielded by a Taoist priest, who became a staple character in vampire cinema. Holding one's breath would temporarily stop them. Eating sticky rice was an antidote to a vampire bite. By creating a separate vampire myth, the Chinese movies have built a new popular image of the vampire in the Orient much as the *Dracula* movies created one in the West.

Interest in the vampire continued in Hong Kong through the 1980s, but appeared to decline significantly through the 1990s. Only a very few, such as *Vampire Combat* (2001), *Tsui Hark's Vampire Hunters* (2002), *My Honey Moon with a Vampire* (2003), *The Twins Effect* (2003), *Twins Effects II* (2004), *Shaolin vs. Evil Dead* (2004), *Shaolin vs. Evil Dead: Ultimate Power* (2006), and *Dating a Vampire* (2006). Over 100 vampire movies have been made in Hong Kong.

Sources:

Buber, Martin, ed. *Chinese Tales: Zhuangzi, Sayings and Parables and Chinese Ghost and Love Stories.* Atlantic Highland, NJ: Humanities Press International, 1991. 235 pp.

de Groot, J. J. M. *The Religious System of China.* 5 vols. Leyden, The Netherlands: E. J. Brill, 1892–1910.

De Visser, M. W. *The Dragon in China and Japan.* Wiesbaden, Germany: Dr. Martin Sändig, 1913, 1969. 242 pp.

Hurwood, Bernhardt J. *Passport to Supernatural: An Occult Compendium from Many Lands.* New York: Taplinger Publishing Company, 1972. 319 pp.

Latsch, Marie-Luise. *Traditional Chinese Festivals.* Singapore: Greaham Brash, 1984. 103 pp.

Liming, Wei. *Chinese Festivals: Traditions, Customs, and Rituals.* Hong Kong: China International Press, 2005. 127 pp.

MacKenzie, Donald A. *Myths of China and Japan*. London: Gresham Publishing Company, 1923. 404 pp.

O'Brien, Daniel. *Spooky Encounters: A Guailo's Guide to Hong Kong Horror*. Manchester, UK: Headpress/Critical Vision, 2003. 191 pp.

Vellutini, John L. "The Vampire in China." *Journal of Vampirology* 6, 1 (1989): 1–10.

Wieger, Leo. *A History of the Religious Beliefs and Philosophical Opinions in China*. 1927. Rept. New York: Paragon Book Reprint Corp., 1969. 774 pp.

Willis, Donald C. "The Fantastic Asian Video Invasion: Hopping Vampires, Annoying Aliens, and Atomic Cats." *Midnight Marquee* 43 (Winter 1992): 4–11.

Willoughby-Meade, G. *Chinese Ghouls and Goblins*. New York: Frederick A. Stokes Co., 1926. 431 pp.

❨ Christianity and Vampires ❩

The belief in vampires preceded the introduction of Christianity into southern and eastern Europe. It seems to have originated independently as a response to unexplained phenomena common to most cultures. Ancient Greek writings tell of the *lamiai,* the *mormolykiai,* and other vampirelike creatures. Independent accounts of vampires emerged and spread among the Slavic people and were passed to their non-Slavic neighbors. Possibly the **Gypsies** brought some belief in vampires from **India** that contributed to the development of the myth. As Christianity spread through the lands of the Mediterranean Basin and then northward across Europe, it encountered these vampire beliefs that had already arisen among the many Pagan peoples. However, vampirism was never high on the Christian agenda and was thus rarely mentioned. Its continued presence was indicated by occasional documents such as an eleventh-century law promulgated by Charlemagne as emperor of the new Holy Roman Empire. The law condemned anyone who promoted the belief in the witch/vampire (specifically in its form as a *strix*), and who on account of that belief caused a person thought to be a vampire to be attacked and killed.

By the end of the first Christian millennium, the Christian Church was still organizationally united and in agreement upon the basic Christian affirmation (as contained in the Nicene Creed) but had already begun to differentiate itself into its primarily Greek (Eastern Orthodox) and Latin (Roman Catholic) branches. The church formally broke in the year 1054 with each side excommunicating the other.

During the second Christian millennium, the two churches completed their conquests through the remaining parts of Europe, especially eastern Europe. Meanwhile, quite apart from the major doctrinal issues that had separated them in the eleventh century, the theology in the two churches began to develop numerous lesser differences. These would become important especially in those areas where the boundaries of the two churches met and wars brought people of one church under the control of **political** leaders of the other. Such a situation arose, for example, in the twelfth century when the predominantly Roman Catholic Hungarians conquered **Transylvania**, then populated by Romanians, the majority of whom were Eastern Orthodox. Slavic but Roman Catholic **Poland** was bounded on the east by Orthodox Russian states. In the Balkans, Roman Catholic Croatia existed beside predominantly Orthodox Serbia.

One divergence between the two churches frequently noted in the vampire literature was their different understanding of the incorruptibility of dead bodies. In the

East, if the soft tissue of a body did not decay quickly once placed in the ground, it was generally considered a sign of evil. That the body refused to disintegrate meant that the earth would, for some reason, not receive it. An incorrupt body became a candidate for vampirism. In the West, quite the opposite was true. The body of a dead saint often did not experience corruption like that of an ordinary body. Not only did it not decay, but it frequently emitted a pleasant odor. It did not stink of putrefaction. These differing understandings of incorruptibility explain in large part the demise of belief in vampires in the Catholic West, and the parallel survival of belief in Orthodox lands, even though the Greek Church officially tried to suppress the belief.

Vampires and Satan: Admittedly, vampires were not a priority issue on the agenda of Christian theologians and thinkers of either church. However, by 1645 when **Leo Allatius** (1586–1669) wrote the first book to treat the subject of vampires systematically, it was obvious that much thought, especially at the parish level, had been devoted to the subject. The vampire had been part of the efforts of the church to eliminate Paganism by treating it as a false religion. The deities of the Pagans were considered unreal, nonexistent. In like measure, the demons of Pagan lore were unreal.

Through the thirteenth and fourteenth centuries, as the Inquisition became a force in the Roman Catholic Church, a noticeable change took place in theological perspectives. A shift occurred in viewing Paganism (or **witchcraft**). It was no longer considered merely a product of the unenlightened imagination, it was the work of **Satan**. Witchcraft was transformed in the popular mind into Satanism. The change of opinion on Satanism also provided an opening for a reconsideration of, for example, the **incubus/succubus** and the vampire as also somehow the work of the devil. By the time Allatius wrote his treatise on the vampire, this changing climate had overtaken the church. Allatius was Greek, but he was also a Roman Catholic rather than an Orthodox believer. He possessed a broad knowledge of both churches. In his *De Graecorum hodie quorundam opinationibus*, the vampire toward which he primarily turned his attention was the *vrykolakas*, the Greek vampire.

Allatius noted that among the Eastern Orthodox Greeks a *noncanon*, that is, an ordinance of uncertain authorship and date, was operative in the sixteenth century. It defined a *vrykolakas* as a dead man who remained whole and incorrupt, who did not follow the normal pattern of disintegration which usually occurred very quickly in a time before embalming. Occasionally, such a *vrykolakas* was found, and it was believed to be the work of the devil. When a person discovered a *vrykolakas*, the local priest was to be summoned. The priest chanted an invocation to the Mother of God and again repeated the services of the dead. The earlier noncanon, however, originated in the period when the church was attacking the belief in vampires as superstition and was designed to reverse some centuries-old beliefs about vampires. It ascribed incidents involving *vrykolakas* to someone seeing a dead person, usually at night, frequently in dreams. Such dreams were the work of the devil. The devil had not caused the dead to rise and attack its **victims**, but deluded the individual with a false dream.

Allatius himself promoted the belief that was gaining dominance in the West through the sixteenth-century: Vampires were real and were themselves the work of the devil. Just as the Inquisition in the previous century had championed the idea that witchcraft was real and that witches actually communed with the devil, so vampires were actually walking around the towns and villages of Europe. They were not the dead returned, they were bodies reanimated by the devil and his minions. Allatius even quoted the witchfinder's bible, the *Malleus Maleficarum* (*The Witch's Hammer*), which noted the three conditions necessary for witchcraft to exist: the devil, a witch, and the permission of God. In like measure, Allatius asserted that for vampires to exist all that was needed was the devil, a dead body, and the permission of God.

The tying of vampirism to the devil by Allatius and his colleagues brought Satan into the vampire equation. Vampirism became another form of Satanism and the vampire the instrument of the devil. Also, his victims were tainted by evil. Like the demons, vampires were alienated from the things of God. They could not exist in the realms of the sacred and would flee from the effective symbols of the true God, such as the **crucifix**, or from holy things, such as holy **water** and the **eucharistic wafer**, which both Orthodox and Roman Catholics believed to be the very body of Christ. In like measure, the offices of the church through the priest were an effective means of stopping the vampire. In the Eastern Orthodox church, the people always invited the priest to participate in their anti-vampire efforts. In its attempt to counter the superstitious beliefs in vampires, the Orthodox church ordered its priests not to participate in such activities, even threatening excommunication.

The Eighteenth-century Vampire Debates: During the seventeenth century, reports, not just of vampires, but of vampire epidemics, began to filter out of eastern Europe, especially Prussia and Poland. These incidents involved cases in which bodies were exhumed and mutilated. The mutilation of the bodies of people buried as Christians and presumably awaiting the resurrection was of utmost and serious concern to Christian intellectuals and church leaders in western Europe. The majority of these reports came from Roman Catholic-dominated lands, the most important from that area of Serbia which had been taken over by Austria in the wake of a fading Ottoman Empire. The cases of **Peter Plogojowitz** and **Arnold Paul** launched a heated debate in the German (both Lutheran and Catholic) universities. In the midst of this debate, Cardinal Schtrattembach, the Roman Catholic bishop of Olmütz, **Germany**, turned to **Rome** for some advice on how to handle the vampire reports. The pope, in turn, called upon the learned archbishop of Trani, **Italy**, **Giuseppe Davanzati**, who spent five years studying the problem before writing his *Dissertazione sopra I Vampiri*, finally published in 1744.

Davanzati was swayed by the more skeptical arguments that had emerged as the consensus in the German debates. He advised the pope that the vampire reports were originating in human fantasies. While these fantasies might possibly be of diabolical **origin**, pastoral attention should be directed to the person reporting the vampire. The bodies of the suspected vampires should be left undisturbed. The church followed Davanzati's wisdom.

Meanwhile, as Davanzati was pursuing his research, so was **Dom Augustin Calmet**. Calmet, known throughout **France** as a Bible scholar, published his *Dissertations sur les Apparitions des Anges des Démons et des Espits, et sur les revenants, et Vampires de Hingrie, de Boheme, de Moravie, et de Silésie* two years after Davanzati. Calmet played devil's advocate to his fellow churchman. He described in some detail the reports of the eastern European vampires and called upon theologians and his scholarly colleagues to give them some serious study. He explored various possibilities concerning the accounts and left open the medieval position that the bodies of suspected vampires were animated by the devil and/or evil spirits. His colleagues in the church did not receive his report favorably. Even members of the Benedictine order, of which he was a member, chided him for giving credence to what amounted to nothing more than children's horror stories. In the third edition of his book, he finally did away with the devilish option and concluded that vampires did not exist. However, by this time his earlier editions had spread far and wide, and had become the basis for translations. Few noted the final position he had reached. Though his colleagues dismissed him, he found broad popular support, and his book went through several printings in France and was translated and published in Germany and England.

The sign of the future came in 1755 and 1756 when in two actions Empress Maria Theresa took the authority of handling the vampire cases out of the hands of parish priests and local authorities and placed it in the hands of Austrian government officials. The clear intent of the law was to stop the disturbance of the graves. During the decades following Maria Theresa's action, the spokespersons of what would become known as the Enlightenment would take over the final stages of the debate and essentially end it with their consensus opinion that vampires were unreal. After a generation in which the likes of Diderot and Voltaire expressed their opinion of vampires, scholars have not found it necessary to refute a belief in the vampire. Calmet became an intellectual relic, though he provided a number of interesting stories from which a popular literary vampire could be created.

Dracula and the Church: Interestingly enough, the first vampire stories—from **Johann Wolfgang von Goethe**'s "The Bride of Corinth" to **Sheridan Le Fanu**'s "Carmilla"—were largely secular works. Religious artifacts and religious characters were almost completely absent. At the end of "Carmilla," as Laura's father began his quest to locate and destroy **Carmilla**, he suggested to Laura that they call upon the local priest. The priest performed certain solemn, but unnamed, rituals which allowed the troubled Laura to **sleep** in peace. However, he did not accompany the men to finally kill Carmilla, though two medical men were present to oversee the act. It was left to **Bram Stoker** and his novel *Dracula* **(1897)** to reintroduce Christianity into the vampire's life. In the very first chapter, as **Jonathan Harker** made his way to **Castle Dracula,** a woman took off a rosary, with an attached **crucifix,** and gave it to him. In spite of his anti-Roman Catholic background, Harker put the rosary around his neck and wore it. Later, an enraged **Dracula** lunged for Harker's neck but quickly withdrew when he touched the rosary. **Abraham Van Helsing,** the pious vampire hunter from Holland, explained that the crucifix was one of several sacred objects whose presence deprived the vampire of its power.

Besides the crucifix, Van Helsing used the eucharistic wafer, the bread consecrated as the body of Christ in the church's communion service (in this case the Roman Catholic mass). He placed the wafers around the openings of the tomb of **Lucy Westenra** and sanitized (destroyed the effectiveness of) the boxes of **native soil** Dracula had brought from his homeland. Most importantly, the wafer burned its imprint into the forehead of the tainted **Mina Murray** after her encounter with Dracula.

In subsequent productions of *Dracula,* the eucharistic wafer largely dropped from the picture. It was used on occasion to sanitize the earth, but only in **Bram Stoker's Dracula** did the scene of Mina's being branded by the wafer become a part of a dramatic presentation. Instead, it was the crucifix that became the religious symbol most frequently used to cause the vampire to lose its **strength** or to harm the vampire.

The Vampire and the Church Since Stoker: Through the twentieth century, the crucifix became a standard part of the vampire hunter's kit. Frequently he would flash it just in time to save himself. On many occasions, heroines were saved from a vampire about to pounce upon them by a shining cross hanging around their neck. At the same time, especially since midcentury, the vampire novel began to show signs of secularization. Some vampires came from outer space or arose as victims of a disease. Such vampires, lacking any negative supernatural origins, were unaffected by the holy objects.

As the century progressed, vampire writers challenged the role of Christianity in the culture. Some expressed their doubts as to its claims to exclusive truth concerning God and the world. Writer **Anne Rice,** for example, very early in her life became a skeptic of Roman Catholicism, in which she was raised. Her vampires, reflecting her nonbelief, were unaffected by Christian symbols. They walked in churches with impunity and handled crucifixes with no negative reaction. In like measure, **Chelsea Quinn Yarbro**'s hero, **St. Germain,** and other **good guy vampires,** were not Satanic; quite the opposite, they were moral agents. The vampires in Yarbro's books had no negative reaction to Christian objects or places.

Vampires in **science fiction** were raised in an alien culture that had never heard of Christianity. They were among the first group of vampires that had no reaction to Christian sacred symbols. The vampires of *The Hunger* by Whitley Strieber and those in **Elaine Bergstrom**'s novels, were unaffected by the cross because they were aliens. Bergstrom's vampires, the Austra family, made their living working in cathedrals repairing stained glass. Other writers affected by the religiously pluralistic culture in the West questioned the value of Christian symbols for people raised in or adhering to another faith. For example, they asked if Jewish symbols served as **protection** from Jewish vampires. In Roman Polanski's *The Fearless Vampire Killers,* or *Pardon Me but Your Teeth Are in My Neck* (1967), one of the more humorous moments came from a Jewish vampire attacking a young girl who tried to protect herself with a cross.

The relation to the sacred in general and Christianity in particular will continue to be a problem for vampire novelists, especially those working in the Christian West. The vampire is a supernatural **gothic** entity whose popular myth dictated its aversion for the crucifix. The literary vampire derives its popularity from the participation of its readers in a world of fantasy and supernatural power. At the same time, an increasing number of novelists do not have a Christian heritage and thus possess no understanding or appreciation of any power derived from Christian symbols. For the foreseeable future, new vampire fiction will be written out of the pull and tug between these traditional and contemporary perspectives.

Sources:

Frayling, Christopher. *Vampyres: Lord Byron to Count Dracula.* London: Faber and Faber, 1991. 429 pp.

Frenschkowski, Marco, "'Ich trinke niemalsö Wein.' Das Blut in der Religionsgeschichte." *Kursiv: Eine Kunstzeitschrift aus Oberösterreich* 4, 3 (1997): 7–13.

Hartnup, Karen. *On the Beliefs of the Greeks: Leo Allatios and Popular Orthodoxy.* Leiden: Brill, 2004. 370 pp.

Summers, Montague. *The Vampire: His Kith and Kin.* London: Routledge, Kegan Paul, Trench, Trubner, & Co., 1928. 356 pp. Rept. New Hyde Park, NY: University Books, 1960. 356 pp.

Churel *see:* India, Vampires in

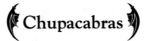

Chupacabras

The chupacabras (literally "goat sucker") is a vampirelike creature that began a reign of terror in Puerto Rico, **Mexico**, and Central America in the mid-1990s. Most accounts picture the creature as what might be described as a cross between a **bat** and a kangaroo. It has hairy arms, glowing red eyes, and bright-colored spine-like appendages that run over the body from the head to the end of the back. Scales, claws, and bat-shaped wings are also common attributes.

The primary **victims** of the chupacabras have been **animals**, specifically chickens and other farm animals, including horses, dogs, cats, and most importantly goats. In the anecdotal stories that have spread throughout Latin America, the creature has been described in ways as to associate it with the vampire. It leaves two puncture wounds on the neck of its victims, it hunts at night, it has batlike wings, it sucks **blood**, and defies the laws of the physical universe. A **crucifix** holds it at bay.

The quick spread of the chupacabra stories in the press and the popular acceptance of the stories among the public has led various authorities to speak against the reality of the creature. Some veterinarians and other authorities called upon to autopsy the bodies of the victims have commented that they have found no special loss of blood, and report the wounds are consistent with the attack of wild dogs or other predatory animals. Norine Dresser, the primary American scholar who has studied the accounts, has judged the chupacabras as a contemporary legend; that is, a popularly told tale that mixes credible details with preposterous elements (the very elements that make them both newsworthy and entertaining). The stories of the chupacabras arose quickly, a sign of the **political/economic** anxieties that have affected the whole Caribbean basin.

Between 1995 and 2005, approximately a dozen chupacabra feature films were made, but after a decade, the idea seemed to have largely run its course. Government officials in those countries where the idea attained currency in the popular culture had largely decided that no such creature existed and the press tired of reporting the latest sightings. While belief still exists, the number of reports have markedly declined since the middle of the first decade of the new century. Chupacabras remain the subject of novels, while speculation on their existence has shifted to UFO enthusiasts.

Sources:

Anaya, R. *Curse of the ChupaCabra*. Albuquerque: University of New Mexico Press, 2006.

Clark, Jerome, and Loren Coleman. *Cryptozoology A to Z*. New York, NY: Fireside, 1999. 270 pp.

Corrales, Scott. *Chupacabras: And Other Mysteries*. Murfreesboro, TN: Greenleaf, 1997. 248 pp.

Downes, Jonathan. *The Island of Paradise—Chupacabra, UFO Crash Retrievals, and Accelerated Evolution on the Island of Puerto Rico*. Exerter, UK: CFZ Press, 2008.

Dresser, Norine. "Chupacabras: A Contemporary Vampire Invasion." A paper presented at Dracula '97: A Centennial Celebration, Los Angeles, August 14–17, 1997.

Heinsohn, Robert. *Chupacabras*. AuthorHouse, 2006. 304 pp.

Cihuacoatl *see:* Mexico, Vampires in

Cihuateteo *see:* Mexico, Vampires in

Cirque du Freak *See* Shan, Darren

Clans, Vampire *see* Vampire: The Eternal Struggle

Club Vampire *see:* Vampire Fandom: United States

Coatlicue *see:* Mexico, Vampires in

Coffins

In both novels and motion pictures, vampires **sleep** in coffins, and as they move from place to place, they transport their coffins with them. The association of vampires and coffins began with the simple fact that vampires were dead, and dead people, by the time of the development of the literary vampire in the nineteenth century, were buried in coffins. It should be noted that much vampire lore originated in an era prior to the use of coffins. Until recent centuries, the use of coffins was limited to those wealthy enough to afford them. The poorer classes would be transported in coffins to the grave-yard, but then the body would be removed and buried in the shroud in which it had been wrapped. The coffin was then available for reuse. One kind of reusable coffin, termed a "slip" coffin, came equipped with hinges on the bottom to allow the body to be dropped into the grave.

Before the seventeenth century, when coffins became common even for the poor, the dead were commonly wrapped in a burial shroud and placed in a relatively shallow grave. In times of epidemics, the dead might be buried quite hastily and in very shallow graves. Such bodies were subject to predator damage, seemingly the source of northern European beliefs that vampires first devour their own extremities. To keep predators away from bodies buried without a coffin, a flat rock could be placed over part or all of the body. The problems of burial were further complicated by winter **weather** and frozen ground that would delay burials for weeks or months until the spring thaw, and by various beliefs in astrology that suggested that some moments were better than others for an auspicious burial.

The practice of putting a **stake** into a vampire's body may have originated as a means of fixing the vampire to the ground without a coffin, rather than attacking the vampire itself. Since keeping the corpse in the ground was one purpose of staking someone, the stake did not have to go through the heart. It could just as appropriately go through the stomach or the back. Also the material from which the stake was made was not as important as its functionality. Thus stakes were made of various kinds of wood or iron.

At the time of the great vampire epidemics in eastern Europe in the early eighteenth century, it was the common practice to bury the dead in coffins. Anti-vampire measures consisted of various actions to keep the vampire, usually designated as a recently deceased member of the community, confined to the coffin. The coffin would be opened and the body staked. In some areas the clothes would be attached to the sides of the coffin in order to hold the body in place. The appendages would be nailed to the sides of the coffin so that the vampire could not eat them. The coffin could then be returned to the grave.

Early literary vampires did not have coffins. Geraldine (from **Samuel Taylor Coleridge**'s "Christabel"), **Lord Ruthven,** and **Varney the Vampyre** had no casket home. **Carmilla** brought no coffin with her, though she was eventually found resting in her crypt at an old chapel. Otherwise, these vampires seemed perfectly comfortable to rest wherever they happened to be.

In **Bram Stoker**'s *Dracula,* (1897) the vampires did not rest in a coffin (as was depicted in the 1931 movie), but he did need to rest on his **native soil.** Thus he transported large crates (not coffins) of soil with him to England, and the desecration of the soil with sacred objects led to his hasty return to his native land. At the end of the novel, **Abraham Van Helsing** entered **Castle Dracula** to destroy the three vampire **brides** who resided at the castle. He found them in their tombs and destroyed them. He also found a large ornate tomb with the word DRACULA written on it. There he laid bits of a **eucharistic wafer**, thus **destroying** it as a resting place for a vampire.

The idea of the vampire resting in a coffin primarily derived from the *Dracula* (1931) movie in which the vampires were shown rising out of their coffins in the basement of the castle. In later movies, the boxes of earth that **Dracula** carried to England tended to be replaced by a coffin partially filled with dirt. Numerous vampire movies made use of a scene in which the vampire awakened and slowly thrust his hand out of the coffin.

While modern novels and movies tended to picture vampires sleeping in coffins, this was not a necessity. The coffin was merely one way to meet the requirement that the vampire rest on native soil. Throughout the twentieth century, the vampire increasingly lost any attachment to native soil, and the coffin was utilized more as a protective device shading the vampire from the **sunlight.** At the same time, the coffin served several additional useful purposes, especially in the movies. As a visual object immediately recognized by the audience, it helped build atmosphere. It also provided comic moments, as in George Hamilton's *Love at First Bite*, with all of the problems inherent in transporting, protecting, and explaining the presence of a coffin. The coffin also supplied a ready means of international transportation for the mobile vampire of the modern world. In the movie *Pale Blood* (1989) the vampire carried a light, unobtrusive, portable "coffin," which he could set up like a tent. Finally, and probably most importantly, the coffin supplied a target for the **vampire hunter** that made locating the vampire during the day far easier.

In developing her modern vampire myth, **Anne Rice** altered the importance of the coffin through the several novels of the "Vampire Chronicles." In **Interview with the Vampire,** the vampire **Lestat de Lioncourt** slept in a coffin, and the night he made Louis a vampire, he forgot to obtain a coffin for him. Thus Louis had to sleep with Lestat as dawn approached. Coffins were a convenience for Rice's vampires, not a necessity. Her vampires could simply return to the earth (as Lestat did for many years) or stay in a sealed chamber protected from the sunlight as the two original vampires (Akasha and Enkil) had done for centuries. Though coffins were not required, most vampires slept in them and only after some years of vampiric existence realized all they needed was a shield of **protection** from the sun's rays. As in Rice, coffins largely disappeared from the world of vampires in *Buffy the Vampire Slayer* and in the "Twilight" series.

Sources:

Barber, Paul. *Vampires, Burial, and Death: Folklore and Reality*. New Haven, CT: Yale University Press, 1988. 236 pp.

Colman, Penny. *Corpses, Coffins, and Crypts: A History of Burial.* New York: Henry Holt and Co., 1997. 227 pp.

Coleridge, Samuel Taylor (1772–1834)

Samuel Taylor Coleridge, a romantic poet and the first to introduce the vampire theme to British **poetry**, was born in Ottery St. Mary, the son of a minister in the Church of England. His father died when Coleridge was nine, and he was sent to Christ's Hospital, London, as a charity pupil. In 1790 he entered Jesus College, Cambridge. He left college briefly in 1793, but returned the following year. There he met fellow poet **Robert Southey,** who would become his lifelong friend. Through Southey he met Sara Fricker, his future wife, and got his first contract to prepare a book of poetry.

In 1797 Coleridge met William Wordsworth, who was credited with bringing Coleridge's poetic genius to the public's attention. The initial result of this friendship was "The Rime of the Ancient Mariner," published in the celebrated *Lyrical Ballads,* which Wordsworth put together. Coleridge wrote almost all of his famous poems during the next five years of his close association with Wordsworth.

Among the poems Coleridge worked on during this creative period was "Christabel." Though never mentioning vampires directly, it is now generally conceded that vampirism was the intended theme of "Christabel," the substantive case having been made by Arthur H. Nethercot in the 1930s. Nethercot argued that the essential vampiric nature of the Lady Geraldine, who was "rescued" after being left in the woods by her kidnappers, was demonstrated by examining her **characteristics**. First, throughout the poem, Christabel was portrayed as a potential **victim** who needed to be shielded from the forces of evil. Geraldine, however, was pictured as a richly clad woman first seen bathing in the moonlight (the element that revived vampires in nineteenth-century vampire tales). Second, as Geraldine approached the door of the castle of Christabel's father, she fainted. After Christabel assisted her across the threshold, she quickly revived. Vampires had to be formally invited into a home the first time they entered. Third, Geraldine then walked by the dog, who let out an uncharacteristically angry moan. It was commonly believed that vampires had negative effects upon **animals**. Coleridge dwelt upon the evening encounter of the two **women**. Christabel showed Geraldine to a place of rest. She opened a bottle of **wine**, which they shared. At Geraldine's suggestion, Christabel undressed, after which Geraldine partially disrobed, revealing her breast and half her side. What did Christabel see? In lines later deleted from the published version, Coleridge noted that Geraldine's appearance was "lean and old and foul of hue." Christabel entered a trance-like state:

> Yet Geraldine nor speaks nor stirs; Ah! what a stricken look was hers! Deep from within she seems half-way To lift some weight with sick assay, And eyes the maid and seeks delay; Then suddenly, as one defied, Collects herself in scorn and pride, And lay down at the Maiden's side!

In a scene with obvious **lesbian** overtones, the two women lay together for an hour and again the animals were affected:

O Geraldine! one hour was thine Thou'st had thy will! By tairn and rill,
The night-birds all that hour were still. But now they are jubilant anew,
From cliff and tower, tu-whoo! tu-whoo!

The next morning, Geraldine awoke refreshed and her lean, old, and foul body was rejuvenated, "That (so it seemed) her girded vests/Grew tight beneath her heaving breasts." Christabel, on the other hand, awoke with a sense of guilt and immediately went to prayer. She then led Geraldine to the audience with her father, the lord of the castle. Geraldine immediately attached herself to Lord Leoline while Christabel had a momentary flashback of Geraldine's body when she first disrobed. She attempted to have her father send Geraldine away, but he was already enraptured, and in the end turned from his daughter and departed with Geraldine at his side.

"Christabel" was composed in two parts, the first being written and published in 1798. A second part was finished around 1800. "Christabel" thus preceded Southey's "Thalaba," the first English-language poem to actually mention the vampire in its text. Also, the imagery of "Christabel" is an obvious and important source of **Sheridan Le Fanu**'s story "Carmilla." After 1802, Coleridge wrote little and drew his income primarily from lecturing and writing critical articles. Most of his life he was addicted to drugs, having been hooked on opium in an attempt to deal with chronic pain and later consuming vast quantities of laudanum. He received some recognition of his literary work in 1824 when he was named a "Royal Associate" of the Royal Society of Literature. He died on July 25, 1834, at the age of 61.

Sources:

Nethercot, Arthur H. *The Road to Tryermaine: A Study of the History, Background, and Purposes of Coleridge's "Christabel."* Chicago: University of Chicago Press, 1939. 230 pp. Rept. New York: Russell & Russell, 1962. 230 pp.

Keesey, Pam, ed. *Daughters of Darkness: Lesbian Vampire Stories.* Pittsburgh/San Francisco: Cleis Press, 1993. 243 pp.

Collectibles, Paraphernalia, and Souvenirs *see:* Paraphernalia, Vampire

Collins, Barnabas

Barnabas Collins was a vampire character introduced into the story line of the daytime **television** soap opera *Dark Shadows*. He went on to become the show's central character and saved it from early cancellation. *Dark Shadows*, the **gothic** tale of the Collins family, had begun in 1966 on ABC's afternoon schedule, however, by early 1967 the show was facing cancellation. Threatened with that fate, producer **Dan Curtis** began to experiment successfully with supernatural elements. Finally, he decided to add a vampire.

Barnabas, played by actor **Jonathan Frid**, made his first appearance in episode 210. Willie Loomis, looking for a hidden treasure, discovered a secret room in the nearby mausoleum which contained a **coffin** secured shut with a chain. Not knowing what he was doing, he released Barnabas from his prison of many decades. In the next episode, Barnabas presented himself at the door of Collinswood, the family estate, as the family's long lost English cousin. He received permission to take up residence in the Old House,

the former family manor. In his search for **blood**, Barnabas discovered Maggie Evans (Kathryn Leigh Scott), the image of his long lost love whom Barnabas vampirized in an attempt to bring her into his world. Barnabas's attacks upon Maggie led to the introduction of Dr. Julia Hoffman (Grayson Hall), a blood specialist. Brought in to deal with Maggie's illness, she discovered Barnabas' nature, but rather than **destroying** him, she fell in love. In her infatuation, she initiated a process to cure him.

At this point, Barnabas's Collins and *Dark Shadows* had become a phenomenon of daytime television. As the audience grew, the decision was made to give Barnabas a history. Through the instrument of a séance, the cast of *Dark Shadows* was thrust into the 1790s to assume the roles of their ancestors or eighteenth-century counterparts. The new story line began with episode 366. In 1795 Barnabas was the son of family patriarch Joshua Collins. As the story developed, the family became host to Andre du Prés and his daughter Josette DuPres Collins (Kathryn Leigh Scott), Barnabas's fiancée, who arrived from their plantation in Martinique for the wedding. Josette was accompanied by her maid, **Angélique Bouchard** (played by Lara Parker, a new addition to the cast), who was a witch. Angélique, in her desire for everything her employers possessed, moved on Barnabas but was repelled. She then turned on Josette and through her **witchcraft** caused Josette to marry Barnabas's uncle Jeremiah Collins instead. Barnabas killed Jeremiah in a duel.

Eventually, Barnabas was tricked into marrying Angélique, but when he discovered her occult actions, he shot her. Believing that she was dying, Angélique cursed Barnabas with the words that set the pattern of his character for the future, "I set a curse on you, Barnabas Collins. You will never rest. And you will never be able to love. Whoever loves you will die. That is my curse and you will live with it through all eternity." As the words died out, a vampire **bat** flew into the room and headed straight for Barnabas's throat. He died from the attack only to arise a vampire. He decided that Josette should join him in his vampiric existence, and began to drain her of blood. Before he could finish the **transformation**, however, Angélique's spirit lured Josette to a cliff, where she fell to her death. Jeremiah Collins having learned of his son's condition, locked him in the mausoleum and chained him up to stop the plague of his vampiric attacks.

With episode 461, the story line returned to the present. Barnabas had been given a history and a complex personality. Besides his blood thirst, he had a moral sensitivity, the ability to show great passion and love, and was the **victim** of great suffering. In Angélique he had an enemy who returned in various guises to thwart his plans for happiness. His adventures would continue for almost 800 more *Dark Shadows* episodes. In 1970 *Dark Shadows* creator/producer Curtis borrowed the cast for a feature movie, *House of Dark Shadows*, at the close of which Barnabas was killed. Thus he did not appear in the 1971 follow-up, *Night of Dark Shadows*. In 1990 Barnabas's story was revived when NBC began a prime-time version of *Dark Shadows*. It covered the basic story line of the emergence of Barnabas Collins (portrayed by **Ben Cross**) in the present and his **origin** in the 1790s prior to its cancellation after only one season.

In 1966 Marilyn Ross (pseudonym of **Daniel Ross**), began what would become 33 *Dark Shadows* novels based upon the television series. Barnabas appeared first in the sixth volume and his name and image dominated it for the remaining titles. The first issue of the comic book *Dark Shadows* (from Gold Key), which included a picture of Barnabas on the cover of most issues, appeared in March 1969. The series continued through 1976. In 1992 a new *Dark Shadows* comic based on the NBC series was initiated by Innovation Comics. In spite of the television series being canceled, Innovation's comic book continued beyond the television story with a fresh story line until Innovation's demise in 1994.

By 1968, Barnabas's image began to appear on a wide variety of products, among the first being the *"Dark Shadows"* Game from gum card, Whitman, and a Halloween costume. Through 1969, the variety of **paraphernalia** included another set of **trading cards**, two jigsaw puzzles, pillows, a poster, and several model kits. Other items appeared over the years, and a new set of memorabilia was generated in response to the 1991 television series.

Collins was only the second vampire of modern history to gain a wide public following. In spite of occasional rumors to the contrary, there appears little likelihood that a new *Dark Shadows* series will come to television, however, the continuation of *Dark Shadows* conventions and the numerous new *Dark Shadows* writings, ensure that Barnabas will have high visibility at least as long as those people who watched the original series on television survive. In early 2010, director Tim Burton confirmed that he was directing a Dark Shadows movie starring Johnny Depp as Barnabas.

Sources:

Hamrick, Craig. *Barnabas & Company: The Cast of the TV Classic Dark Shadows*. Lincoln, NB: iUniverse, Inc., 2003. 276 pp.

Howard, Malia. *Jonathan Frid: An Actor's Curious Journey (A Career Biography)*. Privately printed, 2001.

Scott, Kathryn Leigh. *The Dark Shadows Companion: 25th Anniversary Collection*. Los Angeles: Pomegranate Press, 1990. 208 pp.

———, Jim Pierson, and David Selby. *The Dark Shadows Almanac: Millennium Edition*. Los Angeles: Pomegranate Press, 2000. 271 pp.

Stockel, Shirley, and Victoria Weidner. *A Guide to Collecting "Dark Shadows" Memorabilia*. Florissant, MO: Collinwood Chronicle, 1992. 107 pp.

Thompson, Jeff. *The Television Horrors of Dan Curtis: Dark Shadows, The Night Stalker and Other Productions, 1966–2006*. Jeffersonville, NC: McFarland & Company, 2009. 208 pp.

❨ Collins, Nancy A. (1959–) ❩

Nancy Collins, an Arkansas native and the creator of vampire character Sonia Blue, was born on September 10, 1959 and raised in Arkansas. She has traced her interest in horror to her grandfather's inviting her to join him at the local theater to watch the latest horror movies. He was a devout fan of Boris Karloff. After practicing her writing skills with short stories, Collins suddenly became a hot item in the literary world after her first novel, *Sunglasses After Dark* (1989), received the Bram Stoker Award. The novel introduced heiress Denise Thorne who was raped and vampirized while in **London** and emerged out of the experience as the vampire Sonia Blue. Since adapting to her new existence, she had been searching for the man who attacked her. Blue's adventures would continue in three sequels: *In the Blood, Paint It Black* and *A Dozen Black Roses*. The first three of the Sonia Blue novels were collected in the single volume *Midnight Blue: The Sonia Blue Collection* from White Wolf. *Sunglasses After Dark* was also adapted as a comic book by Verotik.

While best known for her vampire character, Collins has written widely in the horror field. Her short stories have appeared in various anthologies (*The Year's Best Fantasy and Horror, Best New Horror, The Definitive Best of the Horror Show, Splatterpunks*, and *The Best of Pulphouse*), and she is the co-editor of the erotic horror anthologies *Forbidden Acts* and *Dark Love*. Additional novels include *Walking Wolf, Wild Blood*, and *Tempter*, and for two years (1991–93), she scripted DC Comics' *Swamp Thing* comic book series.

While authoring several vampire short stories, Collins returned to the vampire genre in a big way in 2008 with the first volume of a new vampire series directed at teenagers: VAMPS, about life at Bathory Academy, a private school for training the daughters of the finest vampire families. By the end of 2009, three volumes had appeared.

Collins has received the British Fantasy Society's Icarus Award, and is also the founder of the International Horror Critics Guild.

Sources:

Collins, Nancy. *After Dark*. Vamps 3. New York: Harper Teen, 2009. 192 pp.

———. *Cold Turkey*. Holyoke, MA: Crossroads Press, 1992.

———. *A Dozen Black Roses*. Clarkston, GA: White Wolf Game Studio, 1997. 237 pp.

———. *In the Blood*. New York: ROC, 1992. 302 pp.

———. *Midnight Blue: The Sonia Blue Collection*. Stone Mountain, GA: White Wolf Game Studio, 1995. 559 pp. Includes *Sunglasses after Dark, In the Blood*, and *Paint It Black*.

———. *Night Life*. Vamps 2. New York: Harperteen, 2009. 256 pp.

———. *Paint It Black*. London: New English Library, 1995. 253 pp.

———. *Sunglasses After Dark*. New York: Penguin Books, 1989. Rept. New York: New American Library, 1989. 253 pp.

———. *Tempter*. New York: New American Library, 1990. 299 pp. Rept. London: Futura, 1990. 299 pp.

———. *Vamps*. New York: Harperteen, 2008. 256 pp.

Collinsport Players

The Collinsport Players is a fan-led **Dark Shadows** dramatic group founded at the Dark Shadows Festival in Newark, New Jersey, in 1984 by Jeff Thompson and Dr. Laura Brodian, hosts of the festival. Both were already in costume and decided to enliven their hosting chores with a set of improvisational sketches. The positive reaction of the audience led to a formalizing of their activities as the Collinsport Players (named for the town in which the Collins family resided in the **television** show). Improvisation dominated the 1985 performance of a skit entitled *Julia's Trump*. From that point, scripts were written and the cast size increased. *Spelling Bee*, presented in 1985, involved five actors. In 1986, the twentieth anniversary of the premiere of *Dark Shadows*, the group performed *The More Things Change: The Official Twentieth Anniversary Skit*, a major step forward into a full one-act play with some two dozen actors participating.

The Collinsport Players has regularly performed at every annual national Dark Shadows Festival since its initial performance in 1984. It draws its cast from fans around the country. The new scripts each year are sent to the players six weeks ahead of time. They memorize their parts and gather upon their arrival at the festival site for two rehearsals before their performances. The plays have been comedies full of inside jokes.

(Left to right) Jeff Thompson, Jonathan Harrison, Joan Stewart, and Eileen Berger of the Collinsport Players.

Many have spoofed actual episodes of the television series while others have moved in more speculative directions, taking the characters into hypothesized situations. Among the Collinsport Players' most successful comedies, complete with costumes, sound effects, and **music**, have been *Quiet on the Set, The Times They Change, The Loco-Motion, Double Play,* and *A Julia Carol.* In 1993 the first of two volumes of the Players' skits was published by HarmonyRoad Press. Connie Jonas, the press' founder, is a member of the group.

Jeff Thompson, co-founder of the Players and its current producer-director, has been a *Dark Shadows* fan for many years, and has written widely for several of the fanzines. He wrote most of the plays for the Players, one fan-press book on *The Dark Shadows Comic Books,* and in 1990 completed his master's degree program with a thesis on the historical novels of **Daniel Ross,** who wrote 33 *Dark Shadows* novels under the pseudonym Marilyn Ross. Thompson completed his thesis at Tennessee State University, where he teaches English.

The Collinsport Players were among the performers at **Dracula '97: A Centennial Celebration** in Los Angeles. They performed their twenty-fifth annual performance at the Dark Shadows convention held in Elizabeth, New Jersey in 2009.

Sources:

"Barnabas Collins Meet Your Peers." *New York Times* (September 26, 1993): 11.

Thompson, Jeff. *The Dark Shadows Comic Books.* Los Angeles: Joseph Collins Publications, 1984. Revised ed. 1988. 115 pp.

—————. *The Effective Use of Actual Persons and Events in the Historical Novels of Dan Ross.* Nashville, M.A. thesis, Tennessee State University, 1991. 207 pp.

—————. *The Television Horrors of Dan Curtis: Dark Shadows, The Night Stalker, and Other Productions, 1966–2006.* Jeffersonville, NC: McFarland & Company, 2009. 208 pp.

—————, and Connie Jonas, eds. *The Collinsport Players Companion.* 2 vols. Portland, OR: HarmonyRoad Press, 1993–94.

Jeff Thompson, cofounder of the Collinsport Players, on stage in a production of *The More Things Change.*

Comic Books, Vampires in

Comic books emerged as a distinct form of popular literature in the 1930s, arising from the comic strips that had become a standard item in newspapers. The first vampire in a comic seems to have appeared in an early comic book title, *More Fun*. Each issue of *More Fun* carried the continuing stories of Dr. Occult, a ghost detective who fought various supernatural villains. In issue No. 7, Dr. Occult's first major case pitted him against a creature called the "Vampire Master". The story ran for three issues, each installment being one large page. It concluded with the vampire being killed when a knife was plunged into his heart. Before the end of the decade, in the fall of 1939, Batman would encounter a **Transylvanian** vampire, the Monk, in issues 31 and 32 of *Detective Comics*. As more horror stories appeared in the adventure and **crime** comics of the 1940s, response suggested that there was an audience for an all-horror comic book.

In 1948 the American Comics Group issued the first, and one of the most successful, horror comics, *Adventures into the Unknown*. Very quickly vampires found their way onto its pages, and through the early 1950s each issue commonly had at least one vampire story. *Adventures into the Unknown* soon spawned imitators. In 1950 William Grimes and artist Al Feldman of EC Comics began *Crypt of Terror* (later *Tales from the Crypt*) which was quickly joined by the *Vault of Horror* and *Haunt of Fear*. During the next four years, over 100 horror comic book titles joined the pioneering efforts. Among the horror comics of the 1950s were a variety of titles by Atlas Comics (later Marvel Comics) such as *Suspense Comics* (1950–1953), *Mystic* (1951–1957), and *Journey into the Unknown* (1951–1957), each of which carried vampire stories. Avon's *Eerie* No. 8 (August 1953) became the first of many to adapt **Bram Stoker**'s novel ***Dracula* (1897)** to comic book format.

Vampires under Attack: The boom in horror comics did not go unnoticed by the larger society, and attacks upon them began to mount. Psychology spokespersons such as Frederic Wertham (1895–1981) decried the violence and sex he found in some comic books as a direct source of the growing phenomenon of juvenile delinquency and began to demand their suppression. Feeling the intensity of the attack, a number of the comic book publishing firms found it in their best interest to create the Comic Magazine Association of America (CMAA). The CMAA quickly concluded that some form of self-regulation was necessary to prevent government intervention in its business. In 1954 the CMAA issued a Comics Code, which went into effect in October of that year. The code dealt with some broad issues such as glamorizing crime and the graphic portrayal of death and responded to the criticisms of horror comics directly.

At the same time that controversy raged in America, a similar controversy developed in England. In 1955 the Children and Young Persons (Harmful Publications) Act was passed, which led to the disappearance of horror comics from the stores. The bill was renewed in 1965 and is still on the books, one reason that so few horror/vampire comics have originated in the **United Kingdom**. The Comics Code called for the elimination of the words "horror" or "terror" in the title of comic books and forbade the picturing of, among other things, scenes of depravity, sadism, or excessive gruesomeness. One paragraph dealt forcefully with the major characters associated with the horror story.

Thus, in October 1954, **Dracula** and his kin were banished from the pages of the comic book. The only major appearance of a vampire following the im-

Cover art from the comic book *Seduction of the Innocent,* one of the many comic books to feature vampires.

plementation of the code was by Dell Comics, a company that did not formally subscribe to the code, though in large part tried to adhere to it. A single October/December issue of a new title, *Dracula*, appeared in 1962. The story, set in the present time, centered upon an encounter between several Americans and Count Dracula in Transylvania. However promising the first issue might have been, the second never appeared.

Meanwhile, Dracula and his cohorts were discovering a new format by which they could sneak back into the comic book world. In 1958, four years after the implementation of the Comics Code, a new type of magazine, the horror movie fan magazine, arrived on the newsstands. The first, *Famous Monsters of Filmland*, was developed by James Warren and **Forrest J. Ackerman** and published by the Warren Publishing Company. Projected as a movie fanzine, it was not subject to the regulations of the Comics Code, even though it began to include black and white horror comics interspersed with movie stills and feature stories. In 1964 Warren risked the publication of a black and white horror comic, featuring the very characters and scenes specifically banned by the Comics Code, in a new full size (8 1/2" X 11") magazine format.

Technically, *Creepy* was not a comic book, but it reached the same youthful audience. It was so successful that in 1965 it was joined by *Eerie*, which followed a similar format. That same year, vampires crept back into comic books (full color in a standard comic format) through *The Munsters*, a comic book based upon the popular **television** series which featured two vampires, Lily and Grandpa (really Count Dracula), in a comedy format with no visible bloodsucking.

Finally in 1966, Dell decided to release a second issue of *Dracula*. While continuing the numbering of the original issue of 1962, the new issue carried a completely new story line and an entirely new "Dracula" recast in the image of a superhero. The new Dracula character, a descendent of the original Count, had been experimenting with a serum made from the brains of **bats**. After he accidentally consumed some of the potion, he discovered that he had the ability to transform into a bat. In two subsequent issues he moved to the United States, donned a superhero costume, and launched a war on the forces of evil.

In 1969, with rising pressure to revamp the Comics Code and provide some liberalization in its enforcement, Gold Key issued the first new comic books to feature a vampire as the leading figure. Like *The Munsters*, also by Gold Key, **Dark Shadows** was based on a popular television series. It featured the adventures of vampire **Barnabas Collins**. *Dark Shadows* was joined in September by Warren Publishing Company's **Vampirella**. The latter, featuring a sexy female vampire from outer space in stories combining **humor**, horror, and romance, became the most popular and long-lived vampire comic book in the history of the medium.

The Vampire's Return: Finally, bowing to the needs of companies eager to compete with the black and white comic books, CMAA formally revised the Comics Code, effective January 1, 1971. The change also reflected both an awareness of changing times and the inability of the critics of comic book art to produce the evidence to back up the charges leveled at them in the 1950s. The code still discouraged the portrayal of situations that involved, for example, excessive gore, torture, or sadism. However, the important sentence concerning vampires was rewritten to read:

> Vampires, **ghouls**, and **werewolves** shall be permitted to be used when handled in the classic tradition such as Frankenstein, Dracula, and other high caliber literary works written by **Edgar Allan Poe**, Saki (H. H. Munro), Conan Doyle, and other respected authors whose works are read in schools throughout the world.

Marvel Comics responded immediately to the new situation. It launched a line of new horror titles and in 1972 led in the return of the vampire. Joining Warren's *Vampirella* was **The Tomb of Dracula**, which provided a new set of imaginative adventures for Dracula in the modern world. It lasted for 70 issues, had two revivals, and influenced the 1990s, adventures of the Midnight Sons, who united a variety of forces to fight malevolent occultism. That same year, Marvel introduced a new vampire, **Morbius**. After several appearances as a guest villain in other Marvel magazines, Morbius became part of the regular cast appearing in *Vampire Tales* (beginning in 1973), was the leading figure in *Fear* (beginning in February 1974), and in the 1990s was an integral part of the Midnight Sons, a short-lived venture by Marvel into the creation of a horror universe similar to its superhero universe.

The rapidly rising sales in horror comics during the early 1970s slowly leveled off and during the later part of the decade began to decline. While *Vampirella* survived the decade, few others did. The enthusiasm for horror comics had been overwhelmed by the proliferating number of superheroes. As horror comics in general slumped, the vampire comics all but died. *The Tomb of Dracula* was discontinued in 1979, to be followed by six issues of a black and white full-sized comic magazine, which died in 1980. *Vampirella* was issued for the last time in 1981. With two exceptions, no comic book in which a vampire was the leading character was issued through the early and mid-1980s.

In 1981 DC Comics, by no means a major voice in the horror comics field, introduced a new vampire character, Andrew Bennett, in its long-standing horror comic book *The House of Mystery*. His life and adventures were told in a series of episodes under the title **"I ... Vampire"**. Bennett was, according to the story, 400 years old. Four centuries ago he bit his fiance, Mary, who, of course, also became a vampire. She resented what had happened to her, and as a result spent the rest of her existence trying to get even with Bennett and with the world. "I ... Vampire" dominated most (but not all) issues of *House of Mystery* from March 1981 (No. 290) through August 1983 (No. 319). DC had also introduced another vampirelike character, **Man-Bat** who appeared periodically throughout the decade, usually in association with Batman. In 1975 and 1976, DC tried to establish Man-Bat in a comic book of his own, but it lasted for only two issues. A second Man-Bat comic, a one-shot, was issued in December 1984.

Following the demise of the *Tomb of Dracula* in 1979 and its sequel in 1980, Dracula made a number of appearances as a guest villain in various Marvel comics. A definitive encounter occurred in *Doctor Strange* (No. 62, December 1983). In a faceoff with Dracula, the occultist Dr. Stephen Strange performed a magical ritual, the Montesi Formula, which demolished Dracula and supposedly killed all of the vampires in the world. By this single act, Marvel banished the vampire from the Marvel Universe.

The Vampire Revival: After this low point of interest in vampires following Marvel's banishment in 1983, the vampire slowly made a comeback. The situation in the comic book world paralleled that in the movies. The production of vampire movies hit bottom in 1984 when only one, *The Keep*, was released. At the same time the number of new vampire novels dropped to nine in 1983, half the number of 1977.

Meanwhile, radical changes were occurring in the world of comic books. First, and most noticeably, the technology of producing comic books measurably improved. A higher quality paper allowed a more brilliant eye-catching color. Then, as comic book illustrations were being recognized as an art form, artists demanded and got more freedom, most obvious in the disappearance of the box into which cartoon art had traditionally fit. At the same time, the comic book market was shifting to accommodate a new adult readership. No longer were comic books just for

Cover art from Chaos! Comics' *Purgatori*, which features one of the newer breeds of "bad girl" vampires.

children and youth; numerous new titles were developed exclusively for that ever-expanding adult audience that had grown up with comics. Third, the X-rated comic had emerged as part of the new specialty line for the adult reader. Fourth, a significant portion of the new adult-oriented comics were not open-ended series, but miniseries designed to last for a predetermined number of issues, most frequently four. Fifth, to accommodate the new market, a host of new companies, collectively called "the independents," came into existence.

Thus, when the vampire comic began to make its comeback in the 1990s, it did so in a radically new context. The initial issue of *Blood of the Innocent,* the first of the new vampire comics, was released at the beginning of 1986 by WarP Comics. It ran four issues and was followed by *Blood of Dracula* from Apple Comics. Rick Shanklin was the writer of both projects. Marvel, the giant of the comic book industry, entered the picture with its very unconventional vampire title *Blood* (four issues, 1987–88), a good example of the new artistic and technological advances that were setting the standards of the industry. In 1989 Eternity Comics (an imprint of Malibu Graphics) released the first of two four-issue titles, *Dracula* and *Scarlet in Gaslight.* Then in 1990, Innovation (another of the new companies) launched a twelve-issue adaptation of **Anne Rice**'s bestselling novel *The Vampire Lestat.* These six titles heralded the spectacular expansion of vampire comic book publishing, which became evident in the early 1990s. The ten new vampire titles that appeared in 1990 became 23 titles in 1991. In 1992 no fewer than 34 new titles were published, followed by a similar number in 1993.

In 1983 Marvel had killed off all of the vampires and for six years none appeared. At the end of 1989, Morbius reappeared in issue No. 10 (November 1989) of *Dr. Strange: Sorcerer Supreme.* It seemed that he had survived when the other vampires had been killed. He had been returned to his human state before Dr. Strange worked his magic and for a number of years lived a somewhat normal life. On a vacation in **New Orleans** at the end of the decade, however, he encountered the witch Marie Leveau, who changed him back into a vampire. The cover of *Dr. Strange: Sorcerer Supreme* No. 14 (February 1990) announced the return of the vampires to the Marvel Universe. Morbius, after several appearances with Dr. Strange, got his own comic in September 1992.

Innovation's *The Vampire Lestat* featured some of the best artwork in the field, and its success justified the equally well-done series adapting Rice's other vampire novels, **Interview with a Vampire** and **The Queen of the Damned**. Following Innovation's lead were *Big Bad Blood of Dracula* (Apple), *Blood Junkies on Capitol Hill* (Eternity), the adult adaptation of "Carmilla" (Aircel), *Death Dreams of Dracula* (Apple), *Dracula the Impaler* (Comax), *Dracula's Daughter* (Eros), *Ghosts of Dracula* (Eternity), **Richard Matheson**'s *I Am Legend* (Eclipse), *Night's Children* (Fanta Co), **Nosferatu** (Tome), and **The Tomb of Dracula** (Epic). In 1991 Harris Comics acquired the rights to *Vampirella* and revived it with a new story line that picked up the title character ten years after the last episode in the original series. The response led to a new full-color *Vampirella* and a set of reprints from the original series.

An equally expansive year for vampire comics, 1992 had a 50 percent growth in new titles from the previous year. Innovation continued its leadership with its adaptation of the briefly revived television series *Dark Shadows.* Its artwork was rivaled by the equally spectacular Topps Comics production of *Bram Stoker's Dracula* based on the **Francis Ford Coppola** movie. Other new titles included *Blood Is the Harvest* (Eclipse),

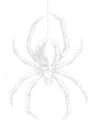

Children of the Night (Night Wynd Enterprises), *Cristian Dark* (Darque Studios), *Dracula in Hell* (Apple), *Dracula, The Suicide Club* (Adventure), *Little Dracula* (Harvey), and *Vampire's Kiss* (Friendly).

By 1992 Marvel Comics was fully involved in the vampire revival. It issued several reprints of its 1970s, success *The Tomb of Dracula* under new titles: *Requiem for Dracula, The Savage Return of Dracula,* and *The Wedding of Dracula.* More importantly, it began several entirely new comics that featured vampires. *Team Titans,* a spin-off of the superhero *New Titans,* included the vampire Night Rider. *The Nightstalkers* was built around **vampire hunters Blade, the Vampire Slayer,** Frank Drake, and Hannibal King, all characters from *The Tomb of Dracula* who had disappeared in 1983. Morbius finally got his own series.

These titles were then integrated through crossover stories with several other horror (but not vampiric) series, including *Ghost Rider, Darkhold,* and *Spirits of Vengeance.* The response was significant enough for Marvel to begin talking about a separate area of the Marvel Universe which dealt with occult issues. In late 1993 Marvel announced its new Universe structure by briefly setting apart these five titles, plus a new title, *Midnight Sons Unlimited,* and the older *Dr. Strange: Sorcerer Supreme* under a distinct Marvel imprint, Midnight Sons, which appeared in the October, November, and December 1993 issues of its several occult titles.

The vampire revival at Marvel proved short lived. As part of a general reorganization of Marvel titles, all of the Midnight Sons series were discontinued in the spring of 1994. The only vampire-related character to survive was Blade, who got his own series, but even it was discontinued the following year after only ten issues, caught in the continued rethinking of Marvel's overall direction as a comic book company. Marvel again largely abandoned the world of horror and vampires, though its characters from *The Tomb of Dracula* would make occasional appearances. Blade's comic series was revived in anticipation of *Blade* the movie starring Wesley Snipes (released in 1998).

A major event in comic book publishing occurred in 1994 with the emergence of the "Bad Girls"—the female superheroes who were both feminine and deadly. Brian Pulido at Chaos! Comics is generally given the credit for producing the first successful bad girl, Lady Death, but she was soon joined by Shi and the revamped Vampirella, introduced in the Harris series, "Vengeance of Vampirella" (1994–96) written by Tom Sniegorski and utilizing a variety of artists. Chaos! Comics soon expanded into the vampire field with its characters Purgatori and Chastity. Collectively the Bad Girl titles from Chaos! and the various "Vampirella" titles (Harris having featured her in a number of miniseries) were notable for their consistency in appearing at the top of the comics sales lists. The Bad Girl phenomenon also opened a market for a variety of new titles with a lead female character, a number of whom were vampires. Other notable vampires included Luxura featured in the comic series "**Vamperotica**" from Brainstorm Comics; *Bethany the Vampfire* (also in a series from Brainstorm); Donna Mia the **succubus** introduced in the horror anthology series "Dark Fantasies: Lady Vampré" (Blackout); Sonia Blue (in *Sunglasses After Dark* from Verotik); and Taboo (*Backlash*, Image).

Quite apart from the Bad Girl titles, the number of new vampire titles continued to multiply through the 1990s. Most notable of the new series was ***Preacher*** by Garth Ennis and Steve Dillon from DC's dark adult Vertigo series, which included the vampire Cassidy as a continuing character. *Wetworks* from Image set a group of modern commandos against the supernatural world of the Balkans that included werewolves and the Blood Queen's Vampire Nation. *Vigil* the female vampire detective created by Arvin Laudermilk and first introduced in 1992, continued her adventures in a number of one shots and miniseries through the 1990s though having to change publishers on several occasions.

At the end of the 1990s, some predicted the vampire's demise as a topic of comics books, but the vampire theme continued unabated. Leading the way was ***Buffy the Vampire Slayer***. Dark Horse began to issue a comic title, which included both new stories and comic versions of selected episodes in September of 1998. The series would continue into 2003 (sixty-three issues), becoming the third-longest vampire comic book series in the English-speaking world. It was also reprinted in several languages in Europe. In 1999, Dark Horse also began the companion *Angel* comic book, but it was discontinued in 2001.

There was some expectation that following the demise of the Buffy and **Angel** television shows that fan interest would dissolve away. Though diminishing somewhat, it continued and eventually IDW picked up the *Angel* franchise. *Buffy/Angel* creator Joss Whedon decided to continue the story line in the two shows through comic books, and in 2007 picked up the story from the last of Angel with a new series of comics from IDW, *Angel: After the Fall*, while the *Buffy* story line was continued in the Season Eight *Buffy the Vampire Slayer* series from Dark Horse. Both series continue as this encyclopedia goes to press.

Succeeding **Anne Rice** as the most popular vampire novel author was **Laurell Hamilton**. After producing more than a dozen novels featuring her monster enforcer character Anita Blake, Hamilton's first vampire novel was brought to comics in 2006 as *Anita Blake Vampire Hunter in Guilty Pleasures,* from Marvel. Hamilton's popularity as a novelist did not displace the most popular writer of vampire comics in the new century, **Steve Niles**. His *30 Days of Night*, a miniseries from IDW became an instant hit and led to a number of sequels as well as additional Niles's horror titles, including several series featuring his vampire detective Cal McDonald. Vampirella remained a popular commodity in the new century. In 2001, Harris Comics began a new Vampirella monthly series, each issue coming with multiple variant and enhanced covers. The series was discontinued after 23 issues, but Vampirella has continued to manifest in a variety of new miniseries and one shots.

The comic book has proved a natural venue for vampires and seems to have settled in as the second main type of character (next to the superhero) in comics. Literally hundreds of new titles featuring vampires appeared in the decade after the Dracula centennial in 1997. *Dracula* remained a popular source book, and over the years more than three dozen adaptations of the novel have appeared as well as recent new editions of the novel with illustrations by prominent graphic artists such as Jae Lee and Ben Templesmith (the original artist used to bring Steve Niles's works to life).

Note: A complete listing of the more than 10,000 comic book issues with vampires published in the twentieth century, compiled by Massimo Introvigne, J. Gordon Melton, and **Robert Eighteen-Bisang**, has been posted at http://www.cesnur.org/2008/vampire_comics.htm.

Sources:

Barker, Martin. *A Haunt of Fears: The Strange History of the British Horror Comics Campaign.* London: Pluto Press, 1984. 227 pp.

Benton, Mike. *Horror Comics: The Illustrated History.* Dallas, TX: Taylor Publishing, 1991. 144 pp.

Glut, Donald R. *The Dracula Book*. Metuchen, NJ: Scarecrow Press, 1975. 388 pp.

Goulart, Ron. *The Encyclopedia of American Comics*. New York: Facts on File, 1990. 408 pp.

Horn, Maurice, ed. *The World Encyclopedia of Comics*. New York: Chelsea House Publishers, 1976. 785 pp.

Melton, J. Gordon. *The Vampire in the Comic Book*. New York: Count Dracula Fan Club, 1993. 36 pp.

Thompson, Jeff. *The Dark Shadows Comic Books*. Los Angeles, CA: Joseph Collins Publications, 1984, 1988. 115 pp.

Cooke, Thomas Potter (1786–1864)

Thomas Potter Cooke was perhaps the most prominent British stage actor in melodrama in the early nineteenth century and the first to play a vampire, **Lord Ruthven**. Orphaned at an early age, he was only ten years old when he joined the Royal Navy. During the next eight years he served aboard the *H.M.S. Raven* and *H.M.S. Prince of Wales*, participated in several battles, was commended for his gallantry, and on one occasion survived a shipwreck. Soon after leaving the navy he joined the London stage. He was quickly recognized as a talented performer. Critics noted that he was handsome and skillful and possessed of a noble bearing.

Cooke was already a veteran of the stage by the time he was selected to take the lead in James R. Planché's *The Vampire or the Bride of the Isles* that opened at the English Opera House (a temporary name assumed by the Lyceum in 1817) on August 9, 1820, only two months after **Charles Nodier's** original adaptation of **John Polidori's**, *The Vampyre* opened in Paris. Plaché had done a hasty translation and adaptation of the French production whose setting in Scotland was retained because of the colorful Scottish dress, the ready availability in the **opera** house's costume room, and Planché's assessment that the audience would not care. They had developed a taste for regular doses of **gothic** melodrama over the preceding generation.

Cooke's performance was outstanding and audiences offered several minutes of applause at the end of his performances. Although there were ten songs included in the script, he did not participate in the musical aspect of the play. Highlighting his movements on stage was a soliloquy detailing Lord Ruthven's lack of self-esteem. During the soliloquy, he noted that he was a demon, walking the earth only to kill and feed, and said, "The little human that remains of heart within this wizard frame, sustained alone by human **blood**, shrinks from the appalling act of planting misery in the bosom of this veteran chieftain (by killing his daughter)." Cooke thus had the opportunity to portray a vampire with a range of emotions that could exercise his abilities. He capped his performance by his sudden disappearance through Planché's vampire trap amidst flames of red **fire**, an effect that stunned the audiences of the period.

Cooke went on to become one of the first English actors to appear in Paris. He traveled to France in 1826 to star in another nonvampire melodrama. However, it appeared that in the wake of **Monsieur Philippe's** (the star in Nordier's vampire play) sudden death in 1824, Cooke briefly assumed his role for a special performance in the summer of 1826.

Cooke's early work in melodrama made him a celebrity in London, and he would go on to a long career that lasted into his seventies. He had a particular love for playing sailors, most notably Sweet William in *Black Eyed Susan* a role he assumed no less than 765 times. He last played the role at the age of 74. He died in 1846.

Coppola, Francis Ford (1939–)

Francis Ford Coppola, director of the 1992 motion picture **Bram Stoker's Dracula**, was born on April 7, 1939, in Detroit, Michigan. In 1962, three years after completing his bachelor's degree at Hofstra University, he went to work for **Roger Corman** at American International Pictures. He served as co-director and co-screenwriter for *The Playgirls and the Bellboy* before directing his first horror films *The Terror* and *Dementia 13* in 1963. That same year he married Eleanor Neil. In 1964 he became the director at Seven Arts and while there also completed a Masters of Fine Arts degree at UCLA (1967). His film *You're a Big Boy Now* was accepted by the school as his master's thesis. He would become the first major American film director to come out of one of the several university film programs that had arisen in post–World War II America. Three years after his graduation he won his first Oscar for his screenplay for *Patton*.

In 1972, he founded the Directors Company with Peter Bogdanovich and William Franklin. That same year he had his first major motion picture, *The Godfather*, for which he won an Oscar for best screenplay (with Mario Puzo). He also won two Oscars for *The Godfather, Part II*: one for best director and one for best screenplay (again with Puzo). His 1979 production *Apocalypse Now* was the first major picture about the Vietnam War. It won the Palme d'Or and the Fipresci Prize from the Cannes Festival. He moved on to do a number of notable films, including *Peggy Sue Got Married* (1986), *Tucker: The Man and His Dream* (1988), and *The Godfather, Part III*.

Coppola thus emerged in the early 1990s as the most acclaimed director ever to turn his attention to the **Dracula** theme. The production began with a screenplay by Jim Hart and with Winona Ryder (who gave Coppola the screenplay) as **Mina Murray**, the female lead. There were budget limitations, and a decision was reached to film the picture entirely at Columbia's studios in Los Angeles. It took 68 days. A basically youthful cast was selected along with Anthony Hopkins, fresh from his Oscar win for best actor for *Silence of the Lambs*, as **Abraham Van Helsing.** His goal was to take the old theme, return to the novel for fresh inspiration, and produce a new movie that would stand out from the prior *Dracula* versions.

The screenplay not only relied upon the **Bram Stoker** novel, but the extensive research on the historical Dracula, the fifteenth-century Romanian prince **Vlad the Impaler** by historians **Raymond T. McNally** and **Radu Florescu**. In order to integrate that new historical material, a rationale for the actions of Dracula (based in part upon unresolved personal issues from the fifteenth century) was injected into the story line from the novel. The movie was also helped by changing guidelines concerning what could be shown on the screen. For example, it was not until 1979 in the **Frank Langella Dracula** that the vital scene from the novel in which Dracula and Mina shared **blood** was incorporated into a film.

Though Coppola had available to him the high-tech special effects developed in the decade since the previous *Dracula*, he chose not to use them. Instead, he returned

Director Francis Ford Coppola's contribution to vampire films was 1992's *Bram Stoker's Dracula*.

to some older tricks of cinematic illusions. Elaborate use of double exposures was employed and miniatures were used instead of matte paintings to provide more depth.

The finished product quickly took its place among the best of the *Dracula* films, though Dracula aficionados were divided on it. The initial response to its opening surprised many, grossing double the original expectations for its first week when it played on almost 2,500 screens. The movie provided Columbia Pictures with its largest opening ever, surpassing *Ghostbusters 2* (1989). It has proved equally popular on video. A rumored sequel, *Van Helsing's Chronicles*, that would have continued the story of the **vampire hunter** with star Anthony Hopkins was never filmed. Coppola has not revised the vampire theme in subsequent films.

Sources:

Bergan, Ronald. *Francis Ford Coppola: Close Up: The Making of His Movies*. New York: Thunder's Mouth Press, 1998. 144 pp.

Biodrowski, Steve. "Coppola's Dracula: Directing the Horror Classic." *Cinefantastique* 23, 4 (December 1992): 32–34.

Coppola, Francis Ford, and James V. Hart. *Bram Stoker's Dracula: The Film and the Legend*. New York: Newmarket Press, 1992. 172 pp.

———, and Eiko Ishioka. *Coppola and Eiko on Bram Stoker's Dracula*. Edited by Susan Dworkin. San Francisco: Collins Publishers, 1992. 96 pp.

Holte, James Craig. *Dracula in the Dark: The Dracula Film Adaptations*. Westport, CT: Greenwood Press, 1997. 161 pp.

Corman, Roger William (1926–)

Roger William Corman, independent film director and producer, was born April 5, 1926, in Detroit, Michigan. Following his service in the U.S. Navy during World War II, he earned an engineering degree at Stanford University. His career in motion pictures began as a messenger boy at 20th Century-Fox in the early 1950s. He worked his way up from screenwriter to director and producer. His first directing job was on *Guns West*, a western for American International Pictures, for whom he would direct and produce for almost two decades. Over the next four decades Corman would direct and/or produce over 100 films. He left AIP to found his own New World Pictures in 1970. At New World Pictures he developed specialized sub-genre films that were distinctive for their formulaic amount of violence, nudity, humor, and social commentary incorporated into each plot. In 1985 Corman established a new distribution company, Concorde Pictures. He currently heads Concorde and New Horizons Home Video.

Corman's films seem to have treated every subject imaginable. They have become known for their quick production on a low budget. At the same time Corman is applauded for the opportunity he gave many young actors and the relative freedom to experiment he gave new directors. Such diverse people as Jack Nicholson and **Francis Ford Coppola** started with Corman. As might be expected, among his more than 100 movies, Corman produced his share of vampire movies, including some of the more important films of the genre.

Corman's first vampire film, which he both directed and produced, was also possibly the first **science fiction** vampire movie. *Not of this Earth* (1957) had humanoid aliens checking out earthlings as possible sources for **blood** for their race. In *Little Shop of Horrors* (1960), later a Broadway musical and a 1980s movie from Warner Bros., the plant in the quaint florist shop was the vampire.

In 1966 Corman acquired footage from a Russian film, *Niebo Zowiet*, around which Curtis Harrington wrote a script. A week of shooting and a new sci-fi vampire, the *Queen of Blood*, emerged. Still an interesting picture, it featured **Forrest J. Ackerman** in a brief role and started assistant director Stephanie Rothman on her directing career. Rothman then directed Corman's next vampire production, *The Velvet Vampire* (1971), which featured a female vampire wreaking damage on the unsuspecting until she encounters a groups of savvy hippies.

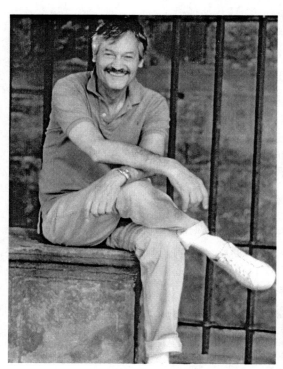

Director Roger Corman.

Corman retired from directing in 1971, but continued to oversee production at his company. Through the remainder of the decade at New World, Corman did not pursue the vampire, there being plenty of other interesting themes to explore. However, through the 1980s New World and its successor Concorde/New Horizons were responsible for a series of vampire movies, including: *Saturday the 14th* (1981), *Hysterical* (1982), *Transylvania 6–5000* (1985), *Vamp* (1986), *Saturday the 14th Strikes Back* (1987), *Not of This Earth* (1987), and *Transylvania Twist* (1989).

Then in 1988, with the noticeable increase in interest in vampires, Corman's Concorde initiated a new effort titled *Dance of the Damned*. The story centered on a stripper with a suicidal impulse who unknowingly took a vampire home. He wanted to know about the experiences he had been denied. The idea worked well enough that it was remade in 1992 as *To Sleep with a Vampire*. The relative success of these two movies led immediately to a third film that combined the **Dracula** myth with the new contemporary vampire popularized by the **Anne Rice** novels. The result, *Dracula Rising*, had a young female art historian encountering Dracula while working in **Transylvania.** As suggested by **Dan Curtis's *Dracula* (1973),** Dracula saw her as the image of his lost love of four centuries earlier. Dracula had originally become a vampire when his love had been executed as a witch. When he finally found her again, his vampiric condition kept him from her.

In 1990 Corman authored his autobiography, which he appropriately titled *How I Made a Hundred Movies in Hollywood and Never Lost a Dime*. After 40 years his companies continue to make movies and given the perspective of four decades, his accomplishments are bringing him some of the recognition he had been denied through most of his career. In 1992 he was awarded the 30th Annual Career Award by **The Dracula Society.**

Sources:

Corman, Roger, with Jim Jerome. *How I Made a Hundred Movies in Hollywood and Never Lost a Dime*. New York: Random House, 1990. 237 pp.

Gray, Beverley. *Roger Corman: Blood-Sucking Vampires, Flesh-Eating Cockroaches, and Driller Killers*. New York: Thunder's Munth Press, 2003.

McGee, Mark Thomas. *Roger Corman: The Best of the Cheap Acts*. Jefferson, NC: McFarland, 1988. 247 pp.

Morris, Gary. *Roger Corman*. Boston: Twayne Publishers, 1985. 165 pp.

Naha, Ed. *The Films of Roger Corman*. New York: Arco Press, 1982. 209 pp.

Shairo, Marc. "*Dracula Rising*: Corman's Count." In *Dracula the Complete Vampire*. New York: Starlog Communications International, 1992, pp. 66–71.

Silver, Alain, and James Ursini. *Roger Corman: Metaphysics on a Shoestring*. Los Angeles: Silman-James Press, 2006. 332 pp.

❮ *Count Dracula* (Television) ❯

Count *Dracula* (1977) was a made-for-television co-production of the British Broadcasting Company and American Public Television. It consisted of three 45-minute segments, and thus was the screen adaptation of *Dracula* with the longest running time.

Count Dracula began with **Jonathan Harker** saying goodbye to **Mina Murray** (now **Lucy Westenra**'s sister), Lucy, and their mother. He traveled to **Castle Dracula** where he had his initial confrontation with **Dracula** (**Louis Jourdan**) and the three female vampire residents. He eventually escaped and returned to England. Lucy was engaged to **Quincey P. Morris**, now transformed from a Texan into a staff person at the American embassy in **London**. Once Dracula began his attack on Lucy, **Dr. John Seward** called **Abraham Van Helsing** to his assistance. Van Helsing arrived, as in the novel, as an elderly foreign expert. He taught the men that supernatural evil existed and that they must unite to fight it.

Lucy finally died, and her post-death activity convinced the men that Van Helsing was correct. They proceeded to Lucy's tomb to finally kill her in one of the most graphic vampire death scenes to that point in time. With Harker back in England and married to Mina, Van Helsing built a united front to kill Dracula. Meanwhile Dracula attacked Mina and forced her to drink his **blood**. The attack made her a full partner in the final drive to kill the vampire.

In the final scenes, Van Helsing and Mina arrived at Castle Dracula only to confront the three **women** who call to Mina as their new sister. Van Helsing protected her before going into the castle to kill the women. The **Gypsies** who brought Dracula's sleeping body back to the castle were fought off in a Western-style gunfight. The last Gypsy got the box to the entrance of the castle where he was stopped. In the end, it was Van Helsing, not the younger men, who pried open the lid of the box and killed Dracula with a **stake**. *Count Dracula*, even more than *El Conde Dracula*, relied on the story of **Bram Stoker**'s novel. Only the more recent ***Bram Stoker's Dracula*** (1992) would, for example, return all of the major characters in the novel to the movie story line. *Count Dracula* also raised the level of realism in the depiction of the vampire's attack and the scenes of the vampire women attacking the baby in the early segment of the movie (which was cut from the American version). *Count Dracula* returned the essential scene in the novel, in which Dracula forced Mina to drink his blood, and the subsequent events in which she was branded with a **eucharistic wafer.** Louis Jourdan assumed the role of Dracula in this version. He brought to the part a suave, continental manner. He was an aristocratic lover, but a man used to getting what he wanted. He seduced women and took them away from the mundane gentlemen with whom they had been paired. Jourdan thus laid the groundwork for the sensual Dracula so effectively portrayed by **Frank Langella** in ***Dracula*** (1979).

Sources:

Holte, James Craig. *Dracula in the Dark: The Dracula Film Adaptations*. Westport, CT: Greenwood Press, 1997. 161 pp.

Waller, Gregory A. *The Living and the Undead: From Stoker's Dracula to Romero's Dawn of the Dead*. Urbana, IL: University of Illinois Press, 1986. 376 pp.

The Count Dracula Society *see:* Vampire Fandom: United States

Count Ken Fan Club *see:* Vampire Fandom: United States

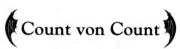

Count von Count

Count von Count is a beloved character in the children's television show *Sesame Street*. He is a vampire modeled on **Bela Lugosi** with **fangs**, a cape, and widow's

peak. Though he has fangs, he has not been seen using them on anyone. Biographical details are sparse, but he is rumored to be a distant relative of Count **Dracula** born on October 9, some 1,832,652 years ago. Like his relative, he lives in a castle with a pet cat and a number of **bats**, enough so he will never lack for enough to count. The Count has had two girlfriends, Countess von Backwards known for counting backwards and more recently Countess Dahling von Dahling. At different time his mother, brother, and grandparents have appeared.

Others suggest that he was the product of the fertile imagination of writer Norman Stiles and brought to life by puppeteer Jerry Nelson (1934–). On the versions of *Sesame Street* internationally, his appearances are facilitated by a number of different puppeteers. He originally appeared in 1972, during the show's fourth American season.

Prior to the appearance of the Count, very few vampire characters in any medium were directed toward children, and none toward preschoolers. The justification for including the vampire puppet was as a tool to teach children about basic numbers and counting. The Count has a love of counting and demonstrates that love by counting anything he sees. In a normal person, his penchant for counting would be a mental disease called arithmomania. On the show his activity is perfectly normal and functional.

After working through some elements of the original character which were upon examination deemed possibly too scary for young children (such as the use of thunder and lightning after he finished a counting session), the Count settled in as a standard character of the show.

The Count has been a ubiquitous character in *Sesame Street* videos and books. He has been the primary character in three videos (now on DVD): *Learning about Numbers* (1986); *Count It Higher* (1988); and *Rock & Roll!* (1990). He has appeared in dozens of Sesame Street books and has been the featured character on titles such as *The Count's Counting Book* (1980); *Count All the Way to Sesame Street* (1985); and *Learn About Counting with the Count* (2006).

Sources:

Anastasio, Dina. *Count All the Way to Sesame Street*. Racine, WI: Western Pub. Co., 1985. 24 pp.

The Count's Counting Book. New York: Random House/Children's Television Workshop, 1980. 14 pp.

Davis, Michael. *Street Gang: The Complete History of Sesame Street*. New York: Viking, 2008. 394 pp.

Freudberg, Judy, and Tony Gaiss. *The Count Counts a Party*. Western Publishing Company, 1980. 26 pp.

Hoults, Amy. *Holiday Countdown with Count Von Count*. Learning Horizons, 2006. 16 pp.

Korr, David. *The Day the Count Stopped Counting*. New York: Western Pub. Co., 1977. 46 pp.

Morrow, Robert W. *Sesame Street and the Reform of Children's Television*. Baltimore, MD: Johns Hopkins University Press, 2006. 226 pp.

St. Pierre, Stephanie. *The Count Counts Scary Things*. New York: CTW Publishing, 1998. 24 pp.

Stiles, Norman. *The Count's Number Parade*. Racine, WI: Western Pub. Co., 1977. 24 pp.

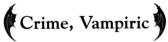

❨ Crime, Vampiric ❩

The great majority of people labeled as "real" vampires during the last two centuries manifested symptoms of what psychologists call hematomania, a **blood** fetish. (Sex-

ual pleasure and other **psychological** needs of persons with this condition are met by the regular consumption of human blood, occasionally in conjunction with the eating of human flesh.) Presumably most of those who regularly drank blood located legal means of obtaining it, usually from a willing donor. Some, however, turned to crime, and a few joined the list of the West's most notorious serial killers. The modern stream of vampiric crime related to hematomania had its precedent in the career of Countess **Elizabeth Bathory** (1560–1614), who allegedly killed more than 600 people for their blood.

The Marquis de Sade and Gilles de Rais are frequently listed among the modern vampiric criminals, but the list of crimes attributed to neither included the drinking of the blood they might have shed. There is a distinction between those who draw pleasure from killing people or from the drawing of blood and those vampiric types who derive pleasure from its consumption. Likewise there is a distinction between people who drink blood for the overpowering pleasure it brings and those who occasionally sip blood (usually of an animal) as part of a religious ritual and believe they draw some supernatural power from the otherwise repulsive act.

Several vampiric killers emerged in the nineteenth century. The earliest reported case was that of a man named Sorgel, a German who killed a man in the forest and drank his blood in an attempt to cure himself of epilepsy. His actions led to his arrest and confinement in an asylum. That same year Antoine Léger killed a 12-year-old girl, drank her blood, and ate her heart. After his execution, Sorgel's brain was examined by pathologists.

A more famous incident involved Sergeant Françoise Bertrand (1824–1849), who was arrested in 1849 in Paris for opening the graves of the dead and eating flesh from the corpses. While termed a vampire by some, he engaged in much more **ghoul**-like behavior, and went on to become the model of one of the more successful novels about **werewolves**, including *The Werewolf of London*. A generation later, in 1886, Henri Blot was arrested for a similar crime. He was caught because he fell into a **sleep**-like **hypnotic** trance after completing his work. He was apprehended quickly; he had violated only two bodies.

The United States has been home to one vampire killer, seaman James Brown. In 1967 Brown was discovered aboard his ship, a fishing boat on its way to Labrador, sucking the blood from the body of a crewman he had murdered. He had already killed and drained another sailor. He was arrested and returned to Boston. Brown was sentenced to life in prison, where he killed at least two more people and drank their blood. Following the second killing, he was sent to the National Asylum in Washington, D.C., where he remained confined in a padded cell until he died.

Fritz Haarmann (1879–1924) is another famous vampiric killer. By the time of his arrest and execution in 1924 in **Germany**, he had killed and cannibalized more than 20 people. However, during the last several years, he also began to bite and suck the blood of his **victims**. Contemporary with Haarmann was **Peter Kürten** (1883–1931), also from Germany. Kürten killed first as a nine-year-old boy. He killed again in 1913. Then in 1929 he began a series of ghoulish crimes in which he stabbed and then mutilated his victims. At the height of his crime spree in August of that year, he killed nine people, mostly young women. His initial excitement at killing someone gave way to a fixation on blood. He began to drink the blood of his victims, continuing even after the blood he consumed made him sick. In one case he bit and drank from the wound. Finally arrested in 1930, he was executed the following year.

Through the twentieth century a number of reports of vampirelike criminals have surfaced. A few, such as **John George Haigh** (1910–1949) and Richard Chase, became famous. Others received no more than passing notice. During the 1940s, Haigh operated out of a home in **London**. There he killed his victims, drained their blood, and then disposed of the bodies in a vat of sulfuric acid. Richard Chase (1950–1980) began his crime spree in Sacramento, California, in December 1977, when he shot and killed a man. The following month, he killed again, and this time he drank his victim's blood. He continued this practice in a string of killings in January, until his arrest at the end of the month. It turned out that as early as 1974, he had killed a cat and drunk its blood. In the following years he killed a number of **animals** and drank their blood in hopes that it would improve his physical health. After his arrest he moved through a complex legal process, including scrutiny of his sanity. Tried and convicted of multiple murders, he was sentenced to death, but cheated the executioner by committing **suicide**.

The most famous case of vampire-related crime in recent years has been that of Roderick Justin "Rod" Ferrell (1980–) and the small "Vampire Clan" he led. Ferrell claimed to be Vesago, a 500-year-old vampire. The product of a teenage marriage that quickly fell apart, his mother abandoned him during his teen years. Shortly thereafter he began to adopt his vampire persona. He was known to spend time in cemeteries through the evening hours. While he became delinquent with schoolwork and attendance, he became active in the role-playing game "Vampire: The Masquerade", through which he came to know a wide range of people interested in vampirism.

In the spring of 1996, Ferrell reconnected by telephone with an old girlfriend, Heather Wendorf, who apparently told Rod that her parents were hurting her and that she wanted him to come get her, but that he would have to kill them to do so. In November 1996, Ferrell and several companions went to Florida, met up with Wendorf, killed her parents, and fled the state. They would later be arrested in Louisiana. He was convicted of murder and sentenced to death in 1998 and currently (2009) awaits execution.

Beginning in the 1990s, the media developed an interest in "vampire" related crime and regularly gave wide coverage to any cases that in any way related to vampiric activity. The advent of the Internet facilitated the wide dissemination of the accounts of such crimes and related court action. While most vampire crimes concern serial killers who in some manner include blood drinking in their crimes, it would also include any crimes in which the killer was motivated by the blood of the victim, any crime committed by someone involved in the vampire subculture, and any crime directed against people who have developed a vampire persona. A reminder that many folk beliefs about vampires survive around the world occurred in 2007 in Guyana when three people were arrested for killing a woman who had wandered into the town of Bare Root. Shortly after she appeared, a resident saw a child with a red mark on her chest, an indication of a "Old Higue," a traditional vampire in the East African-based vampire beliefs of the country. Vampires, there, are women who may shed their skin and fly around drinking the blood of small children and infants. The woman was called out as a possible vampire and several techniques applied to identify her. In the end, she was stabbed and left to die. The woman turned out to be a person suffering from a mental disorder and incapable of rationally responding to the people who initially encountered her. Several vampire-related crimes are reported annually worldwide.

THE VAMPIRE BOOK: THE ENCYCLOPEDIA OF THE UNDEAD

Sources:

Biondi, Ray, and Walt Hecox. *The Dracula Killer*. New York: Pocket Books, 1992. 212 pp.

Brautigam, Rob. "Some Blood Drinkers." *For the Blood Is the Life* 2, 9 (Summer 1991): 12–14.

"Human Vampire." *Fate* 6, 5 (May 1953): 46.

Jones, Aphrodite. *The Embrace*. New York: Pocket Books, 1999. 384 pp.

Linedecker, Clifford L. *The Vampire Killers*. New York: St. Martin's Paperback, 1998. 275 pp.

London, Sondra. *True Vampires: Blood-Sucking Killers Past and Present*. Feral House, 2003. 380 pp.

Monaco, Richard, with Bill Burt. *The Dracula Syndrome*. New York: Avon, 1993. 167 pp.

Ramsland, Katherine. *Piercing the Darkness*. New York: HarperPrism, 1998. 371 pp.

———. *The Vampire Killers*. Posted at TruTV. http://www.trutv.com/library/crime/serial_killers/weird/vampires/1.html. Accessed on April 6, 2010.

Shay, V. B. "James Brown, Vampire." *Fate* 2, 4 (November 1949): 59.

Tuczay, Christa. *Die Herzesser: Dämonische Verbrechen in der Donaumonarchie*. Wien: Seifert 2007.

"Vampire Arrested in Argentina." *Fate* 13, 10 (October 1960): 45.

Volta, Ornella. *The Vampire*. New York: Award Books, 1962. 153 pp.

Waltje, Jörg. *Blood Obsession: Vampires, Serial Murder, And The Popular Imagination*. New York: Peter Lang, 2005. 157 pp.

Croglin Grange, The Vampire of

Among frequently cited incidents involving "real" vampirism, the story of the vampire of Croglin Grange, an old house located in Cumberland, England, has proved very intriguing. An account of the vampire originally appeared in the *Story of My Life* by August Hare, written during the last years of the 1890s. According to Hare, the various episodes occurred around 1875 to 1876. Owned at the time by a family named Fisher, the house was rented to a woman and her two brothers: Amelia, Edward, and Michael Cranswell. During one summer, the district experienced a hot spell, so when the three retired for the night, the woman slept near the window. She shut the window but did not close the shutters. Unable to go to **sleep**, she spotted something approaching that eventually reached the window and began to scratch and then to pick at it, removing a pane. A creature then reached in and unlocked the window. The terrified woman, frozen in fear, waited as a brown face with flaming eyes came to her, grabbed her, and bit her throat.

She screamed, and when her brothers rushed to her rescue, the creature hurriedly left. One brother tended to his sister and the other pursued the creature, which disappeared over a wall by a nearby church. The doctor who later treated the woman suggested a change of scenery, and the brothers took her to Switzerland for an extended visit. The three eventually returned to Croglin Grange. The following spring the creature appeared again. One brother chased it, shot it in the leg, and traced it to a vault in the local cemetery. The next day, accompanied by some townspeople, the brothers entered the vault, which was in complete disarray except for one **coffin**. When they opened the coffin, they found a body with a fresh gunshot wound in the leg. A **bullet** was extracted, and they burned the corpse.

In 1924, Charles G. Harper, basing his assertions on a visit to the area, challenged the Hare book. Harper could find no place named Croglin Grange. Though there were two other buildings, Croglin High Hall and Croglin Low Hall, neither fit the description of Croglin Grange. There was no church, the closest one being over a mile away,

and no vault corresponding to the description of the one opened by the brothers and their neighbors. Harper's own account was challenged at a later date, when F. Clive-Ross visited the area. In interviews with the local residents, he determined that Croglin Low Hall was the house referred to in Hare's story and that a chapel had existed near it for many years, its foundation stones still visible into the 1930s. Clive-Ross seemed to have answered all of Harper's objections.

The Croglin Grange story continued when, in 1968, **psychic** researcher Scott Rogo offered a new challenge. He noted the likeness of the story of the vampire at Croglin Grange to the first chapter of ***Varney the Vampyre***, the popular vampire story originally published in 1847. The accounts, both of which were published in 1929 by **Montague Summers**, are very similar, and it is likely that one is based on the other, according to Rogo. He suggested that the entire Croglin Grange story could be dismissed as a simple hoax.

A final footnote to the controversy: Clive-Ross, later discussed the case again with residents of the area, and was told that there was a significant mistake in Hare's original account: the story took place not in the 1870s, but in the 1680s, almost two centuries earlier. While this fact would definitely place the events prior to the publication of *Varney the Vampyre,* it also pushes the story far enough into the past as to turn it into an unverifiable legend.

Sources:

Dyall, Valentine. "Vampire of Croglin Grange." *Fate* (April 1954): 96–104.
Glut, Donald F. *True Vampires of History.* Secaucus, NJ: Castle Books, 1971. 191 pp.
Hare, Augustine. *Story of My Life.* 6 vols. London: George Allen, 1896–1900.
Harper, Charles C. *Haunted Houses.* Detroit: Tower Books, 1971. 288 pp.
Rogo, Scott. "Second Thoughts on the Vampire of Croglin Grange." *Fate* 21, 6 (June 1968): 44–48.
Summers, Montague. *The Vampire in Europe.* London: Routledge, Kegan Paul, Trench, Trubner, & Co. 1929. 329 pp. Rept. New Hyde Park, NY: University Books, 1962. 329 pp.

Cross *see* Crucifix

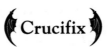

Crucifix

The crucifix, a major symbol of the Christian faith, is a Latin cross with a figure of Jesus on it. It often appears on the end of the rosary, a string of prayer beads. The cross represents Jesus as he was executed on the original Good Friday. The crucifix is used primarily by Christians in the Roman Catholic Church, the several branches of the Eastern Orthodox Church, and other church bodies that follow a similar liturgical style of **Christianity**. In general, Protestant and Free churches do not utilize the crucifix. They prefer a plain cross, sometimes thought of as an empty cross, without the corpus a symbol of the resurrected Christ.

In the first chapter of the novel ***Dracula,*** **(1897)** a woman in **Bistritz, Transylvania**, took a rosary from her neck and gave it to **Jonathan Harker** upon hearing that he was going to visit Count **Dracula**. Harker, a member of the protestantized Church of England, had been taught that such an object was a product of idolatrous thinking. However, he put

it around his neck and left it there. A short time after his arrival at **Castle Dracula**, Dracula made a grab for Harker's throat. Harker reported, "I drew away, and his hand touched the string of beads which held the crucifix. It made an instant change in him, for the fury passed so quickly that I could hardly believe that it was ever there." Having yet to figure out what Dracula was, he wondered about the meaning of the crucifix.

The crucifix played an important role in several other scenes in the novel. One appeared again in the hands of a man aboard the *Demeter*, the ship that brought Dracula to England. He was found tied to the ship's wheel with the crucifix in his hands, the beads wrapped around an arm and a wheel spoke. Later, after **Lucy Westenra** died and while she was experiencing life as a vampire herself, **vampire hunter Abraham Van Helsing** locked her in her tomb for a night with a crucifix and **garlic**, described as things she would not like. In Van Helsing's famous speech in chapter 18, he described the crucifix as one of the things that, like garlic, so afflicted the vampire that the creature had no power. So, when the men burst into the bedroom where Dracula was sharing **blood** with **Mina Murray** (by then Mina Harker), they advanced upon him with their crucifixes raised in front of them. Dracula retreated.

Through the tale *Dracula*, then, the crucifix entered vampire lore as a powerful tool against vampires, especially when confronting one directly. It was not mentioned in historic vampire stories, though many priests who participated in the dispatching of a vampire no doubt wore the crucifix. The emergence of the crucifix came directly from **Bram Stoker**'s combining some popular ideas about the magical use of sacred objects by Roman Catholics and the medieval tradition that identified vampirism with Satanism (through Emily Gerard, Stoker developed the notion that Dracula became a vampire due to his having intercourse with **Satan**). In addition, a significant amount of Roman Catholic piety focused around the crucifix, and among church members it could easily take on not just sacred, but magical, qualities. It was not just a *symbol* of the sacred, but the bearer of the sacred.

If then the vampire was of the realm of Satan, it would withdraw from a crucifix. For Stoker, the presence of the crucifix caused the vampire to lose its supernatural **strength**. Thus, in the case of Harker, Dracula lost his fury; Lucy could not escape her tomb; and when the men burst into Mina's bedroom, the weakened Dracula, faced with overwhelming odds, departed quickly. Following *Dracula,* the crucifix became a standard element of vampire plays, movies, and novels through the twentieth century. A second sacred object, the **eucharistic wafer**, largely dropped out of the picture. However, the crucifix acquired one of the properties Stoker assigned to the wafer. It burned vampire flesh, and left a mark on those tainted with the vampire's bite. Thus the crucifix not only caused the vampire to lose strength, but actually did it harm. If a potential **victim** wore a crucifix, the vampire must find some method of removing it, either through **hypnotic** suggestion or with the help of a human cohort.

While the crucifix was a standard item in the vampire hunter's kit, it was not omnipresent in vampire books and movies. The relation to the holy was among the first elements of the tradition to be challenged as the vampire myth developed. Writers who were not Roman Catholic or even Christian found no meaning in the crucifix and the eucharistic elements and simply dropped them from consideration. However, others, most prominently **Chelsea Quinn Yarbro** and **Anne Rice**, chose to acknowledge the sacred world but essentially deny its power, specifically mentioning the immunity of their vampires to holy objects. Yarbro's vampire, **St. Germain**, existed prior to Christianity and never converted to its beliefs. Rice, writing in Catholic **New Orleans**, created her vampire, **Lestat de Lioncourt**, as a child of Roman Catholics in **France**; and at various points in *Interview with the Vampire* and *The Vampire Lestat*, Roman Catholic supernaturalism was specifically cast aside. Lestat was described, for example, as already an atheist when he was transformed into a vampire. Nevertheless, he called upon those bits of Christianity he remembered, in an attempt to keep the vampire Magnus from him. His efforts were useless. Then, accompanying the bites that made Lestat a vampire, Magnus pronounced the words of consecration from the Mass, "This is my Body, This is my Blood." Like Yarbro, Rice replaced Christianity in her writings with a new, pre-Christian myth that began in ancient Egypt with the original vampire couple, Akasha and Enkil.

The challenge to the effectiveness of the crucifix in vampire novels symbolizes a larger challenge to the role of the supernatural in modern life. It includes a protest against the authority of any particular religion and its claims of truth in a religiously pluralistic world. While the lessening of the role of the supernatural in the novels of Rice and Yarbro has its supporters, the crucifix remains a popular protective object for fictional characters. Consideration of their reaction to sacred objects likely will continue to be a conscious element in the development of new vampire characters in the future.

In *Buffy the Vampire Slayer*, the cross remains an object that can affect vampires negatively, but it obviously does not have the power it has manifested in the past. Possibly the most telling episode relative to the cross was in season four. In "Who Are You," a group of vampires take over a church on a Sunday morning. Standing before the assembled congregation, their leader makes a short speech noting his previous fear of entering such a building and enjoying his discovery that there are no negative effects. As he speaks, a crucifix is displayed prominently in the window above the altar behind the vampire. He closes his speech by noting that the Lord seems to be absent, at least there are no visible effects of his presence. He mockingly informs the congregation that he had come to the church primarily because he had heard that the Lord would be present.

Similarly, in the "**Twilight**" series, the cross is no longer a factor. Author **Stephenie Meyer** is a member of the church of Jesus Christ of Latter-day Saints, a Christian church that does not particularly favor the display of crosses. The vampires of the Twilight saga are affected by neither crosses nor holy **water**.

Sources:

Frayling, Christopher. *Vampyres: Lord Byron to Count Dracula*. London: Faber and Faber, 1991. 429 pp.

Gresh, Lois H. *The Twilight Companion: The Unauthorized Guide to the Series*. St. Martin's Griffin: New York, 2008. 242 pp.

Summers, Montague. *The Vampire: His Kith and Kin*. London: Routledge, Kegan Paul, Trench, Trubner, & Co., 1928. 356 pp. Rept. New Hyde Park, NY: University Books, 1960. 356 pp.

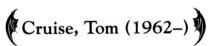

Cruise, Tom (1962–)

Tom Cruise, the actor who portrayed the vampire **Lestat de Lioncourt** in the movie version of **Anne Rice's** *Interview with the Vampire* was born Thomas Cruise

Tom Cruise played Lestat de Lioncourt in the film
Interview with the Vampire.

Mapother on July 3, 1962, in Syracuse, New York. He grew up in New York and New Jersey and began his acting career soon after graduating from high school. His first professional part was a role in a dinner theater production of *Godspell*. Cruise's debut in motion pictures was in 1981 in *Endless Love*, followed by *Taps* and *Losin' It*. He became a star after his performance as a young rich kid left on his own in his family's suburban Chicago home in the comedy *Risky Business*. A series of starring roles followed, including *All the Right Moves*, *Legend*, *Top Gun*, *The Color of Money*, and *Rain Man*, movies in which he worked with many of Hollywood's finest actors and actresses. Cruise took a major step forward with his portrayal of a Vietnam veteran in *Born on the Fourth of July* (1989), which earned him an Academy Award nomination. More recently he has continued his appealing performances in *A Few Good Men* and *The Firm*. In 1993 he was presented with the Actor of the Decade Award at the Chicago International Film Festival.

In the summer of 1993 it was announced that Cruise had been signed to play Lestat in the long-delayed movie version of *Interview with a Vampire*. He was given the part opposite Brad Pitt, who would play Louis. The announcement unleashed a controversy between author **Anne Rice** and the studio, Geffen Films. Rice decried the selection of Cruise, whom she saw as too young, too American, and, most of all, lacking in the primal quality of Lestat. Cruise's career had been a series of almost stereotypical male roles quite different from the character of Lestat. Unlike the traditional vampire, Lestat develops close relationships with other males and shows a number of feminine **characteristics**. Fans were quick to jump to Cruise's defense and to note that he had grown with each part he had played. His fans claimed that his performances in *Rain Man* and *Born on the Fourth of July* demonstrated that he could adapt to many different roles. Cruise reportedly accepted a slight cut in salary for what he saw as a risky part that would test his acting ability. It was the first time he would portray what was considered a dark role. The film was to be completed and released in the fall of 1994, and became one of the largest grossing vampire films of the twentieth century. After seeing the film Anne Rice rescinded her comments and said Cruise did a wonderful job. Cruise did not star in the sequel, **Queen of the Damned**, but has gone one to play in a number of outstanding roles and has remained a center of controversy due to his religious commitments. Rumors periodically surface that he is considering a second attempt to play Lestat, but no manifestation beyond the rumors have appeared to date (2009).

Sources:

Silver, Alan. "The Vampire Cruise?" *DGA Directors Guild of America News* 18, 5 (October–November 1993): 27.

❨ Cullen, Edward ❩

Edward Cullen, whose full name is Edward Anthony Masen Cullen, is **Stephenie Meyer**'s vampire hero throughout her four Twilight book series as well as the unpublished and unfinished manuscript, *Midnight Sun*. Edward is described as lanky, six foot two inches, and boyish looking with bronze untidy hair and green eyes that turned gold/black when he became a vampire. Meyer describes Edward as a "beautiful boy" with a "dazzling face," "flawless lips," and "perfectly ultra white teeth" and compares him to the mythical Greek god Adonis. On Meyer's website, she said that Charlotte Brontë's Mr. Rochester (*Jane Eyre*) and Jane Austen's Mr. Ferrars (*Sense and Sensibility*) were the characters that led her to the name Edward.

Before he became a vampire, Edward was the biological son of Elizabeth and Edward Masen, a successful lawyer. Edward was born on June 20, 1901, and grew up in a moderately wealthy family in Chicago; by 1918, his fairly happy life vanished when the influenza epidemic claimed the lives of both his parents. Edward became stricken as well, but his attending physician, Dr. Carlisle Cullen, saved his life by changing him into a vampire. Edward subsequently became the "adopted son" of Carlisle and Esme Cullen and the brother to Alice and Emmett Cullen as well as Rosalie and Jasper Hale. Edward has been to medical school twice (though he never practiced medicine), and he collects cars as a hobby and enjoys a wide range of **music**.

Edward is often described as very charming and polite. In fact, he retains some of the same mannerisms and outdated speech from his previous life in the early twentieth century. As a vampire, he possesses superhuman speed, agility, and **strength** and is not able to **sleep**. His skin, according to Meyer, is "satin smooth, cool as stone" and sparkles like small diamonds when exposed to **sunlight**. Edward's vampire family renounces human **blood** on moral grounds and instead feeds off **animals**. Edward initially rebelled against this lifestyle, so from 1927 to 1931, he left Carlisle and Esme and limited his hunting of humans to those who were truly evil. His special ability to read other people's minds helped him to avoid killing innocent people for food. But after awhile, the taking of human lives—whether evil or innocent—weighed heavily upon Edward's conscience, and he returned to Esme and Carlisle and resumed their lifestyle.

Edward and his family first moved to Forks, Washington, in 1936. They travelled around frequently until they returned to Forks in 2003, and two years later Edward met **Isabella Swan** or "Bella," a human female only 17 years old. Emotionally, Edward was stagnant or fossilized until Bella came into his life. He fell in love for the first time and was both attracted to Bella yet wanted to kill her. He fought this impulse every moment he was with Bella and became obsessed with her. Yet, Edward was very protective of Bella and put her safety and welfare before anything else. Although their vampire/human relationship had many obstacles, he married Bella on August 12, 2006, and fathered a half human, half vampire daughter through her.

As Edward's character develops through the Twilight series, he experiences many new emotions around Bella. He breaks off the relationship with her because he fears she is not safe around his vampire family and goes through a very dark, reclusive period. He even contemplates **suicide**. Once Edward and Bella reunite, he asks her to marry him.

As his relationship with Bella deepens, he learns to control his thirst for her blood and is able (although somewhat reluctantly) to make love to her on their honeymoon. He also forms an uneasy alliance with Jacob Black, a Quileute Indian who has the ability to transform into a **werewolf** and whose ancestors were once enemies of the Cullens and other vampire families. In the movie *Twilight* and its forthcoming sequels, Edward Cullen is played by British actor Robert Pattinson.

Sources:

Gresh, Lois H. *The Twilight Companion: The Unauthorized Guide to the Series*. St. Martin's Griffin: New York, 2008. 242 pp.

Meyer, Stephenie. *Twilight*. New York: Little, Brown and Company, 2005. 498 pp.

———. *Twilight: The Story Behind Twilight*. Posted at http://www.stepheniemeyer.com/ twilight.html. Accessed on April 6, 2010.

Twilight News Updates. *Cullen, Edward*. October 3, 2006. Posted by http://www.twilightlexicon.com/?p=18. Accessed on April 6, 2010.

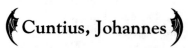 Cult of the Vampire

The Cult of the Vampire was a semi-secret magical group operating in England in the 1990s that built its practice of magic on the model of vampirism. Vampires were pictured as the first outcasts of human society who formed clans and developed techniques for controlling the occult forces of nature. The modern Cult of the Vampire was organized as an initiatory magical order with seven degrees. The neophyte was introduced to the techniques of occult practice through a series of lessons (approximately 25 to each initiatory level). The goal of the training was to learn to conquer death by leaving the physical body. One learned to transcend the body in the third degree level and animal **transformation** is the fourth.

While vampires may use their sorcery when and where they see fit, groups of magicians gather at the time of the new **moon** for ritual and magical workings. The order's lineage, it was claimed, comes from **Transylvania** and was introduced into England in 1888 as the Ordo Anno Mundi. No evidence of the group's continued existence has surfaced since the beginning of the new century.

Sources:

"Cult of the Vampire." *Crimson* 17 (1995): 26.

Mercer, Mick. *Hex Files: The Goth Bible*. Woodstock, NY: Overlook Press, 1997. 229 pp.

Cuntius, Johannes

Henry More (1614–1687) described several vampirelike people in his book *An Antidote Against Atheism*, a volume primarily about **witchcraft**. The case of Johannes Cuntius took place in Pentsch, Silesia, a section of **Poland**, where he had served as an alderman. A fairly wealthy man, he was about 60 years old when one day he was struck by a horse whose shoe was being repaired. Upon recovering from the blow, Cuntius began to complain of his sinfulness. He died a short time later. The night of his death a black cat entered the room and scratched his face.

Between the time of his death and burial, the first reports of an *incubus* were heard. After his burial, the town watchman reported strange noises coming from Cuntius's house almost nightly. Other extraordinary stories were reported from different households. One maidservant, for example, said that she heard someone riding around the house and then into the side of the building, violently shaking it. On different nights, Cuntius appeared and had violent encounters with former acquaintances, friends, and family members. He came to his bedroom and demanded to share the bed with his wife. Like the common revenant (one that returns after death or long absence), he had a physical bodily presence and extraordinary **strength**. On one occasion he was reported to have pulled up two posts set deeply into the ground. However, on other occasions he seemed to operate in non-corporeal form—like a ghost—and disappeared suddenly when a candle was lit in his presence. Cuntius was reported to smell badly and to have especially foul breath. He was said to have once turned milk to **blood**. He defiled the cloth on the church's altar with spots of blood. He sucked the cows dry of blood and attempted to force his attentions not only on his wife but on several women in town. One person he touched reported that his hand felt cold as ice. Several holes, which went down to his **coffin**, appeared at his gravesite. The holes were filled in, but reappeared the next evening.

The townspeople, unable to find any remedy to these occurrences, finally decided to check the graveyard. They dug up several graves. All the bodies were in an advanced state of decay, except for that of Cuntius. Though he had been in the ground for some six months, his body was still soft and pliable. They put a staff in the corpse's hand, and it grasped it. They cut the body and blood gushed forth. A formal judicial hearing was called and a judgment rendered against the corpse. The body was ordered to be burned. When it proved slow to burn, it was cut into small pieces. The executioner reported that the blood was still fresh and pure. After the burning, the figure of Cuntius was never seen again.

Sources:

Glut, Donald G. *True Vampires of History*. New York: H C Publishers, 1971. 191 pp.

More, Henry. *An Antidote Against Atheism*. London: J. Fleshner, 1655. 398 pp.

Curtis, Dan (1927–2006)

Dan Curtis, the producer-director who developed the *Dark Shadows* **television** series, was born in 1928, in Connecticut. His first work in television was as a salesman for MCA. A sports buff, he sold CBS on doing a show called *CBS Golf Classic*, which is best remembered for live microphones that Curtis had the golfers wear; the show won an Emmy Award in 1965. The success of the show helped Curtis become an independent producer. He decided that soap operas were a good field, and began to think about developing a daytime show.

The initial idea for *Dark Shadows* began to take shape after a vivid dream that Curtis had. It concerned a young woman traveling by train to a new job as a governess at an old place in New England. The dream concluded with the girl standing at a railroad station. Curtis described his dream to officials at ABC, and they risked a small budget to begin development. He gathered a team to put together what would become a daytime serial with a **gothic** flavor. Over several years, *Dark Shadows* evolved from the

Director Dan Curtis of *Dark Shadows* fame.

original idea. As the story line matured, it centered on the Collins family of a mythical fishing village called Collinsport, Maine. The young woman from Curtis's dream became Victoria Winters, an orphan in search of her past, which she believed lay in New England. An early story line concerned a man she met on the train as she headed for her new job. He accused one of the Collins family of lying at a trial in which he was convicted and sent to prison. The show went on the air on June 27, 1966. At the time, there was no mention of vampirism or any thought of a vampire character. It was only later that when the show was threatened by low ratings that supernatural elements in the form of ghosts were added. They helped to raise the ratings, but not enough. In the winter of 1966–67, with little hope that the show would survive, Curtis made a radical decision. He had the writers create a vampire character. If the show failed after that, he reasoned, at least he would have had fun. The vampire, **Barnabas Collins**, made his first appearance in April 1967. The response was enormous, and by the summer, both Curtis and ABC realized they had a hit. As the show steadily rose in the ratings, Curtis borrowed the cast and created the first of two movies with MGM based on the show, *House of Dark Shadows* (1970). The following year a second feature, *Night of Dark Shadows*, was produced.

Due to low ratings, the original *Dark Shadows* daytime series ended in 1971, though it went into syndication several years later. Meanwhile, Curtis allowed his interest in vampires to influence his future projects. At the same time he began a fruitful relationship with horror writer **Richard Matheson**, who would write the scripts for a number of Curtis's productions through the decade. In 1972 he worked with ABC to produce *The Night Stalker,* a Matheson script concerning a reporter (Carl Kolchak, played by Darren McGavin) who discovered a vampire operating in Seattle. The show became the most watched made-for-television movie to that date. ABC then had Curtis produce and direct the sequel, *The Night Strangler,* based on "Jack the Ripper" themes. The two movies led to a television series based on the Kolchak character. Curtis and his company, Dan Curtis Productions, went on to produce other television horror movies, including *The Norliss Tapes* (1973) and *Scream of the Wolf* (1974).

Curtis still had an interest in vampires, however, and in 1973 decided to produce a new version of *Dracula*. He chose veteran actor **Jack Palance** as its villain star, and Matheson as his writer. He also wanted to bypass the stage play that had been the basis for both the **Bela Lugosi** movie in 1931 and the more recent **Horror of Dracula** from **Hammer Films**. The script drew on fresh research on **Vlad the Impaler**, the fifteenth-century Wallachian prince thought of as the original **Dracula**. In the end, Curtis's Dracula was driven to reclaim his long-lost love whom he saw reborn in the person of **Jonathan Harker**'s fiance. This need took him to England. At the same time, he was under attack from **vampire hunter Abraham Van Helsing** (played by Nigel Davenport), and their personal battle formed the second dynamic of the script.

In 1975, Curtis brought to television a movie, *Trilogy of Terror,* composed of three of Matheson's short stories. It was followed the next year with a similar horror collection, *Dead of Night,* which included Matheson's story, "No Such Thing as a Vampire." A successful producer who had found his niche in developing made-for-television movies, Curtis reached a new high in the next decade with the production of two very successful TV miniseries. *The Winds of War* (1983) and its sequel, *War and Remembrance* (1988–89), were based on the books of Herman Wouk. Curtis's productions were thus diversified, only occasionally returning to the horror genre. However, the continuing popularity of *Dark Shadows* in syndication suggested the possibility of its revival. In 1990 Curtis sold the idea of a prime-time *Dark Shadows* series to NBC. With a new set and a new cast, a pilot show was filmed. Based on the old series, it began with the awakening of Barnabas Collins and his entrance into the Collins household. From there—while keeping the basic framework of the old series—the story line developed in novel directions. The series aired in early 1991 but, seemingly due to the outbreak of the Gulf War, did not make the ratings cut and was cancelled after only 12 episodes. In the meantime, Innovation Comics began production of a comic book based on the new series. The comic was a success, and the new story line and characters continued into 1994 when Innovation ceased operation.

Curtis continued as a celebrity among the very loyal fans of *Dark Shadows,* but was himself upset that he was remembered more for the series than for some of his other work. He died March 27, 2006 at the age of 78.

Sources:
Dawidziak, Mark. "Dark Shadows." *Cinefantastique* 21, 3 (December 1990): 24–30.

Gross, Edward, and Marc Shapiro. *The Vampire Book: Conversations with the Undead.* East Meadow, NY: Image Books, 1991. 134 pp.

Thompson, Jeffrey. *The Television Horrors of Dan Curtis: Dark Shadows, The Night Stalker and Other Productions, 1966–2006.* Jeffersonville, NC: McFarland & Company, 2009. 208 pp.

❨ Cushing, Peter (1913–1994) ❩

Peter Cushing, a British movie actor known for his portrayal of **Abraham Van Helsing, Dracula**'s main protagonist, was born in 1913 in Kenley, Surrey. His formal stage debut was in *The Middle Watch* in 1935 in a performance at Worthing, though he had done minor roles on stage previously. Cushing worked in 1936 as an assistant stage manager of the New Connaugh Theatre in Worthing, and moved on in 1937 to work as a stage actor in a repertory theater in Southampton. He made his film debut in 1939 in *The Man in the Iron Mask*, directed by James Whale. In 1941 he made *Vigil in the Night* and also made a number of short films in the 1940s as part of the war effort.

Following the war, Cushing moved between stage, movie and television roles; the most noteworthy acclaim coming in the 1954 British television production of *1984*. He was, at the time, regarded as a major British TV star, being featured in productions like "Pride and Prejudice," where he played Darcy.

In 1957 he starred as monster-maker Victor Frankenstein in the first of **Hammer Films**' famous horror series. After the success of *Curse of Frankenstein*, Cushing teamed again with director **Terence Fisher** and opposite **Christopher Lee** in Hammer's 1958 production of *Dracula* (better known under its American title as **Horror of Dracula**). As Van Helsing, Cushing assumed the image of a cultured intellectual who had chosen to confront absolute evil in the person of the vampire. He returned to the role of Van Helsing in one subsequent Hammer *Dracula* movie—*The Brides of Dracula* (1960)—and as a vampire-hunting descendant of Van Helsing in *Dracula A.D. 1972* (1972) and *The Satanic Rites of Dracula*, released in the United States as *Count Dracula and his Vampire Brides* (1973). He also played a Van Helsing relative in the Hammer/Shaw co-production of *The Legend of the Seven Golden Vampires* (also known as *The Seven Brothers Meet Dracula*), which mixed horror and martial arts themes. As the only person to play Van Helsing so many times, Cushing has become the best-known actor associated with the role.

While Cushing became well known for his portrayal of Van Helsing, he was able to play a number of other parts, sometimes appearing in three or four movies a year, and had some success not only in vampire movies but also in a variety of others. He returned to his portrayal of Dr. Frankenstein in several Hammer films with the same theme. (Cushing ultimately played Frankenstein six times). He also played a Van Helsing-like role of an intellectual and/or scientist in horror movies that, when considered alongside his famous Van Helsing roles, reveal Cushing as having continually portrayed a symbol of a stable normal world that turned back the challenges of the chaotic forces of evil. This role was seen in its extreme form in *Twins of Evil*, (Hammer, 1971) in which he played a fanatical witchhunter who actually encountered the supernatural.

Above and beyond his Van Helsing roles, Cushing appeared in several other vampire films, including *The Blood Beast Terror* (1968), *The Vampire Lovers* (Hammer, 1970), *Incense for the Damned* (1970), and *Tender Dracula* (1974). He also teamed with Christo-

Peter Cushing usually portrayed a vampire hunter, but in *Tender Dracula* he played an actor named MacGregor who made his living in horror films.

pher Lee in several nonvampire movies such as *The Creeping Flesh* (1973) and *The House of Long Shadows* (1982), in which Lee, Cushing, and Vincent Price joined in a tribute to the **gothic** "old dark house" film. Possibly his most notable nonvampire appearance was as a villain, Grand Moff Tarkin, in *Star Wars*, though not to be forgotten was his highly successful role as Sherlock Holmes, the first appearance of Holmes in color. Cushing passed away on August 11, 1994.

Note: I am grateful to Uwe Sommerlad, a German movie expert and personal friend of Cushing, who read and commented on an earlier version of this entry.

Sources:

Ambrogio, Anthony. *Peter Cushing*. Austin, TX: Luminary Press, 2009. 232 pp.

Cushing, Peter. *An Autobiography and Past Forgetting*. Baltimore, MD: Midnight Marquee Press, 1999. 255 pp.

Del Vecchio, Deborah, and Tom Johnson. *Peter Cushing: The Gentle Man of Horror and His 91 Films*. Jefferson, NC: McFarland & Company, 1992.

Eyles, Allen, Robert Adkinson, and Nicholas Fry. *The House of Hammer*. London: Lorrimer Publishing Limited, 1973. 127 pp.

Gullo, Christopher. *In All Sincerity … Peter Cushing*. Princeton, NJ: Xlibris, 2004. 420 pp.

Marrero, Robert. *Vampires Hammer Style*. Key West, FL: RGM Publications, 1974. 98 pp.

Miller, David. *The Peter Cushing Companion*. London: Reynolds & Hearn, 2000. 192 pp.

❨Czech Republic and Slovakia, Vampires in the❩

The first historical state in what is now the territory occupied by the Czech Republic and Slovakia was founded by tribes that settled in the mountainous region north of present-day Austria and **Hungary**. The state founded in the seventh century would, two centuries later, be united with the Great Moravian empire, which in 836 C.E. invited Cyril and Methodius, the Christian missionaries, into their land. While among the Czechs and Slovaks, the pair preached and taught the people in their native Slavic language. However, Roman Catholicism, not Eastern Orthodoxy, dominated church life, and Latin, not Old Church Slavonic became the language of worship. The Moravian empire disintegrated early in the tenth century and Slovakia became part of Hungary. After a period under German control, the Czech state reemerged as the Czech (Bohemian) kingdom. Like **Poland,** both the Czechs and the Slovakians became Roman Catholic.

The Bohemian kingdom survived through the Middle Ages but gradually through the sixteenth century came under Austrian hegemony and in the next century was incorporated into the Hapsburg empire. At the end of the eighteenth century, a revival of Czech culture led to a revival of Czech nationalism. Finally, in 1918, at the end of World War I, Czechoslovakia was created as an independent state. That country survived through most of the twentieth century, though 1,000 years of separate political existence had driven a considerable wedge between the Czechs and Slovaks. After World War II, Communist rule replaced the democratic government that had been put in place in 1918. The Communist system was renounced in 1989 and shortly thereafter, Bohemia and Moravia parted with Slovakia. On January 1, 1993, two separate and independent countries, the Czech Republic and Slovakia, emerged.

The Vampire in the Czech Republic and Slovakia: The Czech and Slovakian vampire—called an *upir,* and to a lesser extent, *nelapsi,* in both Czech and Slovak—was a variety of the Slavic vampire. The *upir* was believed to have two hearts and hence two souls. The presence of the second soul would be indicated by a corpse's flexibility, open eyes, two curls in the hair, and a ruddy complexion. Among the earliest anecdotes concerning Czech vampires were two fourteenth-century stories recounted by E. P. Evans in his volume on the *Criminal Prosecution and Capital Punishment of Animals* (1906), as mentioned in Dudley Wright's survey. The first concerned a revenant that terrorized the town of Cadan. The people he attacked seemed destined to become a vampire like him. They retaliated, attacking his corpse and driving a **stake** through it. That remedy proved ineffective and they finally burned him. In 1345, in Lewin, a woman believed to be a witch died. She returned in various beastly forms and attacked villagers. When uncovered in her grave it was reported that she had swallowed her face cloth; when the cloth was pulled out of the grave, it was stained with **blood**. She also was staked, which again proved ineffective. She used the stake as a weapon while walking around town. She was finally destroyed by **fire**.

Writing in 1863, Henry More recorded events that occurred in the late 1500s to **Johannes Cuntius** (or Kunz), a merchant who troubled his family and neighbors following his violent death. Cuntius lived in the town of Pentsch (present-day Horni Benesov). His son lived in Jagerdorf (present-day Krnov) in a part of Moravia dominated by Lutheran Protestants. **Dom Augustin Calmet** included reports of vampires from Bohemia and

Moravia in his famous 1746 treatise. He noted that in 1706 a treatise on vampires, *Magia Posthuma* by Charles Ferdinand de Schertz, was published in Olmutz (Moravia). *Magia Posthuma* related a number of incidents of vampires who made their first appearance as troublesome spirits that would attack their former neighbors and the village livestock. Some of the reports were of classic nightmare attacks accompanied with pain, a feeling of being suffocated, and squeezing around the neck area. Those so attacked would grow pale and fatigued. Other stories centered on poltergeist effects featuring objects being thrown around the house and possessions of the dead person mysteriously moving. One of the earliest and more spectacular cases concerns a man of the Bohemian village of Blow (Blau) in the fourteenth century. As a vampire he called upon his neighbors, and whomever he visited died within eight days. The villagers finally dug up the man's body and drove a **stake** through it. The man, however, laughed at the people and thanked the people for giving him a stick to fend off the dogs. That night he took the stick out of his body and began again to appear to people. After several more deaths occurred, his body was burned. Only then did the visitations end. Schertz, a lawyer, was most concerned with the activity of villagers who would take the law into their hands and mutilate and burn bodies. He argued that in cases of severe disturbances, a legal process should be followed before any bodies were desecrated. Included in the process was the examination of the body of any suspected vampire by physicians and theologians. Destruction of the vampire, by burning, should be carried out as an official act by the public executioner.

Montague Summers was most impressed by the evidence of vampirism detailed by the Count de Cadreras, who early in the 1720s was commissioned by the Austrian emperor to look into events at Haidam, a town near the Hungarian border. The Count investigated a number of cases of people who had been dead for many years (in one case 30 and another 16 years), and who had reportedly returned to attack their relatives. Upon exhumation each still showed the classic signs of delayed decomposition, including the flow of "fresh" blood when cut. With the Count's consent, each was beheaded (or nails driven into the skull) and then burned. The extensive papers reporting these incidents to the emperor survived, as well as a lengthy narrative given by the Count to an official at the University of Fribourg.

It is unlikely that the town of "Haidam" will ever be identified. No place by that name has been recorded. It has been suggested most convincingly that the term derived from the word "haidamak," a Ukrainian term meaning "outlaw" or "freebooter." Haidamak, derived from the Slavic "heyduck," referred to a class of dispossessed who had organized themselves into loose itinerant bands to live off the land. Eventually the Austrian Hapsburg rulers employed them as guardians along their most distant frontiers. This Haidam probably referred to the land of a haidamak rather than a specific town by that name.

As recently as the mid-twentieth century, folklorist Ján Mjartan reported that the belief in vampires was still alive in Slovakia. The vampire was thought to be able to suck the blood of its **victims** (humans and cattle) and often suffocated them. The vampire also was believed capable of killing with a mere glance (evil eye), thus devastating whole villages. Preventing the rise of a suspected vampire was accomplished by placing various objects in the **coffin** (coins, Christian symbols, various herbs, the dead person's belongings), putting poppyseed or millet **seeds** in the body orifices, and nailing the clothes and hair to the coffin. Finally, the head or the heart could be stabbed with an iron wedge, an oak stake, a hat pin, or some thorn such as the **hawthorn**. The body was

carried headfirst to the grave, around which poppyseed or millet was scattered. The seeds also were dropped on the path homeward, and once home various rituals such as washing one's hands and holding them over the stove were followed. The family of the deceased repeated these measures if they proved ineffective the first time.

Contemporary Vampire Lore: As with other Slavic countries, the belief in vampires receded to rural areas of the Czech Republic and Slovakia through the twentieth century. It made a brief appearance in the midst of the Czech cultural revival of the nineteenth century in a famous short story "The Vampire" by Jan Neruda (1834–91). In recent decades, Josef Nesvadba, a Czech psychiatrist, has emerged as an impressive writer of horror fiction. A collection of his stories in English was published in 1982 as *Vampires Ltd*. In the twenty-first century, Czechs and Slovakians have rediscovered **Elizabeth Bathory**, one of the superstars of the vampire world, though they are caught in the middle of promoting her for the sake of tourism while having their most famous citizen vilified as a monster. A few have arisen to seriously look at the defense of Bathory as a victim of Catholic anti-Protestantism, published in the 1980s by Laszlo Nagy. However, as books on Bathory continue to appear, the legend generally wins over history. A variety of publications on Bathory have appeared in the Czech Republic and Slovakia since the fall of the Berlin wall, as have several movies (*Demons Claw*, 2006; *Bathory*, 2008; and *Blood Countess*, 2008).

Sources:

Calmet, Augustine. *The Phantom World*. 2 vols. London: Richard Bentley, 1850. Reprint of English translation of 1746 treatise.

Hrbkova, Sárka B. *Czechoslovak Stories*. Freeport, NY: Books for Libraries Press, 1970. 330 pp.

Nesvadba, Josef. *Vampires Ltd*. Czechoslovakia: Artia Pocket Books, 1982. 225 pp.

Perkowski, Jan L., ed. *Vampires of the Slavs*. Cambridge, MA: Slavica Publishers, 1976. 294 pp.

———. *The Darkling: A Treatise on Slavic Vampirism*. Columbus, OH: Slavica Publishers, 1989. 174 pp.

Summers, Montague. *The Vampire in Europe*. London: Routledge, Kegan Paul, Trench, Trubner, & Co. 1929. 329 pp. Rept. New Hyde Park, NY: University Books, 1961. 329 pp.

Wright, Dudley. *Vampires and Vampirism*. London: William Rider and Sons, 1914, Revised ed.: 1924. Rept. *The Book of Vampires*. New York: Causeway Books, 1973. 217 pp.

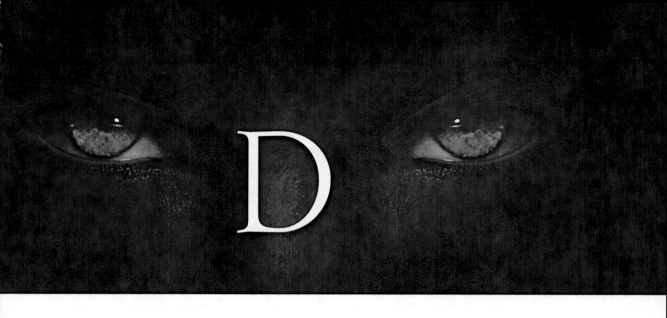

❦ Daniels III, Leslie Noel (1943–) ❧

Leslie Noel Daniels III, author of a series of vampire novels, was born in 1943 in Connecticut. He received his bachelor's degree in 1965 and his master's degree in 1968 from Brown University in Providence, Rhode Island. His master's thesis was written on *Frankenstein*. Daniels has since pursued a career in writing and in music.

During the early 1970s he produced two nonfiction works, both of which touched on the vampire: *Comix: A History of Comic Books in America* (1971) and *Living in Fear: A History of Horror in the Mass Media* (1975). He then edited two anthologies of horror stories: *Dying of Fright* (1976) and *Thirteen Tales of Terror* (1976).

In 1978, in the first of five novels, Daniels introduced a new vampire, **Sebastian de Villanueva** in *The Black Castle*. The book told the story of the origin of Don Sebastian, a brother of a local inquisitor in **Spain** in 1496. The vampire next appeared in sixteenth-century **Mexico** in *The Silver Skull* (1979) and as *Citizen Vampire* (1981), surviving amid the French Revolution. *Yellow Fog* (1986) found Sebastian, now known as Sebastian Newcastle, settled in **London** where he found love in the person of Felicia Lamb and an enemy in Reginald Callender, who was engaged to Felicia until Sebastian stole her away. In the end, Felicia lay dead and Sebastian fled, pursued by Callender. The chase led them to **India** and an encounter with the followers of the goddess **Kali** in the last of the five novels, *No Blood Spilled* (1991).

Since *No Blood Spilled*, Daniels has not returned to the vampire genre. In the new century, he has been best known for his nonfiction writing on the world of comic book super heroes—Batman and Wonder Woman.

Sources:

Daniels, Les. *The Silver Skull*. New York: Charles Scribner's Sons, 1970. Rept. New York: Ace Books, 1983. 234 pp.

———. *The Black Castle*. New York: Charles Scribner's Sons, 1978. Rept. New York: Berkley Books, 1979. 232 pp.

———. *Citizen Vampire*. New York: Charles Scribner's Sons, 1981. 197 pp.

———. *Yellow Fog*. New York: Donald M. Grant, 1986. Rev. ed.: New York: Tor, 1988. 294 pp.

———. *No Blood Spilled*. New York: Tor, 1991. 218 pp.

———. *DC Comics: A Celebration of the World's Favorite Comic Book Heroes*. New York: Watson-Guptill, 2003. 272 pp.

Danis the Dark Productions *see:* Vampire Fandom: United States

Dark Delicacies

America's premier horror/vampire-oriented book store, Dark Delicacies, filled a need in 1995 for a book store serving a national (and even international) clientele. The store specializes in horror fiction and nonfiction books and related movies, jewelry, and **paraphernalia**. Located in Burbank, California, Dark Delicacies is owned by Del Howison and his wife Sue, who opened the store to sell horror in a context largely unadulterated by science fiction and fantasy. Located in proximity to a number of southern California television and film production companies, the store has become a major resource and a site for various documentaries. Authors of new books participate in scheduled book signings held there several times each month.

Del Howison, owner of the Dark Delicacies book store.

Dark Delicacies became one of the principal sponsors of **Dracula '97: A Centennial Celebration,** the grand event commemorating the 100th anniversary of the publication of **Dracula**. The Howisons organized the exhibit area for the event and coordinated the numerous autograph sessions by the authors and celebrity guests. The store has also become the meeting place for various fan groups such as the Phantom Coaches Hearse Society and the Undead Poets Society. The store caters to book collectors and may be contacted through its Website, http://www.darkdel.com/.

As the world of Hollywood filmmaking and horror writing became intertwined, the store became a place for both moviemakers and writers to promote their wares, sponsoring multiple book and DVD signing events monthly. The Howisons have also published several short story anthologies featuring writers who frequent the store. Their anthologies *Dark Delicacies* and *Dark Delicacies II: Fear,* were nominated for the **Bram Stoker** Award, as was their nonfiction reference text, *The Book of Lists: Horror.*

Del Howison has appeared in a number of movies, from cameo appearances to a speaking part in **Don Glut**'s *Blood Scarab* (2008). In the process, Del became the only cinema actor to play **Renfield** multiple times (four in all). Del has also authored a short story, "The Lost Herd." Under the name "Sacrifice," it became the premiere episode of the television anthology series "Fear Itself" on NBC (2008).

Sources:

Howison, Del, and Jeff Gelb. *Dark Delicacies*. New York: Ace, 2007. 368 pp.

———. *Dark Delicacies II: Fear*. New York: Ace, 2008. 336 pp.

———. *Dark Delicacies III: Haunted*. New York: Ace, 2009. 336 pp.

Wallace, Amy, Del Howison, and Scott Bradley. *The Book of Lists: Horror*. New York: Harper Paperbacks, 2008. 432 pp.

❦ *Dark Shadows* (1966–1971; 1991) ❦

*D*ark Shadows began in 1966 as a daytime soap opera on ABC **television**. With low ratings threatening cancellation, the show added supernatural elements to the plot, and then in April 1967 introduced a vampire. This vampire—**Barnabas Collins**—has joined **Dracula** and **Lestat de Lioncourt** as one of the most easily recognizable vampires.

Once Collins was introduced to the show, the ratings turned around and the show became a hit. While the show went off the air in 1971, fans have kept its memory alive to the present day through fan clubs, publications, and conventions.

The Origin of Dark Shadows: *Dark Shadows* began as an idea of producer **Dan Curtis.** The beginning of a story had come to him, according to one account, from a dream in which he saw a young woman with long dark hair. The woman was traveling by train to New England, where she had been offered a job as a governess. After she got off the train, she went to a large "forbidding" house. Curtis approached ABC with the idea of taking his opening and creating a **gothic**-flavored daytime show. He collaborated with Art Wallace in developing the idea, and assembled a production crew that included Robert Costello, Lela Swift, John Sedwick, Sy Tomashoff, and Robert Cobert.

As the story developed, it first centered on Victoria Winters (Alexandra Moltke), the young woman of Curtis's dream. She was an orphan who had been found with a note, "Her name is Victoria. I can no longer care for her." The rest of her name was added because she was found in the wintertime. As she grew up, the orphanage received donations for Victoria's care from Bangor, Maine. On her 20th birthday, Victoria received a offer from a Mrs. Elizabeth Collins Stoddard (Joan Bennett) of Collinsport, Maine, who wished to hire Victoria as a governess for her nephew. This gave her not only had employment, but the possibility of an opportunity to learn about her past.

Collinsport was a small fishing town on the Maine coast. Collinwood, the Collins's family home, was a forty-room mansion built in the 1700s. The family resided in its central structure and had closed both wings of the house. Also on the property was an older house, built in the 1600s and now abandoned.

At Collinwood, the family estate where she was employed, Victoria interacted with the residents. Mrs. Stoddard, the family matriarch, had become a recluse after her husband disappeared eighteen years before. David Collins (David Henesy), her nephew, was nine years old and somewhat of a problem. He had driven off previous governesses

The cast from the 1991 television production of *Dark Shadows*.

by his undisciplined behavior, especially his nasty pranks at their expense. David's father, Roger Collins (Louis Edmonds), had a drinking problem and was generally neglectful of his son. Carolyn Stoddard (Nancy Barrett), Elizabeth's daughter, was a girl enjoying her youthful years and running through a series of loves. The mansion also was home to Matthew Morgan (Thayer David), the caretaker.

The cast was rounded out with several townspeople: Maggie Evans (Kathryn Leigh Scott), a waitress in the local diner who lived with her father Sam (David Ford), an alcoholic artist; Joe Haskell (Joel Crothers), employed by the Collins Fishing Fleet and involved with Carolyn Stoddard; and Burke Devlin (Mitchell Ryan), a businessman Victoria met on the train ride to Collinsport.

Devlin became Winters's first friend and confidant. He was also the focus of the initial storyline, which was built around his reasons for returning to Collinsport after an absence of ten years. He was certain that Roger Collins had lied in court, and Burke had been sent to prison as a result. He wanted revenge. In the tension resulting from his return, Bill Malloy (Frank Schofield), a local man who tried to mediate the situation, was killed. The supernatural element first entered into the *Dark Shadows* story when

Malloy's ghost appeared to Victoria and told her that he had been murdered.

Taping for *Dark Shadows* began on June 13, 1966, and the first episode was aired with little fanfare two weeks later. During the first year of *Dark Shadows*, an additional character appeared, one that would become of long-term importance to the emerging story. As the supernatural element was increasing, a painting over the fireplace in the Old House came alive. The new character turned out to be the ghost of Josette DuPrés Collins (also played by Kathryn Leigh Scott). After a brief appearance in episode 40, she appeared again in episode 126 to protect Victoria from Matthew Morgan, the murderer of Malloy, who had kidnapped her. Morgan died from fright upon seeing Josette, thus resolving that subplot. Afterward, Josette become intricately integrated into the storyline.

The *Dark Shadows* audience was introduced to new supernatural subplots almost weekly. Around the 200th episode, a transition began. First, the original Burke Devlin situation was resolved when Roger Collins confessed to manslaughter and perjury. Then a new character, Willie Loomis, took up residence at Collinwood. Almost immediately Loomis called at-

Cover of *The Dark Shadows Companion*.

tention to a portrait in the foyer of the mansion. It was one of the family ancestors, Barnabas Collins.

The Emergence of Barnabas Collins: Though the addition of supernatural elements improved the show's ratings, ABC executives indicated early in 1967 that *Dark Shadows* was still in danger of being cancelled. Curtis, who had always wanted to do a vampire picture, gambled and decided to add a vampire to the show. Canadian Shakespearean actor **Jonathan Frid** was finally hired for the part. The original idea was to have the vampire jazz up the show, improve its ratings, and then quietly fade away. That plan would soon be discarded.

Barnabas Collins made his first appearance in episode 210 in April of 1967. Willie Loomis discovered a secret room with a chained **coffin** in the family mausoleum. He undid the chains and Barnabas came out of his resting place. In the next episode, he appeared at the front door of Collinwood and confronted the family as their long-lost cousin from England. He moved into the abandoned old house on the estate, and soon the community was plagued by a mysterious illness. The symptoms included fatigue, bite marks, and the loss of **blood**.

As the story unfolded, the audience discovered that Barnabas was a vampire who had lived two centuries earlier. (He actually was the person in the portrait in the mansion.) In his human life at the end of the eighteenth century, he had loved and lost Josette DuPrés, and he still longed for her in his new life at Collinwood. Having noticed

Maggie Evans's resemblance to Josette, he tried to turn her into another Josette. When she refused his advances, he nearly killed her.

By this point in the story, which was being broadcast in the summer of 1967, the ratings had jumped in a spectacular manner—the show became a hit. In a matter of weeks, Jonathan Frid became a star, and quantity of his fan mail soared. Overwhelmingly, the mail was from young women, even teenagers.

Crowds regularly gathered at the entrances to the ABC studio where the show was taped. The first *Dark Shadows* **paraphernalia** appeared. Meanwhile, as the story continued, another new character was introduced— Dr. Julia Hoffman (played by Grayson Hall). Called on to treat Maggie Evans, Hoffman became intrigued with Barnabas, discovered his vampiric nature, and offered to help him overcome it. Initially he accepted her ministrations, but he eventually turned on her. He was about to kill the doctor when the ghost of his beloved sister Sarah appeared to save her.

The Origin of Barnabas Collins: With Sarah making her ghostly presence known to a number of people, the decision was made to hold a seance. During the seance Victoria went into a trance and the lights went out. When the lights returned, she had disappeared and her place had been taken by Phyllis Wick. Victoria woke up in Collinsport in 1795. The scene was now set to relate the story of Barnabas's **origin**. The son of a prominent local landowner, Barnabas traveled to the DuPrés plantation on the island of Martinique. There he began an affair with **Angélique Bouchard** (played by Lara Parker), a beautiful servant girl who, it was later revealed, knew **witchcraft**. Then he met and fell in love with the plantation owner's daughter, Josette, and they made plans to wed. Barnabas broke off the affair with Angélique.

Meanwhile, back in Collinsport, Victoria had found work in the Collins's home as governess to Barnabas's young sister Sarah. The members and acquaintances of the family from the 1960s reappeared as their counterparts in the 1790's storyline. Barnabas returned from the West Indies to prepare for his marriage but did not anticipate that Angélique would use her powers of witchcraft to disrupt the plans. She caused Josette to fall in love with Jeremiah, Barnabas's brother. She then claimed Barnabas for herself. Barnabas, in turn, killed his brother in a duel and turned on Angélique. She cursed him and sent a **bat** to attack him, and Barnabas emerged from the encounter a vampire.

After considering various options, he decided to make Josette his **vampire bride**. Before he could carry through on his plans, Angélique interfered again and caused Josette to commit **suicide**. Barnabas told his father of his condition and asked to be killed. His father could not kill him, but did chain Barnabas in a coffin (which Willie Loomis eventually discovered).

While Barnabas fought Angélique, Victoria had been condemned as a witch. As she was about to be killed, she suddenly reappeared in 1967. Only a few minutes of the seance had passed while she was lost for some months in the 1790s. Barnabas realized that Victoria now knew his identity and decided to court her, but he was immediately distracted by the arrival of Angélique as Cassandra, the new wife of Roger Collins.

New Story Lines: With five half-hour shows to write each week—the equivalent of more than a feature-length movie—story ideas were exhausted at a rapid rate. During 1968, the writers turned to classic nineteenth-century gothic novels for ideas, and during the last three years of the show merged subplots from a variety of horror themes into the ongoing story. The major confrontation between Barnabas and Cassandra, for example, was based around a subplot derived from *Frankenstein*. Late in 1968 Henry James's *The Turn of the Screw* inspired a plot that led to the introduction of the second most popular member of the cast, Quentin Collins (played by David Selby).

The storyline again sent Victoria into the past—this time for good. Thus Elizabeth Stoddard needed another governess for her nephew David. Meanwhile, David and Amy (a young girl visiting at Collinwood) went exploring in one of the unoccupied wings of the house, where they discovered a disconnected telephone. While the children played with the phone, a ghostly voice called them to a room where a gramophone mysteriously played music. The ghost of Quentin (his name derived from James's text) appeared. He attempted to take control of both children, but a female spirit intervened. She blocked Quentin's effect on Amy, but was of little help to David. Eventually Barnabas was drawn in to protect David. In his attempt to contact Quentin, Barnabas was thrown back to 1897 (the year **Bram Stoker**'s novel **Dracula** was published), the time when Quentin actually lived. Barnabas found himself chained in his tomb. One of his ancestors, however, hired **Gypsies,** who discovered the mausoleum and freed Barnabas. Again he arrived at the door as the long-lost cousin from England.

Quentin and Barnabas started as rivals. However, as the story developed, Quentin and his male descendants were cursed—because of this, they would become **werewolves**. In the face of this new reality, Barnabas and Quentin came to some understanding of each other. Each, in turn, was transported back to the present and the story continued.

While based on *Dracula*, from which it drew its understanding of the vampire and the vampire's powers, *Dark Shadows* created the most elaborate and complex alternative to the *Dracula* story in modern mythology. It played to an ever-growing audience from the time Barnabas Collins was added to the storyline to the spring of 1967, and became the most popular soap opera on ABC, pushing the network past CBS and putting it in a position to challenge NBC for the daytime audience. It was estimated that twenty million people were regular viewers. Frid received several thousand letters every week and David Selby only slightly less. Additional thousands of letters were directed to the rest of the cast. The show lasted for two more years before its ratings began to sag and it was finally cancelled. The final show (the 1,245th segment) was aired on April 2, 1971. Many believe that it was not so much a dip in the ratings but the exhaustion of the story that led to its cancellation.

Additional Dark Shadows Vampires: While Barnabas Collins was the dominant vampire of the *Dark Shadows* series, other characters also had a brush with vampirism. The most prominent was Angélique. Following the return of the story to the 1960s from the 1790s, Angélique reappeared in the person of Cassandra Collins, the new wife of Roger Collins. Shortly thereafter, one Nicholas Blair, a warlock claiming to be Cassandra's brother, arrived at Collinwood. When Cassandra got in his way, he used his strong magical powers to turn her into a vampire. Through the ministrations of Dr. Hoffman, Barnabas was temporarily cured of his vampirism. However, Angélique/Cassandra, wanting Barnabas to be with her in her new form, attacked him and turned him back into a vampire. Angélique's plans were foiled, however, when she was set on **fire** by Barnabas. She died screaming as the flames enveloped her.

During Angélique's career as a vampire, she attacked handyman Tom Jennings, who had discovered the location of her coffin. He survived as a vampire for only a few episodes before being staked. The continuing storyline took the cast back to the nineteenth century where a prevampirized Angélique reappeared. After being attacked by Barnabas, a servant, Dirk, was made a vampire. He was soon staked by Edward Collins.

Later, the storyline led Barnabas and the Collins family into an encounter with the Leviathans, old demonic forces in the tradition of H. P. Lovecraft. The Leviathans were responsible for turning him back into a vampire. Among the Leviathans was Audrey, a vampire who made a brief appearance in a single episode. The most notable fact of Audrey's otherwise inconsequential appearance was that she was played by a young Marsha Mason, later to go on to stardom in the movies. Another female vampire at this time was Megan Todd (Marie Wallace), a **victim** of Barnabas. She eventually was staked by Willie Loomis.

Finally, toward the end of the show, Roxanne Drew appeared as a young woman involved in a bizarre experiment to transfer her life force to Angélique. At this point in the story, the major characters were moving between parallel times with the same people but different histories. In real time, Barnabas met Roxanne again as the girlfriend of an astrologer, Sebastian Shaw. She was a vampire and, before being discovered, bit Maggie Evans. Meanwhile, the story shifted to 1840. There Barnabas also met Roxanne and they fell in love.

However, the ever-present and vengeful Angélique killed her. Roxanne then rose as a vampire and was soon cornered in her coffin. She disintegrated in her crypt when a **crucifix** was placed on top of her.

Dark Shadows Books and Paraphernalia: The show had a far reaching effect on popular culture. Under the pseudonym of Marilyn Ross, from 1966 to 1972 **Daniel Ross** authored thirty-three paperback novels developed from the show. In spite of the Comics Code that banned vampires from **comic books** from 1954 to 1971, Gold Key produced the *Dark Shadows* comic books, the first vampire-oriented comics in almost two decades. In 1968–69, *Dark Shadows* paraphernalia began to appear, including the *Dark Shadows Game*, Viewmaster stereo pictures, model kits, jigsaw puzzles, and **trading cards**, to name just a few. A "Dark Shadows" Original Soundtrack Album (1969) was one of four record albums of *Dark Shadows* **music**. "Quentin's Theme," the most popular piece of *Dark Shadows* music, appeared on the first album and was also released as a single. Initially heard on the gramophone in the room where Quentin first appeared, the theme was recorded more than twenty times by various artists.

Dark Shadows in the 1990s: In 1990, NBC announced that it had asked **Dan Curtis**, the creator of *Dark Shadows*, to put together a new cast for a prime-time version of the old soap opera. Ben Cross was chosen to play the vampire Barnabas Collins. His role was strongly reminiscent of Jonathan Frid, the original Barnabas Collins. In spite of his moments of genuine anger and vicious attacks on individuals, Cross's Barnabas was a sensitive, reluctant vampire who allowed hematologist Julia Hoffman to try to cure his vampiric condition. Even though *Dark Shadows* fans gave the new series strong support, it was cancelled after only twleve episodes (thirteen hours of programming) during the second half of the 1990–91 season.

More *Dark Shadows*: The most substantial spin-offs of the television series were two full-length feature movies, *House of Dark Shadows* (1970) and *Night of Dark Shadows*

(1971). These were later made available on video. A short time after its cancellation, the show went into syndicated reruns on independent stations and PBS—the first time that had happened to a daytime soap opera. It was later picked up by the new SCI-FI cable channel. All 1,245 segments were released on VHS video and have now been transferred to DVD by MPI Home Video. Additionally, a variety of specialized videos have been developed from the series including: *Dark Shadows: Behind the Scenes*, *Dark Shadows Bloopers*, *Dark Shadows 35th Anniversary Reunion*, and *Dark Shadows: Vampires and Ghosts*.

Dark Shadows fandom has remained active through the first decade of the twenty-first century. Over a thousand people showed up for Jonathan Frid's appearance at the 2008 annual convention. In response to the continued interest in the series, new books, CDs, and DVDs continue to appear and actors with even a small role on the original series are invited to make appearances at fan gatherings. The fans have also created a continuing market for *Dark Shadows* collectibles and several businesses have arisen to cater to the demand.

Ben Cross as Barnabas Collins in the 1991 remake of *Dark Shadows*.

Sources:

Borzellieri, Frank. *The Physics of Dark Shadows: Time Travel, ESP, and the Laboratory*. New York: Cultural Studies Press, 2008. 90 pp.

Gross, Edward, and Marc Shapiro. *The Vampire Interview Book: Conversations with the Undead*. New York: Image Publishing, 1991. 134 pp.

Parker, Lara. *Dark Shadows: The Salem Branch*. New York: Tor Books, 2006. 288 pp.

Pierson, Jim. *Dark Shadows Resurrected*. Los Angeles: Pomegrante Press, 1992. 175 pp.

Scott, Kathryn Leigh, ed. *The Dark Shadows Companion: 25th Anniversary Collection*. Los Angeles: Pomegranate Press, 1990. 208 pp.

———. *My Scrapbook Memories of Dark Shadows*. Los Angeles: Pomegranate Press, 1986. 152 pp.

———, and Lara Parker. *35th Anniversary Dark Shadows Memories*. Los Angeles: Pomegranate Press, 2001. 276 pp.

———, and Jim Pierson. *Dark Shadows Almanac: Thirtieth Anniversary Tribute*. Los Angeles: Pomegranate Press, 1995. 176 pp.

Thompson, Jeff. *The Television Horrors of Dan Curtis: Dark Shadows, The Night Stalker, and Other Productions, 1966–2006*. Jeffersonville, NC: McFarland & Company, 2009. 208 pp.

❦ Dark Shadows Fandom ❦

After **Dark Shadows,** (1966–1971) the popular daytime **television** soap opera, went off the air, interest in the series stayed alive primarily in the imaginations of teenagers who had rushed home from school to watch it. Several years after ABC-TV's cancellation of the show, fans continued to manifest a high level of devotion to the series. *The World of Dark Shadows* fanzine appeared in 1975 and two years later the first Shadowcon fan convention was organized in San Diego as part of Starcon, a science fiction convention. In 1979 Shadowcon emerged as an independent gathering in Los Angeles, where it continued annually until 1986. Within a few years, the nature of the Shadowcon conventions began to expand and diversify by including all aspects of science fiction, fantasy, and horror. Thus, in 1983, a new organization that had an exclusive focus on *Dark Shadows*, the Dark Shadows Festival, was created by the combined efforts of *The World of Dark Shadows*, *Shadowgram*, and *Inside the Old House*, published by Old House Publishing.

The annual Dark Shadows Festival convention led to the growth of existing *Dark Shadows* fan publications (most prominently *Shadowgram*, edited by Marcy Robin), the founding of new fanzines, and the opening of fan clubs that kept interest alive. Their work came to unexpected fruition in the 1991 when a new version of *Dark Shadows* aired in prime time on NBC-TV. Unfortunately, the new show was canceled after only one season, but not before it led to the creation of a whole new set of *Dark Shadows* books, collectibles, and souvenirs.

Dark Shadows fans find the most effective way to enter the fold is through the Dark Shadows Festival Official Fan Club, which provides contacts for local fan clubs and information on obtaining Dark Shadows books, videos, and **paraphernalia**. The Club was founded in 1982 as the World Federation of Dark Shadows Clubs. It was a coalition of clubs in three countries that publish newsletters and magazines (now all discontinued) dedicated to preserving the memory of the two television series of *Dark Shadows*. The present name was adopted in 1992. The club keeps members informed of the continuing careers of the stars of the two shows, and maintains an active biographical archive, a library of fan club publications, and an archive of *Dark Shadows* paraphernalia. The club may be contacted at PO Box 92, Maplewood, NJ 07040 or through its Website, http://www.darkshadowsfestival.com/. In the 1990s, the club maintained an active list of over 30,000 fans.

For a number of years, *Shadowgram* published by Marcy Robin, and *The World of Dark Shadows* published by Kathleen Resch (both of Temple City, California), served as official periodicals for the club. *Shadowgram* was founded in 1979 by Maria Barbosa and Marcy Robin. The first issue was a two-page sheet reporting on what the major actors from the original *Dark Shadows* series were doing eight years after the series was canceled. It is currently published both as an online publication accessed through Yahoo Groups and a printed fanzine. *The World of Dark Shadows*, edited by Kathy Resch, is now published only rarely, but *Shadowgram: The Official Dark Shadows Newsletter*, edited by Marcy Robin (Box 1766, Temple City, CA 91780-7766), appears quarterly and has emerged as the major *Dark Shadows* news periodical.

The fanzine specializes in reports on the current activities of the cast of both the original and the 1991 television series, information on new *Dark Shadows* paraphernalia and announcements of fan activities. It also reports on the unaired 2004 Dark Shadows pilot for the WB network and on the latest developments in the (as of 2009) planned Tim Burton/Johnny Depp *Dark Shadows* feature film.

Marcy Robin has been active in *Dark Shadows* fandom since the mid-1970s. She participated in the Shadowcon conventions of the 1970s, and in 1983, was among the founders of the Dark Shadows Festival, the group that currently organizes the annual national gatherings of *Dark Shadows* fans. With Kathleen Resch, she has coauthored two books—a novel, *Beginnings: The Island of Ghosts*, and a volume on the series, *Dark Shadows in the Afternoon*.

She has written a number of short stories around the *Dark Shadows* themes, some of which have been gathered into an anthology titled *From the Shadows... Marcy Robin*. She was one of the main contributors to *The Dark Shadows Companion*, a volume celebrating the 25th Anniversary of *Dark Shadows* and assembled by one of the stars, Kathryn Leigh Scott.

In the 1990s, *The World of Dark Shadows*, was the oldest existing fanzine serving the fans of *Dark Shadows*. Its first issue was circulated to thirty people in 1975 by its founder/editor Kathleen Resch; by the early 1990s the subscriber count was over 2,000. Resch has been among the most active leaders in *Dark Shadows* fandom. In the 1970s and 1980s she published a series of fanzines under the collective title of *Dark Shadows Concordance*. Each concordance summarized a particular set of the original episodes. By 1992, concordances were available for episodes 365–700 and 981–1,245. When completed, the concordances covered all of the 1,225 episodes. *Shadows in the 90's* was a concordance of the 1991 prime-time *Dark Shadows* series.

The World of Dark Shadows has also included several anthologies of *Dark Shadows* short stories and novels. Resch contributed a short story, "Edges," to *Decades*. Additional *World of Dark Shadows* anthologies included two volumes under the name *From the Shadows*, one with stories by Marcy Robin and the other by Virginia Waldron; and *Echoes*, a collection edited by Resch. Additional novels from *The World of Dark Shadows* include *Shadowed Beginnings* by Carol Maschke, *Rebirth of the Undead* by Elwood Beaty and D. L. Crabtree, and Lori Paige's two books, *Dark Changeling* and *The Year the Fire Came*. Resch also edited a second *Dark Shadows* fanzine, *Echoes ... from the Past*.

Conventions: The Dark Shadows Festival, founded in 1983, superseded the original Shadowcon gatherings. The first "Fests" were held in San Jose, California, and Newark, New Jersey, in 1983. The latter included a trip to Lyndhurst, the mansion in Tarrytown, New York, that was used as Collinwood in the feature movies *House of Dark Shadows* (1970) and *Night of Dark Shadows* (1971). The two films were then screened for those in attendance. The festival also featured a costume contest, now a regular feature of the annual program coordinated by Marcy Robin. The initial Fests were followed by additional meetings in San Jose and in Dallas, Texas, after which they alternated between the Los Angeles and New York City areas (plus a convention in Las Vegas in 1998). The tenth festival was held in New York and included a tour of New England locations used in the *Dark Shadows* series and films. It featured an appearance by **Jonathan Frid** (the original **Barnabas Collins**), who attended thirteen of the sixteen Fests held through 1993.

The festivals were designed to be fun events for fans to meet and talk to each other, to meet members of the cast, and to have the opportunity to purchase the wide variety of *Dark Shadows* souvenirs and paraphernalia.

Each of the festivals has featured many of the original stars, and the 1990s gatherings in the 1990s also included stars from the 1991 revival series. Since the mid-1980s, Jim Pierson has been the chairman of every Dark Shadows Festival. Pierson, who has authored and coauthored several *Dark Shadows* books, also works for Dan Curtis Productions and MPI Home Video.

Dark Shadows Festival Publications has printed *The Introduction of Barnabas*, a book summarizing the 1967 *Dark Shadows* episodes featuring the vampire Barnabas Collins also includes a variety of documents about the show. It also publishes an annual *Dark Shadows* calendar.

Regional Fan Organizations: Among the many *Dark Shadows* fan activities is a variety of clubs, small publishers, and journals that cooperate with the Dark Shadows Official Fan Club. One of the oldest fan structures is Old House Publishing (11518 Desdemona Dr., Dallas, TX 75228, http://home.earthlink.net/~nardoz/itoh.html) founded in 1978 by Dale Clark. That same year, Clark started *Inside the Old House*, a *Dark Shadows* fanzine. Each issue includes fan fiction, poetry, artwork, biographies of *Dark Shadows* characters, discussions of controversies within the *Dark Shadows* community, a fan letter column, and classified ads of *Dark Shadows* paraphernalia. Clark, a longtime *Dark Shadows* fan, is also the author of eight volumes of the *Dark Shadows Questions and Answers Book* and several *Dark Shadows* novels: *Resolutions in Time*, *Reunion*, *Retribution*, and *Revelations*. Clark was also one of the cofounders of the Dark Shadows Festival.

Through the 1990s, numerous fan clubs and small press publishing endeavors thrived in the *Dark Shadows* fan world. Dark Shadows over Oklahoma was a *Dark Shadows* fan club founded by Brett Hargrove and later led by Letha Roberts. The group gathered monthly, and Roberts edited *The Graveyard Gazette*, the club's newsletter. Harmony Road Press was a small publishing company founded in 1992 specializing in *Dark Shadows* books and periodicals. It was headed by Connie Jonas.

Among its publications were *Christmas in Collinsport*, a seasonal anthology of pictures, poetry, and prose; Anna Shock's collected short stories, *Shadowed Reflections*; and the novels *Masks and Facades* and *A Matter of Trust*, both by Jonas. Jonas also edited *The Music Box*, a *Dark Shadows* fanzine named for the music box owned by *Dark Shadows* character Josette. *The Music Box* featured fiction, art, poetry, and fan news. In 1992 the press announced publication of a single-issue fanzine edited by Travis McKnight, *The Lara Zine*, built around the *Dark Shadows* actress Lara Parker, who played the witch Angélique. Connie Jonas is a member of the **Collinsport Players**, a fan-founded dramatic group that presents skits at the annual Dark Shadows Festival. In 1993, Harmony Road Press published an anthology of scripts of the group's original productions, *The Collinsport Players Companion*, edited by Jeff Thompson and Jonas.

Lone Gull Press was founded in Massachusetts in 1984 by author Lori Paige and artist Jane Lach to publish materials for *Dark Shadows* fans. Their first product was *The Secret of the Chalice*, a fanzine that appeared that same year. They followed with a series of fanzines, including *Tales of Hoffman*, a one-shot publication built around the *Dark Shadows* character Julia Hoffman, and *Cauldron*, of which six issues appeared in 1987 and 1988. In 1988 Paige wrote *Balm in Gilead*. *The Gates of Hell* is the name of a full-length novel that provided the substance for the fanzine of the same name. In addition, Lone Gull published Sharon Wisdom's *Love's Pale Shadow* (1992).

The Long Island Dark Shadows Society was a *Dark Shadows* fan club founded in 1988 by Steven C. Schumacher and Cindy Avitabile Conroy. While active, the club held five meetings each year, which included screenings of *Dark Shadows* videos and discussions of various *Dark Shadows* topics. In 1993 the society reported approximately twenty-five members. The New England Dark Shadows Society was founded in the early

1990s by Ron Janick. The Society held monthly meetings at which *Dark Shadows* videos were screened followed by discussions related to *Dark Shadows*. Also among its activities was an annual visit to Seaview Terrace in Newport, Rhode Island, the house used for exterior shots of Collinwood, the Collins family home, in the 1966–1971 television series. The society published a fanzine titled *Widow's Hill Quarterly*.

The Oregon Dark Shadows Society was founded in 1991 by Connie Jonas, a long-time and active *Dark Shadows* fan, who also edited *The Music Box*, an independent fanzine published by her company, Harmony Road Press. In 1993, the club reported about a dozen members. It gathered monthly to screen video releases of *Dark Shadows* episodes, share fandom gossip, engage in dramatic readings, hold trivia contests, and plan for upcoming *Dark Shadows* events such as the annual Dark Shadows Festival. The group joined the effort that brought the SCI-FI Channel to the Portland area cable system in 1992. The club also published a monthly newsletter, *News & Notes*. Many of the members of the earlier *Dark Shadows* club in Seattle affiliated with the Oregon society.

The Pittsburgh Dark Shadows Fan Club was founded in 1987 for fans of *Dark Shadows* in southwestern Pennsylvania and the nearby counties in Ohio and West Virginia. Although *Shadows of the Night* was used as the name of two different vampire fanzines, founder Dan Silvio edited the one that has served as the official publication of the Pittsburgh Dark Shadows Fan Club. Silvio began *Shadows of the Night* in 1987 and it has continued to the present, both as a printed fanzine and as an e-newsletter. *Shadows of the Night* may be contacted at sotnight@aol.com.

The Wyndcliffe Dark Shadows Society was founded in 1988 by May Sutherland. It began as an effort to publish a newsletter, *Wyndcliffe Watch*, for *Dark Shadows* fans. However, with the help of Sutherland's friends Jane Lach and Lori Paige, founders of Lone Gull Press, the newsletter grew into a full-sized fanzine with the first issue, which appeared in October 1988. The society soon followed. Medallion Press is the society's publishing arm.

Sutherland was also the president of the Seattle/Tacoma Dark Shadows Fan Club, a position she held from March 1989 to May 1992. The club met monthly and lobbied the local public television station to pick up the syndicated *Dark Shadows* reruns.

After KTPS (now KBTC) began carrying the show, the club held fundraisers to support the station. Meanwhile, Sutherland also became head of the West Washington chapter of the Sci-Fi Channel Fan Club.

In 1992, the local club stopped meeting. However, the continuing society and its associated fanzine grew to approximately 250 member/subscribers and includes people from across North America, plus members in Turkey and Japan.

May Sutherland has authored one novel, *Sins of the Fathers*, a *Dark Shadows* story that has the vampire Barnabas Collins under attack from another vampire running loose at his Collinwood estate.

Like all fan communities, clubs and periodicals come and go, and among the defunct fans organizations are Alternate Shadows, a *Dark Shadows* fan club headquartered in Ithaca, New York. It was founded and led by Patrick Garrison and his wife Josette, who also edited a fanzine called *The Parallel Times*. In 1983, 1984, and 1985, the group sponsored the Manhattan Shadows convention, which included a blood donation con-

test. The prize was a dinner in New York City with Jonathan Frid, the actor who originally played the vampire Barnabas Collins in the *Dark Shadows* series. The club disbanded in 1988, and the fanzine was discontinued soon afterward.

The Friends of Dark Shadows began in 1983 under the leadership of Sharida Rizzuto as the New Orleans branch of the International Dark Shadows Society. Rizzuto, who had a broad experience in fanzine publishing, published four issues of *Inside Dark Shadows*. Rizzuto and the New Orleans group then separated from the International Dark Shadows Society and reorganized as the Friends of Dark Shadows. She issued a new fanzine, *The Collinwood Record* (seven issues), and a newsletter, *The Collinwood Journal* (three issues). She was assisted by associate editor Sidney J. Dragon, the group's vice-president. The Friends of Dark Shadows and its periodicals were discontinued in 1987. Rizzuto, however, continued to publish *Dark Shadows* news in another publication, *The Vampire Journal*, now a publication for the Realm of the Vampire organization.

The Dark Shadows Society of Milwaukee was a short-lived *Dark Shadows* fan club founded in 1986 by Lynn L. Gerdes and others in southeastern Wisconsin. The club met for discussions and screenings of *Dark Shadows* episodes. It disbanded in 1989. The Houston Dark Shadows Society was a *Dark Shadows* fan club founded in 1986 by Parker Riggs. It served primarily *Dark Shadows* fans in the Greater Houston, Texas, area, although its membership grew to include fans around the country. The society published *Lone Star Shadows*, a quarterly newsletter edited by Riggs, featuring news of *Dark Shadows* fandom. It ran for 20 issues. Both the club and the magazine were discontinued in 1991.

The Twenty-first Century: As of 2009, *Dark Shadows* fandom is represented by the Central Florida Dark Shadows Fan Club (http://www.cfdsfanclub.com/); *Shadowgram*, the periodical published by Marcy Robin (P.O. Box X, 1766 Temple City, CA 91780-7766); the online *Dark Shadows Journal* (http://www.collinwood.net/); the late longtime fan Craig Hamrick's *Dark Shadows* Online Website (http://www.darkshadowsonline.com/); the *Dark Shadows* DVD Club (http://www.darkshadowsdvd.com/); and, most importantly, the Official *Dark Shadows* Fan Club, which sponsors the annual *Dark Shadows* convention (P. O. Box 92, Maplewood, NJ 07040). Almost legendary *Dark Shadows* fan Marcy Robin also publishes the *Official Dark Shadows Newsletter*.

Sources:

Christmas in Collinsport. Portland, OR: Harmony Road Press, 1992. 45 pp.

Clark, Dale. *Resolutions in Time*. Temple City, CA: Pentagram Press, 1983. 66 pp.

————. *Dark Shadows Questions and Answers*. 8 vols. Dallas: Old House Publishing, 1990–93.

————. *Reunion*. Dallas: Old House Publishing, 1991. 98 pp.

————. *Retribution*. Dallas: Old House Publishing, 1992. 88 pp.

————. *Revelations*. Dallas: Old House Publishing, 1993.

Dresser, Norine. *American Vampires: Fans, Victims, Practitioners*. New York: W. W. Norton & Company, 1989. 255 pp.

"DS Festival Celebrates 10th Anniversary." *Shadowgram* 63 (January 1993): 2–3.

The Introduction of Barnabas. Maplewood, NJ: Dark Shadows Festival, 1988. 144 pp.

Jonas, Connie, and Jeff Thompson, eds. *A Matter of Trust*. Portland, OR: HarmonyRoad Press, 1991. 217 pp.

———— *The Collinsport Players Companion*. Vol. 1. Portland, OR: HarmonyRoad Press, 1993. 108 pp.

———. *Masks and Facades*. Portland, OR: HarmonyRoad Press, 1993. 387 pp.

The Lara Zine. Portland, OR: HarmonyRoad Press, 1993.

Paige, Lori. *Balm in Gilead*. North Riverside, IL: Pandora Publications, 1988.

Resch, Kathleen, ed. *Decades*. Santa Clara, CA: Pentagram Press, 1982.

———, and Marcy Robin. *Beginnings: The Island of Ghosts*. Temple City, CA: The World of Dark Shadows, 1982. 167 pp.

———. *The Dark Shadows Concordance 1840*. Temple City, CA: Pentagram Press, 1987.

———. *The Dark Shadows Concordance 1970 Parallel Time*. Temple City, CA: The World of Dark Shadows, 1988.

———. *The Dark Shadows Concordance 1795*. Temple City, CA: The World of Dark Shadows, 1989.

———. *The Dark Shadows Concordance 1968*. 2 vols. Temple City, CA: The World of Dark Shadows, 1989; 1990.

———. *Dark Shadows in the Afternoon*. East Meadow, NY: Image Publishing, 1991. 109 pp.

Robin, Marcy. *From the Shadows… Marcy Robin*. Ed. by Kathleen Resch. Temple City, CA: Pentagram Press, 1986. 85 pp.

Shock, Anna H. *Shadowed Reflections*. Portland, OR: HarmonyRoad Press, 1993. 40 pp.

Sutherland, May. *Sins of the Fathers*. Tacoma, WA: Medallion Press, 1993.

Thompson, Jeff. "An Overview of Dark Shadows Fandom." *The Southern Fandom Confederation Bulletin* No. 8 (January 1991). 4 pp.

———. "A History of the East Coast Dark Shadows Festivals: 1983–1993." In *The Dark Shadows Festival Memory Book, 1983–1993*. Ed. by Jim Pierson. Maplewood, NJ: Dark Shadows Festival, 1994. 7 pp.

———. *Television Horrors of Dan Curtis: Dark Shadows, The Night Stalker, and Other Productions, 1966–2006*. Jefferson, NC: McFarland, 2009. 200 pp.

Wilson, Marcy. *Crazy Vein*. Tacoma, WA: Medallion Press, 1994.

Wisdom, Sharon. *Love's Pale Shadow*. Sunderland, MA: Lone Gull Press, 1992.

Dark Shadows Festival *see:* Dark Shadows Fandom

Dark Shadows over Oklahoma *see:* Dark Shadows Fandom

Dark Shadows Society of Milwaukee *see:* Dark Shadows Fandom

Davanzati, Giuseppe (1665–1755)

Giuseppe Davanzati, an archbishop of the Roman Catholic Church and vampirologist, was born on August 29, 1665, in Bari, Italy. He first attended the Jesuit College in Bari but left at the age of fifteen to enter the University of Naples. Three years later, his parents having both passed away, he entered the University of Bologna with the idea of becoming a priest. He was a distinguished student in science and mathematics, and upon completion of his course of studies commenced a period of travel using Paris as his home base. At some point he was ordained to the priesthood by the bishop of Salerno. Soon after the turn of the century, Pope Clement XI called him back to Italy to become treasurer of the Sanctuary of St. Nicolas at Bari. Several years later he was entrusted with the particularly difficult and sensitive task of representing the pope in Vienna before the throne of Emperor Charles VI. His success was rewarded by his elevation to the episcopacy as archbishop of Trani, a town north of Bari. He served that post

with distinction until 1745 when Pope Benedict XIV named the aged archbishop patriarch of Alexandria.

Davanzati's years as an archbishop coincided with waves of vampirism reported around Europe in the first half of the eighteenth century. However, he did not encounter the subject until 1738, when he was brought into discussions initiated at the request of Cardinal Schtrattembach, the bishop of Olmütz (**Germany**), who wanted the church's advice. Schtrattembach had been presented official reports on outbreaks of vampirism in various parts of Germany beginning in 1720, highlighted by the account of **Arnold Paul** in Serbia in 1831. Davanzati spent the next few years studying these reports and other pertinent texts, and in 1744 published his *Dissertazione sopra I Vampiri*. Davanzati concluded that the vampire reports were human fantasies—though possibly of a diabolical **origin**. A major part of Davanzati's argument centered on the tendency of the vampire to appear among the illiterate and lower-class peasants—people who were believed to be more easily deceived by such appearances than those who were educated. Davanzati emerged as the leading Italian authority on vampires. His work was reprinted in 1789, and his opinion came to be accepted by most people in power, both within the church and in political control. However, his work was soon overshadowed by the treatise of his learned French colleague, **Dom Augustin Calmet**. Calmet's scholarly work, published just two years after Davanzati's, did not support Davanzati's harsh conclusion. Through Calmet, the subject of vampirism reached both the intellectual community and the policymakers of Europe in ways Davanzati's dismissal of the topic could not. Davanzati died on February 16, 1755.

Sources:

Davanzati, Giuseppe. *Dissertazione sopre I Vampiri*. Naples, Italy: Presso i fratelli Raimondi, 1744. Rept. Bari, Italy: BESA Editrice, 1998. 159 pp. (The first reprint since 1744.)

Imbruglio, Girolamo. *Naples in the Eighteenth Century: The Birth and Death of a Nation State*. Cambridge: Cambridge University Press, 2000. 220 pp.

Introvigne, Massimo. *La strippe di Dracula: Indagine sul vampirismo dall'antichita ai nostri giorni*. Milan: Arnoldo Mondadori Editore, 1997. 474 pp.

Summers, Montague. *The Vampire: His Kith and Kin*. Rept. New York: University Books, 1960. 356 pp.

⸙ de Lioncourt, Lestat ⸙

Lestat de Lioncourt was the central character in the "Vampire Chronicles", several novels by **Anne Rice** that have become key works in the revival of interest in vampires in the 1990s. In the first two novels treating Lestat, Rice gave a detailed description of his two centuries of existence, except for the several decades of childhood and youth before he became a vampire. His physical appearance was summarized in the opening paragraphs of her second vampire book, *The Vampire Lestat* (1985). He was six feet tall with thick blond hair. His eyes were gray (not red) and easily picked up blue or violet from the environment. He had a very expressive face capable of conveying his wide range of strong, even exaggerated emotions, with a mouth that seemed to be a little too big for his face. His skin was white and had a slightly reflective quality. It changed noticeably while he was feeding. When he was hungry, his skin was tight with his veins protruding. After feeding, it appeared more normal, and Lestat had little trouble passing among "normal" humans. The most striking aspect of his physical appearance were his **fingernails**, which looked like glass.

Elsewhere, Rice revealed that Lestat, like all vampires, experienced a significant increase in **strength** from his human form. He developed a pair of canine-like **fangs**. He had some unusual abilities, both telepathic force and **hypnotic power,** but could not change into animal forms (a **bat** or wolf, for instance). He could still see himself in a **mirror** but lost the ability to engage in normal human sex and hence could not procreate. He normally slept in a **coffin.** An atheist before his **transformation,** Lestat had no problem with holy symbols or being in consecrated places. Traditionally, **sunlight** and **fire** hurt vampires, but Lestat communicated his doubts that they could ultimately kill him. He even believed that a **stake** in the heart had little effect.

Lestat's Life: When Lestat first appeared in *Interview with the Vampire* (1976), he was in **New Orleans.** However, his story really began (in *The Vampire Lestat*) in **France** around 1760 during the reign of Louis XVI and Marie Antoinette. Lestat was about 20 years old, the youngest son in a royal family whose estate was in the Auvergne, in rural France. The family was relatively poor and had no money for their sons to attain proper vocational training. Lestat wanted to escape this life and go to Paris. Shortly after finally realizing his dream, he was kidnaped from his sleeping quarters by a vampire named Magnus. Magnus turned

A graveyard set from the movie *Interview with the Vampire.*

Lestat into a vampire and then forced him to oversee the elder vampire's apparent death. In return, Lestat inherited Magnus's fortune.

The first phase of Lestat's vampiric existence centered on Paris. It included a visit by his dying mother, Gabrielle, whom he turned into a vampire. She took to the nocturnal life well, and together they challenged the vampire community of Paris, which had trouble accepting their new way of integrating into human life. After this intense encounter, they traveled around Europe as Lestat sought a senior vampire named Marius. Meanwhile, France was rising in revolt (1789). Lestat's family estate was mobbed and his brothers killed. His father escaped to New Orleans. He and his mother parted and he buried himself in the ground to rest.

A short time later Marius found and revived him and related the account of the beginnings of their lineage of vampirism. Marius's account took Lestat back into ancient Egypt, long before the first pyramid. Egypt was ruled by a couple, Akasha and Enkil. For the good of their people, they were forced to encounter a demon and became vampires. Marius had brought them out of Egypt to save them from total destruction. They were alive, but sat motionless. Lestat had a private encounter with the pair, including sharing **blood** with Akasha, who moved for the first time in several centuries.

Lestat then left Marius and sailed to Louisiana in 1789. In New Orleans he met Louis, whom he turned into a vampire; he wanted Louis's plantation as a home for his father. Lestat also found Claudia, a child whom he turned into a vampire. She could grow mentally but not physically, and her situation became the focus of intense conflict. After several decades of adventures and fighting, Louis and Claudia attempted to kill Lestat.

Lestat was hurt but not killed. He could not get help from the old vampire community in Paris and lived out the nineteenth century in seclusion. In 1929 he buried himself again and had no motivation to awaken until 1984, when he was attracted by the sounds of a rock band, Satan's Night Out. He arose and introduced himself to the group. They handed him a copy of *Interview with a Vampire*, Louis's story of their life together. He reacted by writing his own autobiography, published as *The Vampire Lestat*, the same name adopted by the band. Concurrently, he found success as a rock idol. As a rock performer, he could appear in public as a vampire; people accepted it as part of his public persona.

The sound of Lestat the rocker soon drifted into the frozen northland where Marius had eventually taken Akasha and Enkil. In 1985, Akasha awoke in response to the **music**. She killed Enkil and left the sanctuary to dominate the world and create a new Eden inhabited primarily by a select group of females. She intended to kill off most of the males, though Lestat was a favored individual. She initiated the killing almost immediately, but as Halloween approached, her activity increased.

Lestat had a concert set for San Francisco. Many of the living vampires headed for the concert. After the concert, Akasha forced Lestat to accompany her on one of her massacres. They then journeyed to Sonoma County, California, for what became a final confrontation. Akasha was killed, and her threat ended. The surviving vampires, including Lestat, went to Miami for some rest and relaxation.

In the meantime, Lestat had learned of one David Talbot, the aging leader of the occult research group, the **Talamasca**. His organization had taken an interest in vampires and had sent a researcher to New Orleans to research the truth of the story recounted by Louis in *Interview with a Vampire*. Lestat traveled to **London** to meet Talbot and the unusual pair became friends, though Talbot refused Lestat's offer to become a vampire. While developing his relationship with Talbot, Lestat received an offer from an unusual individual, Raglan James, who wanted to swap bodies with Lestat. Talbot advised against it, but Lestat was intrigued with James and agreed to a temporary exchange. Too late, he learned that James planned to assume his identity and life.

Lestat enlisted Talbot's assistance to track James, and once they found him, they devised a scheme to force a new transfer. In the process Lestat got his body back and Talbot found himself in James's body. In his new relatively young body, Talbot reconsidered Lestat's offer of a vampire's life. The widely traveled Lestat's next adventure took him into the supernatural realms of heaven and hell. Guided by the devil, he found himself confronting the nature of evil, the significance of Christ's life, death, and resurrection, and the often-bloody history of the Church. He traveled backward in time to watch Christ's passion and crucifixion, including the legendary moment when a young woman, Veronica, wiped the sweat from Christ's face and his visage miraculously appeared on her veil. Lestat responded by drinking Christ's blood, stealing the veil, and fleeing back to earth. Memnoch, the devil, tried to prevent him and in their struggle, Lestat lost his left eye.

Lestat returned to Earth where, in Manhattan, he met up with several of his old acquaintances. Talbot listened to him recount the story of his adventure. Dora, the daugh-

ter of one of his **victims** who happened to be a televangelist, took the veil and showed it to her audience as a miraculous sign. Lestat eventually found his way back to New Orleans where he encountered one of the ancient vampires who returned the eye he had lost. He knew that his adventure had been real, but he could not explain the meaning of it all.

As Lestat's story continued in Rice's "Vampire Chronicles", the books themselves became part of the vampire mythology. The first book, *Interview with the Vampire,* was published as Louis's memoirs of Lestat. Lestat then countered with his version of the story in *The Vampire Lestat,* his "autobiography." In the third volume, **The Queen of the Damned** (1988), the modern Lestat had to deal with the situation of becoming a public figure when his story becomes known. *The Tale of the Body Thief* (1992) recounted the story of his adventure with Raglan James, and *Memnoch the Devil* of his adventures in the supernatural realms. After *Memnoch,* Rice announced that he had left her, and that she would not, at least for the near future, be writing about him again.

As a character Lestat caught the imagination of a new generation of vampire enthusiasts in the 1990s. He successfully combined the popular image of the vampire derived from books and movies (e.g., **Lord Ruthven** and **Dracula**) and his own distinct personality. Rice described that uniqueness in terms of androgyny, implying the movement away from culture-bound gender designations and the development of a whole personality that combines strong elements of female and male traits regardless of physiology. In practice, given the intense gender assignments common in Western culture, androgyny is often expressed by a person adopting obvious attributes or expressions of the other sex. Thus, women may adopt male hairstyles, and men may wear feminine dress and makeup. More significantly, androgyny may lead people to develop aspects of their personality that have generally been assigned by the culture to the other sex. Thus, women may develop their assertiveness and men their ability to express their feelings. The current **gothic** subculture has taken the lead in living out an androgynous lifestyle, which is largely owing to Lestat.

Although emphasizing Lestat's androgynous nature, Lestat fans have also emphasized their attraction to his embodiment of typically male attributes. He is a man of strong will and action. He lifted himself up by his own bootstraps; given only a minimal knowledge by his vampiric creator, he taught himself to be a vampire. His discoveries left him with little need of traditions, and he made his own way in the world according to his own rules. "My strength, my refusal to give up, those are the only components of my heart and soul which I can truly identify," he definitively states in *The Tale of the Body Thief*. He faced the problem of his vampiric situation, a condition for which he did not ask, and which imposed a blood thirst upon him. He had to kill to survive, which was evil by human standards. His evolved ethic, though infused with self-interest, led to the choice to feed on the worst of humankind and thus find some moral justification in the necessary search for food.

Lestat in the 1990s: Lestat's central role in the 1990's revival of interest in vampires is illustrated by the numerous places he can be found. He inspired the creation of a gothic rock band, Lestat; a role-playing game, **Vampire: The Masquerade**; and Anne Rice's Vampire Lestat Fan Club. His story has appeared on audiotape and in **comic books,** has been translated into a number of languages (from Romanian to Japanese), and was finally brought to the motion picture screen in 1994.

Lestat in the Twenty-First Century: After Memnock, Rice turned her attention to developing the story of other vampires such as Armand, Pandora, and Victorio. While Lestat was never far from the storyline, he returned to the center of attention in *Blood Canticle* (2003). This book also integrated his story with that of the Mayfairs, a family of witches about which Rice had written several books. In the story, Mona Mayfair is in love with Lestat's close friend, the vampire Tarquin "Quinn" Blackwood. She is, however, dying of a wasting disease. In what she believes is her last hour, she visits her lover's home, where Lestat turns her into a vampire. He also falls in love with the already married Rowan Mayfair.

As a vampire Mona has great strength and manifests anger over the child she bore that had caused her illness. The child is a Taltos, a member of a supernatural race that once inhabited parts of the Scottish highlands. The child has disappeared, and Lestat promises to find it if it is still alive. It is finally found on a remote island, where the Taltos now reside. As the story concludes, the remaining Taltos move to New Orleans where Rowan's husband runs a large medical center, and where they can survive in a relatively happy family situation. Mona and Quinn are able to resume their relationship. In the end, Rowan asks Lestat to turn her, but he refuses.

Blood Canticle was the last of the vampire novels written by Rice, but Lestat has lived on in the movies (*Queen of the Damned* appeared in 2002), and singer Elton John wrote the music for the 2006 broadway production of *Lestat the Musical*.

Sources:

Ramsland, Katherine. *The Vampire Companion: The Official Guide to Anne Rice's The Vampire Chronicles*. New York: Ballantine Books, 1993. 507 pp. Rev. ed.: 1995. 577 pp.

Rice, Anne. *The Vampire Lestat*. New York: Alfred A. Knopf, 1985. 481 pp. Rept. New York: Ballantine Books, 1986. 550 pp.

————. *Interview with the Vampire*. New York: Alfred A. Knopf, 1986. 448 pp. Rept. New York: Ballantine Books, 1987. 346 pp.

————. *The Queen of the Damned*. New York: Alfred A. Knopf, 1988. 448 pp. Rept. New York: Ballantine Books, 1989. 491 pp.

————. *Tale of the Body Thief*. New York: Alfred A. Knopf, 1992. 430 pp. Rept. New York: Ballantine Books, 1993. 435 pp.

————. *Memnoch the Devil*. New York: Alfred A. Knopf, 1994. 354 pp. Rept. New York: Ballantine Books, 1995. 434 pp.

————. *Blood Canticle*. New York: Alfred A. Knopf, 2003. 360 pp.

de Villenueva, Sebastian

The vampire that appeared in a series of five novels by **Les Daniels**, Sebastian de Villenueva originated in fifteenth-century **Spain**. According to the story line, first presented in *The Black Castle* (1978), Sebastian participated in the siege of Malaga in 1487, part of the effort to drive the Moors from Spain. He was killed when a cannon exploded in his face. His body was returned to his castle in northeastern Spain and entombed in a crypt. His brother, still a young man at the time of the siege, had become a monk and eventually was named inquisitor for his home territory.

In the days following his accident, Sebastian went through a set of (undisclosed) "rituals" that made him a vampire. From the cannon explosion, he retained a scar that ran down the left side of his face. He took advantage of his brother's position and regularly visited the cells of the Inquisition where he fed among the prisoners. He claimed that during the first nine years of his life he had never taken a life.

Sebastian was a vampire in the traditional sense, with the familiar variety of powers and limitations. He could transform himself into a **bat** or become **mist**, a form in which he could pass through the smallest crack. He was also subject to the second death: **sunlight, fire,** or a **stake** through the heart; in addition he needed to **sleep** on **native soil.** At the end of *The Black Castle*, Sebastian died in a fire he built in front of his castle. However, his skull was not consumed in the flames and, once severed from his body, rolled into the castle moat. It was later retrieved and taken to **Mexico**, where he was brought back to life to begin a new series of adventures. Aligned with an Aztec priestess, he ended his Mexican sojourn when she transformed him into pure spirit. He reappeared in revolutionary **France** (*Citizen Vampire*, 1981) when an alchemist brought him back from spirit. Sebastian returned once more to the spirit realm, only to assume a body in nineteenth-century England (*Yellow Fog*, 1986) and **India** (*No Blood Spilled*, 1991).

Sources:

Daniels, Les. *The Black Castle*. New York: Charles Scribner's Sons, 1978. Rept. New York: Berkley Books, 1979. 232 pp.

———. *Citizen Vampire*. New York: Charles Scribner's Sons, 1981. 197 pp.

———. *The Silver Skull*. New York: Charles Scribner's Sons, 1970. Rept. New York: Ace Books, 1983. 234 pp.

———. *Yellow Fog*. New York: Tor, Donald M. Grant, 1986. Rev. ed.: New York: Tor, 1988. 294 pp.

———. *No Blood Spilled*. New York: Tor, 1991. 218 pp.

❰ Deane, Hamilton (1880?–1958) ❱

Hamilton Deane, the playwright and director who brought *Dracula* to the stage, was born near Dublin. His family owned an estate adjacent to that of **Bram Stoker's** father, and his mother had been acquainted with Bram Stoker in her youth. Deane entered the theater as a young man, first appearing in 1899 with the Henry Irving Vacation Company (Stoker worked for Henry Irving in London for many years). Even before he formed his own troupe in the early 1920s, Deane had been thinking about bringing *Dracula* to the stage. Unable to find a scriptwriter to take on the project, he wrote it himself in a four-week period of inactivity while he was suffering with a severe cold. He also contacted Florence Stoker, Bram's widow, and negotiated a deal for the dramatic rights.

In order to more easily stage the detailed story, he dropped the book's beginning and ending sections that occurred in **Transylvania.** He transformed **Quincey P. Morris** into a female to accommodate the gender makeup of his company at the time. He also recast the more sinister **Dracula** of the novel into a representative of cultured continental royalty capable of fitting into British society. Deane was the first to dress Dracula in evening clothes and a cape (an **opera** cloak).

Deane submitted his play for government approval in 1924. The license was issued on August 5, but censors insisted that one scene be altered. The death of Dracula at the hands of the men had to be changed so that the hammering of the **stake** was not actu-

Playwright and director Hamilton Deane.

ally shown. Instead, the men were to gather around the **coffin** in such a manner as to block the action from the audience.

When the play opened in Derby, England, Deane assumed the role of **Abraham Van Helsing**, Dracula's archenemy. Fearing that London critics would pan his play, Deane stayed away for three years, but finally risked an opening there on February 14, 1927, at the Little Theatre. Though the reviews were largely unfavorable, the audiences filled the house each night. By the end of the summer he had moved the production to the larger Duke of York's Theatre. Following up on a casual remark by a reporter, Deane pulled off an almost legendary publicity stunt. He hired a nurse to be present at each performance to assist any viewers who reacted badly to the play by fainting or taking ill.

Deane's desire to return to the countryside led to a brief break between himself, Florence Stoker, and one of his backers, Harry Warburton. The split led to Warburton's commissioning, with Stoker's approval, a second version of the play (which opened in September 1927), but proved unsuccessful and soon closed. Deane kept the London company running, but at one point had three different groups performing the play at various locations in the countryside.

People were known to memorize entire scenes and to become so involved with the play that they shouted out lines before the actors could deliver them. In 1927 Horace Liveright bought the American dramatic rights from Florence Stoker and hired newspaperman **John L. Balderston** to edit it for the New York stage. Balderston's editing constituted a full rewriting, though Deane's name has been retained on the publication and on the various revisions of the Balderston version. The **Universal Pictures** movie with **Bela Lugosi** merely increased the demand in England for Deane to keep his production of the play alive.

In 1939 Deane played the role of Dracula for the first time. Later that year he brought his troupe to the Lyceum Theatre, where Stoker had worked when he wrote the play and where he had staged a one-time-only reading of his work in order to establish his dramatic rights. After a brief run of *Dracula* and then of *Hamlet,* the Lyceum closed its doors permanently. During one performance at the Lyceum, Lugosi, who was in the audience, rushed on stage at the close of the play to embrace Deane.

Deane's last performance as Dracula was in 1941 at St. Helen's, Lancashire. After his death late in 1958, his version of the play largely fell into disuse, with most revivalists preferring the Balderston rewrite.

Sources:

Deane, Hamilton, and John L. Balderston. *Dracula: The Vampire Play in Three Acts.* New York: Samuel French, 1927. 113 pp. Various editions.

Dracula (The Original 1931 Shooting Script). Atlantic City, NJ: Magic Image Filmbooks, 1990.

Glut, Donald F. *The Dracula Book*. Metuchen, NJ: Scarecrow Press, 1975. 388 pp.

Skal, David J. *Hollywood Gothic: The Tangled Web of Dracula from Novel to Stage to Screen*. New York: W. W. Norton & Company, 1990. 242 pp.

————, ed. *Dracula: The Ultimate, Illustrated Edition of the World-Famous Vampire Play*. New York: St. Martin's Press, 1993. 153 pp.

Dearg-dul *see:* Ireland, Vampires in

Death of Vampires *see:* Destroying the Vampire

Decapitation

One of the surest and most common means of **destroying the vampire** and making sure it did not return to a semblance of life was to cut off its head. This was clearly illustrated in **Bram Stoker**'s novel, *Dracula*. **Arthur Holmwood, Lucy Westenra**'s fiance, and Lucy's other friends could not bring themselves to cut off Lucy's head after her death. They consented only when Dr. **Abraham Van Helsing** demonstrated to them that Lucy had joined the undead. He and Arthur carried out the decapitation. Van Helsing did not, however, decapitate the three vampire **women** in **Castle Dracula**; they disintegrated before his eyes after he staked them. In like measure, **Dracula** disintegrated after **Jonathan Harker** and **Quincey P. Morris** stabbed him.

Carmilla, the vampire in **Sheridan Le Fanu**'s tale, lost her head as part of the process of being killed, thus continuing the trend in European folklore. Severing the head to destroy a vampire was common throughout **Germany** and Eastern Europe. When a vampire was reported in a village, and its identity determined, the body would be disinterred. Commonly, it then was impaled on a **stake** and its head cut off. Decapitation prevented the head from directing the body in its wanderings. In northern Europe (**Poland** and Germany), the head might be placed between the knees or under the arm. There also were reports of the head being placed under the body and buried separately, so that it could not be returned to the neck and reconnected. It was also possible that the vampire could return with the head held in its arms. In some cultures, the exact instrument for severing the head, a shovel or a sword, was prescribed.

As the vampire was dramatized, the process of decapitation was, as a whole, left behind. It was a much too indelicate means of death to present to a theater audience or show on a movie screen. Nevertheless, it was not forgotten. In the reworking of the vampire legend by **Chelsea Quinn Yarbro**, her hero **St. Germain** feared only two things that would cause the "true death"—**fire** and the severing of the spine (which decapitation would accomplish). In *Blood Games* (1979), he faked the death of his love Olivia as part of a plot to free her from the clutches of her husband. After vampirizing her, she died, but was revived by St. Germain and his helpers. He gave strict instructions to be followed so that the "true death" would not overtake her.

The movies from **Hammer Films** raised horror films to a new level with their depiction of flowing **blood** in full color. As society became more permissive in the last generation, directors responded to audiences' thirst for blood, developing the so-called

"splatter" movies. In this atmosphere, decapitation returned to the vampire myth, not in the traditional manner, but as the climax of a fight or similar intense interaction between two characters. However, in spite of splatter movies, decapitation has remained a rare occurrence, at least for vampires.

In the television series ***Buffy the Vampire Slayer***, decapitation was rarely used, as vampires immediately turned to dust upon dying. Thus, while a vampire might be killed by decapitation, staking was the overwhelmingly preferred method. It was, of course, not possible to copy the model in Dracula of staking a vampire and subsequently decapitating it as further means of preventing its future return. In the **"Twilight"** book series, decapitation still offers the possibility of a vampire's return. The chosen method is thus complete dismemberment and a scattering of body parts in dfferent locations, or even better, cremating them.

Denmark, Vampires in *see:* Scandinavia, Vampires in

The Desert Island Dracula Library

The Desert Island Dracula Library is a specialized line of titles from the British publishing company, Desert Island Books, owned by **Dracula** scholar **Clive Leatherdale**. While Desert Island is by no means limited to Dracula and vampire studies, it has been a special interest of Leatherdale who has himself written several of the outstanding books on the novel *Dracula*. The aim of the Library is to:

- enhance the understanding of Dracula by adding to the critical works already published by the Dracula Library, which includes **Elizabeth Miller**'s *Dracula: The Shade and the Shadow*;
- increase the folkloric appreciation of vampirism by republishing early texts, to stand alongside **Dom Calmet's Treatise on Vampires and Revenants**;
- publish annotated editions of all **Bram Stoker**'s major works, in addition to the two editions already available: *Dracula Unearthed* and *The Jewel of Seven Stars*; and
- make available Stoker's hitherto unpublished works, most of which date from his early years.

Desert Island Books may be reached at http://www.desertislandbooks.com/. Volumes of the Desert Island Dracula Library are distributed in North America by Firebird Distributing (1945 P Street, Eureka, CA 95501). In the 1900s, Desert Island Books was very active in the publishing of material related to Dracula and vampires. Its last major Dracula publication was Elizabeth Miller's *Dracula Sense and Nonsense* in 2000.

Destroying the Vampire

Almost everywhere vampires have been seen as evil, monstrous creatures. Once a vampire was confirmed to be wandering in a neighborhood, people hastened to locate and destroy it. In the most famous vampire novel, *Dracula*, the lengthy process of destroying **Dracula** took up half the novel.

Dracula's death was presaged by the killing of **Lucy Westenra**, whom Dracula had turned into a vampire. Confronted in her crypt, the men who knew her in life put a **stake** through her heart, decapitated her, and filled her mouth with **garlic**. Later, in his speech to the men assembled to kill Dracula (chapter 18), Dr. **Abraham Van Helsing** informed them of the means of destroying vampires:

> … The branch of the wild rose on his **coffin** keep him so that he move not from it; a sacred **bullet** fired into the coffin kill him so that he be true dead, and as for the stake through him, we know already of its peace; or the cut off head that giveth rest. We have seen it with our eyes.

In the end, however, the men deviated from the formula. Dracula was killed with a Bowie knife plunged into his heart by **Quincey P. Morris**; **Jonathan Harker** then carried out the **decapitation**. His body then crumpled to **dust** as everyone watched. Among the sources he used for his novel, **Bram Stoker** referred to Emily Gerard's *The Land Beyond the Forest* as a major source of information on vampires. Concerning the killing of vampires, she had observed in her travels that the vampire:

> … will continue to suck the **blood** of other innocent persons till the spirit has been exorcised by opening the grave of the suspected person, and either driving a stake through the corpse, or else firing a pistol-shot into the coffin. To walk smoking round the grave on each anniversary of the death is also supposed to be effective in confining the vampire. In very obstinate cases of vampirism it is recommended to cut off the head, and replace it in the coffin with the mouth filled with garlic, or to extract the heart and burn it, stewing the ashes over the grave.

She noted further that it was a common practice to lay a thorny branch of the wild rose across the body at the time of burial to prevent a suspected vampire from leaving its coffin.

Folklore Traditions: In his treatment of the methods of destroying the vampire, Stoker reached back into the folklore of Eastern Europe to develop his own myth. While traditions concerning vampires varied widely on some issues, when it came to killing them, there was consensus across cultures from **Greece** and the southern **Slavic** lands to **Poland** and **Russia**. In eastern Europe, vampire activity would be traced to the graveyard and to a particular body, usually that of a recently deceased person, as the suspected vampire. The body would then be disinterred, examined for signs of vampiric activity (lifelike appearance, blood around the mouth), and a determination made that the person was indeed the vampire. Once the designation was made, there was a tendency to treat the corpse at two levels. First, steps

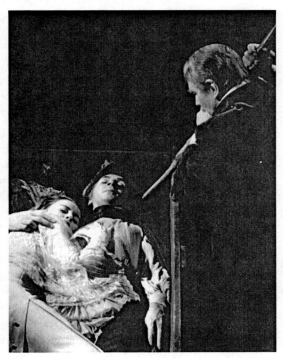

Perhaps the most popular way to destroy a vampire is to thrust a stake through the vampire's heart, as actor Frank Langella does in this 1979 version of *Dracula.*

would be taken to stop its vampiric activity by specific actions against the body. Among the least intrusive would be the firing of a **bullet** into the coffin.

In Eastern Orthodox countries, the local priest might repeat the services for the dead, which in effect would again dispatch the soul on its journey to the realm of the dead. If the coffin was opened, the suspected vampire's clothing might be nailed to the sides of the coffin (away from the mouth area). Commonly, however, the body would be mutilated in one of several ways. It could be staked (with different cultures using materials that varied from an iron stake to a hat pin or local woods). In most cultures the stake did not have to go through the heart and usually was put through the stomach area. In these cases, it was assumed that the stake would hold the body in the ground. At times the body would be turned face downward and then staked. If the stake did not work, the corpse would only dig itself deeper into the earth. Occasionally, the body might have been staked with a nail or pin even before it was buried; in that instance a subsequent opening of the grave would be followed immediately by more drastic activity.

Along with staking, decapitation was common. Among the Kashubian Poles, the severed head might be placed between the legs. If mutilating the body with a stake and decapitating it did not work, the last resort was to burn the body. There are few reports of vampire activity continuing after cremation. It was, of course, this mutilation and cremation of long-dead persons that moved the authorities to suppress belief in vampires in the eighteenth century. Through the early part of that century, the ruling powers not only were receiving accounts of vampire activity but also had to deal with complaints of families against hysterical townspeople who were mutilating the corpses of loved ones.

Thus the authorities, primarily Roman Catholic Austrians, were forced to take action against antivampire attacks on the graveyards. While edicts against mutilating bodies did not end belief in vampires (which persists to this day in some areas), they did slow the reports of vampires and spread skepticism.

The Fictional Vampire: Once the vampire became an object of fiction, its death frequently became the point of the story. Such was not the case in the beginning. Both **Samuel Taylor Coleridge** and **John Polidori**, who respectively wrote the first vampire poem and short story in English, left their vampires free to attack the next **victim**. Polidori did allow his vampire to be killed in quite normal ways by the bandits who attacked **Lord Ruthven** and his traveling companion, but he could always be revived by the light of the full **moon**. **Varney the Vampyre**, after what seemed like endless adventures, finally committed **suicide** by jumping into a volcano. Thus the current conventions concerning the death of vampires have to be traced to the story of "**Carmilla**". Drawing from the folkloric traditions, author **Sheridan Le Fanu** suggested that the vampire should be decapitated, staked, and then burned, and such was the fate of Carmilla. As noted previously, Stoker's characters saw the staking of the corpse as adequate, and thus did not advocate its burning.

The development of staking as a conventional means of destroying the vampire led to two important reinterpretations of the vampire myth. First, by emphasizing that the stake had to be driven into the heart rather than the stomach or back, a change in the myth occurred. The vampire no longer was pinned to the ground. The stake now attacked the heart, the organ that pumped the blood, and "the blood is the life." Second, the vampire, being seen as in some way immortal, could be brought back to life by pulling the stake from the chest.

Crucial to the development of the vampire myth was the movie *Nosferatu, Eine Symphonie des Garuens*. Director Freidrich Wilhelm Murnau, in altering the storyline of *Dracula*, created the idea that the vampire could be killed if a beautiful woman held his attention until dawn. The vampire could not return to his resting place and would be killed by the **sunlight**. The vampire's death in the dawn's light was one of the memorable scenes in the movie. This perspective on the vampire was an addition to the myth. Previously, while the vampire preferred the night, it was not limited to it. Its powers were enhanced during the evening, but Lord Ruthven, Varney, and Dracula all made daytime appearances. Folkloric vampires were nocturnal creatures, but the daylight merely protected the living from them.

There was no hint that daylight killed them. However, once suggested, the negative effects of sunlight became a common element in twentieth-century vampire stories. In the movie *The Mark of a Vampire*, **Bela Lugosi** disintegrated in the presence of sunlight. The effects of sunlight were used effectively in the *Horror of Dracula*, which climaxed as Abraham Van Helsing ripped the draperies from the wall of **Castle Dracula** and caught the vampire in the dawn's early light. **Frank Langella's** *Dracula* **(1979)** was impaled on a ship's hook and hoisted high into the sunlight. Lesser bits of

Drawing of Vlad the Impaler torturing his victims. Vlad is considered by some to be the "real" historical Dracula.

sunlight would do significant damage but not be fatal. In one episode of the **television** series *Forever Knight*, for example, a boy innocently opened a window, and the little beam of light falling on vampire Nick Knight's eyes temporarily blinded him. The **clan** of vampires in the movie *Near Dark*, while able to be active in daylight, received severe burns each time the sunlight penetrated their barriers of drapes and tinfoil.

Modern Vampires: As the myth has been restructured in the twentieth century, vampires face three fatal dangers: a stake in the heart, sunshine, or **fire**. Usually there is also the possibility of being revived by removal of the stake or by a magical ritual, and/or by adding blood to the ashes of someone who had died after being burned in the sun or by fire.

In the face of these assumptions, several prominent contemporary vampire writers have attempted to reinterpret the vampire tale. **Chelsea Quinn Yarbro** has written a series of novels concerning the vampire **St. Germain**. St. Germain was affected by the sun, but not fatally. However, there was the possibility of what was termed the "true death." The vampire would die if his spine was severed or if he was consumed in fire. Stakes could hurt, but unless they cut the spine, he would recover.

Anne Rice thoroughly and systematically demythologized the vampire myth. Her vampires were not affected by many of the traditional forces or objects (especially holy objects) that have plagued other vampires and reduced their powers. Though her vampires were nearly immortal, they could be killed by sunlight or by fire and the subsequent scattering of the ashes.

However, some vampires (those older and closer to Akasha in lineage) were somewhat immune to the sunlight. Rice's vampires also faced a threat over which they had little or no control and of which most were unaware. In Rice's world, vampires were created by the merger of a spirit that moved into Akasha, the first vampire. All vampires remained in some way tied to Akasha, hence whatever happened to her was passed on to them. Were she to be killed and the spirit driven out, all vampires would cease to be.

In the post-Rice era, playing with the vampire myth has become common. One popular variation has been to provide a motivation for the vampire hero/villain to become a daywalker, someone who is immune to the effects of sunlight. His ability to maneuver in daylight make the vampires hunted by the Marvel Comics hero and half-vampire **Blade** envious of him. Blade is, of course, a variation on the **dhampir**, a character in Slavic vampire lore who is the product of a human mother and vampire father, a hybrid child with the power to discern, hunt, and destroy vampires, regardless of the time of day. A *dhampir* is the also the hero in Rebecca York's 2007 novel, *Daywalker*. In 1999, Marvel villainess Baroness Blood, the spouse of **Baron Blood**, discovers a means to become a daywalker using the Holy Grail, and almost succeeds. At about the same time, daywalkers began to appear in Japanese animé/manga. In the popular children's series *Tsukuyomi Moon Phase,* the evil Count Kinkell is able to bend light around himself so it will not consume him. Daywalking vampires also appear in the animé/manga series *Vampire Princess Miyu, Negima,* and *Hellsing.*

In Season Four of the TV series **Buffy the Vampire Slayer**, Buffy is able briefly to realize her desire of a life with the vampire **Angel** when she gains possession of the Gem of Amarra and passes it on to him. A vampire wearing the ring can experience the sunlight unharmed. In the end, however, Angel smashes the ring and continues his business of slaying various denizen of the night. In the **"Twilight"** series of popular novels, the vampires are able to move about in daylight, but have moved to the rainy world of Forks, Washington, to escape the harmful effects of direct sunlight (which Edward Cullen plans to use in his suicide attempt in volume two, *New Moon* (2006).

Sources:

Dorff, Stephen. *Blade*. New York: HarperPaperbacks, 1998. 343 pp.

Glut, Donald F. *The Dracula Book*. Metuchen, NJ: Scarecrow Press, 1975. 388 pp.

Meyer, Stephenie. *New Moon*. Boston: Little, Brown Young Readers, 2006. 576 pp.

Perkowski, Jan L. *The Darkling: A Treatise on Slavic Vampirism*. Columbus, OH: Slavica Publishers, 1989. 174 pp.

Ramsland, Katherine. *The Vampire Companion*. New York: Ballantine Books, 1993. 508 pp.

Yarbro, Chelsea Quinn. *Hotel Transylvania*. New York: St. Martin's Press, 1978. 252 pp.

Dhampir

Gypsies believed that some vampires have an insatiable sexual appetite and will return from the grave to have sex with their widow or a young woman of their choosing. The vampire's continued visits could lead to the woman becoming pregnant. The product of such a union, usually a male, was called a *dhampir*. It was believed that the

dhampir had unusual powers for detecting and **destroying the vampire**—a most important ability. Some modern *dhampirs* among the Gypsies of Eastern Europe placed most of their value in their ability to locate the vampire, which was simply shot with a pistol if located outside of its grave. Some individuals believed to be *dhampirs* supplemented their income by hiring themselves out as **vampire hunters**. The *dhampir* was otherwise a normal member of the Gypsy community, though some people believed that a true *dhampir* possessed a slippery, jelly-like body and lived only a short life—a belief derived from the understanding that vampires have no bones. The powers of the *dhampir* could be passed to a male offspring, and ultimately through a family line. While vampire hunting abilities could be inherited, they could not be learned. Occasionally, since the fall of Communist governments in the southern Balkans, stories of the adventures of a *dhampir* have found their way to newspapers.

As the vampire myth has expanded and the number of variations on it have grown, the *dhampir* has emerged as a character that allows new story lines. The most successful such *dhampir character* is **Blade the Vampire Slayer**, the popular vampire-slaying hero in Marvel comics and the three movie spin-offs. *Dhampirs* have also been featured in the writings of Scott Baker, Millie Devon, **Nancy Collins**, Barb and J. C. Hendee, and Rebecca York.

Sources:

Devon, Millie. *Dhampir: Child of God*. Fairfield, CT: Mystic Rose Books, 1995. 175 pp.

Hendee, Bar, and J. C. Hendee. *Dhampir*. New York: ROC, 2003. 376 pp.

Trigg, E. B. *Gypsy Demons & Divinities: The Magical and Supernatural Practices of the Gypsies*. London: Sheldon Press, 1973. 238 pp.

Vukanovic, T. P. "The Vampire." In Jan L. Perkowski, ed. *Vampires of the Slavs*. Cambridge, MA: Slavica Publishers, 1976, 201–34.

Doyle, Sir Arthur Conan *see:* Holmes, Sherlock

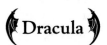

Dracula

Dracula, the title character in **Bram Stoker's** 1897 novel, set the image of the vampire in the popular culture of the twentieth century. Stoker took the rather vague and contradictory picture of the vampire that had emerged from the nineteenth-century literature and earlier times and developed a fascinating, satisfying, and powerful character whose vampiric life assumed mythic status in popular culture.

The Emergence of Dracula: Dracula appeared in print in the very first chapter of Stoker's novel. The reader, however, did not learn until later in the text that the driver who met **Jonathan Harker** at **Borgo Pass** and took him to **Castle Dracula**, was none other than Dracula himself. Harker's diary did note that the driver possessed great **strength**, a "grip of steel." The second chapter opened with Harker entering the castle after his long journey and finally meeting Dracula. He later recorded his impressions in his diary, writing that Dracula was "a tall man, clean shaven save for a long white moustache, and clad in black from head to foot, without a single speck of colour about him anywhere." (It will be noted that this description varies greatly from the common image of Dracula in formal evening dress, an image fostered by **Bela Lugosi** in the American play and the ***Dracula* [1931]** movie.) In excellent English, but with a strange intonation, he spoke one of his most famous lines, "Welcome to my house! Enter freely and of your own will!" After Harker stepped inside, Dracula moved to shake hands. Harker noted that his host had "a strength which made me wince, an effect which was not lessened by the fact that it seemed as cold as ice—more like the hand of a dead than a living man." Over supper Harker had a chance to study Dracula with some leisure and was able to develop a more complete description:

> His face was a strong—a very strong—aquiline with high bridge of the thin nose and peculiarly arched nostrils; with lofty domed forehead, and hair growing scantily round the temples, but profusely elsewhere. His eyebrows were very massive, almost meeting over the nose, and with bushy hair that seemed to curl in its own profusion. The mouth, so far as I could see it under the heavy moustache, was fixed and rather cruel looking, with peculiarly sharp white teeth; these protruded over the lips, whose remarkable ruddiness showed astonishing vitality in a man of his years. For the rest, his ears were pale and the tops extremely pointed; the chin was broad and strong, and the cheeks firm through thin. The general effect was one of extraordinary pallor.

> Hitherto I had noticed the backs of his hands as they lay on his knees in the firelight, and they had seemed rather white and fine; but seeing them now close to me, I could not but notice that they were rather coarse—broad, with squat fingers. Strange to say, there were hairs at the centre of the palm. The nails were long and fine, and cut to a sharp point. As the Count leaned over me and his hands touched me, I could not repress a shudder. It may have been that his breath was rank, but a horrible feeling of nausea came over me, which, do what I would, I could not conceal. The Count, evidently noticing it, drew back; and with a grim sort of smile, which showed more than he had yet done his protuberant teeth, set himself down again on his own side of the fireplace. We were both silent for a while; and as I looked towards the window I saw the first dim streak of the coming dawn. There seemed a strange stillness over everything....

Harker's first encounter with Dracula included what would become basic elements of the vampire's image. He had unusual strength. He had a set of **fangs**, (extended canine teeth). His skin was very pale, and his body was cold to the touch. He had a noticeable case of bad breath. Among the elements that were soon forgotten were the hairy palms of his hands and his sharp **fingernails**. Only in the 1970s did the need for the sharp fingernails return, as movie directors added the scene from the book in which Dracula used his nails to cut his skin so the heroine, **Mina Murray**, could drink his **blood**. An encounter between Dracula and Harker the next day began with Harker noticing the lack of **mirrors** in the castle. Again Dracula's long teeth were evident, but more importantly, Harker noted:

> ... I had hung my shaving glass by the window, and was just beginning to shave... This time there could be no error, for the man was close to me, and I could see him over my shoulder. But there was no reflection of him in the mirror!... but at that instant I saw that the cut had bled a little, and the blood was trickling over my chin. I laid down the razor, turning as I did so

half-round to look for some sticking plaster. When the Count saw my face, his eyes blazed with a sort of demonic fury, and he suddenly made a grab at my throat. I drew away, and his hand touched the string of beads which held the **crucifix**. It made an instant change in him, for the fury passed so quickly that I could hardly believe that it was ever there.

Slowly, Dracula's unusual nature became a matter of grave concern, not just a series of foreign eccentricities. Harker dutifully noted that "I have yet to see the Count eat or drink...." And in light of the bizarre situation in which he had been entrapped, he wondered, "How was it that all the people at **Bistritz** and on the coach had some terrible fear for me? What meant the giving of the crucifix, of the **garlic**, of the wild rose, of the **mountain ash**? Bless that good, good woman who hung the crucifix round my neck...." The next day Harker began to gain some perspective on Dracula. He asked him about **Transylvania**'s history, and Dracula responded with a spirited discourse. Dracula resided in the mountainous borderland of Transylvania, an area that centuries earlier had been turned over to the **Szekelys**, tribes known for their fierceness and effectiveness in warfare. Their role was to protect Hungarian territory from invasion. Dracula spoke as a *boyar,* a feudal lord and member of Hungarian royalty, "We Szekelys have a right to be proud, for in our veins flows the blood of many brave races who fought as the lion fights, for Lordship." In chapter 3, during his encounter with the three **women** who lived in the castle, Harker noted other revealing facts about Dracula. While his cheeks were red with rage, his eyes were blue, but as his rage grew, his eyes also became red with the flames of hell behind them.

The Fictional Dracula and the Historical Dracula: In chapter 3, Dracula also spoke the line that first suggested a tie between him and **Vlad the Impaler**, the original historical Dracula:

> ... who was it but one of my own race who as Voivode crossed the Danube and beat the Turk on his own ground! This was a Dracula indeed. Who was it that his own unworthy brother, when he had fallen, sold his people to the Turk and brought the shame of slavery on them! Was it not this Dracula, indeed, who inspired that other of his race who in a later age again and again brought his forces over the great river into Turkeyland; who, when he was beaten back, came again, and again, and again, though he had come alone from the bloody field where his troops had been slaughtered, since he knew that he alone could ultimately triumph....

Later, in chapter 18, **Abraham Van Helsing** would elaborate on Dracula as Vlad the Impaler, though Vlad was never mentioned by name. Stoker, it seems, constructed his leading character, at least in part, from the historical Dracula. That Dracula was a prince not of Transylvania, but of the neighboring kingdom of Wallachia. Stoker turned the Wallachian prince into a Transylvanian count. The real Dracula's exploits largely occurred south of the Carpathian Mountains, which divided Wallachia and Transylvania, and he only infrequently ventured into Transylvanian lands. The real Dracula was a Romanian, not a Szekely, though given the location chosen by Stoker for Castle Dracula, he was correct to think of his main character as a Szekely. Stoker drew the reader's attention, however, not to the fifteenth-century Dracula and the account of his earthly exploits, but to someone who was meeting daily with Jonathan Harker, and to the way in

which each encounter with Dracula's increasingly weird behavior shattered Harker's conventional understanding of the world. The most mind-boggling event occurred as Harker peered out of the window of his room and observed Dracula outside on the castle wall:

> ... I saw the whole man slowly emerge from the window and begin to crawl down the castle wall over that dreadful abyss, face down, with his cloak spreading out around him like great wings....

As he focused on the count's strange behavior, he put the fragments of his observations together:

> ... I have not yet seen the Count in the daylight. Can it be that he sleeps when others wake, that he may be awake whilst they sleep!

Finally, he made a definitive observation that completed the picture of Dracula as a vampire. In chapter 4, he discovered Dracula in his daytime **sleep**.

> There, in one of the great boxes, of which there were fifty in all, on a pile of newly dug earth, lay the Count! He was either dead or asleep, but I could not say which—for the eyes were open and stony, but without the glassiness of death—and the cheeks had the warmth of life through all their pallor, and the lips were as red as ever. But there was no sign of movement, no pulse, no breath, no beating of the heart. I bent over him, and tried to find any sign of life, but in vain.

> ... There lay the Count, but looking as if his youth had been half-renewed, for the white hair and moustache were changed to dark iron-grey; the cheeks were fuller, and the white skin seemed ruby-red underneath; the mouth was redder than ever, for on the lips were gouts of fresh blood, which trickled from the corners of the mouth and ran over the chin and neck. Even the deep, burning eyes seemed set amongst swollen flesh, for the lids and pouches underneath were bloated. It seemed as if the whole awful creature were simply gorged with blood; he lay like a filthy leech, exhausted in his repletion.

Dracula in England: At the end of the fourth chapter, the storyline of *Dracula* reverted to England, to where the count was en route. Dracula's intention was to move to **London**, and reestablish himself, though to what end was not yet revealed. Leaving Harker to his fate in the castle, and carrying with him fifty boxes of his native soil, Dracula traveled to the Black Sea. There he secretly boarded the *Demeter*, the ship that would take him to his new home. Aboard the *Demeter* he quietly came out of his box each night and fed on the sailors. One by one the men grew weak, and as the journey continued, they died. Finally, off the shore of **Whitby**, a town in northern England, a sudden storm called forth by Dracula blew the ship aground. Dracula transformed himself into a wolf and left the derelict ship. The storyline then shifted to two women, **Lucy Westenra** and Mina Murray, and the men in their lives. Dracula made only fleeting appearances through the rest of the novel. Instead, he hovered as a vague menace, constantly disturbing the natural course of Lucy and Mina's lives and requiring a cadre of men to search out and destroy him.

Dracula attacked Lucy first. He lured her out of her apartment to a seat on the opposite side of the river, where a **suicide** had been memorialized. He proceeded to bite her on the neck and drink her blood. He next appeared outside her room in the form of another animal, a **bat**. Meanwhile, having retrieved his boxes of earth from the *Demeter*, he had them shipped into London, where the novel's action now moved. Dracula distributed the boxes from his main home at his **Carfax** estate to other locations around the city.

Dracula renewed his attacks upon Lucy, who received a transfusion from her doctor **John Seward** after each attack. The men who assisted her, however, failed to realize that they were merely postponing her ordeal and her ultimate death and **transformation** into a vampire. Lucy's death and Van Helsing's demonstration of her vampiric powers welded the men into a unit to fight Dracula. Van Helsing was first able to obtain their assistance in killing Lucy with a **stake**, garlic, and **decapitation**. He then trained the men as **vampire hunters**. In this process, in chapter 18, Van Helsing described Dracula and all his powers and weaknesses. A vampire commands the dead and the **animals**, especially the "meaner things"—rats, bats, owls and foxes. He can disappear at will, reappear in many forms (especially a wolf, a bat, and as a **mist**), and can alter the **weather**. Slightly changing the folk tradition, Van Helsing noted that Dracula preyed not upon the ones *he* loved best, but upon the ones *we* loved best. Dracula cast no shadow, he did not reflect in mirrors, he could see in the dark, and he could not enter anywhere without first being invited.

Dracula had grown strong through his long years of existence. However, his strength was strictly limited during the day. For example, while he could move around during the day, he could transform himself only at the moment of sunrise, high noon, and sunset. He could pass over running tide only at high or low tide. Dracula was somewhat vulnerable. His power was taken away by garlic, various sacred objects (the crucifix, the **eucharistic wafer**), and the wild rose. He could be destroyed by attacking him in his **coffin** with a **bullet** fired into the body, a stake through his body (not necessarily the heart), and decapitation. Van Helsing's (i.e., Stoker's) understanding of Dracula was derived primarily from the folklore of vampires in Transylvania/**Romania** as described by Emily Gerard in her popular travel book, *The Land beyond the Forest* (1885).

Soon after the session where Van Helsing trained the vampire hunters, Dracula attacked and killed **R. N. Renfield,** the madman who had been trying to become Dracula's faithful servant. Then Dracula renewed his attack on Mina that had begun earlier in the book. The men broke into her bedroom and found her drinking Dracula's blood, presumedly the crucial step in becoming a vampire. Those who were merely drained of blood by a vampire simply died. After driving Dracula away, Van Helsing and the men organized by him counterattacked first by sanitizing Dracula's boxes of native soil. All but one of the 50 were found, and in each a piece of the eucharist was placed. While the men were at work, in the daylight hours, Dracula suddenly appeared in his home in Picadilly but fled after a brief confrontation.

With only one box of the refreshing earth left, Dracula returned to his homeland. While he traveled by boat, Van Helsing, Mina, and the men took the train. The final chase led to Dracula's castle. Arriving first, Van Helsing sanitized the castle, including Dracula's tomb. Soon thereafter Dracula appeared, with the other men in hot pursuit. Just as sunset approached, and Dracula's powers were restored, Jonathan Harker and **Quincey P. Morris** killed him by simultaneously decapitating him (Harker) and plunging a bowie knife into his heart (Morris). The centuries-old Dracula crumbled to **dust**.

Dracula in Films, Drama, and Books: *Dracula* was well received by the reading public and both filmmakers and dramatists soon saw its potential. Not long after the book appeared, Stoker moved to assert his rights to any dramatic productions by staging a sin-

gle public performance of *Dracula* in London. Then, after Freidrich Wilhelm Murnau filmed **Nosferatu,** a slightly disguised version of *Dracula,* Florence Stoker asserted her ownership of the dramatic and film rights to her late husband's novel. The initial dramatic rights were sold to **Hamilton Deane** in 1924 and the American rights to Horace Liveright three years later. The film rights to *Dracula* were sold in 1930 to **Universal Pictures,** which in the 1950s passed them to **Hammer Films.** Both the stage and film versions of *Dracula* radically altered the character's image. Deane dropped attributes of Dracula that would prevent his acceptance by middle-class British society. Thus Dracula lost his bad breath, hairy palms, and odd dress. He donned a tuxedo and an **opera** cape and moved into the Harkers's living room. The Universal movie had an even more influential role in reshaping the image. Bela Lugosi's portrayal in the American stage play was succeeded by others, but in the movie he reached millions who never saw the stage play, and what they saw was his suave, aristocratic European manner and pronounced Hungarian accent. He reinforced that image in subsequent films. For many, the Stoker character and Bela Lugosi's representation of him merged to create the public image of Dracula. In future portrayals of Dracula, as frequently as not, the actor who played

Bela Lugosi's cinematic interpretation of Dracula from the 1931 classic film based on the Bram Stoker novel.

Dracula offered his interpretation of the Lugosi/Dracula persona, rather than the character presented in Stoker's novel.

Stoker's novel was reprinted frequently in the following decades. Doubleday brought out the first American edition in 1899. After it entered the public domain, many reprints were published, along with condensed versions and adaptations for **juvenile** audiences. As early as 1972 a version for children, abridged by Nora Kramer, was published by Scholastic Book Services.

At the same time, authors initiated efforts to create new interpretations of this highly intriguing literary figure. Prior to 1960, Dracula seems to have appeared in only one novel, in the 1928 *Kasigli Voyvode* ("The Impaling Vampire") by Turkish writer Ali Riga Seifi. He was the subject of several short stories, such as Ralph Milne Fraley's "Another Dracula," which appeared in the September and October 1930 issues of *Weird Tales.* In 1960 two new Dracula novels, Otto Frederick's *Count Dracula's Canadian Affair* and Dean Owen's *The Brides of Dracula,* were the first of more than 100 Dracula novels that would be published over the next three decades. Memorable among these are the several series of Dracula novels by **Robert Lory** (nine action stories), **Fred Saberhagen** (seven novels), and **Peter Tremayne** (three novels).

Following the success of the Hammer *Dracula* movies, the vampire movie in general, and the *Dracula* vampire movie in particular, made a marked comeback. Over 100 movies have featured Dracula, and many others star vampires who are only thinly-veiled imitations. The first movie that attempted to bring the *Dracula* novel to the screen may have been a silent film made in **Russia** (1920), but no copy has survived. Following *Nosferatu* and the Bela Lugosi film, other versions have included *Dracula* **(Spanish, 1931),** *Horror of Dracula* (1958), *El Conde Dracula* (1970), *Dracula* **(1979),** and *Bram Stoker's Dracula* (1992). Dracula has become the fictional character most often brought to the screen, with the possible exception of **Sherlock Holmes.** Dracula made his first **television** appearance in the 1960s through Bela Lugosi (who made a brief appearance as Dracula on the popular television series *You Asked for It*) and **John Carradine,** who appeared in a NBC production of the play. Other television specials that attempted to dramatize the novel featured **Denholm Elliott** (1971), **Jack Palance** (1973), and **Louis Jourdan** (1977). A comic contemporary Grandpa Count Dracula (portrayed by Al Lewis) was a regular character in the 1964–66 series *The Munsters*. During the 1990–91 season, a more serious and sinister count appeared briefly in his own *Dracula—The Series*. As early as 1953, Dracula was featured in **comic books** in *Eerie*'s (Avon Periodicals) adaptation of the novel. He made several appearances before vampires were banished in 1954 under the conditions of the Comics Code. During the period of banishment, Dell brought out one issue of a *Dracula* comic, but he mostly was limited to guest shots in humorous comics such as *The Adventures of Jerry Lewis* (July-August 1964), *The Adventures of Bob Hope* (October-November 1965), and *Herbie* (September 1966). Dracula did appear in several European and South American comic books, but it was not until the 1970s that he made his comeback in one of the most successful comics of the decade, *The Tomb of Dracula*. In this version, Marvel Comics brought Dracula into the contemporary world in conflict with the descendants of his antagonists in the Stoker novel. He soon got a second Marvel series, *Dracula Lives!*, and made numerous appearances in different Marvel comics as a guest villain. Most recently Dracula was the subject of two comic books from Topps. These grew out of the latest attempt to bring Dracula to the screen in **Francis Ford Coppola**'s *Bram Stoker's Dracula*.

Dracula's image (as portrayed by Lugosi) has been a favorite in merchandising, from candy labels to ads selling various products. Each October before Halloween his face graces greeting cards, posters, buttons, party favors, and miscellaneous **paraphernalia.** Many Dracula statues and dolls, in almost every medium, from artistic to cute, have been produced.

Dracula also has been celebrated in **music**. As early as 1957, "Dinner with Drac" (Cameo, 1957) appeared on a hit record by John Zacherle. A 1950s **humor** album, *Dracula's Greatest Hits*, had parodies of popular hit tunes that had been transformed into songs about Dracula. Dracula made a number of musical appearances through the 1960s and 1970s, primarily in comic situations, but in 1979 there emerged what would become known as the **gothic** subculture. That musical community was launched by the rock band Bauhaus, whose first hit was an eerie piece titled "Bela Lugosi's Dead." The gothic world found the vampire an apt symbol of the dark world they were creating, and Bela Lugosi's Dracula served as a starting point for their funeral dress. **Vlad**, former leader of the gothic band Dark Theater, is a Lugosi/Dracula fan who not only adopted aspects of Lugosi's persona into his own, but also created a shrine to Lugosi in the living room of his home.

The permeation of the culture by Dracula during the last generation led to the formation of clubs and organizations that celebrated and promoted him. These include

The Count Dracula Fan Club, The Count Dracula Society, The Dracula Society, and **The Bram Stoker Society**. As the centennial of the publication of Bram Stoker's *Dracula* approached, Dracula had become one of the most recognizable images in all of popular culture. His popularity provided the base from which other popular vampire figures, such as **Barnabas Collins** and **Lestat de Lioncourt**, could evolve.

Sources:

Davidson, Carol Margaret, ed. *Bram Stoker's Dracula: Sucking through the Century, 1897–1997*. Toronto: Durndun Press, 1997. 432 pp.

Dresser, Norine. *American Vampires: Fans, Victims, Practitioners*. New York: W. W. Norton & Company, 1989. 255 pp.

Glut, Donald F. *The Dracula Book*. Metuchen, NJ: Scarecrow Press, 1975. 388 pp.

Haining, Peter. *The Dracula Centenary Book*. London: Souvenir, 1987. 160 pp. Rpt. as *The Dracula Scrapbook*. Stamford, CT: Longmeadow Press, 1987. 160 pp. Rev. ed.: London: Chancellor Press, 1992. 160 pp.

————. *The Dracula Scrapbook*. New York: Bramwell House, 1976. 176 pp.

Miller, Elizabeth. *Reflections on Dracula: Ten Essays*. White Rock, BC: Transylvania Press, 1997. 226 pp.

Senf, Carol A., *Dracula: Between Tradition and Modernism*. New York: Twayne Publishers, 1998. 132 pp.

Skal, David J. *Hollywood Gothic: The Tangled Web of Dracula from Novel to Stage to Screen*. New York: W. W. Norton & Company, 1990. 242 pp.

Stoker, Bram. *Dracula*. Westminster, London: A. Constable & Co., 1897. 390 pp.

❦ *Dracula* (1931) ❦

In the wake of the success of the stage production of *Dracula* in New York in 1927, producer Horace Liveright (1886–1933) developed touring companies to take the play to various parts of the country. Actor **Bela Lugosi**, who had starred in the New York play, joined the West Coast company and eventually settled in Los Angeles where he could resume his film career. Then in 1930, **Universal Pictures** moved to purchase the film rights for *Dracula* from Florence Stoker. The original asking price, reportedly $200,000, was far too high from the studio's perspective, so Bela Lugosi was cajoled into negotiating Stoker's widow down to a more reasonable amount. Universal eventually got the rights for $40,000 and hired director **Tod Browning** to take charge of the project.

Because of his role in negotiating the rights, Lugosi expected the part of **Dracula** would automatically be offered to him. It was not. Rather, Universal announced that John Wray, who had just had a major part in *All's Quiet on the Western Front*, would play the role. Universal also considered Conrad Veidt (who declined the honor), Ian Keith, William Courtney, Paul Muni, Chester Morris, and Joseph Schildkraut. Not until a few weeks before shooting began did Lugosi secure the part. He sold his services for a special lower fee, and as a result was paid very little money—$3,500 for seven weeks of filming (about half of David Manners salary). Helen Chandler was chosen to play **Mina Murray** (now Mina Seward) and Frances Dale took the part of **Lucy Westenra** (changed to Weston). David Manners assumed the now greatly diminished role of **Jonathan Harker**. The other major part, **R. N. Renfield**, went to Dwight Frye. **Edward Van Sloan**, who had previously played **Abraham Van Helsing**, moved west for the movie part, and the cast was filled out by Herbert Bunston as Dr. **John Seward**. The movie was able to do much that the play could not. The film added the opening segment of the novel in which Jonathan Harker traveled to **Transylvania** and had his initial encounter with Dracula and his three **brides**. This chapter included what many consider the most dramatic moments of the book. However, in the movie, Renfield, not Harker, made the trip to **Castle Dracula**. His experiences there accounted for his "insane" behavior following his return to England. An elaborate set was developed for the memorable scenes in the castle but it was poorly utilized. Browning has been justly criticized for the restricted and flat manner in which he shot Dracula's encounter with his English guest, so ripe with possibilities. In spite of Browning's limitations, however, the scenes that began with Lugosi's opening line, "I am ... Dracula," are among the most memorable, powerful, and influential in horror film. *Dracula* also included a brief scene aboard the *Demeter*, the ship that brought Dracula to England.

Poster art for 1931's *Dracula*.

From this point, the film rejoined the revised version of the **Hamilton Deane/John L. Balderston** play. Dracula had moved to **London** and targeted Mina Seward after previously disposing of Lucy. He abducted her to **Carfax**, now transformed into Carfax Abbey, his London home, but was tracked by Van Helsing, Dr. Seward, and Harker and finally destroyed. As in the play, the closing chapters of the book, describing the return to Transylvania, were deleted. Also, true to the play, at the end Van Helsing stopped the credits and made the famous closing speech on the reality of vampires.

Dracula was set to open on Friday, February 13, 1931, at the Roxy Theater in Manhattan. New York was plastered with blood-red signs. Papers on the West Coast panned the production. The *Los Angeles Times* dubbed it a freak show—a curiosity without the possibility of wide appeal. The New York coverage was mixed. Critics did not like it, but also had to respond to Universal's intense publicity and advertising campaign. The run at the Roxy lasted only eight days. The national release came in March. A silent version was prepared for theaters that had not yet added sound equipment. (Also, to make full use of the expensive set, a Spanish-language version with a completely new cast was filmed simultaneously with the Lugosi English-language version.) The movie opened in Los Angeles with no fanfare because Universal was in the midst of a budget crunch. In spite of its slow start, *Dracula* (the first of what would become a lineage of horror talkies) caught the imagination of the public and became the largest grossing film for Universal that year. For the first time since the Depression had started, the studio, threatened with closing, made a profit.

Today, two generations after its release, some assessment of Universal's *Dracula* is possible. Certainly, it is the most influential vampire film of all time. All subsequent performances of the vampire have been either based upon it or a direct reaction to it.

Edward Van Sloan (left) as Abraham Van Helsing, and Bela Lugosi as Dracula in a promo shot for the 1931 Tod Browning film.

However, its original success did not lead, at least immediately, to a second vampire movie, but to the production of a very different horror movie, *Frankenstein*, and a string of horror movies covering various themes. Additionally, its continued success through the years did not lead to the production of many more vampire movies, which appeared only sporadically until the 1960s. In the 1960s, however, the vampire genre was discovered as a unique creation, not just another variation on the horror genre.

Beginning with **Horror of Dracula** (1958), **Hammer Films**'s remake of *Dracula* starring **Christopher Lee**, the novel *Dracula* has been adapted to the screen more than twenty-five times, the character Dracula has appeared in more than one hundre films, and characters largely based on Dracula have been featured in several hundred more. The more important remakes of the Dracula novel after the first Lee version included **El Conde Dracula** (1970), also with Lee; **Dracula (1973)** with **Jack Palance**; **Count Dracula (1978)** with **Louis Jourdan**; **Dracula (1979)** starring **Frank Langella**;*Nosferatu* (1984); and director **Francis Ford Coppola**'s **Bram Stoker's Dracula** (1992). Ranking with each of these was the delightful satire/comedy *Love at First Bite* (1979), starring George Hamilton. Non-English versions of *Dracula* were produced in Turkey (*Drakula Istanbula*, 1953), Korea (*The Bad Flower*, 1961), Pakistan (*Zinda Laash*, 1967), **Spain** (*El Conde Dracula*, 1970), **Japan** (*Lake of Dracula*, 1970), and **Italy** (*Dracula's Curse*, 2002).

Sources:

Everson, William K. *Classics of the Horror Film*. New York: Citadel Press, 1974. 274 pp.

Glut, Donald. *The Dracula Book*. Metuchen, NJ: Scarecrow Press, 1975. 388 pp.

Holte, James Craig. *Dracula in the Dark: The Dracula Film Adaptations*. Westport, CT: Greenwood Press, 1997. 161 pp.

Madison, Bob, ed. *Dracula: The First Hundred Years*. Baltimore, MD: Midnight Marquee Press, 1997. 322 pp.

MagicImage Filmbooks Presents Dracula (The Original 1931 Shooting Script). Atlantic City, NJ: MagicImage Filmbooks, 1990.

Skal, David J. *Hollywood Gothic: The Tangled Web of Dracula from the Novel to Stage to Screen*. New York: W. W. Norton & Company, 1990. 242 pp.

❨ Dracula (Spanish, 1931) ❩

At the same time **Universal Pictures** produced its famous version of **Dracula** starring **Bela Lugosi**, it produced a second version in Spanish. The Spanish version

Dracula (Carlos Villerias) pours a glass of wine for Jonathan Harker in the 1931 Spanish film *Juan*.

grew out of the studio's decision to respond to the changes brought about by the addition of sound to movies. Universal received a high percentage of its revenue from the foreign distribution of silent films, but talkies in English could threaten revenue because the techniques of dubbing had yet to be perfected. Universal's Czechoslovakian-born executive Paul Kohner suggested a solution to the studio's head, Carl Laemmle, Jr.: shoot foreign language versions of motion pictures simultaneously with the English versions, thus cutting costs by using the sets more than once. Kohner also argued that salaries for foreign actors and actresses were far less than those of Americans. Laemmle appointed Kohner head of foreign productions. The first result was a Spanish version of *The Cat Creeps*, a talkie remake of *The Cat and the Canary*, which Univeral had originally done as a silent film. Released in 1930 as *La Voluntad del Muerto*, it was an overwhelming success in Mexico and made actress Lupita Tovar a star. Kohner decided to make a Spanish version of *Dracula* and moved quickly to secure the youthful Tovar for the lead before she could return to Mexico. He chose Carlos Villarias (or Villar) for the role of **Dracula**, and secured a capable supporting cast with Barry Norton ("Juan" or **Jonathan Harker**), Eduardo Arozamena (**Abraham Van Helsing**), and Pablo Alvarez Rubio (**R. N. Renfield**).

Though it continued to be shown in Latin American countries into the 1950s, the Spanish version of *Dracula* became a largely forgotten entity in the United States. Universal failed to register its copyright of the film and did not make extra copies to preserve it. **Donald F. Glut's** 1975 work on Dracula mentioned it only in passing. In 1977, the American Film Institute attempted to make an archival print, but the only copy available (at the Library of Congress) had a decomposed third reel. In 1989, author **David J. Skal** followed up a rumor that a copy had survived in Cuba. He was able to facilitate the preparation of a copy, which was presented in the United States for the first time since the 1930s. The showing took place on Halloween, 1992 at the University of California at Los Angeles.

The Spanish version followed the same script as the Lugosi version. However, as Skal noted, it was very different in that the more mobile camera movement employed by director George Melford and his shooting team gave it a much livelier quality. Both mood and action were enhanced. It stands as "an almost shot-by-shot scathing critique of the **Browning** (Lugosi) version," said Skal.

The film opened in Mexico City and New York in April 1931 and in Los Angeles in May. It was one of the last Spanish-language films made in Hollywood—such productions being discontinued in the post-Depression business atmosphere. While possibly the superior movie, there is very little chance, given the development of the vampire film, that more than a few film historians and vampire buffs will ever see it. In spite of its being released for home video (later on DVD), and becoming somewhat of a best seller in that media, the film has become a historical curiosity rather than an important and influential film.

Sources:

Holte, James Craig. *Dracula in the Dark: The Dracula Film Adaptations*. Westport, CT: Greenwood Press, 1997. 161 pp.

Skal, David J. *Hollywood Gothic: The Tangled Web of Dracula from the Novel to Stage to Screen*. New York: W. W. Norton & Company, 1990. 242 pp.

Turan, Kenneth. "The Missing 'Dracula.'" *Los Angeles Times* (October 31, 1992).

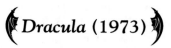 *Dracula* (1973)

In 1973 producer-director **Dan Curtis**, who had great success with vampire **Barnabas Collins** in the daytime **television** series *Dark Shadows*, teamed with screenwriter **Richard Matheson** (best known for his **science fiction** vampire novel *I Am Legend*) to produce a new version of *Dracula* for television. The pair attempted to bypass both the play by **Hamilton Deane** and **John L. Balderston** (the basis for the version of *Dracula* [1931] with **Bela Lugosi**) as well as *Horror of Dracula* and the other **Hammer Films** productions with **Christopher Lee**. At the same time, they were strongly influenced by the work of **Raymond T. McNally** and **Radu Florescu**, who published *In Search of Dracula: A True History of Dracula and Vampire Legends* (1972). This was the first book to highlight the exploits of **Vlad the Impaler**, the historical person who stands, in part, behind the lead character in **Bram Stoker's** novel. Curtis's Dracula was preeminently the fifteenth-century Wallachian ruler and military hero, still alive in the nineteenth century. The painting of him, astride his horse, dominated a room of **Castle Dracula** and in several scenes stole the attention of the camera. In the corner of the painting, a young woman was pictured. This woman was Dracula's true love (or true passion) from the fifteenth century, who had not survived with him into the nineteenth century.

Very early in the movie, Dracula saw a picture of **Jonathan Harker, Mina Murray, Arthur Holmwood,** and **Lucy Westenra.** Lucy looked nearly identical to the woman in the painting, so Dracula immediately decided that he must possess her. His quest for Lucy dominated the action in the first part of the film, while revenge for her death (the second time his love had been taken from him) occupied the remainder of the show. Curtis choose veteran character actor **Jack Palance** as Dracula. The story began with Jonathan Harker (Murray Brown) traveling to **Transylvania.** There he moved through forbidden portions of the castle and discovered Dracula's secret.

As Dracula departed for England, Harker was left behind to be bitten by Dracula's **brides.** In England the action centered on the two women, Lucy (Fiona Lewis) and Mina (Penelope Horner), Lucy's fiance Arthur Holmwood (Simon Ward), and most importantly, **Abraham Van Helsing** (Nigel Davenport). The novel's subplot concerning Dr. **John Seward** and the insane **R. N. Renfield** were pushed aside.

Van Helsing came to the fore after Lucy was bitten by Dracula. It was his task (Holmwood was unable to face his duty) to drive the **stake** into her heart. With his true love dead again, Dracula turned on Mina. Eventually, Van Helsing and Holmwood acted together. They drove Dracula back to Transylvania and followed him to Castle Dracula. One by one they faced and defeated the three vampire brides, Jonathan Harker (who had become a vampire and had to be killed), and finally Dracula himself. Dracula was first weakened by letting in the **sunlight** (as he was killed in *Horror of Dracula*). Then Van Helsing grabbed a spike from a suit of armor and impaled him. Dracula thus suffered the same fate that he was said to have inflicted on so many others.

The Jack Palance/Dan Curtis *Dracula* was viewed by a national television audience and has been cited as a more than competent version of the familiar tale. However, it never gained the following of the Hammer Films and was subsequently eclipsed by the **Frank Langella**/John Badham *Dracula* **(1979)** and *Bram Stoker's Dracula* (1992).

Sources:

Holte, James Craig. *Dracula in the Dark: The Dracula Film Adaptations*. Westport, CT: Greenwood Press, 1997. 161 pp.

Waller, Gregory A. *The Living and the Undead: From Stoker's Dracula to Romero's Dawn of the Dead*. Urbana, IL: University of Illinois Press, 1986. 376 pp.

❦ *Dracula* (1979) ❦

In 1979 **Universal Pictures** replayed a scenario that first occurred a half century before when it again filmed a version of the **Hamilton Deane/John L. Balderston** production of *Dracula, the Vampire Play in Three Acts*. In the original case, Universal purchased the film rights to the play following its successful run on Broadway and in touring companies around the country. In 1978 it reacted to the award-winning Broadway revival of the play starring **Frank Langella**. Universal had stayed away from the wave of quickie vampire movies, the production of which reached a new high in the 1970s, and it turned the new *Dracula* into a lavish production.

The film opened with the wreck of *Demeter,* the ship that transported Dracula to the English town of **Whitby**. These scenes, merely alluded to in the play, were filmed on the coast of Cornwall. Safely on land, Dracula then proceeded to invade the household of Dr. **John Seward** (Donald Pleasence), whom Balderston had turned from a young suitor into the middle-aged father of **Lucy Westenra** (now Lucy Seward). When **Mina Murray** (now Mina Van Helsing) died under mysterious circumstances, Seward called Mina's father, Dr. **Abraham Van Helsing** (played by the equally eminent Laurence Olivier), to assist him in handling the problem of Dracula.

The distinctive difference of the Langella version was its underlying understanding of the relation of **sexuality** and horror. Dracula was the object of horror—the undead. Yet as he entered the Seward household, he did not accomplish his goals by brute force. He fell in love first with Mina and then with Lucy. He won them over when his sensuality attracted their attention, and he then completely seduced them. Dracula's triumph occurred when he invaded Lucy's bedroom and shared his **blood** with her, in as sensual a scene as could be found in any vampire movie. Subsequently Lucy, completely captivated by Dracula's magnetism, rushed off to **Carfax** to join him.

This version of *Dracula* offered a new twist to Dracula's eventual destruction. He attempted to escape England, accompanied by a very willing Lucy, but Van Helsing and the other men were in pursuit. They finally caught up with Dracula on the ship, where he emerged from his **coffin** to battle the forces of good. In the end he was impaled on a hook and hoisted high into the air to be burned to death in the **sunlight.** The film got mixed reviews. Some applauded its sensual quality, while others saw it as an empty parody of the vampire movie. Interestingly enough, it appeared during the same year as the best and most successful of the several *Dracula* spoofs, *Love at First Bite.* In spite of its mixed reception, the Langella film took its place as one of the better and more interesting of the *Dracula* remakes.

Sources:
Allen, Thomas. "Yeh, But Did He Die?" *The Long Island Catholic* (July 26, 1979).
Arnold, James W. "'Dracula'—Another Day at the Blood Bank." *The Catholic Herald Citizen* (August 4, 1979).
Ebert, Roger. "Dracula: Revival of the Undead Hero." *Chicago Sun-Times* (July 8, 1979).
Holte, James Craig. *Dracula in the Dark: The Dracula Film Adaptations.* Westport, CT: Greenwood Press, 1997. 161 pp.
Waller, Gregory A. *The Living and the Undead: From Stoker's Dracula to Romero's Dawn of the Dead.* Urbana, IL: University of Illinois Press, 1986. 376 pp.

Dracula and Company *see:* Vampire Fandom: United States

Dracula (Dell Comics Superhero)

In 1962, Dell Publishing Co., Inc., which did not subscribe to the 1954 Comics Code prohibiting vampires, issued a comic book titled *Dracula* that told the story of a contemporary encounter with a revived **Count Dracula** at his castle in **Transylvania**. The title was discontinued after the first issue. Four years later, however, in November 1966, a new *Dracula* comic book appeared. The initial issue continued the numbering of the previous *Dracula* volume but began what amounted to an entirely new storyline. At **Castle Dracula** in **Transylvania**, a present-day Count Dracula was working in a modern laboratory on a serum derived from **bats** that was to aid in the healing of brain damage. He completed the serum, but some of it accidently dripped into his glass. When he drank from the glass, he was changed into a bat.

In this story, there was no mention of vampires or vampirism. Rather, Count Dracula blamed his problems on vampire bats whose bad image had haunted his family. By removing the superstitions of the bat from his family's name, he had hoped to come out of hiding and lead a productive life. After consuming the serum, Dracula had to alter his plans to aid humanity. As he was contemplating his future, representatives of the new dictatorial government moved in to take over his castle. Dracula then decided to fight the evil he now saw all around him.

He had the ability to change into a bat, and his supersensitive brain could control bats. He began a body-building program and had a new suit made with batlike features. Dracula emerged as a new superhero, which at the time was not yet in vast supply. Count Dracula also moved to the United States and assumed the name Al. U. Card. His first task was to defeat a plan to change the world's **weather**. In the United States he took over an abandoned radar control site as an underground laboratory and headquarters. He also saved a young woman, B. B. Beebbe, who drank some of the formula and became his partner. She called herself Fleeta (from "fliedermaus," German for "bat").

The series survived for three issues in 1966–67 and then was discontinued. In 1972, following the revisions of the Comics Code and the appearance of several successful vampire **comic books**, *Dracula* was revived for a third time and issues 2–4 were reprinted as issues 6–8. However, the character never caught on and after issue 8 the series was discontinued again.

Sources:
Dracula. No. 1–8. New York: Dell Publishing Co., Inc., 1962, 1966–67, 1972–73.
Rovin, Jeff. *The Encyclopedia of Superheroes*. New York: Facts on File, 1986. 443 pp.

The Dracula Fan Club *see:* The Vampire (Real Vampires)

Dracula (Marvel Comics Character)

Immediately after the Comics Code was revised in 1972 (lifting the ban on vampires that had been in effect since 1954), Marvel Comics moved to issue several horror titles that fell within the new guidelines. One of these was a series based on **Count Dracula**. *The Tomb of Dracula*, which devised a completely new set of adventures for the count, and became one of the most successful vampire-oriented **comic books** of the century. The central hero was Frank Drake, a descendant of the count, whose family had abandoned the family estate and anglicized their name. Drake had inherited the family fortune but quickly squandered it. Destitute, his only asset was **Castle Dracula**. As the story opened, Drake traveled to **Transylvania** to see the castle with the idea of either selling it or turning it into a tourist attraction. Accompanying him were his girlfriend Jeanie and another friend, Clifton Graves, who had originally suggested the possible value of the castle.

Wesley Snipes brings the comic book vampire hero Blade to life on the screen.

As they explored the castle, Graves discovered the crypt containing the remains of Dracula, complete with the **stake** in his heart. Graves pulled out the stake, thus awakening the count. Dracula confronted Drake and Jeanie but was driven off by her **silver** compact. While the pair considered the implication of the encounter, Dracula fled to the nearby town to find fresh **blood**. After the townspeople found the body of Dracula's first **victim**, they marched on the castle and set **fire** to it.

Drake, Jeanie, and Graves went back to **London**, and the count followed. Drake sold the Transylvania property but his more immediate problem was that Jeanie had been bitten by Dracula and was now a vampire. During Drake's next confrontation with the count, Jeanie was killed. Distraught, Drake attempted **suicide**. He was stopped by Rachel Van Helsing, granddaughter of **Abraham Van Helsing**, who also had dedicated her life as a **vampire hunter**. Taj, a mute Asian Indian, accompanied her. Rachel Van Helsing carried a crossbow whose wooden arrows amounted to wooden stakes. Together, the three set out to kill Dracula.

They were soon joined by two more vampire fighters, Quincy—not the same Quincy as in the novel—Harker (the son of **Jonathan Harker** and **Mina Murray** mentioned in the last paragraphs of the novel), and **Blade, the Vampire Slayer**, an African American whose mother had been killed by a vampire. A generation older than either Drake or Van Helsing, Harker used a wheelchair equipped with devices such as a weighted net and a cannon that fired poisoned wooden darts. Blade's major weapon was a set of wooden knives. Later in the series, Hannibal King, a detective who had been turned into a vampire, allied himself with the team. He and Blade had their initial encounter not with Dracula, but with **Deacon Frost**, another vampire from Blade's past.

The team fought Dracula for a decade, through seventy issues of **The Tomb of Dracula**. Dracula was portrayed very much as he was in popular lore. He was evil, but with some traits of human feeling, pining over love betrayed and the capture of his son by the forces of good. Drake, Van Helsing, Harker, and Blade fought him with wooden stakes (their most consistently effective tool), the **crucifix**, silver, fire, and daylight. While there were partial victories on both sides, each defeated character recovered to carry the series to its conclusion. For example, very early in the series Dracula was killed, but he was brought back to life. Later in the series he lost his vampiric powers for a time. As was common in Marvel Comics, Dracula made appearances in other Marvel titles (*Dr. Strange, Frankenstein, Thor*) and several of the Marvel characters (*Silver Surfer, Werewolf by Night*) appeared in *The Tomb of Dracula* to offer their services to defeat him.

The Marvel *Dracula* was strongly affected by the Hammer *Dracula* movies in one respect. Those bitten by Dracula died and immediately became vampires. In the novel, they were merely weakened by their first encounter. *The Tomb of Dracula* concluded in issue 70 with what appeared to be Dracula's definitive death. He was killed in a confrontation with Quincy Harker, who impaled him with a silver spoke from his wheelchair. Harker also cut off Dracula's head, stuffed his mouth with **garlic**, and buried both himself and Dracula under stones dislodged from Castle Dracula in an explosion.

However, the Count was quickly revived in the new series of *The Tomb of Dracula* issued by Marvel in a black-and-white magazine format (not covered by the revised Comics Code). When his body was discovered and the silver spoke removed, Dracula was freed for further adventures. He starred in the revived series of *The Tomb of Dracula*, which lasted for six issues. Over the next few years he also made guest appearances as the villain in several Marvel Comics. For example, in 1983 he had a confrontation with Dr. Strange, the super-hero with magical powers. Dr. Strange invoked what was termed the Montesi Formula, a magical incantation designed to destroy all the vampires in the world. Dracula disintegrated in the process. Hannibal King, who had never ingested human blood, was turned back into a normal man by the same process.

By the beginning of the 1990s, the Montesi Formula had weakened and vampires began to reappear in the Marvel Universe. While most of the vampires killed in 1983 remained dead, the old and powerful vampire Dracula was resurrected and made his first appearance in No. 10 of *Dr. Strange Sorcerer Supreme* in November 1989. Then in 1991, the *The Tomb of Dracula* was revived a third time by writer **Marv Wolfman** and artist Gene Colan, for four issues published by Epic Comics, a Marvel subsidiary. The story picked up the lives of Drake and Blade ten years after the death of Dracula at the hands of Quincey Harker. Drake had continued to suffer **psychological** upset as he tried to deal with his own ancestry, his problems with females, and his immediate need to deal with the return of Dracula to life. They put Dracula away again, but the never-dead-for-long vampire would return in 1994 to bedevil Drake and Blade again in their further adventures as the Nightstalkers. Since then, Dracula has been a visiting villain in various Marvel comics.

Sources:

Doctor Strange. No. 62 New York: Marvel Comics, December 1983.

Sienkiewicz, Bill. "Dracula." *The Official Handbook of the Marvel Universe* 2, 17 (August 1987): 10–13.

The Tomb of Dracula. Nos. 1–70. New York: Marvel Comics, 1971–79.

The Tomb of Dracula. Nos. 1–6, New York: Marvel Comics, 1979–80.

The Tomb of Dracula. Nos. 1–4. New York: Epic Comics, 1991–92.

The Dracula Museum *see:* Count Dracula Fan Club

❦ Dracula '97: A Centennial Celebration ❦

Dracula '97: A Centennial Celebration was an international commemoration of the publication of the novel *Dracula* held in Los Angeles from August 14–17, 1997. The largest of the several **Dracula** centennial fests held throughout 1997 and 1998, Dracula '97 attracted more than 600 attendees and more than 100 presenters. It was cosponsored by the American and Canadian chapters of the **Transylvanian Society of Dracula** and the **Count Dracula Fan Club**. The event was chaired by J. Gordon Melton

Kathryn Leigh Scott, who portrayed Maggie Evans in the original *Dark Shadows,* was a featured guest at the Dracula '97 convention.

who was joined on the executive committee by **Elizabeth Miller** and **Dr. Jeanne Youngson.** They, in turn, were assisted by **Chelsea Quinn Yarbro** (literary program), Del and Sue Howison of **Dark Delicacies** (exhibits), Karen Tate (travel), Norman Kaeseberg (stage), Julia Winden Fey (film festival), Mary Tokita (press), and **David Skal** (awards). Norinne Dresser also served on the planning committee.

Elizabeth Miller was in charge of organizing the heart of the gathering, a scholarly conference that included approximately ninety papers that covered the spectrum of issues in vampire and Dracula studies. Included were approximately thirty scholars from outside the United States, including six historians and folklorists from **Romania**. An anthology from the papers was published in 1998. Miller also oversaw Dracula '97's literary contest and edited the volume of winning essays, poems, and short fiction. A wide variety of stars from memorable vampire films and the **television** series *Dark Shadows* were on hand to greet their many fans. Lopita Tovar, who as a 19 year-old starred in the 1931 Spanish *Dracula*, and Carla Laemle, who as a teenager spoke the very first words in the opening scene of **Bela Lugosi**'s *Dracula*, appeared, along with **Hammer Films** stars **Ingrid Pitt**, Veronica Carlson, and Yutte Stinsgaard. Actresses Lara Parker and Kathryn Leigh Scott from the original *Dark Shadows* series also highlighted the Friday evening program. A special salute to Bela Lugosi made up the Thursday evening opening program, featuring reminiscences by Bela Lugosi, Jr.

Honored guests for the event were comedian **Elvira** (media guest of honor), author **Fred Saberhagen** (literary guest of honor), and publisher Robert Eighteen-Bisang (publisher guest of honor). The program was ably chaired by cartoonist Gahan Wilson (toastmaster), lecturer Vincent Hillyer (master of ceremonies), and nightclub owner Blade Rhino (Saturday evening masquerade contest). Awards were presented to a variety of authors, books, and films voted the best in their category and the work of many leaders of vampire fandom was acknowledged. Entertainment ran the spectrum from **drama** (Collinwood Players) and dance (Paul Ebey, Susanne Muldowny) to **music** (Barry Fisher's Dracmaniacs, **Vlad** and the Dark Theatre, and Element). Several additional centennial celebrations were also held in 1997 in North America and Europe, including a large German Dracula centennial conference convened at Wetzlar.

Sources:

Miller, Elizabeth, ed. *Blood Offerings for Dracula: Winning Entries for the Count's Creative Writing Contest.* Los Angeles: Transylvanian Society of Dracula, 1997. 46 pp.

———. "Dracula '97 (Los Angeles, August 14–17, 1997): A Brief Overview." *Transylvanian Journal: Dracula and Vampire Studies* 3, 1 (Fall 1997): 49–54.

———. *Dracula: The Shade and Shadow.* Westcliffe-on-Sea: Desert Island Books, 1998. 256 pp.

❦ *Dracula; or, The Undead* ❧

The initial dramatic presentation of *Dracula* occurred on May 18, 1897, at 10:15 A.M. at the Lyceum Theatre in **London**. This singular performance was staged by author **Bram Stoker** to secure himself the performance copyright from the many writers who were constantly searching for inspirations for new dramatic works for the London stage. Since the Lyceum was fully booked for its regular season's performances, a weekday morning was virtually all the space available. In fact, the performance was not intended as a profit-making performance attracting a large audience, but merely the minimal fulfillment of a legal regulation. It is assumed that the audience was composed of few of the theater staff and some invited friends.

The text for what amounted to a dramatic reading was hastily prepared by Stoker using proof copies of the novel's text. He adapted the text for the stage and made changes he knew would be demanded by Lord Chamberlain, who was charged with the power of censorship over such public performances. There is every reason to believe that his final text was treated liberally as he made it known that no real public performances were to be staged. Only a single copy of the manuscript, now located in the British Museum, survived.

While Stoker's mentor Henry Irving and his star actress Ellen Terry declined to participate in the dramatic reading, Terry's daughter Edith Cragg assumed the role of **Mina Murray**. The program lists a Mr. Jones, probably T. Arthur Jones, as portraying Dracula. Other leading parts were taken by Herbert Passmore (**Jonathan Harker**), Ken Rivington (Dr. **John Seward**), and Tom Reynolds (**Abraham Van Helsing**). There is some disagreement as to whether Kate Gurney or Ida Yeolande played **Lucy Westenra**, as two variations of the playbill exist. The performance lasted for more than four hours.

For those who have tried to comment on the evolving perception of its title character, the manuscript of *Dracula: Or the Undead* has been one of the most obscure texts of Dracula. However, in the mid-1990s, Sylvia Starshine copied the manuscript located in the British Museum and reproduced an edited and annotated edition (1997). On the 100th anniversary of the initial performance a second reading was performed at the Spaniards Inn. The cast included Mitch Davies, Maureen Evans, Suzanne Barbieri, Jo Fletcher, Caroline Jones, Eric Arthur, Gerald Hill, Jason Brooks, and Sylvia Starshine.

An artist's rendition of author Bram Stoker.

Sources:

Stoker, Bram. *Dracula: or The Undead*. Edited by Sylvia Starshine. Nottingham, UK: Pumpkin Books, 1997. 277 pp.

The Dracula Society (UK)

The Dracula Society, the primary organization in the **United Kingdom** keeping the study of **Dracula** alive, was founded in October 1973 by Bernard Davies and Bruce Wightman (d.2009) as a vampire interest group to help facilitate travel to **Romania**. At the time, standard tours were just beginning to respond to tourists who wished to visit sites associated with Dracula. Closer to its home base in **London**, the society sponsors lectures, films, auctions, and parties; its regular meetings are occasions for members to celebrate Dracula and his literary and cinematic cousins. It also arranges visits to nearby locales associated with **gothic** literature, especially the northern England town of **Whitby**, where, in the novel, Dracula landed. The society focuses on Dracula and **Bram Stoker**, but also reaches out to literary vampires in general, associated monsters such as the werewolf and mummies, and folklore.

The society maintains an archive to preserve materials related to Dracula and the gothic theme in literature, the stage, and the cinema. The archives houses the complete papers of **Hamilton Deane**, who brought Dracula to the stage. It also contains the cloak worn by **Christopher Lee** in his screen portrayals of Dracula. Annually, the society makes two awards: The Hamilton Deane Award for the outstanding contribution to the gothic genre in the performing arts and the Children of the Night Award for the most outstanding contribution to the gothic genre in the literary field.

The society adopted the shield of the Voivodes of Wallachia (Dracula's family) as its crest, adding a ribbon with a Latin quote from the third-century Christian theologian Tertullian, "I believe because it is impossible." The society is open to anyone over the age of eighteen; in 1993 it reported approximately 150 members. It may be contacted through the secretary, The Dracula Society, PO Box 30848, London W12 0GY, United Kingdom or through its Internet site at: http://www.thedraculasociety.org.uk/. Members receive *Voices from the Vaults*, the society's quarterly newsletter. The current chairman is co-founder Bernard Davies.

Sources:

Guiley, Rosemary Ellen. *Vampires Among Us*. New York: Pocket Books, 1991. 270 pp.

Dracula—The Series

Dracula—The Series was a short-lived syndicated **television** series starring Geordie Johnson in the title role. The series was set in the contemporary world, with Dracula living as a power broker under the name Alexander Lucard (Dracul spelled backward). He was opposed by three youths. The series did not gain significant ratings from either the public or vampire fans and was canceled after the 1991–92 season.

Sources:

Weaver, Tom. "Cinema Dracula." In *Dracula: The Complete Vampire*. New York: Starlog Communications, 1992, pp. 4–20.

❨ *Dracula:* The Vampire Play in Three Acts ❩

The first vampire story by **John Polidori**, published in 1819, immediately inspired a number of stage adaptations in Paris and **London**. No such wave of enthusiasm followed *Dracula*'s publication in 1897. However, shortly after his novel was published, author **Bram Stoker** did assemble the members of the Lyceum Theatre company and worked with them for a dramatic presentation of the book. That one-time event was held merely to establish Stoker's ownership of the book's plot and dialogue.

The story of Dracula's initial appearance on stage began in 1899 when **Hamilton Deane**, having quit his job as a London bank clerk, made his stage debut with the Henry Irving Vacation Company. There he met Bram Stoker and read *Dracula*. He saw its dramatic potential at once, and concluded that someone should write a stage play based upon it. But Deane had a career to concentrate on, and over the following years he spent his time becoming first a well-known actor and then the head of his own theater company. In 1918 Deane ended a lengthy stay on the New York stage and returned to England; in his suitcase was a copy of *Dracula*. As he moved through the British theatrical world, he approached numerous authors to write the *Dracula* play. He even went so far as to outline the acts and scenes. Most writers gave up in the face of the numerous characters and complicated subplots. Finally, during a period of sickness in 1923, Deane took the suggestion of one of his actresses and started to write the play himself. He became immersed in the new **drama** and finished it in four weeks. He obtained permission from Stoker's widow to use the material. The play debuted in Derby in June 1924.

This production became immensely important in the development of the modern image of the vampire. In the original novel, Dracula was dressed completely in black. He was an aristocrat of arrogant manners, and very bad breath. In contrast, Deane gave Dracula a somewhat sanitized presence. Dracula was dressed in formal evening wear, complete with an **opera** cloak that would further identify him with the **bat**. A cape had been mentioned by Stoker, most dramatically when it spread out as Dracula was crawling on the outside wall of **Castle Dracula**. While Dracula rarely appeared in London, he entered the play ready to match wits with the other characters, especially **Abraham Van Helsing**, rather than simply hovering as a presence backstage. Deane, in his negotiations with Florence Stoker, seemed to have consciously moved away from the image of the film *Nosferatu, Eine Symphonie des Garuens*, in which Dracula was portrayed as a monster of truly odd appearance, not a character that could interact with polite society. To reduce the storyline to manageable proportions, Deane cut out the first section of the book, which took place in **Transylvania**, and allowed the play to open in London in the Hempstead home of **Jonathan Harker**. The play then followed the storyline of the book, except that Dracula was killed at **Carfax**, his British home, instead of being tracked to the Continent. For the original performances, the government licensing agent insisted that Dracula's death not be shown; hence the cast gathered around the **coffin** and blocked the audience's view of the staking.

Deane also wrote what became a noteworthy addendum to the play. After the final act, as members of the audience were preparing to leave, he appeared on stage, still in his Van Helsing persona. He addressed them briefly, apologizing beforehand if the play were to cause nightmares, but then, tongue-in-cheek, warning that there might be

Raymond Huntley, who played Abraham Van Helsing in the stage version of *Dracula*.

such things as vampires. Deane assumed the role of Van Helsing; his future wife, Dora Mary Patrick, played Mina. Edmund Blake became the first actor to play Dracula. He was soon followed by **Raymond Huntley**. The character of **Quincey Morris**, the Texan who courted Lucy, became a woman, ostensibly to create an additional part for a female member of the Deane Theatre Company. Deane's company traveled for three years around England and Scotland. So popular was the play, that it began to push aside other plays in the company's repertoire.

In 1927, Deane decided to risk the play in London. It opened on February 14 at the Little Theatre on the West End. As he had expected, the press reviews were quite hostile. Almost everything about the play was criticized, and Deane thought that it would have a very short run. Instead, the public overrode the critics, and *Dracula* sold out night after night. Over the summer, the production moved to the larger Duke of York's Theatre. Deane turned an off-the-cuff comment by a newspaperman into one of the more famous publicity stunts in theatrical history. He had the Queen Alexandra Hospital send over a nurse who could attend to anyone who fainted from fright during the course of the play. At the end of one performance, a reported thirty-nine members of the audience took advantage of her presence.

A problem developed when Deane decided to take his company back on the road. Wanting to continue the London success, Florence Stoker commissioned a second *Dracula* play. A much inferior drama, it had only a brief run, by which time she had completed an agreement with Deane. About the same time she accepted an offer from New York producer Horace Liveright to stage a version of Deane's play on Broadway. Liveright engaged **John L. Balderston** to do a complete rewrite.

The Balderston version was even further removed from the book. **Lucy Westenra** and **Mina Murray** were collapsed into a single character, Lucy Seward, who became the daughter of Dr. **John Seward**. Seward, one of Lucy's youthful suitors in the novel, became a middle-aged father of a grown daughter. Lucy's other two suitors, Quincey P. Morris and **Arthur Holmwood** (Lord Godalming) completely disappeared. The Balderston play opened in the library of Seward's sanatorium. Huntley, originally offered the Dracula role, declined. The part was given to a little-known actor who could not understand English, **Bela Lugosi**. Bernard H. Jukes came from England to play **R. N. Renfield**. The Balderston production was tried out in New Haven, Connecticut, and then opened formally at the Fulton Theater in New York City on October 5, 1927. The play ran for 241 performances. It reopened in Los Angeles and San Francisco with Lugosi and Jukes joining the West Coast cast. Touring companies were established for the Midwest and the East Coast. The success of the American play led directly to the purchase of its rights by Universal and its translation to the motion picture screen. The Balderston version of *Dracula* was published by Samuel French in 1933 and has since been made available for stage production and screen adaptation.

Meanwhile, Hamilton Deane continued to produce the play in England, the movie version having given it new life. In 1939 he presented it in the Lyceum Theatre in London, the very theater where Bram Stoker had worked when he was writing *Dracula*. These last performances at the Lyceum were made more memorable one evening when Lugosi attended and came on stage to embrace Deane at the play's conclusion. Following *Dracula*'s run, and a brief run of *Hamlet*, the theater closed forever. Deane continued the play in London for two more years.

Dracula was produced by different companies on a number of occasions through the years, but it experienced a major revival in 1977, opening on Broadway October 20th, fifty years after its debut. **Frank Langella** assumed the title role. Equally heralded were the scenery and costumes by Edward Gorey. (Gorey had designed the scenery for the summer theater production of the Nantucket Stage Company on Nantucket Island, Massachusetts.) The new production received two Tony Awards, for best production of a revival and best costume design. It then served as a basis for the 1979 film starring Langella and directed by John Badham. Since its publication by Samuel French, the Deane-Balderston play has been popular for local drama groups and is annually produced by both amateur and semi-professional theaters around the country.

Sources:

Deane, Hamilton, and John L. Balderston. *Dracula: The Vampire Play in Three Acts*. New York: Samuel French, 1933. 112 pp.

Glut, Donald. *The Dracula Book*. Metuchen, NJ: Scarecrow Press, 1975. 388 pp.

Ludlam, Harry. *A Biography of Dracula: The Life Story of Bram Stoker*. London: Fireside Press/W. Foulsham & Co., 1962. 200 pp.

Skal, David J. *Hollywood Gothic: The Tangled Web of Dracula from the Novel to Stage to Screen*. New York: W. W. Norton & Company, 1990. 242 pp.

———, ed. *Dracula: The Ultimate, Illustrated Edition of the World-Famous Vampire Play*. New York: St. Martin's Press, 1993. 153 pp.

❨ Drama, Vampire ❩

Soon after the 1819 publication of **John Polidori**'s **"The Vampyre,"** the vampire was brought to the stage in **France**. There Polidori's dark tale caught the interest of a group of French romantics attracted to the story because they thought it had been written by **Lord Byron**. Before the year was out, it had been translated and published in Paris as *Le Vampire, nouvelle traduite de l'anglais de Lord Byron*. However, for many of these early explorers of the subconscious, the vampire became a fitting symbol of the darker, nightmare side of the inner reality they were discovering. An expanded sequel to the story appeared early in 1820 as *Lord Ruthwen ou les vampires*, authored by Cyprien Bérard. Bérard's colleague **Charles Nodier** was the first to adapt "The Vampyre" for the stage. He merely had to alter the ending of Polidori's story to assure his audience that the forces of good were still in control. In the end, these forces triumphed over the lead antihero, **Lord Ruthven**, who in Nordier's version was killed. His three-act play, *Le*

Vampire, mélodrame en trois actes, opened on June 13, 1820, at the Theatre de la Porte-Saint-Martin in Paris. It was an immediate and somewhat unexpected success and inspired several imitations. It was translated into English by **J. R. Planché** and opened in **London** as *The Vampire; or, The Bride of the Isles*. Later in the decade it would inspire a vampire **opera**, *Der Vampyr*, by German musician **Heinrich August Marschner**. Two days after Nodier's play premiered, a second vampire play, a farce also called *Le Vampire*, opened at the Vaudeville in Paris. This comedic version of Polidori's tale was set in **Hungary** and featured a young suitor mistakenly believed to be a vampire. A short time later, a second comedy, *Les trois Vampires, ou le chair de la lune*, opened at the Varieties. It centered on a young man who imagined that vampires were after him as a result of his reading vampire and ghost stories. In 1820, no less that four vampire plays, all comedies, opened in Paris under the titles *Encore un Vampire; Les Etrennes d'un Vampire; Cadet Buteux, vampire*; and *Le Vampire, mélodrame en trois actes*. The vampire seemed to have run its course with Parisian audiences after a year or two, but in 1822 a new play, *Polichinel Vampire* premiered at the Circus Maurice. The following year a revival of Nodier's play again attracted a crowd at the Porte-Saint-Martin. Among those who attended was the young **Alexandre Dumas**, who was just beginning his literary career. He later would recall his traumatic evening at Nodier's play, where he was seated next to the author, by composing his own stage version of *Le Vampire*. The 1851 production of that play closed out the Parisian phase of Dumas's life.

Over the next few years, writers periodically would fall back on the vampire theme, which always attracted an audience hungry for the supernatural. In England, for example, records have survived of St. John Dorset's *The Vampire: A Tragedy in Three Acts* (1831); **Dion Boucicault**'s *The Vampire* (1852; generally revived under the title, *The Phantom*); George Blink's, *The Vampire Bride* (1834); and Robert Reece's *The Vampire* (1872).

Theatre du Grand Guignol: At the end of the nineteenth century a theatrical innovation in Paris had an immense effect upon the image of the vampire. Max Maurey opened the Theatre du Grand Guignol in 1899. The drama offered at the theater followed the old themes of dark romanticism but treated them in a fresh manner. It attracted numerous working-class people who seemed fascinated with the presentation of gruesome situations and ultrarealistic stage effects, however horrific. The theater developed its own vampire drama called, fittingly, *Le Vampire*. Grand Guignol, slightly tempered by stricter censorship laws, opened in London in 1908. The English version emphasized the **gothic** element in its stage productions. Most importantly, Grand Guignol flourished in both England and France, producing original drama as well as utilizing established horror stories such as **Dracula** and **Edgar Allan Poe**'s tales.

Through the first half of the twentieth century the theater influenced individual motion pictures; but after World War II it became important in the creation of the **Hammer Films** horror classics, beginning with *The Curse of Frankenstein* (1958) and the *Horror of Dracula* (1958).

Dracula Dramatized: The entire thrust of vampire drama had changed in 1897 with the publication of **Dracula** by **Bram Stoker**. During the twentieth century, the overwhelming majority of new vampire plays and dramatic productions would be based on *Dracula*, and the character of Lord Ruthven, who dominated the stage in the nine-

teenth century, would all but disappear. The drama-
tizing of Dracula was initiated immediately after the
publication of the book, Stoker himself taking the
lead with the intention of protecting his rights to his
literary property. Using the cast of the Lyceum Theatre, where he worked, he presented ***Dracula; or,
The Undead*** as a five-act, forty-seven-scene play.
Ellen Terry (1847–1928), the cast's star, portrayed
Mina Murray. Even Stoker described the hastily prepared production, "Dreadful!" Its opening night was
also its last performance. The intricacies of the plot
served as an obstacle to playwrights who might have
wanted to bring the story to the stage. However, in
the years after World War I, an old friend of the
Stoker family, **Hamilton Deane,** then the head of his
own dramatic company, began to think seriously
about a *Dracula* play. He asked a number of acquaintances to give it a try, but was always turned down.
Finally, in 1923 during a period of illness, he accepted
the challenge himself. Four weeks later, he had a finished script. He overcame the book's problem by
deleting the opening and closing chapters in **Transylvania** and **Whitby,** setting all the action in three
scenes in London, and bringing Dracula on stage in
London to interact with his archenemy **Abraham
Van Helsing.** Deane, not at ease in London, and fearing the ridicule of the London critics, opened the play

Bela Lugosi as Dracula in John Balderston's pivotal
stage version of *Dracula,* which opened in 1927.

in rural Derby, England, in June 1924. It was a success, and the public's demands soon
made it the company's most frequently performed play. Finally, on February 14, 1927,
Deane opened his play in London. The public loved his work, and while most critics
panned it, others gave it very high marks. It played at the Little Theatre on the West
End and after several months moved to large facilities at the Duke of York's Theatre. It
ran for 391 performances. Deane then took it back to the countryside where it ran successfully through the 1930s. At one point he had three companies touring with the play.
Soon after *Dracula* opened in London, Horace Liveright purchased the American rights
for the play from Florence Stoker, Bram Stoker's widow. To assist with the delicate negotiations, Liveright had engaged the services of **John L. Balderston,** an American playwright and journalist then living in London. Balderston continued in Liveright's employ
to do extensive rewriting of Deane's play for the American audience. Balderston also
streamlined the plot, eliminating several characters and significantly changing the ones
who remained. Dr. **John Seward,** the youthful suitor of **Lucy Westenra** in the original
story, became the central character in the revised plot as Lucy's father. Mina Murray, the
leading woman in the novel, was eliminated and her role collapsed into that of Lucy,
who also became the love object of **Jonathan Harker.** The Balderston version of *Dracula* opened on Broadway on October 5, 1927, following a brief tryout at the Shubert
Theater in New Haven, Connecticut. **Bela Lugosi** assumed the title role. The play was
an immediate success and played for 33 weeks and 241 performances. Liveright had hes-

itated in developing a touring company to take it around the country but, Deane (who retained a small financial stake in the American enterprise) threatened to write a play based on a vampire other than Dracula and bring it to the United States. Balderston convinced Liveright of the need to send a company on the road. Lugosi joined the West Coast cast that played Los Angeles and San Francisco. The success on the West Coast convinced Liveright to create a second company to tour the East and the Midwest.

The original Deane version of the play significantly affected the image of Dracula and the **appearance of the vampire** in general. Deane domesticated Stoker's Dracula by dressing him in formal evening wear and ridding him of his extreme halitosis. The formal opera cloak, the cape with the high collar, would be clearly identified with the vampire character. Balderston's rewrite of Deane's play, however, was the more influential dramatic version of the novel. It introduced Bela Lugosi, later typecast as Dracula, to the part.

And it was Balderston's version that served as the basis of the 1931 **Universal Pictures** movie and the 1979 remake with **Frank Langella**. Published by Samuel French, the Balderston play became the version to which producers turned when they decided to revive Dracula on the stage. The most notable revival, of course, was the 1977 stage version starring Langella, which inspired Universal's remake.

Dracula Clones, Variations, and Parodies: For a generation after the success of the Balderston play, dramatists did little with the vampire theme, although in England a satire of Deane's play appeared briefly in the 1930s and a musical version surfaced in the 1950s. While a few variations on the Dracula theme were written in the 1960s, generally whenever a vampire play was sought, the Balderston play was revived yet again. The situation did not change until 1970 when suddenly four new vampire plays were published: Bruce Ronald's *Dracula, Baby*; Leon Katz's *Dracula: Sabbat*; Sheldon Allman's *I'm Sorry, the Bridge Is Out, You'll Have to Stay the Night*; and a more obscure *Johnny Appleseed and Dracula*. Since that time almost 50 vampire plays have been published. They vary from one-act plays for high school productions to more serious dramas designed for the Broadway stage. Only a few, such as *The Passion of Dracula* (1977), *Dracula Tyrannus* (1982), and *Vampire Lesbians of Sodom* (1984), have risen above the crowd to receive some national attention. *The Passion of Dracula* opened for a successful run at the Cherry Lane Theatre in New York City on September 30, 1977, just three weeks before the award-winning revival of the Balderston play with Frank Langella opened at the Martin Beck Theatre on October 20th. It was a variant of the Dracula story with Christopher Bernau as Count Dracula and Michael Burg as his archenemy Abraham Van Helsing.

On August 23, 1978, it began a successful run in London. Ron Magid's *Dracula Tyrannus: The Tragical History of Vlad the Impaler* was the first play to use all of the newly available material on the historical Dracula, **Vlad the Impaler**, the fifteenth-century Romanian ruler. It built on the ruler's rivalry for the throne with his cousin Dan. *Vampire Lesbians of Sodom*, whose three acts take the audience on a romp through history from ancient Sodom to Hollywood in the 1920s and modern Las Vegas, is based more upon the **vamp**, the female seductress, than the classical vampire.

Among the lesser-known plays, made available in large part for amateur productions, were several written by Stephen Hotchner and Tim Kelly. In 1975, Hotchner wrote three one-act Dracula plays, *Death at the Crossroads, Escape for Dracula's Castle,* and *The Possession of Lucy Wenstrom.* These were adapted for use at high schools, colleges, and community festivals from a full-length *Dracula* play Hotchner published in 1978 that combined the three one-act plays. During the 1970s Kelly also produced a number of Dracula-based plays, including musical variations such as *Seven Brides for Dracula* (1973) and *Young Dracula; or, the Singing Bat* (1975). Hotchner and Kelly's publisher, Pioneer Drama Service in Denver, Colorado, specialized in plays for amateur productions. The Dramatic Publishing Company of Chicago also published a number of Dracula-based dramas, including the first *I Was a Teen-Age Dracula* by Gene Donovan (1968). These productions characteristically used a lighter treatment of the vampire/Dracula theme and were targeted to younger audiences or people attending less serious entertainment events.

Of the vampire plays written since 1965, the overwhelming majority have been variations on the *Dracula* story, or at the very least have used the word "Dracula" in the title. **"Carmilla"**, comes in a distant second with three plays based on **Sheridan Le Fanu**'s story. During this period the number of vampire plays has steadily increased and, given the heightened interest in vampires at the beginning of the 1990s, there is every reason to believe that new plays will continue to be written.

Vampire Theater: The **gothic** movement that developed in the United States in the late 1970s has had a noticeable influence upon vampire drama. The movement itself was very dramatic, built as it was around bands who used theatrical effects as an integral part of their performances. Possibly the principal examples were those by choreographed by **Vlad**, the Chicago rock musician who headed the band The Dark Theatre.

La Commedia del Sangria was created in 1992 by Tony Sokal as a dramatic company that performs "vampire theatre" and includes a strong element of audience interaction. The company's very metaphysical production examines questions of the vampiric condition (limited immortality) and the existence of God. Some of the actors begin the performance portraying audience members and then enter the stage as an apparent interruption. The production received warm response from people in the vampire subculture who attended to cheer on the vampires each time they bit someone.

Sources:

Deane, Hamilton, and John L. Balderston. *Dracula: The Vampire Play in Three Acts.* New York: Samuel French, 1927. 113 pp.

Donovan, Gene. *I Was a Teen-Age Dracula.* Chicago: Dramatic Publishing Company, 1968. 90 pp.

Dracula (The Original 1931 Shooting Script). Atlantic City, NJ: Magic Image Filmbooks, 1990.

Glut, Donald F. *The Dracula Book.* Metuchen, NJ: Scarecrow Press, 1975. 388 pp.

Hotchner, Stephen. *Dracula.* Denver, CO: Pioneer Drama Service, 1978. 55 pp.

Kelly, Tim. *Young Dracula; or, The Singing Bat.* Denver, CO: Pioneer Drama Service, 1975. 61 pp.

Leonard, William Tolbert. *Theatre: Stage to Screen to Television.* Vol. 1. Metuchen, NJ: Scarecrow Press, 1981.

McCarty, John. *Splatter Movies: Breaking the Last Taboo.* Albany, NY: FantaCo Enterprises, Inc., 1981. 160 pp.

Nelson, Hilda. *Charles Nodier.* New York: Twayne Publishers, 1972. 188 pp.

Oliver, A. Richard. *Charles Nodier: Pilot of Romanticism.* Syracuse, NY: Syracuse University Press, 1964. 276 pp.

Skal, David J. *Hollywood Gothic: The Tangled Web of Dracula from Novel to Stage to Screen.* New York: W. W. Norton & Company, 1990. 242 pp.

Stuart, Roxana. *Stage Blood: Vampires of the Nineteenth-Century Stage.* Bowling Green, OH: Bowling Green University Popular Press, 1994. 377 pp.

❨ Dreyer, Carl Theodor (1889–1968) ❩

Carl Theodor Dreyer, thought by many to be Denmark's greatest film director, was born on February 3, 1889, in Copenhagen. He began his working career in 1909 as a journalist, and in 1911 he married Ebba Larsen. On the side he began writing scripts for a motion picture company, Scandinavisk-Russiske Handelshus, and in 1913 Dreyer quit his job to work for Nordisk Films Kompagni.

Six year later, he was given the opportunity to direct his first film, *Praesidenten (The President),* for which he also wrote the screenplay. Dreyer made several movies in Denmark and Germany but gained prominence with *Du Skal Aere Din Hustru (The Master of the House)* in 1925. He was invited to France to work and there made his notable *La Passion de Jeanne d'Arc* in 1928. Soon after the appearance of *La Passion de Jeanne d'Arc,* the film industry began its transition to sound and it was not until 1932 that Dreyer directed again. His first sound movie remains the one for which he is best remembered.

In 1932 he directed **Vampyr** (released to English-speaking audiences as *The Dream of David Gray*), lauded by some critics as the greatest vampire film of all time. Others have complained of the slow pace of the film, suggesting that it failed as entertainment. Loosely inspired by **Sheridan Le Fanu**'s female vampire story **"Carmilla"**, *Vampyr* implied the horror that surrounded the action on the screen and invited viewers to participate with their imagination.

The story concerned an older female vampire who was preying on the daughter of the owner of the local manor. David Gray, a visitor in the town, discerned the true nature of her malevolence and took the lead in **destroying** her.

Two memorable scenes stood out in Dreyer's communication of horror. In one, early in the picture, a policeman was sitting with his shadow cast on the wall behind him. Suddenly, the shadow started to operate separately from the policeman and walked away. Later, Gray dreamed of his own funeral. He could see out of the casket, which had a small window just above his face. As he awoke and gazed through the opening, the vampire's face appeared looking back at him. Dreyer produced part of the atmosphere of *Vampyr* by shooting much of the film at dawn and at twilight. He also discovered a flour mill where the white **dust** in the air and the white walls added a eerie quality to the scenes photographed there. Dreyer chose amateur actors whose overall appearances, especially their faces, communicated aspects of personality he wished to explore. He brought out their inherent features by the frequent use of closeup shots and little makeup. He sought to create a feeling of uneasiness in his audience, a feeling that would remain even after the conflict of the story had been resolved.

Following the completion of *Vampyr,* Dreyer left filmmaking and resumed his journalism career. He did not make another film until 1942, when he produced a docu-

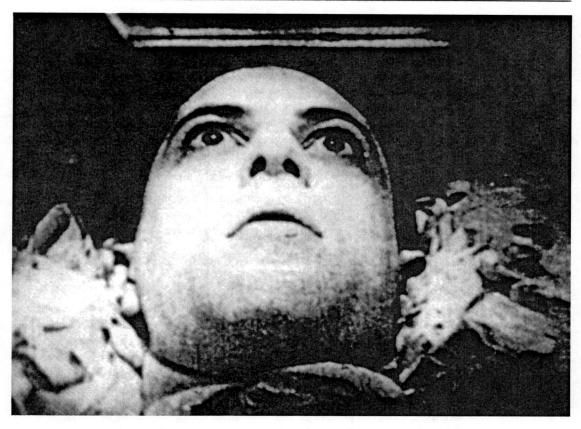

David Gray (Julian West) dreams of his own funeral in one of the most famous scenes from Carl Theodor Dryer's classic film, *Vampyr*.

mentary during World War II. He made a number of films through the 1940s and early 1950s. In 1952 he was given the management of a film theater by the Danish government. His 1955 film, *Ordet*, received the Golden Lion Award. *Vampyr* was his only treatment of the vampire theme.

He died in Copenhagen on March 20, 1968. He spent his last years on a project to make a movie about the life of Christ, but the film was never produced.

Sources:

Bordwell, Carl. *The Films of Carl-Theodor Dreyer*. Berkeley: University of California Press, 1981.

Carney, Raymond. *Speaking the Language of Desire: The Films of Carl Dreyer*. Cambridge: Cambridge University Press, 1989. 363 pp.

Dreyer, Carl Theodor. *Four Screen Plays*. Trans. by Oliver Stallybrass. Bloomington, IN: Indiana University Press, 1970. 312 pp.

Everson, William K. *Classics of the Horror Film*. New York: Citadel Press, 1974. 247 pp.

Thomas, Nicolas. *International Dictionary of Films and Filmmakers. II: Directors*. Chicago: St. James Press, 1991.

Duckula, Count

Count Duckula was a cartoon character introduced in the **United Kingdom** in the 1980s. A cross between **Dracula** and Donald Duck, he lived in modern-day **Transylvania** at Castle Duckula with his servants Igor and Nanny. While coming from a long line of vampire ducks, and feared by the local villagers, Count Duckula was a vegetarian who preferred vegetable juice to **blood**. He wore the requisite evening dress and **opera** cape, but had no **fangs**. He slept in a magical **coffin** that could transport him, and his entire castle, to various parts of the world for his adventures. He had an archenemy in Dr. Von Goosewing, the **vampire hunter**. The unfortunate count was in love with the doctor's niece, Vanna von Goosewing.

Count Duckula was brought to **television** as an animated cartoon series in the United Kingdom in 1988, a series later shown in **America**. Also in 1988, Marvel Comics introduced a *Count Duckula* comic that appeared bi-monthly for fifteen issues.

Sources:

Count Duckula. Nos. 1–15. New York: Marvel Comics, 1988–91.
Drake, Royston. *Duckula: The Vampire Strikes Back*. London: Carnival, 1990. 30 pp.

Dumas, Alexandre (1802–1870)

Alexandre Dumas (Davy de la Pailleterie), prominent French novelist and playwright best remembered for his novels *The Three Musketeers* and *The Count of Monte Cristo,* was born on July 24, 1802, in Villers-Cotterets, France, the son of Thomas Alexandre Dumas Davy de la Pailleterie, a general in Napoleon's army, and Marie Louise Elisabeth Labouret. His father's mother was an African slave. Dumas's father died in prison when his son was four. Dumas showed few outstanding qualities as he was growing up. He had beautiful handwriting and was a good conversationalist, but proved to be a dullard in arithmetic and only average in his other school work.

However, he had a vivid imagination which led him into the theater. Dumas turned to the theater at the age of eighteen after seeing a performance of *Hamlet.* He organized his own drama company for which he wrote material, directed the plays, and often performed. Fired by ambition, he moved to Paris early in 1823, ready to take the city by storm. Interestingly enough, his career was to begin and end with a vampire.

Shortly after Dumas's arrival in Paris, **Charles Nodier's** play, *Le Vampire,* opened for its second run at the Porte-Sainte-Martin theatre. As Dumas was about to sit down for the performance, someone made a comment about his head of bushy red hair. Insulted, he challenged the man to a duel and left the theater. By the time he got to the street, however, he thought better of his actions and, after purchasing a second ticket, returned to the theater through another door. He was seated in the orchestra section next to a well-dressed gentleman, and they conversed until the play began. While Dumas enjoyed the play, the gentleman next to him obviously did not and let his displeasure show. Following the second act, the man stood up and announced he could stand no more. Then, during the third act, the performance was interrupted by some shrill whis-

tles. The gentleman, whom Dumas later learned was none other than Charles Nodier, was ushered from the theater. The evening was to prove a significant one, and Dumas devoted three chapters of his *Memoirs* to a description of his reactions to the play.

Dumas spent the next years reading, writing poetry, and working hard at his job. In 1827 he finished a play, *Christine*, but he had no connections to present it to a producer. Someone suggested that he try to reach Baron Taylor of the Comédie-Française. Taylor was a good friend of Nodier, and even though Dumas had not seen Nodier since the night at *Le Vampire*, he risked sending a letter to the author. He reminded Nodier of the evening and asked for an introduction to Taylor. Nodier arranged an appointment, and Dumas was able to sell Taylor on the play. His literary career was launched. Instead of making the revisions requested by Taylor, however, he wrote a second play, *Henri III et Sa Cour*, which opened on February 10, 1829. With a new job as the librarian to the Duc d'Orleans, he was finally able to mingle with the artistic and intellectual community of Paris. He spent his spare time with a variety of mistresses. Dumas was one of the most successful playwrights in Paris for the rest of the decade. His career was interrupted in 1830 by the emergence of Louis Philippe, who did not like Dumas's republican **political** views.

Dumas took the occasion to absent himself from Paris. Several unsuccessful plays in a row occasioned the writing of the first volume of *The Three Musketeers* in 1844. It was soon followed by *The Count of Monte Cristo*, and a series of very successful adventure novels. The dramatization of *The Three Musketeers* was also well received, and Dumas was again financially successful. He built a large estate, the Château de Monte Cristo. In 1847 the Théâtre Historique was constructed to show his plays.

However, this all came to an end with the revolution of 1848. The theater was closed during the revolution and attendance lagged in the aftermath. His debts mounted. Then on December 2, 1851, Louis Napoleon, the president of France, dismissed the Assembly and launched his coup d'état. Dumas had been desperately trying to recoup his fortunes, but his new plays all failed. Finally, in a last attempt, he turned to the vampire theme he had encountered when he arrived in Paris. On December 30, less than a month after the coup, his version of *Le Vampire* opened at the Ambigu-Comique.

About the same time he also authored a vampire short story, "The Pale Lady" (1848). It was to be his last play for the city he had so loved. Early in 1852 he left for Belgium to get away from his creditors and a government that, once again, did not appreciate his politics. Once in Belgium, he began work on his *Memoirs* and wrote several other books reflecting on his career and travels. He died at the home of his son in Puys, France, on December 5, 1870. Dumas holds a prominent place in nineteenth-century French literature for his fast-paced action novels and the vivid imagination he brought to his writing. He also is important in the development of the modern vampire myth as the last of a generation of great French writers to explore the theme.

Sources:

Dumas, Alexandre. *The Memoirs, Being Extracts from the First Five Volumes.* London: W. H. Allen & Co., 1891. The condensed English edition of the *Memoirs*, published under the title *The Road to Monte Cristo*, eliminated all references to *The Vampyre*.

———, and Frank N. Morlock. *The Return of Lord Ruthven the Vampire.* Encino, CA: Hollywood Comics, 2004.

Gorman, Herbert. *The Incredible Marquis: Alexandre Dumas*. New York: Farrar & Rinehart, Inc., 1929. 466 pp.

Martone, Eric. *Alexandre Dumas's the Vampire: A Novel Based on the Drame Fantastique*. Lincoln, NB: iUniverse. 2003.

Stuart, Roxana. *Stage Blood: Vampires of the Nineteenth-Century Stage*. Bowling Green, OH: Bowling Green University Popular Press, 1994. 377 pp.

Dust

Similar to his ability to transform himself into **animals** or a **mist**, as described in the 1897 novel, **Dracula** also could transform into a cloud of dust. Dr. **Abraham Van Helsing** made reference to the coming and going of the three **women** in **Castle Dracula**. While **Jonathan Harker** looked on, they transformed themselves into a dust form while standing in the moonlight. In his second encounter with the women, Harker saw the moonlight quiver as the dust danced around and then slowly took on a recognizable shape, the three phantomlike images.

Dracula made his first and only appearance in this form during his attacks upon **Lucy Westenra**. The wolf Beserker had broken some of the glass from the window in her room. Then suddenly, the room seemed to fill with "a whole myriad of little specks" blowing in the window and forming themselves into a "pillar of dust" inside the room. She passed out and upon regaining consciousness noticed that the air again was full of these dusty specks.

While a notable element in the novel *Dracula*, this vampiric ability has not been of importance to the twentieth-century conception of the vampire.

The vampire transforming into dust is, of course, separate from the vampire turning to a pile of dust when killed. This later concept appeared at the end of *Dracula* and was used, for example, in the **Hammer** adaptation of the novel, *Horror of Dracula*, in which Dracula burns in the light of the sun. In its sequel, the dust (or ash) is reanimated by dripping fresh **blood** on it. That process would be used in several movies as a means of reviving a deceased vampire. In *Buffy the Vampire Slayer* tevision series, as vampires are killed, they are said to be "dusted," a reference to their immediate disentegration into a pile of ash/dust after being staked or beheaded.

Dynamite Fan Club *see:* Vampire Fandom: United States

Eighteen-Bisang, Robert (1947–)

Robert Eighteen-Bisang, an independent Canadian scholar, is best known as the owner of the world's largest collection of rare vampire books. He resides in Vancouver, where he attended the University of British Columbia. After receiving his bachelor's degree in sociology in 1976, he worked for a time in advertising and marketing.

Eighteen-Bisang began collecting books on **Dracula** and vampires more than a quarter of a century ago. He worked with the likes of rare-book dealers Lloyd W. Currey (in New York) and George Locke (London), and was able to discover hundreds of rare vampire books before other collectors were aware that they existed. Along the way he purchased the core of the vampire collections assembled by Marlene Woods in Longview, Texas, and **Forrest J. Ackerman** in Hollywood.

Eighteen-Bisang's foremost interests are the vampire myth as it appears in literature, popular culture, and in bibliographic research. Over the years, he has shared his knowledge with numerous scholars and collectors. He has written articles for and acted as an advisor to dozens of books—including four annotated editions of *Dracula* and several encyclopedias.

Bram Stoker's Notes for Dracula (2008), which he co-authored with **Elizabeth Miller,** has been received as a core academic text for the study of *Dracula* and vampires, and received glowing reviews. *Famous Monsters of Filmland* nominated his book "the best book of the year" and it won the **Lord Ruthven** Award for "best vampire book of 2008." His expertise has been recognized by invitations to speak across North America and in 1997 he was one of the guests of honor at "Dracula '97" in Los Angeles. He is also the founder of **Transylvania** Press, Inc., the first company to reprint **Bram Stoker's** abridged edition of *Dracula*. His is also credited with the discovery of Hutchinson's colonial edition of *Dracula*, possibly the true first edition of Bram Stoker's macabre fairy tale;

demonstrating that parts of *Dracula* are based on the Jack the Ripper murders of 1888; and proving that one of **Sherlock Holmes**'s cases, "The Adventure of the Illustrious Client," was a rationalized (and, some say, plagiarized!) adaptation of *Dracula*. *University Affairs* recently cited him as one of the leading independent scholars in Canada.

As this encyclopedia goes to press, Eighteen-Bisang is working on two books with **Martin H. Greenberg**—*Sherlock Holmes v. Dracula* and *Vampire Lists*—and a definitive, three-volume vampire bibliography, with J. Gordon Melton.

Sources:

Eighteen-Bisang, Robert. "Dracula, Jack the Ripper and 'A Thirst for Blood.'" *The Jack the Ripper Casebook*, 2008. Posted at http://www.casebook.org/dissertations/rip-thirst.html. Accessed on April 5, 2010.

———."Dracula by Arthur Conan Doyle" in *The Sherlock Holmes Journal* (December 2009).

———."Hutchinson's Colonial Edition of Dracula" Transylvania Press. Posted at http://www.transylvania.com/. Accessed on April 5, 2010.

Doyle, Sir Arthur Conan. *Vampire Stories.* Edited by Robert Eighteen-Bisang and Martin H. Greenberg. New York: Skyhorse Publishing, 2009. 271 p.

Stoker, Bram. *Bram Stoker's Notes for Dracula: A Facsimile Edition.* Edited by Robert Eighteen-Bisang and Elizabeth Miller. Jefferson, NC: McFarland & Co., 2008. 331 p.

Zamprelli, Pascal. "The Indie Scene." *University Affairs / Affaires universitaires* (December 1, 2008).

❨ El Conde Dracula ❩

*E*l *Conde Dracula* (1970) is a Spanish-language movie version of **Bram Stoker's Dracula** made by popular director Jesus Franco. Franco built on the popularity of **Hammer Films**' horror movies and lured Hammer star **Christopher Lee** to play the title role. Lee saw it as an opportunity to play the character as it was described in the original novel (rather than the **Hamilton Deane/John Balderston** stage version), the only exceptions being that there were no hairy palms or elongated ears and fingers. With all of its shortcomings, Lee felt it to be the most faithful to Stoker of any films to that time. Franco opened with **Jonathan Harker**'s (not **R. N. Renfield**'s) trip to **Transylvania**. He returned to the film the final race to Transylvania with its fatal confrontation with **Dracula** in his castle. While making a noticeable attempt to add previously missing elements from the novel, in many significant ways *El Conde Dracula* deviated significantly in much the same manner as previous *Dracula* movies.

Following Jonathan's initial encounter with Dracula, he returned to England and was treated in **Abraham Van Helsing**'s private clinic, where **Dr. John Seward** worked as a mere employee. Dracula appeared and attacked **Lucy Westenra** to the alarm of her fiancé **Quincey P. Morris**, here an English nobleman rather than a Texan. Lucy's fiancé from the novel, **Arthur Holmwood**, did not appear. Unable to save Lucy, Van Helsing and Morris ended her vampiric life with a **stake** and **decapitation.** The men invaded Dracula's estate where they encountered a set of stuffed animals that came alive, presumably at Dracula's command, and eventually drove Dracula away with a **crucifix.** Before returning to Transylvania, Dracula attacked **Mina Murray** on two occasions. The second time, in the clinic, Van Helsing drove him off by burning a cross in the floor with a poker from the room's fireplace. Before he died, the madman Renfield gave them the clue where to find the fleeing Dracula, and Harker and Morris set out to look for him. They entered **Castle Dracula** and killed the three female residents and then drove off the **Gypsies** protecting the body of Dracula asleep in his crate of earth. They killed him by setting him on **fire** and tossing him onto the rocks below the castle.

Waller noted that Franco saw *El Conde Dracula* as a confrontation between youth and age. Lucy, Mina, Jonathan, and Quincey were of one generation and Van Helsing and Dracula of another. Van Helsing, the major voice of maturity, informed the young men of Dracula's true nature, but was pushed aside because of his own knowledge in the black arts. In the end, Van Helsing was left behind as the strong and youthful men journeyed to Transylvania to destroy Dracula. Franco's *El Conde Dracula* was released in English versions as *Count Dracula* and as *Bram Stoker's Count Dracula*.

Sources:

Holte, James Craig. *Dracula in the Dark: The Dracula Film Adaptations*. Westport, CT: Greenwood Press, 1997.

Waller, Gregory A. *The Living and the Undead: From Stoker's Dracula to Romero's Dawn of the Dead*. Urbana, IL: University of Illinois Press, 1986. 376 pp.

Elliott, Denholm Mitchell (1922–1992)

Denholm Mitchell Elliott, one of England's most famous actors, was born May 31, 1922, in **London**, the son of Nina Mitchell and Niles Layman Elliott. Just prior to World War II he attended the Royal Academy of Dramatic Arts but did not make his formal stage debut until 1945 in *The Drunkard*. He made his first movie, *Dear Mr. Prohack*, in 1948. In 1951 he appeared on the New York stage for the first time and made his first Hollywood movie, *Breaking the Sound Barrier*. In 1969 Elliott starred in the title role in the British **television** version of *Dracula*. He has been remembered, at least in England, as one of the more memorable persons to portray the count. The production was one of the most faithful adaptations of the novel, and was noted particularly for the final scene in which **Dracula** disintegrated. Elliott wore a beard for the part.

Following his appearance in *Dracula*, Elliott appeared in numerous movies, both American and British productions, though none of the vampire genre.

Sources:

Elliott, Susan, and Barry Turner. *Denholm Elliott: Quest for Love*. Trafalgar Square, 1996.

Glut, Donald F. *The Dracula Book*. Metuchen, NJ: Scarecrow Press, 1975. 388 pp.

Elrod, P. N.

Patricia Nead Elrod, popular author of vampire novels, began writing at the age of 12. She developed an interest in vampires at a young age while watching vampire movies and especially the **Dark Shadows television** series. During the 1980s she became an active participant in role playing games, particularly one called *Mercenaries, Spies, & Private Eyes*. In 1986 she entered a role-playing module into a *Dragon* magazine contest that eventually was bought and published in the first issue of *Dungeon Adven-*

Popular novelist P. N. Elrod.

tures. This was her first professional publication. Meanwhile, through her role playing, she developed a supernatural character, a vampire detective. At one point she began to write up the game scenario, and it became the first of "The Vampire Files" novels, *Bloodlist*. She quickly followed with *Lifeblood* and *Bloodcircle*. All three novels were published in 1990. Their success prompted the continuation of the series and three more volumes appeared: *Art in the Blood* (1991), *Fire in the Blood* (1991), and *Blood on the Water* (1992). This series features Jack Fleming, a reporter who had been transformed into a vampire. After his **transformation** he became a detective with a nonvampire partner, Charles Escott.

By this time Elrod built her writings around what she thought of as interesting characters, some of whom just happened to be vampires who have to work out their relationship with the "normal" world. One such interesting character, Jonathan Barrett, who had appeared briefly in *Bloodcircle*, became the central figure for a second series which recounted his life after becoming a vampire on the eve of the American Revolution. Having drunk **blood** from a vampire while away at college in England, in an incident he merely thought of as kinky sex, Barrett became a vampire when he was killed shortly after his return to the colonies in **America**. His story of discovering what he had become on awakening from the dead was told in three volumes, the first of which, *Red Death*, appeared in 1993. Meanwhile, Elrod was asked by TRS, Inc., the publishers of the *Ravenloft* role-playing series, to write the autobiography of their main character, the vampire Strahd. *I, Strahd* appeared in 1993, and a sequel, *I Strahd: The War with Azalin* came out in 1998. Through the 1990s Elrod became one of the most recognizable names among vampire fiction writers, and a **P. N. Elrod Fan Club** emerged in 1993. Through it, she kept her growing legion of fans aware of her new writing projects, and with the advent of the Internet the club has been superseded by her website, http://www.vampwriter.com/.

Into the new century she has remained active in writing vampire fiction. She continued the adventures of Jack Fleming in *A Chill in the Blood* (1998), *The Dark Sleep* (1999), *Lady Crymsyn* (2001), *Cold Streets* (2003), *Song in the Dark* (2005), and *The Devil You Know* (2009), with additional titles in the pipeline. In the mid 1990s, she began a series of novels with Nigel Bennett (better known at the time as **LaCroix** in the **Forever Knight** television series). The first one, *Keeper of the King,* appeared in 1996. The novels were based upon the fantasy of a Sir Lancelot-like character having become a vampire. In the first novel the knight, Richard d'Orleans, is brought into the modern age where he meets contemporary challenges while tying up loose ends from his past. It proved popular enough to continue the adventures through sequels, *His Father's Son* (2001) and *Siege Perilous* (2004).

Sources:

Bennett, Nigel, and P. N. Elrod. *Keeper of the King.* Riverdale, New York: Baen, 1996. 400 pp.

————. *His Father's Son.* New York: Baen, 2001. 337 pp.

————. *Siege Perilous.* New York: Baen, 2004. 336 pp.

Elrod, P. N. *Bloodcircle.* New York: Ace Books, 1990. 202 pp.

————. *Bloodlist.* New York: Ace Books, 1990. 200 pp.

————. *Lifeblood.* New York: Ace Books, 1990. 202 pp.

————. *Art in the Blood.* New York: Ace Books, 1991. 195 pp.

————. *Fire in the Blood.* New York: Ace Books, 1991. 198 pp.

————. *Blood on the Water.* New York: Ace Books, 1992. 199 pp.

————. "Partners in Time." *Good Guys Wear Fangs* 1 (May 1992): 1–23.

————. *Red Death.* New York: Ace Books, 1993. 288 pp.

————. *I Strahd: Memoirs of a Vampire.* Lake Geneva, WI: TSR, Inc., 1993. 309 pp.

————. *Death and the Maiden.* New York: Ace Books, 1994. 224 pp.

————. *Death Masque.* New York: Ace Books, 1995. 261 pp.

————. *Dance of Death.* New York: Ace Books, 1996. 340 pp.

————, and Martin H. Greenberg. *The Time of the Vampires.* New York: Daw, 1996. 320 pp.

————. *A Chill in the Blood.* New York: Ace Books, 1998. 327 pp.

————. *I Strahd: The War with Azalin.* Lake Geneva, WI: TSR, Inc., 1998. 310 pp.

————. *The Dark Sleep.* New York: Ace Books, 1999. 359 pp.

————. *Lady Crymsyn.* New York: Ace Books, 2001. 410 pp.

————. *Cold Streets.* New York: Ace Books, 2003. 380 pp.

————. *Song in the Dark* (The Vampire Files). New York: Ace, 2005. 377 pp.

"An Interview with P. N. Elrod." *The Vampire Information Exchange Newsletter* 65 (December 1993): 14.

Elvira

E lvira is the vampirelike persona of actress Cassandra Peterson. Elvira was created in 1981 after Peterson landed a job with KHJ-TV in Los Angeles as hostess for the station's horror movie program, *Movie Macabre.* On May 23, 1982, she hosted a screening of *The Mad Magician,* a 3-D film. In connection with the show, more than 2.7 million pairs of 3-D glasses were distributed, and Elvira became the first person to appear on **television** in 3-D. Shortly thereafter, her new celebrity status was confirmed when she made an appearance on *The Tonight Show,* and Rhino Records released *3-D TV. Movie Macabre* went into syndication. Peterson grew up in Colorado Springs, Colorado, and began her career in show business as a showgirl in Las Vegas. She tried to break into films and television, and obtained a number of bit parts in various movies and TV shows. She tried out for the part of Ginger for *Rescue from Gilligan's Island* (1978), a movie revival of the old television series, but lost out to Judith Baldwin. She had almost decided to quit show business when the offer came to host *Movie Macabre.* The character Elvira evolved over several months. It was created from a host of sources, but obviously drew on popular public images of female vampires such as Morticia Addams (of **The Addams Family**), **Vampirella**, and former television hostess and movie actress **Vampira** (Maila Nurmi). At one point Vampira accused Elvira of stealing her persona and filed suit, but the case was dismissed in court.

The sudden fame in 1982 allowed Elvira to make cameo appearances on several national television shows, and she put together a Halloween-oriented show at the Knott's

Actress Cassandra Peterson as her alter ego, the vamp Elvira.

Berry Farm amusement park. Her television show was nominated for an Emmy award as the best local television show. Since that time Elvira has expanded the range of her appearances. In 1985 she began to appear on *Thriller Theatre,* a series of re-releases on video of old B-movies by LIVE Entertainment. Also in 1985, she received the annual Count Dracula Society Award from the Academy of Science Fiction, Fantasy and Horror Films. In 1986, Marvel Comics began to publish *Elvira's House of Mystery,* which ran for 11 issues. The Elvira Halloween costume became the best selling costume of the 1986 season. In 1987, she made her first appearances in commercials for Coors BeerÆ, becoming the first female celebrity hired to endorse a beer product. To keep up with this variety of activities, Peterson founded Queen B Productions. While no one noticed that Cassandra Peterson (without the Elvira persona) had appeared in a number of films, in 1988 Queen B Productions began work on *Elvira, Mistress of the Dark,* a full-length feature film starring Elvira. The production did not do well as a movie (the distributor, New World Pictures, went out of business soon after its release), but it was shown on prime-time television and did quite well as a video. A single comic book issue was developed from the movie by Marvel Comics.

The production of *Elvira, Mistress of the Dark,* required a sharpening of the image and the development of a story for the character. The movie attempted to explain her appearance by describing Elvira as descending from a line of sorcerers. Her mother had tried to break out of that lineage by marrying a mortal, and Elvira was the product of that union. Eventually, her mother was killed by her brother Vincent, and Elvira was raised in an orphanage. Elvira's following was organized into the Elvira Fan Club (which may be contacted through the Elvira webpage at http://www.elvira.com/fanclub.html). For a number of years, the fan club published a newsletter, *The Elvira Examiner.* Members receive a bumper sticker, poster, decal, and button. The club also offers members a variety of products and **paraphernalia** with Elvira's image, from an annual calendar to T-shirts and pin-up posters. Elvira's image is marketed through Queen B Productions. Through it, a line of Elvira cosmetics was developed. There have been four Elvira **games:** a pinball arcade game, a hand-held computer game, and two computer role-playing games—*Elvira: Mistress of the Dark* (1990) and *Elvira II: The Jaws of Cerberus* (1991). In 1993, a new **comic book** series, *Elvira, Mistress of the Dark,* was launched by Claypool Comics. It ran monthly for 166 issues through February 2007. In 1996 the first of a new set of novels by Elvira and John Paragone appeared.

Peterson has been an activist for animal rights. In 1990 she released a perfume line that was the first to carry the cruelty-free symbol of People for the Ethical Treatment of Animals (PETA); for this she won PETA's Humanitarian Award. She has also appeared in ads decrying the wearing of furs. Elvira was the Media Guest of Honor at **Dracula '97: A Centennial Celebration.** Elvira/Peterson was active through the first decade of the new century with a wide variety of public appearances.

Sources:

Counts, Kyle. "Elvira, Mistress of the Dark." *Cinefantastique* 19, 1/2 (January 1989): 104–07.
Cziraky, Dan. "Elvira." *Femme Fatale* 1, 3 (Winter 1992/93): 6–11, 60.
———. "Mistress of the Dark." *Femme Fatale* 1, 2 (Fall 1992): 34–37.
Elvira, Mistress of the Dark. No. 1–166. Leonia, NJ: Claypool Comics, 1993–2007.
Elvira, with John Paragon. *Transylvania 90210.* New York: Berkley Boulevard Books, 1996. 169 pp.
———. *Camp Vamp.* New York: Berkley Boulevard Books, 1997. 172 pp.
———. *The Boy Who Cried Werewolf.* New York: Berkley Boulevard Books, 1998. 165 pp.
"Shop of Horrors." *The Elvira Examiner* 11 (1993): 2.

Eretik *see:* Russia, Vampires in

Estonia, Vampires in *see:* Baltic States, Vampires in the

Estries

Estries were a Jewish female vampire that emerged during the medieval period. Estries is a French word derived from the *strix*, the Latin word for the screech-owl. The *strix* lies behind the Greek *striges*, the Romanian *strigoi*, and the Italian *strega*, a vampire-witch character. The female *strega*, like the lamia, attacked infants and drained their blood (an early explanation for what is now known a crib death).

Among the earliest references to the estries is found in the writings of the Hasidei Ashkenaz, a twelfth-century pietist movement in Germany, which, after being forced out of Germany, became the source of the Kabbalists of Spain in the fourteenth and fifteenth centuries and ultimately of the Hassidic movement of the eighteenth century in Eastern Europe. The Hasidei Ashkenaz movement was founded by Judah ben Samuel of Regensburg (1140–1217), a.k.a. Judah the Pious, who authored the movement's main text, the *Sefer Hasidim* (Book of the Pious). He identified the estries with creatures spoken of in the Talmud that had been created at twilight on the first Friday (that is, the end of the six days of creation described in Genesis) just before God rested for the first Sabbath. Their bodies were left unfinished, and God never returned to complete them. Among their powers, they had developed the ability to morph into various forms, most notably the cat. Judah the Pious also recounted the story of a woman who fell ill and was cared for by two other women, neither of whom had realized that the person in their care was an estrie. When one of the caring women fell asleep, the estrie moved to attack her. The other cried out, awakening her companion, and together they were able to subdue the vampire.

Three centuries later, Rabbi Menahem Zioni, a fifteenth century kabbalist, identified the estries with those people who built the Tower of Babel (Genesis 11: 4-9). After God destroyed the tower, he transformed those who would climb to God's throne into vampires, werewolves, and other monstrous beings.

The estries could be restrained by imposing of an oath upon them. It was also noted that the exercise of their power was also related to the loosening of their hair. If their hair could be constrained, they could not attack. Salt and bread could be used to counter the effect of an injury from a estrie, while an estrie could recover from the injury inflicted by a human if it could consume bread and salt that had belonged to the person who injured her. If a woman identified as an estrie was buried, her mouth would be stuffed with dirt.

Belief in estries gradually disappeared from Jewish lore and do not appear in the contemporary Jewish community, though remnants of belief in the other Jewish vampire, **Lilith**, still can be found.

Sources:

Dan, Joseph. *The Esoteric Theology of Ashkenazi Hasidism*. Jerusalem: Mosad Bialik, 1968.

Segal, Eliezar. "The Right Vampire?" *Jewish Free Press* (October 25, 2001): 8–9. Posted at http://people.ucalgary.ca/~elsegal/Shokel/011025_Vampires.html. Accessed on April 5, 2010.

Trachtenberg, Joshua. *Jewish Magic and Superstition: A Study in Folk Religion*. New York: Atheneum, 1970.

❨ Eucharistic Wafer ❩

The holiest ritual of **Christianity** is that of Holy Communion or the Eucharist. Especially among the older liturgical churches—the Roman Catholic Church, the Eastern Orthodox Church, and the Church of England (and those Anglican churches in fellowship with it)—is the belief that under the elements of bread and **wine**, the body and **blood** of Christ is somehow mystically present. They are treated as holy objects that embody the sacred. Among most Protestants and Free Church members, the sacramental elements are also considered symbols of the body and blood of Christ. They are handled with respect but are not in themselves holy.

The treatment of the eucharistic elements as holy objects—for Roman Catholics the transubstantiated body and blood of Christ—made them open to various superstitious and magical considerations. At the end of the mass, the worship service in which the bread (usually in the form of small wafers) and wine were consecrated, all the wine was consumed. However, some wafers usually were left on the altar, as was a lighted candle to signal their presence. Such wafers had various uses, and in his famous treatise on vampires, **Dom Augustin Calmet**, a Roman Catholic scholar/priest, related a number of old stories of their involvement in **destroying vampires**. Pope St. Gregory the Great (590–604 C.E.) told the story of two nuns who died in a state of excommunication. At a later date, they were seen at the local church. They departed when the deacon called for any excommunicants to leave. St. Benedict sent some consecrated bread to their former nurse in order that it might be offered for their reconciliation. From that time on the nuns remained quietly in their graves. Gregory also related the story of a Benedictine priest who died after leaving his monastery without permission. He was buried in consecrated land, but the next day his body was found above ground. A consecrated wafer was placed on his breast and his body reinterred. It was also related that St. Basil was buried with a piece of the eucharistic wafer he had saved to be interred with him. He died with it in his mouth. Calmet's stories most likely stand behind **Bram Stoker**'s use of the eucharistic wafer in his novel as an effective weapon against vampires. Vampire expert **Abraham Van Helsing** brought the eucharistic wafer—the Host—with him from his

Roman Catholic parish in Amsterdam. As he was trying to demonstrate that **Lucy Westenra** had in fact become a vampire, he used a crumpled wafer mixed with putty to seal the door to her tomb, first to block her entrance and then to keep her inside until the men could arrive and finally kill her. To defeat **Dracula**, Van Helsing armed each man in his cadre with a wafer that he had placed in an envelope. The men set about their work of sanitizing the boxes of **native soil** that he had brought with him from **Transylvania**. In each box as it was treated, they placed a portion of a wafer. Meanwhile, **Mina Murray** (now Mrs. Harker) had encountered Dracula and had been forced to drink of his blood. She considered herself unclean. Van Helsing tried to comfort her, but to little avail. As the men left to do their work, he took a wafer and placed it on Mina's forehead as a talismanic **protection**. Mina screamed as the wafer branded an image of itself on her skin, leaving a red mark that remained until Dracula was killed at the end of the novel.

In subsequent dramatizations of *Dracula* and other vampire films, the vampire's resting place would on occasion be sanitized with the Eucharist (or in its absence with a **crucifix** or **garlic**). Otherwise, the Eucharist has been used only rarely, while the crucifix has become a standard item in the vampire hunter's kit. The crucifix also absorbed the eucharistic wafer's power to brand the flesh of a vampire or someone bitten by a vampire. Only in the 1992 movie ***Bram Stoker's Dracula*** was the scene of Mina's being burned by a wafer dramatized.

Like the crucifix, the role of the eucharistic wafer in vampire lore has been called into question by more secular writers. The vampires of **Anne Rice**, for example, are not affected by sacred objects. Such is also the case with vampires from outer space and those created by some disease. The modern vampire hero, which has grown out of the writings of **Chelsea Quinn Yarbro**, and of which the leading characters in the novels of **Elaine Bergstrom** are an example, also are not affected by sacred objects. This abandonment of both the crucifix and the eucharistic wafer can be attributed largely to the loss of belief in **Satan** as a force opposing God (or of vampires being evil or Satanic), and to the relativizing of Christianity, which is seen as but one religion among many.

Sources:
Calmet, Dom Augustin. *The Phantom World*. 2 vols. London: Richard Bentley, 1850.

Ewers, Hanns Heinz (1872–1943)

Hanns Heinz Ewers, an enigmatic German nationalist and writer of horror fiction, made several contributions to vampire fiction. He was born in Düsseldorf (where serial killer **Peter Kürten** would later commit his **crimes**) and educated for a legal career which he abandoned for writing. His first noteworthy success was his novel, *Alraune* (1911) which has been adapted as a movie on five occasions, the most recent being a sound version in 1952. Earlier, in the 1907 *The Sorcerer's Apprentice,* he had introduced a character, Frank Braun, who was always getting himself involved in nefarious schemes with horrific and boomerang effects.

Alraune followed the further downward spiral of Frank Braun, who was in debt due to his gambling but had figured a way out. He suggested a project to his uncle (a biologist), hoping that the uncle would take care of his financial debt. The experiment involved the insemination of a young woman with the semen of a sex criminal. They carried out the process of going to the worst part of town, kidnapping a harlot, and artificially inseminating her. The product of the experiment was Alraune, who grew into a beautiful young woman. However, Alraune became a vampire who attacked men sexually and then took their **blood** and soul. Braun became her **victim**, but survived when she died before finishing him off. Braun became a continuing character for Ewers and reappeared in his 1922 novel *Vampir*. In the meantime, during World War I he operated as a German agent in the United States for which he was interned and deported. In the novel, Braun jumped ship in San Francisco during World War I and made his way to New York where he became a writer of propaganda aimed at shifting America's loyalty to Germany. In the process he met up with an old acquaintance, Lotti Levi. The wealthy woman began to make contributions to the German cause, and also went above and beyond by contributing blood to Braun. He had become a vampire who, like Alraune before him, killed and drained the blood of his lovers. Afterward he had no memory of his actions, and the novel ends without his vampirism being resolved.

Ewers authored a number of horror (and gruesome) short stories, but is better known for ending his career as a Nazi sympathizer (though he was not an Anti-Semite). He wrote the official biography of storm trooper Horst Wessel. He also seems to have fallen from Hitler's favor as his writings glamorized some of the older leaders who had also fallen from Hitler's favor. He also was opposed to anti-Semitism (and had pictured Braun's lover in *Vampir* as a pro-German Jew) and felt Jews were as good as Germans racially. After he fell from grace, his books were banned and burned. Even after WWII only a few of his texts have been reprinted.

Sources:

Ewers, Hanns Heinz. *Der Zauberlehrling.* 1907. English edition as *The Sorcerer's Apprentice.*
———. *Alraune.* 1911.
———. *Vampir.* 1922. English edition as *Vampire.*
Frenschkowski, Marco. "Von Schemajah Hillel zu Aaron Wassertrum. Juden und Judentum in der deutschsprachigen phantastischen Literatur." In Thomas Le Blanc and Bettina Twrsnick, Hrg. *Traumreich und Nachtseite. Die deutschsprachige Phantastik zwischen Décadence und Faschismus.* Schriftenreihe und Materialien der Phantastischen Bibliothek Wetzlar 15. Wetzlar: Phantastische Bibliothel, 1995. pp. 126–157.
Kugel, Wilfried. *Der Unverantwortliche: Das Leben des Hanns Heinz Ewers.* Düsseldorf: Grupello, 1992.

❨ Explanations of Vampirism ❩

As reports of vampirism filtered into western and central Europe from the east, along with accounts of otherwise credible western witnesses offering support to the vampire hypothesis, scholars and church leaders attempted to find some explanation. Some simply dismissed the reports as stories of primitive superstitions. Many, however, otherwise unable to fit vampires into their eighteenth-century world view, took the reports seriously. They began to propound various alternative explanations to account for what people had observed, especially the phenomena reported in the case of **Arnold Paul**. Actual reports of vampirism, rather than the general folklore concerning vampires, usually

began with people dying from a lingering disease. After some of these people died, neighbors dug up the corpses and observed a variety of unusual conditions, all signs of continuing life. The bodies had not decayed. The skin had a ruddy complexion and the hair and **fingernails** had continued to grow. Fresh flesh had appeared as the outer layer of skin had peeled off. **Blood** was present around the mouth and in the body when it was cut or punctured. There might be a sexual erection on the bodies of males. If staked, the body reacted as if in pain. Occasionally, when a **stake** was thrust into the body, the corpse was heard to cry out. In northern Europe, reports of chewed-off appendages suggested to observers that vampires fed on themselves before leaving the grave to feed on others.

By far the most popular explanation of vampire reports was premature burial. Many people in the eighteenth and nineteenth centuries knew of catalepsy, a disease in which the person affected took on many of the symptoms of death; on occasion, such people were removed by the undertaker and even buried before they reawakened. Herbert Mayo presented an extensive argument for this thesis in his volume, *On the Truths Contained in Popular Superstitions* (1851). In 1896 theosophist **Franz Hartmann** wrote a book based on widespread accounts of accidental interments. Premature burial remained a popular explanation of vampirism into the twentieth century and **Montague Summers**, in his famous treatise on vampirism, felt the need to devote a number of pages to a discussion of it before making his own case for the reality of the vampire in *The Vampire: His Kith and Kin* (1928). He admitted that cases of premature burial "may have helped to reinforce the tradition of the vampire and the phenomenon of vampirism." As recently as 1972, Anthony Masters also argued for the plausibility of premature burials to account for vampire beliefs.

Others suggested that anomalous incidents of preservation of the body from its normal rate of decay accounted for the state of the exhumed bodies. Perhaps something in the soil or an unusual lack of air or moisture slowed the decay. Possibly the shriek heard when the corpse was staked was the escape of trapped air. Similarly, others suggested that what was being observed was simply the natural decay of the body. Most people were unaware of continued changes in the body after death, such as the loss of rigidity. As debate over the reasons for the vampire epidemics continued, other explanations were offered. For example, one set of literature suggested that some form of disease accounted for the vampire symptoms. High on the list was the plague—sometimes known as black death. An epidemic of the plague occurred simultaneously with a vampire outbreak in East Prussia in 1710. The spread of plague germs could account for the spread of vampire symptoms. During the twentieth century, rabies was offered as a specific explanation of vampirism. People with rabies would bite others and manifest animal-like behavior, and had an unquenchable thirst. There also were outbreaks of rabies in **Hungary**, Saxony, and East Prussia during the eighteenth century. In nineteenth-century New England, families suffering from tuberculosis used vampirism as an explanation after experiencing multiple deaths, and treated the bodies of the deceased accordingly. Most recently, in the 1960s, the disease **porphyria** has been suggested as an explanation of vampire reports. One characteristic of porphyria is an extreme sensitivity to light.

Social explanations were also offered for the spread of vampirism. For example, some noticed that vampire reports came from areas in which the Roman Catholic Church and the Eastern Orthodox churches were in contention for the faith of the people. Others saw the reports as a reaction to national defeat, especially in those areas

taken over by Austria in the seventeenth and eighteenth centuries. Pope Benedict XIV, who ruled in the mid-eighteenth century, believed that his own priests were the problem. They supported and spread the accounts of vampirism in order to get superstitious people to pay them to do exorcisms and additional masses.

The most satisfying explanation of the vampire reports to date has come from cultural historian Paul Barber, who in the 1980s conducted a thorough survey of the original reports. Barber also had the benefit of modern medical knowledge concerning the process of decay of human bodies. He analyzed the arguments against the previously cited explanations; none really explained the broad range of phenomena reported in the vampire stories. Vampires were reported whether the factors cited were present or not. Barber has built a comprehensive case that the various accounts of vampires fairly accurately report what actually was observed. The eighteenth-century observers saw bodies in different states of decay from a perspective of limited understanding of the normal processes of decomposition. They tended to offer both natural and supernatural explanations of the unexpected things that they saw. Barber was able to account for the overwhelming majority of the reported attributes of the bodies observed by the eighteenth-century **vampire hunters**. The hunters had dug up bodies within a few months of their original burial. Some were bodies of people who had died during winter and had been kept in cold storage (which significantly inhibited decomposition) for burial after the spring thaw. He also accounted for such odd phenomena (to modern researchers) as the appendages seen sticking out of graves (usually of bodies buried without **coffins**) and appendages that appeared to have been eaten by the corpse, both of which probably derive from the activity of various animal predators on bodies buried in shallow graves without a coffin.

Conclusion: A consideration of the **strengths** and limitations of many explanations of vampires suggests that the belief in vampirism is a very old and possibly cultural response to an event that happens in all cultures—the untimely death of a loved one as a result of childbirth, accident, or **suicide**, followed by an intense experience of interacting with the recently dead person. Given that belief, there are a variety of events, such as the irregular rate of decay of the soft flesh of corpses, that could be cited as visible "proof" that vampires exist or as factors that on occasion correlate to their presence. Since "unnatural" deaths still occur, and people still have intense experiences with the dead (now usually thought of as encounters with ghosts or apparitions), those people who also believe in vampires can point to those experiences as in some manner substantiating their belief. Thus, these experiences indicate the presence of vampires. Hence, we know vampires exist because of these experiences.

Sources:

Barber, Paul. *Vampires, Burial, and Death: Folklore and Reality.* New Haven, CT: Yale University Press, 1988. 236 pp.

Frayling, Christopher. *Vampyres: Lord Byron to Count Dracula.* London: Faber and Faber, 1991. 429 pp.

Masters, Anthony. *The Natural History of the Vampire.* New York: G. P. Putnam's Sons, 1972. Rept. Berkley Publishing Corporation, 1976. 280 pp.

Summers, Montague. *The Vampire: His Kith and Kin.* London: Routledge, Kegan Paul, Trench, Trubner, & Co., 1928. 356 pp. Rept. New Hyde Park, NY: University Books, 1960. 356 pp.

———. *The Vampire in Europe.* London: Routledge, Kegan Paul, Trench, Trubner, & Co., 1929. 329 pp. Rept. New Hyde Park, NY: University Books, 1961. 329 pp.

F

Fangs

Early in **Bram Stoker's** *Dracula* (1897), at the time of his first encounter with **Dracula, Jonathan Harker** sketched his impressions. Besides Dracula's other prominent physical features, he noted that the vampire's mouth "was fixed and rather cruel-looking, with peculiarly sharp white teeth; these protruded over the lips ..." (chapter 2). Later in that same chapter he reinforced his initial description by referring to Dracula's "protuberant teeth" and as they conversed he could not take his eyes from the smiling count for, "as his lips ran back over his gums, the long, sharp, canine teeth showed out strangely." Thus Stoker wedded what has become one of the most identifiable features of the modern vampire to its most popular representative figure.

Like Dracula, the three **women** in the castle, more recently referred to as the vampire **brides**, also possessed the extended canines. As one of the women approached him, Harker noted not only her bad breath but felt the hard dents of the sharp teeth on his skin. He could see the moonlight illuminate the teeth of the other two women. Stoker reinforced the importance of the teeth in identifying the vampire during Dracula's attacks on **Lucy Westenra**. As her strange illness progressed, the knowledgeable Dr. **Abraham Van Helsing** called attention to "the little punctures on her throat and the ragged exhausted appearance of their edges" (chapter 10). As the end approached, he noted the **transformation** overtaking her signaled by her teeth—her canine teeth looked longer and sharper than the rest. After her death they had grown even longer and sharper. Dracula was not the first vampire to have fangs. In describing the first attack on Flora Bannerworth by **Varney the Vampyre**, author **James Malcolm Rymer**, (writing in the 1840s, a full half century before Dracula,) noted, "With a plunge he seizes her neck in his fang-like teeth—a gush of **blood**, and a hideous sucking noise follows." In examining Flora later, her mother brought a light close by so that "all saw on the side of Flora's neck a small puncture wound; or, rather two, for there was one a little distance from the

Doug Wert bares his fangs in *Dracula Rising*.

other." Laura, the **victim** of "Carmilla," in **Sheridan Le Fanu**'s 1872 tale, had a somewhat different experience. She remembered being attacked as a child and feeling two needles plunging into her chest, but upon examination, there were no visible wounds. Later in the story, Carmilla and Laura were speaking to a wandering peddler who noted that Carmilla had the "sharpest tooth—long thin, pointed, like an owl, like a needle." He offered to cut it off and file it to a dull point so that it would no longer be "the tooth of a fish." Later in a dream, Laura again had the experience of two needles piercing the skin of her neck. The doctor found a little blue spot at that place on her neck. The daughter of General Spielsdorf reported an experience similar to Laura's—a pair of needles piercing her throat. It was finally concluded that both had been attacked by a vampire, who would have—as was well known—two long thin and sharp teeth that would leave a distinguishing puncture wound on its victim.

While both Varney and Dracula possessed extended canine teeth, as **Martin V. Riccardo** has noted, this trait was not yet a permanent feature. When *Dracula* was brought to the screen in 1922's ***Nosferatu, Eine Symphonie des Grauens***, **Graf Orlock**, the Dracula figure, had two rat-like teeth protruding from the front of his mouth, rather than the canines mentioned by Stoker. Then when **Bela Lugosi** turned Dracula into a household word through his performance in the 1931 film, he did so without any fangs. Nor did he ever have protruding teeth in any of his subsequent performances. Dracula was also portrayed by **Lon Chaney**, Jr. (*Son of Dracula*, 1943) and **John Carradine** (*House of Frankenstein*, 1944, and *House of Dracula*, 1945) but neither actor sported fangs. The fangs had appeared twice before Lee, in the 1952 Turkish version of *Dracula*, which did not receive broad distribution, and a 1957 **Roger Corman** film *Blood of Dracula* with a female wolflike vampire. In 1958, in the **Hammer Films** bloodfest **The Horror of Dracula**, did **Christopher Lee** turned to the camera and showed audiences his extended canines. He would repeat this act in subsequent films, and after him many others would do likewise. Thus, while Lugosi (following **Hamilton Deane**'s lead) established the image of the vampire dressed in an evening suit and cape, it was Lee who fixed the image of the fanged vampire in popular culture. Since Lee's portrayal, most (though by no means all) cinematic vampires have shown the required teeth, as did **Barnabas Collins** in the **Dark Shadows television** series late in the 1960s.

Once established, fangs became an artistic convention to call attention to the presence of vampires. Fangs commonly appeared on the cover art of vampire novels, quickly identifying those titles not possessing an obvious vampiric name. They were used in a like manner on comic book covers, Dracula dolls, and Halloween greeting cards. A new feature introduced into recent vampire films and novels has been retractable vampire teeth. Vampires would thus appear normal when interacting with humans, and show their fangs only when angry or about to feed. This development seems to have derived from the favorable reaction to the transformation into a werewolf shown in the Oscar-winning *American Werewolf in London*. Such a dramatic transformation from a normal appearance into a monsterlike figure was graphically portrayed by Grace Jones and her fellow vampires in *Vamp* (1986) and would be followed in a number of movies where close-up shots of a vampire's mouth would show the fangs moving into place for a bite. It became a standard element in the many episodes of **Buffy the Vampire Slayer** and of *Angel*. The appearance of the extended canine teeth accompanied other changes in facial expressions and signaled the emergence of the darker predatory side of the vampire's personality. The conventional canine fangs created a problem for the cinematic vampire. Lee's canine teeth appeared to be used more for ripping flesh than for neatly puncturing the skin and jugular vein. The two holes would be so far apart that the vampire would find it difficult to suck from both holes at the same time. Therefore, it has been common to picture the two holes as being much closer together than the distance between the canine teeth would suggest. This discrepancy, overlooked by most fans, has given feminist interpreters of vampires an opening to find something positive in the male-dominated myth. Penelope Shuttle and Peter Redgrove, for example, suggested that the wounds were not those of a carnivore, but of a viper, a snake. They suggested that the film directors, without consciously knowing what they were doing, were harking back to an ancient myth that associated the beginning of menstruation with a snake's bite. After being bitten by the snake, the girl became a woman and began menstruating; after being bitten by the vampire, the women tended to become more active and sexual. While the vampire myth has been associated with the particular anxieties of teenage males, possibly it also has something subtle to communicate directly to young females. **Twilight** author **Stephenie Meyer** decided to drop the fangs altogether and replaced them with strong piercing teeth, suitable for tearing the flesh rather than puncturing it. They work on the wild animals that are the major food of her vampires.

Sources:

Gresh, Lois H. *The Twilight Companion: The Unauthorized Guide to the Series*. New York: St. Martin's Griffin, 2008. 242 pp.

Riccardo, Martin V. *The Lure of the Vampire*. Chicago: Adams Press, 1983. 67 pp.

Shuttle, Penelope, and Peter Redgrove. *The Wise Wound*. New York: Richard Marek, 1978. 335 pp.

Feehan, Christine

Romance writer Christine Feehan is the author of the Dark series of novels about a vampiric race called the Carpathians. Through 2009, some 18 titles appeared. Feehan was born Christina King, in California, where she also grew to adulthood in a large family. She married Richard Feehan. He first novel, *Dark Prince* appeared in 1999. It was the first of her Dark novels which together form about two-thirds of the novels she has written.

The "Dark" series centers on the lives, struggles, and adventures of a people known as the Carpathians, who in the novels are an ancient race of hominids that live unnoticed within the human community. Live traditional vampires, they live on human **blood** and have extremely long life spans. They can shape shift and have considerable personal strength. Carpathians attempt to feed on humans in such a way as to not kill them and begin to arouse the world to their presence.

In the present, the Carpathians have a problem. In recent centuries, they have been unable to produce children who can survive their first year. It is also the case that it has been more than 500 years since a female has been born. Meanwhile, if unable to connect with a lifemate, male Carpathians lose both their ability to see in color and to feel emotionally. They are only moved emotionally by the rush that comes from killing, however, the price of killing is their transformation into a soulless monster, and a close resemblance to the traditional monster as an undead vampire. Vampires unable to find a mate often commit suicide by walking into the dawning sun. The dilemmas faced by the Carpathian males provides the majority of the material to be explored in Feehan's different novels, most of which center on the story of one particular individual. More recent novels will bring back fan-favorite characters for updating and encores.

Feehan has yet to announce any conclusion to her Dark series. In 2007 her novel *Dark Hunger* was adapted as a manga-style comic book. She maintains an Internet site at http://www.christinefeehan.com/.

Sources:

Feehan, Christine. *Dark Prince*. New York: Love Spell Books, 1999. 314 pp.

———. *Dark Challenge*. New York: Love Spell Books, 2000. 390 pp.

———. *Dark Gold*. New York: Love Spell Books, 2000. 312 pp.

———. *Dark Magic*. New York: Love Spell Books, 2000. 358 pp.

———. *Dark Desire*. New York: Love Spell Books, 2001. 390 pp.

———. *Dark Fire*. New York: Love Spell Books, 2001. 390 pp.

———. *Dark Guardian*. New York: Love Spell Books, 2002. 369 pp.

———. *Dark Legend*. New York: Leisure Books, 2002. 394 pp.

———. *Dark Melody*. New York: Jove Books, 2003. 384 pp.

———. *Dark Salvation*. New York: Jove Books, 2003. 341 pp.

———. *Dark Symphony*. New York: Jove Books, 2003. 341 pp.

———. *Twilight Before Christmas*. New York; Pocket Star Books, 2003.

———. *Dark Destiny*. New York: Love Spell Books, 2004. 383 pp.

———. *Dark Secret*. New York: Berkley, 2005. 383 pp.

———. *Dark Celebration: A Carpathian Reunion*. New York: Berkley, 2006. 372 pp.

———. *Dark Demon*. New York: Jove, 2006. 209 pp.

———. *Dark Hunger*. New York: Berkley, 2007. 208 pp.

———. *Dark Possession*. New York: Berkley Hardcover, 2007. 368 pp.

———. *Dark Curse*. New York: Berkley Hardcover, 2008. 416 pp.

———, and Marjorie M. Liu. *Dark Dreamers*. New York: Leisure Books. 2006.

———, Susan Grant, and Susan Squires. *The Only One*. Leisure Books: New York, Reissue edition, 2003.

———, Maggie Shayne, Emma Holly, & Angela Knight. *Hot Blooded*. New York: Jove Books:, 2005.

Female Vampires *see:* Women as Vampires

Fingernails

When **Jonathan Harker** first encountered **Dracula** early in the novel by **Bram Stoker,** his "nails were long and fine, and cut to a sharp point." Above and beyond the role this description had in emphasizing Dracula's animal-like quality, these nails would become functional later in chapter 21 when they would be used to open a wound in his chest from which he would force **Mina Murray** to drink. The fact that his nails were noticed at all possibly derived from some of the widely circulated reports of the vampires of eastern Europe. Among the **characteristics** that **vampire hunters** looked for in the bodies that they exhumed, in the belief that they were possibly vampires, were nails that appeared to have grown since the burial of the person. Fresh nails, or occasionally no nails at all, were a common item mentioned in reports from **Germany**, and both northern and **southern Slavs**. Fingernails have not been emphasized in most post–Dracula vampires. **Graf Orlock**, the Dracula figure in the 1922 film *Nosferatu, Eine Symphonie des Grauens*, had extended fingers with elongated nails that added to his rodentlike appearance. However, when **Bela Lugosi** brought Dracula into a British home, neither hands nor nails appeared abnormal in any way. Occasionally, however, when only the audience could see him, he stuck his hands in front of him like an animal about to pounce on a prey. After Lugosi, only a few vampires that had been altered into a demonic form had clawlike alterations in the hands, though they appear briefly in *Bram Stoker's Dracula* in 1992, in a scene in which Coppola pays homage to both *Nosferatu* and **Carl Dreyer's** *Vampyr*. Dracula, of course, calls upon his sharp finger nails to cut himself in order to allow the blood to flow for Mina to drink.

Fingernails became a characteristic of the vampire to which **Anne Rice** paid attention in her vam-

Vampires occasionally have very long fingernails, as demonstrated here by Radu (Anders Hove) in the movie *Subspecies*.

pire novels. Louis, **Lestat,** and their companions develop fingernails with a distinctive glassy appearance that once noticed easily distinguish them from the average human. Thus, they would make an effort to hide their fingernails.

Hong Kong movies often (but by no means always) picture the hopping vampires with long fingernails. These not only become part of a menacing appearance when the vampire lunges at someone with his hands protruding forward but can on occasion become a knife-like weapon for stabbing someone.

Sources:

Barber, Paul. *Vampires, Burial, and Death: Folklore and Reality.* New Haven, CT: Yale University Press, 1988. 236 pp.

Finland, Vampires in *see:* Scandinavia, Vampires in

Fire

Though not mentioned by **Abraham Van Helsing,** the voice of knowledge about vampires in **Bram Stoker's** *Dracula,* **(1897)** fire was considered the ultimate means of **destroying a vampire** in eastern European countries. Fire was an ancient symbol of God. For example, God appeared to Moses in the burning bush and once the Hebrews left Egypt, God signaled his presence through a cloud that hovered by day and a fire by night. The fiery destruction of the evil cities of Sodom and Gomorrah was an illustration of God's power. In the book of Revelations, God was pictured as cleansing the earth by fire at the end of time. Fire was thus both destructive and renewing, consuming the old and corrupt and making way for the new and pure.

Throughout the world, fire has been a vital source of light and warmth and integral to food preparation. It was natural for it to take on symbolic and religious meanings. While fire has had a particular meaning and its own rituals in each culture, it has been part of the sacred life of all cultures. In the Mediterranean, the metaphorical description of the soul as a spark of fire added to its sacred quality. Fire also has been used to execute people in some countries—a practice used especially for condemned heretics and witches during the medieval period in Europe. In eastern Europe, from **Bulgaria** and **Romania** to **Russia** and **Poland,** the body of a suspected vampire was burned if lesser means (the **stake,** or **decapitation**) failed to stop it. Throughout Europe, people used a new fire to cure livestock of sickness. When such a fire was to be built, residents would extinguish every individual fire in the village and start two new bonfires a short distance from each other. The people then walked the animals in the village through the new fire, or need fire. Afterwards, they relit the village fires from the embers of the need fire. At times, when a vampire was believed to be attacking cattle and other domestic animals, villagers would resort to a need fire, hoping that would free them from the vampire. It was believed that the fire would cause the vampire to leave the herd and become trapped in the area of the fire, where it then would be devoured by wolves. While not mentioned by Stoker as a way to fight the vampire, fire was used by the author of **Varney the Vampyre** as the ultimate means of death: Varney jumped into the fiery opening of a volcano. Through the twentieth century, this concept of fire has

The Parisian Theatre of the Vampires, as shown in *Interview with the Vampire*, was destroyed by fire.

been picked up in many vampire novels and movies, where it provided a popular option for the vampire's destruction. Torch-carrying villagers attacking the vampire's (or other monster's) lair and burning it to the ground was a common scene in movies of the 1930s and 1940s.

More recently, **St. Germain,** the vampire hero in **Chelsea Quinn Yarbro**'s novels, noted fire as one of two means to experience the "true death" of a vampire. For **Anne Rice**'s vampires, whose **blood** was combustible, fire was almost the only way they could be destroyed. **Lestat de Lioncourt** was introduced to fire soon after he was made a vampire when Magnus, his creator, committed **suicide** by jumping into a fire before he told Lestat much about the vampiric life. Claudia and Louis used fire against Lestat before their leaving for Europe, and later Louis used fire against the Parisian vampire community when he burned their Theatre of the Vampires. Fire had its most prominent role in Rice's third vampire volume, ***Queen of the Damned***, where one character notes that fire is the one weapon that vampires can use against each other, and that is exactly what Akasha the ancient original vampire did. She launched a mission against the vampire community and destroyed many before she was herself destroyed. The effectiveness of fire on vampires is carried forward in more recent vampire productions such as the **Buffy the Vampire Slayer**, *Angel*, and the "Twilight" series. In the movies, it repeatedly has made for an exciting ending to a vampire chase, occasionally by shoving the vampire into a furnace for cremation.

Sources:

Edmans, Karl-Martin. "Fire." In Mircea Eliade, ed. *The Encyclopedia of Religion*. New York: Macmillian Publishing Company, 1987.

Ramsland, Katherine. *The Vampire Companion: The Official Guide to Anne Rice's The Vampire Chronicles*. New York: Ballantine Books, 1993. 507 pp.

Fisher, Terence (1904–1980)

Terence Fisher directed the majority of the classic horror motion pictures produced by **Hammer Films** in the 1950s and 1960s, including three important vampire films. Apprenticed aboard the training ship *H.M.S. Conway* during the late 1920s, he later left the sea and held different jobs until 1930 when he went to work at Shepard's Bush Studios. Because there were no schools to learn the film business at that time, he mastered his chosen trade on the job through the 1930s, primarily as a film editor. It was not until 1948 that he directed his first picture, *A Song for Tomorrow*. As early as 1953 Fisher worked at Hammer Films on its early **science fiction** productions, *Four-Sided Triangle* and *Spaceways*. In 1957 he was paired with screenwriter **Jimmy Sangster** and actors **Peter Cushing** and **Christopher Lee** to do a remake of the classic **Universal Pictures'** film *Frankenstein*. The film was a success, and the four men assembled the next year to do *Dracula*. This film became the most memorable of Fisher's career. Through it and others to follow, Fisher—more than any single person—created the distinctive Hammer style with horror movies in general, and the Dracula/vampire movie in particular. *The Horror of Dracula*, the title by which his first Dracula movie is best known, became spectacularly successful. It put Hammer's films on the map as the premier successor to the Universal horror movies of the 1930s and 1940s. Before turning his task over to a new wave of Hammer directors, Fisher would make more than ten additional Hammer horrors, including *The Mummy* (1959) and *The Curse of the Werewolf*, (1961), and significant sequels to both the *Frankenstein* and *Dracula* features. Other Dracula movies by Fisher included *The Brides of Dracula* (1960) and *Dracula, Prince of Darkness* (1965).

Fisher has been hailed for his genuine contributions to the horror genre. He not only brought Technicolor to the horror movie, but presented the evil deeds of Frankenstein and Dracula and other classic monsters directly to the audience, rather than leaving viewers to imagine the action. Although Fisher put the horrid acts on the screen, he also imposed a moral order that opposed evil and eventually defeated it. Technically, such films as *The Horror of Dracula* did not necessarily break new ground as Fisher developed his new versions of the pre-war black and white movies. He merely used the state of the art technology of the late 1950s and the openings provided by the changing social standards concerning what could be presented to film audiences. Most importantly, Fisher's movies appealed to a new generation of horror fans, and his success seemed to reflect the uniqueness of his subject rather than originality or outstanding directing talent on his part. Fisher is thus remembered as a competent director—but not a great one. In judging Fisher, however, one must also take into account the severe budget constraints that Hammer imposed on him; these included, for example, limiting the lines spoken by Christopher Lee after he became a star (largely because of *The Horror of Dracula*) as a means of reducing what would have been Lee's high salary demands. Fisher retired in 1973 and died of cancer in 1980.

Sources:

Bourgoin, Stephane. *Terence Fisher*. Paris: Edilig, 1984. 127 pp.

Glut, Donald G. *The Dracula Book*. Metuchen, NJ: Scarecrow Press, 1975. 388 pp.

Hutchings, Peter. "Terence Fisher." In Nicolas Thomas, ed. *International Dictionary of Films and Filmmakers*. Vol. 2: *Directors*. Chicago: St. James Press, 1991.

————. *Terence Fisher*. Manchester: Manchester University Press, 2002. 224 pp.

Leggett, Paul. *Terence Fisher: Horror, Myth and Religion*. Jeffersonville, NC: McFarland & Company, 2002. 216 pp.

Pirie, David. *Heritage of Horror: The English Gothic Cinema, 1946–1972*. New York: Avon, 1973. 192 pp.

Quinlan, David. *The Illustrated Guide to Film Directors*. Totowa, NJ: Barnes & Noble Books, 1984. 334 pp.

Florescu, Radu R. (1925–)

Radu R. Florescu is an Eastern European historian who, along with his late colleague **Raymond T. McNally**, has been one of the most prominent scholars calling attention to **Vlad the Impaler**, the historical **Dracula**, and his relationship to the vampire legend. One of his ancestors, Vintila Florescu, was Vlad's contemporary but was a supporter Vlad's brother, Radu the Handsome, who took the Wallachian throne in 1462 at the end of Vlad's reign. Florescu seemed destined for an obscure life as a specialist in eastern European politics and culture. His first book was *The Struggle Against Russia in the Romanian Principalities* (1962). However, in the early 1970s he teamed with his Boston College colleague Raymond T. McNally as the author of *In Search of Dracula* (1972), a popular book on the vampire myth. Their book drew upon the historical data concerning Vlad the Impaler, the fifteenth-century Romanian prince who had been associated with the vampire legend by **Bram Stoker**. Some years previously, McNally had become interested in tracking down any real history behind Stoker's novel. His search led him to Vlad the Impaler; after McNally joined the faculty at Boston College, Florescu discovered that the two shared a mutual interest. In the late 1960s they formed a team with Romanian historians Constantin Giurescu and Matai Cazacu to perform research on Dracula and vampire folklore. It was found that in **Romania**, vampire folklore was not tied to Dracula (until very recently). Stoker possibly learned of Vlad from **Arminius Vambéry**, a Romanian scholar he met in the 1890s in **London**.

In Search of Dracula was designed as a miniature encyclopedic survey of aspects of the Dracula legend. Some reviewers, noting the lack of footnotes concerning the historical Dracula, suggested that Florescu and McNally had made up the details of his life. Those reviews led to their next work, a complete biography of Vlad titled, *Dracula: A Biography of Vlad the Impaler, 1431–76*, published in 1973. This study not only spurred further work on the fifteenth-century prince by Romanian historians but also altered the treatment of Dracula in the movies. Among several such movies, two versions of **Dracula**—the 1973 version with **Jack Palance** and the 1992 version by **Francis Ford Coppola**—emphasized the relationship between Bram Stoker's Dracula and the historical Romanian prince. A number of recent novels, such as the several books by **Peter Tremayne** and Dan Simmons's *Children of the Night*, also built their plot on the connection. In 1976, a Swedish documentary about Vlad, with actor **Christopher Lee,** took Florescu's and McNally's first book as its title.

Florescu continued his productive collaboration with McNally. In 1979, (coinciding with the release of the new version of *Dracula [1979]* with **Frank Langella**), they completed an edited version of *Dracula* under the title, *The Essential "Dracula": A Completely Illustrated and Annotated Edition of Bram Stoker's Classic Novel.* This edition was noteworthy for its extensive use of notes that Stoker made while writing the novel. More recently, Florescu and McNally issued a comprehensive presentation of Vlad's life in its context in the broad sweep of fifteenth-century history, *Dracula, Prince of Many Faces: His Life and Times* (1989). The fall of the Cheshescu government in Romania has allowed increased contact and collaborative activity between Romanian scholars and their Western counterparts. In 1991, building on an idea first proposed in the 1970s by Florescu and McNally, Kurt W. Treptow brought together Romanian, British, and American scholars to create an anthology of contemporary research on Dracula. Florescu contributed a paper to this work called, "Vlad II Dracula and Vlad III Dracula's Military Campaigns in Bulgaria, 1443–1462." Florescu was one of the speakers at **Dracula '97: A Centennial Celebration** in Los Angeles and received an award from the **Transylvanian Society of Dracula** for his contributions to Dracula scholarship. Most recently Florescu has been able to combine his interest in Romanian history with an exploration of his own family's contribution in *General Ioan Emanoil Florescu: Organizer of the Romanian Army* (2007).

Sources:

Florescu, Radu. "Vlad II Dracula and Vlad III Dracula's Military Campaigns in Bulgaria, 1443–1462." In Kurt W. Treptow. *Dracula: Essays on the Life and Times of Vlad Tepes.* New York: Columbia University Press, 1991. pp. 103–16.

———. "What's in a Name: Dracula or Vlad the Impaler?" In Elizabeth Miller, ed. *Dracula: The Shade and Shadow.* Westcliffe-on-Sea: Desert Island Books, 1998. pp. 192–201.

Florescu, Radu, and Raymond T. McNally. *Dracula: A Biography of Vlad the Impaler, 1431–1476.* New York: Hawthorn Books, 1973. 239 pp.

———. "The Dracula Search in Retrospect." *The New England Social Studies Bulletin* 43, 1 (Fall 1985–86).

———. *Dracula, Prince of Many Faces: His Life and Times.* Boston: Little, Brown and Company, 1989. 261 pp.

———. *The Complete Dracula.* Boston: Copley Publishing Group, 1992. 409 pp.

McNally, Raymond T., and Radu Florescu. *In Search of Dracula.* New York: Greenwich, 1972. 223 pp.

———, eds. *The Essential "Dracula": A Completely Illustrated and Annotated Edition of Bram Stoker's Classic Novel.* New York: Mayflower Books, 1979. 320 pp.

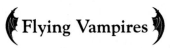

Flying Vampires

Some vampires had the ability to fly. Flying was quite common among Asian vampires. For some, such as the *penanggalan* vampire of **Malaysia**—who flew about as a head and neck and a set of dangling entrails—it was essential. As some Chinese vampires grew older, they transformed into flying creatures. In general, European vampires did not fly, though they were known to levitate. Other vampirelike creatures, such as the *banshee*—the wailing spirit—flew. The European vampire's ability to fly generally was tied to its **transformation** into a creature, such as a bird or **bat.** The ancient Roman *strix,* originally a screech owl, was later identified with the vampiric witches of **Italy.** The

Kiefer Sutherland plays David, the leader of the Lost Boys in the 1987 film. These modern vampires had the ability to fly.

witches were believed to have the power to change into a crow or an owl so they could move about more quickly. Once the vampire was identified with the bat, most thoroughly in the novel ***Dracula* (1897)**, its mobility became greatly extended. The West African vampire, which goes under various names such as the *obayifo* and *asiman* and which reappeared in the Caribbean as the **loogaroo** (Haiti), **sukuyan** (Trinidad), and *asema* (Surinam), regularly changed into a flying ball of light. In this form it could be seen in the night sky. A vampire of this sort, who lived otherwise as a member of the community, would enter the flying state by taking off its skin. After feasting, it often would assume the shape of an animal, at which time it could be chased and, if caught, wounded or killed. Most vampires of twentieth-century literature and motion pictures flew only by making a transformation into a bat. In movies, the bat became a recurring problem to be handled by steadily improving special effects departments. Occasionally the solution would involve the camera taking the bat's perspective so that the audience saw the same view as the bat, but not the bat itself. This bat's-eye view was used effectively in the movies *Innocent Blood* (1992) and *Dracula Rising* (1992).

Those vampires that denied the ability to transform into a bat or other flying creature seemed destined to remain earthbound, and in most cases, have been so limited. The vampires in **Anne Rice**'s novels were an exception. Though without any ability to transform into an animal form, they flew, at least in a limited way. **Lestat de Lioncourt** discovered this when he encountered Magnus (his creator), who picked him up and flew him to the top of a nearby building. The first major movie with vampires flying in their human form was *The Lost Boys* (1987), which included a scene in which two airborne vampires fought each other. More recently police officer Nick Knight, the lead character in the **television** series *Forever Knight*, occasionally took to the air in order to catch a criminal suspect.

For those who saw the vampire more as a supernatural creature, its flying ability represented no great extension of its magical powers. The vampire was frequently linked to witches, who magically flew to their sabbats on a broom. However, as the vampire became a creature of nature, and the vampiric condition related to a disease or a **blood** condition, its ability to fly was seen more as an unbelievable extension of natural powers. In more recent vampire movies and television series, the ability to move at great speed, is demonstrated by Nick St. John in the television series *Moonlight*, Bill Compton the 173-year-old vampire in *True Blood*, and **Edward Cullen** in the movie *Twilight*.

❰ *Forever Knight* ❱

During the 1992–93 **television** season, *Forever Knight* emerged as one of the more popular late-night alternatives to the talk shows. The story was built around Nick Knight, an 800-year-old vampire whose current role was that of a policeman on the Toronto police force. *Forever Knight* first appeared as a two-hour made-for-television movie and pilot for a possible series. Titled *Nick Knight*, it aired on August 20, 1989. In the movie, Nick Knight (Rick Springfield) was a 400-year-old Los Angeles detective assigned to investigate a series of murders in which the **victims** were drained of **blood**. One of the murders occurred in a museum where a goblet that was used to drink blood in an ancient ceremony had been stolen.

Knight was determined to recover his mortal nature. In the meantime he survived on bottled blood. He recognized the murders as possibly having been committed by his old enemy **Lucien LaCroix**, who regularly reappeared as Nick's major obstacle. In the process of investigating the museum murder, Knight met Alyce Hunter, an archaeologist who became his human confidant. She discovered that the goblet was used in a ceremony to cure vampirism. In the end, Knight's investigation led him not to LaCroix, but to Jack Fenner, a bloodmobile attendant and not a vampire, who had been committing the murders because he held a grudge against transients. LaCroix had actually committed only one murder—that in the museum to get the cup. In their initial encounter, LaCroix destroyed the cup. At the end, LaCroix drained Hunter's blood, which set the stage for Knight to destroy LaCroix.

When finally produced as a television series in the 1990s, several changes had occurred, including a new name: *Forever Knight*. The action shifted from Los Angeles to Toronto, and Knight had aged four centuries; his birthdate as a vampire was set in 1228. His real name was changed from Jean-Pierre (mentioned in passing in the earlier movie) to Nicolas de Brabant. As the series proceeded, the story of his past was gradually revealed through flashbacks. In the opening episode, Nicolas (Geraint Wyn Davies), a knight, awakened to find himself turned into a vampire by Lucien LaCroix (Nigel Bennett), who would appear in the flashback scenes throughout the series. He had previously been seduced by Jeannette (Deborah Duchene), a female vampire, and the three had lived together for many years until Nick renounced their vampiric evil and began a search to become mortal again. In the series, Knight worked as a Toronto policeman on the graveyard shift. His sole confidant was Dr. Natalie Lambert (Catherine Disher), a forensic pathologist who was working on a means to transform Knight. The opening episode picked up the story line from the movie concerning the theft of the sacrificial cup at the museum. The story was completed in the second episode, in which Fenner was discovered to be the murderer and both LeCroix and Alyce Hunter were killed. CBS added *Forever Knight* as a weekly entry in its late-night **crime** series, *Crimetime after Primetime*, which was aired against NBC's popular *The Tonight Show*. It garnered a high rating and a loyal audience of vampire fans. However, it disappeared along with all of the *Crimetime* series after CBS signed comedian David Letterman to do his show opposite *The Tonight Show* in August 1993. In the meantime, two fan clubs (the Forever Knight Fan Club and The Official Geraint Wyn Davies Fan Club) and a variety of fanzines began to work for the revival of the show. Their campaign resulted in the show being picked up by TriStar and finding new life in syndication.

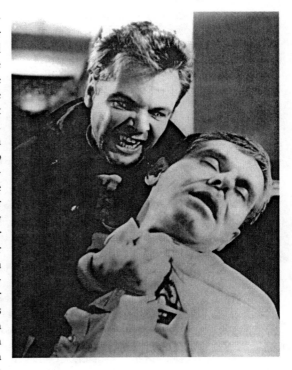

Geraint Wyn Davies as cop/vampire Nick Knight in *Forever Knight.*

At the beginning of the second season, *Forever Knight* found a home on the USA cable network. However fans were disappointed to learn that both John Kepelos and Deborah Duchene would not be returning. Instead, the series introduced several new characters, not too long afterward, it was announced that actors Blue Mankuma, Lisa Ryder, and Ben Bass would assume the roles respectively of Captain Reese (the new precinct commandant), Tracey Vetter (Nick's new partner), and Javier Vachon (a new vampire character). Unfortunately, in spite of a well-organized campaign by the Friends of Forever Knight, the series was permanently cancelled at the end of the third season.

Although there have been no signs of the show being renewed, **Forever Knight fandom** (including an active publishing effort) remained active through the 1990s; reruns of the show appeared on the Sci-Fi Cable Channel, and in 1997, a new set of books based on the *Forever Knight* series began to appear. The television series was notable for its introduction of the game-face, the changed facial appearance of the vampire when s/he is angered or about to feed. This aspect of the vampire was picked up as a central aspect of vampire existence in **Buffy the Vampire Slayer**.

Sources:

Garrett, Susan M. *Forever Knight: Intimations of Mortality.* New York: Berkley Boulevard Books, 1997. 284 pp.

Hathaway-Nayne, Anne. *Forever Knight: These Our Revels*. New York: Berkley Boulevard Books, 1997. 274 pp.

Sizemore, Susan. *Forever Knight: A Stirring of Dust*. New York: Berkley Boulevard Books, 1997. 252 pp.

Strauss, Jon. "Forever Knight." *Epi-log* 36 (November 1993) 4–11; 37 (December 1993): 29–35, 62.

Forever Knight Fandom

In the wake of public response to the **Forever Knight television** series during the 1992–93 season, Lora Haines founded a club for the show's growing number of fans. The club publishes a newsletter, *Feeding Frenzy*, six times a year. Already in 1988, Rosemary Shad had founded The Official Geraint Wyn Davies Fan Club, built around *Forever Knight*'s handsome young star. A variety of fanzines also appeared, including *The Raven*, edited by Amy Hull and Paula Sanders; *Knight Beat*, edited by Barbara Fister-Liltz; *Knightly Tales*, edited by Ann Hull and Bill Hupe; *On the Wings of the Knight*, edited by Jessica Daigneault; and *Forever Net* (drawing on the Forever Knight computer networks). The Geraint Wyn Davies Fan Club is at 4133 Glendale Rd., Woodbridge, VA 22193, http://www.geocities.com/TelevisionCity/1937/book1999b.html. Fan clubs for several of the cast members appeared, including Nigel Bennett, who played LaCroix, Deborah Duchene, who played Jeanette, and John Kepelos, who played Nick Knight's partner, Lt. Don Schanke. Among those most active in *Forever Knight* fandom is Barbara Fister-Liltz, who has a long career in vampire-related fan organizations. She was a leader in the development of **Shadowcon**, an annual **Dark Shadows** convention, and also illustrated several *Dark Shadows* books, including Lori Paige's *Balm in Gilead* and S. M. Brand's *Belinda: A Weekend in New England*. She also founded Pandora Publications, which published a variety of *Dark Shadows* and vampire publications. Fister-Liltz currently lives in Illinois where she works for Special Services Unlimited, distributor of both *Forever Knight* and *Dark Shadows* merchandise.

Forever Knight fandom survived into the new century, but has become almost exclusively found on several Internet sites where fans can continue to discuss the show and offer their own fan fiction that develops new story lines for the characters. The three season series was brought out on DVD in the middle of the decade (2003–06).

Fortune, Dion (1890–1946)

Dion Fortune, occult magician and exponent of the concept of **psychic vampirism,** was born Violet Mary Firth in 1890 in Wales. She supposedly manifested psychic abilities at an early age, which led to an interest in spiritualism, psychoanalysis, and theosophy. Around 1919 she joined the Alpha and Omega chapter of the Stella Matutina, a group loosely affiliated with the Hermetic Order of the Golden Dawn, a ritual magic group. While a member of the order, she took a magical motto, "Deo Non Fortuna" (By God Not Luck), which was later shortened to Dion Fortune, her public name. Five years later she founded the Fraternity of the Inner Light to attract members to the Golden Dawn, but soon split with the order and developed her own version of magical teachings. She claimed contact with the "Inner Planes" of wisdom from which she received the fraternity's teachings. She not only authored the lessons for the fraternity, but penned a number of books, including: *Sane Occultism* (1929), *The Training and Work of an Initiate* (1930), *The Mystical Qabalah* (1936), and *The Sea Priestess* (1938).

In 1930 Fortune published one of her more popular books, *Psychic Self Defense*. The book grew out of her own experiences with a boss who had gained some degree of occult training in **India** and who tried, by occult means, to obtain Fortune's assistance in several nefarious schemes. In her occult work Fortune also had been witness to various incidents of psychic attack, which she was called on to interrupt. Among the elements of a psychic attack were vampirism, nervous exhaustion, and a wasting of the body into a "mere bloodless shell of skin and bones." Fortune propounded an occult perspective on vampirism. She suggested that occult masters had the power to separate their psychic self from their physical body and to attach it to another and to drain that person's energy. Such persons would then unconsciously begin to drain the energy of those around them, especially people with whom they are in an intense emotional relationship. The attack on the psychic self would manifest in what appeared to be bite marks on the physical body, especially around the neck, ear lobes, and breast (of females). It was Fortune's belief that troops from eastern Europe during World War I had several accomplished occultists among them. These occultists, upon their deaths, were able to attach themselves to British soldiers who survived the war and, hence, made their way to England.

Fortune included fictionalized accounts of the incidents of psychic vampirism in *The Secrets of Dr. Taverner*. The story of Fortune's early experience of psychic attack was discussed in some detail in a biographical book by Janine Chapman. Fortune's work on psychic vampirism was picked up by Anton LaVey and integrated in to *The Satanic Bible* (1976). It also underlies much of the discussion on emotional vampirism in recent psychological literature.

Sources:

Chapman, Janine. *Quest for Dion Fortune*. York Beach, ME: Samuel Weiser, 1993. 190 pp.

Fortune, Dion. *Psychic Self Defense: A Study in Occult Pathology and Criminality*. 1930. Rept. London: Aquarian Press, 953. 212 pp.

———. *The Secrets of Dr. Taverner*. 1926. Rept. St. Paul, MN: Llewellyn Publications, 1962. 231 pp.

France, Vampires in

French records supply only a limited number of texts for vampire researchers. Among them are folklore stories of the *melusine*, a creature reminiscent of the classical *lamiai* figure. Melusine reportedly was the daughter of King Elinas and his fairy wife. Angry at her father, she and her sisters turned their magic against their parents. For her actions, her mother turned her into a serpent from the waist down. Melusine would remain this way until she found a man who would marry her on the condition that he would never see her on Saturday (when her serpentlike body reappeared). She found such a person in Raymond of Poitoi, and, once married, she used her magic to help him build a kingdom. The problem emerged when their children arrived—each was deformed. The situation came to a head when one of the children burned an abbey and killed 100 people. In his anger, Raymond revealed that he knew Melusine's secret. She reacted by accepting the curse upon her and realizing that she was condemned to fly through the air in pain until the day of judgment. Until the castle fell, she would appear before the death of each of Raymond's heirs to voice her lament. She thus became the banshee—the wailing spirit of the House of Lusignan. Even after the castle fell to the French crown, people reported that Melusine appeared before the death of a French king. She was not a vampire, but did show the direction in which at least one of the older vampires evolved.

When the idea of the vampire was introduced into France at the end of the seventeenth century, it was an unfamiliar topic. The subject seemed to have been raised initially in 1693 when a Polish priest asked the faculty at the Sorbonne to counsel him on how he should deal with corpses that had been identified as vampires. That same year, newspaper reports of vampires in **Poland** appeared in a French periodical, *Mercure Galant*. A generation later, the *Lettres Juives* (Jewish Letters), published in 1737, included the account of several of the famous Serbian (mistakenly reported as Hungarian) vampire cases. However, the issue of vampirism was not raised for the French public until the 1746 publication of **Dom Augustin Calmet**'s *Dissertations sur les Apparitions des Anges et des Espits, et sur les revenants, et Vampires de Hingrie, de Boheme, de Moravie, et de Silésie*. This treatise by the French Bible scholar continued the vampire debate that had been centered in the German universities. The debate had reached a negative conclusion concerning the existence of vampires, and Calmet called for what he thought of as a more biblical and scientific view, which considered the accounts of vampires in Eastern Europe, and called for further study. While not accepted by his colleagues, the book was a popular success, reprinted in 1747 and 1748, and translated into several foreign languages.

Calmet brought the debate into the Parisian salons, and he soon found a number of detractors. Voltaire reacted sarcastically and spoke of businessmen as the real bloodsuckers. Diderot followed a similar line in his salon of 1767. Only Jean-Jacques Rousseau argued in support of Calmet and his rational approach to the evidence.

French Vampires: No survey of French vampires would be complete without mention of the several historical figures who have been cited as actual vampires. Leading the list was Gilles de Rais (1404–1440). A hero of France, de Rais was a brilliant general who fought with Joan of Arc—but was also a man known to have few equals as a sadistic murderer. He tortured and killed a number of young boys (and a few girls), receiving intense sexual gratification in the process. He also practiced a form of Satanism. It was only with great difficulty that he was brought to trial. Upon conviction, he was strangled and his body burned.

Somewhat different was the Viscount de Moriéve, a French nobleman who, by strange fortune, kept his estates through the period of the French Revolution. Following the revolution he took out his animosity against the common people by executing many of his employees one by one. Eventually he was assassinated. Soon after his burial, a number of young children died unexpectedly. According to reports, they all had vampire marks on them. These accounts continued for some 72 years. Finally, his grandson decided to investigate the charges that his grandfather was a vampire. In the presence of local authorities, he had the vault opened. While other corpses had undergone the expected decomposition, the viscount's corpse was still fresh and free of decay. The face was flushed and there was **blood** in the heart and chest. New nails had grown and the skin was soft.

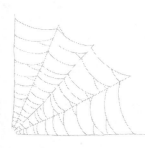

THE VAMPIRE BOOK: THE ENCYCLOPEDIA OF THE UNDEAD

The body was removed from its resting place, and a white thorn was driven into the heart. As blood gushed forth, the corpse made a groaning sound. The remains were then burned. There were no more reports of unusual deaths of children from that day forward. J. A. Middleton, who originally wrote of de Moriée, discovered that he had been born in Persia, married an Indian, and later moved to France as a naturalized citizen. She believed that he had brought his vampirism with him from the East.

While the de Moriéve case carried many of the elements of traditional European vampirism, that of Francois Bertrand did not. During the 1840s Bertrand, a sergeant in the French Army, desecrated a number of graves in Paris before being caught in 1849. After opening graves, he would mutilate bodies in a **ghoul**-like fashion. His story became the basis of a famous novel, *Werewolf of Paris* (1933) by Guy Endore.

The Literary Vampire: France's real contribution to vampire lore came in its nurturing of the literary vampire. Soon after its publication, copies of "The Vampyre" (1819), written by **John Polidori** but mistakenly attributed to **Lord Byron**, arrived in Paris. It was hailed as a great product of Byron and inspired several of the literary elite, most notably **Jean Charles Nodier** who wrote *Le Vampire*, a **drama** based on Polidori's story and featuring his vampire star **Lord Ruthven**. *Le Vampire* led to other Parisian vampire plays, several of them farces, and was translated into English for performance in **London**.

Through Nodier the vampire was introduced into French romantic literature. The romantic exploration of the inner self, often with the assistance of mind-altering drugs, soon encountered the negative aspect of the human psyche. The vampire emerged as a symbol of the dark side of human nature and most of the French romantics utilized it at one point or another. **Théophile Gautier** authored a vampire story, "La Morte Amoureuse" (published in English as "The Beautiful Vampire" and "Clarimonde") in 1836 and a poem titled "Les Taches Jaunes" ("The Yellow Bruises"). Poet Charles Baudeliare wrote several vampire poems including "The Vampire" and "Metamorphoses of the Vampire", both published in 1857. **Alexandre Dumas** brought to an end this generation of romantic interest in the vampire with his short story "The History of the Pale Woman" and his dramatic version of *Le Vampire* (1851). During this era, **Alexey Tolstoy**, the first Russian writer of vampire stories, published his novellas "Upir" and "The Family of the Vukodlak" in French, and they were first circulated and read in the salons of Paris.

Since the mid-nineteenth century, the vampire has appeared only occasionally in French novels. Paul Féval wrote two vampire novels, *Le Vampire* (1867, English translation as *The Vampire Countess*, 2003) and *La Ville Vampire* (1875, English translation as *Vampire City*, 2003). Later novelists included Gustave Lerouge, *La Guerre des Vampires* (1909); Jean Mistler, *Le Vampire* (1944); Maurice Limat, *Moi, Vampire* (1966); Claude Klotz, *Paris Vampire* (1974); and Christine Renard, *La Mante au Fil des Jours* (1977).

In the last generation, the French have picked up on the contemporary vampire craze, and while French authors have not utilized the vampire to anything like the extent of English-speaking countries, a number of French vampire novels have appeared, and their number has been supplemented by the many novels originally written in English, including those by **Stephen King** and **Anne Rice**, that have been translated and published in France. Among the authors producing multiple titles are Jeanne Faivre d'Ardier, Claude Klotz, and Michel Pagel. In addition, a steady supply of texts aimed at

children and teenagers built around the vampire theme continue to appear. Most of the *Buffy the Vampire Slayer* and *Angel* novels were also translated into French.

The Cinematic Vampire: France produced two of the earliest vampire films. *Le Vampire* (1914) was a silent film in which a man attempted to get a vampire bat to kill his wife. *Les Vampires* (1915) was a ten-part serial built around a secret society of super-criminals. It starred Eugene Ayme as Le Grand Vampire (a criminal master, not a real vampire) and Juliet Musidora as Irma Vep (an anagram of vampire). After these early movies, it would be 30 years before the next vampire films were produced. Immediately after World War II, Jean Painleve directed a documentary on *Le Vampire*. It was followed by a short feature that appeared in 1947 as *Les Vampires*. Over the next 20 years, a number of vampire movies were produced in France, most now forgotten. Rising above the crowd was *Et Mourir de Plaisir* (*Blood and Roses*), produced by **Roger Vadim** and starring his wife Annette Vadim as **Carmilla** in this remake of the **Sheridan Le Fanu** tale.

The French movies have become known for continually pushing the amount of overt nudity and sex on the screen. *Et Mourir de Plaisir* paved the way for the work of **Jean Rollin,** the French director who has most frequently utilized the vampire theme. His first feature-length vampire film, *Le Viol du Vampire* (*Rape of the Vampires*), inaugurated a series of increasingly explicit films that have become among the most notable of all vampire motion pictures. *La Viol du Vampire* was followed by *La Nue Vampire* (*The Nude Vampire*, 1969), *Le Frisson des Vampires* (*Sex and the Vampires*, 1970), and *Le Cult de Vampire* (*The Vampire Cult*, 1971). Through the 1970s he produced *Requiem pour un Vampire* (1972), *Levres se Sang* (1974), and *Fascination* (1979). After his 1982 feature, *La Morte-Vivante*, it would be a number of years before he again approached the vampire, but finally in 1995 he returned to the theme in the well-received *Les Deux orphelines vampires* (1995).

Rollin created an era of French vampire movies, but after he moved on to other subjects few French producers have picked up on the theme. Through the late 1980s to the present less than a dozen French vampire movies have been released. The French vampire films include: *Sexandroide* (1987), which combined sex, **science fiction**, and vampires; *Baby Blood* (1990); *Un Vampire au Paradis* (1992); *Trouble Every Day* (2001); *Fiancée of Dracula* (2002); *Blood Mallory* (2002); **Perfume** (2007); and *Les Dents de la nuit* (2008).

Popular Culture: As in North America and the **United Kingdom**, the vampire has entered the popular culture of France, most notably in **comic books**. In the 1970s vampire stories began to appear in such horror comics as *La Maison du Mystere* and *La Manoir des Fantomes*. Among the early independent vampire issues was a 12-part serialization of *Jacula: Fete in la Morgue*, the translation of a 1969 Italian adult comic.

The cover of the menu from the Count Dracula restaurant in Paris, France.

THE VAMPIRE BOOK: THE ENCYCLOPEDIA OF THE UNDEAD

As French comic books developed into some of the best examples of comic book art, vampires periodically appeared, though they were by no means as popular as in the United States. Among the outstanding issues were Philippe Druillet's *Nosferatu* (1989) (also translated into English) and *Le Fils de Dracuella* by J. Ribera (1991) and its sequels.

Among the most noteworthy of French vampire comic books are the two series by Joann Sfar featuring as main characters the Grand Vampire (six volumes, 2001–2005) and the Petit Vampire (six volumes, 1999–2004). The latter series became the basis of a 52-episode animated television series in 2004.

Contemporary French scholars and writers have joined in efforts to educate the public on vampires and vampirism. This interest can be traced to the early 1960s with the publication of two books, Tony Faivre's *Les Vampires* (now an extremely rare volume) and the very popular *Le Vampire* by Ornella Volta, which has been translated into English and Spanish. These initial efforts were followed by such volumes as Roland Villeneuve's *Loups-garous et Vampires* (1963), Francois R. Dumas's *A la Recherche des Vampires* (1976), Robert Ambelain's *La Vampirisme* (1977), Jean-Paul Bourre's *Le cult du vampire aujourd'hui* (1978), Roger Delorme's *Les Vampires Humains* (1979), and Jean-Paul Bourre's *Dracula et les Vampires* (1981). The first wave of French scholarship on the vampire was capped by Jean Marigny's *Le Vampire dans la Littérature anglo-saxonne* (1985). Jacques Finné included an extensive list of additional French vampire titles in his 1986 bibliography. During the 1990s, partially in response to the 1997 Dracula centennial, French scholars expanded their work and produced a number of notable studies. The decade was launched by the likes of Jean Markale's *l'Enigme des vampires* (1991), which was followed by an additional discussion of the vampire phenomena as a whole in *La chair et le sang: vampires et vampirisme* (1997) by Elisabeth Campios and Richard D. Nolane. The discussion of Dracula, his significance and the ties to Prince **Vlad the Impaler**, were carried forward by Denis Buican's *Les Metamorphoses de Dracula* (1993); Matei Cazacu's *l'Historie du Prince Dracula* (1996); and Jean Marigny's *Dracula: figures mythiques* (1997). More recent studies include Sabine Jarrot's *La vampire dans la Littérature du XIX and XX siècle* (2000) and Estelle Valls de Gomis's *Le vampire: enquête autour d'un mythe* (2005).

The broad spectrum of French scholarship on vampires had been showcased in several anthologies of articles, the most notable being *Les Vampires* (1993), papers from a colloquy held at Cerisy, which includes both an introduction and papers by France's two most notable vampire scholars, Jean Marigny and Antoine Faivre, and a bibliographical article on eighteenth-century studies of vampires. Other collections appeared as *Les Vampires* (1995) edited by Jean-Marie Beurq and Bruno Lapeyre, and *Dracula: de la mort a la vie* (1997) compiled by Charle Grivel. Many vampire novels have appeared in the French language, both translations of the more numerous English-language novels, and original novels by French-speaking novelists. Also, in anticipation of the centennial two fine collections of vampire fiction appeared: the first, compiled by Francis Lacassin entitled *Vampires analogie* (1995), includes many of the prominent nineteenth-century writings; the second, by Jean Marigny entitled *Vampires et les Seins* (1997) is a more extensive contemporary collection.

In 2005, Jacques Sirgent, a vampire enthusiast opened the Musées des vampires (Vampire Museum), in a Paris suburb. The Irish ambassador to France graced the open-

ing with an appearance. The museum is open by appointment and those who wish to take a guided tour or attend a movie screening are invited to contact the museum directly.

Sources:

Bourre, Jean-Paul. *Dracula et les Vampires*. Paris: Editions du Rocher, 1981.

Briggs, Katherine. *A Dictionary of Fairies*. London: Penguin Books, 1976. Reprint as: *An Encyclopedia of Fairies, Hobgoblins, Brownies, Bogies, and Other Supernatural Creatures*. New York: Pantheon Books, 1976. 481 pp.

Druillet, Philippe. *Nosferatu*. 1989. Rept. Milwaukee, OR: Dark Horse Comics, 1991.

Feval, Paul. *Vampire City*. Encino, CA: Black Coat Press, 2003. 199 pp.

———. *The Vampire Countess*. Encino, CA: Black Coat Press, 2003. 351 pp.

Finné, Jacques. *Bibliographie de Dracula*. Lausanne, Switz.: L'Age d'Homme, 1986. 215 pp.

Jarrot, Sabine. *La vampire dans la Littérature du XIX and XX siècle*. Paris: l'Harmattan, 2000. 224 pp.

Marigny, Jean. *Le Vampire dans la Littérature anglo-saxonne*. Paris: trese d'état, Didier Erudition, 1985.

Middleton, J. A. *Another Grey Ghost Book*. London: E. Nash, 1914. 320 pp.

Praz, Mario. *The Romantic Agony*. London: Oxford University Press, 1970. 479 pp.

Valls de Gomis, Estelle. *Le vamire: enqulte autour d'un mythe*. Cheminements, 2005. 471 pp.

Les vampires. Paris: Albin Michel, 1993.

Volta, Ornella. *Le Vampire*. Paris: Jean-Jacques Pauvert, 1962. 236 pp. English translation as: *The Vampire*. London: Tandem Books, 1963. 157 pp.

Wilson, Katherine M. "The History of the Word 'Vampire.'" *Journal of the History of Ideas*. 44, 4 (October–December 1985): 577–83.

Frankenstein's Monster

Among the fictional creatures most associated with the vampire was the monster created by Victor Frankenstein. Movies featuring the creatures have been paired on double bills and, on occasion, both monsters have appeared in the same movie. The creatures share a history that goes back to 1816, when Frankenstein's monster was originally created and the vampire underwent a profound alteration. **Elizabeth Miller** has noted a certain appropriateness to the pairing of the vampire and Frankenstein as "both deal with the issues of death and resurrection, creation and transgression, and the blurring of boundaries between life and death." During the week of June 19, 1816, **Lord Byron** called together a group of friends at a villa outside of Geneva, Switzerland. Trapped by a storm, the group, consisting of poet Percy Bysshe Shelley, Byron's physician **John Polidori**, and Shelley's second wife-to-be writer Mary Wollstonecraft, agreed with Byron to create and entertain the group with a "ghost" story. It was Mary Shelley's story that evolved into *Frankenstein* (first published anonymously in 1818). Byron wrote the core of a story that, several years later, Polidori expanded into the first vampire short story. It was published in 1819 as "The Vampyre" under Byron's name.

Frankenstein was the story of a scientist, Victor Frankenstein, who assembled and brought to life a human body composed of the parts of several corpses. Frankenstein, although proud of having discovered a way to restore animation to lifeless matter, was unable to deal with the life he had created and rejected the creature. In return, the creature sought revenge and became the monster he is known as today. Frankenstein's monster differed from the vampire in at least one important respect. Frankenstein was created wholly from Mary Shelley's imagination and was not, like the vampire, based on popular folklore. Thus the expansion of the *Frankenstein* story originated with one novel, while vampire literature drew from a large body of preexisting folk material. There were, of course, sources Shelley drew from to create Frankenstein, such as the early material on robots and the legend of the Golem, a clay figure made by humans and brought to life. Nevertheless, like the literary vampire, Frankenstein's monster provided an important insight into the human situation—and it proved immediately and perennially popular. *Frankenstein* was first brought to the stage in 1823 in England, three years after Polidori's "The Vampyre" inspired several French plays. Soon afterward, several different dramatic versions of *Frankenstein* appeared. However, while there were a number of different vampire stories throughout the nineteenth century, there were no variations on the *Frankenstein* tale, although Shelley's book went through many printings.

Frankenstein came to the screen in 1910 in a silent production by Thomas Edison's film company, but unfortunately no copies have survived. Several other silent movie adaptations were made before the

Poster art from the movie *Abbott and Costello Meet Frankenstein.*

vampire—now in the form of **Dracula**—and Frankenstein were brought together again by **Universal Pictures**. Universal had been revived by the success of *Dracula* (1931). The studio decided that *Frankenstein* was to be the next logical picture and announced that the movie would star **Bela Lugosi** and **Edward Van Sloan** (**Abraham Van Helsing** in *Dracula*). Lugosi, once he understood the nature of his part in the movie refused to go through with it. His part was then given to a young unknown actor, Boris Karloff. The Frankenstein film equaled the success of the Dracula movie and made Karloff a star. In 1933, it was announced that Lugosi would star in *The Return of Frankenstein*, this time as the mad scientist. However, Lugosi decided against that part as well. The movie went into production with Karloff again playing the monster and was released as *The Bride of Frankenstein*. Several other sequels followed. By the 1940s, Universal had also produced horror films featuring **werewolves**. In the 1940s, they began to put several monsters together in different kinds of encounters. In 1944, Dracula (**John Carradine**), Frankenstein, and the Wolfman were united for the first time by Universal in the *House of Frankenstein*. The next year the three returned in the *House of Dracula*. Seeing the end of the monstrous possibilities in 1948, Universal put its three monsters together with its comedy stars Bud Abbott and Lou Costello in *Abbott and Costello Meet Frankenstein* (1948). Following the movie's release, the trio did not appear together on screen for a decade.

Hammer's Revival: The popularity of horror films was at a low ebb in the 1950s. Then **Hammer Films** bought the rights to the Universal monsters and began remaking the classic films in color. They chose Frankenstein as a first effort. *The Curse of Frankenstein* (1957) was so successful that they signed the actor who played the monster, **Christopher Lee**, to portray Dracula. **Peter Cushing**, who portrayed Frankenstein, was signed to play **Abraham Van Helsing** in the next production, released in the United States as the *The Horror of Dracula*. The two pictures were as successful for Hammer as the originals were for Universal, and over the next two decades Hammer became known for its distinctive horror motion pictures. Although Hammer never brought the characters of Dracula and Frankenstein's monster together in the same motion picture, it was a theme with too much potential to neglect. The same year Hammer produced the *Curse of Frankenstein*, a Mexican studio developed its own Dracula/Frankenstein plot that emerged as *El Castillo de los Monstruos (Castle of the Monsters)*. It was a comedy about a newlywed couple who met a number of monsters, including Frankenstein's monster and a vampire. It was followed by a sequel, *Frankenstein, el Vampiro y CIA* (1961). Other meetings of Dracula (or another vampire) and Frankenstein's monster (or a similar creature) occurred in *Sexy Proibitissimo* (1961), *Love Me Quick!* (1964), *Frankenstein's Bloody Terror* (1967), *Mad Monster Party?* (1969), and *La Venganza de las Mujeres Vampiro* (1969). In the 1960s, the comic **television** series, *The Munsters* featured Frankenstein-like character Herman Munster (Fred Gwynne) as head of a family that included a vampiric wife, Lily (Yvonne de Carlo), and Grandpa (Al Lewis). Grandpa revealed, during the course of the series, that he was Count Dracula. In 1966, a movie developed from the show, *Munster, Go Home!* During the 1970s, Frankenstein's monster and Dracula were pitted against each other again in *Dracula vs. Frankenstein* (1970), *Capulina Contra los Monstruos* (1972), *Dracula Contra Frankenstein* (1972), *La Invasion de Los Muertos* (1972), and *Pepito y Chabelo vs. Los Monstruos* (1973). By the early 1970s, however, the Frankenstein/Dracula connection had been largely exhausted, and in the succeeding years only two attempts to reunite them were made: *Dracula tan Exarchia* (1983) and *Howl of the Devil* (1988). The one vampire-Frankenstein connection that has remained was that forged by *The Munsters* television show. In the 1980s, it enjoyed a brief revival in a movie, *The Munsters' Revenge* (1981), and in a new series that ran on television from 1988 to 1991. Then in the 1990s, several new Munster movies with a new cast were made, *Here Come the Munsters* (1995) and *The Munsters Scary Little Christmas* (1996), to be followed by several sentimental documentaries that reunited the cast.

Dracula and Frankenstein in Fiction: Among the more interesting works of fiction featuring Frankenstein's monster during the past generation was a Marvel comic book that appeared during Marvel's rediscovery of horror following the loosening of the restriction on horror titles. The plot of *The Frankenstein Monster* was linked by the monster's search for his creator. In issue No. 8 (November 1973), the monster, now in **Transylvania**, saved a **Gypsy** girl from rape. He was befriended by the girl's mother who promised to help him in his quest. Instead, she tricked Frankenstein into assisting her in freeing Dracula from his tomb. Frankenstein had a brief fight with Dracula, who escaped. Frankenstein then returned to the Gypsy camp only to find it destroyed by villagers who believed the Gypsies had brought the vampire back to them. Angry, Frankenstein challenged the villagers. They overpowered him and were about to burn him at the **stake** when Dracula attacked another village female. As the townspeople turned their attention to catching Dracula, Frankenstein escaped. He tracked the fleeing Dracula to his hiding place and, in a final fight, staked the vampire. Dracula was dead ... at least for the moment.

Novelists who have played with the Frankenstein character in the twentieth century have rarely followed the lead offered by motion pictures and developed new fictional encounters with Dracula. One exception was **Donald Glut** who, in the 1970s, developed a series of new Frankenstein adventures. One, *Frankenstein Meets Dracula* (1977), was written as a sequel to **Bram Stoker's** *Dracula*. Resurrected after his death at the end of the novel, Dracula vowed to take revenge. He attempted to transplant the brain of a descendent of Abraham Van Helsing into the Frankenstein monster's head. However, the monster rejected the idea of the transplant and turned on Dracula. A second novel in the series that included Dracula was never published. The most recent encounter of Frankenstein's monster with Dracula occurred in a set of **juvenile literature** books, the "Fifth Grade Monsters" series by Mel Gilden. In the first volume, *M Is for Monster* (1987), Danny Keegan, a "normal" fifth grader, was introduced to the new kids in class. They include C. D. Bitesky (a vampire), Howie Wolfner (a werewolf), and Elisa and Frankie Stein (who bore more than a passing resemblance to Frankenstein and his bride). Gilden took Danny and the "monsters" through a series of adventures, most with plots that focused on the importance of young people's acceptance of kids who are slightly different. The books also serve as examples for older readers who have problems with monsters and other things that go bump in the night. Dracula, Frankenstein, and the other monsters have been partially tamed in Gilden's books and made a part of our culture as creatures of **humor**.

Sources:

Florescu, Radu. *In Search of Frankenstein: Exploring the Myths Behind Mary Shelley's Monster.* London: Robson Books, 1997. 287 pp.

The Frankenstein Monster. Nos 7–9. New York: Marvel Comics, 1973–74.

Gilden, Mel. *M Is for Monster.* Fifth Grade Monsters No. 1. New York: Avon, 1987. 89 pp.

———. *The Secret of Dinosaur Bog.* Fifth Grade Monsters No. 15. New York: Avon, 1991. 90 pp.

Glut, Donald. *The Frankenstein Catalog.* Jefferson, NC: Mcfarland & Company, 1984. 525 pp.

———. *The Frankenstein Legend: A Tribute to Mary Shelley and Boris Karloff.* Metuchen, NJ: Scarecrow Press, 1973. 372 pp.

———. *Frankenstein Meets Dracula.* London: New English Library, 1977. 140 pp.

Jones, Stephen. *The Illustrated Vampire Movie Guide.* London: Titan Books, 1993. 144 pp.

Miller, Elizabeth. "Dracula and Frankenstein: A Tale of Two Monsters." In Elizabeth Miller. *Reflections on Dracula: Ten Essays.* White Rock, BC: Transylvania Press, 1997. pp. 139–56.

❰ Frid, Jonathan (1924–) ❱

Jonathan Frid, the actor who portrayed vampire **Barnabas Collins** on *Dark Shadows*, the original ABC-TV daytime series, was born in Hamilton, Ontario, Canada. Frid made his stage debut during his teen years in a school production of Sheridan's *The Rivals*. However, it was not until his years in the Canadian Navy during World War II that he made the decision to pursue an acting career. After the war, Frid moved to **London** to attend the Royal Academy of Dramatic Arts. While in England, he appeared in his first film, *The Third Man*. In 1950, Frid moved back to Canada to attend the Toronto Academy of Arts and continue his acting career. He graduated from Yale in 1957 with a master's degree in fine arts with a major in directing. Frid then settled in New York where, for the next decade, he played in several stage productions and was known for his portrayal of a variety of Shakespearean characters. He appeared with Ray Milland in a 1967 touring company production of *Hostile Witness*. After the tour concluded and he returned to New York, Frid made plans to move to California. His career in New York was at a standstill, and he decided to seek a position on the West Coast as a teacher.

Before he had a chance to leave for California, however, he received a call to join the cast of **Dark Shadows**. He interviewed for the part because it was to be only a few weeks work and would provide him some money to start over in his new home. At that point, the show's ratings dropped and ABC threatened cancellation. To boost ratings, the show's producer, **Dan Curtis**, decided to experiment with adding supernatural elements to the story line. He had successfully introduced ghosts and decided to add a vampire. Frid, as vampire Barnabas Collins, began to appear in April 1967. The audience responded, especially women and teenagers (the show was on at 4:00 P.M.), and ratings steadily climbed. By summer, everyone recognized that the show was a hit, and numerous spinoff products for fans began to appear.

Frid played the part of Barnabas Collins for the next four years, until the show was finally canceled in 1971. He also starred in the first of two movies based on the show, *House of Dark Shadows* (1970). At the end of the movie, Barnabas Collins was killed. There were no vampires in the second movie, *Night of Dark Shadows* (1971), which featured other characters from the *Dark Shadows* cast. Although Frid gained star status, he also experienced some degree of typecasting that limited his choice of parts once the show ended.

After he joined the show, Frid's character became the trademark image of *Dark Shadows*. His likeness dominated the publicity materials for the show, including the first *Dark Shadows* movie. More than 30 paperback books were written based on the show by Harlequin author **Daniel Ross**, and nearly all featured Frid's picture on the cover. His representation also graced the covers of most issues of the *Dark Shadows* comic book (the first vampire comic to appear after the lifting of the ban on vampires in 1954). Soon after he joined the show, a Barnabas the Vampire Model Kit was issued, complete with a glow-in-the-dark walking stick.

Following the cancellation of the show, Frid kept a low profile. He tried to distance himself from *Dark Shadows* and the role of Barnabas Collins. He did not want to find himself in a position similar to that of **Bela Lugosi**—trapped in the **Dracula** persona. He took a part on stage in *Murder at the Cathedral* and in two movies: *The Devil's Daughter* (1972), an ABC made-for-television movie, and *Seizure* (1974), director Oliver Stone's first film. Most of Frid's time, however, was devoted to the development of three one-man shows: *Jonathan Frid's Fools & Fiends*, *Shake-*

Jonathan Frid as the vampire Barnabas Collins in the original *Dark Shadows*.

spearean Odyssey, and *Fridiculousness*. He toured the country with the shows, performing readings from Shakespeare, humor, and classic horror pieces by authors such as **Edgar Allan Poe**. In 1986, he joined an all-star cast in a Broadway revival of *Arsenic and Old Lace* and toured with the company the following year.

Frid's association with the show did not go away. *Dark Shadows* went into syndication, and a new audience became delighted with Barnabas Collins. During the 1980s, somewhat surprised (as have been many observers) at the persistence of fan interest in *Dark Shadows*, the Dark Shadows festival (fan conventions) began to be held in 1983. Frid made his first appearance in 1983 and at every festival from then through 1993. Then for many years he did not appear, though he remained the fans' most popular character. His long hiatus ended in 2007 when he starred at the convention and he made back to back appearances in 2008 and 2009.

Sources:

Dawidziak, Mark. "Dark Shadows." *Cinefantastique* 21, 3 (December 1990): 24–28.

Frid, Jonathan. *Barnabas Collins: A Personal Picture Album*. New York: Paperback Library, 1969. 128 pp.

Gross, Edward, and Mark Shapiro. *The Vampire Interview Book: Conversations with the Undead*. New York: Image Publishing, 1991. 134 pp.

Hamrick, Craig. *Barnabas & Company: The Cast of the TV Classic Dark Shadows*. Lincoln, NB: iUniverse, Inc., 2003. 276 pp.

Scott, Kathryn Leigh, Jim Pierson, and David Selby. *The Dark Shadows Almanac: Millennium Edition*. Los Angeles: Pomegranate Press, 2000. 271 pp.

Friends of Dark Shadows *see:* Dark Shadows Fandom

Frost, Deacon

Deacon Frost, a vampire and antagonist of **Blade the Vampire Slayer,** was introduced in the pioneering comic series *Tomb of Dracula* (Marvel, 1972–1980), one of the many characters created by writer Marv Wolfman. The first reference to Deacon Frost occurs in issue No. 13 in which he kills Blade's mother as she is going into labor with him. Frost's bite taints the blood remaining in her and Blade is thus born as a ***dhampir***, his mother's blood passing to him several extra-mundane abilities, including the dhampir's traditional sensitivity to the presence of vampires. Blade also cannot be transformed into a vampire. Deacon Frost had been high on his list of hoped-for targets when he met the cadre of vampire hunters headed by the wheel-chair-bound Quincey Harker (in issue No. 10).

Frost, as originally conceived, was a white-haired but vigorous senior citizen, with a full beard and mustache. He tended to dress in nineteenth-century European garb.

In later appearances in *Tomb of Dracula*, we learn that his vampire career dates to the 1860s when, as a scientist in search of immortality, he injected himself with vampire blood resulting in his transformation into a vampire (No. 53). He turned Hannibal King into a vampire and a vampire hunter. Through the issues of *Tomb of Dracula* in the 1970s, he periodically reappears and broadcasts his grandiose idea of replacing **Dracula** as the Lord of the Vampires. He was endowed with the ability to produce vampire doppelgangers (clones). They were automatically generated after he bit someone. And with a vampire

army of doppelgangers he attacked Blade and King. They ultimately defeated him, and killed Frost. Later one of his doppelgangers showed up and had to be dispatched.

In 1998, Blade emerged again as the star of his own movie in which he again faces off against Deacon Frost (portrayed by Stephen Dorff). The movie begins with Blade's unusual birth. The action moves immediately to a nightclub where the now adult Blade (portrayed by Wesley Snipes) takes on a room full of vampires, whom we later discover are minions of Frost, now appearing as a much younger man, completely clean shaven.

Frost still has grandiose plans, now focused on ruling the various vampire "houses" or clans and becoming a vampire god, La Magra, which he initially accomplishes through performing a magical ritual, that included the slaying of the heads of the 12 vampire houses. With his new status and the powers it confers, he and Blade are set up for their final confrontation. In relatively quick fashion, Blade seemed to have finally killed the vampire by first cutting off his arm and then cutting him in two pieces. Frost, however, is not done, but reassembles the two halves and regenerates a new arm. In the end, he is seemingly killed from darts filled with pure **sunlight**.

Since no vampire seems to ever be killed for good, it was not surprising when Frost and his clones reappeared. In a Blade one-shot comic, *Blade: Cresent City Blues* (1998), Frost reappears, affirms that a previous reappearance was in fact one of his clones, and then proceeds to build a power base in New Orleans. Blade again thwarts Frost's plans, but the vampire ultimately escapes. He reappears again in *Blade: Vampire Hunter* (1999–2000) where he heads for the desert to meet Dracula, who is about to engage in a Rite of Ascension that would greatly expand his powers. Blade arrived in the nick of time and after a lengthy battle again killed Deacon Frost with a stake in the heart. This story was cut short in 2000 and only completed in the new *Tomb of Dracula* Series in 2004.

Sources:

Blade. Nos. 1–12. New York: Marvel, 2007.

Blade: Vampire Hunter. Nos. 1–6. New York: Marvel Comics, 1999–2000.

Christensen, Jeff. "Deacon Frost." The Appendix to the Handbook of the Marvel Universe. Posted at http://www.marvunapp.com/Appendix3/frostdeaconblade.htm. Accessed on April 5, 2010.

Brooks, Eric. "Blade." Marvel Universe. Posted at http://marvel.com/universe/Blade. Accessed on April 5, 2010.

Tomb of Dracula. Nos. 1–70. New York: Marvel Comics, 1972–1979.

Tomb of Dracula. No. 1–4. New York: Marvel 2004–2005.

Games, Vampire

In the late 1960s vampires moved from being of interest to a few horror fans to capturing the popular imagination. Games built around vampirism are one sign that vampires have become an entrenched element in popular culture.

Board Games: The first set of vampire games were board games. The very first was a spin-off from the *Dark Shadows* daytime **television** show. *The "Dark Shadows" Game* was distributed by Whitman in 1968. In the game up to four players race each other through a maze.

The following year, Milton Bradley released *The Barnabas Collins "Dark Shadows" Game*, developed in response to the popular introduction of the vampire **Barnabas Collins** to the cast. Quite distinct from the Whitman game, it required that players assemble a skeleton on a scaffold. The winner got to wear Barnabas's **fangs**.

In the mid-1970s, British horror and vampire fan Stephen Hand, disappointed at the lack of horror-oriented games, created his first board game, Barnabas's. The game featured a set of **vampire hunters** searching **Castle Dracula** for **Dracula** to kill him with a **stake**. In the 1980s, Hand revised the game and introduced ideas for a military game based on **Vlad the Impaler**'s wars.

A few years later it was followed by *The Undead* (1981), designed by Steve Jackson. Based on **Bram Stoker**'s *Dracula*, the game matched one player, who assumed the role of the Count unleashed upon **London** (a map of the city formed the game board), against one or more other players, the vampire hunters. The game could be played as a straight board game or expanded as a role-playing game. The next vampire board game to hit the market was released in 1987 as *The Fury of Dracula*. As with *The Undead*, the players assumed the roles of vampire hunters pitted against one player, who acted as Dracula. The vampire hunters had to find Dracula and kill him before he was able to es-

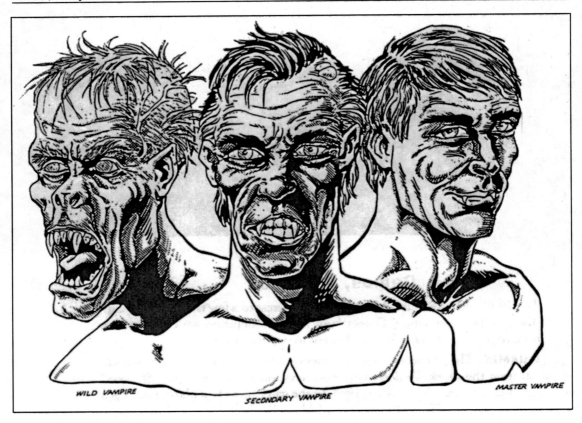

WILD VAMPIRE   SECONDARY VAMPIRE   MASTER VAMPIRE

Vampires of different types inhabit the gaming world of *Vampire Kingdoms*.

tablish vampire accomplices in the cities of Europe (a map of Europe formed the game board). The game gave a slight advantage to Dracula—an advantage that was overcome only if the hunters worked together.

Among the more unique vampire-related games was *Dracula's Bite on the Side*, a dinner table mystery game in the "Murder à la Carte" series. The game was designed as part of an entire evening that included a dinner held to celebrate the 1893 betrothal of Count Dracula's ward, Bella Kashiasu, to Ivan Evenstich. Each of the eight dinner guests became a murder suspect and the evening was spent trying to determine who the murderer might be. As the game proceeded, guests interrogated each other and revealed what they had discovered. At the end of the game, each player guessed the murderer's identity.

Most recently, a board game was released in connection with **Francis Ford Coppola**'s movie, ***Bram Stoker's Dracula*** (1992), by Leading Edge Games. The players in this game assumed the role of one of the vampire hunters from *Dracula*—**Abraham Van Helsing, Jonathan Harker, Quincey P. Morris**, etc. Their goal was to overcome a set of Dracula's servants, such as his **vampire brides** or **Lucy Westenra** as a vampire. Then the players had to defeat the various forms of Dracula to rescue **Mina Murray**, who was trapped in Dracula's clutches.

For many years board games were the only vampire games, but in the 1990s, they were joined by a variety of what have been termed role-playing games.

Role-Playing Games: Today, the most popular vampire-oriented games are role-playing games. Fantasy role-playing games center on an alternative fantasy world that the players enter through their imaginations. They are games of make-believe, in which the players enter the story they simultaneously tell. By telling and playing there is an experience that goes beyond simply listening to someone tell the story.

Some games are led by the "gamemaster," or storyteller, who sets the starting point and guides the course of the game. Prior to the game, each character is assigned a unique combination of helpful attributes (**strength**, dexterity, stamina, intelligence) and talents. For the purpose of the game, the character's traits are quantified on a descriptive character sheet that assigns numerical values to each attribute. Thus, each character starts the game with a unique set of attributes, a variety of weapons, and other appropriate abilities. As the game begins, the characters are placed in situations they get out of through a combination of their own choices and sheer chance (represented by a throw of the dice). The gamemaster describes what has happened after each player's action choice and decides how well the players have either succeeded and prospered or failed and suffered in the quest of their goal.

Each role-playing game has created its own myth that defines the imaginative world in which the game operates. As might be expected, vampires appeared in *Dungeons and Dragons* (D&D), a role-playing game that deals in the widest possible world of fantasy and magic. As early as 1982, a *Ravenloft* module of D&D featuring a vampire, Count Strahd von Zarovich, was written for D&D by Tracyand Laura Hickman. By 1990, this module had grown into an "advanced" variant game with a primary vampire theme based upon the D&D worldview. A new *Ravenloft* game has been designed and written by Bruce Nesmith and Andria Hayday.

Ravenloft is a fictional island continent containing a number of kingdoms. Near its middle is the kingdom of Barovia, the land where Ravenloft Castle is located. Barovia is ruled by Count Strahd. In the past, the count loved a young woman, Tatyana, but she did not return his love and, instead, planned to marry his brother Sergei. Rejected and angry, the count killed Sergei, which, in turn, led to Tatyana's **suicide**. Through an unclear transaction, the count made a pact with "death," and became a vampire. Count Strahd's castle and land were drawn out of the physical world into the etheric plane. *Ravenloft*, like most D&D landscapes, is a magical land. The various domains that surround Barovia are inhabited by a variety of **werewolves, ghouls,** and supernatural creatures, and the various games of *Ravenloft* are built on their interaction. The popularity of the game has led to the publication of a number of spinoff novels based on *Ravenloft* and its inhabitants by authors such as **Elaine Bergstrom** and **P. N. Elrod**. Shortly after vampires invaded *Dungeons and Dragons,* Pacesetter introduced a horror role-playing game in which vampires play a key role.

Chill was built around the myth of the Societas Argenti Viae Eternitata (SAVE), the Eternal Society of the Silver Way. According to the *Chill* story, SAVE was founded in 1844 in Dublin, **Ireland** by a group of scientists led by Dr. Charles O'Boylan. O'Boylan posited the existence of little understood natural laws used by two separate opposing sets of entities who exist in the noncorporeal world. Most importantly, he believed that a

The vampire Methusalah from the role-playing game
Vampire: The Masquerade.

highly disciplined source of evil intruded into the human realm and threatens our safety. Afraid that they could not convince the public of the existence of the evil Unknown, the decision was made to turn SAVE into a secret organization to fight the evil. SAVE kept an archive of its activities in Dublin, Ireland.

The early research of SAVE led to its confrontation with vampires in the Pirin Mountains of **Bulgaria** (1868) and Lucerne, Switzerland (1975). Fighting vampires were a central aspect of SAVE's work. In the 1985 book *Vampires,* by Gali Sanchez and Michael Williams, the *Chill* mythology was continued in a summary of the major cases investigated over the years, in which the goal was the destruction of vampires and vampirelike creatures. The vampires were found in Eastern Europe, the Orient, and **Mexico**. Gamers are invited to assume the persona of one of the ten typical vampire types.

The most popular vampire-oriented role-playing game was entitled **Vampire: The Masquerade**, which has now evolved into Vampire: the Eternal Struggle. The game was created by Mark Rein-Hagen and published in 1991 by White Wolf Game Studio. Its basic myth was called "The Masquerade," a secret realm that began with Cain (the biblical character who, in Genesis 4, killed his brother and was afflicted with an undesignated curse). According to the Masquerade, the curse was eternal life and a craving for **blood**. After wandering in the wilderness for many years, Cain once again lived among mortals and created a city and progeny—a small number of vampires who carried Cain's curse. The city was destroyed, but later generations periodically appeared as a secret force in history. The bulk of existing vampires constitute the sixth generation and their children, and they face pressure to stop creating vampires because it is believed that the vampiric powers diminish as each generation from Cain is created.

The Masquerade myth stated that, beginning in 1435, the Inquisition was able to arrest and kill many of Cain's progeny, "the Kindred." The Inquisition stamped out whole bloodlines by burning them. This period of attack drove the vampire community, which had lived somewhat openly on the edge of human society, completely underground. In 1486, at a global convocation, a secret worldwide network was established. It established the law of the Masquerade, an attempt to convince the world that either all vampires were dead or, better still, they never existed. The Masquerade demanded that all vampires make a reasonable effort at secrecy.

The accumulated wisdom of the nearly immortal vampires was given to intelligent mortals who then turned their attention to the development of science and the suppression of superstition. As a result, the early belief in vampires was crushed. The Masquerade, however, was threatened by the mysticism that arose from a combination of forces—the mysticism of psychedelic drugs, new **music**, and the establishment of the vampire image in popular culture. In the myth, those affected by the new mysticism are ready to believe in the existence of vampires. There is also a generation gap between those vampires who created the Masquerade and understand its necessity and those vampires created in the last century whose brashness, the elder vampires felt, drew unwelcomed attention to the vampire community.

According to the myth of the game, the elder vampires had more powers than the younger vampires. Although the stake was hurtful for both old and young, it was not, by itself, fatal. **Sunlight** and **fire** were the vampires' greatest dangers. Holy objects had no effect, nor did running **water**. The vampires had sharpened senses that aided them in hunting—including the power to impose their will on mortals. The elder vampires could even change their forms.

Vampire: The Masquerade explained that new vampires could be created by having their blood drained and receiving some of the vampire's blood. The new vampires had slightly less power than the vampires who created them. Vampires no longer breathed, but could fake respiration. Their hearts did not beat. The blood they consumed spread through their bodies by osmosis rather than through arteries or veins. It also carried the necessary oxygen. The vampires' wounds healed quickly, however, the stake produced a form of paralysis. The vampire in the game moved in the world of mortals very much like historic nobleman hunters moved among beasts in the forest. The worldwide vampire society thus existed as a parallel society beside that of mortals. The vampires were organized into territorial **clans** ruled by princes. Every major city of the mortal world supported a vampire community and vampires who entered a new city had to present themselves to the powers established there. As *Dungeons & Dragons* spun off a card game, *Magic, the Gathering*, so *Vampire: The Masquerade* led to a card game variation originally published as *Jyhad* and then revised and reissued in 1995 as *Vampire: The Eternal Struggle*. The Camarilla, the international vampire organization, ruled the city's controlling clan and enforced the Masquerade.

Players of *Vampire: The Masquerade* create a character in the imaginary vampire community and gather with others to enact the almost infinite number of possible situations created by the gamemaster/storyteller. The success of *Vampire: The Masquerade* allowed its evolution. In 1993; a live-action version of the game appeared. This version freed the game from the delays caused by the use of dice, which has been replaced with a series of hand signals. The new form of the game allows players to remain in character during virtually all of the game and expands the number of players who can play at one time. **The Camarilla: A Vampire Fan Association** (50 S. Main St., Ste 8, Salt Lake City, UT 84144), an organization based on the *Vampire* mythology, provides a national network of gamers.

Other Vampire-Oriented Role-Playing Games: Although *Vampire* emerged in the early 1990s as the most popular vampire-oriented role-playing game, it was not the only one. Among its competitors is *Vampire Kingdoms* (1991) (created by Kevin Shiembieda), a game within the larger fantasy role-playing world of *Rifts*, published by Palladium Books. *Vampire* centers on life and conflicts within the vampire community, while *Vampire Kingdoms* draws its adventures from the conflicts between vampires and non-vampires, especially Doc Reid and his Vampire Hunters.

Vampires and a one-eyed alien being from the game
Vampire Kingdom.

According to *Vampire Kingdoms*, there are three varieties of the Undead—master vampires, secondary vampires, and wild vampires—which together form a hierarchy of vampiric life. At the top are the master vampires, which appear most like humans. Secondary vampires are somewhat more savage with pale skin, corpse-like bodies, and strange eyes. They are, however, still able to move in human society on a limited basis. The wild vampires are far more ghoulish in appearance, and with their strange appearance, terrible stench, and obvious wildness, instantly communicate their distinctive threat.

In this game, all vampires operate under a super power, the Vampire Intelligence, making them the true Lords of the Undead, described as a monstrous elemental being.

In *Vampire Kingdoms*, since the devastation of the Earth (termed the time of the Rifts), vampires have risen to dominate sections of Mexico, Central America, and **South America**. Old Mexico City is Vampire Central. The area is organized into a set of vampire kingdoms, tribal groupings, and city states.

The Mexico Empire is composed of one vampire intelligence, one master vampire, 1,700 secondary vampires, and some 65,000 humans (the food source). The master vampire runs the kingdom from Mexico City, while the local vampire intelligence lives in Tula, some 70 miles north. Several other vampire kingdoms are also located in the former Mexico.

Human civilization in *Vampire Kingdoms* is centered in the Midwest. Most of the Southwest is wilderness with a handful of scattered settlements located on the sites of the former cities of El Paso, Houston, or San Antonio. Kenneth Reid and his Vampire Hunting Rangers are headquartered at Fort Reid, in what is now northern Mexico. Reid is a human who has undergone bionic reconstruction. He hates vampires and is committed to **destroying** them. Because of his bionic component he is immune to being transformed into a vampire. He is helped by a set of super-hero assistants, both humanoid and otherwise. One, Carlotta the White, is a dragon who usually appears in the form of a beautiful woman.

Another game highlighting vampires was *Nightlife* (1990), designed by L. Lee Cerney and Bradley K. McDevitt and published by Stellar Games. *Nightlife* delves into the world of what is termed "splatterpunk," a reality created by combining the ghoulish terror of *Night of the Living Dead* and the rudeness of Punk Rock. David Scrow, who first defined "splatterpunk" reality, saw previous attempts at horror as being too polite. So splatterpunk attempted to confront the reader or viewer with the gore and revolting nature of the horror world. At the same time as the splatterpunk world was emerging, a modern vampire, usually spelled with a "y" as "vampyre," emerged. This new vampire is sensual, urbane, and the object of sympathy. This type of vampyre appeared in the writing of **Chelsea Quinn Yarbro** and **Anne Rice** and appeared in such movies as **Frank Langella**'s *Dracula* **(1979)** and *The Lost Boys* (1987).

Nightlife fantasizes about characters who live secretly in New York City in the not-too-distant future. They include vampyres, **werewolves**, ghosts, and demons. These "extranatural" creatures together make up the Kin. Their term for humanity is the Herd. In addition to the vampyres who suck human blood, there are several varieties of the Kin that might be termed **psychic vampires**. The Wyghts and the Animates live on human life energy. Each form of the Kin has special abilities, which they term their "edges." Vampyres can, for example, transform into such various shapes as a **bat** or a cloud of **mist**. "Edges" are countered by "flaws," such as the vampyre's problem with sunlight.

In *Nightlife*, vampyres are just one character from among several others. They form the transition to a number of role-playing games in which a vampire character is one of many a player might choose. Typical of these games is *Shadowrun* (1989), a game that fantasizes about the year 2050, a time when technology and human flesh have mixed. Humans interface with computers and bionic people are common. In this world, an awakening of the mystical has occurred and magic has returned as a potent force in human life. A variety of creatures, such as elves and trolls, who survived by assuming human form, have reverted to their more natural appearance. Within this world of human, part-human, and other-than-human life, vampires appear as one of a number of "critters." The vampires are described as diseased humans who have been infected with the Human-Metahuman Vampiric Virus. Vampires consume both the blood and the life energy of their **victims**.

One role-playing game, ***Bram Stoker's Dracula***, capitalized on the popularity of the 1992 movie. The game assumes that following Dracula's death, he left behind a brood of newly created vampires that must be tracked down and defeated. Players choose a character and generate that character's attributes by the throw of the dice. In the game, the vampires have special powers (especially the older ones), but the modern hunter characters have the benefit of high-powered modern weapons—including automatic assault rifles.

Though a few of the role-playing vampire games of the 1990s remain available (as of 2008), *Vampire the Eternal Struggle* was the only one to grow and maintain a continuing playing audience.

Computer Games: During the 1980s, games that could be played on a personal computer, especially the several systems that could be connected to a television screen (Nintendo being the most popular) made sizable inroads into the toy market. By the 1990s, retail stores specializing exclusively in computer games were common in urban areas. The first vampire-oriented computer game appears to have been *Elvira, Mistress of the Dark* (produced by Accolade). It appeared in 1990 and won the game of the year award from Computer Gaming World the following year. The game's success led to a sequel, *Elvira: The Jaws of Cerberus* (1992).

In 1993, the world of computer games discovered vampires. Early that year, three new vampire games appeared: *Dracula Unleashed* (Viacom), *Vampire Master of Darkness* (Game Gear), and *Veil of Darkness* (Strategic Simulations). More significantly, however, Psygnosis Ltd., a British company, released a game based on *Bram Stoker's Dracula*

after nearly two years of development. The game was developed to fit the Mega-CD-Rom system developed by Sega. The system allowed a significant expansion of memory and permitted the inclusion of clips and sound from the film in the game. Versions of the finished game have been released in several formats for various game systems.

As vampire games have developed through the 1990s, they have provided an alternative avenue for speculation about the meaning of being vampiric. The rules of the games, which in the case of the role-playing games constitute book-length publications, have become a forum where ideas about vampiric existence are tested and bartered. The appearance of the number of games based on the vampire myth symbolizes the renewed enthusiastic level of interest in vampires.

Among the electronic games, Castlevania stands out. Castlevania initially appeared in Japan in the mid-1980s. More than two dozen new versions of and sequels to the original game have appeared through the intervening years, each incorporating the latest advances in electronic gaming and then being adapted to different gaming systems. The storyline of the game concerns an ongoing war between the Belmont family of vampire hunters and Dracula. Dracula seems to reappear every century, and it is the charge of the Belmonts to block his plans to dominate the world. BradyGames has published a series of strategy guides to the different Castlevania games.

Twenty-first Century: In the new century, White Wolf emerged as a dominating force in the world of live action role-playing (LARP) games. Its *Vampire: The Requiem* has been an ongoing presence as other vampire role-playing games have come and gone. By the middle of the first decade, it was virtually the only vampire-themed LARP still on the market. The associated card game had also been able to recreate itself continually with expansion decks that offered ever new variations on the basic game.

The two most popular vampire phenomena of the decade—**Buffy the Vampire Slayer** and the **Twilight** books and movies—both spawned a host of cult paraphernalia, including games. Both *Buffy* and its spinoff **Angel** led to the production of jigsaw puzzles, board games, a chess set, and electronic computer games. A short-lived LARP game never really took off, but an associated role-playing card game produced three large sets of trading cards, complete with enhanced variant cards, now valued by collectors.

As the *Twilight* book series was adapted into movies, a similar variety of games appeared—jigsaw puzzles and board games, including a *Twilight* version of the trivia game, *Scene It*. Also, in 2009, several decks of playing cards were issued with a *Twilight* illustration and pictures of the stars on the back of each card. As of 2009, no electronic games based on *Twilight* have appeared, perhaps due to its perceived largely female audience. Meanwhile, action-oriented movies such as *Van Helsing*. The **Underworld** series, **Blood the Last Vampire**, **Vampire Hunter D**, **Blade**, and **Bloodrayne**, have all spawned to new electronic games.

Sources:

Auliffe, Ken R. "Oh, the Horror!" *Garemag* 1, 2 (April/May 1993).

Bergstrom, Elaine. *Tapestry of Lost Souls*. Lake Geneva, WI: TSR, Inc., 1993.

"Bram Stoker's Dracula: The Game." *Dracula* (UK) 9 (September 1993): 36–7.

Campbell, Brian. *Darkness Unveiled*. N.p.: Wizards of the Coast, 1995. 200 pp.

Carella, C. J. *Angel Role-Playing Game Corebook*. Loudonville, NY: Eden Studios, 2003. 254 pp.

———. *Buffy the Vampire Slayer Core Rule Book*. Los Angeles: Eden Studios, 2002. 249 pp.

Elrod, P. N. I, *Strahd: The Memoirs of a Vampire*. Lake Geneva, WI: TSR, Inc., 1993. 309 pp.

Findley, Nigel. *Van Richlen's Guide to Vampires*. Lake Geneva, WI: TSR, Inc., 1991. 95 pp.

Golden, Christie. *Vampire of the Mists*. Lake Geneva, WI: TSR, Inc., 1991. 341 pp.

Koke, Jeff. *Gurps Vampire the Masquerade*. N.P.: Steve Jackson Games, 1993. 192 pp.

Marmell, Ari, Dean Shomshak, and C.A. Suleiman. Vampire: The Requiem. *Stone Mountain*, GA: White Wolf Publishing, 2004. 294 pp.

McCubbin, Chris W. *Vampire: The Masquerade Companion*. N.p.: Steve Jackson Games, 1994. 160 pp.

McDevitt, Bradley K., and L. Lee Cerny. *Nightlife: The Role-Playing Game of Urban Horror*. Swanton, OH: Stellar Games, 1990. 3rd ed.: 1992. 256 pp.

Melton, J. Gordon. "Vampire." *Garemag* 1, 5 (October/November/December 1993): 8–15.

Nakazono, Barry. *Bram Stoker's Dracula Role-Playing Game*. Pasadena, CA: Leading Edge Games, 1993. 182 pp.

Nesmith, Bruce, and Andria Hayday. *Ravenloft*. Lake Geneva, WI: TSR, Inc., 1990. 144 pp.

Rein-Hagen, Mark, et al. *Vampire: The Masquerade*. Stone Mountain, GA: White Wolf, 1991. 263 pp.

———. *Book of the Damned*. Stone Mountain, GA: White Wolf Game Studio, 1993. 138 pp.

Sanchez, Gali, and Michael Williams. *Vampires*. Delevan, WI: Pacesetter Limited of Wisconsin, 1985. 96 pp.

Snead, John. *Buffy the Vampire Slayer Role-Playing Game: The Magic Box*. Loudenville, NY: Eden Studios, 2003. 126 pp.

"White Wolf Games." *Game Shop News* 16 (April 28, 1993): 4–6.

Winninger, Ray. *The Chill Companion*. N.P.: Mayfair Games, 1991. 159 pp.

Garden, Nancy (1938–)

Nancy Garden, an author of books for young people, was born in Boston, Massachusetts and attended Columbia University where she received a bachelor's degree in 1961 and a master's degree the following year. Garden decided to specialize as an author of **juvenile literature** and, in 1969, became a contributing editor for *Junior Scholastic*. She held various positions as an editor through the mid-1970s, and in 1976 became a freelance writer.

Garden has been credited with writing the first book introducing young people to vampirology—from folklore to modern presentations of the vampire in books and motion pictures. Following the publication of Garden's *Vampires* in 1973, other writers attempted to write vampire books for young people, although no other works were as substantial as her original. She also explored a number of related subjects such as **werewolves** and witches.

Most of Garden's early volumes were nonfiction, but in the 1980s she began primarily writing fiction. Among these works are three vampire novels: *Prisoner of Vampires* (1984), *Mystery of the Night Raiders* (1991), and *My Sister, the Vampire* (1992). She has continued as a prolific writer of juvenile fiction into the new century.

Sources:

Garden, Nancy. *Vampires*. Philadelphia: J. P. Lippencott, 1972. 127 pp.

———. *Prisoner of Vampires*. New York: Farrar, Straus, 1984. 213 pp.

———. *Mystery of the Night Raiders*. (Monster Hunters, Case 1). New York Pocket Books, 1991. 167 pp.

———. *My Sister, the Vampire*. New York: Bullseye Books, 1992. 186 pp.

❦ Garlic ❧

Like the **crucifix**, vampires are believed to have an intense aversion to garlic, and thus people have used garlic to keep vampires away. Introduced into the literary realm in **Bram Stoker**'s novel, garlic became central to the developing vampire myth throughout the twentieth century. Garlic was the first treatment Dr. **Abraham Van Helsing** applied in the case of **Lucy Westenra**. Van Helsing had a box of garlic flowers sent from the Netherlands and decorated Lucy's room with them. He hung them around Lucy's neck and told her that there was much virtue in the little flower. The garlic worked until Lucy's mother, not knowing the flowers' purpose, tore them from her neck.

Garlic was a crucial element in killing the vampire. After driving a **stake** through the vampire's body and removing its head, garlic was placed in the mouth. In fact, this was how Van Helsing finally treated Lucy's body. This treatment was effective, however, only for recently created vampires, because the older ones, (**Dracula** and the three **women** in **Castle Dracula**), disintegrated into **dust** once a stake was thrust into their bodies. Stoker got the idea of using garlic following **decapitation** of the vampire from Emily Gerard's *The Land beyond the Forest*. The book suggested that it was the method employed in **Romania** in very obstinate cases of vampirism (i.e., those that had not been cleared up by methods that did not require any mutilation of the body).

Garlic, a member of the lily family, has been used since ancient times as both an herb and a medicine. It developed a reputation as a powerful healing agent, and it was rumored that it possessed some magical powers as a **protection** agent against the plague and various supernatural evils. In southern Slavic regions, it became known as a potent agent against demonic forces, witches, and sorcerers. The Christian St. Andrew was said to be the donor of garlic to humanity.

In the southern Slavic countries and neighboring Romania, garlic was integrated into the vampire myth. It was used in both the detection of and prevention of attacks by vampires. Vampires living incognito in the community could be spotted by their reluctance to eat garlic. In the 1970s, Harry Senn was advised by his Romanian informants that the distribution of garlic during a church service and observation of those who refused to eat their portion was an acceptable manner of detecting a vampire hidden in the community.

Vampires were especially active in these regions around St. Andrew's Eve and **St. George's Eve**. On those days, windows and other openings in the house were anointed with garlic to keep the vampires away. Cattle might also be given a garlic rubdown. In some communities, garlic was mixed with food and fed to cattle before every important holiday. If a recently deceased person was suspected of vampirism, garlic might be stuffed in the deceased's mouth or placed in the **coffin**. If detection and the need to destroy a vampire required exhumation of its body, the vampire might face decapitation and garlic might be placed in the mouth or within the coffin.

Garlic was also prominent in Eastern Europe and was served as the most universal protective devise used against vampires and vampiric entities. It appeared in the folklore of **Mexico**, **South America**, and **China**. Throughout the twentieth century, garlic became one of the most well-known objects associated with vampires. Not a particularly

religious symbol, garlic survived while the crucifix slowly disappeared from the list of anti-vampire weapons. On occasion, as in the book and film *The Lost Boys*, the effectiveness of garlic was denied, but through the 1990s it continued to appear as a viable vampire detection and/or prevention substance.

While continuing as an item in the vampire hunter's arsenal, it has been less used in the twenty-first century and has gradually been discarded under the weight of denials of its efficacy. It was used by Buffy and her friends on the TV show *Buffy and Vampire Slayer*, but infrequently. It is ineffective for the vampires in the book series *Twilight*. Garlic repels the vampires in Charlaine Harris's novels based on the TV series *True Blood*, but is more of a nuisance than harmful, and is not even mentioned in Laura Smith's *Vampire Diaries*.

Sources:

Lehrer, Ernst, and Johanna Lehner. *Folklore and Odysseys of Food and Medicinal Plants*. New York: Tutor Publishing Company, 1962. 128 pp.

Murgoci, Agnes. "The Vampire in Roumania." *Folk-Lore* 27, 5 (1926): 320–49.

Senn, Harry A. *Were-Wolf and Vampire in Romania*. New York: Columbia University Press, 1982. 148 pp.

Garton, Ray (1962–)

Ray Garton, a horror writer who has authored several vampire novels, was the product of a fairly normal upbringing in California. However, in spite of his protestations that he has no particular relationship to either the dark side of life or violence, he has produced a series of novels that open up a dark, violent world. While his first vampire novel was *Seductions* (1984), he has received most attention for two later works, *Live Girls* (1987) and *Lot Lizards* (1991).

Live Girls traced the downward spiral of Davey Owen who was drawn into a porn center off Times Square in New York City only to discover that the "live girls" promised were really undead females who kept their clientele coming back with their very special bite. A deluxe edition of the hard-to-find book was released in 1997 by Cemetery Dance Publications along with a CD recording of **music** inspired by the novel by **Vlad** (of the Dark Theater), under his full name, Scott Vladimir Licina. *Lot Lizards* is set on the West Coast at a rural truck stop which is inhabited by a group of vampires who prey on the truckers who initially accept their advances with offers of sex.

In the twenty-first century, Garton has continued to show some attention to vampires in his Buffy the Vampire Slayer book, *Resurrecting Ravana* (2000), and a new novel *Night Life* (2007), a sequel to *Live Girls*, in which the two main vampire characters have moved from life in the big city to a more prosaic existence in the suburbs.

Garton resides in rural northern California.

Sources:

Garton, Ray. *Seductions*. New York: Pinnacle Books, 1984. 277 pp.

———. *Live Girls*. London: McDonald, Reprint: New York: Pocket Books, 1987. 311 pp. Rept.Cemetery Dance Publications, 1997.

———. *Lot Lizards*. Shingletown, CA: Mark Ziesing, 1991. 188 pp. Reprint: Shingletown, CA: Mark Ziesing, 1991. 188 pp.

―――. *The New Neighbor*. Lynbrook, New York: Charnel House, 1991. 300 pp.

―――. *Resurrecting Ravana*. New York: Pocket Books, 2000. 305 pp.

―――. *Night Life*. Leisure Books: New York, 2007. 338 pp.

❨ Gautier, Théophile (1811–1872) ❩

Pierre Jules Théophile Gautier, a French romantic author, was born in southern France, the son of Antoinette Adélaide Cocard and Jean Pierre Gautier. As a child, he read *Robinson Crusoe*, and at school he associated with Gérard de Nerval (who later translated *Faust* into French).

As a young man, he was affected by E. T. A. Hoffmann's tales and **Goethe's** "The Bride of Corinth." Gautier also became associated with the circle of writers around Victor Hugo. Throughout the early 1830s, he frequented a variety of literary gatherings, including one that gathered at the Hotel Pimodan; famous for its indulgence in opium.

A change in family fortune in the 1830s forced Gautier to work as a journalist; and he worked at it, somewhat unhappily, for the rest of his life. He authored thousands of reviews as a literary, theatre, and art critic. Gautier's long hours of work earned little more than a modest living and few honors during his lifetime. Apart from newspaper work, he wrote many romantic stories, although his role in the larger romantic movement was overshadowed by that of Victor Hugo. His own exploration of the psyche, in part stimulated by the use of opium, gained greater acknowledgement in the years since his death, when Gautier finally took his place among France's outstanding nineteenth-century writers.

Like many other French romantic writers, Gautier found great inspiration in the vampire myth. His earliest and most famous vampire story, *La Morte Amoureuse* (literally, "the dead woman in love") appeared in 1836. An English translation appeared in *The World of Théophile Gautier* in 1907 and was published separately in 1927 as *The Beautiful Vampire*. The story used what was to become a recurring theme in Gautier's fiction. It told of a woman who returned from the dead to vampirize the male subject of the story. In *The Beautiful Vampire*, the dead woman, Clairmonde, made herself so attractive to her male lover, the priest Romuald, that he chose to bleed to death rather than lose her attention.

The theme would reappear, for example in *Aria Marcella*, which was directly inspired by Goethe's "The Bride of Corinth," in which Gautier declared, "No one is truly dead until they are no longer loved." The 1863 novel *The Mummy's Foot* was set among archaeologists in Egypt. In it a mummy, which retained

French writer Théophile Gautier was fascinated by the vampire myth.

the elasticity of living flesh and had "enamel eyes shining with the moist glow of life," was compared to a vampire lying in its tomb dead … yet alive.

Another vampiric story, *Spirite* (1866), used recently popularized spiritualism as the setting. The story told of a man who experienced both the symbolic and actual death of his love. She first became a nun (and thus died to the world) and then physically died. When the woman took her vows, she gave herself to her love and vowed to be his beyond the grave. Contact was made in a séance and she ultimately lured the man to his death.

During the last years of his life, Gautier lived in a Paris suburb, where he died from a heart condition in 1872. Most of his romantic tales have been translated into English.

Sources:

Du Camp, Maxime, and Andrew Lang. *Théophile Gautier*. Honolulu, HI: University Press of the Pacific, 2004. 252 pp.

Gautier, Frederick Caesar de Sumichras. *The Works of Théophile Gautier*. Charleston, SC: Biblio-Life, 2009. 332 pp.

Gautier, Théophile. *The Beautiful Vampire*. London: A. M. Philpot, 1927. 110 pp.

———. *Spirite: Nouvelle fantastique*. Paris: Biblioth?que Charpentier, 1967.

Riffaterre, Hermine. "Love-in-Death: Gautier's 'morte amoureuse.'" In *The Occult in Language and Literature*. New York: New York Literary Forum, 1980, pp. 65–74.

Smith, Albert B. *Théophile Gautier and the Fantastic*. Jackson, MS: University Press of Mississippi, 1977.

Germany, Vampires in

As among the Slavic peoples of Eastern Europe, vampires and vampire-like figures have a long history in Germany, and the first literary and completely fictional presentations of vampires in literature (poems and novels) are in the German language (though vampires in folklore are much older). By the tenthcentury, Slavic expansion had reached into what is today the eastern part of Germany. **Slavs** and Germanic people have mixed together through to the modern era. Thus, vampire figures in the region are difficult to distinguish from those of their neighbors such as the Kushubian people of northern **Poland**.

A well known early vampire-like figure is the *Nachzehrer*. The term is not connected with the German word for night, but rather stands for "he who devours after (his death)." He is also called *Gierrach* or *Gierhals* ("having a ravenous throat"), *Dodelecker* or even *Totenküsser*, and often mentioned in German folklore from the sixteenth to the eighteenth century, though certainly known earlier. Recent researches have shown he was not just known in parts of Germany in contact with Slavic people, but also in western parts as the Eifel. More rarely a dead person is called *Blutsauger* (with dialect variants) or "bloodsucker" (a term also used in popular speech to describe disagreeable people). A special figure is the *Neuntöter* or "killer of nine," who as a child is born already with his teeth or even two rows of teeth, then usually dies quickly, and may catch or grasp others after his death so they die also.

Like the Slavic vampire, the *Nachzehrer* was a revenant (a recently deceased person returned from the grave to attack the living, usually family and village acquaintances). Also like the Slavic vampire, he may have originated from unusual death circumstances.

A person who died suddenly from **suicide** or an accident may in this sense become a *Nachzehrer*. Similar to the *vjesci* of Poland, a child born with a caul (an amniotic membrane that covers the face of some babies) might become a *Nachzehrer*, especially if the caul was red. This figure was also associated with epidemic sickness. When a group of people died from the same disease, survivors often identified the first to die as the cause of the others' death. In the tomb, *Nachtzehrer* (singular and plural of the word are identical) were known for their habit of chewing on their own extremities and clothes or shroud (a belief likely derived from the finding of bodies that had been subject to predator damage or whose gum had quickly disappeared due to decomposition). The activity of the *Nachzehrer* in the grave continued until he ceased consuming his body and his clothes. As a rule, he does not leave his grave, but in a magical way destroys the life of family members who die immediately after him (thus "he who devours after his death").

He is never called a vampire in German texts, a word that became popular only with the Slavic vampire exhumations of the 1730s, though he can be found lying in pools of **blood**. Many ideas connected with the *Nachzehrer* occur only in a small number of texts, but quite often he can be identified from the sucking, chewing and gnawing noises that come from his grave. In the eighteenth century this belief was generally regarded as superstition, and became a subject for scholarly enquiry and naturalist explanations. To prevent the *Nachzehrer* from destroying living people, various preventive measures were proposed. Some people placed a clump of earth under his chin; others placed a coin or stone in his mouth; still others tied a handkerchief tightly around his neck. As a more drastic measure, people cut off the potential *Nachzehrer*'s head, drove a spike into his mouth to pin the head to the ground, or fixed the tongue in place.

In the nineteenth- and even twentieth-century cases of *Nachzehrer* belief, a comparison with vampires became possible. By this time the word and Slavic vampire ideas had become common knowledge. Alfons Schweiggert investigated some *Bluatsauger* (bloodsucker) ideas of Bavaria in the 1980s. He found that *Bluatsauger* were believed to become undead because they were not baptized (Bavaria is a mostly Roman Catholic part of Germany), were involved in witchcraft, lived an immoral life, or committed suicide. They might also have become vampires from eating the meat of an animal killed by a wolf. During the burial process, an **animal** jumping over the grave might have caused a person to return as a vampire. In like measure, Bavarians reported that a nun stepping over a grave could have the same effect. Their appearance is described as pale in color, somewhat resembling a **zombie**. If such a *Bluatsauger* were loosed upon a community, residents were told to stay inside at night, to smear their doors and windows with **garlic**, and place hawthorn around their houses. If members of the community owned a black dog, an extra set of eyes could be painted upon the animal, causing the vampire to flee. To effectively kill the vampire, a **stake** through the heart and garlic in the mouth were recommended. Such beliefs are considered the German equivalents of vampire stories, but it is extremely improbable anything in them is independent of the Slavic vampire tales, or even goes back to pre-nineteenth-century times.

Exhumations of dead people suspected of vampire-like influences on the living happened a number of times as recent as the nineteenth century in Germany, as in Western Prussia 1870–73 (cases of G. Gehrke and Franz von Poblocki, and a few less well-documented ones; the last exhumation in 1913 in the Kreis Putzig, Western Prussia). Of course, both state and ecclesiastical authorities tried to forbid these clandestine exhumations, but without success. Cholera epidemics were sometimes interpreted as influenced by vampires, as in 1855 in Danzig, but it is not quite clear how serious these interpretations were.

The Great Vampire Debate: The beliefs and practices in Germany and Eastern Europe concerning vampire-like figures and vampiric happenings became the subject of several books written as early as the seventeenth century (although none used the term "vampire" in its text). Notable treatises included "De Masticatione Mortuorum" (1679) by Philip Rohr, which discussed the eating habits of the *Nachzehrer*, and Christian Frederic Garmann's "De Miraculis Mortuorum" (1670). In the early eighteenth century, a flood of reports of Eastern European vampires began to filter into Germany, where they prompted a massive debate in the universities. Although Germany did not escape the vampire hysteria (epidemics were reported in East Prussia in 1710, 1721, and 1750), the vampire issue seems to have been initially raised by the widespread newspaper reports of vampire investigations in Serbia in 1725 and especially the 1731–32 investigation of the **Arnold Paul** case. A popularized version of the Arnold Paul case was a bestseller at the 1732 Leipzig book fair. Helping to initiate the debate were theologian Michael Ranft's "De Masticatione Mortuorum in Tumulis Liber" (1728; a German translation appeared 2006) and John Christian Stock's "Dissertio de Cadauveribus Sanguisugis" (1732). The "Philosophicae et Christianae Cogitationes de Vampiris" ("Philosophical and Christian Thoughts on Vampires") by Johann Christian (not Christofer) Harenberg (1739) is still mentioned in **Sheridan Le Fanu**'s "**Carmilla**," who knew this and similar items through the English translation of **Dom Augustin Calmet**'s great work on vampires, translated into English by Henry Christmas (1850). The debate in German scholarly circles centered on various nonsupernatural (or at least nonvampiric) explanations of the phenomena reported by the vampire investigators, especially in the Paul case. Ranft led the attack on the existence of vampires by suggesting that although the dead can influence the living, they could never assume the form of resuscitated corpses. Others assumed that the changes in the corpses (offered as proof of vampirism) could have resulted from perfectly natural alterations due to premature burial, plague or rabies, unnaturally well-preserved corpses, the natural growth of hair and nails after death.

The debate resulted in the relegation of the vampire to the realm of superstition and left scholars with only a single relevant question concerning the vampire: "What causes people to believe in such an unreal entity as the vampire?" The primary dissenting voice, which emerged as the German debate was coming to an end, belonged to the French biblical scholar Dom Calmet. He dissented from his German colleagues simply by leaving the question of the vampire's existence open. Calmet implied the possibility of vampires by suggesting that the very thing that would establish their existence was still lacking: solid proof. Although he did not develop any real argument in favor of vampires, Calmet took the reports very seriously and suggested that vampires were a subject suitable for further consideration by his colleagues. Interestingly enough, while most of the works of his German contemporaries were soon confined to the shelves of a few university libraries, Calmet's work was translated into various languages and reprinted as late as the 1850s (and in English as recently as 1993). Recent research on vampires of the 1720s and 1730s has concentrated on the forensic and medical aspects, but also on the role of the vampire as a successor to the witch as a scapegoat. In the 1730s belief in **witchcraft** had almost disappeared in Germany and Austria, and the vampire stories took over some of its imaginative functions for the public.

The Literary Vampire: Germany and Austria also gave birth to the modern literary vampire. In all probability the first modern piece of vampire literature was a short poem, "Der Vampir" by Heinrich August Ossenfelder (1748). Not strictly a poem about vampires, but much more influential in the development of vampire literature in both Germany and England, was "Lenore" (1774) by Gottfried August Bürger, a ballad about a revenant who returned to claim his love and take her to his grave as his bride. This very well known poem was translated into English by Sir Walter Scott as "William and Helen" (1797); in the eighteenth century, four other translations appeared, such as those by William Taylor (1765–1836) and the Rev. J. Beresford, and also a first parody "Miss Kitty, a Parody on Lenora." **Bram Stoker** quotes it in his story "**Dracula**'s guest" (published posthumously 1914). Even more influential to the popularity of the vampire theme was **Johann Wolfgang von Goethe**'s poem, "Die Braut von Korinth" ("The Bride of Corinth"), originally published in 1797. Goethe emerged as the leading literary figure on the continent, and his attention to the vampire theme legitimized it for others.

What may have been the first vampire novel in any language was written by Ignaz Ferdinand Arnold (1774–1812; he also wrote as Theodor Ferdinand Kajetan Arnold). In his time Arnold was a well known and quite successful musician and writer. He wrote popular novels on crime, conspiracies, conjurers, secret societies, ghosts and other sensationalist subjects. Although never taken as serious literature, his three-volume novel published in 1801 entitled *Der Vampir* (also known as *Der Vampyr*) was noticed in some contemporary catalogues and biographies, but no copy is known to be in existence. Such books were not bought by libraries in the early nineteenth century. *Der Vampir* was probably the first vampire novel ever published, and the vampire is certainly meant in a literal, not a metaphorical sense, as can be concluded from the sensationalist supernaturalism of Arnold's other books. Germany also produced the first monograph on vampires not in folklore, but in literature: Stefan Hock, *Die Vampirsagen und ihre Verwertung in der deutschen Literatur* (1900; reprinted in 2006); by the time this monograph was written Hock was not able to find a copy of Arnold's book. There are other German vampire novels almost as early, for example: *Der Vampyr oder die blutige Hochzeit mit der schönen Kroatin; Eine sonderbare Geschichte vom böhmischen Wiesenpater* (1812); or Theodor Hildebrand(t), *Der Vampyr oder die Todtenbraut. Ein Roman nach neugriechischen Volkssagen* (1828). There is also a tale by Ernst Theodor Amadeus Hoffmann (1776–1822) sometimes mentioned in this context. This story—often called "Aurelia" (1820), though originally without title and part of a larger composition and published in English under a variety of names—is in fact about ghouls, and even has a model in the *Arabian Nights* (Night 351, "Story of Sîdîî Nu'mân").

There has been some argument about another early German vampire story that may have been the first short piece of vampire fiction. An English version of a story "Wake Not the Dead" was published in 1823, and became attributed to the famous German writer Johann Ludwig Tieck. But the story is in fact by Ernst Raupach. It was originally entitled "Laszt die Todten ruhen" ("Let the Dead Rest") and there is a play using the same title. The tale is notable for featuring a female vampire, Brunhilda, who was brought back to life by Walter, a powerful nobleman. Walter was in love, but awoke one evening to find his wife draining his blood. The German version has more clear-cut allusions to the **Elizabeth Bathory** tradition. Another later vampire tale is Edwin Bauer's "Der Baron Vampyr, ein Kulturbild aus der Gegenwart" (1892).

The first really extensive German treatment of vampires in eastern European folk-lore in the nineteenth century was written by Georg Conrad Horst, "Zauber-Bibliothek" Vol. 1 (1821), who stated that even the name of vampires had become little known by then. This certainly changed with the successful romantic opera *Der Vampyr* (1828) by Heinrich Marschner (1795–1861), with a libretto by Wilhelm August Wohlbr‚ck based vaguely on Polidori's "The Vampyre" and more particularly on the play *Der Vampir oder die Totenbraut* (1821), written by Heinrich Ludwig Ritter. The opera is still occasionally performed. It is also discussed in Karl Rosenkranz's very influential *Ästhetik des Häszlichen* (853), together with Goethe's and Lord Byron's (i.e. Polidori's) vampiric texts. Another theoretical and ethnological text of some impact (perhaps even on Stoker, via Arminius Vambéry or other channels) is Wilhelm Mannhardt's *Über Vampirismus* (1859).

The flow of vampire novels and tales in Germany since then never abated. Ferenz Köröshazy, (pseudonym of Seligmann Kohn) wrote *Die Vampyrbraut oder die Wirkungen des bösen Blickes. Aus dem Ungarischen* (1849). Perhaps the most interesting of these nineteenth-century German vampire novels is Hans Wachenhusen (1822–98), *Der Vampyr, Novelle aus Bulgarien* (1878), where the vampire is an evil former Eastern Orthodox priest in pursuit of a young woman, until she is rescued by an English officer. But the real strength of the novel is its careful description of the multicultural society in the late Ottoman empire, which Wachenhusen knew well from travels (and about which he had published many books). **Gypsies** are also mentioned a number of times and have a similar role to those in Stoker's ***Dracula***. Indeed the atmosphere of the novel in some parts is comparable to *Dracula*, though Stoker's is a much more complex tale. In 1860 in "Odds and Ends" there appeared an anonymous short story, "The Mysterious Stranger," translated from German. The story tells of a certain Azzo von Klatka, a nobleman living in the Carpathian Mountains. He attacked the daughter of a neighbor, an Austrian nobleman. She began to weaken and had wounds on her neck. Meanwhile, von Kaltka grew visibly younger. In the end, the victim was forced to drive nails in the vampire's head to kill him.

Elements of this tale may have echoes in *Dracula*; both stories open with a person traveling into the strange territory of the Carpathian Mountains and being impressed by the picturesque scenery. In "The Mysterious Stranger" the travelling knight and his family were startled by the appearance of wolves, but the "stranger" calmed and commanded them (as did Dracula). The stranger is found to live entirely on liquids and appears only in the daytime. Eventually, he is discovered sleeping in an open coffin in a ruined chapel below the castle. One character in the story, Woislaw, an older man who was quite knowledgeable about vampires, may also have inspired Stoker's vampire-hunting character Abraham Van Helsing.

"Psychic vampirism" is more rare in German novels, though the theosophists often wrote about it, influencing e.g. Franz Hartmann's article "Seelenbräute und Vampirismus," (1895), later published as a small book. Ladislaus Stanislaus Reymont, "Der Vampir, Roman" (1914, from the Polish "Wampir") is a story about a weak-willed protagonist who falls victim to a demonic, strong-willed woman in **London**. More important is another tale of psychic vampirism, Georg von der Gabelentz, "Das Rätsel Choriander" (1929). The erotic side of vampirism is most clearly expressed in Toni Schwabe's story, "Der Vampir" (1921).

The German version of the first homosexual vampire novel by German author George Sylvester Viereck, "Das Haus des Vampyrs" (1909) was originally published in

English ("The House of the Vampire", 1907). It was translated into German by the author himself. There also exists an unpublished German drama by Viereck, "Der Vampyr, Schauspiel in 3 Akten" (1905?). Another stylistically elegant vampire story is Leonhard Stein, "Der Vampyr" (1918), where the female vampire can be read as a metaphor of the psychic side of social decline.

Almost nothing from the classic German vampire literature has been translated into English. In these golden years of the German phantasmic tale (1900–30), vampires even became a subject of children's literature: Friedrich Meister, *Der Vampyr, Eine Seegeschichte* (1910). As is to be expected, many novels about vampires are more popular reading than high literature, just, as in many other languages. For example Paul Pitt, whose real name is Paul Oskar Ernst Erttmannwrote "Der Mitternachtsvampir, John Kling's Erinnerungen Bd. 15" (1931). And L. Hackenbroich's "Ein Vampyr. Kriminalroman" (1908) is a non-supernatural crime story.

Stoker's *Dracula* first came out in German in 1908, translated by Heinz Widtmann. By then vampires were firmly established in the German supernatural tale. In 1912 a psychoanalytical analysis of vampire tales appeared, written by Ernest Jones, a follower of Sigmund Freud, entitled *Der Alptraum in seiner Beziehung zu gewissen Formen des mittealterlichen Aberglaubens.*

The undisputed masterpiece of German vampire tales is Karl Hanns Strobl, "Das Grabmal auf dem Père Lachaise" (1913), a short novelette comparable in complexity to "Carmilla". A young scholar is financed by the Countess Anna Feodorowna Wassilska (a character reminiscent of Elizabeth Bathory), if he is willing to live for a year after her death in her tomb, where he is sometimes visited by his fiancée. There he soon encounters strange phenomena. Fed by meals devilishly well prepared by a Tatar servant of the Countess, he quickly finds he cannot leave the tomb, and becomes convinced he is to be the victim of a vampire. But things are more complicated. This subtle tale can be read as a study in personality deteriorization and allows both for a supernatural and a non-supernatural reading.

With the Nazi era, came the end of fantastic literature in Germany, but in the 1970s vampire literature was revived, most of it quite stereotype. But some items deserve mention. Barbara Neuwirth, a successful Austrian writer, has edited an anthology of vampire stories written by German and Austrian female writers, some of them with a feminist approach (*Blasz sei mein Gesicht*, 1988). The Austrian writer Elfriede Jelinek (nobel laureate, 2004) is certainly the most important living writer deeply interested in the vampire motif, which she has used many times (*Die Kinder der Toten*, 1995). And of course many supernatural and fantasy writers in present-day Germany have written vampire tales, sometimes long cycles of novels as with Wolfgang Hohlbein (born 1953) or more rarely cycles of rather sophisticated short stories, as with Christian von Aster (born 1973). Jörg Weigand, *Isabella oder eine ganz besondere Liebe* (1993) who uses the vampire theme for a complex story of Eastern and Western Germany (which became reunited in 1990). Hans Carl Artmann (1921–2000) wrote many satiric pieces such as "Dracula, Dracula" (1966). Especially noticeable has been original juvenile literature on vampires, and among children's authors, Angela Sommer-Bodenburg (born 1948) has emerged as an international favorite. Her series of children's novels starring "the little vampire" Rüdiger who befriends the human child Anton started in 1979, and has been translated into over 30 languages and has sold many millions of copies.

Poster art from the 1931 version of *Dracula*.

As in most western countries, vampires are a beloved part of public imagination. A vampire museum existed for some years in the Gieszen era, but at present is not open to the public. Germany has shared the international vampire fashions from ***Buffy the Vampire Slayer*** to ***Twilight***. But in the late twentieth century and early twenty-first century Germany has produced extensive and substantial scholarship on vampires in folklore, mythology, literature and the arts, none of which has been translated into English so far.

The Cinematic Vampire: Germany reemerged as an important locale for the developing vampire myth in the early twentieth century. In 1922 Prana Films released *Nosferatu, Eine Symphonie des Grauens* directed by Friedrich Wilhelm Murnau. *Nosferatu* was a greatly disguised but recognizable movie adaptation of *Dracula*. It was screened only once before Stoker's widow, Florence, charged Prana Films with literary theft. Meanwhile, as she pursued the case, the financial instability of Prana Films forced it into a receivership. After three years of litigation, Stoker finally won the case and all copies of the film were ordered to be destroyed. In recent years, *Nosferatu* has been hailed as one of the great films of German expressionism and the silent era. However, it could be argued that it had only a minimal role in the development of the modern vampire.

The few copies that survived were hidden and not seen by audiences until the 1960s. By then, Florence Stoker was dead and both the **Bela Lugosi** and **Christopher Lee** versions of *Dracula* were already finished.

Although *Nosferatu* remains the most famous German vampire film, Germany has given the public a number of other important cinematic treatments of the subject. The German vampire emerged in the 1960s in a series of forgettable films including (as released in English) *Cave of the Living Dead* (1964), *Blood Suckers* (1966), and *The Blood Demon* (1967) with Christopher Lee. The 1964 movie *The Vampire of Düsseldorf* told the story of **Peter Kürten**, a true life serial murderer who drank the blood of his victims. It was followed in 1962 by *Tenderness of Wolves* (1973), which treated the vampiric/ghoulish murders of **Fritz Haarmann**, who had murdered some twenty-five boys and consumed their blood.

During the 1970s, Germany was the location for two of the most unique and thoughtful vampire films. *Jonathan* (1970) used vampirism as a parable for the rise of fascism. *Martin* (1976) explored the life of a young, sophisticated vampire who moved from biting to using a razor blade and syringe. Other more recent German vampire movies include *The Werewolf vs. the Vampire Woman* (1970), *The Vampire Happening* (1978), and *A Lovely Monster* (1991).

The Twentieth-Century Literary Vampire: During the last two decades, Germany provided a fruitful environment for the vampire novel. The country has been an ever-present element of horror literature, and numerous vampire short stories appeared in Germany's several horror-fiction magazines. For three decades, a host of contemporary popular fiction writers have mined the vampire cave of legend. They were led by Jason Dark, who wrote more than 300 popular novels including some twenty featuring Dracula and other vampires. His vampire books were published in a series of horror pulps by Bastei-Lübbe Verlag at Bergisch Gladbach. Frederic Collins, who had also written several vampire novels, was the editor of the series. Among the writers who also developed multiple vampire novels for Bastei-Lübbe were: Brian Elliot, Robert Lamont, Frank de Lorca, A. F. Morland, Mike Shadow, and Earl Warren. Many of these names, of course, are pseudonyms; some are house names used by different writers.

Zauberkreis-Verlag and Pabelhaus, both pulp publishers located in Rastatt, also released a set of vampire titles in a horror series. Among the more popular writers for Zauberkreis-Verlag were Maik Caroon, Roger Damon, Marcos Mongo, Dan Schocker, John Spider, and W. J. Tobien. Pabelhaus writers included James R. Buchette, Neal Davenport, Frank Sky, and Hugh Walker. The majority of German vampire novels continue to be published by these three publishing companies.

Sources:

Barber, Paul. *Vampires, Burial, and Death: Folklore and Reality.* New Haven, CT: Yale University Press, 1988.

Freund, Winfried. "Der entzauberte Vampir. Zur parodistischen Rezeption des Grafen Dracula bei H.C. Artmann und Herbert Rosendorfer." In *Rezeptionspragmatik. Beiträge zur Praxis des Lesens.* Gerhard Köpf, ed. Munich, Germany: Fink, 1981, 131–48.

Hamberger, Klaus. *Mortuus non mordet. Dokumente zum Vampirismus 1689–1791.* Wien: Turia und Kant, 1992. A painstakingly edited collection of sources on the vampire exhumations of the 1730s and other eighteenth-century aspects; the most important collection of sources on "original" vampires.

———. *Über Vampirismus: Krankengeschichten und Deutungsmuster 1801–1899*. Vienna, Austria: Turia und Kant, 1992. Vampires and medical history in the nineteenth century.

Hock, Stefan. *Die Vampyrsagen und ihre Verwertung in der deutschen Literatur*. Berlin, Germany: Alexander Duncker, 1900 (the first book on vampires in literature).

Jänsch, Erwin. *Vampir Lexikon*. Augsburg, Germany: Soso, 1995. A popular book, though it has many mistakes.

Klaniczay, Gabor, "The Decline of Witches and Rise of Vampires in the Eighteenth-Century Habsburg Monarchy." *Ethnologia Europaea*17 (1987): 165–180.

Kremer, Peter. *Draculas Vettern. Auf der Suche nach den Spuren des Vampirglaubens in Deutschland*. Düren, Germany: Selbstverlag, 2006.

Kyll, Nikolaus. "Die Bestattung der Toten mit dem Gesicht nach unten. Zu einer Sonderform des Begräbnisses im Trierer Land." *Trierer Zeitschrift für Kunst und Geschichte* 27 (1964): 168–83.

Lambrecht, Karin. "Wiedergänger und Vampire in Ostmitteleuropa: Posthume Verbrennung statt Hexenverfolgung" *Jahrbuch für deutsche und osteuropäische Volkskunde* 37 (1994): 49–77.

Le Blanc, Thomas, Clemens Ruthner, and Bettina Twrsnick, eds. *Draculas Wiederkehr. Tagungsband 1997*. Wetzlar, Germany: Phantastische Bibliothek, 2003.

Martin, Ralf-Peter. *Dracula: Das Leben des Fₗrsten Vlad Tepes*. Frankfurt am Main, Germany: Fischer Taschenbuch Verlag, 1991.

Meurer, Hans. *Der Dunkle Mythos: Blut, Sex and Tod: Die Faszination des Volksglaubens an Vampire*. Schliengen, Germany: Edition Argus, 1996.

Moore, Steven, ed. *The Vampire in Verse: An Anthology*. Chicago: Adams Press, 1985.

Prussmann, Karsten. *Die Dracula-Filme*. Munich, Germany: Wilhelm Heyne Verlag, 1993.

Neu, Peter. "Der Nachzehrer. Ein Beitrag zu Totenbrauchtum und Totenkult in der Eifel im 17. Jahrhundert." *Rheinisch-westfälische Zeitschrift für Volkskunde* 30–31 (1985–86), 225–27.

Pütz, Susanne. *Vampire und ihre Opfer: Der Blutsauger als literarische Figur*. Bielefeld, Germany: Aisthesis Verlag, 1992.

Schroeder, Aribert. *Vampirismus*. Frankfurt am Main, Germany: Akademische Verlagsgesellschaft (Studienreihe Humanitas), 1973.

Schumacher, Katrin. *Femme fantôme: Poetologien und Szenen der Wiedergängerin um 1800/1900*. Tübingen, Germany: Francke, 2007.

Schürmann, Thomas. *Der Nachzehrerglauben in Mitteleuropa*. Marburg, 1990. (The most important study on the subject).

Schweiggert, Alfons, *Wunderwesen zwischen Spessart und Karwendel in Brauchtum, Sage, Märchen*. Weilheim: Stöppel, 1988.

Steiner, Otto. *Vampirleichen*. *Vampirprozesse in Preussen*. Hamburg, Germany: Kriminalistik, 1959.

Tuczay, Christa, and Julia Bertschik, ed. *Poetische Wiedergänger. Deutschsprachige Vampirismus-Diskurse vom Mittelalter bis zur Gegenwart*. Tübingen, Germany: Francke, 2005. The most important collection of studies on vampires in Germany.

❨ Ghouls ❩

The ghoul, a traditional monster frequently associated with the vampire, originated as part of Arabic folklore. It played a part in several tales in the *Arabian Knights*. Ghouls represented a more demonic aspect of the world of jinns, the spirits of Arabic mythology. The Arabic *ghul* (masculine) and *ghulah* (feminine) lived near graves and attacked and ate human corpses. It was also believed that ghouls lived in desolated places where they would attack unsuspecting travelers who mistook the ghoul for a traveling companion and were led astray. Ghul-I-Beában was a particularly monstrous ghoul believed to inhabit the wilderness of Afghanistan and Iran. Marco Polo, reflecting on the

accounts of ghouls he had heard about during his travels, suggested that ghouls, gryphons (an imaginary animal, part eagle, part lion), and good faith were three things people frequently referred to but did not exist.

The ghoul returned to popular culture in the twentieth-century through a multitude of monster movies. New ghouls were similar to vampires because they were re-animated dead people in humanoid form. The ghoul, however, ate human flesh, while the vampire drank **blood**. The ghoul also acted with neither a will nor intellect, and seemed to have somewhat derived from the **zombie**—the figure in Haitian folklore reportedly brought back to life by magic and destined to work in the service of the person who brought it back to "life." One nineteenth-century case, that of François Bertrand, was a popular example of ghoulish behavior. Bertrand, a noncommissioned officer in the French Army, was arrested after he entered and desecrated several tombs in Paris. He was convicted and sentenced to a lengthy term in prison in 1849 after confessing to an overwhelming compulsion to tear the corpses of women and girls to pieces. His story later became the basis of a popular novel, *The Werewolf of Paris* by Guy Endore.

Modern ghouls, really a ghoul/zombie mixture, made definitive appearances in two movies directed by George Romero: *Night of the Living Dead* (1968) and *Dawn of the Dead* (1979). Romero acknowledged that the numerous vampires of **Richard Matheson**'s 1954 novel, *I Am Legend,* inspired his "living dead." *Night of the Living Dead* pictured the dead returning to life by some form of radiation and eating their fellow humans. The ghouls walked slowly, were limited in their actions, and were destroyed by a **bullet** or sharp blow to the head. Although they could be killed relatively easily, in packs they could simply overwhelm individuals and small groups, such as those trapped in the farmhouse in the movie. *Night of the Living Dead* and *Dawn of the Dead* seemed to have inspired a group of Italian movies featuring a variation on Romero's ghoul/zombie as exemplified in Umberto Lenzi's *City of the Walking Dead* (1983).

The ghoul, in a somewhat different form, has been given new life in the 1990s through **Vampire: The Masquerade** the popular role-playing **game**. In the mythology of the game, ghouls are people who have received some vampire blood, hence have attained a degree of immortality, but have not gone through the full Embrace which would make them a vampire. They are servants of the vampires and can be most helpful as they easily move about in the daytime.

The ghoul is a rare creature in Western popular culture, though its cousin the zombieenjoyed extensive revival in the 1990s. It has been integrated into White Wolf's game, *Vampire: The Eternal Struggle,* and a modest number of fictional writings, most designed for a teen or younger audience have appeared. R. L. Stine has written several ghoul stories in his juvenile series.

Sources:

Barber, Richard, and Anne Riches. *A Dictionary of Fabulous Beasts.* New York: Walker and Company, 1971. 167 pp.

Russell, W. M. S., and Claire Russell. "The Social Biology of Werewolves." In J. R. Porter and W. M. S. Russell. *Animals in Folklore.* Totowa, NJ: Rowman & Littlefield, 1978, 143–182.

Waller, George A. *The Living and the Undead: From Stoker's Dracula to Romero's Dawn of the Dead.* Urbana, IL: University of Illinois press, 1986. 378 pp.

Giles, Rupert

Rupert Giles, a major character on the TV series ***Buffy the Vampire Slayer***, was the Watcher who in 1997 was assigned to **Buffy Summers** the new Slayer who had arrived at Sunnydale High School. His cover was to pose as the school librarian, very convenient as it allowed him to accumulate and store a variety of ancient and obscure texts that Buffy and her vampire and demon-hunting associates would need. It was also the perfect place to hold strategy sessions with the students that had gathered around the Slayer. Giles' cool, unflappable, and thoroughly British style contrasted with Buffy's often impulsive and bottom-line approach to her work. Over time, however, they developed a close relationship and she credits him with her maturity.

Giles came from a line of Watchers, which included his father and grandmother. He was a reluctant recruit to the Watcher's ranks, but after time dabbling in the occult, and working in a museum—both of which would provide useful background for his task—he accepted the assignment with Buffy. As her Watcher he provided information, guided the emergence of her own powers and talents, trained her in various fighting skills, and offered magical and other back-up as needed. At times he operated as a substitute for Buffy's largely absent father.

It is Giles who laid out the mythical world in which the Slayer operates in the first two episodes of Buffy and he was usually the one who brought forth the texts that were relevant to the current situation. As the series progresses, and Buffy's friend Willow Rosenberg masters the computer, she begins to rival Giles in knowledge, albeit from a different source.

Once in Sunnydale, he began dating and fell in love with Jenny Calendar, a teacher at the high school. He later learned that she was from the **Gypsy** tribe that cursed **Angel** by giving him back his soul and it was her job to keep an eye on him. When Angel reverted to his evil Angelus-self in season two, Jenny worked to reinstitute his soul, but Angel killed her before she could finish the spell. A short time later, Giles was kidnapped by Angel and tortured. He never really trusted Angel after that incident.

Following the destruction of Sunnydale High School at the end of season three, Giles spent a year unemployed but then purchased an occult shop that became the new headquarters of the Slayer and her friends. He is especially helped by Anya, the former demon who became **Xander Harris**'s girlfriend. Naïve in the ways of the world, she was fascinated with the idea of sales and moneymaking. At one point, Giles ate some enchanted candy supplied by an old acquaintance named Ethan Rayne. As a result, he reverted to his teen consciousness, commits some acts of vandalism and thievery, and had a brief sexual encounter with Buffy's mother Joyce.

As Buffy matured, she became more independent and developed a significant distrust of the Watcher's Council. She eventually cut her ties with the council, but asked Giles to remain her Watcher. He did so for a little while, during which time Buffy's new sister, Dawn, appeared, and Buffy's mother died.

With the death of Joyce, Buffy was left without an income, and slowly developed a mountain of debt. Meanwhile, she sacrificed herself to save Dawn and the world. Giles decided it was time for him to withdraw, and he returned to England just as Willow,

now an accomplished witch, organized Buffy's friends in a great magical action that brought her back from the dead. Upon learning that Buffy had come back, Giles returned to Sunnydale. Though happy to see Buffy again, he denounced Willow's action as the work of an amateur. Having surmised that his presence is blocking Buffy's further growth and independence, he now readied himself to return to England, but before leaving, he gave Buffy a substantial check, enough to pay off her debt and carry her until she could reestablish herself financially.

After Giles left for England, Willow goes on a magical rampage after her lover Tara was killed. Hearing of her destructive activity, Giles returned and allows her to drain him almost to the point of death. His act infused Willow with some positive magical energy and set the stage for Xander to reason her back to her senses, after which Giles took Willow to England for a time of recovery.

In the midst of the final season, Giles returned to Sunnydale for a last time, bringing with him all the potential Slayers for the final battle set up by the First Evil. In the final episode, he was present for the battle at the Hellmouth, and was one of the survivors.

Giles played a role, though never seen, in the last season of **Angel**. He was now in Europe training a host of new Slayers and working with former Sunnydale resident (and comic relief) Andrew Wells, who is in training as a Watcher. Angel contacts Giles in an attempt to find Buffy.

In the comic book season eight of *Buffy*, Giles now heads Buffy's international slaying operations in England. At one point, he recruited the Slayer Faith to assist him in killing a rogue Slayer named Gigi and her colleague Roden, both headed on a highly destructive course. As a result of their actions, Buffy broke relations with Giles, but he continues as an active character in the continuing comic season.

In the wake of the ending of the *Buffy* TV series, Joss Whedon confirmed rumors of a possible BBC follow-up series built around Giles and called *Ripper*. As late as 2007, he reconfirmed that pals for the series were active, but production had not been initiated as of 2009.

Although one of the most popular characters in the show, Giles was among the least featured in the paraphernalia spun off from the show. He appeared on a variety of trading cards, most notably the Men of Sunnydale set from Inkworks (2005), and in several action figures. Meanwhile, librarians appreciated the identification of Giles's occupation and wisdom with his many skills in martial arts and magic, leading some to argue that he had done more to improve the image of the profession than anyone in recent years.

Sources:

Bowers, Cynthia. "Generation Lapse: The Problematic Parenting of Joyce Summers and Rupert Giles." *Slayage: The Online International Journal of Buffy Studies* 2 (2001). http://www.slayageonline.com/essays/slayage2/bowers.htm. Accessed July 15, 2009.

Cullen, John. "Rupert Giles, the Professional-Image Slayer." *American Libraries* 31, 5 (2000): 42.

DeCandido, GraceAnne A. "Bibliographic Good vs. Evil in *Buffy the Vampire Slayer*." *American Libraries* 30.8 (1999): 44–47.

Dupuy, Coralline. "Is Giles Simply Another Dr. Van Helsing? Continuity and Innovation in the Figure of the Watcher in *Buffy the Vampire Slayer*." In *Refractory: A Journal of Entertainment Media* 2 (2003). *Special Issue on Buffy the Vampire Slayer*. Eds. Angela Ndalianis and Felicity Colman. Posted at: http://blogs.arts.unimelb.edu.au/refractory/2003/03/18/is-giles-simply-

another-dr-van-helsing-continuity-innovation-in-the-figure-of-the-watcher-in-buffy-the-vampire-slayer-coralline-dupuy/. Accessed July 15, 2009.

Golden, Christopher, and Nancy Holder. *Buffy the Vampire Slayer: The Watcher's Guide*. New York: Pocket Books, 1998. 298 pp.

Holder, Nancy, with Jeff Mariotte and Maryelizabeth Hart. *Buffy the Vampire Slayer: The Watcher's Guide*. Volume 2. New York: Pocket Books, 2000. 472 pp.

Ruditis, Paul. *Buffy the Vampire Slayer: The Watcher's Guide*. Volume 3. New York: Simon Spotlight, 2004. 359 pp.

Glut, Donald Frank (1944–)

Donald Frank Glut, author and editor of vampire books, was born in Pecos, Texas, the son of Julia and Frank C. Glut. He attended DePaul University for two years (1962–64) and completed his bachelor's degree (1967) at the University of Southern California. Following his graduation, Glut launched a career as a writer and, during the intervening quarter century, has produced numerous horror titles, especially around the **Frankenstein** and **Dracula** themes. Throughout the early 1970s, he authored a series of Frankenstein books including *Frankenstein Lives Again* (Spanish ed. 1971; English ed. 1977), *Terror of Frankenstein* (Spanish ed. 1971; English ed. 1977) and *The Frankenstein Legend: A Tribute to Mary Shelley and Boris Karloff* (1972).

In 1972, Glut produced his first vampire book, *True Vampires of History*. It proved a landmark volume—the first to bring together the accounts of all real (as opposed to legendary) vampires in what was a historical narrative. He followed in 1975 with *The Dracula Book*, a monumental bibliographical work on the character of Dracula as he appeared in the different media, such as books, **comic books**, stage, and film. It was awarded the Montague Summers Award by **The Count Dracula Society**, and became the foundation of all future vampire bibliographical and movie research. In 1977, Glut brought together his two primary loves in a novel, *Frankenstein Meets Dracula* (German edition, 1980).

During the 1970s, Glut contributed articles to numerous comic books including *Eerie, Ghost Rider, The Occult Files of Dr. Spektor*, and **Vampirella**. He created the vampire character Baron Tibor, who appeared in several stories in *The Occult Files of Dr. Spektor*. His novelization of *The Empire Strikes Back* earned him the Galaxy Award in 1980.

Glut continued his interest in Frankenstein and produced *The Frankenstein Catalog* (1984), an updated edition of his prior bibliographical work. He also pursued an interest in dinosaurs and has authored

Author and editor Donald Glut.

a number of titles on that topic, beginning with *The Dinosaur Dictionary* (1972). In the early 1990s, he began compiling a comprehensive work on dinosaurs. His completed work, *Dinosaurs: The Encyclopedia*, published in 1997, was named a outstanding reference source by the American Library Association.

In his youthful years, Glut produced a set of short amateur films about vampires, which became well known among those interested in vampires, though many people had not actually seen the films. Over the years Glut improved his moviemaking skills and, after making a variety of movies over the years, turned to vampires once again and produced a feature film trilogy—*The Erotic Rites of Countess Dracula* (2003), *Countess Dracula's Orgy of Blood* (2004), and *Blood Scarab* (2008)— which present the contemporary story of Elizabeth Bathory's search for a way to live and move about in daylight. In the series she is presented as Count Dracula's widow. At about the same time, Glut assembled all of his early amateur movies into an anthology collection published on DVD as *I Was A Teenage Moviemaker—Don Glut's Amateur Movies* (2006).

Sources:

Glut, Donald F. *True Vampires of History*. New York: H C Publishers, 1971. 191 pp.

———. *The Dracula Book*. Metuchen, NJ: Scarecrow Press, 1975. 388 pp.

———. *Frankenstein Meets Dracula*. London: New English Library, 1977. 140 pp.

———. *Dinosaurs: The Encyclopedia*. Jeffersonville, NC: McFarland & Company, 1997.

Goethe, Johann Wolfgang von (1749–1832)

Johann Wolfgang von Goethe, Germany's most renown man of letters, was born in Frankfurt am Main the son of Katherine Elisabeth Textor and Johann Kaspar Goethe. He entered the University of Leipzig in 1765 to study law. While there, however, he found he was more interested in art and drama and wrote his first plays shortly before a hemorrhage forced his return home in 1768. Goethe finished his law studies at Strasborg in 1771 and established a practice in Frankfurt. These years became a period of intense change in Goethe's world and the beginning of the amazing literary productivity that characterized his life.

In the early 1770s, Goethe began work on *Faust*, the work for which he is most remembered. In fact, he worked on it for much of his life. In 1775, he moved to Weimar at the invitation of Duke Karl August. Although he intended to only stay a few months, he resided there for the rest of his life. In 1784 Goethe began his association with Friedreich Schiller at the University of Jena. The two embarked on a program to give German literature a new degree of seriousness and purpose, a program that met with a remarkable level of success. Goethe's 1796 novel *Wilhelm Meisters Lehrjahre* has been described as the most influential work of fiction in German literature. He completed Part 1 of *Faust* in 1806 and saw its publication two years later.

Although not a romantic, Goethe was the idol of the emerging German romantic movement and his influence was felt by romantics throughout Europe. One work that garnered their appreciation was his 1797 poem, "The Bride of Corinth." It was one of the earliest modern ventures into **poetry** based on the vampire theme.

Often mistakenly cited as being based on a story in Philostratus's *The Life of Apollonius of Tynana*, the poem was in fact based on another story from ancient **Greece** recounted by Phlegon. In it a young woman, Philinnon, returned from the dead to be with her love, Machates.

In his lifetime, Goethe emerged as the most respected man of letters in nineteenth-century Europe. Thus his involvement in the controversy surrounding the publication of the first vampire novella in 1816 was of importance. In that year, **"The Vampyre"**, appeared in a London magazine under the name of **Lord Byron**. Even before Byron could issue a denial of his connection to the story that was actually written by **John Polidori**, Goethe declared it Byron's greatest work. Goethe, therefore, inadvertently lent his prestige to the erroneous ascription of Polidori's tale to Byron, especially in non-English speaking lands. As late as 1830, it was included in the French edition of Byron's collected works.

In the 1820s, Goethe began work on the second part of Faust, which was completed in 1831. He died the following year.

Sources:

Frayling, Christopher. *Vampyres: Lord Byron to Count Dracula*. London: Faber and Faber, 1991. 429 pp.

Williams, John R. *The Life of Goethe: A Critical Biography*. Oxford: Wiley-Blackwell, 2001. 352 pp.

Good Guy Vampires

Margaret L. Carter, a scholar of vampire literature, has defined good guy vampires as vampires who act morally when dealing with mortals, and, as a whole, conform their moral perspective to a human ethical perspective. In order to obtain **blood** without killing or "raping" their **victims**, they will attempt to acquire it from **animals**, blood banks, or willing human donors. A few, like **Vampirella** and **Blade**, use synthetic blood substitutes. Carter also maintains that the good guy vampires retain personality and freedom of choice, and are not so consumed with blood lust that ethical decisions become impossible. Good guy vampires tend to emerge in one of two situations: either they are basically good people who discover themselves trapped in the evil condition—vampirism—and are forced to continually fight against it, or vampirism is pictured as an ethically neutral state, in which vampires can make ethical decisions on how to find their needed sustenance, blood.

In the 1960s, good guy vampires Vampirella and **Barnabas Collins** appeared in popular culture, while literary examples of that time include the **Dracula** of **science fiction** writer **Fred Saberhagen** and **St. Germain**, the hero vampire of the novels of **Chelsea Quinn Yarbro**. Throughout the 1980s, good guy vampires multiplied in literature and media, but most notably reappeared in the 1990s in the person of Nick Knight, the vampire lead of the **television** series, *Forever Knight*. Carter has rightfully pointed out that the good guy vampire is a feature of modern vampire lore that separates it radically from nineteenth-century vampire literature. It is worth noting, however, that the idea of a morally responsible vampire was not really common in twentieth-century literature until after the 1950s. Good guy vampires have been an essential part of the revival of interest

Jessica Hamby (Deborah Ann Woll, left) and Bill Compton (Stephen Moyer) in the successful vampire television series *True Blood*.

in vampires in the 1990s. When in 1992 Mary Ann B. McKinnion announced her intention of starting a fanzine dedicated to good guy vampires, she received encouraging response. For several years she turned out substantial issues annually. *Good Guys Wear Fangs* featured original short stories and **poetry** in which the vampire is a hero.

The good guy vampire found its real home in both romantic fiction and teenage fiction. Good guy vampires became the heroes for writers **Amanda Ashley, Christine Feehan,** and **Charlaine Harris,** whose books were adapted for the HBO television series *True Blood*. And then there are the good guy detectives Jack Fleming in **P. N. Elrod**'s many books, and Henry Fritzroy in the novels of **Tanya Huff.** Simultaneously, in the early episodes of **Buffy the Vampire Slayer**, a good guy vampire, **Angel**, would be introduced as a romantic love interest of the Slayer. In the teen book series **Twilight**, a family of good guy vampires, the Cullens, take center stage with narrator Bella Swan as the main protagonists. Good guy vampires have shown up on many television shows, notably the vampires of *Vampire High*, Nick St. John of *Moonlight*, the two rival vampires in Laura Smith's *Vampire Diaries*, Bill Compton and his vampire friends of *True Blood*, and a number of animée series from Japanese television. Many of the television vampires were aimed at a youthful audience and many were developed from and/or spawned teenage vampire novels.

Sources:

Carter, Margaret L. "What Is a Good Guy Vampire?" *Good Guys Wear Fangs* 1 (May 1992): vi–ix.

Good Guys Wear Fangs. No. 1–. Plymouth, MI: Mary Ann B. McKinnion 1992–.

Greenberg, Martin H. *Vampire Detectives*. New York, NY : DAW Books, 1995. 320pp.

Miller, Elizabeth, and Margaret L. Carter. "Has Dracula Lost His Fangs." In Elizabeth Miller. *Reflections on Dracula: Ten Essays*. White Rock, BC: Transylvania Press, 1997, pp. 25–46.

Good Guys Wear Fangs *see:* Vampire Fandom: United States

Gothic

In literature, the term "gothic" refers to a particular form of the popular romantic novel of the eighteenth century. Gothic novels continued to appear in the nineteenth century and have reemerged in strength as part of the paperback revolution of the last half of the twentieth century. Elizabeth MacAndrew approached the essence of the gothic experience by defining it as the literature of the nightmare. Gothic literature evolved out of explorations of the inner self, with all of its emotive, nonrational, and intuitive aspects.

Thus it emerged as a form of romanticism, but confronted the darker, shadowy side of the self. At its best, gothic works force the reader to consider all that society calls evil in human life.

Gothic novels called into question society's conventional wisdom, especially during the post-Enlightenment period when special emphasis was placed on the rational, orderliness, and control. Gothic authors have challenged the accepted social and intellectual structures of their contemporaries by their presentation of the intense, undeniable, and unavoidable presence of the nonrational, disorder, and chaos. These are most often pictured as uncontrollable forces intruding from the subconscious in the form of supernatural manifestations of the monstrous and horrendous. Gothic literature, as Thompson noted, imposed a sense of *dread*. It created a complex mixture of three distinct elements: *terror*, the threat of physical pain, mutilation, and/or death; *horror*, the direct confrontation with a repulsive evil force or entity; and *the mysterious*, the intuitive realization that the world was far larger than our powers of comprehension could grasp.

To accomplish its self-assigned task, gothic literature developed a set of conventions. Generally, action was placed in out-of-the-ordinary settings. Its very name was taken from the use of medieval settings by its original exponents, stereotypically an old castle. The most dramatic sequences of the story tended to occur at night and often during stormy weather.

Integral to the plot, the characters attempted to function amid an older but disintegrating social order. It was a literary device that subtly interacted with the reader's own sense of disorder. The energy of the story often relied on the combined attack on the naïve innocent and the defenders of the present order by momentarily overwhelming and incomprehensible supernatural forces in the form of ghosts, monsters, or human agents of **Satan**.

The Origins of the Gothic and the Vampire: The birth of gothic fiction is generally cited as the 1763 publication of *The Castle of Otranto* by British writer Horace

Walpole (1717–97). The tale described the interaction of the descendants of Aphonse the Good, a twelfth-century ruler of a small Italian state. His heirs, both the good and the bad, joined some innocent bystanders in struggles to attain their personal goals, only to be diverted by the ghosts that haunted their castle. The success of Walpole's novel inspired other writers to explore the gothic world. Most notable among those authors was Ann Radcliffe, who was often credited with developing the gothic novel into a true literary form through her novels *The Castles of Athlin and Dunbayne* (1789), *A Sicilian Romance* (1790), *The Romance of the Forest* (1791), *The Mysteries of Adolpho* (1794), and *The Italian* (1797).

The popularity of the gothic novel directly led to the famous 1816 gathering of **Lord Byron**, Percy and Mary Shelley, and **John Polidori** in Switzerland. Each was invited to wait out the stormy weather by writing and reading a ghost story to the others. Mary Shelley's contribution was the seed from which *Frankenstein* would grow. Byron wrote a short story that Polidori would later turn into the first modern vampire tale. The effect of the storm was heightened by the group's consumption of laudanum. This typified the role that various consciousness-altering drugs played in stimulating the imagination of romantic authors. The use of laudanum, opium, and/or cocaine produced a dreamlike state so prized by poets and fiction writers of the era that they defined it as the epitome of the creative moment. It also occasionally induced nightmares and encouraged the exploration of the darker side of consciousness.

Once introduced, the vampire became a standard theme in gothic romanticism, especially in **France**. Leading the French exploitation of the vampire was **Jean Charles Emmanuel Nodier**. However, virtually every romantic writer of the nineteenth century from **Samuel Taylor Coleridge** to **Edgar Allan Poe** ultimately used either the vampire or a variation on the vampiric relationship in his or her work. Gothic fiction reached a high point in 1897 with the publication of the great vampire novel, *Dracula*. Like Polidori, **Bram Stoker** brought the Gothic into the contemporary world; but Stoker developed his themes far beyond Polidori. *Dracula* played on traditional gothic themes by placing its opening chapters in a remote castle.

Contemporary **Transylvania** (like contemporary **Greece** in Polidori's story) replaced the older use of medieval settings and effectively took the reader to a strange pre-modern setting. However, Stoker broke convention by bringing the gothic world to the contemporary familiar world of his readers and unleashed evil from a strange land on a conventional British family. Neither the ruling powers, a strong heroic male, nor modern science could slow—much less stop—the spread of that evil. Except for the intervention of the devotee of nonconventional and supernatural wisdom, **Abraham Van Helsing**, the evil would have spread with impunity through the very center of the civilized but unbelieving world. Eventually, of course, Van Helsing was able to organize all the forces of good, including the necessary implements of what most considered an obsolete religion, to defeat **Dracula**.

Throughout the twentieth century, the vampire developed a life of its own. It flew far beyond the realm of the gothic, although it regularly returned to its gothic romantic home. The gothic vampire survived in novels and films, from *Dracula* (1931) to the horror features of **Hammer Films**. The genre experienced a notable revival in the 1960s through the **television** soap opera *Dark Shadows's*. *Dark Shadows'* success and the continued attention given to its basic myth vividly demonstrated the more permanent appeal of gothic realities in contemporary life. *Dark Shadows* was set in the late twentieth century, but action centered on an old mansion in a remote corner of rural New England. Its main characters were members of an old aristocratic family, the Collinses, who symbolized the establishment under attack by the hippie subculture of the time.

Vampire **Barnabas Collins**, and the accompanying supernatural horde that descended on the Collins family, seemed most analogous to the chaotic youthful uprising that was emerging in the very homes of the West Coast's ruling elites.

The 1980s Gothic Movement: Heir to the gothic tradition, mixed with elements from the psychedelic/flower child/rock music subcultures of the 1960s and 1970s, was the gothic countercultural movement that appeared in most urban centers of the U.S. West during the 1980s. The movement's origins can be traced to late 1970s, musical groups in the United Kingdom. It certainly also had its direct precursors in such bands as Black Sabbath and the punk rock music of the 1970s. Possibly the most prominent of those groups was Bauhaus, a rock band formed in 1978. In the following year, the band released the single "Bela Lugosi's Dead," their most popular recording to date. The song was picked up in 1983 for use in the opening sequence of the film version of Whitley Strieber's *The Hunger.* Bauhaus was soon joined by such groups as Siouxsie and the Banshees, The Cult, The Cure, and The Sisters of Mercy.

Together these bands created a variant music called gothic rock or death rock. A circuit of music clubs, most notably The Bat Cave in London, opened to provide a stage for their performances.

Gothic music, as all countercultural forms, articulated an explicit nonconformist stance vis-à-vis the dominant establishment. It opposed narrow sexual mores and traditional established religions. High priests, churches, and congregations were replaced with rock musicians, nightclubs, and fans. The music celebrated the dark, shadowy side of life and had a distinct fascination with death. Its slow, driving sound was frequently described as melancholy, gloomy, even morbid. To those enthralled by the new gothic culture, the vampire is perhaps the single most appropriate image.

In the continuing goth movement, both men and women dress in black. Men seem to be perpetuating vampiric images from **Anne Rice** novels, while women perpetuate what, at first glance, seems to be the persona of Morticia Addams of *The Addams Family,* **Vampira**, and **Elvira**, although some aim for a more Victorian funereal style or a modern vampish look. Vampires, **blood, fangs**, and **bats** have filled the pages of gothic magazines, whether or not vampirism is discussed.

The movement was especially popular in the early 1980s when it spread to the European continent and throughout North America. By the middle of the decade, however, it showed a marked decline in England. Bauhaus disbanded in 1983, although some of its members reformed as Love & Rockets. Most of the clubs that had provided meeting places for gothic aficionados turned their attention to other new trends in popular music, and The Bat Cave closed. To keep the movement alive when the media announced its obituary, one gothic band, Nosferatu, founded The Gothic Society and the periodical *Grimoire.* Through the remainder of the decade *Grimoire* became the new center of a network of gothic bands and fans. Curve, Rosetta Stone, Mortal Coil, Wraith, and Slimelight joined Nosferatu as bands of the gothic scene.

Even as the movement was suffering in England, it was experiencing the early stages of its emergence in the United States. By 1990, a number of gothic bands traveled a circuit of clubs, and fans kept up with the movement through their own fanzines. *Propaganda* was the first of the gothic fanzines to hit the newsstands and offered national (and international) coverage to the emerging gothic movement. Founded by "Propaganda Minister" Fred H. Berger, *Propaganda* provided some structure for "The Underground," as the new gothic subculture referred to itself. The magazine publicized many gothic bands and personalities and provided advertising space for both gothic records and the variety of clothing, jewelry, and paraphernalia demanded by devoted fans. More recently, it produced two gothic videos, *The Trilogy* and *Blood Countess*, the second based upon the life of **Elizabeth Bathory**. In 1992, *Propaganda* was joined on the West Coast by the slick Los Angeles-based magazine *Ghastly*, published by Nosferatu Productions and edited by Jeremy Bai. Nosferatu Productions marketed the gothic subculture through a mail order catalog that included gothic fanzines, compact disc (CDs) and cassettes, cosmetics, clothing, and even condoms. Nosferatu also launched two additional periodicals: *The Oracle*, a monthly newsletter that updates readers on show dates and the latest releases on CD; and *The Cabala*, a fan networking journal.

Through the early 1990s, fans around the United States created a host of gothic fanzines that serviced the growing gothic community, including *The Black Chronicle* from Necronomicon Publishers, *Dark Arts*, *Delirium*, *Dysmetria* from Nosferatu Productions, *Elegia: A Journey into the Gothic*, *Esoterra*, *La Noire D'Immortality*, *Machine Gun Etiquette*, *Permission* , *Terra-X*, *Theatre of the Night*, *Virtue et Morte*, and *Carpe Noctem*.

Gothic writers were second only to the bands in defining the gothic world. The most notable are **Poppy Z. Brite**, author of the novel *Lost Souls*, and Lydia Lunch, an author and recording artist. Among Lunch's writings is a vampire **comic book**, *Bloodsucker* (Eros Comics, 1992). *Nights' Children*, the independent comic art of Wendy Snow-Lang also circulated freely through the gothic subculture.

In the 1990s the majority of large urban centers in the United States developed at least one nightclub that regularly featured gothic music. Most clubs scheduled gothic nights once or twice a week and devoted other evenings to closely related rock music, most often punk and/or industrial rock. Some of the more well known goth rock bands from the early 1990s were Ministry, Shadow Project, Christian Death, This Ascension, The Shroud, The Prophetess, and Death in June. They were joined through the mid-1990s by the likes of Skinny Puppy, Faith & Disease, and Thanatos. Several bands adopted specifically vampiric images, including Astro Vamps, London after Midnight, Lestat, Neither/Neither World,, and Transvision Vamp. In addition, individual musicians adopted stage personae tying them to the vampiric image. They include Eva Van Helsing of The Shroud and Vlad of Nosferatu. Toney Lestat of Wreckage claims to have met the real vampire **Lestat de Lioncourt,** the character featured in the vampire novels of Anne Rice. Toney Lestat adopted his name after Rice made the Lestat character famous.

Gothic music has continued to develop in relation to other trends in rock, especially industrial rock. Besides the bands who self-consciously play to a goth audience, there are others who have adopted much of the dark gothic image aimed at alienated teenagers, while reaching a somewhat different audience. Possibly the best example from the mid-1990s was Marilyn Manson, arguably the most controversial rock musician of the decade with a name constructed with reference to two of the previous generation's most tragic figures. He was able to provoke parental anger unmatched since the Satanic bands of the 1980s.

The Atmospheric Gothic World: Integral to the contemporary gothic world is the dark and eerie atmosphere surrounding those who inhabit it. The presence of that atmosphere, initially created by the music and the decor of the nightclubs, has been furthered by the appearance of the bands and copied by the members of their audiences. Commonly, clothing is black, loose fitting, and revealing, though tight-fitting leather is an acceptable alternative. Hair, if combed, tends to be uncurled, razor cut, and either black or starkly blonde.

Accessories include chain mail and symbolic jewelry (ankhs, crosses, and daggers). Dark clothing combined with pale make-up and dark lipstick presents an overall image of death. A variety of specialty enterprises have arisen to supply the necessary clothing and accessories for the gothic public. Opened in 1988, Siren, a gothic shop in Toronto, was the oldest and best-known retailer of gothic clothing, jewelry, and accessories in North America, but it finally closed in 2005.

Anne Rice's *The Vampire Chronicles* emerged as popular reading material in the gothic world, and her

Morpheus (left) and Grovella Blak were the owners of the gothic and vampire store Siren, which closed in 2005.

leading character Lestat the ideal to emulate. Rice described Lestat as essentially an androgynous being—and for many an essential aspect of the gothic image is androgyny, an ideal of wholeness in which one part of a duality encompasses its opposite. Androgyny can be said to exist when light accepts darkness or pleasure recognizes the role of pain, but the word is most commonly associateded with individuals who blur the social distinctions between what is masculine and feminine. Many members of the gothic bands, especially the males, present a stage persona that make it difficult for the audience to immediately identify them as male or female and choose names with either no gender identification or an opposite one. The androgynous theme was an element present in such pre-gothic rock groups as Twisted Sister and KISS.

As a secondary theme, based in part upon the androgynous ideal, the gothic world has continued a self-conscious critique of the dominant sexual mores of late twentieth-century society. This critique was also present in previous movements such as punk rock. It has been reflected in the names of several gothic bands such as the Andi Sex Gang and Sex Gang Children. Some have noticed that the androgynous ideal (as articulated by Rice and embodied most forcefully in her male characters) was, in many ways, indistinguishable from the value system of the gay community. The homosexual aspect of the gothic world has been presented most clearly in Poppy Z. Brite's writing.

Beyond just a demand for sexual freedom or the acceptance of homosexuality, some gothic music and literature have also argued for the destruction of the taboos that surround sadomasochism (an essentially androgynous activity that explores the pleasure of pain), fetishism, bondage, and other sexual activities still considered perverted even by many who consider themselves otherwise sexually liberated. Among the bands most focused on this message was Sleep Chamber, led by John Zewizz. Zewizz has argued that these various forms of sexual activity—among the most threatening and misunderstood by the general public—are merely a form of foreplay and, alone, are harmless and pleasure-producing. Several periodicals focused on this aspect of the gothic world, most prominently *Blue Blood* and *Euronymous Future Sex*. Possibly the most extreme element of the gothic scene is its celebration of death. The most extreme expression of this is found in the writing and activity of Leilah Wendell at the Westgate Gallery in New Orleans (http://www.westgatenecromantic.com/leilapage.htm).

Through the first decade of the twenty-first century, the goth scene has continued in both England and North America, and to a lesser extent in such places as Australia and Japan. Magazines, goth retail shops, nightclubs, and bands have come and gone, though a few bands such as Alien Sex Fiend, Inkubus Sukkubus, Fields of the Nephilim, and Rosetta Stone have survived in the highly volatile field. The survival of the vampire theme in goth music is no better illustrated than in the CD collection *Vampire Rituals: Gothic Music from the Deepest Depths of Hell* (2006), which included cuts from twelve goth bands/artists.

The goth subculture continues to attract an audience of mostly young adults who see it as both a viable alternative to the mainstream culture of their elders and the pop culture of their contemporaries. Members of the goth movement remain the most marginalized of subcultures, relatively small in numbers but a viable community of like mind and heart. Though Western culture in general has been very tolerant of goths, occasionally they have become victims of hate crimes by those disturbed by the gothic dark demeanor.

Conclusion: The world of vampire enthusiasts fades imperceptibly into that of the gothic subculture. They support each other, although the mainstream of vampire fandom would not share the gloomy atmosphere that pervades the gothic world. Between the two communities, the observer can see the wide variation in the vampire's role in the lives of different people.

Sources:

Baddeley, Gavin. *Goth Chic: A Gothic Guide to Dark Culture*. London: Plexus, 2002. 288 pp.

Bevington, Gregory. "All Aboard the Ghost Train: An Interview with Tony Lestat." *Ghastly* 2 (1992): 24–26.

Brite, Poppy Z. *Lost Souls*. New York: Delacorte Press, 1992. Rept. New York: Dell, 1993. 355 pp.

Duncan, Michelle. "Nosferatu: The Vampire's Cry." *Propaganda* 19 (1992): 8–10.

Goodlad, Lauren M. E., and Michael Bibby, eds. *Goth: Undead Subculture*. Durham, NC: Duke University Press, 2007. 456 pp.

Hart, Paul. "Murphy on Bauhaus: Interview with the Vampire." *Propaganda* 20 (1993): 8–11.

Hodkinson, Paul. *Goth: Identity, Style and Subculture (Dress, Body, Culture)*. Oxford, UK: Berg Publishers, 2002. 288 pp.

Kilpatrick, Nancy. *The Goth Bible: A Compendium for the Darkly Inclined*. New York: St. Martin's Griffin, 2004. 304 pp.

MacAndrew, Elizabeth. *The Gothic Tradition in Fiction*. New York: Columbia University Press, 1979. 289 pp.

Mercer, Mick. *Gothic Rock: Black Book.* London: Omnibus Press, 1988. 95 pp.

———. *Gothic Rock.* Birmingham, UK: Pegesus Publishers, 1991. 178 pp.

Praz, Mario. *The Romantic Agony.* London: Oxford University Press, 1970.

Thompson, G. R. "Introduction: Romanticism and the Gothic Tradition." In *The Gothic Imagination: Essays in Dark Romanticism.* G. R. Thompson, ed. Pullman, WA: Washington State University Press, 1974.

Venter, Julian. *Gothic Charm School: An Essential Guide for Goths and Those Who Love Them.* New York: Harper, 2009. 256 pp.

Gothic Society of Canada *see:* Siren

Gothica *see:* Vampire Fandom: United States

Graham, Heather *see:* Pozzessere, Heather Graham

Greece, Vampires in

Greece is one of the oldest sources for the contemporary vampire legend. Ancient Greek writings record the existence of three vampirelike creatures—the *lamiai*, the *empusai*, and the *mormolykiai*. Also known in Greece was the *strige*, a vampire witch. *Strige* was derived from the Latin *strix*, which originally referred to the screech owl and later to a night-flying demon that attacked and killed infants by sucking their **blood**. The *lamiai* was named after Lamia, who was said to have been a Libyan queen. She was the daughter of Belus and Libya, and, as the story was told, was loved by Zeus, the king of the Greek gods. Hera, Zeus's wife, became jealous and took out her resentment by robbing Lamia of all her children, who had been fathered by Zeus. Unable to strike at Hera, Lamia retired to a cave from where she took out her anger by killing offspring of human mothers, usually by sucking the blood out of the children. Her actions led to her transformation into a hideous beast. (The story of the *mormolykiai* is very similar—they are named after a woman named Mormo, who cannibalized her own children.) Later, Lamia became identified with a class of beings modeled on her, described as coarse-looking women with deformed, serpentlike lower bodies. Their feet were not identical; instead, one was brass and the other was shaped like that of an animal, commonly a goat, donkey, or ox. The *lamiai* were known primarily as demonic beings who sucked the blood from young children; however, they had the power to transform themselves into beautiful young maidens in order to attract and seduce young men. Philostratus included a lengthy account of the *lamiai* in this transformation in the chapter 25 of the fourth book of his *Life of Apollonius.* One of Apollonius's students, Menippus, was attracted to a beautiful rich woman whom he had first encountered as an apparition. In a dream-like state he was told when and where he would find her. The young man fell in love and contemplated marriage. When he related his story to Apollonius, the latter informed his young student that he was being hunted by a serpent. Upon meeting the woman, he told Menippus, "And that you may realize the truth of what I say, this fine bride is one of the vampires (*empusai*), that is to say of those beings whom many regard as *lamiai* and hobgoblins (*mormolykiai*). These beings fall in love, and they are devoted to the delights of Aphrodite, but especially in the flesh of human beings, and they decoy with such delights those whom they mean to devour in their feats." In spite of protestations by

Menippus, Apollonius confronted the *lamiai* with the facts. One by one, the elements of her environment disappeared. She finally admitted her plans and her habit of feeding "upon young and beautiful bodies because their blood is pure and strong." Philostratus called this account the "best-known story of Apollonius." Apuleius, in the very first chapter of the *Golden Ass*, recounted the story of an encounter with a *lamiai* who caught up with her fleeing lover and killed him by first thrusting her sword into his neck, taking all of his blood, and then cutting out his heart.

The people soon lost their fear of the *lamiai* and, even in ancient times, they had simply become a tool for parents to frighten their children. However, when a child dies suddenly from an unknown cause, a saying still popular in Greece suggests that the child has been strangled by the *lamiai*. The *lamiai* were rediscovered in literature in the fifteenth century, when Angelo Poliziano of Florence published a poem, *Lamia* (1492). In 1819, British poet **John Keats** authored a poem with the same name. Since the time of Keats, the *lamiai* have appeared in numerous poems, paintings, sculptures, and musical pieces. For example, August Enna authored an **opera** called *Lamia*, which was first performed in Antwerp, Belgium, in 1899. Poems on the same theme were written by Edward MacDowell (1888), Arthur Symons (1920), Frederick Zeck (1926), Robert Graves (1964), and Peter Davidson (1977). Among recent novels featuring the *lamiai* were the four books of J. N. Williamson—*Death Coach* (1981), *Death School* (1981), *Death Angel* (1982), and *Death Doctor* (1982)—featuring the character of Lamia Zacharias. More recently, Tim Powers's novel, *The Stress of Her Regard* (1989), took place in early nineteenth-century England and featured a *lamia* interacting with Keats, **Lord Byron**, **John Polidori**, Mary Godwin, and Percy Shelley.

The Vrykolakas: Although the *lamiai*, *empusai*, and *mormolykiai*, were known for drinking blood, they were not vampires in the same sense as those of eastern Europe. They were spirit beings rather than revivified corpses (revenants). The ancient Greeks, however, did have a class of revenants, *vrykolakas*, which would develop into true vampires. The term was derived from the older Slavic compound term *vblk'b dlaka*, which originally meant "wolf-pelt wearer". The term developed among the southern Slavs, from whom it probably passed to the Greeks.

The best description of revenants in ancient Greek literature appears in a story told by Phlegon, a freed man who lived in the time of the Roman Emperor Hadrian. It seems that Philinnon, the daughter of Demostratus and Charito, some six months after her death, had been observed entering the room of Machates, a young man staying in the parents' guest-chamber. A servant told the couple about seeing their daughter, but when they peeped into the guest-chamber, they could not ascertain who Machates was entertaining. The next morning Charito told Machates about her daughter's death. He admitted that Philinnon was the name of the girl in his room. He then produced the ring she had given him and a breast band she had left behind. The parents recognized both as possessions of their late daughter. When the girl returned that evening, the parents stepped into the room and to see their daughter. She reproached them for interrupting her visits with Machates and said she had been granted three nights with him.

However, because of their meddling, she would now die again. Sure enough, Philinnon again became a corpse. At this point, Phlegon entered the picture as a witness. As town official, he was called upon to keep order as word of Philinnon's return spread through the community that night. He led an examination of her burial vault, finding the gifts she had taken away from her first visit to Machates—but no body. The townspeople turned to a local wise man who advised that the body be burned and appropriate purification rituals and propitiatory rites to the deities be observed.

This basic story of the returned dead contains some unique aspects of the later Greek *vrykolakas* account. Once discovered, the body was, for example, characteristically burned, rather than decapitated or staked through the heart. The ancient revenant was not yet a vampire, or even an object of much fear. The revenant often returned to complete unfinished business with a spouse, a family member, or someone close to him or her in life. On this early account of a brief visit by a revenant, more elaborate accounts would build. In later centuries, stories would be told of much lengthier visits and of *vrykolakas* who resumed life in the family.

Occasionally, there would be a report of a revenant who went to a location where he was unknown, and where he then remarried and fathered children. One of the oldest reports of the *vrykolakas* was written by the French botanist Pitton de Tournefort. While on the island of Mykonos in the year 1700, he heard of a man who had recently died and yet had been reported walking about town generally making a nuisance of himself. After various noninvasive remedies failed, on the ninth day after his burial the body was disinterred and the heart removed and burned. The troubles did not stop. The townspeople tried sticking swords into the grave since it was a common belief that sharp objects prevented vampires from rising. At one point, an Albanian visitor to the island suggested that the problem was the sticking of "Christian" swords in the top of the grave, since the cross shape of the sword would prevent the devil who was animating the corpse from leaving. He suggested using Turkish swords. It did not help. In the end, on January 1, 1701, the corpse was consumed in a fire.

Greece produced the first modern writer on vampires, Leone Allacci (commonly known as **Leo Allatius**). In 1645, he authored *De Graecorum hodie quorundam opinationibus*, a volume on the beliefs of the Greek people, in which he discussed the *vrykolakas* at great length. Early in the twentieth century, John Cuthbert Lawson spent considerable time investigating the *vrykolakas* in Greek folklore. He noted its development in three stages, beginning with that of pre-Christian times, represented by Phlegon's account. In that account, the return was by divine consent for a specific purpose. Lawson also found, in the ancient Greek texts, an underlying belief in revenant status as a punishment for human failure. In the likes of Euripides and Aeschylus, Lawson noted instances when people were cursed with an incorruptible body, meaning that in death the individual would be denied communion with those on the other side of the grave. Thus, the ancient Greek writers entertained a concept of the "undead." Lawson noted three circumstances that would predispose an individual to become a *vrykolakas*. First, there could be the curse of a parent or someone who an individual had failed, such as that placed by Oedipus against his undutiful son. Oedipus called upon Tartarus (the place of the dead) to refuse to receive the son and to drive him forth from his place of final rest. Second, one might become undead because of a evil or dishonorable act, most notably against one's family, such as the murder of a kinsman or adultery with a sister- or brother-in-law. Third, the dead might join the undead by dying violently or by not being buried. The popular belief in *vrykolakas* was taken into the doctrinal perspective of the Greek Orthodox

Church as it became the dominant force in Greek religious life in the first millennium C.E. The church developed a teaching both about the dead whose bodies remain uncorrupted and about true revenants, those who are resuscitated and return to life. Concerning the former, the church taught that a curse could in fact prevent the natural decay of the body which at the same time became a barrier to the progress of the soul. However, the curses pronounced by parents and others took second place to the "curse" pronounced by the church in its act of excommunication (which effectively denied the victim the saving sacraments of the church). Stories of the accursed dead whose bodies did not decay gradually became the basis of a belief that excommunication produced physical results. Reports of changes in the bodies of excommunicated individuals who later had their excommunication lifted joined the popular hagiography of the church.

When it came to the *vrykolakas*, the church seemed plainly embarrassed but had to deal with what many thought, even in ancient times, to be illusionary. At times the documents spoke of the devil stirring up the imagination of people who believed that a dead person had come to visit. In the face of persisting accounts, however, the church developed an explanation, claiming that the devil inhabited the body of the dead and caused it to move. However, such occurrences tended to be tied to the activities of mediums, in a manner reminiscent of the biblical story of the woman at Endor (1 Samuel 28).

Thus, as the church came to dominate Greek religious life, it proposed that the dead might become *vrykolakas* if they died in an excommunicated state, if they were buried without the proper church rites, or if they died a violent death. To these it added two other causes: stillborn children or those who were born on one of the great church festivals. These causes expanded the earlier Greek notions of those who died under a familial curse or in great sin. The Christianization of the Slavic and Balkan peoples effectively began toward the end of the first Christian millennium and made impressive gains during the tenth through the twelfth centuries. As the Eastern Orthodox Church gained dominance in **Russia, Romania, Hungary**, and among the **southern Slavs**, beliefs from those countries flowed back into Greece and began to alter still further the understanding of the revenant, transforming it into a true vampire. The significant concept was that of the werewolf. It was from the Slavs that the word *vrykolakas*, derived from an old Slavic term for wolfpelt, was adopted as the Greek designation for a resuscitated corpse.

Some Slavic people believed that **werewolves** became vampires after they died. Lawson argued that the Slavonic term came into Greece to describe the werewolf (a term he still found in use in a few places at the beginning of the twentieth century), but gradually came to designate the revenant or vampire. The Greeks also absorbed a Slavic view of the possible vicious nature of vampires. The ancient Greek revenant was essentially benign and returned primarily to complete some unfinished family business. On occasion it committed an act of vengeance, but always one that most would consider logical. It did not enact chaotic violence.

Gradually, the view that vampires were characteristically vicious came to dominate Greek thought about the *vrykolakas*. The vampire's vicious nature was focused in its bloodthirstiness and its wanton nature. The Slavic vampire also characteristically returned to work its violence upon those closest to it. A popular form of cursing one's enemy was to say, "May the earth not receive you" or "May the earth spew you forth."

THE VAMPIRE BOOK: THE ENCYCLOPEDIA OF THE UNDEAD

In effect, one was suggesting that the accursed person return as a vampire and wreak havoc on his or her nearest and dearest.

The *Callicantzaros*: One other type of vampire existed in Greece. The *callicantzaros* was a peculiar kind of vampire that was discussed at some length by Leo Allatius in his 1645 treatise, *De Graecorum hodie quorundam opinationibus*. The *callicantzaros* was related to the extraordinary sanctity ascribed to the Christian holy days at Christmas time. Children born during the period after Christmas ending with the Epiphany or Twelfth Night (the evening when the Three Wise Men are supposed to have arrived at Bethlehem to present their gifts to the baby Jesus) are considered unlucky. They were described as feast-blasted and believed to be destined to become vampires after their death.

The *callicantzaros* was also distinct among vampires in that its activities were limited to Christmas Day and the week or 12 days afterward. During the rest of the year it traveled in some vague netherworld. It was distinguished by its manic behavior and extended **fingernails**. It would seize people with its talons and tear them to pieces. Reports on the *callicantzaros* vary widely as to its appearance, possibly related to the state of maturity of the person deemed to be a future vampire. The *callicantzaros* had an effect upon everyday life, as any person born during the forbidden period was viewed with some degree of hostility. Parents would fear that these children would act out vampiric fantasies as they grew up and would harm their brothers and sisters.

The Modern Literary Vampire: These legends propagated the Greek idea of the vampire, which was still alive at the time British, French, and German writers began, to explore the vampire theme in poems, stories, and stage productions. As vampire literature developed, the early authors established an association between Greece and the vampire. **Goethe**, for example, set his 1797 poem, "The Bride of Corinth," in Greece. Then John Keats drew upon ancient Greek sources for his poem "The Lamia" (1819). And John Polidori placed much of the action for **"The Vampyre"** (1819) in Greece.

In the nineteenth and twentieth centuries, numerous observers discovered that belief in the *vrykolakas* was still alive in rural Greece. In 1835, William Martin Leake's *Travels in North Greece* contained several accounts of the disposal of bodies believed to be *vrykolakas*. Lawson's study, previously noted, recounted many anecdotes he had retrieved in his field work. And as recently as the 1960s, G. F. Abbott, Richard Blum, Eva Blum, and their staff had no problem collecting reports of Greeks who had encountered a *vrykolakas*. Though mentioned by Lawson, Abbott and the Blums both reported multiple stories that suggested people became *vrykolakas* because animals, such as cats, jumped over the bodies between the time of death and burial. Abbott recounted a story of the body of a suspected *vrykolakas* being scalded with boiling **water** rather than burned.

Greece stands as one of the oldest and most important centers for vampire lore. Its idea of the vampire, having passed through a complicated process of development, remains strong today and continues as a resource for understanding the impact of the vampire myth. In addition, Greece also has contributed significantly to the emerging image of the modern fictional vampire.

Sources:

Abbott, G. F. *Macedonian Folklore*. Chicago: Argonaut, Inc. Publishers, 1909. 273 pp.

Apuleius. *The Golden Ass*. Translation by W. Adlington. London: William Heineman, 1935. Numerous editions.

Barber, Paul. *Vampires, Burial, and Death: Folklore and Reality*. New Haven, CT: Yale University Press, 1988. 236 pp.

Blum, Richard, and Eva Blum. *The Dangerous Hour: The Lore of Crisis and Mystery in Rural Greece*. London: Chatto & Windus, 1970. 410 pp.

Calmet, Dom Augustin. *Dissertations sur les Apparitions des Anges des Démons et des Espits, et sur les revenants, et Vampires de Hingrie, de Boheme, de Moravie, et de Silésie*. Paris, 1746. Rept. *The Phantom World*. 2 vols. London: Richard Bentley, 1850.

Fontenrose, Joseph. *Python: A Study of Delphic Myth and Its Origins*. Berkeley, CA: University of California Press, 1959. 616 pp.

Horton, George B. *Home of Nymphs and Vampires: The Isles of Greece*. Indianapolis: The Bobb-Merrill Company, 1929. 219 pp.

Lawson, John Cuthbert. *Modern Greek Folklore and Ancient Greek Religion*. 1910. Rept. New Hyde Park, NY: University Books, 1964. 610 pp.

Leake, William Martin. *Travels in Northern Greece*. 4 vols. 1835. Rept. Amsterdam: Adolf M. Hakkert, 1967.

Philostratus. *The Life of Apollonius of Tyana*. Translation by F. C. Conybeare. London: William Heineman, 1912. Various editions.

Powers, Tim. *The Stress of Her Regard*. New York: Charnel House, 1989. Rept. New York: Ace Books, 1989. 410 pp.

Reid, Jane Davidson. *The Oxford Guide to Classical Mythology in the Arts, 1300–1990s*. New York: Oxford University Press, 1993. 1,310 pp.

Summers, Montague. *The Vampire: His Kith and Kin*. London: Routledge, Kegan Paul, Trench, Trubner & Co., 1928. Rept. New York: University Books, 1960. 356 pp.

❨ Greenberg, Martin H. (1941–) ❩

Political scientist and anthologist Martin H. Greenberg has prepared a number of anthologies of vampire short fiction. Born and raised in Miami, he attended Miami University, and after graduation pursued graduate work at the University of Connecticut, from where he received both his master's and doctorate degrees in Political Science in 1965 and 1969 respectively. He accepted a position at the University of Wisconsin-Green Bay and became chairman of the department in 1971. In 1972 he moved back to his home state to work at Florida International University in Miami.

As a young man, Greenberg became interested in science fiction and as early as 1974 coedited his first anthology (with Patricia Warrick), *Political Science Fiction*. Since that time he has been involved in the editing of more than fifty similar books, convinced that science fiction is the most important literary genre of the modern age. For his anthologies, he deliberately sought works that integrated the insights of social science with fiction.

In the late 1980s, Greenberg began to look at horror fiction in general and vampire fiction in particular, producing such collections as *Back from the Dead*, *Cults of Horror*, and *Devil Worshippers*. The first strictly vampire anthology, *Vamps* (1987), looked at the role of **women** as exemplified in vampire literature. He also became fascinated with the durability of the vampire in the face of the demise of other monster types in the late twentieth century. As the centennial of the publication of **Dracula** approached in 1997, Greenberg worked with Lawrence Schimel in producing a four-volume set of regional American vampire stories. Since then he has edited a number of anthologies including

Single White Vampire Seeks Same (2001, with Brittany A. Koren), *The Repentant* (2003, with Brian Thompson), and *Better Off Undead* (2008, with Daniel M. Hoyt). Most recently he worked with Robert Eighteen-Bisang compiling *The Vampire Stories of Sir Arthur Conan Doyle* (2009).

Sources:

Asimov, Isaac, Martin H. Greenberg, and Charles G. Waugh. *Young Monsters*. New York: Harper & Row, 1985. 213 pp.

Greenberg, Martin H. *Dracula: Prince of Darkness*. New York: DAW Books, 1992. 316 pp.

———. *A Taste for Blood*. New York: Barnes & Noble. 1992. 589 pp.

———, ed. *Celebrity Vampires*. New York: DAW Books, 1995. 318 pp.

———. *Vampire Detectives*. New York, NY : DAW Books, 1995. 320 pp.

Greenberg, Martin H., and Brittany A. Koren, eds. *Single White Vampire Seeks Same*. New York: DAW Books, 2001. 317 pp.

———, and Charles G. Waugh, eds. *Vamps*. New York: DAW Books, 1987. 365 pp.

Schimel, Lawrence, and Martin Greenberg, eds. *Blood Lines: Vampire Stories from New England*. Nashville, TN: Cumberland House, 1997. 224 pp.

———. *Fields of Blood: Vampire Stories from the Heartland*. Nashville, TN: Cumberland House, 1998. 208 pp.

———. *Southern Blood: Vampire Stories from the American South*. Nashville, TN: Cumberland House, 1997. 203 pp.

———. *Streets of Blood: Vampire Stories from New York City*. Nashville, TN: Cumberland House, 1998. 231 pp.

Thomsen, Brian M., and Martin H. Greenberg, eds. *The Repentant*. New York: DAW Books, 2003. 313 pp.

Weinberg, Robert, Stefan R. Dziemianowicz, and Martin Greenberg. *Weird Vampire Tales: 30 Blood-Chilling Stories from the Weird Fiction Pulps*. New York: Gramercy Books, 1992. 442 pp.

———. *100 Vicious Little Vampire Stories*. New York: Barnes & Noble, 1995. 588 pp.

———. *Rivals of Dracula*. New York: Barnes & Noble, 1996. 377 pp.

Yolen, Jane, and Martin H. Greenberg. *Vampires*. New York: HarperTrophy, 1991. 228 pp.

❨ Gypsies, Vampires and the ❩

I n the opening chapters of **Bram Stoker**'s novel *Dracula*, **Jonathan Harker** discovered that he was a prisoner in **Castle Dracula**, but he was given hope by the appearance of a band of Gypsies:

> A band of Szgany have come to the castle, and are encamped in the courtyard. These Szgany are gypsies; I have notes of them in my book. They are peculiar to this part of the world, though allied to the ordinary gypsies all the world over. There are thousands of them in Hungary and Transylvania who are almost outside all law. They attach themselves as a rule to some great noble or boyar, and call themselves by his name. They are fearless and without religion, save superstition, and they talk only their own varieties of the many tongues.

He soon discovered that the Gypsies were allied to the Count. The letters he attempted to have the Gypsies mail for him were returned to **Dracula**. The Gypsies were overseeing the preparation of the boxes of **native soil** that Dracula took to England.

The Gypsies then reappeared at the end of the novel, accompanying the fleeing Dracula on his return to his castle. In the end, they stepped aside and allowed their vampire master to be killed by **Abraham Van Helsing** and his cohorts.

The Emergence of the Gypsies: Since the fourteenth century, the Gypsies have formed a distinct ethnic minority group in the Balkan countries. Within the next two centuries, they were found across all of Europe. While they received their name from an early hypothesis that placed their origin in Egypt, it is now known that they originated in India and were related to similar nomadic tribes that survive to this day in northern India. At some point, around 1000 C.E., some of these tribes wandered westward. A large group settled for a period in Turkey and incorporated many words from that country into their distinctive Romany language. Crossing the Bosporous, the Gypsies found their way to Serbia and traveled as far north as Bohemia through the fourteenth century. They were noted as being in Crete as early as 1322. In the next century, a short time before the emergence of **Vlad Dracul** and **Vlad** the Impaler as rulers in Wallachia, they moved into what are now Romania and Hungary. The Gypsies fanned out across Europe throughout the next century. They were in Russia and Poland, eventually making their way to France and Great Britain.

In Romania and Hungary, Gypsies were often enslaved and persecuted. Their nomadic, nonliterary culture left them vulnerable to accusations of wrongdoing, and they became known not only as traveling entertainers but as thieves, con artists, and stealers of infants; despised minority groups in Europe faced the latter charge quite often. During World War II, the Nazis attempted an extermination of the Gypsies as a "final solution" to what they had defined as "the Gypsy problem."

Gypsies and the Supernatural: Gypsies developed a sophisticated and complicated supernatural religious world view, made more difficult to describe by the diversity of the different bands in various countries and the reluctance of Gypsies to talk to outsiders about their most sacred beliefs. Only the most diligent and persistent effort by a small band of scholars yielded a picture of the Gypsies' world view, which varied from country to country. Gypsy theology affirmed the existence of *o Del* (literally, the God), who appeared one day on Earth (the Earth being the eternally present uncreated world). Beside *o Del*, the principle of Good, was *o Bengh*, or Evil; *o Del* and *o Bengh* competed in the creation of humanity.

O Bengh formed two statuettes out of earth, and *o Del* breathed life into them. Because there was no written text, the account differed from tribe to tribe. The expanded world of the Gypsies was alive with the forces of Good and Evil contending with each other throughout nature. Wise Gypsies learned to read the signs and omens to make the forces work for them and to prevent evil forces from doing them harm.

Gypsies kept a living relationship with the dead (some have called it a cult of the dead), to whom they had a great loyalty. Gypsies regularly left offerings of food, especially milk, so the dead would protect living family members. E. B. Trigg, in *Gypsy Demons & Divinities: The Magical and Supernatural Practices of the Gypsies*, described this practice as a form of worshiping vampire gods, which he compared to the activity of Indian worshipers toward the vampire figures of their mythology.

What happened to the dead? Among the Gypsies of the Balkans, there was a belief that the soul entered a world very much like this one, except there was no death. Bosnian

ᴛʜᴇ Vᴀᴍᴘɪʀᴇ Bᴏᴏᴋ: ᴛʜᴇ Eɴᴄʏᴄʟᴏᴘᴇᴅɪᴀ ᴏꜰ ᴛʜᴇ Uɴᴅᴇᴀᴅ

Gypsies, influenced by Islam, believed in a literal paradise, a land of milk and honey. Others, however, believed that the soul hovered around the grave and resided in the corpse. As such, the soul might grow restless and the corpse might develop a desire to return to this world. To keep the dead content, funeral rites were elaborate and families made annual visits to the grave sites. Within this larger world there was ample room for the living dead, or vampires. This belief was found among Gypsies across Europe, but was especially pronounced, as might be expected, in **Hungary**, **Romania**, and the **Slavic** lands.

Questions have been posed as to the origins of Gypsy vampire beliefs. In **India**, the Gypsies' land of origin, there were a variety of acknowledged vampire creatures. For example, the *bhuta*, found in western India, was believed to be the soul of a man who died in an untimely fashion (such as an accident or **suicide**). The bhuta wandered around at night, and among its attributes was the ability to animate dead bodies, which in turn attacked the living in ghoulish fashion. In northern India, from whence the Gypsies probably started their journey to the West, the *brahmaparusha* was a vampirelike creature who was pictured with a head encircled by intestines and a skull filled with **blood** from which it drank. Gypsies also had a belief in Sara, the Black Virgin, a figure derived from the bloodthirsty goddess **Kali**. Thus, Gypsies may have brought a belief in vampires, or at least a disposition to believe in them, to the Balkan Peninsula. Once in the area, however, they obviously interacted with the native populations and developed the belief of what became a variety of the Slavic vampire.

The Gypsy vampire was called a *mulo* (or *mullo*; plural, *mulé*), literally "one who is dead." Gypsies viewed death essentially as unnatural, hence any death was an affront and viewed as being caused by evil forces attacking the individual. Thus, any individual—but especially anyone who died an untimely death (by suicide or an accident)—might become a vampire and search out the person or persons who caused the death. Given the clannish nature of Gypsy life, these people were most likely those close to the deceased. Prime candidates would be relatives who did not destroy the belongings of the deceased (according to Gypsy custom) but kept them for themselves. The vampire also might have a grudge against anyone who did not properly observe the elaborate burial and funeral rites.

The vampire usually appeared quite normal, but often could be detected by some sign in its physical body. For example, the creature might have a finger missing, or have animal-like appendages. Easier to detect was the vampire that took on a horrific appearance and could only be viewed under special conditions. Vampires might be seen at any time of day or night, though some believed them to be strictly nocturnal creatures. Others thought that vampires could appear precisely at noon when they would cast no shadow. Slavic and **German** Gypsies believed that vampires had no bones in their bodies, a belief based upon the observation that a vampire's bones are often left behind in the grave.

Gypsies believed that vampires engaged in various forms of malicious activity upon their return from the dead. They attacked relatives and attempted to suck their blood. They destroyed property and became a general nuisance by throwing things around and making noises in the night. Male vampires were known to have a strong sexual appetite and returned from the dead to have sexual relations with a wife, girlfriend, or other women. Female vampires were thought to be able to return from the dead and assume a normal life, even to the point of marrying—but would exhaust her husband with her endless sexual demands. Gypsies thought that **animals** and, on occasion, even plants be-

Christian gypsies believed that the crucifix would repel a vampire, much as this one being used on actor Christopher Lee.

came vampires. Dead snakes, horses, chickens, dogs, cats, and sheep were reported as returning as vampires, especially in Bosnia. In Slavic lands it was thought that if an animal such as a cat jumped over a corpse prior to burial, the corpse would become a vampire. Gypsies believed that the animal might become a vampire at the time of its death. Plants such as the pumpkin or watermelon could, if kept in the house too long, begin to stir, make noises, and show a trace of blood; they would then cause trouble, in a limited way, for both people and cattle. In the most extreme cases, family tools might become vampires. The wooden knot for a yoke or the wooden rods for binding sheaves of wheat became vampires if left undone for more than three years.

It was believed that action could be taken to prevent a dead person from returning as a vampire. As a first step, the **victim** of a vampire called upon a **_dhampir_**, the son of a vampire. Gypsies believed that intercourse between a vampire and his widow might produce a male offspring. This child would develop unusual powers for detecting vampires, and a _dhampir_ might actually hire out his services in the case of vampire attacks. There was some belief that the _dhampir_ had a jellylike body (because some thought that vampires had no bones) and hence would have a shorter life span. Many Gypsies thought that iron had special powers to keep away evil. To ward off vampires, at the time of burial a steel needle was driven into the heart of the corpse, and bits of steel were placed in the mouth, over the ears and nose, and between the fingers. The heel of the shoe could be removed and **hawthorn** placed in the sock, or a hawthorn **stake** could be driven through the leg. If a vampire was loose in a village, one might find **protection** in different charms, such as a necklace with an iron nail. A ring of thorn could be set around one's living quarters. Christian Gypsies used a **crucifix**. Slavic Gypsies prized the presence of a set of twins, one male and one female, who were born on a Saturday and who were willing to wear their underclothes inside out. Such people could scare off vampires immediately, it was believed.

The grave site might be the focus of a suspected vampire. Gypsies have been known to drive stakes of ash or hawthorn into a grave, or pour boiling **water** over it. In more problematic cases, **coffins** were opened and the corpse examined to see if it had shifted in the coffin or had not properly decomposed. In the case of a body thought to be a vampire, Gypsies followed the practices of their neighbors: having the prayers for the dead recited; staking it in either the stomach, heart, or head; or resort to **decapitation** and/or, in extreme cases, cremation.

The need to destroy the vampire was slight among some Gypsies who believed its life span was only forty days. However, some granted it a longer life and sought specific means to kill it. An iron needle in the stomach often would be enough. In Eastern Or-

thodox countries, such as Romania, holy water would be thrown on the vampire. If these less intrusive means did not work, Gypsies might resort to more conventional weapons. If captured, a vampire might be nailed to a piece of wood. If one was available, a *dhampir* might be called upon to carry out the destruction. Black dogs and wolves were known to attack vampires, and some Romanian Gypsies believed that white wolves stayed around the grave sites to attack vampires; otherwise the world would be overrun with the dead.

Numerous reports on the *mulo* have been collected and show significant variance among geographically separated Gypsy groups. There has been some speculation that their vampire beliefs originated in India, from whence the Gypsies themselves seemed to have derived. India had a rich vampiric lore.

The legends have become differentiated over the centuries as Gypsies dispersed around Europe and North America and interacted with various local cultures.

Conclusion: The belief in vampires has survived among Gypsies, but, like all supernatural beliefs, it has shown signs of disappearing. In particular, the strength of this belief has been affected by secular schooling, modern burial practices, and governments hostile to actions taken in response to vampires, such as the mutilation of bodies.

Sources:

Clebert, Jean-Paul. *The Gypsies*. Harmondsworth, Middlesex, U.K.: Penguin Books, 1963. 282 pp.

Leland, G. G. *Gypsy Sorcery*. New York Tower Books, n.d. 267 pp.

Trigg, E. B. *Gypsy Demons & Divinities: The Magical and Supernatural Practices of the Gypsies*. London: Sheldon Press, 1973. 238 pp.

Vukanovic, T. P. "The Vampire." In *Vampires of the Slavs*. Jan L. Perkowski, ed. Cambridge, MA: Slavica Publishers, 1976, 201–234.

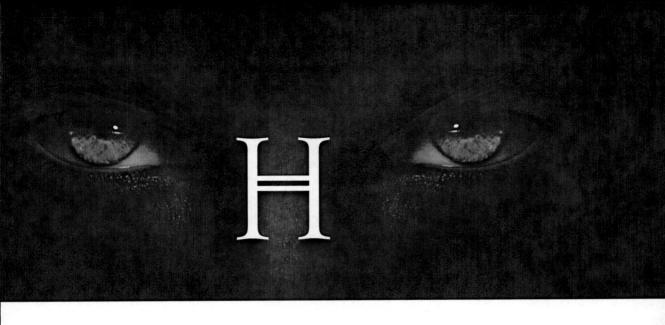

Haarmann, Fritz (1879–1925)

Fritz Haarmann, the so-called Vampire of Hanover, (**Germany**), is one of several prominent persons often cited as an actual modern vampire. Born on October 24, 1879 in Hanover, Haarmann grew up in fear of his father. He joined the army as a young man and after a period of service returned to Hanover. However, he soon was arrested for child molestation. Sentenced to a mental institution, he escaped and went to Switzerland. Thus began a period of his life when he lived on the streets, surviving off of petty **crime** interspersed with arrests and brief stays in jail. After World War I, he seemed to have switched sides and joined the police department as an informer and spy. Haarmann was homosexual. He picked up young men off the street and invited them to his home. There he engaged in sex and on occasion (five or more times a year) killed them. Arrested in 1919, he spent nine months in jail for engaging in illegal sex. After his release, he met Hans Grans, who became his lover and partner in crime. During the early 1920s, Haarmann's crimes became even more grisly. He began to bite the throats of his **victims** and drink their **blood**.

In 1924 the discovery of the remains of several of Haarmann's victims and the persistent pleas of the parents of several young men who had disappeared initiated an investigation that eventually led police to Haarmann. Arrested that year on sex charges, Haarmann sat in jail as his living quarters were searched. The corpses of more than 20 bodies were found. Faced with the most incriminating evidence—clothing identified as belonging to one of his victims—Haarmann finally confessed and implicated Grans. The subsequent trial proved a gruesome affair. Haarmann was formally charged with 24 murders, but was believed to have killed more than 50 people. He testified and related accounts of many of his activities, including cannibalism. During part of this time, he worked as a butcher and claimed to have sold the meat of several of his victims to his customers. Convicted, he was sentenced to death and executed by **de-**

capitation on April 15, 1925. Grans was imprisoned for life. His brain was sent to Göttingen University for study.

Haarmann was not a vampire in the traditional folkloric sense. He was a disturbed individual with a blood fetish that found expression during the rape and murder of his victims. As such, his crimes fit more into the history of serial murder than with the folkloric or literary vampire. The movie *Tenderness of the Wolves* (1974) was inspired by the Haarmann case. Since that time, Haarmann has been the subject of several television documentaries, usually as a representative serial killer.

Sources:

Glut, Donald F. *True Vampires of History.* New York: H C Publishers, 1971. 191 pp.

Lessing, Theodore. *Haarmann̈—Die Geschichte eines Werwolfs,* 1925. English translation by Mo Croasdale: "The Story of a Werewolf." In *Monsters of Weimar.* London: Nemesis Books, 1993: pp. 11–156.

Volta, Ornella. *The Vampire.* New York: Award Books, 1962. 153 pp.

❨ Haigh, John George (1910–1949) ❩

John George Haigh, the so-called Vampire of **London** and one of several persons frequently cited as an actual modern vampire, was born into a strict Plymouth Brethren family in England. The Plymouth Brethren were a fundamentalist Protestant group, and Haigh's parents passed on to him a strong image of the suffering of Christ on the cross and his bleeding—the saving power of his **blood** being an important part of that image. It was also reported that his mother had a strong belief in prophetic dreams.

As a young man, Haigh left the Plymouth Brethren and joined the Church of England, but his heritage stayed with him. He had a revelation that he should begin to drink his own urine, a practice based upon his unique interpretation of two biblical passages, Proverbs 5:15 and John 7:38. He also had a recurring dream of a forest of crosses that transformed into trees dripping with blood. At one tree, a man collected a bowl of blood. Haigh would feel drained of energy and the man would offer him the bowl of blood to drink. But before he could drink, Haigh would awaken. He concluded from this dream that he needed to drink blood to restore his vitality. Haigh established a laboratory in his own home, where he lured his designated **victims**. There he would kill them, drain their blood, and dispose of their bodies in a vat of sulfuric acid. He was finally arrested when he tried to pawn the fur coat of one elderly female victim. Haigh was confident that he could not be tried and convicted without a corpse to confirm death. However, upon investigating his laboratory, the police found several body parts the acid failed to dissolve, including a victim's teeth, which were identified by their unusual dental work. At his trial, Haigh confessed to the nine murders, claiming that they had been religious acts and that the consumption of blood was necessary to his attaining eternal life. He was convicted and hanged on August 10, 1949. Haigh left his clothing to the London Wax Museum and, for some years, a wax model of Haigh stood in Madame Tussaud's House of Horrors.

As with most of the modern cases of vampirism, Haigh was not a vampire in either the traditional folkloric sense or the modern literary variety. He was a disturbed man whose problems were expressed in a religious format, which included an obsession with blood. His history of **crime** fits more properly with accounts of serial killers than that of vampires.

Sources:

Dunboyne, Lord. *The Trial of John George Haigh.* Notable Trial Series 78. London: William Hodge, 1953.

Glut, Donald F. *True Vampires of History.* New York: H C Publishers, 1971. 191 pp.

La Bern, A. *Haigh: the Mind of a Murderer.* London: W. H. Allen, 1974.

Volta, Ornella. *The Vampire.* New York: Award Books, 1962. 153 pp.

Haining, Peter Alexander (1940–)

Peter Alexander Haining, anthologist of vampire literature, was born April 2, 1940, at Enfield, England, and began his adult life as a journalist in Essex. He was assigned to investigate a graveyard desecration, which the local rector claimed had been done by Satanists. His work on the case generated within him an interest in the occult and black magic and led him to co-author *Devil Worship in Britain* with colleague A. V. Sellwood. This 1964 book became the first in a prolific line of books that Haining wrote or, in most cases, edited. Among his early anthologies was *The Craft of Terror*, a 1966 collection of extracts from **gothic** horror novels that set the stage for *The Midnight People* (1968; issued in the United States as *Vampires at Midnight*), a collection of vampire stories. Haining suggested that vampires were unique among evil monsters in that they were based on fact (i.e., the folklore and legends from countries around the world). Thus, he combined the fictional selections with several accounts of real vampires.

Throughout the 1970s and 1980s, Haining edited a new anthology of occult and/or horror material once or twice a year, occasionally moving into the mystery realm. He returned to vampires in 1976 with *The Dracula Scrapbook*, an illustrated survey of **Dracula** in fact and fiction. In 1985 he compiled *Vampire: Chilling Tales of the Undead*, an anthology of vampire fiction. Among his most recent anthologies is one devoted to a celebration of **vampire hunters**.

In 1987, he compiled a second volume on Dracula, *The Dracula Centenary Book*. It was reissued in 1992 as *The Dracula Scrapbook*, though it is completely different from the 1976 volume with the same title. Behind *The Dracula Centenary Book* was Haining's assumption that the unnamed year in which **Bram Stoker** set the novel ***Dracula* (1897)** was 1887. That year is at best questionable, as most Dracula scholars now agree that the year was 1893. Whatever the support for 1887 as the year of Dracula's arrival in England, the assumption provided an excuse to publish one of the better Dracula anthologies.

In the new century, Haining compiled a very useful reference volume, *A Dictionary of Vampires* (2001), and assembled a collection of Bram Stoker's short stories characterized by their not being in a previous anthology and their relating in some way to the novel *Dracula*.

Sources:

Ashley, Mike. *Who's Who in Horror and Fantasy Fiction.* London: Elm Tree Books, 1977.

Haining, Peter, ed. *The Midnight People*. London: Leslie Frewin Publishers, 1968. Rept. London: Everest Books, 1975. 255 pp. Reprint as: *Vampires at Midnight*. New York: Grosset & Dunlap, 1970. 255 pp.

———. *The Dracula Scrapbook*. New York: Bramwell House, 1976. 176 pp.

———. *Vampire: Chilling Tales of the Undead*. London: W. H. Allen, 1985. 240 pp.

———. *The Dracula Centenary Book*. London: Souvenir Press, 1987. Revised ed. as: *The Dracula Scrapbook*. London: Chancellor Press, 1992. 160 pp.

———. *The Vampire Omnibus*. London: Orion, 1995. 496 pp.

———. *The Vampire Hunters' Casebook*. London: Warner Books, 1996. 363 pp.

———, and Peter Tremayne. *The Un-Dead: The Legend of Bram Stoker and Dracula*. London: Constable, 1997. 199 pp.

———, ed. *A Dictionary of Vampires*. London: Robert Hale, 2001. 256 pp.

Stoker, Bram. *Shades of Dracula*. Edited by Peter Haining. Berkeley, CA: Apocryphile Press, 2006. 208 pp.

Hamilton, Laurell K. (1963–)

Laurell K. Hamilton is the author of an ongoing series of novels built around an alternative history in which the United States, and especially the futuristic St. Louis, Missouri, have altered society so that vampires and **werewolves** have been accepted into the social order. Through the 1990s, the series steadily gained an ever-increasing readership and Hamilton's books rose to the top of the vampire genre market.

Hamilton was born Laurell Kaye Klein on February 19, 1963, in rural Arkansas. Raised in a Christian Holiness environment, she began writing horror fiction as a youth. She then attended Marion College (now Indiana Wesleyan University) where she enrolled in a creative writing program. She left it as her instructor was offended by her writing about both vampires and other horrors. With a prediction that her writing would never amount to anything, she finished her college education in the biology department. After college, with her husband Gary Hamilton, she moved to suburban St. Louis. In 1992, she saw her first novel, *Nightseer*, published. The first of the vampire/horror novels appeared the following year.

The key person in the new social order of alternate St. Louis in Hamilton's novels is Anita Blake, described as an animator and **vampire hunter**. Blake is a good example of what in comic book publishing is now termed a "Bad Girl," a woman who is able to keep up with the best of the superheroes, but is at the same time completely feminine and attractive to her male contemporaries. In Blake's case, both a vampire and a werewolf are after her, and not to satiate their thirst and hunger.

In the novels, Blake earns her living by reanimating the dead and facilitating the gaining of important information from them. She also operates as a vampire hunter when the situation calls for it. At all times she is an intimate of the vampires and werewolves who live in St. Louis. Hamilton had noticed that in mystery novels female detectives did not get to do any of the fighting that their male counterparts enjoyed, and so she made sure that Anita did not lack violent encounters.

Hamilton's first novel, *Nightseer* (1992), did not bring much notice, but the first of her Anita Blake novels, *Guilty Pleasures* (1993), took off and led to six sequels over the next five years. By the end of decade she had become one of the most noted writers in the vampire genre. The early novels were brought out in omnibus volumes by the Science

Fiction Fan Club. A Laurell K. Hamilton Fan Club flourished. Much to the delight of fans, Hamilton continued to produce new Anita Black adventures through the first decade of the new century, with seventeen on the shelves by 2009, and others in the pipeline.

Meanwhile in 2006, a graphic arts adaptation of the initial Anita Blake novel, *Guilty Pleasures* was brought out as a cooperative venture by Dabel Brothers Productions and Marvel Comics. The monthly comic was drawn by Brett Booth from a script produced by Stacie M. Ritchie from Hamilton's text. The comic books were regularly gathered into graphic novels. After a brief hiatus following issue No. 6 in 2007, the monthly issues resumed from Marvel with Ron Lim and Jess Ruffner as artist and writer. Along with *Guilty Pleasures*, Marvel also released a unique Anita Blake story, *First Death*, a prequel to *Guilty Pleasures*, which told the back story for Blake. It was written by Jonathon Green, and drawn by Wellington Alves. In 2009, Marvel released a new Anita Blake series, *The Laughing Corpse*.

As of 2009, Hamilton remains at the top of the list of those writer best known for their vampire related novels, though like most of them she writes other novels as well. She tries to maintain contact with a large readership through her Webpage at http://www.laurellkhamilton.org/. She is assisted in this process by the Laurell K. Hamilton Fan Club. It publishes the quarterly *News To Die For Newsletter*, and may be contacted at http://www.laurellkhamilton.org/fanclub.htm.

Sources:

Hamilton, Laurell K. *Guilty Pleasures*. Anita Blake, Vampire Hunter, Book 1. New York: Ace Books, 1993. 265 pp.

————. *The Laughing Corpse*. Anita Blake, Vampire Hunter, Book 2. New York: Ace Books, 1994. 293 pp.

————. *Circus of the Damned*. Anita Blake, Vampire Hunter, Book 3. New York: Ace Books, 1995. 329 pp.

————. *Bloody Bones*. Anita Blake, Vampire Hunter, Book 5. New York: Ace Books, 1996. 370 pp.

————. *The Lunatic Cafe*. Anita Blake, Vampire Hunter, Book 4. New York: Ace Books, 1996. 369 pp.

————. *The Killing Dance*. Anita Blake, Vampire Hunter, Book 6. New York: Ace Books, 1997. 287 pp.

————. *Blue Moon*. Anita Blake, Vampire Hunter, Book 8. New York: Ace Books, 1998. 418 pp.

————. *Burnt Offerings*. Anita Blake, Vampire Hunter, Book 7. New York: Ace Books, 1998. 392 pp.

————. *Obsidian Butterfly*. Anita Blake, Vampire Hunter, Book 9. New York: Ace Books, 2000. 386 pp.

————. *Narcissus in Chains*. Anita Blake, Vampire Hunter, Book 10. New York: Berkley Books, 2001. 424 pp.

————. *Cerulean Seas*. Anita Blake, Vampire Hunter, Book 11. New York: Berkley Pub Group, 2003. 416 pp.

————. *Incubus Dreams*. Anita Blake, Vampire Hunter, Book 12. New York: Berkley Pub Group, 2004. 658 pp.

————. *Danse Macabre*. Anita Blake, Vampire Hunter, Book 14. New York: Berkley, 2006. 483 pp.

————. *Micah*. Anita Blake, Vampire Hunter, Book 13. New York: Jove, 2006. 280 pp.

————. *The Harlequin*. Anita Blake, Vampire Hunter, Book 15. New York: Penguin Group, 2007. 422 pp.

————. *Blood Noir*. Anita Blake, Vampire Hunter, Book 16. New York: Berkley Books, 2008.

————. *Skin Trade*. Anita Blake, Vampire Hunter, Book 17. New York: Berkley Hardcover, 2009. 496 pp.

❨ Hammer Films ❩

Hammer Films, the film studio whose horror movies in the 1960s brought a new dimension to the vampire myth, was founded in 1948 by Will Hammer and Sir John Carreras. Largely based upon public response to its horror movies, Hammer became the most successful British film company in the generation after World War II. Hammer burst upon the scene after the film industry had neglected the horror genre for several decades—partly out of censorship considerations and partly from its own conservative nature. Hammer's openness to the horror film was due in large part to Carreras's understanding of the company's credo: Motion pictures should first and foremost simply entertain and tell a good story. Beginning as a small, relatively poor company with limited capital, Hammer Films turned out low-budget "B" movies following patterns set in Hollywood. A **television** series, however, became the catalyst for major changes for the company.

In the 1950s, British television produced the successful **science fiction** series, *The Quatermass Experiment*, built around the character of Bernard Quatermass. He was a scientist who sent a rocket into space only to have it return with a new form of alien life that took over the body of the surviving astronaut. Hammer brought Quatermass to the screen in 1955 in *The Quatermass Xperiment*. This was quickly followed by *X the Unknown* (1956) and *Quatermass II* (1957). The success of these science fiction "monster" movies suggested that new films with classical horror themes might be equally successful. **Universal Pictures,** which owned the motion picture rights to both *Frankenstein* and *Dracula* at that time, was essentially separating itself from producing horror movies. The owners worked out a deal by which the company sold the rights to *Dracula* and *Frankenstein* to Hammer.

In creating the new horror features, Hammer drew upon a French and British stage tradition originally developed at the Theatre du Grand Guignol in Paris. Grand Guignol emphasized the shock value of presenting gruesome and terrifying scenes to the audience realistically. Vampires were a standard fare of these stage productions. Hammer horrors were in full color. **Blood** flowed freely and monstrous acts were fully portrayed on screen—not merely implied for the audience to imagine. Hammer then assembled one of the more famous teams ever to work on what would become a series of horror pictures: director **Terence Fisher**, screenwriter **Jimmy Sangster**, and actors **Christopher Lee** and **Peter Cushing**. Their first picture was *The Curse of Frankenstein*, a new version in Technicolor of Mary Shelley's original *Frankenstein*. It differed markedly from the older Universal version in its graphic depiction of **Frankenstein's monster's** violence, now in full color.

The same team plunged immediately into a second classic horror volume, *Dracula*, better known under its American title, ***The Horror of Dracula*** (1958). Sangster and Fisher decided not to use the play upon which Universal's *Dracula* (1931) was based; they also deviated rather freely from **Bram Stoker**'s story, which was transformed into the final battle of a long-standing war between **Abraham Van Helsing** (goodness) and **Dracula** (evil). The first **victim** of this war, at least in the segment seen by the audience, was **Jonathan Harker**, who arrived at **Castle Dracula** as a secret Van Helsing operative. After he was turned into a vampire, Van Helsing was forced to kill him. The next victim was **Lucy Westenra** (now called Lucy Holmwood). Before Van Helsing finally defeated Dracula, the war almost claimed the life of **Mina Murray** (now known as Mina Holmwood).

The Horror of Dracula was even more influenced by Grand Guignol than was *The Curse of Frankenstein*. Its graphic presentation of gore began with memorable opening frames of dripping red blood and was highlighted by Christopher Lee's showing his **fangs** to the audience just before bending over a yielding Mina whom he held tightly in his arms. Vampiric **sexuality** also was more overt, with the biting as a metaphor for the sex act. Dracula unleashed all of the chaotic life forces, most powerfully symbolized by sex, that society tried to suppress and science attempted to understand and control.

Like *The Curse of Frankenstein*, *The Horror of Dracula* was an immense success. It made Christopher Lee an international star in ways his portrayal of Frankenstein's monster had not. And as would be true of other Draculas, Lee's fans tended to be women, a high percentage of them teenagers. Hammer moved quickly to capitalize on both of its successes, but in the long run *Dracula* proved to be the more lucrative theme. As Hammer moved ahead with its next vampire (and other horror) movies, it began to encounter problems from censors. It had purchased the rights to *I Am Legend*, a classic vampire book, and hired its author, **Richard Matheson,** to work on the screenplay. However, the censor's office let it be known that the movie would be banned in England, and Hammer stopped filming. The subsequent banning of **Mario Bava**'s Italian-made *Black Sunday* served to inform Hammer of strict limits to what could, for the moment, be put on the screen; thus, for a brief period the company postponed new considerations of the vampire motif. In its second Dracula movie, *The Brides of Dracula* (1960), Dracula did not actually appear, though David Peel was present as the Dracula-like Baron Meinster. Meinster succeeded where Dracula failed in his biting of Van Helsing (Cushing); but Van Helsing cauterized the wound, thus preventing the vampire's affliction from infecting him. Before the successful team from *The Horror of Dracula* was reassembled, however, Hammer produced the first of its movies with a female vampire, the *Kiss of the Vampire* (1962), starring Clifford Evans, Edward de Souza, Isobel Black, and Noel Williams as the vampire.

Lee made his return as Dracula in *Dracula, Prince of Darkness* (1965). To establish continuity, director Terence Fisher began the new film with footage from the end of *The Horror of Dracula*. The film also developed one of a series of creative ways to resurrect the dead count. In this case, Dracula's servant killed a man whose blood was allowed to drip on Dracula's ashes. This sequel was memorable both for Lee's impressive performance (though he had few lines) and for the graphic staking of Barbara Shelley by a group of monks, made possible by some easing of the standards of censorship through the decade.

In *Dracula Has Risen from the Grave* (1968), Dracula was resurrected by a priest who allowed his blood to drip on the count's frozen body. (Dracula had died by drowning in an icy pond in *Dracula Prince of Darkness*.) Meanwhile, Fisher had moved on to other projects and did not direct this film, which marked the beginning of the downward trend that would characterize future vampire movies that Hammer assigned to less-experienced directors. The most memorable scene was Dracula pulling the **stake** from his own body (a scene Christopher Lee protested at the time). There also was an increasingly explicit depiction of sexual themes. In *Dracula Prince of Darkness*, Dracula embraced the passive Mina as he bit her. But in *Dracula Has Risen from the Grave*, the vampire's female

A scene from Hammer Films' *Taste the Blood of Dracula.*

victims/lovers began to react to the count, signaling their participation in the event and experiencing a sexual thrill from it. The sexual give-and-take of the vampire's bite became even more graphic in *Taste the Blood of Dracula* (1970), which brought the count back to Victorian England. In the film, a member of the British royalty witnessed Count Dracula's demise, as depicted in *Dracula Has Risen from the Grave*, and collected some of his blood and several of his personal possessions. In a magic ceremony, he attempted to revive Dracula by drinking his blood. Dracula arose, but at the cost of his benefactor's life. Meanwhile, several men who had been privy to the process of resurrecting Dracula stole his ring and cloak. Dracula proceeded to attack the men by way of their two female children. The interaction of Dracula and his female victims suggested a conscious use of vampirism as a symbol responding to new attitudes about sexuality that developed in the late 1960s.

Immediately after *Taste the Blood of Dracula*, Lee began filming *Scars of Dracula* (1971) under the direction of **Roy Ward Baker**. The story was set in **Castle Dracula**, where a young man, his girlfriend, and several others were exploring. Dracula began to kill them one by one until only the young man stood as a barrier to the woman, the real object of the vampire's quest. The story of Dracula and the woman, however, became a subplot set in the parentheses of Dracula's encounter with a more transcendental force—nature. At the beginning of the movie Dracula was awakened by a bolt of lightning that struck his **coffin**. In the end he was killed by a similar bolt that struck a metal spike he had intended to use on the remaining live male.

Hammer's most intense attention to vampirism came during the years 1970 to 1972. The studio produced six films, which necessitated going beyond mere variations on the Dracula story. The first choice for a new thrust was **Sheridan Le Fanu**'s story, "Carmilla." *Vampire Lovers* (1970), possibly the most faithful adaptation of "Carmilla," opened with the awakening of the vampire **Carmilla** Karnstein (who assumed an anagram of her name, Mircalla). She had returned to Karnstein Castle in the present, where she was introduced to the social world. She first attracted and then vampirized Laura, the subject of the original story, and then Emma, an acquaintance. Before she was able to kill Emma, however, her work was discovered and a group of male **vampire hunters** tracked her down in the chapel and killed her. *Vampire Lovers* reached a new level of sexual explicitness and visual gore. The amply endowed **Ingrid Pitt** played Mircalla, who seduced Laura (Pippa Steele) and Emma (Madeleine Smith) in scenes with **lesbian** overtones. Following the trend set in the *Dracula* movies, the film continued the depiction of blood and violence, especially in the opening and closing scenes during which the vampire was killed.

Carmilla inspired a second film, *Lust for a Vampire* (1971), a film that gave Jimmy Sangster the opportunity to move from his screenwriting role to directing. The movie, with its standard emphasis on graphic violence, opened with one of the more memorable horror scenes. Mircalla/Carmilla (now played by Yutte Stengaard), Count Karnstein (Mike Raven), and his wife were all awakened by the blood of a sacrificial victim killed over their graves. The revived Mircalla then turned to several males as her victims (rather than her usual female ones); but as the deaths mounted, the villagers discovered her vampirism and killed her and the Karnstein family in a **fire**. Ingrid Pitt returned to the screen for her second vampire role in 1971 as **Elizabeth Bathory** in *Countess Dracula*. The film centered on Bathory's last years, when she attempted to vampirize teenagers (both male and female) of their youth so that her own beauty and youthful appearance would remain intact. The voluptuous Pitt, transforming back and forth from the aging countess to the rejuvenated vampire, made the film work.

The trend toward violence seemed to peak in the second of the 1971 vampire releases, *Vampire Circus*. Set in Serbia in 1810, Count Mitterhouse (Robert Tayman), a vampire, was revived and set out to seek revenge on the town he held responsible for his death a century before. The instruments of his revenge were circus performers who had set up their tents to entertain the townspeople. However, the performers soon joined the count in murdering the town's leading citizens. The bloody murders set the stage for a closing battle scene with aroused villagers attacking the circus. The film ended with Mitterhouse being staked and decapitated.

On the heels of its 1971 successes, Hammer exploited the Dracula theme again with *Dracula A.D. 1972*, which attempted to bring Dracula into the contemporary world. The film did not deal with the role that Dracula might assume in the complex modern world; rather, it moved a Victorian plot into a contemporary setting. The story concerned Dracula's emergence among a group of young people in the early 1970s. Constantly encountering hostile, unfamiliar structures that left him ineffective in the present-day world, Dracula vampirized several of the youngsters and used them as his instruments. **Peter Cushing** returned in his Van Helsing role as the vampire hunter—a dedicated descendent of the original—to track Dracula to his death.

The second 1972 offering to vampire fans was *Captain Kronos, Vampire Hunter*, the story of a young hero who traveled the country searching out and disposing of vampires. Based in part on American cowboy heroes, Kronos arrived complete with an assistant—for some comic relief. The film's failure at the box office not only canceled Hammer's plans for a new series based on Kronos, but in fact, highlighted a significant aspect of the vampire myth. The myth was about vampires and all that they symbolize, not necessarily the destruction of evil.

The 1972 *Twins of Evil* returned to the story of Carmilla for inspiration. Hammer selected twins Mary and Madeline Collinson to play Mary and Freida Gelhorn. The two were unleashed by Count Karnstein on the local village to avenge the death of the Karnstein family. The spread of the vampire epidemic attracted the Van Helsing-like Gustav Weil (played by Peter Cushing) to mount a crusade to destroy all the vampires. As the plot unfolded, the movie pictured two opposing and ambiguous forces: the vampire and the overly zealous, puritanical vampire hunter—who was himself tainted with evil. The conflict resulted in the death of Count Karnstein and the vampires, along with Weil

Hammer Films tried to bring the Dracula myth into the modern age with *Dracula A.D. 1972*, which starred Christopher Lee as Dracula. Stephanie Beacham is in the background.

and some of his cohorts. The twins were relatively innocent bystanders, and one escaped (the other was killed).

Lee's final appearance in the Hammer *Dracula* movies occurred in *The Satanic Rites of Dracula* (1973), also known as *Count Dracula and His Vampire Bride*. Again the scene was contemporary **London**, where an aging Van Helsing was consulted by Scotland Yard on a black magic group that had come to their attention. His investigation led him, however, to Dracula, who had emerged as a real estate dealer and was surrounded by a group of corrupt (but not vampirized) businessmen. Because of his partners, Drac-

ula escaped Van Helsing's first attack, which utilized—for some inexplicable reason—a silver **bullet** (a werewolf remedy). With the aid of his granddaughter, Van Helsing continued the attack. This movie revived an old folk remedy for conquering vampires, as Dracula was led into a **hawthorn** bush. The vampire world created by Hammer was finally exhausted with a cooperative project between the studio and Shaw Brothers, a massive movie production company in Hong Kong.

Directed by Roy Ward Baker, *The Legend of the Seven Golden Vampires* (1974) (also known as *The Seven Brothers Meet Dracula*) had Abraham Van Helsing (again portrayed by Peter Cushing) traveling to **China** to find the elusive Dracula. Early in the film, Van Helsing met Hsu Tien-an, the local vampire hunter. In China, both vampire and vampire hunters naturally knew martial arts, and the film emerged as a feeble attempt to merge the two genres. Needless to say, the film was a commercial failure.

By 1974, at the time it authorized the filming of *The Legend of the Seven Golden Vampires*, Hammer Films was in financial trouble. It had hoped that its exploitation of the martial arts theme, added to its tried-and-true vampire theme, would be a great success. Instead, the combination had quite the opposite effect. Warner Bros., which had distributed many of Hammer's films in **America**, refused to release this one; and in the end the Chinese vampires merely speeded Hammer's swift move into bankruptcy in 1975. An era of vampire movies was over. The studio had explored the vampire theme for a generation. Its movies inspired a worldwide boom in vampire (and horror) movies in the 1960s as many directors attempted to copy the Hammer successes. But hampered by low budgets and even lower production values, they rarely reached Hammer's proficiency.

Hammer was then moved into receivership. In 1975 it was purchased by Ray Skeggs, who set about restructuring the business. The main product of this period was two 1980s television series. The Hammer *House of Horror* aired thirteen episodes in 1980 and its follow-up, the Hammer **House of Mystery and Suspense** aired thirteen episodes from 1984–86. After the series, the company seemed moribund. Occasionally announcements of projects that never appeared or rumors of productions circulated, but nothing made it to the screen.

Then in 2007, Dutch producer John De Mol purchased the Hammer Films rights which brought him ownership of some 300 Hammer films. De Mol's company set plans to restart the studio and produce two to three movies (horror or thrillers) each year. The first new film under the hammer banner was made in 2008. The vampire film *Beyond the Rave*, premiered free online exclusively on MySpace in April 2008. It came out as a twenty-part serial, with each episode lasting four minutes. Since its original run, the episodes have been available on YouTube. The story concerned a soldier on his last night before shipping out to war. Ed goes searching for his former girlfriend Jen at a rave party led by the mysterious Melech, who turns out to be the leader of a growing vampire community. To get through the evening he must deal both with some mean drug dealers and seductive vampires neither of who have his well being in mind.

As this encyclopedia goes to press, it is yet to be seen if Hammer will return as a force in the horror or vampire entertainment realm. Meanwhile, since the mid 1970s, the memory of Hammer has been kept alive by it fans.

Hammer Fandom: The devoted fans of Hammer Films have organized and created a world of fanzines and collectibles, which in the 1990s was given focus by the

Hammer Horror Collector's Network based in Campbell, California, and supported by the continuing Hammer Films. Since the mid-1970s, a series of Hammer-related periodicals have appeared including *The House of Hammer, Hammer Horror,* (which ran for seven issues in 1995), *Little Shoppe of Horrors, The House that Hammer Built, Dark Terrors,* and *Behind the Screams.* These have been superseded by Hammer's significant presence on the **Internet**, sites easily located with any search engine.

The most valued items by collectors are the various movie posters and theater cards, including the ones produced for the non-English releases, and the various novelizations of the later movies that appeared in the 1970s. Among the vampire titles with accompanying novels are *Vampire Lovers, Countess Dracula, Scars of Dracula, Lust for a Vampire,* and *Kronos* (a.k.a. *Captain Kronos, Vampire Hunter*). However, over the years a wide variety of products have been produced just for the continuing legion of fans. Topping the list are **trading cards**, a set of which appeared in 1975 and 1976 from Topps called Shock Theater. These were not widely distributed and are among the most valued items for collectors. There have been two sets—Hammer Horror I and Hammer Horror II—that included posters art and stills from different movies, more than half from the vampire titles. There is also a set of playing cards with stills from the Hammer movies. Since 1997 when a 40th Anniversary set of trading cards appeared, at least three additional sets have manifested the continued fan interest.

There are a variety of histories of Hammer, and several stars, most notably Christopher Lee and Peter Cushing, produced autobiographies. Ingrid Pitt, who has her own fan club (Pitt of Horror, P. O. Box 403, Richmond, Surrey, UK TW10 6FW) completed a light-hearted but well-written and researched survey of vampirism. And musical fans can track down *Dracula: Classical Scores from Hammer Horror,* released by Silva on vinyl in 1989 and on CD in 1993.

Sources:

Eyles, Allen, Robert Adkinson, and Nicolas Fry, eds. *The House of Horror: The Story of Hammer Films.* London: Lorrimer Publishing Ltd., 1973. 127 pp.

Flynn, John L. *Cinematic Vampires.* Jefferson, NC: McFarland and Company, 1992. 320 pp.

Hutchings, Peter. *Hammer and Beyond: The British Horror Film.* Manchester: Manchester University Press, 1993. 193 pp.

Jewel, John. *Lips of Blood: An Illustrated Guide to Hammer's Dracula Movies Starring Christopher Lee.* London: Glitter Books, 2002. 136 pp.

Marrero, Robert. *Horrors of Hammer.* Florida: RGM Publications, 1984. 131 pp.

Maxford, Howard. *Hammer, House of Horror: Behind the Screams.* London: B. T. Batsford, 1996. 192 pp.

McCarty, John. *Hammer Films.* Pocket Essentials. Harpenden, Herts., UK: Pocket Essentials, 2002. 95 pp.

Meikle, Denis. *A History of Hammer: The Rise and Fall of the House of Hammer, 1949–1979.* Lanham, MD: Scarecrow Press, 2001. 420 pp.

Miller, Mark A. *Christopher Lee and Peter Cushing and Horror Cinema: A Filmography of Their 22 Collaborations.* Jefferson, NC: McFarland and Company, 1995. 437 pp.

Pohle, Robert W., Jr., and Douglas C. Hart. *The Films of Christopher Lee.* Metuchen, NJ: Scarecrow Press, 1983. 227 pp.

Svekla, Gary J., and Susan Svekla, eds. *Memories of Hammer.* Baltimore: Luminary Press, 2002. 256 pp.

❮ Harker, Jonathan ❯

At the beginning of ***Bram Stoker's Dracula***, Jonathan Harker arrived in **Bistritz, Romania**, in the midst of a journey to **Castle Dracula**. Upon his arrival at the Golden Krone Hotel, a note from Count Dracula awaited him. He was to go to the **Borgo Pass**, where a carriage from the castle would pick him up. When people learned of his destination to the castle, they were frightened and concerned for his welfare, and one lady gave him a rosary with a **crucifix** to wear. He was taken to Borgo Pass and then transported to Castle Dracula, where **Dracula** invited him in. Harker ignored the unusual appearance and manner of the count as he ate that evening. The next afternoon as he explored the castle, he noticed the lack of **mirrors**. He and Dracula spoke of England and worked to complete Dracula's purchase of **Carfax**, a house in the **London** suburb of Purfleet.

The next day, the visit to Castle Dracula took on a strange and even sinister quality. As Harker shaved, Dracula suddenly appeared behind him. Dracula knocked the mirror aside, but not before Harker noticed that the image of Dracula behind him was not reflected in the mirror. He also noticed that Dracula recoiled from the crucifix. Harker began to catalog the strange occurrences day by day and concluded that for some reason he was being held prisoner. He tried to act as if the visit was normal, but then was ordered to write a series of letters telling his employer that he was extending his visit.

Harker became convinced of Dracula's supernatural nature as he watched him crawl down the outside wall of the castle. He subsequently encountered the other residents of the castle, the vampire **brides**, three **women** who attacked him only to be thwarted at the last moment by Dracula's sudden appearance. As he pondered his condition and strategized ways to flee, he noticed that a band of **Gypsies** had arrived. He escaped from his room and roamed through the castle. He found the count lying in a box of earth and considered killing him, but he did not. A second time he approached Dracula, immobile in his vampire **sleep**, but again found himself unable to complete the kill. Dracula escaped and left Harker behind in the castle.

Somehow Harker finally escaped and made his way to Budapest, where he became a patient at the Hospital of St. Joseph and St. Mary. The sisters who ran the hospital informed his fiance, **Mina Murray**, of his arrival. Mina left England, in spite of the declining health of her friend, **Lucy Westenra**, to go to Budapest where she and Harker were married.

Upon their return to England, they were informed of Lucy's death, and Harker met Dr. **Abraham Van Helsing**, who had been called in as a consultant in her case. By adding the journal of his experiences in Castle Dracula to the data on Lucy's death, a picture of what was occurring began to emerge. Also, he had spotted Dracula walking around London. Once Harker recovered his health and his sense of sanity, he and Mina worked together to compile and correlate information on Dracula's activities. Harker then traveled into London to locate and track the movement of the boxes of earth Dracula had brought with him from the castle. Harker attended the meeting at which Van Helsing organized an informal committee, and he was the first to answer Van Helsing's call for a commitment to destroy Dracula. Harker joined in the search for the boxes of earth, unaware that Mina was at that very moment under attack. He had believed her fatigue to be caused by stress. Several days later, he was at home with Mina when Dracula arrived. Dracula put Harker to sleep while he proceeded to exchange **blood** with Mina, a process interrupted by the timely arrival of the other men. They succeeded in driving Dracula away.

Harker accompanied Van Helsing on the final chase back to Castle Dracula. He traveled the last leg of the journey on horseback, along with associate **Arthur Holmwood**, and arrived with the others just as the box containing Dracula's body was deposited in front of the castle. With **Quincey P. Morris**, he approached the box and used a large knife to slit Dracula's throat. At the same moment, Morris plunged his Bowie knife into Dracula's heart. In the fracas that concluded with Dracula's death, Morris was killed. Harker and Mina went on to live happily, and named their first child after Morris. Seven years after killing Dracula, the couple returned to **Transylvania**, where many of the memories of their life converged.

It has been suggested that the character of Jonathan Harker was based upon Joseph Harker, a young artist who worked at the Lyceum Theatre where **Bram Stoker** was employed. Harker worked with a team of designers that created the stage setting for the theater's production of *Macbeth*. Stoker had known Harker's father, a character actor who had been kind to Stoker in his earlier years. When the job was completed, Stoker returned the favors shown him by helping Harker establish himself independently as an artist.

As *Dracula* was brought to the stage and screen, Harker's role in the story frequently suffered, though not as much as the character of Quincey P. Morris, who was cut out completely to simplify the complex plot for dramatic presentation. In the stage versions, Harker's important opening trip to Transylvania was deleted. When that segment of the novel was returned to the script in the movie version of ***Dracula* (1931)** with **Bela Lugosi**, **R. N. Renfield**—not Harker—made the trip to Castle Dracula. In ***Horror of Dracula*** (1958) with **Christopher Lee**, he arrived at Castle Dracula not as a naive real estate dealer, but as a secret agent in league with Van Helsing. However, he was attacked and killed early in the course of events, before Van Helsing could arrive to assist him. Only in **Francis Ford Coppola's** *Bram Stoker's Dracula* did Harker (played by Keanu Reeves) have the central role he played in the novel from the opening chapter to the final death of Dracula at his hand.

Sources:
Haining, Peter. "The Origin of Jonathan Harker." *CDFC (Count Dracula Fan Club) Special*: 3–4.

HarmonyRoad Press *see:* Dark Shadows Fandom

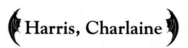

Harris, Charlaine

Charlaine is the popular author of a series of vampire novels set in rural Louisiana that in 2007 were turned into a popular **television** series, *True Blood*, on Home Box Office (HBO). The series takes it named from the premise that vampires have been able to become a public segment of human society because they have discovered a substitute for the **blood** they needed to survive, which is bottled and distributed under the label, True Blood.

Harris was born and raised in Tunica, Mississippi, the daughter of a librarian mother and school principal father. She attended Southwestern (now Rhodes) College in Memphis, and later settled in southern Arkansas with her husband, where she attended writing classes at the University of Missouri-St. Louis. She had begun writing in her youth, but only after settling into family life did she turn to writing novels and find a publisher to accept them for publication. Her first novel appeared in 1981. She later published two successful series before turning to write the Southern Vampire series at the end of the 1990s. The first of the vampire novels, *Dead until Dark*, appeared in 2001. At least one new novel in the series has appeared annually. The series contained some good storytelling and a raucous sense of humor.

Dead until Dark introduced Sookie Stackhouse, a waitress in a small Louisiana community, Bon Temps, and her vampire mate, Bill Compton, a Civil War veteran who was turned into a vampire as he made his way home at the end of war. Sookie is a telepath who can read people's minds, an ability setting up numerous situations when their thoughts and their words diverge widely. As the reader is introduced to Sookie, vampires have entered the mainstream, taking a place in contemporary society. They are opposed by some who believe them to be an alien, evil species. They are supported by vampire rights activists. Sookie has a live-and-let-live approach. Then she meets Bill Compton, whose thoughts she cannot read. Around him she can have some peace and quiet. One evening after he had come to the restaurant where she works, she discovered him under attack from some people who wanted to rob him of his blood. Vampire blood is a hot if illegal substance, which has a powerful effect on humans. She saved Bill who had been immobilized under a chain of silver.

The television series follows Sookie Stackhouse (Anna Paquin) as a waitress at Merlotte's, the restaurant in Bon Temps, owned by Sam Merlotte (Sam Trammell), who turns out to be a shapeshifter. Bill Compton (Stephen Moyer), the handsome 173-year-old vampire has returned to Bon Temps to inherit the family property after his last remaining human relative has died. The main story line of the first season concerned the murders of several women all connected to Sookie's brother, Jason (Ryan Kwanten), including his grandmother. Three young women—Maudette Pickens, Dawn Green, and Amy Burley—were all strangled shortly after having been alone with Jason. Though Detective Bellefleur had little doubt that Jason was the killer, the town sheriff did not suspect him. Jason's and Sookie's grandmother was murdered shortly afterward. At the end of the season it was revealed that Arlene Fowler's fiance, Rene Lenier, was actually a man named Drew Marshall who created a fake identity and had been killing women he considers "fang-bangers." The vampire in Harris's books are organized into a hierarchical society with their own system of laws. Local areas are administered by a sheriff and larger areas by a queen or king. As a whole, the vampires are very traditional. They are bound to the night, have retractable **fangs** that leave marks on their victims, and have extra (if not extraordinary) **strength**. Many are **good guys**, but others are more traditionally bad. Vampires are opposed by the the anti-vampire religious movement called the Fellowship of the Sun.

Subsequent volumes (eight in all as of 2009) in the Sookie Stackhouse saga continue her misadventures as a human telepath working with the vampire community, who prize her ability to find bad guys that try to mess with them. At the same time she

Anna Camp (right) plays Sarah Newlin in the television series *True Blood* Here she is in a scene with Ryan Kwanten, playing Jason.

develops relations with the **werewolf** shapeshifters, especially when she has problems with Bill. At the same time, Bill is not the only vampire who finds her attractive.

Harris's vampire books have been among the most heralded in the paranormal romance field. With the success of the HBO series, it appears that her characters will be making numerous additional appearances. Harris maintains a Internet presence at http://www.charlaineharris.com/.

Sources:

"Charlaine Harris: Putting the Bite on Cozy Mysteries." Crescent Blues (2001). Posted at http://www.crescentblues.com/4_4issue/int_charlaine_harris.shtml. Accessed on April 8, 2010.

Hall, Robert L. "Cozies With Teeth!: An interview with Charlaine Harris." Southern Scribe (2004). Posted at http://www.southernscribe.com/zine/authors/Harris_Charlaine.htm. Accessed on April 8, 2010

Harris, Charlene, and Toni L.P. Packer, eds. *Dead Until Dark*. Southern Vampire Mysteries, Book 1. New York: Ace Books, 2001. 260 pp.

———. *Living Dead in Dallas*. Southern Vampire Mysteries, Book 2. New York: Ace Books, 2002. 262 pp.

———. *Club Dead*. Southern Vampire Mysteries, Book 3. New York: Ace Books, 2003. 258 pp.

———. *Dead in Dixie*. New York: Science Fiction Book Club, 2003. 612 pp.

———. *Dead to the World*. Southern Vampire Mysteries, Book 4. New York: Ace Books, 2004. 291 pp.

———. *Dead as a Doornail*. Southern Vampire Mysteries, Book 5. New York: Ace Books, 2005. 295 pp.

———. *Dead by Day*. New York: Science Fiction Book Club, 2005. 419 pp.

———. *Definitely Dead*. Southern Vampire Mysteries, Book 6. New York: Ace Books, 2006. 324 pp.

Harris, Charlaine. *All Together Dead*. Southern Vampire Mysteries, Book 7, 2007. 323 pp.

———. *Many Bloody Returns: Tales of Birthdays with Bite*. Ace Books: New York, 2007. 355 pp.

———. *Dead and Gone*. Southern Vampire Mysteries, Book 9. New York: Ace Books, 2009. 320 pp.

———. *From Dead To Worse*. Southern Vampire Mysteries, Book 8. New York: Ace Books, 2009. 336 pp.

Harris, Xander

Xander Harris (Nicholas Brendon), short for Alexander LaVelle Harris, a main character in the *Buffy the Vampire Slayer* TV series, grew up in Sunnydale, California, the town in which the show was set. He was a childhood friend of **Willow Rosenberg** and both were sophomores at Sunnydale High School when **Buffy Summers** transferred from Los Angeles. He learned of Buffy's calling to the fight against vampires soon after her transfer and, along with Willow, insisted on joining the crusade. He had no particular skills or intelligence to offer, but became Buffy's faithful friend and supporter.

Xander had a variety of relationships with women, most disastrous. His longest high school relationship was with **Cordelia Chase**, their attraction being an enigma among Cordelia's former friends, the more wealthy and trendy girls. He eventually built a reputation for falling for women who turned out to be demons. In season three, he encountered Anyanka, a vengeance demon, who had dedicated the last thousand years to granting wishes of revenge to women who had been wronged by their man. She showed up in Sunnydale after Xander cheated on Cordelia with Willow. In the process of granting a wish to Cordelia, she was transformed into the human Anya (Emma Caulfield). She eventually started dating Xander, and they remained a twosome, off and on, for the rest of the series.

Xander helped Buffy defeat Sunnydale's demonic mayor at the end of season three. Afterwards, he does not attempt to enter college, but spends a year trying to find himself. He lived with his parents and worked at a series of jobs. Anya had left before the final battle at the school, but later returned and she and Xander began an affair that led to his asking her to marry him. By this time he had gotten a more permanent job in construction.

At the beginning of season five, **Dracula** briefly visited to Sunnydale, and Xander became one of his first victims, spending most of the episode as his servant. His real crisis came later, however, as the marriage with Anya approached. In the end, he got cold feet and left her at the altar. In her humiliation and anger, she once again became a vengeance demon, though after only a short time, she sought to become human again. His own maturity was shown when he argued Willow out of destroying the world in her anger over her girlfriend Tara's death.

Xander remained loyal to Buffy to the end and during the last season it cost him his eye. He faced the last battle over the Hellmouth with an eye patch. He survived the final battle, but Anya did not. During the final season of *Angel*, Xander was mentioned as being in Africa working with recently activated slayers. He moved to Scotland for the season eight comic book where he (as of 2009) works closely with Buffy at the central headquarters of her international vampire fighting organization. Buffy appreciates the fact that even though Xander never developed any special talents or powers, he was always there to assist and never left her for even a short time.

Xander was overshadowed in popularity through the series by **Angel** and **Spike**, though he remained a constant presence. As Buffy paraphernalia began to appear, he was a ubiquitous presence in the **trading cards**, and the subject of a set of action figures.

Sources:

Battis, Jes. "'This carpenter can drywall you into the next century': Xander Harris as Hero, Big Brother and Male-In-Progress." In Jes Battis. *Blood Relations: Chosen Families in* Buffy the Vampire Slayer *and* Angel. Jefferson, NC: McFarland, 2005: 44–66.

Camron, Marc. "The Importance of Being the Zeppo: Xander, Gender Identity and Hybridity in *Buffy the Vampire Slayer*." *Slayage: The Online International Journal of Buffy Studies* 23 (2007). Posted at http://slayageonline.com/essays/slayage23/Camron.htm. Accessed on April 8, 2010.

Golden, Christopher, and Nancy Holder. *Buffy the Vampire Slayer: The Watcher's Guide*. New York: Pocket Books, 1998. 298 pp.

Holder, Nancy, with Jeff Mariotte and Maryelizabeth Hart. *Buffy the Vampire Slayer: The Watcher's Guide*. Volume 2. New York: Pocket Books, 2000. 472 pp.

McKeon, J. Michael. "'Love the One You're With': Developing Xander." In Emily Dial-Driver, Sally Emmons-Featherston, Jim Ford and Carolyn Anne Taylor, eds. *The Truth of* Buffy: *Essays on Fiction Illuminating Reality*. Jefferson, NC: McFarland, 2008: pp. 131–141.

Ruditis, Paul. *Buffy the Vampire Slayer: The Watcher's Guide*. Volume 3. New York: Simon Spotlight, 2004. 359 pp.

❨ Harrison, Kim ❩

Kim Harrison, is a pen name used by writer Dawn Cook, the author of young adult fantasy novels, who in 2004 began a new series of books about Rachel Morgan, a witch and agent for a security force who keeps the supernatural creatures of Cincinnati in line. Cook, the only daughter among her parents' many children, became a tomboy in self defense. She grew up near Ann Arbor, Michigan. She majored in science in college, and after graduation married and settled down in South Carolina, where she continues to reside. She has two children. In the process she became a devotee of both romantic novels, the world of fantasy and **science fiction**, and Clint Eastwood movies. Prior to 2009, she tried to keep the two identities Cook and Harrison separate.

The Kim Harrison novels center on a fictional Cincinnati where a science-fiction/fantasy world makes romance possible. In the not too distant future, the Inderland has become visible. It is the realm in which vampires, witches, **werewolves**, and other supernatural creatures have existed on the edge of human awareness. A tomato virus that proved fatal only to humans, wiped out most of the human race, and ultimately brought the Inderlanders into the open. In Cincinnati, the Inderlanders reside in an area known as the Hollows.

Rachel Morgan, the heroine featured in Harrison's books, is a witch who works for Inderland Security. While the Federal Inderland Bureau (managed by humans) has ultimate charge of controlling Inderland-human interaction, Inderland Security (run by Inderlanders) has charge of any matters that mystify the FIB. Tired of her job, Morgan found a way to sever her contract with IS and become an independent bounty hunter, with a vampire named Ivy Tamwood and a Pixie named Jenks as her partners. As she pursues her supernatural villains, she constantly has to be alert for Ivy who really wants to bite the boss and turn her into a mere minion. She also has to contend with Kisten, her boyfriend, who is also a vampire. (Ivy got her own story in "Undead in the Garden of Good and Evil," a short story in the anthology, *Dates from Hell*.) Rachel Morgan made her first appearance in *Dead Witch Walking* in 2004. By 2009, she had invited readers along on seven adventures that included tracking down a drug dealer and a serial killer, dealing with a war between vampires and werewolves, and facing off against a spectrum of demons (who smudged her aura). More adventures were waiting in the wings.

Still in her first decade as a published author, Harrison has won several awards for her books from both her romance and fantasy/science fiction colleagues. She maintains a Web presence at http://www.kimharrison.net/.

Sources:

Harrison, Kim. *Dead Witch Walking*. The Hollows, Book 1. New York: HarperTorch, 2004. 416 pp.

————. *Every Which Way but Dead*. The Hollows, Book 3. New York: HarperTorch, 2005. 501 pp.

————. *The Good, the Bad, and the Undead*. The Hollows, Book 2. New York: HarperTorch, 2005. 453 pp.

————. *A Fistful of Charms*. The Hollows, Book 4. New York: HarperTorch, 2006. 554 pp.

————, Lynsay Sands, Kelley Armstrong, & Lori Handeland. *Dates from Hell*. Rept. New York: Avon Books, 2006. 404 pp.

————, Lynsay Sands, Vicki Pettersson, and Marjorie M. Liu. *Holidays Are Hell*. Harper: New York, 2007. 384 pp.

————. *For a Few Demons More*. The Hollows, Book 5. New York: HarperCollins, 2007. 456 pp.

————. *The Outlaw Demon Wails*. The Hollows, Book 6. New York: Eos, 2008. 464 pp.

————. *White Witch, Black Curse*. The Hollows, Book 7. New York: Eos, 2009. 512 pp.

"Kim Harrison: Secret Identity." Locus Online. Posted at http://www.locusmag.com/Perspectives/2009/05/kim-harrison-secret-identity.html. Accessed on April 8, 2010.

❨ Hartmann, Franz (1838–1912) ❩

Franz Hartmann, theosophist and author on the occult, was born November 22, 1838, in Bavaria, **Germany**. Through his mother, he claimed to be descended from Irish nobility. He became a physician and moved to the United States to practice his profession. In **America**, he encountered spiritualism and in the late 1870s became associated with the newly founded Theosophical Society. The international headquarters of the society was established in Adyar, **India**, in the early 1880s and Hartmann was invited to stay for a period. In 1884 he published his first major work, the sympathetic *Report of Observations During Nine Months' Stay at the Headquarters of the Theosophical Society at Adyar (Madras), India*. His report was largely lost in the furor that was to follow the next year when Richard Hodgson published his devastating attack upon theosophical leader Madame H. P. Blavatsky, claiming that all the unusual occurrences that had been reported around her were the result of fraud. The Hodgson Report forced Blavatsky into a period of retirement in England, and Hartmann accompanied her back to Europe. He had meanwhile been working on his next book, *Magic, Black and White* (1885).

Hartmann later left Blavatsky in England and returned to his native Bavaria. There, he claimed, he encountered a secret order of occultists, Rosicrucians. He served as the president of the Theosophical Society in Germany for a brief period, but soon left to found his own independent group. It was during this period that Hartmann became interested in vampirism. He investigated several cases of contemporary vampirism and reported them in a series of articles in occult journals. From these investigations, Hartmann developed a theory of **psychic vampirism**. He came to believe that vampires were real but were not bloodsucking revenants. They were better described as a force field of subhuman intelligence that acted instinctively, not rationally. Hartmann saw the vampiric force as more malignant than evil. He supported this theory with his report of a young serving boy who had exhibited classic signs of a vampire attack. The boy was emaciated to the point of physical collapse, yet had an insatiable appetite. He reported that a force had settled on his chest, during which time he became paralyzed and unable to cry out. He claimed the force had sucked the life out of him. His employer attended to the boy during one of these attacks and reported that he had grasped an invisible yet tangible gelatinlike substance resting on the boy's chest. Hartmann concluded that the man had encountered ectoplasm, a mysterious substance that was alleged to stream from the bodies of spiritualist mediums during séances.

In 1895, Hartmann authored a book about the phenomena surrounding premature burial. He developed a theory put forth earlier by **Z. J. Piérart**, a French psychical researcher in the 1860s, concerning the astral body. Piérart hypothesized that when a person was buried alive, the astral body (a ghostly double of the physical body, which many occultists believe to be an essential component of every individual) separated from the physical body. The astral body would vampirize others (taking both **blood** and life) and thus nourish the living body in the tomb; hence the lifelike **characteristics** of many exhumed corpses. Hartmann ascribed this theory to Paracelsus (1493–1541), the sixteenth-century alchemist. Hartmann took the theory one step further, suggesting that the astral body could be severed completely from the physical and thus continue as a free-floating, earthbound vampire spirit. He cited one case in which a young man committed **suicide** after being rejected by the woman he loved. Following the man's death, Hartmann believed, his astral form attached itself to the woman and began to suck the life out of her.

Hartmann's cases have become classic reports of actual modern vampires (and as such were reprinted in the volumes by **Montague Summers** and **Donald Glut**), though his theories generally have been discarded except within a few occult circles. Occult theories of the intangible "astral body" and of "ectoplasm" provide an explanation by referring to phenomena equally elusive and as much in need of explanation as vampirism. Most modern theories of psychic vampirism view it as a report on the social interaction of living persons.

Hartmann wrote a number of occult books. After the turn of the century, he spent much of his time wandering in the Untersberg Mountains near Salzberg. He died August 7, 1912, in Kepten, Bavaria.

Sources:

Glut, Donald F. *True Vampires of History*. New York: H C Publishers, 1971. 191 pp.

The hawthorn is a small, thorny tree of the rose family that once symbolized hope and was also considered a powerful charm against witches and sorcerers.

Hartmann, Franz. *Premature Burial*. London: 1896.

———. "An Authenticated Vampire Story." *Occult Review* (September 1909).

———. "A Miller of D———." *Occult Review* 9, 5 (November 1924): 258–259.

———. "A Modern Case of Vampirism." Reprint in Donald F. Glut. *True Vampires of History*. New York: H C Publishers, 1971: 128–131.

Rogo, Scott. "In-depth Analysis of the Vampire Legend." *Fate* 21, 9 (September 1968): 70–77.

Summers, Montague. *The Vampire in Europe*. London: Routledge, Kegan Paul, Trench, Trubner, & Co., 1929. 329 pp. Rept. New Hyde Park, NY: University Books, 1960. 329 pp.

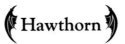 **Hawthorn**

The hawthorn (*Crataegus oxyacantha*), a small tree of the rose family, was prevalent throughout southern Europe. The plant is also known as the whitethorn and is typical of a number of related thorn bushes (wild mountain rose, blackthorn) that are substituted for hawthorn in different locations. In ancient times, hawthorn was used both as a symbol of hope and as a charm against **witchcraft** and sorcery. As such, it was often placed in the cradles of infants. As a **protection** against witchcraft, people might build a barrier of hawthorn around their house or doorway. The Greeks placed pieces of hawthorn in the casements of houses to prevent the entrance of witches. In

Christopher Lee, as Dracula, suffers a fatal encounter with a hawthorn bush in the film
The Satanic Rites of Dracula.

Bohemia, hawthorn was put on the thresholds of the cow houses, also to prevent witches from entering. The anti-witchcraft use of hawthorn easily transferred to the closely related vampire. The hawthorn united two ancient practices. First, to protect one's home or another place, people commonly erected a symbolic barrier such as a hawthorn bush. While unable to stop or even slow down the usual physical forces, hawthorn was believed to be capable of blocking intruding supernatural forces or spirits. Second, hawthorn was thought by many to have a sacred quality as it was one of several plants designated as the bush from which Christ's crown of thorns was made.

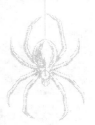

Hawthorn branches were variously placed on the outside of a **coffin**, in the corpse's sock, or on top of the corpse.

In Bosnia, a particular twist to the hawthorn legend developed. When visiting the home where a person had just died, women placed a small piece of hawthorn behind their headcloth, and then threw the twig away on their way home. If the deceased person was a vampire, it would focus its attention upon the hawthorn rather than follow the woman home. According to the **Bram Stoker** character, Dr. **Abraham Van Helsing**, a branch of wild rose on the coffin would keep a vampire confined inside. Stoker probably learned of this practice from Emily Gerard. Her book, *Land Beyond the Forest* (a major source for *Dracula* [1897]), stated that the people of **Transylvania** often "lay the thorny branch of a wild rose bush across the body to prevent it from leaving the coffin." In spite of Stoker's use of it, the thorn did not attain a prominent role in modern literary and movie vampire lore. The hawthorn made a brief appearance at the end of **Hammer Films**'s *The Satanic Rites of Dracula*, in which **Christopher Lee** as **Dracula** was destroyed by being trapped in a hawthorn bush.

In addition to the plant's thorn and bush applications, among the **southern Slavs**, the wood of the hawthorn or blackthorn was to be used in the **stake** that impaled the vampire's corpse. It might be hammered through the head, heart, or stomach.

Sources:

Gerard, Emily. *Land Beyond the Forest*. 2 vols. New York: Harper & Brothers, 1888.

Lehner, Ernst, and Johanna Lehner. *Folklore and Symbolism of Flowers, Plants and Trees*. New York: Tudor Publishing Company, 1960. 128 pp.

Perkowski, Jan L. *The Darkling: A Treatise on Slavic Vampirism*. Columbus, OH: Slavica Publishers, 1989. 169 pp.

Porteous, Alexander. *Forest Folklore, Mythology, and Romance*. London: George Allen & Unwin, 1928. 319 pp. Rept. Detroit: Singing Tree Press, 1968. 314 pp.

Summers, Montague. *The Vampire in Europe*. London: Routledge, Kegan Paul, Trench, Trubner, & Co., 1929. 329 pp.

Held, Eric S. *see:* Vampire Fandom: United States

❨ The Highgate Vampire ❩

One of the more interesting interludes in vampire history concerns events that took place at a cemetery in the Highgate section of **London** during the years 1967 to 1983. The cemetery, officially called the Cemetery of St. James, was consecrated by the bishop of London in 1839, four days before Queen Victoria's 20th birthday. It gained some association through its slightly disguised use by **Bram Stoker** as the burial place of **Lucy Westenra**, after her death (as a result of **Dracula**'s attacks). The modern story of vampires at Highgate began with reports of a phantomlike entity seen in the cemetery in the evenings. While rumors of a ghost circulated, occultist and head of the **Vampire Research Society**, Sean Manchester received the account of schoolgirl Elizabeth Wojdyla and her friend, who claimed to have seen some graves open and the dead rise from them. Wojdyla also reported having nightmares in which something evil tried to come into her bedroom. Over several years, Manchester collected similar accounts of unusual

The Highgate Vampire was sighted several times at the cemetery's North Gate.

sightings associated with the cemetery. In 1969 Wojdyla's nightmares returned, except now the malevolent figure actually came into her room. She had developed the symptoms of pernicious **anemia** and on her neck were two small wounds suggestive of a classic vampire's bite. Manchester and Elizabeth's boyfriend treated her as a **victim** of vampirism and filled her room with **garlic**, **crucifixes**, and holy **water**. She soon improved. Meanwhile, various people continued to add new reports of seeing a ghostly being in the cemetery.

Because they were of a common sort, no one probably would have heard of the Highgate reports had not signs been found that the cemetery and a nearby park were being used for rituals that involved the killing of **animals**. Some of the dead animals had been drained of **blood**, and the local newspaper asked in its headline, "Does a Wampyr Walk in Highgate?" Manchester then reported that he had been contacted by another woman who had the same symptoms as Wojdyla. The young woman, followed while sleepwalking, led Manchester to a cluster of burial vaults in the cemetery. Manchester told the press that he believed a genuine vampire existed at Highgate and should be dealt with accordingly. The newspaper story and a subsequent feature spot on the independent Thames TV led to the cemetery becoming a gathering point of the curious.

A group of amateur filmmakers used it as the site for a film, *Vampires by Night*. On Friday, March 13, 1970, before an assembled crowd of onlookers, Manchester and two cohorts entered the vault where three empty **coffins** were found. They lined the coffins with garlic, and in each they placed a cross. The vaults were sprinkled with salt (used for exorcisms) and holy water.

Events turned nasty in August when the body of a young woman was found at the cemetery. It appeared that someone had treated the corpse as a vampire and had decapitated and tried to burn it. An enraged citizenry demanded that the authorities protect the bodies of loved ones from abuse. Before the month was out, the police arrested two men who claimed to be **vampire hunters**. The men were a factor in the souring relationship between Manchester and the police. But while the police were distracted by the amateur vampire hunters, Manchester had quietly entered another vault and discovered what he believed was a real vampire. Rather than mutilating the body (a crime in England), he read an exorcism and sealed the vault with cement permeated with pieces of garlic.

In the summer of 1970, David Farrant, another amateur vampire hunter, entered the field. He claimed to have seen the vampire and went hunting for it with a **stake** and crucifix—but was arrested. He later became a convert to a form of Satanism. He was later convicted on two charges of breaking into tombs at Highgate. In 1978 he denounced the vampire as a hoax he had created by himself in 1970. Manchester quickly responded, noting that the reports originated prior to Farrant's involvement and that he was not privy to the incidents that had made the Highgate vampire so newsworthy.

Meanwhile, in 1977, Manchester began an investigation of a mansion near Highgate Cemetery that had a reputation of being haunted. On several occasions Manchester and his associates entered the house. In the basement they found a coffin, which they dragged into the backyard. Opening the casket, Manchester saw the same vampire he had seen seven years before in Highgate Cemetery. This time he conducted an exorcism by staking the body, which disintegrated into a slimy, foul-smelling substance, and burned the coffin. He had destroyed the Highgate Vampire. Soon after this incident, the mansion was demolished and an apartment house was erected in its place.

The consequences from the Highgate Vampire did not end with its death, however. In 1980 reports of dead animals found drained of blood began to appear in Finchley. Manchester believed that a vampire created by the bite of the Highgate Vampire was the cause. He contacted many of the people he had met in 1970 and eventually targeted a woman he called Lusia as the culprit. He discovered that Lusia had died and been buried in Great Northern London Cemetery, and he had dreams in which she came to him. One autumn evening in 1982, Manchester entered the cemetery. There he encountered a large, spiderlike creature about the size of a cat. He drove a stake through it. As dawn approached, it metamorphosed into Lusia—she had only now truly died. He returned her remains to the grave, thus ending the case of the Highgate Vampire. Manchester wrote an account of his perspective on *The Highgate Vampire* (1985; Revised 1991), upon which he expanded in the *The Vampire Hunter's Handbook* (1997), and the Vampire Research Society offers a cassette tape concerning the incident. Meanwhile, David Farrant founded The Highgate Vampire Society (http://www.davidfarrant.org/) and has continued to present his side of the story in a series of booklets, the most recent appearing in 2002.

Sources:

Farrant, David. *Beyond the Highgate Vampire*. London: British Psychic and Occult Society, 1991. Third revised ed. London: British Psychic and Occult Society, 2002. 63 pp.

———. *The Vampire Syndrome: The Truth Behind the Highgate Vampire Legend*. London: Mutiny! Press, 2000. 65 pp.

In Highgate Cemetery. London: Friends of Highgate Cemetery, 1992. 20 pp.

Manchester, Sean. "The Highgate Vampire." In Peter Underwood, ed. *The Vampire's Bedside Companion: The Amazing World of Vampires in Fact and Fiction*. London: Leslie Frewin, 1975. pp. 81–121.

———. *The Highgate Vampire*. London: British Occult Society, 1985. 172 pp. Revised ed. London: Gothic Press, 1991. 190 pp.

———. *The Vampire Hunter's Handbook*. London: Gothic Press, 1997. 96 pp.

Thompson, Paul B. "The Highgate Vampire." *Pursuit* 16, 3. Rept. *Fate* (May 1985): 74–80.

Holder, Nancy

Nancy Holder is the prolific author of a set of novels and several nonfiction books related to the popular vampire **television** series *Buffy the Vampire Slayer* and *Angel*. She was born Nancy Lindsay Jones in Los Altos, California on August 29, 1953. Her father was a navy officer, and she grew up in California and **Japan**. She left school at sixteen to study ballet in Germany, but several years later returned to California and studied communications at the University of California— San Diego, graduating summa cum laude. Her daughter Belle Claire Christine Holder was born in 1996.

Holder published her first novel in 1983 under her family name. Then just as the *Buffy the Vampire Slayer* series began its television run, she was invited as one of the authors who would write the spin-off novels, both original stories and adaptations of the episodes of the series. Almost half of those novels with be co-authored with friend and colleague Christopher Golden, including the *Sunnydale Year Book*, while several were also written with Jeff Mariotte. In one sense, novels that are part of franchises are hardly the place where a fiction writer shows their greatest creativity as they must be developed according to strict guidelines of, in this case, the television show, and on what any given character may or may not be or do. At the same time, however, such writing demands a set of special skills to be able to write with a creative edge and in an entertaining fashion while maintaining the guidelines. Holder has shown a special ability in this regard, and, in addition to Buffy and **Angel**, has written for a variety of television franchises. In between these assignments, she has been able to produce additional novels on self chosen topics.

She and Golden also co-wrote the first volume of the *Buffy the Vampire Slayer Watcher's Guide*, the first of several semi-official books about the show. Holder joined with her colleagues Jeff Mariotte and Maryelizabeth Hart to produce Volume 2 of the *Watchers Guide* and *Angel the Casefiles*. In the process of doing the many novels and working on the Watcher's guides, she became somewhat of an expert on the show and was invited to contribute essays to two of the nonfiction anthologies on *Buffy* and *Angel*. She was one of the featured speakers at the Slayage scholars conference in Nashville in 2004.

Holder is a four-time winner of the Bram Stoker Award given by the Horror Writer Association for superior achievement in horror writing, a sign of the respect for Holder among her professional colleagues. She occasionally teaches courses in writing and on occasion on *Buffy the Vampire Slayer* at the University of California—San Diego. She maintains her Internet presence at http://www.nancyholder.com/.

Sources:

Fiction

Golden, Christopher, and Nancy Holder. *Buffy the Vampire Slayer: Halloween Rain*. New York: Archway/Pocket Books, 1997. 162 pp.

———. *Buffy the Vampire Slayer: Blooded*. New York: Archway/Pocket Books, 1998. 274 pp.

———. *Buffy the Vampire Slayer. Child of the Hunt*. New York: Pocket Books, 1998. 324 pp.

———. *Buffy the Vampire Slayer: The Gamekeeper Trilogy*. Science Fiction Book Club, 1999. 724 pp.

———. *Buffy the Vampire Slayer: Ghost Roads*. Book Two: The Gatekeeper Trilogy. New York: Pocket Books, 1999. 398 pp.

———. *Buffy the Vampire Slayer: Immortal*. New York: Pocket Books, 1999. 309 pp.

———. *Buffy the Vampire Slayer: Out of the Madhouse*. New York: Pocket Books, 1999. 367 pp.

———. *Buffy the Vampire Slayer: Sons of Entropy*. New York: Pocket Books, 1999. 317 pp.

———. *Sunnydale High Yearbook*. New York: Pocket Books, 1999. 91 pp.

———. *Spike and Dru: Pretty Maids All in a Row*. New York: Pocket Books, 2000. 305 pp.

———. *Buffy the Vampire Slayer: Oz: Into the Wild*. New York: Pocket Books, 2002. 278 pp.

———. *Buffy the Vampire Slayer: The Wisdom of War*. New York: Simon Pulse, 2002. 401 pp.

Guran, Paula. "Interview: Nancy Holder: Staying on Target." Dark Echo Horror (1998). Posted at http://www.darkecho.com/darkecho/archives/holder.html. Accessed on April 8, 2010.

Holder, Nancy. *Buffy the Vampire Slayer: The Angel Chronicles*. Vol. I. New York: Archway/Pocket Books, 1998. 208 pp.

———. *Buffy the Vampire Slayer: The Angel Chronicles*. Vol. III. New York: Archway/Pocket Books, 1999. 180 pp.

———. *Angel: City Of*. New York: Archway/Pocket Books, 1999. 177 pp.

———. *Angel: Not Forgotten*. New York: Pocket Pulse, 2000. 243 pp.

———. *Buffy the Vampire Slayer: The Evil that Men Do*. New York: Archway/Pocket Books, 2000. 335 pp.

———. *Buffy the Vampire Slayer: The Book of Fours*. New York: Pocket Books, 2001. 336 pp.

———. *Buffy the Vampire Slayer: The Journals of Rupert Giles*. Vol. I. New York: Simon Pulse, 2002. 191 pp.

———. *Buffy the Vampire Slayer: Blood and Fog*. NY: Simon Pulse, 2003. 291 pp.

———. *Buffy the Vampire Slayer/Angel: Heat*. NY: Spotlight, 2004. 456 pp.

———. *Buffy the Vampire Slayer: Keep Me in Mind*. NY: Simon Spotlight Entertainment, 2005. 256 pp.

———. *Buffy the Vampire Slayer: Queen of the Slayers*. NY: Simon Spotlight Entertainment, 2005. 320 pp.

———. *Buffy the Vampire Slayer: Carnival of Souls*. NY: Simon Spotlight Entertainment, 2006. 302 pp.

———, and Jeff Mariotte. *Buffy the Vampire Slayer/Angel: Unseen: The Burning*. New York: Pocket Books, 2001. 274 pp.

———, and Jeff Mariotte. *Buffy the Vampire Slayer/Angel: Unseen: Door to Alternity*. New York: Pocket Books, 2001. 301 pp.

———, and Jeff Mariotte. *Buffy the Vampire Slayer/Angel: Unseen: Long Way Home*. New York: Pocket Books, 2001. 288 pp.

———, and Jeff Mariotte. *Angel: Endangered Species*. New York: Simon Pulse, 2002. 276 pp.

Nonfiction

Golden, Christopher, and Nancy Holder. *Buffy the Vampire Slayer: The Watcher's Guide*. NY: Pocket Books, 1998. 298 pp.

Holder, Nancy. "Death Becomes Him: Blondie Bear." In Yeffeth, Glenn, ed. *Five Seasons of Angel: Science Fiction and Fantasy Writers Discuss Their Favorite Vampire*. Dallas, TX: Benbella Books, 2004: 143–66.

———. "Slayers of the Last Arc." In *Seven Seasons of Buffy: Science Fiction and Fantasy Writers Discuss Their Favorite Television Show*. Dallas, TX: Benbella Books, 2003: 195–205.

Holder, Nancy, with Jeff Mariotte and Maryelizabeth Hart. *Buffy the Vampire Slayer: The Watcher's Guide*. *Volume 2*. New York: Pocket Books, 2000. 472 pp.

———, with Jeff Mariotte and Maryelizabeth Hart. *Angel: The Casefiles*. Vol. *1*. NY: Simon Pulse, 2002. 405 pp.

Holmes, Sherlock

Dracula and Sherlock Holmes vie with each other as the most popular fictional character in the English-speaking world. ***Dracula* (1897)** is the single novel most frequently made into a movie, while Sherlock Holmes, the subject of 56 short stories and four novels, is the character most frequently brought to the screen (with **Dracula** a close second). Both have been the subject of many more additional books and stories by authors who use one or the other as their central figure.

The Sussex Vampire: Sherlock Holmes had only one brush with a vampire. The short story, "The Adventure of the Sussex Vampire" appeared in the January 1924 issue of the *Strand Magazine,* just six months before the dramatic version of *Dracula* written by **Hamilton Deane** opened in rural England. The story began with an inquiry concerning vampires, to which Holmes made what has become one of his more famous lines, "Rubbish, Watson, rubbish! What have we to do with walking corpses who can only be held in their grave by **stakes** driven through their hearts? It's pure lunacy." Watson reminded him that vampirism might take the form of a living person sucking the **blood** of someone younger in order to retain his or her youth (a probable reference to the case of **Elizabeth Bathory**). Their client, Robert Ferguson, related an incident in which his wife was found apparently biting the neck of their infant son and immediately afterwards was seen with blood on her mouth. To Holmes the idea of a vampire, even the more human one described by Watson, was absurd. "Such things do not happen in criminal practice in England." But, Holmes asked rhetorically, "Could not a bleeding wound be sucked for other than vampiric reasons?" Holmes simply thought of the alternative, that the mother was in fact sucking poison from a wound the child had received from his older jealous stepbrother.

While *Dracula* was enjoying success on the stage throughout the country, "The Adventure of the Sussex Vampire" received its first dramatization in a 1929–30 British radio series of *The Adventures of Sherlock Holmes*, prepared for broadcast by Edith Meiser. Her version would be the one most frequently used when other adaptations were made, such as the first American radio dramatization in 1936 and the Basil Rathbone/Nigel Bruce portrayals in 1939–40 and 1941–42. The first **television** adaptations occurred in the fall of 1964 for the BBC. Most recently, the story has become the subject of two movies: *Sherlock Holmes in Caracas* (Venezuela, 1992) and *Sherlock Holmes: The Last Vampire* (**United Kingdom**, 1992), the latter being a made-for-television movie in the Jeremy Brett/Edward Hardwicke series of Sherlock Holmes stories.

Holmes Meets Dracula: Over the decades there have been several attempts to link Sherlock Holmes to the Dracula story. For instance, Sherlockians have entertained themselves with a debate that Dr. **Abraham Van Helsing** was in fact Sherlock Holmes in disguise. Purists, however, have rejected such a notion. Since both Sherlock Holmes and Dracula were pictured by their creators, Arthur Conan Doyle and **Bram Stoker**, as contemporaries in the Victorian world of the late nineteenth century, it was inevitable that, in view of the recent revived interest in each, someone would suggest their interaction. A hint of what was to come appeared in 1976 when Nicholas Meyer added Bram Stoker as a character in *The West End Horror,* a new Sherlock Holmes story. Two years later, two different authors picked up on the suggestion.

Loren D. Estleman, writing as Holmes's chronicler Dr. John H. Watson, authored *Sherlock Holmes vs. Dracula: The Adventures of the Sanguinary Count.* What would happen if Holmes were called in to solve the case of the *Demeter,* the ship that brought Dracula to **London** but then was found mysteriously wrecked at **Whitby** with all its crew dead. And then while working on the case, Holmes's interest was drawn to the accounts of the "Bloofer Lady," **Lucy Westenra** as a vampire preying on the local children of Hamstead Heath. The great detective followed his clues as he became involved in the events of the original novel and was led to his own confrontation with Dracula.

Estleman closely followed the characterizations of the creators of Holmes and Dracula: Holmes was good; Dracula was the epitome of evil. Not so for **Fred Saberhagen**. In his series of novels, Saberhagen saw Dracula as a misunderstood and maligned figure, the **victim** of the ignorant and malicious Dr. **John Seward**. In the second of his series of novels, *The Holmes-Dracula Files,* Saberhagen brought the two characters together, but had to accommodate the plot to the reversal already made in *The Dracula Tape* (1975). The story revolved around a plot to destroy London during Queen Victoria's Jubilee celebration. The story was complicated by Dracula's being hit on the head, resulting in a case of amnesia. He could not remember who he was, not even his vampiric nature. To add a little color, he and Holmes were the spitting image of each other, even Holmes's companion Dr. Watson had trouble telling them apart. Could they, however, pool their resources to defeat the evil Dr. Seward? After the double-barreled blast from Estleman and Saberhagen, it wasn't until the 1980s that Dracula and Holmes would again be brought together. They had a brief encounter in *Dracula's Diary* (1982), in which Dracula made a scenic tour of Victorian characters. Then, in the early stages of the vampire's return to **comic books** in 1987, Dracula was pitted against several of his Victorian contemporaries, from Jack the Ripper to Sherlock Holmes. On the centennial of "A Study in Scarlet," the first Holmes story, Martin Powell published *Scarlet in Gaslight,* a four-issue series that began with Holmes's traditional nemesis, Professor Moriarty, traveling to **Transylvania** to make common cause with Dracula. Holmes had been drawn into the count's domain, however, by the mother of Lucy Westenra, who had begun to show mysterious symptoms of fatigue and blood loss. Holmes was sharp enough to trace Dracula in Lucy's bedroom in Whitby. In the end, however, he was unable to prevent her death.

Meanwhile, Moriarty had developed a plot to release a plague of vampires on London, though his alliance with Dracula had fallen apart. Eventually, Dracula and Holmes united to stop the professor. Dracula only wanted to have the now vampiric Lucy at his side. He was thwarted when she was killed (the true death) in the final encounters in

London. The main characters survived, to meet one last time at the famous falls in Switzerland where Holmes faked his own death and, with relish, Dracula killed Moriarty. In *The Dracula Caper* (1988, the eighth in the Time Wars series by Simon Hawke), Holmes does not appear, but Doyle teams with Bram Stoker to save the world from Dracula. The most recent encounter between Holmes and Dracula found but a small audience of Holmes enthusiasts. Published in a limited edition, it quickly sold out. In *The Tangled Skein*, author David Stuart Davies picked up the plot of "The Hound of the Baskervilles," one of the most famous Holmes stories. Stapleton, the villain of the earlier story, returned to continue his evil, but was soon surpassed by a series of bloody murders that served to bring Dr. Van Helsing into Holmes's territory. The two were forced to unite their efforts to deal with both Stapleton and Dracula.

The possible encounter of Sherlock Holmes and a vampire has just been too tantalizing to leave alone; several authors have picked up the challenge of keeping Holmes true to Doyle's character while sending him off to pit his mind against the irrational. Val Andrews's *Sherlock Holmes and the Longacre Vampire* begins with a series of unusual murders occasioned by, or at least associated with, the opening of *Dracula* in Henry Irving's theatre (which, of course, never occurred). Holmes must move in to discover what lies behind the seemingly vampire-caused deaths. In Stephen Seitz's *Sherlock Holmes and the Plague of Dracula*, **Mina Murray** engages Holmes's services to locate **Jonathan Harker**, her future husband who has disappeared during his trip to Transylvania. Holmes must go east to encounter Dracula and bring his client's lost love back home.

Sources:

Andrews, Val. *Sherlock Holmes and the Longacre Vampire*. London: Breese Books, 2001. 125 pp.

Cox, Greg. *The Transylvanian Library: A Consumer's Guide to Vampire Fiction*. San Bernardino, CA: Borgo Press, 1993. 264 pp.

Doyle, Arthur Conan. *The Annotated Sherlock Holmes*. 2 vols. New York: Clarkson N. Potter, 1967.

Eyles, Allen. *Sherlock Holmes: A Centenary Celebration*. London: John Murray, 1986. 141 pp.

Geare, Michael, and Michael Corby. *Dracula's Dairy*. New York: Beaufort Books, 1982. 153 pp.

Godfrey, Robert. "'Tangled Skein' Heading for the Big Screen." *Sherlock Holmes Gazette* 8 (Autumn 1993): 36–37.

Hawke, Simon. *The Dracula Caper*. Time War No. 8. New York: Berkley Ace, 1988. 212 pp.

Jones, Kevin. *The Carfax Syndrome: Being a Study of Vampirism in the Canoin*. New York: Magico Magazine, 1964. 18 pp.

Saberhagen, Fred. *The Holmes-Dracula File*. New York: Ace Books, 1978. 249 pp.

Scarlet in Gaslight. 4 vols. Newbury Park, CA: Eternity Comics, 1987–88.

Seitz, Steven. *Sherlock Holmes and the Plague of Dracula*. Shaftsbury, CT: Mountainside Press, 2006. 208 pp.

Watson, John H. (pseudonym of Loren D. Estleman). *Sherlock Holmes vs. Dracula: The Adventure of the Sanguinary Count*. New York: Doubleday & Company, 1978. 211 pp. Rept. New York: Penguin Books, 1979. 214 pp.

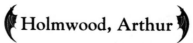

Holmwood, Arthur

The Honorable Arthur Holmwood, one of the leading characters in **Bram Stoker**'s novel, **Dracula, (1897)** was first mentioned in chapter five as **Lucy Westenra**'s true love, and soon afterward he asked Lucy to marry him. He was tied to two other characters, Dr. **John Seward** and **Quincey P. Morris**, with whom he had traveled to various parts of the world. Holmwood did not participate in much of the early action of the novel because his father's illness called him from Lucy's side. Later in the novel, following his father's death, he became the new Lord Godalming.

Holmwood appeared in **Whitby** soon after Lucy's first encounter with **Dracula**. He called Seward to examine her, and gave her one of the needed transfusions. He also joined in the futile watch before Dracula's last attack. Just before her death, as she was turning into a vampire, Lucy tried to attack him, but he was saved by **Abraham Van Helsing**, who had been called in as a consultant by Seward. Holmwood was hesitant in responding to Van Helsing's call to treat Lucy as a vampire, but he finally joined Van Helsing, Seward, and Morris in trapping and killing her. With Van Helsing at his side, he drove the **stake** into her body and assisted in removing her head and filling her mouth with **garlic**.

Becoming an integral part of the team to search out and destroy Dracula, Holmwood entered **Carfax** to sanitize Dracula's home base of the vampire's influence. He also went into south and west **London** with Morris to seek out Dracula's other resting places. He traveled with **Mina Murray** and the team to **Transylvania** and was present in the final confrontation near the castle when both Dracula and Morris were killed. In the movement of the novel to the stage and screen, Holmwood has received quite varied treatment. He, like Morris, was dropped from the stage play as a superfluous character. And, as might be expected, he did not appear with **Bela Lugosi** in *Dracula* **(1931),** which was based on the play. However, he came to the center in the ***The Horror of Dracula*** (1957) as the husband of Mina and brother of Lucy. In that movie, the Holmwood household became the target of Dracula's attack in England. He was also present in **Francis Ford Coppola**'s ***Bram Stoker's Dracula***, where his part (portrayed by Cary Elwes) most closely approximated his role in the novel.

Sources:

Holte, James Craig. *Dracula in the Dark: The Dracula Film Adaptations*. Westport, CT: Greenwood Press, 1997. 161 pp.

Waller, Gregory A. *The Living and the Undead: From Stoker's Dracula to Romero's Dawn of the Dead*. Urbana, IL: University of Illinois Press, 1986. 376 pp.

❮ Homosexuality and the Vampire ❯

The vampire, especially in its literary and cinematic form, mixed elements of horror and **sexuality**. To many, it became a symbol of the release of the powerful emotional energies believed to be bottled up by restrictions on sexual behavior common to many societies. Homosexual behavior had always been suppressed during the centuries of Christian dominance of the West, and thus, it could be expected that in the heightened sensuality associated with vampirism, some homosexual elements might be present—and such has been the case. Literary critics have long noted a homosexual aspect among the very first pieces of vampire literature.

Samuel Taylor Coleridge's "Christabel", the first vampire poem in English, portended a theme that would reappear in vampire literature—**lesbian vampire** relationships. The poem centers upon the vampiric relationship of Christabel and Geraldine, the vampire. It became the inspiration for "Carmilla", the 1872 short story by **Sheridan Le Fanu**, in which the sexual element was even more pronounced. As other female vampires appeared in succeeding decades, primarily in short stories, the lesbian element often hovered in the background.

However, while there was a recurring lesbian presence in vampire literature, the same could not be said of male homosexuality. The male vampires of the nineteenth century—from **Lord Ruthven** to **Varney the Vampyre** to **Dracula**—invariably sank their teeth into female **victims**. This strict male heterosexuality was emphasized in *Dracula* **(1897)** the first major work to include male vampire victims. **Jonathan Harker** was not touched by Dracula, but remained behind as a feast for his vampire **brides** when Dracula departed for **London**. Nor did Dracula view any of **Lucy Westenra**'s suitors as additional sources of **blood**; he turned rather to **Mina Murray**. His several confrontations with the men were only in terms of physical combat. In the movies, one could also note the absence of male vampires attacking male victims. When the plot called for such men-on-men attacks, they were always mediated by modern medicine, in the form of needles and transfusions (as in *The Return of Dr. X* and *Blood of the Vampire*) or by way of an animal (as in *The Devil Bat*). Not until the sexual revolution of the 1960s did a male homosexual vampire appear. The first gay vampire movie, a pornographic production, was *Does Dracula Really Suck?* (also released as *Dracula Sucks* and as *Dracula and the Boys*). During the 1970s several additional titles with gay vampires appeared: *Sons of Satan* (1973), *Tenderness of Wolves* (1973), and an Italian film, *Il Cavaliere Costante Nicosia Demoniaco Ovvero Dracula in Brianza* (1975). Of these, only *Tenderness of Wolves* was released to the general public. The movie was devoted to the case of **Fritz Haarmann,** a homosexual serial killer who murdered a number of young boys and drank their blood. Two additional gay vampire movies also appeared in the filmographies: *Gayracula* (1983) and the undated *Love Bites* (1993). There is a small selection of x-rated movies with a vampire theme such as *The Vampire of Budapest* (1995).

In 2007, the first gay-oriented vampire television series, *The Lair*, aired on here!, a gay television network. Developed from the successful series *Dante's Cove*, *The Lair* was built around a nightclub that gave its name to the series. The club is home to a group of vampires that includes Colin (Dylan Vox), who manages the club and Damian (Peter Stickles), the group's leader. Action centers on the vulnerability of the club from law enforcement and the press discovering the dangers to those who wander in unsuspecting of the club's true nature.

The first season (six episodes) aired in 2007, season two (thirteen episodes) in 2008, and the third season in 2009. The first two season were released on DVD.

In literature, gay and lesbian vampires have made relatively few appearances. The first writer to become known for his gay vampire writings was Jeffrey N. McMahan. His first book, *Somewhere in the Night*, a Lambda Literary Award winner, was a collection of short horror stories that included several vampire tales. He also introduced the character of Andrew, a gay vampire who went on to become the subject of a novel, *Vampires Anonymous*, in which a modern-day **vampire hunter** and a vampire recovery group seek to cure individuals of vampirism. Andrew and the vampire community, however, see no need to be cured. The most significant expression of a vampiric gay relationship came not from a gay

writer, but in several novels by **Anne Rice**. Her first novel, ***Interview with the Vampire***, featured the intense relationship between Louis and **Lestat de Lioncourt**, the homosexual connotations of which were not missed by reviewers. Rice was not attempting to highlight sexual orientation issues so much as gender issues—specifically, androgyny. However, this idea of male androgyny has frequently masked a more central concern for homosexuality or bisexuality. Lestat was pictured as one who easily bonded with males and frequently cried. Yet, when he briefly switched bodies with mortal, Raglan James, he raped a woman. In several of Rice's novels, male vampires could not have "normal" intercourse—their sex organs being dysfunctional. She suggested, however, that the experience of biting and sucking blood was a far superior form of sex; the mutual sharing of blood by two vampires was an act analogous to intercourse. The Rice novels have been a source for the modern **gothic** rock movement, whose fans value the androgynous ideal and have opened their circles to homosexuality and other sexual expressions, such as transvestism and sadomasochism.

In the wake of Rice's popularity in the gay/lesbian community, a host of novels and short story collections have appeared specifically geared for a lesbian and gay audience. Emerging in the first decade of the twenty-first century as a gay vampire writer is Michael Schiefelbein. Schiefelbein uses his years of training for the priesthood and his ultimate rejection of the Roman Catholic Church (and the church of him) as the emotional hook into the continuing stories of Victor Decimus, a Roman officer who served in Palestine at the time of Jesus. When Jesus rejected him, he became a vampire and now spends his time corrupting devout young men (mostly in monastic setting) and thereby undermining the Church that grew from Jesus's life. The adventures began with *Vampire Vow* (2001) and have continued in *Vampire Thrall* (2003) and *Vampire Transgression* (2006), with future stories in the works.

Lesbian readers found their vampire interests best expressed by African American writer Jewelle Gomez whose *Gilda Stories* (1991) has been recognized from beyond the lesbian and gay communities. It traces the story of a lesbian vampire who began life as a slave in Mississippi in the 1850s. She ran away from serfdom and each chapter allows the reader to see her maturation and development once she is introduced to vampiric existence. While the short story has become the most prominent focus of lesbian vampires, additional novels include *Virago* (1990) and *Bloodsong* (1997) by Karen Marie Christa Minns, *Shadows after Dark* (1992) by Ouida Crozier, *Scarlet Thirst* (2002) by Crin Claxton, and *Soapsuds* (2005) by Finola Hughes and Digby Diehl.

Gays and lesbians interested in vampires founded two organizations in the early 1990s (though neither survived for many years). Bite Me in the Coffin Not in the Closet Fan Club was a vampire fan organization for gay and lesbian people who have an interest in vampires and vampirism. Founder Jeff Flaster of Middletown, New York, also edited the club's monthly fanzine, which published short fiction for and about gay and lesbian vampires, contact information for members, and other items of interest. Also operating for a few years in the early 1990s was the Secret Room, a Texas-based organization for gay/lesbian/bisexual fans of the ***Dark Shadows* television** series. Lesbian and gay interest in vampires is currently given focus on the Internet at the Queer Vampires site, http://www.queerhorror.com/Qvamp/.

Sources:

Bowen, Gary. *Diary of a Vampire*. New York: Rhinoceros, 1995. 232 pp.

Claxton, Crin. *Scarlet Thirst*. London: Diva Books, 2002. 270 pp.

Gomez, Jewelle. Ithaca. *The Gilda Stories*. New York: Firebrand Books, 1991. 252 pp.

Hughes, Finola, and Digby Diehl. *Soapsuds*. New York: Ballantine Books, 2005. 384 pp.

Jones, Stephen. *The Illustrated Vampire Movie Guide*. London: Titan Books, 1993. 144 pp.

Keesey, Pam. *Vamps: An Illustrated History of the Femme Fatale*. San Francisco, CA: Cleis Press, 1997. 171 pp.

McMahan, Jeffrey N. *Somewhere in the Night*. Boston, MA: Alyson Publications, 1989. 182 pp.

———. *Vampires Anonymous*. Boston, MA: Alyson Publications, 1992. 253 pp.

Ramsland, Katherine. *The Vampire Companion*. New York: Ballantine Books, 1993. 506 pp.

Rice, Anne. *Interview with the Vampire*. New York: Alfred A. Knopf, 1976.

Rowe, Michael, and Thomas S. Roche, eds. *Sins of Darkness: Tales of Men, Blood, and Immortality*. Pittsburgh: Cleis Press, 1996. 173 pp.

Schiefelbein, Michael. *Vampire Vow*. Los Angeles: Alyson Publications, 2001. 203 pp.

———. *Blood Brothers*. Los Angeles: Alyson Publications, 2002. 220 pp.

———. *Vampire Thrall*. Los Angeles: Alyson Publications, 2003. 302 pp.

———. *Vampire Transgression*. New York: St Martin's Press, 2006.

The Horror of Dracula

Second only to the **Bela Lugosi** version of *Dracula* (**1931**) in setting the image of Dracula in contemporary popular culture was the first of the **Hammer Films** *Dracula* movies starring **Christopher Lee**. Originally released as *Dracula* (1958), it subsequently was released in the United States as *The Horror of Dracula*, the title commonly used to distinguish it not only from the other *Dracula* movies, but from the host of Christopher Lee Dracula/vampire films. The movement of Hammer Films into the horror market has become one of the most famous stories in motion picture history. *The Horror of Dracula* came on the heels of the company's success with a new version of *Frankenstein*, and utilized the following team: Christopher Lee as Dracula; **Peter Cushing** as **Abraham Van Helsing**; and **Terence Fisher** and **Jimmy Sangster** as director and screenwriter, respectively.

While having the 1931 **Universal Pictures** production as a persistent reference point, *The Horror of Dracula* attempted to reinterpret the story and return to the **Bram Stoker** novel for inspiration (though it deviated from both the novel and the previous movie in important ways). The story opened with **Jonathan Harker** (John Van Eyssen) coming to **Castle Dracula** not as a real estate agent, but as Dracula's new librarian. Here, prior to Dracula's appearance, he encountered a young woman dressed in nightclothes. It soon was revealed that he was an undercover agent and had, in fact, come to Castle Dracula as Van Helsing's assistant to kill Dracula. Harker was attacked and bitten by the woman (Valerie Gaunt), whom he in turn killed. But in the process he became a vampire himself. (*The Horror of Dracula* popularized the assumption that a single bite by a vampire was all that was necessary for one to become a vampire—an opinion not proposed in Stoker's novel.) In this movie, Dracula escaped before Van Helsing arrived at Castle Dracula to check on his co-conspirator. Discovering that Harker had been compromised, Van Helsing was forced to **stake** him, and he returned to England to begin a one-on-one confrontation with Dracula, which was the true subject of the film.

Dracula beat Van Helsing to England, where a new configuration of Stoker's familiar characters had been created. Gone were Dr. **John Seward**, **R. N. Renfield**, and **Quincey P. Morris**. **Arthur Holmwood** (Michael Gough) emerged as the dominant male. Rather than a suitor of **Lucy Westenra** (Carol Marsh), however, he was married to **Mina Murray** (Melissa Stribling), and Lucy was recast as his sister (and Harker's fiance). Lucy also was the primary object of Dracula's interest, he having taken her picture from Harker before leaving the castle. Van Helsing discovered that Lucy already had been bitten and was vampirizing others, so he took the lead in killing her. An angry Dracula then attacked Mina.

In the final scene, Holmwood and Van Helsing chased Dracula back to his home. Dracula had discarded Mina in an open grave and was burying her when the **hunters** arrived. Arthur went to his wife's side while Van Helsing chased Dracula into his castle. Dracula had all but defeated Van Helsing, but, as so many villains before him, he paused to experience a very human moment of satisfaction. In that moment, Van Helsing recovered and, pushing the vampire aside, he rushed across the room and pulled the draperies from the window, allowing **sunlight** to stream into the room. The sunlight, which was fatal to vampires, caught Dracula's foot and quickly burned it. Grabbing a **crucifix**, Van Helsing pushed Dracula farther into the light, which then completely consumed him. Dracula's ashes blew away in the wind, leaving only his large ring. (The ring and ashes would become important in future Hammer *Dracula* sequels, though there seems no reason to believe that Fisher had a sequel in mind when completing the *The Horror of Dracula*.) By the same sunlight that killed Dracula, Mina was cured of her vampirism, and she and her husband were happily reunited.

Two elements contributed to the success of *The Horror of Dracula*. First, the movie presented a new openness toward **sexuality**. There is every reason to believe that the interpretation of the **psychological perspectives on vampire mythology**, such as that offered by Ernest Jones's now classic study *On the Nightmare* (1931), underlay the movie's presentation. That sexual element began with Harker's encounter with one of Dracula's **brides**. While Harker drew her to what he thought was a protective embrace, she gleefully took full advantage of the situation and bit him, a scene that has been the object of various psychological interpretations relative to teenage sexual awakening. That interpretation was reinforced by his subsequent attack on the woman with his stake. Harker's naive actions, of course, prove fatal.

Dracula was just as sexual as his vampire bride. He seduced the women he bit with kisses and gained their loving attention before he sank his teeth in their neck. As David J. Hogan, in *Dark Romance: Sexuality in the Horror Film*, notes, "When he (Lee) bites a young lovely's throat he is not merely feeding, but experiencing (and inducing) a moment of orgasmic ecstasy." Lee would go on from the *The Horror of Dracula* to become an international star and, like Lugosi, to develop a large and loyal female following.

The second element of success of *The Horror of Dracula* was that it was the first *Dracula* movie to be made in Technicolor. It made full use of red liquids from the still little understood **blood** dripping on a crypt during the opening credits to its more appropriate reappearances throughout the picture. Color added a new dimension to the horror movie and secured its revival in the 1960s. Color also cooperated with the heightened level of freedom concerning what could be pictured on the screen. In 1931, Dracula never showed his **fangs** or bit anyone on camera. However, Lee regularly showed his teeth and had no problem offering the women his vampire kiss.

Sources:

Hogan, David J. *Dark Romance: Sexuality in the Horror Film.* Jefferson, NC: McFarland & Company, 1986. 334 pp.

Holte, James Craig. *Dracula in the Dark: The Dracula Film Adaptations.* Westport, CT: Greenwood Press, 1997. 161 pp.

Jones, Ernest. *On the Nightmare.* New York: Liveright Publishing Company, 1951. 374 pp. Originally published in 1931.

Ursini, James, and Alain Silver. *The Vampire Film: From Nosferatu to Bram Stoker's Dracula.* New York: Limelight Editions, 2004. 342 pp.

Waller, Gregory A. *The Living and the Undead: From Stoker's Dracula to Romero's Dawn of the Undead.* Urbana, IL: University of Illinois Press, 1986. 376 pp.

❦ Hour of the Wolf ❦

Although few critics actually associate Swedish writer and director Ingmar Bergman with vampires, *Hour of the Wolf* (1968) recalls images of **Universal Pictures's Dracula (1931)**. The Swedish movie is in black and white with English subtitles and a running time of approximately 90 minutes. Visual references in *Hour of the Wolf* from *Frankenstein, Dracula, The Bride of Frankenstein, The Birds*, and *Psycho* abound along with eerie castle interiors resembling Hollywood's **gothic** era. *The Hour of the Wolf* is one of Bergman's "darker" films, a nightmarish descent into death, vampires, and **sexuality**; its extreme contrast of intense light and dark shadows is a reminder of the German Expressionist style of earlier Hollywood horror movies. As a few Bergman biographers have pointed out, one of the movie's characters, the archivist Lindhorst (Georg Rydeberg), bears a striking resemblance to **Bela Lugosi**'s **Dracula**.

Hour of the Wolf is an allegory about a personality disintegration of a creative artist. The story revolves around Johan (Max von Sydow), a painter who lives on a remote island with his wife Alma (Liv Ullmann). Johan struggles with nightmares and personal demons and even attempts to kill Alma (the story is told from her point of view). The couple is invited to wine and dinner by the island's owner, Baron von Merkens (Erland Josephson), who lives in a neighboring castle. But the guests appear to be references to monsters from classic horror movies: the Baron's face recalls contours in Boris Karloff's **Frankenstein monster**, an old woman peels off her face to reveal a decomposing skull and gaping eye sockets resembling Mrs. Bates's corpse in *Psycho*, and Lindhorst's dark widow's peak, sinister gleaming eyes, and malevolent grin are a match for Lugosi's Count Dracula. There's a reference to **fangs** during the dinner-table conversation, and a quick shot of Lindhorst flapping his "wings" among a flock of birds.

As one of the most influential and acclaimed artists of modern cinema, Bergman (1918–2007) directed and/or wrote close to 67 films during his lifetime. Some of his memorable pictures include *Wild Strawberries* (1957), *Through a Glass Darkly* (1961), *Persona* (1966), and *Cries and Whispers* (1972). *Hour of the Wolf*, or *Vargtimmen* in Swedish, was originally titled *The Cannibals*, perhaps referring to the castle's residents feasting on Johan's blood. The movie was later referenced in another vampire film, *The Hunger* (1983).

Sources:

Gervais, Marc. *Ingmar Bergman: Magician and Prophet.* Montreal: McGill-Queen's University Press, 1999. 257 pp.

Milne, Tom. "Review of Hour of the Wolf from Time Out." 1968. *Bergmanorma: The Magic Works of Ingmar Bergman.* Posted at www.Bergmanorama.webs.com. Accessed on April 8, 2010.

Scheider, Dan. "Hour Of The Wolf by Ingmar Bergman." *Alternative Film Guide.* Posted at http://www.altfg.com/blog/film-reviews/hour-of-the-wolf-ingmar-bergman/. Accessed on April 8, 2010.

Wood, Robin. *Ingmar Bergman.* New York: Frederick A. Praeger, Inc., 1969. 191 pp.

Houston Dark Shadows Society *see:* Dark Shadows Fandom

Huff, Tanya (1957–)

Tanya Huff, a Canadian writer and author of several **science fiction**/fantasy novel series and preeminently of two series of vampire novels, was born in Halifax, Nova Scotia, and attended Ryerson Polytechnical Institute where she earned an associate's degree in Radio and Television Arts. In the mid-1980s she opened Bakka, now Toronto's main science fiction book store, and turned to writing during her spare time. Her first published works were children's fantasy fiction stories.

Huff endeared herself to vampire fans with the series of novels about detective Vicki Nelson, formerly a police officer who had been forced to retire due to failing eyesight. In her first advent, *Blood Price*, she becomes involved in a case in which a serial killer is leaving bodies scattered around Toronto drained of **blood**. She soon encountered Henry Fitzroy, an illegitimate son of King Henry VIII and a vampire now living in Canada. Fitzroy was brought out of his private world by the killing, which he attributed to a young vampire in the throes of a feeding frenzy. Their work together to solve the case would lead to their sharing both their bedroom and a series of adventures into the supernatural.

Fitzroy is similar to traditional vampires except, since he is not evil, Huff saw no reason for religious symbols like the cross to harm him, and equally could see no reason that he should defy the laws of physics by creating no reflection in the mirror. After the fourth Nelson/Fitzroy novel in 1993, rumors flew around that Huff was abandoning her characters and for five years nothing more was heard of her. However, in 1997, they again appeared, much to the delight of Huff's fans. Then in 2007, the novels were adapted for two seasons on television that aired in the spring and fall of 2007 under the title *Blood Ties*. The DVDs of the series were released in 2009. Meanwhile, Huff launched a new series of novels built around Tony Foster, Fitzroy's former donor and gay lover. In this series he has moved to Vancouver to take a job in television, interestingly on a show about a vampire detective. The first of the trilogy, *Smoke and Shadows* appeared in 2004, to be followed by *Smoke and Mirrors* (2005) and *Smoke and Ashes* (2006).

Sources:

Harrell, Megan. "Interview with Tanya Huff." Foxfire News. Posted at http://firefox.org/news/articles/258/1/Interview-with-Tanya-Huff/Page1.html. Accessed on April 8, 2010.

Mel Brooks's *Dracula: Dead and Loving It* is a prime example of vampire humor. Leslie Neilsen played the hapless Count Dracula.

Huff, Tanya. *Blood Price*. New York: Daw Books, 1991. 272 pp.
———. *Blood Trail*. New York: Daw Books, 1992. 304 pp.
———. *Blood Lines*. New York: Daw Books, 1993. 271 pp.
———. *Blood Pact*. New York: Daw Books, 1993. 332 pp.
———. *Blood Debt*. New York: Daw Books, 1997. 330 pp.
———. *Smoke and Mirrors*. New York: DAW, 2004. 374 pp.
———. *Smoke and Shadows*. New York: DAW, 2004. 375 pp.
———. *Smoke and Ashes*. New York: DAW, 2006. 400 pp.
———. *Blood Bank*. DAW, 2008. 336 pp.

Humor, Vampire

To some, the stage vampire was essentially humorous, and the thought of being lampooned in the press was partially responsible for keeping **Hamilton Deane** from bringing his original *Dracula* play, which had been quite successful in rural England, to

London. In fact, a comedic version of the Deane play, *Dracula, the Comedy of the Vampire*, appeared at various locations around Europe in the 1930s. With his knowledge of the theater, Deane could have expected some amount of fun to be had at his play's expense. A century earlier, **Charles Nodier** brought the vampire to the stage in Paris. Within a few months, several other vampire plays, all farces and most comments upon his play, opened in competing Parisian theaters. The fact that vampire humor first appeared on stage was an indication of its future. Vampires as objects of humor made their primary appearance on the stage, and more recently in motion pictures, rather than in novels. Vampire books usually have been horror stories with only very rare hints of humor. Meanwhile, a stereotypical vampire was gradually created in the successive productions of *Dracula*, Hamilton Deane's original play in England (1924), and the portrayals of **Bela Lugosi** in the American play in 1927 and **Universal Pictures**' movie version in 1931. The creation of the vampire's image on the stage and screen provided the context for future opportunities to lampoon that image. To a much lesser extent, vampire fiction was not tied to the Lugosi vampire, while even the most variant vampire movie had to use the stereotypical Dracula as its starting point.

The spread of popular vampire humor awaited the creation of the widely recognized stereotypical cinematic vampire by Bela Lugosi in the 1930s. The first major attempt to exploit the humorous possibilities of Lugosi's **Dracula** occurred in the 1948 *Abbott and Costello Meet Frankenstein*. The plot of the movie revolved around Dracula's attempt to steal comedian Lou Costello's brain and place it in the head of **Franken-stein's monster**. Lugosi returned to his Dracula role for the spoof, which in retrospect received high marks as one of Abbott and Costello's best movies. It was said to be far superior to *Abbott and Costello Meet Dr. Jekyll and Mr. Hyde* (1953), in which an unnamed actor made a cameo appearance as Dracula.

The 1950s: Mainstream vampire humor in the 1950s was limited to two movies and a play. Early in the decade, Lugosi traveled to England to portray another vampire, Count Von Housen, in one of the series of Old Mother Riley comedies. *Mother Riley Meets the Vampire* (1952; a.k.a. *My Son the Vampire*) was one of his less remembered roles. Lugosi's stereotyping as a horror actor drastically limited the roles offered him as he aged and led him to construct a 1954 Las Vegas stage production, "The Bela Lugosi Review", in which he was forced to play a spoof of the part he had made famous. In the second 1950s comedic vampire movie, *The Bowery Boys Meet the Monsters*, the vampire was secondary to the plot, which featured one of the Bowery Boys (Huntz Hall) being turned into a **werewolf**. More important than both of these movies was the first new vampire play in several decades. *I Was a Teenage Dracula*, a three-act mystery by Gene Donovan, heralded some 40 sub-

Halloween greeting cards specialize in vampire humor.

sequent plays featuring Dracula for high school and other amateur productions, the great majority of which were comedies.

The 1960s: The 1960s saw the production of one of the best comic vampire movies ever made, Roman Polanski's *The Fearless Vampire Killers* or *Pardon Me, But Your Teeth Are in My Neck* (1967). Polanski's film (originally called *Dance of the Vampires*) concerned the antics of two **vampire hunters**, Professor Ambronsius and his assistant (played by Polanski), as they tracked down the villainous Count Von Krolock (Ferdy Mayne). Among the more memorable scenes was a bizarre dance sequence from which the movie took its name.

However, the comic vampire really found a home on two **television** series, *The Addams Family* and *The Munsters*. Both shows attempted to place the classical "monsters," including several vampirelike characters, in an ordinary, "normal" middle-class American setting, and both ran through the 1964/65 and 1965/66 seasons. Both shows inspired early **comic books** that introduced the comic vampire to that medium. The Munsters, which featured a thinly disguised Count Dracula, led to a movie, *Munster Go Home!* (1966). The **gothic** soap opera *Dark Shadows* became a hit daytime show on NBC during the last years of the decade. Among the items created as a result of the show was possibly the first vampire joke book, *Barnabas Collins in a Funny Vein*, published in 1969. A second *Dark Shadows* joke book appeared in 1981, *Die Laughing*, compiled by Barbara Fister-Liltz and Kathy Resch. A comedy **drama** featuring the Transylvanian Count included several plays simply entitled *Dracula* that originally were staged in 1965 and 1966, respectively.

The 1970s: The 1970s opened with a new vampire play, *I'm Sorry, the Bridge Is Out, You'll Have to Spend the Night*, a musical comedy featuring the songs of Sheldon Allman and Bob Pickett. Allman had made a record titled *Sing Along with Drac*, which included such memorable titles as "Children's Day at the Morgue" and "Fangs for the Memory." Pickett had been the Dracula voice in the 1962 album *The Monster Mash*, which included not only the title song but "Blood Bank Blues" and "Transylvania Twist." The spoof opened in Los Angeles on April 28, 1970 at the Coronet Theatre. It featured several of the classic Universal monsters and included the insect-eating **R. N. Renfield**, from *Dracula*, who had his solo moment with a song called "Flies."

Several other vampire plays made their initial appearance in the 1970s. Both *Count Dracula* or *A Musical Mania for Transylvania* and *Monster Soup* or *That Thing in My Neck Is a Tooth* were staged in 1974. They were joined by *The Vampire's Bride* or *The Perils of Cinderella* (1979) later in the decade. The decade closed with what generally has been considered the best of the many comedy vampire movies, *Love at First Bite* (1979). George Hamilton played a modern Dracula in prerevolutionary **Romania**. As the movie opened, Dracula played the piano. The howls of the wolves grew louder and louder, and, in a slightly altered version of one of Bela Lugosi's famous lines, he shouted out, "Children of the night, shut up!" Forced out of his castle by the Communist government, he took the opportunity to search out a New York fashion model (Susan Saint James), with whose picture he had fallen in love. There he met Saint James's psychiatrist, a descendant of **Abraham Van Helsing** (Richard Benjamin). The movie was a delightful mixture of hilarious one-liners and humorous situations, such as Dracula waking up in the midst of a funeral service in an African American church.

Bela Lugosi played the Dracula-like Count Von Housen in the comedy *My Son the Vampire*.

Possibly second in popularity only to *Love at First Bite* as a humorous treatment of the vampire theme was *Andy Warhol's Dracula* (a.k.a. *Blood for Dracula*, an Italian production in which Dracula traveled to **Italy** looking for the **blood** of "wirgins.") The humor centers upon his comment on modern society and the inability to find a virtuous (sexually pure) young woman—a fact graphically displayed by his regurgitating every time he got blood from an apparently virginal female. In 1977, the first family of television comic horror, *The Addams Family*, returned with a full length movie, *Halloween with the Addams Family*, but response was disappointing. An adult sexually oriented comedy, *Dracula Blows His Cool* (1979), was produced in West **Germany** and dubbed in English for an American audience.

In 1974, Phil Hirsch and Paul Laikin compiled a new collection of vampire humor in *Vampire Jokes and Cartoons*. The 1970s also marked the appearance of **juvenile vampire literature**, specifically designed for children and teens. Overwhelmingly, the approach to the vampire in children's books was very light (using vampires to teach tolerance for children who were different) to comedic. One of the more comic and delightful vampire characters for kids was **Bunnicula** (1979), a vegetarian vampire rabbit who slept during the day and attacked vegetables to suck out the juice at night. The rabbit presaged **Count Duckula** of the late 1980s.

The 1980s and 1990s: Vampire humor prospered in the 1980s with movies leading the way. By far the best of the comic films (harking back to Andy Warhol's movie) was *Once Bitten*, in which a female vampire (Lauren Hutton) went in search of a male virgin in Hollywood. Unlike the Warhol vampire, Hutton quickly found the inexperienced Mark Kendall (Jim Carrey) and began to vampirize him. His attempts to discover what was happening to him and then extract himself from the vampire's clutches provided the setting for the hilarity. Other comic vampire movies of the decade included *I Married a Vampire* (1984), *Who Is Afraid of Dracula?* (1985), *Transylvania 6–5000* (1985), and *Transylvania Twist* (1989). During the 1980s, **Elvira**, the vampiric television horror show hostess, burst onto the national scene as a comic personality who combined features of the **vamp** with a Marilyn Monroe-type dumbness. Elvira attracted a devoted following and had her own fan club. She also developed a line of cosmetics and inspired a Halloween look-alike costume and a **comic book**. In 1988, she starred in her first feature-length movie, *Elvira, Mistress of the Dark*.

Developing in the 1980s and coming into their own in the 1990s were vampire Halloween greeting cards. As Halloween emerged as one of urban **America**'s most celebrated holidays, it dropped much of its earlier role as a harvest festival and became a time for fun for youngsters. Vampires and **bats** have been perennial Halloween characters. In response, the greeting card industry produced hundreds of cards featuring the vampire, most built around vampire-oriented one-liners, to send to friends at Halloween. Accompanying the cards were many cartoon vampire party products. These Halloween products illustrated most clearly the severe stereotyping of the vampire image. Vampires could be quickly recognized (and distinguished from witches, ghosts, or other monsters) by their **fangs**, cape, widow's peak, and accompanying bats.

The 1980s also saw the flowering of vampire literature for children and youth. A large percentage of the more than 50 titles were humorous, though serious horror stories for teenagers also were produced. Typical of the comedic literature were the many titles of Victor G. Ambrus. Written for younger children, Ambrus developed a comical Dracula (complete with cartoon illustrations), who in his initial appearance in *Count, Dracula* (1980), was content to teach children to count. *Dracula's Bedtime Storybook* (1981) had Dracula romping through British literature with Frankenstein's monster, Dr. Jekyll and Mr. Hyde, and **Sherlock Holmes**. A series of new titles continued into the 1990s. For older children, in addition to the further adventures of Bunnicula, there were such titles as Judi Miller's *A Vampire Named Murray*, the story of a vampire cousin from "Vulgaria" who came to live with the Kaufmans. Murray was allergic to human blood, but loved V-8 juice (and could warm up to vegetable soup). Murray did stand-up comedy for the kids, and they loved him. But the neighbors thought he was too different, and they wanted him to leave town.

The 1980s ended, and the 1990s began as the interest in vampires reached an all-time high. From 1980 through 1993, the number of vampire novels doubled and the number of vampire short stories and comic books multiplied several times. Thus, it was fitting that the period should be capped with a doubling of the number of vampire joke books. In 1986 Charles Keller finished his compilation of *Count Draculations: Monster*

Riddles, followed in 1991 by Gordon Hill's *The Vampire Joke Book*, 64 pages of riddles. "Why did Dracula become a vegetarian? Because he couldn't bear stakes," was typical fare for Keller and Hill. The next year, **Jeanne Youngson**, president of the Count Dracula Fan Club, compiled *The World's Best Vampire Jokes*. For example: "Why do vampires have such a tough time? Some people never give a sucker an even break," or "What do you get when you cross a woolen scarf with a vampire? A very warm pain in the neck." James Howe followed Hill and Youngson in 1993 with the *Bunnicula Fun Book* (1993), combining jokes with fun things for children.

Vampire humor continued, but at a decreased level in the first decade of the new century. While a few vampire movies and television shows had their funny moments, as a whole comedy was a significant part of either world, even in those movies and shows made for youth and children. Vampire humor primarily survived in new collections of vampire jokes and Halloween greeting cards.

Legendary Dracula actor Christopher Lee hams it up with *Saturday Night Live* cast members Jane Curtin and John Belushi.

Sources:

Barnabas Collins in a Funny Vein. New York: Paperback Library, 1969.

Fister-liltz, Barbara, and Kathy Resch, eds. *Die Laughing*. North Riverside, IL: Phoenix Publications, 1981. 28 pp.

Hawkins, Colin, and Jacqui Hawkins. *Vampires Joke Book*. London: Picture Lions, 2001. 24 pp.

Hill, Gordon. *The Vampire Joke Book*. London: Foulsham, 1991. 64 pp.

Hirsch, Phil, and Paul Laikin, eds. *Vampire Jokes and Cartoons*. New York: Pyramid Books, 1974.

Howe, James. *Bunnicula Fun Book*. New York: Morrow Junior Books, 1993. 164 pp.

———, and Louis Phillips. *Bunnicula's Long-lasting Laugh-alouds: A Book of Jokes & Riddles to Tickle Your Bunny Bone!* Bunnicula Activity Books. New York: Little Simon, 1999. 48 pp.

Keller, Charles. *Count Draculations: Monster Riddles*. New York: Little Simon (Simon & Schuster), 1986.

Vania, Count Trans L. *The Vampire Joke Books*. New York: Pinnacle Books, 1995. 155 pp.

Woo, Diane. *Werewolf, Ghost, and Vampire Jokes You Can Sink Your Teeth Into*. New York: Tor Classics, 2009.

Youngson, Jeanne. *The World's Best Vampire Jokes*. New York: Dracula Press, 1992.

❨ Hungary, Vampires in ❩

Hungary, **Bela Lugosi**'s native country, has a special place in the history of vampires. Vampire historian **Montague Summers** opened his discussion of the vampire in Hungary by observing, "Hungary, it may not untruly be said, shares with **Greece** and Slovakia the reputation of being that particular region of the world which is most terribly infested by the Vampire and where he is seen at his ugliest and worst." **Bram Stoker's *Dracula* (1897)** opened with **Jonathan Harker**'s trip through Hungary. Harker saw Budapest as the place that marked his leaving the (civilized) West and entering the East. He proceeded through Hungary into northeast **Transylvania**, then a part of Hungary dominated by the **Szekelys**, a Hungarian people known for their fighting ability. (Dracula was identified as a Szekely.) In the face of Stoker and Summers, and before **Dom Augustin Calmet**, Hungarian scholars have argued that the identification of Hungary and vampires was a serious mistake of Western scholars ignorant of Hungarian history. To reach some perspective on this controversy, a brief look at Hungarian history is necessary.

The Emergence of Hungary: The history of modern Hungary began in the late ninth century when the Magyar people occupied the Carpathian Basin. They had moved into the area from the region around the Volga and Kama rivers. They spoke a Finnish-Ugrian language, not Slavic. Their conquest of the land was assisted by Christian allies and, during the tenth century, the Christianization of the Magyars began in earnest. In 1000 C.E., Pope Sylvester crowned István, the first Hungarian king. Later in that century, when the Christians split into Roman Catholic and Eastern Orthodox branches, the Hungarians adhered to the Roman church.

István's descendants moved into Transylvania gradually but had incorporated the area into Hungary by the end of the thirteenth century. The Hungarian rulers established a system by which only Hungarians controlled the land. A Magyar tribe, the Szekleys were given control of the mountain land in the northeast in return for their serving as a buffer between Hungary and any potential enemies to the east. The Romanian people of Transylvania were at the bottom of the social ladder. Above them were the Germans, who were invited into cities in southern Transylvania. In return for their skills in building the economy, the Germans were given a number of special privileges. By the fourteenth century, many Romanians had left Transylvania for Wallachia, south of the Carpathians, where they created the core of what would become the modern state of **Romania**. Following the death of the last of István's descendants to wear the crown of Hungary, it was ruled by foreign kings invited into the country by the nobles. The height of prosperity for the nation came in the late fifteenth century when Matthias Corvinus (1458–1490), a Romanian ethnic and contemporary of Wallachian prince **Vlad the Impaler**, ruled. He built his summer capital at **Visegrád** one of the most palatial centers in eastern Europe. Hungarian independence ended essentially at the battle of Mohács in 1526, which sealed the Turkish conquest of the land. During the years of Turkish conquest, while Islam was not imposed, Roman Catholic worship was forbidden. The Reformed Church was allowed, however, and remains a relatively strong body to the present. Transylvania existed as a land with an atmosphere of relative religious freedom, and both Calvinist Protestantism and Unitarianism made significant inroads. Unitarianism made significant gains at the end of the sixteenth century following the death of Roman Catholic Cardinal Bathory at the Battle of Selimbar (1599). The Szekelys were excommunicated and as a group turned to Unitarianism.

The Turks dominated the area until 1686 when they were defeated at the battle of Buda. Hungary was absorbed into the Hapsburg empire and Roman Catholicism rebuilt. The Austrian armies would soon push farther south into Serbia, parts of which were absorbed into the Hungarian province.

The eighteenth century was characterized by the lengthy rulerships of Karoly III (1711–1740) and Maria Theresa (1740–1780). Hungarian efforts for independence, signaled by the short-lived revolution in 1848, led to the creation in 1867 of Austria-Hungary. Austria-Hungary survived for a half century, but then entered World War I on **Germany's** side. In 1919 Austria-Hungary was split into two nations and the large segments of Hungary inhabited by non-Hungarian ethnic minorities were given to Romania, Serbia, and Czechoslovakia. Most importantly, Transylvania was transferred to Romania, a matter of continued tension between the two countries. Hungary was left a smaller but ethnically homogeneous land almost entirely composed of people of Hungarian ethnicity but with a small but measurable number of **Gypsies.** After the wars, Hungary was ruled by Miklós Horthy, a dictator who brought Hungary into an alliance with Hitler and Germany as World War II began. After the war, in 1948, the country was taken over and ruled by Communists until the changes of the 1990s led to the creation of a democratic state.

The Vampire Epidemics: Following the Austrian conquest of Hungary and regions south, reports of vampires began to filter into western Europe. The most significant of these concerned events during 1725–32, their importance due in large measure to

Vlad the Impaler was imprisoned in Visegrad, Hungary, possibly in Solomonís tower, shown here.

the extensive investigations of the reported incidents carried on by Austrian officials. The cases of **Peter Plogojowitz** and **Arnold Paul** especially became the focus of a lengthy debate in the German universities. Different versions of the incidents identified the locations of the vampire epidemics as Hungary rather than (more properly) a Serbian province of the Austrian province of Hungary. The debate was summarized in two important treatises, the first of which, *Dissertazione sopre I Vampiri* by Archbishop **Giuseppe Davanzati,** assumed a skeptical attitude. The second, Dom Augustin Calmet's *Dissertations sur les Apparitiones des Anges des Démons et des Espits, et sur les revenants, et Vampires de Hingrie, de Boheme, de Moravie, et de Silésie,* took a much more accepting attitude.

Calmet's work was soon translated and published in German (1752) and in English (1759) and spread the image of eastern Europe as the home of the vampire. While Calmet featured vampire cases in Silesia (**Poland**), Bohemia, and Moravia (Czechoslovakia), the "Hungarian" cases of Paul and Plogojowitz were the most spectacular and best documented. The image of Hungary as a land of vampires was reinforced by Stoker and Summers, and later by both **Raymond T. McNally** and **Leonard Wolf,** who suggested that the Hungarian word *vampir* was the source of the English word vampire. That theory has more recently been countered by Katerina Wilson, who argued that the first appearance of the word "vampir" in print in Hungarian postdates the first published use of the term in most Western languages by more than a century (actually by some 50 years). The question remains open, however, in that it is highly possible that someone (for example, a German-speaking person in Hungary in the early eighteenth century) might have picked up the term in conversation and transmitted it to the West.

Meanwhile, Hungarian scholars confronted the issue. As early as 1854, Roman Catholic bishop and scholar Arnold Ipolyi assembled the first broad description of the beliefs of pre-Christian Hungary. In the course of his treatise he emphasized that there was no belief in vampires among the Hungarians. That observation was also made by other scholars, who wrote their articles and treatises in Hungarian destined never to be translated into Western languages. In current times, the case was again presented by Tekla Dömötör, whose book *Hungarian Folk Beliefs* was translated and published in English in 1982. He asserted, "There is no place in Hungarian folk beliefs for the vampire who rises forth from dead bodies and sucks the **blood** of the living." The conclusions of the Hungarian scholars have been reinforced by the observations of Western researchers, who have had to concede that few reports of vampires have come from Hungary. Most also assert, however, that in Hungarians' interaction with the Gypsies and their Slavic neighbors, such beliefs likely did drift into the rural regions.

Vampirelike Creatures in Hungary: Having denied the existence of the vampire in Hungarian folk culture, the Hungarian scholars from Ipolyi to Dömötör also detailed belief in a vampirelike being, the *lidérc*. The *lidérc* was an **incubus/succubus** figure that took on a number of shapes. It could appear as a woman or a man, an **animal**, or a shining light. Interestingly, the *lidérc* did not have the power of **transformation**, but rather was believed to exist in all its shapes at once. Through its magical powers, it caused the human observer to see one form or another. As an incubus/succubus it attacked **victims** and killed them by exhaustion. It loved them to death. Defensive measures against the *lidérc* included the placing of garters on the bedroom doorknob and the use of the ubiquitous **garlic**. Hungarians also noted a belief in the *nora*, an invisible being described by those to whom he appeared as small, humanoid, bald, and running on all fours. He was said to jump on his victims and suck on their breasts. Victims included the same type of person who in Slavic cultures was destined for vampirism, namely the immoral and irreverent. As a result of the *nora*, the breast area swelled. The antidote was to smear garlic on the breasts.

Sources:

Calmet, Dom Augustine. *The Phantom World.* 2 vols. London: Richard Bentley, 1746, 1850.
Dömötör, Tekla. *Hungarian Folk Beliefs.* Bloomington, IN: Indiana University Press, 1982.
Kabdebo, Thomas. *Hungary.* Santa Barbara, CA: Clio Press, 1980. 280 pp.
McNally, Raymond T. *A Clutch of Vampires.* New York: Bell Publishing Company, 1974. 255 pp.
Summers, Montague. *The Vampire in Europe.* New Hyde Park, NY: University Books, 1961. 329 pp.
"Vampires in Hungary." *International Vampire* 1, 4 (Summer 1991).
Wilson, Katherine M. "The History of the Word 'Vampire.'" *Journal of the History of Ideas* 64, 4 (October–December 1985): 577–83.

❨ Huntley, Raymond (1902–1990) ❩

Raymond Huntley, who had a long career on the British stage during the twentieth century, portrayed **Dracula** in the original **Hamilton Deane** play and thus became the first stage actor to assume the role. Born just after the turn of the century, the 22-year-

old Huntley was already assuming co-starring roles. Deane took the "star" role in his production, that of **vampire hunter** Professor **Abraham Van Helsing,** and gave the title but lesser role of Dracula to Huntley. He first performed the role in the town of Morecambe; it was not until 1927 that the production came to **London.** As Dracula, Huntley dressed in formal evening clothes, a cape with a high collar, and a wig with gray streaks that gave Huntley a rather devilish appearance. The play had enjoyed great success in theaters around the country, but opened to mixed reviews in London. It was not high **drama,** but was entertaining theater that attracted large audiences. Huntley shared in the varied opinions of reviewers, one of whom mistook Huntley's makeup for a mask.

Huntley would play Dracula for Deane for many years, and in 1928 was offered the role in the American production. He wanted more money than was being offered and as a result the part went to a young Hungarian expatriate, **Bela Lugosi.** Huntley eventually came to **America** to join the cast of the play touring the cities along the Eastern seaboard. He was angered when he was forced to wear green makeup for the part, and happy to return to England to resume his stage acting career. He missed the role in the movie, although **Universal Pictures** had no problem using him as their bargaining chip to force Lugosi to accept a very small salary for playing Dracula in the film.

Huntley escaped the typecasting that afflicted Lugosi following his stage and screen performances, and he enjoyed a long and successful career as an actor on the London stage. He also appeared in various films such as *Room at the Top* and *Young Winston.*

Sources:

Skal, David. *Hollywood Gothic: The Tangled Web of Dracula from Novel to Stage to Screen.* New York: W. W. Norton & Co., 1990. 242 pp.

❨ Hurwood, Bernhardt J. (1926–1987) ❩

Bernhardt J. Hurwood is a popular author of books on vampires and the supernatural. Born in New York City, he graduated from Northwestern University in 1949, his education having been interrupted by his service in the U.S. Merchant Marine from 1945 to 1947. He held a variety of jobs through the 1950s but emerged in 1962 as a full-time writer. Hurwood's first book, *Terror by Night,* was published in 1963.

While his literary career covered many subjects, two topics dominated his writing—sex and the supernatural. In 1965 he published his first collection of supernatural stories, *Monsters Galore,* which was followed by *Monsters and Nightmares* (1967), *Vampires, Werewolves and Ghouls* (1968), *Ghosts, Ghouls and Other Horrors* (1971), *Haunted Houses* (1972), *Vampires, Werewolves, and Other Demons* (1972), *Chilling Ghost Stories* (1973), and *Eerie Tales of Terror and Dread* (1973). Most of these are **juvenile** volumes, and some, such as *Vampires, Werewolves and Other Demons,* featured true stories to introduce the younger audience to classic reports of vampirism and lycanthropy. Along the way, he wrote *Passport to the Supernatural,* a popular book for adults on supernatural themes (i.e., ghosts, vampires, and **werewolves**) as they have been experienced around the world.

With all of his attention on the supernatural, which included significant emphasis on vampires, Hurwood also wrote four books primarily on vampires. The first, *Dra-*

cutwig (1969), was a novel written under the pen name Mallory T. Knight. The book concerned the problem of a young girl, who happened to be Dracula's daughter, with a very thin body similar to then-popular model Twiggy, trying to make it in a high-profile modeling world. *Terror by Night* (1976), reissued as *The Vampire Papers* and *The Monstrous Undead*, written under Hurwood's real name, dealt with the sexual and psychopathic aspects of both vampirism and lycanthropy. Chapters treated such topics as necrophilia, cannibalism, **blood** rituals, and premature burial. Published three years later, *By Blood Alone* (1979) was Hurwood's best vampire novel. The story concerned conversations between psychiatrist Edgar A. Wallman and his vampire patient Zachary Lucius Sexton. The elderly Sexton was suffering from boredom (the perennial problem of the immortals). He asked Wallman why he could not commit **suicide**. Wallman approached Sexton as a man suffering from a delusion and thus attempted to cure him of his dysfunctional fantasy rather than dealing with the reality of the situation. The volume was noteworthy for using the sessions between his two characters as a vehicle to convey all the information he had gleaned from his readings about vampires. Finally, in 1981 Hurwood authored *Vampires*, a light survey of vampire lore covering the **origins** of vampires, **Vlad the Impaler**, vampire folklore, and the modern literary and cinema vampire. Hurwood continued to write until shortly before his death from cancer in 1987.

Sources:

Hurwood, bernhardt J. *Vampires, Werewolves and Ghouls*. New York: Ace Books, 1968.
———— (as Mallory T. Knight). *Dracutwig*. New York: Award Books, 1969. 156 pp.
————. *Passport to the Supernatural*. New York: Taplinger Publishing Company, 1972. 319 pp.
————. *Vampires, Werewolves and Other Demons*. New York: Scholastic Book Services, 1972. 112 pp.
————. *By Blood Alone*. New York: Charter, 1979. 245 pp.
————. *Vampires*. New York: Quick Fox, 1981. 179 pp.

Hypnotic Powers

In many books and movies, the vampire possessed hypnotic powers. **Jonathan Harker** discovered this the day he attempted to kill **Dracula**. Dracula was lying in his box of earth in his vampire **sleep** when Harker threatened him with a shovel. However, the vampire turned his head, and as his eyes fell on Harker, the sight paralyzed the man. Instead of delivering a fatal wound, Harker merely grazed Dracula's head with the shovel he wielded.

The vampire's hypnotic hold on a person was even stronger after it had first bitten the **victim**. Dracula's hypnotic powers were evident, for example, when he lured **Lucy Westenra** from her bedroom in **Whitby** across the bridge to a meeting place on the other side of the river. Nothing that her protectors did after that time prevented Dracula's access to her. Again, Dracula appeared to have put **Mina Murray** into a trance after first attacking her. She was not aware of what she was doing in the crucial encounter with Dracula in her bedroom, when he forced her to drink from the **blood** flowing from his chest. Also at that moment, as vampire expert **Abraham Van Helsing** observed, "Jonathan is in a stupor such as we know the Vampire can produce." When Mina came to her senses, she pronounced herself unclean. Van Helsing was later able to used the hypnotic link between Mina and Dracula. He hypnotized Mina, and while

in a trance she was able to give him information on Dracula's progress on the return trip to his castle.

Hypnotic powers were not evident in the accounts of the folkloric vampire. However, it often attacked at night while its victims slept, and there were a number of accounts in which people awoke with the vampire hovering over them. In like measure, the nineteenth-century literary vampire did not use any hypnotic powers. **Varney the Vampyre** stole into victims' rooms as they slept. **Carmilla** seduced them with her charm and beauty. Since *Dracula* (1897), however, the vampire's hypnotic energy has been an essential part of its power. The look could be used to call victims from their bedrooms or to get them to open the door and let the vampire into the room. With suggestion, victims could get rid of barriers such as **garlic** or a **crucifix** that blocked his access. Frequently it appeared as a simple exercise in power, as the vampire forced an unwilling victim to walk across the room to meet a set of gleaming teeth, or as it hypnotized a third party to assist him in seizing his victim. On occasion, a vampire like Diedre Griffith in Karen Taylor's *Blood Secrets*, would use its hypnotic powers to make a person forget the encounter. Such a situation arose in the 1988 comedy *My Best Friend Is a Vampire*, when the youthful Jeremy Capello must hypnotize his friend Ralph so he can forget his close brush with death. Other vampires like **Count Yorga**, uses their hypnotic abilities to seduce their next victim, and still others, such as vampire cop Nick Knight (*Forever Knight*) uses it to get his way and cover the fact that he is a vampire. The hypnotic glare of **Bela Lugosi** into the camera remains one of the memorable moments of the movie version *Dracula*, and the success of those who followed him in that part often was related to their ability to copy that intense look.

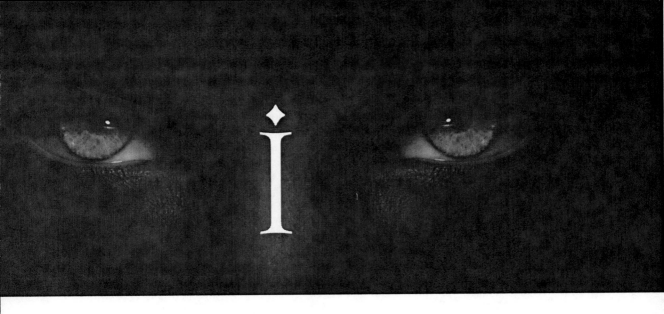

❲ *I … Vampire* ❳

❝I … Vampire" was a popular series of vampire stories that appeared in *The House of Mystery*, a **comic book** published by DC Comics in the 1980s. The series began in the March 1981 issue (No. 290) and appeared periodically through the August 1983 issue (No. 319). "I … Vampire" told the story of Lord Andrew Bennett who was raised during the Elizabethan Era in England of the late sixteenth century. Bennett was a hero of the Spanish War and a well-known figure at court. Then in 1591 he was bitten by a *dearg-dul*, a type of vampire found in **Ireland**, and became a vampire himself. He was in love with Mary Seward, personal handmaiden to the queen. When she discovered his condition, she wanted to spend eternity with him and demanded that he make her a vampire. As a vampire, she felt superior to the human race and could rule the world, an idea Bennett rejected. She left him and he vowed to find her and save her soul, which he had despoiled. Although he had a thirst for **blood**, Bennett had sworn off human blood. Their conflict continued into the 1980s and provided the tension for the stories of the series. Mary built an international organization to seek control of the planet.

The organization, the Blood Red Moon, commanded a large number of vampires that operated as Mary's agents. Bennett had a difficult time killing them because most of the things that hurt them were dangerous to him. Their conflict climaxed in a rush to gain what was termed the Russian Formula. The Russians discovered that vampirism was caused by a virus. Taking the formula made one a new kind of vampire, with all the vampiric powers (**strength, transformation,** etc.) but free from the limitations of the undead and able to live on common human food rather than blood. After Bennett secured and took some of the formula, he was able to walk in the **sunlight**. He discovered Mary's headquarters and prepared to destroy her and her sleeping vampire cohorts. As he went to do this, however, he suddenly found himself unable to move. He learned too late that the formula was designed to create new vampires who were free of bloodlust and was not meant to be consumed by those who were already vampires. Although alive and conscious, Bennett could feel his body sink into rigor mortis.

As Bennett lay dying, Mary bit Bennett's human girlfriend, Deborah Dancer. It seemed that his final damnation was to know that she had become Mary's willing servant. However, Deborah had already taken the Russian Formula and was instead transformed into the new kind of vampire. She fought Mary and dragged her body into the sunlight, where Mary perished. Deborah returned to the dying Bennett to inform him of Mary's death and of her love. Thus, "I ... Vampire" ends with Bennett dying in peace and Deborah living on as the new kind of vampire.

Sources:

The House of Mystery. Nos. 290–319. New York: DC Comics, 1981–83.

Incubus/Succubus

The incubus was a demon figure closely associated with the vampire. The incubus was known for its habit of invading a woman's bedroom at night, lying on top of her so that its weight was quite evident on her chest, and forcing her to have sex. The succubus, the female counterpart of the incubus, attacked men in the same way. The experience of the incubus/succubus attack varied from extreme pleasure to absolute terror. It was, as psychotherapist Ernest Jones noted, the same spectrum of experiences described in modern literature between the erotic dream and the nightmare. The incubus/succubus resembled a vampire in that it attacked people at night while they slept. It often attacked a person night after night, like the vampire of the **Gypsies**, leaving its **victim** exhausted. However, it differed from the vampire in that it neither sucked **blood** nor stole the life energy.

The incubus seemed to have originated in the ancient practice of incubation, where a person went to the temple of a deity and slept there overnight. During the course of the evening, the person would have contact with the deity. Often that contact involved sexual intercourse, either in a dream or with one of the very human representatives of the deity. This practice was at the root of several religious practices, including temple prostitution. The most successful incubation religion was connected with Aesculapius, a healing god who specialized in, among other things, curing sterility. Christianity, which equated the Pagan deities with devilish demons, viewed the practice of intercourse with the deity as a form of demonic activity.

Through the centuries, two main opinions on the origin of incubi and succubi competed with each other. Some saw them as dreams, figments of the fantasy life of the person who experienced their visitations. Others argued for the objective existence of the demons, contending that they were instruments of the devil. By the fifteenth century, church leaders, especially those connected with the Inquisition, favored the latter explanation and tied the demonic activity of incubi and succubi to witchcraft. The great instrument of the witchhunters, *Malleus Maleficarum* (*Witches Hammer*), assumed that all witches willingly submitted to incubi.

The objective existence of the incubus/succubus was supported by Thomas Aquinas in the thirteenth century; he argued that children could even be conceived

through the intercourse of a woman with an incubus. He believed that a demon could change form and appear as a succubus for a man and an incubus for a woman. Some thinkers argued that succubi collected male semen then, in the form of an incubus, deposit it in a female. Nuns seemed a particular target of incubi, as demons seemed to delight in pestering those who strove to live the holy life. The idea of the objective existence of incubi and succubi held sway until the seventeenth century, when a trend toward a more subjective understanding became noticeable.

Ernest Jones, a Freudian psychologist, tied the incubus/succubus and the vampire together as two expressions of repressed sexual feelings. The vampire was seen as the more intense of the two. Because of the similarities of vampires and incubi/succubi, various forms of the latter often appear on lists of different vampires around the world such as the *follets* (French), *duendes* (Spanish), *alpes* (German), and *folletti* (Italian). Closely related to the incubus was the *mare* (Old Teutonic), *mara* (**Scandinavian**) or *mora* (Slavic), a demon of the nightmare.

Jan L. Perkowski noted that stories of the Slavic vampire also included elements of what appeared to be the *mora*. He considered these as vampire accounts that had experienced demon contamination. He carefully distinguished the vampire (an enlivened corpse) and the *mora* (a spherical shaped spirit), and he criticized vampirologists such as **Montague Summers**, Dudley Wright, and Gabriel Ronay for confusing the two. He also criticized Jones on much the same ground. While acknowledging that the vampire and *mora* shared a like mode of attack and generally attacked the same kind of victim (someone asleep), the vampire phenomenon was to be distinguished in that it centered on the corpse while the *mora* phenomenon had no such objective reference and was centered entirely upon the victim who survived the demon's attack.

The incubus and succubus have been the subject of a variety of movies that span a wide spectrum of emphasis on the close relationship of these demons to the vampire. Between 1965 and 2005, there were six feature movies simply entitled *Incubus*, while in about the same time frame there more than a dozen named *Succubus* or a minor variation— *Succubus: The Motion Picture* (1999) or *Succubus the Demon* (2006). The film *Incubus* (1965) starring William Shatner is distinguished as being the only movie with all dialogue in the artificial language Esperanto.

Sources:

Jones, Ernest. *On the Nightmare*. New York: Liveright Publishing Corporation, 1951.

Perkowski, Jan L. *The Darkling: A Treatise on Slavic Vampirism*. Columbus, OH: Slavica Publishers, 1989. 169 pp.

Robbins, Rossell Hope. *The Encyclopedia of Witchcraft and Demonology*. New York: Crown Publishers, 1959. 571 pp.

India, Vampires in

Among the vast number of deities and supernatural entities found in India's religious world were a number that possessed vampiric **characteristics** and were noted in the vampire literature. They merge into a wide variety of demonic entities that more closely resemble ghosts, **ghouls**, living witches and sorcerers. The Indian vampire and vampiric entities appeared in ancient Indian texts, and some have speculated that India was one place where belief in vampires originated and from there spread to surrounding lands.

There was certainly evidence that the **Gypsies** brought a form of vampire belief from India with them when they migrated westward. In ancient Hinduism (the dominant religion of India), creation was portrayed as beginning with the formation of a golden egg (cosmic intelligence). Visible creation resulted from the division of the egg into the heavens, the earth, and the twenty-one regions of the cosmos. These twenty-one regions of the cosmos were roughly divided into three zones, one of which was the Tala, or subterranean region, the abode of the chthonian entities including ogres, spectres, and demons.

The most well-known of the vampiric beings from the Tala were the *rakshasas* (feminine, *rakshasis*), generally described as ogres and demons who lived in cemeteries and disturbed the affairs of people by disrupting rituals and interrupting devotions. The slaying of infants was among their most loathsome actions. The *rakshasas* came in a variety of forms, some male and some female, some more humanoid and some half animal. Hanuman, the deity that appeared in the form of a monkey, was reported to have observed *rakshasas* in every imaginable shape when he entered the city of Lanka as an envoy of Ramam. The *rakshasas* were characters in many Indian epics, such as the *Mahabharata* and the *Ramayana* (which contains the Hanuman episode), and many of the deities and mythical heroes gained their reputation by slaying *rakshasas*. The *rakshasas* were cited as vampires because of some of their characteristics. For example, they were nocturnal wanderers of the night. They had a fearsome appearance with elongated **fangs**. Texts described them as *asra-pa* or *asrk-pa* (literally: drinkers of **blood**). Like the Greek *lamiai*, they sought pregnant female **victims** and were known to attack infants. The natural enemy of the *rakshasas* was *Agni*, the dispeller of darkness and officiator at sacrificial ritual, and people called on *Agni* to destroy or ward off demons.

Closely associated with the *rakshasas* were the *yatu-dhana* (or *hatu-dhana*), sorcerers who devoured the remains left by the *rakshasas*. On occasion the term *yatu-dhana* was used interchangeably with *rakshasas*. Also frequently mentioned with the *rakshasas*, but even lower on the scale of beings, were the *pisachas* (literally: the eaters of raw flesh), also described as hideous in appearance, repellant, and bloodthirsty. The texts described them as flesh-eating ghouls and the source of malignant disease. In the *Puranas*, a set of Hindu writings, the *pisachas* were described as the products of the anger of the deity Brahma.

> After creating gods, demons (asuras), ancestors, and humankind, Brahma became afflicted with hunger, and they began to eat his body, for they were raksasas and yaksas. When Brahma saw them he was displeased, and his hair fell out and became serpents. And when he saw the serpents he was angry, and the creatures born of his anger were the fierce flesh-eating *pisachas*. Thus Brahma created cruel creatures and gentle creatures, dharma and adharma, truth and falsehood.

Also possessing some vampiric characteristics were the *bhuta*, the souls of the dead, specifically those who had died an untimely death, had been insane, or had been born deformed. They wandered the night and appeared as dark shadows, flickering lights, or misty apparitions. On occasion they would enter a corpse and lead it in its ghoulish state to devour living persons. The *brahmaparusha* was a similar entity known in northern India.

Bhutas lived around cremation grounds, old ruins, and other abandoned locations, and in deserts. They might undergo a **transformation** into either owls or **bats**. The owl had a special place in Indian mythology. It was considered unlucky to hear the owl's hoot, possibly fatal if heard in a burial ground. Owl flesh could be used in black magic rituals. *Bhutas* were the ever-present evil spirits and were considered dangerous for a wide variety of reasons. They ate filthy food and were always thirsty. They liked milk and would attack babies who had just fed. They could enter the body through various orifices and possess a person. While the *bhutas* might act in a vampirish way on occasion, they generally were seen as simply malevolent beings.

The Indian demon-like figures possibly closest to the Western vampire were the *vetalas*, or *betails*, spirits that inhabited and animated the bodies of the dead. A *betail* was the central character in *The Vetala-Pachisi*, a classic piece of Indian literature comparable to Chaucer's *Canterbury Tales* or the *Arabian Nights*. Originally translated and published in English in the mid-nineteenth century, a new translation of 11 of what he deemed were the most interesting of the stories was made by **Sir Richard F. Burton** and published in 1870 under the title *Vikram and the Vampire*. *The Vetala-Pachisi* described the encounter of King Vikram with a *betail* who told him a series of tales. Vikram, like King Arthur, was an actual person who lived in the first century C.E. and became a magnet for many tales and fables. In the book, a yogi cajoled Vikram to spend an evening with him in the cemetery. He then asked Vikram to bring him a body he would find some four miles to the south at another burial ground. The body, the yogi told him, would be hanging on a mimosa tree. The body turned out to be a *betail*. Vikram encountered great difficulty in getting the vampire to accompany him back to the yogi, but finally succeeded through his persistence. To entertain them on the return trip, the *betail* told a series of stories that form the body of the book.

When they reached the cemetery with the yogi, the king found him invoking **Kali**. He was surrounded by the host of demons from Indian lore, including the *rakshasas*, the *bhutas* (who had assumed various beastly shapes), and the *betails*. The yogi led them to the shrine of the goddess Kali. There Vikram killed the yogi who was about to kill him. As a boon, the gods granted him fame.

A survey of Indian vampiric entities would be incomplete without further mention of the goddess Kali, often associated with Siva as a consort. She was a dark goddess, usually pictured as having black skin. She had a terrible and frightening appearance, wearing parts of the human body as ornaments. Her favorite places were the battlefield, where she became drunk on the blood of her victims, and the burial/cremation ground. In *Vikram and the Vampire*, Kali appeared in the shrine located at the cemetery, and as Vikram entered he saw her:

> There stood Smashana-Kali, the goddess, in her most horrible form. She was a naked and a very black woman, with half-severed head, partly cut and partly painted, resting on her shoulder; and her tongue lolled out from her wide yawning mouth; her eyes were red like those of a drunkard; and her eyebrows were of the same colour; her thick coarse hair hung like a mantle to her knees.

Burton comments on this passage:

Not being able to find victims, this pleasant deity, to satisfy her thirst for the curious juice, cut her own throat that the blood might spout up into her mouth.

Other Vampiric Entities: Throughout India, among the various ethnic/linguistic groups, there were a multitude of ghosts, demons, and evil spirits who lived in or near cemeteries and cremation locations and who bore some resemblance to the vampires of Europe. Many fooled others by assuming the form of a living person. They reverted to a horrible demonic appearance just before attacking their victims. For example, in Gujarat there were the *churels*, **women** who died an unnatural death (in western India the churel was also known as a *jakhin, jakhai, mukai, nagulai,* and *alvantin*). If such a woman had been treated badly by her family, she would return to harass them and to dry up the blood of the male family members. Such a woman could become a *dakini*, an associate of the goddess Kali, and a partaker in her vampirish and ghoulish activities. If a young man was tempted by the *churel* and ate of the food she offered, she would keep him with her until dawn and return him to his village a grey-haired old man. The *churel* had one noticeable feature that gave her away—her feet were turned backwards so her heel was in front and her toes in back.

Women at the time of childbirth and their infants were given great attention by family and friends. A woman who died in childbirth was likely to become a ghost. To prevent that from occurring, the family would bury rather than cremate the body. They would then fix four nails in the ground at the corners of the burial spot and plant red flowers on top of the grave. A woman who died in childbirth was also buried in a special place (the exact spot differing in various sections of India). For example, the corpse could be carried outside the house by a side door and buried within the shadow of the house by the noontime sun. It was believed that by not using the front door, the *churel* would be unable to find her way home. Some used iron nails in the house's threshold and sprinkled millet **seeds** on the road to the burying ground. As in eastern Europe, the *churel* must count the seeds, a task that kept her busy until daybreak. In the Punjab, a woman who died in childbirth would have nails driven through her hands and feet, red pepper placed in her eyes, and a chain wrapped around her feet. Others broke the legs above the ankles and turned the feet around backward, bound the big toes together, or simply bound the feet with iron rings.

Among the most interesting vampires were the *chedipe* (literally: prostitute), a type of sorceress in the Godavari area. The *chedipe* was pictured as riding a tiger through the night. Unclothed, she entered the home of a sleeping man and sucked his blood out of his toe. Using a form of hypnotism, she put the others in the household into a trance-like sleep so that they were unaware of her presence. In the morning, the man would awaken but feel drained of energy and somewhat intoxicated. If he did not seek treatment for his condition, the *chedipe* would return. On occasion the *chedipe* would attack men in the jungle in the form of a tiger with a human leg.

Devendra P. Varma has made a case that the vampire deities of the ancient Hindus are the source of vampire beliefs in Europe. He asserted that such beliefs were carried by the Arab caravans over the Great Silk Route from the Indus Valley into the Mediterranean Basin. They probably arrived in **Greece** around the first century C.E. This theory, while entirely possible, has yet to be developed in the depth necessary to place

The Vampire Book: The Encyclopedia of the Undead

it beside alternative theories that project multiple **origins** of vampiric myth in different cultures to meet a set of fairly universal needs.

Sources:

The Baital-Pachisi; or, The Twenty-five Tales of a Demon. Ed. by Duncan Forbes. London: Crosby, Lockwood, 1857.

Burton, Richard, trans. *Vikram and the Vampire; or, Tales of Hindu Devilry.* 1870, 1893. Rpt.: New York: Dover Publications, 1969. 243 pp.

Crooke, William. *Religion and Folklore of Northern India.* Humphrey Milford: Oxford University Press, 1926. 471 pp.

Danielou, Alain. *Hindu Polytheism.* New York: Bollingen Foundation, 1964. 537 pp.

Enthoven, R. E. *The Folklore of Bombay.* Oxford: Clarendon Press, 1924. 353 pp.

Harding, Elizabeth A. *Kali: The Black Goddess of Dakshineswar.* Lake Worth, FL: Nicolas-Hays, 1993. 352 pp.

Kingsley, David. *Hindu Goddesses: Visions of the Divine Feminine in the Hindu Religious Tradition.* Berkeley, CA: University of California Press, 1986. 281 pp.

MacDonell, A. A. *Vedic Mythology.* Strassburg, Germany: Verlag von Karl J. Trübner, 1897. 189 pp.

Sutherland, Gail Hinich. *The Disguises of the Demon: The Development of the Yaksa in Hinduism and Buddhism.* Albany, NY: State University of New York Press, 1991. 233 pp.

Thurston, Edgar. *Omens and Superstitions of Southern India.* New York: McBride, Nast & Company, 1912. 320 pp.

Trigg, E. B. *Gypsy Demons & Divinities: The Magical and Supernatural Practices of the Gypsies.* London: Sheldon Press, 1973. 238 pp.

Varna, Devendra P. "The Vampire in Legend, Lore, and Literature." Introduction to *Varney the Vampyre.* Devendra P. Varna, ed. New York: Arno Press, 1970.

Walker, Benjamin. *The Hindu World: An Encyclopedia Survey of Hinduism.* New York: Frederick A. Praeger, 1986. 281 pp.

International Vampire

International Vampire was one of the higher quality periodicals of the 1990s published for fans of vampires. It was founded in 1991 by its editor, Rob Brautigam, a resident of Amsterdam, Netherlands. Each issue contained well-researched articles of vampire history and folklore, notices of various fan organizations and periodicals, and book reviews. After some six years, it was discontinued. Several people interested in vampires established sites on the Internet in the early 1990s and as the decade came to a close the established sites were numbered in the thousands. For the vampire enthusiast, they provide constant entertainment and are a source of vast amounts of information. But, given the amateur nature of most sites, like fanzines and fan clubs, they have a tendency to be ephemeral, quite surprising given the cost and time needed to maintain a home page. However, on any given day, one can get on the web and, using any of the major search engines, immediately find more sites than they can absorb in a sitting.

For both the neophyte and the experienced Internet user, a very good place to start is Candy Cosner's Vampire Junction site (http://www.afn.org/~vampires/links .html). Cosner, a longtime vampire fan, started Vampire Junction as a fanzine in the early 1990s and gradually made the transition from printed to electronic media in the

middle of the decade. Even though some areas on the site are devoted to Cosner's special interests (poetry, short fiction), she makes a real contribution with the more than 600 "Links to All Things Vampiric," giving leads to almost any area of vampire interest. The sites for chat rooms, fan clubs, or specific topics are listed alphabetically to facilitate locating them. To help narrow down the bewildering number of choices, she has called attention to the "better" sites and warns people when they are about to enter an exclusively commercial site.

The Vampire Junction has also pulled together the sites related to the more popular specialized interests—**Anne Rice**, *Buffy the Vampire Slayer*, *Forever Knight*, *Vampire: The Masquerade*, *Dark Shadows*, *Vampirella*, and vampire literature/writers—so one does not have to go searching through the entire list to find their favorite topic or miss sites because their name doesn't reveal their content.

A second general interest vampire site is Pathway to Darkness (http://www.pathwaytodarkness.com/). Along with sections containing interactive opportunities, selections of vampire fiction, and reviews of vampire movies and games, this site has a direct link to "Count Duckula's Vampire Films" at http://www.uncc.edu/~ltrobert/vampfilm.htm, the best list of vampire films currently existing on the Internet. Count Duckula is further cross-referenced to the Internet Movie Database (www.imdb.com), which offers additional information about any particular film.

Amid the hundreds of vampire films, the Hammer movies have inspired the most noticeable community of fans. **Hammer Films** has an official web page (www.hammerfilms.com), but, Greg Turnbull's Hammer Horror (http://www.firstlevel.com/homepages/hammer/) is another excellent source of information. The site is especially directed to collectors but also has space for fans to chat about Hammer and keep up with the stars of the movies, especially the beautiful cadre of Hammer women. One of Hammer's biggest stars, Ingrid Pitt, has her own fan club with associated internet presence, The Pitt of Horror (www.pittofhorror.com).

The oldest, strongest and most loyal fans of a vampire television show are the devotees of *Dark Shadows*, which has an extensive Internet presence. Few pages provide a better starting point for exploring the cyber world of *Dark Shadows* than the Dark Shadows Frequently Asked Questions Page (http://members.aol.com/tchoate1/ds/faq.htm). There are pictures and facts, but mostly there are links that cover publications and collectibles, the show's stars, videos of the television show, and fan news.

For Buffy, one could do worse than begin at the unofficial *Buffy the Vampire Slayer* site (http://www.geocities.com/TelevisionCity/Set/9329/index.html).

It contains pictures, episode summaries (and even complete scripts of shows), interactive activities, those ever-present rumors to be dispelled, and a host of additional information on the top vampire television show of the 1990s. Links to the other *Buffy* sites are divided between the very best "banner sites" and all the rest.

A similar site for *Forever Knight* is the Internet Traveler's Guide to *Forever Knight* (http://www.geocities.com/Hollywood/8125/). It offers not only the requisite pictures, episode summaries and information for trivia buffs, but a set of links to even more *Forever Knight* sites. Topping the list of topics for vampire buffs are the Anne Rice sites that include everything from the fan clubs of the stars of *Interview with the Vampire* to travel guides for New Orleans. Here is one area in which the official site is very well done and one cannot go wrong starting with The Anne Rice Official Site (www.anne-rice.inter.net/). Rice has participated in its preparation and keeps her many fans updated on her writing projects as well as answering questions put to her. There is also an archive of past issues of her newsletter. The one drawback is the lack of links to unofficial sites, but that single oversight is ably handled by Dracula's Daughter, one site that does not give away its content with its name; (http://users. aol.com/mishian/DD/DD.html). It vies with Rice's site in attempting to post the latest news. From it one can find their way to the additional fan sites. Dracula's Daughter is particularly useful for collectors of Rice's books (which have now been reproduced in a variety of media).

For Vampire: The Masquerade, start with The Vampire Archive (http://www.monterey.edu/staff/ StoneRob/world/Vampire/). It is one of the larger sites with comprehensive coverage of the game and its variations. One can learn about the intricate mythology underlying the game and survey the vast amount literature that has been produced to enhance play.

Vampirella is the hottest vampire in the comic book world and Scott's page (http://www.abs.net/~scor pion/legion/htmls/legion.html) is among the best of the fan sites. It risks being buried among several hun-

Cover art from the comic *Purgatori.*

dred sites devoted entirely to reproducing one or a few *Vampirella* comic book covers or *Vampirella* trading cards. Scott's site covers the recent Harris Comics issues, the Scarlet Legion Fan Club, the *Vampirella* film, as well as including liberal amounts of *Vampirella* art. The other hot comic book vampires, Purgatori and Chastity, are from Chaos! Comics (www.chaoscomics.com/).

To research **Dracula**, the world's best-known vampire, go to the interrelated sites of gothic scholar Elizabeth Miller (www.ucs.mun.ca/~emiller/) and the Canadian Chapter of the **Transylvanian Society of Dracula**, which she heads (www.ucs.mun .ca/~emiller/tsd.htm). Segments of the sites focus on serious consideration of Dracula and vampire studies and other parts take a more lighthearted approach to the subject. From these sites one can look up Web pages on **Transylvania**, the novel **Dracula**, and some of the organizations with which TSD has close ties, such as the Dracula Society in England, Transylvania Press, and Desert Island Books. But also look for references to Vampire Legends of Rhode Island, Stone & Wing: Bat Motif Jewelry, the Haunted Bookshop (Australia), the Ooga Booga Page, another very comprehensive site, Vampyres Only (http://www.vampyres-only.com//) and Evil Eyes (in French). Also, for a full text of the novel, go to http://www.literature.org/Works/Bram-Stoker/dracula/.

Gothic fiction forms a large area of interest for vampire fans. Two sites come to the fore in providing information about vampire novels and their authors, Dark Echo (www.darkecho.com) and the Dark Side of the Net (www.gothic.com). The latter also carries links to the whole gothic world, including vampire comic books. Horror Net (www.horrornet.com) carries an extensive listing of home pages and email addresses of horror writers (including many who are best known for their vampire novels).

For almost all of the sites mentioned above, another almost equally valuable Internet address could have been given, but these sites are easily accessed and serve as open doors to surfing the Internet. From them you can explore the subject of vampires from almost any angle and perspective. You can look at pictures, download fiction, buy a wide assortment of **paraphernalia**, and learn about vampire life. You also have the opportunity to chat endlessly with other people interested in vampires in general or your favorite vampire in particular, and more than a few people who claim to be vampires themselves. And every indication seems to suggest that in the near future the opportunities to learn about vampires and interact with others of like mind will only grow.

Interview with the Vampire

*I*nterview with the Vampire, the first vampire novel by **Anne Rice**, appeared in 1976. As sequels were produced in the late 1980s, it became known as the first volume of a saga, The Vampire Chronicles. In 1994 a movie based upon it starring **Tom Cruise**, Brad Pitt, Kirsten Dunst, and Antonio Banderas became one of the largest-grossing films of that year. The book introduced one of the most important contemporary vampire characters, **Lestat de Lioncourt**, and has gone on to become the second best-selling vampire novel of all time, second only to **Bram Stoker**'s *Dracula*. The novel is presented as a story-within-a-story. Louis (Pitt), a 200-year-old vampire, met with a journalist to tell his story and try to prove the truth of his tale. Louis's story began when he became a vampire in colonial Louisiana. In the midst of a period of despair, he was found by Lestat (Cruise), a vampire who had come to Louisiana from **France**. Once changed, the two lived at Louis' plantation outside **New Orleans** until the slaves figured out that their master had become a creature of the night and drove them away. They then established themselves in the city where Lestat indulged himself and Louis worried about killing humans in order to survive.

A short time later the pair was joined by Claudia (Dunst), a five-year-old orphan child whom Louis made into a vampire. Seven years afterward, resentful that she had been trapped in the body of a child, Claudia attempted to kill Lestat, and she and Louis left for Europe. In Paris, they encountered a group of vampires who operated out of a theater, using the facilities as their home and the draw from the shows as income. Louis was very much impressed with one of their number, **Armand** (Banderas). Afraid of being abandoned, Claudia demanded that Louis create a vampire out of a childless woman, Madeleine, to act as Claudia's surrogate mother.

All was fine until the group at the Theatre of the Vampires discovered that Claudia had attempted and nearly succeeded in killing their benefactor Lestat, who had provided them with the theater. They kidnapped Louis, Claudia, and Madeleine, and locked the two females in a room where they were consumed in the morning sun. Louis was confined to a **coffin**, but released by Armand. In retaliation, he set **fire** to the theater and killed most of the vampires. He then left with Armand and had a meeting with Lestat in New Orleans.

Interview with the Vampire explores numerous themes relevant to the vampire myth: **sexuality** in general and **homosexuality** in particular, the role of community in vampiric

Lestat de Lioncourt (Tom Cruise) prepares to take a victim in *Interview with the Vampire*.

existence, the nature of vampirism in a secular age, and the morality of murder. All of the strong characters in the book are male, with the exception of the child Claudia. The vampires, however, live in a communal setting quite distinct from most previous vampires who were overwhelmingly loners. Rice's vampires have no problem with religious symbols and know nothing of God or a sacred space. Lestat, who emerges from the novel as the most appealing character, has little thought for taking life if that is the way he will survive. With the exception of Claudia, the main characters in *Interview with the Vampire* would reappear multiple times in the succeeding novels.

The novel has been translated into a number of languages, including most of the European languages, and Chinese and Japanese. It has been reproduced on cassette tape and CD and in a number of deluxe and souvenir editions. Fans of the book and its sequels gathered annually through the 1990s in New Orleans for a Halloween party put on by the **Anne Rice Vampire Lestat Fan Club.**

Sources:

Ramsland, Katherine. *The Vampire Companion: The Official Guide to Anne Rice's The Vampire Chronicles.* New York: Ballantine Books, 1993. 507 pp.

Brad Pitt made his mark as Louis de Pointe du Lac in the film version of *Interview with the Vampire*.

Rice, Anne. *Interview with the Vampire*. New York: Alfred A. Knopf, 1976. 372 pp. Rept. New York: Ballantine, 1979. 346 pp.

Ireland, Vampires in

Ireland, like its neighbor the **United Kingdom,** does not have a rich vampire lore, in spite of a mythology that contains numerous stories of preternatural beings and contact between the living and the dead in the form of ghosts and revenants. **Montague Summers** spoke of an Irish vampire, the *dearg-dul*, but supplied little information about it. Irish folklorists found no mention of it in the folklore they compiled. The most famous vampire tale was that of "The Blood-Drawing Ghost," collected and published by Jeremiah Curtin in 1882. It told the story of a young woman named Kate. She was one of three women whom a man from County Cork was thinking of marrying.

To test the women, he placed his cane at the entrance of the tomb of a recently deceased person and then challenged them to fetch it. Only Kate accepted the challenge.

Upon arriving at the tomb, she encountered the dead man who forced her to take him into town. There he drew **blood** from three young men who subsequently died. He mixed the blood with oatmeal he had forced Kate to prepare. While he devoured his meal, Kate secretly hid her portion. Unaware that she had not eaten her oatmeal, the "vampire" confided in her that the blood-oatmeal mixture would have brought the men back to life. As they were returning to his tomb, the "vampire" told Kate of a fortune in gold to be found in a nearby field.

The next day, the three young men were found. Kate then struck a bargain with their parents. She offered to bring them back to life if she could marry the oldest one and if the land where she knew the gold was located could be deeded to her. Deed in hand, she took the oatmeal she had hidden and put some in the mouth of each man. They all quickly recovered from the vampire's attack.

With her future husband, she dug up the gold and the wealthy couple lived a long life and passed their wealth to their children.

Dudley Wright, in *Vampires and Vampirism*, mentioned a female vampire who lured people to her by her beauty. She supposedly resided in the graveyard at Waterford near Strongbow's Tower. Summers conducted one of his rare personal investigations only to discover that there was no Strongbow's Tower near Waterford. He suggested that Wright made a mistaken reference to another structure, Reginald's Tower, but upon checking with authorities on Irish lore, was told that no vampire legends were known about Reginald's Tower. As a final explanation, Summers suggested that Wright's story was a confused version of a story told of the Anglo-Saxon conquest of Waterford after which a frog (not native to Ireland) was found and interred in Reginald's Tower.

In 1925, R. S. Breene reported another Irish story concerning a priest who died and was properly buried. Upon their return trip from the graveside, mourners from the funeral parlor met a priest on the road and were upset to discover that it was the man they had just buried. He differed only in that he had pale skin, wide-open glittering eyes, and prominent long white teeth.

They went immediately to the farmhouse of the priest's mother. They found her lying on the floor. It seemed that shortly before the funeral party arrived she had heard a knock at the door. Looking outside she saw her son. She made note of the pale complexion and the prominent teeth. Fear overcame her and rather than letting him in, she fainted.

The Literary Vampire: Ireland gave birth to two of the most famous vampire authors, **Sheridan Le Fanu,** who wrote the novella, **"Carmilla"** and **Bram Stoker,** the author of *Dracula.* Le Fanu drew on his Irish homeland for his early stories, but both men had moved to England by the time they wrote their most famous vampire stories, which they set in continental Europe.

The vampire rarely appeared in Irish literature. One appearance that attained a relative level of fame occurred in James Joyce's *Ulysses* (1922), which used vampire imagery. The vampire first appeared early in the novel when Stephen, the main character, spoke of the moon kissing the ocean: "He the moon comes, pale vampire, through storm her eyes, has bat sails bloodying the sea, mouth to her mouth." He makes later reference to the "… potency of vampires mouth to mouth." Joyce injected the vampire into his very complex ruminations on divinity, creativity, and **sexuality.** In another reference, Stephen spoke of the vampire man's involvement with chic women. Finally, Stephen identified God as the "Black panther vampire." Joyce seemed to be settling on an image of the creative Father god as a vampire who preyed upon his **victims**—virgin women. The insertion of the virgin assisted Joyce in making the point that creation was also inherently a destructive process. In any case, the several brief references to the vampire supplied Joyce's literary critics with the substance for a lively debate.

The tradition of Irish vampire lore is celebrated today in the work of the **The Bram Stoker Society** and an associated group, The Bram Stoker Club.

The society attempts to promote the status of Bram Stoker's writings, especially *Dracula,* and to call attention to Irish **gothic** literature in general. It sponsors an annual school each summer.

Sources:

Cheng, Vincent J. "Stephen Dedalus and the Black Panther Vampire." *James Joyce Quarterly* 24, 2 (Winter 1987): 161–76.

Curtin, Jeremiah. *Tales of the Fairies and of the Ghost World Collected from the Oral Tradition in South-West Munster.* 1882. Rept. New York: Lemma Publishing Corporation, 1970. 198 pp.

Kelly, Sean, ed. *Irish Folk and Fairy Tales.* New York: Gallery Press, 1982. 367 pp.

Summers, Montague. *The Vampire in Europe.* London: Routledge, Kegan Paul, Trench, Trubner, & Co., 1929. 319 pp. Rept. New Hyde Park, NY: University Books, 1961. 329 pp.

Wright, Dudley. *Vampires and Vampirism.* 1914, Rev. ed. 1924. Rept. *The Book of Vampires.* New York: Causeway Books, 973. 217 pp.

Italian History, Vampires in *see:* Rome, Vampires in Ancient

❨ Italy, Vampires in ❩

In Italy, the vampire phenomenon took on a modern identity when a "vampiric plague" hit Serbia and other lands in Eastern Europe in the seventeenth century. Italians contributed to the animated international debate that began on the nature of this phenomenon, which ultimately contributed to and inspired nineteenth-century vampire literature. Within the debate various positions reflective of different theological and ideological positions were articulated throughout the centuries.

As the vampiric plague was beginning, a Franciscan from Pavia, Ludovico Maria Sinistrari (1622–1701), included vampirism in a study of demonic phenomena, *De Daemonialitate, et Incubis, et Succubis*, and offered a theological interpretation of them. Far from the contemporary rationalism of the Enlightenment that emerged in the following century, he thought of vampires as creatures that had not originated from Adam (i.e., humanity). While they had a rational soul equal to humans, their corporeal dimension was of a completely different, perfect nature. He thus enforced the idea that vampires were creatures that parallel human beings rather than opposite, chthonious, underground beings. (The oddness of Sinistrari's views may be because his study was a hoax. It was reportedly written in the nineteenth-century by Isidore Lisieux, which would account for the fact that the study was not mentioned by Italian authors through the 1700s.) Credit for initiating the modern view of vampirism is usually given to J. H.

Zedler, whose *Grosses volständige Universal-Lexicon aller Wissenschaften und Künste*, (1745) saw vampirism as a superstition used to explain what were in reality certain diseases. However, two years earlier, in his 1743 *Dissertazione sopra i vampiri*, Cardinal **Giuseppe Davanzati**, noticing that the belief in vampires mostly occurred in rural and less-populated areas of the world, labeled vampirism as simply the "fruit of imagination," arguing that such a belief was not found in the metropolitan milieus of Western Europe.

Davanzati's work was looked upon with favor by the then Pope Benedict XIV who as Prospero Lambertini (1675–1758) wrote what remained for many years the standard Roman Catholic sourcebook on miracles and the supernatural, *De servorum Dei beatifications et Beatorum canonizations* (Rome, 1934). As pope, he reprimanded some Polish bishops who were making their belief in vampires too public. While the first edition of his book did not deal with vampires, the second edition added two pages punctuating his negative conclusions on the subject.

Nevertheless, reports of vampirism became a more widespread phenomenon in the mid-eighteenth century throughout the central and eastern parts of Europe. Accounts that were documented in *Traité sur les apparitions et sur les vampires ou le revenans d'Hongire, de Moravie* (1749) by French Benedectine scholar **Dom Augustin Calmet** became a source of inspiration for vampire novels throughout the following centuries. Gerhard van Swieten's *Remarques sur les vampirisme* (1755) suggested that vampirism was a superstition generated out of ignorance. The opinion recanted Calmet's tales and represented the triumph of the scientific rationalism that predominated in the culture of the late eighteenth century.

The Literary Vampire: In the early nineteenth century, the first literary works on vampires and vampirism began to appear, mostly in Northern Europe. Reportedly, a vampire-oriented literary tradition also began in early nineteenth-century Italy with the **opera** *Il Vampiro* by A. De Gasperini (first presented in Turin in 1801), however, a copy of the opera has never been found in Italian libraries and there is some doubt it ever existed.

Romanticism, a popular literary movement that reflected on inner human experience, itself enforced a mythic image of the vampire with its emphasis on the symbology of **blood**, the night, melancholy, and the "erotic tenderness for corpses." Mostly in the northern part of Europe, from superstitious popular belief, vampirism was introduced to the literate metropolitan milieu through the literary works of Novalis, **Goethe**, and **John Keats**. In 1819 **John Polidori** created **Lord Ruthven**, the protagonist in his short story, "**The Vampyre**" (translated into Italian as "Il Vampiro" in the twentieth century). Vampires especially began to appear in French and Russian literature, in the works of **Charles Nodier**, Charles Baudelaire, **Alexandre Dumas**, **Alexey Tolstoy**, and Nikolai Gògol.

The first Romance to be published in Italy, *Il Vampiro*, written by Franco Mistrali, appeared in 1869. Mistrali's story, which takes place in Monaco in 1862, was centered on blood and incestuous lovers. It presented the vampire in a literary, decadent, and aristocratic manner that was influenced by the contemporary literature of Keats, Goethe, Polidori, and **Lord Byron**. The historical folkloric connotations of vampirism, as documented at the time of the vampiric plague, became the subject of *Vampiro*, a novel written in 1908 by Enrico Boni. It was perhaps the only work that illustrated the popular universe of superstition and fears of the rural culture.

A naturalist approach to the phenomenon was found in the work of Luigi Capuana, *Un Vampiro* (1904; 2nd ed., 1907). The author aimed at an objective description of facts that could be explained scientifically (vampirism as an hallucination), although some skepticism remained at the end of the novel. In 1907, the same year as the second edition of Capuana's *Un Vampiro* was Daniele Oberto Marrama published *Il Dottore nero* (translation: *The Black Doctor*).

Significant works on vampires in the following decades included Nino Savarese's *I ridestati del cimitero* (translation: *The Reawakened of the Cemetery*, 1932) Tommaso Landolfi's *Il racconto del lupo mannaro* (translation: *The Tale of the Werewolf*, 1939), *Racconto d'autunno* (translation: *Fall Tale*, 1947), Bacchelli's *Ultimo licantropo* (translation: *The Last Lycanthrope*, 1947), and Guadalberto Titta's *Il cane nero* (translation: *The Black Dog*, 1964). As can be discerned from the titles, vampires and **werewolves** were closely associated in the writings of the Italian authors.

Poster art from the 1998 Italian event celebrating the vampire.

In the wake of the successful Italian movies *I Vampiri* in 1957 by Riccardo Freda, *Tempi duri per i Vampiri* (*Uncle Was a Vampire*) in 1959 by Stefano Steno, and **Mario Bava**'s movies in the 1960s, a new wave of commercial vampire horror literature emerged in the form of series, such as *I Romanzi del Terrore*, *KKK Classici dell'orrore*, and *I Racconti di Dracula* (translation: Dracula's Stories). The most renowned author of a series was Gaetano Sorrentino (a.k.a. Max Dave). In contrast with the commercial literature of those years, a more sophisticated image of vampires appeared in the novels of the authors of these last decades, such as the grotesque and comic vampire (with a benign social criticism) in *Il mio amico Draculone* (translation: *My Friend Draculone*) by Luigi Pellizzetti in 1970 and Italo Calvino's vampire in *Il Castello dei destini incrociati* (translation: *The Castle of Crossed Destinies*). There were several works that featured an "existential trickster" representing the ambiguity of life in contrast to death. Also published in the same period was Giovanni Fontana's *Tarocco Meccanico* (translation: *Mecanic Tarot*), where the vampire was used as a literary image in the game of oxymora and metaphors that constitute the author's "romanzo sonoro" (sound romance).

By this time, the traditional stereotype of the vampire had been replaced by sophisticated, metaphorical images that expressed undefinable images. A new connotation of this archetype, in a total break with the tradition, was developed in *Anemia* by Alberto Abruzzese (1984). Here the protagonist was a highly-placed officer of the Communist Party who, in his everyday life, gradually discovered, through a series of initiation-like psychological fears and physical changes, his real identity as a vampire. He had to accept his metamorphosis to maintain the balance needed to stand the rhythm of his ordinary life. The play seems to be a commentary on the difficulty of the old Italian Communist Party in adapting to the changes that transformed it into the post-communist Democrat Party of the Left.

Another original approach to the vampire theme can be found in the novels of Furio Jesi (1941–80). He presented a playful vampire in a short story for children "La casa incantata" ["The Enchanted House"]), published posthumously in 1982, but his major contribution was *L'ultima notte* (translation: *The Last Night*). An expert in mythology and anthropology, Jesi described vampires as mythological archetypes symbolizing life, drawing on pre-Christian and Oriental traditions (Mesopotamia, ancient **Mexico**, **Greece**, **Tibet**, and **India**). Dracula himself was used as a symbol of fertility and the endless flow of planetary existence, while the mission of these vampires was to reconquer the earth and human species that were heading toward ecological destruction.

Finally, vampires themselves revealed their identity in Gianfranco Manfredi's collection *Ultimi vampiri* (translation: *The Last Vampires*) (1987). In the several novels of the series, *I figli del fiume* (translation: *The Children of the River*), *La guarigione* (translation: Recovery), *Il metodo vago* (translation: *The Vague Method*), and *Il pipistrello di Versailles* (translation: *Versailles Bat*), the surviving "last vampires" described their historical experience throughout the centuries living side by side with humans, coping with their tricks, and finally, being defeated by them. Here some of the major events that radically changed the course of human history, (such as the Lutheran Reformation and the Spanish Inquisition—a consequence of the vampiric plague—Versailles and Waterloo) were explained from the perspective of the vampires.

Vampire Poetry: It was within two avant-garde artistic movements, the Scapigliatura and Futurism, in the late nineteenth and early twentieth century respectively, that an Italian vampire **poetry** developed. The central topic in this poetry was the **vamp**, the seductive and fatal vampire woman, caught in her erotic and most aggressive dimension.

These images were heavily inherited by late romanticism and French poetry, in particular the poems of Baudelaire (*Les Métamorphoses du Vampire, Le Vampire, La Fontaine de Sang*). Within the Scapigliatura movement, the most popular poets to write of vampires were Nicola Maciarello, Arrigo Boito (1842–1918), Amilcare Ponchielli, Ugo Tarchetti, Achille Torelli (1841–1922), and Olindo Guerrini. The most influential Futurist poet was Filippo Tommaso Marinetti (1876–1944).

In the decades following the 1920s, with the exhaustion of the Futurist movement, Italian poetry drew little inspiration from vampirism. In mid-century, authors such as Aldo Palazzeschi and Dino Campana only vaguely alluded to vampires in their work. Since the 1970s however, the *lamiai*, a Greek vampire entity, appeared in Giovanni Fontana's *Le Lamie del labirinto* (translation: *The Labyrinth Lamias*). In the tradition of the "sound romance," *Tarocco Meccanico* developed the image of the vampire as a metaphorical, artistic, and poetic function.

Religious scholar Massimo Introvigne is a Dracula researcher and founder of the Italian branch of the Transylvanian Society of Dracula.

The Cinematic Vampire: At the same time that Stefano Steno's vampire comedy *Tempi Duri per i Vampiri* was released in 1959, there also appeared Riccardo Freda's *I Vampiri* (*The Devil's Commandment*) (1957), and *Caltiki, il mostro immortale* (*Caltiki, the Immortal Monster*) (1959), which brought fame to special photography cameraman Mario Bava. Bava went from being a mere cameraman to directing more than 20 movies distinguished by his use of haunting baroque imagery. Bava's most important and representative works included: *La Maschera del Demonio* (a.k.a. *The Mask of Satan, Black Sunday,* and *Revenge of the Vampire*), 1961; *Ercole al centro della terra* (a.k.a. *Hercules in the Haunted World*) also in 1961, where he mastered colour special effects; *La Frusta e il corpo* (*The Whip and the Body*), 1963; *I tre volti della paura* (*Black Sabbath*) also in 1963, a series of three short stories; "Sei donne per l'assassino" ("Blood and Black Lace"), 1964; and "Terrore nello spazio" ("Planet of the Vampires"), 1965. Bava's influence spread internationally and was evident in such movies as Giorgio Ferroni's *La notte dei diavoli* (1971), Ray Danton's *Hannah, Queen of the Vampires,* Paolo Solvay's *Il plenilunio delle vergini,* and the later features from **Hammer Films.** Some Italian vampire actors should also be mentioned because of the successful roles they played. Many of Bava's movies starred **Barbara Steele,** who became the horror vamp of Italian movies. In 1963 she played in *La danza macabra* (directed by Antonio Margheriti); in 1965 she was in Mario

Caiano's *Gli amanti d'oltretomba* (*The Faceless Monster*), and appeared in Michael Reeve's *La Sorella di Satana* (*Revenge of the Blood Beast*). A specialized Italian vampire was Walter Brandi who played in Piero Regnoli's *L'ultima preda del vampiro* (*The Playgirls and the Vampire*), 1960; Renato Polselli's *L'Amante del vampiro* (*The Vampire and the Ballerina*); and Roberto Mauri's *La Strage dei Vampiri* (*Slaughter of the Vampires*), 1962. Finally, Giacomo Gentiomo's *Maciste contro il vampiro* (*Goliath and the Vampires*), 1961, should be mentioned because its style also manifests traces of Bava's influence. (Bava's son was also responsible for *Fantaghirò*, a fantasy series whose star character was a young girl in a fantasy medieval world who hunts witches, ogres, and occasionally, like **Buffy the Vampire Slayer**, tracks down vampire-like creatures. *Fantaghirò* ran for five seasons on Italian television (1991–95), and was syndicated in several countries (not including the United States.)

The Contemporary Scene: After a heyday in the 1960s, the Italian cinematic vampire fell into disfavor and has since made only infrequent appearances. Movies include *Fracchia contro Dracula* (1985), *Anemia* (1986, an adaptation of the Abruzzese novel whose showings were limited to several experimental theaters), *Vampire a Venezia* (1988), and the 1990 remake of *La maschera del Demonio*. Throughout the 1980s, the Italian literary vampire merged with the Western Europe and North American vampire. Many novels originally written and published in English have now been translated and published in Italy. Italians have also continued to write about vampires both in popular works and more serious fiction. Among the most prominent of the new Italian authors to contribute to the tradition is Patrizia Valduga, notable for the originality of her work. In 1991, she authored *Donna di dolori* (translation: *Woman of Pain*) in which the vampires appeared to remind the reader of the horrors of the twentieth century.

Scholarship on vampires has blossomed in the 1990s. Among prominent studies published during the decade are Marinella Lorinza's *Nel dedalo del drago* (1993); Vito Teti's, *La Melanconia del Vampiro: mito, storia, immaginario* (1994); Carla Corradi Musi's *vampiri europei e vampiri dell'area sciamanica* (1995); Mario Barzaghi, *Il vampiro o il sentimento della modernita* (1996); Massimo Centini's *Dracula un Mito Immortale* (1997); and Massimo Introvigne's *La Stripe di Dracul: Indagine sul vampirirismo dall'antiochita al nostri giorni* (1997).

In 1995, Introvigne, a religious studies scholar, founded the Italian chapter of the **Transylvanian Society of Dracula** (c/o Dr. Massimo Introvigne Via Confienza 19, 10121 Torino), the historical and cultural association of people interested in vampire lore and Dracula studies. Introvigne has a significant collection of vampire books, and the Society cooperated with television producer Riccardo Mazzoni in his staging of "Dracula 1998," the Italian celebration of the Dracula centennial. Centered on a museum display in Milan in the spring, the program included a number of invited guests and several commemorative publications including a substantial survey of the Italian vampire and a new edition of artist Guido Crepax's *Conde Dracula*, one of the finest graphic arts versions of the novel.

Many Italians were introduced to vampires through **comic books** in which vampires began to appear in the 1960s, and vampire stories were soon standard fare in the horror anthologies. While Italian publishers translated and republished many American comics (**Vampirella**, **Morbius**, Rune, etc.), Italians were the most prolific among European nations in generating their own characters and stories. Among early independent vampire titles was **Jacula**, an adult vampire comic featuring a female vampire, reminiscent of the Bad Girl vampires of the 1990s. *Jacula* went on to become the single longest-lasting vampire series ever published, running for 327 issues over a fourteen-year period (1969–82). In the wake of *Jacula*'s success, several imitations were issued, including the almost equally successful, *Zora*, which ran for 235 issues (1973–85).

Through the years Italian comics gave Dracula (both **Count Dracula** and **Vlad the Impaler**) ample treatment. Other aristocratic Eastern European vampires included Bela Rakosi, who invaded the American West in the 1970s series, *Zagor*. Zagor, though having no experience with vampires, figured out their weaknesses and dispatched Rakosi on two different occasions. Vampires frequently appear as guest villains in several Italian adventure comics with a horror slant. Even toward the end of the twentieth century, vampire comics were as popular as ever.

Sources:

Agazzi, Renato. *Il mito del vampiro in Europa*. Poggibonsi: Antonio Lalli, 1979. 257 pp.

Guariento, Steve. "Bava Fever! Italian Gothic, Italian Camp, Italian Psychos (1966–72)" *Samhain* 37 (May/June 1993): 22–26.

Giovannini, Fabio. *Il libro dei vampiri: Dal mito di Dracula alla presenza quotidiana*. Bari: Edizioni Dedalo, 1997. 246 pp.

Introvigne, Massimo. *La stirpe di Dracula: Indagine sul vampirismo dall'antichita ai nostri giorni*. Milan: Arnoldo Mondadori Editore, 1997. 474 pp.

Pattison, Barrie. *The Seal of Dracula*. New York: Bounty Books, 1975. 136 pp.

Raucci, Vincenzo. *Bram Stoker's Dracula 1897–1997*. Monza: Penguin's Editions, 1997. 64 pp.

Rossignoli Emilio de. *Io credo nei vampiri*. Luciano Ferriani, 1961. 379 pp.

Tardiola, Giuseppe. *Il Vampiro nella Letteratura Italiana*. Rome: De Rubeis, 1991. 89 pp.

Vampiri: Miti, legende, letteratura, cinema, fumetti, multimedialità. Milano: Casa Editrice Nord, 1998. 159 pp.

❨ Ivan the Terrible (1530–1584) ❩

Ivan the Terrible was the first czar of Russia. His arbitrary and cruel behavior led to his comparison with **Vlad the Impaler,** the historical **Dracula.** Ivan inherited the title of Grand Duke of Moscovy when he was three and grew up watching the leading families (the boyars) of his land lead the countries through a period of chaos as they fought among themselves for bits of power. He was seventeen when a Chosen Council emerged to bring about reform. Although they succeeded in ending the chaos, Ivan continually fought with them over a multitude of administrative matters. In 1564, in frustration, he suddenly abdicated. When the people demanded his return, he was able to dictate the terms of his reinstatement and gain almost absolute power.

He moved quickly to establish his own ruling elite, the *Oprichnina*, which wrested much of the remaining power from the boyars.

Ivan's reign of two decades was marked, in part, by his conquest of the lands along the Volga River and his movement into Siberia, as well as by a disastrous war in which he unsuccessfully tried to capture Livonia (today Estonia). He is most remembered however, not for his political actions, but for his personal conduct. In his desire to establish a strong central Russian government, he was quick to punish (and even execute) many who challenged his rule or in any way showed disrespect for what he considered his ex-

Ivan the Terrible, who has been compared to Vlad the Impaler.

alted status. He manifested symptoms of extreme paranoia and had a quick and fiery temper. In 1580, in a moment of rage, he killed his own son, a prospective heir.

Outstanding among the traits remembered by his contemporaries, Ivan possessed a dark sense of humor, quite similar to that attributed to Vlad. It often characterized the tortures and executions of those who became the objects of his rage. As one historian, S. K. Rosovetskii, has noted, many of the stories told about Ivan were variations of those originally ascribed to Vlad a century earlier. For example, there was a Romanian folk story about the leading citizens of the town of **Tirgoviste**, Dracula's capital. The citizens had mocked Dracula's brother. In revenge, he rounded up the leading citizens (the boyars) following Easter Day celebrations and, in their fine clothes, he marched them off to work on building **Castle Dracula**. Ivan, it was reported, did something quite similar in the town of Volgoda when the people slighted him on Easter morning. He rounded them up, still dressed in their Easter finery, to build a new city wall for the town.

Possibly the most famous Dracula story told of Ivan concerned the Turkish envoy who refused to remove his hat in Dracula's presence. Dracula, in turn, had the man's hat nailed to the top of his head. Ivan, it was reported, did the same thing to an Italian diplomat (or in an alternative account, to a French ambassador).

Ivan, like Vlad, often turned on powerful figures in Russian society and humiliated them to prevent their return to the dignity of their offices. The story was told, for example, of his attack on Pimen, the Russian Orthodox metropolitan of Novgorod. He stripped Pimen of his church vestments, had him dressed as a strolling minstrel (an occupation denounced by the church), then staged a mock wedding in which Pimen was married to a mare. Presenting the defrocked prelate with the signs of his new status, a bagpipe and a lyre, Ivan sent him from the city.

Ivan differed from Vlad in his sexual appetite. He was a polygamist with seven wives and as many as 50 concubines. He also left his immediate successors with a very mixed inheritance. Although he had expanded the territory of Russia, he left behind a bankrupt country, and discontent with his rule grew steadily. Ivan, however, died quietly in the middle of a chess game on March 18, 1584.

Sources:

de Madariaga, Isabel. *Ivan the Terrible*. New Haven: Yale University Press, 2006. 256 pp.

Parrie, Maureen. *The Image of Ivan the Terrible in Russian Folklore*. London: Cambridge University Press, 1987. 269 pp.

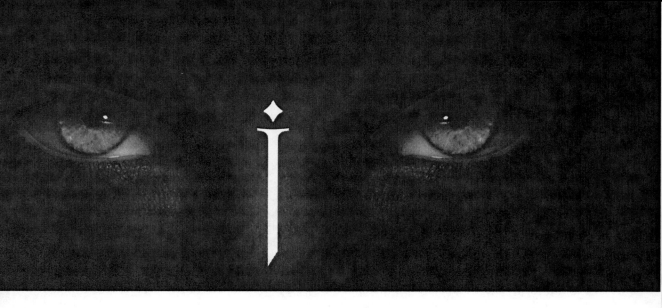

Jacula

An Italian adult comic book of the 1970s and possibly the most successful vampire comic book of all time, *Jacula* ran for 327 issues from 1968 to 1982, and then an additional 129 reprint issues from 1982 to 1984. The comic took its name from the female vampire whose adventures were featured in its pages. According to the storyline, Jacula became a vampire after being bitten by another vampire in 1835 in **Transylvania**. She eventually became so proficient (learning, for example, to live unscathed in **sunlight**) that she was elected as the vampire queen. According to the mythology of the stories, vampires are in a league with the devil (**Satan**), who uses them in pursuit of his long-term goal: to discover Jesus Christ's grave and thus prove to the world that his resurrection is a myth. Quite apart from Satan's plan, however, Jacula had a number of remarkable adventures, often with the assistance of her mortal lover Carlo Verdier, including encounters with **Frankenstein's monster**, Jack the Ripper, and the Marquis de Sade.

Jacula was created by a group of comic artists who operated collectively as Studio Giolitti and was published by Erregi (later Ediperiodici). The publisher was continually harassed because of, by 1960s standards, the slightly pornographic nature of the publication (Jacula was more often than not pictured sans clothing). Public protest eventually brought the series to an end. The title character gave her name to an Italian experimental progressive rock band also founded in 1968 in Milan. The band included Antonio Bartoccetti, Doris Norton (also known as Fiamma Dello Spirito), Charles Tiring, and Franz Porthenzy.

Sources:

Bram Stoker's Dracula, 1897–1997. Monza: Penguin's Editions, 1997. 61 pp.

Giovannini, Fabio. *Il libro dei vampiri: Dal mito di Dracula alla presenza quotidiana*. Bari: edizioni Dedalo, 1997. 246 pp.

Vampiri!: Miti, leggende, letteratura, cinema, fumetti, multimedialita. Milan: Editrice nord, 1998. 158 pp.

Japan, Vampires in

The varied creatures of Japanese folklore did not include a classical bloodsucking vampire. Possibly the most vampirelike of the numerous mythological beings was the *kappa*. Described as fabulous creatures of the **waters**—rivers, ponds, lakes, and the sea—the *kappas* penetrated the Japanese culture and now appear in fiction, cartoons, toys, and art. The *kappa* was first widely written about in the eighteenth century. It was described as an unattractive, humanlike child with greenish-yellow skin, webbed fingers and toes, and somewhat like a monkey with a long nose and round eyes. It had a shell similar to a tortoise and smelled fishy. It had a concave head that held water. If the water in its head spilled, the *kappa* would lose its **strength**. The *kappas* operated from the edge of the water in which they lived. Many stories related attempts by *kappas* to grab horses and cows, drag them into the water, and suck their **blood** through their anuses (the main trait that has earned *kappas* some recognition as vampires). However, they have been known to leave the water to steal melons and cucumbers, rape women, and to attack people for their livers. People would propitiate the *kappas* by writing the names of their family members on a cucumber and throwing it into the river where the kappas lived.

The *kappas* were viewed as part of the rural landscape. They were not attacked by humans, but on occasion *kappas* attempted to strike deals with them. Such a relationship was illustrated in the story of "The Kappa of Fukiura." The *kappa* near Fukiura was a troublesome creature until one day it lost an arm trying to attack a horse. A farmer retrieved the arm, and that night the *kappa* approached the farmer to ask for its return. Rebuffed at first, the *kappa* finally convinced the farmer to return the arm by promising that it would never again hurt any of the villagers. From that time forward, as reported by the villagers, the *kappa* would warn them by saying, "Don't let the children go out to the beach, for the guest is coming." The guest was another *kappa*, not bound by the Kappa of Fukiura's agreement.

Another popular story of the *kappas* told of one who lived at Koda Pond. A man left his horse tied by the pond. A *kappa* tried to pull the horse into the pond, but the horse bolted and ran home. The *kappa* spilled its water, lost its strength, and was carried to the stable. The man later found his horse along with the *kappa*. Caught in a weakened condition, the *kappa* bargained with the man, "If you prepare a feast in your home, I will certainly lend you necessary bowls." From that time on, whenever the man got ready to hold a feast, the *kappa* would bring bowls. After the feast the bowls would be set out and the *kappa* would retrieve them.

Apart from the *kappa*, the Japanese had another interesting folktale. The "Vampire Cat of Nabeshima" told the story of Prince Nabeshima and his beautiful concubine Otoyo. One night a large vampire cat broke into Otoyo's room and killed her in the traditional manner. It disposed of her body and assumed her form. As Otoyo, the cat began to sap the life out of the prince each night while guards strangely fell asleep. Finally, one young guard was able to stay awake and saw the vampire in the form of the young girl. As the guard stood by, the girl was unable to approach the prince, who, then slowly recovered. Finally, it was deduced that the girl was a malevolent spirit who had targeted the prince. The young man, with several guards, went to the girl's apartment. The vampire escaped, however, and removed itself to the hill country. From there, reports of its work were soon received. The prince organized a great hunt, and the vampire was finally killed. The story has been made into a play, **The Vampire Cat** (1918), and a movie, *Hiroku Kaibyoden* (1969).

Contemporary Japanese Vampires: The Japanese, while lacking an extensive vampire lore, have in the last generation absorbed the European vampire myth and contributed to it, primarily through the film industry. Their contemporary vampire is called a *kyuketsuki*. As early as 1956 a film with a vampire theme, *Kyuketsuki Ga*, was released. It concerned a series of murders in which all the **victims** had **fang** marks on their necks, but in the end, the killer turned out not to be a vampire. Some years later the director of *Kyuketsuki Ga* worked on another film, *Onna Kyuketsuki* (1959), which told of a real vampire who kidnapped the wife of an atomic scientist. Among Japan's 1960s vampire movies was *Kuroneko* (1968), which built upon the vampire cat legend. A woman and her daughter were raped and murdered by a group of samurai. They returned from the grave as vampires who could transform themselves into black cats and attack their murderers. In *Yokai Daisenso*, a provincial governor was possessed by a bloodsucking Babylonian demon, an early signal of the coming absorption of Western elements in the Japanese movies.

Hammer Films' vampire movies inspired the 1970 *Chi i Suu Ningyo* (*The Night of the Vampire*) and the 1971 *Chi o Suu Me* (released in the West as *Lake of Dracula*), both directed by Michio Yamamoto. **Dracula** made his first appearance in Japan in the 1970s. In *Kyuketsuki Dorakyura Kobe ni Arawaru: Akuma wa Onna wo Utsukushiku Suru* (literally: *Vampire Dracula Comes to Kobe: Evil Makes a Woman Beautiful*) (1979), Dracula discovered that a reincarnation of the woman he loved lived in Kobe, Japan. In 1980, *Dracula*, a full-length animated movie based on the Marvel Comics characters in the very successful **The Tomb of Dracula**, was the first of a number of excellent cartoon vampire features out of Japan. It was followed by *Vampire Hunter D* (1985) and *Vampire Princess Miyu* (1988), some of the most watched of the Japanese features in the West. In *The Legend of the Eight Samurai* (1984), director Kinji Fukasaku offered a Japanese version of the **Elizabeth Bathory** story in which an evil princess bathes in blood to keep her youth. The vampire theme was carried into the 1990s with such movies as *Tale of a Vampire*, directed by Shimako Sato and based upon the **Edgar Allan Poe** poem, "Annabel Lee." By the end of the 1990s, manga, the Japanese comic books, and anime, the animated version of comic art, had found an audience, and amid the hundreds of titles making their way to the West were a representative number of vampire titles. The more successful manga had originated as anime or were made into anime. Through the first decade of the twenty-first century a number of vampire-oriented television series for children and youth appeared, most animated, including *Descendants of Darkness* (2001), *Hellsing* (2002), *Vampiyan Kids* (2002–03), *Lunar Legend Tsukihime* (2003), *Bloodhound: Vampire Gigilo* (2004), *Moon Phase* (2004–2005), *Karin* (Japan 2005), *Trinity Blood* (Japan 2005), *Blood +* (2005–06), *Nigema!?* (2006–07), *Black Blood Brothers* (2006–2008), and *Rosario + Vampire* (2008). Translated and transferred to DVDs, these television shows were later released in West, along with their related comic books.

After *Vampire Hunter D* appeared, its became recognized as one of the finest vampire films of all time, and both its writer Hideyuki Kikuchi and artist Yoshitaka Amano

were recognized for their talents. Kikuchi went on to write a series of *Vampire Hunter D* novels and Amano illustrated the movie's sequel *Vampire Hunter D: Bloodlust* (2000), and the covers of the novels. Currently, Digital Manga Publishing and Hideyuki Kikuchi are overseeing a project to adapt and publish all of the *Vampire Hunter D* novels into a manga format.

Sources:

Amano, Yoshitaka. *The Art of Vampire Hunter D: Bloodlust*. Screenplay by Yoshiaki Kawajiri. San Diego: IDW Publishing, July 2006.
———. *The Art of Vampire Hunter D*. Milwaukie, OR: DH Press, 2007. 200 pp.
———. *Coffin: The Art of Vampire Hunter D*. Milwaukie, OR: DH Press, 2007. 200 pp.
Dorson, Richard M. *Folk Legends of Japan*. Rutland, VT: Charles E. Tuttle Company, 1962. 256 pp.
Hurwood, Bernhardt J. *Passport to the Supernatural: An Occult Compendium from All Ages and Many Lands*. New York: Taplinger Publishing Company, 1972. 319 pp.
Jones, Stephen. *The Illustrated Vampire Movie Guide*. London: Titan Books, 1993. 144 pp.
Van Etten, Gerard. *The Vampire Cat: A Play in One Act from the Japanese Legend of the Nebeshima Cat*. Chicago: Dramatic Publishing Company, 1918. 16 pp.

Java, Vampires in

The Javanese shared much of their mythology with **Malaysia** and the rest of Indonesia. Included in that mythology was the belief in the *pontianak*. The *pontianak* was a bansheelike creature that flew through the night in the form of a bird. It could be heard wailing in the evening breeze as it sat in the forest trees. It was described variously as a woman who died a virgin (de Wit) or a woman who died giving birth (Kennedy). In both cases, it appeared as beautiful young **women** and attacked men whom it emasculated. De Wit noted that the *pontianak* appeared fairer than any love-goddess. Such creatures would embrace a man, but immediately withdraw after a single kiss. In the process they revealed the hole in their backs, which had been covered by the long tresses of hair. The man had to grab the hair and pull out a single strand, or he would be vampirized by the woman. If he failed, he would soon die; if he succeeded, he would live a long and happy life.

The *pontianak* also attacked babies and sucked their **blood** out of jealousy over the happiness of the mother. Infants who were stillborn or who died soon after birth of an unknown cause would be thought of as **victims** of a *pontianak*.

Sources:

de Wit, Augusta. *Java: Facts and Fancies*. The Hague: W. P. van Stockum, 1912. Rept. Singapore: Oxford University Press, 1984. 321 pp.
Kennedy, Raymond. *The Ageless Indies*. New York: John Day Company, 1942. 208 pp.

Jourdan, Louis (1921–)

Louis Jourdan, an actor known for his starring role in a made-for-television production, **Count Dracula** (1978), was born in Marseilles, France. He made his first movie in 1940 in a French production, *Le Corsaire*. After World War II he came to the United States and appeared in *The Paradine Case* (1946), which was followed by many appearances on stage and screen.

In 1978 Jourdan starred in his first vampire role as Count **Dracula** in the BBC production of the **Bram Stoker** novel. The lengthy production (two-and-a-half hours) is remembered as one of the more faithful reenactments of the original work. It included the famous scene in which **Jonathan Harker** saw Dracula crawling down the walls of his castle. The movie was noted for its emphasis on **drama**, and tension rather than **blood** and violence. A sexual element was present, but because *Count Dracula* was produced for television, there was no nudity. Jourdan played the role in a manner similar to **Frank Langella** (then starring in the Broadway revival of the play), as a suave, continental romantic hero. Women swooned in ecstacy when he bit them. After his Dracula role, Jourdan went on to star in several other movies, including the James Bond movie *Octopussy*, (1983) and *The Return of the Swamp Thing* (1989). He currently (2009) lives in retirement in Vielle, in southern France.

Sources:

Holte, James Craig. *Dracula in the Dark: The Dracula Film Adaptations*. Westport, CT: Greenwood Press, 1997. 161 pp.

Jones, Stephen. *The Illustrated Vampire Movie Guide*. London: Titan Books, 1993. 144 pp.

Waller, Gregory A. *The Living and the Undead: From Stoker's Dracula to Romero's Dawn of the Dead*. Urbana, IL: University of Illinois Press, 1986. 376 pp.

Journal of Vampirology

From 1984 to 1990 the field of vampire studies had what closely resembled a scholarly journal. The 18 issues of the *Journal of Vampirology* contained a variety of well-researched articles on vampire history and folklore. Editor John L. Vellutini of San Francisco wrote more than half of the articles, and the journal reflected both his interests and his expertise. Although serious students of the field read the publication, their number was too small to keep the journal in print.

Juvenile Literature

Vampire fiction was exclusively an adult literature until the appearance of horror **comic books** in the 1940s. In the wake of the controversy over the hypothesized harmful content of comic books in the 1950s (which had the effect of banishing the vampire from their pages for two decades), there was no support for expanding the scope of juvenile literature in general by the inclusion of vampire stories.

The ban on vampires in comic books began to be lifted in the late 1960s with the appearance of **Dark Shadows** and **Vampirella**, and was done away with completely in 1971. That same year, the first novel written specifically for young people that included a vampire theme was published. *Danger on Vampire Trail* was No. 50 in the very popular Hardy Boys series of mystery books. The youthful detectives were tracking some credit card thieves, whom they traced to a remote location called Vampire Trail. The site

recently had been renamed following reported attacks by **bats**, and on an exploration of the trail the Hardys found a dead vampire bat, seemingly far away from his natural habitat. However, in the end, they found no vampires, and the bat turned out to have been imported from Central America simply to scare locals away from the crooks' hideout.

The 1970s: The real introduction of the juvenile audience to the subject came in 1973 with the publication of **Nancy Garden**'s nonfiction *Vampires*. Based in large part on two books by **Montague Summers** and the research of **Radu Florescu** and **Raymond T. McNally**, Garden presented a broad survey of vampire lore, the literary and cinematic vampire, and the real **Dracula, Vlad the Impaler**. The obvious popularity of the vampire during the decade prompted two similar nonfiction vampire books by Thomas Aylesworth and the Ronans. That same year, the first juvenile vampire novel, Vic Crume's *The Mystery of Vampire Castle*, a novelization of the Walt Disney movie of the same name, concerned a 12-year-old amateur movie producer-director Alfie Booth, who had decided to spend his summer making a Dracula movie. In the process, Alfie and his brother ran into several jewelry thieves whose eventual detection and capture supplied the real **drama** of the movie. It was not until the last half of the decade that the initial real bloodsucking vampires made their appearance. Among books aimed at a high school audience, evil vampires bared their teeth in Steven Otfinoski's *Village of Vampires* (1978). The novel's hero, Dr. John Lawrence, his daughter Sandy, and assistant Paul Ross had journeyed to the village of Taaxacola, **Mexico**, where cows had begun to die of a strange malady. Several years before, Lawrence had been in the village to administer a serum to the cattle, which had been under attack from vampire bats. Upon his return, however, he discovered that the entire village now had been turned into vampires. It became the Lawrence party's task to kill them in the traditional manner (**stake** through the heart). In the end, the men had to rescue Sandy as she also was about to be made into a vampire. In Kin Platt's *Dracula Go Home!*, a 1979 comic novel, Larry Carter, a high schooler working at his aunt's hotel during summer vacation, checked a Mr. A. L. R. Claud from Belgrade into a room. The man was pale and wore a black suit with a large hat. He asked for room 13. Larry was sure that Mr. Claud was a vampire and set out to find the proof. In the end, he was found not to be a vampire but a jewel thief who had returned to town to recover stolen merchandise.

For the younger audience still in elementary school, a more benign vampire strolled across the pages of a host of books. For example, in 1979 Deborah Howe and her husband James Howe introduced possibly the most lovable vampire of all time, the vegetarian vampire rabbit **Bunnicula**. Bunnicula, who was given his name after having been found in the theater during a Dracula movie, was the pet of Pete and Toby Monroe. The rabbit was the third animal in a home that included Harold the dog and Chester the cat. Bunnicula was a strange rabbit; he slept all day and, instead of two bunny teeth in front, he had two **fangs**.

It was Chester who first spotted the rabbit leaving his cage at night to raid the refrigerator. The next morning the Monroes discovered a white tomato from which all the juice and color (and life) had been sucked. It was the knowledgeable Chester, who spent all of his spare time reading books, who was the first to determine that Bunnicula was a vampire. Having made his discovery, Chester proceeded to block Bunnicula's path to the kitchen with a **garlic** barrier. Bunnicula almost starved until Harold, concluding that Bunnicula was causing no harm, intervened and smuggled him into the kitchen.

Bunnicula proved as popular as he was lovable, and his story was made into a movie for children's **television**. Through the 1980s he returned in a series of stories, beginning with the 1983 volume, *The Celery Stalks at Midnight*. For the youngest audience, a vampire literature developed out of the popular televison show *Sesame Street*, one of the most heralded products of the Public Broadcasting Network. The show specialized in the socialization of preschool children and the teaching of basic knowledge such as the alphabet and numbers. Soon after the show began, the teaching of numbers became the special domain of Count von Count, a puppet version of a **Bela Lugosi**—like vampire complete with widow's peak and fangs. Through the 1970s, the Count made such tapes as *The Count Counts* (1975) and was the subject of several books, including *The Counting Book* (1971), *The Count's Poem* (1976), *The Day the Count Stopped Counting* (1977), and *The Count's Number Parade* (1977).

The 1980s: The 1980s saw the development of a full range of vampire literature for all ages. Literature for the youngest children was launched with the continuing volumes featuring **Count von Count** of *Sesame Street*. He began the decade with *The Count's Counting Book* (1980). When the book's cover was opened, the Count and his castle popped up to say, "Aha! Another wonderful day to count on." He then counted various things in his atmospheric neighborhood. In 1981 he followed with *The Count Counts a Party* and other items through the decade. For elementary school young people, several popular vampire series joined the Bunnicula titles. In 1982 the first volume of Ann Jungman's series featuring Vlad the Drac, another vegetarian vampire, appeared.

That same year in **Germany**, Angela Sommer-Bodenburg published the first of her four books featuring the young vampire Rudolph Sackville-Bagg, Rudolph's vampire sister Anna, and their human friend Tony Noodleman. These were promptly translated into English and published in the United States as *My Friend the Vampire*, *The Vampire Moves In*, *The Vampire on the Farm*, and *The Vampire Takes a Trip*. Typical of children's literature, the vampire was a somewhat sympathetic character, at worst a mischievous boy, with the primary elements of horror hovering in the background. *The Vampire Moves In*, for instance, revolved around Rudolph's move into the family storage bin in the basement of the apartment building where Tony's family lived. He had been kicked out of his own family vault because of his fraternizing with humans. The plot centered on the problems created by the vampire's presence, not the least of which was the terrible smell that began to radiate from the vampire's **coffin** and the presence of the undead.

A third series that began later in the decade by author Mel Gilden featured the "fifth grade monsters." In the opening volume, *M Is for Monster*, Danny Keegan began a new school year as a fifth grader. His major problem was bully Stevie Brickwald. However, when he got to school he discovered four new classmates. One possessed a huge mane of hair and slightly pointed ears. His name was Howie Wolfner. A brother and sister team by the name Elsie and Frankie Stein each had metal bolts coming out of the side of their necks. Finally there was the short, fanged kid with slicked–back hair, a black suit, white bow tie, and a satin-lined cape. His name was C. D. Bitesky, whose family came from **Transylvania**. C. D. carried a Thermos bottle from which he frequently sipped a red liquid that he termed the "fluid of life," and he had a pet bat named Spike.

After an initial hesitancy, Danny became friends with these different but nonetheless special people, and within a few years their adventures would fill 15 volumes with

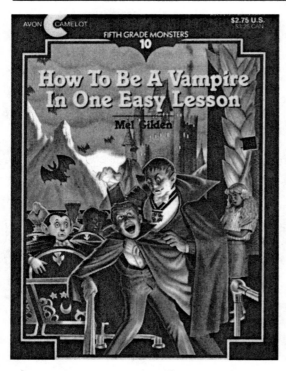

AVON CAMELOT $2.75 U.S. $3.25 CAN.

FIFTH GRADE MONSTERS
10

How To Be A Vampire In One Easy Lesson

Mel Gilden

Author Mel Gilden wrote a series of books featuring
"The Fifth Grade Monsters," which of course
included several vampires.

no end in sight. C. D. was especially featured in volume 10, *How to be a Vampire in One Easy Lesson* (1990), in which the persistent Stevie Brickwald tried to make friends with the "monsters" and asked C.D. to make him a vampire. C. D. first invited him to his home where his parents started to teach Stevie Romanian history. The impatient Stevie learned that he must meet the Count, C. D.'s patriarchal uncle, who lived in the basement of the local theater, appropriately named **Carfax** Palace. When Stevie appeared at school the next day dressed in a crumpled tuxedo, following his private session with the Count, he announced that he was a "freelance vampire first class." However, Stevie wished to use his newfound "will" to keep him from having to go to school, but his teacher and the principal finally persuaded him that he was not a vampire.

The final series aimed at elementary school young people to appear in the 1980s was written by Ann Hodgman. Her first volume, *There's a Batwing in My Lunchbox*, was published by Avon in 1988. The young people's vampire, while borrowing from the more traditional character of horror fiction, to some extent had his (and it has almost exclusively been a male) fangs pulled. He was a good person—definitely not the sinister figure of the adult novels or the movies. Absent from the youthful vampire book was any hint of horror, any factor that might lead to the young reader having nightmares. He was never pictured as biting anyone, though there were oblique references, and of course, no harm resulted from a vegetarian like Bunnicula biting a plant. Placed within the context of the young person's world, the vampire was either a lovable pet, a comic figure, or more likely, a somewhat out-of-the-ordinary classmate who can become, in spite of his differences, a close friend.

As the number of titles for elementary school children expanded, so did the number aimed at high schoolers. Typical of these was *The Initiation* by Robert Brunn (1982). The story concerned Adam Maxwell, a student at Blair Prep School. Adam had a problem—he was a misfit. He was totally unappreciative of the elitism and snobbery so evident among both his classmates and the students of nearby Abbott, a girls school similar to Blair. Both were founded by a Transylvanian couple, Isadore and Bella Esterhaus. Adam soon met his counterpart at Abbott, Loren Winters. Four days after his arrival to the school, Adam found a body in one of the school lockers. Loren had witnessed one of her classmates leaving campus with a man who was reported dead the next day.

Together Adam and Loren attempted to figure out the situation they were in. The focus of their search led to an initiation ceremony that occurred during the biweekly mixers promoted by the two schools. Selected students were invited to the basement to be inducted into "a serious organization." Blindfolded and paired with an initiator of the opposite sex, they were attacked in the dark, and all that could be heard was a "wet slurping noise." In the 1970s, the vampire had received some recognition from the new respect given to classic horror and **gothic** fiction within the academic community—a respect reflected in the addition of such stories to elementary and high school curricula. By the 1980s **Bram Stoker's** *Dracula* **(1897)** was recognized as such a classic piece of horror literature, and condensed versions of *Dracula* designed for a juvenile audience began to appear.

In the early 1970s, a black-and-white comic version of *Dracula* (1973) became the first juvenile adaptation of the story, and a version for children had been published in 1976 as *Paint Me the Story of Dracula*. Then, at the beginning of the decade, Delacote Press released Alice and Joel Schick's color comic book version of *Dracula*. Several years later, Stephanie Spinner and illustrator Jim Spence prepared a condensed version, often reprinted, for elementary schoolers. In addition, a juvenile version of **John Polidori's** original vampire story, "The Vampyre", appeared in England in 1986.

The 1990s: Through the 1980s, the production rate of new vampire-oriented juvenile literature had steadily increased. That increase did not stop in the early 1990s. In the 1980s, some 50 titles were published. In the three years of 1990 to 1992, over 35 titles appeared. Series begun in the 1980s by Mel Gilden, Ann Hodgman, and James Howe continued, and a new series for high schoolers, *The Vampire Diaries* by L. J. Smith, explored the triangle of the vampire brothers Damon and Stefan, and the girl Elena whom they both desired and who must decide between them. For the youngest vampire fans, a pop-up version of *Dracula* was published by Gallery Books in 1990. Preschoolers could start their learning process with Alan Benjamin's *Let's Count, Dracula* (1991).

During the 1980s two vampire stories were included in the "Choose Your Own Adventure" series. A third such vampire volume, *Vampire Invaders* by Edward Packard, appeared as No. 118 in the series in 1991. Additionally, several general juvenile horror series added a vampire novel. Carl Laymon's *Nightmare Lake*, for example, appeared as No. 11 in Dell's *Twilight* series. Bert, Eliot, and his sister Sammi on an island vacation, discovered a skeleton after which their dog removed a stick protruding from its rib cage. The children reported their discovery to the police, but upon their return to the island, the skeleton had disappeared. The mystery increased when two bodies were found in a canoe. One had a bloody wound on his neck and, as was later determined, had died from loss of **blood**. The other person awoke in a state of near hysteria and complained of an attack by a bat. The emergence of vampire believers and skeptics set the stage for the final revelation of the true vampire in their midst.

Among the outstanding new novels was Annette Curtis Klause's *The Silver Kiss*, centered upon the experience of Zoë, a young girl with a fatally ill mother and an emotionally distant father, who tried to protect her from the reality of death. Her loneliness opened her to a relationship with Simon, a vampire. Simon had grown up in Cromwellian England. A business acquaintance of his father introduced vampirism to the family and chose Simon's older brother Christopher as his first **victim**. Christopher disappeared for many years, but at one point returned to attack his brother Simon, now a young man, and to transform him into a vampire. He also learned that Christopher had killed their mother. Simon was determined to hunt down and kill his brother.

That drive had brought him to **America** in the 1930s. Meanwhile, between her seemingly immortal friend who was ready for a final encounter with his brother and her

dying mother, Zoë overcame her father's protecting her from the reality of death and arrived at some understanding of its role in life. Of a lighter nature was *Great Uncle Dracula* by Jayne Harvey, a modern-day parable for children who feel they just do not fit in. It was the story of Emily Normal, a third grader who moved with her father and brother from Plainville to Transylvania, U.S.A., to live with her uncle. Soon after she arrived for her first day at school, she realized that Transylvania was a creepy place: all the girls dressed in black and claimed to be witches; the class pets were tarantulas; her teacher's name was Ms. Vampira and the principal was Frank N. Stein. Emily just did not fit in. She had always done well as a speller, but the "spell"-ing bee did not concern "spelling" words but doing magic "spells." She did make friends, however, and soon found herself at a party. But the party turned into a disaster when Emily fell on the birthday cake while playing pin the tail on the rat. Emily finally got her chance, however, in the gross face contest. Angry at being called names since her arrival at school, she won the contest by the face she made just as she shouted out, "I am not a weirdo." She was awarded the prize for making the grossest face anyone in Transylvania could remember.

Through the 1990s and the first decade of the new century, vampire story books for children and novels for youth proliferated. For the youngest, the most prominent books featured *Mona the Vampire* (by Hiawyn Oram and Sonia Hollyman), later to become an animated television program. Young readers could get into the *Monster Manor* series by Paul Martin and Manu Boiseau or *My Sister the Vampire* by Sienna Mercer. Slightly older readers could find the *Vampirates* series by Justin Somper, the *Vampire Plagues* series by Sebastian Rooke, and the *Vampire Beach* series by Alex Duvall.

Richie Tankersley Cusack's *Buffy the Vampire Slayer* (1992), the novelization of the movie, heralded the series of Buffy novels that would begin to appear after the television show, originally pitched at a high school audience but found a much broader appeal. At its height in the middle of the next decade, more than fifteen Buffy novels, some completely new stories, some novelizations of episode screenplays, were appearing.

Buffy the Vampire Slayer identified a youth market for vampire novels and a number of authors responded to it. As the new century began, several series written for a junior high school and high school readership shared the spotlight with Buffy in the juvenile vampire market. Leading off the decade was Amelia Atwatter-Rhodes whose *In the Forests of the Night* (1999) was the first of a half dozen books built around vampires and associated creatures. Among the most successful of the new vampire authors was Darren O'Shaughnessy who wrote the *Cirque Du Freak* series under the pen name Darren Shan. His dozen novels traced the adventures of a young Darren Shan who must adjust to life as a half-vampire.

High school vampire fans could assuage their thirst with the *House of Night* series of mother/daughter team **PC and Kristin Cast**, the *Vampire Kisses* series by Ellen Schreiber, The *Vampire Academy* series of Richelle Meade, the *Bloodline* series by Katy Cary, the *Lords of Darkness* series by L. G. Burbank, or the *Morganville Vampires* series of Rachel Caine.

By far the most successful post-Buffy vampire books were the *Twilight* series by **Stephanie Meyer** which trace the story of a high school girl, **Bella Swan**, who by her own definition was clumsy and lacked self assurance in the extreme. She meets the love of her life, a vampire classmate, **Edward Cullen**. *Twilight* was made into the largest grossing vampire movie of all time and was followed by its equally successful sequel *New Moon*, with plans to make movies of the remaining volumes in the book series as this encyclopedia goes to press.

Among the notable fallouts of the success of the *Twilight* series was the revival of the 1990s' *Vampire Diaries* series by **Laura Smith**.

Sources:

Nonfiction

Atwater-Rhodes, Amelia. *In the Forests of the Night*. New York: Delacorte, 1999. 144 pp.

Austin, R. G. *Vampires, Spies and Alien Beings*. New York: Archway/Pocket Books, 1982. 120 pp.

Aylesworth, Thomas G. *The Story of Vampires*. Middletown, CT: Weekly Reader Books, 1977. 85 pp. Rept. Middletown CT: Xerox Education Publications, 1977. 85 pp.

Burbank, L. G. *The Souless*. Vol. 1 *Lords of Darkness*. Palm Beach, FL: Medallion Press, 2004. 384 pp.

Duvall, Alex. *Vampire Beach: Bloodlust*. London: Red Fox Book, 2006. 233 pp.

Garden, Nancy. *Vampires*. Philadelphia: J. B. Lippencott Company, 1973. 127 pp.

Gelman, Rita Golden, and Nancy Lamb. *Vampires and Other Creatures of the Night*. New York: Scholastic, Inc., 1991. 74 pp.

McHargue, Georgess. *Meet the Vampire*. Philadelphia: J. B. Lippencott Company, 1976. Rept. New York: Laurel Leaf Books, 1983. 106 pp.

Martin, Paul, and Manu Boisteau. *Monster Manor: Beatice Spells*. New York: Volo/Hyperion Books for Children, 2003. 82 pp.

Oram, Hiawyn, and Sonia Hollyman. *Mona the Vampire and the Big Brown Bap Monster*. London: Orchard Books, 2004. 64 pp.

Ronan, Margaret, and Eve Ronan. *Curse of the Vampires*. New York: Scholastic Book Services, 1979. 89 pp.

Schreiber, Ellen. *Vampire Kisses*. New York: HarperCollins Juvenile Books, 2003. 208 pp.

Somper, Justin. *Demons of the Ocean*. Vampirates 1. London: Simon & Schuster Children's Books, 2005. 298 pp.

Fiction

Benjamin, Alan. *Let's Count, Dracula*. A Chubby Board Book. New York: Simon & Schuster, 1992. 16 pp.

Brunn, Robert. *The Initiation*. New York: Dell, 1982. 154 pp.

Cooney, Caroline. *The Cheerleader*. New York: Scholastic, 1991. 179 pp.

———. *The Return of the Vampire*. New York: Scholastic, 1992. 166 pp.

The Counting Book. New York: Random House, 1971.

The Count's Counting Book. New York: Random House/Children's Television Workshop, 1980. 14 pp.

Crume, Vic. *The Mystery in Dracula's Castle*. New York: Scholastic Book Services, 1973. 111 pp.

Cusick, Richie Tankersley. *Vampire*. New York: Pocket Books, 1991. 214 pp.

———. *Buffy the Vampire Slayer*. New York: Pocket Books, 1992. 183 pp.

Dixon, Franklin W. *Danger on Vampire Trail*. The Hardy Boys, Vol. 50. New York: Grosset & Dunlap, 1971. 175 pp.

Garden, Nancy. *Prisoner of Vampires*. New York: Farrar, Strauss, and Giroux, 1984. 213 pp.

———. *Mystery of the Night Raiders*. (Monster Hunters Case, 1) New York: Pocket Books, 1987, 1991.

———. *My Sister, the Vampire*. New York: Alfred A. Knopf, 1992. 186 pp.

Gilden, Mel. *Born to Howl*. New York: Avon, 1987. 91 pp.

———. *How to Be a Vampire in One Easy Lesson*. New York: Avon, 1990. 91 pp.

Harvey, James. *Great Uncle Dracula*. New York: Random House, 1992. 77 pp.

Hodgman, Ann. *My Babysitter Has Fangs*. New York: Pocket Books, 1992. 137 pp.

————. *My Babysitter Bites Again*. New York: Pocket Books, 1993. 135 pp.

Howe, Deborah, and James Howe. *Bunnicula*. New York: Atheneum Publishers, 1979. Rept. New York: Avon, 1980. 98 pp.

Korr, David. *The Day the Count Stopped Counting*. New York: Western Publishing Company, 1977. 46 pp.

Packard, Edward. *Space Vampire*. Choose Your Own Adventure, No. 71. New York: Bantam Books, 1987. 118 pp.

————. *Vampire Invaders*. Choose Your Own Adventure, No. 118. New York: Bantam Books, 1991. 111 pp.

Polidori, John. *The Vampyre*. Retold by David Campton. London: Beaver/Arrow, 1986. Rept. New York: Barron's Educational Series, 1988. 139 pp.

Sommer-Bodenburg, Angela. *Der Kleine Vampir*. Reinbek bei Hamburg, Germany: Rowohlt Taschenbuch Verlag, 1982. Reprint as, *My Friend the Vampire*. Trans. by Sarah Gibson. New York: E. P. Dutton, 1982. Rept. New York: Penguin, 1991. 131 pp.

————. *Der kliene Vampir zeiht um*. Reinbek bei Hamburg, Germany: Rowohlt Taschenbuch Verlag, 1982. Reprinted as: *The Vampire Moves In*. New York: E. P. Dutton, 1982. 155 pp. Rept. New York: Minstrel/Pocket Books, 1986. 155 pp.

————. *Der kleine Vampir auf dem Bauerhof*. Reinbek bei Hamburg, Germany: Rowohlt Taschenbuch Verlag, 1983. Reprinted as: *The Vampire on the Farm*. New York: E. P. Dutton, 1990. 136 pp. Rept. New York: Minstrel/Pocket Books, 1990. 135 pp.

————. *The Vampire Takes a Trip*. New York: E. P. Dutton, 1985.

Spinner, Stephanie. *Dracula*. New York: Random House, 1982.

Stiles, Norman. *The Count's Number Parade*. Racine, WI: Western, 1977. 24 pp.

Stoker, Bram. *Dracula*. Adapted by Stephanie Spinner. New York: Step-Up Adventures/Random House, 1982. 94 pp.

Kali

A major deity in the mythology of **India**, Among other characteristics, Kali was known for her thirst for **blood**. Kali first appeared in Indian writings around the sixth century C.E. in invocations calling for her assistance in war. In these early texts she was described as having **fangs**, wearing a garland of corpses, and living at the cremation ground.

Several centuries later, in the *Bhagavat-purana*, she and her cohorts, the *dakinis*, turned on a band of thieves, decapitated them, got drunk on their blood, and played a game of tossing the heads around. Other writings called for her temples to be built away from the villages near the cremation grounds.

Kali made her most famous appearance in the *Devi-mahatmya*, where she joined the goddess Durga in fighting the demon Raktabija. Raktabija had the ability to reproduce himself with each drop of spilled blood; thus, in fighting him successfully, Durga found herself being overwhelmed by Raktabija clones.

Kali rescued Durga by vampirizing Raktabija and eating the duplicates. Kali came to be seen by some as Durga's wrathful aspect. Kali also appeared as a consort of the god Siva. They engaged in fierce dance. Pictorially, Kali was usually shown on top of Siva's prone body in the dominant position as they engaged in sexual intercourse.

Kali had an ambiguous relationship to the world. On the one hand she destroyed demons and thus brought order. However, she also served as a representation of forces that threatened social order and stability by her blood-drunkenness and subsequent frenzied activity.

Kali became the dominant deity within Tantric Hinduism, where she was praised as the original form of things and the origin of all that exists. She was termed Creatrix, Protectress, and Destructress. In Tantra, the way of salvation was through the sensual delights of the world—those things usually forbidden to a devout Hindu—such as alcohol

Kali, the bloodthirsty Hindu deity.

and sex. Kali represented the ultimate forbidden realities, and was thus to be taken into the self and overcome in what amounted to a ritual of salvation. She taught that life fed on death, that death was inevitable for all beings, and that in the acceptance of these truths—by confronting Kali in the cremation grounds and thus demonstrating courage equal to her terrible nature—there was liberation. Kali, like many vampire-deities, symbolized the disorder that continually appeared amid all attempts to create order. Life was ultimately untamable and unpredictable.

Kali survived among the **Gypsies**, who had migrated from India to Europe in the Middle Ages, as Sara, the Black Goddess. However, her vampiric aspects were much mediated by the mixture of Kali with an interesting French Christian myth. According to the story, the three Marys of the New Testament traveled to **France** where they were met by Sara, a Gypsy who assisted them in their landing. They baptized Sara and preached the gospel to her people. The Gypsies hold a celebration on May 24–25 each year at Saintes-Maries-de-la-Mer, the small French village where the events are believed to have occurred. A statue to Sara was placed in the crypt of the church where the Gypsies have kept their annual vigil.

Sources:

Chatterji, Shoma. *Goddess Kali of Kolkata.* New Delhi: UBS Publishers' Distributors, 2005. 140 pp.

Clébert, Jean-Paul. *The Gypsies.* Harmondsworth, UK: Penguin Books, 1967. 282 pp.

Harding, Elizabeth A. *Kali: The Black Goddess of Dakshineswar.* Lake Worth, FL: Nicolas-Hays, 1993. 352 pp.

Kindler, Babji Bob. *Twenty-four Aspects of Mother Kali.* Greenville, NY: SRV Associations, 1996. 226 pp.

Kinsley, David. *Hindu Goddesses: Visions of the Divine Feminine in the Hindu Religious Tradition.* Berkeley, CA: University of California Press, 1986. 281 pp.

Kalogridis, Jeanne (1954–)

Jeanne Kalogridis, the author of a series of novels based on Dracula, grew up in Florida with an interest in books and language. She attributes her love of reading as a response to her less-than-ideal childhood, during which she found that fantasy provided an escape from the unpleasant present, and horror a safe means of confronting fear, pain, and death. After earning a bachelor's degree in Russian, she attended graduate school at the University of South Florida where she received a master's degree in Linguistics in 1980.

Afterward, she did postgraduate work at Georgetown University and taught English as a Second Language at American University. After teaching for eight years, she decided to begin writing full time. For more than a decade she wrote quite successfully under a pseudonym, then in the mid-1990s decided to publish under her own name.

Kalogridis was particularly affected by reading **Dracula**, and reread it several times. She also read biographies of **Vlad the Impaler**. When she finally went to write about the Dracula family, she modeled her **Dracula** after Vlad. In the Dracula trilogy through which she began to introduce herself to the reading public, she focuses on the idea of Dracula having a covenant with his human family that has been kept alive over the centuries. The first of the novels, *Covenant with the Vampire* (1994), introduces Dracula's family some 50 years prior to the events in **Bram Stoker**'s *Dracula* According to Kalogridis's novel, at the castle of Prince Vlad, Vlad's great-nephew Arkady has recently taken over the job of managing the thriving; busy estate. Arkady is honored to care for his beloved though eccentric great-uncle … until he begins to realize what is expected of him in his new role. Dracula's family are bound by a covenant to serve Dracula and to protect him, meaning that Arkady must provide his great-uncle with **victims** to satisfy his needs, or Vlad will kill those Arkady loves.

The covenant traps him into becoming an accessory to murder and sadistic torture. When Arkady discovers his newborn son has been designated as Dracula's successor, Arkady decides that he must oppose Dracula and save his son. The scene is set for the battle that continues in the two sequels, *Children of the Vampire* (1995) and *Lord of the Vampires* (1996).

Since her Dracula trilogy, Kalogridis has written a number of books, but has not returned to a vampire theme.

Sources:

Kalogridis, Jeanne. *Covenant with the Vampire: The Diaries of the Family Dracula*. New York: Delacorte Press, 1994. 324 pp. Rept. New York: Dell, 1995. 352 pp.

———. *Children of the Vampire: The Diaries of the Family Dracula*. New York: Delacorte Press, 1995. 301 pp. Rept. New York: Delacorte, 1995. 324 pp.

———. *Lord of the Vampires*. New York: Delacorte Press, 1996. 347 pp.

Kaplan, Stephen *see:* Vampire Research Center

Kappa *see:* Japan, Vampires in

❨ Keats, John (1795–1821) ❩

J ohn Keats, British romantic poet, was born in London, the son of Frances Jennings and Thomas Keats. His father, a livery-stable keeper, was killed in 1804 after a fall from a horse. His mother remarried, but it proved an unhappy union and she soon separated. She died in 1810 from tuberculosis. It was as his mother's condition worsened that Keats, never the scholarly type, began to read widely. He especially liked the Greek myths. After his mother's death he was apprenticed to a surgeon and in 1814 moved to London to study at the joint school of St. Thomas and Guy's Hospitals. He passed his examination in 1816 and began a career as a surgeon.

During his years in school in London, poetry came to dominate his leisure time. He was still in his teens when he wrote his first poems, and in 1815 he produced "On First Looking into Chapman's Homer," still hailed as one of the finest sonnets in the English language. About this time he met Leigh Hunt, also a poet, who introduced Keats into various literary circles. Keats's volume of verse was published in 1817. While the book did not do well, he decided to halt his surgical career to seek a quiet existence pursuing his poetry. Through the rest of the year he produced "Endymion," "Ode to Psyche," "Ode to a Nightingale," and one of his most enduring efforts "Ode on a Grecian Urn." Through 1819 he worked on "Otho the Great," "Hyperion," "The Eve of Saint Agnes," and "Lamia".

With "Lamia" he picked up the vampire theme then becoming popular in Western literature. Interestingly enough, he began working on the poem soon after the publication of **John Polidori**'s "The Vampyre" (the first piece of vampire fiction in English), in the *New Monthly Magazine*. At this time, Keats was under some financial strain, and his love affair with Fanny Brawne was having its ups and downs. He also had developed a full-blown case of tuberculosis, a wasting disease that occasioned the periodic spitting up of blood.

Keats's "Lamia" derived from the ancient account of the *lamiai*, the **Greek** vampire-like demons described by Philostratus in his *Life of Apollonius*. The story told of a *lamia* attempting to seduce a young man of Corinth. As he was about to marry the *lamia*, who would have turned on him and killed him, the wise Apollonius intervened. He unmasked her for what she was, and as he pointed out the illusionary environment she had created, its beauty faded away. She, of course, then departed. As Keats did not read Greek, and no English translation of the *Life of Apollonius* had been published, he had to rely upon **Richard Francis Burton**'s version of the story in his *Anatomy of Melancholy*.

Crucial to Burton's retelling was his deletion of a crucial sentence in Philostratus's text, "… she admitted she was a vampire and was fattening up Menippus (Lucius) with pleasure before devouring his body, for it was her habit to feed upon young and beautiful bodies because their **blood** was pure and strong." Burton presented a somewhat sanitized *lamia*, but Keats metaphorically pulled her **fangs** even farther. To best understand "The Lamia," one must view the story, as **James B. Twitchell** and other critics have done, as Keats's having adopted the vampire theme as a metaphor of human relations seen as the interchange of life-giving energies. In the process, Philostratus's story is changed considerably. According to Keats, in her thirst for love, the *lamia* dropped her traditional serpentlike form and moved into Lucius's human world. Lucius responded by becoming vampiric and attempting to gain some of the *lamia*'s former powers. Thus, Keats pictured the *lamia* using powers of psychic vampirism, drawing on Lucius's love as her metaphorical life-blood. In return, Lucius also became a vampire, willing to drain all from the *lamia* to gain new powers. Keats noted that Lucius had "drunk her beauty up." At this juncture Apollonius appeared. He recognized the *lamia* and, over Lucius's protests, drove her away. Without her, Lucius soon died.

Some critics of Keats's poetry have suggested that an even more unambiguous vampire existed in his poetry. In "La Belle Dame sans Merci," also composed in 1819, a knight met a lady with whom he became entranced. She fed him exotic foods and told him she loved him. He visited her underground home, where her mood changed to one of sadness. As the knight slept, he saw pale warriors and was told that he was soon to join them. After his awakening, while "palely loitering," he encountered the narrator of the poem. There the poem ended.

As early as 1948, critic Edwin R. Clapp suggested that the unnamed female, the title character in "La Belle Dame sans Merci," was best understood as a vampire. Clapp, for example, noted the likeness of the **victim** of Polidori's vampire ("There was no color upon her cheek, not even upon her lip."), with images developed by Keats ("pale were the lips I saw/Pale were the lips I kiss'd …"). Critic James B. Twitchell, picking up on Clapp, suggested that Keats had joined **Samuel Taylor Coleridge** in expanding upon the *lamia* myth and liberating it from the past. The *lamia* became a very real character and the encounter of the male with the female who had no pity, a somewhat universal experience. More detailed analysis of the poem easily led to Freudian interpretations such as the one suggested by Ernest Jones, which tied the vampire-*lamia* myth to the initiation of adolescent males into the mysteries of **sexuality**.

Twitchell suggested that the *lamia* theme subtly reappeared in much of Keats's poetry, though "The Lamia" and "La Belle Dame sans Merci" were its best examples. Keats, of course, went on to write many more poems, but in 1820, his health took a decided downward turn. He died February 23, 1821, in Rome.

Sources:

Capp, Edwin R. "La Belle Dame as Vampire." *Philological Quarterly* 27, 4 (October 1948): 89–92.

Jones, Ernest. *On the Nightmare*. 1931. Rept. New York: Liveright, 1971. 374 pp.

Keats, John. *The Complete Poetry of John Keats*. George R. Elliott, ed. New York: Macmillan Company, 1927. 457 pp.

Twitchell, James B. *The Living Dead: A Study of the Vampire in Romantic Literature*. Durham, NC: Duke University Press, 1981. 219 pp.

Kenyon, Sherrilyn (1965–)

Sherrilyn Kenyon, the author of multi-volume "Dark Hunter" vampire series was born and raised in Columbus, Georgia. She began writing during her grammar school years and actually won a writing contest in third grade and another the following year. Writing provided an escape from an abusive family situation, and she was only seven when she wrote a "novel," a horror story reflecting her life at home. She was an early devotee of movies with horror and paranormal themes.

Unable to afford her first choice for college, the Savannah College of Art and Design, Kenyon attended the local state college and majored in English, hoping to be admitted into the creative writing program. Several physical problems blocked her admission to both the creative writing and the journalism programs. She wound up with an interdisciplinary degree in history, language, and classical studies. About this time, the untimely death of her older brother took away her desire to write, which only returned several years later.

In the early 1990s, she sold her first novel, *Born of Night*, which was soon followed by several others. But she encountered a period where she was unable to sell anything and she battled personal problems, which drove her to the brink of giving up on a writing career for a second time. Then, in 1998, she sold a book that appeared under the

pseudonym of Kinley MacGregor. She signed up with a new agent and began circulating her first vampire book. Unfortunately, it arrived in New York just as many publishing houses had decided to shy away from vampire novels despite the fact that there was no sign that the market for them had diminished. The **Dracula** centennial had passed and *Buffy the Vampire Slayer* had yet to manifest its potential. It took several years to finally sell her novel, *Fantasy Lover*, which was finally published in 2002.

Fantasy Lover was a success and Kenyon was able to develop a series of interconnected books which became known as the "Dark Hunters" series. They draw directly upon her classical studies and revolve around a group of human protectors who shield people from supernatural predators sent by the ancient Greek gods. The three types of protectors include the Dark-Hunters who protect the night, Dream-Hunters who protect the subconscious and unconscious, and Were-Hunters who protect the outer reaches of our world. Among the supernatural predators are the vampires, who in Kenyon's world are called Daimons. Daimons are unique (relative to traditional fictional vampires) in that they can only live 27 years, the result of a curse that the god Apollo placed on them. To extend its life, a Daimon must steal a human soul. But Apollo's sister Artemis established the Dark-Hunters whose job is to kill the Daimons and free any human souls before they die.

Over the next seven years, Kenyon would write 19 "Dark Hunter" novels (most but not all with vampires), including one published as an e-book. As the series took off, she also published a number of "Dark Hunter" short stories that appeared in various romance anthologies. Most of the novels center on a particular Dark Hunter, the women in his life, and the particular personal problems he has to solve as he goes about slaying the evil vampires. Kenyon also coauthored *The Dark Hunter Companion*, a nonfiction guide to the Dark Hunter universe and its inhabitants.

In what became a complete reversal of her situation in the mid 1990s, she has become a very successful, best-selling, award-winning author who has been able to shape a very different approach to vampires. She is also among the minority of authors in the romance field to portray primarily evil vampires. Kenyon continues to produce projects and future "Dark Hunter" novels; she also maintains an expansive Internet site (http:// www.dailyinquisitor.com/sherrilyn/). Though primarily known for her "Dark Hunter" vampire novels, she has written a variety of other books including some well-received nonfiction titles.

Sources:

Kenyon, Sherrilyn. *Fantasy Lover*. New York: St. Martin's Paperbacks, 2002.

———. *Night Pleasures*. New York: St. Martin's Paperbacks, 2002.

———. *Dance with the Devil*. New York: St. Martin's Paperbacks, 2003.

———. *Night Embrace*. New York: St. Martin's Paperbacks, 2003.

———. *Night Play*. New York: St. Martin's Paperbacks, 2004.

———. *Kiss of the Night*. New York: St. Martin's Paperbacks, 2004.

———. *Seize the Night*. New York: St. Martin's Paperbacks, 2005.

———. *Sins of the Night*. New York: St. Martin's Paperbacks, 2005.

———. *Unleash the Night*. New York: St. Martin's Paperbacks, 2005.

———. *Dark Side of the Moon*. New York: St. Martin's Press, 2006.

———. *Devil May Cry*. New York: St. Martin's Press, 2007.

———. *The Dream-Hunter/i>*. New York: St. Martin's Paperbacks, 2007.

———. *Upon the Midnight Clear*. New York: St. Martin's Paperback, 2007.

———. *One Silent Night*. New York: St. Martin's Press, 2008.

———. *Dream Chaser*. New York: St. Martin's Paperback, 2008.

———. *Acheron*. New York: St. Martin's Press, 2008.

———. *Dream Warrior*. New York: St. Martin's Press, 2009.

———. *Bad Moon Rising*. New York: St. Martin's Press, 2009.

———, and Alethea Kontin. *The Dark-Hunter Companion*. New York: St. Martin's Griffin, 2007.

Killing the Vampire *see:* Vampire Research Center

 Kilpatrick, Nancy (1946–)

N ancy Kilpatrick, a horror writer, who also writes under the pseudonym Amarantha Knight, was born in Philadelphia and attended Temple University. In 1985 she moved to Canada and took a position at George Brown College in Toronto. As her writing career took off in the mid-1990s, she has remained in the Canada, and now lives in Montreal.

Kilpatrick began with short stories as many fiction writers do; she was granted the Arthur Ellis Award in 1992 for her story "Mantrap," and was a finalist for a **Bram Stoker** Award in 1993. Her short stories have appeared in a number of vampire story anthologies. Her first novel, *Near Death*, was also a finalist for the Bram Stoker Award, and set the precedent for a list of vampire fiction that would appear over the next few years, including *Sex and the Single Vampire* and *Endorphins*. As Amaranth Knight, Kilpatrick has also written a series of adult erotic novels based on classic horror tales under the collective title "The Darker Passions," the first being *The Darker Passions: **Dracula***, followed by, among others, *The Darker Passions: **Carmilla***.

Her initial novel, *Near Death*, would generate three sequels which have been republished as the "Power in the Blood" series—*Children of the Night* (1996), *Reborn* (1998), and *Bloodlover* (2000).

Her novelization of the Dracula musical, *Dracul* appeared in 1998.

As a person who identifies with the goth lifestyle, Kilpatrick put together a questionnaire for her fellow goths that became the basis of a nonfiction book, *The Goth Bible* (2004). She also teaches several courses in writing on the Internet.

Sources:

Kilpatrick, Nancy. *The Darker Passions: Dracula*. New York: Masquerade Books, 1993. 309 pp.

———. *Love Bites*. New York: Masquerade Books, 1994. 202 pp.

———. *Near Death*. New York: Pocket Books, 1994. 295 pp.

———. *Sex and the Single Vampire*. Leesburg, VA: TAL, 1994. 49 pp.

———. *Child of the Night*. London: Raven Books, 1996. 314 pp.

——— (as Amarantha Knight). *The Darker Passions: Carmilla*. New York: Masquerade Books, 1997. 335 pp.

———. *Endorphins*. Norfolk, VA: Macabre, Inc., 1997. 84 pp.

———. *Reborn*. Nottingham, UK: Pumpkin Books, 1998. 280 pp.

———. *Bloodlover*. Toronto: Baskerville Books, 2000. 273 pp.

———. *The Vampire Stories of Nancy Kilpatrick*. Oakville, ON: Mosaic Press, 2000. 171 pp.

———. *The Goth Bible: A Compendium for the Darkly Inclined*. New York: St. Martin's Griffin, 2004. 304 pp.

❨ *Kindred: The Embraced* ❩

The role-playing **game *Vampire: The Masquerade*** (now known as ***Vampire: The Eternal Struggle*)** was brought to **television** in 1996 in a short-lived series, *Kindred: The Embraced*. Although it only lasted for a few weeks, those unfamiliar with the mythology of the game had a chance to see the vampiric world of vampire clans, working with each other in a city under the leadership of a prince and a conclave of clan leaders. As the story developed, Julian Luna (Mark Frankel), the vampire prince of San Francisco, was being hounded by a police officer, Frank Kohanek (Thomas Howell). Kohanek believed that Luna was a mobster, but in the meantime had begun to date one of his former lovers. Slowly he was made aware that she was a vampire.

While keeping Kohanek at arm's length, Luna also has problems with ambitious clan leaders, one of whom, Eddie Furio (Brian Thompson), the leader of the Brujah clan, wanted to become prince and was working to dethrone Luna.

Furio killed the leader of the Gangrel clan, who also worked as Luna's personal bodyguard, and Luna feared that if he did not bring the killer to justice, a clan war might occur. He called upon the other clan leaders (including the Ventrue, Toreador, and Nosferatu clans) to stop Furio.

Kindred only included five of the many clans represented in *Vampire: The Masquerade*, but each of the leaders served as an example of the distinctive characteristics of each type of clan. In the first episode, the conclave of clan leaders had to deal with a vampire who disobeyed the law and shared information about vampires with a mortal, thus breaking the Masquerade. The conclave called for a blood hunt, the legal killing of a fellow vampire. In the meantime, Luna was pursuing a course that allowed vampires to infiltrate mortal society and blend with it as much as possible. Subsequent episodes began to detail the **political** intrigue and **blood**-drinking proclivities that are the major factors of vampire life.

The series was subsequently released in VHS and DVD formats.

❨ King, Stephen (1947–) ❩

Since the mid-1970s Stephen King has been America's premiere horror fiction writer. He was born in Portland, Maine, the son of Nellie Ruth Pillsbury and Donald King. As a child, he began to write science fiction short stories, and at the age of 12 submitted his first stories to *Fantastic* and the *Magazine of Fantasy and Science Fiction*. King graduated from the University of Maine in 1970. His first published story, "The Glass Floor," appeared in *Startling Mystery Stories* in 1967, while he was still in college.

Unable to obtain a job as an English teacher, King started working in an industrial laundry. During this period he wrote a number of short stories, and in 1972 began working on his first book, *Carrie*, eventually published by Doubleday & Company. King then turned his attention to a vampire tale originally called "Second Coming," but later renamed "Jerusalem's Lot." The story was published in 1975 as *Salem's Lot*. Meanwhile King was working on his subsequent novels, *The Shining* (1977) and *The Stand* (1978).

In 1976, *Salem's Lot* was nominated for a World Fantasy Award in the best-novel category. That same year, *Carrie* was released as a movie starring Sissy Spacek. King, a very fertile storyteller, also began to publish material under a pseudonym, Richard Bachman; the first title, *Rage*, appeared in 1977. He also published a second vampire short story, "One for the Road," that year.

During the 1980s, King enjoyed immense success. In his novels he has attempted to explore the vast world of horror and terror, and by choice has rarely returned to a theme once treated. Thus, after one successful vampire volume, he has not returned to the topic for a book, though he published a vampire novella story, "The Night Flier," in 1988. Meanwhile, several of his novels flirted with vampirism. The most obvious was *The Tommyknockers* (1987), which featured an alien vampire.

In 1979 *Salem's Lot* was made into a **television** miniseries under the direction of Tobe Hooper, and a sequel (not based on King's writing), *Return to Salem's Lot*, appeared in 1987. *Salem's Lot*, this time starring Rob Lowe, was remade in 2004 under the direction of Mikael Solomon. *The Tommyknockers* was brought to the screen (for television) in 1993, and *The Night Flier* in 1997.

King has continued to write about two novels annually, his output only slowing slightly following the accident in 1999 that almost killed him. He did not return to the vampire theme in the 1990s. Vampires reappear in his fiction, however, in 2003 in *Wolves of the Calla*. Its sequel *Song of Susannah* (2004) features psychic or emotional vampires. The most notable of the vampire characters is Dandelo (a.k.a. Joe Collins) who almost succeeds in killing Roland, the hero of the series.

Since 1985, when it was it revealed that he had written the Richard Bachman books, King's name has appeared on new printings of them. As might be expected, King has received a numerous awards for his writing including eight **Bram Stoker** awards and a Lifetime Achievement Award (2003) bestowed by his colleagues in the Horror Writers' Association.

Sources:

Hoppenstand, Gary, and Ray B. Browne. *The Gothic World of Stephen King: Landscape of Nightmares*. Bowling Green, OH: Bowling Green State University Popular Press, 1987. 143 pp.

King, Stephen. *Salem's Lot*. New York: Doubleday & Company, 1975. 439 pp.

———. "One for the Road." In *Maine Magazine* (March/April 1977). Reprinted in *Vamps*. Greenberg, Martin H., and Charles G. Waugh, eds. New York: Daw Books, 1987, 12–30.

———. "Jerusalem's Lot." In *Night Shift*. Garden City, NY: Doubleday & Company, 1978.

———. *Tommyknockers*. New York: G. P. Putnam's Sons, 1987. 558 pp.

———. "The Night Flier." In *Prime Evil*. Douglas E. Winter, ed. New York: New American Library, 1988.

Reino, Joseph. *Stephen King: The First Decade, Carrie to Pet Semitary*. Boston, MA: Twayne Publishers, 1988.

Straub, Peter. "Meeting Stevie." In *Fear Itself: The Horror Fiction of Stephen King*. San Francisco: Underwood-Miller, 1982. 255 pp.

Wiater, Stanley, Christopher Golden, and Hank Wagner. *The Complete Stephen King Universe: A Guide to the Worlds of Stephen King*. New York: St. Martin's Griffin, 2006. 432 pp.

Winter, Douglas E. *Stephen King: The Art of Darkness*. New York: New American Library, 1984.

Kürten, Peter (1883–1931)

Often cited as a real vampire, Peter Kürten—the so-called Düsseldorf Vampire—was a serial killer who operated in **Germany** from 1929 to 1930. He was born in Mulheim, Germany, one of ten children, the son of an alcoholic, brutal father. He lived part of his youthful years with the town dogcatcher and found enjoyment killing the unclaimed dogs. Kürten was only nine when he first killed a person. He pushed a playmate into the water and then repeated the act with a second boy who attempted to save the first.

His next known attempt at homicide was eight years later when he tried to rape and kill a young woman. He was sent to jail for four years for his unsuccessful effort. He lived on the streets after his release from prison, but a year later was back in jail for a series of thefts and burglaries. He would later claim to have killed two of his prisonmates by poisoning. In 1913 back on the street in Düsseldorf, he killed again. He murdered a ten-year-old girl.

He cut her throat with a knife and reportedly experienced an orgasm as the **blood** spurted out.

It was not until 1929 that Kürten began the series of crimes that were to earn him his place in criminal history. In February of that year, he attempted the murder of one woman and succeeded in the murder of two children, one male and one female, all by stabbing. His attempts at murder, often unsuccessful, baffled the police. Their mistaken conclusions about the crimes caused a mentally ill man to be convicted of the murder of the boy Kürten had actually killed.

That summer, he was more successful, killing nine people in August alone. He continued his killing through the winter of 1929–30. In May he attempted the strangling death of a young woman and then inexplicably stopped and let her go.

She identified him, and he was arrested. During his crime spree, he had thoroughly confused the police by continually changing his method of killing.

Any doubt about his guilt was only removed when he began his confession and accurately related the circumstances of each crime. He was convicted and executed by decapitation on July 2, 1931.

Kürten was certainly not a vampire in any traditional sense. Superficially, he demonstrated a vampiric trait in his obsession with blood, but he was like neither the vampire of folklore nor that of the modern literary and cinematic tradition. His history of vampire-like **crime** fits more properly into the history of serial murder. Kürten's life inspired two movies, *M* (1931) and *Le Vampire de Düsseldorf* (1964). More recently, Anthony Neilson authored a fictional account of Kürten entitled *Normal: The Düsseldorf Ripper* (1991), which was adapted by Czech director Julius Sevcik to the screen as *Angels Gone* (2009).

Sources:

Glut, Donald F. *True Vampires of History*. New York: H C Publishers, 1971. 191 pp.

Godwin, George. *Peter Kürten: A Study in Sadism*. London: Heineman Medical Books, 1938, 1945. 58 pp. Rept. "Kürten—The Vampire of Düsseldorf." In *Monsters of Weimar*. London: Nemesis Books, 1993, pp. 159–289.

Volta, Ornella. *The Vampire*. New York: Award Books, 1962. 153 pp.

Wagner, Margaret Seaton. *The Monster of Dusseldorf: The Life and Trial of Peter Kurten*. London: Faber & Faber, 1932.

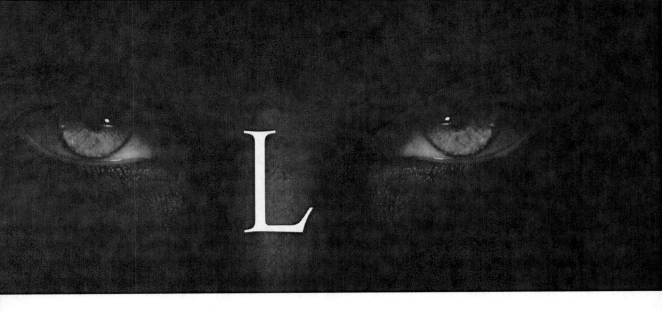

❨ LaCroix, Lucien ❩

LaCroix is a vampire and centuries-long companion of Nick Knight, the detective star of the **television** series *Forever Knight*. Like Knight, LaCroix first appeared in the made-for-television movie, *Nick Knight* (1989), where he had originally turned Knight into a vampire some 400 years ago. However, Knight had rejected the life of killing that the two had shared and broke with his creator/mentor. He began a search for his lost mortality and LaCroix continually foiled his attempts.

In the 1880s, Knight had participated in an archeological dig where he hoped to recover a jade goblet reportedly used in a ritual to cure vampirism. He had one such goblet, but two were required. One-hundred years later, he had become a policeman in Los Angeles. One evening he was called to the museum where a watchman had been killed and drained of **blood**. He would later learn that LaCroix had arrived in Los Angeles, bitten the watchman, and stole the matching goblet.

LaCroix made Nick aware that he had come to town by taking a job as a radio announcer called the Nightcrawler. Tracked down by Nick, he offered him a choice, the goblet or the life of Alyce Hunter, a staff person at the museum. As Knight tried to protect Hunter, LaCroix destroyed the goblet. Then, in the ensuing fight, Knight killed LaCroix by impaling him.

In 1991, the characters from *Nick Knight* were given a fresh start in a television series, *Forever Knight* now set in Toronto. Nick, short for his real name, Nicolas, was a young soldier who returned from the crusades in the year 1228. He spent the evening with a young woman, Jeanette, and woke to discover that he was a vampire, having been transformed by LaCroix (Nigel Bennett). Over the next centuries, LaCroix, Jeanette, and Nicolas had numerous adventures. LaCroix repeatedly reminded Nick what he really was, and when Nick refused the entreaties of people to become a vampire, LaCroix would step in and turn them. LaCroix also stepped in to protect Nick when a member of the Enforcers, a vampire organization dedicated to keeping the existence of vampires unknown, targeted him for possible elimination.

However, LaCroix usually assumed the role of Knight's nemesis, especially when Nick was about to discover a new means of becoming human again. For example, in 1916, in San Francisco, Knight decided to test the powers of acupuncture to make him normal. While he lay covered with needles, LaCroix killed the owner of the acupuncture shop. Again, in 1966, Knight was in East **Germany** searching for the Aberat, a book with rumored spells that could cure vampirism. LaCroix found the book first and, as Knight watched helplessly, consumed it in flames.

LaCroix remained a continuing character through the three seasons of *Forever Knight*, and in 1997 appeared in a novel trilogy based on the series.

Sources:

Garrett, Susan M. *Forever Knight: Intimations of Immortality*. New York: Boulevard Books, 1997. 284 pp.

Nayne, Anne Hathaway. *Forever Knight: These Our Revels*. New York: Boulevard Books, 1997. 274 pp.

Sizemore, Susan. *Forever Knight: A Stirring of Dust*. New York: Boulevard Books, 1997. 252 pp.

Strauss, Jon. "Forever Knight." *Epi-log* 36 (November 1993) 4–11; 37 (December 1993): 29–35, 62.

Lamiai *see:* Greece, Vampires in

Langella, Frank (1940–)

Frank Langella, star of the 1979 film version of *Dracula,* was born in Bayonne, New Jersey. His parents were Frank Langella, a businessman, and Ruth Weil, a magazine editor. He attended Syracuse University and in 1959 was awarded the Syracuse Critics Award as Best Actor. He went on to study acting, dance, and voice with private teachers and launched a career that has included both acting and theatrical management. Langella made his stage debut in 1960 in *The Pajama Game* at the Erie Playhouse. In 1963 he made his New York debut in *The Immoralist* at the Bouwerie Lane Theatre. That same year he became one of the original members of the Lincoln Center repertory training company.

In 1967 Langella first appeared in the title role of *Dracula* at the Berkshire Theatre Festival. Three years later he made his film debut in *The Twelve Chairs*, a part that would be followed by more notable roles in *Diary of a Mad Housewife* and *The Deadly Trap*. In 1977, he attained a new level of recognition as the star in the revival of the **Hamilton Deane/John L. Balderston** version of *Dracula*, which in 1978 received two Tony Awards. He was later chosen to star in the movie version of *Dracula* directed by John Badham.

An accomplished actor, Langella brought a new depth and dimension to a part that had become rather narrowly stereotyped. Langella had reflected upon the Count's character. **Dracula** would, he assumed, carry himself as a member of royalty who was on the one hand (in the presence of females) gracious and mannered, but on the other hand, ruled and commanded and used to having his own way. He also understood Dracula's problem with immortality. While an extended life gave him wisdom beyond his

contemporaries, it also brought a great weariness. In possibly the most important element of his perform- ance, in large part attributable to the changing times, Langella highlighted the sensual and sexual elements of his relationship to **Lucy Westenra** (renamed Lucy Seward), the main character in the Deane/Balderston play. As Dracula, Langella would not only act with defensiveness when attacked, but also as a jealous lover. Langella clearly understood the relationship between Dracula and **women**. In reflecting on the role, he noted:

> … the women have to *want* to make love with Count Dracula. And he must want to make love to them as a man loves a woman … not as a vampire goes after **blood**. The things that go on between Dracula and his women must be the re- sult of her needs as well as his. Something is calling her, and it's not **fangs**, or his wolf's eyes.

Langella created the most appealing and human Dracula since **Bela Lugosi**. He played the character not as a traditional monster, but as a creature of a dif- ferent species. Dracula was not so much cruel and evil as operating out of his very different nature. Langella took his place as one of the most memorable actors to assume the role of Dracula, though, for the sake of his career, he was able to walk away from the part and

Frank Langella as the aristocratic and sensual Dracula in the 1979 version of *Dracula*.

avoid being typecast. Thus, unlike that of Bela Lugosi and **Christopher Lee**, Langella's portrayal consumed only a few years of his lengthy career. He followed his success as Drac- ula with other movies and with additional success on the stage. In 1980 he was able to return to Broadway as Salieri in the highly acclaimed *Amadeus*. Langella has continued to play a wide variety of roles on stage, with occasional movie roles. In 1981 he assumed the title role of Dracula's contemporary in a **television** production of **Sherlock Holmes**. He returned to this role in 1987 in *Sherlock's Last Case* in New York and Washington, D.C. In 2007, he won a Tony Award for Best Performance by a Leading Actor in a Play for his portrayal of Richard Nixon in "Frost/Nixon." He subsequently played the same part in the movie adaptation for which he received an Academy Award nomination.

Sources:

Ebert, Roger. "Dracula: Revival of the Undead Hero." *Chicago Sun-Times* (July 8, 1979).

Holte, James Craig. *Dracula in the Dark: The Dracula Film Adaptations*. Westport, CT: Greenwood Press, 1997. 161 pp.

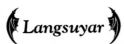

Langsuyar

The *langsuyar* was the most prominent of the several vampires of **Malaysia**. The *lang- suyar* was described as a beautiful woman who reacted strongly to the loss of her

stillborn baby. She flew into the trees and became a night demon that attacked and sucked the **blood** of other **women**'s children. The first *langsuyar* became the source of a class of vampire beings. If a woman died as a result of childbirth, she was a candidate to become a *langsuyar*. To prevent such an occurrence, the body would be treated with a needle in the palm of the hand, eggs under the arms, and glass beads in the mouth. On occasion, *langsuyars* assumed a somewhat normal village life. They would marry and have children—and feed off of others in the evening. They had long hair that covered a hole in their neck through which they sucked blood.

As reported by Walter William Skeat, the *langsuyar* had a counterpart in the **pontianak**, a stillborn child who became a vampire. However, in much of Indonesia (such as in **Java**), what was termed a *langsuyar* in Malaysia was also called a *pontianak*. In the 1950s, Catay-Keris Productions began to make a series of films about the Malaysian *langsuyar*, but designated the star a *pontianak*, after the broader use of the term.

Sources:

Skeat, Walter William. *Malay Magic: An Introduction to the Folklore and Popular Religion of the Malay Peninsula*. London: Macmillan and Co., 1900. 685 pp. Rept. New York: Barnes & Noble, 1966. 685 pp.

❦ Le Fanu, Sheridan (1814–1873) ❧

Joseph Thomas Sheridan Le Fanu, poet and author of short stories in the horror genre, was born on August 28, 1814, in Dublin, **Ireland**. His father was chaplain of the Royal Hiberian Military School, and Le Fanu was born on its premises. His great-uncle was the heralded Irish dramatist Richard Brimsley Sheridan. At age 14, the young Sheridan composed a long Irish poem, which launched his literary career.

Le Fanu's formal literary career began in 1838 when "The Ghost and the Bone-Setter" was published in the *Dublin University Magazine*. Over the next 15 years he wrote 23 stories and two novels. Most of these were set in Ireland and focused on aspects of the Irish character. With few exceptions, they have generally been judged as mediocre, in part due to Le Fanu's inability to relate to the Irish masses, whom he tended to stereotype because of the religious disagreements that separated him from them. However, he did begin his venture into supernatural horror, and in one of his stories, "Strange Event in the Life of Schalken the Painter," he touched on themes later developed in his most famous work, "Carmilla."

In 1861 Le Fanu purchased the *Dublin University Magazine*, which he edited for the next eight years. During the early 1860s Le Fanu wrote four novels. He continued to write novels for the rest of his life, but they never gained a popular audience. It was his short stories that brought him public attention. The year 1866 was a watershed year for Le Fanu; seven of his short stories appeared in Charles Dickens's *All the Year Round*, among the most prestigious periodicals in England, launching an era of production of some masterful short literary pieces. At this time he was becoming increasingly pessimistic about life in general and the course of Irish politics in particular. He seems to have drawn on the negative aspects of his own life to write some of the great supernatural horror tales of the period.

Critics agree that the stories published in his collection *In a Glass Darkly* (1872) are his best stories, though they would disagree on which one is actually *the* best. However, the one that has attained the highest level of fame, even after long neglect of Le Fanu's work, is "Carmilla." "Carmilla," only the third vampire story in English, is still one of the best. It told the story of Laura, the daughter of an Austrian civil servant named Karnstein, who was attacked by a female vampire variously named **Carmilla**, Mircalla, and Millarca. The story traced Laura's early childhood encounter with Carmilla, an experience almost forgotten until the vampire reappeared when Laura was in her late teens. In the end, the **victims** and their family tracked Carmilla to her resting place and destroyed her. First published in several parts in *Dark Blue* magazine (December 1871 to March 1872), "Carmilla" provided a major building block of the modern vampire myth. It was read by **Bram Stoker**, a later resident of Dublin and, like Le Fanu, a graduate of Trinity College.

After his death in Dublin on February 7, 1873, Le Fanu's reputation drifted into almost a century of obscurity, although he had as fans such writers as Henry James and Dorothy Sayers. A major reason for his neglect by the literary elite seems to be the subject of his writing. For many decades the great majority of

Joseph Thomas Sheridan Le Fanu, author of the short story "Carmilla."

literary critics held supernatural horror fiction in disdain, and thus neglected its more able writers. As **gothic** fiction came into its own in the last half of the twentieth century, critical reappraisal of the genre quickly followed. The new era of appreciation of Le Fanu really began in 1964 when E. F. Bleiler completed an edited edition of the *Best Ghost Stories of J. S. Le Fanu*, published by Dover. Then in 1977, under the editorship of **Devendra P. Varma**, Arno Press released the 52 volume *Collected Works of Joseph Sheridan Le Fanu*.

A journal for *Le Fanu Studies* may be contacted through the website http://www.js lefanu.com/lefanustudies.html. It is among vampire fans, however, that Le Fanu is most remembered. Next to *Dracula* **(1897)**, "Carmilla" has become the single vampire story most frequently brought to the screen, and, like *Dracula*, it has inspired other stories of its leading vampire characters. Among the film versions of "Carmilla" are *Blood and Roses* (1961), *Blood and Black Lace* (1964), and *The Vampire Lovers* (1970).

One of its best adaptations is a made-for-television version entitled *Carmilla* that was presented in 1989 on Showtime's *Nightmare Classics*. Additional versions, all entitled simply Carmilla, and more or less true to the original story, were made in 1999, 2000, and 2009. It has often been said that *Vampyr*, the classic vampire movie directed by **Carl Theodor Dreyer**, was based on "Carmilla," but, except for being a story with a female vampire, it bears little resemblance to "Carmilla." Le Fanu wrote a second, lesser-known story at least suggestive of vampirism, "The Room in the Dragon Volant," which was made into a movie, *The Inn of the Flying Dragon* (originally *Ondskans Vardshus*), in 1981.

Sources:

Browne, Nelson. *Sheridan Le Fanu*. London: Arthur Barker, 1951. 135 pp.

Crawford, Gary William. *J. Sheridan Le Fanu: A Bio-Bibliography*. Westport, CT: Greenwood Press, 1995. The author maintains a Web page on Le Fanu at http://www.jslefanu.com/.

Le Fanu, J. Sheridan. *Best Ghost Stories of J. S. Le Fanu*. Edited by E. F. Bleiler. New York: Dover Publications, 1964.

———. *Collected Works of Joseph Sheridan Le Fanu*. Edited by Devendra P. Varma. 52 vols. New York: Arno Press, 1977.

———. *Collected Works of Joseph Sheridan Le Fanu*. BiblioLife, 2008. 468 pp.

McCormack, W. J. *Sheridan Le Fanu and Victorian Ireland*. Oxford: Clarendon Press, 1980. 310 pp.

Leatherdale, Clive (1949–)

Clive Leatherdale, an English writer and publisher, first read *Dracula* **(1897)** in his teens and has returned to it many times since. His professional interest in the novel began in 1982 when, having completed a Ph.D. in Arabian history, he felt free at last to grapple with Dracula's hidden meanings. *Dracula: The Novel and the Legend* (1985) was the result, a work that explored the novel's sexual, Freudian, biblical, occult, and **political** aspects. This book has never been out of print and has been translated into Italian and French editions. Various other works on **Dracula** and **Bram Stoker** followed, culminating in 1998 with *Dracula Unearthed*, an edition of the novel that contains 3,500 textual notes and annotations. Leatherdale is also the owner/publisher of Desert Island Books and several books authored by him have been published as part of his company's **Desert Island Dracula Library**. Leatherdale announced plans to do a book that tackled what he considers to be popular misconceptions regarding Dracula, but *Dracula Unearthed* has turned out to be his last book on the subject. His colleague **Elizabeth Miller**, with whom he has kept a close working relationship, did complete a book length volume of common errors concerning *Dracula*. Meanwhile, Leatherdale has pursued his additional wide interests. He has backpacked around much of the world, has lived in Saudi Arabia, China, and Korea, and written histories or travel books on all three countries. He has also written a work on education and numerous books on sports.

Sources:

Leatherdale, Clive. *Dracula: The Novel and the Legend—A Study of Bram Stoker's Gothic Masterpiece*. 1985. Rept. Westcliff-on-Sea, UK: Desert Island Books, 1993.

———. *The Origins of Dracula—The Background to Bram Stoker's Gothic Masterpiece*. 1987. Rept. Westcliff-on-Sea, UK: Desert Island Books, 1995.

———, ed. *The Jewel of Seven Stars*. Westcliff-on-Sea, UK: Desert Island Books, 1996.

———, ed. *Dracula Unearthed*. 1998. Westcliff-on-Sea, UK: Desert Island Books, 1998.

Lee, Christopher (1922–)

Actor Christopher Lee, who, after **Bela Lugosi**, is most often identified with portraying the vampire **Dracula**, has played the Count in more different motion pictures than anyone. He was born on May 27, 1922, in **London**, England, and later attended Wellington College. In 1947 he signed a contract with J. Arthur Rank, which led to his first film appearance in *Corridor of Blood*. Thus began one of the most active screen careers, which by the mid-1980s saw Lee with parts in more than 130 movies.

His career rose steadily through the 1950s to 1957 when he was brought together with three other people at **Hammer Films** who altered his life dramatically. Responding to the success of several **science fiction**/horror movies, Hammer obtained the motion picture rights to some of **Universal Pictures'** classic monster movies and hired **Terence Fisher**, **Jimmy Sangster**, **Peter Cushing**, and Lee to film a new version of *Frankenstein*. Lee starred as **Frankenstein's monster** in the highly successful *The Curse of Frankenstein* (1957). The four were called together the following year to do a remake of **Dracula (1897)**, best known as **The Horror of Dracula**. Although *The Curse of Frankenstein*, in Lee's words, "started it all," it was *The Horror of Dracula* that made Lee a star and put Hammer on the map as the new king of on-the-screen horror.

Changes in technology and in public mores allowed Lee to present a much different Dracula. Most noticeably, Lee was more directly a creature of horror, dropping much of the image of the suave continental gentleman perpetuated by Lugosi. Unlike Lugosi, Lee had **fangs**, that he showed to the audience, and he attacked his female **victims** on camera. Lacking any clear direction from the production staff, Lee developed Dracula as a complex human who had great positive qualities—leadership, charm, intelligence, and sensuality—coupled with a savage and ferocious streak that would lead to his eventual downfall. Dracula also had a tragic quality, his undead immortality.

The Horror of Dracula was an unexpected success, but it would be some years before Lee would return to the role. Meanwhile, he went to **Italy** to make a comedic vampire movie, *Tempi duri per I Vampiri* (*Hard Times for Vampires*), and Lee has insisted that the vampire he portrayed was not Dracula, but a Baron Rodrigo. He then returned to Hammer for further work on the first round of the Universal horror series as Kharis in *The Mummy* (1960). Moving back to Italy, he worked with director **Mario Bava**, for whom he played the vampire Lico, whom Hercules confronts in the underworld.

While Lee was working on the continent, Hammer had made its first movie about **Carmilla**, the vampire in **Sheridan Le Fanu's** 1872 tale of the same name. Lee was then invited to assume the part of Count Ludwig Karnstein in the 1963 Spanish version of the story, *La Maledicion de los Karnsteins* (a.k.a. *Terror in the Crypt*). It would be another five years before Lee returned to Hammer, where, together with Fisher and Sangster, he made his next Dracula movie. *Drac-*

Christopher Lee as Dracula, the role for which he is most famous.

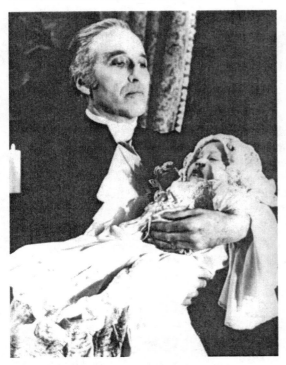

Christopher Lee's last appearance in a vampire movie was in the French comedy *Dracula and Son*.

ula, Prince of Darkness began with the final scene from *The Horror of Dracula*, in which **Abraham Van Helsing** killed Dracula. Dracula was revived by the pouring of **blood** on his ashes.

For Lee, this second Dracula movie was unique in that he never spoke a line, merely grunted and groaned. Whereas *The Horror of Dracula* had made Lee a star, the series of movies made during the seven years beginning in 1966, when *Dracula, Prince of Darkness* was filmed, forever identified him with the role. Most of these—*Dracula Has Risen from the Grave* (1969), *Taste the Blood of Dracula* (1970), *The Scars of Dracula* (1970), *Dracula A.D. 1972* (1972), and *The Satanic Rites of Dracula*, aka *Count Dracula and His Vampire Brides* (1973)—were panned by the critics but found an appreciative audience among the growing legion of vampire fans.

While Lee was turning out the series of Hammer movies, two historians, **Raymond T. McNally** and **Radu Florescu**, were researching the historical Dracula, the Romanian ruler **Vlad the Impaler**. Their first report on their research appeared in 1972 as *In Search of Dracula*. In 1974 a Swedish production crew filmed a documentary based on the book and bearing the same title. Lee was selected to narrate the movie and to appear in scenes as Vlad.

Lee believed that each of the Hammer films moved him further and further from the Dracula of **Bram Stoker**'s novel. For example, *Dracula Has Risen from His Grave* contained a scene in which Lee pulled a **stake** out of his own heart, an action he considered at the time completely out of character. Thus, in 1970 he jumped at the chance to star in Jesus Franco's version of the Dracula story, **El Conde Dracula**. Unlike previous versions, Franco's *Dracula* made a place for all of the novel's main characters, and during the opening scenes stayed relatively close to the book.

The script soon began to deviate, however, and in the end wandered far from the text (attributed partly to an extremely low budget). In one aspect, Lee was very happy with the film; it allowed him to portray Dracula as he was pictured in the book, although Lee lacked the hairy palms and the elongated ears and fingers. Lee did bring out Dracula's progressively more youthful appearance as he drained the blood of **Lucy Westenra** and **Mina Murray**. Franco's film soon entered the ranks of the forgotten movies, although high marks were given to Pedro Portabella, who made a film about the making of *El Conde Dracula*. Portabella's *Vampir* was acclaimed as an artistic meditation on death. Lee starred in the final scenes, in which he described Dracula's death and read the last chapter of the novel, in which Dracula was killed.

Lee's last appearance in a vampire movie was as Dracula in the 1976 film, *Dracula and Son* (a French comedy originally released as *Dracula pere et Fils*). Lee had played

enough different roles to stave off the terror of any actor, typecasting, but at this point he swore off vampire movies altogether. He had supporting parts in *The Private Life of Sherlock Holmes* (1970) and *Hannie Caulder* (1972) and the title role as the villain in the James Bond movie *Man with the Golden Gun* (1974). He went on to have significant character roles in a variety of films, such as *Airport 77* (1976), *Return to Witch Mountain* (1977), and *1941* (1979). He also appeared in the film *Cyber Eden* (1994), an Italian science fiction production.

Lee wrote an initial autobiography, *Tall, Dark, and Gruesome* (1977, revised edition 2009) which he revised on several occasions, before producing a new autobiography, *Lord of Misrule: The Autobiography of Christopher Lee*, in 2004. He also worked with both **Michael Parry** and **Peter Haining** on anthologies of horror stories. He also contributed numerous comments to Robert W. Pohle, Jr., and Douglas C. Hart's study of *The Films of Christopher Lee*, and an afterward to Tom Johnson and Mark Miller's 2004 filmography of his films.

Sources:

Haining, Peter, ed. *More of Christopher Lee's New Chamber of Horrors*. London: Mayflower, 1976. 159 pp.

Johnson, Tom, and Mark A. Miller. *The Christopher Lee Filmography: All Theatrical Releases, 1948–2003*. Jeffersonville, NC: McFarland & Company, 2004. 480 pp.

———, and Michel Parry. *Christopher Lee's X. Certificate*. 2 vols. London: 1975. Reprinted as *From the Archives of Evil*. New York: Warner Books, 1976. 205 pp.

———. *Tall, Dark and Gruesome: An Autobiography*. London: W. H. Allen, 1977. Rev. ed.: London: Victor Gollancz, 1997. 320 pp. Rept. Baltimore, MD: Midnight Marquee Press, 2009. 320 pp.

Lee, Christopher. *Christopher's Lee Treasury of Terror*. Secaucus, NJ: Chartwell Books, 1988. 663 pp.

Kelley, Bill. "Christopher Lee: King of the Counts." In *Dracula: The Complete Vampire*. Special issue of *Starlog Movie Magazine Presents*. No.6. New York: Starlog Communications, 1992: pp. 44–53.

———. "What Dracula Is Up To." *Imagi-Movies* 1, 2 (Winter 1993–1994): 46–48.

———. *Lord of Misrule: The Autobiography of Christopher Lee*. London: Orion Publishing, 2004. 4,448 pp.

Pohle, Robert W., Jr., and Douglas C. Hart. *The Films of Christopher Lee*. Metuchen, NJ: Scarecrow Press, 1983. 227 pp.

Rigby, Jonathan. *Christopher Lee: The Authorised Screen History*. Reynolds & Hearn, 2007. 304 pp.

Lee, Tanith (1947–)

Tanith Lee, a British writer of dark fantasy, began writing children's books, and in 1975 her first novel for adults, *The Birthgrave*, appeared. Born and educated in **London**, after secondary school Lee studied art and held various jobs before becoming a writer. Her best work takes themes from horror, fantasy, and **science fiction**, and integrates a feminist **vision** and a dark twist, which provides the vehicle for exploring some of the larger issues to which Lee speaks (the nature of morality, the individual's sense of control of their life, etc.). She has attained some degree of fame for her retelling of children's stories with an adult twist in her *Red As Blood* or *Tales from the Sisters Grimmer* (1983).

Vampiric themes began to appear quite early in her writings, such as *Kill the Dead* (1980) and especially *Sabella: or the Bloodstone* (1980).

Sabella Quay, a resident of Mars, had at the age of 11 found a plum-sized stone with a ring at one end, which she later began to wear all the time. When she was 14 she had her first sexual encounter, and then killed the boy. Out of the experience she came to understand that she really was not human. Not of the undead, she lived a nocturnal existence because her **blood** was vulnerable to the rays of the sun. She finally learned not to kill the men with whom she had sex and took blood primarily from the deer in the nearby countryside. At one point her Aunt Cassi had figured out that Sabella was a vampire, and left her niece a jeweled **crucifix**. However, Sabella settled into a nice existence with her lover Jace from whom she takes blood and whom she allows to dominate her, realizing that the **victim** has to be stronger than the oppressor, or he dies.

Possibly Lee's most important vampire fiction is the "Blood Opera" series, *Dark Dance* (1992), *Personal Darkness* (1993), and *Darkness, 1* (1994), which reveal the life of the Scarabae. The story begins as Rachaela Day, a seemingly normal and unexceptional woman, is called to her family home, where she meets her ageless relative and is seduced by the handsome Adamus (whom her mother had told her to avoid). She soon learns that she is part of a plan to perpetuate the family. The three volumes follow Rachaela and her daughter Ruth's efforts to cope with their heritage.

Lee has won numerous awards for her writings, including the World Fantasy Convention Award on two occasions. Additional vampire writings include *The Beautiful Biting Machine* (1984) and *The Blood of Roses* (1990). She has not returned to the vampire theme since the 1990s.

Sources:

Lee, Tanith. *Volkkavaar*. New York: DAW Books, 1977. 192 pp. Rept. London: Arrow Books, 1988. 202 pp.

———. *Darkness, 1*. London: Little Brown, 1978. Rept. New York: St. Martin's Press, 1994. 408 pp.

———. *Kill the Dead*. New York: DAW Books, 1980. 172 pp.

———. *Sabella: or the Blood Stone*. New York: DAW Books, 1980. 157 pp. Reprinted in *Sometimes, After Sunset*. Garden City, NY: Nelson Doubleday, 1980. 140 pp. Rept. London: Unwin, 1987.

———. *The Beautiful Biting Machine*. New Castle, VA: Cheap Street, 1984. 43 pp.

———. *The Blood of Roses*. London: Century Publishing, 1990. 678 pp.

———. *Dark Dance*. London: MacDonald, 1992. Rept. New York: Dell/Abyss, 1992. 409 pp. Rept. New York: Warner, 1994.

———. *Personal Darkness*. (Blood Opera 2) London: Little, Brown, 1993. 435 pp. Rept. New York: Dell, 1993. 389 pp.

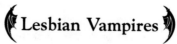

Lesbian Vampires

The incidents of lesbian vampiric relationships, which appeared first in the literary vampire tradition during the nineteenth century and more recently in the cinema, further illustrate the essential sexual nature of the vampire's relationship with its **victim**. The lesbian vampire can also be seen as a special case of both the **homosexual vampire** and **women as vampires**. The earliest vampires were probably female, such as the Malaysian **langsuyar** and the Greek *lamiai*.

The historical reference for the lesbian vampire is **Elizabeth Bathory**, the so-called **blood** countess, who lived in the seventeenth century and whose story **Bram Stoker** used to develop the character of **Dracula**. The story of Bathory suggested several unique ideas about vampires not connected with the historical Dracula, **Vlad the Impaler**. As **Radu Florescu** and **Raymond T. McNally** have noted, in the Stoker novel, Dracula was seen as a Hungarian (not a Romanian), he drank blood, he grew younger as he drank blood, and he existed in an erotic atmosphere. Although none of these attributes could be derived from the story of Vlad, they all were descriptive of Elizabeth Bathory. She was related to Hungarian royalty, and she killed hundreds of young girls, whose blood she drained. Several who survived her torture sessions testified that she bathed in human blood to retain and restore her youth.

Although few have considered Bathory a lesbian, her victims were almost exclusively young women. She was assisted in her **crimes** by her Aunt Klara, who has been described as a lesbian who liked to dress in male clothing and "play men's games." As the vampire became the subject of modern literature, and the vampiric relationship became a means of illustrating erotic situations, the attraction of females to those of their own gender frequently appeared. On occasion this relationship was reciprocal, but more often than not it was a form of rape in which the vampire, generally a woman possessed of some social status or power, attacked or seduced a woman of no status, such as a student or a maid.

From "Christabel" to "Carmilla": At the beginning of the English-language literary vampire tradition, lesbianism arose in **Samuel Taylor Coleridge**'s poem "Christabel" (1816). Among the first poems about vampires, "Christabel" featured an "attack" upon the title character by Geraldine, the vampiric figure. Geraldine first appeared in the woods near the castle of Christabel's father and told a story of having been brought there by kidnappers. Christabel invited Geraldine to take shelter in the castle. They shared a bottle of **wine**. Then, at Geraldine's suggestion, Christabel undressed and got into bed. Geraldine joined her guest.

Whatever passed between them, more implied than stated, the morning found Geraldine refreshed and restored, "fairer yet! and yet more fair!" Christabel arose with a perplexity of mind and a deep sense of having sinned and went immediately to prayer. Christabel nevertheless took Geraldine to her father. Unfortunately, Geraldine beguiled the naive Sir Leoline, who ultimately dismissed his daughter and left with the vampire.

Later in the nineteenth century, the most famous vampire story with lesbian overtones was penned by Irish writer **Sheridan Le Fanu**. "Carmilla," next to *Dracula* the vampire story most often brought to the screen, concerned Millarca Karnstein (also known by two other names made by scrambling the letters of her name—**Carmilla** and Mircalla), who attacked young women to suck their blood. "Carmilla" can be seen, in part, as an attempt to rewrite "Christabel" in prose form. Early in the story the vampire was stranded near a castle and was invited inside by the unsuspecting residents. Once accepted, she targeted nineteen-year-old Laura, the daughter of the retired Austrian official who had purchased the castle some years before. Carmilla began to "seduce" her hostess.

At one point Laura recalled, "She used to place her pretty arms around my neck, draw me to her, and laying her cheek to mine, murmur with her lips near my ear.... And when she had spoken such a rhapsody, she would press me more closely in her trembling embrace, and her lips in soft kisses glow upon my cheek." Laura would try to pull

Ingrid Pitt as the legendary Carmilla Karnstein, hovers over a young female victim in *Vampire Lovers*, one of the many vampire films with lesbian overtones.

away, but found herself without energy. She later described the strange nature of their relationship as simultaneously one of adoration and abhorrence. Later, Carmilla was tracked down and killed before she could kill Laura, but not before she had killed the daughter of a neighbor, General Speilsdorf.

Lesbian Vampires in the Movies: With vampirism as a metaphor for sexual behavior, a variety of sexual actions could be pictured on the screen in vampire movies. At a time when explicit lesbian behavior was banned from the movies, vampirism offered a means for women to relate to each other. Contemporary lesbian writers such as Bonnie Zimmerman and Pam Keesey have traced the first lesbian vampire to *Dracula's Daughter*, a 1936 **Universal Pictures** production. Countess Zaleska (Gloria Holden) satiates her lust by drinking the blood of a series of beautiful models.

It was more than two decades later before another female vampire attacking female victims appeared on the screen. In 1957, *Blood of Dracula* (released in England as *Blood Is My Heritage*) pictured a teenage vampire (Sandra Harrison) attacking her classmates at an all-girls boarding school. That same year, the first of a series of movies based loosely upon the life of Countess Elizabeth Bathory appeared. In *Lust of the Vampire* (a.k.a. *I, Vampiri*) a doctor periodically stole the blood of women to give to the Countess in order to preserve her youthful appearance. **Mario Bava** filmed this early Italian entry in the vampire/horror field.

By far the most acclaimed of the several movies inspired by the Bathory legend is *Daughters of Darkness* (1971), in which a young couple met the still lively and beautiful Countess Bathory in a contemporary Belgian hotel. They were seduced and attacked by Bathory and her female traveling companion. The husband turned out to be a sadist, and the wife and Bathory combined forces to kill him. Although *Daughters of Darkness* was the most critically acclaimed of the Bathory films, the blood countess' most memorable appearance was that portrayed by **Ingrid Pitt** in **Hammer Films'** *Countess Dracula* (1972). The film was produced at a time when Hammer was allowing more nudity and explicitly sexual situations to invade its movies.

"Carmilla" inspired a host of films, possibly the best being the first, **Roger Vadim's** *Blood and Roses* (1960), made to showcase his then wife Annette Stroyberg. The story also underlies Hammer Films' Karnstein Trilogy: *Vampire Lovers* (1970), *Lust for a Vampire* (1971), and *Twins of Evil* (1971). Such movies can be considered lesbian movies only by the most liberal of standards. They starred glamorous female stars, and their male direction and screenplays suggested something more closely approaching a male fantasy of lesbianism. Also, the movies of **Jean Rollin** frequently included lesbian char-

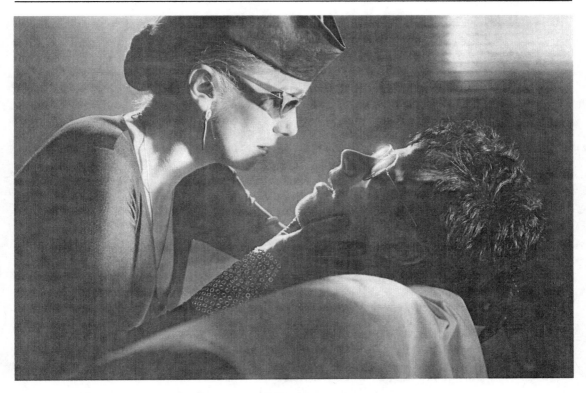

Catherine Deneuve (left) plays an alien vampire in *The Hunger*.

acters pictured in much the same manner as pornographic movies that picture women
engaged in sex scenes shot entirely for a male audience.

More closely portraying a lesbian relationship in a manner acceptable to lesbians
was *Vampyres* (1974), which concerned the murder of a lesbian couple by a homopho-
bic man. The two return from the dead as a lesbian vampire couple and work together
attacking male victims. *The Hunger*, basically the story of an alien vampire and her
human male lovers, has found an appreciative lesbian audience for the scene in which
the vampire (Catherine Deneuve) seduced the doctor (Susan Sarandon), whom she
contacted in hope of finding a cure for her lovers' swift aging. Two other lesbian vampire movies, *Mark of Lilith* (1986) and *Because the Dawn* (1988), both explore the possibility of using the vampire image in a positive way for women.

Recent Additions: The growth of the lesbian subculture in the 1980s led to the
production of significant new literature consciously written by lesbians for lesbians. Several volumes stand out. Pam Keesey has assembled two collections of lesbian vampire
short fiction in *Daughters of Darkness* (1993) and *Dark Angels* (1995). The earlier volume included a chapter from the single piece of African-American lesbian vampire fiction, Jewelle Gomez's *The Gilda Stories* (1991). Gilda was a vampire who was born into
slavery and learned to survive over the decades in a world dominated by white males.

THE VAMPIRE BOOK: THE ENCYCLOPEDIA OF THE UNDEAD

Virago, Karen Marie Christa Minns's first vampire novel, explored the relationship of a lesbian couple attacked by a vampire college teacher.

In contrast to the many male gay vampire books and anthologies that have appeared in recent years, only a few lesbian vampire novels have been published over the last decade, such as Crin Clazxton's *Scarlet Thirst* (2002) and Finola Hughes and Digby Diehl's *Soapsuds* (2005), leaving the short story as the most prominent place for new lesbian vampire literature At the same time, there have been few lesbian vampire relations pictured on film, apart from the made-for-males female-on-female sex scenes in some adult movies. Possibly the most notable lesbian themed vampire movie since the beginning of the new century is *Eternal* (2004) staring Caroline Neron as a modern day Elizabeth Bathory. The most prominent vampire-related lesbian character on television was **Willow Rosenberg**, the witch and vampire fighting companion on *Buffy the Vampire Slayer*, who emerged as a lesbian halfway through the series.

Sources:

Clazxton, Crin. *Scarlet Thirst*. Diva Books, 2002.

De Moss, Bianca. *Blood Sisters: Lesbian Vampire Tales*. Los Angeles: Alyson Books, 2006. 280 pp.

Gomez, Jewelle. *The Gilda Stories*. Ithaca, NY: Firebrand Books, 1991. 252 pp.

Hughes, Finola, and Digby Diehl. *Soapsuds*. New York: Ballantine Books, 2005.

Keesey, Pam. *Daughter of Darkness: Lesbian Vampire Stories*. Pittsburgh/San Francisco: Cleis Press, 1993. 243 pp.

———. *Dark Angels: Lesbian Vampire Stories*. Pittsburgh/San Francisco: Cleis Press, 1995.

———. *Vamps: An Illustrated History of the Femme Fatale*. San Francisco, CA: Cleis Press, 1997. 171 pp.

Kuhn, Annette, with Susannah Radstone, eds. *The Women's Companion to International Film*. London: Virago, 1990. 464 pp. Reprinted as *Women in Film: An International Guide*. New York: Fawcett Columbine, 1991. 500 pp.

Minns, Karen Marie Christa. *Virago*. Tallahassee, FL: Naiad Press, 1990. 181 pp.

———. *Bloodsong*. Irving, CA: Bluestocking Books, 1997. 221 pp.

Tan, Cecilia. *Women of the Bite: Lesbian Vampire Erotica*. Los Angeles: Alyson Press, 2009. 275 pp.

Weiss, Andrea. *Vampires and Violets: Lesbianism in the Cinema*. London: Pandora Press, 1991. 184 pp.

Zimmerman, Bonnie. "Daughters of Darkness: The Lesbian Vampire on Film." In Barry Keith Grant, ed., *Planks of Reason*. Metuchen, NJ: Scarecrow Press, 1984: 153–63.

Lestat de Lioncourt *see:* de Lioncourt, Lestat

Liderc *see:* Hungary, Vampires in

Lilith

Lilith, one of the most famous figures in Hebrew folklore, originated as a storm demon and later became identified with the night. She was one of a group of Sumerian vampire demons that included *Lillu*, *Ardat Lili*, and *Irdu Lili*. She appeared in the Babylonian *Gilgamesh Epic* (approximately 2000 B.C.E.) as a vampire harlot who was unable to bear children and whose breasts were dry. She was pictured as a beautiful young girl with owl's feet (indicative of her nocturnal life). In the *Gilgamesh Epic*, Lilith escaped from her home near the Euphrates River and settled in the desert. In this regard, she earned a place in the Hebrew Bible (the Christian Old Testament). Isaiah, in describing God's day of vengeance, during which the land will be turned into a desert, proclaimed that as a sign of the desolation, "Lilith shall repose there and find her place of rest" (Isaiah 34:14).

Lilith reappeared in the Talmud, where a more interesting story was told of her as the wife of the biblical Adam. Lilith was described as Adam's first wife. They had a disagreement over who would be in the dominant position during sexual intercourse. When Adam insisted upon being on top, Lilith used her magical knowledge to fly away to the Red Sea, an abode of demons. She took many lovers and had many offspring, called the *lilim*. There she met three angels sent by God—Senoy, Sansenoy, and Semangelof—with whom she worked out an agreement. She claimed vampiric powers over babies, but agreed to stay away from any babies protected with an amulet bearing the names of the three angels.

Once more attracted to Adam, Lilith returned to haunt him. After he and Eve (his second wife) were expelled from the Garden of Eden, Lilith and her cohorts, all in the form of an **incubus/succubus**, attacked them, thus causing Adam to father many demons and Eve to mother still more. Out of this legend, Lilith came to be regarded in Hebrew lore much more as a succubus than a vampire, and men were warned against sleeping in a house alone lest Lilith overtake them. Lilith (a name that in popular thought came to be attached to a whole class of demonic beings) were noted as being especially hateful of the normal sexual mating of the individuals they attacked as succubi and incubi. They took out their anger on the human children of such mating by sucking their **blood** and strangling them. They also added any complication possible to **women** attempting to have children—barrenness, miscarriages, and so forth. Thus, Lilith came to resemble a range of vampirelike beings that became particularly visible at the time of childbirth and whose presence was used to explain any problems or unexpected deaths. As a result, those who believed in the Lilith developed elaborate rituals to banish them from their homes. The exorcism of Lilith and any accompanying demons often took the form of a writ of divorce sending them forth naked into the night.

The myth of Lilith (the singular entity, as opposed to the whole class of demons) was well established in the Jewish community during the centuries of the early Christian era. She remained an item of popular lore, although little was written about her from the time the Talmud was compiled (sixth century C.E.) until the tenth century. Her biography was expanded in elaborate (and somewhat contradictory) detail in the writings of the early Hassidic fathers. In the *Zohar*, the most influential Hassidic text, Lilith was described as a succubus, with nocturnal emissions cited as the visible sign of her presence. Demons that plagued humanity were thought to be the product of such unions. She also attacked human babies, especially those born of couples who engaged in intercourse in improper fashion. Children who laughed in their **sleep** were believed to be playing with Lilith, and hence in danger of dying at her hand. During this period, Lilith's vampiric nature was deemphasized; rather, she was described as killing children in order to steal their soul.

The stories about Lilith multiplied during the Middle Ages. She was, for example, identified as one of the two women who came before King Solomon for him to decide which one was the mother of a child they both claimed. Elsewhere she was identified as the Queen of Sheba. Strong belief in her presence was found among more conservative elements in the Jewish community into the nineteenth century, and elements of the belief can be seen to the present time. In the 1970s, **Marv Wolfman**, the

writer for Marvel Comics's *The Tomb of Dracula* drew on the Lilith myth to create an new character, **Lilith, the Daughter of Dracula**. She was killed along with all of the other vampires in the Marvel universe in 1983. Then in 1992, a new realm of the Marvel Universe, primarily populated by superheroes, was created around interaction with an evil supernatural realm. A new Lilith character appeared as the key figure leading the invasion of the supernatural into modern society. Through the mid-1990s, she was opposed by the Midnight Sons in several titles of Marvel **comic books**. Lilith has also been brought into the mythology of the role-playing **game**, in which the **origin** of vampirism is ascribed to the biblical Caine Lilith as the first wife of Adam, is seen as the mother of a child Ennoia who at a later point become a vampire and the mother of a new vampire clan, the Gangrel.

Sources:

Brown, Robert G. *The Book of Lilith*. Lulu.com, 2007. 240 pp.

Graves, Robert, and Raphael Patai. *Hebrew Myths: The Book of Genesis*. Garden City, NY: Doubleday & Company, 1964. 311 pp.

Hurwitz, Siegmund. *Lilith—The First Eve: Historical and Psychological Aspects of the Dark Feminine*. Einsiedeln, Switz.: Daimon Publishers, 1992. 262 pp.

Koltuv, Barbara Black. *The Book of Lilith*. Lake Worth, FL: Nicolas-Hays, 224 pp.

Patai, Raphael. *The Hebrew Goddess*. New York: Ktav Publishing House. 349 pp.

❧ Lilith, The Daughter of Dracula ❧

Lilith, the daughter of **Dracula**, is a Marvel Comics character introduced in 1974. Her name was, at least in part, suggested by **Lilith**, the vampirelike creature from Hebrew folklore. Lilith made her initial appearance in the June 1974 issue of *Giant-Size Chillers*, a **comic book** that picked up and expanded the story of Dracula from Marvel's very successful *The Tomb of Dracula*. Lilith's story began in Belfast, **Ireland**, where young Angel O'Hara and her new husband were breaking the news of their marriage and her pregnancy to her father. He lost his temper and hit the young man, who was killed by the blow. Reacting to the event, for a moment Angel wished her father dead. As her anger rose, a misty light floated into the house and moved into Angel. Suddenly she was transformed into Lilith, who had invaded and taken over her body. The redheaded, green-eyed Angel now stood before her father as a dark-haired, red-eyed Lilith. She was dressed in a skin-tight black suit with a cape and a stylized **bat** image on her forehead. Her immediate impulse was to feed, and Angel's father was the food supply before her. Lilith next turned to revenge. She sought out **vampire** hunter Quincy Harker and tried to drain his **blood**. He would be found later, barely alive.

In the Marvel Universe, Lilith was the daughter of the fifteenth-century wife of **Vlad the Impaler**, Kicked out of the palace by Vlad, her mother turned the baby girl over to a **Gypsy** woman and then committed **suicide**. Vlad later killed the Gypsy's husband and son. In revenge, the woman, a witch, turned the child into a vampire, but with a difference. She could walk in the daylight, and the **crucifix** would not affect her. Also, when she died, her soul would move on to take over a new body. Her purpose in life was to destroy her father. At one point, in the nineteenth century, she and her father agreed to go their separate ways and see each other no more. They did not meet again until the

1940s, at which time Quincy Harker killed her. Again revived, she returned in the 1970s, at which time she suggested that she and her father join forces and jointly rule the world. **Dracula** rejected the proposal.

Nothing more was heard of Lilith until the Fall 1977 issue of *Marvel Preview* (No. 12), which revealed that Lilith/Angel had moved to New York and was living with a man, Martin Gold. As Angel, her pregnancy was beginning to show, but as Lilith she ventured out to feed. Her story continued in the November 1978 issue of *The Tomb of Dracula* (No. 67). Dracula moved to New York. Intuiting the presence of his daughter, he followed her to Gold's apartment. He had lost his vampiric powers and had come to get her to bite him again. She not only turned him down, she attacked him but carefully avoided biting him. As he swore his revenge, she called for the **animals** and the **weather** to torment him. At that point Dracula was near the end of the first phase of his Marvel career. In 1979 he faced his last battles, recovered his vampiric powers and returned to leadership of the undead, only to be killed by Quincy Harker.

Dracula was never ultimately killed, of course, and he revived again in time to appear in the new series of *The Tomb of Dracula,* begun as an adult-oriented magazine without Comics Code approval. In the June 1980 issue (No. 5), Lilith returned and sought the help of Viktor Benzel to help her kill Dracula. Benzel carried out a magical process that separated Angel and Lilith. She then traveled to **Castle Dracula** and confronted her father. She had the advantage as she could use the cross and holy **water** against him. But in the end she could not bring herself to murder her father.

After this encounter with Dracula, Lilith adopted the name Lilith Drake and settled in the south of **France**. In 1983 (*Doctor Strange*, No. 62), Dr. Stephen Strange, the sorcerer, used a magical spell called the Montesi Formula to destroy Dracula, Lilith, and all other vampires throughout the world.

After the Montesi formula weakened, Dracula and a variety of vampires, including Lilith, were reborn. Consumed by bloodlust, she sought the assistance of various Marvel villains to build a vampire army. It would finally be defeated by Spider-Man and Hannibal King (*Spider-Man Unlimited*, No. 20, 1998). In Marvel's miniseries, *Dracula: Lord of the Undead* (1998), Lilith fought Dracula and with the aid of two human cohorts was able to infest him with a deadly virus. Dracula was only able to survive by drinking the blood of a corpse, which would cause him to lose the respect of the other vampires. Most recently (2005), Lilith joined Nick Fury's Howling Commandos as one of its supernatural agents.

Sources:

Doctor Strange. No. 62. New York: Marvel Comics, December 1983.

Dracula: Lord of the Undead. Nos. 1–3. New York: Marvel Comics, 1998.

Giant-Size Chillers. Vol. 1. New York: Marvel Comics, 1974.

Christiansen, Jeff. "Lilith." The Appendix to the Handbook of the Marvel Universe. Posted at http://www.marvunapp.com/Appendix/lilithdod.htm. Accessed on April 9, 2010.

Marvel Review. No. 12. New York: Marvel Comics, 1977.

Nick Fury's Howling Commandos. No. 1–6. New York: Marvel Comics, 2005–2006.

Redondo, Nestor. "Lilith." *The Official Handbook of the Marvel Universe* 2, 18 (October 1987): 23–24.

Spider-Man Unlimited. No. 20. New York: Marvel Comics, 1998.

The Tomb of Dracula. Nos. 1–70. New York: Marvel Comics, 1971–79.

Lindpainter, Peter Josef von (1791–1856)

Peter Josef von Lindpainter, a German musician who also adapted the vampire for the German stage, was a violinist who had studied at Augsburg and Munich prior to becoming the music director of the Isarton Theater in 1812. In 1819 he moved on to Stuttgart as the Kapellmeister of the city's orchestra, where he would remain for the rest of his life. Throughout his long career he was among the country's most honored conductors, although he was known more for his technical proficiency and dramatic effects rather than originality. He spent a period in the 1850s as the guest conductor of the New Philharmonic Society in **London**.

During his long life, he composed 28 **operas**, *Der Vampyr* being among the two or three most successful. He set the plot in **France** and named his vampire character Graf (or Count) Aubri. In the plot, Aubri convinced the father of Isolde, the object of his desire, to break off her engagement to her love, Graf Hippolyte, and allow him to marry her. In the end, Hippolyte fatally wounded him, but as he lay dying, he made Hippolyte swear not to reveal his death until midnight. He had still hoped to prey on Isolde, but she protected herself by claiming God's **protection**. As his time ran out, without the needed **blood**, Aubri died.

When it first appeared, several months after the vampire opera of **Heinrich Marschner**, Lindpainter's production competed successfully with the other *Der Vampyr*, but it was forgotten through most of the twentieth century until the vampire revival of the 1980s aroused interest in both composers.

Lobishomen The *lobishomen* was a mythological creature found in the folklore of **South America**, primarily Brazil, and has often appeared on lists of vampires. However, *lobishomens*, which originally derived from Portuguese mythology, were not vampires; they were Portuguese **werewolves**. In the **Blade** movies, vampires are groups in family lines each with a common name and tattoo design particular to itself. One of the twelve vampire tribes is the Lobishomen Tribe, who are linked to werewolves from Brazil. It appears that the original Lobishomen were killed by a werewolf and returned as vampires.

Sources:

Gallop, Rodney. *Portugal: A Book of Folk-Ways*. Cambridge: Cambridge University Press, 1936. 291 pp.

Sales, Herberto. *O Lobisomen Contos Folcloricos: Lobisomens, Sacis, Botos e Maes-d'Agua, Ingenuas e Eternus Historias da Alma Brasileira*. Rio de Janeiro: Ediouro Grupa Coquetel, 1975. 105 pp.

Lithuania, Vampires in *see:* Baltic States, Vampires in the

London After Midnight

Frequently cited in histories of the horror movie as the first American vampire motion picture, *London After Midnight* (1927) remains important as a pioneering force in future American treatment of the vampire theme. *London After Midnight* came during the fruitful period of collaboration between director **Tod Browning** and character actor **Lon Chaney**, who had first worked together in 1919 on *The Wicked Darling Law*, and again in 1921 for *Outside the Law* and in 1925 on *The Unholy Three*. In 1925, Chaney returned to **Universal Pictures** for one of his most memorable roles, *The Phantom of the Opera* (1925). Chaney and Browning were united for the last time at MGM in 1927 for *London After Midnight*, based upon a short story by Browning called "The Hypnotist", the title under which *London After Midnight* was released in England in response to British sensitivity.

The movie's story line began approximately five years after a death had occurred in a haunted house. Inspector Burke of Scotland Yard had become convinced that the death was a murder, not an accident or **suicide**. He had two suspects, one a friend and the other a nephew of the deceased. He suggested to them that the murder was done by a vampire. The inspector, played by Chaney, then assumed the role of a vampire, for which he had prepared his own elaborate makeup. His actions as the vampire forced the guilty party to reveal his guilt at which time Chaney revealed his double identity. Although all the major elements of the vampire legend were incorporated into the film, in the end, of course, the vampire was explained away as a masquerade. The movie mixed the horror and mystery genres, but in the end was a mystery movie. It was one of Chaney's last movies and one of the last silent horror films before the major studios moved into sound. Chaney had died by the time Browning made a sound version of *London After Midnight* in 1935 under the title *Mark of the Vampire*. In the later version, the Chaney part was divided between **Bela Lugosi** (the vampire) and Lionel Atwill (the inspector).

A fire at one of MGM's vaults in the 1960s appears to have destroyed the last surviving print of *London After Midnight*, and as vampire fandom grew beginning in the 1970s, the film assumed a somewhat mythical status as a classic Chaney picture. *Mark of the Vampire* had made Universal a considerable amount of money. Stills from the picture indicated that Chaney did his usual fine job of weird and grotesque makeup with thin wires that made his eyes bulge. Chaney's animal-like teeth, shown on the poster for the movie, made speech impossible.

There has been no way to appraise Browning's directorial skills on the movie. Then, in 2002, Turner Movie Classics commissioned Rick Schmidlin to restore the movie using the original script and a set of still photographs assembled from the collections at the Academy of Motion Picture Arts and Sciences, the Fairbanks Center for Motion Picture Studies, the Margaret Herrick Library, and the University of Southern California Cinema-Television Library. An original musical score was added by Robert Israel. This new version was subsequently released on DVD as part of *The Lon Chaney Collection*. One leading **gothic** rock band paid homage to the movie by adopting it as the name of their band. London After Midnight was founded by Sean Brennan in 1987.

Sources:

Clarens, Carlos. *Horror Movies: An Illustrated Survey*. London: Secker & Warburg, 1968. 264 pp.

Coolidge-Rust, Marie. *London After Midnight*. New York: Grosset and Dunlap, 1928. 261 pp.

Flynn, John L. *Cinematic Vampires*. Jefferson, NC: McFarland Company, 1992. 320 pp.

Gebert, Michael. "Mike's 'London After Midnight' Myths Page." *The Lon Chaney Home Page*.
    Posted at http://www.michaelgebert.com/lam/lam1.html. Accessed on April 9, 2010.

Gifford, Denis. *A Pictorial History of Horror Movies*. London: Hamlyn, 1973. 216 pp.

Jones, Stephen. *The Illustrated Vampire Movie Guide*. London: Titan Books, 1991. 144 pp.

London After Midnight. New York: Cornwall Books, 1985. 178 pp.

"London After Midnight: Revelations in Black." *Ghastly* 2 (1992): 9–12.

Sweeney, Gary. "Film Review: London After Midnight." *The Midnight Palace*. Posted at http://www.midnightpalace.com/index.php?option=com_content&task=view&id=62. Accessed on April 9, 2010.

London, Dracula's Nineteenth-Century

London, the capital of what is today known as the **United Kingdom** (England, Scotland, Wales, and Northern **Ireland**), was one of three major sites of action in **Bram Stoker's *Dracula* (1897)**. Some of the sites mentioned by Stoker were entirely fictitious locations, but many were quite real, although a few have disappeared or changed names since the novel appeared in 1897, and some were slightly disguised by Stoker.

Action in the novel began with **Jonathan Harker** traveling to **Transylvania** to make arrangements for **Dracula's** move to England. The focus of their negotiations was an estate in the London suburb of Purfleet. Purfleet is a real place located on the north bank of the Thames River, downstream from London. Semi-industrialized and almost a suburb today, in the 1890s it was a quiet rural Essex Village some ten miles beyond the fringe of London's East End. **Carfax**, the estate in Purfleet, had about 20 acres surrounded by a stone wall. On the land was an old house, dating to medieval times, and nearby a chapel. Stoker, through his character Harker, suggested that the name Carfax was a derivative of *quartre face*, referring to its four walls being aligned with the cardinal points of the compass. From his reading of *The Oxford Dictionary of Etymology*, **Leonard Wolf** has suggested that the name derived from the Anglo-Norman term *carfuks*, the significance being that it was a place where four roads met. Wolf further noted, quite correctly, that **suicides** were buried at crossroads and that people who committed suicide were often thought to return as vampires.

Dracula traveled to England by ship along with the **native soil** so necessary for his survival. He landed at **Whitby** and from there had the dirt shipped to his estate. It arrived from Whitby via rail into King's Cross Station, a very real location, the southern terminus of the Great Northern Railway (which connected London with points north, including Whitby). From there they were then taken to Carfax by Messrs. Carter, Paterson & Co., a real cartage firm that was founded in 1860 and continued to operate in London during Stoker's time. It was a prosperous firm with headquarters on Gorwell Road in London. In Stoker's day, Purfleet was connected to central London by London, Tilbury and Southend Railway, which had its terminus at Fenchurch Street. The characters in *Dracula* could thus travel from Purfleet to central London in about 30 minutes.

Once in England, Dracula began an attack upon **Lucy Westenra**, his first **victim**, while she was still in Whitby, the northern town where Dracula initially arrived. However, the action soon moved to London. The Westenra fictional home, Hillingham, was a large mansion, reflecting a relatively wealthy family. The kitchen was in back, there were several bedrooms on the second floor, and maids' rooms presumably occupied the third floor. It was probably located in the Haverstock Hills neighborhood on the slopes leading to Hampstead, and not too far from the Zoological Gardens. When Dr. **Abraham Van Helsing** arrived on the scene, he stayed at several of the city's finer hotels, including The Great Eastern Hotel on Liverpool Street and the Berkeley at Berkeley Street and Piccadilly.

In one of Dracula's earliest actions, he helped the wolf Bersicker escape from the Zoological Gardens. The Gardens were located in the northeast corner of Regent's Park, one of London's largest parks. The wolves' cage was on the edge of the zoo near the lions' house. Bersicker had only a short distance to travel to reach the Westenra home. The Harker residence was located outside of London, in Exeter. His law office was in Devonshire. At one point they came into London to attend the funeral of Harker's former employee, Mr. Hawkins. Before returning to their home, they strolled from Hyde Park to Piccadilly, where the novel's action periodically returned, and stopped in front of Guillano's, one of the most fashionable court jewelers in London. (Later, its premises were replaced by one of the shops given extended frontage of the Park Lane Hotel.) Here they saw Dracula, appearing much younger than when Harker last saw him in the castle in Transylvania.

In the meantime, Lucy had died and was buried at what Stoker described as "a lordly death-house in a lonely churchyard away from teeming London; where the air is fresh and the sun rises over Hampstead Hill." He spoke of the churchyard (or cemetery) at Kingstead. There was no Hampstead Hill or King-

Publicity photo from the film *Mark of the Vampire*, which was a remake of the silent classic *London after Midnight*.

stead, and it was not clear which site Stoker had in mind as Lucy's resting place. **Raymond T. McNally** and **Radu Florescu** have suggested that he in fact was referring to Highgate Hill and the relatively well known Highgate Cemetery, which fits the basic description of Lucy's resting place (one with impressive burial mausoleums and away from London). The cemetery was the only such structure near Jack Straw's Castle, a still-existing inn located on Hampstead Heath, where Dr. Van Helsing and the other men dined before going to Lucy's grave to put the **stake** in her heart. Once inside the cemetery, they found their way to Lucy's resting place. Evidence suggested that it was actually in the Old Ground or Western Cemetery, probably in a somewhat secluded location near the middle of the cemetery. Afterwards, they found their way to a still-existing pub, The Spaniards Inn, and there caught a cab back into London.

Following the settling of Lucy's situation, and the organization of Mina and the men into a covenanted group to destroy Dracula, Dr. **John Seward**'s house near Purfleet increasingly became the center of the group's campaign to defeat Dracula. Seward lived at his private asylum, which was actually located next door to Carfax. Their efforts would take them back to London as Dracula had distributed his boxes of dirt around the city. Of the original 50 boxes, six were carried to the east end to 197 Chicksand Street, Mile End New Town. This detached portion of Mile End was entirely surrounded by Spitalfields, just off Brick Lane in the heart of Jack the Ripper territory. Three of Ripper's murders were com-

Jack Straw's Castle in London, where Abraham Van Helsing dined in *Dracula*.

mitted just a few blocks away. (Stoker began writing *Dracula* just a year or so after the panic over the Ripper murders and in the preface he wrote for the 1898 Icelandic edition of *Dracula* made reference to them.) Part of Chicksand Street still exists today.

Another six of the boxes were dropped south of the Thames, on Jamaica Lane, a fictitious location. While there is no Jamaica Lane, there is a Jamaica Road, the main artery in Bermondsey, a warehouse district of London just east of Walworth, on the south side of the river. Nine boxes were delivered to a house in London's fashionable West End, on the street called Piccadilly, a residence located near the end of the street farthest away from Piccadilly Circus, the popular shopping area where a number of streets converge and which today is a theater/nightclub spot. As early as 1973, the building at 138–139 Piccadilly was suggested as the location of Dracula's residence in an article by Art Ronnie in the *Los Angeles Herald Examiner*. Interestingly, this building has been the London headquarters of **Universal Pictures**. In the 1890s, the building existed as two separate houses. Bernard Davies, cofounder and chairman of **The Dracula Society**, has suggested that 138 Piccadilly possessed the correct architectural and stylistic details as described in the novel, including a bow window, iron-railed balcony, and a backyard. Dracula finally left London and England from the docks along the Thames aboard the *Czarina Catherine*, a fictitious ship.

The house on the right with the bay windows is 138 Piccadilly, which scholars of Bram Stoker's work have identified as one of Dracula's houses in London.

Sources:

Stoker, Bram. *The Annotated Dracula.* Edited by Leonard Wolf. New York: Ballantine Books, 1975. 362 pp.

———. *The Essential Dracula.* Edited by Raymond McNally and Radu Florescu. New York: Mayflower Books, 1979. 320 pp.

Lone Gull Press *see:* Dark Shadows Fandom

Long Island Dark Shadows Society *see:* Dark Shadows Fandom

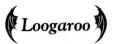

Loogaroo

The *loogaroo* was a vampire entity found in the folklore of Haiti and other islands of the West Indies, including Grenada. The word *loogaroo* is a corruption of the French *loup-garou,* which refers to **werewolves**. The *loogaroo* arose as slaves from West **Africa** appropriated French demonology and mixed it with African vampirology. The *loogaroo* was quite similar to the *obayifo* of the Ashanti and the *asiman* of Dahomey.

Loogaroos were people, usually old **women**, who had made a pact with the devil. In return for certain magical powers, they agreed to bring the devil some warm **blood** each night. To accomplish this task, they removed their skins, which were hidden on the so-called Jumbie tree, the silk-cotton tree. Then, in the form of a fiery ball of light, they would roam across the land in search of blood. In their spirit form they could enter any habitation. Those from whom they took blood would awaken in a tired and fatigued condition. Although *loogaroos* could enter any dwelling, some **protection** was afforded by scattering rice or sand before the door. The *loogaroo*, supposedly, had to stop and count each grain before continuing on its way.

Sources:

Summers, Montague. *The Vampire: His Kith and Kin.* London: Routledge, Kegan Paul, Trench, Trubner, & Co., 1928. 356 pp. Rept. New Hyde Park, NY: University Books, 1960. 356 pp.

The Lord Ruthven Assembly

The Lord Ruthven Assembly (LRA) was founded in 1988 as a scholarly organization dedicated to the serious pursuit of scholarship on and research of the vampire/revenant figure in a variety of disciplines. Most of its members are active participants in the International Association for the Fantastic in the Arts (IAFA), which has recognized the Assembly as a special interest group within its association. Its annual meeting is held during the annual conference of the IAFA, when several sessions of academic papers are offered.

The LRA originated out of the desire of the "vampire people" who attended the IAFA's annual conference to get together to discuss common interests. Spearheading the formation of the Assembly was Lloyd Worley of the University of Northern Colorado who became the founding president. Other original officers include Veronica Hollinger, Allienne R. Becker, and Lillian Heldreth. The decision was made to name the Assembly after author **John Polidori**'s **Lord Ruthven**, the first vampire in English prose fiction.

As of 1998, serving the Assembly are President Stacie Hanes and Secretary Kathy Davis-Patterson, both of Kent State University. Historian **Radu Florescu** has been named an honorary president and Lloyd Worley is the honorary founding president. The Lord Ruthven Assembly may be contacted through its secretary, Kathy Davis-Patterson, at kdavis@tusc.kent.edu.

Sources:

Lord Ruthven Assembly. Posted at http://home.earthlink.net/~lt._dahlquist/lordruthven.htm. Accessed on April 8, 2010.

Lory, Robert Edward (1936–)

Robert Edward Lory, a **science fiction** and fantasy writer, was born in Troy, New York, the son of Dorothy Doughty and Edward Austin Lory. He attended Harper College (now the State University of New York, Binghamton), from which he received a bachelor's degree in 1961.

Lory's first stories were published in the early 1960s in such magazines as *Fantasy and Science Fiction* and *If.* His first book, *Eyes of Bolsk,* appeared in 1969. Then in 1973 and 1974 he completed a popular series of nine books based on the **Dracula** legend. The first, *Dracula Returns,* had Dr. Damien Harmon and his assistant Cam (Cameron Sanchez) traveling to **Romania**, where they were guided to Dracula's crypt by one of his cohorts, a woman named Ktara. Dracula was resting there. "His thick hair was combed neatly back, not a single strand out of place. His sharp angular cheek and bone structure, combined with the thick brows that nearly met at the bridge of his Roman nose, gave the face a dignified nobility. He appeared to be in his late forties or early fifties. And his clothing—formal, impeccable black-tie attire—was perfectly pressed." The major flaw in his appearance was a **stake** that had been driven through his heart.

Harmon had previously implanted a small device near his own heart that controlled a second small device with a sliver of wood that he inserted next to Dracula's heart. The device allowed him to move the sliver of wood in and out of Dracula's heart. The stake was removed and Dracula awoke. He turned to Harmon ready to attack, only to clutch his chest and drop to the floor. Harmon's device gave him control, and he planned to use Dracula in his war against evil. Dracula was transported back to New York and upon awakening was presented with a bottle of synthetic **blood** for his immediate nourishment.

Harmon informed Dracula that he must subsist on the synthetic blood or nothing. The first target of Dracula unleashed was a **crime** syndicate. In the eight subsequent volumes Dracula traveled the world and encountered various natural and supernatural enemies, from practitioners of voodoo and **witchcraft** to the mummy and a legion of killer vampire **bats.** Lory retained the image of Dracula as projected earlier in this century by **Bela Lugosi,** but Lory's Dracula was compelled to become a force for good. Lory's fast-moving action stories thus form a transition to the **"good guy" vampires** of **Fred Saberhagen** and **Chelsea Quinn Yarbro** that appeared a few years later. Lory has admitted to little purpose in his writing beyond that ascribed to Arthur Conan Doyle—to "tell a whopping good tale."

The popular Dracula series has been translated into several foreign languages. After the completion of the Dracula series, Lory began a fantasy series based upon the signs of the horoscope. His last books were published in the mid-1970s.

Sources:

Ashley, Mike. *Who's Who in Horror and Fantasy Fiction.* London: Elm Tree Books, 1977. 240 pp.

Lory, Robert. *Dracula Returns.* New York: Pinnacle Books, 1973. 124 pp.

———. *Dracula's Brothers.* New York: Pinnacle Books, 1973. 186 pp.

———. *Dracula's Gold.* New York: Pinnacle Books, 1973. 182 pp.

———. *The Hand of Dracula.* New York: Pinnacle Books, 1973. 224 pp.

———. *Dracula's Lost World.* New York: Pinnacle Books, 1974. 181 pp.

———. *The Drums of Dracula.* New York: Pinnacle Books, 1974. 189 pp.

———. *The Witching of Dracula.* New York: Pinnacle Books, 1974. 177 pp.

———. *Challenge to Dracula.* New York: Pinnacle Books, 1975. 180 pp.

———. *Dracula's Disciple.* New York: Pinnacle Books, 1975. 179 pp.

Loyalists of the Vampire Realm International Vampires Association *see:* Vampire Fandom: United States

❨ Lugosi, Bela (1882–1956) ❩

Bela Lugosi, the actor most identified with the image of **Dracula** and the vampire in the public mind, was born Bela Blasko on October 20, 1882, in Lugos, **Hungary**. At the time of his birth, Lugos was part of the Austro-Hungarian empire and was located some 50 miles from **Transylvania**. Lugosi attended school locally.

Lugosi was still quite young when a traveling theater company came to Lugos and he gave up ideas of entering a profession for a life on the stage. He began to write and stage amateur productions and in 1893 left school for good. He also left home looking for an acting job; not finding any, he held various jobs as a laborer in the mines, a factory, and on the railroad.

When he had the opportunity to act, his first experiences were negative. His lack of education made him appear stupid. He began a self-education program and read voraciously. His first formal stage role was as Count Konigsegg in *Ocskay Brigaderos* (*Brigadier General Ocskay*) in 1902. The following year he played Gecko, Svengali's servant, in *Trilby*, his first part in a horror production. During this time he tried out a number of stage names, but finally settled on Lugosi, meaning "one from Lugos." In 1910 he starred in *Romeo and Juliet*, for which he received good reviews, and went on to become a featured actor on the Hungarian stage. In 1911 he moved to Budapest to work at the Hungarian Royal Theatre

A publicity shot of Bela Lugosi in character as Dracula.

and two years later joined the National Theatre of Budapest; although his salary increased, the young actor he was not given any starring roles.

Lugosi's acting career was interrupted by World War I. He returned to the theater in 1917. That same year he risked his career by taking a job with the Star Film Company and appeared in his first film, *The Leopard*. For the film he adopted a new stage name, Arisztid Olt. His second role was in *Az Elet Kiralya*, based on *The Picture of Dorian Gray*. He starred in a variety of films until the chaos following the end of the war forced him to leave Hungary. He settled in **Germany** where he appeared in several movies, including *Sklaven Fremdes Willens* (*Slave of a Foreign Will*) and *Der Januskopf* (based on *Dr. Jekyll and Mr. Hyde*).

There was a tendency to cast Lugosi in the role of the villain, although his last role was that of a romantic lead in *Der Tanz auf dem Vulkan*. Banned from Hungary because of his political views, in 1920 he decided to immigrate to the United States. He barely escaped death when his identity was discovered by some Hungarian crew members of the ship on which he traversed the Atlantic. Although an illegal alien, he was granted political asylum and allowed to work. He organized a Hungarian repertory company, which played to the Hungarian-American community.

THE VAMPIRE BOOK: THE ENCYCLOPEDIA OF THE UNDEAD

He got a break in 1922 when he was offered a part in *The Red Poppy*—if he could learn the part. Unable to speak English, he nevertheless memorized the part and opened to his first English-speaking audience in December 1922 at the Greenwich Village Theatre. Lugosi received far better reviews than the play, which ran for only six weeks on Broadway before closing. *The Red Poppy* led to Lugosi's first Hollywood movie part as the villain in *The Silent Command* (1923), an action spy movie.

Unable to obtain further roles in Hollywood, in spite of positive reviews, Lugosi returned to New York and made several movies. He also appeared in several plays and made it back to Broadway briefly in *Arabesque*. The events that were to change his career and life forever can be traced to 1927.

That year, the **Hamilton Deane** version of the play *Dracula* opened in London. Producer Horace Liveright perceived some possibilities for the play in the United States and negotiated the purchase of the American rights. He also had **John L. Balderston** do a thorough rewrite of the script. Director John D. Williams, familiar with Lugosi's work in other plays, cast him in the title role. He fit the part Balderston had created as if it were made for him. His face, especially his eyes, his hand movements, and his Hun-

Bela Legosi in full Dracula garb in one of his many vampire films.

garian accent contributed greatly to the success of the play, which opened October 2, 1927, at the Fulton Theater. It played for forty weeks on Broadway, after which several companies took it on the road.

Lugosi continued his part with the West Coast production of *Dracula*. Back in southern California, he picked up several small movie parts. In 1929, an eventful year, he made his talkie debut in *Prisoners* and he worked with director **Tod Browning** on *The Thirteenth Chair*. In 1930 **Universal Pictures** purchased the motion picture rights to *Dracula*. The company used Lugosi to negotiate the agreement with **Bram Stoker**'s widow, and he was somewhat insulted when not automatically given the part. Rather, Lugosi was among five men considered for the role. Browning wanted **Lon Chaney**, but he died soon after Universal finished its negotiations with Florence Stoker. Lugosi was finally signed for $500 a week. His hardest job was to adapt the part he had played hundreds of time on the stage to the film medium.

Dracula opened on February 14, 1931, and became an immediate, though somewhat unexpected, hit. The film would influence all vampire films that came after it, and Lugosi's **Dracula** would be the standard against which all later vampires were judged. Lugosi became a star, with ninety-seven percent of his fan mail coming from women. He responded by suggesting that generations of subjection had given women a masochistic interest, an enjoyment of suffering experienced vicariously on the screen. Lugosi moved from *Dracula* to portray an Eastern mystic in a Charlie Chan movie, *The Black Camel*,

Bela Legosi menaces three young women.

and then began shooting for *Frankenstein*. The monster proved to be a part not made for him, so he was replaced by Boris Karloff and instead starred in *Murders in the Rue Morgue*, where he did well as a mad scientist. He drifted from Universal in 1932 to make *White Zombies*, in which he played a sorcerer, and returned to the stage in Los Angeles in a horror play, *Murdered Alive*. By this time, he had already been hit by the actor's nemesis—typecasting. Studios continually offered him parts to bring terror to the audience.

In 1933, Lugosi returned to New York for a brief (and last) appearance on Broadway as the villain in *Murder of the Vanities*. He went from Broadway to a vaudeville touring company in which he played *Dracula*. He periodically returned to the part in summer stock whenever his film work was light. In 1934 he made one of his better movies when Universal teamed him with Boris Karloff in *The Black Cat*. At the end of the year both Lugosi and Browning moved over to MGM to team up again in *Mark of the Vampire*. Lugosi played Count Mora in the remake of Browning's silent film, **London After Midnight**. During the rest of the decade into the early 1940s, Lugosi played in a variety of horror movies and appeared as the villain in non-horror flicks, mostly mysteries. Of these, his team-up with Boris Karloff and Basil Rathbone in *Son of Frankenstein* (1939) is possibly the most memorable. Publicity for *The Devil Bat* (1941), a routine mystery, made use of Lugosi's identification with the vampire in its advertising.

Through the early 1940s Lugosi made as many as five movies a year, overwhelmingly in villain or monster roles. He played a Dracula-like role in the comedy *Spooks Run Wild* (1941) and finally portrayed Frankenstein in *Frankenstein Versus the Wolfman* (1943). He played his first genuine vampire role since *Dracula* in Columbia Pictures' *Return of the Vampire* (1944). Lugosi was cast as Armand Tesla, a vampire hardly distinguishable from Dracula, and, as might be expected, Universal filed suit against Columbia for infringement upon its rights. In 1948 Lugosi returned to Universal for his next vampire role. The horror theme having largely run its course, as many at Universal thought, the idea emerged to get the major monsters together with the studio's comic stars, Bud Abbott and Lou Costello, for a monster spoof. Lugosi re-created his Dracula role for *Abbott and Costello Meet Frankenstein*. He played the part with as much dignity as possible and must have enjoyed it somewhat, as he did it a second time for Abbott and Costello's **television** show in 1950.

The downturn in horror movies left Lugosi out of a job. He did some television and in 1950 began to make personal appearances at movie theaters showing his old horror films. In 1951 he traveled to England to do a new production of *Dracula*, but the play flopped and he found himself without enough money to get back to the States. A friend arranged for him to do his next movie, *Old Mother Riley Meets the Vampire* (a.k.a. *My Son the Vampire*), released in 1952. (Mother Riley was a character in a series of British comedies.) Lugosi's return to America was less than spectacular. His ability to get parts was very limited, and a downward slide landed him in a drug rehabilitation program in 1955. Lugosi made a few more films and then in 1956 was hired by director Edward Wood, Jr., to play a vampire for his quickie movie, *Plan 9 from Outer Space*. He and **Vampira** were to play a pair of vampires raised from their graves by outer space aliens. A week after shooting began, on August 16, 1956, Lugosi died. Another actor, doing scenes with the vampire cape pulled across his face, filled in for Lugosi for the rest of the film. *Plan 9* has since become known as one of the worst films of all time and has a substantial cult following.

Lugosi's last years were years of loneliness and abandonment by the industry for which he had worked all his life. He did not live to see the acclaim of a new generation of fans who had an appreciation for the horror genre and understood his contribution to it. Only in the last generation, with the revival of the horror movie in general and the vampire movie in particular, has Lugosi's impact been understood.

Sources:

Bojarski, Richard. *The Films of Bela Lugosi*. Secaucus, NJ: Citadel Press, 1980. 256 pp.

Copner, Mike, and Buddy Barnett. "Bela Lugosi Then and Now!" Special issue of *Videosonic Arts* 1 (1990).

Cremer, Robert. *Lugosi: The Man Behind the Cape*. Chicago: Henry Regnery Company, 1976.

Lennig, Arthur. *The Count: The Life and Films of Bela "Dracula" Lugosi*. New York: G. P. Putnam's Sons, 1974. Revised ed. as *The Immortal Count: The Life and Films of Bela Lugosi*. Lexington, KY: University Press of Kentucky, 2003. 560 pp.

Magic Image Filmbooks Presents Dracula (The Original 1931 Shooting Script). Atlantic City, NJ: Magic Image Filmbooks, 1990.

Pirie, David. *The Vampire Cinema*. London: Hamlyn, 1977. 176 pp.

Rhodes, Gary D., and Richard Sheffield. *Bela Lugosi-Dreams and Nightmares*. Collectables Press, 2007. 352 pp.

Skal, David J. *Hollywood Gothic: The Tangled Web of Dracula from Novel to Stage to Screen*. New York: W. W. Norton & Company, 1990. 242 pp.

Svehla, Gary J., and Susan Svehla, eds. *Bela Lugosi*. Baltimore, MD: Midnight Marquee Press, 1995. 311 pp.

Lumley, Brian (1937–)

Brian Lumley, author of the *Necroscope* series of vampire books, was born on December 2, 1937, in Horden, Durham, England. Trained as a lawyer, he joined the British army in the 1950s and served in Germany and in Cyprus. He was in Cyprus when he began to write seriously, and the island inspired his first professional short story, "The Cyprus Shell." It and others were collected to make his first book, *The Caller of the Black*, published by Arkham House in 1970. Arkham House specialized in books in the H. P. Lovecraft horror tradition. Lumley adopted the Lovecraft myth of *cthulhu*, the idea of ancient demonic forces that had been pushed aside by the forces of civilization but lay just beneath the surface of civilization awaiting any opportunity to return to power. This myth stood behind his first novels, *The Burrowers Beneath* (1974) and *Beneath the Moors* (1974), and most of his subsequent writings.

In 1986 *Necroscope* was published, the first book in what has become one of the most popular series of vampire books. The series tells the story of Harry Keogh, a necroscope (someone who can speak to the dead). Scottish-born Keogh was the son of a psychic-sensitive Russian émigré. As he grew up, he discovered that he not only had his mother's sensitivity, but that his psychic talents were even more extraordinary. He was able to contact the dead in their graves. In Lumley's alternative world, the dead moved into a new state of immobility and incorporeality, but retained a continued existence through conscious mental processes. Their relationship to Keogh allowed them an outlet to the world. Thus, they loved and respected him.

Keogh's talents pushed him into the world of espionage. He was pitted against Boris Dragosani, a ghoulish necromancer who dissected dead bodies with his hands to gain information by holding their various body parts. Dragosani killed the head of the psychic branch of British intelligence to gain the secrets of their work with people of psychic ability. Keogh decided he had to kill Dragosani, but at the time was unaware of the real threat; Dragosani had developed a relationship with a powerful vampire named Thibor Frenczy. The battle with Frenczy and Dragosani became the prelude to an ongoing battle with the vampiric world that unfolded in the subsequent volumes of the Necroscope series—*Vamphyri!* (1988), *The Source* (1989), *Deadspeak* (1990), and *Deadspawn* (1991). The story continued in a second

The *Necroscope* comic book was based on the Brian Lumley novel of the same name.

series, *Vampire World*, three volumes of which appeared. Lumley continued to work on his vampire mythos through 2001 and then took a break for several years but has continued with two volumes in 2009. In these later volumes, Harry Keogh's place has been taken by a new necroscope, Scott St. John. The entire Necroscope library currently consists of some fifteen volumes, including the collections of related short stories.

Sources:

Ashley, Mike. *Who's Who in Horror and Fantasy Fiction.* London: Elm Tree Books, 1977. 240 pp.

Lumley, Brian. *Necroscope.* London: Grafton, 1988. Rept. New York: TOR, 1988. 505 pp.

———. *Necroscope II. Wamphyri.* London: Grafton, 1988. Rept. *Necroscope II. Vamphyri.* New York: TOR, 1989. 470 pp.

———. *Necroscope III. The Source.* London: Grafton, 1989. Rept. New York: TOR, 1989. 505 pp.

———. *Necroscope IV. Deadspeak.* London: Kinnell, 1990. Rept. New York: TOR, 1990. 487 pp.

———. *Necroscope V. Deadspawn.* London: Grafton, 1991. Rept. New York: TOR, 1991. 602 pp.

———. *Blood Brothers. Vampire Worlds 1.* New York: TOR, 1992. 408 pp. Rept. London: ROC, 1992. 741 pp.

———. *Vampire World III: Bloodwars.* London: ROC, 1993. Reprinted as *Bloodwars. Vampire World III.* New York: TOR, 1994. 760 pp.

———. *Vampire World II: The Last Aerie.* London: ROC, 1993. Reprinted as *The Last Aerie. Vampire Worlds 2.* New York: TOR, 1993. 758 pp.

———. *Necroscope: The Lost Years.* New York: TOR, 1995. 415 pp.

———. *Necroscope: Resurgence. The Lost Years, Volume Two.* New York: TOR, 1996. 414 pp.

———. *Necroscope Avengers.* New York: TOR, 2001. 445 pp.

———. *Necroscope: Defilers.* New York: Tor Books, 2001. 640 pp.

———. *Harry Keogh: Necroscope and Other Weird Heroes!* New York: Tor Books, 2005. 320 pp.

———. *Necroscope: The Touch.* New York: Tor Books, 2007. 512 pp.

———. *Necroscope: Harry and the Pirates: and Other Tales from the Lost Years.* New York: Tor Books, 2009. 192 pp.

———, and Bob Eggleton. *A Coven of Vampires.* Subterranean Press, 2007. 210 pp.

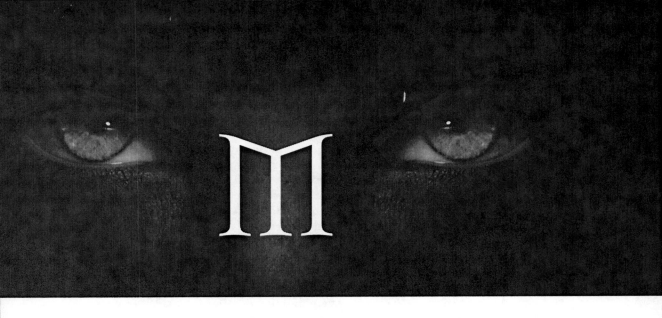

M

Malaysia, Vampires in

Western observers who began to look at the magical/religious world of Malaysians in the nineteenth century discovered belief in several vampire-like beings, somewhat analogous to the *lamiai* of the mythology of **Greece**. These beliefs have survived to this day in spite of the overlay of Hindu and Islamic thought that has come to dominate the religious life of the peninsula. Vampires still inhabit the very lively world of the average Malaysian.

The Vampire in Malaysian Folklore: There are two beings closely related to the Greek *lamiai*: the *langsuyar* and the *pontianak*. The former was described as a banshee-like **flying** demon. The original *langsuyar* was a woman of extreme beauty who bore a stillborn baby. When told of the condition of the child, she recoiled from the shock. Suddenly, she clapped her hands and flew away into a nearby tree. She was seen from time to time and identified by her green robe, her long **fingernails** (considered a mark of beauty in Malaysian society), and her ankle-length black hair. The hair concealed an opening in her neck through which she sucked the **blood** of children. The first *langsuyar* then gave way to groups of similar beings. Later *langsuyars* were flesh eaters with a particular fondness for fish (a staple of the Malaysian diet).

If a woman died either in childbirth or in the 40 days immediately following (during which time she was considered unclean), it was believed she might become a *langsuyar*. To prevent that from occurring, her family placed glass beads in her mouth (which stopped any banshee-like shrieks). To prevent her from flying, they would place eggs under her arms and a needle in the palm of each hand. However, it was also possible to tame a *langsuyar* by capturing it, cutting off its hair and nails, and stuffing them into the hole in the neck. In that case, the *langsuyar* became domesticated and could live in human society somewhat normally. Reports have been collected claiming that such *langsuyars* came into villages, married, and bore children.

However, their new life ended usually at a village party when they began to dance. Suddenly, they would revert to their more spirit-like form and fly off to the jungle, leaving husband and child behind.

The **origin** of the *pontianak* was directly linked to that of the *langsuyar*—it was the creature's stillborn child. It was believed to take the form of a night owl. To prevent a deceased baby from becoming a *pontianak*, it was treated somewhat like its mother, with beads, eggs, and needles. As with the *langsuyar*, there were specific words to be spoken when "laying" a possible *pontianak*. Walter William Skeat, the main authority on Malaysian mythology, noted some confusion between the *langsuyar* and the *pontianak*. Both could appear as a night owl, both were addressed in invocations as if they were the same, and both mother and child were treated alike to prevent them from becoming a vampire after their death. This confusion has been somewhat cleared up by noting that in parts of Malaysia and throughout much of Indonesia, in places such as **Java**, what Skeat described as the *langsuyar*, the female vampire, was called a *pontianak*. The *penanggalan* was a third vampire-like creature in Malaysian folklore. According to tradition, it originated with a woman in the midst of performing *dudok bertapa*, a penance ceremony. She was sitting in a large wooden vat used for holding the vinegar derived from the sap of the palm tree.

In the midst of her ceremony, a man found her and asked her what she was doing. Startled, she moved to leave, and did so with such force that her head separated from her body, and with the entrails of her stomach trailing behind, she flew off into a nearby tree. That severed head with the dangling stomach attached below it became an evil spirit. It appears on the rooftops of the homes where children are being born. It whines a high-pitched sound and tries to get to the child to suck its blood.

Writing in the early 1800s, P. J. Begbie described the *penanggalan* as an evil spirit that possessed a woman and turned her into a sorcerer. When it wished to travel, it would detach its head and, with its entrails trailing behind, fly off in pursuit of food in the form of the blood of both the living and dead. He also told the story of a man with two wives, one of dark and one of light skin. He was told that they were both *penanggalans*. The man did not believe it, so to test them he watched one night and saw them leave to feed. He then switched their bodies. When they returned, they attached their heads to the wrong body. When the king was presented with this irrefutable proof of their evil nature, both were executed.

An alternate version of the story stated that the *penanggalan* originated from a woman who had been using magic arts and finally learned how to fly. At that time her head and neck were separated from her body, and with her intestines dangling, she took up her abode in a tree. From there she flew from house to house to suck the blood of not only babies but also mothers giving birth. To protect the birthing site, the leaves of the *jeruju* (a kind of thistle) were hung around the house and thorns stuck in any blood that was spilled. As might be expected, blood and other juices dripped from the dangling intestines, and should such drippings fall on anyone, they would immediately fall ill.

Two other blood-drinking entities, the *polong* and the *pelesit*, were closely related in Malaysian lore. The former appeared in the form of a very small female creature (about one inch in height) and the latter as a house cricket. The *polong* operated somewhat like a witch's familiar in traditional Western mythology. It could be attracted by

gathering the blood of a murder victim in a bottle over which a seven-day (some say 14-day) ritual was performed. Then one waited for the sound of young birds chirping, a sign that the *polong* had taken up residence in the bottle. The *polong* was fed by cutting a finger, inserting it in the bottle, and allowing the *polong* to suck the blood. (In the West, the witch's familiar was said to suckle from a hidden protuberance on the witch's body—a witch's teat). In return for a daily supply of blood, the *polong* was available to do a variety of tasks, including attacking one's enemies. If one was attacked by a *polong,* which was signaled by various kinds of wild ravings, wise men were called in to exorcise it and to attempt to discover who sent it to torment the victim. Deaths were occasionally attributed to the attack of a *polong* who remained unexorcised.

The *pelesit* generally accompanied the *polong* in its travels and arrived before it. If the *polong* was sent to attack someone, the *pelesit* would first attempt to enter the body of the victim and, in a sense, prepare the way for the *polong.* Walter William Skeat reported a rather gruesome method of creating a *pelesit.* The potential owner dug up a recently deceased infant. The infant's corpse was carried to an ant hill. After a while the child would cry out and at that moment its tongue would have to be bitten off. The tongue was then dipped in specially prepared coconut oil and buried for three nights.

After the third night the tongue turned into a *pelesit.* The Chewong were among the many peoples in the very diverse population of Malaysia. They possessed their own mythology, which included the existence of many spirits collectively called the *bas.* There were various kinds of *bas,* some of which will attack humans under certain circumstances. The usual food of the *bas* was a *ruwai,* roughly translated as soul or life or vitality. Their preferred prey was the wild pig, and the *bas* set invisible traps to snare the pig's *ruwai.* Sometimes a human *ruwai* was caught in the trap, and in such a case the *bas* would eat the human spirit/soul. The *bas* might also encounter a human *ruwai* when it was traveling about during a person's dreams. *Bas* usually did not attack humans or approach human places of habitation. They knew fire as a sign of human presence, and a person in the woods who encountered a *bas* could build a fire and the *bas* would depart.

On rare occasions, *bas* were thought to attack humans. They attacked in different ways, although most sought only the *ruwai.* For example, the *eng banka,* the ghost of a dead dog that inhabited swamp areas, would steal a *ruwai.* If it was not recovered, the victim died within a few days; someone who suddenly became ill and died a few days later was seen as the victim of an *eng banka.* The *maneden,* which lived in the wild pandanus plant, differed quite a bit from the *eng banka.* It attacked humans who cut the plant in which it resided by biting them and sucking their blood. It attached itself to the elbow of men or the breast nipples of women. To stop the attack the person had to give the *bas* a substitute, such as the oily nut from the hodj nut tree. Thus, the attack of the *eng banka* was a variety of psychic vampirism and that of the *maneden* a more literal vampiric attack.

The Modern Malaysian Vampire: It was not until after World War II that the film industry (always under strict British control) began to develop. Shaw Brothers, a firm based in Hong Kong, established Malay Film Productions in 1947. It was soon joined by Catay-Keris Productions. In their drive to compete with Western films, which dominated the market, the Malaysians sought particularly Malaysian themes and locales for their films. The Malaysian vampire thus entered the film world, one of the first such

films being *Pontianak* in 1956. In this film, Maria Menado played a hunchbacked young woman made beautiful by magic. After her husband was bitten by a snake and she sucked his blood to get the poison out, she was turned into a vampire, the *pontianak*. The vampire movies drew on the broad use of the term *pontianak* throughout Indonesia and always pictured the vampire as a young and beautiful woman. The stories told in the movies were made plausible to viewers by the numerous reports from Malaysians who claimed to actually know a vampire who was living a more or less normal life as a wife and mother. During the late 1950s and 1960s, Catay-Keris eventually produced a series of six movies featuring a *pontianak*. The original Catay-Keris film has been lost and no known copies exist, but several of the others such as *Pontianak Gua Musang* (1964) and a later movie also called simply *Pontianak* (1975) have been released in the video CD format still popular in southeast Asia. After the Shaw Brothers closed their Malaysian operation in the 1960s, few horror movies were made in Malaysia. The film industry largely disappeared in the mid 1970s.

When Malaysian films began to be made again in the 1990s, a series of restrictions had been placed on the books, primarily to guide Muslim censors in reviewing Hollywood movies. Among the characters banned from the screen were vampires and monsters, who could only appear in dream sequences. The first attempt to make a horror movie within the stated guidelines was the popular *Pontianak Sundal Malam* (2001). Its success opened the door both to more vampire movies and a loosening of the restrictions. As the industry revived, a new series of pontianak films have appeared such as *Pontianak Harum Sundal Malam* (2004) and its sequel and *Pontianak Menjerit* (2005).

Sources:

Begbie, P. J. *The Malayan Peninsula*. Vepery Mission Press, 1834. Rept. Kuala Lumpur: Oxford University Press, 1967. 523 pp.

Howell, Signe. *Society and Cosmos: Chewong of Peninsular Malaysia*. Singapore: Oxford University Press, 1984. 294 pp.

Kennedy, Raymond. *The Ageless Indies*. New York: John Day Company, 1942. 208 pp.

Laughlin, Will. "Braineater." Posted at http://www.braineater.com/. Accessed August 15, 2009.

Lent, John A. *The Asian Film Industry*. Austin: University of Texas Press, 1990. 310 pp.

Skeat, Walter William. *Malay Magic: An Introduction to the Folklore and Popular Religion of the Malay Peninsula*. London: Macmillan and Co., 1900. 685 pp. Rept. New York: Barnes & Noble, 1966. 685 pp.

Skeat, Walter William, and Charles Otto Blagden. *Pagan Races of the Malay Peninsula*. 2 vols. New York: Macmillan and Company, 1906. Rept. New York: Barnes & Noble, 1966.

Winstedt, Richard. *The Malay Magician Being Shaman, Saiva, and Sufi*. London: Routledge and Kegan Paul, 1961. 180 pp.

Man-Bat

Man-Bat is a vampire-like character introduced in the 1970s by DC Comics as the stiff guidelines of the 1954 Comics Code were being relaxed. Created by Frank Robins, Man-Bat made his initial appearance in *Detective Comics* (No. 400) in early 1970. The original story concerned Kirk Langstrom, an expert on nocturnal mammals at the museum in Gotham City, the home of superhero **Batman**. Langstrom had become obsessed with the idea of besting Batman in some way. In seeking to accomplish his goal, he concocted a serum made from the glands of **bats**. The serum gave him a natural sonar power and the supersensitive hearing abilities associated with bats. There was an unwanted side effect—he began to transform into a giant bat creature.

Langstrom was trying to find some way out of his predicament when thieves broke into the museum. Batman was about to be defeated by the thieves when Man-Bat showed up to help. In their next encounter, Man-Bat attempted to steal drugs that he hoped would reverse his condition. At the time, Langstrom was engaged, his marriage was approaching, and he was trapped in his bat form.

His fiance, Francine, took some of the serum as an act of love and thus joined Langstrom in his batlike existence. With Batman's help they both received an antidote and returned to human form.

Their story appeared to be over. However, there was enough reader reaction to include several new Man-Bat stories in future issues of *Detective Comics*. In No. 429, Francine was bitten by a vampire bat and became a vampire she-bat. Her vampiric side was cured by a complete blood transfusion. Meanwhile, Langstrom had continued his research and attained the ability to turn into Man-Bat at will by taking some pills. He became a crime fighter like Batman. In this capacity he earned a large reward that left him independently wealthy. At the end of 1975, DC Comics tried to test their new character, who seemed to have a large following, with his own **comic book**. The first issue of *Man-Bat* appeared in December 1975. In it, Langstrom was called upon to deal with super criminal Baron Tyme, who had discovered a means to control Francine and use her to commit crimes.

Tyme's intervention reactivated Francine's vampirism. The new comic book was short lived, however, and after only two issues, Man-Bat returned to *Detective Comics*. Over the next decade, Man-Bat made sporadic appearances to interact with Batman (for example, in *Batman Family* No. 18 in 1978 and *Batman* No. 348 in 1982) and occasionally with other DC characters, such as Superman (*DC Comics Presents* No. 335 in 1981). In 1984 a second attempt was made to revive Man-Bat in a separate publication. The original Man-Bat stories from *Detective Comics* were reprinted, but only one issue appeared, and Man-Bat returned to a secondary role in the ongoing DC cast.

Through the 1990s to the present, Man-Bat has made periodic appearances and, in the hands of new artists John Bolton and Kelley Jones, developed a more sinister appearance. He has also been involved in more stories which have pushed him to the edge of human society. In "Final Night of the Man-Bat," for example, Doug Moench and Jones placed Man-Bat in a Gotham City that had lost its sunlight and Batman had to save Man-Bat from losing his humanity altogether and becoming a killer.

In the middle of the first decade of the new century, Batman is apparently killed in a story line called the "Final Crisis," though the people of Gotham only know that he has disappeared and seemingly abandoned them. While a power struggle begins to fill Batman's place, Langstrom is struggling with the possibility of changing into Man-Bat and killing his wife as a tragic result. His wife disappears and, while searching for her, Langstrom is captured by the villainous Doctor Phosphorus, from whom he learns that he no longer needs the serum to make the change into Man-Bar. When the opportunity arises, he changes in order to save his wife from Phosphorus's evil designs.

Man-Bat has proved popular enough to remain an active character in Batman's comic book world and to make the jump to television beginning with *Batman: The Animated Series* (1992–1995). There have been several Man-Bat action figures.

Sources:

Delano, Jamie, and John Bolton. *Batman Manbat.* No. 1–3. New York: DC Comics, 1995.

Man-Bat. DC Comics. Nos. 1–2 (December 1975/January 1976,–February/March 1976).

Man-Bat. DC Comics. No. 1 (1984).

Man-Bat. DC Comics. Nos. 1–6 (June 2006–October 2006).

Moench, Doug et al. "Darkest Night of the Man-Bat." *Batman* 536–68 (November 1996–January 1998).

Manchester, Sean *see:* Vampire Research Society

The Manor of the Devil

The Manor of the Devil (*La Manoir du Diable*), also known as *The Haunted Castle* and *The Devil's Manor*, is the very first vampire film. The first practical motion picture camera was produced by Louis and Augustus Lumière in the 1890s, and at that time the average movie lasted slightly over one minute. In 1896, the Lumière brothers worked with George Méliès, a magician fascinated with the new medium, to produce an original vampire film.

Using some 195 feet of film, *The Manor of the Devil* was over three minutes long. The Devil in the form of a vampire bat flies into the window of a castle. He circles the room and then transforms into Mephistopheles (portrayed by Méliès). He produces a large caldron and a number of people (from witches to beautiful young girls) pour forth until suddenly a man appears brandishing a cross. Mephistopheles immediately vanishes in a puff of smoke.

Méliès continued to make numerous pictures, only a few of which have survived. He is best known today for his film picturing a rocket heading to the moon.

Sources:

Flynn, John L. *Cinematic Vampires: The Living Dead on Film and Television, from the Devil's Castle (1896), to Bram Stoker's Dracula (1992).* Jefferson, NC: McFarland & Company, 1992. 320 pp.

Mara *see:* Scandinavia, Vampires in

Marryat, Florence (1837–1899)

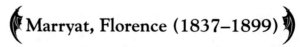

Florence Marryat, a popular British author and spiritualist, wrote approximately ninety novels and more than 100 short stories in her lifetime. She is primarily remembered today, however, for *There Is No Death* (1891) and *The Spirit World* (1894), her two books in support of the mediums of the late nineteenth century, many of whom had been charged with faking their séances. As a novelist, she wrote for a female audience, including such titles as *Love's Conflict, Too Good for Him, Her Lord and Master, Forever and Ever,* and *The Girls of Feversham.*

Marryat also made her mark on the vampire world. The same year that saw the publication of **Bram Stoker**'s *Dracula* (1897) celebrated the publication of Marryat's *The Blood of a Vampire*, a 345-page novel about a psychic vampire, Harriett Brandt. Marryat looked to the then-British colony of Jamaica for the origin of her vampire. In the story, Brandt's father had been kicked out of medical school in Switzerland prior to moving to Jamaica where he pursued a career as a mad scientist. The natives were the victims of his torturous experiments. Her mother, a black woman, was a witch, as evil as her mad-scientist husband. At one point her mother had been bitten by a vampire bat and had developed a taste for **blood**.

While Brandt was a child, the black people rose up and killed her parents and Brandt was raised in a convent school. When she came of age, she inherited her father's considerable estate, and left Jamaica to see Europe for the first time. When she settled in among the Brits vacationing in a resort town in Belgium, she was as yet unaware of her vampiric nature. The first victim was the baby of a woman who befriended Brandt at the hotel. Eventually Brandt married, and from her husband gradually became aware of her vampiric state, although not in time to keep him from slowly declining and dying. After his death, unable to control her vampirism, she committed **suicide**.

Marryat's novel is a study in contrasts, and completely different in approach to the vampire and novel of Stoker. The vampire Brandt lacks **Dracula**'s **strength**, being as much a victim as those whose death she unwittingly causes. Missing from the story are the explorations of **sexuality** and power that provide the tension in *Dracula* and the plot moves so slowly it can lose the reader's interest even before the nature and source of Brandt's peculiar psychic vampirism is discovered.

Sources:

Marryat, Florence. *The Blood of the Vampire*. London: Hutchinson & Co., 1897. 345 pp. Reprinted. Kansas City, MO: Valancourt Books, 2009.

Marschner, Heinrich August (1795–1861)

Heinrich August Marschner, the author of the first vampire **opera**, was born on August 16, 1795, in Zittau, Germany. He manifested an early talent for music but left home at eighteen to pursue law at the University at Leipzig. Fortunately, one of his professors recognized his true talents and convinced him to drop out of law. Marschner moved to Vienna, where he met Beethoven and wrote his first operas. In 1823 he became music director at the opera house at Dresden.

Four years later he moved back to Leipzig. By the time of his return to Leipzig, the vampire had become an item of fascination for French artists and that interest was being felt in **Germany**. Thus, in 1828, while in Leipzig, Marschner wrote his opera *Der Vampyr*. The finished piece was a collaborative product. The libretto was written by Wilhelm August Wohlbrück, Marschner's brother-in-law. It was based on **Charles Nodier**'s very successful stage play that had first brought the vampire to Parisian theater audiences. Nodier's work was in turn based on **John Polidori**'s "The Vampyre". The opera opened with a gathering of witches. **Lord Ruthven** appeared and was told that he had twenty-four hours to locate three **victims**. Janthe, the first of his three victims-to-be, soon ar-

rived, and she and the vampire departed into the vampire's cave where he killed her. Janthe's father then killed Ruthven, but he was revived when his friend Aubry placed him in the moonlight. (Moonlight, a theme introduced by Polidori, was retained in the nineteenth-century works based on "The Vampyre," but disappeared from the twentieth-century lore.)

The next scene was the home of Malwina, the young woman with whom Aubry was in love. They were prevented from consummating their love, however, as Malwina's father had promised his daughter to the Earl of Marsden—that is, Ruthven. Aubry could not expose Ruthven because he had taken an oath never to reveal Ruthven's vampiric condition. On his way to the wedding, Ruthven located his third victim, Emmy, the daughter of a peasant. After killing Emmy he headed for another needed feeding. Unable to prevent the wedding by his best arguments, Aubry finally broke his oath and revealed Ruthven's true nature.

Cosmic forces took over, and Ruthven was struck by lightning and fell into the pits of hell. The opera ended with the wedding guests singing a closing song thanking God.

Der Vampyr opened in Leipzig on March 29, 1829. The opera was a great success and was taken on the road. It opened in London in August and ran for some sixty performances at the Lyceum Theater, the same theater that later played such a central role in **Bram Stoker**'s career and the site of the original dramatization of *Dracula*. In 1831 Marschner continued his career at Hanover, where he wrote his most critically acclaimed work, *Hans Heiling*. In 1859 he was pensioned as Hanover's general music director. He died two years later on December 14, 1861. The town erected a monument to him in 1877.

Der Vampyr has been revived only rarely since the 1820s; however, in 1992 the BBC sponsored a modern production of it. The new production, entitled *Der Vampyr—A Soap Opera*, utilized Marschner's music but had a completely new libretto written by Charles Hart that transferred the setting to modern London. Lord Ruthven became Ripley the Vampyr. (His part was sung by Omar Ebrahim.) The outline of the old plot survived, however, and Ripley, after several bloody scenes that would satisfy any vampire enthusiast, received his just reward in the presence of the wedding guests. The new version of *Der Vampyr* has been released on a Virgin Classics compact disc.

William Marshall as Blacula in *Scream, Blacula, Scream*.

Sources:

Brautigam, Rob. "Der Vampyr." *International Vampire* 1, 4 (Summer 1991): 8–10.

———. "The Vampyr—A Soap Opera." *International Vampire* 10 (1993): 5.

Palmer, A. Dean. *Heinrich August Marschner: 1795–1861*. Ann Arbor, MI: UMI Research Press, 1980. 591 pp.

❦ Marshall, William B. (1924–2003) ❦

Wingilliam B. Marshall, Shakespearean actor and star of two vampire movies, was born on August 19, 1924, in Gary, Indiana. Early career highlights included successful performances in the title roles in *Oedipus Rex* and *Othello* in the 1960s. These parts led to movie roles as a Haitian patriot leader in *Lydia Bailey* and a nubian in *Demetrios and the Gladiators*. In the early 1970s, as movies aimed at an African-American audience became a growth industry, producer Joseph T. Naar at Power Productions began a search for someone to play a black vampire lead in a movie he was putting together. Marshall, six feet five inches tall, fit the part in a most impressive manner. Not used to playing stereotypical black characters, he assumed some direct responsibility for the final creation of the character, Prince Mamuwalde, cursed by **Dracula** to become Blacula. He transformed the title role, which had the potential for degenerating into a parody of both vampires and black people, into a serious dramatic part. He was responsible for developing the character of Prince Mamuwalde into an antislavery freedom fighter.

Blacula (1972) was successful enough to lead to one sequel, *Scream, Blacula, Scream.* (1973). Although Marshall was eager to continue his portrayal of Blacula in further movies, the production company, American International, dropped the idea.

Sources:

Glut, Donald F. *The Dracula Book*. Metuchen, NJ: Scarecrow Press, 1975. 388 pp.

❦ Matheson, Richard (1926–) ❦

Richard Matheson, a screenwriter and science fiction/horror novelist, was born in Allendale, New Jersey. His first publications were science fiction stories, although it has been noted that at least a hint of horror has been part of his writing from the beginning. His first sale was a short story, "Born of Man and Woman" (1950), which then became the title of his first book (1954), a collection of his stories. His first vampire short story, "Drink My Red Blood", appeared in 1951 and has been frequently reprinted. It was three years later that he completed the novel that has been hailed as one of the classics of the vampire genre, *I Am Legend* (1954).

I Am Legend recounted the problem caused by a new bacterium that created an isotonic solution in human blood from which it lived. It slowly turned humans into vampires. As the story developed, Robert Neville, who was immune to the bacteria, survived as the only untainted human. Most of the action took place at Neville's fortified home. He was

William Marshall as Blacula.

Will Smith is a doctor trying to find a cure for a gruesome plague in *I Am Legend*.

opposed by his former neighbor, Ben Cortland, who led the vampire hordes in their search for fresh **blood**. As the bacteria invaded the body, they caused the canine teeth to elongate and turned the skin a pale gray-white color. The bacteria were killed by the light of the sun and by **garlic**, and thus those infected adopted the habits of traditional vampires. Cortland was nearly unkillable. He survived **bullets**, knife wounds, and other normally fatal traumas. The bacteria immediately sealed wounds. However, if a person was staked, the **stake** kept the wound open and the bacteria died. At the end of the story, humans developed a vaccine that killed the germ.

Matheson occasionally returned to the vampire theme in his stories, including "The Funeral" (1955) and "No Such Thing as a Vampire" (1959), and he went on in his lengthy career to write several horror screenplays. His 1956 novel, *The Incredible Shrinking Man*, was made into a movie in 1957. He adapted several of **Edgar Allan Poe**'s stories for the screen for producer **Roger Corman**. His novel *Bid Time Return* (1975) won the Howard Award as the best fantasy novel of the year.

I Am Legend has been adapted to the screen three times, but without the use of Matheson's own screenplay. First, an Italian production, released in America as *The Last Man on Earth* (1964), starred Vincent Price.

Then, *I Am Legend* served as the basis for the 1971 American production *The Omega Man*, starring Charlton Heston; however, in this latter production, the vampire theme was largely eliminated. The vampire theme was somewhat revived in the third attempt to bring *I Am Legend* to the screen (2007) starring Will Smith.

In 1968 Matheson's "No Such Thing as a Vampire" was brought to the **television** screen as an episode of the BBC's Late Night Horror Show. Then in 1971 Matheson began a period of creative work with producer/director **Dan Curtis**. His first effort was a screenplay for *The Night Stalker*. Matheson's story of a vampire-hunting reporter became the most-watched made-for-television movie up to that time. On the heels of that success he wrote the screenplay for Curtis's new production of **Dracula (1973)** starring

Jack Palance in the title role. Then, in 1975 and 1977 Matheson's short stories became the basis for two made-for-television movies, *Trilogy of Terror* and *Dead of Night*. The latter, directed by Curtis as the pilot for a never-produced series, brought *No Such Thing as a Vampire* to the screen again as one of three stories.

In 1989 the Horror Writers of America gave Matheson the first of two **Bram Stoker** Awards for the best volume of collected fiction for his *Richard Matheson: Collected Stories*. The following year they presented him with the award for lifetime achievement. In 2006, Gauntlet Press, a publishing house specializing in editions for collectors, released a collection of Matheson's vampire writing under the title *Bloodlines*.

Sources:

Ashley, Mike. *Who's Who in Horror and Fantasy Fiction*. London: Elm Tree Books, 1977. 240 pp.
Matheson, Richard. "Drink My Red Blood." *Imagination* (April 1951). Rept. as "Blood Son." In *A Feast of Blood*. Charles M. Collins, ed. New York: Avon, 1967. Rept. as "Drink My Blood." In *The Midnight People*. Peter Haining, ed. New York: Popular Library, 1968. Rept. in *A Clutch of Vampires*. Raymond T. McNally, ed. New York: Bell Publishing Company, 1974, pp. 223–34.
———. *I Am Legend*. New York: Fawcett, 1954. 175 pp. Rept. New York: Berkley Publishing Company, 1971. 174 pp.
Matheson, Richard, and Mark Dawidziak. *Bloodlines: Richard Matheson's Dracula, I Am Legend and Other Vampire Stories*. Colorado, CO: Gauntlet Press, 2006. 420 pp.
Pickersgill, Frederick, ed. *No Such Thing as a Vampire*. London: Corgi, 1964. 126 pp.
Rovin, Jeff. *The Encyclopedia of Super Villains*. New York: Facts on File, 1987. 416 pp.
Wiater, Stanley, Matthew Bradley, and Paul Stuve. *The Twilight and Other Zones: The Dark Worlds of Richard Matheson*. New York: Citadel Press, 2009. 352 pp.

❦ McNally, Raymond T. (1931–2003) ❦

Raymond T. McNally, a leading historian and scholar on vampires in folklore and fiction and expert on **Vlad the Impaler**—the historical **Dracula**—was born on May 15, 1931, in Cleveland, Ohio, the son of Marie Kinkoff and Michael Joseph McNally. After completing his education, McNally took a position as instructor at John Carroll University in his hometown. He moved on to Boston College in Chestnut Hill, Massachusetts, in 1958. In 1961 he was named an American Exchange Scholar to the USSR and spent the year at the University of Leningrad. From 1964 to 1974 he also served as director of Boston College's Slavic and East European Center. He was appointed full professor in 1970.

After joining the faculty at Boston College he met **Radu R. Florescu**, a Romanian historian with whom he shared an interest in Dracula and vampire lore.

They formed a team to do research on the historical Dracula, a fifteenth-century ruler named Vlad the Impaler, and his relationship to the novel by **Bram Stoker**. In 1967 McNally was one of a party of men who discovered and explored the authentic **Castle Dracula**. His continued collaboration with Florescu proved fruitful, its first product being *In Search of Dracula* (1972), one of the early nonfiction works on Dracula and the first to offer details about the obscure Vlad the Impaler. It became a popular bestseller. The following year, they completed a more scholarly biography, *Dracula: A Biography of Vlad the Impaler, 1431–1476*. These books have become two of the most

Vampire folklore scholar Raymond T. McNally.

influential works for people interested in vampires. **Christopher Lee**, the actor most identified at the time with the dramatic role of Dracula, starred in a documentary film based on the two books, *In Search of Dracula* (1976), made by a Swedish film company. Later books and movies have incorporated data from the two volumes as part of the Dracula storyline.

McNally followed the success of the two volumes with an anthology of vampire writings (both fiction and nonfiction), *A Clutch of Vampires: These Being among the Best from History and Literature* (1974). Through the 1970s he continued to work with Florescu, and in 1979 they completed a new edition of Stoker's novel, *The Essential Dracula: A Completely Illustrated and Annotated Edition of Bram Stoker's Classic Novel*. Meanwhile, McNally had also become fascinated with **Elizabeth Bathory**, the other historical personage who stood behind the Dracula myth. Bathory, a Czechoslovakian countess, was (like Vlad) not a vampire, but she did kill many young girls and it was said that she would bathe in their **blood**, a practice she thought would preserve her youth. *Dracula Was a Woman: In Search of the Blood Countess of Transylvania* appeared in 1983. Two decades of work on the historical Dracula led to the publication of *Dracula, Prince of Many Faces: His Life and Times* (1989), a comprehensive attempt to put the life story of Vlad the Impaler into the broad context of fifteenth-century European history.

In the early 1970s, while researching and writing their first books, McNally and Florescu had suggested some collaborative work between British, Romanian, and American scholars interested in Vlad and Dracula. The fall of the Romanian dictatorship in 1990 has allowed such an endeavor to proceed. The first product was an edited volume, *Dracula: Essays on the Life and Times of Vlad Tepes*, to which McNally contributed an essay, "An Historical Appraisal of the Image of Vlad Tepes in Contemporary Romanian Folklore." McNally continued as a leading figure in the field through the 1990s. A new addition of his landmark volume coauthored with Radu Florescu, *In Search of Dracula* was released in 1994. He was a presenter at both the World Dracula Conference in **Romania** in 1995 and at **Dracula '97: A Centennial Celebration** in Los Angeles, at which the **Transylvanian Society of Dracula** gave him an award for his historical scholarship. He was an active member of the **Lord Ruthven Assembly**, and was named one of its honorary presidents. In 1997 he completed a new annotated version of Dracula on CD, *Dracula: Truth and Terror*.

During the last decade of his life, McNally received the accolades of his colleagues for his work in putting the study of *Dracula* on the academic agenda, while at the same time there was a growing critique of his early work that suggested that he had significantly overstated the case for identifying Count Dracula with Prince Vlad Dracula, as well as over emphasizing the role of Elizabeth Bathory on Bram Stoker and the writing

of *Dracula*. Most recently, Dracula scholars Robert Eighteen-Bisang and Elizabeth Miller praised McNally for his role in making Stoker's notes on *Dracula*, long hidden away in the Rosenbach Museum and Library in Philadelphia, known to the world of Dracula scholars; at the same time, they criticizedhim for his role in spreading the false impression that Vlad was the model for Count Dracula.

During his many years at Boston College, McNally founded and headed the school's Russian and East European Center (1964). In 1995, he joined with his colleague Donald Carlisle, in founding the Balkan Studies Institute, also based at Boston College.

Sources:

Florescu, Radu, and Raymond T. McNally. *The Complete Dracula*. Boston: Copley Publishing Group, 1992. 409 pp. (A combined publication of *In Search of Dracula* and *Dracula; A Biography of Vlad the Impaler*.)

———. *Dracula: A Biography of Vlad the Impaler, 1431–1476*. New York: Hawthorn Books, 1973. 239 pp.

———. *Dracula, Prince of Many Faces: His Life and Times*. Boston: Little, Brown and Company, 1989. 261 pp.

McNally, Raymond T. *A Clutch of Vampires: These Being among the Best from History and Literature*. New York: Bell Publishing Company, 1974. 255 pp.

———. *Dracula Was a Woman: In Search of the Blood Countess of Transylvania*. New York: McGraw-Hill, 1983. 254 pp. Rept. London: Hamlyn Paperback, 1983. 254 pp.

———. "An Historical Appraisal of the Image of Vlad Tepes in Contemporary Romanian Folklore." In *Dracula: Essays on the Life and Times of Vlad Tepes*. New York: Columbia University Press, 1991. 336 pp.

McNally, Raymond T., and Radu Florescu. *In Search of Dracula*. New York: Greenwich, 1972. 223 pp. Rev. ed. as: *In Search of Dracula: Twenty Years Later*. Boston: Houghton, Mifflin, 1994. 297 pp.

———, eds. *The Essential "Dracula": A Completely Illustrated and Annotated Edition of Bram Stoker's Classic Novel*. New York: Mayflower Books, 1979. 320 pp.

Stoker, Bram. *Notes for Dracula*. Annotated and transcribed by Robert Eighteen-Bisang and Elizabeth Miller. Jeffersonviile, NC: McFarland & Company, 2008. 331 pp.

Melrose Abbey, The Vampire of

One of the famous cases of an actual vampire was chronicled by twelfth-century writer **William of Newburgh**. His account of a vampire that haunted Melrose Abbey in England began with a priest who neglected his holy vows and office and devoted his days to frivolous activity. Following his death, he came out of his grave and tried to enter the cloister at the monastery. Failing on several occasions, he began to wander through the countryside. He found his way to the bedside of a lady to whom he had been chaplain. His several visits to her prompted her to report the incidents to the brothers at the monastery.

Several of the brothers set up a watch at the graveyard where the priest was buried. As his companions sought relief from the chilly air by a fire, one monk kept watch and saw the dead priest arise from the grave and approach him. He hit the dead priest with a battle axe and forced him back into the grave. The earth opened to receive the corpse, closed over it, and gave the appearance of having been undisturbed.

When the three who had been warming themselves returned, they listened to and believed the account of the monk who reported his encounter with the body of the dead priest. At the break of day they opened the grave. There they found the corpse. It bore the mark of the wound previously reported by the monk, and the **coffin** was swimming in **blood**. They burned the body and scattered the ashes.

Sources:

Glut, Donald G. *True Vampires of History*. New York: H C Publishers, 1971. 191 pp.

Newburgh, William of. *Historie rerum anglicanum usque ad annum*. 1198. In *Chonicles of the reigns of Stephen, Henry II, and Richard I*. R. Howlett, ed. London: Roll series no. 82, 1884–1989.

Mexico, Vampires in

Accounts of vampires in Mexico can be traced as far back as the ancient Maya, whose territory centered on what is now Guatemala but also reached north into the Yucatan peninsula and the southern part of present-day Mexico.

This was the territory of the vampire **bats**, which were incorporated into the mythology of the Maya. *Camazotz,* the fierce cave god of the Mayan underworld, was known from his appearance in the *Popol Vol* and his representations in Mayan art.

In the *Popol Vol,* two brothers entered the underworld to avenge the death of their father. To accomplish their task, they had to pass through a number of obstacles, one of which was the Bat House. They were first attacked by a horde of bats and then by *Camazotz* himself. *Camazotz* was pictured as a manbat with a sharp nose and large teeth and claws. At one point, one of the brothers stuck his head out of their hiding place and *Camazotz* quickly decapitated him. The head was then used as the ball in a game. The decapitated brother obtained a substitute head, and the brothers eventually played the game and won.

Camazotz, with his sharp nose and large teeth and claws, was a popularly feared figure among the Mayans, and numerous representations appeared in Mayan art. *Camazotz* served two diverse purposes. He was integral to the basic agricultural myth built around the cycle of growing maize. In his descent, he brought death to the maize grain at the time it was buried in the earth, a necessary step leading to its rebirth in the harvest. He was also a feared, bloodthirsty god of the caves. People avoided places believed to be his dwelling place.

The Aztecs: From the elaborate mythology of the Aztecs, whose territory was north of the Mayas's lands, came several vampire deities. Among those cited as vampiric was the lord of the underworld, the region of the dead; however, he appeared to have been more a devourer of the souls of the dead than a vampiric figure. Nevertheless, a set of vampire-like figures was evident in the goddesses related to the "earth lady," *Tlalteuctli,* the personification of the rock and soil upon which humans lived. *Tlalteuctli* was also a terror-producing figure. Never pictured as a woman, she was shown as a huge toad with **blood** covering her jaws. Several of the female figures that surrounded the earth lady shared a common hideousness and thirst for blood: *Coatlicue,* "serpent skirt"; *Cihuacoatl,* "snake woman"; *Itzpapalotl,* "obsidian knife butterfly"; and the *cihuateteo*. These goddesses were also known as the *cihuapipiltin,* or princesses.

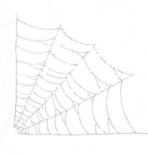

Coatlicue was described as black, dirty, disheveled, and ugly. A statue of her survived and has been placed in the National Museum in Mexico City. It has a skirt of snakes and a necklace of hands and hearts with a skull-shaped pendant. The head is missing and in its stead is a stream of gushing blood that becomes two rattlesnake heads.

Cihuacoatl was the ancient goddess of Culhuacan, but after the fifteenth century her worship was centered in Xochimilco. Her appearance was terrifying—stringy hair, her mouth open to receive **victims,** and two knives gracing her forehead. However, she had the ability to change herself into a beautiful young woman who, like vampire demons in many lands, enticed young men to their doom. They had sexual relations with her, only to wither away and die afterward. *Cihuacoatl* survived into this century both as the Virgin of Guadalupe in Roman Catholic lore and as La Llorona, the Weeping Woman, in popular folklore. As such she could be heard at night weeping for her dead children. *Cihuacoatl* represented the hunger of the gods for human victims, and state prisoners were regularly sacrificed to satisfy her need for blood. *Itzpapalotl*, not as specifically vampiric as the other two, was a personification of the ritual sacrificial knife.

The *cihuateteo* were the most vampiric of all the Aztec deities. They originated from **women** who died in childbirth. They had once been mortal, had struggled with the child, and had succeeded in holding it until both died in the struggle. Thus, they attained the status of warrior. As demonic figures, the *cihuateteo* very much resembled such other vampiric figures as the *lamiai* of ancient **Greece** or the **langsuyar** of **Malaysia.** The *cihuateteo* wandered the night and attacked children, leaving them paralyzed or otherwise diseased. They held counsel with other *cihuateteos* at local crossroads. Food offerings were placed at crossroads in structures dedicated to the *cihuateteos* so that they would gorge themselves and not attack the children; also, if the vampiric beings remained at the crossroads until morning, they would be killed by the **sunlight.** In recent years the *cihuateteos* have been described as having white faces and chalk-covered arms and hands. They wear the costume of Tlazolteotl, the goddess of all sorcery, lust, and evil.

The *Tlahuelpuchi*: The Aztecan culture was largely destroyed by the European invasion and the religious conquest of the land by Roman Catholicism. The goddesses continued somewhat, however, transformed in the popular imagination into witches that survived under different names. They were called **bruja** (feminine) or *brujo* (masculine) by the Spanish and *tlahuelpuchi*, the blood-sucking witch, by the descendants of the Aztecs.

The *tlahuelpuchi* was a person (most often a woman) believed to possess the power to transform itself into one of several **animals** and in that form attack and suck the blood of infants or, on rare occasions, children and adults. The *tlahuelpuchi* drew elements from both the ancient Aztec goddesses and the witches of **Spain,** who had the power to transform themselves into animals and liked to suck the blood of infants. The most common animal into which the witches transformed themselves was a turkey, but animals as varied as fleas, cats, dogs, and buzzards were reported. Such witches lived incognito in their communities, and witches became objects of fear, especially among couples with infants.

The *tlahuelpuchi* was born a witch and had no control over her condition, which remained with her for life. Since the condition was a chance occurrence of birth, the witch could not pass her condition to another. There was no way to tell if a person was a witch until she reached puberty. The power of **transformation** arrived with the first

menses. At that time the young witch also developed an insatiable thirst for human blood. That a person was a witch would soon become known to relatives, of course, but out of shame and fear, they would seek to conceal the fact. A witch would kill anyone who revealed her identity, but would otherwise not attack kinspeople. The *tlahuelpuchi* had to have blood at least once a month and some as much as four times a month.

On the last Saturday of every month, the *tlahuelpuchi* entered the kitchen of her dwelling and performed a magical rite. She lighted a fire made of special substances and then transformed into an animal, usually a dog.

Her lower legs and feet were left behind in the form of a cross. Upon her return from feeding, she retransformed into a human and reattached her appendages. The witch could, on occasion, be known by the limp developed from her regular transformations. Occasionally, the witch might attack children, adults, or the livestock of a person they had quarreled with.

The *tlahuelpuchi* also had **hypnotic power** over individuals and could cause them to kill themselves, primarily by having them walk to a high place and jump to their death. They might also attack livestock of people they wished to harm. Thus, particular kinds of evil that affected people were routinely attributed to the witches in their midst.

Protection from witches was most ensured by use of the ubiquitous **garlic**. Wrapped in a tortilla, cloves of garlic might be placed in the clothes of an infant. In the absence of garlic, an onion could be substituted.

Bright metal was also considered effective, and parents sometimes placed a machete or a box of pins under their infant's crib. Pins or other metal objects might be fashioned into a cross. Parents also used clear **water**, **mirror**s, or holy medals. Infant deaths were attributable to parents having relaxed their vigilance in protecting their child.

On occasion, people reported seeing a witch in animal form. It was spotted and distinguished from other animals by the phosphorous illumination it emitted. There would often follow an attempt to kill it, either by stoning and clubbing (to avoid direct physical contact), but more often than not, the witch escaped by changing form. On vary rare occasions, a woman in the community was called out as a *tlahuelpuchi*. If the accusation was accepted by a group of people, that person would be attacked in her home and clubbed and/or stoned to death. Afterward, the sense organs, including the fingers, were removed, and the body, unburied, was disposed of in a deserted spot.

Belief in the *tlahuelpuchi* has continued to the present day in rural Mexico. As recently as 1954 the state of Tlaxcala passed a law requiring that infants reportedly killed by **witchcraft** had to be referred to medical authorities. Researchers Hugo G. Nutini and John M. Roberts, working in the same state in the 1960s, had no trouble gathering numerous tales of witchcraft.

The Cinematic Vampire: Today, Mexico's prolific movie industry has become well known, and vampire enthusiasts have made note of the large number of vampire movies from Mexico, many of them featuring U.S. actors. The Mexican vampire image was strongly influenced by the **Universal Pictures**'s Spanish-language rendition of **Dracula (Spanish, 1931)** starring Carlos Villarias and Lupita Tovar. This American-made version circulated freely in Mexico in the years prior to World War II and directly influenced the image of the vampire in the emerging urban culture.

Lupita Tovar (right) as Mina Murray in the 1931 Spanish-language production of *Dracula*, which was filmed in Mexico. Also shown is Eduardo Arozamena as Abraham Van Helsing.

The vampire arrived in force in 1957 when German Robles starred as the vampire Count Lavud in three vampire movies: *El Vampiro* (*The Vampire*), *El Ataud del Vampiro* (*The Vampire's Coffin*), and a comedy inspired by the earlier movies, *El Castillo de los Monstruos* (*Castle of the Monsters*). Count Lavud, obviously influenced by **Bela Lugosi**, was pictured as a suave Hungarian nobleman. In the first movie he was killed with a **stake** that subsequently was removed to allow him further life in the second.

Robles secured his claim as Mexico's first vampire star in 1959 by starring in a twelve-part serial as a bearded descendant of the prophet Nostradamus who had become a vampire. Subsequently, the serial was recut into four feature-length movies: *La Maldición de Nostradamus* (*The Curse of Nostradamus*), *Nostradamus y el Destructor de Monstruos* (*The Monster Demolisher*), *Nostradamus, El Genii de las Tinieblas* (*The Genie of Darkness*), and *La Sangre de Nostradamus* (*The Blood of Nostradamus*). (To avoid certain Mexican government film regulations, films were often made as serials and then quickly recut into feature films.) These features were released in the United States by **Roger Corman**'s American International Pictures. Robles also played a vampire in the Argentine film *El Vampiro Aechecha* (*The Lurching Vampire*, 1959). His final appearance was in *Los Vampiros de Coyoacan* (1973), in which he played the hero instead of a vampire.

Robles's success quickly led to an exploitation of the market. Alfonso Corona Blake made his first vampire movie, *El Mundo de los Vampiros* (*World of the Vampires*) in 1960. Two years later Blake was one of the directors called upon to work on the movies of the masked wrestler-turned-actor **Santo**. He directed Santo's first vampire movie, *Santo Contra las Mujeres Vampiro* (*Samson vs. the Vampire Women*). Santo emerged as one of Mexico's favorite movie characters and over two decades fought a variety of supernatural villains. In 1967 he battled **Dracula** in *Santo en el Tesoro de Dracula* which was also made in an adult version as *El Vampiro y el Sexo*. The vampire women returned in 1969 in *Santo en la Venganza de las Mujeres Vampiros*.

Frederico Curiel, the director of *Santo en la Venganza de las Mujeres Vampiros*, had emerged in 1959 as the director of the Nostradamus films. In 1967 he directed *El Imperio de Dracula* (*The Empire of Dracula*) and the following year *Las Vampiras*, one of **John Carradine**'s last films. He was joined as an important director of vampire titles by Miguel Morayta, who was responsible for *El Vampiro Sangriento* (*The Bloody Vampire*, 1961) and *La Invasion de los Vampiros* (*The Invasion of the Vampires*, 1962).

The vampire as a theme in Mexican cinema peaked in the 1960s. During the early 1970s the last of the Santo vampire movies, *Santo y Blue Demon Contra Dracula y el Hombre Lobo*, appeared. Rene Cardona, who had directed *Santo y el Tesoro del Dracula*, continued his work in *Santo Contra Cazadores de Cabezas* (1970), *La Invasion de los Muertos* (1972), and the two comedies *Capulina Contra Los Vampiros* (1972) and *Capulina Contra Los Monstruos* (1972). He was followed by Juan Lopez, who directed *Mary, Mary Bloody Mary* (1975) and *Alucarda* (*Sisters of Satan*, 1975). Few new vampire films appeared through the remainder of the decade. From being a center of the vampire cinema in the 1960s, Mexico seems to have largely abandoned the genre through the 1980s and into the 1990s, though a number of the Mexican masked wrestlers adopted a vampire persona. The vampire theme re-emerged briefly at the end of the 1990s when Mexican moviemakers jumped on the **chupacabra** bandwagon with movies such as *Ataca el Chupacabras* (1996) and *Chupacabras* (2000).

Sources:

Fentome, Steve. "Mexi-Monster Meltdown!" *Monster International* 2 (1992): 4–13.

Nutini, Hugo G., and John M. Roberts. *Bloodsucking Witchcraft: An Epistemological Study of Anthropomorphic Supernaturalism in Rural Tlaxcala*. Tucson: University of Arizona Press, 1993. 476 pp.

Summers, Montague. *The Vampire: His Kith and Kin*. London: Routledge, Kegan Paul, Trench, Trubner, & Co., 1928. 356 pp. Rept. New Hyde Park, NY: University Books, 1960. 356 pp.

Meyer, Stephenie (1973–)

Stephenie Meyer is the author of the **Twilight** series, four novels about a teenage girl's romance with a vampire. The novels were published by Little, Brown and Company beginning with *Twilight* (2005), and followed by *New Moon* (2006), *Eclipse* (2007), and *Breaking Dawn* (2008). A fifth manuscript, *Midnight Sun*, was the expected companion to *Twilight* but was never published; Meyer completed only the first twelve chapters of *Midnight Sun* before it was illegally leaked on the Internet. The incomplete and unfinished manuscript is now posted on Meyer's website www.StephenieMeyer.com.

Stephenie Meyer was born on Christmas Eve 1973 in Hartford, Connecticut, although her family moved to Phoenix, Arizona, when she was four years old. She was one of six children and was raised as a member of the Church of Jesus Christ of Latter-Day Saints (commonly known as Mormons). She attended Brigham Young University as an English literature major and was graduated in 1997. Meyer and her husband Christian Patrick Meyer were married in 1994; she was a homemaker and mother to three sons before she embarked upon her first book.

Meyer has said that she received her inspiration for *Twilight* on June 6, 2003, when she had a "very vivid dream" of an average girl and a young attractive male vampire having an intense conversation in the woods. That dream eventually became Chapter 13 "Confessions" in *Twilight*. Meyer has stated that she had no interest in vampire literature prior to writing *Twilight* and hadn't even read **Bram Stoker's *Dracula***. And she has viewed only parts of the movies ***Interview with the Vampire*** and *Lost Boys*, since she generally avoids R-rated films as a follower of the Mormon faith.

Although Meyer doesn't write overtly Mormon literature, she has said that her religious upbringing has filtered into her stories. She avoids any type of sexual explicitness in her writing; in fact, her books' appeal lies in "their fine moral hygiene" according to *Time* magazine. "What makes Meyer's books so distinctive is that they're about the erotics of abstinence," the magazine explained. And the theme of free agency or individual choice throughout her books also draws from Mormon doctrine.

Her science fiction novel, *The Host* (2008), follows *Twilight*'s themes of love and choice and also includes nonhuman creatures. *The Host* is set in the near future on Earth, which is inhabited by parasitic aliens who take over the bodies of humans and annihilate their hosts' personalities.

Sources:

Beahm, George. *Bedazzled: Stephenie Meyer and the Twilight Phenomenon*. Nevada City, CA: Underwood Books, 2009. 248 pp.

Burton, Ryan. *Female Force: Stephenie Meyer*. No. 1. n.p.: Blue Water Comics, 2009. 32 pp.

Grossman, Lev. "Stephenie Meyer: A New J. K. Rowling?" *Time* (April 24, 2008). http://www.time.com/time/0,8816,173483,00.html.

Irwin, Megan. "Stephenie Meyer's Vampire Romance Novels Made a Mormon Mom an International Sensation." *Phoenix New Times* (July 12, 2007).

Kirschling, Gregory. "Stephenie Meyer's 'Twilight' Zone." *Entertainment Weekly* 10 (August 2007). Posted at http://www.ew.com/ew/article/0,,20049578,00.html. Accessed March 19, 2009.

Meyer, Stephenie. *Twilight*. Boston: Little, Brown Young Readers, 2005. 512 pp.

———. *New Moon*. Boston: Little, Brown Young Readers, 2006. 576 pp.

———. *Eclipse*. Boston: Little, Brown Young Readers, 2007. 629 pp.

———. *Breaking Dawn*. Boston: Little, Brown Young Readers, 2008. 754 pp.

❨ Midnight Sons ❩

At the end of 1983, Marvel Comics killed off all of the vampires in the Marvel Universe, especially those that had survived from the popular 1970s series ***The Tomb of Dracula***. The means chosen for their demise was the use of a magical operation called the Montesi Formula by occultist Dr. Stephen Strange, as told in *Doctor Strange*, No. 62,

December 1983. In that process, Hannibal King, who had been a vampire character introduced in *The Tomb of Dracula*, was returned to normal life. Almost no vampire appeared in any Marvel **comic book**s for the next six years.

By the end of the 1980s, however, it had become obvious that the horror theme in general and the vampire theme in particular had a large and growing audience among readers of comic books. Marvel, the largest of the comic book companies, addressed this growing public by reintroducing the vampire in November 1989, when **Morbius** burst upon the pages in Issue 10 of a relatively new series, *Dr. Strange: Sorcerer Supreme*. Four issues later, in February of 1992, Marvel announced the return of vampires to the Marvel Universe, their return made possible by a weakening of the Montesi Formula. At the same time, Hannibal King found himself transforming back into a vampire.

The full effects of the reversal of the Montesi Formula became evident in 1992, when Marvel initiated the creation of a new region of the Marvel Universe populated primarily with superheroes. Marvel brought together some of its older titles, to which were added several brand new titles in a shared story line called the "Midnight Sons." The idea of the Midnight Sons recalls the February 1976 issue of *Marvel Premiere* (No. 28), in which Morbius and Ghost Rider joined Swamp-Ooze and the Werewolf by Night in the Legion of Monsters.

The older heroes incorporated into the Midnight Sons were Ghost Rider (Daniel Ketch), Johnny Blaze, Vengeance (Michael Badilino), the Nightstalkers (Frank Drake, Hannibal King, and Blade), and the Darkhold Redeemers (Louise Hastings, Sam Buchanan, Victoria Montesi, and the sorcerer Modred). Morbius was also revived and given his own series. **Blade the Vampire Slayer**, Frank Drake, and Hannibal King, the three vampire fighters from *The Tomb of Dracula* series in the 1970s, were dusted off and given their own story line as *The Nightstalkers*. The Nightstalkers operated as a detective agency in contemporary Boston.

The Midnight Sons now lived on the edge of reality where the occult and supernatural, in their most sinister form, were a constant threat.

The story of the Midnight Sons officially began in fall 1992 in a six-part story carried in a variety of Marvel titles: *Ghost Rider* (No. 28), *Spirits of Vengeance* (No. 1), *Morbius* (No. 1), *Darkhold* (No. 1), *Nightstalkers* (No. 1), and *Ghost Rider* (No. 31). The lead characters of these titles comprise The Nine, who together protect this world from crumbling under the pressure of the supernatural evil world. The initial story pitted The Nine against **Lilith**, Queen of Evil and Mother of Demons, a sorceress of obscure origin based upon the ancient Semitic demonic personage, and not to be confused with **Lilith, the Daughter of Dracula**, who had appeared in previous Marvel vampire comic books. As the Midnight Sons combined to defeat the forces of evil called together by Lilith, they discovered their own questions about one another. They especially questioned the legitimacy of Morbius and Hannibal King, vampires who were not that different from some of the entities from the evil world. Their inability to work with one another except when attacked has led to both independent and interrelated stories during the first year of the Midnight Sons.

A favorable response to the Midnight Sons was immediately noticeable, and in April 1993 Marvel added a seventh title, *Midnight Sons Unlimited*, and soon afterward began to reprint the old Morbius stories in a new series, *Morbius Revisited*. Then, in October 1993, Marvel moved to promote the Midnight Sons by giving them their own unified Marvel imprint introduced with a seventeen-part story, "Siege of Darkness," the first part of which appeared in *Nightstalkers* (No. 14). The Midnight Sons who survived the "Siege of Darkness" (several were killed) became a more united team. "Siege of Darkness" was printed complete with its own dagger-like logo and firmly established a supernatural realm on the edge of the old Marvel Universe of super (but very human) heroes and villains. The development of this separate supernatural Marvel realm also recognized the problems encountered by the superheroes (the main characters in the Marvel universe) whenever they had to deal with supernatural evil.

As part of its promotion of the new imprint, Marvel issued a Midnight Sons dagger logo pin and a new *Ghost Rider and the Midnight Sons Magazine*. Soon after the conclusion of "Siege of Darkness," *Nightstalkers* was discontinued. Hannibal King and Frank Drake were killed in its final issue.

Blade survived and continued in his own new title, *Blade, the Vampire Hunter* that lasted for ten issues into 1995. Within a short time, all of the Midnight Sons titles were discontinued as Marvel went through a major reorganization in the mid-1990s.

After several years without any titles featuring their vampire characters, In 1997, a new *Blade* comic appeared, heralding the revival of the series in conjunction with the release of the *Blade* movie with Wesley Snipes in 1998.

Interestingly enough, also in 1998, Hannibal King was brought back from the dead (and **Marv Wolfman** from his other projects) in a new story for the longstanding *Journey into Mystery* series, an anthology series that had King operating as a detective out of an office in New York City.

After essentially disappearing from the Marvel Universe, the Nightstalkers reappeared in a highly revised context in *Blade: Trinity*, the third Blade movie. The Nightstalkers were formed by Whistler, Blade's colleague from the first two movies, and are now led by his daughter Abigail Whistler (portrayed by Jessica Biel). They include only one of the old Nightstalkers, Hannibal King (portrayed by Ryan Reynolds). In the story, Dracula captures King and threatens to turn him into a vampire, the rescue attempt setting up the final battle between Blade and the first vampire.

Sources:

Blade, the Vampire Hunter. Nos. 1–10. New York: Marvel Comics, 1994–95.

Ghost Rider and the Midnight Sons Magazine. Nos. 1—. New York: Marvel Comics, 1993—.

Melton, J. Gordon. *The Vampire in the Comic Book*. New York: Count Dracula Fan Club, 1993. 32 pp.

Midnight Sons Unlimited. Nos. 1–9. New York: Marvel Comics, 1993–95.

Morbius the Living Vampire. Nos. 1–32. New York: Marvel Comics, 1992–95.

Nightstalkers. Nos. 1–18. New York: Marvel Comics, 1992–94.

Wolfman, Marv. "The Long Cold Kill!" *Journey into Mystery*, Pt. 1. 520 (May 1998); Pt. 2. 521 (June 1998).

Midnight to Midnight *see:* Vampire Fandom: United States

Miller, Elizabeth Ann (1939–)

Elizabeth Miller, who emerged in the 1990s as one of the most widely hailed ***Dracula*** scholars, was born in St. John's, Newfoundland. She taught in the English Department at Memorial University of Newfoundland for over thirty years. In 1991 she received the University President's Award for Distinguished Teaching. Upon her retirement, the university named her Professor Emeritus.

With Nicolae Paduraru, Miller co-organized the first World **Dracula** Congress, held in **Romania** in 1995, and, along with Jeanne Youngson and J. Gordon Melton, **Dracula '97: A Centennial Celebration**. She founded the Canadian chapter of the **Transylvanian Society of Dracula**, and at the 1995 World Dracula Conference, held in Romania, she was made a baroness of the House of Dracula.

Since the early 1990s, Miller has become the most productive scholar in the area of Dracula and vampire studies. She has published seven books, including *Reflections on Dracula* (1997), *Dracula: Sense & Nonsense* (2000, 2006), *A Dracula Handbook* (2004) and **Bram Stoker**'s Notes for Dracula: A Facsimile Edition (with Robert Eighteen-Bisang, 2008). She is editor of the *Journal of Dracula Studies*. *Dracula: Sense and Nonsense* became a watershed volume in Dracula studies by compiling the information from two decades of scholarly research and providing a new plateau from which further scholarly discourse could proceed.

Bram Stoker's Notes for Dracula: A Facsimile Edition received the **Lord Ruthven** Award as the best nonfiction title in vampire studies of 2009.

Miller has lectured widely at a variety of venues across North America and Europe. From Vancouver to Bucharest, she has been interviewed for many television documentaries, including ones for National Geographic, the Discovery Channel, PBS, BBC, and ABC's *20/20*. Her expertise is frequently sought for articles on the subject and she has been widely quoted in, among others, *The New York Times*, *U.S. News & World Report*, the *Chicago Tribune*, and *The Wall Street Journal*.

Miller maintains two authoritative and expansive Dracula websites as well as a blog, all accessible through www.blooferland.com. She currently resides in Toronto.

Elizabeth Miller, founder of the Canadian chapter of the Transylvanian Society of Dracula.

Sources:

Bram Stoker's Notes for Dracula. Annotated and transcribed by Robert Eighteen-Bisang and Elizabeth Miller. Jeffersonville, NC: McFarland & Company, 2008. 331 pp.

Miller, Elizabeth. *Reflections on Dracula: Ten Essays*. White Rock, BC: Transylvania Press, 1997. 226 pp.

———, ed. *Dracula: The Shade and the Shadow*. Westcliff-on-Sea: UK: Desert Island Books, 1998. 256 pp.

———. *Dracula*. New York: Parkstone Press, 2001. 238 pp.

———. *A Dracula Handbook*. Philadelphia: ExLibris, 2004. 200 pp.

———. *Bram Stoker's Dracula: A Documentary Volume*. Dictionary of Literary Biography, #304. Detroit: Thomson Gale, 2005. 392 pp. Rpt. *Bram Stoker's Dracula: A Documentary Journey into Vampire Country and the Dracula Phenomenon*. New York: Pegasus, 2009. 392 pp.

———. *Dracula: Sense & Nonsense*. Southend-on-Sea, UK: Desert Island Books, 2000. Rev. ed., 2006. 256 pp.

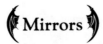 Miller, Linda Lael (1949–)

Linda Lael Miller, a popular writer of romance literature, was born Linda Lael in Spokane, Washington. She married shortly after high school and worked as a clerk-typist for a number of years before becoming a writer of women's books. Her first book, *Fletcher's Woman*, appeared in 1983. She found a growing readership and produced more than twenty romance novels by the end of the decade. Her 1987 book, *Wanton Angel*, won the Romantic Times Award for the Most Sensual Historical Romance Book of the Year.

In the wake of **Anne Rice**'s success, which proved that books about vampires could find a readership among fans of romance novels, Miller produced her first vampire novel, *Forever and the Night*. It became one of the first books on the subject to be marketed as a romance title. A best-seller, it told the story of Aidan Tremayne, a handsome twenty-two-year-old young man with black hair and blue eyes. In 1782 he began an affair with a woman named Lisette who turned out to be an ancient female vampire from Atlantis. During one of their love-making sessions, she bit him and then shared her **blood** with him. He became an undead creature, but unlike most vampires he was tortured by the remnant of humanity that remained alive in him. He later moved to Connecticut and there in the modern world met Neely Wallace, a woman that a gypsy predicted would be either his salvation or ultimate damnation. He also had a sister Mauve, who was turned into a vampire.

Forever and the Night concentrated on the story of Tremayne and Wallace, but in the wake of its success, subsequent novels developed the accounts of Mauve and the other vampires with whom they were associated. While Miller's was by no means the first **gothic** romance novel (a tradition that dates at least as far back as author **Florence Marryat** in the 1890s), the response to Miller's book led to a flurry of vampire romance novels that has continued to the present. She has not returned to the vampire theme since her four novels in the mid-1990s.

Sources:

Miller, Linda Lael. *Forever and the Night*. New York: Berkley Books, 1993. 338 pp.

———. *For All Eternity*. New York: Berkley Books, 1994. 341 pp.

———. *Time without End*. New York: Berkley Books, 1995. 357 pp.

———. *Tonight and Always*. New York: Berkley Books, 1996. 339 pp.

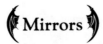 Mirrors

The now-popular idea that vampires cast no reflection in a mirror (and often have an intense aversion to them) seems to have first been put forward in **Bram Stoker**'s

novel, *Dracula*. Soon after his arrival at **Castle Dracula**, **Jonathan Harker** observed that the building was devoid of mirrors. When **Dracula** silently came into Harker's room while he was shaving, Harker noticed that Dracula, who was standing behind him, did not appear in the shaving mirror as he should have. Dracula complained that mirrors were objects of human vanity, and, seizing the shaving mirror, he broke it.

When the novel was brought to the stage and the episode in Castle Dracula deleted, the incident of the mirror was transformed into a confrontation between Dracula and Dr. **Abraham Van Helsing**. The mirror incident does not seem to have any precedent in either vampire folklore or the earlier vampire short stories and **dramas**, although Stoker seemed to have been aware of folklore about mirrors. Mirrors were seen as somehow revealing a person's spiritual double, the soul. In seeing themselves revealed in a mirror, individuals found confirmation that there was a soul and that hence life went on. They also found in the reflection a new source of anxiety, as the mirror could be used to affect the soul negatively.

The notion that the image in the mirror was somehow the soul was the source of the idea that breaking a mirror brought seven years' bad luck. Breaking the mirror also damaged the soul.

Thus, one could speculate that the vampire had no soul, had nothing to reflect in the mirror. The mirror forced the vampire to confront the nature of his/her existence as the undead, neither living nor dead. On occasion, in both vampire fiction and the cinema, the idea of nonreflection in mirrors has been extended to film, that is, the vampire would not appear in photographs if developed.

In her popular reinterpretation of the vampire myth, **Anne Rice** dropped Stoker's mirror convention. She argued in part that although vampires have certain "supernatural" attributes, they existed in the same physical universe as mortals and generally had to conform to the same physical laws, including those of optics. Hence, in *Interview with the Vampire* and *Vampire Lestat,* Louis and **Lestat de Lioncourt,** respectively, saw themselves in a mirror and experienced a moment of self-revelation about their new vampire image. (Of course, Rice's vampires didn't follow *all* physical laws since they had the ability to fly.)

During the 1990s, vampire writers and movies have moved back and forth on the problem of mirrors, and the related problem of capturing the image of the vampire on film, television, or with the new digital cameras. Some, for example the vampires of **"The Twilight Series"** and the books of **L. A. Banks** can see and be seen in mirrors. Meanwhile, most still cannot, including those of television series such as *Buffy the Vampire Slayer* and *Being Human*, and the popular books of **Charlaine Harris** and **Laurell K. Hamilton.**

Sources:

Goldberg, Benjamin. *The Mirror and Man*. Charlottesville, VA: University Press of Virginia, 1985. 260 pp.

Ramsland, Katherine. *The Vampire Companion*. New York: Ballantine Books, 1993. 507 pp.

The Miss Lucy Westenra Society of the Undead *see:* Vampire Fandom: United States

Mist

In **Bram Stoker's** *Dracula*, Dr. **Abraham Van Helsing**, the vampire authority, suggested that vampires could transform into a mist, although their ability to travel very far in this form was quite limited. **Dracula** adopted this form to conceal himself on the ship *Demeter* while traveling to England. In this form, he could move with ease in and out of the box in which he rested. Van Helsing, acknowledging this ability, sealed the door of the vault of the vampirized **Lucy Westenra's** resting place with a putty containing flakes of a **eucharistic wafer** so not the tiniest space was left for her to escape. He later sealed the door to **Castle Dracula** in a similar manner.

Dracula's primary appearances in the form of mist were during his attacks on **Mina Murray**. In Murray's record of the first attack, she noted that she saw a thin streak of white mist that moved across the lawn. It seemed to have a sentience and vitality all its own. The mist started to move into the room, not through the window, but through the joinings of the door. The mist concentrated into a cloud out of which Dracula emerged. Several days later, when the men finally figured out that Murray was under attack, they went to her room and found her drinking Dracula's **blood**. They moved toward him with **crucifix**es in hand, but he turned back into mist and disappeared under the door.

The idea of the vampire transforming into mist was a minor concept in folklore, but it was occasionally mentioned as a logical means for the vampire to leave and return from the grave without disturbing the topsoil that covered the **coffin**. The idea of such a **transformation** was often made when small holes apparently leading downward to the coffin lid appeared on the top of the grave.

In a famous moment from the fifth season of *Buffy the Vampire Slayer*, Buffy staked Dracula and then apparently left his Sunnydale lair. After a moment, Dracula began to reform from a mist. Buffy then quickly reentered the scene to **stake** him a second time, noting that she was aware of Dracula's ability to revive from mist because she had watched him do this in the movies.

Miyu, Vampire Princess

Vampire Princess Miyu, a highly successful vampire character from **Japan**, made her initial impressive appearance in a popular four-episode video released in 1988 and translated into English in 1990. Created by graphic artist Narumi Kakinouchi, Miyu is a member of a vampire clan who serve a peculiar role in the realm dividing the natural and supernatural worlds.

According to the myth, the Shinma, the gods and demons, abandoned the natural world to human beings in the historical past. They now reside in the Dark, a distant netherworld, and it is left to the vampire clan to guard the barrier between the two worlds. In the present, one group of Shinma decide to return to earth. Miyu, as the present guardian of the gateway between the worlds, has the task of tracking down these Shinma and returning them to their sleep state in the netherworld.

To accomplish her task, Miyu's aging was halted and she is not affected, as are most vampires, by **sunlight**, **garlic**, or religious symbols. She moves among humans as a beautiful young girl but must pick and choose people who will serve as her food source. Early in her Shinma-fighting career, Miyu encounters Himiko, a spiritualist who attempts to exorcise a young girl possessed by a Raen, a Shinma. Miyu intervenes when Himiko's efforts prove unavailing, and the two became associates. Miyu also works with Vampire Princess Yui.

After the success of the video, Miyu became the subject of many **comic books,** the first of which was translated into English in 1995 as the beginning of the series *Vampire Miyu.* In October 1997 Japanese **television** began airing a twenty-six-episode Princess Miyu television show.

The Japanese manga of Princess Miyu was published by Antarctic Press in 1995, but the series was discontinued after only six issues. It was subsequently picked up by Studio Ironcat which began a long run in 1997. The comic series was later reprinted as trade paperbacks.

The original animé series was issued in English on VHS and more recently on DVD. Tokyopop released the television series on six DVDs in 2003.

Sources:

Kakinouchi, Naumi. *Vampire Miyu.* Nos. 1–6. San Antonio, TX: Antarctic Press, 1995–96.
———. *New Vampire Miyu.* Kuni Kamura, trans. Fredericksburg, VA: Studio Ironcat, 1997–2000. 5 vols.

Mongolia, Vampires in *see:* Tibet, Vampires in

Moon

Because the vampire is a nocturnal creature, one might expect it to have a special relationship to the moon, as **John Polidori** certainly assumed in his original vampire tale, "The Vampyre," published in 1819. **Lord Ruthven,** the vampire, was killed in the course of the story. However, he was taken out to the pinnacle of a nearby hill so that his body could be exposed to the "first cold ray of the moon that rose after his death." The moon's rays revived the vampire. This idea of the moon's effect on a vampire was picked up by writers and dramatists who built on Polidori's tale through the first half of the nineteenth century.

James Malcolm Rymer followed Polidori's lead in **Varney the Vampyre,** and through the words of Chillingworth, a man wise in such matters, explained to his readers the nature of the vampire's resurrection. In chapter 4 of the story Varney was shot, and mortally so, but Chillingworth warned:

> With regard to these vampyres, it is believed by those who are inclined to give credence to so dreadful a superstition, that they always endeavor to make their feast of **blood,** for the revival of their bodily powers, on some evening immediately preceding a full moon, because if any accident befalls them, such as, being shot, or otherwise killed or wounded, they can recover by lying down somewhere where the full moon's rays will fall upon them.

In the next chapter Rymer vividly describes the effects of the moon:

As the moonbeams, in consequence of the luminary rising higher and higher in the heavens, came to touch the figure that lay extended on the rising ground, a perceptible movement took place in it. The limbs appeared to tremble, and although it did not rise up, the whole body gave signs of vitality.

Immediately afterward Varney arose and escaped from his pursuers. **Bram Stoker** departed from this fictional convention. In ***Dracula***, the moon was used for atmosphere, but possessed no supernatural qualities. In the first chapter, for example, the moonlight provided added emphasis to Dracula's command over the wolves. Later, in chapter 4, the three **women** who resided in **Castle Dracula** made their appearance in the **dust** dancing in the moonbeams. Subsequent authors of vampire fiction followed Stoker's lead; it was the deadly sun, not the moon (except as it was an important element in the larger nocturnal environment), that became a significant element of vampire lore.

The idea of the moon reviving a vampire was not repeated in the movies until 1945, in *The Vampire's Ghost*, a movie loosely based on Polidori's "The Vampyre." Meanwhile, the moon became closely associated with **werewolves,** as it is the full moon that often triggers the transformation of the werewolf from his human into his wolf form. In the artwork accompanying contemporary fiction, the use of the moon on the cover very frequently indicates to the potential reader that the book has werewolf characters.

Sources:

Steiger, Brad. *The Werewolf Book: The Encyclopedia of Shape-Shifting Beings.* Detroit, MI: Visible Ink Press, 1999. 432 pp.

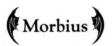

Morbius

Morbius, a Marvel Comics vampire character introduced in 1971, was the first original vampire introduced after revision of the Comics Code allowed vampires once again to appear in **comic books,** from which they had been banished in 1954. Michael Morbius, according to the story, was an outstanding biologist whose work had won him the Nobel Prize. He was engaged to be married. However, he had contracted a rare blood disease. As his condition worsened, he began to work on a cure. He developed a serum from vampire bat blood and treated himself with electric shock. His efforts finally stopped the effects of the disease, but he experienced unwanted side effects; he grew **fangs** and developed an intense thirst for **blood,** which led to him vampirizing his best friend. He also developed some superpowers, including the standard heightened **strength** and **flying** ability because his bones became hollow.

Morbius was introduced in issue No. 101 of *Amazing Spider-Man* (1971) and his encounter with Spider-Man launched a series of battles with various Marvel superheroes. He was able to survive battles against the Bestial Lizard and the Human Torch and then took on the X-Team in the pages of *Marvel Team-Up* (No. 3 and No. 4). In *Marvel Team-Up,* after defeating Iceman and the Avenging Angel, he was bested by Cyclops. In the X-Men laboratory he was treated by the X-Team scientist Professor X, but the experimental enzyme merely confirmed Morbius's status as the Living Vampire.

Morbius quickly escaped to begin his many adventures, in most of which he fought villains more evil than himself while searching for ways to meet his need for blood without killing the innocent. Periodically he turned his attention to finding a cure for his condition.

In 1973 Morbius was established in the new Marvel magazine-size *Vampire Tales*, the first issue of which appeared in the fall. Then in February 1974, in issue No. 19, Morbius became the featured character of *Fear*, and for the next few years the Morbius stories appeared simultaneously in the two comics. *Vampire Tales* lasted eleven issues through June 1975, and *Fear* concluded its Morbius story with issue No. 31 in December 1975 with Morbius flying off to possible future adventures.

In 1976 his adventures resumed. He appeared in issue No. 15 of *Marvel Two-in-One* to fight The Thing. He squared off against **Blade the Vampire Slayer** in issue No. 8 of *Marvel Preview*. In 1980, in issue No. 38 of the *Spectacular Spider-Man*, Morbius was finally cured. He had drunk some of Spider-Man's radioactive blood and was then struck by lightning, which drained him of his vampiric powers. He later devised a serum that returned him to a normal human life. He was brought to trial for his multiple murders, but acquitted when judged insane. It seemed the end of the story, and Morbius faded into oblivion during the 1980s, especially after Marvel killed off all its vampires in December 1983.

After many years' absence, Morbius made a dramatic reappearance in November 1989 in issue No. 10 of *Dr. Strange: Sorcerer Supreme*. Issue No. 14 in February 1990 revealed the events of Morbius's missing years. After living normally for several years, he had gone on a vacation to **New Orleans**.

One evening he met a beautiful woman named Marie and went home with her. He discovered that she was actually Marie Laveau, who had kept herself young with the blood of vampires. Since there were no more true vampires, she was aging again. She treated him with an intense but less than fatal electric shock, causing him to again become a vampire. He went on to battle Dr. Strange, who had accidently become the instrument allowing vampires to return to the real world.

In September 1992, with vampires returning and supernatural evil on the rise, those characters most capable of interacting with the supernatural were brought together in a new realm of the Marvel Universe. Those who were to oppose the supernatural were designated the Midnight Sons. They included old Marvel heroes such as Ghost Rider and **Blade the Vampire Slayer**. Morbius joined the Midnight Sons with the first issue of his own comic book, *Morbius, the Living Vampire*. The initial adventure of Morbius and the other Midnight Sons set them against a union of evil entities led by **Lilith**, Queen of Evil and Mother of Demons. Their conflicts late in 1993 led to the demise of the Darkhold and The Nightstalkers, but Morbius continued his life on the edge of the world of good and evil, a reluctant vampire with a conscience and a bloodthirst. In his most recent adventures, he has fought a new round in his continuing struggle with Spider-Man (1997).

In the new century, Morbius has made relatively few appearances in Marvel Comics, engaging in a time of wandering in search of a cure for his condition. To this end, at one point, he sought out a scientist, Dr. Andrea Jansen, only to discover that she had joined the international conspiratorial organization known as Hydra, and aligned with the villainous Crown. Morbius was taken prisoner and experimented upon. Later freed by Blade and Spider-Man, in his blood lust, he bit Blade before fleeing.

A very different re-imagined version of Morbius appeared in *Ultimate Spider-Man* No. 95 (2006). The new Morbius was a real vampire who origins reached back to the brother of **Dracula**. Struggling against his vampire nature, the Ultimate Morbius became a vampire slayer, though because he is also a vampire his motives are immediately called into question whenever he appears. Such is the case with his first meeting with Spider-Man in the Ultimate Universe. Vampires are attacking a young man, and it is not clear on whose side Morbius is fighting.

Sources:

Benton, Mike. *Horror Comics: The Illustrated History*. Dallas, TX: Taylor Publishing Company, 1991. 144 pp.

Fear. Nos. 20–31. New York: Marvel Comics, 1973–1974.

Ghost Rider and the Midnight Sons Magazine. No. 1. New York: Marvel Comics, 1993.

Mackie, Howard, and Claudio Castilini. "Vampire's Kiss." *Spider-Man* 77 (February 1997).

Marvel Preview. Marvel Comics. No. 8. New York: Marvel Comics, Fall 1976.

Morbius, the Living Vampire. Nos. 1–32. New York: Marvel Comics, 1992–1995.

Ultimate Spider-Man. No. 95 New York: Marvel Comics, 2006.

Mormolykiai *see:* Greece, Vampires in

Moroi/Moroaica *see:* Romania, Vampires in

❨ Morris, Quincey P. ❩

Quincey P. Morris was one of the leading characters in *Dracula*, the 1897 novel by **Bram Stoker**. Prior to the time of action covered by the novel, he had been a friend of both **Arthur Holmwood** and **John Seward**, the three having been together in Korea, and he and Holmwood having traveled together in South America and the South Seas. Morris was the only American character in the novel, first appearing in chapter 5 (along with Seward and Holmwood) as a suitor of **Lucy Westenra**. His desires for Lucy lead to concern for her declining health and then commitment to the conspiracy to destroy **Dracula**. He was first described in a letter from Lucy to her friend **Mina Murray**:

> … He is such a nice fellow, an American from Texas, and he looks so young and so fresh, that it seems almost impossible that he has been so many places and has had such adventures…. Mr. Morris doesn't always speak slang— that is to say he never does so to strangers or before them, for he is really well educated and has exquisite manners—but he found out that it amused me to hear him talk American slang, and when ever I was present, and there was no one to be shocked, he said such funny things.

He proposed to Lucy, but she was already engaged to Arthur Holmwood. She kissed him, and he offered his friendship and departed. He reappeared later (chapter 12) at Holmwood's request to check on Lucy's failing health (she had been bitten by Dracula). He arrived just in time to donate his blood. In the subsequent discussion of Lucy's condition, Morris, from his experience in **South America**, was able to introduce the idea of a **vampire bat**. Of course, his story of a big bat that could bring down a cow was not factual; the several species of vampire bats are small, and no one bat can drink enough to do more harm than mildly irritate a cow. Put in the mouth of Morris, however, the speech served an important literary purpose, with Stoker tying the bat and the vampire together in his plot. **Abraham Van Helsing** later reinforces Morris's statements.

Morris assumed the task of patrolling the outside of the house to stop any "bat" from reaching Lucy. Once Lucy died and it was determined that she had been transformed into a vampire, Van Helsing recruited Morris to join a group of men who set out to drive the prescribed **stake** through her heart. He was present for the driving of the stake, but stepped outside as Van Helsing and Holmwood cut off her head and stuffed the mouth with **garlic**. After this event he became an integral part of the effort to kill Dracula. He joined the group as they entered **Carfax** to sanitize the earth upon which Dracula slept. The four men then split into two groups, with Holmwood and Morris going to find Dracula's other hideaways in **London**.

Morris rejoined the other group as it prepared to track Dracula back to his castle in **Transylvania**. Morris arrived on horseback as everyone converged on the entrance to the castle. Dracula was carried in, resting in a box of his **native soil**, as the evening was fast approaching. When Dracula awakened, Morris and **Jonathan Harker** killed him. Morris plunged his Bowie knife into Dracula's heart as Harker decapitated him. Unfortunately, in the fight to reach Dracula's box, Morris was wounded, and a few minutes later he died. His last words to Mina were, "I am only too happy to have been of service!" Mina and Jonathan named their son after him.

As *Dracula* made its way from the novel to the stage to the screen, the character of Morris suffered greatly. As the novel was condensed, the Morris character was the first to be dropped. **Hamilton Deane** deleted him as a Texan from the British play and gave his name to a female character, ostensively to create a part for a member of his theater company. However, Morris remained absent from the American play and from the several *Dracula* movies beginning with the **Bela Lugosi** version in 1931. He reappeared in *El Conde Dracula* (1970), Jesus Franco's Spanish version, but as a British nobleman replacing Arthur Holmwood, who did not appear. In the 1977 **Count Dracula**, Morris was also Lucy's fiancé, but as a staff person at the American embassy in London. Not until **Francis Ford Coppola**'s 1992 feature, **Bram Stoker's Dracula**, did Morris's character, as he appeared in the book, finally make an appearance. He also appeared in *Dracula: Pages from a Virgin's Diary*, the ballet version of *Dracula* directed by Guy Maddin (2002).

In recognition of his being slighted in the stage and screen productions, one group of Dracula enthusiasts formed the Quincey P. Morris Dracula Society. In addition, Mina Murray and Jonathan Harker's son, Quincey (named for Morris) was a leading character in Marvel Comics' **The Tomb of Dracula** in the 1970s.

With the burgeoning of vampire literature in the 1990s, it was inevitable that Morris would make additional appearances. Among the more notable are Norman Partridge's short story, "Do Not Hasten to Bid Me Adieu," which appeared in the 1994 *Love in Vein* collection assembled by Poppy Z. Brite, and P. N. Elrod's novel *Quincey Morris, Vampire*. Justin Gustainis has launched a mystery series featuring a descendant of Morris, also named Quincey.

Sources:

Elrod, P. N. *Quincey Morris, Vampire.* New York: Baen, 2001. 336 pp.

Partridge, Norman. "Do Not Hasten to Bid Me Adieu." In *Love in Vein*. Poppy Z. Brite, ed. New York: HarperPrism, 1994: 3–24.

Moss, Stephanie

Stephanie Moss, a professor of English with a specialization in fantasy and horror literature, received her doctorate from the University of South Florida where she is a member of the faculty of the English Department. For the International Conference on the Fantastic Arts in 1992, she wrote "The Prostitute in Dracula" and has presented a series of papers that have since earned her acclaim as a **Dracula** scholar. She has been actively involved in **The Lord Ruthven Assembly**, serving a term as secretary. In 1995 she was among the presenters at the World Dracula Conference in **Romania** and spoke at **Dracula '97: A Centennial Celebration** in Los Angeles. She has continued as an active Dracula scholar into the new century.

Sources:

Moss, Stephanie. "The Psychiatrist's Couch: Hypnosis, Hysteria, and Proto-Freudian Performance in Dracula." In *Bram Stoker's Dracula: Sucking Through the Century, 1897–1997*. Carol Davison, ed. Toronto: Dundurn Press, 1997, pp. 123–46.

———. "Stoker and Victorian Periodicals." A paper presented at the Stoker Undead Conference held on the occasion of Bram Stoker's 150th birthday at Boston College, Boston, Massachusetts, November 8–9, 1997.

———. "Psychical Research and Psychoanalysis: Bram Stoker and the Early Freudian Investigation into Hysteria." In *Dracula: The Shade and the Shadow*. Elizabeth Miller, ed. Westcliff-on-Sea, UK: Desert Island Books, 1998.

———. "Dracula and the Blair Witch Project." A paper presented at the Second World Dracula Congress held at Poiana Brasov, Transylvania, Romania, May 25–28, 2000.

Mountain Ash

In the third chapter of **Dracula**, while **Jonathan Harker** was trying to determine his situation, he asked rhetorically, "What meant the giving of the **crucifix**, of the **garlic**, of the wild rose, of the mountain rose?" The modern reader has come to know these four items as devices for **protection against vampires**. Mountain ash is a member of the rose family and is also known in northern Europe and the British Isles as the rowan. **Bram Stoker** probably knew of the traditional use of the mountain ash as protection against **witchcraft**, in much the same manner as **hawthorn** was used throughout southern Europe. A rowan tree was often planted in churchyards and at the door of homesteads as a warning against evil spirits and was sometimes pruned so it became an arch over the barn door to protect the farm animals. It was particularly effective in conjunction with a red thread, and in the Scottish highlands women often used a piece of twisted red silk around their fingers along with a necklace of rowan berries.

In Scandinavia it was also known as Thor's Helper, a designation derived from a story in which the tree helped him escape a flood caused by the Frost Giants.

Sources:

McNeil, F. Marian. *Scottish Folklore and Folk Belief*. Vol. 1, *The Silver Bough*. Glasgow: William Maclellan, 1957, 1977. 220 pp.

Porteous, Alexander. *Forest Folklore, Mythology, and Romance*. London: George Allen & Unwin, 1928. 319 pp.

Mulo *see:* Gypsies, Vampires and the

❨ *The Munsters* ❩

The Munsters emerged in 1964 as one of two new situation comedies in the fall **television** season featuring a cast of "monstrous" characters attempting to live as an otherwise normal family. Included in the Munster family were two vampires, Lily (played by Yvonne De Carlo) and Grandpa (Al Lewis), who in the course of the series was revealed to be none other than Count **Dracula**. The family was completed by the **Frankenstein**ish Herman (Fred Gwynne) and the children, the wolfish Eddie (Butch Patrick) and the very "normal" Marilyn (Beverly Owens). Herman worked in a mortuary owned by classic horror actor **John Carradine**. *The Munsters* ran for two seasons. It gave birth to a **comic book** from Gold Key that ran for sixteen issues from January 1965 to January 1968. The original cast joined in a movie, *Munster! Go Home*, released in 1966, in which John Carradine assumed a different role as the family's butler.

A second movie—*The Munsters' Revenge*—was made for television and aired February 27, 1981. It included the major stars—Fred Gwynne, Yvonne De Carlo, and Al Lewis. The series was revived for the 1988 season as *The Munsters Today*, starring John Shuck (Herman), Lee Meriweather (Lily), and Howard Morton (Grandpa). In spite of bad reviews by fans of the original series, its seventy-two episodes carried it into 1991.

Possibly the most vampiric of all *The Munsters* shows was the animated sequel *Mini-Munsters*, which played in 1973 for the *Saturday Superstar Movie* on ABC. The story concerned a Dracula-like relative sending two teenagers, Igor (a Frankenstein-like monster) and Lucretia (a vampire), to stay with the Munster family.

Originally, *The Munsters* ran opposite the ABC series **The Addams Family**. Both were popular in their original format and both have had numerous spin-offs in the form of movies, comic books, and other **paraphernalia**. The Munsters and the Addams tended to appeal to the same set of fans, and in the 1990s, some fans of the two shows banded together to form The Munsters and Addams Family Fan Club (http://www.geocities.com/tmafc/).

The mid-1990s saw a new wave of Munsters nostalgia. A **trading card** series, The Munsters Collection, was issued by Kayro-Vue Productions in 1996, and the following year at the annual ComicCon International in San Diego, a new *Munsters* comic book was launched.

As a result of this new wave of interest there were also two new Munster movies *Here Come the Munsters* (1995) and *The Munsters's Scary Little Christmas* (1996).

A documentary on the show entitled *The Munsters—America's First Family of Fright* ran on national television in 2003.

Sources:

Anchors, William E., Jr. "The Munsters." *Epi-log* 37 (December 1993): 36–43, 63.

Cox, Stephen. *The Munsters: Television's First Family of Fright*. Chicago: Contemporary Books, 1989. 174.

———. *The Munsters: A Trip Down Mockingbird Lane*. Back Stage Books, 2006. 204 pp.

Jones, Stephen. *The Illustrated Vampire Movie Guide*. London: Titan Books, 193. 144 pp.

The Munsters. Nos. 1–16. New York: Gold Key Comics, 1965–68.

The Munsters. Nos. 1–4. Bethel, CT: TV Comics, 1997–98.

Peel, John. *The Addams Family and Munsters Program Guide.* Virgin: London, 1996. 240 pp.

The Munsters and the Addams Family Fan Club *see:* Vampire Fandom: United States

❨ Murray (Harker), Mina ❩

Mina (short for Wilhelmina) Murray, one of the leading characters in **Bram Stoker's** *Dracula*, made her first appearance in the book through correspondence with her long-time friend **Lucy Westenra.** As with Lucy, Stoker said very little about Mina's physical appearance, but she was obviously an attractive young woman in her twenties.

She was engaged to **Jonathan Harker,** who at the beginning of the novel had traveled to **Transylvania** to arrange for the sale of some property to Count **Dracula.** While she was awaiting his return, she joined Lucy in **Whitby** for a vacation together. The visit went well until Lucy began to sleepwalk. One night in the middle of the night, Mina found Lucy sleepwalking on the East Cliff and thought she saw someone with her. Taking Lucy home, she noticed that her friend had two small prick marks on her neck. Mina began to worry about Lucy and about Jonathan, who had yet to return from Transylvania or write to explain his delay.

Finally, a letter concerning Harker arrived. He was in the Hospital of St. Joseph and St. Mary in Budapest recovering from his experiences in **Castle Dracula.** Mina dropped everything and went to Budapest, where she married Jonathan without further delay. She and Jonathan returned to England, where they learned of Lucy's death.

Abraham Van Helsing, who had been brought into Lucy's case as a consultant while Mina was in **Hungary,** immediately engaged Mina in his search for information concerning the vampire that caused Lucy's death. Mina was interested in how Lucy's death and Jonathan's condition were related. She volunteered to transcribe Dr. **John Seward**'s diary concerning the events leading to Lucy's death. She was present when Van Helsing organized the men to destroy Dracula. To Jonathan's relief, having completed the transcription work, Mina initially agreed to "hold back" and let the men do the work of actually killing Dracula.

However, Mina began to have the same symptoms as Lucy before her death. She grew pale and complained of fatigue. During her major encounter with Dracula, **mist** floated through the cracks in the door and filled her room. The mist formed a whirling cloud. Mina saw the two red eyes and white face she had seen while with Lucy. Meanwhile, as Mina's fatigue increased, the men went about the work of discovering the locations of Dracula's resting places.

The men finally realized that Dracula was attacking Mina and hurried to her room. Dracula had entered some moments earlier and, while Jonathan slept, told Mina that she was to become "flesh of my flesh; **blood** of my blood; kin of my kin; my bountiful wine-press for a while; and shall be later on my companion and my helper." He then opened a wound in his chest with his sharp **fingernails** and forced Mina to drink the blood. He pushed her aside and turned his attention to the men as they rushed into the room; they

Amy Yasbeck portrayed a voluptuous—and funny—
Mina Murray in the comedy *Dracula: Dead and
Loving It.*

held him at bay with a **eucharistic wafer** and a **crucifix**. Dracula turned into mist and escaped. Mina had the marks of his teeth on her neck, and her own teeth had become more prominent, a sign that she was in the process of becoming a vampire. Van Helsing, wishing to protect her, touched her forehead with the wafer. Unexpectedly, it burned its impression into her forehead as if it was a branding iron.

Left behind while the men destroyed Dracula's resting places in **London**, Mina suggested that Van Helsing hypnotize her. In her hypnotic state, she revealed that Dracula had left England on a ship. Mina traveled with the men as they chased him to **Castle Dracula** for a final confrontation.

When the last encounter with Dracula began, Mina was en route to the castle with Van Helsing. When they arrived, Van Helsing drew a protective circle around Mina at the edge of which he placed pieces of the eucharistic host.

Among the entities who tried, unsuccessfully, to invade the circle were the three vampire brides who lived in the castle. During the daylight hours, Mina remained in the circle while Van Helsing went into the castle to kill the three vampires, sanitize Dracula's tomb, and make the castle inhospitable to any "undead." The next day Mina and Van Helsing made their way some distance from (but still in view of) the castle to a spot safe from wolves, and again Van Helsing drew a circle. From their protected cover, they saw Dracula approach in his box with a band of **Gypsies**. Close behind were the men in hot pursuit. In front of the castle Dracula was finally killed. The spot on Mina's forehead disappeared, and she and Jonathan returned to England.

Mina on Film and Stage: As the primary female character in *Dracula*, Mina generally had a prominent part in both stage and screen versions of the book. Only in the American version of the play by **John L. Balderston** did Mina disappear and have her character combined with Lucy. In the **Frank Langella** movie version, **Dracula (1979)**, her role was reversed with that of Lucy. Winona Ryder played Mina in **Bram Stoker's Dracula**, the movie that most closely approximated Stoker's original story. Ryder's portrayal deviated from the book most clearly in the movie's subplot about her romantic interest in the youthful-appearing Dracula.

Mina was one of the most appealing of Stoker's characters and almost always appears in the cinema remakes of the novel, though occasionally conflated with Lucy Westenra. She also appears in a variety of stories claiming to be sequels to *Dracula* or later adventures of the count. Alan Moore included her in his graphic novel, *League of Extraordinary Gentlemen*, and she was depicted as a vampire in the cinematic adaptation (2003). Fred Saberhagen sends Dracula to assist a distressed descendent of Mina in *An Old Friend of the Family* (1987).

Mina was the main subject of several books: Elaine Bergstrom's *Mina* (1994) and *Bound by Blood* (1998) and Dotie Bellamy's *The Letters of Mina Harker* (1998), among others. She was a significant character in Freda Warrington's *Dracula the Undead* (1997), Victor Kellerher's *Into the Dark* (1999), Kimberley Zagoren's *Mina's Journal* (2002), and the sequel to *Dracula* by Dacre Stoker & Ian Holt, *Dracula: The Un-Dead* (2009).

Sources:

Bellamy, Dotie. *The Letters of Mina Harker.* West Stockbridge, MA: Lingo Books/Hard Press, 1998. 221 pp.

Bergstrom, Elaine. *Blood to Blood: The Dracula Story Continues.* New York: Ace, 2000. 309 pp.

———— (as Marie Kiralay). *Mina.* New York: Berkley Books, 1994. 325 pp.

Kellerher, Victor. *Into the Dark.* Victoria, Australia: Viking, 1999. 393 pp.

Warrington, Freda. *Dracula the Undead.* New York: Penguin Books, 1997. 300 pp.

Zagoren, Kimberley. *Mina's Journal.* San Jose, CA: Writer Club Press, 2002. 178 pp.

Music, Vampire

More than 100 vampire songs appeared in contemporary music in the 1990s, ranging from the superlative to the execrable. Such a spectrum of accomplishment is not surprising, because the same variation occurs in literature, film, and art. What is new and different is the sudden high concentration of rock and roll songs devoted to this subject. No other genre has managed that kind of output.

Perhaps the vampire music trend could be attributed both to the conservative backlash in society and to the fact that rock and roll almost became establishment. When rock tunes began showing up in Muzak, the limits had to be tested further. The few avenues remaining in the antisocial realm were the occult, excessive vulgarity, and nonstandard, bizarre chord changes. Vampires as a musical topic was ripe for picking.

The Vampire in Rock Music: Vampire songs can be separated into five groups: those with obvious vampire lyrics, those obliquely vampiric, those allegedly vampiric, those in which vampires are mentioned, and those found on the soundtracks to vampire films. Obvious lyrics contain references to **blood**-drinking, the "undead," nocturnal existence, famous vampires, or other vampire traits. There is no doubt in the listener's mind regarding the subject at hand. Oblique lyrics are metaphorical, hinting at nocturnal activities, a "**victim**" being drained, or predatory hunger for another person. Alleged lyrics involve vampires, identified through either the title or some other means; the nature of the music (for example thrash metal or hardcore punk), however, makes it impossible to decipher what is being sung. Songs in which vampires are mentioned have as their main focus something else, often sex, but make references to vampirism. Vampire film soundtracks are often totally instrumental, but occasionally they include a song that falls into one of the other categories.

Vampire Music with Obvious Lyrics: One of the earliest examples of vampire rock comes from the New York Rock and Roll Ensemble's 1972 album *New York Rock and Roll Ensemble* (Atco Records). Entitled "Gravedigger," the song wanders from the

gravedigger's point of view to that of the female vampire and back again. Other than this weakness, the narrative carries nicely, relating the gravedigger's fascination for the woman entombed: "Her lips are painted red/And it looks like she's been fed/And there's a smile upon her face...." Siouxsie and the Banshees were a product of England's late-1970s punk rock movement. Their angular music is filled with jarring images, and "We Hunger," from *Hyaena* (1984, Geffen Records), equates vampires with sucking leeches, rust, corrosion, and rotting **seeds**—at best a very mixed bag of metaphors. The song is quite direct, employing such phases as "belching foul breath," "your destructive kiss death" (Siouxsie often slams words together like dancers at a concert), and "the thirst from a vampire bite." Concrete Blonde's 1990 album *Bloodletting* contains not one but three vampire songs. The title cut, also known parenthetically as "The Vampire Song," sounds as if it was influenced by **Anne Rice**. References to **New Orleans**, gardens at night, blood drunkenness, and killing run through the song. The chorus even states, "O you were a vampire and baby/I'm walking dead." Also on the *Bloodletting* album, "The Beast" compares love to a vampire and other creatures. Singer-songwriter Johnette Napolitano's dim view of romance is summed up in these lyrics: "Love is the leech, sucking you up/Love is a vampire, drunk on your blood/Love is the beast that will tear out your heart." Although superficial, one of the cleverest of vampire songs is "**Bela Lugosi**'s Dead" by Bauhaus, from their *Teeny* album (Small Wonders Records, 1979). The song is a pastiche of verbal and musical images. Even if it hadn't been used in the opening segment of "The Hunger," it would still be a vampire song. Here we find black capes back on the rack, **bats** who have left the bell tower, and victims who have been bled. The opening line of the chorus, "Bela Lugosi's dead" is immediately followed by the repetitive "undead, undead, undead." Unfortunately the concept is not developed beyond these scant images. But lead singer Peter Murphy's deep and plaintive voice creates an eerie aura of otherworldliness that carries the song.

Shockmeister extraordinaire Alice Cooper, the Bela Lugosi of rock and roll, and the singer who virtually began an entire subset of rock and roll devoted to theatrical horror as a concert form, has recorded only two obvious vampire songs to date—"Fresh Blood" on the 1983 Warner Bros. album *Da Da*, and "Dangerous Tonight" on the 1991 Epic Records album *Hey Stoopid*. "Fresh Blood" works at an emotional level, with lyrics referring to "a sanguinary feast" and victims dying "of some **anemia**." Among the singer's victims are "showgirls, businessmen in suits in the midnight rain ... bad girls and cops on the beat...." A key line is "just detained her and drained her on the spot." But the music is not up to Cooper's customarily creepy standard; instead, it rattles along like a skeleton trying to keep up at a dance. By contrast, "Dangerous Tonight" has a menacing blend of elements that add up to an effective threat, and it marked a resurgence for the Master of the Macabre. The music is high-energy heavy metal and the lyrics, "Take another bite/it'll be alright/what's wrong will soon feel right/Dangerous tonight" and "take another sip" letting "a little drip on your thigh," among others, provide a sensuous and snarling serenade.

By sheer weight of numbers, the heavy metal genre of rock and roll has contributed the most vampire songs to the market. On the Metal Blade label, the Houston group Helstar produced a 1989 album entitled *Nosferatu*. One doesn't find a more obvious title than this. *Nosferatu* is a virtual rock **opera** on **Frank Langella**'s version of **Dracula** (1979). For a speed metal band, Helstar manages some poignant acoustic passages. The songs are punctuated by sound bites of dialogue from the movie.

Helstar's best song is "**Harker**'s Tale," a thickly woven monologue that follows the original **Dracula** story only loosely. Harker warns the listener against "the Prince of Hell," presenting gory details such as, "The host upon his forehead/Then I heard a hellish howl/As it burned into his flesh...." The throng assembled to kill Dracula is instead decimated: "A sea of broken bodies marks the spot/Where he has been/The bloodless cadavers/Here sucked dry of their sins...." Helstar's "Rhapsody in Black" is a thickly textured statement from a vampire that declares, "I am the dark/That puts the light to shame" and refers to dawn as, "the only enemy/That time has placed on me." Although uneven at times, Helstar clearly demonstrates poetic inspiration. In "The Curse Has Passed Away" the narrator crawls through "halls of darkness" with a **stake** to destroy the vampire, referred to as "my feudal tyrant." We are provided the details lacking in so many other vampire songs: "His body crumbled into **dust**/Then passed before my sight/Remaining only his cloak and ring by its side/A look of peace not seen before/Upon his face I saw last...." Although not syntactically correct, the lyrics are faithful in detail to **Bram Stoker**'s *Dracula*.

In "To Sleep, Per Chance to Scream" (a pun on a Shakespearean line) there is the crackerjack line, "Eternal youth with one puncture." Regarding Shakespeare, there is one bit of metaphoric language that occurs in vampire songs that may or may not be deliberately planted. In Shakespeare's time, "to die" meant sexual consummation. In rock lyrics, the verb "fall" is used in such a way that a similar inference can be drawn. In "Suck It And See," Grim Reaper sings "I hope she don't make me fall too soon..." and in "The Beast" Concrete Blonde sings, "The monster wants out of you/Paws you and claws you/You try not to fall...." Given the construction of the lines, almost no other interpretation seems possible.

Grim Reaper's "Night of the Vampire," from their 1987 RCA album *Rock You to Hell*, works at the level of a visceral discovery that some bogeyman does exist after all: "If you think you're safe at midnight/That's the last thing you could do/He'll be looking for that nightmare bite/He could be coming after you." The chorus, "Night of the vampire, he's only looking for your life," misses all of the splendid menace available to the truly inspired.

Perhaps the penultimate vampire rock song is "Blood Banquet," created by the ludicrously named Mighty Sphincter for their 1986 album *New Manson Family* on the Placebo label:

> I have existed for centuries Living in castles built of your fears And from behind this mortal mask I carry out this deadly task In order to revive myself I plunge into the stream of life That drains into the scarlet seas And holds the red wines of immortality.

Here the vampiric singer summarizes his existence in eight lines. "Living in castles built of your fears" is psychologically insightful, and the last three lines, although they may be metaphorically ungainly, are at least consistently liquid. The singer/guitarist Doug Clark's dark, rich vocals deliver the song with a delicate balance of ennui and menace.

Vampire Music with Oblique Lyrics: Sting's 1985 "Moon over Bourbon Street" (*Dream of the Blue Turtles*, A&M Records) was, according to the liner notes, inspired by Anne Rice's *Interview with the Vampire*.

More coherent than most other songs in the genre, it is a first-person lament by a night prowler: "I pray everyday to be strong/For I know what I do must be wrong...." The singer is eloquent on his affliction: "The brim of my hat hides the eye of a beast/I've the face of a sinner but the hands of a priest...." "Forget Me Not," from Bad English's eponymous 1989 Epic Records album, was a well-selected first single release from the band. This one says, "A thousand lifetimes long ago/We made a promise we would not let go/And so I come for you tonight/And we live again before we lose each other...." The scanning is not precise, as in much rock music, but the imagery is vividly seductive. Aside from the vampiric flavor of the lyrics, veteran rocker John Waite's rendering of the song, full of angst and longing, contributes to its overall impact.

Probably Siouxsie and the Banshees's finest effort lyrically is "The Sweetest Chill," from the 1986 *Tinderbox* (Geffen Records). Here, a vampiric message may be gleaned from references such as "fingers like a fountain of needles/Shines along my spine/And rain down so divine." Siouxsie's "Night Shift," from 1981's *Ju Ju* (Polydor), is an awkward and oblique monologue from a male vampire ("a happy go lucky chap/Always dressed in black...") in what sounds like the local morgue. Once again the point of view wanders from one person to another.

"Sick Things" by Alice Cooper (1973, *Billion Dollar Babies*, Warner Bros.) is more successful as a vampire song than his "Fresh Blood," although it is only obliquely vampiric. The lyrics refer to eating and biting, with an appetite presumably for the audience. When he sings, "I love you Things I see as much as you love me," Alice makes the declaration sound threatening. The song is about feeding off the sickness and derangement of the audience to inspire Alice to even more outlandish behavior and music. Similarly, "I Love the Dead" is more vampiric musically than "Fresh Blood." "Blood and Roses" by the Smithereens (1986, *Especially for You*, Enigma) has more going for it vampirically than merely sharing the name of a **Roger Vadim** film. With lyrics like "I try to love but it comes out wrong/I try to live where I don't belong/I close my eyes and I see blood and roses," the song evokes mental images of Phillinon and **"Carmilla"** and "La Belle Dame sans Merci". The seductress in the song can fall in love and get married, but she can't change her nature enough to quite fit in.

Alleged Vampire Music: Alice Cooper's "I Love The Dead" (1973, *Billion Dollar Babies*, Warner Bros.) is a tour de force, opening with a vaguely oriental musical motif and dripping with menace: "I love the dead/Before they're cold...." The song must be placed in the "alleged" vampire category because a good case could be made for it as a necrophiliac's rhapsody. Should we choose vampirism, the lines still apply: "While friends and lovers mourn your silly grave/I have other uses for you, darling...." These two lines, central to the skimpy lyric, are not just sung, but delivered to us laden with innuendo. There is a smirking chuckle just before the word "silly," and the second line is wrapped in multiple meanings, doubtlessly conglomerated from the purring threats of a hundred movie femmes fatales.

"Blood Lust" by Blood Feast, a thrash metal band, can be partially grasped, but "Vampire" is not so much sung as spat and screeched. The group plays at breakneck speed from beginning to end. If there is a point to either of these songs, most listeners will miss it.

Music that Mentions Vampires: Bobby "Boris" Pickett & The Crypt Kickers's" Monster Mash" (initially a number one single from 1962, currently available on *Elvira's*

Haunted Hits, Rhino Records) was a comedy hit, sung in a Boris Karloff voice. It is a musical cartoon, taking off on the dance crazes of the time. Dracula is referred to three times in the song, lastly as a rival to "Boris": "Out from his **coffin** Drac's voice did ring/Seems like he was troubled by just one thing/He opened the lid and shook his fist and said/'What ever happened to my Transylvanian Twist'?" Not quite so amusing is the Yugoslavian band Laibach's, cover version of the Rolling Stones's "Sympathy for the Devil" (1988, Restless/Mute Records). The first verse is sung in a vaguely eastern European accent mimicking Bela Lugosi, in a context in which the words could apply to a vampire as much as to **Satan**. Beyond that point the accent becomes Russian, appropriate to the "Anastasia" references, and the song takes on political overtones.

Songs from Vampire Movie Soundtracks: Most vampire movie soundtracks consist of loosely connected mood pieces, sometimes extremely tongue-in-cheek. For the most part, moviemakers relied on classical music performed by studio orchestras. "Swan Lake" for ***Dracula* (1931)** was the first such instance. The most widely known impression of the vampire—formally attired in evening clothes and elegant cape—arose from theater and movie producers's need to explain the music. Filmmakers thought that audiences would not understand the rationale for the music unless they were told where it came from. Hence, when **Tod Browning** made *Dracula* (1931), "Swan Lake" was established as the main song when Dracula and several of the other main characters spent a night at the ballet.

Innocent Blood provides comedic touches with its soundtrack by concentrating on the music appropriate to the milieu: Italian East Coast Mafia.

Several Frank Sinatra tunes well within the characters's interests and context are used. From "I Got You Under My Skin" to "That Old Black Magic," the music provides a sensuous and lighthearted background to the often frenetic images.

"Good Times" by INXS and Jimmy Barnes and "People Are Strange" by Echo and the Bunnymen are two selections from 1987's *The Lost Boys*, one of the most popular vampire movies of the 1980s. The theme was one of youth and alienation for two brothers in the "murder capital" of the U.S. The music is theirs, full of hope and disaffection at the same time. "(My Future's So Bright) I Gotta Wear Shades" by Timbuk 3 (1988, *My Best Friend Is a Vampire*) is in the same youthful vein, but it takes a lighter approach because the movie is a light comedy.

The songs on the *Son of Dracula* (1974, Rapple Records) soundtrack have the bouncy sweetness that infected the popular music scene in the early 1970s. "Without You" and "Jump into the Fire" got considerable airplay given their origin on the soundtrack of a vampire film. "Without You" is a poignant song that laments life without a particular loved one. Harry Nilsson sings it, on the edge of weeping: "I can't live/If living is without you," and "No I can't forget this evening/Or your face as you were leaving…. You always smile but in your eyes your sorrow shows…." In the movie, Nilsson, as Count Downe, abdicates the throne of the Draculas in favor of his human love, Amber.

Pop diva Mariah Carey released a new version of the song in 1994 that robbed the song of much of its original poignancy.

The soundtrack of ***Dracula* (1979)** bears the unmistakable mark of famous conductor John Williams. In several cases, selections could have been used in *Star Wars*

Count Downe (actor/singer Harry Nilsson) menaces merlin the Magician (ex-Beatle Ringo Starr) in the music-filled film *Son of Dracula*.

(Williams's most famous movie score) with the same effect. Williams repeats the theme in several selections.

In literature, vampires are often romantic or at least adventurous beings.

Their lives are far from ordinary. Rock and roll treatments, on the other hand, concentrate on the morbid, without much romance. Intense gore seems to be the thing that gets the most attention.

The New Gothic Movement: A special slice of rock and roll is reserved for the **gothic** movement. Heir to the classic gothic tradition, mixed with elements from the psychedelic/flower child/rock music subcultures of the 1960s and 1970s, was the gothic counter-cultural movement that appeared in most urban centers of the West during the 1980s. The movement's origins can be traced to late 1970s musical groups in the United Kingdom. It certainly also had its direct precursors in such bands as Black Sabbath and the punk rock music of the 1970s. Possibly the most prominent of those groups was Bauhaus and the previously mentioned single, "Bela Lugosi's Dead," their most popular recording to date. Bauhaus was soon joined by such groups as Siouxsie and the Ban-

shees, The Cult, The Cure, and The Sisters of Mercy. Together these bands created a variant music called gothic rock or death rock. A circuit of music clubs, most notably The Bat Cave in London, opened to provide a stage for their performances.

Gothic music, as all counter-cultural forms, articulated an explicit nonconformist stance vis-à-vis the dominant establishment. It opposed narrow sexual mores and traditional established religions. High priests, churches, and congregations were replaced with rock musicians, night clubs, and fans. The music celebrated the dark, shadowy side of life and had a distinct fascination with death. Its slow, driving sound was frequently described as melancholy, gloomy, even morbid. Those enthralled by the new gothic culture found the vampire the single most appropriate image for the movement. Both men and women dress in black. Men seem to be perpetuating vampiric images from Anne Rice novels, while women perpetuate what, at first glance, seems to be the persona of Morticia Addams of **The Addams Family**, **Vampira**, and **Elvira**, although some aim for a more Victorian funereal style or a modern vampish look. Vampires, blood and **fangs**, and **bats** fill the pages of gothic magazines, whether or not vampirism is discussed.

The movement was especially popular in the early 1980s when it spread to the European continent and throughout North America. By the middle of the decade, however, it showed a marked decline in England. Bauhaus disbanded in 1983, although some of its members reformed as Love & Rockets. Most of the clubs that had provided meeting places for gothic aficionados turned their attention to other new trends in popular music, and The Bat Cave closed. To keep the movement alive when the media announced its obituary, one gothic band, Nosferatu, founded The Gothic Society and the periodical *Grimoire*, which became the new center of a network of bands and fans. Curve, Rosetta Stone, Mortal Coil, Wraith, and Slimelight joined Nosferatu as bands of the gothic scene.

Even as the movement was suffering in England, it was experiencing the early stages of its emergence in the United States. By 1990, a number of gothic bands traveled a circuit of clubs, and fans kept up with the movement through their own fanzines. *Propaganda* was the first of the gothic fanzines to hit the newsstands and offer national (and international) coverage to the emerging gothic movement. Founded by "Propaganda Minister" Fred H. Berger, *Propaganda* provided some structure for "the Underground," as the new gothic subculture referred to itself. The magazine publicized many gothic bands and personalities and provided advertising space for both gothic records and the variety of clothing, jewelry, and **paraphernalia** demanded by devoted fans. More recently, it produced two gothic videos, *The Trilogy* and *Blood Countess*, the second based upon the life of **Elizabeth Bathory**.

In 1992, *Propaganda* was joined on the West Coast by the slick Los Angeles-based magazine *Ghastly*. The magazine was published by Nosferatu Productions and edited by Tara and Jeremy Bai. More so than *Propaganda*, Nosferatu Productions markets the gothic subculture through a mail order catalog that includes gothic fanzines, compact disc (CDs) and cassettes, cosmetics, clothing, and even condoms. Nosferatu has also launched two additional periodicals: *The Oracle*, a monthly newsletter that updates readers on show dates and the latest releases on CD; and *The Cabala*, a fan networking journal.

The majority of large urban centers in the United States now have at least one nightclub that regularly features gothic music. Many clubs schedule gothic nights once or twice a week and devote other evenings to closely related music such as punk or industrial rock.

A large number of contemporary bands play gothic music. Some of the more well-known are Ministry, Shadow Project, Christian Death, This Ascension, The Shroud, and Death in June. Several bands have adopted specifically vampiric images, including Astro Vamps, **Lestat**, Neither/Neither World, London after Midnight, and Transvision Vamp. In addition, individual musicians have adopted a stage persona tying them to the vampiric image. They include Eva **Van Helsing** of The Shroud and **Vlad** of Nosferatu. Toney Lestat of Wreckage claims to have met the real vampire **Lestat de Lioncourt**, the character featured in the vampire novels of Anne Rice. Toney Lestat adopted his name after Rice made the Lestat character famous.

Through the first decade of the twenty-first century, the goth scene has continued in both England and North America, and to a lesser extent in such places as Australia and Japan. Bands have come and gone, though a few such as Alien Sex Fiend, Inkubus Sukkubus, Fields of the Nephilim, and Rosetta Stone have survived in the highly volatile field. Goth rock still exists, with groups such as the Fields of the Nephilim still active, but both goth rock and the entire gothic scene have markedly declined. Yet, even in the midst of that larger decline, Theatres des Vampires, an Italian gothic metal band, appeared at the end of the 1990s and has specialized in vampire-themed songs through several albums. A new gothic band, Nox Arcana, formed in 2003, released its Dracula homage album *Transylvania* in 2005. The survival of the vampire theme in goth music is no better illustrated than in the CD collection *Vampire Rituals: Gothic Music from the Deepest Depths of Hell* (2006), that included cuts from twelve goth bands/artists.

Beyond Rock and Roll: In non-rock and roll genres, there are scant pickings. Perhaps the only modern folk song about vampires is Claudia Schmidt's "Vampire," from *Midwestern Heart* (Flying Fish Records, 1981).

It says: "Far below the world is lying unaware/My soul is crying Vampire ... this is my song." A reasonably good couplet can be found in the song's last verse: "Life's not life if you must lose it/Death's not death if you refuse it...."

The Vampire in Classical Music: Classical music was, from its beginnings, devoted to church-related themes. Until our modern age, musicians were in the employ of church or king, beholden to royal sponsors, and their duties would have precluded experimentation. Gradually, over a period of many years, mainstream classical music lost most of its religious edge. During the early nineteenth century, at the height of the romantic movement's fascination with the vampire, one German musician, **Heinrich August Marschner**, wrote a vampire opera, *Der Vampyr* (1829), one of only two known, the other being *Lamia*, by August Enna, first performed in 1899 in Brussels, Belgium.

The nineteenth century saw the development of the "tone poem," which is programmatic in content—there is a subject depicted by the music—though it was never as popular a form as the symphony or the concerto. Among programmatic works, a few dark subjects emerged, but only a few. Hector Berlioz's "Symphony Fantastique" (1830) concludes with a witches's sabbath. Much of Berlioz's work was a radical breakthrough for its time. Franz Liszt's "Mephisto Waltz" (1861) is based on a simple folktale in which the devil grabs a violin at a village dance and plays seductive melodies. In Saint Saens's "Danse Macabre" (1874) death plays the violin as skeletons dance at midnight.

The revels end at dawn. Modest Mussorgsky's "Night on Bald Mountain" (1877) evokes Halloween night, when evil spirits are free to roam (immortalized in Walt Disney's animated film *Fantasia*). The mountain in question is Mt. Triglav, near Kiev in the Soviet Union; the action occurring on St. John's Eve (or Midsummers Eve, June 23rd) and Mussorgsky explained it as describing "a subterranean din of unearthly voices." Once again, the evil celebration disperses when dawn breaks.

Through the first decade of the twenty-first century, several notable trends could be noticed in vampire-related music. First, the great output of this music as seen in the 1990s has passed. Vampire-themed songs continue to appear but at a significantly reduced rate. Second, most of the gothic bands that developed a vampire persona no longer exist and the few that do seem to have moved beyond goth rock into new and evolving forms of music appearing in the rock scene. Quite apart from the goth scene, there are several rock bands that have adopted a vampire persona (Vampire Weekend, Vampire Moose), but are not doing vampire-themed music.

Even as gothic rock declined, several large musical productions built around Dracula appeared. The decade began with the release on VHS of Richard Ouzounian's *Dracula: A Chamber Musical* (1997), originally produced to celebrate the Dracula Centennial. Two years later, the Winnipeg Ballet staged a production of Guy Maudin's *Dracula: Pages from a Virgin Diary* (2002), which was soon after released on DVD. Additional productions include: Sergei Kvitko's *Dracula* (CD, 2005) written for the Riverwalk Theatre's production of the play, *Dracula*; "Dracula Opera Rock," by PFM, the music for a rock opera version of "Dracula" staged in Rome (2006); and the music by Christopher J. Orton for the off-Broadway musical *Dracula* (released on CD in 2007). Pierre Henry, a French composer known for his pioneering efforts with electronic music, also released his *Dracula* album in 2003.

As a matter of course, a number of Dracula and vampire movies produced worthy sound tracks. Among the more notable: the new sound track produced for the 1922 film *Nosferatu* by Type-O-Negative for a 2007 re-release of the movie on DVD, and the new compositions written by Philip Glass in 1999 for the 1931 *Dracula*.

Sources:

Kilpatrick, Nancy. *The Goth Bible: A Compendium for the Darkly Inclined*. New York: St. Martin's Griffin, 2004. 304 pp.

Mercer, Mick. *Gothic Rock*. Los Angeles: Cleopatra Records, 1994.

Steele, Valerie, and Jennifer Park. *Gothic: Dark Glamour*. New Haven, CT: Yale University Press, 2008. 180 pp.

Thompson, Dave. *The Dark Reign of Gothic Rock: In The Reptile House with The Sisters of Mercy, Bauhaus and The Cure*. London: Helter Skelter Publishing, 2002. 288 pp.

❮ Myanmar, Vampires in ❯

Myanmar, known until 1989 as Burma, is a Southeast Asian country bounded by India and Bangladesh on the west, China on the north, and Laos and Cambodia on the east. The Myanmars settled the land in the ninth century and over the next century established an independent country. It has been variously part of the Chinese, British, and Japanese empires; it emerged as an independent nation following World

War II. The Myanmars are primarily Buddhist and tend to cremate their dead; thus, they do not have a strong tradition of revenants. The culture does have a large pantheon of deities and supernatural entities, however, along with a rich tradition of ghosts and demonic beings.

The most malevolent of the ghosts, the *thaye* and *tasei*, were beings that, because of their evil earthly life, were condemned to their disembodied state until they had worked out their karmic difficulties and were eventually reborn into another body. These disembodied ghosts, at times, took on a kind of visible materiality. When seen, they were tall, dark, and possessed huge ears, a large tongue, and tusk-like teeth. They resided near villages at the local cemeteries. On occasion they assumed **characteristics** of vampires and **ghoul**s and fed on corpses or went into the village to attack living people. More frequently, they were seen as the cause of minor illnesses. They entered town either at high noon or after dark.

In the folklore, **protection** from ghosts was provided by a *lehpwe*, an amulet for a variety of purposes. One such amulet consisted of a drawing of an elephant made from the letters of the Myanmar alphabet.

In earlier centuries tattooing of the body in the area between the navel and the knee was popular. There were also specific rituals to banish ghosts from a village, both brief ones for individual use and longer ones for the community.

Sources:

Spiro, Melford E. *Burmese Supernaturalism*. Philadelphia: Institute for the Study of Human Issues, 1978. 300 pp.

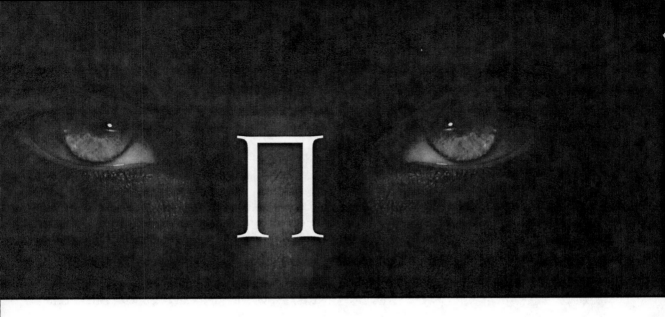

Nachzehrer *see:* Germany, Vampires in

Name, The Vampire's

In his story "Carmilla", author **Sheridan Le Fanu** assigned a unique characteristic to vampires: they must choose a name that, "if not his or her real one, should at least reproduce, without the omission or addition of a single letter, those, as we say, anagrammatically, which compose it." **Carmilla** was originally named Millarca and was also known as Mircalla. This characteristic was unique to Le Fanu's vampire. Although others have not employed Le Fanu's stipulation concerning the vampire's name, noted sequels to **Dracula,** the leading character frequently called himself Count (or Dr. or Mr.) "Alucard," Dracula's name spelled backward, such as in *Son of Dracula* (1943). Other variations of Dracula included Dr. Aluca, or, in the Dell *Dracula* **comic book,** *Al U. Card.*

Sources:
Le Fanu, Sheridan. "Carmilla." 1872. Reprinted in Les Shepard, ed. *The Dracula Book of Great Vampire Stories*. New York: Jove, 1978: 15–99.

Native Soil

In the folklore of eastern Europe, vampires were believed to be the revived body of a recently deceased member of the community. They resided in their graves at the local graveyard. They were commonly surrounded by their native soil, but no special mention was made of it. Nor was there mention of native soil in the early vampire fiction, such as **John Polidori**'s, "The Vampyre"; *Varney the Vampyre*; or **Sheridan Le Fanu**'s, "Carmilla". The idea of a need for native soil came from the imagination of **Bram Stoker**.

In *Son of Dracula* Lon Chaney Jr.'s vampire character was known as Count Alucard, which is Dracula spelled backwards.

As a desperate **Jonathan Harker** began to explore **Castle Dracula**, he discovered the Count laying in a box filled with newly dug earth; other boxes of soil were nearby. Harker returned to his room in great fear. Later, he again went to the room with the box and discovered **Dracula** bloated with **blood** from a recent feeding. For a second time Harker was unable to take decisive action and the boxes, with the vampire in one of them, were shipped to England. After landing in England, Dracula retrieved the boxes and had them sent to a number of locations in the greater **London** area. **Vampire hunter Abraham Van Helsing** discovered that Dracula needed the native soil as his resting place, and that attacking his resting place was an effective means of **destroying** him. Of the 50 boxes, 49 were located and filled with **eucharistic wafers**, thus making them inhospitable to the vampire. Dracula escaped in the last box and returned to **Transylvania**, where he was later killed.

The transportation of Dracula's native soil to England also served a useful purpose in what many critics saw as an underlying theme in *Dracula* **(1897)**—the fear that existed in civilized Englishmen (Stoker's first audience) concerning the invasion of their society by representatives of the "uncivilized" cultures they had conquered. Stephen D. Arata spoke of this fear of reverse colonization—a fear prominent in late nineteenth-century British fiction. Thus, one could view Van Helsing's gathering of the men to fight Dracula as the organization of an army, called to defend home and hearth, that launched an attack on foreign soil in the form of the 50 boxes of earth.

In spite of these possible meanings of the native soil in *Dracula*, later writers saw it more narrowly as a necessary attribute/limitation on the vampire. Mystically, the vampire drew **strength** from it. Many contemporary writers such as **Anne Rice** simply dropped the idea; it limited the mobility of vampires too much. Possibly the modern vampire most tied to his native soil has been **P. N. Elrod**'s hero vampire Jack Fleming. Others, however, allowed a more literal reading of the Dracula myth to influence their development of a new variation of the myth. **Chelsea Quinn Yarbro** developed the most unique variation of the native soil myth. Her hero **St. Germain** had special shoes with hollow heels where native soil was placed. Thus he was in constant touch with that vivifying element.

Sources:

Arata, Stephen D. "The Occidental Tourist: Dracula and the Anxiety of Reverse Colonization." *Victorian Studies* 33, 4 (Summer 1990): 621–45.

Elrod, P. N. *Bloodlist*. New York: Ace Books, 1990. 200 pp.

Senf, Carol A. *The Vampire in Nineteenth-Century English Literature*. Bowling Green, OH: Bowling Green State University Popular Press, 1988. 204 pp.

Yarbro, Chelsea Quinn. *Hotel Transylvania*. New York: St. Martin's Press, 1979. Rept. New York: New American Library, 1979. 408 pp.

Near Dark

*N*ear Dark (1987) is a contemporary vampire story set against a Western landscape. The Kathryn Bigelow-directed film about a marauding band of psychopathic vampires alternates sadistic **humor** with a vampire girl-meets-boy romance against a background of truck stops, oil rigs, run-down motels, and dry empty towns. Bigelow co-wrote *Near Dark* with Eric Red (writer of the 1986 violent fable *The Hitcher*), and the German electronic music group Tangerine Dreams provided the movie's original score. Other vampire Westerns—namely, *Curse of the Undead* (1959) and *Billy the Kid versus Dracula* (1966)—had preceded *Near Dark*, but Bigelow's film was set in the modern-day West.

The movie opens in Heartland, USA, where Mae (Jenny Wright) needs a lift home one night and Caleb Colton (Adrian Pasdar) is happy to oblige. But Mae is a vampire; Caleb asks for a kiss, and she bites his neck. As the sun rises, Caleb grows sick and he stumbles through a cornfield and is picked up by an RV with Mae in it. Caleb spends the day sleeping in the RV with Mae and her "family" of vampire outlaws: Jesse Hooker (Lance Henriksen), Severen (Bill Paxton), Diamondback (Jenette Goldstein), and Homer (Joshua John Miller). Mae tries to teach Caleb to kill for blood, but he won't do it. Mae's vampire family determines to get Caleb to kill humans so they go on a grotesque killing spree in a bar. But Caleb still won't kill. The vampires seek shelter in a motel, and they're awakened when the police knock on the door and a bloody Bonnie and Clyde-type shootout follows.

Later, Caleb's father transfuses some of his own blood into Caleb so his son becomes human again. But when Caleb's sister Sara is missing, Caleb mounts a horse and is confronted by the vampire family. The sun comes up, burning all the other vampires. In a surprise twist, Caleb transfuses some of his blood into Mae, and she becomes human again.

According to Bigelow (who recently won an Oscar for directing the acclaimed *The Hurt Locker*), *Near Dark* invents its own vampire mythology. The traditional religious symbols used to battle vampires—crosses, holy **water**, and the Bible—are not apparent although the movie makes sly references to them. The film also omits the standard clichés like **garlic**, **stakes**, silver bullets, and even **fangs**, but **sunlight** definitely burns and destroys the vampires. *Near Dark*'s vampires are immortal and possess rapid healing powers as well. But the notion that a blood transfusion can "cure" the vampire condition appears, by some, to be too improbable and not in line with **Bram Stoker**'s ideas. Bigelow explained that the transfusion is a way to reclaim Caleb and Mae and allow the two young characters to love each other.

Near Dark was released in theaters in October 1987 by the now defunct DeLaurentis Entertainment Group (DEG). The movie's debut closely followed the release of *The Lost Boys* (1987), a similar tale of a young man's adventures among a clan of vampire outlaws. But DEG was teetering on bankruptcy, and *Near Dark* lasted only two weeks in theaters. HBO Home Video subsequently released the movie in video format, and over the years, *Near Dark* has enjoyed a sizeable underground cult following. Lionsgate Home Entertainment released the Blu-ray version of *Near Dark* in November 2009, which includes the documentary, *Living in Darkness*. Platinum Dunes, a production company that specializes in horror films, recently planned a *Near Dark* remake but called it off because the story was "too similar" to **Twilight**.

Sources:

"The 80's Movie Gateway: *Near Dark*." (March 2000). Posted at http://www.fast-rewind.com/near-dark.htm. Accessed on April 10, 2010.

"Exclusive: *Near Dark* Remake Is Off." (December 12, 2008). Posted at http://www.famousmonstersoffilmland.com/near-dark-postponed-indefinitely. Accessed on April 10, 2010.

Felsher, Michael. *Near Dark: Pray for Daylight*. Troy, MI: Anchor Bay Entertainment, Inc., 2002. 10 pp.

Wilmington, Michael. "Sexy Horror Arrives *Near Dark*." *Los Angeles Times*, p. 10. (October 9, 1987).

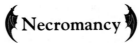

Necromancy

Abraham **Van Helsing**, the wise vampire expert in **Bram Stoker**'s novel **Dracula** (1897) noted, in his halting English, that vampires "have still the aids of necromancy, which is, as his etymology imply, the divination by the dead, and all the dead that he can come nigh to are for him to command." Necromancy was a form of divining the future through the use of the dead, most specifically dead bodies. Necromancy was specifically condemned in the Jewish Bible (Deuteronomy 18:11), though it is not altogether clear what form was being practiced. It possibly involved the calling up of the spirit or shade of the deceased as was done when Saul attempted to communicate with Samuel (I Samuel 28). By Stoker's time, the term necromancy referred specifically to calling forth the dead from the grave to obtain otherwise unavailable information, especially about the future. From the Middle Ages to the present, artists have produced drawings of such necromanic activity. Necromancy involved a corpse, but was also seen as communication with the spirit/soul of the dead person, which appeared before the magician in a ghostly but bodily form—what theosophists termed the astral body.

In the mid-nineteenth century, the United States, England, and much of continental Europe were swept by the movement called spiritualism. Spiritualism was built around the practice of mediumship, the communication with the spirits of the dead. Spiritualism was several steps removed from traditional necromancy, however, although its practitioners were called necromancers by many religious critics. The identification of spiritualism and necromancy was common in Stoker's time.

Sources:

Cavendish, Richard. *The Black Arts*. New York: G. P. Putnam's Sons, 1967. 373 pp.

de Givry, Emil Grillot. *Picture Museum of Sorcery, Magic and Alchemy*. New Hyde Park, NY: University Books, 1963. 395 pp.

Kieckhefer, Richard. *Forbidden Rites: A Necromancer's Manual of the Fifteenth Century*. University Park, Pa.: Pennsylvania State University Press, 1998. 384 pp.

Nefarious *see:* Vampire Fandom: United States

Nepal, Vampires in *see:* Tibet, Vampires in

New England Dark Shadows Society *see:* Dark Shadows Fandom

New Moon *see:* The Twilight Saga: New Moon

New Orleans

Since it has been introduced as a home for vampires, New Orleans has emerged as the true American vampire city. While many different American cities, especially New York and Los Angeles, have provided locations for vampire stories, none has become so identified with the nocturnal creatures as has the Crescent City. The association is not from a history of vampire incidents in the city's folklore. There is certainly a vampire figure, the fifollet in the folklore of the African Americans of Louisiana, and the **loogaroo**, a variation on the West African vampire found among the Haitian slaves who came into the city in the early nineteenth century, but only two vampire stories can actually be traced to the city. One of those involved two serial killers in the 1930s who drank **blood** from their **victims** before killing them. The city's reputation for vampires has purely modern roots, and can be found in the writings of **Anne Rice**, especially *Interview with a Vampire*, the second most popular vampire book of all time, which sets much of the action in New Orleans. Throughout the 1990s, a number of other authors have also enjoyed success with New Orleans vampires.

New Orleans is a unique place on the American landscape, and an appropriate setting for vampires. It was the center of voodoo, a religion practiced in secret during the night by the slaves who built a different culture in order to survive away from their homeland. New Orleans also stands as a foreign enclave within a country dominated by English-speaking British influence. In the French Quarter, New Orleans is also a land separated from the present by its unique architecture and heritage. The recognition of the old European setting as providing an appropriately **"gothic"** setting was heralded in the *Son of Dracula*, set in rural Louisiana near New Orleans.

Interview with the Vampire tells the story of Louis, an eighteenth-century New Orleans vampire, raised on a plantation near the city, who is brought into the nightlife by the vampire **Lestat**. They try living on the plantation for a time, but the slaves soon figure out what is occurring in the mansion house and force the pair into the anonymity of city. By the 1790s, when Louis is made a vampire, New Orleans had spread far beyond the old French Quarter, and provided ample food for the thirsty pair. Its bawdy nightlife also provided cover for their nefarious activities. It is here that they find the little girl Claudia and make her a vampire.

Claudia and Louis left New Orleans in 1862 after trying to kill Lestat. However, after Claudia's death in Paris later that year, he and his new companion, **Armand**, finally settled in New Orleans after living in New York for a number of years. While there Louis again met with Lestat before moving on, leaving Armand behind. In 1929, Lestat went underground in New Orleans where he would remain in a vampiric **sleep** for many decades. Armand remained in New Orleans through the twentieth century and is the one found by Daniel Molloy when he comes looking for Louis. Louis had given his now-famous interview to Molloy, who had published it under the pseudonym Anne Rice.

While Armand and Daniel were busy with their relationship, Lestat was awakened by the rock **music** of a band rehearsing not far from the cemetery in which he lay asleep. Awakened by the music, he made his way to the band's room and soon began his new career as a rock star. The publication of his autobiography, *The Vampire Lestat*,

brings Jesse, the employee of the occult studies organization, the **Talamasca**, to New Orleans where she finds the home where Louis and Claudia had lived and the several items that Claudia had hidden and left behind.

Once Lestat leaves New Orleans in 1985, the city is less essential to the "The Vampire Chronicles," the action shifting to California, Miami, New York, and the world beyond. However, after Lestat's visit to heaven and hell, he returns to New Orleans and resides in St. Elizabeth's, the former orphanage on Napoleon Street (an actual building once owned by Rice).

Rice, of course, is not the only vampire fiction writer to place her novels in New Orleans. In 1982, George R. R. Martin brought Josiah Yorke to the Crescent City on his 1850s river boat, the *Fevre Dream*. There he found the vampire community for which he had been searching. Damon Julian had led a group of vampires from Portugal in the 1750s. Using the city as their headquarters, they moved along the river among the slaves whom they treated as their personal food supply. Yorke presented his blood substitute which would allow vampires to stop killing and integrate into human society. Julian rejected his plan and their conflict would provide the action for the rest of the novel.

Nancy Collins, author of the highly acclaimed series of novels featuring the vampire Sonia Blue and a resident of New Orleans, finally brought her character to New Orleans in the second volume of the series, *In the Blood*. Sonja had been made a vampire in a most brutal manner by a vampire named Morgan and had set out to find and kill him. Upon her return to the United States, she settled in New Orleans. Pangloss, the old vampire who had made Morgan, wanted to find Sonja. Palmer, the private detective Pangloss hired to track her, caught up with her in the French Quarter, where Pangloss happened to keep an apartment. While soaking up the atmosphere, they would come to know each other, and from there they would launch the next phase of Sonja's search for Morgan.

The character was born in New Orleans, in a room over a bar in the French quarter, the result of the union of his mother Jessy, a teenager infatuated with vampires, and Zillah, a 100-year-old vampire who gave her more than she bargained for. From their one night stand in the mid-1970s, and Jessy's subsequent death-giving birth, Nothing emerged as the central character in **Poppy Z. Brite**'s *Lost Souls* (1992). The orphan Nothing was taken to live with a "normal" couple in Maryland, far from New Orleans, but his **origin** was stronger than the loving environment of his youth. As a teenager he ran away from home and began the pilgrimage which would lead him to his father and then to his birthplace where his history would suddenly catch up with him.

In the early 1990s, Carnifax is a vampire who has integrated himself into New Orleans society and become a viable candidate for governor. Only a **werewolf**, Desiree Cupio, the lead character in Daniel Presedo's **comic book** series *Dream Wolves*, recognizes him for what he is. Many years before he had fallen in love with Desiree's mother, sired a child, and also had killed the one he loved. When they finally meet, they are infatuated with each other, and only slowly recognize their prior connections. Their adventures lead them around the French Quarter until they converge on Desiree's aunt's house where the truth is revealed.

In 1993, **Blade the Vampire Slayer** squares off against his reappearing nemesis **Deacon Frost** in New Orleans, where with the assistance of Hannibal King and Brother

Voodoo, he blocks Frost's attempt to take over a local industry though the good guys were unable to finish off the evil vampire.

In 1994, the story of New Orleans vampires were recreated for followers of the role-playing **game Vampire: The Masquerade.** The story begins with Doran, a Frenchman turned into a vampire in 1471. He settled in what was to become New Orleans in 1705 and as the vampire community of the city grew, fought for his place in the moonlight, his main competitor over the centuries being Spanish vampire Simon de Cosa. He led the city's Kindred until after World War II when he announced his grandiose plan for a new time in which vampires and mortals could live side by side. Some did not like his idea and in 1955 he was assassinated. Today the city is led by a new prince, Marcel.

New Orleans's reputation as the vampire city was kept alive through the 1990s by numerous vampire fans who flocked to the city and joined in the various tours of the locations featured in the Anne Rice novels (and the movie *Interview with a Vampire*) or take the midnight tour exploring the French Quarter's vampiric heritage. The most dedicated come at the end of October for the annual Halloween Coven Party sponsored by Anne Rice's Vampire Lestat Fan Club.

The Anne Rice Vampire Lestat Fan Club dissolved in 2000. In 2004, following the death of her husband, Rice announced that she was leaving New Orleans and put the last property she owned in the Garden District up for sale. She had by this time written the last of her vampire novels, *Blood Canticle* (2003) and moved on to other themes.

New Orleans was changed significantly by Hurricane Katrina that struck the city in August 2005. Much of the city was flooded, though the French Quarter remained above water and the Garden District was less affected than other parts of the city. As the city rebounded, the vampire aspect of life began to reappear, beginning with the nightly vampire tours that focused on the French Quarter and the Garden District. Tours to Oak Alley, the plantation outside the city which was used as a location in *Interview with a Vampire* have also returned. In 2008-09, the movie version of **Darren Shan**'s *Cirque du Freak, The Vampire's Assistant*, was shot in New Orleans, though the novel does not specify it as the story's setting.

In 2006, some former members of the Rice Fan Club approached Rice about restarting the club, in part as an effort to assist the city to recover. The first of the new gatherings occurred in 2007, and in successive years have broadened their appeal. The 2009 event was announced as the "True Blood and Gold Ball." Through and since the disaster of Katrina, New Orleans has remained a favorite location for fiction writers to set their novels. Just before Katrina struck, Andrew Fox had set his two novels, *Fat White Vampire Blues* (2003) and *Bride of the Fat White Vampire* (2004), in the city.

More recently, his work has been joined by the various titles of Shannon Drake/Heather Grahams such as *Under the Blood Red Moon* (1999) and *Kiss of Darkness* (2006); Lynn Viehl's *When Angels Burn* (2005); Denise Wilkinson's *Isabella St. Clair: Vamp of New Orleans, the Vieux Carre* (2007); Adrian Phoenix's *A Rush of Wings* (2009), to mention a few. Pete Callahan's self-published novel, *Vampire in New Orleans* carries the story line through the Katrina event. In her seventh vampire novel, *All Together Dead*, **Charlaine Harris** features a new character, Sophie-Anne Leclerq, the vampire queen of Louisiana, who resides in post-Katrina New Orleans. The **L. A. Banks**'s novels, while basically operating out of Philadelphia, frequently mention New Orleans as

places the characters have either come from or visited, while the more recent novels such as *The Wicked* (2007) and *The Shadows* (2008) reflect on Katrina.

Sources:

Brite, Poppy Z. *Lost Souls*. New York: Asylum/Delacorte, 1992. 359 pp.

Callahan, Peter. *Vampire in New Orleans*. New Orleans: self published, 2007.

Collins, Nancy. *Midnight Blue: The Sonja Blue Collection*. Clarkston, GA: White Wolf Game Studio, 1995. 559 pp.

Fox, Andrew. *Fat White Vampire Blues*. New York: Ballantine Books, 2003. 334 pp.

————. *Bride of the Fat White Vampire*. New York: Ballantine Books, 2004. 429 pp. tp.

Golden, Christopher, and Gene Colan. *Blade*. New York: Marvel, 1993.

Graham, Heather (pseudonym of Heather Graham Pozzessere). *Blood Red*. Don Mills, ON: Mira Books, 2007. 347 pp.

Harris, Charlaine. *All Together Dead*. Southern Vampire Mysteries, Book 7. 2007. 323 pp.

Marmel, Ari, and C. A. Suleiman. *City of the Damned: New Orleans*. Stone Mountain, GA: White Wolf Publishing, 2005. 144 pp.

Martin, George R. R., *Fevre Dream*. New York: Poseidon Press, 1982. 350 pp.

Nordan. Frances. *New Orleans Vampires*. New Orleans: California Concepts, 2001. 143 pp.

Presedo, Daniel. *Dream Wolves*. First series. No. 103. London Night Studios, 1993–94. *Dream Wolves*. Second series. No. 108. Baton Rouge, LA: Drameon Studios, 1994–95.

Ramsland, Katherine. *The Vampire Companion: The Official Guide to Anne Rice's The Vampire Chronicles*. New York: Ballantine Books, 1993. 507 pp.

Rice, Anne. *Interview with the Vampire*. New York: Alfred A. Knopf, 1976. 372 pp.

————. *The Vampire Lestat*. New York: Alfred A. Knopf, 1985. 481 pp.

————. *Queen of the Damned*. New York: Alfred A. Knopf, 1988. 448 pp.

————. *Memnoch the Devil*. New York: Alfred A. Knopf, 1994. 354 pp.

————. *Pandora*. New York: Alfred A. Knopf, 1998. 353 pp.

Richardson, Beverly. "Vampire City: A Visit to New Orleans." *The Borgo Post* (Transylvanian Society of Dracula-Canadian Chapter) 3, 5 (June 1998): 2.

Roshell, Patricia Ann. *New Orleans by Night*. Stone Mountain, GA: White Wolf Game Studio, 1994. 125 pp.

Smith, Kalila Katherine. *Journey Into Darkness ... Ghosts & Vampires of New Orleans*. New Orleans: DeSimeon, 1998.

Wilkinson, Denise M. Snellgrove. *Isabella St. Clair: Vamp of New Orleans, the Vieux Carre*. Baltimore, MD: PublishAmerica, 2007. 220 pp.

❨ Newman, Kim (1959–) ❩

Kim Newman, the author of the award-winning vampire novel *Anno-Dracula*, was born in London in 1959, but was brought up in Somerset. He attended the University of Sussex where he majored in English. At the end of the 1970s, he moved to London and began his career working in the theater and cabaret circles. He finished his first play, *Another England*, in 1980 which, along with a few others over the years, were produced by the Sheep Worrying Theatre Group, at the Arts Centre, Bridgewater. To bolster his income, Newman also played the kazoo in a cabaret band.

In the early 1980s he also wrote several short stories, some of which were published, and numerous scripts for radio and **television**. His first book, *Ghastly Beyond Belief: The Science Fiction and Fantasy Book of Quotations*, written with Neil Gaiman, appeared in 1985. Over the next decade he contributed widely to various literary reference books and his broad knowledge of the horror field led to his first award-winning book, *Horror: 100 Best Books* (with Stephen Jones, 1988), which received the Bram Stoker Award as the year's Best Non-fiction Title. Additional reference titles include *Nightmare Movies: A Critical History of the Horror Film Since 1968* (1988) and the *BFI Companion to Horror* (1996).

Newman's first vampire novel, *Bad Dreams*, appeared in 1990, and over the next few years he established himself in the horror field as a fiction writer of note. His talent was confirmed in 1992 with the appearance of the alternative history volume *Anno-Dracula*, which hypothesized a future for England if the characters in **Bram Stoker**'s novel had been real and if Dracula had won. The volume won three awards: The Children of the Night Award (**The Dracula Society**) for Best Novel (1992); the fiction award of **The Lord Ruthven Assembly** (1994); and the International Horror Critics' Guild Award for Best Novel (1994). It was followed by a sequel, *The Bloody Red Baron* (1994), which followed an alternative history through World War I.

In the meantime, under the pseudonym Jack Yeovil, Newman has written a set of novels including several based on the Warhammer **games**. Of his Yeovil novels, three feature vampires: *Warhammer: Drachenfels* (1989), *Orgy of the Blood Parasites* (1994), and *Warhammer: Genevieve Undead* (1993).

Sources:

Newman, Kim. *Nightmare Movies: A Critical History of the Horror Film Since 1968*. London: Bloomsbury, 1988.

———. *Bad Dreams*. London: Simon & Schuster, 1990. Rept. New York: Carroll & Graf, 1991. 316 pp. Rept. London: Grafton, 1992. 316 pp.

———. *Anno-Dracula*. London: Simon & Schuster, 1992. 359 pp. Rept. New York: Carroll & Graf, 1993.

———. *Warhammer: Drachenfels*. Brighton, East Sussex, UK: GW Books, 1989. 247 pp. Rept. London: Boxtree, 1993. 257 pp.

———. *Warhammer: Genevieve Undead*. London: Boxtree Limited, 1993. 357 pp.

———, ed. *BFI Companion to Horror*. UK: Cassell Academic, 1996.

———. *The Bloody Red Baron*. New York: Carroll & Graf, 1995. 358 pp.

———. *Dead Travel Fast*. New York: Dinoship, 2005. 321 pp.

———. *Orgy of the Blood Parasites*. London: Pocket Books, 1994. 224 pp.

———, and Neil Gaiman. *Ghastly Beyond Belief: The Science Fiction and Fantasy Book of Quotations*. London: Arrow, 1985.

❦ *The Night Stalker* ❦

The Night Stalker was a highly successful made-for-**television** vampire movie produced by **Dan Curtis** in the wake of his successful vampire-oriented soap opera, **Dark Shadows**. The story concerned a luckless reporter, Carl Kolchak, (Darren McGavin) who encountered a vampire named Janos Skorzeny (Barry Atwater) who was killing showgirls in Las Vegas. He tried to convince his editor and the police of the vampiric nature of the killer, but in their disbelief he was left to confront the bloodsucker by himself. The show was notable in that it received the highest rating of any made-for-television movie to that date and led to *The Night Stalker* television series, in which

Kolchak tracked down a variety of creatures of the night including a vampire created by Skorzeny who subsequently moved to Los Angeles. **Richard Matheson** wrote the screenplay for the debut episode, which aired January 11, 1972 on ABC. The original novel by Jeff Rice, upon which the movie was based, was published in 1974. Kolchak has been kept alive into the new century in reprint editions of the original novels and new graphic novel adventures from Moonstone publishing. The original television movie and series are available on DVD.

Sources:

Dawidziak, Mark. *The Night Stalker Companion: A 25th Anniversary Tribute.* Beverley Hills, CA: Pomegranate Press, 1997. 206 pp.

Rice, Jeff. *The Night Stalker.* New York: Pocket Books, 1974. 192 pp. Rept. In *The Kolchak Papers: The Original Novels.* Chicago: Moonstone (November 21, 2007).

Nightlore *see:* Vampire Fandom: United States

Darren McGavin as reporter Carl Kolchak in *The Night Stalker*.

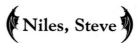

Niles, Steve

Steve Niles burst upon the **comic book** world in 2002 with his successful comic book series *30 Days of Night*. Written by Niles, with the collaboration of artist Ben Templesmith, the story opined about happenings when a small town in remote Alaska where there was a month without **sunlight** was cutoff and attacked by vampires. Niles's story of the horrific zombie-like vampires was perfectly complemented by Templesmith's rendering of a night world where the only whiteness was the vampires' mouths of sharp teeth.

Niles was born in Jackson, New Jersey, on June 21, 1965. He grew up in suburban Washington, D.C., in an environment informed by comic books and punk rock. For a short period he was in a punk rock band. He also credits Washington's television horror host Count Gore De Vol, as influencing his interest in vampire lore.

In the late-1980s, while still in Washington, Niles formed Arcane Comix, an independent graphic arts publishing concern, through which he published several works he edited. At the beginning of the 1990s he moved to California and began to write for different comics publishing houses most notably Fantaco/Tundra and Eclipse Comics. Then at the beginning of the twentieth century, he began working with IDW, a new comic book publisher based in San Diego. Niles had done a four-issue adaptation of **Richard Matheson**'s *I Am Legend* for Eclipse. His first work for IDW became the collection of the four issues to produce a black-and-white graphic novel (1991). *30 Days of Night* then became the IDW's first comic book series—a series of a mere three issues.

The series became an immediate success and heralded the birth of a new force in horror writing (while at the same time serving as a notable start to Templesmith, who was working his first job as a comic artist). The pair moved on to work together in two further series *Criminal Macabre* (for Dark Horse) and *Dark Days*. *Criminal Macabre* centered on the drug-addicted detective Cal McDonald who operates in a world inhabited by **ghouls** and vampires. He eventually becomes a vampire himself. Niles had introduced the character in some stories that appeared in his Arcane Comix anthologies and later in the Dark Horse anthology *Dark Horse Presents*. In 2002, Niles had issued two Cal McDonald novels, *Savage Membrane* and *Guns, Drugs and Monsters*. The novels set the stage for further comics, the 2003 Dark Horse series with Templesmith, a 2004 sequel, *Last Train to Deadsville* (Image), and a 2005 series *Supernatural Freak Machine: A Cal McDonald Mystery* (IDW).

Meanwhile, the success of *30 Days of Night* led to its first sequel, *Dark Days*. By this time, Niles had become a star within the horror writing community, and he has gone on to write a series of successful comics while the writing of numerous *30 Days of Night* miniseries sequels have been turned over to new writers and artists. Niles would do two *Annuals* (2004, 2005); *30 Days of Night: Return to Barrow* (2004); *30 Days of Night: Dead Space* (2006); and *30 Days of Night: Eben and Stella* (2007). Meanwhile, other writers tried their hand with *30 Days of Night: Spreading the Disease* (2006) and *30 Days of Night: Dust to Dust* (2008). Additional vampire titles among the many works Niles has written include *Aleister Arcane* (2004), *The Cryptics* (2006), and *City of Others*, a zombie story with vampires (2007).

In 2007, *30 Days of Night* finally made it to the screen as a successful horror movie. By 2009, it had emerged as the twelfth highest grossing vampire movie in history. A sequel and a *Criminal Macabre* movie remain a possibility. That same year, *I Am Legend* was made into a movie starring Will Smith. Niles counts Richard Matheson as the single greatest influence on his writing career and jumped at the chance to participate in the promotional comic *I Am Legend: Awakening*, produced by DC Vertigo and distributed at the San Diego Comicon. The movie also led to a third printing of his IDW graphic novel of *I Am Legend*.

Sources:

Bostaph, Melissa. "Interview with Steve Niles." Dread Central.com. Posted at http://www.dread-central.com/interviews/niles-steve-30-days-night. Accessed on April 10, 2010.

Niles, Steve. *Guns, Drugs, and Monsters*. San Diego, CA: IDW Publishing, 2002. 197 pp.

———. *Dial M for Murder: a Collection of Cal McDonald Mystery Stories*. San Diego: IDW Publishing, 2003. 192 pp.

———. *Guns, Drugs, and Monsters*. Book 2: Cal McDonald, Monster Hunter. New York: iBooks, Inc., 2005. 224 pp.

———. *Savage Membrane*. New York: iBooks, 2005. 199 pp.

———. *Criminal Macabre: The Complete Cal McDonald Stories*. Milwaukie, OR: Dark Horse Comics, 2007. 419 pp.

———, and Jeff Mariotte. *30 Days of Night: Rumors of the Undead*. New York: Pocket Star Books, 2006. 401 pp.

———. *Immortal Remains: 30 Days of Night*. New York: Pocket Star Books, 2007. 384 pp.

Njetop *see:* Poland, Vampires in

Nodier, Charles (1780–1844)

Jean Charles Nodier, a dramatist who introduced the vampire theme to the French stage, was born on April 29, 1780, in Basancon, France. As a young man he began his writing career and became politically involved. In 1818, Nodier settled in Paris where he remained for the rest of his life. That same year, *Jean Shogar*, his first novel, was published. In Paris he became associated with several authors who were exploring what, in the post–Freudian world, would be known as the subconscious. His literary works began to explore the world of dreams, and included some attention to the nightmare. The larger movement would become known as the romantic movement and was seen as a distinct reaction to the limitations of the rationalism typified by Voltaire and his colleagues of the previous generation.

Nodier had just settled into his life in Paris when, in April 1819, **John Polidori**'s short story "The Vampyre," appeared in the *New Monthly Magazine*. The story attracted considerable attention, in part because of its initial attribution to **Lord Byron**. Nodier was asked to write a review of it. He saw in the tale the expression of a widespread need in his generation to relieve its boredom through the experience of the outrageous and fantastic. The review was the first manifestation of a love-hate relationship with the vampire. Although Nodier seemed fascinated with it, he also saw a need, as an up-and-coming leader in Parisian literary and intellectual circles, to show a certain disdain. He did recognize its importance and termed the legend of the vampire "the most important of all our superstitions." In an 1819 article, he called his readers' attention to the stories of people who confessed to being vampires and doing horrible things during their sleeping hours.

In 1820, his colleague Cyprien Bérard's two-volume sequel to "The Vampyre," *Lord Ruthven ou Les Vampires*, was published anonymously but included an introductory article by Nodier. Many then assumed that Nodier had written both **Lord Ruthven** tales. After some investigation, Bérard's authorship was discovered. Meanwhile, Nodier was at work on his own vampire production, a stage melodrama called *Le Vampire*, (Pierre François Carmouche and Achille de Jouffroy collaborated on the piece). In *Le Vampire*, Nodier presented his own interpretation of Lord Ruthven, the lead character in Polidori's tale.

Ruthven was introduced as the hero who had saved the life of Sir Aubrey. Aubrey believed him dead, but when Ruthven arrived on the scene to marry Malvina, Aubrey's sister, he was welcomed. Meanwhile, Ruthven was shot while attending the wedding feast of Lovette and Edgar after Edgar had been angered at Ruthven's attempts to seduce his wife-to-be. Again, Aubrey thought Ruthven was dying and swore not to tell Malvina about his actions. As Aubrey was about to tell Malvina about her fiance's death, Ruthven suddenly appeared and reminded Aubrey of his oath. Aubrey was momentarily lost in the conflict between his duty and his oath, and Ruthven moved on to the church with his prospective **bride**, Malvina. Ruthven was foiled only in the last moment when Aubrey came to his senses and interrupted the service.

Le Vampire opened on June 13, 1819, at the Theatre de la Porte-Saint-Martin. Despite mixed reviews, some by his **political** detractors, Nodier's **drama** was an immediate success. The text of the play was soon published and also found a popular audience. In the wake of the immense audience reaction, two other vampire plays soon opened at competing theatres—as did several comical and satirical plays lampooning it. *Le Vampire* had a long and successful run; in 1823, it was revived for a second long run with the same stars,

Monsieur Phillipe and Madame Dorval. **Alexandre Dumas** attended the revival. He included a lengthy account of the performance in his memoirs, and the play would later inspire his own vampire drama in the 1850s. Nodier returned to the subjects of nightmares and vampires in his opium-inspired 1821 story, *Smarra; ou, Les Demons de la Nuit*. Opium, he believed, provided a gate to another world—the realm of dreams and nightmares. *Smarra* told the story of Lorenzo, who experienced an encounter with a vampire. However, the vampire was not Lord Ruthven, the almost human creature who mingled in society and delighted in destroying others, but more of a spirit-like creature of the dream world.

Among Nodier's Paris acquaintances in the early 1820s was the youthful Victor Hugo, who published his first novel, a **gothic** horror story titled *Hans de'Islande*, in 1823. *Hans de'Islande* (*Hans of Iceland*) featured a central character who consumed the **blood** of his **victims**, but did so by gathering and then drinking the blood in a skull as an act of revenge. Although Nodier tried to validate the horror fantasy realm as a reasonable one for a neophyte writer to explore, Hugo explicitly denounced *Le Vampire* in a review of the play's opening. Nodier had the opportunity to review *Hans de'Islande* and gave it a sympathetic review, calling attention to Hugo's latent talent.

In 1824, in recognition of his work (especially that devoted to the vampire theme), Nodier was appointed curator of the Bibliotheque de l'Arsenal, one of Paris's outstanding libraries. He later founded a salon where the literary world gathered and he authored a number of works, the best being his many short stories that explored the fantasy world of dreams, both good and bad. A 13-volume collected work was published during the years 1832–1841. In 1833, he was elected to the French Academy. He died January 27, 1844. Throughout the nineteenth century, many writers were inspired by Nodier's fantastic tales and he eventually found a new audience in the French surrealists. Recently, *Le Vampire* and other of Nodier's dramatic works were reprinted in the "Textes Littéraires Francais" series. An English translation of his vampire play is available on the Internet at http://www.munseys.com/diskone/vampnod.pdf.

Sources:

Nelson, Hilda. *Charles Nodier*. New York: Twayne Publishers, 1972. 188 pp.

Nodier, Charles. *Le Vampire*. Edition critique par Ginette Picat-Guinoiseau. Geneva: Librairie Droz S. A., 1990. 255 pp.

Oliver, A. Richard. *Charles Nodier: Pilot of Romanticism*. Syracuse, NY: Syracuse University Press, 1964. 276 pp.

Pavicevic, Mylena. *Charles Nodier et le Theme du Vampire*. Ottawa, ON: Biblioteque Nationale du Canada, 1988.

Stuart, Roxana. *Stage Blood: Vampires of the 19th-Century Stage*. Bowling Green, OH: Bowling Green University Popular Press, 1994. 377 pp.

Nora *see:* Hungary, Vampires in

Norway, Vampires in *see:* Scandinavia, Vampires in

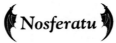

Nosferatu

Nosferatu is a modern word derived from Old Slavonic word, *nesufur-atu*, borrowed from the Greek *nosophoros*, a "plague carrier." Vampires were associated in the pop-

The frightening and disturbing Graf Orlock (Max Schreck) in *Nosferatu, Eine Symphonie des Grauens.*

ular mind with the spread of disease (such as tuberculosis whose cause was otherwise unknown) and by, extension with the idea of spreading the infection of vampirism through its bite. It is not a Romanian word, and it is not found in Romanian dictionaries. It was originally a technical term in the old Slavonic that filtered into common speech. It has erroneously been reported to mean "undead," a concept developed by **Bram Stoker** for *Dracula* **(1897)**, and elsewhere as a reference to the devil. It appears to have entered literature through the popular travelogue of Emily Gerard's *The Land Beyond the Forest* (1885) in which she said, "More decidedly evil is the *nosferatu*, or vampire, in which every Romanian peasant believes as he does in heaven or hell." From Gerard, Stoker picked up the term for *Dracula*. In his famous determinative speech on the vampire in chapter 18, **Abraham Van Helsing** said, "The *nosferatu* do not die like the bee when he stings once. He is only stronger; and being stronger, have yet more power to work evil." The term, though used by Stoker, is not prominent.

The term first gained real prominence when it was used by Freidrich Wilhelm Murnau in his attempt to create a disguised version of *Dracula* for the screen. Murnau's film, ***Nosferatu, Eine Symphonie des Grauens***, made the term part of the popular language about vampires, especially after its rediscovery in the 1960s and the new release in 1972. Over the last several decades, it has commonly appeared in novels and films as a term synonymous with the vampire. In his two books about vampires, **Leonard Wolf** relied on Gerard, repeated her mistakes, and then contributed one of his own when he said in his *The Annotated Dracula* that *nosferatu* was a Romanian word meaning "not dead."

Sources:

Gerard, Emily. *The Land Beyond the Forest*. 1885. 2 vols. Edinburgh & London: Will Blackwood & Sons, 1888.

Senn, Harry A. *Were-Wolf and Vampire in Romania*. New York: Columbia University Press, 1982. 148 pp.

Stoker, Bram. *The Annotated Dracula*. Edited by Leonard Wolf. New York: Clarkson N. Porter, 1974. Rept. New York: Ballantine, 1976. 362 pp.

Wolf, Leonard. *A Dream of Dracula: In Search of the Living Dead*. Boston, MA: Little Brown, 1972. Rept. New York: Popular Library, 1977. 326 pp.

❨ *Nosferatu, Eine Symphonie des Grauens* ❩

The earliest surviving film based on **Dracula (1897)** is *Nosferatu, Eine Symphonie des Grauens* (*Nosferatu, a Symphony of Horrors*), an unauthorized 1922 adaptation of **Bram Stoker**'s novel by Prana-Film, a German company founded in 1921. The movie was the only finished product of the company. One of the company's co-directors, Albin Grau, was a spiritualist and familiar with *Dracula*. He saw the book's possibilities for presentation as a powerful motion picture. Grau hired Friedrich Wilhelm Murnau (1888–1931) as director and Henrik Galeen as screenwriter.

Murnau and Galeen proceeded to make a very loose adaptation of *Dracula*. The title was changed to *Nosferatu*, a term derived from an Old Slavonic word, *nosufur-atu*, a word borrowed from the Greek and tied to the concept of carrying a plague. The location for the latter part of the story was changed to Bremen, **Germany**, and set in 1838, the year of an actual outbreak of the plague in that city. The **Dracula** character's appearance was altered to appear rodent-like, and his persona tied to the rats who gathered in great numbers in Bremen when he arrived.

In the screenplay, Murnau made a variety of additional changes, including the names of all of the leading characters. Dracula was transformed into **Graf Orlock**, played by **Max Schreck**. Orlock was developed into a monstrous figure with exaggerated features—a bald head, long, claw-like **fingernails**. His pair of vampire **fangs**, rather than being elongated canines, protruded from the very front of his mouth, like a rat's teeth. He walked with a slow labored gait and wore a long coat. He was closer to the vampire of Eastern European folklore than Stoker's *Dracula*, but his distinct appearance meant that he was unable to easily move among normal society in the manner of Dracula. Thus, Orlock became, to some extent, a very different character.

In *Nosferatu* **Jonathan Harker** (renamed Waldemar Hutter and played by Gustav von Wangenheim) left his wife **Mina Murray** (renamed Ellen Hutter and played by Greta Schroeder-Matray) to travel to **Transylvania** to conduct the sale of a house next door to their home in Germany. Hutter was taken to a bridge and left there. Upon crossing the bridge, it was as if he had entered a new world. A coach with a mysterious driver

met him to take him to Orlock's castle. In his bedroom at Orlock's castle, Hutter was bitten by Orlock, while back in Bremen Ellen simultaneously cried out Hutter's name. The next day, Hutter discovered Orlock's **coffin**, but it was too late—the vampire was already on his way to Germany.

While Orlock traveled to Germany, the major characters (soon to assemble in Bremen) were shown acting independently of each other. First, Hutter escaped but was hospitalized. Hutter's boss, **R. N. Renfield** (renamed Knock, played by Alexander Granach), went mad and was confined to an asylum. Professor **Abraham Van Helsing** (renamed Bulwar, played by John Gottow) experimented in his laboratory with a meat-eating plant, a "vampire of the vegetable kingdom." Orlock killed the crew on the ship that was carrying him to Bremen.

Upon the Count's arrival in Bremen, a plague broke out in the city caused by the rats Orlock controlled. Hutter arrived with a book he had taken from the castle. It suggested that the way to defeat a vampire was through the sacrifice of a virtuous woman who allowed the vampire to remain with her until dawn. In the end, Orlock attached himself to Ellen's neck and stayed until the **sunlight** destroyed him. Ellen died from the sacrifice, and immediately the plague abated.

Later Controversy: *Nosferatu, Eine Symphonie des Grauens* premiered in the Marble Gardens of the Berlin Zoological Gardens in March 1922. The movie received good reviews initially. However, Prana-Film was financially unstable and unpaid creditors soon asserted themselves. Several weeks later, Florence Stoker, the widow of Bram Stoker, received a copy of the announcement of the film's premier. She immediately joined the British Incorporated Society of Authors and turned to it for assistance. Because Prana-Film had neglected either to ask permission to use her late husband's book or to pay her for using it, the society represented her. It presented the matter to its German lawyer. By June, the company was in receivership and it was clear that no money would result from pursuing the case. However, the society continued to press the matter because of its implications for later cases.

The case with the receivers, Deutsch-Amerikansch Film Union, dragged on for several years. Florence Stoker asked for the destruction of all copies of the film. The matter was finally settled in July 1925, when all copies owned by the German receivers were destroyed. However, in October of that year, she was contacted by a new organization in England. The Film Society solicited her support for its private screenings of "classic" movies. On its first list was *Nosferatu* by Murnau. She now had a dispute with the society, which initially refused to cancel its showing or tell her where they had obtained a copy of the film.

In 1928, **Universal Pictures** purchased the film rights of *Dracula*. As owners of the film rights, they then granted the Film Society the privilege of showing *Nosferatu*. Florence Stoker protested, and in 1929, the Film Society turned over its copy to her for destruction. Later that year, copies appeared in the United States in New York and Detroit under the title *Nosferatu the Vampire*. In 1930, these copies were turned over to Universal to also be destroyed.

After Florence Stoker's death in 1937, various versions of the film became available, though there was little demand for it. In the 1960s, a condensed version was aired on **television** as part of *Silents Please*, a show based on old silent movies. In this version,

the characters' names were changed back to those in the Stoker novel and the name of the movie was changed to *Dracula*. This version was then released by Entertainment Films under the title *Terror of Dracula*. In 1972, Blackhawk Films released the original film to the collectors' market under the title *Nosferatu the Vampire* and the *Silents Please* version as *Dracula*. In spite of the destruction of most of the copies of the original *Nosferatu*, one copy did survive, and a restored version of the film was finally screened in 1984 at the Berlin Film Festival and has since become commonly available.

A sound remake of *Nosferatu, Die Zwolfte Stunde: Eine Nacht Des Grauens*, appeared in 1930 by Deutsche Film and was probably made without Murnau's knowledge. The film gives a reference to "artistic adaptation" by a Dr. Waldemar Roger who apparently re-edited the original film with some of Murnau's discarded footage and then added a dance scene and a death mass. The censors later cut the death mass due to religious objections, but unlike the original, the film ended on a happy note.

In 1979, a remake of *Nosferatu* was produced. *Nosferatu: The Vampyre* featured Klaus Kinski in the title role. The new movie was written, produced, and directed by Werner Herzog. Although it kept the distinctive aspects of the original story line, it more clearly acknowledged its basis as a version of *Dracula*, in part by using the names of the characters in Stoker's novel.

Nosferatu: The Vampyre was one of three important vampire movies released in 1979. The other two were *Love at First Bite*, the Dracula spoof with George Hamilton, and the **Frank Langella** version of **Dracula (1979).** The movie inspired a novel based on the screenplay, and a phonographic recording of the movie soundtrack was issued.

In 2000, director E. Elias Merhige's *Shadow of the Vampire* told the saga of the making of Murnau's 1922 original *Nosferatu* with one crucial change: Max Schreck was an actual vampire. According to Merhige's version, Murnau (John Malkovich) secretly hired Schreck (Willem Dafoe), a sniveling rodent-like demon in a long coat who occasionally lunches on the film's cast and crew. One of the movie's producers was Nicolas Cage.

Sources:

Ashbury, Roy. *Nosferatu*. London: York Press, 2001. 86 pp.

"Classic Horror Movies with The Missing Link," Posted at http://www.classichorror.free-online.co.uk/index.htm. Accessed on April 10, 2010.

Glut, Don. *The Dracula Book*. Metuchen, NJ: Scarecrow Press, 1975. 388 pp.

Holte, James Craig. *Dracula in the Dark: The Dracula Film Adaptations*. Westport, CT: Greenwood Press, 1997. 161 pp.

Leous, Gus. "Enigmatic Max Schreck." *Newsfinder: A Literary Favour to World Culture*. Posted at http://www.newsfinder.org/site/more/enigmatic_max_schreck/. Accessed on April 10, 2010.

Prawer, S. S. *Nosferatu: Phantom der Nacht*. Ser.: BFI Film Classics. British Film Institute, 2004. 96 pp.

Skal, David J. *Hollywood Gothic: The Tangled Web of Dracula from Novel to Stage to Screen*.

Obayifo *see:* Africa, Vampires in
Old House Publishing *see:* Dark Shadows Fandom

Oldman, Gary (1958–)

Gary Oldman, the actor who portrayed the title role in **Francis Ford Coppola**'s production of *Bram Stoker's Dracula*, was born in London, England. His dramatic career began at age 17 when he applied for a position at a theatre near his home. After hearing him read a passage from Shakespeare, the theatre's director assumed a mentor's role for Oldman. Once he broke into movies, Oldman quickly became known within the professional community for his ability and the wide range of characters he portrayed. He played Sid Vicious in *Sid and Nancy*; Joe Orton in *Prick Up Your Ears*; and Lee Harvey Oswald in Oliver Stone's *JFK*.

The role of **Dracula** allowed Oldman to show the broad range of his acting abilities, as he had to portray the variant personas into which Dracula transformed. He was first Prince **Vlad the Impaler**, the young warrior who won the war but, in a nasty twist of fate, lost his love. He was then the aged nobleman, the undead ruler of **Castle Dracula**. Once in England, Dracula's **animal** persona came to the fore, first as a monstrous wolflike creature (harking back to the identification of vampires and **werewolves** in Slavic folklore) that attacked **Lucy Westenra**, then as a batlike creature that opposed the men united against him. Meanwhile, he periodically reappeared as the handsome young suitor of **Mina Murray** that vied for her love until she married **Jonathan Harker**. The very nature of the part prevented Oldman from being typecast in the role. Since *Bram Stoker's Dracula*, Oldman has remained active starring or co-starring in two to three movies annually.

Sources:
Rohrer, Trish Deitch. "Gary Oldman." *Entertainment Weekly* No. 145 (November 20, 1992): 32–34.

Gary Oldman (with Winona Ryder) as Dracula in
Bram Stoker's Dracula.

Onyx *see:* Vampire Fandom: United States

Opera

Following the publication of **John Polidori**'s initial vampire story, and its popularization by being adapted for the stage in **France**, it was also adapted for the stage in **Germany** by Heinrich Ludwig Ritter under the title *Der Vampyr, oder die todten Braut* in 1821. It was this German play that then became the basis of the script written by Wilhelm August Wohlbrück, which Heinrick August Marshner (1795–1861) turned into the first vampire opera. *Der Vampyr* premiered in Leipzig on March 28, 1828.

Following Ritter's lead, the Wohlbrück script has **Lord Ruthven** meet the (**Satan**-like) Vampyrmeister to beg for more time on earth. He is given a deal—he can have three more years if he brings the Vampyrmeister three virgin **brides**. He celebrates his first kill with a light song about the joy of killing. He then kills Emmy and goes after Malwine as his third. Introduced to Malwine's family as the Earl von Marsden, he attempts to draw the young woman away from Aubrey her true love. Aubry is helpless because of an oath previously made to Lord Ruthven, which, if he breaks, will cause him to become a vampire. However, Ruthven is ultimately thwarted.

Marshner's work was quickly followed by a similar adaptation, also named *Der Vampyr*, by **Peter Josef von Lindpainter** (1791–1856). The script, by Caesar Max Heigel, follows closely the plot of **Charles Nodier**'s prior Parisian production, even though the characters' names are shifted around. The vampire has, for example, become known as Graf Aubri. Lindpainter's opera has been largely forgotten, while Marshner's was produced for the first time in England in 1829, and in recent decades in London in 1976. In 1992 the British Broadcasting Company filmed a version of the opera (with a new script by Charles Hart), which played on American **television** and has been released on CD and video. Marshner's opera was also revived for a performance in Boston in 1980. (A list of recent public performances can be found http://www.operone.de/opern/vampyr.html.)

Following the German productions of the 1820s, the genre seems to have exhausted itself as a subject for opera. However, there were a number of attempts to turn the vampire play into a musical. Various productions added songs and Gilbert and Sullivan produced their own vampire operetta, *Ruddigore*, which enjoyed a successful run after its opening in January of 1887. Like all of their work, *Ruddigore* was a satire, in this case of **Dion Boucicault**'s *The Vampire*. Throughout the twentieth century, a host of Dracula musicals have been written and staged, including *Seven Brides for Dracula* by Tim Kelly and Larry Nestor, *Count Dracula, or A Musical Mania from Transylvania* by

Lawrence O'Dwyer (1974), *Dracula* by Kingsley Day (1978), and *My Fair Dracula* by William Lockwood and Franklyn J. Wyka (1996). However, opera seems to be the one contemporary media that has chosen not to take a bite out of the Vampire Lord.

Sources:

Stuart, Roxanne. *Stage Blood: Vampires of the 19th-Century Stage*. Bowling Green, OH: Bowling Green State University Popular Press, 1984. 377 pp.

Order of the Vampyre

The Order of the Vampyre is part of the Temple of Set, a religious institution dedicated to and consecrated by Set, an ancient Egyptian god who was later adapted into the "**Satan**" of the Jewish and Christian traditions. Hence, the Temple of Set is popularly known as a "Satanic" religion, although its initiates consider themselves "Setians," a more precise description. The Temple was founded in 1975 by priests of the Church of Satan (founded in 1966) who had decided to carry forward the serious work of the Church in a more historic, less anti-Christian context. Like its parent body, the Temple of Set is a strictly ethical and law-abiding institution. It is configured as an "umbrella" organization that has a number of specialized "orders" whose members concentrate on specific areas of research and black magic applications of the results of that research. It views vampirism as a kind of extension of human consciousness into extremes of human desires and behavior. It is the purpose of the Order of the Vampyre not merely to illustrate (or caricature) these extremes, as artists and novelists regularly do, but rather to identify and understand them. These extremes are the "rages of the raw human soul" that have been all but completely suppressed by the mind's fear of looking deep within itself.

Initiates of the order are encouraged to apply aspects of the "vampyric existence" to their conscious existence. They become, in effect, "vampires" who are sensitive in the extreme to the pleasure and pain of life and very much aware of how different they are compared to "normal" humanity. In this process, the initiates do not drink the **blood** of or otherwise harm humans or other **animals** in any way. Rather, an initiate sees, hears, feels, and lives acutely—both positively and negatively. They bring to bear extraordinary powers of imagination and visualization as well as creation and appreciation of thematic art, **music**, and literature. Thus, like vampires of fiction, the initiate is more vital than humanity in general.

The environment of the Order of the Vampyre is described as exhilarating, but also stressful and hence not appropriate for many people—not even the majority of Setians. Admission to the order is by invitation only to Setians who have attained at least the standing of Adept II within the Temple of Set. Membership is international, and the order holds meetings and activities on its own and in conjunction with the regional, national, and international conclaves of the Temple of Set. The Order is currently led by Lady Lilith Aquino, the wife of Michael Aquino, the founder of the Temple of Set, and Magister William T. Butch. The order may be contacted through the office of the Temple of Set at PO Box 470307, San Francisco, CA 94147. It has an Internet presence at http://www.xeper.org/ovampyre/.

Sources:

Aleiss, Angela. "Vampires: The Bloody Truth." Religion News Service, November 18, 2000.

Beliefnet. Posted at http://www.beliefnet.com/Faiths/2000/11/Vampires-The-Bloody-Truth.aspx. Accessed on April 10, 1010.

The Crystal Tablet of Set. San Francisco, CA: Temple of Set, 1989.

Dresser, Norine. *American Vampires: Fans, Victims, Practitioners.* New York: W. W. Norton & Company, 1989. 255 pp.

❨ Ordo Strigoi Vii ❩

The Ordo Strigoi Vii is a loosely organized vampire association founded by Father Sebastian (b. Aaron Todd Hoyt), a.k.a. Father Sebastiaan Tod Van Houten. According to Sabastiaan, he learned about vampires in the mid-1990s while working a Renaissance Faire. A Romanian associate at the faire gave him a copy of *The Vampire Bible* published by the **Temple of the Vampire** but hinted at a Romanian origin for a vampire he beheaded. Following his contact's death in 1996, Sebastian founded the Ordo Strigoi.

Father Sebastiaan and the Ordo Strigoi Vii have roots in the role-playing **game** community. Sebastian was involved with a role-playing group called the "The Long Black Veil" which mixed the writings of **Vampire: the Masquerade** and then fellow-gamer **Michelle Belanger**. In the early days of the Ordo Strigoi Vii, he took the rules of players in *Vampire: the Masquerade* and published them as a set of guidelines for real vampires. These rules were later extensively edited by Belanger and emerged as the Black Veil, a set of rules now widely acknowledged by contemporary self-identified vampires.

As Sebastiaan played at being a vampire and learned about reputedly real vampires, he began to organize a vampire community in New York, using the name The Sanguinarium as an umbrella name. The Sanguinarium, which slowly morphed into the Ordo Strigoi Vii, began to network with vampires and vampire groups across the United States.

While resembling the Temple of the Vampire in some aspects, Sebastiaan tried to create a much more open and accessible group. He modeled it on a think tank where people could gather do discuss their vampiric nature. He also absented himself for periods of time so it did not become centered on him. Members seek development of their potential and personal evolution and work at cultivating "the dragon," an individual's highest potential. Members also attempt contact with disembodied entities, the "strigoi morte," former human beings who now survive as something like a ghost or thought-form. Included among these disembodied entities is a collective thought-form called Elorath. Though not a deity, Elorath has some deific characteristics. The Ordo Strigoi Vii believe that vampire are pre-selected by specific characteristics, but basically are made, as they work to develop their vampire nature.

Father Sebastiaan currently (2009) resides in Paris, France. He has authored one book, with vampire researcher Katherine Ramsland, that was sold with a metal replica of the modified ankh with a **bat** that is the symbol of the Ordo Strigoi Vii.

Sources:

Laycock, Joseph. *Vampires Today: The Truth about Modern Vampirism.* Westport. CT: Praeger, 2009. 200 pp.

Sebastiaan, Father. *Vampyre Almanac 2000*. New York: The Sanguinarian, 2000. 144 pp.
———, and Katherine Ramsland. *Vampire Almanac: 1998–1999 Edition*. New York: Endless
    Night, 1998. 180 pp.

Oregon Dark Shadows Society   *see:* Dark Shadows Fandom

Origins of the Vampire

How did vampires originate? If vampires did (or do) exist, where did they come from?
The answers to these questions have varied widely as the vampire has appeared in
the folklore of different countries and various fiction writers have speculated on the nature of vampirism.

The Folkloric Vampire: The vampire figure in folklore emerged as an answer to
otherwise unsolvable problems within culture. The vampire was seen as the cause of
certain unexplainable evils, accounted for the appearance of some extraordinary occurrences within the society, and was often cited as the end product of immoral behavior.
The earliest vampires seem to have originated as an explanation of problems in childbirth. For example, the *langsuyar*—the primary vampire figure of **Malaysia**—was a beautiful young woman who had given birth to a stillborn child. Upon hearing of her child's
fate, she clapped her hands and flew away into the trees. Henceforth, she attacked children and sucked their **blood**. A similar tale was told of the *lamiai*, the original vampire
of **Greece**. Just as tales of vampires were inspired by childbirth problems, they also originated from unusual circumstances surrounding births. Children who were different at
birth were considered to be vampire candidates. For example, among the Kashubian
people of **Poland**, children born with a membrane cap on their heads or with two teeth
were likely to become vampires unless dealt with properly while growing up.

Similarly, some vampires stories originated from problems surrounding the death
of a loved one. In eastern Europe, vampires were individuals who returned from the
grave to attack their spouses, their immediate families, and possibly other acquaintances
in the village. Symptoms of vampiric attack included nightmares, apparitions of the
dead, and the death of family members by a wasting disease (such as tuberculosis). Some
of the symptoms point to the vampire as a product of the grieving process, especially the
continued ties of the living to the dead, often taking the form of unfinished emotional
business. Thus, vampires were seen as originating from the failure of the family (in a
time before the existence of funeral parlors) to perform the funeral and burial rites with
exacting precision. A common event that allegedly led to the creation of a vampire was
allowing an **animal** such as a cat to jump over the body of a dead person prior to burial.

Vampirism was also caused by unexpected and sudden violent deaths, either from
accidents or **suicides**. Suicides were also part of a larger class of vampires that existed as
a result of the immoral behavior of the person who became a vampire. The vampire
served as an instrument of social control for the moral leaders of the community. Thus,
people who stepped outside of the moral and religious boundaries of the community not
only jeopardized their souls, but might become vampires. A potential vampire committed evil acts, among them suicide, and anyone guilty of great evil, especially of an anti-
social nature, was thought likely to become a vampire after death. In some Christian

countries, notably **Russia** and Greece, heresy could also lead to vampirism. The heretic was one type of person who died in a state of excommunication from the church. Excommunication could be pronounced for a number of unforgiven sins from actions directly attacking the church to more common immoralities such as adultery or murder. Heresy was also associated in some cultures with **witchcraft**, defined as consorting with **Satan** and/or the working of malevolent antisocial magic. Witches who practiced their craft in their earthly lives might become vampires after their deaths.

Vampire Contamination: After the first vampire was created, a community of vampires might soon follow. When a particular vampire figure, such as the original *lamiai*, took its place in the mythology of a people as a lesser deity or demon, they sometimes multiplied into a set of similar beings. Thus, Greek mythology posed the existence of numerous *lamiai*, a class of demonic entities. They were assumed to exist as part of the larger supernatural environment and, as such, the question of their origin was never raised. Also, such demonic entities did not create new vampires by attacking people. Their **victims** might suffer either physical harm or death as the result of the vampire's assault, but they did not become vampires. Things were quite different in eastern Europe. There, vampires were former members of the community. Vampires could draw other members of the community into their vampiric existence by contaminating former family and neighbors, usually by biting them. In the famous case of **Arnold Paul**, the vampiric state was passed by meat from cows that had been bitten by Paul.

The Literary Vampire: In the nineteenth century, the vampire figure was wrenched from its rural social context in eastern Europe and brought into the relatively secularized culture of western European cities. It was introduced into the romantic imagination of writers cut off from the mythological context in which the vampire originated. Those writers had to recreate a new context from the few bits of knowledge they possessed. In examining the few vampire cases at their disposal, most prominently the Arnold Paul case, they learned that vampires were created by people being bitten by other vampires.

The imaginary vampire of nineteenth-century romanticism was an isolated individual. Unlike the Eastern European vampire, the literary vampire did not exist in a village culture as a symbol warning residents of the dangerous and devilish life outside the boundaries of approved village life. The imaginary vampire was a victim of irresistible supernatural attack. Against their wills, they were overwhelmed by the vampiric state and, much like drug addicts, forced to live lives built around their blood lust. The majority of beliefs associated with the origins of vampires were irrelevant to the creators of the literary vampire, although on occasion one element might be picked up to give a novel twist to a vampire tale.

Underlying much of the modern vampire lore was the belief that vampires attacked humans and, through that attack, drew victims into their world. Again, like drug addicts might share an addiction and turn others into addicts, so the vampire infected nonvampires with their condition. Writers have generally suggested that vampires primarily, if not exclusively, created new vampires by their bites. The radical simplification of the vampire myth can be seen in *Dracula* (1897), especially its treatment on the stage and screen. **Bram Stoker** did not deal directly with the problem of **Dracula**'s origin as a vampire. In Dr. **Abraham Van Helsing** famous speech in chapter 18, where he described in some detail the nature of the vampire, he suggested that Dracula became a vampire because he "had dealings with the Evil One." More important, however, was his ability to transform people into vampires. Dracula's bite was a necessary part of that transmission, but, of itself, not sufficient. **Jonathan Harker** was bitten a number of times by the three vampire **women**, but did not become a vampire. On the other hand, **Lucy Westenra** did turn into a vampire and **Mina Murray** was in the process of being transformed into a vampire when the men interrupted Dracula. In the key scene in chapter 21, Dracula, having previously drunk Mina's blood, forced her to drink his. Thus, in *Dracula* new vampires originated not from the bite of the vampire but by an exchange of blood.

Bram Stoker had little material to draw upon in considering this point. The question was avoided by **John Polidori** in his original vampire story. ***Varney the Vampyre***, the subject of the 1840s novel, became a vampire as punishment for accidently killing his son, but the actual manner of **transformation** was not revealed. **Sheridan Le Fanu** was familiar with the folkloric tradition and suggested suicide as the cause of new vampires, but saw the death of a person previously bitten by a vampire as the basic means of spreading vampirism. His anti-heroine, **Carmilla** was the product of a vampire's bite.

In the rewriting of *Dracula* for screen and stage, the scene from the book during which Mina consumed Dracula's blood was deleted. It was considered too risqué, but without it some other means had to be found to transmit the vampiric state. Thus came the suggestion that merely the vampire's bite transmitted the condition—the common assumption in most vampire novels and movies. At times, vampires required multiple bites or the bite had to take enough blood to cause the death of the victim. While most vampire books and movies have not dealt with the question of vampire origins apart from the passing of the vampiric condition through the bite of a preexisting vampire, occasionally writers have attempted to create a vampire myth that covers the origin of the first vampire.

Among the more intriguing of recent origin stories was that told by **Anne Rice** in the third of her "Vampire Chronicles," ***The Queen of the Damned***. Akasha and her husband Enkil ruled as queen and king of ancient Egypt. At one point Akasha had two witches, Maharet and Mekere, brought to her court. They allowed her to see the world of spirits, but then one of the spirits, Amel, attacked her. Akasha turned on the two witches and in her rage ordered them raped publicly and then banished. However, both Akasha and Enkil were intrigued by the spirit world and began to explore it on their own. Meanwhile, an uprising occurred and the rulers were seriously wounded. Akasha's soul escaped from her body temporarily only to encounter the spirit Amel who joined himself to her. Her soul reentered her body and brought Amel with it. Fused with her brain and heart, the presence of Amel turned her into a vampire. She, in turn, passed the vampiric condition to Enkil and to their steward Khayman by the more traditional bite. All other vampires in the book, who originated from a vampire's bite, have a lineage that can ultimately be traced to these three first vampires.

The Vampire Bat: In chapter 12 of *Dracula*, Bram Stoker suggested, but did not  develop, the idea that vampire **bats** might ultimately be the cause of vampirism. **Quincey P. Morris** delivered a brief oration on his encounter with vampire bats in **South America**. Although vampire bats made numerous appearances in vampire lore—primarily as humans temporarily transformed into animal form—few writers developed the idea of vampirism originating with vampire bats.

Most prominent among the few stories in which vampirism originated with a bat was *Dark Shadows*. The *Dark Shadows* story line, took **Barnabas Collins** back to 1795 to his origin as a vampire. Spurning the witch Angelique's love for him, Barnabas wound up in a fight with her and shot her. Wounded and near death, she cursed Barnabas and a bat attacked him. He died from the bite and arose from the grave as a vampire. Subsequently, Barnabas created other vampires in the common manner—by biting them and draining their blood to the point of death.

The Science Fiction Vampire: A final option concerning the origin of vampires was derived from **science fiction**. As early as 1942 in his short story "Asylum," A. E. van Vogt suggested that vampires were an alien race who originated in outer space. The most successful of the **comic book** vampires, *Vampirella*, was a space alien. She originated on the planet Drakulon and came to earth to escape her dying planet. Ultimately, in the *Vampirella* story line, even Dracula was revealed to be an alien.

Science fiction also suggested a second origin for the vampire: disease. Not incompatible with either vampire bats or outer space aliens, disease (either in the form of germs or altered blood chemistry) provided a nonsupernatural explanation of the vampire's existence—an opinion demanded by many secularized readers or theater-goers. Disease explained the vampire's strange behavior, from its nocturnal existence to the "allergy" to **garlic** to its blood lust. This idea was explored most prominently in **Richard Matheson**'s *I Am Legend*. In the end, however, the science fiction space vampire was like its supernatural cousin. Whatever its origin, the vampire was the bearer—at least potentially—of its condition to anyone it attacked, and the vampire's bite was the most common way to spread vampirism.

Sources:

Ramsland, Katherine. *The Vampire Companion*. New York: Ballantine Books, 1993. 508 pp.

Rice, Anne. *The Queen of the Damned*. New York: Alfred A. Knopf, 1988. 448 pp.

Perkowski, Jan L. *The Darkling: A Treatise on Slavic Vampirism*. Columbus, OH: Slavica Publishers, 1989. 174 pp.

Scott, Kathryn Leigh, ed. *The Dark Shadows Companion: 25th Anniversary Collection*. Los Angeles: Pomegranate Press, 1990. 208 pp.

Summers, Montague. *The Vampire: His Kith and Kin*. London: Routledge, Kegan Paul, Trench, Trubner, & Co., 1928. 356 pp. Rept. New Hyde Park, NY: University Books, 1960. 356 pp.

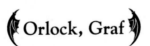 Orlock, Graf

The vampire Graf (or Count) Orlock (variously spelled Orlok, Orlac, or Orloc) first appeared in the 1922 German silent film *Nosferatu, Eine Symphonie des Grauens*. *Nosferatu* was a thinly veiled adaptation of **Bram Stoker**'s *Dracula* **(1897)**, but Prana-Films, the film's production company, neglected to gain permission from the author's widow to produce the movie. Director Frederich W. Murnau, changed the title, the setting, and the names of all of the leading characters of the novel. While keeping the basic story line, he thought he had altered it enough to be protected against charges of plagiarism. Such was not the case, however, and the film had only limited screenings before legal action was taken against it and most copies were destroyed. However, enough survived to alter the image of the vampire through the twentieth century.

Graf Orlock (Max Schreck), the Dracula-like vampire from the classic film *Nosferatu*.

Although British playwright **Hamilton Deane** made **Dracula** a character that could blend into proper British society—he wore formal evening clothes and showed few effects of having experienced death—Murnau made Count Orlock a far greater object of horror. Murnau, it seemed, drew on the tradition of European folklore to create a vampire who suffered from the effects of his encounter with death. Graf Orlock was given a rodent-like appearance with two **fangs** placed close together in the front of his mouth rather than elongated canine teeth. He was bald and his face was distorted into a parody of humanness. His fingers were extended and given a claw-like quality—a feature that was exaggerated through the course of the movie. He moved with slow deliberate steps.

Orlock assumed several **characteristics** not highlighted in *Dracula*. Dracula had some control over **animals**, especially wolves and **bats**. Orlock also had that control, but was focused on rats; wherever he chose to go, plague bearing rats were sure to congregate. Murnau changed the setting of his movie to Bremen in 1838 (rather than the 1890s) to coincide with the outbreak of plague in that town. Another key difference was that of **sunlight**. Dracula, while a creature of the night, could move about in the daytime. Orlock, on the other hand, was adversely affected by sunlight and could not be exposed to it at all. Also unlike Dracula, Orlock did cast a shadow and his image was reflected in glass. Murnau developed the idea that the vampire could be most effectively attacked if a virtuous woman held him enthralled at her side until sunrise. Orlock was thus finally killed by lingering in a woman's bedroom until the sun disintegrated him.

The Return of Orlock: Because of the lengthy legal proceedings during Florence Stoker's life, copies of *Nosferatu* did not begin to circulate until the 1960s. (However, enough was known about its plot that it possibly affected the ending of **Hammer Films'** first *Dracula* production, **The Horror of Dracula** (1958). (In that film, **Van Helsing** killed Dracula by exposing him to the morning sun by pulling the shade from a window.) The Orlock character did not make another appearance until 1979 when *Nosferatu: The Vampyre*, a remake of the first movie was made (Klaus Kinski assumed the title role). The new movie was written, produced, and directed by Werner Herzog. Although it kept the distinctive aspects of the original *Nosferatu* story line, it more clearly acknowledged its basis as a version of *Dracula*—in part by using the names of the characters in Stoker's novel. Orlock did not appear again until 1991 when three different **comic book** companies, operating in the midst of a revival of interest in the vampire, issued comic books inspired by his character. The first of these was issued by Tome Press and was a straight adaptation of the 1922 movie. *Nosferatu* by Dark Horse Comics was the translation of an apocalyptic vampire tale by French writer Philippe Druillet with an Orlocklike character, but little obvious relationship to *Dracula*. Druillet's work also appeared in a German translation.

The most ambitious of the three projects came from Millennium Publications, which issued a four-part series called *Nosferatu*. Author Mark Ellis provided a complete story of Graf Orlock's existence quite different from the *Dracula* legend and brought Orlock's menace into the present day. Graf Orlock was an eleventh-century nobleman whose estate was in the Carpathians. After Orlock became a vampire, he was eventually killed and his body sealed in the castle. An English knight returning from the crusades stopped at the castle. His squire freed Orlock, who was once again able to move about in human society. In the process the knight, William Longsword, was bitten. Following that incident, Orlock expressed his nature by causing wars and sending plagues. Longsword, who fought Orlock over the centuries, finally caught up with him in contemporary Brooklyn, where a group of plague **victims** had been discovered. The story led to a final conflagration, but not before Orlock passed along his undead condition. The Orlock character, like Dracula, has entered the public domain, and it would be difficult to predict where he might again arise. Sporadically, a character based on the Orlock figure will make brief cameo-like appearances in both horror and non-horror contexts.

Sources:

Druillet, Philip. *Nosferatu*. Milwaukee, OR: Dark Horse Comics, 1991.

Hollywood Gothic. New York: W. W. Norton & Company, 1990. 242 pp.

Monette, Paul. *Nosferatu: the Vampyre*. New York: Avon Books, 1979. 172 pp.

Nosferatu: A Symphony of Shadows, a Symphony of Shudders. Nos. 1–2. Plymouth, MI: Tome Press, 1991.

Nosferatu: Plague of Terror. No. 1–4 St. Paul, MN: Millennium Comics, 1991–92.

Outer Space Vampires *see:* Science Fiction and the Vampire

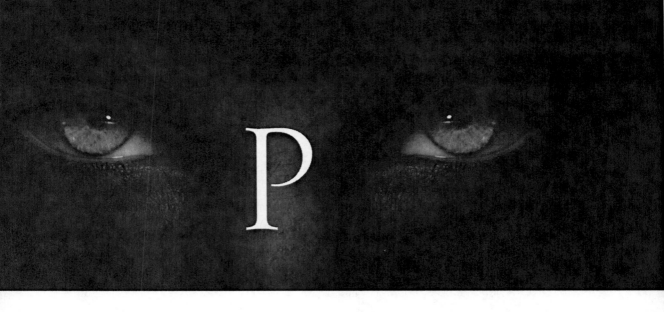

P

P. N. Elrod Fan Club *see:* Vampire Fandom United States

Palance, Jack (1928–2006)

Jack Palance, who played the title role in the made-for-television movie ***Dracula*** **(1973)** was born Vladimir Palahnuik on February 18, 1928, in Lattimer, Pennsylvania. In 1947 he made his Broadway debut and three years later appeared in his first Hollywood movie, *Panic in the Streets*. He became famous following his appearance in *Shane*. For his role as the villain, he won an Oscar nomination as best supporting actor, the second time he had received that honor.

Palance's movie career was largely determined by his physical build (he had a brief career in professional boxing), his distinctive voice, and the plastic surgery he received following the crash of his airplane during World War II. He quickly emerged as a one of Hollywood's great heavies. It limited his starring roles, but he became famous as one of the industry's outstanding character actors. Therefore, he was a natural consideration for the title role as Dracula when **Dan Curtis**, fresh on the heels of his successful vampire-oriented ***Dark Shadows*** series, decided to make a new version of ***Dracula***. Curtis's *Dracula* was the first remake of the classic tale following the introduction of **Vlad the Impaler**, (also known as **Vlad Dracul**).

Palance portrayed a Dracula who had lost his love four centuries before, but rediscovered her in the person of **Lucy Westenra**, whose picture was carried by **Jonathan Harker** when he appears at **Castle Dracula** at the beginning of the film. Leaving Harker to be attacked by the **women** at the castle, Dracula went in search of his lost love. He turned her into a vampire, but she was killed by **Abraham Van Helsing** and her fiancé **Arthur Holmwood**. Enraged, Dracula sought revenge by attacking **Mina Murray**, Harker's fiancé. Dracula was chased back to his castle and finally destroyed.

Jack Palance as Dracula.

The Palance version first aired on CBS on February 8, 1974, and was then released to theaters in Europe. It subsequently took its place as one of the finer versions of *Dracula* and has been released on both VHS and DVD. Palance continued with his active career, which included hosting the popular television series *Ripley's Believe It or Not*. He died in 2006.

Sources:

Holte, James Craig. *Dracula in the Dark: The Dracula Film Adaptations*. Westport, CT: Greenwood Press, 1997. 161 pp.

Jones, Stephen. *The Illustrated Vampire Movie Guide*. London: Titan Books, 1993. 144 pp.

Paraphernalia, Vampire

As the vampire entered popular culture during the 1960s, a host of items were manufactured to promote and exploit the interest. Actually the first such item seems to have appeared in 1928 at the 250th performance of the stage play of **Dracula** in London. Everyone who attended was given an envelope, which they were told not to open until after the performance. The envelope contained a copy of *Dracula's Guest*, a collection of short stories by **Bram Stoker**, and a small rubber-band-powered bat that flew into the air when released.

Movies have always been a great source of collectible items—posters, movie cards, publicity packets, and photographs, even souvenir booklets—so such items were common with vampire movies. It wasn't until 1966, however, in connection with **Hammer Films**, *Dracula, Prince of Darkness*, that special items were produced specifically as advertising gimmicks for a vampire movie. Patrons attending the movie (usually shown as a double feature with another Hammer production, *Plague of the Zombies*), were given vampire **fangs** and a zombie mask.

In 1968, manufacturers began to recognize the existence of a vampire-oriented public for whom a variety of such items could be created and marketed. This recognition came in the wake of the success of vampire **Barnabas Collins** on the **gothic television** soap opera **Dark Shadows**. In 1968, Barnabas and *Dark Shadows* provided the theme for a new board **game**, Viewmaster 3-D reels, and a Halloween mask and costume. In 1969 a veritable flood of new *Dark Shadows* products were released, including several records, a second board game, jigsaw puzzles, model kits, a magic slate, and pillows. The success of *Dark Shadows* memorabilia led to the production of other vampire items either specifically for Halloween (from plastic fangs to greeting cards) or to both build and exploit the market generated by various vampire movies. In 1992 a line of approximately 100 products (including **trading cards**, T-shirts, computer games, jewelry, and miniature statuettes) was developed for release in connection with **Francis Ford Coppola's** *Bram Stoker's Dracula*.

During the 1970s, while most vampire paraphernalia was produced in connection with either *Dark Shadows* (which still has a large, well-organized fan network) or with particular motion pictures, the vampire image was adopted by a number of products that ranged from breakfast cereal to candy. The spread of products dominated by a vampire image also coincided with the adoption of the vampire theme in advertising. Examples of this included ads in which a vampire recommended a product like mouthwash, and one in which a **victim** was rescued by a garden poison that killed insects dressed like **Bela Lugosi**.

Halloween Paraphernalia: The most popular vampire items have been produced for Halloween—one of the most widely celebrated holidays in North America. The merchandising of Halloween tripled between 1983 and 1993, and by the early 1990s, it was second only to Christmas in terms of the number of people who decorated their homes. The vampire has become an integral part of the Halloween celebration and merchants carry a wide variety of vampire products to respond to public demand. Leading the list are vampire costumes, both those based on the older Bela Lugosi image and some newer figures such as Barnabas Collins and horror hostess **Elvira**. Besides complete costumes there are vampire masks and wigs and a wide selection of make-up. Elvira has marketed a line of cosmetics, and several companies produce vampire teeth, artificial **blood**, and make-up. For the party planner, there are vampire-oriented supplies including placemats, posters, hanging bats, and window and wall decorations. One set of party items pictured the popular cartoon cat Garfield in vampire regalia.

Halloween greeting cards began to make an impact in the 1980s and by 1993 Halloween was ranked eighth among greeting card sales—an estimated thirty-five million cards were sent in 1992. By 2009, Halloween greeting card sales reached $350,000. Vampire greeting cards are largely humorous, often including a basic set of one-liners and riddles. The cards, designed for a quick immediate impact, indicate how stereotypical the vampire image has become—vampires are invariably shown with a cape and two fangs and, more often than not, in association with **vampire bats**. To a lesser extent vampires have appeared on postcards; there is a set of cards with movie stills from *Dracula* **(1931)** and an eleven-card set (of an originally projected series of twenty-four cards) from *Dark Shadows* (1987).

Halloween candy has also become a multi-million dollar business currently growing at about two percent per year. In recent years, among the vampire oriented candy products that reached the market were *Frankford Vampire Bites*, *Gummi Mummies* (they came in a **coffin** that became a coin bank), *Creepy Coffin* (with a chocolate vampire), *Count Crunch*, and *Vambite*.

The vampire has become an integral part of the Halloween celebration in the United States, as illustrated in this greeting card.

Toys: Trading cards are closely associated with **comic books**. Apart from the vampires that have appeared in collections of cards picturing a host of monsters, possibly the first vampire trading cards were the two sets of *Dark Shadows* cards marketed by the Philadelphia Chewing Gum Company at the end of the 1960s. Both the first or "pink" series and the second or "green" series included sixty-six scenes from the television show. Imagine, Inc. issued a new *Dark Shadows* set in 1993 with sixty-two cards from the 1960s television series. Topps produced two card sets in association with vampire-oriented movies: **The Addams Family** (1991, one hundred cards) and **Bram Stoker's Dracula** (1992, one hundred cards). In addition to the one hundred-card set made for *Bram Stoker's Dracula*, there was an additional sixteen-card set distributed with the four-issue comic book of the movie published by Topps. In 1992, Acid Rain Studios, which had produced a number of vampire comic books, also issued a fifty-card black-and-white trading card set.

Vampire toys began with the *Dark Shadows* games, jigsaw puzzle, Viewmaster set, magic slate, and model kits in 1968 and 1969. Over the last twenty-five years, however, the most popular items have been the numerous vampire dolls and statues. Vampires have been reproduced in every possible medium. There was a vampire teddy bear, plastic statuettes of the characters from *The Addams Family* and **The Munsters**, and, of course, **Dracula**, the most reproduced figure. Dracula was occasionally placed in a coffin with a movable lid. In 1990, Funny Toys Corporation marketed "Dracula in Coffin,"

A female vampire as drawn by comic book artist Wendy Snow-Lang.

a vampire in evening dress in a battery powered coffin that opened and closed with an eerie noise. In the early 1990s, **Universal Pictures** released action figures of the popular *Teenage Mutant Ninja Turtles* that portrayed the four turtles as four of the classic monsters from Universal movies; Donatello was the Dracula figure. These figures were just one of a line of items licensed by Universal using the Bela Lugosi Dracula image.

Apparel: Since the 1960s, teeshirts have become the daily wear of many people, and shirts bearing the advertising of a wide number of products have been marketed. As might be expected, vampires have found their way onto such shirts. Elvira's Queen B Productions has produced both T-shirts and sweatshirts. A variety of T-shirts with scenes from the movie and the comic book appeared in connection with *Bram Stoker's Dracula*. Recent *Dark Shadows* T-shirts had scenes from the 1990s (rather than the 1960s) television series.

The ease of producing T-shirt illustrations made it easy for smaller producers to get into the market. **Vlad**, the leader of the rock band Dark Theater, has a T-shirt line, as does independent cartoonist Wendy Snow-Lang. At the opposite end of the economic scale, *Bram Stoker's Dracula* products included a bustier version marketed through Macy's ($1,500), a tie with a wolf symbol, boxer shorts, and red laced underpants with rosebud appliqué.

The more affluent can purchase vampire jewelry. One of the more popular items is a reproduction of the ring worn by Barnabas Collins in the 1960s television series. Wristwatches have been produced with designs from both the 1960s and 1990 *Dark Shadows* television series and *Bram Stoker's Dracula*. *Bram Stoker's Dracula* also led to the production of a set of broaches in the form of a bat, a bug, and a spider and a vampire red lipstick in a $500 bejeweled coffin-shaped lipstick holder. Among the most unusual items was an ornament suitable for a necklace or bracelet that contained dirt from **Castle Dracula**.

Miscellaneous Items: The number and variety of vampire-oriented paraphernalia are extensive. *Dark Shadows* products alone included pillows, a **music** box, a Barnabas Collins walking cane, lunch box, keychains, drinking mugs, and calendars. Count Chocula cereal, introduced in the 1970s, is still popular. There are lapel buttons with witty vampire one-liners and even a vampire condom.

No discussion of vampire products would be complete without mentioning the several anti-vampire kits. The first such kit was alleged to have been produced by Nicolas Plomdeur, a gunmaker in Liege, Belgium, in the mid-nineteenth century. His kit included a real pistol made in the shape of a latin cross, a silver **bullet**, a wooden spike, powder flask, and a clove of **garlic**. The only known surviving example of the Plomdeur kit is owned by Val Forgett of the Navy Arms Company. A similar kit can be found in the Mercer Museum at Doylestown, Pennsylvania. This kit's wooden box contains a pistol, two silver bullets, a cross attached to a wooden **stake**, a magnifying glass, some garlic, and several "serums" especially formulated by the manufacturer of the kit, reputedly a Dr. Ernest Blomberg. The kit was reportedly designed for nineteenth-century English-speaking travelers going to Eastern Europe.

Finally, for the most intense vampire enthusiasts, Death, Inc. of San Francisco, California, has offered a full "Vampire Line" of coffins.

The Twenty-first Century: Since the 1990s, an overwhelming amount of new vampire paraphernalia has been produced in association with successful movies and television seres. Above and beyond the usual promotional materials, *Bram Stoker's Dracula* (1992) had a variety of games, jewelry, and clothing associated with it, as did *Interview with the Vampire* two years later. Both were, however, far eclipsed by the merchandising that developed from the seven-year run of **Buffy the Vampire Slayer** and the spinoff **Angel**, which ran for five years. Both the amount and variety of items with logos and pictures of the stars on them expanded exponentially. Many of the items are specifically related to the content of the movie or television show, such as the Tru Blood drink featured in HBO's *True Blood* television series, and the glasses from which to drink the blood substitute; or the replica of the vampire hero's necklace from CBS's *Moonlight* series.

The merchandizing associated with *Buffy* carried through the middle of the first decade of the new century, but it was eclipsed beginning in 2008 by the extensive amount of paraphernalia developed in relation to the four books and the movie adaptations of **The Twilight Series** of **Stephenie Meyer**. The majority of items directed toward *Twilight* fans are specifically aimed for use by its largely teenage and female

audience. Marketing for *Twilight* varies somewhat in that the many items are largely manufactured by one company which specializes in a reaching the fan base rather than a set of companies that specialized in the type of merchandise being produced (jewelry, trading cards, action figures, games, or clothing). Also, with the rise of the Internet, are guides to collecting are nonexistent. The availability of different items is totally tied to direct sales, thus guides to items not immediately available—about which a collector would like to know and for which a collector might search—are not being created. Among the rare exceptions is Jeff Allendar's House of Checklists (http://nslists.com/jachlist.htm), which gives extensive information on trading cards sets, including all the vampire cards.

Conclusion: The number of different places where the vampire image can now be found is further proof of its significant penetration into the popular culture. The fact that so many products for children and young adults now feature vampires indicate that its popularity will only expand as the next generation matures after experiencing the vampire in such a positive manner.

(For more information on specific categories of paraphernalia, see separate entries in this book, including **comic books, music,** and **games.**)

Sources:

Broeske, Pat H. "See the Movie, Buy the Automobile Air Freshener." *New York Times* (December 6, 1992): 12.

Jones, Del. "Holiday Is a Business Treat." *USA Today* (October 29, 1993): 1–2.

Ramsland, Katherine. "Dr. Blomberg Anti-Vampire Kit." *Dead of Night* No. 6 (Summer 1990): 48.

"Recession Won't Carve into Halloween Spending." *SP Daily News*, October 21, 2009. Posted at http://www.cspnet.com/ME2/Audiences/dirmod.asp?sid=&nm=&type=Publishing&mod=Publications%3A%3AArticle&mid=8F3A7027421841978F18BE895F87F791&tier=4&id=CBA7591C6C73457FADDE72AA8BDB1E4C&AudID=6CB610EEADF24F2F87B4FCDF31DC45E1. Accessed November 15, 2009.

Spangenberger, Phil. "Vampire-Killing Kit." *Guns & Ammo* 33, 10 (October 1989): 72–73, 127.

Stockel, Shirley, and Victoria Weidner. *A Guide to Collecting "Dark Shadows" Memorabilia.* Florissant, MO: Collinwood Chronicle, 1992. 107 pp.

Parry, Michael (1947–)

Michael Parry, a British horror writer and anthologist, was born on October 7, 1947, in Brussels, Belgium. His entry into the horror field came through the cinema. As a teenager, he began to write film reviews of horror movies and news stories in the field. In 1969, he wrote and produced *Hex,* a short surrealistic film that used a black magic theme. His first book was a novel based on the screenplay of the **Hammer Films** vampire movie, *Countess Dracula* (1971), about Countess **Elizabeth Bathory**. Although most of his work has been western novels, throughout the 1970s and 1980s he produced a series of anthologies of horror fiction. His anthologies—many which included vampire stories—were notable for the knowledge Parry demonstrated of the vast field of horror short fiction. Two of these anthologies, *Christopher Lee's X Certificate* (1975) and *The Great Villains* (1976) were done with **Christopher Lee**, the contemporary actor most identified with the role of **Dracula**. His most famous vampire book was *Rivals of Drac-*

ula (1977), which, along with **Les Shepard**'s *Dracula Book of Great Vampire Stories* (1977) made the most important vampire short stories available to a growing audience of vampire enthusiasts.

Sources:

Ashley, Mike. *Who's Who in Horror and Fantasy Fiction*. London: Elm Tree Books, 1977. 240 pp.
Parry, Michel. *Countess Dracula*. London: Sphere Books, 1971. Rept. New York: Beagle Books, 1971. 140 pp.
———. *Rivals of Dracula*. London: Corgi Books, 1977. 190 pp.

❦ Paul (Paole), Arnold ❦

Arnold Paul (or Paole) was the subject of one of the most famous eighteenth-century vampire cases. In the late seventeenth century and into the eighteenth century there was a spate of attacks in central Europe that were attributed to vampires. These cases in general, and the Paul case in particular, were one of the causes of a revival of interest in vampires in England and **France** in the early nineteenth century.

Paul's birthdate is unknown, but it seems he was born in the early 1700s in Medvegia, north of Belgrade, in an area of Serbia that was at that time part of the Austrian Empire. He served in the army in what was "Turkish Serbia" and then returned home in the spring of 1727. Paul purchased several acres of land and settled down to farming. Soon afterwards, he became engaged to a young woman from a neighboring farm. Although he was considered a good natured and honest person, some of the townspeople noted that he sometimes tended to be gloomy.

Paul told his fiancée that his problem stemmed from his war days. While he was in service in Turkish Serbia, he said, he had been visited and attacked by a vampire. According to Paul, he killed the vampire after following it to its grave, ate some of the dirt from the vampire's tomb, and bathed his wounds in the **blood** of the vampire to cleanse himself of the effects of the attack. However, he was fearful of having been tainted by the attack. A week later, Paul died as the result of a fatal accident. He was buried immediately.

However, three weeks after his burial, there were reports that Paul had appeared around town. After four people who made reports died, there was panic in the community. Community leaders felt it was best to disinter the body to determine if Paul was a vampire. So, forty days after Paul was buried, the grave was opened. Two military surgeons were present. The lid was removed from the **coffin** and the witnesses found a body that appeared as if it had just recently died. What was apparently new skin was evident under a layer of dead skin, and the nails had continued to grow. They pierced the body and blood flowed out of the corpse. It was determined by those present that Paul was indeed a vampire. To destroy the vampire, they drove a **stake** into his body was, and he was heard to utter a loud groan. His head was severed and his body burned. Although the case could have ended there, it did not. The four other people who had died were treated in the same way in case they were also vampires.

Three years later, in 1731, in the same area, some seventeen people died of the symptoms of vampirism in a matter of three months. No action was taken until one victim, a young girl, claimed that a man named Milo, who had recently died, had attacked her in the middle of the night. Word of this second wave of vampirism reached Vienna, and the Austrian Emperor ordered an inquiry to be conducted by Regimental Field Surgeon Johannes Fluckinger. Soon after, Fluckinger traveled to Medvegia to gather accounts of what had occurred. When Milo's body was disinterred, it had the same characteristics as that of Arnold Paul. Milo's body was then staked and burned. An inquiry into the reason that the vampirism that had been eradicated in 1727 had returned led to the determination that Paul had vampirized several cows that the recently dead had fed on. Under Fluckinger's orders, the townspeople dug up the bodies of all who had died in recent months. It was found that, of the forty bodies that were disinterred, seventeen were in the same preserved state. They were all staked and burned.

Fluckinger wrote a full report of his activities and presented it to the emperor early in 1732. His report was soon published and became a bestseller. As early as March 1732, accounts of Paul and the Medvegia vampires were circulated in the periodicals of France and England. Because the case was so well documented and became the focus of many studies and reflections about vampires. Arnold Paul became the most famous "vampire" of the era. It is also noteworthy that the Paul case was instrumental in shaping the conclusions reached by both **Dom Augustin Calmet** and **Giuseppe Davanzati**, two Roman Catholic scholars who prepared books on vampirism in the middle of the century.

Sources:
Barber, Paul. *Vampires, Burial, and Death: Folklore and Reality.* New Haven, CT: Yale University Press, 1988. 236 pp.

Frayling, Christopher. *Vampyres: Lord Byron to Count Dracula.* London: Faber and Faber, 1991. 429 pp.

Hamberger, Klaus. *Mortuus non mordet. Dokumente zum Vampirismus 1689–1791.* Wien: Turia und Kant 1992. This painstakingly edited collection of sources on the vampire exhumations of the 1730s and related eighteenth-century phenomena is the one most important collection of sources on "original" vampires. This is the only edition using the relevant archives themselves.

Summers, Montague. *Vampires in Europe.* London: Routledge, Kegan Paul, Trench, Trubner, & Co., 1929. 329 pp. Rept. New Hyde Park, NY: University Books, 1961. 329 pp.

Pelesit *see:* Malaysia, Vampires in

Penanggalan *see:* Malaysia, Vampires in

Perfume

*P*erfume: The Story of a Murderer, one of the most unique of modern vampire novels, was released in Germany as *Das Perfum* in 1985. Its author was Patrick Susskind (b. 1949) The novel concerns one Jean-Baptiste Grenouille, an eighteenth-century Frenchman born with no body odor of his own, who discovers that he possesses a most developed sense of smell. As he gains a wider range of olfactory experiences, he was drawn to a young woman with a beautiful odor. He kills her attempting to capture it.

Grenouille eventually found his way to the great perfume maker Baldini of Paris, who begins giving him a formal education in creating perfumes. Grenouille later perfects

his art, capturing the essence of various flowering plants while at Grasse, the center of the perfume industry. But his goal is to devise a technique for capturing the essence of humans, and when he succeeds, he concocts a scheme to make the ultimate perfumes from the combined essences of a number of beautiful women. This action of stealing the life essence of his victims is essentially vampiric in nature. The end result, the perfume, also makes him capable of using it to manipulate those around him, most notably those who arrest, try and convict him and then the crowd which gathers to watch his execution. In the end, all, including the father of one of his victims, declare him innocent. He, however, remains an empty shell of a human being.

The novel was successful internationally and has remained in print in several languages. In 2006, a film adaptation, *Perfume: The Story of a Murderer*, was released. Cowritten and directed by Tom Tykwer, it starred Ben Whishaw and Dustin Hoffman.

Sources:

Suskind, Patrick. *Perfume*. New York: Alfred A. Knopf, 1986. 255 pp.

Peterson, Cassandra *see:* Elvira

Philippe, Monsieur (?–1824)

Monsieur Philippe, the stage name of actor Emmanuel de la Villenie, was probably the first person to portray a vampire on stage. He enacted the part of Rutwen (the name assumed by the character **Lord Ruthven**) in **Jean Charles Emmanuel Nodier**'s *Le Vampire* which opened in Paris in 1820. Believing it was **Lord Byron**'s work, Nodier had adapted **John Polidori**'s *The Vampyre*, the original piece of vampire prose fiction, as a **drama**.

Philippe had made a name for himself in several roles, including that of Wallace in Pixérécourt's *Le Chefs écossais* in 1819 prior to being tapped for the lead in Nodier's play. His lead in *Le Vampire* merely elevated his life as a stage star. One commentator noted that he had become the first star assuming fatal roles, and that playing the vampire had brought him great prestige. Even **Alexandre Dumas** who attended a performance soon after arriving in Paris, saw him as "the representation of the pure-blooded melodrama." *Le vampire* moved the action in Polidori's story to Scotland, the traditional home of Lord Byron's family. Monsieur Philippe portrayed Rutwen, pronounced Rootwen, due to Nordier's misunderstanding of the pronunciation of Polidori's character Ruthven (which is pronounced "riv-ven"). Rutwen was introduced as an attractive and seductive young man possessed of **hypnotic** eyes, yet he was also a murderer who had killed many women over the centuries. He was a passionate lover, but his love brought death. The combination of Philippe's handsome face, his emotive portrayal of Rutwen, and Nordier's presentation of the vampire as a complex tragic figure, drew the Parisian theater-goers like the strongest magnet.

After a long run with *Le Vampire*, Philippe continued his success on the stage in Boirie's *Les Duex Forcats* (1922), but what appeared to be the beginning of a long-acclaimed career was suddenly cut short on October 16, 1924, when Philippe was found dead. He appeared to be the victim of what was at the time called "apoplexy." The local priest refused to grant him the church's rites and a riot occurred at the funeral by infuriated colleagues and fans.

Sources:

Stuart, Roxana. *Stage Blood: Vampires of the 19th-Century Stage*. Bowling Green, OH: Bowling Green State University Popular Press, 1994. 377 pp.

Philippines, Vampires in the

The modern Philippines is a country composed of numerous peoples whose belief systems survive, some in a rather secularized form, in spite of several centuries of Islamic and Christian missions and the development of a host of modern indigenous religions. The tribes of the Philippine Islands had an elaborate mythology, which included demonic beings, dragons, were-animals, giants, **ghouls**, and vampires. The Capiz section of the island of Panay was especially associated with the vampire, where many were believed to reside.

Of the vampire-like creatures, the *aswang* was by far the most well known throughout the Islands. The term *aswang* was used to describe a set of different creatures that were analogous to vampires, **werewolves**, ghouls, and witches, and in the folklore literature could be found under any one of those headings.

The **flying** *aswang*, or the bloodsucker, usually appeared as a beautiful maiden who engaged in vampiric activities at night, always returning home to resume her normal life before dawn. Some women have an ointment that they rub on their body prior to their nocturnal activities. The ointment was the source of their supernatural abilities. In its vampiric state, the *aswang* became a large bird that flew through the sky crying out *kakak* or *kikak*. It would land on the roof of a prospective **victim**'s house and let down a long tongue with a sharp point. The point was used to prick the jugular vein, and the **blood** was sucked up through the hollow tongue's tubular structure. Children were told stories of the possibility of being attacked by an *aswang*. Once filled with blood, the *aswang* resembled a pregnant woman. Upon returning home she fed her children, who suckled at her breast. The *aswang*'s supernatural powers ceased either with its washing off the ointment or the coming of dawn.

The *aswang* was a common bugaboo parents used to keep children in line. A large percentage of Filipinos grew up with at least some belief in its existence. The strength of this belief was documented quite vividly in the 1950s when it was used against a group of insurgents (the Huk or *Hukbalahap*) during the presidency of Magsaysay, a Philippine leader strongly supported by the American government. American advisors to Magsaysay convinced him to create a psychological warfare unit to counter the efforts of Huk leaders to win people away from their support of the central government. Among the efforts of this unit, noted in General E. G. Lansdale's *account, was an attempt to convince a Huk unit to abandon a position in fear of an* aswang's *attack.*

The operation began with a rumor planted in a community threatened by Huk attack. People were told that a vampire had moved into the area. The Huk were barricaded at the top of a nearby hill. They soon became aware of the rumor that was spreading through the area. Several days later, the psychological warfare unit was able to capture a Huk soldier and kill him by draining his blood. They made two puncture wounds on

his neck and left him on the road near the hill where he would be found. When he was found, the Huk believed their dead comrade to be a victim of the *aswang*. The next day all of the Huk troops left.

Building on Lansdale's account, Norine Dresser noted that in the late 1980s she found the story of the *aswang* and the Huk and other tales of the *aswang* were still very much alive in the Filipino immigrant community in California. They told her the old stories of the vampire creatures and she discovered that several of her informants still believed in the *aswang*. They also reflected on the long range effect of the 1950s incident that many local people, not just the Huks, attributed to a vampire. Once the Huks left, people began to wonder who the *aswang*'s next victims would be. Some started wearing **garlic** necklaces. Some left the area and their abandoned land was taken over by the government and used in its land redistribution programs.

Despite the fear caused by the incident, everyone recognized its effectiveness in destroying the Huks's support among the people.

One tale told by the Isneg people related the **origin** of the vampire, which they called *danag*. According to the story, several people were in the fields planting their crops when a woman cut her finger. Another woman sucked the wound and thereby discovered that she liked the taste of blood. She went on sucking until she had taken all of the blood. The story concluded by noting that the blood sucking replaced farming.

The Tagalog people spoke of a vampire called the *mandurugo* about which they told the story of "The Girl with Many Loves." The young woman was described as one of the most beautiful to live in the land. She married at the age of sixteen. Her husband, a husky youth, withered away in less than a year. After his death, she married again, with the same result. She married a third time and then a fourth. The fourth husband, having been warned, feigned sleep one night holding a knife in his hand. Soon after midnight he felt a presence over him and then a prick on his neck. He stuck the knife into the creature on top of him. He heard a screech and the flapping of wings. The next day his bride was found dead some distance from the house with a knife wound in her chest.

As the Philippine film industry developed after World War II, the vampire became a subject of its attention. Given the large Roman Catholic influence in the Islands, however, the films tended to relate more to the European vampire than the *aswang* or associated Philippine vampire characters. Beginning in the 1960s, a number of inexpensive B-movies were made in the Philippines by American companies, including some of the most forgettable in the horror and vampire genres. Due to a variety of copyright, trademark, and trade agreement obstacles, many of the Philippine movies have never been released in the United States.

Sources:

Dresser, Norine. *American Vampires: Fans, Victims, Practitioners*. New York: W. W. Norton & Company, 1989. 255 pp.

Lansdale, Edward Geary. *In the Midst of Wars*. New York: Harper & Row, 1972. 386 pp.

Lopez, Mellie Leandicho. *A Handbook of Philippine Folklore*. Diliman, Quezon City: The University of the Philippines Press 2006.

Ramos, Maximo D. *Creatures of Philippine Lower Mythology*. Manila: University of the Philippines Press, 1971. 390 pp.

❨ Piérart, Z. J. (?–1878) ❩

French psychical researcher on vampirism Z. J. Piérart emerged into prominence in the 1850s as spiritualism swept across France. Under the leadership of Alan Kardec, French spiritualism became the first branch of the movement to accept reincarnation as part of its belief system. Piérart became the leader of the smaller opposition group of spiritualists that did not accept the idea. A professor at the College of Maubeuge, he founded a spiritualist journal, *La Revue Spiritualiste*, in 1858.

Piérart's rejection of reincarnation led directly to his consideration of vampires. Spiritualists in general had argued against reincarnation as they claimed to be in contact with the spirits of the dead—even those who had been dead for many years—an impossibility if the spirit had been reincarnated and lost its former earthly identity.

Piérart became interested in the problem of psychic attack. In a series of articles, he proposed a theory of psychic vampirism suggesting that vampires were the astral bodies (the ghostly double of the spiritual body that spiritualists had proposed as an essential component of each person and one cause of ghostly apparitions of the dead) of either incarcerated individuals or the dead that were revitalizing themselves on the living. He first proposed the idea that the astral body was forcefully ejected from the body of a person buried alive, and that it vampirized the living to nourish the body in the tomb.

While Piérart's theories had some predecessors, especially sixteenth-century Paracelsus, his work pioneered modern psychical concern with the phenomenon of vampirism. It opened the discussion of the possibility of a paranormal draining of an individual's energy by a spiritual agent. It would later be further developed by Theosophist **Franz Hartmann**.

Piérart's work also preceded the development of psychical research as a science and his work was soon superseded by more detailed considerations of the nature of ghosts and theories of astral (body) projection. In 1873, Piérart's journal was suppressed by the French government responding to clerical pressure against spiritualism. He spent his last years as the secretary to Baron du Potet de Sennevoy, who had pioneered research on animal magnetism.

Sources:

Melton, J. Gordon, ed. *Encyclopedia of Occultism and Parapsychology*. 5th ed. Detroit, MI: Gale Research Company, 2001.

Rogo, Scott. "In-depth Analysis of the Vampire Legend." *Fate* 21, 9 (September 1968): 70–7.

❨ Pike, Christopher ❩

Christopher Pike is the pseudonym of Kevin McFadden (1961–) one of the most popular writers of **juvenile literature** today. Few biographical details are known about the author, but he was born in Brooklyn and held various jobs while practicing his writing skills and trying to sell his first books. He did not have much success until an editor at a publishing company suggested that he try his hand at writing for a younger audience. The result was *Slumber Party* (1985), his first novel, which was well received and led to additional titles. By 1989 Pike had published seven books.

Pike specializes in mystery/suspense and the supernatural, not avoiding pure horror stories, aimed at adolescents making their transition to adulthood. He describes violent activity in some graphic detail. The primary characters are teenagers and the subtext of the stories generally follows some of the major concerns of teen existence. Among his best-selling books are the titles in the *Spooksville* series featuring stories set in the mythical town of Springville where spooky things occur all the time. The continuing characters—Sally, Adam, and Watch—explore the range of the sinister supernatural.

During the 1990s, Pike had occasionally turned to the vampire theme, the first time in his book *Monster* (1992). Even adults appreciated his six-part story of Alisa Perne, the youthful vampire in the series of novels, *The Last Vampire*. Alisa was an ancient vampire living as a high school student in contemporary Los Angeles. Her mate, Yaksha, who had originally forced her into the vampiric life, saved his own life by promising to kill all of the vampires he had made. Now, 5,000 years later, he had largely completed his task—only Alisa remained. Her mission became assisting the nearly invulnerable Yaksha to die, while preventing him from killing her.

The solution to that dilemma set the stage for the various adventures throughout the novels.

In 1994 Pike published *The Midnight Club* about a group of terminally ill teens at a hospice called Rotterdam House. Five of the residents began to meet together at midnight to tell stories. Then one night the members of the Midnight Club created a pact that the first to die would make an attempt to contact the others from wherever he or she was in the great beyond. In 1996, some youthful readers of *The Midnight Club* founded their own Midnight Club on the Internet. The club has evolved into the Christopher Pike Fan Club accessed through the author's homepage on the Internet. Those who join the club are invited to take the name of one of Pike's characters.

In 2009, *The Last Vampire* series was reissued as a two-volume set, *The Thirst*.

Sources:

Pike, Christopher. *Monster*. New York: Archway/Pocket Books, 1992. 182 pp.
———. *The Last Vampire*. New York: Archway/Pocket Books, 1994. 198 pp.
———. *The Last Vampire 2: Black Blood*. New York: Archway/Pocket Books, 1994. 196 pp.
———. *The Last Vampire 3: Red Dice*. New York: Archway/Pocket Books, 1995. 193 pp.
———. *The Last Vampire 4: Phantom*. New York: Archway/Pocket Books, 1996. 179 pp.
———. *The Last Vampire 5: Evil Thirst*. New York: Archway/Pocket Books, 1996. 179 pp.
———. *The Last Vampire 6: Creatures of Forever*. New York: Archway/Pocket Books, 1996. 181 pp.
———. *Night of the Vampire: Spooksville 9*. New York: Ministrel Books/Pocket Books, 1997. 102 pp.
———. *The Last Vampire: Collector's Edition*. Vol. 1. New York: Archway/Pocket Books, 1998. 198 pp.

Pisachas *see:* India, Vampires in

❦ Pitt, Ingrid (1943–) ❦

Ingrid Pitt, an actress who became known for her portrayal of female vampires in the 1970s, was born Natasha Petrovana on a train heading from Germany to a concentration camp in Poland. She grew up in East Berlin, and as a young woman, she escaped

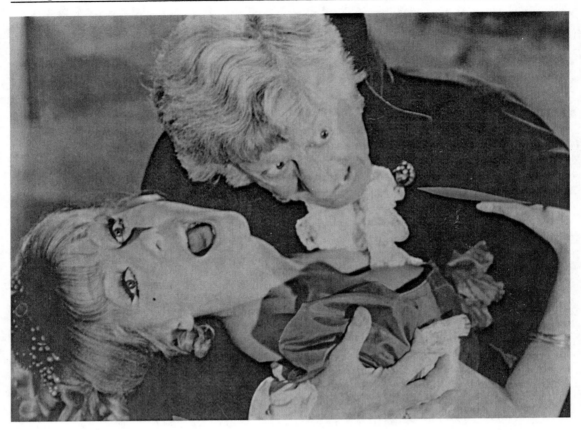

Ingrid Pitt is about to become a vampire's lunch in *The House that Dripped Blood*.

to the West to become a model and actress and married the man who had helped her during her flight.

Pitt made her first horror movie in 1964, *The Sound of Horror*, a Spanish production. Following her appearance in *Where Eagles Dare* (1969), she was discovered by Jimmy Carreras of **Hammer Films**. Her two films for Hammer established her fame and her identification with vampirism.

Her first Hammer movie, *The Vampire Lovers*, was based on **Sheridan Le Fanu**'s story, **"Carmilla"**. The increasingly permissive standards for movies allowed a degree of nudity and a more direct presentation of lesbianism than had been possible. As Carmilla, Pitt successively vampirized Pippa Steele, Madeline Smith, and Kate O'Mara, after which she was tracked down and beheaded by **Peter Cushing**. While her same-sex scenes were most frequently described as **lesbian**, Pitt did not see it that way, believing that vampires had no specific gender.

There was little doubt that Pitt's popularity was due to her glamorous appearance and nude scenes. She was offered a variety of vampire scripts, which she turned down because she felt they were little more than sexploitation movies. However, she soon returned to Hammer to make her second movie, *Countess Dracula* (1971), based on the life of Countess **Elizabeth Bathory**. Pitt took her portrayal very seriously, and her research included a trip to Eastern Europe to visit Bathory's castle. The dynamic story of the Bathory legend involved her bathing in **blood** to restore her youth. The aging countess believed she was rejuvenated by the blood, and one of the more memorable scenes in vampire movies was that of Pitt coming out of her bath with the blood dripping off of her body.

Pitt would take on one more vampire role, a comic spoof, "The Cloak", which appeared as a segment of the horror anthology *The House that Dripped Blood* (1971). After appearing in several other movies in the early 1970s, she moved behind the camera to start writing. Pitt participated in her husband's production company in Argentina, during which time she wrote a novel, *The Cuckoo Run* (1980) and a nonfiction work, *The Perons* (1982).

From the early 1980s to the present, she has concentrated on writing and producing, with only a few guest appearances acting in movies and on television.

There is an active Ingrid Pitt fan club, the Pitt of Horror, also accessed through the Pitt of Horror Website, http://www.pittofhorror.com/), which makes available a wide variety of items related to Pitt and Hammer. To celebrate the **Dracula** centennial, Pitt made a number of personal appearances and was the cinema guest of honor at **Dracula '97: A Centennial Celebration** in Los Angeles. Her book, *The Ingrid Pitt Bedside Companion for Vampire Lovers,* appeared in 1998. She continues to be active in the British fan scene.

Sources:

Hallenbeck, Bruce C. "Countess Dracula." *Femme Fatales* 1, 3 (Winter 1992/93): 52–5.

"Ingrid Pitt: A Profile." *For the Blood Is the Life* 2, 10 (Autumn 1991): 17.

Pitt, Ingrid. *The Ingrid Pitt Bedside Companion for Vampire Lovers.* London: BT Batsford, 1998. 192 pp.

———. *Life's a Scream: Autobiography of Ingrid Pitt.* London: William Heinemann, 1999. 320 pp.

Rept. *Ingrid Pitt: Darkness before Dawn.* Baltimore, MD: Luminary Press, 2005. 320 pp.

Pittsburgh Dark Shadows Fan Club *see:* Dark Shadows Fandom

Planché, James Robinson (1796–1880)

James Robinson Planché, popular British dramatist, produced his first successful burlesque at the age of twenty-two. That production launched a career that, while centering on the writing and translating of various dramas (most of a comedic nature), found him working in many varied capacities. Thus, for many of the plays on which he worked, he was the producer, manager, and/or costume designer. In addition, he occasionally wrote libretti for operas and songs for vaudeville.

Planché became involved in the world of vampires in 1820 in response to their popularity on the French stage following **Charles Nodier**'s production of *Le Vampire*. He adapted Nodier's play for the London stage. *The Vampire* or *The Bride of the Isles*, opened at the Lyceum Theater on August 9, 1820. Because the theater had a ready collection

of Scottish clothing, Planché set the action in Scotland (one land not readily associated with vampires). The play was most remembered, however, for the trap door though which the vampire, **Lord Ruthven** (played by **Thomas Potter Cooke**), could disappear. It became known in the theater as the "vampire trap." The many-faceted Planché had a lifelong interest in heraldry, and many consider his *The History of British Costumes* (1834) his most permanent contribution. His writing was a strong influence on W.S. Gilbert (of the team Gilbert and Sullivan).

Sources:

Glut, Don. *The Dracula Book*. Metuchen, NJ: Scarecrow Press, 1975. 388 pp.

Kunitz, Stanley J., ed. *British Authors of the Nineteenth Century*. New York: H. W. Wilson Company, 1936. 677 pp.

Planché, J. R. *Plays*. edited by Donald Roy. Cambridge: Cambridge University Press, 1986., pp. 43–68.

———. *Recollections and Reflections*. 2 vols. London: Tinsley Brother, 1872.

———. *The Vampire* or, *The Bride of the Isles*. London: John Lownes, 1820.

Stuart, Roxana. *Stage Blood: Vampires of the 19th-Century Stage*. Bowling Green, OH: Bowling Green University Popular Press, 1994. 377 pp.

Plogojowitz, Peter

One of the more famous historical vampires, Peter Plogojowitz lived in Kisolova, a small village in Austrian-occupied Serbia, an area officially incorporated into the province of **Hungary**. The town of Kisolova was not far from Medvegia, the home of **Arnold Paul**, another famous "vampire," whose case occurred at the same time.

Plogojowitz died in September 1728 at the age of sixty-two. But three days later in the middle of the night he returned to his home and asked his son for food, then left. Two evenings later he reappeared and again asked for food. When the son refused, he was found dead the next day. At roughly the same time, several villagers became ill with exhaustion, diagnosed with an excessive loss of blood. They claimed that they had been visited by Plogojowitz in a dream and that he bit them on the neck and sucked their blood. All in all, nine persons mysteriously died of this strange illness during the following week.

When the chief magistrate sent a report of the deaths to the commander of the Imperial forces, the commander responded with a visit to the village. He demanded that the graves of all the recently dead be opened. Astonishingly, they found that body of Plogojowitz was less like a corpse than a man in a trance, breathing very gently. His eyes were open, his flesh plump, and his complexion ruddy. His hair and nails appeared to have grown since his burial and fresh skin was found just below the scarf. Most importantly, his mouth was smeared with fresh **blood**.

The commander quickly concluded that Plogojowitz was a vampire. The executioner who came to Kisolova with the commander drove a **stake** through the body. When he did, blood gushed from the wound and from the orifices of the body. The body was then burned. None of the other bodies manifested signs of vampirism, but to protect them, and the other villagers, **garlic** and whitethorn were placed in their graves and their bodies were returned to the ground.

The story was reported by the Marquis d'Argens in his *Lettres Juives,* which was quickly translated into an English version in 1729. Even though his story was not as well known as the incidents that began with Arnold Paul, the Plogojowitz case was a major element in the European vampire controversy of the 1730s.

Sources:

Barber, Paul. *Vampires, Burial, and Death: Folklore and Reality.* New Haven, CT: Yale University Press, 1988. 236 pp.

Hamberger, Klaus. *Mortuus non mordet. Dokumente zum Vampirismus 1689–1791.* Wien: Turia und Kant 1992. This painstakingly edited collection of sources on the vampire exhumations of the 1730s and related eighteenth-century phenomena is the one most important collection of sources on "original" vampires. This is the only edition using the relevant archives themselves.

Summers, Montague. *The Vampire in Europe.* London: Routledge, Kegan Paul, Trench, Trubner & Co., 1929. 329 pp. Rept. New Hyde Park, NY: University Books, 1961. 329 pp.

❨ Poe, Edgar Allan (1809–1849) ❩

American writer Edgar Allan Poe was born in Boston, Massachusetts, the son of David Poe, Jr. and Elizabeth Arnold Hopkins. His parents, both actors, died of tuberculosis in 1811. Young Edgar then lived with John Allan, a merchant, and incorporated his benefactor's name into his own. He entered the University of Virginia in 1826, but after a falling out with John Allan he dropped out and joined the army. His first book, a collection of his poems, was published in 1827 shortly after his tenure in the army began. In 1830, after a brief reconciliation with John Allan, Poe was sent to West Point, but was expelled for disobedient behavior. In 1831 he moved to take a newspaper job in Baltimore, and while there met an aunt who had been previously unknown to him. In 1835, he married her daughter Virginia Clemm and remained married to her for twelve years, until her death in 1847. During those years, he moved from one job to another, drinking heavily, and always in debt. He himself died while on a drinking binge, and his body was found in a gutter. His literary executor wrote a scurrilous biography that turned many people against Poe through the rest of the nineteenth century, though it did not stop his rising fame, which grew both in North America and Europe. He was well-known in France and Germany in the late nineteenth century.

Rediscovered in this century, Poe found an extensive and appreciative new readership for both his **poetry** and short stories, many of which have been turned into movies. While Poe explored many areas of the **gothic** world, he never specifically wrote a vampire story. Contemporary critics, however, have found widespread use of a vampire or *lamiai*-like character in his various writings. Amid the actual vampirism encountered in the literature of the early nineteenth century, historians studying the period have noted that many writers considered a more metaphorical or psychic vampirism in which the vampire-like character sucks the life force or psychic energy from another, usually a person close to them. As early as the 1930s, D. H. Lawrence recognized such a theme in Poe's work.

More recently James B. Twitchell carried Lawrence's position even farther and argued that "the development of the vampire analogy was one of Poe's central artistic concerns." Twitchell saw the vampire (or *lamiai,* since his vampires were usually female) theme in a number of Poe's stories, particularly "Bernice," "Morella," "Ligeia," "The Oval Portrait," and "The Fall of the House of Usher." In "Bernice," Poe told the story of a man originally in a weakened condition who seemed to grow more robust as his cousin Bernice declined and finally died. In the end, however, it was Bernice who became the vampire, a fact signaled by her paleness, lifeless eyes, and prominent teeth.

The narrator of the story became increasingly afraid and after Bernice died, he went to the grave to slay the vampire by pulling her teeth.

Bernice was but the first of the supposed female vampires created by Poe.

Morella, in a story written shortly after "Bernice," bled the narrator of her story of his willpower. She also possessed the vampire's identifying marks: cold hands, **hypnotic** eyes, and a bloodless face. In like measure, the title character in "Ligeia" (1938) possessed a *lamiai*'s likeness with her cold hands, pale appearance, prominent teeth, and hypnotic eyes. In these first three stories, suggested Twitchell, Poe used the vampiric theme to highlight a form of relationship between lovers. He returned to the theme in "The Fall of the House of Usher" in which the vampiric exchange of energy occurred between siblings. Finally, in "The Oval Portrait," Poe wove a fascinating story of an artist who destroyed those around him by his all-consuming passion with his work. The story concerned an artist who was painting the portrait of his beautiful wife, not noticing that as he painted she grew weaker and weaker. He concluded his work by declaring it the essence of life itself. He eventually found his wife dead, completely drained of life.

Twitchell's interpretations highlighted, if not a central theme, certainly an important and somewhat neglected secondary motif in Poe, a motif all the more significant due to its widespread use in the writings of so many of Poe's prominent contemporaries.

Sources:

Bailey, J. O. "What Happens in 'The Fall of the House of Usher'?" *American Literature* 35 (1964): 445–466.

Barnes, Nigel. *A Dream within a Dream: The Life of Edgar Allan Poe*. London: Peter Owen, 2009. 272 pp.

Blythe, Hal, and Charlie Sweet. "Poe's Satiric Use of Vampirism in 'Bernice.'" *Poe Studies* 14, 1 (June 1981): 23–24.

Kendall, Lyle H., Jr. "The Vampire Motif in 'The Fall of the House of Usher.'" *College English* 24 (1963) 450–453.

Kiessling, Nicolas. "Variations of Vampirism." *Poe Studies* 14, 1 (June 1981): 14.

Poe, Edgar Allan. *The Complete Works*. Ed. by James A Harrison. New York: T. Y. Crowell, 1902. The stories considered above have been frequently reprinted in various collections.

Richmond, Lee. "Edgar Allan Poe's 'Morella': Vampire of Volition." *Studies in Short Fiction* 9 (1972): 93–94.

Twitchell, James. *The Living Dead: A Study of the Vampire in Romantic Literature*. Durham, NC: Duke University Press, 1981. 219 pp.

———. "Poe's 'The Oval Portrait' and the Vampire Motif." *Studies in Short Fiction* 14, 4 (Fall 1977): 387–393.

Zumbach, Frank T. E. A. *Poe. Eine Biographie*. Düsseldorf, Zürich: Rev. ed. Artemis & Winkler, 1999.

Poetry, Vampires in

It is not surprising that writers found poetry a natural vehicle of expression for the vampire theme. Poetry speaks with some facility to the intense passions and dark concerns that have been suppressed by conventional society. It relates the central human needs of love and community (family) commonly celebrated by society with other key concerns of death and **sexuality**. The latter concerns, while just as important to human life, are often neglected and the emotions attached to them denied, while discussion of them has been pushed to the fringe of social discourse.

The vampire, especially after its unreality was established by Enlightenment science, became an ideal vehicle for writers to express their own complex feelings and to illustrate their personally frightening experiences. The dead-yet-alive vampire, blending into the shadows of society, obsessed with **blood** (and other body fluids), embodies the darker but no less real side of human existence. Given any of the commonly accepted positive human virtues/emotions, the literary vampire immediately juxtaposed in his or her person both the lights and shadows of the author's life.

The Vampire in Germany: The emergence of the modern literary vampire began with the exploration of the vampiric theme in the poetry of **Germany**. More than a generation prior to **John Polidori**'s famous 1819 novella, **"The Vampyre"**, poets were reacting to the intense debate on the subject of vampirism that took place in the German universities in the mid-eighteenth century. Possibly the first such poem was "Der Vampir" written by Heinrich August Ossenfelder:

My dear young maiden clingeth Unbending, fast and firm To all the long-held teaching Of a mother ever true; As in vampires unmortal Folk on the Theyse's portal Heyduck-like do believe.

But my Christian thou dost dally, And wilt my loving parry Till I myself avenging To a vampire's health a-drinking Him toast in pale tockay.

And as softly thou art sleeping To thee shall I come creeping And thy life's blood drain away.

And so shalt thou be trembling For thus shall I be kissing And death's threshold thou'lt be crossing With fear, in my cold arms.

And last shall I thee question Compared to such instruction What are a mother's charms?

Many similar poems show up in the collections of other poets. More important than any of these specifically vampire poems, however, was Gottfried August Bürger's "Lenora." "Lenora" told the story of William, a young man who died but came back to claim his bride. Arriving in the middle of the night, he called his unsuspecting Lenora to travel with him to their bridal bower. She responded:

"Say on, where is our bridal hall? Where, how the nuptial bower? Far, far from here! Still, cool, and small, Where storms do never lower.

Hast room for me. For me and thee.

Come up and dress and mount with me! The wedding guests are waiting No more of this debating!"

After a ride across the country at breakneck speed, William spoke again:

"In somber gloom we near the tomb With song and wailing tearful! Come, open stands the bridal room, Though all around look fearful.

Come sexton, quick! Come with the choir, Our bridal song with reed and lyre! Come, priest, and say the blessing, Nor wait for our confessing."

The couple rode into the graveyard:

High reared the steed and wildly neighed; Fire from his nostrils started.

And lo! from underneath the maid The earth to 'dmit them parted.

While not a vampire poem, "Lenora" does play upon the themes of love and death, which are so essential to the vampire's life. Denounced by the literary critics, it nevertheless found a popular following. In the 1790s it was translated into English by William Taylor of Norwich and for several years circulated around Norwich as a favored topic for poetry reading/discussion groups, then a widespread entertainment event. Sir Walter Scott heard of "Lenora" from the discussions of Taylor's as yet unpublished poem and went about securing a copy of the original German text. Upon reading it, he too became enthusiastic and chose to make his own translation of the ballad the initial publication of his lengthy literary career. Published the same year as Taylor's translation, it became by far the more popular version. The importance of "Lenora" was further demonstrated by the fact that at least three additional translations were made in 1796 alone and others in subsequent years.

In Germany, "Lenora" inspired what has been traditionally called the first vampire poem, "The **Bride** of Corinth" ("Die Braut von Korinth"), in 1797 by **Johann Wolfgang von Goethe**. In most later commentaries on the vampire in literature, Goethe was said to have based his poem on the account from ancient **Greece** of the encounter of the philosopher Apollonius with a *lamiai*. However, it is, in fact, a retelling of another story; that of Philinnon as related by Phlegon. Goethe's version told of a young man who had traveled to Athens to claim his bride, the daughter of his father's comrade.

Shown into a guest room after his travels by the woman of the house, he was surprised by the arrival of a beautiful young woman at his door. He noted her paleness, but nevertheless invited her in. She wanted a lock of his hair. He offered her **wine**, but she would not drink until midnight, at which time she assumed a new vitality. As dawn approached, the mother heard the activity of the two lovers and burst into the room. The girl turned out to be the recently deceased daughter of the family. She had returned from her grave to find that her love had denied her. Before she left, she told the young man that he would soon join her in death, and asked her mother to see that their bodies were burned. She had been given an ineffective Christian burial, and was now roaming the land without the peace of death.

The Vampire in England: "Lenora" and "The Bride of Corinth" became standard reading for the emerging Romantic movement and the poets who were exploring their inner consciousness. Both Shelley and **Lord Byron** were enthusiastic about it, and "Lenora" directly influenced **Samuel Taylor Coleridge** and **Robert Southey** who shared the honors for producing the first vampire poems in English. Geraldine, the vampiric figure in Coleridge's 1801 poem "Christabel," was never identified as a vampire, but did, as Arthur H. Nethercot effectively argued, have many of the **characteristics**. The first

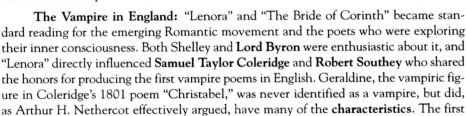

hint that something was wrong with Geraldine was revealed as Christabel assisted Geraldine, who had appeared outside the castle walls, into her castle home:

> The lady Geraldine sank, belike through pain, And Christabel with might
> and main Lifted her up, a weary weight, Over the threshold of the gate:
> Then the lady rose again, And moved, as she were not in pain.

Coleridge seemed to be making reference to the vampire's inability to enter a home without first being invited, now a standard aspect of vampire lore. Then Christabel's father's dog gave an uncharacteristic "angry" moan as Geraldine passed; vampires have a strange effect on **animals**. As Christabel showed her guest to a place of rest, Geraldine noted that the midnight hour was hers.

The two women lay together, and Christabel took Geraldine in her arms.

During Geraldine's hour, Christabel entered a trance-like state while all the nightbirds quieted their chirping. The following morning, Christabel awoke refreshed as one who had "drunken deep of all the blessedness of sleep!" While Coleridge must be credited with writing the first English vampire poem, Southey was the first to introduce a traditional vampire as a character in one of his poems. In the poem "Thalaba the Destroyer" the hero Thalaba had a brief encounter with a vampire, his recently deceased bride Oneiza who had died on their wedding day. He was forced to kill her anew by thrusting a lance through her. Southey based his addition of the vampire character to his poem upon reading accounts of the Eastern European vampires—the same ones that had, a half century earlier, caused the debate over vampires in Germany.

Once introduced to British poetry, the vampire made a number of appearances throughout the early nineteenth century. Possibly the first poem dedicated to the vampire was John Stagg's "The Vampyre" published in his 1810 collection *The Minstrel of the North*. Like Southey, Stagg derived the material for his poem from reading the Eastern European vampire reports. It related a vampire's attack on Herman, the young husband of Gertrude. Herman was under attack from his recently deceased friend Sigismund:

> From the drear mansions of the tomb, From the low regions of the dead,
> The ghost of Sigismund doth roam,

> And dreadful haunts me in my bed! There vested in infernal guise, By means
> to me not understood, Close to my side the goblin lies, And drinks away my
> vital blood!

As he predicted, Herman died that night, and a frightened Gertrude saw Sigismund at their house. The next day, Sigismund's tomb was opened and his body was found "Still warm as life, and undecay'd." The townspeople drove a **stake** through the body of both Sigismund and Herman.

Stagg was followed by Lord Byron's "The Gaiour," the story of an "infidel," a term for non-Muslims in Islamic lands. As an infidel, the story's hero was cursed by a Muslim to become a vampire and roam the earth sucking the blood of those closest to him. **John Keats**'s "Lamia" (1819) drew inspiration from the ancient account of Apollonius and the *lamiai*, though the translation he used lacked the key original reference to the vampire. In Keats's poem, the *lamiai* established a vampiric relationship, a form of psychic vampirism, with Lucius, her human love.

Keats also drew on the vampiric relationship in several other poems such as "La Belle Dame sans Merci". After Keats, however, the vampire appeared only rarely in English literature. Henry Thomas Liddell, a youthful James Clark Maxwell, and Arthur Symons were among the authors who made the few British contributions to the genre between the romantics and the 1897 effort of poet laureate Rudyard Kipling. Kipling's brief "The Vampire" was a lament to the "rag and a bone and a hank of hair," that is, the "woman who did not care" for the man who worshipped her. Kipling's poem was inspired by a painting of a beautiful woman looking down on the man who had died out of love unreturned. It was memorable as a defiant statement about the **vamp**, the non-supernatural *femme fatale*, the subject of numerous silent movies, epitomized by the characters portrayed by actress **Theda Bara**.

The French Poetic Vampire: In **France**, the vampire emerged after the 1819 novella by Polidori. It found its most expansive expression in **drama**, there being no fewer than five French vampire plays within two years. During the nineteenth century, however, the short story was the primary vehicle for the vampire's French apparitions. Few poets made reference to the vampire. Among these was **Théophile Gautier**, more notable for his vampire stories, but who in 1844 also wrote "Les Taches Jaunes." A man who had lost his love sat alone and noted:

> But there are yellow bruises on my body And violet stains; Though no white vampire come with lips blood-crimsoned To suck my veins!

And then he asked:

> Oh, fondest of my loves, from that far heaven Where thou must be, Hast thou returned to pay the debt of kisses Thou owest me?

A decade later, when Charles Baudelaire began his probings of human experience, he dedicated his poems, including his vampire poems, to Gautier.

Baudelaire succeeded in outraging even French society in the mid-nineteenth century. His "The Vampyre" and "Les Metamorphoses du Vampire," which appeared in the 1857 collection *Les Fluers du Mal*, earned him a trial for obscenity. In the latter, for example, he described the morning-after relationship of a man and woman. The man lamented:

> When out of all my bones she had sucked the marrow And as I turned to her, in the act to harrow My senses in one kiss, to end her chatter, I saw the gourd that was filled with foul matter!

The New Wave of Vampire Poetry: During the twentieth century the vampire made an increasing number of appearances. Notable among the poems early in the century was the Irish writer James Joyce's brief vampire poem embedded in *Ulysses*:

> On swift sail flaming From storm and south He comes, pale vampire Mouth to my mouth.

In this brief poem Joyce draws on the flying Dutchman legend as treated in Richard Wagner's **opera**, to which Joyce added mention of the vampire, an image that he uses in several places in *Ulysses*. Wagner, in turn, had been inspired by *Der Vampir*, the opera by **Heinrich August Marschner**. Joyce's fellow countryman, magician, and poet William Butler Yeats, also penned a brief vampire verse titled "Oil and Blood":

In tombs of gold and lapis lazuli Bodies of holy men and women exude Miraculous oil, odour of violet.

But under heavy loads of trampled clay Lie bodies of the vampires full of blood: Their shrouds are bloody and their lips are wet.

During the twentieth century, American poets appropriated the vampire, and as the century progresses, they seem to have become the largest community of poets to make use of it. Among the first was Conrad Aiken. He initially composed a poem, "La Belle Morte," inspired by Gautier's "La Morte Amoureuse," but his "The Vampire" (published in 1914) was a delightful piece of light verse:

She rose among us where we lay.

She wept, we put our work away She chilled our laughter, stilled our play; And spread a silence there.

And darkness shot across the sky, And once, and twice, we heard her cry; And saw her lift white hands on high And toss her troubled hair.

Aiken described the beautiful vampire who had affected all (at least all of the males) who saw her:

"Her eyes have feasted on the dead, And small and shapely is her head, And dark and small her mouth," they said, "And beautiful to kiss; Her mouth is sinister and red As blood in moonlight is."

During the pulp era, as the horror short story in general, and the vampire short story in particular, found a new audience, the number of vampire poems showed a marked increase. But it was nothing to compare with the flood of vampire poems that have appeared since World War II. During the last generation, with the development of a noticeable vampire subculture and the rise of vampire fanzines, a flurry of poetic efforts have responded to a community that lives for the vampire and finds its inspiration in the shadowy side of life. More than half of all the vampire poems ever written have been published since 1970. They are regularly featured in various vampire magazines, from such purely literary magazines as **Margaret Louise Carter**'s, *Vampire's Crypt* to the more general periodicals such as *Realm of the Vampire, Bloodlines, Fresh Blood, Onyx, Shadowdance,* and *Nefarious.*

Contemporary vampire poems, as poetry in general, tend to be short and revel in images and the feelings of the poet. They stand in sharp contrast to the epic storytelling verse of the nineteenth century. Also, the contemporary poets celebrate the vampire and the dark images of life in the evening, whereas nineteenth-century poets tended to operate in the sunlight and to point the finger of moral judgment—or at the very least the righteous indignation of a wronged lover—at the vampires who inhabited their imaginations. Common to both the newer and the older poetry is the use of the vampire as a metaphor to highlight the different levels of power assumed as lovers come together, and the willingness of the more dominant partner to take from the other and leave them empty. Some of the distinct flavor of the poetry of this generation, as well as the continuing common theme, was vividly illustrated in a poem by Ryan Spingola that appeared in *Nefarious* (1993):

I was never what you wanted but my blood will serve your purpose quench your hunger for a short time use me, I give you my life and soul they mean nothing to me now you always had my soul Since that day long ago now you don't want it my blood is all you want you'll take it and leave me lying on the cold floor to die alone and drained of my very life

The vampire revival of the 1990s provided space for poetry on vampires, whose rich imagery supplies poets with endless quantities of inspiration.

Serving as an early venue for the new vampire-oriented poets was Preternatural Press, located in Silver Spring, Maryland, which published a number of volumes through the mid 1990s and beginning in 1990 issued an annual periodical, *Rouge et Noir: Les poemes des Vampires*. *Rouge et Noir* was succeeded by *Dreams of Decadence: Vampire Poetry and Fiction*, a literary magazine that appeared in 1995, soon picked up national distribution, and continued to appear as late as 2002. Along with the more serious efforts at poetry represented by *Rouge et Noir* and *Dreams of Decadence*, poetry served as a vehicle for humor, nowhere more vividly demonstrated than in the three massive self-published volumes by Vlad Tepic, a.k.a. Count Flapula.

In the new century, poetry like many things vampiric, shifted to the Internet. Few indeed were publications such as Maria Alexander and Christina Kiplinger Johns's *Biting Midnight: A Feast of Darksome Verse* (2002). Instead, on the Internet, vampire poety has found a home and a number of sites and many works are featured on the poetry pages of the Vampire Legacy Society, the Realms of Darkness, and the Vampire Forum. Several more-or-less ephemeral poetry groups have operated under the name Undead Poets Society. While yet to make the impact of fiction writers, vampire poets have kept their art very much alive.

Note: Vampire fans are in debt to the Count **Dracula** Fan Club (now the **Vampire Empire**) and compiler Steven Moore for the publication *The Vampire Verse: An Anthology*. It is a comprehensive collection of vampire-oriented poems up to the modern era, with a sampling of contemporary verse. It also has an extensive **bibliography** of additional contemporary vampire poems.

Germany and Austria also have a significant tradition of vampire poems, some quite serious, some parodies and even limericks. A collection of such texts is found in Simone Frieling, Hrg., *Von Fledermäusen und Vampiren. Geschichten und Gedichte* (Frankfurt am Main and Leipzig, Germany: Insel-Verlag, 2003).

Sources:

Alexander, Marie, and Christina Kiplinger Johns. *Biting Midnight: A Feast of Darksome Verse*. Anaheim, CA: Medium Rare Books, 2002. 119 pp.

Carter, Margaret L., ed. *Daymares from the Crypt: Macabre Verse*. San Diego, CA: The Author, 1981. 13 pp.

Martin, Timothy P. "Joyce and Wagner's Pale Vampire." *James Joyce Quarterly* 24, 4 (Summer 1986): 491–496.

Moore, Steven. *The Vampire in Verse: An Anthology*. New York: Dracula Press, 1985. 196 pp.

Nethercot, Arthur H. *The Road to Tryermaine*. Chicago: University of Chicago Press, 1939. 230 pp. Rept. New York: Russell & Russell, 1962. 230 pp.

Praz, Mario. *The Romantic Agony*. London: Oxford University Press, 1970. 479 pp.

Reed, Meg, and Chad Hensley, eds. *Rouge et Noir: Les poemes des Vampires*. 2 vols. Long Beach, CA: Preternatural Productions, 1991.

Spriggs, Robin, and Brent L. Glenn. *The Dracula Poems: A Poetic Encounter with the Lord of Vampires*. Murrayviille, GA: Circle Myth Press, 1992. 122 pp.

Stewart, W. Gregory. *Blood Like Wine.…* Silver Spring, MD: Preternatural Press, 1996.

Tepid, Vlad (Count Flapula) (pseudonym of John Jacobs). *Count Flapula's Monster Songbook*. Arlington, VA: self-published, 2001. 283 pp.

———. *Count Flapula's Scary Songbook*. Arlington, VA: self-published, 2001. 291 pp.

———. *Count Flapula's Vampire Songbook*. Arlington, VA: self-published, 2001.

Twitchell, James. *The Living Dead: A Study of the Vampire in Romantic Literature*. Durham, NC: Duke University Press, 1981. 219 pp.

Whitehead, Gwendolyn. "The Vampire in Nineteenth-Century Literature." *The University of Mississippi Studies in English* 8 (1990): 243–248.

Youngson, Jeanne. *The Further Perils of Dracula*. Chicago: Adams Press, 1979. 50 pp.

Poland, Vampires in

The Polish vampire is a variety of the vampire of the **Slavs**, with which it shares most essential features. Poland as a national group emerged from the union of some twenty west Slavic tribes including the Polonians (from which the country's name was derived), the Vistulans, the Silesians, the East Pomeranians, and the Mazovians. These tribes originally inhabited the Oder and Vistula River valleys. A significant boost was given to Polish self-identity in the tenth century with the founding of the Piast dynasty. Over the centuries it has found itself caught between the expansionist plans of the Germans and the Russians. Poland reached its greatest expansion in the seventeenth century, but at other times—following reverses on the battlefield—it almost ceased to exist.

Christianity was introduced to Poland in the late ninth century, and from the beginning, the Roman Catholic Church was dominant. As early as 969 C.E. a bishop was appointed to Krakow. Because of the allegiance of the people to Roman Catholicism, many of the beliefs about death and burial that pervaded the mythology of the southern Slavs were absent from Polish folklore.

Most importantly, unlike Eastern Orthodoxy, Roman Catholicism did not believe that the body of those who died outside of the rites of the church would remain incorrupt. There was some indication that beliefs about the witch/vampire *strix* of Roman **origins** filtered into Poland during the years immediately after the country's conversion to Christianity.

The Polish Vampire: Much of our knowledge of the Polish vampire derives from the field work of Jan L. Perkowski among the Kashubs (northern Poles) of Canada, where belief in vampires remains alive to the present day.

Perkowski's research both confirmed previous work and documented some modern developments. The common words for vampire in Poland were *upi—r* or *upier* (male) and *upierzyca* (female), a variation on the root Slavic word *opyrbi*, and alternatively *opji* or *wupji*. (*Upior/Upiorzyca* were borrowed from the Ukranian language probably in the fifteenth century.) A second word **vjesci** (variously spelled *Vjeszczi* was also popular, and occasionally the term *njetop* was used. The future vampire was destined to its fate from birth. Infants born with a membrane cap (caul) on their heads would become a *vjesci* and those born with two teeth would become a *upier/upierzyca* (or *wupji*).

The vampiric career of the future *vjesci* could be diverted by removing the cap, drying it, grinding it into a powder (or burning it), and feeding it (or its ashes) to the child when he or she was seven years old. Perkowski noted that modern Kashubs tended not to separate the two types of vampires.

Those destined to become vampires led otherwise normal lives, but they were noted to have a hyperactive personality and a red face. There was a saying among the Kashubs, "as red as a vampire." Also at the critical period, the time of their death, the future vampire would refuse final rites and the pastoral role of the priest. The body of a person suspected of becoming a vampire had to be watched carefully, for it was believed that the person did not truly die.

Hence, the body cooled very slowly, retained its color, and did not stiffen. Spots of **blood** often appeared around the face and/or **fingernails**.

After midnight, according to belief, it awakened and began to eat its own clothes and flesh. It then visited its relatives and sucked their blood. After visiting its relatives, it would go to the local church and ring the church bell. Those who heard the bell were destined to be the vampire's next **victims**.

Several precautions could be taken to prevent the future vampire from rising. First, the sign of the cross was made over its mouth. A **crucifix** or coin was placed in its mouth. A block might be placed under the chin to prevent it from reaching the burial clothes. The vampire was also blocked by certain obstacles. For example, a net might be put in the **coffin** based on the belief that the vampire would have to untie the knots before ascending. In like measure, a bag of sand or poppy **seeds** would be placed in the coffin in the belief that the vampire would have to count all of the grains of sand or all of the seed before arising from the tomb. Added precaution was afforded by scattering sand or seeds on the route from the grave to the family's house.

If, in spite of all precautions, a vampire managed to arise and attack the community, its tomb had to be opened and the body finally laid to rest. A nail could be driven through its forehead. However, the more common practice was **decapitation** of the corpse after which the severed head was placed between the corpse's feet. At the time the head was severed, blood from the wound would be given to any who had fallen ill as a result of the vampire's attack. The blood caused their recovery.

As late as 1870, in the town of Neustatt-an-der-Rheda (today known as Wejherowo) in Pomerania (northwest Poland), prominent citizen Franz von Poblocki died of consumption (tuberculosis). Two weeks later, his son Anton died. Other relatives also became ill and complained of nightmares. The surviving family members suspected vampirism and they hired a local vampire expert, Johann Dzigielski, to assist them. He decapitated the son who was then buried with his head placed between his legs. Over the objections of the local priest, the body of von Poblocki was exhumed and decapitated in like manner.

The priest complained to the authorities who arrested Dzigielski. He was tried and sentenced to four months in jail. He was released only when the family appealed the decision and found an understanding judge.

Polish Folklore Tales: Along with the accounts of actual vampires within the community, the Poles had a set of folktales about vampires that were told as a means of reinforcing community mores. One example, collected by Marion Moore Coleman, was called "The Vampire Princess." It told of Jacob, a poor man, and a king whose daughter had become a vampire. To earn money to feed his own daughters, Jacob agreed to assist the king. An old man gave him instructions, which Jacob followed to the letter. The final step involved Jacob entering the tomb of the princess when she left it, writing the name of the Holy Trinity inside of the coffin, and sprinkling it with holy **water**. As a result of his action, the princess was laid to rest and Jacob was amply rewarded by the grateful monarch. Among the community beliefs promoted by the story were the need to rely on the wisdom of elders, the efficacy of the church's means of grace, and the rewards that come to people for virtuous action.

Jan L. Perkowski has noted that belief in vampires, at least in their immediate presence, has been decreasing among the Canadian Kashubs he studied.

Among the important cultural factors leading to the loss of belief was the depersonalization of the birth and death process in hospitals and funeral homes. The preparation of the body in funeral homes broke the intimate dynamic between the deceased and the community and made the detection of the potential vampire difficult. Additionally, the Kashubs were surrounded by and participated in a larger culture that does not support a belief in vampires.

Sources:

Bratigam, Rob. "Vampire of Roslasin." *International Vampire* 1, 1 (Fall 1990): 4–5.

Coleman, Marion Moore, comp. *A World Remembered: Tales and Lore of the Polish Land.* Cheshire, CT: Cherry Hill Books, 1965. 229 pp.

Perkowski, Jan L., ed. *Vampires of the Slavs.* Cambridge, MA: Slavica Publishers, 1976. 294 pp.

———. *The Darkling: A Treatise on Slavic Vampirism.* Columbus, OH: Slavica Publishers, 1989. 174 pp.

Polidori, John (1795–1821)

John Polidori was the author of "The Vampyre," the first modern vampire story. Polidori attended Edinburgh University from which he received his medical degree at the age of nineteen. He wrote his thesis in 1815 on the nightmare. Polidori, however, had ambitions to be a writer and thus was delighted to be invited to be the traveling companion of **Lord Byron**, who was leaving England for a tour of continental Europe in the spring of 1816. In Geneva, they were joined by Claire Clairmont, Mary Godwin, and Percy Shelley.

Several days later, occasioned in part by bad weather that limited their movements, Byron suggested that each person begin a "ghost" story. He primed the pump somewhat by reading some tales from *Fantasmagoriana* to the small group. One evening, each began a story, but Mary Godwin was the only one who took the project seriously. Her story eventually grew into the novel *Frankenstein*. Polidori began a story about a skull-headed lady who was punished for peeking through a keyhole, but like the rest, soon lost interest in developing it very far.

Polidori kept a journal of his experiences in Europe, including some detailed notes on the evening of the storytelling, and most importantly, a synopsis of Byron's story. It concerned two friends traveling in **Greece**, where one of them died. Before his death,

however, he extracted an oath from the other that he reveal nothing about the conditions leading to his death.

Upon his return to England, he discovered his dead friend very much alive and having an affair with his sister. Byron saw no future in his story and so abandoned it.

Polidori took the plot of Byron's summer tale and developed it into a short story of his own. **"The Vampyre"** was published in the April 1819 issue of *New Monthly Magazine*. He took at least a light swing at Byron in his choice of the name of the vampire, **Lord Ruthven**, the name chosen by Byron's former lover Caroline Lamb to lampoon Byron in her novel, *Glenarvon*. The story was published under Lord Byron's name, which caused it to receive far more immediate attention than it otherwise would have gotten.

Goethe pronounced it Byron's best, and it was quickly translated into French and hailed as a new Byron masterpiece. The May issue of *New Monthly Magazine* included Polidori's explanation of the circumstances surrounding the writing of "The Vampyre," and Byron wrote a letter to *Gallignani's Magazine* in Paris, but by then it was too late. The *New Monthly Magazine*'s owner continued his insistence that he had published an original Byron story, and emphasized the assertion by publishing it separately as a booklet also under Byron's name.

One can only speculate what might have happened had the story been published under Polidori's name. It launched the first wave of interest in the vampire and went on to become, with the exception of **Dracula**, the most influential vampire tale of all time. The young Parisian romantics immediately saw its potential. Cyprien Bérard wrote a lengthy sequel detailing further adventures of its vampire character, *Lord Ruthwen ou Les Vampires* (1820). **Charles Nodier**, who wrote the preface to the French translation of "The Vampyre," turned the plot into a three act play. The play launched a theatrical fad that saw five Paris playhouses offering vampire productions by the end of the year. Lord Ruthven periodically reappeared during the next thirty years, his last ventures being recounted by **Alexandre Dumas** in 1852.

Unfortunately, Polidori did not live to see the far-reaching results of his story. His life took a negative turn and in 1821 he committed **suicide**. He was twenty-six years old.

Sources:

Bleiler, E. F. , ed. *Three Gothic Novels*. New York: Dover Publications, 1966. 291 pp.

Hanson, Robert R. *A Profile of John Polidori with a New Edition of The Vampyre*. Columbus, OH: Ph.D. dissertation, Ohio State University, 1966.

Macdonald, D. L. *Poor Polidori: A Critical Biography of the Author of "The Vampire."* Toronto: University of Toronto Press, 1991. 333 pp.

Polidori, John. *Ernestus Berchtold, or the Modern Oedipus*. London: Longman, Hurst, Rees, Orme, and Brown, 1819. 275 pp.

———. "The Vampyre." *New Monthly Magazine* (April 1819).

Senf, Carol A. "Polidori's *The Vampyre*: Combining the Gothic with Realism." *North Dakota Quarterly* 56, 1 (Winter 1988): 197–208.

———. *The Diary of John Polidori*. William Michael Rosetti, ed. London: Elkin Mathew, 1911. 228 pp. Rpt. Ithaca NY: Cornell University Library, 2009. 246 pp.

Switzer, Richard. "Lord Ruthwen and the Vampires." *The French Review* 19, 2 (December 1955): 107–12.

Twitchell, James B. *The Living Dead: A Study of the Vampire in Romantic Literature*. Durham, NC: Duke University Press, 1981. 219 pp.

Political/Economic Vampires

The description of a vampire as a creature who attacks people and saps their life's **blood** easily lends itself to various metaphorical extensions. Some of the most popular have been in the political realm in which governments and other powerful social structures have been seen as vampires sucking the life out of people over whom they rule or have some control. This political and economic usage of vampires and vampirism was obscured by the dominance of **psychological** interpretations of vampirism, which directed attention to the personal psychological forces operating in vampire accounts. However, the political element inherent in vampirism has also been recognized almost from the entrance of the word "vampire" into Western Europe.

Shortly after the introduction of the word "vampire" in an English publication in 1732, (an account of the investigation of **Arnold Paul** in Serbia), *The Gentleman's Magazine* of May 1832 carried a satirical article treating the Paul story as a metaphor of appalling social conditions. A decade later, a more serious utilization of the vampire as a political metaphor occurred in *Observations on the Revolution of 1688* (written in 1688, but published in 1741), which noted:

> Our Merchants indeed, bring money into their country, but it is said, there is another Set of Men amongst us who have as great an Address in sending out again to foreign Countries without any returns for it, which defeats the Industry of the Merchant. These are the Vampires of the Publick, and Riflers of the Kingdom.

A few years later, in 1764 Voltaire, in his *Philosophical Dictionary*, writing in response to the many vampires reported to exist in Eastern Europe, sarcastically responded:

> We never heard a word of vampires in London, nor even Paris. I confess that in both these cities there are stock-jobbers, brokers, and men of business, who sucked the blood of the people in broad daylight; but they were not dead, though corrupted. These true suckers lived not in cemeteries, but in very agreeable palaces.

Communism and the Vampire: The most famous use of the vampire image in political rhetoric came in the nineteenth century in the writings of Karl Marx. Marx borrowed the image from his colleague Frederick Engels, who had made a passing reference to the "vampire property-holding" class in *The Condition of the Working Class in England*. Marx commandeered the image and turned it into an integral element of his condemnation of the bourgeoisie (middle class). The bourgeoisie supported the capitalist system—the very system that had it in its grip.

Thus Marx could speak of British industry as vampire-like, living by sucking blood, or the French middle class stealing the life of the peasant. In France the system had "become a vampire that sucks out its the peasant's blood and brains and throws them to the alchemist's cauldron of capital." As Chris Baldick noted, for Marx, the essential vampiric relationship was between capital and labor. Capital sucks the life out of living labor and changed it into things of value, such as commodities. He contrasted living labor (the working class) with dead labor (raw products and machinery). Living labor was sentenced to be ruled by the "dead" products of its past work.

Karl Marx, who is thought of as the first "political vampire," is buried, appropriately enough, in London's vampire-infested Highgate Cemetery.

These products did not serve living labor, but living labor served the products it had created. Its service provided the means to obtain the products (which made up the wealth of the middle and upper class). Very early in *Capital* Marx stated, "Capital is dead labour which, vampirelike, lives only by sucking living labour, and lives the more, the more labour it sucks."

Dracula and Xenophobia: Recent comment on the novel *Dracula*, especially that of Stephen D. Arata, emphasized the social comment **Bram Stoker** more or less consciously embedded in his novel. *Dracula*, like other British novels of the period, expressed the fear that had developed as the British Empire declined: as the civilized world declined, Great Britain, and by extension Western Europe and North America, were under the threat of reverse colonization from the earth's "primitive" outposts. Stoker was well known for placing his **gothic** setting at a distant place, rather than pushing his storyline into the distant past. In the person of Dracula, he brought the wild unknown of the East, of **Transylvania**, to contemporary **London**.

Arata convincingly argued that Stoker held Transylvania as a fresh and appropriate symbol of the strife believed to be inherent in the interaction of the races of Eastern Europe and the Middle East. **Dracula** was not like **Lord Ruthven** or **Carmilla**—merely another decadent member of displaced royalty. He was a warrior in a land that pitted warriors against each other as a matter of course. His intentions were always domination and conquest. The coming of vampirism could bring the racial heterogeneity (and the racial strife inherent within it) to Great Britain. After figuring out what Dracula was and what he intended by his purchase of property in London, **Jonathan Harker** lamented his role in introducing Dracula to the city's teeming millions. He would conquer the land and foul the blood of the British race; the threat to the body was also a threat to the body politic.

The central problem for Stoker was a form of Victorian racism and the threatened pollution that the savage races, represented by the figure of Dracula, brought. After Dracula bit **Mina Murray**, she became "unclean." The boxes of foreign earth he brought to England had to be "sanitized." The untouchable Dracula was also sexually virile, capable of making any number of offspring, while British men by contrast were unproductive. Unlike the mothers, the fathers of the major characters were not mentioned, the only exception being **Arthur Holmwood**'s father, who died during the course of the novel. Only at the end, after Dracula was killed, did Harker symbolize the father of a new generation with a pure racial heritage.

The Contemporary Vampire: Throughout the twentieth century, the vampire has become a stock image utilized internationally by political cartoonists and commentators to describe the objects of their hostile political commentary. In recent decades, war, fascism, and even the country of Ghana have been labeled as vampiric entities. One recent vivid example of such usage of the vampire metaphor appeared in the wake of the fall of Communism in Russia and Eastern Europe at the end of the 1980s and the proclamation by then U.S. President George Bush of a "New World Order."

This term had previously entered the language through its use by a wide variety of political utopians from which it had acquired a number of controversial connotations. It sparked a variety of negative comment. The most virulent of the opposition, claiming that a New World Order amounts to the arrival of a world government, organized the Police Against the New World Order and launched Operation Vampire Killer 2000. Its program consists of a step-by-step plan to inform police, the military, and other law enforcement units about the New World Order and thus prevent their cooperation with it.

Sources:

Arata, Stephen D. "The Occidental Tourist: Dracula and the Anxiety of Reverse Colonization." *Victorian Studies* 33, 4 (Summer 1990): 621–45.

Baldick, Chris. *In Frankenstein's Shadow*. Oxford: Clarendon Press, 1987. 207 pp.

Engels, Frederick. *The Conditions of the Working Class in England*. (1845). In *Karl Marx and Frederick Engels on Britain*. Moscow: Foreign Languages Publishing House, 1953.

Frimpong-Ansah, J. H. *The Vampire State in Africa: The Political Economy of Decline in Ghana*. London: J. Curry, 1991. 205 pp.

Marx, Karl. *Capital*. New York: Appleton, 1889. 816 pp.

McCabe, Joseph. *What War and Militarism Cost: A Realistic Survey of the Vampire of the Human Race and the Supreme Enemy of Human Progress*. Girard, KS: Haldeman-Julius, 1938. 31 pp.

Operation Vampire Killer 2000: American Police Action for Stopping the Program for World Government Rule. Phoenix, AZ: American Citizens & Lawmen Assoc., 1992. 73 pp.

Reiman, Guenter. *The Vampire Economy: Doing Business under Fascism*. New York: Vanguard Press, 1939. 350 pp.

Voltaire. *Philosophical Dictionary*. 1764. Rept. New York: Alfred A. Knopf, 1924. 316 pp.

Wilson, Katharina M. "The History of the Word 'Vampire.'" *Journal of the History of Ideas* 44, 4 (October-December 1985): 577–83.

Polong *see:* Malaysia, Vampires in

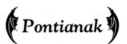

Pontianak

The *pontianak* was a type of vampire found in **Malaysia, Java,** and throughout much of Indonesia. In Malaysia it was paired with the ***langsuyar***, another Malaysian vampire, with whom it shared a common **origin**. The Malaysian *langsuyar* was originally a woman who gave birth to a stillborn child. The *pontianak* was that stillborn child.

As a vampire, it appeared as a night owl. To keep a dead infant from becoming a vampire, it was treated in a manner similar to a woman who died in childbirth: needles were placed in the palms of the hands, eggs were placed under the arms, and beads were placed in the mouth.

In Java and throughout the rest of Indonesia, the *langsuyar* and *pontianak* changed places, and the *pontianak* referred to the female night ***flying vampire***. Raymond Kennedy

found the Javanese speaking of the *pontianak* as a banshee who wailed in the night breeze for the child she had lost at birth. Augusta De Wit, also in Java, found that the *pontianak* was thought to be the spirit of a dead virgin. She seduced young men but as they embraced, she revealed the hole in her back. She would break the embrace after a single kiss and pronounce a death sentence on the man. He would die soon afterward if he did not grab her long hair and succeed in loosening a single strand.

In Malaysia, the following charm might also be said:

O Pontianak the Stillborn May you be struck dead by the soil from the grave-mound.

Thus (we) cut the bamboo joints, the long and the short, To cook therein the liver of the Jin (Demon) Pontianak.

By the grace of "There is no God but God"

Of the several Malaysian vampire spirit beings, the *pontianak* was the only one seen as a *jin* or *genie*, a type of spirit in Islamic mythology. In the mid-1950s Catay-Keris Productions began to make a series of movies based upon the *pontianak* as the beautiful female of Indonesian lore. Abandoned for a generation in the 1970s, the *Pontianak* returned to popularity in the new century.

Sources:

De Wit, Augusta. *Java: Facts and Fancies*. The Hague: W. P. van Stockum, 1912. Rept. Singapore: Oxford University Press, 1984. 321 pp.

Kennedy, Raymond. *The Ageless Indies*. New York: John Day Company, 1942. 208 pp.

Skeat, Walter William. *Malay Magic*. New York: Macmillan and Company, 1900. 685 pp. Rept. New York: Barnes & Noble, 1966. 685 pp.

Winstedt, Richard. *The Malay Magician Being Shaman, Saiva, and Sufi*. London: Routledge and Kegan Paul, 1961.

❨ Porphyria ❩

The little-known disease porphyria is actually a collective name for seven little known diseases, first identified during the nineteenth century. They were such rare diseases that only through the twentieth century have the different varieties been pinpointed and described. Collectively, the porphyrias are metabolic disorders caused by an enzyme deficiency that inhibits the synthesis of heme, the more extreme forms of the disease are characterized by an extreme sensitivity to light. The name porphyria comes from the Greek *porphyros*, meaning reddish-purple, and refers to a substance prominent in the blood and urine of a person with porphyria.

As early as 1964, L. Illis, in the article "On Porphyria and the Aetiology of Werewolves" suggested that porphyria could account for the reports of **werewolves**. In 1985, David Dolphin, in a paper presented to the American Association for the Advancement of Science, suggested that porphyria might underlie the reports of vampires. He noted that one treatment for porphyria was the injection of heme. Dolphin hypothesized that it was possible that people suffering from porphyria in past centuries attempted to drink the **blood** of others as a means of alleviating their symptoms. His idea received wide publicity and was seriously debated for a brief period.

Among those who critiqued Dolphin's theory was Paul Barber. First, Barber noted that there was no evidence that drinking blood would have any effect on the symptoms of the disease. Barber argued quite succinctly that Dolphin's theory only fit the situation if one did not look at the data too closely and had little respect for the powers of observation of the people who made the reports. The reports did not describe people who had the symptoms of porphyria, many of them related to the descriptions of corpses, not living persons, or to disembodied ghosts.

The coverage given the porphyria hypothesis in the popular press was a matter of great distress to many patients suffering from porphyria. *The Los Angeles Times,* for example, provided broad coverage as did many of the tabloids. Dr. Jerome Marmorstein, a physician from California, convinced the *Times* to do follow-up coverage countering the effects of its initial article. Norine Dresser, who has written the most extensive report of the debate, contacted the Porphyria Foundation and discovered a range of negative reactions experienced by people as a result of publicity connecting them to vampirism. Their distress was heightened by several popular **television** shows built on the possibility of a porphyria patient exhibiting vampiric behavior patterns.

The debate over porphyria lasted for several years, but Dolphin's hypothesis was eventually discarded altogether. It has no viable exponents at present. Meanwhile, the porphyria symptoms obviously resonate with the descriptions of lycanthropy. There are several studies in English and a number of in German expressing this idea.

Sources:

Barber, Paul. *Vampires, Burial, and Death: Folklore and Reality.* New Haven, CT: Yale University Press, 1988. 236 pp.

Dean, Geoffrey. *The Porphyrias.* Philadelphia: J. P. Lippencott, 1963. 118 pp.

Dresser, Norine. *American Vampires: Fans, Victims, Practitioners.* New York: W. W. Norton & Company, 1989. 255 pp.

Evans, Tammy. *Porphyria: The Woman Who Has the Vampire Disease.* Far Hills, NJ: New Horizon Press, 1997. 288 pp.

Illis, L. "On Porphyria and the Aetiology of Werewolves." *Proceedings of the Royal Society of Medicine* 57 (January 1964): 23–26. In *A Lycanthropy Reader: Werewolves in Western Culture.* Charlotte F. Otten, ed. Syracuse, NY: Syracuse University Press, 1986, pp. 195–199.

Pozzessere, Heather Graham (1953–)

Heather Graham Pozzessere is the name of a popular paranormal romance writer who writes under two pen names, Heather Graham and Shannon Drake, with most of her vampire titles appearing under the latter. Pozzessere was born Heather Graham in 1953 in Miami, Florida and later attended the University of South Florida. She married and worked a variety of jobs while raising a family. After the birth of her third child, she withdrew from outside employment and stayed at home. She also began to write. She sold her first book, *When Next We Love,* in 1982. She subsequently wrote novels in the romance, science fiction, and horror genres, but had her major success in romance. She was a founding member of the Florida chapter of Romance Writers of America. She began hosting the annual *Romantic Times* Vampire Ball, a charity affair, in 1999.

Because of her wide popularity, she was chosen to write the launch books for the Dell's Ecstasy Supreme line, Silhouette's Shadows line, and Harlequin's imprint, Mira Books. Her books have been translated into approximately twenty languages.

Very early in her career, Pozzessere authored her first vampire novel, *This Rough Magic* (1988), somewhat lost amid the many ephemeral Silhouette titles. Then, after authoring a number of books, Pozzessere wrote her first vampire novel under her pen name Shannon Drake, *Beneath a Blood Red Moon*, at the end of the 1990s. For what would become a six-volume series, Pozzessere created the vampire character Maggie Montgomery who runs a clothing boutique in **New Orleans**' French Quarter. She found herself drawn to a police detective named Sean Canady, with whom she feels a deep connection. But he has come into her life while investigating a murder in the French Quarter. A **blood** trail from the victim ended at Maggie's shop. To solve the murder, she had to reveal her secret identity to him.

In the sequel, Maggie and Sean take second place to Lucien, the King of the Vampires, who has been attracted to travel writer Jade MacGregor. They had met in Scotland, where he saved her from an attack by other vampires. The vampire followed her to New Orleans, where Lucien had to risk his secret identity to continue to assist her. Each of the remaining four titles takes the reader to a different exciting setting such as Venice, Italy or Salem, Massachusetts, focusing on another couple, while reintroducing the characters from the earlier novels.

Pozzesssere revives the vampire world of her Shannon Drake series in the most recent novels written as Heather Graham for Mira Books. She returns to her favorite New Orleans setting and invites characters from the past to attend to the two new characters who will become the focus of each novel. In *Kiss of Darkness* (2006), for example, Maggie and Sean Canady (now married) and Lucien reappear to assist Jessica and Byron (the latter a vampire hunter just awakening to the existence of "good" vampires).

Sources:

Drake, Shannon. *Beneath a Blood Red Moon*. New York: Zebra Books/Kensington, 1999. 383 pp.

———. *When Darkness Falls*. New York: Zebra Books/Kensington, 2000. 428 pp.

———. *Deep Midnight*. New York: Zebra Books/Kensington, 2001. 478 pp.

———. *Realm of Shadows*. New York: Zebra Books/Kensington, 2002. 396 pp.

———. *The Awakening*. New York: Zebra Books/Kensington, 2003. 384 pp.

———. *Dead by Dusk*. New York: Zebra Books, 2005. 379 pp.

Graham, Heather. *Kiss of Darkness*. Don Mills, ON: Mira Books, 2006. 395 pp.

———. *Blood Red*. Don Mills, ON: Mira Books, 2007. 347 pp. Romance.

Pozzessere, Heather Graham. *This Rough Magic*. Silhouette Intimate Moments 260. New York: Silhouette Books, 1988. 251 pp.

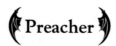

Preacher

Through the 1990s, DC Comics has nurtured its Vertigo series, comics written for an adult audience that have featured a variety of horror titles. Among the series' top entries is *Preacher*, written and drawn by the team of Garth Ennis and Steve Dillon. The series is named after Jesse Custer, a preacher who had become possessed by Genesis, a new entity created by the mating of an angel and a demon. Genesis had great **strength**, but lacked willpower. In his possessed state, Jesse has the power to speak the

Word and bend people to his desires. Jesse is driven into a number of situations by his knowledge that God has retired from running the universe. He seeks God to call him to account for this patent neglect of creation.

Jesse is accompanied by two friends/colleagues, Tulip, his girlfriend, and Proinsas Cassidy, a vampire from **Ireland**. Born in 1900, as a young man, Cassidy joined the cause of Irish freedom from British rule. At one point, during Easter week of 1916, Cassidy's brother Billy pulled him from the fight, and the pair headed for home. On the way, Cassidy was attacked by a bog monster who pulled him into the **water**. The next day when he struggled out of the water, he began to burn in the sun. He quickly understood his survival meant staying in the water until nightfall.

Without a teacher, Cassidy learned what it meant to be a vampire by trial and error. As he mastered his new existence, he decided to immigrate to **America** where no one would know him. In New York, a city that never **sleeps**, he attached himself to the late-night pub crowd. After running across a copy of *Dracula*, he finally gained a better understanding of what had happened to him. (Cassidy's story is told in issue Nos. 30–33 of *Preacher*.) Over the eight decades of existence Cassidy has developed few long-term relationships, having discovered the issue mortals have with his eternal youth.

However, he has involved himself with Jesse and Tulip, and they continually find themselves getting each other out of potentially fatal situations. Cassidy is almost invincible. He has been shot, stabbed with knives, and decapitated. And when appendages were severed, they eventually grew back. The sun remains his one major enemy. He needs a regular intake of **blood**, but also enjoys alcohol, some drugs, and tobacco.

Preacher ran for sixty-six issues, and was quickly reprinted in trade paperback editions. There were also five related one-shot special issues and a spin-off series, *Saint of Killers*, which was void of vampires. There have been several attempts at turning the series into a movie, and several variant scripts produced, but none have been put into production.

Sources:

Kitson, Niall. "Rebel Yells: Genre Hybridity and Irishness in Garth Ennis & Steve Dillon's Preacher." *The Irish Journal of Gothic and Horror Studies* 2 (March 2007). Posted at http://irish-gothichorrorjournal.homestead.com/. Accessed August 15, 2009.

Preacher. Nos. 1–66. New York: DC Comics, 1995–2000.

Premature Burial *see:* Explanations of Vampirism

❨ Protection against Vampires ❩

Coinciding with the emergence of the belief in vampires was the designation of methods of protecting oneself from them. In the West, the vampire first appeared as a threat to infants and to mothers at the time of birth, and the best protection available was the use of magic. The earliest barriers known to have been used against vampire attacks were magical words and acts, which survived in the more recent use of prayer and Bible quotes. In the first century, Ovid left an account of an ancient ritual to protect a child, which included touching the door where the infant resided with a branch of a plant, sprinkling the entrance of the house with **water**, and killing a pig that was offered to the *strix* (vampire) as alternative food. The words spoken during this ritual included:

Birds of the night (i.e., the *strix*), spare the entrails of the boy. For a small **victim** (the pig) falls. Take heart for heart, I pray, entrails for entrails. This life we give you in place of a better one.

After the pronunciation of the formula, the house was further secured with thorn branches at the window. This ancient account of warding off the attack of a vampire mentions one of the several most common items that served to protect people from vampires: the thorn. The **hawthorn**, in part because of its association with the story of Jesus's death, was the most common across Southern Europe, but other thorns were used as magical barriers against both vampires and witches. Both the obvious problems that the wild thorn bush had presented to humans and its many values when properly utilized suggested the extension of its role into the supernatural realm. And, in fact, it was reported as an anti-witch and anti-vampire shield not only in Europe, but in Asia and the Americas.

Possibly even more than thorns, the pungent herb **garlic**, which was utilized as both a medicine and a food flavoring, was also a protective device used to ward off witches and vampires. Garlic was found in all parts of the world, particularly in the warmer climates, and everywhere found its way onto the list of anti-vampire items. Garlic's inherent value as a medicine, coupled with its strong offensive smell, suggest its power to drive away the forces of evil.

The other ubiquitous protective device against vampires was **seeds**. All around the world people scattered seeds between themselves and the suspected vampire as a barrier. Vampires were thought to be fascinated with counting seeds, be they mustard, millet, grass, linen, carrot, poppy, or rice.

The seeds might be scattered in the **coffin**, over the grave, on the path between the grave site and the village, or around a home that the vampire might enter. The vampire would either have to count the seeds slowly, one per year, or be caught in a situation of having to collect and count enough seeds that it could not finish its task before dawn.

In Europe, especially since medieval times, objects sacred to **Christianity**, most commonly the **crucifix**, the **eucharistic wafer**, and holy **water**, have been cited as effective protective devices. Vampires were identified with the realm of the devil, and **Satan** and his minions could not exist in the presence of the holy. Mere priests, also being sinners, were not considered completely holy whereas the cross and eucharistic host were symbolic of the very presence of God. In Latin American countries, sacred pendants were attached to a child's bed clothes. In Eastern Orthodox countries, an icon (such as a holy picture) had the same sacred value as a crucifix.

Around the world, several other sacred objects have been noted, but were not prominent in non-Christian societies. Here the vampire, indeed the whole realm of evil, was not seen in such polarized categories as it was in the Christian world. (In an early episode of *Buffy the Vampire Slayer*, Buffy's friend Willow [whose parents were Jewish] wonders if and how she could make use of the cross against vampires, a question raised previously in several movies such as *Love at First Bite* [1979]. The idea expresses the problem of affirming the particularly of the sacred in a more pluralistic religious setting.) The use of holy objects that banished the unholy also led to a consideration of various purifying agents. The most universal was **fire**. Fire, while destructive, cleansed. It was a major agent in **destroying the vampire**, but could also be used to drive the vampire away. From accounts around the world, numerous items have been used to ward off vampiric evil. Some are purely defensive, forming a barrier between the vampire and its potential victim.

Others create an aura or atmosphere that the vampire would avoid. A few were more offensive and would actually harm the vampire. Typical of the defensive protective devices would be the many things that could be placed in a bedroom to ward off a vampire. Shoes turned around, a **mirror** placed by the door, and a broom put behind a door all served in one or more cultures as a vampire barrier.

Items with illumination or smell, such as candles or garlic, were usually the best to create a protective atmosphere. However, metal—typically pieces of iron, placed under or near a baby's crib—was thought to keep vampires away in many diverse cultures. Iron, when used as a structural feature could form a strong physical barrier for it was substance that vampires avoid. To a lesser extent, **silver** was used in a similar manner. Needles, knives, and scissors were also placed near the bed to be used against the vampire in the advent of an attack.

Protection against the Modern Vampire: With the secularization of the vampire myth in the late twentieth century, most of the prophylactic attributes of traditional protective items were lost. Recent vampires have been affected little by holy objects, thorns or seeds. Garlic alone remained an almost universal item that vampires were believed to avoid, and only a minority of contemporary Westerners used garlic with any regularity. Modern novels left victims with few protections from the onslaught of a vampire. Even fire, also still universally avoided by vampires, rarely occurred in modern society in a form useful to stave off a vampire's effort to reach its victim. Modern vampires generally have extra **strength**, but can be overcome by a group of people.

In recent novels and films, victims have had little to protect them should a vampire single them out. The only forces holding the vampire in check were: a possible moral commitment not to kill; or rational consideration, to be discrete, that kept a vampire from leaving a trail of **blood**-drained bodies to be found by authorities who would then discern the vampire's existence.

Some help survives. Taoist magical formulas written on paper and stuck to the forehead of a Chinese vampire has been a standard feature of Hong Kong movies. In the British television series *Being Human*, the Jewish werewolf found that the Star of David he wore around his neck kept the evil vampires at bay. The cross still works occasionally, but is less and less effective all the time.

Psychic Vampirism Among the most popular theories to explain the persistency and universality of vampire myths, the idea of psychic vampirism traced the belief in the vampire to various occult, psychic, or paranormal phenomena. Such **explanations** have their **origin** in folktales that identified the vampiric entity as a ghostly figure rather than a resuscitated body—or even further back to ancient times and the earliest vampire-like figures who were described as evil gods or demons, such as the *lamiai* of **Greece**. Such entities were closely related to the medieval **incubus/succubus**.

Psychic explanations of vampirism emerged in the nineteenth century on the heels of psychical research, a scientific discipline that assigned itself the task of investigating experiences formerly assigned to the realm of the occult or supernatural. It attempted to discern which experiences were illusional, which had ready psychological

explanations, and which were paranormal or psychic. Psychical research borrowed many terms from spiritualism and occultism as a part of its early working language. While vampirism was not the most popular topic for discussion among spiritualists and occultists, it appeared occasionally and seemed to need an explanation from the perspective of the occult worldview.

Astral Vampirism: Among ritual magicians and theosophists, vampirism was explained as due to the astral body. It was their understanding that each person had not only a physical body, but a second body, usually invisible, which was often seen separating from the physical body at the moment of death. This astral body accounted for such phenomena as ghosts and out-of-body experiences. Henry Steel Olcott, the first president of the Theosophical Society, speculated that occasionally when a person was buried, the person was not really dead, but in a catatonic or trance-like state, still barely alive. Citing the experience of yogis who could slow their breathing to an indiscernible rate and survive without air for many weeks, Olcott surmised that a person could survive for long periods in the grave. In the meantime, the person would send his or her astral double to suck the **blood** or life force from the living and thus gain nourishment. This explanation, to Olcott, seemed to explain why a body that had been buried for weeks or months would be dug up and appear as if it had recently gorged itself on blood. It was his belief that the blood or life force swallowed by the astral form passed immediately to the organs of the physical body lying in the tomb, and then the astral body quickly returned to that corpse.

Olcott also commented on the practice of burning the corpse of a suspected vampire. He argued that vampirism, and the possibility of premature burial and vampirism, made cremation the preferable means of disposing of the physical remains of the deceased. Cremation severed the link between the astral and physical body and prevented the possibility of vampirism. Olcott's original observations, including his preference for cremation, were later expanded on by other prominent theosophical writers such as Charles W. Leadbeater, Arthur E. Powell, and **Franz Hartmann**.

Hartmann traced the astral vampirism theory back to the alchemist Paracelsus (1493–1541), though Olcott and his mentor, H. P. Blavatsky, seemed to have developed the theosophical position directly from the work of pioneer psychical researcher **Z. J. Piérart**. Hartmann, who related several vampire stories in the pages of the *Occult Review*, developed his own variation of astral vampirism in his theory of an "astral tumour." He saw the vampire as a force field of subhuman intelligence that acted out of instinct rather than any rational thought. He differed from Olcott by suggesting that the vampire was malignant, but since it lacked any intelligence, was not morally evil.

Two modern versions of the astral vampirism hypothesis have been articulated. In the 1960s parapsychologist Scott Rogo formulated a theory based upon broad reading in both vampire and psychic literature and attention to some of the more exotic psychic occurrences. He posed the definition of a vampire as "a certain kind of haunting which results in an abnormal loss of vitality through no recognized channel." Vampirism was not due to a living agent, but to a disassociated portion of the human that remains intact and capable of some degree of human consciousness after death. This remnant eventually dissipated, but that disintegration was postponed by its ability to take life from the living. **Martin V. Riccardo**, founder of the Vampire Studies network, suggested that astral vampirism may account for many of the reports of vampirism. He focused, however, upon the activity of individuals who sent their astral bodies to attack their sleeping neighbors. Riccardo cited a detailed case reported by occultist **Dion Fortune**, author of a volume on the prevention of various negative occult experiences, *Psychic Self-Defense*. Fortune discovered that some of her neighbors shared a nightmare attack attributed to the same person. Fortune confronted the person, who admitted to having magical powers and to harming others.

Vampiric Entities: Among the "I AM" Ascended Masters groups that have grown out of the original work of Guy Ballard, a somewhat different emphasis on the vampire theme has been evident. These groups posited the idea that over the centuries, humankind created a large number of what were termed "mass entities." Through calling up negative realities, thinking about them, and feeling violently about them, they called these mass entities into existence. Every time a person gave attention to one of these mass entities, it drew **strength** from that individual and became more powerful in altering the course of humanity. The legion of mass entities went under names like war, pestilence, and fear.

These mass entities acted like vampires and, as one of the Masters speaking to the members of the Bridge to Freedom asserted, it was the task of those related to the Ascended Masters and their cause to dissolve the "vampire activity of the mass humanly created entities." The work of dissolution was accomplished through decreeing, the particular process of prayer utilized by the "I AM"-related groups.

The Church Universal and Triumphant under the leadership of its Ascended Masters Messenger Elizabeth Clare Prophet, identified a number of disincarnate mass entities, including drug and tobacco entities, insanity entities, sex entities, and entities aligned against the church. One set of entities was termed Halloween entities, which included the horror entity named Dracula (female) or Draculus (male). The church has given its members a ritual of exorcism of these entities.

Magnetic Vampirism: The most common form of psychic vampirism, however, did not involve an astral body. Magnetic vampirism was the sapping of life force by one person from another. The idea of magnetic vampirism was based on the commonly reported experience of a loss of vitality caused by simply being in the presence of certain people. Hartmann referred to psychic sponges—people who unconsciously vampirized every sensitive person with whom they came into contact. He believed such a person was possessed by a vampiric entity who continually drained both the energy of its possessed host and all of his or her acquaintances. Scott Rogo, author of "In-depth Analysis of the Vampire Legend," cited the case of clairvoyant Mollie Flancher who, because of some unrelated condition, was kept under careful observation for many years.

It was noted that any animals that she attempted to keep as pets soon died, and those close to her speculated that she had sapped them of their psychic energy.

Anton LaVey (1930–1997), founder of the Church of Satan, taught church members about psychic vampirism and how to avoid it as a key element in the Church's ego development program.

Psychic vampirism made a significant comeback in the 1990s. A new movement of real vampires, the Sanguinarians, became visible and were identified by their con-

sumption of blood. As the new phase of the real vampire movement developed, however, it became evident that the great majority did not drink blood or had abandoned the practice for a number of reasons, including the transmission of blood diseases. At this point, voices favoring psychic vampirism came to the fore, and long-time Ohio vampire Michelle Belanger emerged as their primary spokesperson.

Note: There are many instances of tales of alleged psychic vampirism in theosophical literature in its early phase. These are collected in Marco Frenschkowski, "Okkultismus und Phantastik. Eine Studie zu ihrem Verhältnis am Beispiel der Helena P. Blavatsky," *Das schwarze Geheimnis. Magazin zur unheimlich-phantastischen Literatur* 4 (1999): 53-104, No. 78 in the United States.

Sources:

"Address by Believed Archangel Zadkiel." *The Bridge* 7, 7 (October 1958): 16–23.

Belanger, Michelle A. *Psychic Vampire Codex: Manual of Magick & Energy Work.* York Beach, ME: Weiser Books, 2004. 284 pp.

———. *Sacred Hunger.* Lulu.com, 2005. 142 pp.

———. *Vampires in Their Own Words: An Anthology of Vampire Voices.* York Beach, ME, Weiser Books: 2007. 288 pp.

Fortune, Dion. *Psychic Self-Defense.* London: Aquarian Press, 1952. 212 pp.

Hartmann, Franz. "Vampires." *Borderland* (London) 3, 3 (July 1896).

Hort, Barbara E. *Unholy Hungers: Encountering the Psychic Vampire in Ourselves & Others.* Boston: Shambhala, 1996. 264 pp.

LaVey, Anton Szandor. *The Satanic Bible.* New York: Avon, 1969. "Names of Disincarnate Entities and Possessing Demons." Livingston, MT: Church Universal and Triumphant, 1987. 2 pp.

Leadbeater, Charles W. *The Astral Plane: Its Scenery Inhabitants, and Phenomena.* London: Theosophical Publishing House, 1915. 183 pp.

Olcott, H. S. *The Vampire.* Adyar, Madras, India: Theosophical Publishing House, 1920. 19 pp.

Powell, Arthur E. *The Etheric Double and Allied Phenomena.* Wheaton, IL: Theosophical Publishing House, 1925, 1969.

———. *The Astral Body and Other Astral Phenomena.* Wheaton, IL: Theosophical Publishing House, 1927, 1973. 265 pp.

Ravensdale, Tom, and James Morgan. *The Psychology of Witchcraft.* New York: Arco Publishing Company, 1974. 200 pp.

Rogo, Scott. "In-depth Analysis of the Vampire Legend." *Fate* (September 1968): 70–7.

Slate, Joe H. *Psychic Vampires.* St. Paul, MN: Llewellyn Publications, 2002. 243 pp.

Psychological Perspectives on Vampire Mythology

Through the twentieth century the psychological element of the vampire myth repeatedly captured the attention, even fascination, of psychological researchers. The widespread presence of the vampire image in human cultures led some psychologists to call the vampire an archetype—an intrapsychic psychological structure grounded in the collective unconscious. The differing major psychoanalytic interpretations help us understand the compelling fascination with narratives and images grounded in vampire mythology. This mythology rests on central metaphors of the mysterious power of human **blood**, images of the undead, forbidden and sexualized longings, and the ancient idea that evil is often hard to detect in the light of day. Humans have long felt that there is a sense in which evil operates like a contagious disease, spreading through defilement caused by direct contact with a carrier of a supernatural "toxin."

Freudian Perspectives: Prior to Freud's development of psychoanalysis, even sophisticated psychologies tended to associate the realm of the undead with premodern demonological mythologies. Freudian thought legitimized the human fantasies of the undead as a topic for serious scientific research. Freud developed a modern map of the unconscious, which he saw as a repository of denied desires, impulses, and wishes of a sexual and sometimes destructively aggressive nature. In **sleep** we view the unconscious as a landscape inhabited by those aspects of life that go on living, the realm of the undead spoken through dreams. According to Freudian psychoanalysis, vampire narratives express in complex form the fascination—both natural and unnatural—which the living take in death and the dead. From Freud's point of view, "All human experiences of morbid dread signify the presence of repressed sexual and aggressive wishes, and in vampirism we see these repressed wishes becoming plainly visible." Freudians emphasize the ways in which ambivalence permeates vampire stories. Death wishes coexist with the longing for immortality. Greed and sadistic aggression coexist with a compulsively possessive expression of desire. Images of deep and shared guilt coexist with those of virginal innocence and vulnerability.

Freud and his followers noted the ways in which vampire stories reflect the unconscious world of polymorphous perverse infantile **sexuality**. From a Freudian point of view it is particularly striking that in **Bram Stoker's *Dracula***, all the traditional mythical traits of the vampire are blended in such a way that it reflects the Oedipus complex. Count **Dracula** is seen as a father figure of enormous power and the entire story one of incest, necrophilia, and sadistic acting out of oral and anal fixations. According to Freud, the Oedipus complex emerges between the ages of three and five and is responsible for much unconscious guilt. Oedipal rivalry with fathers causes castration anxiety in males. Both males and females experience feelings of aggression toward the parent of the same sex and feelings of possessive erotic desire toward the parent of the opposite sex. Since conscious awareness of these feelings and associated wishes raises the anxiety level of the child to unacceptable levels, ego defenses come into play to prevent the conscious mind from becoming aware of these dangerous impulses. From the Freudian point of view, it is the function of dreams to disguise these wishes into more acceptable forms that will not wake the dreamer from sleep. Thus, a competent dream interpretation can trace dream images back to the unacceptable Oedipal wishes that underlie them. Following this belief, the vampire image is a fantasy image related to these wishes.

A classical Freudian interpretation of the vampire legend, therefore, seeks to discern the same denied Oedipal wishes in the story. Here the blending of sexuality and aggression in the vampire attack is seen as suggestive of the child's interpretation of the primal scene (the parents having sexual intercourse). That is, the male child often fantasizes sexual contact between his parents as causing harm to the mother. From this point of view, Count Dracula's relationship to his group of female vampires can be interpreted as an image of the father-daughter acting out of repressed incestuous strivings that continue to hold the daughter under the power of the father's spell.

Werewolves, "pit bulls from the pounds of hell," are another image of this same father-daughter tryst. The immature female whose own agency and autonomy are undeveloped, secretly agrees to the father's continuing narcissistic claims to power over her life.

Clearly, Freud and his early followers were right in their assumption that the vampire myth was grounded in archaic images of repressed longings and fears. However, the classical Freudian interpretation—while containing some helpful insights—was a gross oversimplification of the psychological contents of vampire narratives. Carl Jung offered the first powerful alternative to early Freudian views.

Jungian Perspectives: Jungian psychoanalysts point to the worldwide interest in the vampire as evidence of its archetypal nature. From a Jungian perspective, the myriad varieties of vampire narratives found cross-culturally throughout history indicate that these images are not merely by-products of personal experience but are grounded in species-wide psychological structures. In other words, vampire images reflect significant experiences and issues that are universal in human lives around the world. In short, there is something about the vampire that we already understand intuitively—with the knowledge coming from deep within our psyche.

Jung believed that the vampire image could be understood as an expression of what he termed the "shadow," those aspects of the self that the conscious ego was unable to recognize. Some aspects of the shadow were positive. But usually the shadow contained repressed wishes, anti-social impulses, morally questionable motives, childish fantasies of a grandiose nature, and other traits felt to be shameful. As Jung put it:

> The shadow is a moral problem that challenges the whole ego-personality, for no one can become conscious of the shadow without considerable moral effort.

> To become conscious of it involves recognizing the dark aspects of the personality as present and real.

The vampire could be seen as a projection of that aspect of the personality, which according to the conscious mind should be dead but nevertheless lives. In this way Jung interpreted the vampire as an unconscious complex that could gain control over the psyche, taking over the conscious mind like an enchantment or spell. And even when we were not overwhelmed by this unconscious complex, its presence led us to project the content of the complex onto characters in a vampire narrative. Of social importance, the image of the vampire in popular culture serves us as a useful scapegoat since—through the mechanism of projection—the vampire allows us to disown the negative aspects of our personalities. As Daryl Coats noted:

> Dracula treats Mina Harker the way **Jonathan Harker** would like to treat her but is scared to do so. Dracula treats Lucy the way her fiance would like to treat her. The vampiric Lucy can respond to men the way the non-vampiric Lucy could not.

This Jungian interpretation of the vampire image provided significant insight into the enormous popularity of vampire stories. From this point of view, a vampire lives within each of us. We project this inner reality on both male and female persons, members of other "tribes" and ethnic groups. We all have a dim awareness that this demonic yet tragic figure is real. However, we usually fail to grasp that this outer image is an expression of an inner reality—a reality that is elusive, threatening to self and others, and that can be effectively engaged only through a combination of empathy and heroic effort.

Jung did not limit his discussion to what would be an oversimplification by suggesting that vampiric traits in others result entirely from our projections.

THE VAMPIRE BOOK: THE ENCYCLOPEDIA OF THE UNDEAD

He observed that auto-erotic, autistic, or otherwise narcissistic personality traits can result in a personality that is in fact predatory, anti-social, and parasitic on the life energy of others. In contemporary psychology and psychiatry this type of personality is called a "narcissistic personality disorder." This clinical syndrome contains the most important clues to the psychological reality represented in the vampire image.

Otto Kernberg noted that narcissistic personalities are characterized by a "very inflated concept of themselves and an inordinate need for tribute from others." Capable of only a shallow emotional life they have difficulty experiencing any empathy for the feelings of others. Their ability to enjoy life, except for their experiences of their own grandiose fantasies and the tributes that they can manipulate others into giving them, is severely limited.

They easily become restless and bored unless new sources are feeding their self esteem. They envy what others possess and tend to idealize the few people from whom they desire food for their narcissistic needs. They depreciate and treat with contempt any from whom they do not expect nurturance. According to Kernberg, "their relationships with other people are clearly exploitative and parasitic." Kernberg's description of the narcissistic personality sounds as if it were crafted to describe vampires:

> It is as if they feel they have the right to control and possess others and to exploit them without guilt feelings—and behind the surface, which very often is charming and engaging, one senses coldness and ruthlessness.

Jungian interpreters often highlight the parallels between the vampire image and the characteristics of narcissistic psychopathology. Daryl Coats, for example, has noted that the vampire is both narcissistic and autistic. He emphasizes that the vampire experiences "narcissistic self-destruction as a result of their intensely selfish desires." Jungian analyst Julia McAfee has focused on the vampire as an image of the shadow of the narcissistic mother.

The narcissistic mother, while appearing on the surface to have good will and a nurturing attitude toward the child, in fact drains the energy of the child and weakens the child through subtle (and not so subtle) emotional exploitation.

This pattern provides insight into the psychological experiences that underlie the numerous folktales of vampires preying on children. As we shall see below, vampiric parents have always been a widespread human phenomenon—and there is reason to believe that the incidence of such predatory behavior toward children is increasing.

The Vampire and the Culture of Narcissism: Although Jung and subsequent Jungian interpreters have noted these and other narcissistic aspects of vampire myths, they did not adequately explore narcissistic psychopathology, the chief psychological dynamic underlying vampire narratives and the major reason for the current burgeoning fascination with the vampire image. However, others assumed the lead in psychoanalytic research into pathological narcissism and its social formation as a "culture of narcissism." In his book, *The Culture of Narcissism*, Christopher Lasch diagnosed the rapidly spreading climate of moral self-absorption that has emerged in the wake of modernization and secularization. Our contemporary penchant for narcissistic self-indulgence has resulted from the eclipse of the Protestant work ethic with its emphasis on

public involvement and community values. Lasch also noted that contemporary alterations in culture also indicated a fundamental shift in our psychological development.

Peter Homans, building on Lasch's insight, suggested "that the dominant or modal personality of our culture has shifted to a narcissistic psychological organization." He tied this recent phenomenon to the process of a gradual erosion of a religious view of the world. Homans further noted that the collapse of the Protestant ethic as a bulwark against pathological self-involvement was only the last in a long line of cultural and religious developments leading to today's increasing narcissism. Here we begin to discern the chief psychological dynamic underlying the increasing popularity of vampire images and narratives. "If our society is a culture of narcissistic self-involvement, then the vampire image is a perfect icon to express the psychological character configuration underlying it."

Vampirism and Narcissistic Psychopathology—Perspectives from Psychoanalytic Self Psychology: Both Lasch and Homans have emphasized the importance of the contribution of psychoanalytic self psychology in their analysis of the culture of narcissism. They built upon the insights of such theorists as Alice Miller, D. W. Winnicott, Heinz Kohut, and Ernest Wolf who, in their analysis of narcissistic pathology, provide a more adequate understanding of the vampiric metaphor, its myth, and meaning in contemporary culture. Psychoanalyst Alice Miller has written extensively on the ways in which narcissistic mothers prey on their children. In her best-selling *The Drama of the Gifted Child* and other books Miller describes in depth the ways in which an emotionally immature mother can reverse the appropriate flow of nurturing—expecting the child to be whatever the parent needs for the parent's own satisfaction. This creates in the child a compliant but false self—an empty shell that, though it appears to be functional and successful, is in fact covering an extremely enfeebled, needy, and fragile core.

D. W. Winnicott, famed British psychoanalyst, wrote extensively on the concept of the false self, which developed in response to an inadequately nurturant early emotional environment. It was, however, psychoanalyst Heinz Kohut who became the chief interpreter of narcissistic personalities. The work of Kohut, Wolf, and their colleagues offers us the best understanding of the psychodynamics that underlie the vampire narratives. What goes wrong to cause an individual to develop a narcissistic personality disorder? As Kohut emphasized, the development of a "normal" personality requires a creative interplay between the innate potentials of the child's self and the emotional environment that is created by those who are the primary caregivers of the child. The emerging self of the child contains infantile potentials for mature self-esteem and a cohesive sense of the self. But the environment of the child must evoke and support the development of those potentials if the self of the child is to mature into a centered and vigorous personality. Among the essentials of an adequate nurturing environment are: idealizable adults who will allow intimacy and an empowering merger with their calmness, and nurturant significant others who will "mirror" the child (i.e., recognize and affirm the independence and value of the child's emerging self).

Kohut asserted that an inadequate nurturing environment causes significant damage in the form of "narcissistic wounds." The development of the self is arrested and the emerging self is left in a weakened condition in an ongoing struggle with overwhelming longings and unmet emotional needs. When normal development is disturbed in this way, the resulting state of emotional disequilibrium necessitates that the individual seek

to compensate for the resulting deficit or weakness in the structure of the self. Therefore, the person who has not successfully built a psychological internal structure remains pathologically needy and dependent upon others to perform functions he or she cannot execute. Others must be "used" in various ways to bolster a fragile sense of self and to attempt to fill an inner emptiness. This primal dependency is at the root of "vampiric" predatory patterns in relationships.

Symptoms resulting from such emotional disturbances have characteristic features. Patients often report feeling depressed, depleted, and drained of energy. They report feelings of emptiness, dulled emotions, inhibited initiative, and not being completely real. At work they may find themselves constricted in creativity and unproductive. In social interaction they may have difficulty in forming and sustaining interpersonal relationships. They may become involved in delinquent and anti-social activities. They often lack empathy for the feelings and needs of others, have attacks of uncontrolled rage or pathological lying. Often a person with such narcissistic wounds will become hypochondriacally preoccupied with bodily states. They will experience bodily sensations of being cold, drained, and empty. These clinical descriptions, of course, parallel some of the major symptoms of the **victims** of vampires as described in vampire narratives. However, we shall see below that the tie between narcissistic pathology and the vampire is much tighter than merely sharing the same set of symptoms.

Narcissistic wounds and resulting pathology manifests in a wide spectrum of clinical syndromes ranging from psychosis to narcissistic character disorders. Several narcissistic disorders described by Kohut and Wolf are relevant for an inquiry into the vampire myth. What they denoted as the "mirror-hungry personalities" is of special importance. Mirror-hungry personalities "thirst for self objects whose confirming and admiring responses will nourish their famished self." Because of their deep-felt lack of worth and self esteem, these persons have a compulsive need to evoke the attention and energy of others. A few establish relationships that fuel their needs for long periods, but they also engage in a constant search for new sources or supplies of emotional nourishment. Even genuinely loving, accepting, and nurturing responses quickly become experienced as inadequate.

Thus, Wolf elaborates:

Despite their discomfort about their need to display themselves and despite their sometimes severe stage fright and shame they must go on trying to find new self objects whose attention and recognition they seek to induce.

Such mirror-hungry personalities often manifest arrogant superiority. If this arrogance is not affirmed and accepted they will often withdraw into what self psychologists call "a grandiose retreat" seeking refuge in isolation in order to shore up their self esteem. Kohut and Wolf have noted that such personalities may result either from a lack of mirroring attention in childhood or from a problem with the parent's attempts to give such attention. For example, when a parent gives a child attention, the parent may fail to align that attention to the immediate needs of the child. Instead, the parent may claim the child's attention not to nurture the child, but to bolster the parent's enfeebled self by reenforcing the dependence of the child on the parent. In any case, the child does not receive the kind of mirroring attention that allows for the development

of an independent and vigorous self. The intense infantile needs for adequate mirroring will persist in the unconscious of the adult in the form of deep and compulsive longings.

It should be clear from the above description that the powerful appeal of vampire narratives grow out of the human experience of mirror-hunger both in parent and child. When this psychologically archaic hunger for affirmation is seen in the parent, it results in predatory emotional exploitation of the child. Such exploitation is an increasingly widespread experience and undoubtedly lies behind the growing fascination with the vampire image. It is these "vampiric parents" that were noted above in the work of Julia McAfee and Alice Miller.

The dynamics of mirror-hunger also helps us to understand the combination of grandiosity and immortality in the vampire mythology. When the child does not experience adequate mirroring, its infantile grandiosity cannot be transformed into a mature psychological structure identified by its more realistic sense of self-esteem. Adult untransformed grandiosity makes unrealistic claims on others. There are accompanying fantasies of being able to fly, being invisible, being able to change shape at will—all capacities of a vampire. That the vampire does not, and cannot die can be seen as the way in which grandiose feelings of invulnerability take possession of the mirror-hungry person when archaic needs break through into consciousness. The more disappointment experienced by the mirror-hungry person, the more they resort to the grandiose retreat from social involvement.

What is Dracula's remote castle on the top of a difficult to reach mountain if it is not a "grandiose retreat?" Dracula is not satisfied in his isolation. His hunger drives him in search for someone to fulfill his longings. So the retreat does not satisfy, but intensifies the experience of chronic emptiness and longing, and eventually to another expedition to find "new blood." The effect of a vampiric visitation is clearly experienced as a drain of energy on the part of the prey, along with a kind of claustrophobic suffocation resulting from the "depletion" of the blood. Mirror-hungry personalities often manifest a kind of "counter-dependency." That is, they will often seek to avoid expressions of emotional need and dependency.

Underlying this reluctance to admit chronic unmet needs to self or others is the fear of a disastrous, even fatal, depletion of the person who is seen as a potential source of gratification. Thus we can understand Count Dracula's ambivalence with regard to his claiming Mina as one of the undead. If she is exploited, then she is depleted and no longer an adequate source. Therefore the prospect of "having" can be experienced simultaneously as a threat of "losing." Self psychologists often refer to such fears of destroying the nourishing self object as one of the reasons for the "defense against self object longings." A person may feel, "my needs for mirroring and narcissistic supplies are monstrous—if I gratify them, they may destroy you. Therefore I must not let myself be aware of these toxic needs." This escape into denial is paralleled in the Dracula's daylight retreat into his **native soil** (mother earth) brought from **Transylvania** and placed in his residence at **Carfax**.

While the vampire sleeps during the daylight of consciousness, in the enclosure of unconsciousness—symbolized by the **coffin**—he sleeps unaware of his unmet longings for maternal nurture. This dynamic illustrates the central conflict of the vampire drama. There is both desperation for an infusion of emotional nutriments, "lifeblood," if the fragmentation of the self is to be avoided—and revulsion at the "monstrous" neediness that this desperate longing manifests in the inner emotional life. Although the conscious mind may repress awareness of these urges, we can see here that in the vampiric personality narcissistic rage and related envy manifests in a compulsive desire to seek the destruction of the independent life of the other. The other has been experienced as possessing "the Good," life, energy, well-being, attention, etc. The envying person experiences emptiness within, intolerable longing for something that will fill the void, and the desire to take the other's "life" from them—thereby hoping to gain enough "nutriments" to avoid the disintegration of the self.

This self psychological interpretation sheds some useful light on the elements of sexuality so integral to the vampire narratives. A hallmark of vampire mythology has been the powerful erotic imagery accompanying the vampire attack. The sexual contact portrayed in these stories utilizes images of the innocent virginal woman or youth becoming the target of compulsive bloodlust (e.g., narratives that merge engagement in sexual intercourse with the acquisition of bite wounds to the throat and breast). Sexuality and aggression fuse in a manner that leads to the infection and death of the victim. Psychologically speaking, narcissistic wounds often lead the individual to seek narcissistic nourishment through sexual activity. A facade of sexual attraction and genital sexual behavior masks a quest for what Freudians have called oral (not genital) gratification. The compulsive quality of this sexual behavior is grounded in the individual's narcissistic psychopathology. Today this pathology is widely understood to be the emotional foundation of sexual addictions. The Dracula story captures this combination of apparently erotic behaviors that are, in fact, expressions of a deep inner emptiness, not human affection.

The Social Psychology of Intergroup Hate: The Vampire Image and the Mechanism of Scapegoating: It would be a mistake to assume that the psychological importance of the image of the vampire relates only to intrapsychic, familial, and small group interpersonal interactions. The projection of this image onto other social groups is undoubtedly one of the powerful psychosocial mechanisms that fuel malignant racism, anti-Semitism, sexism, and other expressions of scapegoating with resultant hate crimes.

In the dynamic of scapegoating, we find someone or some group that can be used as a receptacle for the projection of the vampiric image. Then the scapegoat can be blamed, cast out of the community, and/or persecuted with various degrees of violence. This externalization of the vampiric image enables the person or "in-group" to feel better—guiltless or "cleansed." As a social dynamic such scapegoating both allocates blame and seems to "inoculate" against further disappointments by evicting or eliminating the cause of one's "disease." Racist rhetoric is frequently fueled by the projection of the image of the vampire onto other social groups. An example of this recently became international news when a leader of an American Black Muslim group publicly characterized Jewish people as "bloodsuckers," imaging them as parasites draining the lifeblood of the black community. The projection of this image enables the dehumanization of its target group—allowing the rationalizations needed to justify ruthless racial discrimination and violence.

Such racist rhetoric is usually grounded in what self psychologists call "narcissistic rage". Narcissistic rage differs from anger or "righteous indignation." Anger always seeks positive changes in relationship in a context of justice and potential reconciliation—not the destruction of the other party. Narcissistic rage seeks the utter destruction of the independent personhood of the other—either through death or ruthless enslave-

ment and exploitation. Thus the vampire within projects its image onto the other—thereby justifying its own predatory intentions.

Conclusions—Emptiness, Envy, and the Vampiric Personality: In surveying the development of the major psychoanalytic perspectives on the vampire, the attempt was made to trace the manner in which each school of thought, out of its understanding of fundamental psychodynamic processes, sought to interpret vampirism. Each of these perspectives contributed to the understanding of the rich mythological and symbolic narratives of vampire lore and one by one built the foundation upon which rests the more promising contemporary interpretation by self psychology, which views the vampire as a primary icon representing essential aspects of narcissistic psychopathology. Self psychology calls attention to the significance of inner emptiness, the longing for emotional nutriments that can prevent disintegration of the self, and the resulting envy that sees such nutriments (the Good) in others and wishes to take it from them. Contemporary psychoanalytic self psychology in the tradition of Heinz Kohut and Ernest Wolf, in offering a more complete psychological understanding of the origins, major forms, and manifestations of such vampiric psychological illness, also provides the necessary therapeutic insights and techniques needed if healing of vampiric and vampirized personalities is to occur.

Sources:

Bourguignin, Andre. "Vampirism and Autovampirism." In *Social Dynamics of Antisocial Behavior.* L.B. Schesinger and E. Revitch, eds. Chicago: Charles C. Thomas, 1983: 278–301.

Coats, Daryl R. "Jung and the Irish Vampires." *Journal of Vampirology* 2,4 (1986): 20–27.

Henderson, D. James, "Exorcism, Possession, and the Dracula Cult: A Synopsis of Object-Relations Psychology." *Bulletin of the Menninger Clinic* 40, 6 (November 1976): 603–628.

Homans, Peter. *The Ability to Mourn: Disillusionment and the Social Origins of Psychoanalysis.* Chicago: University of Chicago Press, 1989.

Jones, Ernest. *On the Nightmare.* Hogarth Press, 1931. Rev. ed.: New York: Liveright Publishing Corporation, 1951.

Jung, C. G. *Civilization in Transition.* Vol. 10, *The Collected Works of C. G. Jung.* Princeton, NJ: Princeton University Press, 1962.

Kohut, Heinz and Wolf, Ernest S. "The Disorders of the Self and Their Treatment: An Outline." *The International Journal of Psycho-Analysis.* 59, 4 (1978): 413–425.

Lasch, Christopher. *The Culture of Narcissism: American Life in an Age of Diminishing Expectations.* New York: W.W. Norton & Co., Inc., 1979.

Lee, Ronald, and Martin Colby J. *Psychotherapy after Kohut: A Textbook of Self Psychology.* Hillsdale N.J.: The Analytic Press, 1991.

McAfee, Julia. *The Vampire Archetype and Vampiric Relationships.* Evanston, IL: The C.G. Jung Institute of Chicago, 1991.

Millon, Theodore. "Narcissistic Personality: The Egotistic Pattern." In *Disorders of Personality: DSM–III, Axis II.* New York: John Wiley and Sons, 1981.

Noll, Richard. *Vampires, Werewolves, and Demons: Twentieth-Century Reports on the Psychiatric Literature.* New York: Brunner/Mazel, 1992.

Richardson, Maurice. "The Psychoanalysis of Ghost Stories." *The Twentieth-Century* 166 (1959): 427.

Twitchell, J. B. "The Vampire Myth." *American Imago* 37,1 (Spring 1980): 83–92.

Ulanov, Ann and Barry Ulanov. *Cinderella and Her Sisters: The Envied and the Envying.* Philadelphia: The Westminster Press, 1983.

Wolf, Ernest S. *Treating the Self: Elements of Clinical Self Psychology.* New York: Guilford Press, 1988.

❨ Pulp Magazines, Vampires in the ❩

Essential to the spread of the vampire as an object of popular myth in the twentieth century was the pulp magazines, mass circulation periodicals named for the cheap pulpwood paper on which they were printed. They were the successors of the "penny dreadful" of the nineteenth century and, in an age before television, filled a significant gap in the entertainment industry. The earliest pulps provided readers with a wide variety of genre fiction, including detective, western, jungle, and action/adventure.

Occasionally they would print a "different" or "off trail" story, the avenue by which the then-highly questionable horror tales slipped into the pulp market.

All-Story Magazine was among the first to feature such "different" stories. Beginning in 1919, *The Thrill Book* specialized in "strange, bizarre, occult, mysterious, tales," the harbinger of the first true all-horror pulp, *Weird Tales*, which made its appearance in 1923. *Weird Tales* dominated the tiny market through the 1920s. It was joined by *Ghost Stories* in 1926, and following the creation of a broad public by the **Universal Pictures** movies in the early 1930s, additional titles appeared. *Strange Tales of Mystery and Terror* hit the stands in 1931 as direct competition for *Weird Tales*, and they were soon joined by Popular Publications' *Dime Mystery* (1933), *Terror Tales* (1934), and *Horror Stories* (1935). *Terror Tales* and *Horror Stories* specialized in what was termed the shudder tale, in which hapless **victims** were terrorized by mad scientists and/or psychotics masquerading as model citizens.

Through the 1930s a number of horror titles were created to meet a burgeoning public demand. The vampire slowly emerged as a subject of horror fiction. Horror great H. P. Lovecraft may have introduced the vampire theme into pulp fiction with his story "The Hound", which appeared in the February 1924 issue of *Weird Tales*. "The Hound" is however, not a true vampire tale. Lovecraft later penned "The Shunned House" about a quite interesting "collective" vampire. It was written 1924 but not printed until 1928 in a separate booklet by W. Paul Cook, though not bound at that time. The story also appeared in *Weird Tales* October 1937. Vampirism also plays a minor role in Lovecraft's "The Case of Charles Dexter Ward," written in 1927, but not published until 1941.

Lovecraft aside, the first true pulp vampire story seems to have been "The Vampire of Oakdale Ridge" by Robert W. Sneddon in the December 1926 issue of *Ghost Stories*. Beginning in 1927 with "The Man Who Cast No Shadow" by Seabury Quinn and the reprinting of "Dracula's Guest" by **Bram Stoker**, *Weird Tales* began to offer a steady stream of vampire tales. Quinn's character was typical of early twentieth-century vampires. Based in part on **Dracula**, he possessed the same hairy palms and lacked a **mirror** image.

Quinn set his Transylvanian Count Czerny against his popular detective figure Jules de Grandin. The first era of vampire tales culminated in two of the best pulp stories: "A Rendezvous in Averoigne" by Clark Ashton Smith and "Placide's Wife" by Kirk Mashburn, both of which appeared in *Weird Tales* contemporaneously with the release of Universal Pictures' **Dracula (1931)**.

The decade following the success of **Bela Lugosi**'s *Dracula* saw the publication of numerous vampire stories by a group of authors who emerged as the collective heirs of the **Edgar Allan Poe** tradition of horror.

Poster art from the classic vampire film *House of Dracula*.

Typical of these new authors, Robert E. Howard, famous as the creator of Conan the Barbarian, had his "The Horror from the Mound" published in *Weird Tales* in 1932. Like other vampires to appear later in the Conan adventures, his first vampire was a loathsome powerful monster who could be destroyed only in a one-on-one fight with cowpuncher Steve Brill.

Among the most heralded and reprinted of the 1930s vampire pulp fiction, *I, the Vampire* was an early work by science fiction great Henry Kuttner. He set his suave vampire, Cevalier Futaine, in contemporary Hollywood where he arrived from **France** to play a role in a new film, *Red Thirst*. Robert Bloch, a prolific horror writer who reached his zenith of fame with the novel *Psycho*, began in the 1930s pulps. Among his memorable early tales was "The Cloak", which appeared in *Unknown Worlds* in 1939. This story built upon the premise of a cloak that transformed the wearer into a vampire.

The best "typical" vampire tale from the pulps may very well be "Revelations in Black" by Carl Jacobi. It appeared in *Weird Tales* in April of 1933 and was reprinted in the Arkham House volume of that name in 1947.

Pulp fiction continued through World War II but experienced a noticeable decline by the end of the 1940s. The publishers of *Weird Tales* finally went bankrupt in

1954, and the pulps gave way to newsstand magazines devoted to fantasy, science fiction, and horror such as *The Magazine of Fantasy and Science Fiction* and *Fantastic Stories of the Imagination*. Over the years several vampire anthologies have lifted stories from the pulps, and by far the best collection appeared in *Weird Vampire Tales* (1992), edited by Robert Weinberg, Stefan R. Dziemianowicz, and **Martin H. Greenberg**.

Sources:

Carter, Margaret L. *The Vampire in Literature: A Critical Bibliography*. Ann Arbor, MI: UMI Research Press, 1989. 135 pp.

Parnell, Frank H., with Mike Ashley. *Monthly Terrors: An Index to the Weird Fantasy Magazines Published in the United States and Great Britain*. Westport, CT: Greenwood Press, 1985. 602 pp.

Sullivan, Jack, ed. *The Penguin Encyclopedia of Horror and the Supernatural*. New York: Viking, 1986. 482 pp.

Weinberg, Robert, Stefan R. Dziemianowicz, and Martin H. Greenberg, eds. *Weird Vampire Tales: Thirty Chilling Stories from the Weird Fiction Pulps*. New York: Gramercy Books, 1992. 442 pp.

❮ The Queen of the Damned ❯

The Queen of the Damned is the title of the third volume in **Anne Rice**'s "The Vampire Chronicles" and the designation of Akasha, the original vampire who ruled as a queen in ancient Egypt, more than six millennia ago. Although Akasha first appears in *The Vampire Lestat* (1985), she became the subject of *The Queen of the Damned* (1988) which recounts the story of the **origin** of Rice's vampires and the return of the queen in 1985 with a grandiose scheme to take over the world.

Akasha ruled beside her weaker husband Enkil and became known for her lack of tolerance of those who thought differently than she did. While she showed some enlightened rulings, she also had a dark side expressed in her desire to experience the supernatural. In that endeavor she had two young female witches brought to her court to demonstrate their contact with the spirit world. The antics of the spirit Amel caused the pair to receive some severe punishment.

Mad at Akasha, Amel attacked Khayman, the court's chief steward, and the priests were unable to exorcise his dwelling. Meanwhile those opposed to Akasha and Enkil assassinated the pair. As she lay bleeding, Akasha's soul escaped but was seized by Amel. Binding himself to her soul, Amel then entered her body with which he fused, thus creating a new entity, and the first vampire. Akasha's body healed almost immediately and she shared her **blood** (and, as it turned out, the presence of Amel) with Enkil. He also healed miraculously.

They sought a cure to their vampiric condition, but the witches informed them that the only way they could end the possession by Amel was to kill themselves. They discovered that Amel had a tremendous thirst. They killed many and in the process created additional vampires. Then they noticed that as the number of vampires increased, their hunger decreased, and eventually they had no need for blood at all. Once they reached that state, they remained together, but as living statues. In this condition, they gained legendary status in the vampire community as "those who must be kept." They were preserved and protected by vampire guardians who were aware that somehow their existence was dependent upon the two.

The tie between Akasha and Enkil and all other vampires was made abundantly clear when suddenly several millennia ago, vampires everywhere were severely burned, many fatally. When one new vampire, Marius, was sent to Egypt, he discovered that the person whose responsibility it was to guard the pair had grown tired of his job and placed them in the sun. Akasha begged Marius to take her to Europe. He then became the new guardian, and she became the impersonal observer of the world, projecting her consciousness from her body and utilizing the eyes of others, both vampires and mortals.

Over the years, she was visited by only a few outsiders. Marius had allowed his new love, Pandora, to drink from Akasha. At another time, while visiting Marius, **Lestat** made his way to the underground shrine room where the two were located. He awakened Akasha and they embraced and exchanged blood. Suddenly Enkil awoke and separated them. Only Marius's appearance saved Lestat from being killed.

Then in 1985, Akasha was awakened by Lestat's **music**. She then sucked the life out of Enkil and initiated her plan of world domination. She set out to destroy most of the males (both mortal and vampire) and to establish an Eden in which the **women**, but especially Akasha herself, would reign. Along the way, she invited Lestat to join her and took him on one of her killing sprees. However, she targeted the two witches who had been the instrument leading to her vampirism. Maharet and Mekare were present at a gathering of vampires in Sonoma, California, strategizing about the deaths Akasha had caused. When Akasha appeared, but before she could act, Mekare pushed her through a glass wall. She was decapitated, and Maharet moved immediately to isolate the heart and brain of the fallen queen. Both were passed to Mekare who quickly devoured them. In the eating of Akasha's organs, the essence of Amel passed to Mekare and she became the nexus of the life force flowing through the vampire community. With Akasha destroyed, undead life could return to some degree of normalcy.

The Queen of the Damned was brought to the screen in 2002 in a production with Stuart Townsend as Lestat and Akasha played by rhythm and blues singer Aaliyah. Already possessed of a strong following as a singer, this movie was seen as a major step in turning her into a major movie star. Unfortunately, she died in a plane crash before the movie was released. Though far behind *Interview with the Vampire* in appeal, the movie went on to become one of the top twenty vampire films in gross receipts.

Sources:

Ramsland, Katherine. *The Vampire Companion: The Official Guide to Anne Rice's The Vampire Chronicles.* New York: Ballantine Books, 1993. 507 pp.

Rice, Anne. *The Queen of the Damned.* New York: Alfred A. Knopf, 1988. 448 pp. Rept. New York: Ballantine Books, 1989. 491 pp.

———. *The Vampire Lestat.* New York: Alfred A. Knopf, 1985. 481 pp. Rept. New York: Ballantine Books, 1986. 550 pp.

Rakshasas *see:* India, Vampires in

Ramsland, Katherine (1953–)

Katherine Ramsland is a philosopher who has emerged as a major interpreter of **Anne Rice**'s writings. Born in Ann Arbor, Michigan, Ramsland attended Northern Arizona University, where she received her bachelor's degree in 1978; Duquesne University, where she received her master's degree in 1979; and Rutgers University, where she received her doctorate in 1984. Following her graduation, she began teaching in the philosophy department at Rutgers and wrote her first book on the Danish existentialist philosopher, Soren Kirkegaard, entitled *Engaging the Immediate: Applying Kirkegaard's Indirect Communication to Psychotherapy* (1988).

During the 1980s she became acquainted with Anne Rice and saw in her a subject worthy of her time and scholarly interpretation. Even though Ramsland had been working in a genre field, she was able to reach a mass audience. Over several years, she produced *Prism of the Night,* which became the first of a series of books on Rice that have ranged from *The Anne Rice Trivia Book* to the collection of scholarly papers assembled for *The Anne Rice Reader.* In the process of her writings and scholarship, Ramsland gained an in-depth familiarity with Rice's vampire books and had become privy to many considerations that underlay the novels. She brought all that she had learned together in the massive volume, *The Vampire Companion: The Official Guide to Anne Rice's The Vampire Chronicles* (1993). She also prepared a similar volume on Rice's **Witchcraft** novels.

In 1997, Ramsland's interest in vampires led to her becoming editor of a short-lived periodical, *The Vampyre Magazine,* published by Sabertooth, Inc. She had by this time become intrigued by the phenomenon of real vampires, which led to the very successful volume *Piercing the Darkness* (1998), which highlighted her adventures into the darker sides of the community. In the new century, an interest in crime appeared that led to a number of books. The two interests merged in her book, the *Science of Vampires* (2002), and a lengthy article, "The Vampire Killers" for the TruTV Crime Library (posted at http://www.trutv.com/library/crime/serial_killers/weird/vampires/1.html). Ramsland currently teaches forensic psychology at DeSales University in Center Valley, Pennsylvania.

Sources:

Ramsland, Katherine. *Prism in the Night: A Biography of Anne Rice.* New York: Dutton, 1991. 385 pp. Rept. New York: Plume Books, 1992.

———. *The Vampire Companion: The Official Guide to Anne Rice's The Vampire Chronicles.* New York: Ballantine Books, 1993. 507 pp. Revised. 1995. 577 pp.

———. *The Anne Rice Trivia Book.* New York: Ballantine Books, 1994. 244 pp.

———. *The Witches Companion: The Official Guide to Anne Rice's "Lives of the Mayfair Witches."* New York: Ballantine Books, 1994.

———. *The Anne Rice Reader.* New York: Ballantine Books, 1997. 359 pp.

———. *Piercing the Darkness.* New York: HarperPrism, 1998. 371 pp.

———. *The Science of Vampires.* New York: Berkley Boulevard Books, 2002. 276 pp.

Real Vampires *see:* The Vampire (Real Vampires)

Realm of the Vampire *see:* Vampire Fandom: United States

❨ Redcaps ❩

Redcaps were malevolent spirits found in the lowlands of Scotland (now part of the **United Kingdom**). They haunted abandoned sites, especially places where violent deeds had been committed. Their connection to vampirism seems to have come from their carrying a cap that had been dyed red with human **blood**. At every opportunity the redcap would re-dye the cap in blood.

Sources:

Briggs, Katherine. *An Encyclopedia of Fairies*. New York: Pantheon Books, 1976. 481 pp.

❨ Renfield, R. N. ❩

R. N. Renfield was one of the major characters in **Bram Stoker**'s novel *Dracula* (1897). At the beginning of the novel, Renfield was confined to the lunatic asylum managed by Dr. **John Seward**. Apart from demonstrating a set of unusual symptoms, no history of or specific reason for his confinement was given. When first described, Seward praised Renfield for his love of **animals**, however, he revised his opinion somewhat after Renfield ate them in order to absorb their life. Seward then coined a new term to describe him: zoophagous, or life-eating.

Renfield's symptoms took a radical turn just at the time **Dracula** made the move from **Whitby** to **London**. Renfield announced to his attendant, "I don't want to talk to you: you don't count now; the Master is at hand." Seward initially interpreted his words as the sign of a religious mania. The next day he made the first of several attempts to escape and headed toward **Carfax**, where Dracula had deposited his boxes of earth. Captured, he was returned to the asylum, but escaped again several days later.

Seward's attention was diverted from Renfield for several weeks as he treated **Lucy Westenra**. However, one evening Renfield escaped and broke into the doctor's study. He attacked Seward with a knife, and dropped to the floor to lick up the drops of **blood** that had fallen from the cut. Again several weeks passed during which time Lucy died and it was determined that she was a vampire. Almost forgotten again in the concern for Lucy, Renfield called Seward to come to his cell. He spoke sanely to Seward and the men who accompanied him, Dr. **Abraham Van Helsing**, **Quincey P. Morris**, and **Arthur Holmwood**. Later that day Seward and Renfield had a long conversation, and Seward determined that Dracula had been with him. The following day, it was found that Renfield had been attacked in his cell. Seward and Van Helsing attended him, and Renfield described Dracula's attack. He mentioned **Mina Murray**'s (now Harker) name as he lay dying. From his words, Van Helsing determined that Mina was under attack, and the men left Renfield to save her. They broke into her bedroom just in time as she and Dracula were sharing each other's blood.

The character of Renfield, the mad man—one of the most vivid and interesting in the novel—has been given quite varied treatment in the several stage and screen adaptations, though most often he was used to promote atmosphere or as comic relief. Dwight Frye was especially remembered for his frantic portrayal of Renfield in **Universal Pictures'** *Dracula* (1931).

The presence of Renfield, however, vividly portrayed the intense evil represented by the vampire. Supernatural **explanations** vie, even in the modern secular world, with scientific "**psychological**" explanations that have no need to appeal to either the sacred or preternatural. In the end, even Dr. Seward agreed that the psychological explanations were inadequate, and he joined Van Helsing on the crusade to destroy the vampire.

Renfield has become the subject of several works designed as comments and sequels on Dracula. Kyle Garrett (pseudonym of Gary Reed) led the way in 1994 with a three issue **comic book** series about Renfield that told the story of Dracula from Renfield's perspective. Both Tim Lucas in *The Book of Renfield* (2005) and Barbara Hambly in *Renfield: Slave of Dracula* (2006) have imagined a more sympathetic Renfield as the victim of Dracula who did what he could to fend off the over-powering vampire.

Sources:

Garrett, Kyle, and Galen Showman. *Renfield.* Caliber Comics, 1994. 103 pp.

Hambly, Barbara. *Renfield: Slave of Dracula.* New York: Berkley Publishing Group, 2006. 306 pp.

Lucas, Tim. *The Book of Renfield: A Gospel of Dracula.* New York: Touchstone, 2005. 406 pp.

Waller, Gregory A. *The Living and the Undead: From Stoker's Dracula to Romero's Dawn of the Dead.* Urbana, IL: University of Illinois Press, 1986. 376 pp.

Riccardo, Martin V. (1952–)

Martin V. Riccardo, a writer, researcher, hypnotist, and lecturer on vampires, is the founder of Vampire Studies. He grew up in the Chicago Metropolitan Area and graduated with a Bachelor of Science degree from the University of Illinois in 1974. Originally created as the Vampire Studies Society in Chicago, Illinois, in 1977, Vampire Studies ("Society" was dropped from the name in 1990) was designed as a means for vampire enthusiasts to share information on the subject. It was the first vampire-oriented fan club to use the word vampire in its title. Riccardo had initially developed an interest in the subject several years earlier when he had heard a lecture by **Leonard Wolf,** author of *A Dream of Dracula.* After some extensive research on the subject, he began lecturing on vampires in 1976.

In 1977, Vampire Studies began publishing *The Journal of Vampirism,* one of the first periodicals devoted to vampires in folklore, fiction, film, and fact. The journal published nonfiction articles, book and movie reviews, news reports, fiction, **humor,** cartoons, and **poetry.** A primary interest of the journal was reports of vampires and vampire attacks. The journal folded in 1979 after six issues. While being the center of vampire fandom in Chicago, Riccardo built a large correspondence network and was himself an active member in many of the vampire-oriented fan clubs. He also built a large collection of vampire books, magazines, and **comic books.** Among the members, contributors, and correspondents to Vampire Studies were Dorothy Nixon and Eric Held, who later founded the Vampire Information Exchange. Jan L. Perkowski, a **Slavic** studies scholar from the University of Virginia and an authority on the Slavic vampire, was also a contributor to *The Journal of Vampirism,* as was Dr. **Jeanne Youngson,** founder of the Count Dracula Fan Club, now known as the **Vampire Empire.**

In 1983, Riccardo saw the publication of two vampire books: *Vampires Unearthed,* the first comprehensive **bibliography** of vampire literature and filmography, has become

Vampire studies founder Martin V. Riccardo.

the basis of all vampire bibliographic work since; *The Lure of the Vampire* was a collection of Riccardo's essays. Through the 1980s and 1990s, Riccardo has also written a number of articles on vampires for various vampire and occult periodicals. He coined the term "astral vampirism" to refer to a form of **psychic vampirism** in which the astral body or ghost form left the physical body for the purpose of draining **blood** or vital energy. During the early 1990s he concentrated his research on vampire dreams and fantasies. Riccardo does not believe that there are Dracula-like creatures but does believe in the process of **psychic vampirism** in the sense that people can suck the energy or life force from others.

After *The Journal of Vampirism* folded, Riccardo continued to stay in contact with the subscribers and others interested in the varied issues related to vampires. Over the years he received thousands of letters from individuals interested in vampires, and reporting their experiences of them. Letters he had received through his correspondence network first suggested a line of research he pursued through the mid-1990s on dream experiences. The work resulted in his book, *Liquid Dreams of Vampires* (1996). Riccardo is a hypnotist by profession. From 1984 to 1985 he edited *Hypno-News of Chicagoland*. He also has an interest in the larger occult world and in 1981 founded the Ghost Re-

search Society. For six years in the 1980s he hosted the Midwest Ghost Expo, a yearly convention for ghost researchers and enthusiasts. He also has coordinated programs on a variety of occult topics from reincarnation to ancient Egypt.

In the 1990s, Riccardo hosted the Vampire Fan Forums, gatherings of fans and personalities in the vampire world for lectures, discussions, and fun. He is a popular lecturer on vampires and the occult in Greater Chicago. He received the Count's Award for Meritorious Service at **Dracula '97: A Centennial Celebration** for his many years of work in building vampire fandom.

Sources:

"The Lure of Martin V. Riccardo." Special issue of *The Vampire Information Exchange Newsletter* 53 (April 1991).

Ricardo, Martin V. *Mystical Consciousness*. Chicago: MVR Books, 1977.

———. "The Persistent Vampire." *Fate* (July 1978): 74–81.

———. *The Lure of the Vampire*. Chicago: Adams Press, 1983. 67 pp.

———. *Vampires Unearthed*. New York: Garland Publishing, 1983. 135 pp.

———. "Vampires—An Unearthly Reality." *Fate* (February 1993): 61–70.

———. *Liquid Dreams of Vampires*. St. Paul, MN: Llewellyn Publications, 1996. 252 pp.

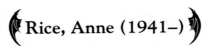

Rice, Anne (1941–)

A mong the people who have contributed to the significant increase of interest in the vampire in the last generation, few rank with writer Anne Rice. Her major vampire character, **Lestat de Lioncourt**, who was introduced in her 1976 book, *Interview with the Vampire*, has taken his place beside **Bram Stoker's Dracula** and *Dark Shadows'* **Barnabas Collins** as one of the three major literary figures molding the image of the contemporary vampire.

Rice was born Howard Allen Frances O'Brien in the Irish community in **New Orleans,** Louisiana, and changed her name to Anne shortly after starting school. During her late teens she grew increasingly skeptical of the teachings of the Roman Catholic Church in which she had been raised. She not only rejected the unique place of the Roman Church among other religious bodies, but also pronounced her disbelief in its major affirmations of the divine work of Jesus Christ and the existence of God. She replaced her childhood religious teachings with a rational ethical system, an integral element in her reworking of the vampire tradition. Both Rice and her poet husband Stan Rice began writing professionally during the early 1960s, but he was the first to receive recognition. In 1970 he won the Joseph Henry Jackson Award for poetry. Rice sold her first story, "October 4, 1948," in 1965, but it was not until 1973 that she felt ready to quit her job in order to write full time.

The Vampire Chronicles: As early as 1969 Rice had written a short story that she called "Interview with the Vampire." In 1973 she turned it into a novel and attempted to sell it. Following several rejections, Alfred A. Knopf bought it, and it was published in 1976. The book became an unexpected success and has remained in print both in hardback and paperback. Her second novel, *The Feast of All Saints*, was published by Simon & Schuster three years later, and a third, *Cry to Heaven*, appeared in 1982.

Anne Rice, author of the wildly popular "Vampire Chronicles" series.

Meanwhile another side of Rice emerged in a series of novels published under a pseudonym, A. N. Roquelaure. *The Claiming of Sleeping Beauty* (1983), *Beauty's Punishment* (1984), and *Beauty's Release: The Continued Erotic Adventures of Sleeping Beauty* (1985) were adult erotic fantasy novels. The sado-masochistic theme in the Roquelaure novels carried over into the more conventional novels published under a second pseudonym, Anne Rambling. In the midst of the release of these novels, her important vampire short story appeared in *Redbook* in 1984, "The Master of Rambling Gate." Rice returned to the vampire theme in 1985 with *The Vampire Lestat*, the most heralded of what was to become the "Vampire Chronicles" series. This volume further developed the character of Lestat introduced in her earlier work.

He emerged as a strong secular individualist who took to the vampire's life quite naturally. Born into the lesser aristocracy, he defied the vampire establishment in Paris and decided to make his own way in the world. A man of action who rarely rested in indecision, he was also deeply affected by poetry and **music** and freely showed his emotions. Rice described him as both an androgynous ideal and an expression of the man she would be if she were male. Like Rice, Lestat rejected his Catholic past and had no aversion to the religious weapons traditionally used against his kind. Seeking moral justification for his need to feed on fresh **blood**, he began to develop a vampire ethic, selecting those who had done some great wrong as his **victims**.

The success of *The Vampire Lestat* led to demands for more, and Rice responded with **The Queen of the Damned** (1988). Like the previous volumes, it became a bestseller and soon found its way into a paperback edition. Previously, *Interview with the Vampire* had also appeared in an audio cassette version (1986), and the publishers moved quickly to license audio versions of *The Queen of the Damned* (1988) and *The Vampire Lestat* (1989).

Rice was now a recognized author and her writing was regularly the subject of serious literary critics. She continued to produce at a steady rate and successively completed *The Mummy* (1989), *The Witching Hour* (1990), and *Lasher* (1993). In the meantime, further adventures of Lestat appeared in the fourth volume of the Vampire Chronicles, *The Tale of the Body Thief* (1992), released on audio cassette simultaneously with its hardback edition. In 1991 **Katherine Ramsland** finished her biography of Rice, entitled *Prism of the Night*, and moved on to compile a comprehensive reference volume, *The Vampire Companion: The Official Guide to Anne Rice's Vampire Chronicles* (1993).

No sooner did Ramsland's volume appear that a fifth volume of the "Vampire Chronicles," *Memnoch the Devil* took Lestat into the supernatural realms of heaven and hell (after which Ramsland issued a revised edition). Memnoch was not as well received as the previous volumes, as it story tended to subordinate plot to philosophical musings on theological issues. After the publication of *Memnoch*, Rice announced that Lestat had left her and, to the disappointment of his fans, that there would be no more Lestat novels. However, she soon returned to the vampire theme with *Pandora* (immediately available on cassette and CD), the first of several volumes following the other characters in the "Vampire Chronicles."

Lestat's Vampire Culture: Rice's novels have permeated the culture like no other recent vampire writings. Lestat was honored by a **gothic** rock band that took his name as their own and the androgynous ideal has been adopted by the gothic subculture. In 1988 a group of women in New Orleans founded an Anne Rice Fan Club. Rice approved the effort but suggested that a reference to Lestat be added to the club's name. It emerged as the Anne Rice's Vampire Lestat Fan Club. Two years later, Innovation Corporation picked up the **comic book** rights to *The Vampire Lestat*, which it issued as a 12-part series. A similar release of *Interview with the Vampire* and *The Queen of the Damned* followed in 1991 (though Innovation unfortunately folded before the final issue of *Queen of the Damned* could be released). Her short story "The Master of Rambling Gate" was also issued in 1991. Innovation brought together one of the finest teams in comic book art to produce the three. Innovation also released three issues of *The Vampire Companion*, a fanzine in comic book format, which included stories about Rice's vampire books, Innovation's artists, and the process of producing the comic adaptations.

In 1976 Paramount bought the rights to *Interview with the Vampire*. The rights had a ten-year option, which expired in 1986. The rights reverted to Rice, and she, in turn, sold them to Lorimar along with the rights to *The Vampire Lestat* and *The Queen of the Damned*. Lorimar sold its rights to *Interview with the Vampire* to Warner Bros., which then passed them on to Geffen Pictures. In 1993 Geffen announced that it would begin the filming under Neil Jordan's direction. The studio signed **Tom Cruise** to play Lestat and Brad Pitt to play Louis, the vampire who is interviewed in the story. Rice, who had earlier envisioned Rutger Hauer as the perfect Lestat, reacted emotionally to the choice of Cruise, whom she saw as devoid of the androgyny so definitive of her favorite vampire character. However, when she finally previewed the film in 1994, she retracted all she had said and praised Cruise for his success in bringing Lestat to the screen. *Interview* went on to be one of the largest-grossing films of the decade.

There is every reason to believe that, in spite of Rice's ending the Lestat stories, that he and his fellow vampires will remain a popular reference point for the vampire community for many years to come. *Interview with a Vampire* went on to become one of the best-selling vampire books of all time (second only to Dracula) and was translated into a number of foreign languages. A second period of intense attention on her vampire universe began to manifest in 1998, when two new novels, *The Vampire Armand*, and *Pandora* appeared. They were quickly followed by *Victorio the Vampire* (1999), *Merrick* (2000), *Blood and Gold* (2001), *Blackwood Farm* (2002), and *Blood Canticle* (2003). The last two brought both the Vampire Chronicles and the series of books on the Mayfair Witches to a culmination.

Even as she was finishing these last novels, Rice was undergoing a period of intense religious ferment which included a renewed faith in Christ and active membership in the Roman Catholic Church (beginning in 1998). In 2000, she quietly saw to the disband-

ing of the Anne Rice Vampire Lestat Fan Club and the discontinuance of the annual Halloween parties. In 2004, she announced her return to her Catholic faith to her fans and the general public, followed the next year with a new novel, *Christ the Lord, Out of Egypt,* the first of a trilogy on the Life of Christ. Most recently, she has talked about her religious pilgrimage in the autobiographical *Called Out of Darkness: A Spiritual Confession* (2008).

Meanwhile, Rice also made a very public move away from New Orleans, where she had been a very active participant in the city's political and economic life, in 2004. She sold the last of her property holding prior to the disaster of Hurricane Katrina. She quickly emerged as an advocate of relief to those hurt by the flooding and assistance for rebuilding. As part of her effort, she gave her blessing to some of the leaders in the former fan club to reopen it and again begin holding the annual Halloween event.

Sources:

"Anne Rice" In *Contemporary Literary Criticism.* Edited by Daniel G. Marowski and Roger Matuz. Vol. 41. Detroit, MI: Gale Research Company, 1987.

Frankel, Martha. "Interview with the Author of Interview with the Vampire." *Movieline* 5,5 (January/February 1994): 58–62, 96–97.

Ramsland, Katherine. *Prism in the Night: A Biography of Anne Rice.* New York: Dutton, 1991. 385 pp.

———. *The Vampire Companion: The Official Guide to Anne Rice's The Vampire Chronicles.* New York: Ballantine Books, 1993. 507 pp.

Rice, Anne. "The Master of Rambling Gate." *Redbook* (February 1984): 50–58. Rept. Bryon Preiss, ed. *The Ultimate Dracula.* New York: Dell, 1991, 15–46. Rept. Richard Dalby, ed. *Vampire Stories.* Secaucus, NJ: Castle Books, 1993. pp. 189–203.

———. *The Vampire Lestat.* New York: Alfred A. Knopf, 1985. 481 pp. Rept. New York: Ballantine Books, 1986. 550 pp.

———, *Interview with the Vampire.* New York: Alfred A. Knopf, 1986. 448 pp. Rept. New York: Ballantine Books, 1987. 346 pp.

———. *The Queen of the Damned.* New York: Alfred A. Knopf, 1988. 448 pp. Rept. New York: Ballantine Books, 1989.

———. *Tale of the Body Thief.* New York: Alfred A. Knopf, 1992. 430 pp. Rept. New York: Ballantine Books, 1993.

———. *Memnoch the Devil.* New York: Alfred A. Knopf, 1995. 354 pp.

———. *Pandora.* New York: Alfred A. Knopf, 1996. 353 pp.

———. *The Vampire Armand.* New York: Alfred A. Knopf, 1998. 388 pp.

———. *Vittorio the Vampire.* New York: Alfred A. Knopf, 1999. 292 pp.

———. *Merrick.* New York: Alfred A. Knopf, 2000. 307 pp.

———. *Blood and Gold.* New York: Alfred A. Knopf, 2001. 471 pp.

———. *Blackwood Farm.* New York: Alfred A. Knopf, 2002. 528 pp.

———. *Blood Canticle.* New York: Alfred A. Knopf, 2003. 360 pp.

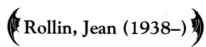 Rollin, Jean (1938–)

Jean Rollin, a French horror movie director, is best known for his production of a number of adult erotic vampire films, beginning with *La Reine des Vampires* (*Queen of the Vampires*) in 1967. Rollin entered the film industry as a teenager in 1955 as an assistant director working on animated films. A short time later he produced his first film, a short

entitled *Le Amours Jaunes*. In 1965 he met American producer Sam Selsky. Selsky asked him to put together a half-hour short to run with one of his already produced films. The resulting *Le Reine des Vampires* proved superior to the feature with which it ran and led Selsky to support Rollin's first feature film, *Voil des Vampires* (*Rape of the Vampires*), which met with relative commercial success. In this film, into which most of *Le Reine des Vampires* was edited, he established what was to be the hallmark of his subsequent work—a preference for visual effects that carry the film's message and dominate the often weak story lines. His first feature, in fact, has a rather flimsy plot about the attempt to free two **women** from a vampire's curse. It enjoyed success, in large part, because of the sexual scenes—the audiences reacted to a decade of rather strict censorship during the reign of Charles de Gaulle.

Rollin followed the success of his first work with his first color feature, in 1969 *La Nue Vampire* (released in English as *The Nude Vampire* or *The Naked Vampire*) and in 1970 one of his more heralded productions, *Le Frisson des Vampires* (released in English as *Sex and the Vampire* or *Vampire Thrills*). *Le Frisson des Vampires* concerned a young couple who encounter the vampire Isolde, who makes her first appearance in a suit of chain mail and thigh-high leather boots. Again the visual imagery overshadowed the plot, and Rollin saturated the audience with his portrayal of vampirism as a perverse form of **sexuality**.

By the time of his third film he had assembled a group of specialists who assisted him through the 1970s in a series of low-budget productions. He regularly returned to the vampire theme feeling that vampirism provided an effective vehicle for portraying erotic themes. In 1971 he directed *Le Cult du Vampire*, followed in 1972 by *Requim pour un Vampire* (also released as *Vierges et Vampires* and *Caged Virgins*). Rollin also directed a number of horror and adult features. In 1974 he produced *Levres de Sang* (*Lips of Blood*) and followed it in 1979 with *Fascination* and in 1982 with *La Morte-Vivante*. *Fascination* featured a cult of vampire women (a theme Rollin had used in earlier films) that conducted ritual sacrifices of men in a remote castle home. His last vampire movie concerned a dead woman revived as the result of a chemical waste spillage. She began attacking people to drink their **blood**, an appetite that grew stronger as the film progressed. In his spare time Rollin authored several horror-fantasy novels.

He continued to make movies through the 1980s and into the 1990s and currently lives in Paris. In the 1990s he returned to the vampire theme with *The Vampire Orphanes* (1996) that told the story of two girls who were blind orphans by day but turned into and bloodthirsty vampires by night. He also released a oversized volume of essays on his vampire movies illustrated with numerous stills. His most recent encounter with vampires, *La fiancée de Dracula* (2000) has a **vampire hunter** tracking down **Dracula**'s vampire descendents in the contemporary world.

Sources:

"Blood Poetry: The Cinema of Jean Rollin." Special issue of *Kinoeye: New Perspectives on European Cinema* 2, 7 (April 2002). Posted at http://www.kinoeye.org/index_02_07.php. Accessed on April 11, 2010.

Flynn, John L. *Cinematic Vampires: The Living Dead on Film, Television, from The Devils Castle (1896) to Bram Stoker's Dracula (1992)*. Jefferson, ND: McFarland & Company, 1992. 320 pp.

"Lust at First Bite." *The Dark Side* (July 1992): 5–10.

Pirie, David. *The Vampire Cinema*. London: Hamlyn, 1977. 175 pp.

Rollin, Jean. *Virgins & Vampires*. Edited by Peter Blumenstock. Schwenningen, Germany: Crippled Dick Hot Wax, 1997. 153 pp.

❨ Romance Literature, Vampires in ❩

According to the Romance Writer of America, the romance novel is defined by the prominence of two elements: a central love story, in which two individuals fall in love and struggle to make the relationship work, and a story line ultimately brought to an emotionally satisfying and optimistic (that is happy) ending, meaning that their relationship is rewarded with emotional justice and unconditional love. The story requires a strong female character who is searching, however consciously, for an ideal romantic love and whose feelings about the men she encounters are in the foreground as the novel proceeds. The male figure may approach any of a spectrum of ideals and is often pictured as larger than life relative to strength, courage, will, handsomeness, recklessness, ability to bear suffering, knowledge of women, and/or mystery.

Romance novels are written by women for a female audience, though a few men (usually writing under a female penname) have proven successful masters of the genre. The primary story line is usually the female character's account of events and in many cases is written in the first person.

The romance genre is often traced to the eighteenth century and the novel *Pamela, or Virtue Rewarded* by Samuel Richardson (1740), one of the earliest popular novels to have a story line written from the woman's point-of-view. Romantic writing was further popularized in the nineteenth century, Jane Austen being a noteworthy exemplar. Such novels both accepted the social roles into which women were pushed while providing an element of escape in romantic adventures. The genre blossomed in the twentieth century with British writers such as Barbara Cartland (1901–2000), who wrote over 700 novels, and Georgette Heyer (1902–1974), who invented the regency romance. Their careers blossomed in the 1930s and continued until shortly before their deaths.

The British company Mills and Boon was the first publisher specializing in romance titles, and Harlequin Enterprises, a Canadian publisher, emerged as their North American equivalent. Both companies initially specialized in historical romances, historical settings providing some rationale for the perpetuation of what many post World War II readers began to see as outmoded emphases on traditional sexual mores. The success of the new romance novels with a modern setting pioneered by Avon Publishing, in the 1970s, led to the growth of the field in the 1980s and 1990s. By the beginning of the twenty-first century, romance novels accounted for about half of all the new paperback book sales in North America—much to the distain of both writers and publishers in other fields. The most important romance publishing imprints include Avon, Dorchester, Kensington/Zebra, Dell, Berkley, Love Spell, and of course Harlequin (and its imprints Mira and Silhouette).

The vampire theme in romance writing emerged in the 1970s with the burgeoning of **gothic** romance. The new wave of vampire novels in the early 1970s appear to have been occasioned by the success of the television show **Dark Shadows** and the accompanying singular phenomenon of **Daniel Ross**, who wrote numerous romance novels under the pseudonym Marilyn Ross. He began to produce original stories (all quickly written) using the characters and settings of the popular television show late in 1966. The first six (1966–68) featured Victoria Winters, but with the addition of the vampire **Barnabas Collins**, by the end of 1968 the stories moved to him and the women in his life. Ross would go on to author more than twenty additional *Dark Shadows* novels during the next three years.

In the wake of the popularity of *Dark Shadows*, writers of gothic romances found that dropping vampires into their novels was relatively easy. In the three years of 1969–1971, more than a dozen romance novels appeared including titles by Dorothea Nile (a penname of Michael Avallone), Barbara Michaels, Virginia Coffman, Elna Stone, and Florence Stevenson. Ross would even contribute one non-*Dark Shadows* novel under another of his pseudonyms, Clarissa Ross, while Stevenson would go on to write additional vampire romance novels into the 1980s.

Through the 1980s, vampires would show up sporadically in the occasional romance novel, but would not again enjoy anything like the presence it manifested during the early 1970s until the mid-1990s. By this time, the romance genre had expanded to the point that numerous subdivisions had emerged, among them the paranormal romance. Paranormal romance was envisioned as encompassing a variety of phenomena— ghosts, witches, **werewolves**, time travelers, and vampires. Most importantly, **Anne Rice**, whose novels were seen by many as approaching the romance genre, was enjoying great success, and **Laurell Hamilton** was emerging into prominence.

Heralding the new wave of vampire romance novels was Lori Herter, who issued four vampire romance novels in the early 1990s, and Maggie Shayne who issued her first vampire romance in 1993. Then in 1994–95, following the release of the movie version of Rice's *Interview with the Vampire*, more than a dozen vampire-related romance novels suddenly appeared. **Maggie Shayne** (a.k.a. Margaret Benson) was already producing a vampire romance series and would now be joined by **Linda Lael Miller** and **Amanda Ashley** (a.k.a. Madeline Baker). Miller's *For All Eternity* and Ashley's *Embrace the Night* launched two new series. While a number of popular romance writers would attempt a vampire novel, Miller and Ashley would began to redefine the field, suggesting vampire romances as more than just another form of paranormal romance.

By the end of the 1990s, however, editors at the different houses specializing in romance novels diverged significantly in their view of the vampire. Some felt that the vampire was a passing fad and that its time had come and gone. Others, noting continuing high sales figures and the popularity of *Buffy the Vampire Slayer*, continued to accept and even solicit new vampire novels. In 1999 the appearance of two very successful vampire series was initiated by **Christine Feehan**, and Shannon Drake (a.k.a. **Heather Graham Pozzessere**).

Through the early years of the new century, publishers one-by-one recognized that vampires had carved out a secure niche in the expanding romance field. At the same time, writers unable to find a publisher took their novels to publish-on-demand (POD) publishers and issued their books in both electronic and trade paperback formats. A few writers who began with POD houses such as Ellora's Cave were able to jump to one of the larger romance houses. By the end of the decade, more than fifty writers, almost all women, had written and published multiple vampire titles. A few, like **Charlaine Harris,** became superstars, but a number became well known for their writing of vampire

novels—**Nina Bangs**, **Mary Janice Davidson**, **Sherrilyn Kenyon**, Katie MacAleister; **Lynsay Sands**, Susan Sizemore, Kerrelyn Sparks, Susan Squires, and **J. R. Ward**.

At the same time several romance writers had been able to adapt their vampire novels toward a high school and even junior high school audience. The field had been opened by *Buffy the Vampire Slayer* and its many spinoff novels (at one point eighteen annually). The novels of **Stephenie Meyer, P. C. and Kristin Cast,** and Elle Schreiber opened the vampire realm to young women, which previously had almost exclusively been inhabited by young males. In the wake of the success of Stephenie Meyer's *Twilight* series, an early young adult romance series, The Vampire Diaries series written by **Lisa Jane Smith** in the 1990s, was reprinted and was adapted into a hit **television** show.

The romance field is served by Romantic Writers of America (RLA), its primary professional organization, and *Romantic Times* (RT), the primary trade magazine. Amid a variety of romance awards given annually by various organizations, those offered by RWA and RT are the most coveted. Romantic Writers of America has, since 1982 given annual awards (known since 1990 as the Rita Awards) for excellence in the field. Authors of vampire romances were recognized only recently by the Ritas, which have been awarded to Maggie Shayne (2005), Kresley Cole (2007), and J. R. Ward (2008). In 2007, Linda Lael Miller won the RLA's Nora Roberts Lifetime Achievement Award.

RT began issuing awards in 1987, the first for the years 1986–87. Initially issued to authors for a body of work, RT added a second award for best books in 1995. The first writer known primarily for her vampire-oriented titles to be honored was Heather Graham (Pozzessere), who received awards in 1988–89, 1991–92, and 2000. In the mid-1990s, fantasy was added as a category, and Maggie Shayne (1995, 1998, and 2000) and Linda Lael Miller (1997) received awards. Madeline Baker (a.k.a. Amanda Ashley) and Christine Feehan received awards in 1999 and 2003.

In 2004, Paranormal Romance was first recognized with separate three awards. Among the early recipients were Kelley Armstrong (2004) who has written primarily of a **werewolves** (but ones who live in a world also inhabited by vampires), and Susan Sizemore (2005). For the first time, in 2006, Vampire Paranormal Romance was recognized as a separate category, the first award for career achievement going to J. R. Ward. That same year, the number of categories was significantly increased, in recognition of both the growth of the field and the emergence of new subgenres, and both Charlaine Harris and Linda Lael Miller were also recognized in other categories.

In 2007, the number of categories would be radically cut back, and the vampire and paranormal categories collapsed into a single Paranormal award, received by Angela Knight largely for her werewolf/vampire crossover novels. The same award would go to the writing team of C. T. Adams and Cathy Clamp, who wrote both a vampire and a werewolf series. Heather Graham and Keri Arthur also received awards in other categories.

When RT began its awards for best books in 1995, Fantasy was an established category, and the first award went to Susan Krinard for her vampire book, *Prince of Dreams*. Maggie Shayne would receive the award in 1997. In 2000 an award for best Vampire Paranormal romance was added, and again Christine Feehan won the first and the second in 2001. In 2002, the award went to Sherrilyn Kenyon, though Feehan won for Best Historical Paranormal Fantasy. In 2003, the Vampire award went to Susan Sizemore, with additional Paranormal awards to Kelley Armstrong and Thea Devine.

In 2004, best vampire novel went to **Mary Janice Davidson** with additional awards to Kim Harrison and Angela Knight. Sherrilyn Kenyon walked away with the Best Vampire book of 2005, with additional recognition of a vampire title going to C.T. Adams and Cathy Clamp. J. R Ward had the best Vampire title in 2006 with additional vampire titles by Angela Knight also receiving an award. Ward again won the vampire award in 2007, additional vampire books also receiving awards included books by P.C. Cast and Kristin Cast, Kim Harrison, and Jeaniene Frost. Michele Bardsley won her first award for her vampire novel in 2008, with Paranormal awards going to Mary Janice Davidson, Sherrilyn Kenyon, and Jeanne C. Stein. In 2007, RT had given its first award to the best in the Silhouette Nocturne series. In 2008, that award went to Anna Rice for her vampire title.

Sources:

"About the Romance Genre." Romance Writers of America. Posted at http://www.rwanational .org/cs/the_romance_genre. Accessed on April 11, 2010.

Coffman, Virginia. *The Vampire of Moura*. New York: Ace Books, 1970. 265 pp.

Davidson, Mary Janice. *Undead and Unwed*. New York: Berkley Sensation, 2004. 277 pp.

Gideon, Nancy. *Midnight Kiss*. New York: Pinnacle Books, 1994. 411 pp.

———. *Midnight Temptation*. New York: Pinnacle Books, 1994. 380 pp.

Herter, Lori. *Obsession*. New York: Berkley Books, 1991. 278 pp.

James, Stephanie (pseudonym of Jayne Ann Krentz). *Nightwalker*. Silhouette Desire 163. New York: Silhouette Books, 1984. 186 pp.

MacAlister, Katie. *A Girl's Guide to Vampires*. New York: Love Spell, 2003. 374 pp.

Michaels, Barbara. *The Dark on the Other Side*. Greenwich, CT: Fawcett Crest, 1970. 224 pp.

Nile, Dorothea (pseudonym of Michael Avallone). *The Vampire Cameo*. New York: Lancer, 1968. 190 pp.

Shayne, Maggie. *Twilight Phantasies*. *Silhouette Shadows 18*. New York: Silhouette Books, 1993. 251 pp.

Sands, Lynsay. *Single White Vampire*. New York: Love Spell, 2003. 369 pp.

Stevenson, Florence. *The Curse of Concullens*. New York: World Publishing Company, 1970. 143 pp.

Ward, J. R. *Dark Lover*. Black Dagger Brotherhood, Book 1. New York: Signet, 2005. 416 pp.

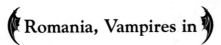

Romania, Vampires in

No country is as identified with vampires as Romania. A land of rich folklore concerning vampires, its reputation was really established by **Bram Stoker**, whose novel *Dracula* **(1897)** began and ended in **Transylvania**. Though at the time Transylvania was a part of **Hungary**, it is now a part of Romania. Recent scholarship has confirmed that the title of Stoker's novel was a reference to **Vlad the Impaler**, a fifteenth-century prince of Wallachia, a section of modern Romania that lies south of the Carpathian Mountains. Stoker derived much of his knowledge of Transylvania, where he located **Castle Dracula**, from Emily Gerard's *The Land Beyond the Forest* (1888). Gerard was a Scottish woman who had married a Polish officer serving the Austrian army. As a brigade commander, he was stationed in Transylvania in the 1880s. The couple resided in Sibiu and Brasov. In describing the several supernatural entities encountered in her research on practices surrounding death, she wrote:

More decidedly evil is the *nosferatu*, or vampire, in which every Romanian peasant believes as firmly as he does in heaven or hell. There are two sorts of vampires, living and dead. The living vampire is generally the illegitimate offspring of two illegitimate persons; but even a flawless pedigree will not insure anyone against the intrusion of a vampire into the family vault, since every person killed by a nosferatu becomes likewise a vampire after death, and will continue to suck the **blood** of other innocent persons till the spirit has been exorcised by opening the grave of the suspected person, and either driving a **stake** through the corpse, or else firing a pistol-shot into the **coffin**. To walk smoking around the grave on each anniversary of the death is also supposed to be effective in confining the vampire. In very obstinate cases of vampirism it is recommended to cut off the head, and replace it in the coffin with the mouth filled with **garlic**, or to extract the heart and burn it, strewing its ashes over the grave. (p. 185)

Romanian concepts concerning the vampire are strongly related to folk beliefs of the **Slavic vampire** in general, though the Romanians, in spite of being largely surrounded by Slavic peoples are not themselves Slavic. Romanians locate their **origins** in ancient Dacia, a Roman province that emerged in Transylvania and the surrounding territories after Trajan's capture of the land in the second century C.E.. He also brought in thousands of colonists in the sparsely settled area. As the colonists and the indigenous people intermarried, a new ethnic community was born. This new community spoke a form of Latin—the basis for modern Romanian. Their subsequent history, especially over the next century is a matter of great controversy between Romanians and their neighbors, a controversy difficult to resolve due to the paucity of archeological evidence.

Following the abandonment of the territory at the end of the third century, Transylvania became the target of various invaders, including the early Slavic tribes. In the seventh-century it was absorbed into the Bulgar Empire. Though some Romanians had become Christians as early as the fourth century, the systematic conversion of the land began in the ninth century soon after the conversion of the Bulgarians under the brothers Cyril and Methodius. The Romanian church eventually aligned itself to Eastern Orthodoxy under Bulgarian Episcopal authority.

At the end of the tenth century, the Magyars (present-day Hungarians) included Transylvania in their expanding kingdom. The Hungarians were Roman Catholics, and they imposed their faith in the newly conquered land. They also encouraged immigration by, among others, the **Szekleys**, a branch of Magyars, and Germans. During the thirteenth century, seizing upon a moment of weakened Hungarian

Bran Castle in Brasov, Romania, which the Romanian government once touted as Castle Dracula.

The Golden Krone (Crown) Hotel in Bistritz, Romania, where Jonathan Harker stopped to eat on his way to Dracula's Castle.

authority in Transylvania, a number of Romanian Transylvanians migrated eastward and southward over the Carpathian Mountains and found the kingdoms of Moldavia and Wallachia. An Eastern Orthodox bishop was established a century later in Wallachia. From that time to the present day, Transylvania would be an item of contention between **Hungary** and Wallachia (which grew into the present-day Romania). Ecclesiastically, both Roman Catholics and Eastern Orthodox would compete for the faith of the people.

No sooner had Wallachia and Moldavia been established than a new force arose in the area. The Ottoman Empire expanded into the Balkans and began the steady march across the peninsula that would carry it to the very gates of Vienna in the early sixteenth century. During the fourteenth century Hungary and the Turks vied for hegemony in Wallachia, thus providing a context for a prince of Wallachia by the name of Vlad to travel to the court of the Emperor Sigismund where he would join the Order of the Dragon, pledged to defend Christian lands against the invading Muslims. The Wallachian prince would become known as **Vlad Dracul** (1390?–1447). He in turn would be succeeded by his son, Vlad the Impaler (1431–1476), known as **Dracula**.

Vlad the Impaler is remembered today in Romania as a great patriot and a key person in the development of the Romanian nation. After Vlad's death, Wallachia fell increasingly under Turkish hegemony, and Moldavia soon followed suit. Through the 1530s the Turkish army moved through Transylvania to conquer the Hungarian capital in 1541. The remainder of the Hungarian land fell under the control of the Austrian Hapsburg empire. The incorporation of the Romanian kingdoms into the Turkish empire allowed a degree of religious freedom, and Protestantism made a number of inroads, particularly in Transylvania. Contemporary scholars have emphasized that none of the vampire legends from Romania or the surrounding countries portrays Vlad the Impaler as a vampire. In the German and some Slavic manuscripts, Vlad's cruelty and his identification as Dracula and devil was emphasized, however, Dracula as a vampire was a modern literary creation.

In the seventeenth century, the Hapsburgs began to drive the Ottomans from Europe, and by the end of the century assumed dominance of Transylvania and began to impose a Roman Catholic establishment. Transylvania remained a semiautonomous region until 1863 when it was formally unified with Hungary. For over a century Moldavia survived amid Russians, Greeks, and Turks, each fighting for control until a united Romania came into existence in 1861. Through a series of annexations at the beginning and end of World War I, including that of Transylvania in 1920, Romania, in roughly its present size, came into existence. The Romanian majority exists side-by-side with a significant Hungarian minority in Transylvania, and the Romanian Orthodox Church competes with a strong Roman Catholic and persistent Protestant presence.

The Vampire in Romania: The Romanian vampire, in spite of the distinct ethnic origin of the Romanians, is a variation of the Slavic vampire. However, like the vampire in each of the other Slavic regions, the vampire in Romania has acquired some distinguishing elements. That distinctiveness begins with the major term used to label vampires, as found by Harry Senn in his field work in the 1970s. *Strigoi* (female, *strigoaica*) is closely related to the Romanian word *striga* (a witch), which in turn was derived from the Latin *strix*, the word for a screech owl that was extended to refer to a demon that attacked children at night. A second term, *moroi* (female, *moroaica*), also spelled *murony* in older sources, seems to be the common term in Wallachia, as *strigoi* is in Transylvania. The Romanians also distinguish between the *strigoi vii* (plural, *strigoi*), or live vampire, and the *strigoi mort* (plural, *strigoi morti*), or dead vampire. The *strigoi vii* are witches who are destined to become vampires after death and who can send out their souls and/or bodies at night to cavort with the *strigoi mort*.

The live vampires tend to merge in thought with the *striga* (witches), who have the power to send their spirits and bodies to meet at night with other witches. The dead vampires are, of course, the reanimated bodies of the dead who return to life to disturb and suck the blood of their family, livestock, and—if unchecked—their neighbors. The *strigoi mort* was a variation of the Slavic vampire, although the Romanians were not **Slavs** and used a Latin word to designate their vampire. The *strigoi* was discovered by an unusual occurrence either at their birth or death, and a living *strigoi* was a person who was born with either a caul or a little tail. A *strigoi vii* may become a *strigoi mort*, as well as other people who died irregularly by **suicide** or an accident. Romanians also use the term *vircolac*, but almost exclusively to describe the old mythological wolflike creature who devoured the sun and **moon**.

The closely related terms *pricolici* or *tricolici* were also wolves. *Virolac* is a variation of the Greek *vrykolakas* or the Serbo-Croatian *vukodlak*. Agnes Murgoci, who worked in

Vlad the Impaler's court in Bucharest.

Romania in the 1920s, found that they still connected the term with its pre-vampiric mythological meaning of a creature who devours the sun and moon. At times when the moon appears reddish, it was believed to be the blood of the *vircolac* flowing over the moon's face. More definitive work was pursued by Harry Senn in Transylvania in the 1970s. He found that popular use of the *vircolac* distinguished it from the *strigoi*. The term *vircolac* described a person who periodically changed into one of several **animals**, usually a pig, dog, or wolf. As such it was much closer to the popular concept of **werewolves** than vampires. *Nosferatu* is an archaic Old Slavonic term apparently derived from *nosufuratu*, from the Greek *nosophoros*, "plague carrier."

From the religious context, the word passed into popular usage. It has been variously and mistakenly cited as a Romanian word meaning either "undead" (Wolf) or the devil (Senn). Through the twentieth century it seems to have dropped from use in Romania. Stoker's use of the term derived from Gerard. It was used by Friedrich Wilhelm Murnau in his attempt to disguise his movie, ***Nosferatu, Eine Symphonie des Grauens*** from Dracula. He tied the story to the great plague that hit Bremen, **Germany**, in 1838.

In Romania the vampire was believed to come into existence first and foremost as the product of an irregular birth, and any number of conditions have been reported

that could predispose a person to become a vampire. Children born out of wedlock, born with a caul, or who died before baptism could become vampires. Pregnant **women** who did not eat salt or who have allowed themselves to be gazed upon by a vampire could bear a vampiric child. The seventh child of the same sex in one family was likely to have a tail and become a vampire. Though children with an irregular birth were the prime candidates of vampirism, anyone could become a vampire if bitten by one. Other potential vampires included people who led wicked lives (including men who swore falsely), witches (who had relations with the devil), a corpse over whom a cat had jumped, or a person who committed suicide.

The presence of vampires was usually first noticed when several unexpected deaths in a family and/or of livestock followed the death of either a family member or of someone suspected of being a vampire. The vampire might, on occasion, appear to the family, and female vampires were known to return to their children. The home of a suspected vampire often was disturbed by the its activity, either in throwing things around (poltergeist) or getting into the food supplies. The vampire would first attack the family and its livestock and then move on to others in the village. If not destroyed it might move on to more distant villages and even other countries, where it could reassume a normal role in society. Vampires were especially active on the eve of **St. George's Day** (either April 23 or May 5), the day witches and vampires gathered at the edge of the villages to plan their nefarious activities for the next year. Villagers would take special precautions to ward off the influences of supernatural beings on that evening. Stoker's character **Jonathan Harker** made the last leg of his journey and finally arrived at Castle Dracula on St. George's Eve. Vampires and witches were also active on St. Andrew's Day. St. Andrew was the patron of wolves and the donor of garlic. In many areas of Romania, vampires were believed to become most active on St. Andrew's Eve, and continued to be active through the winter, and ceased their period of activity at Epiphany (in January), Easter, or St. George's Day.

St. George's Day was and is celebrated throughout much of Europe on April 23, hence the Eve of St. George would be the evening of April 22. St. Andrew's day is November 11, and the eve immediately precedes it. Romania which was on the old Julian Calendar, was 12 days behind the modern Gregorian calendar. Thus in Stoker's day, St. George's Day would have been celebrated in Romania on what was the evening of May 4 in western Europe. Likewise, St. Andrew's Eve would have been the evening of November 23–24. The lag time between the Julian and our Gregorian calendar increases one day every century.

The grave of a suspected vampire would be examined for telltale signs. Often a small hole would be found in the ground near the tombstone, a hole by which the vampire could enter and leave the coffin. If there was reason to believe someone was a vampire, the grave was opened. Those opening the coffin would expect to find the corpse red in the face. Often the face would be turned downward and fresh blood on it or, on occasion, cornmeal. One foot might have retracted into a corner of the coffin. Senn reported that a vampire in the community could be detected by distributing garlic at church and watching to see who did not eat.

It was the common practice of Romanians to open the graves of the deceased three years after the death of a child, four or five years after the death of a young person and seven years after an adult's death. Normally, only a skeleton would be found, which would be washed and returned to the grave. If, however, the body had not decayed, it was treated as if it were a vampire.

There were a wide variety of precautions that could be taken to prevent a person either from becoming a vampire or doing any damage if they did become one. A caul might be removed from the face of a newborn and quickly destroyed before it was eaten. Careful and exacting preparation of the body of the recently dead also prevented their becoming a vampire. The thorny branch of the wild rose might be placed in the tomb. Garlic was also very useful in driving away vampires. On St. Andrew's Eve and St. George's Eve, the windows (and other openings of the house) were anointed with garlic, and the cows would be given a garlic rubdown. Once the vampire was in the tomb, distaffs might be driven into the ground above the grave upon which the vampire would impale itself if it were to rise.

On the anniversary of the death of a suspected vampire, the family walked around the grave. Once a vampire began an attack on the community and its identity was discerned, the vampire had to be destroyed. Emily Gerard, author of *The Land Beyond the Forest*, found the emergence of a relatively new tradition in nineteenth-century reports in which a vampire might be killed by firing a **bullet** into the **coffin.** The preferred method, however, was to drive a **stake** into the body, followed by **decapitation**, and the placing of garlic in the mouth prior to reburial. This method was adopted by Stoker in *Dracula* as a means of **destroying** the vampiric nature that had taken over **Lucy Westenra**'s body. In Romania, the staking could be done with various materials, including iron or wood, and the stake was impaled either in the heart or the navel. Instead of decapitation, the body could also be turned face downward and reversed in the coffin. Millet **seeds** might be placed in the coffin to delay the vampire, who must first go through a lengthy process of eating the millet before rising from the grave. An even more thorough process might be followed in the case of a vampire resistant to other preventive measures. The body might be taken from the grave to the woods and dismembered. First, the heart and liver were removed, and then piece by piece the body was burned. The ashes could then be mixed with **water** and given to afflicted family members as a curative for the vampire's attack.

Vampire Folktales: The Romanian vampire has also become the subject of a number of folktales. Folklorists have noticed that many relate to the cases of couples in which one has recently died. Frequently reprinted was the story of "The Girl and the Vampire" (which also exists in a Russian variant) in which the boy committed suicide following his failure to gain the marriage blessing of his girlfriend's parents. As a result of his manner of death, he became a vam-

Vlad the Impaler's tower at his palace in Tirgoviste, Romania.

pire and began to visit the girl at night. The girl spoke with a wise elder woman in the village who instructed her to attach a thread to his shirt. She then traced the thread, which led to the graveyard and disappeared into the grave of her late boyfriend.

The vampire continued to visit the girl, and they continued their sexual liaison, when her parents died. She refused the vampire's request for her to tell what she had seen the night she followed him to the graveyard, and the girl soon also died. She was buried according to the wise woman's instruction. A flower grew from her grave, which was seen by the son of the emperor. He ordered it dug up and brought to his castle. There, in the evening, it turned into a maiden. Eventually she and the emperor's son were wed. Sometime later, she accompanied her husband to church and had an encounter with the vampire. He followed her into church where she hid behind an icon, which then fell on the vampire and destroyed him. The story served as a discouragement to out-of-wedlock sexual relations while at the same time reaffirming the wisdom of older people and upholding the church as a bastion against evil. Similar values were affirmed in other stories.

It was once the case, according to one folktale that "vampires were as common as leaves of grass, or berries in a pail." They have, however, become more rare and confined to the rural areas. In the mid-1970s Harry Senn had little trouble locating vampire accounts in a variety of Romanian locations. Admittedly, however, the vampire suffered during recent decades from both the spread of public education and the hostility of the government to tales of the supernatural. The importance of vampires in the overall folk belief of Romanians was also demonstrated in a recent study of a Wallachian immigrant community in **Scandinavia**.

Conclusion: The *strigoi morti,* the Romanian vampire conformed in large part to the popular image of the vampire. It was a revenant of the deceased. It had powers to product poltergeist-like phenomena, especially the bringing to life of common household objects. It was seen as capricious, mischievous, and very debilitating. However, the vampire's attack was rarely seen as fatal. Also, it rarely involved the literal biting and draining of blood from its **victim** (the crux of the distortion of the vampire's image in films in the eyes of Romanian folklorists). The *strigoi* usually drained the vital energy of a victim by a process of **psychic vampirism**. The description of the *strigoi's* attack, described in vivid metaphorical language, was often taken in a literal sense by non-Slavic interpreters who then misunderstood the nature of the Slavic vampire.

Of contemporary note, Mircea Eliade, the outstanding Romanian scholar of world religion, was fascinated with vampires, and among his first books was a vampire novel, *Dominisoara Christina* ("Miss Christina"). This obscure work was rediscovered years later by Eliade fans in France and Italy and republished in both countries.

In the 1990s, Romania became the focus of vampire tourism, and several tour companies emerged to support vampire related visits, especially in October. A new Dracula hotel in the **Borgo Pass** was created to serve Dracula-thirsty visitors. Attempting to provide a more nuanced appropriation of Romania's vampire-related culture was the **Transylvanian Society of Dracula**, which annually sponsors a scholarly seminar on a folklore-related subject. The country has also tried to promote itself as the site for movies, the most notable ones being the half dozen *Subspecies* vampire movies produced by Full Moon in the 1990s.

Sources:

Eliade, Micea. *Domnisoara Christina* Bucharest, 1935. French edition as: *Mademoiselle Christiana.* Paris: Editions de l'Herne, 1978. Italian edition as: *Signorina Christiana.* Milan: Jaca Book, 1984.

Gerard, Emily. *The Land Beyond the Forest.* 2 vols. London: Will Blackwood & Sons, 1888.

Kreuter, Peter Mario. *Der Vampirglaube in Südosteuropa: Studien zur Genese, Bedeutung und Funktion. Rumänien und der Balkanraum.* Berlin: Weidler, 2001.

Murgoci, Agnes. "The Vampire in Romania." *Folk-Lore* 27, 5 (1926): 320–349.

Perkowski, Jan L. *The Darkling: A Treatise on Slavic Vampirism.* Columbus, OH: Slavica Publishers, 1989. 174 pp.

———, ed. *Vampires of the Slavs.* Cambridge, MA: Slavica Publishers, 1976. 294 pp.

Schierup, Carl-Ulrik. "Why Are Vampires Still Alive?: Wallachian Immigrants in Scandinavia." *Ethnos* 51, 3–4 (1986): 173–198.

Senn, Harry A. *Were-Wolf and Vampire in Romania.* New York: Columbia University Pres, 1982. 148 pp.

Summers, Montague. *The Vampire in Europe.* 1929. New Hyde Park, NY: University Books, 1961. 329 pp.

❦ Rome, Vampires in ❦

Ancient Rome did not have as developed a mythology of vampirism as did **Greece**, though the idea was by no means absent. It was not an attribute of the returning dead but of living witches. The idea of a vampirelike entity apparently came from the need to account for the unexpected deaths of infants, a need that had produced the *lamiai* of ancient Greece. The Romans spoke of the *strix*, a night demon that attacked infants and drained their **blood**. The *strix* was identified with the screech owl. The term survived in Greece as *striges* in **Romania** as *strigoi* and in **Italy** as *strega*. First-century C.E. Roman poet Ovid described a witch in the fourth book of his work, *Fasti:*

> They **fly** by night and look for children without nurses, snatch them from their cradles and defile their bodies. They are said to lacerate the entrails of infants with their beaks, and they have their throats full of the blood they have drunk. They are called striges.

He also recounted a ritual performed as an invocation to the ancient deity *Carna,* the goddess of flesh, to protect an infant boy from the *strix:*

> Immediately she (Carna) touches the door-posts three times in succession with a spray of arbutus (a plant); three times she marks the threshold with arbutus spray. She sprinkles the entrance with **water** (and the water contained a drug). She holds the bloody entrails of a pig, two months old, and thus speaks: "Birds of the night, spare the entrails of the boy. For a small boy a small **victim** falls. Take heart for heart, I pray, entrails for entrails. This life we give you in place of a better one."

The functionary completed the ritual by placing a white thorn branch in the window of the house. The child would then be safe. From the *strix* developed the concept of the *strega,* a witch, usually a woman, who was believed to have the power to change her form and fly around at night in the form of a bird. She also sucked human blood and possessed a poisonous breath. Petronius in his *Satyricon* left one story of an encounter

The movie *Subspecies*, starring Anders Hove as Radu, was the first vampire movie made in post-Ceausescu Romania.

with the *stregas*. The host of a dinner party told his guests that while he was at the home of a friend, comforting her on the loss of her son, several witches gathered outside the house and created a disturbance. In the home at the time was a muscular young man who volunteered to quiet the witches. He went outside, sword in hand. A few moments later the man returned and fell on the bed. He was black and blue all over and the witches had disappeared.

The rest of the group returned to their task of consoling the mother. However, when she went in to view her son, all she found was a clump of straw. The witches had carried off the boy, and the young man who battled them never recovered. The *strega* continued as part of the popular culture and spread through the old Roman Empire. As late as the ninth century, Charlemagne, who established the new Holy Roman Empire, decreed capital punishment for anyone who believed that another person was a *strix*, and because of that belief attacked, burned, and/or cannibalized that person. It appears that such was the manner of disposing of people believed to be witches.

By the end of the fifteenth century, the witch had been demonized and turned into a Satanist by the Inquisition. People believed to be *stregas* were arrested, tried, and

executed in Italy during the centuries of the witch-hunts. In the interrogations of the suspected witches, the inquisitors had them confess to practices commonly associated with the *stregas,* including the vampirizing of babies. Between 1460 and 1525 some ten books were published on **witchcraft** by Italians. Among these was a brief volume, *Strix,* written by Gianfrancesco Pico della Mirandola and published in Bologna in 1523.

The book grew out of concern over recent accusations of witchcraft that had occurred at Brecia in 1518 and at Sondrio in 1523, though the picture of the *stregas* presented by Mirandola was more complete (he was drawing on common beliefs about witches) than any of the confessions at the recent trials. The accused at Brecia and Sondrio, for example, did not confess to incidents of attacking babies and sucking their blood, though Mirandola was concerned with *stregas* committing such **crimes.** The beliefs articulated by Mirandola were common in the Renaissance and would remain a dominant opinion of the religious and intellectual leaders for the next several centuries. By the eighteenth century, Italians had joined the rest of Europe in doubting the existence of such supernatural evil as was supposedly perpetrated by witches and vampires. Remnants of the belief in *strega* seem to have continued to the present day. Surviving fragments of belief and practice reportedly were rediscovered by C. G. Leland in the nineteenth century and through him have passed into the modern Wiccan revival.

Note: On the modern literary and cinematic vampire, see the entry "Italy, Vampires in."

Sources:

Burke, Peter. "Witchcraft and Magic in Renaissance Italy: Gianfrancesco Pico and His *Strix.*" In Sydney Anglo, ed. *The Damned Art: Essays in the Literature of Witchcraft.* London: Routledge & Kegan Paul, 1977: 32–52.

Burriss, Eli Edward. *Taboo, Magic, Spirits: A Study of Primitive Elements in Roman Religion.* New York: Macmillan Company, 1931. 250 pp.

Frenschkowski, Marco. "Vampire in Mythologie und Folklore." In: Thomas Le Blanc, Clemens Ruthner, and Bettina Twsrsnick, eds. *Draculas Wiederkehr. Tagungsband 1997,* Wetzlar: Phantastische Bibliothek, 2003: 28–58.

Summers, Montague. *The Vampire: His Kith and Kin.* London: Routledge, Kegan Paul, Trench, Trubner, & Co., 1928. 356 pp. Rept. New Hyde Park, NY: University Books, 1960. 356 pp.

———. *The Vampire in Europe.* London: Routledge, Kegan Paul, Trench, Trubner, & Co., 1929. 329 pp. Rept. New Hyde Park, NY: University Books, 1961. 329 pp.

❦ Ross, Daniel (1912–1995) ❦

Novelist William Edward Daniel Ross wrote 33 books inspired by the **Dark Shadows** **television** program and movies. In 1930 Ross began his career as the manager of an acting company with which he also acted. Very early in his professional life, he was awarded the Dominion Drama Festival Prize for Playwriting.

During the 1960s he turned his attention to writing, and through his long career become one of the most prolific writers of **gothic,** romantic, historical, and western fiction under 21 different pseudonyms. His first novel, *Summer Season,* appeared in 1962 under the pseudonym Jane Rossiter. His output reached an all-time high in 1967 when over twenty novels appeared as paperback volumes. Besides his 358 novels, he wrote

Daniel Ross, author of nearly three dozen books inspired by the *Dark Shadows* television series.

some 600 short stories, many of them mysteries that have appeared in such publications as *The Saint Mystery Magazine*, *The Chaplain*, and *Mike Shayne Mystery Magazine*. In the mid-1960s, Ross began to produce gothic fiction under the names Clarissa Ross and Marilyn Ross. Under the latter name, in December 1966 he saw the publication of the first of the thirty-three *Dark Shadows* volumes that appeared during the next six years. The novels, with such names as *The Curse of Collinswood*, *The Phantom and Barnabas Collins*, and *Barnabas, Quentin, and the Vampire Beauty*, featured some of the *Dark Shadows* TV characters in new situations created by Ross. At one point, over a fourteen-month stretch, these novels appeared monthly. **Barnabas Collins**, the popular vampire added to the show in the spring of 1967, did not appear in the first five novels. However, after he became the popular center of the show, subsequent printings of the novels included his picture on the covers. The last volumes continued to appear for some months after the show was canceled. A special volume, Ross's movie tie-in *House of Dark Shadows*, included a photo section. A thirty-fourth volume, *Barnabas, Quentin, and the Mad Ghoul*, was plotted by Ross and scheduled but never published.

While working on the *Dark Shadows* series, Ross wrote two other vampire novels under the pseudonym Clarissa Ross, *Secret of the Pale Lover* (1969) and *The Corridors of Fear* (1971). After the completion of the *Dark Shadows* series for Paperback Library, Ross published another vampire novel as Marilyn Ross, *The Vampire Contessa* (1974). He continued his heavy output into the mid-1980s under such names as Marilyn Carter, Rose Dana, Ruth Dorset, Ann Gilmer, Ellen Randolph, Jane Rossiter, and Dana Ross. In 1989 he completed a play titled *Phantom Wedding*. He considered himself primarily an "entertainer" and "storyteller," and has developed a large following. His writings are collected and preserved at Boston University. In 1988 he was given an honorary doctorate of letters from the University of New Brunswick. Ross passed away on November 1, 1995.

Sources:

Freeman, Alan. "You May Not Know Him, but He Wrote 322 Novels." *Wall Street Journal* 12 (January 1987): 1.

Ross, Dan (as Clarissa Ross). *The Corridors of Fear.* New York: Avon, 1971. 172 pp.

——— (as Clarissa Ross). *The Secret of the Pale Lover.* New York: Magnum Books, 1969. 222 pp.

——— (as Marilyn Ross). *The Vampire Contessa.* New York: Pinnacle Books, 1974. 181 pp.

MacLeod, Hilary. "Dan Ross Is a Busy Man." *Canadian Author and Bookman* (February 1986): 4–5.

Stockel, Shirley, and Victoria Weidner. *A Guide to Collecting "Dark Shadows" Memorabilia.* Edited by Robert Finocchio. Florissant, MO: Collinwood Chronicle, 1992. 107 pp.

Thompson, Jeffrey D. *The Effective Use of Actual Persons and Events in the Historical Novels of Dan Ross*. Nashville, TN: M.A. thesis, Tennessee University Press, 1988. 207 pp.

Ross, Marilyn *see:* Daniel Ross

Russia, Vampires in

The former Soviet Union, including Russia, Siberia, the Ukraine, and Byelorussia, has been one of the homelands of the **Slavic vampire**. The first mention of the word "vampir" in a Slavic document was in a Russian one, *The Book of Prophecy* written in 1047 C.E. for Vladimir Jaroslav, Prince of Novgorod, in northwest Russia. The text was written in what is generally thought of as proto-Russian, a form of the language that had evolved from the older, common Slavonic language but had not yet become distinctive Russian language of the modern era. The text gave a priest the unsavory label "Upir Lichy," literally "wicked vampire" or "extortionate vampire," an unscrupulous prelate. The term—if not the concept—was most likely introduced from the **southern Slavs**, possibly the Bulgarians. The Russians of Kiev had adopted Eastern **Christianity** in 988 C.E. and had drawn heavily on **Bulgaria** for Christian leadership.

Those areas of Russia under Prince Vladimir, centered around the city of Kiev (the Ukraine), accepted Christianity in 988, at which time Vladimir declared war on paganism. Christianity then spread from Kiev northward and westward. For several centuries Christianity existed side by side with existing tribal faiths, but became an integral part of the amalgamation of the tribal cultures into unified states. The invasion of Mongols in the 1240s, including their destruction of Kiev, and their decade of rule, led to a shift of power to Novgorod under Alexander Nevsky. During the fourteenth century, power began to shift to the princedom of Muskovy and the chief Christian cleric established himself in Moscow, though still titled as the metropolitan of "Kiev and all Rus." Westernmost Russia, including the Ukraine and Byelorussia, came under the expanded Lithuanian empire. Thus modern Russia emerged by pushing back the Mongols in the East and the Lithuanians (and Poles) in the West. While the state fought back foreign territorial rivals, Orthodox Christianity was in the very process of driving out the pre-Christian religions. That process was accompanied by the rise of new heretical religious movements, some being amalgamations of Christian and pagan practices. With the emergence of a strong central state in Moscow in the fourteenth century, the state periodically moved against dissident movements. Surviving through this entire period into modern times were people who practiced (or who were believed to practice) magic. They were known as witches and sorcerers.

During the long reign of Vasili II in the mid-fifteenth century, vast changes occurred in Russia, including an expansion of its territory. In 1448, following the breakup of the Roman Catholic and Eastern Orthodox union to combat Islam, and just five years before the fall of Constantinople, the bishop in Moscow declared his autonomous status. There followed a period of expansion, both secular and ecclesiastical. The Russian church assumed many of the prerogatives formerly held by Constantinople, and early in the sixteenth-century there arose the concept of Moscow as the "third **Rome**," the new center of Christian faith. Under Ivan III the Great, territorial expansion reached new heights with the incorporation of Finland and movement to the east across the Urals. Thus the stage was set for the expansion into the Volga River valley under **Ivan the Terrible**, and the incorporation of Siberia and lands all the way to the Pacific Ocean in the seventeenth century. During the several centuries of Romanov rule, Russia continued westward into the **Baltic states**, Byelorussia, and the Ukraine, though its most impressive conquests were southward to the Caspian Sea and the Persian border. By the time of the Russian revolution in 1917, the country had assumed the proportions it has today.

The Russian revolution of 1917 brought the Union of Soviet Socialist Republics (USSR) into existence. The USSR collapsed in December 1991 and has been replaced by the Commonwealth of Independent States (CIS), though a number of the former Soviet states did not join the CIS and chose to become new and independent countries. This essay deals with the lands of the CIS, primarily Russia, Byelorussia, and the Ukraine.

The Russian Vampire: In modern Russia the most common term for a vampire is *uppyr*, a term probably borrowed from the Ukrainian *upyr*. In Russia, the idea of the vampire became closely associated with that of the witch or sorcerer, which in turn had been tied to the concept of heresy. Heresy is defined as the deviation on matters considered essential to orthodox faith, in this case, Eastern Orthodox Christianity. This idea can be viewed as an extension of the Eastern Orthodox belief that a body would not decay normally if death occurred when the individual was outside the communion of the church. The person could be in an excommunicated state due either to immoral behavior or to heresy. Thus a heretic (i.e., *eretik*, or, in related dialects and languages, *eretnik*, *eretica*, *eretnica*, or *erestun*) might become a vampire after death. In Russian thought, the relationship between heresy and the existence of vampires was simply strengthened to the point of identifying one with the other.

The person who was a heretic in this life might become a vampire after death. The most likely heretic to turn into a vampire was the practitioner of magic, under a variety of names—*kudesnik*, *porcelnik*, *koldun*, or *snaxar*. The method of **transformation** into a vampire varied widely.

An *eretik* was also associated with sorcery, a practice that also led to one's becoming a vampire. Over the years and across the very large territory comprising Russia, the *eretik* assumed a number of additional connotations. At time it referred to members of the many sectarian groups that drew people from the true faith. It also referred to witches who had sold their soul to the devil. The vampire *eretik* possessed an evil eye that could draw a person caught in the vampire's gaze into the grave. Dmitrij Zelenin has traced the emergence of the *eretik* vampire from the fight conducted by the Orthodox against the medieval religious sectarians. Sectarians were designated *inovercy* (i.e., persons who adhere to a different faith). Upon death the *inovercy* were associated with the *zaloznye pokojniki*, or unclean dead, and thus were not buried in cemeteries. They had died without confession and thus were seen as dying in sin. Since they did not believe in the true God, possibly they had served the devil, and hence were considered sorcerers.

Eretiks generally were destroyed by the use of an aspen **stake** driven into the back or by **fire**. In the Olonecian region, accounts suggested that any person, including a pious Christian, could become a vampire if a sorcerer entered and took over the body at the moment of death. The peasant would appear to have recovered, but in fact had become a *erestuny* (vampire) who would begin to feed on members of the family. People in the nearby village would start to die mysteriously. In the Elatomsk district of east-central Russia, there were even reports of the *ereticy*—**women** who sold their soul to the devil. After their death, these women roamed the earth in an attempt to turn people from the true faith. They might be found near graveyards, as they slept at night in the graves of the impious. They could be identified by their appearance at the local bath-house, where they made an unseemly noise.

Vampire Folktales: The vampire has been the subject of many Russian folk stories collected in the nineteenth and early twentieth centuries beginning with the work of A. N. Afanasyev in the 1860s. As was common with many folktales, they served to promote community values and encouraged specific kinds of behavior. The tale "Death at the Wedding," for example, related the adventure of a soldier proud of his service to God and the emperor. When he returned to his home town on a visit, he encountered a sorcerer/vampire. Unknowingly, the soldier took the vampire to a wedding, where the vampire began to drain the **blood** of the newlyweds. Horrified, the soldier nevertheless engaged the sorcerer in conversation until he discovered the secret of stopping him. First, he stole some of the blood the vampire had collected into two vials and poured the blood back into the wounds the vampire had made on the couple's bodies. He next led the villagers out to the cemetery, where they dug up the vampire's body and burned it. The soldier was generously rewarded for his actions and his display of courage in service to God and emperor.

The dispatch of the Russian vampire followed traditional means known throughout Slavic countries. The body of a suspected vampire was first disinterred. Often a **stake** (aspen was a preferred wood) was driven through the heart. Sometimes the body would be burned (Afanesyev's account mentioned that aspen wood was used in the cremation of the vampire). In the account from the Olonecian region, the corpse was whipped before the stake was driven through the heart.

The Vampire in Russian Literature: During the nineteenth century, the vampire entered the world of Russian literature, seemingly through the popularity of the German romantic stories of E. T. A. Hoffmann and the writings of **Goethe**. In the 1840s **Alexey K. Tolstoy** (1817–1875) combined the vampire of popular Russian folklore with the literary vampire that had emerged in **Germany** and **France**. His two stories, "Upyr" and "The Family of the Vourdalak," became classics of both the horror genre and Russian literature. The latter was brought to the movie screen by Italian producer **Mario Bava** as part of his horror anthology *Black Sabbath*. More recently, "The Family of the Vourdalak" has become the subject of a Russian-made movie released in the United States as *Father, Santa Claus Has Died* (1992).

At least two other Russian vampire stories have been translated and given worldwide distribution, "Vij" (or "Viv") by Nikolai Gogol and "Phantoms" by Ivan Turgenev. The former became the basis of two movies, *La Maschera del Demonio* (released in the United States as *Black Sunday*), also directed by Mario Bava, and a 1990 remake with the same name by Mario's son Lamberto Bava. A Russian version of *Vij* was filmed in 1967. What was possibly the first vampire film, *The Secret of House No. 5*, was made in Russia in 1912. An unauthorized version of **Dracula (1897)**, the first screen adaptation of the **Bram Stoker** novel, was filmed in Russia two years before **Nosferatu, Eine Symphonie des Grauens**, the more famous film by Freidrich Wilhelm Murnau. However, the vampire has not been a consistent topic for movies in Russia over the years.

Russia was heard from in 1998 when Sergei Lukyanenko released the first of his series of supernatural novels, *Night Watch*, which portrayed a very different Moscow than that seen by the tourist. The hero, Anton Gorodetsky, is an agent for the *Night Watch*, an unusual "police" force that protects humanity from a spectrum of supernatural creates, both good and bad, including vampires, **werewolves, incubi/succubi,** and witches. *Night Watch* was quickly followed by *Day Watch, Twilight Watch,* and *The Last Watch.* The first two novels were made into movies and found a ready audience across Europe and North America.

Sources:

Coxwell, C. Fillingham. *Siberian and Other Folk-Tales*. London: C. W. Daniel Company, 1925. 1,056 pp. Rept. New York: AMS Press, 1983. 1056 pp.

Lukyanenko, Sergei. *The Night Watch*. London: William Heineman, 2006. 489 pp.

Oinas, Felix J. "Heretics as Vampires and Demons in Russia." *Slavic and East European Journal* 22, 4 (Winter 1978): 433–441.

Perkowski, Jan L., ed. *Vampires of the Slavs*. Cambridge, MA: Slavica Publishers, 1976. 294 pp.

———. *The Darkling: A Treatise on Slavic Vampirism*. Columbus, OH: Slavica Publishers, 1989. 174 pp.

Ralston, William Ralston Shedden. *The Songs of the Russian People*. 1872. Rept. New York: Haskell House, 1970. 447 pp.

———. *Russian Folk-tales*. London: Smith, Elder, 1873. Rept. New York: Arno Press, 1977. 382 pp.

Summers, Montague. *The Vampire in Europe*. London: Routledge, Kegan Paul, Trench, Trubner, & Co, 1929. 329 pp. Rept. New Hyde Park, NY: University Books, 1961. 329 pp.

Zelenin, Dmitrij. *Russische (ostslavische) Volkskunde*. Berlin, Leipzig: De Gruyter, 1927.

Ruthven, Lord

Eight decades before anyone had heard of **Dracula**, the vampire Lord Ruthven was created by **John Polidori** and introduced to the world in the first vampire short story, "The Vampyre," published in 1819. Within a few years, Lord Ruthven would appear on both the Paris and **London** stage and inspire a generation of literary activity. "The Vampyre," derived from a story fragment written by **Lord Byron**, was developed by Polidori after his break with Byron, who served as the model for the leading character. The story concerned Aubrey, a wealthy young man who became friends with Lord Ruthven, a mysterious stranger who entered London society. Ruthven was pale in complexion and somewhat cold in demeanor, but a favorite of the women. He freely loaned money to people to use at the gaming tables, but those who accepted his money generally lost it and were led further into debt and eventual degradation.

As Polidori accompanied Byron on a continental journey, so Aubrey traveled to **Rome** with Ruthven in the story. Here he became upset at Ruthven's attempts to seduce the young daughter of an acquaintance. Unable to stop his course of action, Aubrey left Ruthven and went on to **Greece** without him. In Greece he found himself attracted to Ianthe, the daughter of the innkeeper. It was she who introduced him (and the reader) to the legend of the vampire. While Aubrey lost himself in his new relationship and the visiting of the local sights, Ruthven arrived. A short time later, Ianthe was attacked and killed by a vampire. Aubrey, recovering from his loss and not yet connecting Ruthven and the vampire, rejoined him to travel around Greece. As they journeyed across the country, they were attacked by bandits. Ruthven was killed in the attack, but before he died, he made Aubrey swear to conceal the manner of his death and of any **crimes** he might have committed for the period of a year and a day. The bandits carried Ruthven's body to a nearby site where it would be exposed to the **moon**'s light. Aubrey returned to London and along the way began to realize that Ruthven destroyed all upon whom he showered his favors, especially the women who became his lovers. Upon Aubrey's return to London, Ruthven reappeared and reminded him of his promise of silence. Aubrey had a nervous breakdown and while he was recovering, Ruthven ingratiated himself with the sister. They were engaged to be married, and Aubrey, because of his oath, felt unable to prevent the occurrence. The marriage took place on the day the oath ran out, but not in time to prevent Ruthven from killing the sister and disappearing to work his evil elsewhere.

Polidori developed Lord Ruthven from elements of European folklore that had become well known across Europe after the vampire epidemics of the previous century. In his introduction, Polidori refers specifically to the **Arnold Paul** vampire scare and the survey of vampirism written by **Dom Augustin Calmet**. And while the vampire had been the subject of some German and British poems, Polidori, as noted by Carol Senf, took the crude entity of European folklore and transformed it into a complex and interesting character, the first vampire in English fiction. No longer was the vampire simply a mindless demonic force unleashed on humankind, but a real person—albeit a resurrected one—capable of moving unnoticed in human society and picking and choosing **victims**. He was not an impersonal evil entity, but a moral degenerate dominated by evil motives, and a subject about whom negative moral judgments were proper.

Because "The Vampyre" originally appeared under Byron's name, it attracted much more attention than it might have otherwise. In **France**, before the matter of its authorship was cleared up, it was widely reviewed and greatly affected many of the new generation of romantic writers. Playwright **Charles Nodier** was asked to review it and wrote the preface to the French edition. His friend Cyprien Bérard wrote a two-volume sequel to the story, *Lord Ruthwen ou les Vampires*, which appeared early in 1820. Because it was published anonymously, many ascribed it to Nodier; however, Nodier wrote his own version of the Ruthven story in *Le Vampire*, the first vampire **drama**, which opened in Paris in the summer of 1820. In Nodier's tale, Ruthven finally was forced to face the fatal consequences of his evil life. Within two months, **James R. Planché** adapted *Le Vampire* and brought Lord Ruthven to the London stage in *The Vampire, or, The Bride of the Isles*. Meanwhile, back in Paris, Lord Ruthven appeared in four other vampire plays—two serious melodrama, two comedic—before the year was out. He made his debut in **Germany** in 1829 in an **opera**, *Der Vampyr,* by **Heinrich August Marschner**.

Before he left Paris and retired to Belgium, Lord Ruthven made his last appearance on the Parisian stage in 1852 in **Alexandre Dumas**'s final work. After Dumas's play, Lord Ruthven went into retirement as a character to be succeeded by **Varney the Vampyre**, **Carmilla**, and **Dracula**. He would not be rediscovered until 1945. Ruthven served as the initial inspiration for a movie, *The Vampire's Ghost*, produced by Republic Pictures. However, by the time the script was developed the story line little resembled the original, and its leading character had only the vaguest likeness to Lord Ruthven. Lord Ruthven also made a brief appearance when *Vampire Tales*, the Marvel **comic book**, adapted "The Vampyre" in its first issue in 1973.

The most recent revival of Lord Ruthven, a new version of Marschner's opera, appeared on BBC **television** in 1992. In *Der Vampyr—A Soap Opera*, Ruthven was now a modern Londoner and his name had been changed to Ripley the Vampyr.

Sources:

Goulart, Ron. "The Vampire." *Vampire Tales* 1 (1973): 35–48.

Macdonald, D. L. *Poor Polidori: A Critical Biography of the Author of 'The Vampire.* Toronto: University of Toronto Press, 1991. 333 pp.

Rymer, James Malcolm (1804–1884)

James Malcolm Rymer, the author of **Varney the Vampyre**, was born in Scotland. He emerged out of obscurity in 1842 as the editor of the quite respectable *Queen's Magazine*. Prior to that time he had been a civil engineer, surveyor, and mechanical draftsman. As he became a successful writer he dropped these prior occupations. In 1842, he authored an article for *Queen's Magazine* in which he made disparaging remarks about popular fiction written for the working masses. However, the next year, *Queen's Magazine* failed, and he became the editor of *Lloyd's Penny Weekly Miscellany*. Cheap popular fiction, the so-called "penny dreadful," had emerged in England in the 1830s. The penny dreadfuls were of two basic kinds—magazines that cost a penny and specialized in serialized popular novels, and novels published in sections that sold for a penny each.

Ostensibly for adults, by the 1850s the market was directed primarily at children. As Rymer wrote under a variety of pseudonyms, it is not known when he first began to write popular fiction, but in 1841 he authored a very popular novel, *The Black Monk*. His most popular pseudonyms were Malcolm J. Errym and Malcolm J. Merry. The most popular book written largely by Rymer was *Varney the Vampyre; or A Feast of Blood: A Romance*. It appeared in the mid-1840s and in the end ran to 220 chapters and 868 pages. The chapters were then collected in a single volume (1847) and continued to sell for the next 15 years. The idea for *Varney* seems to have been an 1840 reprinting of **John Polidori**'s "The Vampyre" by the *Romanticist's and Novelist's Library* in a penny dreadful format. *Varney* included most of Polidori's distinctive opinions about vampires.

Since *Varney* was issued anonymously, for many years there was some doubt as to the real author. **Montague Summers** believed it to be Thomas P. Prest, author of *Sweeney Todd*, the best known of the penny dreadfuls. However, in 1963, Louis James, who had inherited several of Rymer's own scrapbooks, found conclusive evidence of Rymer's authorship of the majority of the work. It was common for different writers to work on various sections of long-running serials such as *Varney*, and other writers might have been employed to write new chapters. (That fact might account for its often uneven style and its contradictory statements about the lead character.) Rymer continued to write for Lloyd until 1853, when he was employed by another popular penny dreadful publisher, John Dicks. From 1858 to 1864 he wrote for *Reynolds' Miscellany,* and in 1866 wrote for the *London Miscellany*.

Sources:

Anglo, Michael. *Penny Dreadfuls and other Victorian Horrors*. London: Jupiter, 1977. 125 pp.

Bleiler, E. F. "A Note on Authorship" In *Varney the Vampire*. New York: Dover Publications, 1932.

Frayling, Christopher. *Vampyres: Lord Byron to Count Dracula*. London: Faber and Faber, 1991. 429 pp.

James, Louis. *Fiction for the Working Man, 1830–1850*. London: Oxford University Press, 1963. 226 pp.

Johannsen, Albert. *The House of Beadle and Adams and Its Dime and Nickel Novels*. 3 vols. Norman, OK: University of Oklahoma Press, 1950.

Saberhagen, Frederick Thomas (1930–)

Frederick Thomas Saberhagen is a science fiction writer and author of a series of novels expanding upon the **Dracula** theme. He became a freelance writer in 1962 and his first novel, *The Golden People*, was published by Ace Books in 1964. It was followed by *The Water of Thought* (1965) and a number of short stories. In 1967 Saberhagen took a job as an assistant editor with *Encyclopedia Britannica*, a position he held for six years before returning to full-time writing.

In 1967, *Beserker*, a set of short stories and the first book in what was to become the "Beserker" series, began to establish Saberhagen as a leading science fiction writer. The "beserkers" are self-programming and self-replicating robotic spacecraft engineered to kill anything that still lives by their creators, a race long-since dead. The appearance of these mechanical demonic forces drives the divided intelligent life forms to unite against them. In the process, the beserkers become a stimulus to increased progress, which possibly would have not have been made otherwise.

Saberhagen's work is characterized by the blend of science, in which he shows a solid grounding, with mythic and legendary materials. Integrating the two provides him a base for metaphysical speculation. The "Beserker" series, for example, became the vehicle for a lengthy treatment of the role of evil in human life.

In the mid-1970s, Saberhagen stepped out of his science fiction world to publish the first of seven novels using with the Dracula theme. These novels started with the interesting hypothesis that Dracula was in fact the hero in the events that took place in **Bram Stoker**'s novel. In the first volume in the series, *The Dracula Tape* (1975), Dracula is telling his story into a tape recorder. He takes the reader step-by-step through the story, explaining how he tried not to vampirize **Jonathan Harker**, but to protect him. He justified his actions regarding **Lucy Westenra** as a reaction to **Abraham Van Hels-**

ing who, in his ignorance of blood types, was killing her by his transfusions. In the end, her only hope was to be turned into a vampire. His involvement with Lucy led to his falling in love with **Mina Murray**, who was, at that point, married to Harker. This theme reappeared in later volumes in the series.

The Dracula Tape received mixed reviews, especially with Saberhagen's science fiction fans, but gained an audience among vampire/Dracula enthusiasts. It initiated what has become a new approach to the vampire myth. By treating Dracula sympathetically, Saberhagen enlarged the myth in such a way that it could speak to the contemporary need for individuals to develop an understanding of others who are very different. It also opened the possibility of making the vampire a hero, not just an anti-hero.

Dracula as a hero allowed a broad new expanse into which he could be introduced. Saberhagen first developed an obvious theme, the possible encounter of Dracula with his contemporary, **Sherlock Holmes**. In *The Holmes-Dracula File*, the two joined forces to prevent the introduction of plague-bearing rats into London during Queen Victoria's Diamond Jubilee celebrations. Continuing the attack upon the heroes of Stoker's *Dracula*, Saberhagen introduced **John Seward** (the character from the original novel) into *The Holmes-Dracula File* as the villain behind the dastardly plot.

Dracula's feelings for Mina Murray, who made a brief appearance in the Holmes story to reaffirm her love for Dracula, served as the basis for the third volume, *An Old Friend of the Family* (1979). Dracula had developed a means by which Mina and her descendants could contact him should they need him. The need arose in the late 1970s in Chicago, Saberhagen's hometown.

Summoned by Judy Southerland, Dracula, using the pseudonym of Dr. Emile Corday, arrived to find that the incidents experienced by Mina's descendants merely masked a plot directed against him by Morgan, a redheaded vampiress who resented Dracula's influence on the vampire community. After defeating Morgan, Dracula settled in the United States.

In the fourth novel, Dracula changed his name to *Thorn* (1980) and became involved in a conspiracy to steal a painting that turned out to be a portrait of Helen Hundayi. She was, according to the story, Dracula's first wife. In *Dominion* (1982) Dracula, now known as Talisman, encountered Nimue, the Lady of the Lake, who was attempting to bring the master magician, Falerin, to the fore as the supreme ruler. Dracula had an ally in Ambrosius (known to the world as Merlin), whose magical power was needed to finally defeat Nimue.

The sixth of Saberhagen's Dracula novels appeared in 1990. *A Matter of Taste* returned Dracula, now known as Matthew Maule, to Chicago where he had settled as the Southerland family's Uncle Matthew. The story concerned an attempt by Dracula's vampire enemies to kill him. Very early, Dracula was poisoned and lay near death in his bed. The Southerlands protected him against his foes until he could recover and defeat them decisively. This novel also had Dracula recounting the story of his **origins**—an inventive tale of Prince Dracula becoming a vampire. In *A Question of Time* (1992), Dracula joined forces with detective Joe Keogh to fight Edgar Tyrell, a menacing vampire who seemed able to affect time itself. And the series has continued.

Saberhagen's Dracula appeared on the heels of **William Edward Daniel Ross**'s **Dark Shadows** novels, but took Ross's sympathetic treatment of the vampire one step further. *The Dracula Tape* was followed by **Anne Rice's** *Interview with the Vampire*, which also had the vampire telling his story into a tape recorder. Saberhagen's Dracula differed strongly, however, from both the *Dark Shadows* and Anne Rice vampires. Unlike **Barnabas Collins**, Dracula had no problem with his vampire state, no anguish about his uncontrollable drive, and no wish to change. Unlike Rice's Louis and **Lestat de Lioncourt**, Saberhagen's Dracula manifested little ambiguity in his situation. Dracula was a hero whose moral situation was rather clear—he had found the means to handle most of the questions that would be raised about his preying upon the human race.

While producing the Dracula novels, Saberhagen continued to publish science fiction novels at a steady pace, and during the 1970s he also began to write fantasy novels, most prominently the "Swords" and "Lost Swords" series. He edited anthologies on chess, *Pawn to Infinity* (1982), and archaeology, *A Spadeful of Spacetime* (1981) as well.

Saberhagen's Dracula novels brought him to the attention of **Francis Ford Coppola**, and he was chosen, along with coauthor James V. Hart, to write the novelization of Coppola's screenplay for **Bram Stoker's Dracula**.

Saberhagen continued his Dracula series through the mid-1990s with *Séance for a Vampire* (1994) and *A Sharpness in the Neck* (1996), and into the new century with *A Coldness in the Blood* (2002). He was the literary guest of honor at **Dracula '97: A Centennial Celebration** at which he was honored by the **Transylvanian Society of Dracula** for his Dracula series.

Sources:

Saberhagen, Fred. *The Dracula Tape*. New York: Paperback Library, 1975. 206 pp.

———. *The Holmes-Dracula File*. New York: Ace Books, 1978. 249 pp.

———. *An Old Friend of the Family*. New York: Ace Books, 1979. Rept. New York: TOR, 1987. 247 pp.

———. *Thorn*. New York: Ace Books, 1980. 347 pp.

———. *Dominion*. New York: TOR, 1982. 320 pp.

———. *A Matter of Taste*. New York: TOR, 1990. 284 pp.

———. *A Question of Time*. New York: TOR, 1992. 278 pp.

———. and James V. Hart. *Bram Stoker's Dracula*. New York: New American Library, 1992. 298 pp.

———. *Séance for a Vampire*. New York: TOR, 1994. 285 pp.

———. *A Sharpness in the Neck:* New York: TOR, 1996. 349 pp.

———. *A Coldness in the Blood*. New York: TOR, 2002. 383 pp.

Smith, Curtis C., ed. *Twentieth-Century Science-Fiction Writers*. Chicago: St. James Press, 1986. 933 pp.

Wilgus, Neal. "Saberhagen's New Dracula: The Vampire as Hero." In *Discovering Modern Horror Fiction*. Darrel Schweitzer, ed. San Bernardino, CA: Borgo Press, 1987: 92–8.

❦ St. George's Day ❦

S t. George's Day (April 24 or May 6, depending upon calendars) is a feast day on the calendar of the Eastern Orthodox Church in **Romania**, including **Transylvania**. It was usually the day when flocks of sheep were first driven to pasture from their winter home. In the novel **Dracula**, **Jonathan Harker** arrived in **Bistritz** on the eve of St. George's Day and was told by a woman, "It is the eve of St. George's Day. Do you know that to-night, when the clock strikes midnight, all the evil things in the world will have full sway?" The woman begged Harker to wait a day or two before leaving for his meeting with Dracula.

Emily Gerard, a major source of information used by **Bram Stoker** in researching Transylvania, noted that St. George's Day was among the most important of the year, and one that had a number of occult associations. At midnight, the witches would gather for their sabbath and peasants would put up such barriers as **hawthorn** or **garlic** to protect their homes and stables against the witches. Many would sleep with their **animals** in an all-night vigil. Even more than All Saints Eve, St. George's Day was thought to be the time of the most activity of the spirits of the dead.

Harry Senn recorded the story from Cluj (called by its German name, Klausenburgh, in *Dracula*). One year, a cart wheel appeared in town on the eve of St. George's Day. It was tied to the wall of a house. Two days later the wheel disappeared, and in its place hung a woman recognized as being from a neighboring village. She was soon identified as a witch (*strigoaica*).

Sources:

Gerard, Emily. *The Land beyond the Forest*. 2 vols. London: Will Blackwood & Sons, 1888.

Senn, Harry A. *Were-Wolf and Vampire in Romania*. New York: Columbia University Pres, 1982. 148 pp.

❧ Saint-Germain ❧

Saint-Germain, the central figure in a series of novels by **Chelsea Quinn Yarbro** is a 4,000-year-old vampire, Yarbro developed Saint-Germain from a historical personage, the Count de Saint Germain, a mysterious individual and reputed alchemist who lived in eighteenth-century France. He moved in cultured circles of his day, composed music, and was fluent in several languages. The count was a prince from **Transylvania**, whose real name was Francis Ragoczy according to most sources. His money came from international trade, possibly centered on jewels. The few accounts of his life suggested that he was of medium height, wore black and white, rarely ate in public (even at his own parties), claimed extraordinary powers (including an age of several thousand years), and encouraged an aura of mystery about the details of his life. In the historical Saint-Germain, Yarbro found someone who closely fit her evolving image of what a vampire should be. She made Saint-Germain her central character by merely using the facts about him in a vampire mythic context.

At the same time, Yarbro was consciously reworking the **Dracula** myth as it had developed through the twentieth century. She approached the vampire logically and saw many problems in the tradition. First, she removed the overlay of medieval **Christianity**, which left very little "evil" in the vampire's character. In his bite he shared a moment of sexual bliss and had the power to grant a degree of immortality. Second, she decided that the vampire would need to be quite intelligent to survive in what was a hostile environment and would find creative and entertaining ways to spend the centuries of time.

Yarbro also found the essence of vampirism to be the act of taking the **blood**, the intimacy of contact, and the "life" that came from it—rather than the nourishment of the blood's ingredients. Thus the bite became a sexual act.

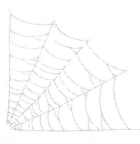

Yarbro introduced Saint-Germain in *Hotel Transylvania* (1978), a novel set in eighteenth-century France. This historical romance revolves around the relationship of Saint-Germain and a young woman, Madelaine de Montalia. Some years earlier, Madelaine's father had promised her to a group of Satanists with whom he had become involved. As she and Saint-Germain were falling in love, the coven of devil worshippers began to put pressure on her father to live up to his bargain and turn her over to them for their own cultic purposes.

Hotel Transylvania slowly revealed facts about Saint-Germain, though an alert reader might guess what was coming when, early in the first chapter, he repeated Dracula's famous line, "I do not drink **wine**." Saint-Germain was a vampire, but a vampire of a different breed. In conversations with Madelaine, Saint-Germain slowly revealed his nature. He was many centuries old. As a vampire he needed only small quantities of blood to survive and would normally take only a wineglass full. Contrary to popular opinion, he was not affected by sacred objects, such as the **crucifix**. He could walk freely on consecrated ground. He was negatively affected by running **water** and **sunlight**, but drew **strength** from his **native soil**. He had constructed shoes with hollow heels and soles into which he put the earth that countered the effect of running water and allowed him to walk around in daylight. Among his few superhuman abilities was his strength, which he amply demonstrated in his final confrontation with the coven of Satanists.

Saint-Germain possessed very human emotions, though time had taught him to stay above most affairs of humans. He had developed his own set of morals, especially concerning attacks on individuals for his blood supply.

Periodically, however, he had fallen in love, as he did with Madelaine in *Hotel Transylvania*. His love affairs revealed his quite different **sexuality**—while he could participate in most sexual activity, he could not have an erection. The bite, however, was a more than adequate substitute for him and for his sexual partner. Sexual relations were limited in that they could not occur between two vampires. Thus if an affair between a vampire and human progressed to the point that the human became a vampire, the affair would necessarily end. They could, and often did, remain friends, but the affair was not part of their immortal existence.

The centuries-old saga of Saint-Germain has been laid out in the subsequent novels, the second of which, *The Palace* (1979) was set in fifteenth-century Florence and the third, *Blood Games* in **Rome** under Nero. In each of these, Saint-Germain confronted life-and-death experiences that forced discussion of the possibility of the "true death." Vampires could be killed by the severing of the spine (such as when the head is cut off) and by being consumed in **fire**.

The Palace also introduced Saint-Germain's former lover and present-day colleague, Atta Olivia Clemens, and the account of her **origin** was spelled out in *Blood Games*. She had been forced into a marriage with an influential Roman official who had ambitions to become emperor. He was also somewhat of a pervert, and forced her to have relations with many men while he watched. Then she met Saint-Germain, and he arranged for her to escape her husband's power and become a vampire. He created a new vampire by drinking too much blood from someone or allowing them to drink of his blood.

While the origin of Saint-Germain was never fully revealed, Yarbro did construct a history for him. He was born 4,000 years ago, in what is today Transylvania, of Proto-Etruscan stock. His people had a vampiric priesthood and, as he was born in the winter (the dark of the year in agricultural societies), he was initiated into the priesthood. Some details of this priesthood were provided in the *Path of the Eclipse*. The protector god of his people was a vampire, and the priests also were vampires. Saint-Germain had been initiated, but before he could assume his position, he was captured and taken into slavery. He served very successfully in the army of his captors, for which he was rewarded with execution. Saint-Germain, however, survived because his executioners did not know they had to either decapitate him or burn his body.

More recent volumes have brought Saint-Germain into the twentieth century in Nazi **Germany** (*Tempting Fate*, 1982) and in various other modern situations (*The Saint-Germain Chronicles*, 1983). In the meantime, Olivia has continued her career quite apart from Saint-Germain, though they occasioanlly make contact through correspondence. During the time of the Emperor Justinian, she moved from Rome to Constantinople and before her return to Rome in 1214 C.E. had lived for a time in Tyre (in the Holy Land). She left Rome for France in the seventeenth century where, following an adventure with the famous Musketeer d'Artagnan, she has drifted in obscurity.

By 2009, Yarbro had produced twenty-two Saint-Germain novels and two volumes of Saint-Germain short stories, the latter volumes showing no diminution in quality. In addition to these works, there have been an additional three Olivia and two Madelaine volumes. Yarbro's novels have been consistently characterized by well-thought-out plots and set in thoroughly researched historical settings.

Yarbro received the Bram Stoker Lifetime Achievement Award at the meeting of the Horror Writers Association, June 12-14, 2009, in Burbank, California.

Sources:

Yarbro, Chelsea Quinn. *Cautionary Tales*. Garden City, NY: Doubleday & Co., 1978. 204 pp.

————. *Hotel Transylvania*. New York: St. Martin's Press, 1978. 252 pp.

————. *The Palace*. New York: St. Martin's Press, 1978. 376 pp.

————. *Path of the Eclipse*. New York: St. Martin's Press, 1981. 433 pp.

————. *Tempting Fate*. New York: St. Martin's Press, 1982.

————. *The Saint-Germain Chronicles*. New York: Timescape Books, 1983. 181 pp.

————. *A Mortal Glamor*. New York: Bantam Books, 1985. 308 pp.

————. *Out of the House of Life*. New York: Tor Books, 1990. 446 pp.

————. *Better in the Dark*. New York: Tor Books, 1993. 412 pp.

————. *Darker Jewels*. New York: Tor Books, 1993. 398 pp.

————. *The Vampire Stories of Chelsea Quinn Yarbro*. White Rock, BC: Transylvania Press, 1994. 324 pp.

————. *Mansions of Darkness*. New York: Tor Books, 1996. 427 pp.

————. *Come Twilight*. New York, Tor Books, 2000. 479 pp.

————. *A Feast in Exile*. New York: Tor Books, 2001. 496 pp.

————. *Night Blooming*. New York: Warner Books, 2002. 429 pp.

————. *Midnight Harvest*. New York: Warner Book, 2003. 434 pp.

————. *In the Face of Death*. Dallas, TX: Benbella Books, 2004. 288 pp.

————. *Dark of the Sun*. New York: Tor Books, 2005. 464 pp.

————. *States of Grace*. New York: Tor Books, 2005. 332 pp.

————. *Roman Dusk*.New York: Tor Books, 2006. 362 pp.

———. *Borne in Blood.* New York: Tor Books, 2007. 368 pp.

———. *A Dangerous Climate.* New York: Tor Books, 2008. 384 pp.

———. *Saint-Germain: Memoirs* Elder Signs Press, 2008. 256 pp.

———. *Burning Shadows.* New York: Tor Books, 2009. 354 pp.

❨ Sands, Lynsay ❩

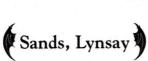

Canadian romance author Lynsay Sands was born in Leamington, Ontario, grew up in southern Ontario, and studied at the University of Windsor. She emerged as a romance author following her first book, *The Deed*, released in 1997, but did not distinguish herself from the mass of other romance writers until the middle of the next decade (2003) with the first of her vampire novels, *Single White Vampire.* This and her subsequent novels about the Argeneaus, a family of modern vampires, became known for the humor she injected into the stories.

The stories center on a nuclear vampire family, a mother Marguerite, three sons (Lucien, Bastien, and Etienne), and a daughter (Lissianna). Later, members of the extended family are introduced, all hundreds of years old, and having problems facing the modern world. Cousin Vincent is an actor living in Los Angeles. The Argeneau family traces their lineage back to Alexandria and Ramses who emerge in the sixteenth century B.C.E. and get caught in Pompeii when Vesuvius erupted in 79 C.E. Sands traces vampirism back to Atlantis and the fabled scientific advances that rival those of the twenty-first century. Atlantean scientists discovered nanos, microscopic entities that could be injected into the bloodstream where they lived and reproduced. The nanos live off of blood. Once in the body, on the good side, they help to constantly regenerate one's body by repairing organs and any damage due to accidents and aging. The body, however, cannot manufacture blood at a rate to meet the needs of the hungry nanos. Hence the descendants of the original Atlanteans, to whom the nanos have been passed, need to regularly ingest more **blood**.

Apart from the scientific nature of their origin, Sands's vampires are fairly traditional—they have great **strength**, have to avoid **sunlight**, need blood regularly, possess **fangs**, and even sleep in **coffins**.

While *Single White Vampire* was the first of the twelve volumes published by Sands, she now tells her new fans to read the novels as she intended them to appear, beginning with *A Quick Bite* (2005) and proceeding to *Love Bites* (2004) before *Single White Vampire* and the fourth novel *Tall, Dark and Hungry* (2004). Most recently, she has begun a subseries within the series built around a group of vampires commissioned by the vampire powers-that-be to hunt rogue vampires, who have broken the laws of the vampire community. Secondarily, they investigate cases of mortals learning of the existence of vampires, who exist in a secret world shielded from the knowledge of the larger human community.

Sands has also participated in several anthologies of vampire stories: *His Immortal Embrace* (2003), *Dates from Hell* (2006), and *Holidays Are Hell* (2007).

Sources:

"Interview–Lynsay Sands." *Darque Review.* http://darquereviews.blogspot.com/2007/11/interview-lynsay-sands.html. Accessed September 15, 2009.

Sands, Lynsay. *Single White Vampire*. New York: Love Spell, 2003. 369 pp.

———. *Tall, Dark and Hungry*. New York: Love Spell, 2004. 372 pp.

———. *Love Bites*. New York: Love Spell, 2004. 373 pp.

———. *A Quick Bite*. New York: Avon, 2005. 360 pp.

———. *A Bite to Remember*. New York: Love Spell, 2006. 384 pp.

———. *Bite Me If You Can*. New York: Avon, 2007. 384 pp.

———. *The Accidental Vampire*. New York: Love Spell, 2008. 372 pp.

———. *Vampire, Interrupted*. New York: Avon, 2008. 384 pp.

———. *Vampires Are Forever*. New York: Love Spell, 2008. 341 pp.

———. *The Immortal Hunter*. New York: Avon, 2009. 368 pp.

———. *The Renegade Hunter*. New York: Avon, 2009. 384 pp.

———. *The Rogue Hunter*. New York: Avon, 2009. 384 pp.

Sangster, Jimmy (1927–)

Jimmy Sangster, a screenwriter for many of the **Hammer Films**' horror movies of the 1950s and 1960s, was born in North Wales. He dropped out of school at the age of fifteen and after the war entered the movie world as a production manager. In 1956 he was given his first opportunity as a screenwriter for *A Man on the Beach*. Next he teamed with director **Terence Fisher** and actors **Christopher Lee** and **Peter Cushing** for the first of two trendsetting Hammer horror films, *The Curse of Frankenstein*. In 1958 the four reassembled for their most memorable effort: *Dracula* (released in America as **The Horror of Dracula**). Sangster's screenplay for the **The Horror of Dracula** altered the story considerably from both the earlier *Dracula* **(1931)** movie with **Bela Lugosi** and the original book. It set vampire hunter **Abraham Van Helsing** in a singular fight with **Dracula**. The story climaxed when Van Helsing killed Dracula by tearing the curtain from the wall and allowing the sun to burn the vampire to ashes.

The following year Sangster wrote the screenplay for Universal/Eros for the production of *The Blood of the Vampire* (also known as *The Demon with the Bloody Hands*). While he returned to Hammer to work on several scripts, it was not until 1960 that he worked again with Fisher and Cushing (minus Lee) to do *The Brides of Dracula*, Hammer's sequel to the *The Horror of Dracula*. Like Lee, Dracula did not appear in *The Brides of Dracula*, a story concerning Baron Meinster, memorable for biting Cushing, who survived by cauterizing the wound.

Through the 1960s Sangster worked on a variety of films as the screenwriter, but also as the producer. He worked on *The Nanny* (1965) and *The Anniversary* (1968), two films starring Bette Davis in some of her most memorable macabre roles. In 1970 he emerged as the screenwriter, producer, and director of the Hammer production of *The Horror of Frankenstein*. Upon completion of *Frankenstein*, he assumed the role of director for the next horror/vampire effort, *Lust for a Vampire*, one of the Hammer **Carmilla** films. It would be his last vampire film.

Through the 1970s and 1980s Sangster continued to work on horror films. He came to the United States and participated in a number of **television** productions, including work with actor/host **Jack Palance** on the *Ripley's Believe It or Not* series. While not wanting to be remembered only as a "Hammer writer," he became best known for his efforts on the several Hammer vampire and Frankenstein movies. He effectively scripted the **gothic** mood by setting his scenes at nighttime, showing his characters in their steady degeneration, and building an atmosphere saturated with illusion and unexpected terror.

Sangster remained active through the 1990s, and co-wrote the screenplay for *Flashback—Mörderische Ferien*, a horror movie released in 2000.

Sources:

Ashley, Mike. *Who's Who in Horror and Fantasy Fiction*. London: Elm Tree Books, 1977. 240 pp.

Vinson, James, ed. *The International Dictionary of Films and Filmmakers*. Volume IV: *Writers and Production Artists*. Chicago: St. James Press, 1988.

Santo

As in America, in Mexico there is a tradition of masked heroes, though of a much different nature. For more than two decades (1958–1982) the most popular masked fighter of evil, Santo, strolled across the motion picture screen attacking monsters and vampires. Santo was created and played by Rodolfo Gizmán Huerta (1915–1984). Huerta, in the persona of Santo, originally attained hero status as a wrestler and became well known throughout the country following World War II. In the ring, Huerta never appeared without his silver mask, the essential element in his costume.

As a movie star, Santo was sometimes confused with another masked character, El Médico Asesino. Santo's first movie was *Cerebro del Mal*, filmed in Cuba just before the revolution. This initial movie included El Incógnito (played by Fernando Osés), also a masked hero character. A second movie, *Cargamento Blanco*, was shot at the same time and, in finished form, even included some footage from the first movie. The movies were not released, however. In September 1960 the comic book-like *Santo, el Enmascarado de Plata* began weekly publication. It furthered Santo's popularity and prompted the release of the two Cuban motion pictures early in 1961. That same year Santo made four additional movies beginning with *Santo Contra los Zombies*. In order to keep the costs down, some of Santo's movies were shot as three twenty-minute segments at Estúdios América, which charged cheaper rates than the large movie studios but which was limited by government regulations to short features. Each segment was given a different name and originally shown on different days.

Later they would be put together as a single feature.

In 1962 Santo appeared in the first of his several vampire features, *Santo Contra las Mujeres Vampiro*, directed by Alfonso Corona Blake and released in the United States as *Samson vs. the Vampire Women*. While Santo would fight a variety of monsters, he was frequently bedeviled by vampires, their next appearance being in *Santo Contra el Baron Brakola* (1965). Baron Brakola was modeled on **Bela Lugosi**, and stills of Lugosi were used in advertisements of the film.

In 1967 Santo met **Dracula** in *Santo un el Tesoro de Dracula*, the first of his technicolor vampire films, which also was released in an adult version as *El Vampiro y el Sexo*. By this time the character had taken on a new quality, having transformed from a simple untutored wrestler/part-time fighter of evil into a superscientist who, for example, in *Santo en el Tesoro de Dracula* invented a time machine. He also acquired the adoration of females, especially in the adult versions of his movies. Over the years Santo fought vampires in *Santo y Blue Demon Contra los Monstruos* (1969), *Santo en la Venganza de las Mujeres Vampiros* (1969), *Santo y Blue Demon Contra Dracula y el Hombre Lobo* (1971), and *Chanoc y el Hijo del Santo Contra Los Vampiros Asesinos* (1981). In the last movie, the aging Santo made only a brief appearance—viewed as an attempt to pass his career to his son.

In spite of the low production values and hastily written scripts (with action often improvised as it was shot), Santo became a national star in Mexico and his films were released to an adoring audience across Latin America and other Spanish-speaking countries. They were among the few Mexican movies able to break through the control American and British film companies held over the international film distribution market.

Sources:

Cotter, Robert Mitchel "Bobb". *The Mexican Masked Wrestler and Monster Filmography*. Jefferson-ville, NC: McFarland & Company, 2008. 216 pp.

Fenton, Steve. "Mexi-Monster Meltdown." *Monster International* 2 (October 1992): 4–13.

Glut, Donald G. *The Dracula Book*. Metuchen, NJ: Scarecrow Press, 1975. 388 pp.

Green, Doyle. *Mexploitation Cinema: A Critical History of Mexican Vampire, Wrestler, Ape-man and Similar Films, 1957–1977*. Jeffersonville, NC: McFarland & Company, 2005. 202 pp.

Higuchi, Horacio. "The Traveling Monster Hunter." *Monster International* 2 (October 1992): 20–31.

Sara the Black Virgin *see:* Kali

Satan

Most modern novelists and screenwriters have agreed that vampires usually were created by the bite of another vampire. However, that left them with a question, "Where did the first vampire come from?" Satanism emerged as the primary answer. The suggestion of Satanism was supported by **Bram Stoker**. In his novel **Dracula**, Stoker had his spokesperson, Dr. **Abraham Van Helsing**, offer the following reflection upon his vampire adversary:

> The Draculas were, says Arminius, a great and noble race, though now and again were scions who were held by their coevals to have dealings with the Evil One. They learned his secrets in the **Scholomance**, amongst the mountains over Lake Hermannstadt, where the devil claims the tenth scholar as his due.

Stoker directly developed his theory that vampirism was ultimately related to Satanism from Emily Gerard's book *The Land beyond the Forest*. The book spoke of the scholomance as a school somewhere in the heart of the mountains of **Transylvania**. There the devil himself taught the secrets of nature and magic. Ten scholars attended at any given time. Payment for the schooling came in the form of one scholar, who remained behind to serve the devil after classes were over. Lake Hermannstadt was near present-day Sibiu.

Raymond T. McNally and **Radu R. Florescu** have noted that at the town of Paltinis Pietrele, near Sibiu, was a place called *pietrele lui Solomon* (the rocks of Solomon). Wandering students stopped here to swear their oaths to Solomon (the wise king of the

Bible), who was believed to know the secrets of alchemy. They suggest that Gerard had heard of this spot and reported on it in a somewhat garbled manner, thus creating a story about the mythical scholomance. While largely ignored in post-*Dracula* fiction, several recent novels (Drake/Andersson, Warrington—see Sources) have developed the scholomance theme.

Quite different from Stoker's reading of Gerard, there was a much stronger and older tradition that tied vampirism to Satanism. Among the **Slavs**, it was believed that the vampire existed in the realm outside of the acceptance of God and the church. Vampires originated among people who were witches (worshippers of Satan), people who had committed **suicide**, or those who were excommunicated. In **Russia**, the vampire was called *eretik* (heretic: a person who has departed from the true faith of Orthodox **Christianity**). People outside the realm of the church were thought to be dealing with the devil.

Unacceptable to God, the vampire was unable to deal with the sacred on earth. It could not stand the presence of holy objects such as the **crucifix** or the **eucharistic host**. It stayed away from churches. It was condemned to live in the darkness. After death, the vampire was rejected by the Earth, and, according to the theology of the Eastern Church, its body would remain intact and incorruptible.

While most stage and film productions about **Dracula** neglect the question of his **origin** as a vampire, Stoker's brief mention of his family's dealings with the devil was part of a fresh mythical presentation of Dracula by **Francis Ford Coppola** in his movie *Bram Stoker's Dracula.* Drawing upon McNally and Florescu's modern accounts of **Vlad the Impaler,** the historical character who, in part, stands behind the fictional Dracula, Coppola pictured Vlad fighting the Turks. Wrongly informed that Vlad had lost the battle, his wife Elizabeth committed suicide. The church refused to hold her funeral or allow her to be buried in holy ground. Her soul could not be saved; she was damned. Vlad was so much in love with her that in his grief he rejected God. He plunged his sword into the cross in the chapel, and drank the **blood** that flowed from it. He vowed to return from the grave accompanied by the powers of darkness to avenge his love's untimely death.

The movement of the vampire myth into modern pluralistic and secular culture has created noticeable changes in the myth. Non-Christian writers have tended to place the vampire in a completely secular realm (vampirism as a disease) or to create a supernatural myth not based on Christian presuppositions or the existence of the devil. Such alternative myths are most evident in the novels of **Chelsea Quinn Yarbro** and **Anne Rice**.

Rice, in particular, has used her presentation of vampires as a means to struggle with her own Roman Catholic background, aspects of which, including any belief in the devil, she had rejected. In *Interview with the Vampire*, the new vampire Louis believed that he was a child of the devil and hence eternally damned. However, he soon realized that he knew nothing of the devil. He questioned one of the Parisian vampires and was told that neither God nor the devil existed. Louis eventually accepted this view of the devil's nonexistence as a step toward realizing his own responsibility for his life—the bad parts of which could not be accounted for by reference to supernatural evil.

On the other hand, novelist Traci Briery has made effective use of the Satanic myth. In *The Vampire Memoirs*, she created the story of Agyar, the original vampire. Several thousand years ago, Agyar began a quest for immortality. His journey took him through bizarre and horrible rituals to distant places, including hell. He received im-

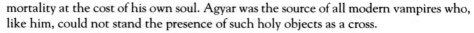

mortality at the cost of his own soul. Agyar was the source of all modern vampires who, like him, could not stand the presence of such holy objects as a cross.

Where vampires have a secularized or heroic existence, they have been set against Satanism and its followers. Yarbro had her vampire hero **Saint-Germain** confront a group of Satanists who had been promised his lady love.

In the movie *Dracula's Widow*, Vanessa, the wife of the late Dracula, attacked and killed a group of Satanists in modern-day Hollywood.

It is worthy to note that "Dracul," commonly translated as "dragon," also may be translated as "devil"; such an association has been used on occasion to tie the historical Dracula, Vlad the Impaler, to Satanism and hence to vampirism.

Mention should be made of an old tradition in Europe, dating at least to the fifteenth century, of a "devil's school." In the German tradition, it usually is located in Salamanca or Toledo (in Spain), while in Norway it is located at Wittemburg (Germany). In the devil's school, Satan teaches black magic, and claims one pupil from every class.

Sources:

Briery, Traci. *The Vampire Memoirs*. New York: Zebra Books, 1991. 431 pp.

Coppola, Francis Ford, and James V. Hart. *Bram Stoker's Dracula: The Film and the Legend*. New York: Newmarket Press, 1992. 172 pp. Rept. London: Pan Books, 1992. 172 pp.

Drake, Asa (pseudonym for Dean Andersson). *Crimson Kisses*. New York: Avon, 1981. 292 pp. Rev. and exp. ed. as Andersson, Dean. *I Am Dracula*. New York: Zebra, 1993. 350 pp.

Rice, Anne. *Interview with the Vampire*. New York: Alfred A. Knopf, 1986. 448 pp. Rept. New York: Ballantine Books, 1987. 346 pp.

Stoker, Bram. *The Essential Dracula*. Raymond McNally and Radu Florescu, eds. New York: Mayflower Books, 1979. 320 pp.

Warrington, Freda. *Dracula the Undead*. New York: Penguin Books, 1997. 300 pp.

Scandinavia, Vampires in

Geographically, Scandinavia consists of three countries of northern Europe: Norway, Sweden, and Finland. Historically and culturally, it also generally includes Denmark and Iceland. Linguistically, each of these country's languages includes strong elements of Old Norse, the common language of the Scandinavian Vikings. The vampire, though present, was not a prominent element in Viking folklore and did not become one in subsequent Scandinavian folk traditions.

Rosalie H. Wax, author of *Magic, Fate and History: The Changing Ethos of the Vikings* pointed out that in the old Scandinavian literature, matter was conceived as substantial, and semitransparent ghostly figures were nonexistent. There was a tradition of ghosts, however, some friendly and some harmful. The latter had greater interaction with the world, more like revenants than ghosts. At times revenants behaved, at least superficially, like a vampire or a **ghoul**, and usually were treated in ways reminiscent of the vampires of Eastern Europe, by a **stake** and **decapitation**. They also have been reported as vampires in some of the popular surveys of vampires around the world.

In the *Eyrbyggia Saga* of Iceland, for example, Thorolf, an early settler of the island, reappeared after his burial. Cattle that went near his tomb became mad and died.

His hauntings at home caused his wife's death. His wanderings were stopped for a while by the removal of his body to a new location. But he returned and, finally, his new tomb was opened and his body burned and ashes scattered. The *Grettis Saga* reported the decapitation of Karr, another Icelander, whose head was laid at his thigh, and of Glam, who was both decapitated and burned. Glam was a strong man who hated his former employer, killing his cattle and driving off members of his household. Glam finally was beaten in a fight with a visiting hero, Grettir. Ancient Danish records told of Mith-othin, a juggler who had earned the wrath of Odin. He fled to Finland but was killed by the Finns. However, in death, he operated from the barrow where his body was laid. Deaths of people near his barrow and sicknesses that spread through the populace were attributed to his taking revenge. To stop his bloody deeds, the people beheaded and staked him.

More central to Scandinavian belief was a *mara*, the nightmare. A *mara* was seen as a beautiful woman but was in fact a troll. She came to people as they slept and lay upon their breast so that they could neither draw a breath nor move a limb. She would attempt to put her finger in the **victim**'s mouth and count the teeth. If she was given time to do her counting, the victim usually died. According to some sources, a *mara* was an unknown person in love with its victim. She also was known to attack the horses and ride one all night so that it would be found in its stable the next morning all sweaty. Steps could be taken against the nightmare spirit, including the spreading of **seeds** around the house, turning shoes the wrong way at the side of the bed, and placing a scythe on the front of the bed.

A knife or sharp instrument was the most effective means of killing or driving away the *mara*. It has been suggested that a vampire appears in the *Kalevala*, the ancient saga of Finland. Over the threshold of the Abode of the Dead in the saga stood *Surma*, the personification of violent death. *Surma* was ready to seize any imprudent person who wandered too near to him and to devour the victim with his notable set of teeth. *Surma* was a horrible figure, but does not appear to have been a vampire.

Modern Scandinavia: The tradition of the substantial dead returning to interact with the living has continued into the twentieth century.

It includes stories of the return of dead lovers (a la Berger's "Lenore") and the gathering of the dead in church buildings to hold their own worship services. More to the point, there were traditions of the dead returning because they had committed **suicide**, because they were overly greedy, or because they wanted to revenge themselves on the living.

Children who were murdered or who died before baptism also returned. There was an evil woman of Ris, Denmark, who walked around after her death. Following a very old tradition, a wooden **stake** was stuck into the earth above her grave and thrust through her body, thus pinning her to the ground. In order to prevent the dead from arising, people would throw soil in the grave or place needles in the soles of the feet. More recently, a tradition emerged of shooting the corpse with a **bullet** made of **silver**. The treatment of revenants in Scandinavia points to the common ways of dealing with non-vampiric revenants and its continuity with similar practices carried out against the vampire in eastern Europe.

One popular story, "Gronnskjegg" (the Vampire or, better translated, the Ghoul) has been collected across Norway. In the story a young girl married an unknown man

with a green beard. On returning home she discovered that her new husband had eaten corpses from the local church graveyard. Later he appeared to her in the form of different relatives and questioned her. When he appeared in the form of her mother, she told all that she knew of him, and he killed her.

Sources:

Craigie, William A. *Scandinavian Folklore: Illustrations of the Traditional Beliefs of the Northern Peoples*. Detroit, MI: Singing Tree Press, 1970. 554 pp.

Hodne, Ornulf. *The Type of the Norwegian Folktale*. Oslo, Norway: Universitetforlaget, 1984. 400 pp.

Kvideland, Reimond, and Henning K. Sehmsdorf, eds. *Scandinavian Folk Belief and Legend*. Minneapolis, MN: University of Minnesota Press, 1986. 429 pp.

MacCulloch, J. A. *The Celtic and Scandinavian Religions*. London: Hutchinson's University Library, 1948. 180 pp.

Wax, Rosalie H. *Magic, Fate and History: The Changing Ethos of the Vikings*. Lawrence, KS: Coronado Press, 1969. 186 pp.

Wright, Dudley. *Vampires and Vampirism*. 1914, 1924. Rept. *The Book of Vampires*. 1924. Rept. New York: Causeway Books, 1973. 217 pp.

Schiefelbein, Michael

Michael Schiefelbein, a pastor in the United Church of Christ, is the author of a series of gay-oriented vampire books. He was born and raised in Topeka, Kansas, and attended a Roman Catholic high school and then spent ten years going through the training necessary to become a Catholic priest. As his training proceeded he eventually came to grips with his self-identity as a gay person and was studying in Rome when he dropped plans for a priestly career. He enrolled in the English department at the University of Maryland from which he received his Ph.D. in the early 1990s, and became a professor in the literature and languages department of Christian Brothers University in Memphis, Tennessee.

While in Memphis, he decided to leave the Catholic Church and join the United Church of Christ (UCC), a Protestant denomination that has been open to sexually active gay and lesbian clergy in its leadership ranks. He attended and graduated from Memphis Theological Seminary (a Presbyterian school) and in 2006, was ordained as a UCC minister. He subsequently he moved to Modesto, California, and became the pastor of College Avenue Congregational Church.

While a professor at Christian Brothers University, where among other courses he taught creative writing, the first of his vampire novels was published. *Vampire Vow* follows the evnts in the life of Victor, a soldier posted to Galilee after the Roman overrun of the region. There he met and fell in love with a young man named Joshu, later known as Jesus the Christ. When Joshu rejected his advances, Victor moved in an entirely different direction—he became a vampire. He began a search for a partner who would carry him through the centuries. Carrying a torch for the one who rejected him, he attempted to undermine and subvert Joshu's God. One way of accomplishing his goal was to join monasteries, whose members were concerned with Victor's rare skin condition that required him to stay out of sunlight. Once in the monastery, he proceeded to subvert the monks sexually and then drain them of their blood.

Victor emerged as a vicious amoral creature, but one that could have the readers hoping for his survival and even at times cheering him on. A cordial reception led to his reappearance in a two of the sequels. *Vampire Vow* carried Victor from first-century Palestine to the contemporary world. In the second, *Vampire Thrall*, he is in Rome anf finds a new lover in the person of Paul, with whom he is assigned to complete the artwork for an illuminated Bible. Paul is eventually turned, and in the third novel of the series, *Vampire Transgression*, he and Victor move to Paul's old home in Kansas. Their life together transgresses the rules of Schiefelbein's vampire world, and the powers that be compete with agents of the church in attempting to take down the two vampire lovers.

Schiefelbein's work emerged as the first multi-volume vampire series with **homosexuality** as a major subtext of note. As this volume goes to press, Schiefelbein has announced a fourth volume in the series, *Vampire Maker*, to be released in 2010.

Sources:

Schiefelbein, Michael. *Vampire Thrall*. Los Angeles: Alyson Publications, 2003. 302 pp.

———. *Vampire Transgression*. New York: St Martin's Press, 2006. 268 pp.

———. *Vampire Vow*. Los Angeles: Alyson Publications, 2001. 203 pp.

Scholomance

In suggesting an **origin** for **Dracula**'s vampirism, **Bram Stoker** drew upon an old folklore tradition of **Transylvania**, as passed to him in the writings of Emily Gerard, of the scholomance, or school of solomonari.

Traditional Romanian society recognized the existence of solomonari, or wise ones, considered successors of the biblical King Solomon and bearers of his wisdom. Some folklorists have considered them a continuing structure from the old Pagan priests of pre-Christian **Romania**. The solomonari were basically wizards whose primary ability was affecting the weather, which they accomplish through their power over the balauri, or dragons. By riding the dragon in the sky they bring rain or drought. The solomonari were thus the Romanian equivalent of the shaman.

According to Romanian tradition, the future solomonari was recognized by certain signs. He must first of all have been born with a caitza (or caul), have a membrane cap, and have a tail. As he grows to manhood, the future solomonari will be a large person with red eyes and red hair and a wrinkled forehead. He will wear white clothes and will arrive in a village as a wandering beggar. Around his neck will be the "bag of the solomonari" in which he keeps his magical instruments, including an iron ax (to break up the sky ice thus producing hailstones), a bridle shaped from birch used to capture the dragon, his magical "book" from which he "reads" the charms used to master the dragons.

The solomonari reportedly are trained at the scholomance, hidden at an unknown location variously said to be located in the mountains, the underground, or the other world. As a teenager, the future solomonari is kidnaped by an older wizard and taken to the school. There he will remain for a number of years (varying from seven to twenty) and undergo a series of initiations (the only character in Romanian folklore described as involved in initiations). At any given time there are no more than ten students in the school, or scoala balaurilor. The teacher is a dragon or the devil. The curriculum con-

sists of a series of difficult physical tests and the mastery of nature. The magician must learn the language of the **animals** and the ability to transform into different animal forms. Students receive their own "book" at the end of their training, described as a stone talisman with nine mysterious letters in it. In any given situation, the solomonari concentrates on the book, and from it discerns what he should do.

Note: For this entry, I am also grateful for material passed to me by Romanian folklorist Silvia Chitamia.

Sources:

Birlea, Ovidiu. *Mica enciclopedie a povestilor romanesti (A Little Encyclopedia of Romanian Folk Tales).* Bucharesti: Ed. Stuntifrca si enciclopedia, 1976.

Candrea, I. A. "Preminte Solomon." *Cercetari folclorice. (Journal of Folkloric Research)* (Bucharesti) 1 (1947): 94–106.

Schreck, Max (1879–1936)

Max Schreck was a German character actor chosen to play Count **Orlock**, the **Dracula** figure in F. W. Murnau's classic silent film ***Nosferatu: Eine Symphonie des Grauens*** (1922). His last name, Schreck, which means "terror" in German, was his actual name and not a stage pseudonym. He became an actor for Max Reinhardt, a prominent theatrical producer in pre-World War I Germany, where he most likely had come to the attention of director and screenwriter Henrik Galeen. While he played many parts, none are as memorable as his single performance in *Nosferatu.*

In the film, Schreck portrayed Dracula as a repulsive rodent-like creature. Dracula's **fangs** became two teeth in the center of his mouth. All of his facial features from his nose to his ears were exaggerated. His head was bald. His **hypnotic** eyes were surrounded by dark makeup. His fingers were not simply long, but elongated. He walked in a stiff halting manner. The grotesque characterization was also further distorted by the use of Schreck's shadow which (in spite of the fact that vampires as nocturnal soulless creatures are not supposed to have shadows) emphasized the horrific features. However, he did have a reflection in the **mirror.**

The idea of Dracula as rodent was carried through by associating Count Orlock with rats and an outbreak of the plague that had occurred in Bremen, Germany, in the 1830s. As an interpretation, it was most effective, but essentially a dead end as far as the vampire character was concerned, relating it to traditional inhuman monsters rather than the suave and very human seducer and sexual predator that would come to the fore in the British stage and American film versions.

Schreck's interpretation of Dracula would be revived in the 1970s by Klaus Kinski for the remake *Nosferatu: The Vampyre* (1979) and its Italian sequel, *Vampire in Venice* (1988). Writer **Stephen King** also adopted a Schreck-like vampire for his villain in *Salem's Lot,* and it inspired the character of Radu, the evil vampire in the *Subspecies* video series.

E. Elias Merhige's movie *Shadow of the Vampire* (2000) cast Willem Dafoe as Max Schreck, who portrayed an actual vampire hired to star in Murnau's original version of *Nosferatu.*

Schreck would go on and play a variety of parts in close to thirty films during the remaining fourteen years of his life, but none as noteworthy as his single performance

Max Schreck in his most famous role as the terrifying vampire Graf Orlock in *Nosferatu*.

in the one film which was suppressed during his lifetime and would bring him fame only a generation after his death. In 2008, German author Stefan Eickhoff wrote the first biography of Schreck, *Max Schreck—Gespenstertheater*, published in Munich.

Sources:

Holte, James Craig. *Dracula in the Dark: The Dracula Film Adaptations*. Westport, CT: Greenwood Press, 1997. 161 pp.

Skal, David. *Hollywood Gothic: The Tangled Web of Dracula from Novel to Stage to Screen*. New York: W. W. Norton & Co., 1990. 242 pp.

Ursini, James, and Alain Silver. *The Vampire Film: From Nosferatu to Bram Stoker's Dracula*. New York: Limelight Editions, 2004. 342 pp.

❦ Science Fiction and the Vampire ❦

As the vampire myth developed and went through a rationalizing/secularizing process, various authors have posed alternative, nonsupernatural theories for the **origin** of vampires—from disease to altered **blood** chemistry. Eventually, at the height of interest

Atom Age Vampire (1963) is a prime example of blending science fiction with the vampire myth.

in flying saucers in the 1950s, it was inevitable that the idea of vampires as space aliens would be posed. However, such an idea had a number of precursors. In 1894, for example, H. G. Wells, in his story "The Flowering of the Strange Orchid," had explored the possibility of a space alien taking over a human body in order to live off the life energies of others. This theme was picked up in the **pulp magazines** in such stories as Sewell Wright's "Vampires of Space" and C. L. Moore's "Black Thirst." A true bloodthirsty space alien seems to have first appeared in 1942 in A. E. Van Vogt's story, "Asylum." Van Vogt's villains were a pair of aliens who arrived on earth in a spaceship. They lived for thousands of years by preying on the life forms of different planets. On earth, they encountered reporter William Dreegh, who eventually was able to stifle their invasion.

By the mid-1950s, interest in flying saucers was on the rise and science fiction had begun to blossom. **Richard Matheson,** who had written both horror and science fiction for many years, was the first to explore the traditional vampire theme in popular science fiction. In *I Am Legend*, Matheson, who had authored several vampire stories, created an end-of-the-world situation in which the hero, Robert Neville, was the only human left. The others had either been killed or turned into vampires. During bat-

Vincent Price (left) plays the title role in *The Last Man on Earth*, costarring Emma Danieli.

tle with the vampires, Neville had to figure out which parts of the old vampire myth were accurate and, hence, which weapons would work against them. *I Am Legend* was made into a movie three times—*The Last Man on Earth* (1964), *The Omega Man* (1971) and *I Am Legend* (2007)—and in each the vampirism was played down, as was the meaning of the title of Matheson's original work.

After Matheson, the mixture of science fiction and vampires occurred occasionally, mostly in short stories. Among the several novels on this theme, the more notable included Colin Wilson's *The Space Vampires* (1976); **Tanith Lee**'s *Sabella, or The Blood Stone* (1980); Brian Aldiss's *Dracula Unbound* (1991); and Robert Frezza's *McLennon's Syndrome*. Two *Star Trek* novels with a vampire theme have been published, but neither appears to have been made into an episode of the popular **television** show. However, the major presence of alien vampires would be felt in the movies.

The Space Vampire in the Movies: By 1954 **Universal Pictures** had a waning interest in the classic monsters it had made famous in the 1930. Their last scenes were played out in *Abbott and Costello Meet Dr. Jekyll and Mr. Hyde*, in which **Dracula** made a cameo appearance. However, a variety of companies were exploiting the classic monsters—including the vampire—within the context of science fiction motion pictures;

these were the hot new items on the agenda, especially for companies specializing in "B" movies. The questions they posed their youthful audiences included: What if vampires are real, and are space aliens? What if earth is being invaded by space aliens who came to drain either our blood or our life force, or both? How should we react to a space alien vampire? The first science fiction movie to explore these questions was the 1951 production from RKO Radio Pictures, *The Thing from Another World* (remade in 1982 as *The Thing*). It starred James Arness as an alien creature (actually an eight-foot vegetable) who needed blood to reproduce. The Thing was discovered in the Arctic snow by a research team and the military eventually had to be brought in to stop the threat. Six years later **Roger Corman** produced and directed *Not of This Earth* (remade in 1988), which saw a humanoid from the dying planet Davanna settle in a small town to search out the viability of human blood as a replacement for that of their own race.

Not of This Earth was soon followed by United Artists' *It! The Terror from Beyond Space* (1958). *It!* began with Colonel Carruthers, the sole survivor of a space expedition to Mars, being arrested by the commander of his rescue ship, who suspected him of cannibalizing his crew in order to survive. On the way home, with Carruthers in lock-up, members of the crew were mysteriously murdered by It. The commander finally realized his error and was able to isolate the vampiric alien in a cargo chamber. All the survivors donned space suits and the oxygen was let out of the ship, thus killing the creature. *It! The Vampire from Beyond Space* became the direct inspiration for the 1979 classic space horror movie *Alien* (which dropped the original's vampire theme).

The last of the 1950s space alien vampire movies would become by far the most famous and financially successful. *Plan 9 from Outer Space* (1959) began with **Bela Lugosi** leaving the grave of his recently deceased wife, played by television horror movie hostess **Vampira**. A ray flashed down from outer space reviving Vampira, who then attacked the attendants who were about to bury her body. Next she killed the police inspector who arrived to examine the bodies of the grave diggers. The scene then changed to an invasion of flying saucers over Los Angeles. Eros and Tanna, who led the invasion, announced "Plan 9," their intention to revive all of the dead on earth and use them as their instrument to take over the planet. The forces of good organized to counter the invasion, and in the end the space people were repulsed.

Plan 9 from Outer Space became famous after being placed at or near the top of several lists of the world's worst movies. The product of director Edward D. Wood, Jr., famous for his quick production of cheap movies, the film was "unintentionally" hilarious for its errors of production. In the graveyard scene, for example, cardboard tombstones swayed when accidentally touched, a cement floor was visible under the cemetery grass, and a mattress (to cushion a fall) could be seen. *Plan 9* also was notable as Bela Lugosi's last film.

Wood seems to have integrated some brief footage of Lugosi that originally had been shot for another movie. The brief segments of actual Lugosi scenes were each shown several times. Lugosi died before *Plan 9* could be finished, and a body double stood in for him. In the later parts of the movie, this stand-in wore Lugosi's cape and walked before the camera in a sinister fashion with his arm raised over his face.

It! and *Plan 9*, the flying saucer movies, were soon followed by a set of movies thematically tied together by the early space explorations.

The infamous Ed Wood (left), who directed the laughably bad science fiction vampire film, *Plan 9 from Outer Space*. To his immediate right is actreall Maila Nurmi, who plays Vampira in the film.

In *First Man into Space* (1959), an astronaut's body was taken over by a space creature. Upon his return to earth, the vampiric creature needed blood and began killing to get it. He broke into a blood bank, but finally was cornered in a decompression tank and killed.

The space alien vampire theme continued through the 1960s, beginning with **Mario Bava**'s *Planet of the Vampires* (originally entitled *Terrore nello Spazio*). The story concerned a spaceship commanded by Captain Mark Markary (played by Barry Sullivan) forced to land on the planet Aura. Here, Markary discovered another ship whose crew was dead. The dead rose, their bodies inhabited by disembodied residents of Aura who had turned them into vampires, and attacked Markary's crew. Once Markary discovered what was occurring, he and two of his crew escaped. Then he realized that the two crew members already had been vampirized and would invade a defenseless earth. The movie ended before he decided what course of action he should follow.

Planet of the Vampires was followed the next year by one of the better space vampire movies, *Queen of Blood*, with a rather impressive cast of John Saxon, Basil Rathbone, and a youthful Dennis Hopper. The story was constructed from a Russian film, the footage of which had been purchased by Roger Corman. The star was a beautiful woman called the Queen of Mars, who had been invited back to earth by members of a United States spaceship. On the return trip the captain discovered that she was a vampire and was killing off the crew one by one. Her weakness, however, was a hemophiliac condition. Cut in a struggle with a crew member, she bled to death.

In the mid-1970s, occult author Colin Wilson tried his hand at the vampire theme in his novel, *The Space Vampires* (1976), a volume originally marketed as a science fic-

tion novel. The novel also fit within the theme of **psychic vampirism,** as the creatures drained their **victims'** "life force" rather than their blood (as the carrier of life energy). The novel was set in 2080. A spacecraft encountered another mysterious craft housing several bodies in lifelike condition that were alive and were vampires.

In the early 1980s Tobe Hooper saw the possibilities of Wilson's novel for the screen and began an adaptation that was released in the United States as *Lifeforce* in 1985. It changed the setting to 1986, to coincide with the return of Halley's comet. In the movie, the action was centered around the relationship between Commander Carlson, who found the space vampires, and the single female vampire. Hooper also added a typical vampire feature—having the vampire killed by a **stake** through her energy center (a feature absent from the novel).

Science Fiction Vampires in Comic Books: The several space vampires who appeared on the movie screen in the 1960s were eclipsed by the most famous one of all, Vampirella. She appeared originally not in a movie, but as a **comic book** character created by **Forrest J. Ackerman** and James Warren, the owner of Warren Publishing Company. Ackerman would go on to become the original writer for *Vampirella*, the most successful vampire comic book of all time. Vampirella was distinguished by being the first space vampire who was the heroine of the story rather than the villain. She hailed from the dying planet Drakulon and came to earth where blood was readily available. She tried not to kill to obtain blood and was remorseful when she had to take a life to survive.

Vampirella was partially inspired by the title character from another Mario Bava movie, *Barbarella.* She was a young, sexy, scantily-clad female.

As the plot was developed through the 1970s, even Dracula was discovered to be a former resident of Drakulon, who had left for earth many centuries ago.

Vampirella became one of the most successful comic books of the 1970s and during the 1990s has enjoyed a new wave of success in the hands of Harris Comics.

Contemporaneously with Colin Wilson's novel, a science fiction story with a vampire theme came briefly to the world of comic books in a short-lived series, *Planet of the Vampires*. The story concerned space explorers who had returned to earth after a long stay on Mars. They found the people divided into two factions following a devastating nuclear war: one faction was centered in the former New York City; the other was in the countryside. The city people had taken cover under a dome. It protected them somewhat, but they lacked immunity to diseases that had developed as a result of the war. The outsiders, on the other hand, had developed a natural resistance. The city dwellers captured outsiders, from whom they drained blood to be used for a serum. The vampires were the machines created by the city dwellers to forcefully take the blood of any outsiders who could be caught.

Planet of the Vampires, published by Atlas Comics, lasted only three issues. Its demise left *Vampirella* the only comic book with a space vampire theme. Once *Vampirella* was discontinued, space vampires largely disappeared, except for *Lifeforce.* With the new wave of vampire comics of the 1990s, the space alien vampire was revived, primarily in the adaptation of movies to comic book format. In 1990, *Plan 9 from Outer Space* was adapted in a single issue from Malibu Comics. The following year *I Am Legend* (which had been made into a movie twice, in 1964 and 1971) appeared in three issues, and a sequel to *Plan 9 from Outer Space* lasted for three issues, though the vampire element had been deleted from the storyline.

Vampirella was revived in 1991 (with reprints of the 1970s stories) and a series with new stories began in 1992. *Vampirella* was the only space vampire among the new wave of comic book vampires in the early 1990s.

The Twenty-first Century: Amid the vampire boom of the 1990s that continues through the first decade of the new century, the lack of science fiction vampires has been noticeable. Glimpses of the future (*Ultraviolet, Vampire Hunter D: Bloodlust*) have been more apparent than flights to outer space (*Dracula 2000, Bloodsuckers*) or mad scientific experiments (*Blade II*). The same could be said of comic books where, in the futuristic *Frey*, Joss Whedon introduces a vampire slayer far in the future. Of course, the movie version of *The League of Extraordinary Gentlemen* draws on an old science fiction theme, Captain Nemo's famous submarine, which is juxaposed with a vampire. One can always look to animé for horror-science fiction crossovers and recent examples would include *Vampire Wars, Trinity Blood,* and *Blood the Last Vampire*.

One science fiction theme that has become popular has to do with the development of a blood substitute that allows vampires to rejoin human society. With the substitute they no longer have to kill humans to survive nor do they have to rely on animal blood. This theme begins with Vampirella who discovers such a substitute soon after her arrival from outer space. In *Sundown: The Vampire in Retreat* (1990), the reformed vampires of the town of Purgatory drink an ill-colored blood substitute as part of the program of pacifism toward humans. **Batman** became a vampire in the graphic novel series by Doug Mench, and in *Batman: Bloodstorm*.(1994) tried ot deal with his bloodlust through use of a blood substitute.

In *Dr. Who: Vampire Science* (1997), Jonathan Blum and Kate Orman send the fabled time lord Dr. Who up against vampires who are engaging in genetic engineering to find a new source of blood. In the Canadian movies, *Karmina* (1996) and *Karmina 2* (2000), the vampires of Montreal have invented a potion that allowed them to exist among humans as one of of them, but also allowed them to revert rather quickly to their vampiric state. In the movie trilogy featuring the half-vampire **Blade the Vampire Slayer**, the title character also consumes a blood substitute. In *The Breed* (2001), the blood substitute allows the futuristic vampires to avoid falling victim to the blood lust that turns them into irrational killers, a problem preventing their integrating into human society, while in the *Daybreakers* (2010), a plague has turned most humans into vampires and a blood substitute is the only way to prevent starvation.

In the novels of **Charlaine Harris**, the Japanese have invented a blood substitute that allowed vampires to mainstream while retaining all their vampiric powers and limitations. This theme is carried into the televion adaptation of the books, *True Blood*, named for the blood substituite. In Brian Meehl's young adult novel *Suck it Up* (2008) the main character, Morning McCobb, dines on a blood substitute made from Soy called Blood Lite.

Sources:

Aldiss, Brian. *Dracula Unbound*. New York: Harpercollins, 1991.

Blum, Jonathan, and Kate Orman. *Doctor Who: Vampire Science*. London: BBC Books, 1997. 283 pp.

Frezza, Robert. *McLennon's Syndrome*. New York: Ballantine Books/Del Rey, 1993. 313 pp.

Harris, Charlaine. *Dead until Dark*. Southern Vampire Mysteries, Book 1. New York: Ace Books, 2001. 260 pp.

Jones, Stephen. *The Illustrated Vampire Movie Guide*. London: Titan Books, 1993. 144 pp.

Lee, Tanith. *Sabella, or the Blood Stone*. New York: DAW Books, 1980. 157 pp.

Matheson, Richard. *I Am Legend*. New York: Fawcett, 1954. 175 pp.

Meehl, Brian. *Suck It Up*. New York: Delacorte Books for Young Readers, 2009. 336 pp.

Moench, Doug, and Kelley Jones. *Batman: Bloodstorm*. New York: DC Comics, 1994.

Planet of Vampires. 3 issues. New York: Atlas Comics, 1975.

Rhodes, Natasha. *Blade: Trinity*. UK: Black Flame, 2004. 416 pp.

Scapperotti, Dan. "Tobe Hooper on *Lifeforce*: The Director of *Poltergeist* Films Colin Wilson's *Space Vampires*. *Cinefantastique* 15, 3 (July 1985): 6–8.

Vampirella. 1–112. New York: Warren Publishing Co.,1969–83.

Vampirella: Morning in America. New York: Harris Publications, 1991.

Wilson, Colin. *Space Vampires*. New York: Random House, 1976. 214 pp. Rept. *Life Force*. New York: Warner Books, 1985. 220 pp.

Screem in the Dark Fan Club *see:* Vlad

The Secret Order of the Undead *see:* Vampire Fandom: United States

The Secret Room *see:* Vampire Fandom: United States

Seeds

The folklore of Europe reported the use of seeds as a protective measure against vampires. The kinds of seeds varied from place to place, but most frequently mentioned was mustard seed, a very small seed that Jesus spoke of in one of his parables in the Christian New Testament of the Bible. Seeds of millet (a name used to refer to several grasses and grains), were most popular, but those of linen, carrot, and rice were also used. Seeds might be placed in the **coffin** to entertain the vampire, but more commonly were spread over the grave site and along the road leading from the cemetery to the village or family home of the deceased.

The idea behind the use of seeds, and on occasion a knotted cloth or fish net, was to take the vampire's attention away from his intended **victim** in town. It was thought that the vampire was required to collect and count each seed before he could come to town and do any damage. Most often, he was able to count only one seed a year. Thus, a handful of mustard seeds could, if one accepted the logic of its use, prevent the vampire's return for an indefinite period.

Selene Selene was a fictional vampire city featured in *La Ville vampire*, an 1875 novel by French writer Paul Féval (1816–87). As the novel was not published in English until 2003, it has remained largely unknown among modern vampire enthusiasts, who have been concentrated within the English-speaking world. Féval's vampires were unique in having a tounge with a tip sharp enough to open wounds from which they could suck **blood**. They also had a power to duplicate themselves using the bodies of other people and **animals**.

Féval located Selene in Yugoslavia, north of Belgrade, close to the site of the village where **Arnold Paul** lived, subject of one of the most famous vampire incidents dur-

ing the eighteenth century. During the hour approaching noon, the cover that shrouded the city would become visible. As one approached the mysterious Selene, the environment changed suddenly—the green vegetation faded away and the sky turned dark. The city was a conglomeration of architectural styles centered around a spiral pyramidal temple. Among its statues was a set showing women being clawed to death by a tiger. The city was inhabited by famous personages of past centuries who were now vampires.

In the somewhat satirical novel, a group arrived in the city in search of a vampire. They carried an iron ladle, some coal, a small portable stove, candles, and smelling salts. They were accompanied by a surgeon who resided in a town near the vampire's home, who had lost two daughters to the creatures. The group entered the village and upon locating the vampire they had targeted, and using the smelling salts to counter the stench, the surgeon removed the vampire's heart with the iron ladle and burned it on the stove. The vampire died and his heart was reduced to ashes. The clock sounded, and other vampires began to rise. The group, carrying the ashes of the vampire's heart, retreated from the city. They used the ashes to escape the hunger and wrath of the city's vampire inhabitants. The ash, when sprinkled on vampires, caused them to explode with a bluish flash.

La Ville vampire was one of the pre-***Dracula*** attempts to play with the vampire legends then alive in Western Europe, prior to the time when the major elements of the literary vampire had been firmly established. It incorporated pieces of Eastern European folklore, especially the practice of burning the suspected vampire's heart, but, like most fictional works of the time, included elements that were not in the modern vampire myth—such as other vampires reacting to the ashes of the dead vampire's heart.

Sources:

Féval, Paul. *La Ville vampire*. Paris: 1875. *Vampire City*. Brian Stableford, trans. Encino, CA: Black Coat Press, 2003. 200 pp.

Manguel, Alberto, and Gianni Guadalupi. *The Dictionary of Imaginary Places*. San Diego, CA: Harcourt, Brace, Jovanovitch, Publishers, 1987. 454 pp.

Seward, John

Dr. John Seward, one of the leading characters in **Bram Stoker's *Dracula***, appeared early in the story as a suitor of **Lucy Westenra**. In a letter to her friend **Mina Murray** (chapter 5), Lucy described Seward:

> He is a doctor and really clever. Just fancy! He is only nine and twenty, and he has an immense lunatic asylum all under his own care. Mr. Holmwood introduced him to me, and he called here to see us, and often comes now. I think he is one of the most resolute men I ever saw, and yet the most calm. He seems absolutely imperturbable. I can fancy what a wonderful power he must have over his patients.

Previously, Seward had been a friend of **Arthur Holmwood** and **Quincey P. Morris**, with whom he had traveled in the Orient. At the asylum, he was giving a significant amount of attention to patient **R. N. Renfield**, who displayed some unusual symptoms. Renfield wanted to consume various **animals** in an attempt to take in their lives. Seward called this unique form of madness "zoophagous" or life-eating. After **Dracula** headed for England, Renfield began to react to his movements. Seward dutifully recorded the changes in Renfield's behavior, but had no understanding of their cause.

While attracted to Lucy, he was shut out of her life by her choice of Holmwood (Lord Godalming), but was called back into the plot as Lucy's health failed. Unable to find any cause, he called in his mentor, **Abraham Van Helsing** of Amsterdam, to consult on the case. Initially Van Helsing was stumped but immediately recognized that Lucy needed **blood**. Seward participated in giving her a transfusion, and while Van Helsing traveled back and forth to Holland, Seward watched over Lucy's progress and recorded her decline.

After Lucy's death, he became one in the team under Van Helsing who sought out and destroyed Dracula and was present when Lucy's body was staked. Seward eventually understood the relationship between Renfield and Dracula and began the process of deciphering his actions. He introduced Van Helsing to Renfield and was present when Renfield connected Dracula to Mina. In fact, he was with the other men who rushed to her bedroom to save her from the vampire's attack.

He then went to Dracula's base at **Carfax** and his house in Piccadilly to destroy the boxes of Transylvanian earth. Once it was discovered that Dracula had escaped England and fled to **Transylvania**, Seward joined the rush to **Castle Dracula**. In the final push to get to the castle, the team split up and Seward traveled by horse with Morris. He arrived immediately after the **Gypsies** had deposited the box of earth containing Dracula's body before the castle doors. Rifle in hand, he held the Gypsies back while Morris and **Jonathan Harker** killed the vampire.

In the later dramatic and cinematic productions of *Dracula,* unlike the other characters, Seward almost always survived. In the **drama** by **Hamilton Deane** and **John L. Balderston**, he became the father of (rather than the suitor of) Lucy Westenra, an alteration also evident in the several movies based upon play. Possibly the most interesting twist on Seward's character came in **Fred Saberhagen**'s novels, *The Dracula Tape* (1975) and especially *The Holmes-Dracula File* (1978), in which Seward emerged as one of the villains. That idea was seconded by **Kim Newman**, who transformed Seward into Jack the Ripper in his novel *Anno Dracula* (1992).

Sexuality and the Vampire

Essential to understanding the appeal of the vampire is its sexual nature. While it frequently has been pointed out that traditional vampires cannot engage in "normal" sexual activity, the vampire is not necessarily asexual. As twentieth-century scholars turned their attention to the vampire, both in folklore and literature, underlying sexual themes quickly became evident. The sexual nature of vampirism formed an underlying theme in *Dracula,* but it was disguised in such a way that it was hidden from the literary censors of the day, the consciousness of the public, and probably from the awareness (as many critics argued) of author **Bram Stoker** himself. Carol Fry, for example, suggested that vampirism was in fact a form of "surrogate sexual intercourse."

Sexuality in *Dracula*: The sexual nature of vampirism is first seen in *Dracula* during **Jonathan Harker**'s encounter with the three **vampire brides** residing in Castle

Dracula. Harker confronted them as extremely appealing sex objects who embody an element of danger. Harker noted, "I felt in my heart a wicked, burning desire that they would kiss me with their red lips" (chapter 3). Stoker went on to describe the three as sensual predators and their vampire's bite as a kiss. One of the **women** anticipated the object of their desire, "He is young and strong; there are kisses for us all." And as they approached, Harker waited in delightful anticipation.

Attention in the novel then switched to the two "good" women, **Lucy Westenra** and **Mina Murray**. Lucy, as the subject of the attention of three men, reveled in their obvious desire of her before she chose **Arthur Holmwood**, the future Lord Godalming, as her betrothed. Mina, to the contrary, was in love with Jonathan and pined in loneliness while he was lost in the wilds of **Transylvania**. While preparing for her wedding, however, Lucy was distracted by the presence of **Dracula**. While on a seaside vacation in **Whitby**, Lucy began sleepwalking. One evening, Lucy was discovered by Mina in her nightclothes across the river. As Mina approached, she could see a figure bending over Lucy. Dracula left as Mina approached, but she found Lucy with her lips parted and breathing heavily. Thus began Lucy's slow **transfor-**

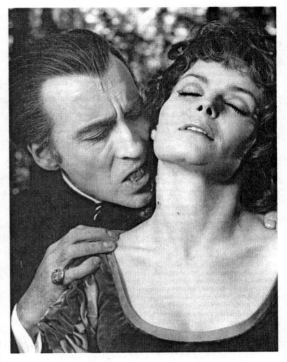

Christopher Lee shows how to be a sexy vampire in *Taste the Blood of Dracula.*

mation from the virtuous and proper, if somewhat frivolous, young lady, into what Judith Weissman termed a "sexual monster." By day she was faint and listless, but by night she took on a most unladylike voluptuousness.

Shortly before her death, she asked Arthur to kiss her, and when he leaned toward her, she attempted to bite him. Stoker's understanding, however unconscious, of the sexual nature of the vampiric attack became most clear in the **blood** transfusions that were given to Lucy in the attempt to save her life. Arthur, who never was able to consummate his love for Lucy, suggested that in the sharing of blood he had, in the eyes of God, married her. The older and wiser **Abraham Van Helsing** rejected the idea, given the sexual connotation for himself and the others who also gave her blood. But by this time, the women's sexual interest in Dracula was firmly established and led directly to the most sexual scene in the book.

Having given Lucy her peace (and, by implication, returned her virtue) in the act of staking and decapitating her, the men called together by Van Helsing to rid the world of Dracula, were slow to awaken to his real target—Mina.

When they finally became aware of this, they rushed to Mina's bedroom. There, they found Dracula sitting on her bed forcing her to drink from a cut on his chest. Dracula turned angrily to those who had interrupted him. "His eyes flamed red with devilish passion...." Once Dracula was driven away and Mina came to her senses, she realized that she had been violated. She declared herself unclean and vowed that she would "kiss" her husband no more.

The Sexual Vampire of Folklore: While there is little evidence that Stoker was intimately aware of Eastern European vampire lore, he could have found considerable evidence of the vampire's sexual nature—particularly in the folklore of the **Gypsies** and their neighbors, the **Southern Slavs**. For example, corpses dug up as suspected vampires occasionally were reported to have an erection. Gypsies thought of the vampire as a sexual entity. The male vampire was believed to have such an intense sexual drive that his sexual need alone was sufficient to bring him back from the grave. His first act usually was a return to his widow, with whom he engaged in sexual intercourse. Nightly visits could ensue and continue over a period of time, with the wife becoming exhausted and emaciated. In more than a few cases, the widow was known to become pregnant and bear a child by her vampire husband. The resulting child, called a *dhampir*, was a highly valued personage deemed to have unusual powers to diagnose vampirism and to destroy vampires attacking the community.

In some cases the vampire would return to a woman with whom he had been in love, but with whom he had never consummated that love. The woman would then be invited to return with him to the grave where they could share their love through eternity. The idea of the dead returning to claim a living lover was a popular topic in European folklore. By far the most famous literary piece illustrating the theme was Gottfried August Bürger's ballad "Lenore," known in English by Sir Walter Scott's translation.

The folklore of **Russia** also described the vampire as a sexual being. Among the ways in which it made itself known was to appear in a village as a handsome young stranger. Circulating among the young people in the evening, the vampire lured unsuspecting women to their doom. Russian admonitions for young people to listen to their elders and stay close to home are reminiscent of the ancient story from **Greece**, which tells of Apollonius, who saved one of his students from the allure of the *lamiai*, whom he was about to marry.

The *langsuyar* of **Malaysia** was also a sexual being. A female vampire, she was often pictured as a desirable young woman who could marry and bear children. *Langsuyars* were believed to be able to live somewhat normally in a village for many years, revealed only by their inadvertent involvement in an activity that disclosed their identity.

The Modern Literary Vampire: While overt sexual activity was not present in *Dracula*, sexual themes were manifest in the vampire literature of the previous century. The original vampire poem written by **Goethe**, "The Bride of Corinth," drew upon the story from ancient Greece concerning a young woman who had died a virgin. She returned from the dead to her parents' home to have sexual experiences with a young man staying temporarily in the guest room. The strong sexual relationship at the heart of **Samuel Taylor Coleridge**'s "Christabel" was expanded in **"Carmilla"**, the popular vampire story by **Sheridan Le Fanu**.

In the story, Carmilla Karnstein moved into the castle home of Laura, her proposed **victim**. She did not immediately attack Laura, but proceeded to build a relationship more befitting a lover. Laura experienced the same positive and negative feelings that Harker had felt toward the three women in Castle Dracula. As she put it:

Now the truth is, I felt unaccountably toward the beautiful stranger. I did feel, as she said, "drawn towards her," but there was also something of repulsion. In this ambiguous feeling, however, the sense of attraction immensely prevailed. She interested and won me; she was so beautiful and so indescribably engaging.

Carmilla went about her assault upon Laura while inducing her to be cooperative. She would draw Laura to her with pretty words and embraces and gently press her lips to Laura's cheek. She would take Laura's hand while at the same time locking her gaze on her eyes and breathing with such passion that it embarrassed the naive Laura. So attracted was Laura to Carmilla, that only slowly did she come to the realization that her lovely friend was a vampire.

The Sensuous Vampire on Stage and Screen: Carol Fry, author of the article "Fictional Conventions and Sexuality in *Dracula*", has properly pointed out that Dracula was in part a stereotypical character of popular nineteenth-century literature, the rake. The rake appeared in stories to torment and distress the pure women of proper society. The rake was to some extent the male counterpart of the **vamp**; however, the consequences of falling victim to a seductive male were far more serious for a woman than they were for a man victimized by a seductive woman. The man who loved and left was thought to have left behind a tainted woman. Just as a state of "moral depravity" contaminated the fallen woman, so vampirism infected the one bitten.

The vampire's victim became like him and preyed on others. The fallen woman might became a vamp, professional or not, who in turn led men to engage in her immoral ways.

Once brought to the stage, Dracula's rakish nature was heightened. No longer hovering in the background as in the novel, he was invited into the living rooms of his intended victims. In this seemingly safe setting, he went about his nefarious business, though what he actually did had to be construed from the dialogue of those who would kill him. Only after the play was brought to the screen, and the public reacted to **Bela Lugosi**, did some understanding of the romantic appeal of this supposed monster become evident to a widespread audience. However, not until the 1950s would the vampire, in the person of **Christopher Lee**, be given a set of **fangs** and allowed to bite his victims on screen.

Interestingly, the obvious sexuality of the vampire was first portrayed on screen by a female vampire. In retrospect, the scene in *Dracula's Daughter* (1936) in which the female vampire seduced the young model was far more charged with sexuality than any played by Lugosi. A quarter of a century later, **Roger Vadim** brought an overtly sensual vampire to the screen in his version of "Carmilla," *Blood and Roses* (1960). In 1967 French director **Jean Rollin** produced the first of a series of semipornographic features, *Le Viol du Vampire* (released in English as *The Vampire's Rape*). The story centered around two women who believed that they were cursed by a vampire to follow his bloodsucking life. The sexuality of "Carmilla" was even more graphically pictured in *The Vampire Lovers*, **Hammer Films**' 1970 production, in which the unclad Carmilla and Laura romped freely around their bedroom.

From these and similar early soft-core productions, two quite different sets of vampire films developed. On the one hand, there were pornographic vampire films that featured nudity and sex. Among the earliest was *Dracula (The Dirty Old Man)* (1969), in which Count Alucard kidnapped naked virgins to fulfill his sexual and vampiric needs.

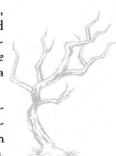

Gloria Holden (right) stars as a sexy vampire femme with Otto Kruger in *Dracula's Daughter.*

Spanish director Jesus Franco produced *La Countess aux Seins Nus* (1973) (released in video in the United States as *Erotikill*), in which Countess Irena Karnstein (a character derived from Carmilla) killed her victims in an act of fellatio. (These scenes were cut from the American version.) The trend toward pornographic vampire movies culminated in 1979 with *Dracula Sucks* (also released as *Lust at First Bite*), a remake of *Dracula,* that closely followed the 1931 movie. It starred Jamie Gillis as Dracula. The more interesting 1980s adult vampire movies include *Dracula Exotica* (1981), also starring Gillis; *Gayracula* (1983), a **homosexual** film; *Sexandroide* (1987); *Out for Blood* (1990); *Princess of the Night* (1990); and *Wanda Does Transylvania* (1990).

Most of these were shot in both hard-core and soft-core versions. Until the 1990s, the pornographic vampire movies were relatively few in number and poorly distributed. With the arrival of the Internet and the burgeoning of the adult film industry in the 1990s, the number of vampire-themed adult movies of the most explicit nature also increased. By the end of the first decade of the new century, more than 100 had been made, including an adaptation of *Dracula,* by Mario Salieri, and a half dozen building off the popularity of the **television** show *Buffy the Vampire Slayer.*

The Vampire in Love: Of far more importance in redefining the contemporary vampire were the novels and films that transformed the evil monster of previous generations into a romantic lover. The new vampire hero owed much to **Chelsea Quinn Yarbro's Saint-Germain**. In a series of novels beginning with *Hotel Transylvania* (1978), Saint-Germain emerged not as a monster, but as a man of moral worth, extraordinary intellect, and captivating sensuality. He even occasionally fell in love. He was unable to have ordinary sexual relations because he could not have an erection. However, his bite conveyed an intense experience of sexual bliss that women found to be a more than adequate alternative.

At the time Yarbro was finishing *Hotel Transylvania*, a new stage production, ***Dracula: The Vampire Play in Three Acts***, had become a hit on Broadway. The play was the first dramatic production of *Dracula* to reintroduce the scene in which Dracula forced Mina to drink from his blood.

The scene, a rape-like experience in the novel, had been transformed into one of seduction. In 1979 the larger populace was introduced to this more sensual Dracula when **Frank Langella** recreated his stage role for the motion picture screen. He presented Dracula as not only a suave foreign nobleman, but as a debonair, attractive male who drew his victims to him by the sheer power of his sexual presence. The scenes in which Lucy, over the objections of her elders, rushed to **Carfax** to join her lover and drink his blood completed a transformation of Dracula from mere monster into a hero who lived up to the movie's billing: "Throughout history he has filled the hearts of men with *terror*, and the hearts of women with *desire*." Langella's Dracula directly informed the 1992 production of **Bram Stoker's Dracula** under the writing and direction of **Francis Ford Coppola**.

Coppola not only brought the vampire into proper society but turned him into a handsome young man who, with his money and foreign elegance, was able to seduce the betrothed Mina from her wimpish fiancé. He returned the final blood drinking scene to her bedroom, revealed Dracula at his most human, and made their lovemaking the sensual climax of the movie's love story subplot, which Coppola had added to explain Dracula's otherwise irrational acts against the British family he had assaulted. The transformation of the vampire into a hero lover was a primary element in the overall permeation of the vampire myth into the culture of late twentieth century **America** (which included the emergence of the vampire in **humor** and the vampire as moral example). As such, the contemporary vampire has had to deal with a variety of sexual patterns.

Television detective Nick Knight developed an ongoing relationship with a researcher who was trying to cure him. Mara McCuniff, the centuries-old vampire of Traci Briery's *The Vampire Memoirs*, was overtaken by her sexual urges for three days each month at the time of the full **moon**. In *Domination*, Michael Cecilone placed his vampires in the world of sadomasochism. Lori Herter's romance novels elevated the vampire as the object of female fantasies.

The response to the conscious development of the vampire as a sexual being has almost guaranteed future exploration in fictional works. *Prisoners of the Night*, a periodical of vampire fiction that appeared annually for several years in the 1990s, focused on sexuality in several issues. Editor Mary Ann B. McKinnon added an impetus to exploring the theme in her fanzine, *Good Guys Wear Fangs*, which covers **good guy vampires**, most of them romantic heroes.

Sexual tension was a constant element in the highly susccessful *Buffy the Vampire Slayer* television series, which featured high school and young adult characters discovering their sexuality and major characters developing relationships with vampires (both good guys and bad boys), **werewolves**, and demons. Meanwhile, both **Anne Rice** and **Laurell K. Hamilton** were accused of upping the sexual content in their later vampire novels as a device to keep their readership despite laggingstorylines.

The entrance of the vampire into **romance literature**, with romance novels now claiming half of the paperback book market, has made the sexually attractive male vampire (both the good guys and the bad boy vampire), a prominent character in popular fiction. The overwhelming number of plots place a desirable female human into a partially forbidden relationship with a handsome vampire. The human-vampire romances came into their own in the 1990s with the writings of Lori Herter, **Maggie Shayne**, **Linda Lael Miller**, and **Amanda Ashley**, who set the statge for the explosion of vampire paranormal romances in the new century. Possibly the most successful of the new romance writers is **Charlaine Harris**, whose vampire stories center on a waitress who finds true love after rescuing a vampire from some people out to steal his blood and subsequently become desirable to other vampires.

Through the first decade of the new century, romance novels became increasingly explicit in their sexual content. The more extreme examples (avoided by the major romance houses) were described as the female equivalent of the most explicit male adult literature.

From adult romance novels, the love theme found its way into young adult novels, an early example being **Lisa Jane Smith**'s "Vampire Diaries" series in the 1990s. The romance theme in young adult novels reached a new height a decade later in *Twilight* and its sequels from **Stephenie Meyer**. Meyer's heroine, a high school girl, finds her true love in a handsome vampire, though not without being challenged by her attraction to a werewolf. Bella Swan and her vampire love object William Cullen must make a range of decisions about limiting their expression of their sexual attraction to each other before their marriage (which does not occur until the fourth and last volume of the series).

Such sexualizing and romanticizing of the vampire, while departing from the common image of the vampire as mere monster, has not been foreign to the creature itself.

From the beginning, a seductive sexuality has existed as an element of the literary vampire, comingling with that of the monstrous, and goes far to explain the vampire's appeal relative to its monstrous cousins.

Sources:

Ballion, Luc Richard, and Scott Bowen. *Vampire Seduction Handbook: Have the Most Thrilling Love of Your Life*. New York: Skyhorse Publishing, 2009. 243 pp.

Bentley, C. F. "The Monster in the Bedroom: Sexual Symbolism in Bram Stoker's *Dracula*." *Literature and Psychology* 22, 1 (1972): 27–34.

Fry, Carol L. "Fictional Conventions and Sexuality in *Dracula*." *The Victorian Newsletter* 42 (1972): 20–22.

Roth, Phyllis A. "Suddenly Sexual Women in Bram Stoker's *Dracula Literature and Psychology* 27, 3 (1977): 113–121.

Shuter, Michael. "Sex among the Coffins, or, Lust at First Bite with William Margold." *Draculina* 17 (December 1993): 32–34.

Stevenson, John Allen. "A Vampire in the Mirror: The Sexuality of Dracula." *PMLA: Publications of the Modern Language Association of America* 103, 2 (March 1988): 139–149.

Trigg, E. B. *Gypsy Demons and Divinities: The Magical and Supernatural Practices of the Gypsies.* London: Sheldon Press, 1973. 238 pp.

Waller, Gregory A. *The Living and the Undead: From Stoker's Dracula to Romero's Dawn of the Dead.* Urbana, IL: University of Illinois Press, 1986. 376 pp.

Weiss, Andrea. *Vampires and Violets: Lesbians in Film.* New York: Penguin Books, 1993. 184 pp.

Weissman, Judith. *Half Savage and Hardy and Free: Women and Rural Radicalism in the Nineteenth-Century Novel.* Middletown, CT: Wesleyan University Press, 1987. 342 pp.

Shadowcon *see:* Dark Shadows Fandom

Shadowdance *see:* Vampire Fandom: United States

Shadowgram *see:* Dark Shadows Fandom

Shadows of the Night *see:* Dark Shadows Fandom

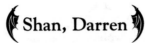

Shan, Darren

Darren Shan is the pen name of Darren O'Shaughnessy as well as the name of the main character in O'Shaughnessy's "Cirque du Freak" juvenile vampire novels, the first of which jumped to the movie screen in 2009 as *The Vampire's Apprentice.*

O'Shaughnessy was born in London on July 2, 1972, and lived there for the first six years of his life, after which his parents moved to Ireland where he grew up and continues to reside. He returned to England to study sociology and English at Roehampton Univerity in London. After a few years working for a cable television company, he became a full-time writer in 1995.

He had started writing as a teenager, and wrote several novels, not published, while in college. His first published book hit the book stores in 1999. Shortly thereafter the first of the "Cirque du Freak" novels, the *The Saga of Darren Shan*, appeared. It proved successful and was reprinted in the United States under the title *Cirque du Freak* the following year. O'Shaughnessy discovered that he liked writing for the younger crowd, and a growing body of fans seemed to enjoy probing his world of unique vampires. Beginning with *The Vampire's Assistant*, the second book in the series, he averaged three titles a year. The final volume (No. 12) appeared in 2004.

The saga of Darren Shan began when he visits a freak show with his friend Steve. Steve discoved that one of the show's personnel, a Mr. Crepsley, is in fact a vampire. Meanwhile, Darren steals a spider (because of a longtime fascination with arachnids) and a flute to train and control it. Unfortunately, at one point, Darren loses control of the spider, which fatally bites Steve. Darren appeals to Mr. Crepsley who has the antidote to the spider's venom that will save Steve. His price is that Darren becomes his assistant. He subsequently helps fake Darren's death, and after Darren's funeral and burial, he digs up his future assistant. Darren is now a *dhampir*-like "half-vampire," similar to **Blade the Vampire Slayer,** and ready to live his next years in the world of vampires.

The vampires of "Cirque du Freak" are not the undead. O'Shaughnessy wished to create what to him were more realistic vampires. They are alive and could be killed by various means. They differ from humans in that they age slowly, with lifespans at least ten times that of humans. They are strong and fast. The oldest vampire character in the series, Paris Skyle, is a **Dracula**-like vampire who is some 800 years old. Vampires fit across the same range of personality as humans and may thus be good, bad or somewhere in between. Vampire possess long sharp **fingernails** which they use for a variety of feats. Most importantly, the nails assist their feeding. They will cut into a human vein and suck small quantities of **blood**. The vampire's saliva has a healing effect and will close the cut made for feeding. The sharp nails replace the need for **fangs**.

Normally, O'Shaughnessy's vampires will drink only enough blood to survive for a short time, thus avoiding taking the life of their victims. Vampires are negatively affected by **sunlight**, but can move about in the day if they stay indoors or in the shade. They may consume **garlic**, cast a shadow and can be seen in **mirrors**, but cannot be photographed. They can survive on animal blood, but prefer that of humans. On the other hand, vampire blood is poisonous to humans.

Not being the undead, the vampires in O'Shaughnessy's books are deterred with neither **crucifix** nor holy **water**. They had dropped any religion followed in their pre-vampire existence, and now relate to a new pantheon of deities. They have a belief in the afterlife, and will be born as wolves in Paradise. They believe the first vampire evolved from wolves. Vampires cannot transform into various **animals** or mist. On the other hand, they have some telepathic powers that allow them to communicate with other vampires and locate humans by following thought patterns.

As O'Shaughnessy envisions it, there is a vampire society that is ruled hierarchically. The society values tradition, honor, and personal pride. Among their traditions is the avoidance of using weapons that work with projectiles. If they fight, it is up close and personal with weapons such as swords or the traditional Japanese weapon, the shuriken, the small blade familiar from Japanese ninja movies. At one end of the spectrum of vampire society are the evil vampires, distinguished by their pattern of drinking all of their victim's blood (and in the process taking a part of their victim's spirit also). These evil vampires, called "vampaneze," are rogue vampires out to destroy their more benevolent kin. The fight against the vampaneze takes up much of the plot of the last half of the Cirque du Freak novels. O'Shaughnessy's vampires carry signs of their battles. While their saliva heals, it does not do so miraculously, and scars remain. Many are thus disfigured and not the beautiful creatures that inhabit the vampire world of a **Stephanie Meyer** or **Anne Rice**.

As Darren Shan, O'Shaughnessy cemented his place as one of the top writers for young people in the U.K. by following his very successful vampire series with "The Demonata" a series about demons. Meanwhile, his *Cirque du Freak* was translated into a variety of languages including Japanese and Chinese. His success also allowed him the leisure to write novels for an adult audience, three of which appeared in the wake of his "Demonata" series. O'Shaughnessy resides in rural Ireland. Shanville, O'Shaughnessy's website, is found at http://www.darrenshan.com/.

Sources:

Rowe, Beverly. "An Interview with Darren Shan." Posted at http://www.myshelf.com/babetoteen/ 01/shan.htm. Accessed October 15, 2009.

"Cirque du Freak" Series

Shan, Darren. *Cirque du Freak: A Living Nightmare*. London: Collins, 2000. 183 pp. Boston, MA: Little, Brown. 2001.

———. *Vampire's Assistant*. London: Collins, 2000. 168 pp. Boston, MA: Little, Brown. 2001.

———. *Trials of Death*. London: Collins, 2001. 167 pp. Boston, MA: Little, Brown. 2003.

———. *Tunnels of Blood*. London: Collins, 2001. 162 pp. Boston, MA: Little, Brown. 2002.

———. *Vampire Mountain*. London: Collins, 2001. 162 pp. Boston, MA: Little, Brown. 2002.

———. *The Vampire Prince*. London: Collins, 2002. 161 pp. Boston, MA: Little, Brown. 2002.

———. *Allies of the Night*. London: Collins, 2002. 186 pp. Boston, MA: Little, Brown. 2004.

———. *Hunters of the Dusk*. London: Collins, 2002. 177 pp. Boston, MA: Little, Brown. 2004.

———. *Killers of the Dawn*. London: Collins, 2003. 167 pp. Boston, MA: Little, Brown. 2005.

———. *The Lake of Souls*. London: Collins, 2003. 220 pp. Boston, MA: Little, Brown. 2005.

———. *Lord of the Shadows*. London: Collins, 2004. 197 pp.

———. *Lord Loss*. Boston, MA: Little, Brown. 2005.

———. *Demon Thief*. Boston, MA: Little, Brown. 2006.

———. *Lord of Shadows*. Boston, MA: Little, Brown. 2006.

———. *Slawter*. Boston, MA: Little, Brown. 2006.

———. *Blood Beast*. Boston, MA: Little, Brown. 2007.

———. *Bec*. Boston, MA: Little, Brown. 2007.

———. *Death's Shadow*. Boston, MA: Little, Brown. 2008.

———. *Demon Apocalypse*. Boston, MA: Little, Brown. 2008.

———. *Dark Calling*. Boston, MA: Little, Brown. 2009.

———. *Wolf Island*. Boston, MA: Little, Brown. 2009.

———. *The Thin Executioner*. Boston, MA: Little, Brown. 2010.

———. *Procession of the Dead*. Boston, MA: Little, Brown. 2010.

———. *Hell's Horizon*. Boston, MA: Little, Brown. 2010.

———. *Hell's Heroes*. Boston, MA: Little, Brown. 2010.

Shepard, Leslie Alan (1917–2004)

Leslie Alan Shepard, author and founder of the **Bram Stoker Society**, began his professional life as a technician for documentary films. He produced and directed a number of films through the 1950s. In 1958–59 he spent time in **India** studying yoga and Hindu metaphysics. Since his return from Asia, he has been active with the Hindu community in England.

In the 1970s, Shepard spearheaded the recognition in **Ireland** of the work of **Bram Stoker**, both as the acting manager for dramatist Henry Irving and as an Irish author of importance. Shepard's compilation of vampire short fiction, *The Dracula Book of Great Vampire Stories*, was published in 1977. He also collected Stoker first editions, autographs, and other memorabilia, and in 1980, he was a founder of the Bram Stoker Society, a literary society to support the recognition of Stoker and other Irish **gothic** authors such as **Sheridan Le Fanu** (1814–1873) and Lord Dunsany (1878–1957). Soon after the founding of the society, Shepard produced a companion volume to his earlier work, *The Dracula Book of Great Horror Stories* (1981). His collection of Stoker material is now on permanent display at the Writers Museum, Parnell Square, in Dublin.

During the late 1970s Shepard began what is possibly his most important literary effort, as author/editor of the *Encyclopedia of Occultism and Parapsychology* (1978). By its third edition (1991), the encyclopedia had grown into a substantive reference work, far surpassing others in the field. With the fourth edition, he passed the writing and ed-

Leslie Shepard, founder of the Bram Stoker Society.

itorial dutires to J. Gordon Melton who produced the two last editions. While working on the first edition, Shepard also authored *How to Protect Yourself against Black Magic and Witchcraft* (1978).

As an officer with the Bram Stoker Society, Shepard produced an important article concerning the causes of Stoker's death for the *Bram Stoker Society Journal* and a monograph on Stoker in Dublin. He died on August 20, 2004 at Blackrock, County Dublin.

Sources:

Krishna, Gopi. *Living with Kundalini: The Autobiography of Gopi Krishna*. Leslie A. Shepard, ed. Boston: Shambhala, 1993.

"Leslie Shepard: Writer, Editor, Film-Maker and Collector." *The Independent* (September 14, 2004). Posted at http://www.independent.co.uk/news/obituaries/leslie-shepard-550467.html. Accessed September 15, 2009.

Shepard, Leslie A. *The Dracula Book of Great Vampire Stories*. New York: Citadel Press, 1977. Rept. New York: Jove/HBJ, 1978. 316 pp.

———. *Encyclopedia of Occultism and Parapsychology*. 2 vols. Detroit: Gale Research Company, 1978. 3rd ed.: 1991.

———. *How to Protect Yourself against Black Magic and Witchcraft*. New York: Citadel Press, 1978. 162 pp.

———, ed. *The Dracula Book of Great Horror Stories*. New York: Citadel Press, 1981. 288 pp.

———. "The Library of Bram Stoker." *Bram Stoker Society Journal*. 4 (1992): 28–34.

———. "A Note on the Death Certificate of Bram Stoker." *Bram Stoker Society Journal*. 4 (1992): 34–6. Reprinted in *Bram Stoker's Dracula: Sucking through the Century, 1897–1997*. Carol Margaret Davidson and Paul Simpson-Housley, eds. Toronto: Dundurn Press, 1997: 411–416.

———. 'Bram Stoker's Dublin." *Bram Stoker Society Journal* 5 (1993): 9–13.

———. *Bram Stoker: Irish Theatre Manager and Author*. Dublin: Impact Publications, 1994. 20 pp.

Shtriga *see:* Southern Slavs, Vampires and the

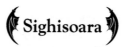

Sighisoara

Sighisoara was the birthplace of **Vlad the Impaler**, the historical **Dracula**. Sighisoara is a small town in south central **Transylvania**. A former Roman town, it was settled by Germans in 1150 C.E. Burned down by the Tartars in 1241, it emerged in the fifteenth century as one of the strongest fortified centers of Hungarian rule. In 1430, **Vlad Dracul** was sent there as commander of the guard and Vlad the Impaler was born (probably in 1430 or 1431) in the home in which Vlad Dracul resided. The family lived in the house until 1436, when Vlad Dracul became the prince of Wallachia and moved to **Tirgoviste**. That home survived the vicissitudes of time, and in

1976 it was designated a part of the Romanian national heritage. The restoration that followed uncovered frescoes decorating the walls—one of which is believed to picture Dracula.

Sources:

Mackenzie, Andrew. *Dracula Country*. London: Arthur Barker, 1977. 176 pp.

Sikkim, Vampires in *see:* Tibet, Vampires in

Silver

The real birthplace of Vlad the Impaler in Sighisoara, Romania.

In the opening chapters of her first vampire book, *Dead until Dark* (2001), author **Charlaine Harris** has her heroine waitress Sookie Stackhouse attracted to vampire Bill Compton. One evening after he has come to the restaurant where she works, she discovers him under attack from some people who would rob him of his **blood**. She has to save Bill after he has been immobilized under a chain of silver. The silver has the effect of burning the vampire's flesh even as it drains his/her strength. Harris's introduction of silver into her vampire mythos is a contemporary borrowing from the modern **werewolf** mythos.

The use of silver bullets against werewolves, popularized in the many werewolf movies, may harken back to a single incident that occurred in rural southern **France** in 1764. A series of murders that included several sheep herders led to rumors of a "loup-garou" or werewolf. Soldiers searching for the creature shot and wounded it, and the murders ceased for several months. Then, they began to reoccur. One of the locals who hunted the creature, Jean Chastel, used silver bullets in his weapon. His shots brought it down. The dead beast was displayed in the town before its burial. Chastel's gun remains on display and the locals still tell the story of the Beast of Le Gevaudan. In addition, Paul Barber found two instances, one in Serbia and one in **Germany**, in which silver as used against werewolves was also said to be effective against vampires. More generally the use of silver is traced to Scotland, however, where it was believed that silver should be used when shooting at Scottish witches who had transformed into an animal form.

Silver is almost never mentioned in vampire literature through the nineteenth and twentieth centuries up to the 1970s. There is a connection, however slight, in that many **crucifix**es, popularly used to repel vampires, were made of silver. In the secularized mid-twentieth century, it appears that some began to look to the crucifix's silver, rather than the sacredness of the symbol, as the effective element in its ability to repel vampires. Otherwise, silver was missing from *Dracula* and other classic vampire tales. As the werewolf was brought to the screen, beginning with *The Werewolf of London* in

1935, however, the major method proposed from killing a werewolf was a silver bullet. Simultaneously, the silver bullet was attaining additional fame as the weapon of choice by the Western hero, the Lone Ranger (introduced to radio in 1933, the movies in 1938, and television in 1949).

The introduction of silver into contemporary vampire lore appears to have been through the movies. In 1972, **Hammer Films** released *Dracula 1972 A.D.* By this time, **Dracula** had already been killed a number of times and each time by a different instrument. As the movie proceeded, the current vampire expert, Lawrence Van Helsing, noted the diversity of instruments able to destroy the vampire—the cross, the bible, the holy water, etc. As he completed his list, he suddenly injected a new agent into the discussion—silver, especially in the form of a knife with a silver blade. The film's conclusion has Van Helsing stabbing Dracula with just such a knife. Two years later, the original **Abraham van Helsing**, now in China, tells his new cohorts that among the ways that a vampire can be destroyed is driving a silver shaft through the heart. In the end, most of the vampires including Dracula are killed by staking, but alas, not with silver.

Silver will reemerge as a tool to fight vampires in the stories of **Blade the Vampire Slayer**, one of the characters created by **Marv Wolfman** for Marvel comics *Tomb of Dracula* series. Blade had an early mentor by the name of Jamal Afari (a character created by Chris Claremont) who trained him to fight vampires. When they met, Afari was dispatching vampires with a silver cane. Blade later developed ebony throwing knives as his main weapon, but gradually added a set of silver-based products as his character was later remolded in superhero fashion. Of course, when Blade jumped to the screen (1998), he was armed with the knowledge that vampires were quite vulnerable to silver and thus **stake**s, swords, and knives, and even a mace-like spray of silver and **garlic** were viable weapons. The silver theme was also prominent throughout the two sequels.

In the 1996 movie, *From Dusk to Dawn*, the characters discuss using silver against vampires, but lacking any to use, discarded the idea. In *Dracula 2000* (2000), Dracula manifests a seemingly irrational dislike to silver, which at the end of the movie is shown to be derived from Dracula's true identity as Judas Iscariot who betrayed Jesus for thirty pieces of silver.

Relating silver to vampires was also facilitated by the development of movies/novels in which vampires and werewolves both appeared. As early as 1979, jokes would be made about the ineffectiveness of silver bullets shot into vampires, in the George Hamilton movie, *Love at First Bite*. In 1993, **Laurell K. Hamilton** introduced her vampire hunter character Anita Blake into a modern St. Louis where both vampires and werewolves are coming into the open. In Hamilton's first novel, *Guilty Pleasures*, the assassin Edward showed Anita a new way to kill vampires, involving injections of silver nitrate while they sleep.

Through the 1990s, the use of silver was integral to the World of Darkness **games** from White Wolf, especially the *Werewolf: The Apocalypse* game launched in 1992. Silver nitrate bullets become a popular weapon that a vampire can use against werewolves. This theme is carried forward in the first of the *Underworld* (2003) movies in which the vampires are at war with werewolves and carry guns with silver nitrate bullets. The silver theme is also an element in a variety of romance novels that feature both vampires and werewolves, most notably those of Carrie Vaughn, but remains primarily an anti-werewolf substance. Almost all of these novels have been written in the first decade of the new century.

Silver does not play a role in the vampire worlds created by **Anne Rice**, Joss Whedon (***Buffy the Vampire Slayer, Angel***), or **Stephenie Meyer**. Apart from these very popular vampire realms, however, it may be stated that since the mid-1990s, vampires have been increasingly viewed as vulnerable to silver, while silver has taken its place as another element in the vampire profile with which authors can play. Silver is also a popular substance for making jewelry, and since the 1990s, silver anti-vampire jewelry, especially necklaces, has enjoyed a new popularity.

Sources:

Barber, Paul. *Vampires, Burial, and Death: Folklore and Reality.* New Haven, CT: Yale University Press, 1988. 236 pp.

Claremont, Chris, and Tony DeZuniga. "The Night Jesse Harper Died." *Marvel Preview* 3 (September 1975): 1-51.

Clark, Jerome. *Unexplained!* Detroit: Visible Ink Press, 1999: pp 218-20.

Dorff, Stephen. *Blade.* New York: HarperPaperbacks, 1998. 343 pp.

Hamilton, Laurell. *Guilty Pleasures.* New York: Ace Books, 1993. 265 pp.

Harris, Charlaine. *Dead until Dark.* New York: Ace Books, 2001. 260 pp.

Joslin, Lyndon W. *Count Dracula Goes to the Movies: Stoker's Novel Adapted, 1922–1995.* Jefferson, NC: McFarland & Company, 1999. 237 pp.

Kane, Tim. *Changing Vampire of Film and Television: A Critical Study of the Growth of a Genre.* Jeffersonville, NC: McFarland & Company, 2006. 232 pp.

Vaughn, Carrie. *Kitty and the Midnight Hour.* New York: Warner Books, 2005. 272 pp.

Skal, David J. (1952–)

David J. Skal, writer and film historian.

David J. Skal, an American writer and film historian, is best known for his series of books on the **gothic**/horror tradition in film and literature. Skal attended Ohio University in Athens, Ohio, where he earned his bachelor's degree in general studies in 1974. His scholarship on the horror genre was brought to public attention by his 1990 study of **Dracula**'s appearances in various media, *Hollywood Gothic*, touted as the most detailed published work of Dracula's movement from the 1893 novel to the stage and screen. The book includes the full story of the campaign by **Bram Stoker**'s widow, Florence, to destroy all prints of the German silent film **Nosferatu** (1922), which infringed her copyright, as well as the first in-depth account of **Universal Pictures**' Spanish-language version of *Dracula*, for which Skal located a crucial missing reel in Havana, thus making possible the film's complete restoration.

Skal followed his initial success with a series of additional books, including *The Monster Show: A Cultural History of Horror* (1993), *Dark Carnival* (1995), a biography of **Tod Browning** coauthored with Elias Savada, and *V Is for Vampire* (1996), which established Skal as one of the leading cultural historians in his field. As the Dracula centennial approached he worked to complete his contributions (along with those of Nina Auerbach) to the *Norton Critical Edition of Dracula* and he worked on **Dracula '97: A Centennial Celebration** held in Los Angeles in 1997. For **television**, he scripted the A&E "Biography" documentary on the life of **Bela Lugosi**. His most recent publications include *Vampires: Encounters with the Undead* (2006), a collection of vampire stories from the nineteenth and twentieth centuries, and *Romancing the Vampire: Collectors Vault* (2009). His nonfiction has been nominated for both the Hugo and Bram Stoker Awards.

Sources:

Skal, David. *Hollywood Gothic: The Tangled Web of Dracula from Novel to Stage to Screen*. New York: W. W. Norton & Company, 1990. 243 pp.

———. *The Monster Show: A Cultural History of Horror*. New York: W. W. Norton & Co., 1993. 432 pp.

———. *Dark Carnival: The Secret World of Tod Browning, Hollywood's Master of the Macabre*. New York: Doubleday and Company, 1995. 359 pp.

———. *V Is for Vampire: The A–Z Guide to Everything Undead*. New York: Plume/Penguin, 1996. 288 pp.

———. *Vampires: Encounters With the Undead*. New York: Black Dog & Leventhal Publishers, 2006. 592 pp.

———. *Romancing the Vampire: Collectors Vault*. Florence, AL: Whitman Publishing, 2009. 144 pp.

Skin, Vampire

The vampire is a revenant, the recently deceased raised to a new existence as the undead. As such, the vampire has been described as extremely pale—the paleness being a sign both of lack of **blood** and the lack of **sunlight**. The deathlike appearance is often accompanied with sunken eyes and the withdrawal of skin around the teeth. (This paleness and related characteristics refers to vampires of European origin. African vampires were not, for example, revenants.) **Jonathan Harker** would summarize his description of **Dracula**'s face by noting, "The general effect was one of extraordinary pallor." The pallor would temporarily leave the vampire immediately after feeding. In European folklore, the bodies of suspected vampires would appear to have "ruddy cheeks" when their body was uncovered. The new color (along with what appeared to be fresh blood exiting the mouth and/or nose) was a sign that the body was in fact that of a vampire.

As the vampire made the transition to the stage, the appearance of the skin occasionally remained an issue. David Skal noted that **Bela Lugosi** wore a green-hued makeup when he played Dracula in 1927–28 on stage in New York. The color suggested both decay and toxicity. By the time the vampire began to appear in color movies, its traditionally pale skin had been abandoned, as it seemed to be of greater concern that the vampire be able to fit into normal society, even to join the beautiful people. Overwhelmingly, the cinema vampires show no skin characteristics that would set them apart from the humans among whom they live. The primary exceptions are those vampires in the Count Orlok tradition

who not only have a deathly pallor but an otherwise odd appearance (pointed ears, prominent rat-like **fangs**) that would prevent their integrating in normal society.

Among the important exceptions are the works of **Anne Rice**, whose main vampire character, **Lestat de Lioncourt**, describes his appearance thusly, "My vampiric nature shows through in my excessively white and reflecting skin, that it is necessary to powder for its exposure to all the objectives, whatever they are." Before feeding, the skin would be taut, and his veins would protrude somewhat. After feeding it looked more normal. As the **gothic** movement of the twentieth century emerged, many goths wished to effect a vampire-like appearance, and Lestat was a popular model. The pale skin was created with make-up, and an overall effect established with dark red lip color and heavily applied eye make-up.

The subject of the vampire's skin was raised anew by **Stephenie Meyer** in her **"Twilight series"**. Her vampires are extremely attractive, possessing skin that is hard and cold to the touch, with an alabaster-like appearance. They are normally pale, but will show some ruddiness after feeding. The paleness of Meyer's vampires does not carry with it a sense of death and decay, as with the revenant. In stark distinction, their skin sparkles when exposed to the sun. This characteristic leads them to avoid the public when the sun is shining and the sky unclouded.

Sources:

Baddeley, Gavin. *Goth Chic: A Gothic Guide to Dark Culture.* London: Plexus, 2002. 288 pp.
Meyer, Stephenie. *Twilight.* Boston: Little, Brown Young Readers, 2005. 512 pp.
Rice, Anne. *The Vampire Lestat.* New York: Alfred A. Knopf, 1985. 481 pp.
Skal, David J. *Hollywood Gothic: The Tangled Web of Dracula from Novel to Stage to Screen.* New York: W. W. Norton & Company, 1990. 243 pp.

Slavs, Vampires and the

While vampires and vampirelike creatures appeared in the mythology of many of the world's peoples, nowhere were they more prevalent than among the Slavs of eastern and central Europe. Because of their belief in vampires, the Slavs experienced several panic-stricken "vampire" outbreaks in the late seventeenth and early eighteenth centuries that resulted in the opening and desecration of numerous graves. This belief system brought the vampire to the attention of the West and led directly to the development of the contemporary vampire myth.

The Slavic people include most eastern Europeans, from **Russia** to **Bulgaria**, from Serbia to the **Czech Republic** and **Poland**. Pouring into the region between the Danube and the Adriatic Sea, the people known collectively as the **southern Slavs** created several countries—Serbia, Croatia, Bosnia and Herzegovina, and Macedonia. In the midst of the Slavic lands are two non-Slavic countries, **Romania** and **Hungary**, though each has shared much of its language and lore with its Slavic neighbors. **Gypsies** have been a persistent minority throughout the Slavic lands, though much of the Gypsy community was decimated by the Nazi holocaust.

The exact origin of the Slavs is a matter of continuing historical debate, but most scholars agree that they came from river valleys north of the Black Sea and were closely associated with the Iranians, with whom they shared a religious perspective that gave a central place to a sun deity. At some point prior to the eighth century C.E., the Slavs, made up of numerous tribes, migrated north and west into the lands they now inhabit. Once settled in their new homes, they began to unite into national groups.

The most important event to give direction to the Slavs was the introduction of Christianity. Initial penetration of the church into Slavic lands began as soon as the Slavs occupied the lands formerly in the hands of the Byzantine empire. However, systematic conversion attempts emerged as an outcome of the extensive reforms instituted during the long reign of Charlemagne (768–814). Charlemagne saw to the development of missions among the Moravians and the Croatians and had a bishop placed at Salzburg to further the Christianization of the Slavs. Most Slavs, however, recognize the work of the brothers Cyril (827–869) and Methodius (825–885) as the real beginning of Slavic Christianity. The brothers developed a Slavic alphabet capable of expressing all of the sounds in the Slavic language in its various dialects.

They borrowed letters from Greek, Hebrew, and Armenian and created a new literary language that included Greek loan-words and new Slavic words that expressed some of the subleties of Greek. This new literary language, most closely resembling Old Bulgarian, became Old Church Slavonic and influenced the various new national languages (from Bulgarian and Serbian to Polish and Russian) that were beginning to emerge from the older common language of the Slavic tribes. Cyril and Methodius translated the Bible and Greek liturgy into Old Church Slavonic. Out of their missions grew the several national eastern Orthodox communions, autonomous churches affiliated with the Ecumenical Patriarch in Constantinople (now Istanbul), the spiritual (though not administrative) head of eastern Orthodoxy.

Through the ninth and tenth centuries, the Eastern Orthodox church and the Western Roman church engaged in a fight over policy and administrative matters that were to lead to their break and mutual excommunication of each other in 1054 C.E. That break had immense significance for the Slavic people, as the Bulgarians, the Russians, and the Serbians adhered to the Eastern church, while the Poles, Czechs, and Croatians gave their loyalties to the Roman church. This split had great significance in the development of vampire lore, as the two churches disagreed over their understanding of the noncorruption of the body of a dead person. In the West, the noncorruption of the body of some saintly people was seen as an additional sign of their sanctity, while in the East, the incorruptibility of the body was viewed as a sign of God's disfavor resting upon the dead person, and hence, the likelihood of the individual's becoming a vampire. Paradoxically, the Church, especially in Russia, also knows the idea of the incorruptibility of the bodies of the saints. **Dom Augustin Calmet** and others discuss the differences (e.g. the smell: the saints don't stink).

Origin of the Slavic Vampire: Jan L. Perkowski, who has done the most thorough study of Slavic vampirism, concluded that it originated in the Balkans. Beginning around the ninth century, speculation on vampires evolved as a result of the confrontation between pre-Christian Paganism and **Christianity**. Bogomilism, a dualistic religion with roots in Iran that emerged in Macedonia in the tenth century, added yet another element to the developing concept. Eventually Christianity won over the other religions, and Pagan and Bogomil ideas, including the belief in vampires, survived as elements of pop-

ular demonology. (Perkowski's reconstruction has been challenged by others who have found that it lacks evidence.) As the concept of the vampire evolved in Slavic mythology, several terms emerged to designate it.

(*Note:* The discussion of terminology quickly brings even the most accomplished scholar into an area of possible confusion, simply because of the dynamic nature of language in which words are constantly shifting in meaning or connotation. There is a major disagreement among authorities over the primacy of older Slavic origins or Turkish origins. Perkowski favors a Slavic origin and his approach has been accepted as a framework for this discussion.)

The most widely used term was one or the other of many variants of the original Slavic term that lay behind our modern word *vampire*, which seems to have evolved from the common form *obyri* or *obiri*. Each language group has a cognate form of the older root word—*upirina* (Serbian and Croatian), *upirbi* (Ukrainian), *up'r* (Byelo-Russian, Czech, Slovak), *upi-r* (Polish), *wupji* (Kashubian), **lampir** (Bosnian), and **vampir** (Bulgarian, also *vbpir*, *vepir*, or *vapir*. There is a wide range of opinion on the origin of the root term *opyrb*, an unsolvable problem because the history of the early Slavic tribes has been lost.

The second popular term, especially among the Greeks and southern Slavs is *vrykolakas* (which, like vampire, possessed a number of forms in the different Slavic languages). This term seems to have derived from the older Serbian compound word, *vblkb* plus *dlaka*, meaning one who wore wolf pelts. Perkowski argues that the term designated someone who wore a wolfskin in a ritual situation. By the thirteenth century, when the word first appeared in a written text, the earlier meaning had been dropped and *vlbkod-laci* referred to a mythological monster who chased the clouds and ate the sun and **moon** (causing eclipses). Still later, by the sixteenth century, it had come to refer to vampires and as such had passed into both Greek and Romanian culture. The older southern Slavic term appears today as *vrykolakas* (Greek), *vircolac* (Romanian), *vbkolak* (Macedonian, Bulgarian), and *vukodlak* (Serbo-Croatian, sometimes shortened to *kudlak*). Because of the root meaning of the term, *vudkolak* has become part of the discussion of the relation of **werewolves** and the vampire.

Three other words have assumed some importance in the literature as designations of the vampire. *Strigoi* (female: *strigoaica*) is the popular Romanian word for witch. Harry Senn, author of *Were-Wolf and Vampire in Romania*, found a variant, *strigoi mort* (dead witch), as a common term for a vampire. *Strigoi* is derived from the Latin *strix* (screech owl) that had also come to refer to a night demon that attacked children. Russians commonly replaced *up'r*, their older Slavic term for a vampire, with *eretik* (or *heretic*), a Greek ecclesiastical word for one who has departed from the true faith. **Vjesci** (alternate spellings *vjeszczi* and *vjeszcey*) is a term employed by the Kashubs of northern Poland.

The Slavic Vampire: The vampire found its place within the world view of the people of eastern and central Europe. It was associated with death and was an entity to be avoided. However, it was not the all-pervasive symbol of evil it would come to be in nineteenth-century western European literature. Within the prescientific world of village life, the role of the vampire was to explain various forms of unpredicted and undeserved evil that befell people.

The Slavic vampire differed considerably from the popular image of the creature that evolved in twentieth-century novels and movies. First, it generally appeared without any prior contact with another vampire. The vampire was the product of an irregularity in the community life, most commonly a problem with the process of either death and burial or of birth. People who met a violent death, which cut them off from the normal completion of their live could become vampires. Thus, people who committed **suicide** or died as the result of an accident might become vampires. Most Slavic cultures had a precise set of ritualized activities to be followed after someone's death and even for some days following the interment of the body. Deviation from that procedure could result in the deceased becoming a vampire. In a community where the church was integral to social life, and deviation from the church a matter of serious concern, to die in a state of excommunication was seen as a cause of vampirism.

Vampirism also could result from problems associated with birth. For example, most Slavic communities had certain days of the year when intercourse was frowned upon. Children conceived by parents who had violated such taboos could become vampires. Bulgarians believed that an infant who died before it was baptized could become a *ustrel*, a vampire that would attack and drink the **blood** of cows and sheep. Among the Kashubs, a child born with teeth or with a membrane cap (a caul) on its head could become a vampire after its death.

Thus, Slavic society offered many reasons why vampires could appear. Of course, part of the horror felt toward vampires was the possibility of its passing on its condition to others. The vampire tended to attack its family, neighbors, friends, and people with whom it had unfinished business. Those attacked assumed the possibility of also becoming a vampire. The belief that a number of community members might become vampires contemporaneously brought on waves of vampire hysteria experienced in Slavic communities.

In the cases where a deceased person was suspected of becoming a vampire, a wide variety of pre-burial actions were reportedly taken as precautions.

Among the most widespread was the placing of various materials into the **coffin** that were believed to inhibit a vampire's activity. Religious objects such as the **crucifix** were the most common. Such plants as the **mountain ash** were believed to stop the vampire from leaving its grave.

Since vampires had a fascination with counting, **seeds** (millet or poppyseed) were spilled in the grave, on top of the grave, and on the road from the graveyard. The vampire slowly counted the seeds before it assumed the privilege of engaging in any vampiric activity. On occasion, in more extreme cases, the body might be pierced with thorns or a **stake**, different groups having preferences for wood (**hawthorn**, aspen, or oak) or iron.

Believing that vampires would first attack and eat their burial garments every effort was made to keep the clothes away from the corpse's mouth. A wooden block might be placed under the chin, or the clothes might be nailed to the side of the coffin.

While there were many possible causes for the creation of a vampire, the existence of one became apparent through the negative effects of its activities. Most commonly, the unexplained death of sheep and cattle (a community's food supply) was attributed to vampires. Strange experiences of the kind usually studied by parapsychologists also suggested the presence of vampires. Included in the stories of vampires were accounts of poltergeist activity, the visitation of a **incubus/succubus**, or the appearance of the specter

of a recently deceased person to a relative or friend. The sudden illness or death of a person, especially a relative or friend, soon after the death of an individual suggested that the person had become a vampire. Vampires also were associated with epidemics.

Once the suggestion that a community was under attack by a vampire was taken seriously by several residents, the discovery and designation of the vampire proceeded. The most likely candidate was a person who had recently died, especially in the previous forty days. (Derived from the forty days between Jesus's death and ascension.) The body of the suspected vampire might then be exhumed and examined for characteristic signs. The body of a vampire was believed to appear lifelike and to show signs of continued growth and change. It would possess pliable joints and blood would ooze from its mouth or other body openings. It might have swelled up like a drum filled with blood. Its hair may have continued to grow and new **fingernails** may have appeared.

When the supposed vampire was located, it had to be destroyed. **Destroying the vampire** usually involved action against the corpse—most commonly, the body was staked using a variety of wood or metal materials. The stake was driven into the head, heart, or stomach. In some instances **decapitation** might occur. The Kashub people placed the severed head between the feet of the corpse before reburial. In the most extreme cases, the body was destroyed by burning. These actions were accompanied, where the services of a priest could be obtained, by such ritual activity as the repeating of the funeral service, the sprinkling of holy **water**, or even an exorcism.

While the belief in vampires was quite widespread, especially in rural eastern Europe, the cases of a community detecting a vampire and taking action against the corpse of the suspect were relatively rare. This was true especially after the widely reported incidents of vampires in the eighteenth century and the subsequent institution of legal penalties, both secular and ecclesiastical, against people who desecrated the bodies of the dead. However, besides the reports of contemporary vampires, a large body of vampire folktales set in the indefinite past circulated in Slavic lands. Like Aesop's fables, these stories functioned as moral tales to teach behavioral norms to members of the community. Among the more famous was one titled simply "The Vampire," originally collected by A. N. Afanasyev in Russia in the nineteenth century. It told of a young girl, Marusia, who became infatuated with a handsome young man who ventured into her town. He was rich, personable, and mannered, but he was also a vampire. Even after she discovered his nature, she did not act, and as a result several members of her family died. She finally learned what to do from her grandmother. The story offered the listener a number of guidelines. For example, it taught that wisdom was to be sought from one's elders, and that young people should beware attractive strangers, as they might be the source of evil. Other stories offered similar advice.

The Slavic Vampire Today: Folklorists such as Harry Senn have had little difficulty collecting vampire stories, both folktales and accounts of the apparent actual vampires, among Slavic populations throughout the twentieth century, though increasingly they have had to travel to the more isolated rural communities to find such accounts. Governments hostile to any form of supernaturalism have had a marked influence on the loss of belief in vampires, effectively eradicating most such beliefs in the urban areas and among more educated persons. Also assisting in the decline of belief has been the rise of the modern undertaker, who has assumed the burial functions previously done by the family of the deceased. The removal of the burial ceremony from the people has caused a certain distancing from the experience of death, which has contributed to the decline of many beliefs about human interaction with the dead.

Sources:

Dvornik, Francis. *The Slavs: Their Early History and Civilization*. Boston: American Academy of Arts and Sciences, 1956. 394 pp.

Perkowski, Jan L., ed. *Vampires of the Slavs*. Cambridge, MA: Slavica Publishers, 1976. 294 pp.

———. *The Darkling: A Treatise on Slavic Vampirism*. Columbus, OH: Slavica Publishers, 1989. 174 pp.

———. *Vampire Lore: From Writings of Jan Louis Perkowski*. Bloomington, Indiana: Slavica 2006. 610 pp.

Senn, Harry. *Were-Wolf and Vampire in Romania*. New York: Columbia University Press, 1982. 148 pp.

Summers, Montague. *The Vampire in Europe*. New York: Routledge, Kegan Paul, Trench, Trubner, & Co., 1929. 329 pp. Rept. New Hyde Park, NY: University Books, 1961. 329 pp.

Wilson, Katherina M. "The History of the Word 'Vampire.'" *Journal of the History of Ideas* 46, 4 (October-December 1985): 577–583.

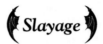

Slayage

Slayage refers to an academic journal, Internet site, and community of scholars devoted to the study of ***Buffy the Vampire Slayer, Angel*** and, increasingly, to the whole body of work produced by Joss Whedon, termed the Whedonverse. *Slayage: The Online International Journal of Buffy Studies* emerged in stages in 2001, the brainchild of two English professors, David Lavery of Middle Tennessee State University and Rhonda V. Wilcox of Gordon College (Barnesville, Georgia). As they gathered essays for a book, *Fighting the Forces: What's at Stake in Buffy the Vampire Slayer*, they discovered that two additional books on *Buffy* were in the works and realized that their interest in the popular television show was shared by a large number of their scholarly colleagues—even more than had been manifested around other pop culture phenomena such as *Star Trek* or *The X-Files*. Using the online journal of *Xena* studies as a model, they created a quarterly journal for *Buffy* studies which continues to the present.

Further interest in studies on *Buffy* was manifested in an international conference held at East Anglia University in Norwich, England, in the fall of 2002, attended by scholars from more than twenty countries. Beginning in 2004, *Slayage* began sponsoring biannual conferences, the first of which brought some four hundred scholars to Nashville. Subsequent conferences were held at Gordon College in Georgia (2006), and Henderson State University, Arkadelphia, Arkansas (2008). Plans were made for a fourth conference to be held in St. Augustine, Florida, in 2010. Late in 2008, the Whedon Studies Association was formed as a legal non-profit educational organization devoted to the study of Whedon and his associates.

Slayage ties together an interdisciplinary network of scholars united initially by their mutual appreciation of the *Buffy the Vampire Slayer* series, and which has faded only slightly by the demise of the series and its offshoot, *Angel*. Scholarly comment, based in academic television and movies studies and English, has reached out to include

perspectives from sociology, anthropology, philosophy and religious studies. The end result has been that by 2009, over half of all the scholarly articles ever written on vampires, and a significant percentage of the scholarly books, have been devoted to the work product of Joss Whedon. In the wake of the formation of the association, the title of the journal was changed to *Slayage: The Journal of the Whedon Studies Association*.

Slayage has also published a still growing encyclopedia of *Buffy* studies, and annually presents the Mr. Pointy Awards (the folksy name given the **stake** inherited by Buffy from her sister slayer Kendra in the series).

Sources:

Adams, Michael. *Slayer Slang: A Buffy the Vampire Slayer Lexicon*. Oxford: Oxford University Press, 2003. 308 pp.

Encyclopedia of Buffy Studies. Posted at http://slayageonline.com/EBS/.

Jowett, Lorna. *Sex and the Slayer: A Gender Studies Primer for the Buffy Fan*. Middletown, CT: Wesleyan University Press, 2005. 254 pp.

Kaveney, Roz, ed. *Reading the Vampire Slayer*. London: Tauris Parke Publishing, 2001. 271 pp.

Koontz, K. Dale. *Faith and Choice in the Works of Joss Whedon*. Jefferson, NC: McFarland & Company, 2008. 231 pp.

Levine, Elana, and Lisa Parks, eds. *Undead TV: Essays on Buffy the Vampire Slayer*. Durham, NC: Duke University Press, 2007. 209 pp.

Pateman, Matthew. *The Aesthetics of Culture in Buffy the Vampire Slayer*. Jeffersonville, NC: McFarland & Company, 2006. 288 pp.

South, James, ed. *Buffy the Vampire Slayer and Philosophy*. LaSalle, IL: Open Court, 2003. 335 pp.

Stevenson, Gregory. *Televised Morality: The Case of Buffy the Vampire Slayer*. Lanham, MD: Hamilton Books, 2004.

Wilcox, Rhonda. *Why Buffy Matters: The Art of Buffy the Vampire Slayer*. London: I. B. Tauris & Company, 2005. 246 pp.

———, and David Lavery, eds. *Fighting the Forces: What's at Stake in Buffy the Vampire Slayer*. Lanham, MD: Rowman & Littlefield Publishers, 2002. 290 pp.

Sleep, Vampire

In the last chapter of ***Dracula***, **Abraham Van Helsing** entered **Castle Dracula** to kill the three **women** residents who would later be referred to the **vampire brides**. When he found them, he saw they were in their "vampire sleep." The term was unique to *Dracula*, though since that time it has been used by other writers. Without naming it, **Bram Stoker** described the state of sleep into which vampires fell in chapter 4, when **Jonathan Harker** discovered **Dracula** resting in one of the boxes of his **native soil**. He observed:

> He was either dead or asleep, I could not say which—for the eyes were open and stoney, but without the glassiness of death—and the cheeks had the warmth of life through all their pallor, and the lips were as red as ever. But there was no sign of movement, no pulse, no breath, no beating of the heart. I bent over him and tried to find any sign of life, but in vain.

Dracula appeared to need periods of rest, which he took primarily during the day. At such times he gave himself to this deathlike sleep, becoming completely vulnerable. The second time that Harker found Dracula in this state, he grabbed a shovel and hit him in the head, making a deep gash above the vampire's forehead. While vulnerable

and appearing dead, Dracula had some degree of consciousness. As Harker was about to hit him with the shovel, he turned his head and looked at Harker, who, upon seeing Dracula react to his intent, dropped the shovel and fled.

The fact that the vampire may fall into a deep sleeplike state at the coming of dawn has been combined with its aversion to **sunlight** to create tension in some vampire novels and movies. Dracula could appear during the day, and some recent vampires have shown this ability (most notably those of ***Twilight***), but many more recent vampires suffer from the sun and prefer to sleep during the day (***Buffy the Vampire Slayer***, *Moonlight*, *Blood Ties*, *True Blood*). **Anne Rice**'s vampires could, for example, enter this deathlike sleep but still have the power to move their arms to protect themselves. The *True Blood* vampires can be up during the day, but must stay out of the sun.

Sources:
Ramsland, Katherine. *The Vampire Companion*. New York: Ballantine Books, 1993. 507 pp.

Slovakia, *see:* Czech Republic and Slovakia, Vampires in the

❧ Smith, Lisa Jane ❧

L isa Jane (L. J.) Smith is an author of books for children and young adults. She graduated from the University of California, Santa Barbara with a degree in experimental psychology and later received teaching credentials from San Francisco State University in elementary education and special education. She abandoned school teaching, however, to write fiction, and in 1987 saw her first book, *The Night of the Solstice*, published. She subsequently became the very successful author of the "Vampire Diaries" series, four volumes of which appeared in 1991.

The first volume of The Vampire Diaries, *The Awakening*, introduces Elena Gilbert, a popular and intelligent high schooler in Mystic Fall, a small town in Virginia. She is in grief from the recent loss of her father but finds an outlet in a new boy at school, Stefan Salvatore. The mysterious Salvatore turns out to be a youthful looking vampire, who was only seventeen when turned. Stefan had been a vampire since the Italian Renaissance. He has a slightly older brother, Damon, also a vampire, with whom he has a love-hate relationship. Stefan, a **good guy vampire**, has found a way to survive without taking human **blood**, while Damon is the bad boy vampire who acts out the role of an amoral predator. The brothers were transformed into vampires by a mutual love, Katherine, a young vampire now deceased. Elena's relationship with the two vampires begins over her resemblance to Katehrine and eventually leads to her death at the end of volume two of Smith's books. She awakens as a vampire herself at the beginning of volume three.

Smith's vampires generally follow the traditional myth of the literary vampire. People become vampires by drinking a vampire's blood, and which they must regularly ingest blood to survive. They burn in **sunlight**, but wear a ring that allows them to walk about in daylight. They are very quick in moving about. They can be killed by a **stake** to the heart. They show a reflection in a **mirror**, are not affected by **garlic** or sacred symbols. They are able to control people's memories so that victims do not remember an attack.

In 2009, in the wake of the success of **Buffy the Vampire Slayer** and **Stephenie Meyer's Twililght Series**, the WB Channel brought The Vampire Diaries to television as a primetime series. Nina Dobrev portrayed Elena Gilbert, with Paul Wesley and Ian Somerhalder as the brothers Stefan and Damon Salvatore respectively.

Several years after the original Vampire Diaries were published, Smith returned to the vampire theme in a new series, "Dark Visions" (1994–1995), in which Kaitlyn, an artist with some precognitive abilities, develops a telepathic link with a brooding loner named Gabriel. Gabriel turns out to be a psychic vampire who drains the life-force of those around him to survive. Kaitlyn must choose between the dark one Gabriel, or the good option, a healer named Rob.

Smith finished out the 1990s with a nine-volume series, "Night World", in which she created a fantasy universe in which the normal world of her main characters is enlivened by the presence of vampires, witches, and shapeshifters. The characters of the Night World have two basic rules—do not tell the humans that they exist and do not fall in love with a human. Not all of the nine novels focus on vampires, but vampires are present in each and integral to the plot in several—such as the first one, appropriately named *Vampire Secret*. James a vampire, has fallen for a classmate Poppy, who has contracted a fatal illness. Having broken a basic rule of falling for a human, he must now decide whether or not to make her a vampire.

In the wake of the new success of the Vampire Diaries, Smith has projected three new volumes in a new series called "The Vampire Diaries: The Return," the first of which, *Nightfall*, appeared in 2009. In it she chose to pick up the story line shortly after the end of volume 4. Smith maintains a webpage at http://www.ljanesmith.net/index.php.

Sources:

"An Interview with Novelist L. J. Smith." *Forbidden Tales*. 1996. Posted at http://www.night-world.net/witchlight/forbiddentales.htm. Accessed Octiber 15, 2009.

"Vampire Diaries" Series by Lisa Jane Smith
The Awakening. New York: HarperCollins, 1991. 311 pp.
The Struggle. New York: HarperCollins, 1991. 313 pp.
The Fury. New York: HarperCollins, 1991. 309 pp.
Dark Reunion. New York: HarperCollins, 1992. 311 pp.
Nightfall . New York: HarperTeen, 2009. 592 pp.
Shadow Souls. New York: HarperTeen, 2010. 512 pp.

"Dark Visions" Series by Lisa Jane Smith
The Passion. New York: Archway/Pocket Books, 1994. 211 pp.
The Possessed. New York: Archway/Pocket Books, 1995. 212 pp.
The Strange Power. New York: Archway/Pocket Books, 1995. 230 pp.
Dark Visions: Collectors Edition. New York: Archway/Pocket Books, 1998. 653 pp.

"Night World" Series by Lisa Jane Smith
Huntress. New York: Archway/Pocket Books, 1996. 226 pp.
Secret Vampire. New York: Archway/Pocket Books, 1996. 228 pp.
Black Dawn. New York: Archway/Pocket Books, 1997. 227 pp.
Witchlight. New York: Archway/Pocket Books, 1998. 227 pp.

Soil *see:* Native Soil

Somtow, S. P.

S. P. Somtow, the pseudonym of Thai-America writer Somtow Sucharitkul, was born in Bangkok in 1952. He started writing early in life and his first published piece, a poem entitled "Kith of Infinity," was written when he was eleven years old. It was seen by actress Shirley McLaine in the *Bangkok Post*. who, moved by its expression of alienation, and under the impression that it had been written by an ancient dead sage, reprinted it in her autobiographical book, *Don't Fall Off the Mountain*. Somtow was educated in Switzerland where his uncle, a member of the diplomatic corps for **Thailand**, was stationed. He attended St. Catherine's College in Cambridge, Massachusetts, from which he received both his bachelor's and master's degrees.

Before Somtow was a writer, he was a musician. He composed numerous musical selections and was the director of the Bangkok Opera Society (1977–78). In 1978 he was the director of the Asian Composer's Conference-Festival held in Bangkok. During the 1990s he has returned to music and wrote a ballet, *Khaki*, which was premiered at a royal command performance in Bangkok.

Somtow began writing science fiction in the 1970s and following the appearance of his novel, *Starship and Haiku* (1981), published a series of novels under his given name. *Starship and Haiku* won the Locus Award for Best First Novel and Somtow won the John W. Campbell Award as Best New Science Fiction Writer. His first vampire novel, *Vampire Junction* (1984), heralded as one of the finer examples of the genre, appeared as the first novel under his pseudonym. Recently it was cited by the Varma Gothic Literary Society as "an outstanding contribution to **gothic** literature in the twentieth century." The novel traces the career of Timmy Valentine, a young boy made a vampire just as Vesuvius erupts and destroys his hometown.

Amazingly he has been able to survive, and has reappeared throughout history with his beautiful boyish voice. In the contemporary world he is a charismatic rock star. *Vampire Junction* prompted the writing of two sequels, *Valentine* (1992) and *Veritas* (1995).

Somtow has roamed across genres, and has written an outstanding werewolf novel, *Moondance*. He last returned to the vampire genre in the **juvenile novel**, *The Vampire's Beautiful Daughter* (1997).

In the new century, Somtow's musical side has come to the fore. Though continuing to write fiction, he is now the director of the Siam Philharmonic Orchestra and has written operas for its associated Bangkok Opera. In 2008, he announced that *Vampire Junction* was being adapted into an opera.

Sources:

Somtow, S. P. *Vampire Junction*. Norfolk, VA: Donning, 1984. 280 pp. Rept: New York: Berkley Books, 1985. 362 pp. Rept: New York: TOR, 1991.

———. *Riverrun*. New York: Avon, 1991. 259 pp.

———. *Forest of the Night*. New York: AvoNova, 1992. 258 pp.

———. *Valentine*. New York: Gollantz, 1992. 384 pp. Rept: New York: TOR, 1992. 373 pp. Reprint: New York: TOR, 1992. 373 pp.

———. *Veritas*. White Rock, BC: Transylvania Press, 1995. 333 pp. Boxed Rept: New York. TOR, 1995. 352 pp.

THE VAMPIRE BOOK: THE ENCYCLOPEDIA OF THE UNDEAD

———. *Riverrun Trilogy. Riverrun, Armorica, Yestern.* Clarkston, GA: White Wolf Publishing, 1996. 580 pp.

———. *The Vampire's Beautiful Daughter.* Athenaeum Books for Young Readers, 1997. 116 pp.

❧ South America, Vampires in ❧

South America has not been an area rich in vampire lore, however, the fact that vampire **bats** are native to the continent suggests that some recognition of vampirism would have appeared in the continent's folklore—and such is the case.

The *Asema*: Among the South American vampires, for example, was the *asema* of Surinam. The *asema* was very much like the **loogaroo** of Haiti and the *sukuyan* of Trinidad—all three were derived from the vampire/witch of West **Africa**. The asema took the form of an old man or woman who lived a normal community life during the daylight hours, but a quite different secret existence after dark. At night, it had the ability to transform into a vampire.

It did so by taking off its skin and becoming a ball of blue light. In that form, it is said that the *asema* flew through the air, entered houses in the village, and sucked the **blood** of its **victims**. If it liked the blood, it would continue taking it until the person died. Also, as with the *loogaroo*, **garlic** was the best **protection** against the *asema*. Herbs might be taken to turn the blood bitter so the *asema* would not like it, a practice noted in both Haiti and Africa. Further protection came from scattering rice or sesame **seeds** outside the door.

The seeds would be mixed with the nails of a ground owl. The *asema* had to pick up the seeds before entering, but because of the nails it would continually drop them. If it remained at its task until dawn, the **sunlight** killed it.

Those who were suspected of being an *asema* were placed under surveyance. Their identity could be determined by watching them take off their skin. The skin was then treated with salt or pepper so that it shrank, and the vampire could not get back into it.

The *Lobishomen*: From Brazil, accounts of the **lobishomen** have survived, described as a small, stumpy, and hunchbacked monkey-like being. It had a yellow face, bloodless lips, black teeth, a bushy beard, and plush-covered feet. It attacked females and caused them to become nymphomaniacs. It would become vulnerable when drunk on blood, thus making it easier to catch. It could then be crucified on a tree. The *lobishomen* was not a vampire, however, but the Portuguese form of a **werewolf**. It was created through **witchcraft** or from parents who were improperly cohabiting (incest). Its werewolf-like nature appeared about the time of puberty when it left home and, for the first time, assumed the form of one of several **animals**. From that time on, usually on Tuesday and Thursdays, it assumed an animal form. In its human form, it could be identified by a yellowish tinge to its skin and blisters on its hands from running in the woods. The werewolf condition could only be stopped if the *lobishomen* was cut with steel. Care had to be taken not to touch the werewolf's blood, however, because it was fatal. The fact of its **transformation** into different animals tied the werewolf to the **bruxa**, the Portuguese witch, who was the more vampire-like entity in Portuguese mythology.

The Cinematic Vampire: The vampire made periodic appearances in the movies of South America, primarily in Argentina and Brazil. The first South American vampire movie was *El Vampiro Negro* (1953) directed by Roman Vinoly. It was based upon the true case of **Peter Kürten**, the vampire of Düsseldorf. It was almost two decades later before a second film, *El Vampiro Archecha*, a joint Argentine-Mexican picture, was produced. This movie was notable for its inclusion of German Robles in the cast.

Brazil produced its first vampire film in 1969/70. The movie was *Um Sonho de Vampiros* (In English: *A Vampire's Dream*), a comedy about a doctor who had to choose between death or vampirism. Others released through the decade include *O Macabro Dr. Scivano* (1971), *Quem tem Medo de Lobishomem* (1974), and *A Deusa de Marmore Escrava do Diabo* (1978).

Quem tem Medo de Lobishomem has been commonly reported in vampire filmographies because of the misunderstanding that the *lobishomen* was a vampire rather than a werewolf. Over the last quarter century, only a very few vampire movies have been made in South America: *As Sete Vampiros* (In English: *The Seven Vampires*, 1986), *Sangre eternal* (*Eternal Blood*, 2002), *Tremendo Amanecer* (*Tremendous Dawn*, 2004), and *Mala Carne* (*Carnal*, 2004).

Sources:

Brautigam, Rob. "Asema: The Vampires of Surinam." *International Vampire* 1, 1 (1990): 16–17.

Gallop, Rodney. *Portugal: A Book of Folk-Ways*. Cambridge: Cambridge University Press, 1936. 291 pp.

Volta, Ornella. *The Vampire*. London: Tandem Books, 1965. 159 pp.

Southern Slavs, Vampires and the

The region consisting of what was formerly Yugoslavia and Albania, now comprises eight countries of diverse religious, ethnic, and linguistic backgrounds. Although very diverse in some respects, these eight nations share a common folk heritage that becomes quite evident upon examination of the reports of vampires and vampire beliefs in the area. Thus, it became fitting to treat vampires and vampirism in these lands as a whole phenomenon.

Background: Albania traced its history to ancient Illyria, a Roman province which reached from present-day Albania north and east across Croatia to **Romania**. Beginning in the fourth-century C.E., it was successfully invaded and occupied by Goths, Bulgars, Slavs, and Normans, successively.

Albanians, much like Romanians, asserted their Roman ties. In the twelfth century, Albania was conquered by the Ottoman Turks and remained in the empire until after World War I. As a legacy, the retreating Ottoman rulers left a population that had primarily been converted to Islam. Albania gained a measure of independence following World War I but was occupied by **Italy** during World War II. After the war, it became an independent nation. Under dictator Enver Hoxha, it was an independent Communist nation with a repressive government that was officially atheist and hostile to religion. Following Hoxha's death the country regained some degree of freedom.

Today, the majority of ethnic Albanians live outside the boundaries of their homeland. There is a small but important Albanian community in the United States, and many live in Italy. The largest number of Albanians outside of Albania live in Serbia and constitute more than ninety percent of the new country of Kosovo.

Yugoslavia was created in 1918, following World War I, as a centralized state uniting the former independent countries of Serbia, Bosnia and Herzegovina, Croatia, and Montenegro. To these countries a part of Macedonia, previously a part of the Ottoman Empire, and Slovenia, a part of the Austrian (Hapsburg) Empire, were added to the new country. Slavic tribes had first moved into the Balkan peninsula in the sixth century and by the eighth century had established themselves as the dominant influence in the area. Some unity was brought by the expansive Bulgar Empire at the beginning of the tenth century, which controlled most of present-day Serbia, Macedonia and Bosnia-Herzegovina.

Christianity moved into the Balkans in strength through the ninth century. Following the division of the Christian movement in 1054 C.E., Serbia, Montenegro, and Macedonia became largely Eastern Orthodox while Croatia and Slovenia were Roman Catholic. Bosnia-Herzegovina was split between the two groups of Christians with a significant Moslem minority. The Bosnia Muslims derive largely from the surviving remnants of the Bogomils, who had persisted to the time of the Turkish conquest and chose Islam over both Orthodoxy or Catholicism.

In 1389 the Turks defeated the combined Slavic forces at the Battle of Kosovo, following which the Ottoman Empire established itself across the southern Balkans. Only Slovenia, controlled by the Germanic Kingdom (and after the thirteenth century the Austrian) remained free of Ottoman control. During the years of Muslim control, proselytization occurred most strongly in Bosnia and Croatia. At the end of the seventeenth century the Hapsburgs pushed further south across Croatia to the Sava River which flowed into the Danube at Belgrade. This territory was formally ceded to Austria in 1699. Through the next two centuries the line between the Ottoman and Hapsburg Empire continued to fluctuate. Serbians began to assert their political independence which was formally granted in 1878.

Following World War II, strongman Josef Broz Tito ruled Yugoslavia until his death in 1980. A decade of weakened central control led to the break-up of the country at the end of the decade. Six separate countries emerged in the early 1990s, and one more in the first decade of the new century.

The Southern Slavic Vampire: The southern Slavic vampire was a variation of the **vampire of the Slavs**, and the beliefs and practices related to it were influenced by those of their neighbors in every direction. The lands of the former Yugoslavia have been cited as the most likely land of **origin** of the Slavic vampire. Jan L. Perkowski has suggested that the peculiar shape assumed by the vampire originated through a combination of Pagan and Bogomil beliefs (religious ideas dominant in the region at the end of the tenth century) that were pushed aside by the conquest of Christianity, though he has found little support for his hypothesis. In any case, through the centuries, Christian leaders attempted to destroy the belief in vampires, but were often forced to accommodate them as they remained strong among the people. Islam proved quite accommodating to the belief in vampires.

Perkowski also traced the origin of the modern word "vampire" to an old Slavic form *obyrbi* or *obirbi*. Among the various Slavic groups and their neighbors, different forms of the word evolved. Dominant in the region in the modern era was *upirina*, a Serbo-Croatian word. The word *vampir*, with the addition of an "m" sound, was also present, and in Bosnia **lampir** was used. Also present was *vukodlak* (Croatian) or *vurvu-lak* (Albanian), words similar to the Greek designation of the vampire, *vrykolakas*. *Vukodlak* was often shortened to *kudlak*. In the late nineteenth century, in Istria near the Italian border, a *kudlak* was believed to be attached to each clan. It was considered an evil being that attacked people at night. It was opposed by another entity, the *krsnik*, which often interrupted a *kudlak's* attack and fought it.

In addition to the more ubiquitous words, the term *tenatz* has been found in Montenegro. This was used interchangeably with *lampir*, the local variation on *vampir*. It was believed to be the body of a deceased person that had been taken over by evil spirits. The *tenatz* wandered the night and sucked the **blood** of the sleeping. They transformed themselves into mice to reenter their burial place. A primary means of detecting a vampire in Montenegro was to take a black horse to the cemetery.

The horse would be repelled by the grave of the vampire and refuse to walk across it. Once detected, the body would be disinterred and if, upon further determination, the **vampire hunters** decided it was a vampire, the corpse would be impaled with a **stake** and burned.

In Croatia one also might find *kosac, prikosac, tenjac,* and *lupi manari* as terms for a vampire. Albanian names for a vampire included *kukuthi* or *lugat*. The *strigon* (Slovenian) and **shtriga** (Albanian, Macedonian) are blood-sucking witches related to the Romanian *strigoi*. Another blood-sucking witch related to the *strigoi* was the *vjeshtitza* (also spelled *veshtitza*) During her field work in Montenegro early in this century, M. Edith Durham discovered that people no longer believed that *vjeshtitza* existed but retained a rich lore about them.

Vjeshtitza were older **women** who were hostile to men, other women, and all children. Possessed by an evil spirit, the sleeping witch's soul wandered at night and inhabited either a moth or a fly. Using the **flying** animal, the witch entered into the homes of neighbors and sucked the blood of **victims**. The victim, over a period of time, grew pale, developed a fever, and died. The witches were especially powerful during the first week of March, and protective measures would be taken against them. The protective ceremony, performed the first day of March each year, included the stirring the ashes in the family hearth with two horns, which were then stuck into the ash heap. **Garlic** was also a common protective substance.

The vampire was a revenant, a body that returned from the grave with some semblance of life. Some believed that it was a body inhabited by an evil spirit. A person was believed to become a vampire in several ways, but a sudden, unexpected, and/or violent accidental death, a wasting sickness, or **suicide** were seen as primary causes. M. Edith Durham, for example, recorded the story in Bosnia of an epidemic of vampirism associated with a typhus epidemic. Vampirism was also associated, in a day prior to professional undertakers, with the need to follow a prescribed process of preparation of the body of a deceased person and its subsequent burial. Irregularities in the process could cause a person to turn into a vampire. In particular, it had to be watched so that **animals,** especially cats, did not jump over the body prior to burial. In Macedonia, if a cat did jump over the body, the corpse would then be pierced with two needles. Vampirism was also assumed to be contagious—an attack by a vampire would lead to vampirism.

The *shtriga* and *vjeshtitza* were blood-sucking witches.

Although not revenants, the witches were members of the community believed to be living incognito. They were difficult to identify, although a sure sign was a young girl's hair turning white. *Shtriga* attacked in the night, usually in the form of an animal such as a moth, fly, or bee. In fact, the word *shtriga* was derived from the Latin *strix*, screech owl, that referred to a flying demon that attacked in the night. The Albanian *shtriga* could be detected by placing a cross made with pig bones on the church door when it was crowded with people. The witch was unable to leave the church and would be seen running around the church trying to find a safe exit.

The *shtrega* traveled at night and, often in the form of an animal, attacked people and sucked their blood. If a *shtriga* was sighted, it could be followed and positively identified because it had to stop and vomit up the blood it had sucked. The vomited blood could then be used to make an amulet to protect one from **witchcraft** and vampirism.

The *strigon* of Slovenia was also a bloodsucking witch. The term was derived from the Latin *striga* (witch), which in turn was derived from *strix*, originally a screech owl that was perceived as a demon that attacked infants in the night. The term was also used more generally to describe a vampire.

Slovenian historian Baron Jan Vajkart Valvasor (1641–1693) recounted the killing of a *strigon* in Istria (western Slovenia). A person who was the suspected vampire had recently died and was seen by several people walking around the town. His suspected vampirism was reported by his wife after he returned home and had sexual relations with her. The *strigon* was killed by a **stake** made of **hawthorn** driven into its stomach while a priest read an exorcism. The corpse was then decapitated. All the while, the corpse reacted as if it were alive—it recoiled as the stake was driven in, cried while the exorcism was pronounced, and screamed out as its head was severed. After the **decapitation**, it bled profusely.

Vampires attacked people it had strong emotional attachments to—both positive (family and friends) and negative (those with whom it had quarreled in life)—and sucked their blood. A sure sign of a vampire was an outbreak of various kinds of contagious illnesses. People who became sick and died from what were then unknown causes were often considered victims of vampiric activity. The vampire could also attack the village livestock in a similar manner.

The southern Slavic vampire was, like that among the **Gypsies**, capable of having sex with a spouse or lover. Durham related the story of a girl in Montenegro who was forced to marry the man chosen by her parents rather than her true love. Her beloved left the country and, in his despair, died. He returned from the grave as a vampire and visited the girl who eventually became pregnant by him. In appearance, the child closely resembled the deceased man.

The villagers were frustrated because the man had died abroad, and thus they could not destroy him. Bodies of males uncovered in the search for a vampire would often have an erect sex organ.

The existence of a vampire could be detected by a variety of means. In Montenegro, for example, a black horse (in Albania, a white horse was used) would be led to a local cemetery—the horse would be repelled by a vampire's grave. The horse usually had to be ridden by a boy who had not yet experienced puberty or a virginal girl. In Croatia, there were reports of strange animal sounds coming from the grave of someone later determined to be a vampire. The body was then disinterred. The discovery of a body turned face down or bloated to the point that the skin was stretched like a drum indicated that the correct body had been uncovered. If only bones remained in the grave, it was not considered a vampire. The Serbians and Bosnians shared the belief with Gypsies in the **dhampir**, the son of a vampire. The offspring of a vampire was considered to have the power to both see and destroy his father and other vampires. In Macedonia, there was the belief in the power of people born on Saturday. Such Sabbatarians, as they were termed, were thought to have a great influence over vampires including the power to lure them into traps where they could be destroyed. On Saturdays, the Sabbatarians could see and kill vampires.

For average people, **protection** from vampires was secured by barricading their homes with thorn bushes (an old remedy for witches).

Once discovered, the vampire could be rendered harmless or destroyed by the traditional means of fixing the body to the ground with a stake and/or decapitation. In the most severe cases, the body might be dismembered or burned. In general, a priest was asked to be present to repeat the funeral prayers over the person who was perceived to be dying a second time. (As part of an attempt to stop the mutilation of dead bodies, the church in Serbia and Montenegro threatened any priest who cooperated in such activity with excommunication.) In both Montenegro and Albania, it was believed that a vampire could be stopped by hamstringing the corpse. G. F. Abbott reported observing the destruction of a vampire by scalding it with boiling **water** and driving a long nail in its navel. The body was returned to the ground and the grave covered with millet **seeds** so if the vampire was not destroyed, it would waste its time counting the millet until dawn. In Croatia, it was believed that a stake driven into the ground over the grave prevented the vampire from rising. In Serbia, a white-thorn or hawthorn stake or other sharp objects might be stuck into the ground over a vampire, or a sickle placed over the neck of the corpse when it was reburied.

It was common among the southern Slavs (as among the Greeks) to dig up bodies some years after their burial, to cleanse the bones, and rebury them in a permanent location. It was important that the soft tissue be completely decomposed by that time—delays in decomposition were cause for concern and could lead to suggestions of vampirism.

The Vampire Epidemics, 1727–1732: The beliefs and practices of the southern Slavs concerning vampires were brought to the attention of western Europe primarily through two spectacular cases that were publicized due to official inquiries into the cases by Austrian authorities. Both cases occurred in a region of Serbia north of Belgrade that had been taken over by Austria from the Ottoman Empire at the end of the seventeenth century and, subsequently, incorporated into the Hungarian province. One incident began with the sudden death of **Peter Plogojowitz**. He was seen by his family several nights after his death. Shortly thereafter, Plogojowitz appeared to several people in their dreams. In one week, nine people died of no known cause. When the local army com-

mander arrived to investigate, Plogojowitz's body was taken from the grave. It was found to be as fresh as it had been when buried. The eyes were open and the complexion was ruddy. His mouth was smeared with fresh blood. Fresh skin appeared just below an old layer of dead skin he appeared to be shedding, and his hair and nails had grown. It was concluded that he was a vampire. Plogojowitz's body was staked and burned.

More famous than the Plogojowitz incident was the case of **Arnold Paul**. Paul lived in the village of Medvegia (spelled in numerous ways in different sources), Serbia, north of Paracin. He told his neighbors that while he had been serving in the army in Turkey, he had been bitten by a vampire. A week later he died. Several weeks after his death, people began to report seeing him, and four such people died. On the fortieth day after his burial, the grave was opened and he was found in a lifelike condition. When his body was cut, he bled freely. When staked, it was later reported that he groaned aloud. He and the four people he reportedly vampirized were decapitated and their bodies burned.

The Arnold Paul case should have ended with his funeral pyre. However, in 1731, some seventeen people in the village died of an unknown cause. Vampirism was suggested. Word of the unusual occurrences reached all the way to Vienna, and the emperor ordered an official inquiry. Following the arrival of Johannes Fluckinger in Medvegia, the body of a new suspected vampire was disinterred. He was also found to be in a healthy state. After some further investigation, it was discovered that Paul had vampirized several cows. Those who ate the meat from the cows were infected with a vampiric condition. The bodies of the recently dead were then disinterred and all were staked and burned.

Fluckinger returned to Vienna and presented the emperor with a complete report. During 1732, the report and several journalistic versions of it became bestsellers throughout Europe. The two cases became the basis of a heated debate in German universities, and after a decade of arguing, the participants concluded that vampires did not exist. However, the debate spurred the interest of **Dom Augustin Calmet**, a French biblical scholar, who, in 1746, completed a most important treatise on the subject published in England as *The Phantom World*.

The fame of Plogojowitz and Paul should have focused attention on Serbia and the southern Slavic countries. Instead, from mere geographical ignorance, many involved in the debate placed the occurrences in **Hungary**, and thus Hungary—which has the least vampire mythology of all the Eastern European countries—became known for vampirism. As a result, scrutiny of vampire beliefs was directed away from Serbia and its southern Slavic neighbors. The misdirection given vampire phenomena by Calmet was reinforced by the writings of **Montague Summers** and number of writers on vampires who essentially copied him.

The vampire has had a long and interesting history in what is now the independent country of Slovenia. Largely Roman Catholic in background, the country existed for many centuries as an Austrian province; however, south of the Drava River, especially in rural areas, Slovenes resisted Germanization and retained their own language and folklore. One of the earliest books to deal with vampires was Count Valvasor's *Die Ehre des Herzogthums Krain* (1689), which told the story of Grando, a peasant of the district of Kranj. A quiet man in life, in death Grando began to attack his neighbors and his body was ordered exhumed. His body was found with ruddy complexion and he appeared to have a smile on his face. A priest called upon the vampire to look to his savior Jesus

Christ, at which the body took on a sad expression and tears were flowing down his cheek. The body was then decapitated and reburied. A more general account of vampires in the region was given in the famous 1734 travelogue, *The Travels of Three English Gentlemen*.

Modern Vampires among the Southern Slavs: Vampire beliefs have continued into the twentieth century, in spite of several generations of hostile governments that denounced both religion and superstitions. Folklorists have had no trouble locating vampire stories. The depth and persistence of the vampire belief was vividly illustrated in a most unexpected manner early in 1993, in the midst of the most violent era experienced directly by Serbia following the break-up of the former Yugoslavia. During that year, a man made a number of appearances on Serbia's state-controlled television station at the height of the country's conflict. He, in all seriousness, argued that at the moment when final destruction threatened the Serbian nation, a fleet of vampires would arise from the cemeteries to defeat Serbia's enemies.

In preparation for this event, he advised viewers to keep a supply of garlic at hand lest the vampires attack them by mistake.

Sources:

Abbott, G. F. *Macedonian Folklore*. Chicago: Argonaut Inc., 1969. 372 pp.

Barber, Paul. *Vampires, Burial, and Death: Folklore and Reality*. New Haven, CT: Yale University Press, 1988. 236 pp.

D'Assier, Adolphe. *Posthumous Humanity: A Study of Phantoms*. San Diego, CA: Wizards Bookshelf, 1981. 360 pp.

Durham, M. Edith. "Of Magic, Witches and Vampires in the Balkans." *Man* 121 (December 1923): 189–192.

Kinzer, Stephen. "At Root of Mayhem: A Bizarre Dream World Called Serbia." *Star Tribune* (Minneapolis) (May 16, 1993): 11A.

Perkowski, Jan L. *The Darkling: A Treatise on Slavic Vampirism*. Columbus, OH: Slavica Publishers, 1989. 174 pp.

————, ed. *Vampires of the Slavs*. Cambridge, MA: Slavica Publishers, 1976. 294 pp.

Petrovitch, Woislav M. *Hero Tales and Legends of the Serbians*. London: George G. Harrap, 1914. 393 pp. Rept. New York: Kraus Reprint Co., 1972. 393 pp.

❨ Southey, Robert (1774–1843) ❩

Robert Southey was a British poet and writer who was among the first to introduce the vampire theme into English literature. While attending Oxford University, he met **Samuel Taylor Coleridge**, who became a lifelong friend, mentor, and supporter. Toward the end of the 1790s, Southey's health failed and he moved to Portugal to recuperate. While there he completed his first major work, a long poem titled *Thalaba the Destroyer*.

Thalaba was to be the first of a series of epic poems drawing upon the mythologies of different cultures and portraying the fight of good over evil. It was in the midst of his story that he came face to face with the vampire.

Southey was inspired to write *Thalaba* by the *Arabian Tales*, which mentioned the Domdaniel, a training school for evil magicians. In the story, set in Arabia, the title character lived in exile with his mother. His father and kinspeople had been slain by the evil magicians. The magicians resided in a cavern where they kept his father's sword—which was to be the instrument of their destruction. Thalaba's life turned into a quest to find the cavern, retrieve the sword, and avenge his father.

In the midst of his quest (in Book VII of the poem), Thalaba sought shelter from the rain in the chamber of the tombs and there had a brief encounter with a vampire. The vampire was none other than his **bride** Oneiza, who had recently died, on their wedding day. Oneiza's body had been reanimated by an invading demonic force. Her cheeks were livid, her lips were blue, and her eyes possessed a terrible brightness. Thalaba grasped a lance and:

> … through the vampire corpse He thrust his lance; it fell, And howling with the wound, Its fiendish tenant fled.

Immediately afterward, Oneiza's spirit appeared and urged Thalaba to continue his great quest. In evoking the vampire, Southey demonstrated his awareness of the vampire tales from continental Europe. He mentioned the outbreaks of vampirism on the continent early in the eighteenth century in his notes, especially the case of **Arnold Paul** in Serbia, and more recent cases in **Greece**. In relating the case

Writer Robert Southey incorporated vampirism into many of his works.

of the vampire Oneiza, Southey assumed the Greek notion that a vampire was a corpse inhabited by an evil spirit. Equally important for Southey were the translations of the German poem "Lenore," which had been published in English by William Taylor in 1796, and adapted in a more popular form by Sir Walter Scott later that same year.

Even before finishing *Thalaba,* Southey wrote a ballad titled "The Old Woman of Berkeley." The title character was a witch who possessed the **characteristics** of a *lamiai,* the ancient Greek vampire-like creature who preyed upon infants. As she herself was made to say:

> From sleeping babes I have sucked the breath, And breaking by charms the sleep of death, I have call'd the dead from their graves.

Thus, Southey vied with Coleridge for the distinction of having introduced the vampire into English literature. Coleridge's poem, "Christabel," was published before *Thalaba,* and while most agree that it was a vampire poem, Coleridge never identified it as such. After Southey introduced the vampire to the English-speaking public, he did not linger over the vampire myth or further develop **gothic** themes. He did, however, go on to become one of England's finer writers, the author of numerous poems and prose works of history and biography. In general, his prose writing received better reviews than his poetry, although he was credited with expanding the number of metrical patterns available to poets who came after him.

Sources:

Haller, William. *The Early Life of Robert Southey, 1774–1803*. New York: Columbia University Press, 1917. 353 pp.

Pratt, Lynda. *Robert Southey and the Contexts of English Romanticism*. Farnham, Surrey, UK: Ashgate Publishing, 2006. 267 pp.

Southey, Robert. *The Poetical Works of Robert Southey*. Paris: A. and W. Galignani, 1829. 718 pp.

Speck, W. A. *Robert Southey: Entire Man of Letters*. New Haven, CT: Yale University Press, 2006. 336 pp.

Spain, Vampires in

Spain, geographically separated from the Eastern European home of the Slavic vampire, has been largely devoid of vampire reports in its folklore tradition, although there has been a strong presence of **witchcraft**. Like the witch in ancient **Rome**, medieval **Italy** (*strega*), and **Portugal** (*bruxa*), the witch in medieval Spain was believed to have the power to transform into various **animal** forms, to steal infants, and to vampirize children. Vampirism of children, for example, figured prominently in a lengthy trial at Logrono in the fall of 1610. A century earlier, one of the leading Roman Catholic spokespersons on witchcraft, Fray Martin Castenega, cited vampirism as one of the evil actions in which witches engaged. Spain did not participate significantly in either the vampire debates of the eighteenth century or the development of the literary vampire of the nineteenth century. However, in the post-World War II world of the cinematic vampire, Spain has played a strong role.

The Cinematic Vampire: The vampire in Spanish films emerged at the end of the 1960s just as the Italian and Mexican vampire movies were at their peak. The first Spanish vampire film seems to have been *Parque de Juegos* (*Park of Games*), a 1963 production based on a Ray Bradbury story. It stood alone until 1968, when *La Marca del Hombe Lobo* (*The Mark of the Wolfman*) and *Malenka la Vampira* (a joint Spanish-Italian production released in English as *Fangs of the Living Dead*) appeared.

Fangs of the Living Dead introduced director Amando de Ossoio who, through the 1970s, became one of the most prolific instigators of vampire films. He successively directed *La Noche del Terror Ciego* (*Tombs of the Blind Dead*, 1971), *El Ataque de los Muertos sin Ojos* (*Return of the Evil Dead*, 1973), *La Noche de los Brujos* (*Night of the Sorcerers*, 1973), *El Buque Maldito* (*Horror of the Zombies*, 1974), and *La Noche de las Saviotas* (*Night of the Seagulls*, 1975). He is most remembered for introducing the blind vampires in *La Noche del Terror Ciego*, which centered upon the Knights Templars, a religious order whose members were blinded and murdered in the thirteenth century. They returned in two of Ossorio's other films to attack people they located with their acute hearing.

In 1970, Leon Klimovsky, an experienced Spanish director, joined veteran werewolf star Paul Naschy to produce his first vampire movie, *La Noche de Walpurgis* (*The Werewolf vs. the Vampire Woman*). In this fifth in a series of werewolf movies for Naschy, his character, Count Waldemar Daninsky, attacked the vampire witch Countess Waldessa. Klimovsky then made *La Orgia Nocturna de los Vampiros* (*The Vampire's Night Orgy*, 1973), *La Saga de las Draculas* (*The Dracula Saga*, 1973), and *El Extrano Amor de los Vampiros* (*Strange Love of the Vampires*, 1974). Naschy first encountered a vampire in

Dracula vs. Frankenstein (1969), one of the earlier Daninsky films. He would later slip out of his werewolf role to play **Dracula** in *Le Gran Amor del Conde Dracula* (*Dracula's Great Love*, 1972). In 2004, director Don Glut coaxed Naschy out of retirement to make his first appearance in an American movie, *Countess Dracula's Orgy of Blood.*

By far the most renowned of Spain's vampire filmmakers was Jesus Franco, Spain's equivalent of Italy's **Mario Bava**. In his first vampire film, Franco cajoled **Hammer Films** star **Christopher Lee** to Spain to do a remake of *Dracula*. Lee was intrigued by the opportunity to play a more faithful Dracula than he had been allowed to perform in England. The result was the film *El Conde Dracula* (1970), which had a script (and a characterization of Dracula) that followed the book more closely than either the **Universal Pictures** or Hammer productions. No one realized at the time, given the movie's slow and ponderous pace, that this would be Franco's best vampire movie.

That same year Franco also made *Vampyros Lesbos die erbin des Dracula*, his version of the **Elizabeth Bathory** story, which was more typical of the adult erotic vampire movies Franco was famous for making. The German version, released in 1971, included heightened levels of sex and violence, both of which

Publicity photo from the film *La fille de Dracula* ("Dracula's Daughter") by Spanish filmmaker Jesus Franco.

were toned down for the Spanish and English-language versions. He followed in 1972 with *La Fille de Dracula* (*Dracula's Daughter*), another adult erotic movie that began with the death of Dracula and followed the adventures of his female offspring. Also that year, he filmed *Dracula contra Frankenstein*, which continued his vampire series while launching a three-film Frankenstein series. In the initial film, Dr. Frankenstein revived Dracula to create a vampire horde as part of a plan to take over the world.

In 1973, Franco moved on to make his version of the **"Carmilla"** story, *La Comtesse aux Seins Nus*, an x-rated story of Countess Irina Karnstein, a voiceless descendent of Carmilla who attacked men and killed them through fellatio. The heightened element of **sexuality** was the only thing of value in this film, and much of the sexual content was deleted in various ways for the different markets. Only the nudity remained in the American video version, finally released as *Erotikill*. Following these six movies, Franco seemed to have exhausted the vampire theme. He turned to other topics and continued to release a large number of movies annually. However, these six films—the one notable effort with Lee and the five erotic films—were enough to establish him in the vampire cinema hall of fame and provide Spanish vampire films with a distinctive image.

After an intense period of releasing vampire movies, Spanish filmmakers, like their colleagues in neighboring countries, reacted to the pressure from American movies and largely abandoned the vampire (and horror) theme. Only one vampire film, *Tiempos duros para Dracula* (1976) was made during the last half of the decade. Naschy, who has continued his werewolf series, revived the vampire twice in the 1980s. *El Returno del Hombre Lobo* (released in English as *The Craving*), the ninth wolfman movie, pitted Daninsky against Elizabeth Bathory and her cohorts. Then, in 1982, Naschy made a children's movie, *Buenas Noches, Senor Monstruo*, which included Dracula and other famous monsters. Of the several vampire movies made in Spain since the beginning of the 1990s, two feature films, *Killer Barbys* (1996) and its sequel *Killer Barbys vs. Dracula* (2002), have received the most widespread distribution. Both were directed by Jesus Franco.

Sources:

Baroja, Julio Caro. *The World of the Witches*. Chicago: University of Chicago Press, 1965. 313 pp.

Henningsen, Gustav. *The Witches' Advocate: Basque Witchcraft and the Spanish Inquisition (1910–1614)*. Reno, NV: University of Nevada Press, 1980. 607 pp.

Jones, Stephen. *The Illustrated Vampire Movie Guide*. London: Titan Books, 1993. 144 pp.

Pattison, Barrie. *The Seal of Dracula*. New York: Bounty Books, 1975. 136 pp.

Tohill, Cathal, and Peter Tombs. *Immortal Tales: Sex and Horror Cinema in Europe, 1956–1984*. London: Primitive Press, 1994. 272 pp.

Spider

Beginning in 1931, the Spider, a character created by author Grant Stockbridge (pseudonym of Norvell Page), emerged as one of the most popular heroes of **pulp magazine** fiction. Two years later, his popular adventures supported the formation of a monthly magazine, *The Spider*, with episodes that would be gathered at a later date and reissued in books. The Spider dedicated itself to the task of killing criminals and worked as a vigilante outside of the law and public approval. In 1935, on the heels of the popularity of **Bela Lugosi's** *Dracula* **(1931)**, the Spider encountered one of its most horrendous foes, the Vampire King, and began the process of **destroying** this evil royalty.

The Spider was the secret identity of wealthy businessman Richard Wentworth. After donning a free-flowing uniform complete with hood and cape, a bullet-proof vest, false teeth, and mask, Wentworth turned into a crime fighter on the streets of New York City. The Spider's major assets were agility, intelligence, and determination. It was strong and acquitted itself quite well in hand-to-hand fighting. Its major weapon, above and beyond normal weapons like handguns, was a gun that squirted a gooey liquid that formed a web, entrapping its target. Unlike modern superheroes, the Spider had no supernormal powers. It did have a sidekick, Ram Singh from India, who served as his ultimate back-up system.

The Vampire King, the 1930s equivalent of the super villain, was a monster from **South America**. It is modelled not on the European vampire, but on the *camazotz*, the Mayan bat god/demon who made its most memorable appearance in the ancient text, *Popol Vuh*. It appeared as a large bat-man with exaggerated and somewhat grotesque features, including huge ears, wings, and claw-like hands with slender, elongated fingers. It did not possess supernatural powers and could not, for example, change his outward form. It was adept at **flying** and had great physical **strength**. The Vampire King's greatest asset, however, was the control over a large flock of **vampire bats**, which he could command to attack. Two South American natives accompanied him and used poisonous darts. Two huge half man/half animal monsters also accompanied him—a pig-man and an armadillo-man.

The final confrontation between the Spider and the Vampire King occurred after the Spider's capture. While the Vampire King conversed with the crime bosses to negotiate control of their North American enterprises, it drank the Spider's **blood**, which had been drained into a chalice. The Vampire King offered the criminals a sip as a means of sealing their evil pact. The Spider recovered just in time and his comrades appeared to assist it. The fight that ensued led to the Vampire King's destruction.

The Spider was brought to the screen in several Saturday matinee serials of the 1930s, but the Vampire King was not among its movie foes. Although a major source for contemporary superheroes, and seemingly a direct inspiration for Spiderman, the Spider was all but forgotten except with a few movie buffs, when, in 1991, he was revived by Eclipse Books in a new **comic book** series.

Sources:

Harmon, Jim, and Donald F. Glut. *The Great Movie Serials: Their Sound and Fury*. Garden City, NY: Doubleday & Company, 1972. 384 pp.

The Spider: Reign of the Vampire King. 1–3. Forestville, CA: Eclipse Books, 1991–1992.

Stockbridge, Grant. *Death Reign of the Vampire King: a Spider Novel*. London: Mews Books, 1935, 1976. 128 pp. Rept. New York: Carroll & Graf, 1992. 319 pp.

Spike

Spike, also known as William the Bloody, was a vampire character from the ***Buffy the Vampire Slayer*** television series, portrayed by James Marsters. He made his initial appearance in season two, arriving in town as one episode closed. Later, however, he became—along with his female cohort Drusilla—one of the show's more popular villains. He hung around long after his initial story line was exhausted and emerged as one of the leading ongoing characters on the show. After the *Buffy* series ended, a place was found for him on the *Buffy* spin-off show ***Angel***.

Spike's life before his arrival in Sunnydale, California, (Buffy's hometown) was told in various episodes of *Buffy*. He emerged as a young poet in London, England, at some point in the late nineteenth century. He got his nickname, William the Bloody, from friends who thought his poetry was "Bloody awful," but was saved from a life of bad reviews by Drusilla, the slightly deranged vampire who turned him. He then met the evil Angel (before he was cursed with the return of his soul), and was thus trained in the vampire life by the one known as Angelus. Angel aside, however, while developing his close relationship with Drusilla, Spike turned on those who had complained that they had rather have a railroad spike driven through their head than listen to his poetry. From his acts of revenge, he adopted the name by which he became known. He seemed to enjoy killing people.

Spike often bragged about killing two slayers (one in China in 1900 and another, named Nikki Wood, in 1977 in New York) and came to Sunnydale to kill number three. He wore a black jacket which he took from the second slayer. He had at least one encounter with **Dracula**, who tossed Spike's autographed copy of **Bram Stoker**'s novel into a fire. Spike claimed that Dracula owed him eleven pounds for the lost book. He also came to Sunnydale (the sight of the Hellmouth, the entrance to the hell realms) in an attempt to find healing for Drusilla, who had been hurt while under attack from a mob.

By the time Spike and Drusilla arrived in Sunnydale, Spike had taken on the persona of a punk rocker. His love of killing was immediately manifested when he attacked a group of people at Sunnydale High School and almost got to Buffy. He then aligned with Angel, but broke with him when Angel (now reverted to his evil side) attempted to make Drusilla his lover. The ups and downs of his relationship with Drusilla became a subplot of season three, and eventually took him from the city.

Spike returned to Sunnydale in a quest to find the Gem of Amarra, a ring with the power to make any vampire immune to **sunlight**. His effort was thwarted, however, and he was eventually taken captive by the Initiative, a secret government agency that was tracking and fighting the various kinds of creatures that Buffy opposed. It planted a microchip in Spike that prevented him from biting (or otherwise hurting) any human. Once freed of their control, he turned to Buffy for assistance. Over the next year, he assisted Buffy friends, but also betrayed them on occasion—constantly searching for a way to get the chip removed. He also fell in love with Buffy, only to have her constantly reject him. She was horrified to discover that he had a robot double of her upon which to exercise his fantasies.

A significant change in Buffy and Spike's relationship began when he refused to disclose the identity of Buffy's sister Dawn as the "Key" which the demon goddess glory was seeking. He then aligned with Buffy friends to continue the fight against vampires in the period after Buffy's death at the end of season five and prior her resurrection in season six. His unusual status as a member of the close circle around Buffy allowed him to become Buffy's confidant. It is to Spike that Buffy revealed that she had been in a heavenly state while dead and was unhappy with her friends for bringing her back. While still grieving her situation, Buffy began a sexual relationship with Spike, notable for its violence . Buffy finally ended the relationship, considering it unsatisfying. Unwilling to accept being cut off, Spike attempted to rape Buffy. Finally, realizing that in his present condition he could never have Buffy, he departed Sunnydale for a remote location where he found a shaman who was capable of giving him his soul (the major component being a conscience).

As the only vampire other than Angel with a soul, Spike returned to Sunnydale ready to make things right with Buffy and to assist her with the last battle with the ultimate opponent, the First Evil. Meanwhile, while trying to establish some trust, his new conscience forces him to deal with guilt over his past actions. Buffy finally took him in and oversaw his recovery. She also facilitated the removal of his chip. He then had to withstand the attention of the son of the slayer Nikki Wood, whom he had killed, and who, as the new principal of Sunnydale High, had aligned with Buffy.

While not renewing their sexual relationship, Spike and Buffy became close emotionally. In the final battle with the horde of vampires emerging from the Hellmouth, Buffy trusted Spike with the key action. He wore a magical amulet, and in an act of self-sacrifice, allowed its energy to radiate from him to destroy the horde and close the Hellmouth. In the process, Spike was consumed along with all of Sunnydale. Just before Spike died, Buffy professed her love for him.

As had been demonstrated throughout the *Buffy* and *Angel* series, it was difficult to kill a vampire with any finality. Thus, it was not surprising that, given Spike's popularity, he reappeared on the continuing *Angel* series. He was resurrected by another amulet, but initially manifested as a ghost-like being. He haunted the law firm Wolfram and Hart, whose Los Angeles office has been taken over by Angel and his new group of

colleagues. After some time, he was finally reembodied. His rivalry with Angel gave him an ambiguous role, but he truly aligned with Angel only after one of his team, a woman called Fred (short for Winifred) was killed by a demon Illyria, who took over her body. In the final episode, Spike joined Angel in the battle to sever, at least temporarily, the Senior Partners of Wolfram and Hart's positioning on earth , by destroying the Circle of the Black Thorn, their major point of access.

That Spike ended his television appearances on *Angel* has had serious implications for the continuation of the character in the post-television **comic books**. While both Spike and Angel have had cameo appearances in the season eight series of *Buffy the Vampire Slayer* comics from Dark Horse Comics, Spike's major adventures have been in the *Angel* comics from IDW Publishing. In *Angel: After the Fall*, the official comics continuing the television storyline, we learn that both Spike and Angel survived the battle that was just beginning as the television series ended, but that the city of Los Angeles now exists in a hell dimension. As Angel regrouped, Spike took up residence in Beverly Hills, where he and Illyria were living outwardly as Demon Lords, while assisting humans to escape life in Los Angeles, and joining Angel's efforts to bring down his fellow demon lords. Spike also continued to protect Illyria, because she possessed the essence of Fred, and hence the possibility of her resurrection.

As Spike's character increased in popularity, he began to appear on all of the **paraphernalia** that developed out of the television series. He was pictured on numerous **trading cards**, had his own action figures, and eventually, as noted above, his own comic books (from IDW). Spike has also prompted significant comment from scholars studying *Buffy* and *Angel*.

Sources:

Amy-Chin, Dee. and Milly Williamson, eds. *The Vampire Spike in Text and Fandom: Unsettling Oppositions in Buffy the Vampire Slayer. European Journal of Cultural Studies:* 8, 3 (August 2005).

Holder, Nancy, with Jeff Mariotte and Maryelizabeth Hart. *Buffy the Vampire Slayer: The Watcher's Guide.* Vol. 2. New York: Pocket Books, 2000. 472 pp.

Ruditis, Paul. *Buffy the Vampire Slayer: The Watcher's Guide.* Vol 3. New York: Simon Spotlight, 2004. 359 pp.

Stafford, Nikki. *Bite Me! The Unofficial Guide to Buffy the Vampire Slayer.* Toronto: ECW Press, 2007. 397 pp.

Topping, Keith. *Hollywood Vampire: A Revised and Updated Unofficial and Unauthorized Guide to Angel.* London: Virgin, 2001. 280 pp.

———. *The Complete Slayer: An Unofficial and Unauthorised Guide to Every Episode of "Buffy the Vampire Slayer."* London: Virgin, 2004. 704 pp.

Yeffeth, Glenn, ed. *Five Seasons of Angel: Science Fiction and Fantasy Writers Discuss Their Favorite Vampire.* Dallas, TX: Benbella Books, 2004. 216 pp.

Stake

The best known way to kill a vampire is by staking it in the heart. This method was prescribed by **Sheridan Le Fanu** in his novella, **"Carmilla,"** and was a remedy later lauded by **Bram Stoker** for his novel, *Dracula*, and repeated in numerous vampire movies.

Christopher Lee falls through the ice in *Dracula, Prince of Darkness*.

The idea of staking the corpse of a suspected vampire or revenant was quite an ancient practice. It was found across Europe and originated in an era prior to the widespread use of **coffins**. The corpses of persons suspected of returning from their graves would be staked as a means of keeping them attached to the ground below their body. Stakes might be driven through the stomach (far easier to penetrate than the heart area, which required penetration of the rib cage). The body might also be turned face down and the stake driven through the back. In some areas, an iron stake or long needle might be used, while in others not only was wood used but the actual wood to be used prescribed. Ash, aspen (a common wood across northern Europe), juniper, and/or **hawthorn** were noted in the literature. Additionally, a stake might be driven into the ground over the grave as a way to block the vampire's rising.

Once coffins were in popular use, the purpose of staking changed somewhat. Where previously the object of the staking was to fix the body to the ground, the purpose of the staking became a frontal assault upon the corpse itself. By attacking the heart, the organ that pumped the **blood**, the bloodsucking vampire could be killed. Staking the heart was somewhat analogous to the practice of driving nails into a vampire's head.

In many Russian stories, it was noted that the stake had to be driven in with a single stroke—a second stroke would reanimate the vampire. This method seems to be derived from a belief in old Slavic tales that advised elimination of enemies, of whatever sort, with one blow.

In Bram Stoker's *Dracula*, **Lucy Westenra** was finally laid to rest by the dual process of thrusting a stake in her heart and **decapitation**. A similar process was used for the three **vampire brides** who resided in **Castle Dracula**. However, Dracula himself was killed by decapitation and a knife plunged into his chest. The idea of staking the vampire became fixed in the modern vampire myth in the play by **Hamilton Deane**, which deviated from the novel by having the men who tracked Dracula to **Carfax** destroy the vampire by staking him. That action was repeated in the **Universal Pictures** version of *Dracula* (1931) starring **Bela Lugosi**.

The prominence of the stake led to much speculation in various novels and movies concerning the rationale for the use of wooden stakes. For most, the stake simply did brute physical damage to the heart. Others believed that the vampire was directly affected by wood. For some, the stake finally killed the vampire, while others saw it as a mere temporary measure. Thus, the removal of the stake became a means of reviving the vampire for a literary or movie sequel. **Robert Edward Lory** made one of the more novel uses of the stake. In his novels, his hero Dr. Damien Hough placed a small wooden sliver into Dracula's body before reviving him. Thus, if Dracula failed to obey Hough or attacked him, the sliver would be thrust into Dracula's heart returning him to his deathlike state. One of the more (unintentionally) comic moments in vampire movies occurred in *Dracula Has Risen from His Grave* (1968) when **Christopher Lee** pulled a stake from his own heart.

Sources:

Barber, Paul. *Vampires, Burial, and Death: Folklore and Reality*. New Haven, CT: Yale University Press, 1988. 236 pp.

Steele, Barbara (1938–)

Barbara Steele, a horror movie star of the 1960s and 1970s, was born in Liverpool, England. After acting in several movies, *Sapphire* (1958) and *Bachelor of Hearts* (1958), she moved to Hollywood to work for 20th Century Fox. In the early 1960s, with Hollywood writers on strike, she traveled to Italy where she found work starring in director **Mario Bava**'s first movie, *La Maschera de Demonio* (released in English as *Black Sunday*), based on Nikolai Gogol's short story "The Vig". This single movie, which happened to be a vampire feature, made her a horror star and soon became her most famous role, the seventeenth-century vampiric witch Princess Asa and her double, Princess Katia. The story began with the whipping and execution of the princess and her consort. Princess Asa, as played by Steele, defiantly showed her anger until a mask lined with spikes was driven into her face. The scene then abruptly changed to the nineteenth century. Two travelers were stranded in front of a castle ruin where their carriage broke down. They explored the castle and discovered the crypt that housed Princess Asa's body.

One of the travelers removed the mask and a cross that had been placed in the body. When an accidental cut allowed the traveler's **blood** to drop on the corpse, Princess Asa and her lover were revived. Meanwhile, the other traveler met Princess Katia, the witch's great granddaughter. The situation was thus created for the renewed confronta-

Barbara steele as the vampire princess in the film *Black Sunday.*

tion between good and evil, represented by Steele's two characters, which provided the main plot of the film. Within the larger context, however, Steele brought the plot to life by her embodiment of a number of ambiguities: beauty hiding decay and sensuality in the midst of horror.

In 1961, Steele briefly returned to Hollywood to play Vincent Price's wife in **Roger Corman**'s *The Pit and the Pendulum.* She played an unfaithful wife trying to drive her husband mad. Although she received good reviews in the United States, Steele returned to Europe to appear in a string of horror movies during the next few years, including *The Horrible Dr.*

Hitchcock (1962), *The Ghost* (1962), and *I Lunghi Capelli della Morte* (1964). Along the way, she also appeared in a number of non-horror movies, the most prominent were Federico's Fellini's *8 1/2* (1962) and *Young Torless* (1966) with German director Volker Schlondorff. Her work in these films, however, was overshadowed by her horror roles and the adulation showered upon her by horror fans.

Of her horror roles during the 1960s, five were in vampire movies: *Castle of Blood* (1964), *Terror Creatures from the Grave* (1965), *Nightmare Castle* (1965), *An Angel for Satan* (1966), and *Revenge of the Blood Beast* (1966). *Castle of Blood,* based on a story by **Edgar Allan Poe**, took place in a castle inhabited by spirits of the dead, one of whom was played by Steele. These spirits appeared every November 2 to re-experience their deaths and to obtain the blood of the living, a prerequisite if they hoped to return the following year. In *Nightmare Castle,* Steele played a murdered wife who returned to avenge herself against her former husband. The vampiric theme was evident also in *The Horrible Dr. Hitchcock* (1962). The movie's title character attempted to drain Steele's blood to allow another woman to stay young.

After completing *Revenge of the Blood Beast,* Steele married James Poe and began a period of relative inactivity, although in 1968 she took a part in *The Crimson Cult.* She had hoped to get the lead in *They Shoot Horses, Don't They?* for which her husband wrote the screenplay, but the part was given to Susannah York. During the 1980s, Steele became acquainted with producer **Dan Curtis** and assumed roles in his popular television miniseries, *The Winds of War* (1983) and *War and Remembrance* (1988–1989). She served as the associate producer of the former and a producer of the latter. Steele's work led to her most recent role in a vampire production. In 1990, Curtis sold the idea of bringing the very successful daytime soap opera of the 1960s, **Dark Shadows**, back to **television** as a 1991 prime-time series. **Ben Cross** was chosen to play vampire **Barnabas Collins**, and Steele was given the role of Dr. Julia Hoffman, the physician who tried to cure him of his vampiric condition. In the process, Dr. Hoffman fell in love with Collins. The show featured a 1790s storyline in which Steele portrayed another character, Natalie DuPrés. Unfortunately, the new *Dark Shadows* series was canceled after only twelve episodes.

Steele has expressed some ambiguous feelings about her horror career.

She would prefer to be remembered for all of her acting roles, but has acknowledged the fame that her image as a "scream queen" brought to her.

Essentially retired by the end of the 1990s, she has done but one movie since the beginning of the new century, a small part in the vampire flick, *Her Morbid Desires* (2008).

Sources:

Deitrich, Christopher, and Peter Beckman. "Barbara Steele." *Imagi-Movies* (Winter 1993/94): 34–43; Part 2: 1, 3 (Spring 1994).

Miller, Mark A. "Barbara Steele." *Filmfax* 19 (March 1990): 63–71, 94.

Stoker, Abraham "Bram" (1847–1912)

Bram Stoker was the author of **Dracula**, the key work in the development of the modern literary myth of the vampire. He was born in Dublin, **Ireland** and at the age of sixteen, he entered Trinity College at Dublin University. Stoker joined the Philosophical Society where he authored his first essay, "Sensationalism in Fiction and Society." He later became president of the Philosophical Society and auditor of the Historical Society. He graduated with a bachelor's degree and honors in science (1870) and, as his father before him, went to work as a civil servant at Dublin Castle. He continued as a part-time student at Dublin and eventually earned his master's degree (1875).

Stoker's favorable impression of British actor Henry Irving, who appeared locally with a traveling drama company, led him to offer his services to the *Dublin Evening Mail* as a drama critic, without pay. As his reviews began to appear in various papers, he was welcomed into Dublin social circles and soon met the Wildes, the parents of Oscar Wilde. In 1873, he was offered the editorship of a new newspaper, the *Irish Echo* (later renamed *Halfpenny Press*), part-time and without pay. The paper did not succeed, and, early in 1874, he resigned. From that point on, Stoker found his major entertainment in the theatre. He also began to write his first pieces of fiction, short stories, and serials, which were published in the local newspapers. His first bit of horror writing, "The Chain of Destiny," appeared as a serial in the *Shamrock* in 1875.

In 1878, Henry Irving took over the management of the Lyceum and invited Stoker to London as the theatre manager, and the Irving-Stoker partnership was to last until Irving's death in 1905. During these first years in London, Stoker found the time to author his first book of fiction, a collection of children's stories, *Under the Sunset*, published in 1882.

Bram Stoker.

Actor and theater manager Henry Irving was Bram Stoker's friend and mentor.

Toward the end of the 1880s, amid his duties at the Lyceum, he increased his writing efforts. The result was his first novel, appeared first as a serial in *The People* in 1889 and was published in book form the following year.

The story of *The Snake's Pass* centered on the legendary Shleenanaher, an opening to the sea in the mountain of Knockcalltecrore in western Ireland.

In 1890, Stoker began work on what was to become the watershed piece in the development of the literary vampire. Meanwhile, he wrote several short stories and two short novels. The novels, *The Watter's Mou* and *The Shoulder of Shasta*, are largely forgotten today. However, his short stories, especially "The Squaw," have survived and are still read by horror enthusiasts.

Stoker's decision to write *Dracula* seems to have been occasioned by a nightmare, in which he experienced a vampire rising from a tomb. He had read **Sheridan Le Fanu's "Carmilla"**, first published in 1872, several years before and had rounded out his knowledge with numerous discussions on the supernatural. To these he added his own research and modeled his main character on a fifteenth-century Transylvanian nobleman. He also decided, probably suggested by Wilkie Collins's *The Moonstone*, to tell the story through the eyes of several different characters. In the end, the story was told through a variety of documents, from diaries to letters to newspaper clippings.

Published in 1897, there was little to suggest that Stoker considered *Dracula* more than a good horror story. He received mixed reviews. Some loved it as a powerful piece of gloomy fascination. Others denounced it for its excessive strangeness and complained of its crudity. Very few recognized its importance and compared it to *Frankenstein*. None realized that Stoker had risen to a literary height to which he would never return—but then very few authors even approached the peak Stoker had attained.

About the time of the publication of *Dracula*, Stoker led a four-hour reading of its text. This odd event was presented, complete with announcements of the **drama** version, *Dracula, or The Un-dead*, to be presented at the Lyceum, to protect the plot and dialogue from literary theft. He had members of the Lyceum company join him in the performance, which was the only dramatic presentation of *Dracula* during his lifetime.

The year after *Dracula* was published, Stoker's career took a downward turn. A fire swept through the Lyceum destroying most of its costumes, props, and equipment. Irving's health, already failing, began to worsen. The theatre was turned over to a syndicate and, in 1902, closed for good. Irving died in 1905. Stoker turned to writing and produced a series of novels: *Miss Betty* (1898), *The Mystery of the Sea* (1902), *The Jewel of the Seven Stars* (1903), *The Man* (1905), and *The Lady of the Shroud* (1909). Of these,

The Lady of the Shroud was possibly the most successful. It reached a twentieth printing by 1934. *The Jewel of the Seven Stars* would later became the inspiration for two motion pictures: *Blood of the Mummy's Tomb* (1971) and *The Awakening* (1980). Of his later writings, Stoker put his most strenuous efforts into his two-volume tribute to his late boss, *The Personal Reminiscences of Henry Irving* (1906). His last books were the nonfiction *Famous Impostors* (1910), which included some interesting sketches of inherently interesting people, and *The Lair of the White Worm* (1911). *The Lair of the White Worm* has enjoyed some success over the years, and was reprinted in popular, inexpensive paperback editions in 1925, 1945, 1961, and most recently in 1989, in conjunction with the British motion picture adaptation directed by Ken Russell in 1992.

Only with great difficulty did Stoker write his last books. In 1905, his health took a decidedly downward turn. That year he had a stroke and soon developed Bright's disease, which affects the kidneys. His condition steadily deteriorated until his death at his home on April 12, 1912. Stoker's biographer Daniel Farson, a great nephew, first suggested that Stoker had died of tertiary syphilis. His conclusions were strongly refuted by Dracula scholar **Leslie Shepard**, but have recently been reaffirmed by writers **Peter Haining** and **Peter Tremayne**.

Possibly the most important of his post-*Dracula* literary products, a collection of short stories titled *Dracula's Guest, and Other Weird Stories* (1914), was published by his widow shortly after his death. She claimed that "Dracula's Guest" was actually a chapter deleted from *Dracula* by the publishers, who felt that the original manuscript was too long.

Stoker was not a wealthy man when he died, and his wife, Florence, was often hard pressed for money. She inherited Stoker's copyrights and had the periodic income from book sales. Then in 1921, Freidrich Wilhelm Murnau decided to make a film version of *Dracula*. He adapted it freely by, among other things, changing its setting to **Germany** and altering the names of several characters. For example, Dracula became **Graf Orlock**. Although he gave Stoker and the book due credit, Murnau neglected to obtain copyright permission. Florence Stoker sued and finally won. The German court ordered all copies of the film destroyed (although, fortunately, one copy survived). In the meantime, playwright **Hamilton Deane** obtained permission to adapt the novel to the stage. The play opened in June, 1924 in Derby and, after many performances around England and Scotland, finally opened in London in 1927.

Through Deane, Florence Stoker lived to see the success of *Dracula* first on stage then in the 1931 filming of a revised version of Deane's play starring **Bela Lugosi**. After her death in 1937, *Dracula* went on to become the single literary piece most frequently adapted for the motion picture screen (over 30

Bram Stoker's home in London, where he lived while he was writing *Dracula*.

A small plaque identifies Stoker's hom in London.

times), and its lead character the single literary figure most portrayed on the screen, other than **Sherlock Holmes**. The most recent film adaptation, ***Bram Stoker's Dracula***, directed by **Francis Ford Coppola**, appeared in 1992. In 1987, the Horror Writers of America instituted a set of annual awards for writings in their field, which they named after Bram Stoker.

Sources:

Belford, Barbara. *Bram Stoker: A Biography of the Author of Dracula*. New York: Alfred A. Knopf, 1996. 381 pp.

Bleiler, E. F., ed. *Supernatural Fiction Writers: Fantasy and Horror*. New York: Charles Scribner's Sons, 1985. 1,169 pp.

Dalby, Richard. *Bram Stoker: A Bibliography of First Editions*. London: Dracula Press, 1983. 81 pp.

Farson, Daniel. *The Man Who Wrote Dracula: A Biography of Bram Stoker*. New York: St. Martin, 1976. 240 pp.

Haining, Peter, and Peter Tremayne. *The Un-Dead*. London: Constable, 1997. 199 pp.

Ludlam, Harry. *A Biography of Dracula: The Life Story of Bram Stoker*. London: Fireside Press/W. Foulsham & Co., 1962. 200 pp.

Roth, Phyllis. *Bram Stoker*. Boston: Twayne, 1982. 167 pp.

Shepard, Leslie. "A Note on the Death Certificate of Bram Stoker." *The Bram Stoker Society Journal* 4 (1992): 35–36.

———. "A Note on the Death Certificate of Bram Stoker." *Bram Stoker Society Journal*. 4 (1992): 34–36.

———. "The Library of Bram Stoker." *Bram Stoker Society Journal.* 4 (1992): 28–34.

———. "Bram Stoker's Dublin." *Bram Stoker Society Journal* 5 (1993): 9–13.

———. *Bram Stoker: Irish Theatre Manager and Author.* Dublin: Impact Publications, 1994. 20 pp.

Stoker, Bram. *Under the Sunset.* London: Sampson Low, Marston, Searle, and Rivington, 1882. 190 pp.

———. *Dracula.* London: Constable, 1897. 390 pp. Rept. New York: Doubleday and McClure, 1899. 378 pp.

———. *The Jewel of the Seven Stars.* London: Heineman, 1903. 337 pp. Rept. New York: Amereon House, 1990. 307 pp.

———. *The Lair of the White Worm.* London: William Rider and Sons, 1911. 328 pp.

———. *Dracula's Guest and Other Weird Stories.* London: George Routledge & Sons, 1914. 200 pp. Rept. *Dracula's Guest.* New York: Zebra Books, 1978. 193 pp.

———. *Shades of Dracula.* Peter Haining, ed. Berkeley, CA: Apocryphile Press, 2006. 208 pp.

Whitelaw, Nancy. *Bram Stoker: Author of Dracula.* Greensboro, NC: Morgan Reynolds, 1998. 112 pp.

Strega *see:* Italy, Vampires in

Strength, Physical

Among the more notable attributes of the vampire is its superhuman strength. **Lord Ruthven**, in **John Polidori**'s **"The Vampyre"** was described as one "whose strength seemed superhuman." **Sheridan Le Fanu** noted, "One sign of the vampire is the power of the hand. The slender hand of Mircalla (i.e., **Carmilla**) closed like a vice of steel on the General's wrist when he raised his hatchet to strike. But its power is not confined to its grasp: It leaves a numbness in the limb it seizes, which is, slowly, if ever, recovered from." In **Bram Stoker**'s novel, among **Jonathan Harker**'s early observations was the great strength in the hand of the driver (later known to be **Dracula**) who took him to **Castle Dracula**. His strength was most clearly pictured by the man's ability to pick up one of the **women** who resided in the castle and toss her aside with ease. Later, in his speech on the nature of the vampire to the men who were to join him in tracking and killing Dracula, **Abraham Van Helsing** described the vampire as having the strength of twenty men (chapter 18). He also noted that **garlic**, such sacred objects as the **crucifix**, and **sunlight** take away the vampire's strength. The strength also often wanes when the vampire has not fed for a long period.

The vampires of folklore had no particular strength, however, people feared their unknown and supernatural realm. The folklore accounts portray a vampire who frequently fled when confronted and who was unable to resist a group set on its destruction. It generally attacked one **victim** at a time, usually a weaker relative (wife, child, or infant).

However, an emphasis upon the vampire's strength has proved a most useful attribute in modern novels and the cinema. The vampire shared this characteristic with other monsters. As vampires moved into society and encountered humans, its strength contributed to a certain arrogance, because vampires knew that no mere mortal could overcome them in a fair fight. Thus, **vampire hunters**, also mere mortals, had to use not only all of their reason and cleverness, but the additional power of supernatural good (holy objects), and often had to work in concert with a group. Vampire hunters fre-

quently had to seek out the vampire's resting place in the day when, in its **vampire sleep**, it was temporarily void of strength.

Many modern vampires have been stripped of their supernatural attributes, such as the power to transform into such different forms as **mist** or **animals**, but have retained their superhuman strength. This strength, along with a lengthened life span, was among the few benefits of the vampiric state granted to the undead.

Strige *see:* Greece, Vampires in

Strigoi/Strigoaica *see:* Romania, Vampires in

Strigon *see:* Southern Slavs, Vampires and the

Succubus *see:* Incubus/Succubus

Suicide

Suicide was one of the acts universally associated with vampirism. In cultures as varied as in **Russia**, **Romania**, West **Africa**, and **China**, suicide was considered an individual's pathway into vampirism. In the West in Jewish, Christian, and Muslim cultures, suicide has traditionally been considered a sin. In most other cultures suicide was frowned upon in an equivalent manner. **Japan** has generally been considered unique in its designation of a form of suicide called *hari-kari*, as a means of reversing the dishonor that initially led to the suicide.

Suicide was among the anti-social actions a person could commit that caused vampirism. In Eastern Europe, those actions included being a quarrelsome person, a drunkard, or associated with heresy or sorcery/**witchcraft**. In each society, there were activities considered a threat to the community's well-being that branded a person as different. While these varied considerably from culture to culture, suicide was most ubiquitous in its condemnation.

Suicide signaled the existence of extreme unresolved tension in the social fabric of a community. It was viewed as evidence of the family's and the community's inability to socialize an individual, as well as a statement by the individual of complete disregard for the community's existence and its prescribed rituals. The community, in turn, showed its disapproval in its treatment of the suicide's corpse. In the West, it was often denied Christian burial and its soul considered outside of the realm of salvation (the subject had committed mortal sin without benefit of confession and forgiveness prior to death). Those who committed suicide were buried at a crossroads or at a distance from the village. The corpse might even be thrown in a river to be carried away by the current.

Those who committed suicide died leaving unfinished business with relatives and close acquaintances. They left people with unresolved grief, which became a factor, sometimes unspoken, in the survivors' personalities for the rest of their lives. Their corpses often returned to the living in dreams and as apparitions. They were the subjects of nightmares, and families and friends occasionally felt under attack from the presence of them. The deceased became a vampire, and actions had to be taken to break the con-

nection that allowed the dead to disturb the living. The various actions taken against a corpse could be viewed as a means of emotional release for the survivors. The break in the connection was first attempted with harmless actions of **protection,** but, if ineffective, those efforts moved to a more serious level with mutilation (with a **stake**) or complete destruction (by **fire**) of the corpse.

Novelists and screenwriters have utilized suicide in their consideration of the problems faced by vampires who have found themselves bored with their long life, displaced in time, or have concluded that their vampire state is immoral.

Immediately after becoming a vampire, for example, **Lestat de Lioncourt** (the continuing character in **Anne Rice**'s vampire novels) had to witness the suicide (by fire) of the vampire who had made him. Eventually, **Armand,** the leader of the Parisian community eventually committed suicide by basking in the **sunlight.** Placing oneself in the open as the dawn approaches is the suicide method of choice for vampires, as recently exemplified by Boya (in the 1996 movie *Blood and Donuts*) and Countess Maria Viroslav in Kathryn Reines's *The Kiss* (1996). Toward the end of *Memnoch the Devil,* the fifth of the "Vampire Chronicles" of Anne Rice, Armand walks into the sunlight out of his intense religious feelings after seeing Veronica's veil that Lestat had returned with after his adventure in heaven and hell.

Both the Cevaillier Futaine (the vampire in Henry Kuttner's 1937 pulp short story, "I, the Vampire" and **Batman** (in the alternative universe Batman story *Batman: Bloodstorm)* committed suicide by leaving their sleeping place open for someone they knew would come in to kill them, Possibly the most ingeneous suicide device was devised for Yaksha, the original vampire in **Christopher Pike**'s *The Last Vampire* series. Yaksha had made a deal to redeem himself by killing all of the vampires and then himself. He saved his former lover for last. She rigged a set of explosives in a room that would kill both of them but then cleverly concealed a shield that would protect her at the crucial moment. Yaksha was killed but she survived.

In the second season of *True Blood* (the **television** series drawing on the novels of **Charlaine Harris**), Godric, the sheriff of Dallas, commited suicide by standing in the open on a building to greet the morning sun as Sookie Stackhouse watches.

Sources:

Barber, Paul. *Vampires, Burial, and Death: Folklore and Reality.* New Haven, CT: Yale University Press, 1988. 236 pp.

Moench, Doug, et al. *Batman: Bloodstorm.* New York: DC Comics, 1994.

Perkowski, Jan L. *The Darkling: A Treatise on Slavic Vampirism.* Columbus, OH: Slavica Publishers, 1989. 174 pp.

Pike, Christopher. *The Last Vampire.* New York: Archway/Pocket Book, 1994. 198 pp.

Reines, Kathryn. *The Kiss.* New York: Avon Books, 1996. 293 pp.

Senn, Harry A. *Were-Wolf and Vampire in Romania.* New York: Columbia University Press, 1982. 148 pp.

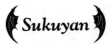

Sukuyan

The *sukuyan* was the vampire entity found on the Caribbean island of Trinidad. It resembled the **loogaroo** of Haiti, and in Trinidad the terms *sukuyan* and *loogaroo* (also pronounced *nigawu* or *legawu*) were often used interchangeably. It was also similar to the *asema* of Surinam and probably originated from the *aziman*, the vampire of the Fo people of Dahomey in West **Africa**. Melville Herskovits recorded a tale of a man in Trinidad who was informed that his late wife was a vampire. The deceased had not only taken the husband's **blood** but was visiting the homes of his neighbors. She was discovered drugging his tea each night. One night he only pretended to drink his tea and:

> … he went to bed, feigning to sleep. Then he heard her call
>
> 'Kin, 'kin, you no know me?' 'Kin, 'kin, you no hear what your mistress say? 'Kin, 'kin, come off, come off!
>
> She took off her skin and put it behind the large water barrel.
>
> Twice she leaped and then went through the roof. As the man watched this, he said to himself, "My wife, that what she do?" The sky seemed afire, and the room was very light. He salted the inside of the skin thoroughly, then put it in place behind the water barrel where she had left it. When she returned before break of day, she tried to get back in her skin but could not because the salt burned her.
>
> 'Kin, go on. 'Kin, you no know me? 'Kin, you no hear what your mistress say?
>
> This was repeated three times, and each line was spoken three times.
>
> "Skin squinch, he draw, can't go on, he burning he." So the woman put away the skin, wrapped herself up in a blanket, and lay down under the bed.

The husband reported her to the authorities, and she was seized and identified as a *sukuyan*. She was tried, condemned to death, and executed by being covered in tar and set afire.

The vampire was seen as a member of the community who lived during the day as an ordinary person but left its skin at night and, as a ball of light, traveled about looking for blood. People could be protected from an attack by a number of means. They could mark their doors and windows with crosses. A pair of scissors and a **mirror** fixed above the door inside of the house also offered **protection**. A broom placed upside down behind the door rendered a *sukuyan* powerless to do its work. If caught, the *sukuyan* usually underwent a **transformation** into one of several **animals**, and without its skin, would thus be unable to resume its human form.

Sources:

Herskovits, Melville J., and Frances S. Herskovits. *Trinidad Village*. New York: Alfred A. Knopf, 1947. 351 pp. Rept. New York: Castle Books, 1964. 351 pp.

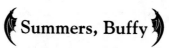

Summers, Buffy

Buffy Summers is the vampire slayer who was the main protagonist of the ***Buffy the Vampire Slayer*** movie (1992) and **television** series, which lasted for seven seasons, five on the WB Network (1997–2001) and two in the UPN Network (2001–2003). She has subsequently appeared in season eight, the continuing story of her post-television years in **comic book** form.

THE VAMPIRE BOOK: THE ENCYCLOPEDIA OF THE UNDEAD

Buffy was born Buffy Anne Summers, in California, on (according to her tombstone) January 19, 1981, the daughter of Hank and Joyce Summers (Kristine Sutherland). Little is known of her life prior to her entering Hemery High School in Los Angeles where she became a cheerleader and was eventually named both Prom Princess and Fiesta Queen.

During her first year at Hemery, Buffy (Kristy Swanson) was approached by a man named Merrick (Donald Sutherland), who informed her that she was the "chosen one," the new slayer of vampires; he was sent to be her watcher and to train her. She reluctantly began to accept her role. Eventually, she was forced to square off against Lothos (Rutger Hauer), the main vampire in town. She was able to kill him, but their confrontation led to a fire that consumed the high school gym. In the wake of the fire, Buffy was expelled and her parents separated. Buffy moved with her mother, a dealer in exotic art, to Sunnydale, California, where she tried to begin a new life as a sophomore at the local high school.

The television series took up the story with Buffy (now portrayed by Sarah Michelle Geller) beginning her sophomore year at Sunnydale High School. She soon became aware of people dying in ways that she recognized. She also met Rupert Giles (Anthony Stewart Head), the school's librarian, whose job provided cover for his real role as Buffy's watcher. Over the next years, he trained and mentored her. She made two new friends, Willow Rosenberg (Allison Hannigan) and Xander Harris (Nicholas Brendon), neither in the "in" crowd. Willow would become Buffy's best friend, and later use her computer skills and magical talents to assist Buffy in her slaying activities. Buffy was invited into the circle of beautiful people led by Cordelia Chase (Charisma Carpenter), but chose to keep her friendships with Willow and Xander. Cordelia soon learned the truth about vampires and demons firsthand, and was brought into the inner circle somewhat against her wishes.

The kids from the high school gathered at the Bronze, the local nightclub for teens. An encounter with vampires outside the club occasioned Buffy meeting **Angel** (David Boreancz), a good guy vampire, with whom she fell in love. During the second season, she lost her virginity to him. He, however, existed under a curse. Vampires are normally soulless revenants, but Angel had been given his soul, and with it, a conscience. The curse is that should he experience a moment of true happiness, as occurred making love to Buffy, he would lose his soul. He transformed into his vicious former self, Angelus, and Buffy was forced to send him to hell. By this time, Buffy had already experienced death, if only for a few minutes, and her death triggered the emergence of her successor, Kendra (Bianca Lawson). Kendra's relatively brief career as a slayer led to the appearance of Faith (Eliza Dushku).

Buffy fought a series of vampires and demons, the first major one being the Master, who killed her at the end of season one. Gradually, a set of continuing vampire antagonists would emerge, most notably Darla (Julie Benz), **Spike** (James Marsters) and Drusilla (Juliet Landau).

Buffy's high school years would culminate in a monumental battle at Sunnydale High School in which the forces of evil organized around Sunnydale's mayor (Harry Groener), who had allied with Faith, who had become a rogue slayer. The battle ended with the mayor's death and the high school being blown up. After the victory, Angel de-

parted to Los Angeles to begin a new life away from Buffy. Cordelia followed him and soon joined his supernatural detective agency.

Buffy and her Sunnydale cohorts, affectionately called the Scooby Gang (a reference to the group of cartoon character teenagers who solve crimes with their dog, Scooby Doo) continued to fight the evil that seemed to be focused on Sunnydale, which is set upon the Hellmouth, the entranceway to the hell realm. In the absence of Angel, Buffy developed a relationship with Riley Finn (Marc Blucas), a soldier who worked with the Initiative, a secret government project that was attempting to respond to the presence of vampires and demons. She cooperated with the Initiative for a short time, but learned that it had created a dangerous experimental Frankenstein-like entity, Adam (George Hertzberg), who was a bigger threat than anything the Initiative was opposing. Using Willow's developing magical powers, Buffy united her resources to take him down.

Buffy began season five with an encounter with **Dracula**, with whom she exchanges **blood**, before destroying him in the typical tongue-in-cheek style that had come to characterize her. The next morning, Buffy awakened to find that she had a sister, Dawn (Michelle Trachtenberg) and that all of her friends had been given the memories of her life as if she had been in the Summers's home all along. Much of season five was spent battling Glory (Clare Kramer), a deity from the hell dimension who was searching for the Key, a mystical artifact that would break down the barriers separating the different dimensions and allow her to return and reign in her own dimension, at a significant cost to the earthly dimension. Buffy finally figured out that Dawn was the Key. Her attempt to understand the nature of Dawn and to protect her led her to embrace the fact that "death is her gift." At the end of season five, Buffy sacrifices herself to save Dawn (and the world) from Glory's attempt to destroy the separate dimensions.

Early in season six, Buffy was brought back to life by her friend Willow by working a magical spell. Because of their knowledge of Angel, Willow and Xander believed Buffy was in the hell dimension. But she was actually in a heavenly place, which she did not want to leave. In the despair and alienation following her resurrection, she began to develop a relationship with Spike. The evil vampire had been tamed by the Initiative who placed a chip in his head that prevented him from harming any human. The intense sexual relationship that develops between Buffy and Spike, often violent, was fueled by Spike's attempt to replace Angel in Buffy's heart. When his love was rebuffed, he attempted to rape her. Their relationship destroyed, he left town to do what was necessary to make himself acceptable to her. Meanwhile, Willow, who had realized that she was a lesbian and had developed a relationship with Tara (Amber Benson), goes through a period of fighting her addiction to magic. But, as Willow's magical prowess had increased, Tara was killed during an unsuccessful attempt to kill Buffy. Willow's grief sent her into a dark period that culminated in her threat to destroy the world with her powers. Ultimately, Xander brought Willow back from the brink.

Buffy began season seven with a new more positive outlook—for Dawn's sake. Buffy now has to face her greatest enemy yet, the First Evil. The fight would in the end focus on the Hellmouth, with a horde of vampires attempting to move through the opening to return to control of the earth dimension. In this final battle, Buffy was joined by Faith (who had found some redemption through Angel's efforts) and Spike, who has regained his soul and returned to win Buffy's trust and love. Of the old gang, only Giles

was missing, as he had returned to his native England. Most importantly, she was joined by a number of potential slayers-in-training whom she nurtured and with whom she shared her powers.

In the final episode, like the Spartans at Thermopylae, she led the small Scooby Gang, now bolstered with the new cadre of slayers, against a massive wave of vampires who rose up through the Hellmouth. They won the battle, but at the cost of the town of Sunnydale (i.e. Santa Barbara, California). The key to their success was Spike, who wore a magical amulet and incinerated himself in a process that destroyed the attacking vampires and closed the Hellmouth. Before he died, Buffy professed her love for him. He knew he did not have her love, but had won her respect.

After the end of the television show, Spike re-emerged as a spirit creature on the spin-off television show *Angel*. After he recoved a body, the two searched for Buffy and at one point saw her from a distance, in Rome.

Throughout the run of the television show, Dark Horse Comics had published a comic book that included both adaptations of story lines from the series and completely new stories. That series went on to become the second longest running English-language vampire comic book (surpassed only by **Vampirella**). But the comic only survived for a short time after the discontinuation of the television show. Then in 2007, Dark Horse, in cooperation with Joss Whedon, the show's creator, began issuing a new comic book that officially constitutes season eight of *Buffy the Vampire Slayer*. In this new comic books series (which continues to appear as this encyclopedia goes to press), Buffy has emerged as the head of a command center in Scotland that is the nexus of an international anti-vampire and demon organization. Of her former close associates, she has contact with Xander, who is in Scotland with her and Giles, who is in England. Willow has continued to emerge as an ever more powerful magical force, and the slayers who survived the battle in Sunnydale are scattered around Europe and North America.

The destruction of Sunnydale did not go unnoticed, and government authorities now brand Buffy and her associates as a terrorist organization. Buffy's real enemy however is Twilight, a person who wants to destroy Buffy and the new legion of slayer as a threat to humanity. Those loyal to Twilight include the witch Amy Madison (a former classmate of Buffy's from Sunnydale, portrayed by Elizabeth Anne Allen), and her former boyfriend, Riley Finn.

Buffy became one of the most popular and influential characters in the popular culture community focused on vampires, and has inspired a number of vampire slayer characters in more recent books, movies, and television shows. Joss Whedon indicated that he created Buffy in reaction to the popular stereotype of the dim-witted female victim in teen-oriented horror movies. Buffy emerged as both attractive and believable. As the show became successful, Sarah Michelle Geller's image graced the covers of numerous fan magazines and appeared on a spectrum of **paraphernalia** from lunch boxes to cell phone covers, to clothing and jewelry. Meanwhile, the character became the subject of intense scholarly scrutiny.

Sources:

Durand, Kevin K., ed. *Buffy Meets the Academy: Essays on the Episodes and Scripts as Texts*. Jeffersonville, NC: McFarland & Company, 2009.

Golden, Christopher, and Nancy Holder. *Buffy the Vampire Slayer: The Watcher's Guide*. New York: Pocket Books, 1998. 298 pp.

Golden, Christopher, Stephen R. Bissette, and Thomas E. Sniegoski. *Buffy the Vampire Slayer: The Monster Book*. New York: Pocket Books, 2000. 370 pp.

Holder, Nancy, with Jeff Mariotte and Maryelizabeth Hart. *Buffy the Vampire Slayer: The Watcher's Guide*. Vol. 2. New York: Pocket Books, 2000. 472 pp.

Ruditis, Paul. *Buffy the Vampire Slayer: The Watcher's Guide*. Vol. 3. New York: Simon Spotlight, 2004. 359 pp.

Stafford, Nikki. *Bite Me! The Unofficial Guide to Buffy the Vampire Slayer*. Toronto: ECW Press, 2007. 397 pp.

Topping, Keith. *The Complete Slayer: An Unofficial and Unauthorised Guide to Every Episode of "Buffy the Vampire Slayer."* London: Virgin, 2004. 704 pp.

Wilcox, Rhonda V., and David Lavery, eds. *Fighting the Forces: What's at Stake in Buffy the Vampire Slayer*. Lanham, MD: Rowman & Littlefield Publishers, 2002. 290 pp.

Summers, Montague (1880–1948)

Alphonsus Joseph-Mary Augustus Montague Summers was the author of a number of important books on the supernatural including several classic studies on vampires. Very early in his life, he began reading many of the more obscure writings by English fiction writers, including those of the **gothic** genre.

In 1899, Summers entered Trinity College and pursued a course toward the Anglican ministry. He went on to Lichfield Theological College where he received his bachelor's degree (1905) and master's degree (1906). He was ordained as a deacon in 1908 and assigned to a parish in a Bristol suburb.

While there, he was charged and tried for pederasty but was found not guilty.

In the wake of the trial, however, he left the Church of England and became a Roman Catholic. At some point—whether before or after he left the Church of England was not altogether clear—he was ordained to the priesthood. He was briefly assigned to a parish in London, but in 1911, moved from the parish into teaching school.

During his teaching years, Summers gathered an outstanding collection of books in various languages (many of which he learned) on occultism and the supernatural, from magic and **witchcraft** to vampires and **werewolves**. He also became an enthusiastic fan of Restoration drama and was one of the founders of The Phoenix, a society established to revive Restoration plays, many of a somewhat risque nature. After fifteen years as an instructor in various schools, Summers moved to Oxford and began the period of scholarly writings that was to make him a memorable author of works on the occult and related fields. His first important work, *The History of Witchcraft and Demonology*, appeared the year he retired from teaching.

Largely because of his choice of topics, his books sold well and Summers was able to make a living from his writings.

The first years of his Oxford period focused on his study of vampirism. In 1928, Summers finished his broad survey, *The Vampire: His Kith and Kin*, in which he traced the presence of vampires and vampire-like creatures in the folklore around the world, from ancient times to the present. He also surveyed the rise of the literary and dramatic vampire. Summers's broad mastery of the mythological, folkloric, anthropological, and historical material on the vampire (a mastery rarely equaled) has been obscured by his own Catholic supernaturalism. On several occasions he expressed his opinion of the evil reality of the vampire, an opinion very much out of step with his secular colleagues.

The following year Summers published his equally valuable *The Vampire in Europe*, which focused on various vampire accounts in Europe (especially Eastern Europe) where the legend found its most complete development. Summers combined his reading of the diverse literature with personal observations formulated from visits to some of the more important centers where vampire belief had survived. Summers completed two volumes of a country-by-country report on vampire lore. While they superseded a number of particular areas, the volumes remain standard sources for vampire studies.

During the 1930s, Summers continued his prodigious output and successively published: *The Werewolf* (1933), a companion volume to his vampire studies; *The Restoration Theatre* (1934); *A Popular History of Witchcraft* (1937); and *The Gothic Quest: A History of the Gothic Novel* (1938), an enthusiastic

Noted vampire expert Montague Summers.

history of gothic fiction. In the 1940s, he added *Witchcraft and Black Magic* (1946). His last book, *The Physical Phenomena of Mysticism*, was published posthumously in 1950.

During the last twenty years of his life, Summers also edited numerous volumes.

He released new editions of some of the most important texts on witchcraft and several anthologies of ghost stories. Toward the end of his life, he produced an autobiographical volume, *The Galantry Show*, which was eventually published in 1980. Beginning in 1956, many of Summers's works, including the two vampire books, were reprinted in American editions.

Summers remains an enigma. A defender of a traditional supernatural Catholic faith, he was the target of numerous rumors concerning homosexuality and his seeming fascination with those very subjects which he, on the one hand condemned, and on the other, spent so much time mastering.

Sources:

Frank, Frederick S. *Montague Summers: A Bibliographical Portrait*. Metuchen, NJ: Scarecrow Press, 1988. 277 pp.

Frenschkowski, Marco. "Keine spitzen Zähne. Von der interkulturellen Vergleichbarkeit mythologischer Konzepte: das Beispiel des Vampirs." In *Poetische Wiedergänger. Deutschsprachige Vampirismus-Diskurse vom Mittelalter bis zur Gegenwart*. Julia Bertschik and Christa A. Tuczay, eds. Tübingen, Germany: Francke 2005: 43–59.

Jerome, Joseph. *Montague Summers: A Memoir*. London: Cecil and Amelia Woolf, 1965. 105 pp.

Morrow, Felix. "The Quest for Montague Summers." In Montague Summers, *The Vampire: His Kith and Kin*. New Hyde Park, NY: University Books, 1960: xiii–xx.

Smith, Timothy d'Arch. *A Bibliography of the Works of Montague Summers*. New Hyde Park, NY: University Books, 1964. 164 pp.

Summers, Montague. *The Vampire: His Kith and Kin*. London: Routledge, Kegan Paul, Trench, Trubner & Co., 1928. 356 pp. Rept. New Hyde Park, NY: University Books, 1960. 356 pp.

———. *The Vampire in Europe*. London: Routledge, Kegan Paul, Trench, Trubner & Co., 1929. 329 pp. Rept. New Hyde Park, NY: University Books, 1961. 329 pp.

———. *The Gothic Quest: a History of the Gothic Novel*. 1938. Rept. London: Fortune Press, 1950. 443 pp.

———. *The Werewolf*. London: Kegan Paul, Trench, Trubner & Co., 1933. Rept. New York: Bell Publishing Company, 1966. 307 pp.

———. *The Galantry Show*. London: Cecil Woolf, 1980. 259 pp.

Sunlight

Today, vampires are commonly portrayed as nocturnal creatures with a great aversion to sunlight. But such was not always the case. In the folklore of many cultures, the vampire was able to infiltrate society and return to some semblance of normal life. In nineteenth-century literature, vampires moved about freely during the day. For example, in "Christabel", the early vampiric poem by **Samuel Taylor Coleridge**, Geraldine the vampire was discovered outside the castle by Christabel late at night. She invited Geraldine to her room where the two passed the rest of the night in bed. Geraldine awakened the next morning, refreshed and ready to meet Christabel's father. In like measure, **Lord Ruthven**, **Varney the Vampyre**, and **Carmilla** maneuvered easily through the day, though they preferred the night.

Concerning **Dracula, Abraham Van Helsing** noted:

His power ceases, as does that of all things, at the coming of day.

Only at certain times can he have limited freedom. If he be not at the place whither he is bound, he can only change himself at noon or at exact sunrise and sunset. These things are we told, and in this record of ours we have proof by inference.

As the men prepared to destroy Dracula's earth-filled boxes, Van Helsing warned that Dracula might appear in his Piccadilly residence, but given his diminished powers, they might be able to cope with him as a group. As predicted, Dracula appeared late one afternoon. **Jonathan Harker** attacked him with a knife and Van Helsing with a **crucifix**. The weakened Dracula escaped by jumping out of the window onto the ground and crossing the yard to the stable and into the city.

The contemporary understanding of the nocturnal nature of the vampire seems to have derived from the 1922 silent movie *Nosferatu, Eine Symphonie des Grauens*. This early unauthorized attempt to bring *Dracula* to the screen made numerous changes in the story in the hope of disguising it.

The characters' names were changed and the location moved to **Germany**. In addition, **Graf Orlock** (the vampire) was transformed into a totally nocturnal creature, and a new method of killing him was introduced. Director Freidrich Wilhelm Murnau introduced a mythical volume, *The Book of the Vampires*, as a source of new wisdom concerning the creatures. The heroine, Ellen Hutter (**Mina Murray** in the novel), read that if a pure woman spent the night with the vampire, holding him at her side until dawn, the vampire would perish in the light. She decided to sacrifice herself for the good of all. Graf Orlock, who had moved next door, already had his eye on Ellen so he soon found his way to her bedroom. He sunk his teeth into her throat and there remained until sunrise. He noticed that he had lingered too long only after his fate was sealed. In one of the more memorable moments, he realized his imminent death just prior to his dissolving into a puff of smoke.

The transition in emphasis made by *Nosferatu* had been prepared by the opening chapters of *Dracula* in which Jonathan Harker, perceiving the nocturnal activities of the Count, noted in his diary, "I have not yet seen the Count in the daylight. Can it be that he sleeps when others wake that he may be awake whilst they sleep!" While *Nosferatu* emerged as an important film, it was for all practical purposes not available until the 1960s, and thus may have had less effect on the development of the vampire's image than many suspect. On the contrary, **Bela Lugosi**'s 1943 *The Return of the Vampire* was widely circulated. Here the sunlight was the instrument of the vampire Armand Tesla's death—it melted Tesla's face.

Having been introduced as a potent and deadly force, sunlight arose as a preferred instrument of death in two of the most important screen adaptations of the Dracula legend. In *The Horror of Dracula* (1958), **Abraham Van Helsing (Peter Cushing)** was nearly beaten by Dracula (**Christopher Lee**) as the pair fought in the castle. However, Dracula paused to savor the moment just long enough for Van Helsing to spring free and rip the drapes from the window. The direct sunlight, like acid, caught Dracula's foot, which quickly dissolved. Recovering his advantage, Van Helsing used his **crucifix** to force Dracula fully into the sunlight where he disintegrated into a heap of ash.

In *Dracula* (1979), **Frank Langella** (as Dracula) fled to the ship that would take him and Lucy Seward (**Lucy Westenra** in the novel) away from England. Van Helsing and **John Seward** thwarted his plans when they reached the ship. In the final fight scene, Dracula impaled Van Helsing and was about to win when he was suddenly caught on a hook and heaved into the sunlight high above the ship.

While sunlight can be an instrument of death and the preferred agent on those rare occasions in which a vampire commits **suicide**), it has been used primarily to define the realm of activity and set the boundary of action for vampire characters in movies and novels. The rising and setting sun prescribed the period of the vampire's activity, and an approaching dawn created a moment of tension as the vampire rushed back to its resting place. It is of some trivial interest that in the **television** show, *Dracula—The Series*, the vampire wore a special skin lotion that blocked the sun and, thus, he was able to go out in the daylight. This idea has also been used in several previous pieces of vampire fiction. As vampire characters have multiplied, the aversion to the sun has a been among the most common traits that novelists and screenwriters have retained. There are some popular exceptions, including the vampires of **Stephenie Meyer**'s "Twilight" series of books and the movies made from them, and the British television series *Being Human*.

In several **comic book** series, the search to find a formula to overcome the inability to "walk" in the daylight has become an element in plots. **Blade the Vampire Slayer**, introduced into Marvel Comics in the early seventies, was a half-vampire who

could walk (and therefore hunt) in the daytime. In the third movie about the slayer , *Blade Trinity* (2005), the vampires resurrect Dracula to oppose Blade and produced a set of new vampires who can walk in the daylight. The first Baron Blood, another Marvel character, used a special cosmetic treatment that allowed him to withstand sunlight and hence remain active during the day. The third Baron Blood, Kenneth Crichton, has to oppose the Baroness Blood, who used him to obtain the Holy Grail, from which she derived an immunity to sunlight. At one point, DC's vampire character Andrew Bennett (who was featured in the series **"I ... Vampire,"** faced opposition from his old nemisis (and girlfriend) Mary Seward. Along the way he took what was known as the Russian formula, which briefly gave him the ability to walk in the sunlight. It also led to his death, although not before Mary was destroyed.

Movie director **Donald Glut** produced a film trilogy built around the story of **Elizabeth Bathory**. In the third movie, *Blood Scarab* (2008), Bathory steals a mummy as part of a scheme to make a deal with an Egyptian goddess so that she will have the ability to move about in daylight.

❨ Swan, Isabella Marie ❩

Isabella Marie Swan, also known as Bella or Bells, is **Stephenie Meyer**'s heroine and main narrator throughout the four-book **"Twilight"** series. Bella is described as slender, five foot four inches and fair skinned, with long, straight dark brown hair, brown eyes, and a thin nose. On her website (www.StephenieMeyer.com), Meyer said that she named her female heroine Isabella because she loved the character "like a daughter" and always wanted to give that name to a daughter of her own.

Bella was born on September 13, 1987, and is the only child of Renee and Charlie Swan. She was born in Forks, Washington and her parents divorced when she was six months old. Bella and her mother moved to Phoenix, Arizona, and when Renee remarried Phil Dwyer, Bella moved back to Forks to be with her father.

Meyer describes Bella as extremely accident prone and clumsy. Bella avoids sports and dancing; she occasionally bites her fingernails and feels as if she doesn't "fit in" with any social group although she easily makes friends with a few people in Forks. Meyer describes Bella as having a "quiet strength"; she is a bookworm who likes to cook and draw as well as take care of her parents by housekeeping and shopping. Like her vampire boyfriend **Edward Cullen**, Bella is a loner and says she finds her "true place" only when

Kristen Stewart plays Bella Swan in the "Twilight" series movies.

she is transformed into a vampire and thus becomes a bona-fide member of the Cullens and their extended family.

Bella's strongest quality is that her mind is closed to Edward's abilities to read her thoughts. This unusual skill—Bella is apparently the only human whose mind is beyond Edward's powers—later serves as a "shield" that she can extend to protect her child and others around her. She also has a penchant for danger and habitually stumbles into situations that put her own life at risk. When Edward breaks off the relationship with Bella in *New Moon*, she decides to deliberately place herself in danger just so she can "hear" his voice. Ironically, these risky situations bring Edward and Bella closer as he repeatedly saves her life and vows to protect her.

Bella's character experiences several changes as the "Twilight" series progresses. She graduates from high school and begins to assert her newfound adulthood and gradually grows more confident about herself and her relationship with Edward. When she turns into a vampire in *Breaking Dawn*, she is no longer clumsy and discovers her own physical agility. Meyer has explained that although Bella is physically weaker than others, she eventually develops into one of the most powerful characters in the "Twilight" series. In the movie ***Twilight*** and its sequels, Bella is played by actress Kristen Stewart.

Sources:

Irwin, Megan. "Stephenie Meyer's Vampire Romance Novels Made a Mormon Mom an International Sensation." *Phoenix New Times* (July 12, 2007).

Personal Correspondence. Twilight_News_Updates, April 18, 2006.

Vaz, Mark Cotta. *Twilight: The Complete Illustrated Movie Companion*. Little, Brown and Company: New York, Boston, 2008. 142 pp.

Sweden, Vampires in *see:* Scandinavia, Vampires in

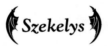

Szekelys

In describing himself to **Jonathan Harker**, **Dracula** took the label *Szekely*. "We *Szekelys* have a right to be proud," he asserted as an opening for a lengthy discourse on the role of his people in the history of **Transylvania**. As he continued, he began to discuss the Draculas, "about one of my own race who crossed the Danube and beat the Turk on his own ground" (chapter 3). This discourse raises many of the questions concerning the relationship of Dracula, the fictional character created by **Bram Stoker**, and the medieval Romanian ruler, **Vlad the Impaler**.

The *Szekelys* (or *Szeklers*) was a distinct group that emerged in Transylvania from among the Hungarian tribes, which moved into the area at the end of the ninth century. Others suggest an independent **origin**, possibly a lost group of Bulgars who had invaded the area in the seventh century. Szekelys claim a pre-Hungarian origin. Originally they settled in southeastern Transylvania, but in 1224 C.E., they migrated northward and relocated in the eastern mountains. The Szekelys formed a first line of defense for the Hungarians who controlled the Transylvanian plain to their west, and they developed a reputation for their bravery and fierceness in battle. They participated in the establishment of the Union of Three Nations in 1437 that set the Hungarians, Szekelys, and

Germans as a controlling majority and made room for the Roman Catholic, Reformed, and Lutheran churches. That same agreement disenfranchised the Romanians and excluded their Eastern Orthodox faith.

After identifying Dracula as a Szekely, Stoker positioned his castle near **Borgo Pass**, a location in Szekely-dominated land in northeastern Transylvania near the Ukrainian border. Stoker thus quite properly sent Harker into the best place to find a Szekely nobleman. The problem arose in identifying this Szekely nobleman, Count Dracula, with the historical ruler of Wallachia, Prince Vlad the Impaler, or Dracula (the son of **Vlad Dracul**).

If Stoker also intended to see his character as a fictionalized version of Vlad, he had hopelessly confused two historical realities. Vlad the Impaler, though born in southern Transylvania, was a Romanian and ruled in Wallachia, the area across the Carpathian Mountains to the south of Transylvania. He was neither Hungarian nor a Szekely. His castle was located near Curtea de Arges in Wallachia, nowhere near Borgo Pass. Most likely, Stoker saw Hungarian and Romanian history and folklore in less than precise terms and borrowed elements from each (as well as other sources) in creating the fictional world inhabited by his vampire creation. The problem of identifying Vlad the Impaler as both a Szkeley warrior and a Wallachian prince was amply illustrated in the opening scenes of the film ***Bram Stoker's Dracula***, which hopelessly confused Romanian geography by trying to integrate the story of Vlad with that of Dracula.

Sources:

Cadzow, John F., Andrew Ludanyi, and Louis J. Elteto. *Transylvania: The Roots of Ethnic Conflict.* Kent, OH: Kent State University Press, 1983. 368 pp.

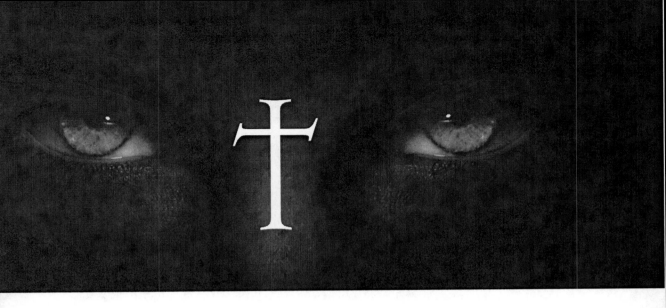

Talamasca

The Talamasca is a semi-secret organization operating in the world of **Anne Rice's** "The Vampire Chronicles." Created in 758 C.E., the Talamasca studies supernatural (or what today is termed paranormal) activity. Over the years it has documented a wide variety of phenomena, including vampires. Researchers on vampires make a special effort to collect items that "vampires" have left behind, and so their files on vampires date to the early Middle Ages. The organization has offices around the world, and the collected data from its investigations are sent to the central files in the **United Kingdom**.

Through much of the last half of the twentieth century, the organization has been headed by David Talbot, its superior general. He welcomed Jesse, the mortal descendent of a worldwide family that originated with two ancient vampires, Maharet and Mekare, and in 1985 sent her on a mission to **New Orleans** to track down the truth behind a recently published book, *Interview with the Vampire*, which was reportedly the true story of an eighteenth-century New Orleans vampire. Jesse had attracted the attention of the Talamasca after a **London** tabloid had done an article on her **psychic** abilities. In New Orleans she was able to locate the house in which vampires Louis, **Lestat,** and Claudia lived, and located some items Claudia had left behind in a secret place in the wall. Unfortunately for her, the organization called her off the case just as she was getting caught up in her investigation.

Shortly thereafter, she read the recently published book, *The Vampire Lestat,* written by a rock musician who claimed to be the Lestat mentioned in *Interview with the Vampire*. While attending his concert in San Francisco she figured out that he really was a vampire. Before she was able to do anything with her new knowledge, another vampire, noting her connection with the Talamasca, attacked her. Her neck was broken, and her life was saved by being transformed into a vampire.

After her recovery, and the passing of an immediate crisis caused by the attempt of Akasha, the so-called **Queen of the Damned**, to take over the vampire community, Jesse placed Lestat in contact with Talbot. Unlike the vampire who had attacked Jesse, Lestat was fascinated with the Talamasca and even with the possibility of being a subject of study. He went to England to meet with Talbot and after getting to know him, offered him the Dark Gift (of being turned into a vampire). Talbot, already seventy-four years old, declined, but then went on to become involved with Lestat in the affair of the body thief.

Lestat was contacted by Raglan James who proposed that he and Lestat switch bodies for a brief time. Talbot was against the idea, but Lestat wanted to give it a try. Unfortunately, as soon as James got into Lestat's body, he decided to keep the body, steal Lestat's assets, and leave Lestat in his mortal state. Lestat then turned to Talbot and the Talamasca for help. They devised a plan to track James and knock him out of Lestat's body. In the final confrontation, a three-way body exchange took place, and Talbot wound up in James's youthful body. With his new body he was much more open to Lestat's bestowal of the Dark Gift. Talbot's involvement in this adventure broke the organization's rule against involvement with the subjects of its studies and Talbot's own rule about talking with a vampire.

After assuming James's body and becoming a vampire, Talbot retired from the Talamasca. Thus he was available to be with Lestat when he returned from his adventure in heaven and hell and recorded his account. Most recently, Talbot has gone to Paris where he has convinced the vampire Pandora to tell him her life story.

Sources:

Ramsland, Katherine. *The Vampire Companion: The Official Guide to Anne Rice's The Vampire Chronicles*. New York: Ballantine Books, 1993. 507 pp.

Rice, Anne. *The Vampire Lestat*. New York: Alfred A. Knopf, 1985. 481 pp. Rept. New York: Ballantine Books, 1986. 550 pp.

———. *The Queen of the Damned*. New York: Alfred A. Knopf, 1988. 448 pp. Rept. New York: Ballantine Books, 1989. 491 pp.

———. *Memnoch the Devil*. New York: Alfred A. Knopf, 1994. 354 pp. Rept. New York: Ballantine Books, 1995. 434 pp.

———. *Pandora*. New York: Alfred A. Knopf, 1998. 353 pp.

❨ *Talamaur* ❩

The *talamaur* was the vampirelike creature of the Banks Islands in the South Pacific. The people of Banks Island had a strong belief in the possibility of lively intercourse with the ghosts of the dead. While some feared the dead, others welcomed interaction with the spirit world. There was also a strong belief that the soul of a living person, a *tarunga*, could separate from the body and wander about, a belief often verified in dream experiences. The *talamaur* was described as a soul or *tarunga* that went out and ate the soul or life still lingering around the body of the corpse of a recently deceased person. It also described the **ghoul**-like behavior of a living person who would eat a corpse with the understanding that the ghost of the dead person would become a close companion of the *talamaur* and would use his ghostly power against anyone to whom he was directed. If people in the village felt afflicted, and if they developed a sense of dread in the presence of one of their

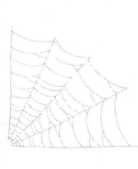

neighbors, that neighbor would be suspected of being a *talamaur*. It was no crime to be a *talamaur*, and it was the practice of some to actually project the image of being a one.

R. H. Codrington, the main source of information on the creature, told the story of one woman who claimed to be a *talamaur*, and on the occasion of a death in the village bragged that she would visit and eat the corpse that evening. Friends of the dead person watched to protect the body. During the course of the evening, they heard some scratching noises close to the corpse. One person threw a stone toward the noise. The next day the woman who claimed to be the *talamaur* had a bruise on her arm, which she said came from being hit while eating the corpse.

Sources:
Codrington, R. H. *The Melanesians: Studies in Their Anthropology and Folk-lore*. Oxford: Clarendon Press, 1891, 1969. 419 pp.

Teeth *see:* Fangs

Tehran Vampire

There being few vampires in Islamic culture, the appearance of an individual known as the Tehran Vampire was unexpected. However, like most modern vampire criminals, Ali Reza Khoshruy Kuran Kordiyeh was similar to almost all of the contemporary Western vampire criminals, in that he was a serial killer. He differed in that he did not drink the **blood** of his **victims** because he killed them by staking them.

The twenty-eight-year-old Kordiyeh worked as a taxi driver and in the evenings cruised West Tehran where he picked up young women. He began his killing spree in March 1997 and before he was caught a few months later he had killed no less than nine people, including one mother and her nine-year-old daughter. He raped his victims and then killed and **staked** them. He generally tried to dispose of the bodies by burning them (not a functional solution, as burning bodies is a difficult process). He was finally caught when identified from sketches generated by two women who escaped him. The discovery of incriminating blood stains in his taxi led to his confession.

In an unusual breach of policy, Iranian officials leaked the time and place of Kordiyeh's execution on August 13, 1997. Not only were the relatives of the victims on hand, but a crowd of over 10,000 gathered. While the crowd shouted insults, the relatives were allowed to deliver their share of the 214 lashes to which he had been sentenced. Afterward he was hung.

Sources:
Valinejad, Adshin. "Iran Flogs, Hangs Serial Killer Known as 'The Vampire.'" *USA Today* (August 14, 1997): 11A.

Television, Vampires on

It was in the late 1940s that regularly-scheduled television programs emerged in the United States, and early programming was based on well-established radio shows of the

day. The *Texaco Star Theater* on NBC featured comedian Milton Berle, and it was on this variety series that the vampire was first introduced to American households. A live broadcast on September 27, 1949 featured **Bela Lugosi** as one of the guest stars, and although not called **Dracula** by name, he appeared in one sketch dressed as the iconic vampire. Lugosi fared well in unfamiliar comedic territory, but after he flubbed a punch line, Berle ad-libbed, "You kill people on the screen and you also kill jokes!" In 1953 Lugosi again appeared as Dracula on the audience-driven show *You Asked for It,* where he performed a "weird vampire **bat** illusion." Lugosi rose from a **coffin**, hypnotized a girl, and then, after placing her within a magic cabinet of sorts, transformed her into a bat. Afterwards he promoted the 3-D film *Phantom Ghoul* and a television series called *Dr. Acula,* neither of which ended up being produced.

Dracula on Television: Following the initial TV appearances by Lugosi, *Dracula,* the novel and the character, periodically reappeared in both new productions and unrelated series. The first adaptation of the novel aired live on NBC in 1956 as part of the series *Matinee Theatre.* This version was based on the 1931 film and starred **John Carradine**, who had previously played the Count on stage as well as in the films *House of Frankenstein* (1944) and *House of Dracula* (1945). British actor Denholm Elliott starred in a 1968 UK adaptation of Dracula that aired as part of the series *Mystery and Imagination*. Although this version began its story in **Whitby**, with only a flashback to the happenings in **Transylvania**, it did include several scenes from the novel that had been left out by previous adaptations. A year later, in what was quite possibly the first televised foreign-language adaptation of the novel, Gianni Lunadei starred as Dracula in the Argentina-produced miniseries *Hay que matar a Drácula.*

The Canadian series *Purple Playhouse* aired its version of *Dracula* on the CBC in 1973. It starred Norman Welsh as the Count, and like many early adaptations, this version had the look of a televised stage play. But it was also in this year that **Dark Shadows** creator **Dan Curtis** helmed a televised movie written by **Richard Matheson** that starred **Jack Palance**. This was the first adaptation to be influenced by the historical work on **Vlad the Impaler** by **Raymond T. McNally** and **Radu Florescu**. It also was the first to incorporate the search for lost love as a motivation for Dracula returning to England. A few years later in 1977, **Louis Jourdan** starred in a full-length BBC production entitled **Count Dracula**, written by Gerald Savory who also adapted his screenplay into a tie-in novel. It aired in the United States as part of the *Great Performances* series on PBS, and this lengthy two-and-a-half hour production was the first to closely follow the original novel.

Subsequently, *Dracula* continued to be adapted in new and interesting ways, although in some cases, only the character names remained while the stories themselves strayed far from the source material. In 1979, *The Curse of Dracula* aired in weekly 20-minute installments as part of *Cliffhangers,* an hourly series based on the format of early movie serials. In this story, Dracula lived in modern-day San Francisco, covertly as a college professor of East European History. After the series was cancelled, all ten chapters were edited together as a two-hour TV movie entitled *The World of Dracula.*

Also in 1979, the kid-friendly and Emmy award-winning telefilm *The Halloween That Almost Wasn't* aired on ABC. It featured Judd Hirsch as Count Dracula who, in an attempt to save Halloween, seeks the help of his monster friends the Mummy, Warren the **Werewolf**, Zabaar the Zombie, and **Frankenstein's Monster**. In 1980 Marvel

Comics commissioned a TV-movie based on their popular **Tomb of Dracula comic book** series, which briefly aired under the title *Dracula: Sovereign of the Damned*. Also in that year, the Showtime Network aired *Passion of Dracula*, adapted from the tongue-in-cheek off-Broadway play from the late seventies.

In 1980, ABC took a similar comedic approach with *Mr. and Mrs. Dracula*, which had the Count and his family trying to adjust to life in America after being ousted from their castle in Transylvania. Viewer response to the pilot episode was tepid, and although a partially-recast version aired again in 1981, the sitcom wasn't picked up by the network. A more traditional adaptation aired in 1982 on the series *HBO Live!* and starred **Frank Langella**, who reprised his role from the *Dracula* stage play. In **Japan**, the short-lived 1982 anime series *Don Dracula* aired on TV Tokyo, and had the titular character moving to Japan along with his daughter Chocola and their servant Igor. A total of eight episodes were produced, only half of which went to air as it was quickly cancelled after the sponsoring company went bankrupt.

Dracula appeared often as a guest villain in television shows such as *Get Smart* (1968), *The Monkeys* (1968), *Night Gallery* (1971), and *Happy Days* (1981). He also appeared in animated series such as *The Beatles* (1965), *The All-New Popeye Hour* (1978), *Challenge of the Super Friends* (1978), *The Fonz and the Happy Days Gang* (1980), *The New Scooby-Doo Mysteries* (1984), and *Ghostbusters* (1986). The 1970 series *Sabrina and the Groovie Goolies*, which ran for sixteen episodes on CBS, featured Sabrina the teenage witch and her cousins, the Groovie Goolies. They all resided at Horrible Hall, a haunted boarding house, run by Count Dracula. The show also featured the vampiress Bella La Ghostly, a telephone switchboard operator, and Batso and Ratso, young vampire twins who liked to cause all sorts of trouble. In 1971, Sabrina was spun-off into her own series, as were her cousins, who reappeared in *The Groovie Goolies* show, which ran for an additional season.

The Count was often cast alongside other classic movie monsters, such as in the 1979 cartoon series *Spider-Woman*. In the episode "Dracula's Revenge," villagers in Grumania find the crypt of Count Dracula, who rises from the grave and soon adds both the Wolf Man and the Frankenstein Monster to his entourage. Inexplicably, the Count creates other vampires by shooting a laser from his fingertips, while the Wolf Man shoots lasers from his eyes to create other lycans. The Frankenstein Monster, not to be outdone, uses the bolts on his neck to shoot lasers to create more like him. The three also appeared in *Spider-Man and His Amazing Friends* (1983), but this time, Dracula is aided by Frankenstein (a robot) and the "Wolf Thing." As in all other cases, the gruesome threesome is foiled in the end. Dracula also appeared in the short-lived animated series *Drak Pack* (1980–82) and in *The Comic Strip* (1987).

Another children's television series, the Canadian-produced *Hilarious House of Frightenstein* (1971), featured the adventures of the mad scientist Count Frightenstein, the thirteenth son of Count Dracula, and his green-skinned assistant Igor. This sketch-based series showcased the talents of Billy Van, who played several characters aside from the Count, including Grizelda (the ghastly gourmet cook), Bwana Clyde Batty (a nineteenth-century British explorer) and the Wolfman, most likely based on the famous DJ Wolfman Jack. Vincent Price also appeared in each episode, where he introduced sketches and occasionally recited intentionally bad (but often funny) poetry. Since its initial run, the series has aired in syndication across Canada and in some parts of the United States, and recently a few episodes have become available on DVD.

Another long-forgotten series now available on DVD is *The Monster Squad*, which aired for 13 episodes on NBC beginning in 1976. It featured Dracula, the Wolfman and Frankenstein's monster, three wax statues inadvertently brought to life by Walt, a criminology student working as a night watchmen at a wax museum. The monsters, in order to atone for their past misdeeds, decide to become crime fighters. In 1988 a British cartoon series was launched, built around a leading character that was a mixture of Donald Duck and Dracula. Count Duckula became a popular children's comedic character as a vegetarian vampire, and **Count Duckula** would run for sixty-five episodes. The series came to the United States and has been aired on cable channels.

The Count continued his reign in 1990 as Alexander Lucard in the short-lived TV series **Dracula: The Series**. Here again Dracula is in the modern world, this time as a billionaire businessman whose real identity has been discovered by three teenagers and their vampire-hunting uncle. In 1991 the FOX Kids channel's animated adventure *Little Dracula* featured a younger protagonist in his quest to become a great vampire just like his Dad. In that same year, the animated adventure *Draculito, mon saigneur* aired on French television for twenty-six episodes.

In 2000, the CBC aired *Dracula: A Chamber Musical*—a Shakespeare Festival production with no bats or **blood**, but a lot of singing. In another updated version of the novel, produced in Italy in 2002, Count Vladislav Tepes relocated to modern-day Budapest in an attempt to leave the superstitious world of Transylvania behind him. In 2006, a German adaptation with Marc Warren as Dracula certainly had a unique take on the story. **Arthur Holmwood**, soon to be married to **Lucy Westenra**, desperately seeks a cure for his syphilis infection. He summons Dracula to **London**, having heard that the Romanian Count possesses extraordinary powers, but of course Dracula has his own agenda, and soon begins to wreak havoc on the local population. In that same year, the British series *Young Dracula* aired on CBBC (the BBC's channel for kids) and lasted two seasons. The story followed the Dracula family as they relocated to a small town in Britain, and was loosely based on the children's book by Michael Lawrence.

More recently, the very loosely-based British series *Demons* (2009) followed the last descendent of the **Van Helsing** line, Luke Rutherford, as he fights against the dark forces of the world with the assistance of Mina Harker, a blind concert pianist well-versed on demons, zombies, werewolves and vampires.

Vampire Television Series: It was in the 1960s that vampires first became featured in a continued leading role, with two of the most famous and successful series having launched in 1964. ABC brought Charles Addams's *New Yorker* cartoon series to television as **The Addams Family**, which featured Carolyn Jones as the vampiric Morticia Addams. CBS also created a new oddball family, **The Munsters**, with characters based on the classic monsters from early **Universal Pictures** horror films. This series featured two vampires, Yvonne de Carlo as Lily Munster, and Al Lewis as Grandpa (who, over the course of the series, was revealed to be, in fact, Count Dracula). Both series were similar in tone, with each family believing they were typical suburbanites, not quite understanding why everyone around them found their habits so peculiar. Both ran for two seasons, yet proved popular enough to spawn several progeny.

In 1973, NBC took an animated version of the Addams family on the road in a haunted RV, a series that ran for two seasons, although the second simply re-aired the original 16 episodes. *The Munsters Today*, essentially a 1988 sequel to the original series, updated the cast and the time period, with the characters remaining the same. The premise: back in the 1960s, one of Grandpa's experiments with a **sleep** machine went horribly wrong, and the entire family ended up in suspended animation.

Twenty years later, a developer looking to turn the house into a parking lot accidentally awakens the family, who now find themselves in similar comedic situations in a new era. After the success of the 1991 *Addams Family* feature film, ABC brought the family back to television in 1992 for a new animated series that ran for three seasons. Both this and the earlier animated *Addams Family* series were geared toward a more youthful demographic, with much of the macabre nature toned down for a Saturday-morning audience. In 1998, the clan returned to a live-action format in *The New Addams Family*, a Canadian-produced series that updated the original story into current times. It ran for a successful two seasons, and two episodes featured John Astin, the original Gomez Addams, as Grampapa Addams.

Audiences in the year 1966 said good-bye to the Addams and Munster families, and hello to the Collins clan, in a show that was to become a television enigma. Producer Dan Curtis sold ABC on a **gothic** daytime soap opera that he called *Dark Shadows*. But the original show did not do well, so in an attempt to boost ratings and avoid cancellation, Curtis introduced a supernatural element, and ghosts soon began to inhabit the Collinwood mansion. But with the introduction of vampire **Barnabas Collins** nine months into the show run, *Dark Shadows* finally became a huge success. It ran for more than 1,200 episodes, and found many viewers among teenagers who rushed home from school to watch it in its afternoon time slot. The series ended its network run in 1971, and during that time the Collins family also faced werewolves, witches, and warlocks, with stories taking place in parallel dimensions and even different time periods. Truly a ground-breaking series, the popularity of the original *Dark Shadows* has since been kept alive through fan clubs, fanzines, and annual conventions.

Although the immortal Count Dracula made several appearances on television over the next twenty years, it wasn't until the early 1990s that other vampires would once again be featured in a continued leading role. Fitting, then, that the decade that saw the beginning of a resurgence of vampires on television was initiated by the same creature that popularized them twenty-five years earlier. In 1991, *Dark Shadows* reappeared on network television in a new lavish prime-time series that starred Ben Cross as Barnabas Collins. While hailed by vampire enthusiasts, and especially the still organized *Dark Shadows* fans, it failed to find a sufficient audience and was cancelled after only one season.

In 1992, the Canadian-German-American television series ***Forever Knight*** made its debut, and told the story of 800-year-old vampire Nick Knight (played by Geraint Wyn Davies), a Toronto police detective trying to hide his vampiric nature while seeking redemption for his past misdeeds. It was an early example of the vampire-as-romantic-hero, seen so often in the twentieth and twenty-first centuries. The series originated as a 1989 made-for-television movie that starred Rick Springfield as a vampire cop in Los Angeles, and although meant to be a pilot for a television series, it was never optioned at the time. However, the show was recast and the story relocated to

Toronto, and found a home at CBS as part of their new *Crime Time after Prime Time* lineup, which aired each evening as an alternative to NBC's popular *The Tonight Show*. The series, although popular with fans, had trouble staying on the air during its three-season run, and ultimately ended in 1996. In that same year, the popularity of White Wolf Game Studio's **Vampire: The Masquerade** role-playing **game** led to a loosely-based television series called *Kindred: The Embraced*. Produced by Aaron Spelling, some called this FOX series a cross between *The Godfather* and *Melrose Place*, and failing to find an audience, it was cancelled after eight episodes.

The daytime soap opera *Port Charles*, a spin-off of the long-running series *General Hospital*, debuted in the summer of 1997. Initially focused on doctors and interns at a medical school, it ultimately took a page from *Dark Shadows* and began to include some gothic and supernatural elements, such as vampires and life after death. About half way into its run, it abandoned the standard open-ended writing style of most soaps, and adopted thirteen-week story arcs much like those found in the Spanish *telenovelas*. Ultimately these changes weren't enough to pull in high ratings, and it was cancelled in 2003, unintentionally ending the series with a cliffhanger episode.

Buffy the Vampire Slayer, by far the most successful vampire-oriented television series to date, aired on the WB and UPN networks from 1997 to 2003. Developed from the 1992 movie that met with decidedly mixed reviews, the series featured Sarah Michelle Gellar as a high school cheerleader selected as the chosen vampire slayer for her generation, fighting supernatural creatures with the help of several classmates and her librarian "watcher." Airing for 145 episodes over seven seasons, *Buffy* has since become a cultural phenomenon; it spawned the spin-off TV series *Angel*, inspired hundreds of novels, magazines and comic books, and has even graced the halls of academia, becoming a hot topic of discussion amongst scholars of popular culture. Development began in 2001 for an animated series based on the live action show, however no network was interested at the time. Yet FOX still tried shopping it around even as late as 2004, when a pilot was produced that included the voices of most of the original cast members. Buffy's love interest **Angel** (David Boreanaz), the vampire-with-a-soul, was a regular on *Buffy the Vampire Slayer* until the end of season three. In 1999 the spin-off series *Angel* premiered, where the titular vampire relocated to Los Angeles in search of redemption, vowing to "help the helpless." Darker in tone than its precursor, *Angel* had a successful run over five seasons, but was unexpectedly cancelled in 2004.

The *Buffyverse* proved so popular that in 2007, four years after the show completed its original network run, Dark Horse Comics began publishing *Buffy the Vampire Slayer Season Eight*, a canonical continuation of the original television series in comic book form, which itself has also spawned several limited-series spin-offs. Much like *Buffy*, the *Angel* universe proved so popular that it inspired a number of books, comics and other merchandise, and recently found renewed life in the canonical comic book series *Angel: After the Fall* from IDW Publishing.

Thanks to the popularity of *Buffy* and *Angel*, networks soon expanded their lineup of vampire television series, but most haven't garnered the same critical praise as their predecessors, with many lasting only one season. In 2006, a short-lived spin-off of the *Blade* movie trilogy featured Kirk "Sticky Fingaz" Jones in the role made popular by Wesley Snipes. *Blade: The Series* had the **vampire hunter** teaming up with a veteran of the

Iraq war as she investigated her brother's mysterious death. The year 2007 would be a banner year for new vampire television series, including the animated *Blood +* as well as the gay-themed *Dante's Cove* and *The Lair*. Also in that year, two new series featured a mixture of vampires and crime drama, two genres seeming perfectly suited for one another, as shown by the previous success of both *Forever Knight* and *Angel*.

The series *Blood Ties*, based on the novels by **Tanya Huff**, had private investigator Vicki Nelson teamed up with vampire Henry Fitzroy, as she investigated supernatural events in Toronto. The equally-popular *Moonlight* starred Alex O'Loughlin as Mick St. John, a vampire and private investigator in Los Angeles, who falls in love with a mortal woman. But as with many vampire series, these were both cancelled even though they had quickly established an avid fan base, many of whom are still crying for more from their beloved bloodsuckers.

HBO's *True Blood*, loosely based on *The Southern Vampire Mysteries* series of novels by **Charlaine Harris**, has quickly rivaled *Buffy* in terms of popularity and cultural impact. The premise is that after the creation of synthetic blood, vampires are now "out of the coffin" and live freely and openly among humans. One such vampire, the 173-year-old Bill Compton (Stephen Moyer), soon finds himself in the company of telepathic barmaid Sookie Stackhouse (Anna

(Left to right) Ian Somerhalder as Damon Salvatore, Paul Wesley as Stefan Salvatore, and Nina Dobrev as Elena Gilbert in the television series *Vampire Diaries*.

Paquin), and they become romantically involved as the series progresses. The show was a runaway hit for HBO, who greenlit a third season that began production in late 2009. Hot on its tail and aimed toward a younger audience, *The Vampire Diaries*, based on the series of books by **L. J. Smith**, made its debut in the fall of 2009. The series premiere was the most-watched launch ever on the CW network to date, with an estimated 4.8 million viewers in the United States.

The resurgence in the popularity of vampires on television has not been limited to North America. In 1991, the Brazilian soap opera *Vamp* began its run, telling the story of the invasion of vampires into a pacific town called the Bay of Angels. In late 1992, serial opera *The Vampyr: A Soap Opera* aired for five episodes on the BBC, an updated version of *Der Vampyr* (1828), a German romantic opera that itself was based on "The Vampyre" (1819) by **John William Polidori**. Other series included the German production *Der Kleine Vampir* (1993); the Cantonese series *Vampire Expert* (1995); the British series *Ultraviolet* (1998); the Japanese series *My Date with a Vampire* (1998); the Brazilian production *O Beijo do Vampiro* (2002); and the Korean series *Hello Franceska* (2005). In 2008, the British series *Being Human* followed a vampire, a ghost, and a werewolf as they shared a flat in modern-day Bristol. Having achieved strong ratings since its premiere, the series has been greenlit for a second season.

Over the past decade, the Japanese television market has seen a major increase in vampire-themed series. Although some have been live action, most are anime series based on manga publications, the most popular of which have also been translated into English and have aired in North America. These include: *Vampire Princess Miyu* (1997), *Descendants of Darkness* (2000), *Hellsing* (2003), *Lunar Legend Tsukihime* (2003), *Tsukuyomi: Moon Phase* (2004), and *Karin* (2005). A more adult-themed manga publication, *Negima! Magister Negi Magi*, has inspired the anime series *Negima!* (2005), an alternate retelling called *Negima!?* (2006), and the live-action series *Negima!!* (2007). Other titles available on DVD that have not yet been televised in North America include *Rosario + Vampire* (2008) and *Vampire Knight* (2008). The series *Trinity Blood* (2005) and *Black Blood Brothers* (2006) were both based on novellas that also inspired popular manga adaptations. Other anime series not directly based on manga include *NightWalker* (1998), *Vampiyan Kids* (2001), and *Legend of Duo* (2004).

Made-for-Television Movies: During the last three decades, feature-length movies produced specifically for the television audience, rather than being released to theaters, became a growing portion of all movies produced. Among the first such movies was **The Night Stalker**, produced by Dan Curtis in 1972. Much like his *Dark Shadows* series, it became the highest rated television show aired to that date. The story followed reporter Carl Kolchak (Darren McGavin) as he investigated a series of gruesome murders, ultimately discovering and then killing a vampire. The success of the movie led to a second telefilm, *The Night Strangler* (1973), followed by *Kolchak: The Night Stalker* series in 1974; it pitted the intrepid reporter against a variety of supernatural elements. One of the first episodes had Kolchak following the trail of a vampire in Las Vegas, herself a victim of Janos Skorzeny, the vampire from *The Night Stalker* telefilm. The series lasted for one season, and was "reimagined" in a short-lived 2005 series that bore little resemblance to the original story.

Dan Curtis worked with Richard Matheson on the script for both Kolchak movies, as well as his version of **Dracula (1973)**. In 1976, the two teamed up once again for *Dead of Night*, which dramatized three of Matheson's stories. One of them, "No Such Thing as a Vampire," told the story of Professor Gheria who tried to kill his wife by creating the impression that she was wasting away due to a vampire's attack. This story was first adapted in the UK as part of the "Late Night Horror" BBC television series in 1968.

Even before *The Night Stalker*, the popular series *The Munsters* led to the production of a made-for-television movie in 1966. *Munster, Go Home!* was made on the heels of the cancellation of the original series, and was intended as a pilot for a new series featuring the family in England. Ultimately the networks weren't interested, so instead it was released theatrically as a stand-alone film. A second television movie, *The Munsters Revenge*, reunited most of the original cast members, and aired on NBC in 1981. Similarly, NBC had earlier attempted to revive the *Addams Family* franchise in 1977 with *Halloween with the New Addams Family*, again reuniting most of the original cast members, but it also failed to recapture the magic of the original series.

The 1970s ended with a handful of noteworthy movies, some of which were pilots for series that were never picked up by the networks. One of these was *The Norliss Tapes*, produced for NBC and directed by Dan Curtis in 1973. It told the story of David Norliss (Roy Thinnes), an author researching a book aimed to debunk supernatural oc-

currences, yet he ultimately crossed paths with a group of modern-day vampires. A second pilot, *Vampire*, aired on ABC in 1979, and starred Richard Lynch as the vampire Prince Anton Voytek. Not so much a blood-and-**fangs** story as it was a tale of revenge, the movie concluded with an open ending, but was never picked up as a series. In that same year, Tobe Hooper directed the dramatic version of **Stephen King**'s early vampire novel *Salem's Lot* for CBS, where vampires invade a small town in New England. An unrelated sequel, *A Return to Salem's Lot*, was briefly released theatrically in 1987, while an updated version of the original story was produced for television in 2004.

More recent made-for-television vampire movies include: *Desire, the Vampire* (1982), *The Midnight Hour* (1985), *Nightlife* (1989), *Daughters of Darkness* (1990), *Shadow Zone: The Undead Express* (1996), *Dracula 3000* (2004), *Bloodsuckers* (2005), and *The Librarian: The Curse of the Judas Chalice* (2008). One of the most unique telefilms to date was **London After Midnight**, a 2002 reconstruction of the lost 1927 **Tod Browning** film. Director Rick Schmidlin utilized some 200 still photographs to recreate the movie, and based the intertitles on the original shooting script.

The cable channel IFC teamed up with Lionsgate Entertainment Corporation to produce a made-for-television movie based on the *Anita Blake: Vampire Hunter* series of books by **Laurell K. Hamilton**. Produced as a pilot for a potential series, the film will air in 2010.

Other Vampire Productions: In addition to the vampire-oriented series and made-for-TV movies, the undead proved popular enough to be written into non-vampire series. Many early appearances played for **humor** and usually had the supernatural element explained away, as found in such series as *Get Smart* (1965), *Gilligan's Island* (1966), and *F Troop* (1967). Among the more notable episodes that treated vampires a little more seriously were those that were part of: *Adventure Inc.*, *Blue Murder*, *CSI: Crime Scene Investigation*, *Diagnosis Murder*, *The Dresden Files*, *Dr. Who*, *The Man from U.N.C.L.E.*, *Nash Bridges*, *Nip/Tuck*, *Quantum Leap*, *St. Elsewhere*, *Starsky & Hutch*, *Superboy*, *Supernatural* and **The X Files**.

As comic books expanded into the television medium, so too did their vampire characters. Marvel's fourth animated *Spider-Man* series (1994–98) had several episodes featuring **Morbius**, the living vampire. However, due to restrictions in place by FOX, no traditional vampires were to be part of the series. So the creators had to include a modified Morbius character, one who subsisted on plasma rather than blood, and who drained his victims through the suckers on his hands. This is reminiscent of the pseudovampire episode "Man Trap" from the original *Star Trek* series, where a creature uses suckers on its hands to drain the salt from the bodies of its victims. Other vampires eventually appeared on *Spider-Man* in name only; none were ever shown biting their victims on the neck. The animated HBO series *Spawn* (1999) featured a vampire during the third season, while on the WB network *Batman: The Animated Series* (2004–08) showcased the DC character **Man-Bat** on several occasions. In 2009, Marvel's psychic vampire Selene, a sorceress and mutant, appeared in the season one finale of *Wolverine and the X-Men* that aired on the Nicktoons Network.

Television anthology series, which ran a new story each week, also had a tendency to air episodes that featured vampires. These series included: *Alfred Hitchcock Presents, Are You Afraid of the Dark?*, *Friday the 13th*, *The Hunger*, *Mystery and Imagination*, *Night*

Gallery, The Ray Bradbury Theater, Tales from the Crypt, Tales from the Darkside and *The Twilight Zone.* The most well-known female vampire in literature, **Carmilla**, has also made rare appearances on television. The British series Mystery and Imagination first dramatized the story in 1966, and in 1989 "Carmilla" was updated and presented in the Showtime series *Nightmare Classics.* The late 1980s also saw television movie adaptations in both Spain and France.

Prior to *Buffy the Vampire Slayer,* with few exceptions, the vampire tended to remain just on the edge of television culture, not having the strength to hold a continuing spot on prime-time television. But that has all changed. Over the past decade, vampires have experienced a population explosion like none other. From the horrific to the romantic, the undead are now firmly entrenched within our television airwaves, much to the delight of their avid fans.

The Internet: Over the past decade, broadcasters have increasingly used the Internet to create awareness for new vampire series, leading up to the official television launch. A rising trend has been to produce *webisodes* that feature new content created solely for the Internet. These video clips, usually two to four minutes in length, often feature character back stories, prequel scenes, and other tales falling within the canon of the show.

The most successful viral marketing campaign to date is for the HBO series *True Blood.* Several hilarious videos released to the Internet were often fake news segments pertaining to the premise of the series, where vampires are "out of the coffin" and living freely among human beings. Leading up to the launch of *The Vampire Diaries,* the CW produced a four-part webisode series entitled *A Darker Truth,* where vampire hunter Jason Harris followed the trail of Stephan Salvatore, whom he believed was responsible for his sister's death. The MTV show *Valemont* began as a short series of webisodes that aired on both MTV and MTV.com, while the Canadian series *Sanctuary* started out as eight webisodes in 2007, and was subsequently picked up as a traditional television series by the SyFy channel.

Hammer Films also used this medium to return to feature film production, releasing *Beyond the Rave* in 2008 as a series of short video installments. Two short films based in the *30 Days of Night* universe, *Blood Trails,* and *Dust to Dust,* were released as a series of webisodes through FEARnet. Emerging filmmakers as well as everyday fans of the genre are also using the Internet to broadcast their vampire stories. Early Web series included *Vampire Trucker* and *Too Shy To Be a Vampire,* and more recent series include *Bleed, 3 Vampires, Vampire Killers, Bleeder* and *Transylvania Television.*

Sources:

Jones, Stephen. *The Illustrated Vampire Movie Guide.* London: Titan, 1993. 144 pp.
Muir, John Kenneth. *Terror Television.* Jefferson, NC: McFarland, 2001. 675 pp.
Terrace, Vincent. *Encyclopedia of Television.* 3 vols. New York: New York Zoetrope, 1985.

❲ Temple of the Vampire ❳

The Temple of the Vampire is a religious organization that practices the religion of Vampirism. According to the temple, its faith is an ancient religion that has, through the centuries, been known by many names including the Order of the Dragon, the Temple of the Dragon, and the Temple of the Vampire Dragon Goddess Tiamat (ancient Sumeria). The modern public temple has attempted to locate those people who might be of the Blood—those who have realized their difference from the mass of humanity, who resonate with the Dark of the Night, who recognize themselves as predators, who know there is something more to life, and who wish to possess it.

According to the Temple, vampires exist as the predators of humans. Vampires emerge out of humanity and represent the next stage in evolution. Theirs is the religion of the elite—the rulers. They believe that vampires created the religions of the world to ensure humanity's basic docility. The basic perspective of the temple is summarized in "The Vampire Creed":

> I am a Vampire. I worship my ego and I worship my life, for I am the only God that is. I am proud that I am a predatory **animal** and I honor my animal instincts. I exalt my rational mind and hold no belief that is in defiance of reason. I recognize the difference between the world of truth and fantasy. I acknowledge the fact that survival is the highest law. I acknowledge the Powers of Darkness to be hidden natural laws through which I work my magic. I know that my beliefs in Ritual are fantasy but the magic is real, and I respect and acknowledge the results of my magic. I realize there is no heaven as there is no hell, and I view death as the destroyer of life. Therefore I will make the most of life here and now. I am a Vampire. Bow down before me.

Today's vampire exists in a double reality. What is termed the Daytime self is a material skeptic who laughs at superstition. The Nightside self practices magical and ritual acts. Through the techniques taught by the Temple, the vampire learns to move in the world of magical fantasy and there begins to realize the traditional powers of the vampire (from shapeshifting to **hypnotic power** to physical immortality). The strengthening of the Nightside self, in which the individual's will is connected with the cosmic Powers of Darkness, leads to changes in the Dayside world in conformity to the Nightside realities. Vampiric rituals allow contact with the Undead Gods and lead to the sacred act of Vampiric communion. Membership in the temple is international and is organized in several levels. The Lifetime Member is one who has made a first step in contact and made a material donation to the temple.

After making application and being accepted, the Lifetime Member becomes an Active Member. After some degree of results in development of one's vampiric powers, advancement to the level of Vampire Predator and entrance into the Second Circle of the Outer Temple is acknowledged. Further advancement may lead to becoming a Vampire Priest/ess. The priesthood has access to the innermost levels of temple knowledge—the hidden teachings. The Temple publishes *The Vampire Bible*, a manual of fundamental magical lore, available to lifetime members. It also issues a biennial publication, *Bloodlines: The Vampire Temple Journal* and the monthly *Lifeforce: The International Vampire Forum*.

Sources:

Aleiss, Angela. "Vampires: The Bloody Truth." Religion News Service, November 18, 2000. *Beliefnet*. Posted at http://www.beliefnet.com/Faiths/2000/11/Vampires-The-Bloody-Truth.aspx. Accessed on April 8, 2010. *Lifeforce*. Vol 1. Lacy, WA: Temple of the Vampire, 1993.

Tenatz *see:* Southern Slavs, Vampires and the

Thailand, Vampires in

Pre-Buddhist Thailand had a significant mythology that survived into the twentieth century as a form of spirit worship. The spirits, which have a minor place in Buddhist thought, nevertheless find a certain compatibility with the dominant Buddhism. The spirits were known collectively as the *phi*. The *phi* were numerous and have never been fully catalogued. They were analogous to the ghosts, goblins, elves, and fairies of western Europe. Many were malevolent and haunted different structures. Every family had a private tutelary spirit that, if neglected, would bring ill fortune to the family members. Among the *phi* who were believed to inhabit the countryside were the ghosts of people killed by **animals, women** who died in childbirth, people who died and did not have proper funeral rites, and those who died suddenly and unexpectedly. These were the sources of various forms of attacks including vampirism. They bit, scratched, and caused disease.

The *Phi Song Nang* were similar to the **pontianak** of **Java** and Indonesia. They appeared as beautiful young women and attacked and vampirized young men. The ways of the *phi* were known to the various occult practitioners, from sorcerers to mediums. The *maw du*, a seer, would be called in cases of a person who had been attacked by a *phi*. The *maw dus* used various spells and incantation to get rid of the *phi*. They also sold charms to prevent the attack of the *phi*. Some entre into the Thai world of vampires was offered in the 2005 movie *Vampires: the Turning*.

Sources:
Graham, W. A. *Siam*. 2 vols. London: The de la More Press, 1924.

Tibet, Vampires in

Tibet, like **India** and **China**, possessed a rich pantheon of supernatural entities, and many had some vampiric characteristics. Many of these were shared with such neighboring nations as Nepal, Sikkim, and Mongolia. Among the most visible of the vampiric entities were the so-called Wrathful Deities who appeared in *The Tibetan Book of the Dead*. This volume described what Tibetan Buddhists believed would be experienced by individuals in the days immediately following their death. During these days, the deceased generally wandered into an area dominated by karma (the law of consequences) where the higher impulses of the heart gave way to the reasonings of the brain centers. The heart impulses were personified by the Peaceful Deities. The brain reasonings were personified by the Wrathful Deities.

Contemporary writers on Tibetan Buddhism have generally emphasized that the deities were not objectively real, but were the products of the person picturing aspects of the self. However, in traditional Buddhist lore, they were pictured as part of a true supernatural realm. The Wrathful Deities, also called the 58 **blood**-drinking deities, were believed to begin their appearance on the eighth day after the deceased passed into the post-death realm. For example, the blood-drinking deities of the Vajra order appeared on the ninth day. Here the intellect was represented by Bhagavan Vajra-Heruka. In one hand he held a human scalp. He was embraced by his mother, Vajra-Krotishaurima, whose right hand held a red shell filled with blood that she placed at her son's mouth.

On the next day, one encountered Ratna-Heruka, who appeared like Vajra-Heruka, but was yellow rather than blue. The red Padma-Heruka appeared on the eleventh day. On the twelfth day, the blood-drinking deities of the Lotus Order were encountered. On the thirteenth day, the eight Kerimas were encountered.

These deities had the heads of various **animals** and engaged in different vampiric and ghoulish actions. One, the Dark-Green Ghasmari, for example, held a scalp filled with blood that she stirred with a *dorje* (a holy object) then drank from it. Other similar deities appeared daily throughout the fourteenth day. The dying person was given instructions on relating to the deities and prayers to acknowledge them. Individuals were also told to call upon the name of their own guru and their personal deity to sustain them in the loneliness of the after-death realms. It should be noted that these deities did not attack the individual who encountered them, rather they were pictured as general representations of vampiric actions previously committed by the deceased.

Devendra P. Varma, author of *The Vampire in Legend, Lore, and Literature* has called attention to Yama, the Tibetan Lord of Death, who, like the Nepalese Lord of Death and the Mongolian God of Time, subsisted by drinking the blood of sleeping people. The Tibetan god had a green face and a blue-green body. In his clawed hand he held the Wheel of Life. The Nepalese god had three blood-shot eyes with flames issuing from his eyebrows and thunder and lightning from his nostrils. In his hands, he carried a sword and a cup of blood. He was decorated with human skulls. The Mongolian god, with his prominent canine teeth, was seen amidst a storm over a bloody sea. There was also a belief in the pursuit of the living by the dead. The dead were cremated, in part, to prevent the soul from attempting to re-enter it. The soul after death, like person before death, became the object of ritual, in this case to keep it from interacting improperly with the realm of the living.

A Sikkim Vampire: Varma has also recorded one case of nonlegendary vampirism in Tibet's neighbor Sikkim. In the early eighteenth century, Princess Pedi Wangmo, the monarch's half-sister, plotted to kill her half-brother. With the assistance of a Tibetan doctor, she bled Chador Namgyal to death and drank his blood. She escaped the palace but was soon caught. Both she and her accomplice were killed. It was believed, by some, that after death she became a vampire. Her story was recounted in a fresco in a monastery in Sinon near Mt. Kanchenjunga.

Sources:

Evans-Wentz, W. Y. *The Tibetan Book of the Dead; or, The After-Death Experiences on the Bardo Plane, according to Lama Kazi Dawa-Samdup's English Rendering.* 1927. Rept. New York: Causeway Books, 1973.

Varma, Devendra P. "The Vampire in Legend, Lore, and Literature." Introduction to *Varney the Vampyre.* New York: Arco Press, 1970.

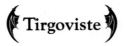

Tirgoviste

Tirgoviste, the former capital of Wallachia and the section of modern **Romania** south of the Carpathian Mountains, was the location of the palace where **Dracula** resided during his years as the prince of Wallachia. The capital of Wallachia was moved to Tir-

A statue of Vlad the Impaler in Tirgoviste, Romania.

goviste from Curtea de Arges in 1415 and there, Mircea the Old, one of Dracula's ancestors, erected the palace that became the seat of power for the prince. During the next century and a half, numerous claimants to the throne briefly resided at Tirgoviste in the unstable situation created by the varying fortunes of Wallachia's powerful neighbors.

Vlad the Impaler, the historical Dracula, first moved to Tirgoviste in 1436 when his father, **Vlad Dracul,** became the prince of Wallachia. He lived there only six years before he was sent to live among the Turks as a hostage to ensure his father's goodwill toward the Ottoman Empire. Vlad returned to Tirgoviste for a brief month in October 1448, when he attempted to assume the throne following the death of his father. He was driven from Tirgoviste by Vladislav II and fled to Moldavia. It was not until Vladislav turned on his Hungarian sponsors and fought against John Hunyadi that Vlad became the Hungarian candidate to hold the throne. He again took up residence in his childhood home in the spring of 1456.

Vlad would rule only six years, but he filled those years with a lifetime of adventure and earned his title, Tepes, or "the Impaler." The yard in front of the palace became the site of numerous executions by impalement. Vlad had the Chinda (Sunset) Tower built adjacent to the palace to provide an observation post for viewing the work of the

THE VAMPIRE BOOK: THE ENCYCLOPEDIA OF THE UNDEAD

The ruins of Vlad the Impaler's palace in Tirgoviste.

executioners. The first notable event of his brief reign probably occurred on Easter of 1459. He invited the many boyars (feudal land owners) to an Easter feast. After they spent the day eating and drinking, Vlad had his soldiers surround the palace, and he arrested the boyars and their families. The elders were immediately killed, but the remainder were marched away to Curtea de Arges to build Vlad's mountain castle.

Vlad's six years of rule culminated at the gates of Tirgoviste in June 1462. For two months, he had fought a losing battle across Wallachia. The Turkish army, led by Mohammed II (1432–1481), arrived at Tirgoviste only to find the impaled bodies of all the Turks who had been taken prisoner. Mohammed II turned back and returned to Adrianople. Vlad followed the retreating army and constantly harassed it. However, Mohammed II gave his army to Vlad's brother Radu cel Frumos who had gained the support of the remaining boyars. Radu chased Vlad to his castle north of Curtea de Arges and, finally, out of the country.

Vlad lived as a prisoner of the Hungarians for more than a decade. He gradually gained the support of King Matthias for his return to the Wallachian's throne. Vlad returned to Tirgoviste in 1476. His stay was short. He moved on to Bucharest just one week later. In December of that year, the Turkish army attacked and the boyars turned on Vlad and killed him. The exact fate of his body is unknown. Tirgoviste remained the capital of Wallachia until 1660 when it was officially relocated to Bucharest. In the 1990s, it began to develop as a tourist site. Vlad's Tower has been opened as a museum, and visitors may wander through the palace grounds. Statues of Vlad may be found in nearby parks.

Sources:

Florescu, Radu, and Raymond T. McNally. *Dracula: A Biography of Vlad the Impaler, 1413–1476.* New York: Hawthorn Books, 1973. 239 pp.

———. *Dracula: Prince of Many Faces: His Life and Times.* Boston: Little, Brown and Company, 1989. 261 pp.

Mackenzie, Andrew. *Dracula Country.* London: Arthur Barker, 1977. 176 pp.

Treptow, Kurt W., ed. *Dracula: Essays on the Life and Times of Vlad Tepes.* New York: Columbia University Press, 1991. 336 pp.

Tlahuelpuchi *see:* Mexico, Vampires in

Tolstoy, Alexey Konstantinovitch (1817–1875)

Alexey Konstantinovitch Tolstoy, the nineteenth-century Russian writer who introduced the vampire into Russian literature, was born in St. Petersburg, **Russia**. Tolstoy was educated at home and, at the age of 16, entered government service at the Moscow Archives of the Ministry of Foreign Affairs. While in Moscow, he was able to study at Moscow University where he absorbed German idealistic philosophy. He received his diploma from the university in 1835.

At the beginning of his literary career, influenced by E. T. A. Hoffmann's tales, Tolstoy wrote several fantastic/horror stories, the first of which was "Upyr" ("The Vampire"). "Upyr" was the story of a young couple, Runevsky and Dasha. The story opened in nineteenth-century Moscow with a group at a ball. Runevsky conversed with a pale young man, Rybarenko, on the subject of vampires. He predicted that if Dasha went to visit her grandmother she would die. Eventually, after a series of adventures and some visionary experiences, Runevsky learned the truth. The problem in Dasha's family stemmed from previous generations, to an unfaithful wife who killed her husband. As he was dying, he pronounced a curse of madness and vampirism upon her and their heirs. She eventually went insane and committed **suicide**. Dasha's grandmother inherited the curse. As a vampire, she had already killed Dasha's mother and was prepared to kill Dasha. In the end he became a believer in the supernatural, although Dasha dismissed everything that happened and believed a more naturalistic explanation.

Tolstoy first read the story at one of the local salons and then, after passing a censor, had it published under the pseudonym Krasnorogsky in 1841. It was followed by a second supernatural tale, "The Reunion After Three-Hundred Years," a ghost story. Tolstoy returned to the vampiric theme in his third story, "The Family of the Vurkodlak". (The *vurkodlak* was the vampire of the **southern Slavs**.) Written in French, it began with the Congress of Vienna in 1815 where the Marquis d'Urfé entertained some aristocratic friends with his story. While traveling through Serbia, d'Urfé stopped for the night. The family he stayed with was upset as the father had left to fight the Turks. Be-

fore he left, d'Urfé told the family to beware if the father returned in less than ten days—it was a sign that he had become a *vurkodlak* and should be impaled with an aspen **stake**. Almost ten days passed before the father returned. The older son was about to kill him but was overruled by the family, although the father refused to eat or drink and otherwise behaved strangely. The father then attacked the family, including the daughter to whom d'Urfé had been attracted. D'Urfé continued on his journey but returned to the village some months later. He was told that the entire family had become vampires. He sought out the young girl but soon discovered that, in fact, she was now a vampire. He barely escaped from the family.

After writing "The Family of the Vurkodlak," which was not published during his lifetime, Tolstoy wrote a fourth supernatural story, "Amena." These four stories formed a prologue to his formal literary career that was really thought to have begun when he started writing **poetry** in the late 1840s. The high point of his career as a poet came in the late 1850s, the period after his service in the Crimean War (1855–1856). In 1861, he resigned from the Imperial Court and devoted the rest of his life to his writing. Tolstoy has been hard to classify, as his works do not readily fit into any of the major schools of nineteenth-century Russian writing. A loner, he rarely participated in the literary circles of his time, and, after leaving the court, settled on his estate in the Ukraine. Tolstoy approved of some Westernization but did not like the more radical activists. He did inject the vampire theme into Russian writing, a theme that would later be picked up by Nicol Gogol and Ivan Turgenev. In 1960, Italian director **Mario Bava** brought "The Family of the Vurkodlak" to the screen as one of three Russian stories in his *La Maschera del Demonio* (released in the United States as *Black Sunday*). Boris Karloff, who narrated the breaks between the stories, also played the father who had become a *vurkodlak*. English editions of Tolstoy's stories were published in 1969.

Sources:

Dalton, Margaret. *A. K. Tolstoy.* New York: Twayne Publishers, 1972. 171 pp.

Ingham, Norman W. *E. T. A. Hoffmann's Reception in Russia.* Würzburg, Germany: Jal-Verlag, 1974: 244–250.

Tolstoy, Alexis. *Vampires: Stories of the Supernatural.* Translation by Fedor Nikannov. New York: Hawthorn Books, 1969. 183 pp.

❴ *The Tomb of Dracula* ❵

*T*he Tomb of Dracula is second only to **Vampirella** as the most successful vampire-oriented **comic book** series of all time. Vampires were banned from comic books in 1954 by the Comics Code, but a revised code in 1971 allowed vampires if they were presented in a manner similar to the vampires of classic **gothic** literature. Marvel Comics responded to the change immediately by resurrecting **Dracula** and setting his new adventures in the 1970s. A familiar cast, composed of the descendants of the characters of **Bram Stoker's** 1897 novel, were assembled to fight him. Reflecting the changing times, a major female character, Rachel Van Helsing, was an active vampire fighter armed with a crossbow. **Blade, the Vampire Slayer,** an **African American,** also joined the team.

The Tomb of Dracula characters were soon integrated into the Marvel Comics alternate world. Dracula, Blade, and Hannibal King, another original character introduced in the series, began to appear in various Marvel titles (*Dr. Strange, Marvel Premiere, Frankenstein,* and *Thor*) and characters from other titles appeared in *The Tomb of Dracula* (*Werewolf by Night* and the *Silver Surfer*). *The Tomb of Dracula* was developed under the guidance of writer **Marv Wolfman**, who created the new characters, and artist Gene Colan. It would be reprinted in England under the title *Dracula Lives* (in black-and-white), translated into Spanish and Italian, and inspire a Japanese feature-length animated video.

It was finally cancelled after seventy issues, though it found a brief continuance for six issues in a black-and-white magazine format. One story in each issue continued the Dracula saga. However, Wolfman and Colan moved on to other projects and through the 1980s, Marvel lost interest in horror fiction. Only in the 1990s was a new attempt to integrate horror into the Marvel Universe attempted. During the early 1990s, Wolfman and Colan revived the story line from their successful series in a revived four-part set, *The Tomb of Dracula* (1991–92), from Marvel subsidiary Epic Comics. The story picked up the life of Frank Drake and Blade the Vampire Slayer a decade after the killing of Dracula at the end of the original series (and the demise of all Marvel vampires in 1983). Dracula had made his initial return several years previously in *Dr. Strange Sorcerer Supreme* (No. 10) and now wished to take revenge on Drake and his loved ones.

Subsequently, in 1992, as vampires were enjoying what proved to be a temporary return to the Marvel Universe, various individual issues of the original series were reprinted as one-shots under the titles *Requiem for Dracula, The Savage Return of Dracula,* and *The Wedding of Dracula. The Tomb of Dracula* one-shots heralded the return of several characters from *The Tomb of Dracula,* including Blade, Hannibal King, and Frank Drake, who were given new life as partners in a present-day Boston detective agency. They were known as *The Nightstalkers,* an anti-vampire/anti-demonic force team. Their adventures appeared in 17 issues, in which they worked with other like-minded crusaders collectively called the Midnight Sons. At the end of *The Nightstalkers* Issue No. 17, Drake and King were killed. Blade survived in a new series for several years, has made subsequent appearances in other Marvel titles, and was featured in the three *Blade* movies starring Wesley Snipes. In 1998 Hannibal King was brought back from the dead for some additional interaction with Dracula, including an appearance in the third of the Blade movies.

From 2003 to 2005, Marvel comics reprinted all the *Tomb of Dracula* stories in black and white in four large volumes as part of its "Essential" reprint series, the *Essential Tomb of Dracula.*

Sources:

Essential Tomb of Dracula. Vols. 1–4. New York: Marvel, 2003–2005.
The Tomb of Dracula. No. 1–70. New York: Marvel Comics, 1971–79.
The Tomb of Dracula. No. 104. New York: Epic Comics, 1991–1992.

❨ Trading Cards, the Vampire on ❩

Trading cards, offered as premiums for various products (especially bubble gum) grew increasingly popular in the years after World War II, with those picturing sports fig-

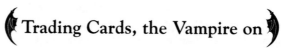

ures from professional baseball and football taking the lead. Then in the 1960s, non-sports cards began to come into their own and it was in this era that vampires first appeared on them, although a few actors who had portrayed vampires had been pictured earlier. It is interesting to note that sports cards have included non-sport themes as part of their huge 400-plus card sets in recent years. In that light, in 1995, Topps's Stadium Club football cards included a ***Vampirella*** Nightmare subset, and more recently Allen & Ginter in Baseball included "authors" like **Bram Stoker** (2008) and "myths" such as the vampire and **chupacabra** (2009) in their baseball cards.

Humor had provided a popular format for trading cards, and humor became the vehicle for introducing the vampire to the media. As early as 1959, Bubbles, Inc. put a vampire card in their series Funny Monsters (You'll Die Laughing) with the caption that posed the question: "What have you got in a red perfume that smells like **blood**?" Topps, a major trading card company, entered the field that same year with a picture of **Dracula** in their Funny Valentines set. The trend continued through the 1960s with vampires being featured on Topps's Monster Laffs Midgees (1963), Monster Greeting Cards (1965), and Monster Laffs (1966). One greeting noted, "You have a great heart—too bad there's a **stake** in it." While giving way to other formats, humorous cards would continue to appear, and the vampire theme dominated Topps's series of Wacky Packages produced in the 1970s and 1980s (especially the 1985 set). Cartoon representations of **Bela Lugosi** and **Christopher Lee** were featured on humorists Gahen Wilson's 1990 Monster Baseball trading card set.

Horror movies emerged as a popular theme for trading cards in the 1960s and possibly the first vampires in that decade were in the 1961 NuCard set that included cards from the 1950s movies *The Horror of Dracula* and *Blood of Dracula*. Two years later the vampires were given more space in the Famous Monsters set from Rosen Gum Co.

The two original themes that introduced vampires to trading cards came together in the first set of cards to feature vampires, the Munsters Mumbles set (Leaf Brands, 1964), created from the popular **television** show *The Munsters*. The set included 72 cards featuring Grandpa Dracula and Lily Munster with black and white stills from the show and an accompanying humorous caption. Card 37, for example, pictured Grandpa next to a clock asking, "It's midnight, Lily, what's for breakfast?" Or, card 12 featured Grandpa observing young Eddie Munster, "This kid plays like he's out for blood." Before the end of the decade, the popular television show *Dark Shadows* inspired two sets of cards from Philadelphia Chewing Gum Company featuring the cast and its vampire **Barnabas Collins**, with black and white stills. The 1968 set was produced without captions and the 1969 set was produced with captions.

During the 1970s, with black and white cards largely a thing of the past, Marvel Comics began to issue cards picturing covers of their highly successful **comic books**. The first Marvel vampire appeared in the 1974 series that included a cover from *The Tomb of Dracula* (No. 21). However, overall, vampires and horror were not a popular topic during the 1970s and relatively few appeared, with the exception of a new format known as the vampire card stickers. The picture on these cards could be peeled off and stuck anywhere the owner (presumably a teenager) desired, such as a notebook or the door to a bedroom or locker. The next Marvel set, the Marvel Comic Book Heroes (1975) from Topps, were stickers, and included both Dracula (complaining that "Flying

A scene from the movie *Blood of Dracula,* which was featured on a series of trading cards from NuCards in 1961.

drives me bats.") and Marvel's new vampire character **Morbius** (asking, "Which way to the blood bank?").

Topps produced the decade's most unusual set, the Monster Initials cards, each of which had two large letters that pictured a monster (including many vampires). After collecting a selection of cards, the letters, which were also stickers, could be removed to spell words that could be placed on school notebooks or other personal objects. And one of Topps's most successful sets, the Wacky Packages, variations of which would continue to appear through the 1980s, included vampires on a can of "Bloodweiser" and "Fang Edward." For the collector, the most desirable and rarest of the decade's vampire cards were the two mid-decade sets called Shock Theatre, which featured stills from the two Christopher Lee **Hammer Films** movies, *Frankenstein* and *Horror of Dracula*, with humorous captions.

These fifty-one-card sets were printed as test sets (for the United States in 1975 and England the next year) but never widely distributed. They were of relatively high quality and included many pictures of the vampire superstars of the period. Topps would continue to dominate the trading card market through the 1980s although, like the vampire in the comics, the vampire in trading cards all but disappeared through the decade. Topps's Farout Iron-ons, a variation on the sticker card, opened the decade with a "Dracula for President" card, and the Garbage Pail Kids set (1986) included the likes of "Haunted Hollis" and "Batty Barney." However, it was not until the 1990s that vampire trading cards (indeed non-sports trading cards of all kinds) would significantly penetrate the popular culture.

Even if you set aside those cards tied to the popular role-playing card game **Vampire: The Eternal Struggle** (originally released as *Jyhad*), which with its several expansion sets now includes more than 2,000 vampire-related cards, still more than 90 percent of all of the vampire cards and sets ever produced have appeared since the beginning of the 1990s.

The new wave of vampire cards saw an improved quality of both the paper stock upon which the cards were printed and enhanced printing techniques. In fact, so good was the reproduction, that cards began to be presented as art objects in and of themselves, and a number of graphic artists allowed their fantasy art to be reproduced as card sets. Various card companies played with different materials including metal for making cards, and different methods of highlighting backgrounds (holograms, for example) were used for premium variants and chase cards. **Chaos! Comics** takes credit for introducing the chromium trading cards first used on the Lady Death set in 1994. Subsequent Lady Death chromium sets also included cards with Chastity, Purgatori, and the other vampires from Chaos! titles. In a few cases, such as the chase cards for the 1996 Munsters sets, shapes were radically varied.

The 1990s also saw the introduction of a number of different size variations from the standard trading card size. Previously, in the 1960s, a few miniaturized cards had appeared, but cards in the 1970s were enlarged to several different sizes from the standard to the 5-by-7-inch colossal cards.

Media led the way in the 1990s with cards based on movies and television. Heralding the new era of vampire trading cards was a 100-card set from Topps with stills from **Bram Stoker's Dracula**, the card set appearing as the movie was released in the fall of 1992. The high-quality set was supplemented with a 16-card set that was distributed simultaneously with the Bram Stoker's *Dracula* comic book, also published by Topps. A year later a similar set of 60 cards was released to celebrate the enduring popularity of the original television series *Dark Shadows* and its vampire Barnabas Collins. Not to be outdone, *The Munsters*, having enjoyed a revival on television that lasted into the early 1990s, became the subject of a new set of 90 cards from Kayro-Vue Productions in 1996, heralding a new comic book series that began in 1997.

A nostalgia similar to that shown for *Dark Shadows* would also be repeated in similar sets celebrating two decades of Hammer Films horror movies (1957–1974). In 1995 and 1996, Cornerstone Communications released two Hammer Horror series, each with

81 cards (individual sheets for saving standard size trading cards have slots for nine cards per sheet). While covering the whole range of horror movies produced by Hammer Films (*The Curse of Frankenstein, The Mummy, The Wolfman*), approximately half of the cards covered Hammer's vampire movies that retained their fan following a quarter of a century after their initial release. Even before the Hammer Horror trading cards, Heritage Toy and Game published The Famous Hammer Playing Cards, which again covered a wide range of Hammer horror but played to the vampire titles.

By the beginning of the 1990s, comic book stores had become the major distributors for non-sports trading cards, and it is not surprising to find a variety of vampire card sets being a spin-off of successful comic books. The most successful vampire comic character of the decade was Vampirella, who appeared in a host of miniseries. In 1995, Topps published the first of four Vampirella sets: the 91-card Visions of Vampirella set. Trading cards as artwork was a significant subtheme of the set, which featured the cover art from both the Warren era Vampirella comics (1970s) and the newer titles from Harris Comics, supplemented by original, never-before-published art that Harris had accumulated. The original set was quickly followed with a seventy-two-card set in a larger size, the Vampirella Gallery, which followed the Visions of Vampirella format with art from both the Warren and Harris eras. The third set, Vampirella Master Visions, tested the new market for colossal cards featuring multiple cards from popular Harris artists John Bolton, Amanda Conner, Joe Lago, Joe Quesada, and Jimmy Palmiotti. A fourth set, returning to standard size, featured the artwork of Joe Jusko from the *Vampirella: Blood Lust* comic book miniseries.

The initial Vampirella sets explored ways of enticing collectors. In the standard cards, the word Vampirella was printed in red, however, a rarer matching set had the word Vampirella printed in gold. Each set had a number of even rarer chase cards which in the gallery set were printed on a chromium layer. The Vision of Vampirella had a second oversized subset of Vampirella pin-up art, while the Gallery set featured an extremely rare single hologram card featuring artwork by legendary Vampirella artist José Gonzalez.

While Marvel's commitment to its vampire-related characters waxes and wanes; throughout the 1990s it has included the **vampire hunters** known as the Midnight Sons in its annual sets of trading cards. Beginning in 1992, the Marvel Universe annual issues from Sky Box have had cards for Morbius and **Blade the Vampire Slayer**, and with less consistency, **Lilith** and Blackout (another Marvel vampire). The most spectacular art appeared in the Siege of Darkness and Fall from Grace subsets for the 1994 Marvel Universe. Each subset of nine cards could be assembled into a larger picture of Morbius, Blade, and their supernatural allies and enemies.

Another successful comic book that served as a launching pad for trading cards was Wetworks from Image, who produced two card sets in 1995 (Aegis Entertainment, 107 cards plus chase cards) and 1996 (Cards International, eight cards). Wetworks was also regularly included in the different Wildstorm sets (drawing on a number of related Image series) through the mid-1990s. Brainstorm Comics was launched with the very successful *Vamperotica* series starring the sexy "Bad Girl" Luxura. In 1994 and 1995, Brainstorm published two Vamperotica sets of 18 cards each (which assembled into a large poster of Luxura). A more impressive 90-card chromium set was released in 1996.

Some of the finest trading cards, judged solely on their artistic merits, came from the many horror and fantasy artists who moved into the trading card market, many turning sets of their artwork into collections of fantasy art. In most cases, the sets put out by artists such as Chris Achilleos, Bernie Wrightson, Boris Vellejo, Greg Hildebrandt, Brom, DeVitio, Bob Eggleston, and Mike Plogg, included only a few vampire-related pictures in what was primarily a set of fantasy art. In many cases the vampire pieces were familiar, having previously appeared as covers or illustrations for vampire books and/or comic books. Bob Eggleston's card set included the cover of both the books and comic books of **Brian Lumley**'s *Necroscope* series. Boris Vellejo's Dracula card had been the cover of TOR's edition of *Dracula*. And Greg Hildebrandt's Dracula cards from his "30 Years of Magic" set had previously illustrated images from two **juvenile** versions of the novel.

Premier graphic artist John Bolton, whose art has been very much in demand throughout the industry, created two sets exclusively of vampire-related art. Though relatively small, with only 12 and 13 cards respectively, his two Vampire Theatre sets were some of the finest trading cards ever published. In like manner, Steve Woron and Don Paresi, two artists who operate out of Illustration Studio in Connecticut and have specialized in drawing fantasy females, have adapted their work for several vampire-related sets, Vampires and Vixens (1993) and Vampyres: Predators of Eternity (1995), and have included vampire cards in other sets. Each individual card is a piece of art in and of itself.

The thousands of vampire trading cards published in the 1990s made it possible for card collectors specializing in the single topic of vampires to emerge, and companies continued to produce trading cards for them to collect. Then at the end of the 1990s, the emergence of the television show **Buffy the Vampire Slayer** occasioned the significant expansion of the collecting realm for vampire trading cards. In 1998, Inkworks began issuing its very successful *Buffy the Vampire Slayer* cards adding card sets for each season of *Angel* in 2001. Cards sets for each season were followed by various retrospect card sets built around particular themes, all capped with the reprinting of the seven seasons of Buffy cards in a special edition complete with **coffin**-shaped card box. In the end, Inkworks would produce some eighteen sets notable for their many premium cards. As was happening with other card sets based on movies and television shows, costume cards featuring pieces of costumes seen on the show became among the most sought after and hard to get chase cards. These cards have continued to hold their value after the show's demise, not commonly done among by trading cards, some of the most ephemeral of pop culture items.

The *Buffy* and *Angel* cards dominated the decade, which saw a multiplication of vampire-oriented cards, both new sets and individual cards in non-vampire sets. However, by 2008, the publication of new *Buffy* sets had ended, and Inkworks, shortly before its succumbing to larger economic pressures and going out of business, issued a series of cards drawn from the first movie of **Stephenie Meyer**'s popular *Twilight* series. The *Twilight* cards surpassed *Buffy*'s popularity and sold out immediately. Inkworks had underestimated the demand, and under-produced. The cards skyrocketed in value, and NECA, a company that specializes in movie-related merchandise, which already had a license for a whole range of *Twilight* paraphernalia, picked up the license for the *Twilight* trading cards. They reissued the first *Twilight* set (minus a few of the chase cards), which also soon sold out, produced the second set (related to the second twilight movie, **The Twilight Saga: New Moon**), and will issue future *Twilight*-related sets. Meanwhile, nu-

merous *Twilight*-related promo cards (difficult to collect) have appeared from widely scattered sources.

Free when initially distributed, often at a particular comic-book or fan convention, they immediately became valued collector's items.

The popularity of *Buffy* and *Twilight*, set the stage for new cards sets commemorating the popular vampires of Hammer Films, *Dark Shadows, the Munsters,* and *Vampirella.* Trading cards are an international phenomenon, and can be found throughout the English-speaking world, across Europe from France to Russia, and very popular in Japan. A number of series have appeared relative to Japanese anime/manga, including popular sets related to *Vampire Princess Miyu* and *Blood the Last Vampire.* Most popular has been the artwork of Yoshitaka Amano, who drew the images for *Vampire Hunter D.*

Unique additions to the world of vampire cards are the popular sketch cards, one of a kind trading cards hand-drawn by artists either as premiums for popular cards sets or as freelance works marketed directly to collectors, usually through various comic and fan conventions. In the 1990s, a few companies tried to market odd-shaped cards. Among the vampire cards, were a selected number of coffin-shaped cards, including one vampire set. As a whole, these were not well received, as they are difficult to fit into the plastic sheets in which collectors most commonly store trading cards, and have disappeared from the market.

Note: This entry was developed from the author's own collection of trading cards and with the helpful reflections of Lee Scott of Salt Lake City, also a collector. Information on vampire related trading-card sets may be found at Jeff Allendar's House of Checklists (http://nslists.com/jachlist.htm).

Transformation

The vampire traditionally could transform itself into various **animals**, particularly a **bat**, a wolf, or a dog. It could also transform into a **dust**-like cloud or a **mist**. This attribute was often referred to as shape-shifting, and vampires figures often graded into shape-shifters, a particular kind of demon entity in European mythologies. It was also an attribute often tied to **witchcraft**. In the novel by **Bram Stoker**, **Dracula**'s first recorded transformations were observed by **Jonathan Harker** but occurred in such a manner that neither Harker (nor the reader) realized what was happening. During the course of the novel, Dracula transformed into a wolf (to leave the ship that had wrecked at **Whitby**,) a bat (throughout the novel), and as mist (in order to enter **Mina Murray**'s bedroom). In one of his encounters with the three vampire **brides** in **Castle Dracula**, Harker noted that they appeared to him first as a swirl of dust in the moonlight. Twenty-five years prior to Dracula, the transformation of the vampire into an animal had also been an integral part of **Sheridan Le Fanu**'s story "Carmilla." In that story, **Carmilla** transformed into a cat on several occasions.

The ability of vampires to transform into animals was part of the folklore of the majority of countries that include a vampire figure. The Japanese, for example, had a well-known tale of a vampire who assumed the form of the wife of Prince Nabeshima and then transformed into a cat to hunt her **victims**. In various countries in eastern Europe,

the **Slavic** vampire could transform into a wide variety of animals, and on rare occasions, even some plants and farm implements. The ancient Roman vampire often appeared as a bird, a crow, or screech owl. Their transformation into wolves tied vampires to **werewolves**, the exact relationship being a matter of scholarly disagreement.

In *Dracula,* **(1897) Abraham Van Helsing** also proposed the idea that vampire transformations were facilitated at certain hours. Dracula could change into various forms during the evening at will. However, during the daylight hours he could change only at noon, or exactly at sunrise and sunset. Most likely, Stoker borrowed this idea from Emily Gerard, who reported that Romanians believed that specific times of the day had special significance. Among these were the "exact hour of noon," a precarious time because an evil spirit, Pripolniza, was active. The idea of special powers tied to certain times of the day was dropped by subsequent writers using the vampire theme.

More recent novels and movies have disagreed on the issue of the vampire's power of transformation. The many remakes of *Dracula* have been fairly consistent with his ability to transform into an animal, at least a bat. In 1992's **Bram Stoker's Dracula**, his ability to transform was a major sub-theme of the plot. However, the influential novels by **Chelsea Quinn Yarbro** and **Anne Rice** have denied the vampire's ability to transform, as have the more recent novels of **P. N. Elrod** and **Elaine Bergstrom**. Yarbro, even more than Rice, stripped her vampires of most of their supernatural abilities, although they were left with great **strength** and a long life.

The trend initiated by Rice and Yarbro carried over into many books and motion pictures that have stepped back from Dracula and created other vampire characters who exist in a contemporary setting. Thus, transformation has not been an element in the life of the vampires in such movies as *Vamp* (1986), **Near Dark** (1987), *The Lost Boys* (1987), *Innocent Blood* (1992), **Bloodrayne** (2005), *30 Days of Night* (2007), or *Let the Right One In* (2008). Movies such as *Van Helsing* (2004), the popular **Underworld** movie trilogy, and the several *Twilight* (2009) movies featured werewolves who transformed from human to animal, while the vampires more or less stayed in human form.

The vampires in **television** series such as **Forever Knight, Buffy the Vampire Slayer**, *Moonlight*, *Blood Ties*, or *Being Human* did not shift into animal forms. The series *True Blood* has included shapeshifters as an integral part of the story, but they are not vampires.

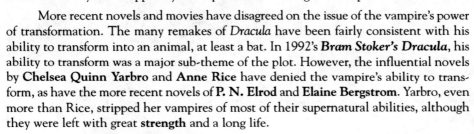

Transylvania

Transylvania (literally, "the land beyond the forest") is the area of north central **Romania** most identified in the public mind with vampires. Its reputation derives from being designated as the home of **Dracula** in **Bram Stoker**'s novel. At the beginning of *Dracula* **(1897), Jonathan Harker** traveled from Budapest, **Hungary** into northern Transylvania, then a part of the Austro-Hungarian Empire. He described the land as one of great beauty but a wild and little known place. His final destination was **Castle Dracula**, a location not noted on any map. Although Harker's destination was a fictional site, the land he moved through was very real. Stoker had never been to Transylvania but had read about it in books at the British Museum, particularly Emily

Black Church in Brasov, Transylvania (Romania), in the shadow of which Vlad the Impaler committed some of the atrocities for which he is so well known.

Gerard's *Land Beyond the Forest*. Transylvania was the center of a powerful state in the first century C.E. The territory was partially conquered by Trajan in 106 C.E.

Over the next several centuries, the merger of the Roman and native people created the distinctive people known today as the Romanians. **Christianity** of a Roman Latin variety made its initial entrance into the area at this time, although over the centuries the Romanians aligned themselves with the Eastern Orthodox Church headquartered in Constantinople. The area was subject to numerous invasions, more or less successful, by a variety of nomadic people. Most importantly, in the tenth century, incursions and eventually conquest by the Hungarians began.

By the thirteenth century, Hungary claimed hegemony in Transylvania, although the various divisions continued to be ruled by the local territorial lords, the voevades. The Hungarians engaged in several acts of social engineering. First, they persuaded the *Szekely* people of western Transylvania to move into the mountainous area in the east and assume the task of border control. The Szekelys emerged as great warriors. Secondly, to improve the economy, the Hungarians invited Germans into southern Transylvania and gave them generous tax benefits. Although they originated from throughout **Germany**, these people became known as the Saxons. They were most prominent in the towns that controlled the mountain passes between Transylvania and Wallachia, located immediately south of the Carpathians. (Today, many of the towns of Transylvania have three names—one each in German, Hungarian, and Romanian.) By the fourteenth century, there were four main groups in Transylvania: Hungarians, Hungarian-speaking Szekelys, Saxons, and Romanians. The Romanians, although a majority of the population, were the conquered people, and measures to suppress them began in earnest.

The Roman Catholic Hungarians launched systematic conversion efforts directed at the Orthodox population. Specific laws were passed to disenfranchise the Romanians, culminating in the 1366 ruling that called into question the traditional status of any Romanian aristocracy who refused to become Roman Catholic and whose loyalty to the Hungarian crown was questionable. Hungary's increasingly oppressive controlled many Romanians to cross the mountains into Moldavia and Wallachia.

The migration south promoted the organization of an independent central government in Wallachia in the fourteenth century, although by the next century, it found itself in a constant battle with the Hungarians to the north and the Turks to the south, both of whom wanted to control it. It was in that tension that **Vlad Dracul** came to the Wallachian throne in 1436. He came to the throne at the same time that John Hunyadi, an outstanding Romanian, emerged in Transylvania. Hunyadi became the governor of Transylvania and his power rivaled that of the king. Hunyadi's reputation promoted the cause of his son, Matthias who, at a point of weakness in the Hungarian royal family, became king of Hungary in 1458. Vlad Dracul opposed Hunyadi and was killed in 1447.

Prior to ascending to the throne, Vlad Dracul was the commander of the guard in Transylvania. He settled in **Sighisoara** around 1430 and, a short time after his arrival, his son (also named Vlad) was born. The son, later to become known as **Vlad the Impaler**, was too young to succeed his father in 1447, but eventually gained the throne within months of Hunyadi's death in 1456. As the ruler of Wallachia he claimed the Transylvanian districts of Amlas and Fagaras. More importantly, he moved against the Saxon merchants of Sibiu (for housing his relatives who were claimants to his throne) and Brasov (whose mercantile policies worked against Vlad's attempt to build the Wallachian economy).

Vlad the Impaler, the historical Dracula, was Wallachian (although he was born in Transylvania), and most of the activities he was famous for occurred there. Bram Stoker placed the fictional Count Dracula in northeastern Transylvania. To arrive at Castle Dracula, Jonathan Harker passed through Klausenburgh (Clug-Napoca) and traveled to **Bistritz** (Bistrita). This section of Transylvania was correctly identified as territory traditionally ruled by the Szekelys and thus he identified Count Dracula as a member of the traditional ruling class. The issue was confused as Stoker attempted to merge the fictional Count Dracula with Vlad the Impaler, the man known for his battles against the Turks and the "bravest of the sons of the 'land beyond the forest.'" Stoker also identified Dracula as the arch vampire. Transylvanian vampire lore was merely a variation of the vampire beliefs found throughout Romania and shared by neighboring groups of **Slavs** and **Gypsies**. Historically, the land had no particular reputation as a home to vampires.

Today, Transylvania has become a major tourist attraction, drawing people not only for skiing in the Carpathian Mountains and the **wine**, but for Dracula buffs. There is now a Count Dracula Hotel at the middle of the **Borgo Pass** that hosts a variety of tours and events annually. The Golden Krone (Crown) Hotel in Bistriz serves the same meal eaten by Jonathan Harker in *Dracula*. Vlad the Impaler's birthplace in Sighisoara and his palace in **Tirgoviste** provide stopping places for tourists heading northward from Bucharest, and

further development seems inevitable. Transylvania's reputation as a home to vampires has been furthered by numerous novelists and movies such as *Transylvania 6-5000* (1985), *Love at First Bite* (1979), and the various adaptations of *Dracula*.

Sources:

Bodea, Cornelia, and Virgil Candea. *Transylvania in the History of the Romanians*. New York: Columbia University Press, 1982. 181 pp.

Florescu, Radu R., and Raymond T. McNally. *Dracula: Prince of Many Faces*. Boston, MA: Little, Brown and Company, 1989. 261 pp.

Mackenzie, Andrew. *Dracula Country*. London: Arthur Barker, 1977. 176 pp.

Mehedinti, S. *What Is Transylvania?* Miami Beach, FL: Romanian Historical Studies, 1986. 121 pp.

Miller, Elizabeth. "Typing Transylvania." In Elizabeth Miller. *Reflections on Dracula: Ten Essays*. White Rock, BC: Transylvania Press, 1997: 47–68.

Walker, Gerald, and Lorraine Wright. "Locating Dracula: Contextualizing the Geography of Transylvania." In Carold Margaret Davison, ed. *Bram Stoker's Dracula: Sucking through the Century, 1897–1997*. Toronto: Durndun Press, 1997: 49–74.

Transylvania Press *see:* Eighteen-Bisang, Robert

Transylvanian Society of Dracula

The Transylvanian Society of Dracula (TSD), a cultural historical organization, was founded in the early 1990s by a group of leading Romanian historians, ethnographers, folklorists, tourist experts, writers, and artists, as well as non-Romanian experts in the field. Its goal has been the interpretation of Romanian history and folklore, especially as it relates to the fifteenth-century ruler **Vlad the Impaler** (the historical Dracula) and Romanian folklore concerning vampires. The group also attempts to identify dracularian traces of the myth in the folklore of other countries around the world. The founding president of the society was Nicolae Paduraru (1932–2009), who for many years had been an official with the Romanian Ministry of Tourism. He also was the general administrator of Count Dracula Treasures, Ltd.

The society organizes tours of various sites in southern **Romania** associated with Vlad the Impaler and those in **Transylvania** (in the northern area of Romania) associated with the novel *Dracula* **(1897).** Some 300 people attended the World Dracula Congress sponsored by the Society in Romania in 1995, an event that marked its worldwide expansion. The American and Canadian chapters were founded during that week, headed by Drs. J. Gordon Melton and **Elizabeth Miller** respectively. Dr. Massimo Introvigne, who attended the Congress subsequently formed an Italian chapter. There is also a chapter in **Japan** and several chapters in other European countries.

In 1997, the American and Canadian chapters, along with the Count Dracula Fan Club, sponsored **Dracula '97: A Centennial Celebration** the international Dracula commemorative event, August 14–17, 1997, in Los Angeles. Some 20 countries, including a delegation from Romania, attended and more than 90 scholarly papers were presented on **Dracula** and vampire studies. The various chapters sponsor different events, among which, the several Romanian chapters organize a symposium in Transylvania each May, on the anniversary of **Jonathan Harker** arrival at **Castle Dracula**. The international Society sponsored the second Dracula World Congress, Dracula 2000, held at Poiana Brasov, Transylvania, the site of Vlad the Impaler's attack upon the German Transylvanian community during his reign of Wallachia in the fifteenth century. The theme of the Congress was "Redefining the Diabolic from the Perspective of Contemporary Society." The Society has continued to sponsor conferences in Romania at least annually in the years of the new century, as well as promoting tours of Dracula sites each October around Halloween through the Company of Mysterious Journeys, http://www.mysteriousjourneys.com/. It offers a variety of Dracula-related products through Count Dracula Treasures, http://www.draculatreasures.com/.

Outside of Romania, the most active chapter has been the Canadian chapter headed by Dr. Elizabeth Miller. It issues the *Journal of Dracula Studies*, and may be contacted through its webpage at http://www.ucs.mun.ca/~emiller/trans_soc_dracula.html or its mailing address, 2309-397 Front St W., Toronto ON, Canada M5V 3S1. The Italian chapter can be contacted by writing to Dr. Massimo Introvigne at cesnur_to@virgilio.it. It posts the electronic news bulletins of the TSD on its website at http://www.cesnur.org/Dracula.htm#Anchor-49575.

Tremayne, Peter (1943–)

Peter Tremayne is the pseudonym of Peter Berresford Ellis when writing horror, fantasy, and **science fiction** works. His first fictional book as Peter Tremayne, *The Hound of Frankenstein*, was one of two books he completed in 1977. The second, *Dracula Unborn* (released in the U.S. as *Bloodright: Memoirs of Mircea, Son of Dracula*) was the first of his Dracula series. Heavily influenced by the writings on **Vlad the Impaler** by **Radu Florescu** and **Raymond T. McNally**, Tremayne wrote his novel as the long-lost "Memoirs of Mircea, Son of Dracula." Mircea, who had been born in, but raised outside of, **Romania**, returned to discover his vampiric heritage and meet his father.

The second vampire novel, *The Revenge of Dracula*, followed a year later. Again, Tremayne employed the device of the discovery of formerly lost memoirs. This volume told the story of a nineteenth-century Englishman who discovered a jade dragon statuette. Afterward, he had a number of strange dreams, including one about a **Dracula** figure. He traveled to **Transylvania** and upon his return had to be committed to an insane asylum. Tremayne's last novel, *Dracula My Love* (1980), was built around the memoirs of Morag, a Scottish governess who moved to **Castle Dracula** and fell in love with the Count, the first person she encountered who treated her with a sense of dignity. This final novel departed from the first two novels in that Dracula was portrayed very positively and sympathetically. Thus, for his last vampire novel, Tremayne participated in the trend to create a vampire hero initiated by **Fred Saberhagen** and **Chelsea Quinn Yarbro**. Ellis continues to write, producing several books annually. He last returned to the Dracula theme in a nonfiction book with coauthor **Peter Haining**, *The Undead*, published in 1997.

Sources:

Haining, Peter, and Peter Tremayne. *The Undead: The Legend of Bram Stoker and Dracula*. London: Constable, 1997. 199 pp.

Tremayne, Peter. *Dracula Unborn*. London: Bailey Brothers and Swinfen, 1977. Rept. London: Corgi, 1977. 222 pp. Reprinted as *Bloodright: Memoirs of Mircea, Son of Dracula*. New York: Walker & Co., 1979. 222 pp. Reprinted as *Bloodright*. New York: Dell, 1980. 251 pp.

———. *The Revenge of Dracula*. Folkstone: Bailey Brothers and Swiften, 1978. Rept. New York: Walker & Co., 1979. Rept. London: Magnum Books, 1980. 203 pp.

———. *Dracula My Love*. London: Bailey Brothers and Swinfen, 1980. Rept. London: Magnum Books, 1980. 203 pp.

❲ TWILIGHT ❳

TWILIGHT is the name under which individuals involved in vampirism along with people who have a serious and academic interest in it have gathered to engage in serious discussion about the nature of vampirism and the issues dominating the new vampire community. TWILIGHT was founded in September of 2007 by a vampire known by his public name Daemonox, he is currently (2009) assisted by another vampire known as Merticus. TWILIGHT happens as a roaming event held two to three times annually as expenses allow. To date all the events have been in the United States, but sites in other countries are under consideration.

Participation in TWILIGHT's events are by invitation following thorough screening, in order to ensure the events, quality, integrity, and success. The immediate goal of TWILIGHT is to engage the vampire community in serious discussion, knowledge exchange, and social networking. A longer term goal is transform TWILIGHT into a roaming event across the United States and beyond.

TWILIGHT conferences I-III were held in Los Angeles, Atlanta, and Seattle. Future conferences are in the planning stages as this encyclopedia goes to press. TWILIGHT has a webpage at http://www.meetup.com/twilight/.

Sources:

Laycock, Joseph. *Vampires Today: The Truth about Modern Vampirism*. Westport. CT: Praeger, 2009. 200 pp.

❲ Twilight (Movie) ❳

The movie *Twilight* was based upon the first novel of the same name in the four-book "Twilight" series by author **Stephenie Meyer**. The novel was adapted for the screen by Melissa Rosenberg (co-executive producer and writer on TV's *The O.C.* and *Dexter*) and directed by Catherine Hardwicke (*Lords of Dogtown* and *The Nativity Story*). The movie stars Kristin Stewart as 17-year-old **Isabella (Bella) Swan** and Robert Pattinson as Bella's vampire boyfriend **Edward Cullen**. The movie cost an estimated $37 million and was released in U.S. theaters by Summit Entertainment on November 21, 2008.

The movie *Twilight*, which follows the novel's basic story line and essential themes, begins when teenager Bella Swan leaves Phoenix, Arizona, to move to the small town of Forks, Washington, to live with her father, Charlie. At Forks High School, she finds herself drawn to a mysterious classmate, Edward Cullen, who is a 108-year-old vampire but is physically only seventeen years old. Although Edward discourages the romance at first, he soon falls in love with Bella and allows himself to be with her, knowing he can't live without her. Edward and his family are "vegetarian vampires" who feed off **animal** rather than human **blood.** But the arrival of three nomadic vampires, James, Victoria, and Laurent, puts Bella's life in danger because they feed off humans. Edward and his family, Alice, Carlisle, Esme, Jasper, Emmett and Rosalie, attempt to save Bella by fighting to keep the lethal tracker James from killing her.

Meyer's novel was first optioned by Paramount Pictures' MTV Films in April 2004. According to director Hardwicke, Paramount's screenplay was substantially different from the original novel, with Bella introduced as a star athlete. When Paramount's rights to the project were about to expire, Summit Entertainment pursued it. Screenwriter Rosenberg attempted to stay as close to the book as possible but had to condense the dialogue and combine some of the characters. As Hardwicke explained, "So we kept to the [novel's] spirit. But there are changes." Meyer worked closely with Summit during the script's development. She drew up a list of rules for her vampire world that could not be changed and made her own suggestions on the script.

In an MTV interview, Rosenberg explained that *Brokeback Mountain* (2005), the story of two gay cowboys who fall in love, actually provided her with a great model of poignancy and forbidden love between Bella and Edward. Rosenberg remained true to *Twilight's* emotions and spirit but did change a number of the novel's key passages. The villainous vampires (Victoria, James, and Laurent) were introduced much earlier in the film than in the book. The movie's scenes of dinner at the Cullen's house and Bella and Edward jumping out to the treetops were not in the book. Likewise, the novel's scene in the biology room where the students do blood typing and Bella faints is not in the movie. In the book, Bella reveals that she knows he is a vampire while in Edward's car driving back from Port Angeles, but the movie instead provides a more visually dynamic setting of a lush forest and meadow.

Principal photography for *Twilight* took forty-four days. Portland and Vernonia, Oregon, served as locations for the Forks, Washington, setting of the novel, and St. Helens, Oregon, stood in for the small town of Port Angeles. A year after its initial release, the film grossed $191 million in North America and more than $384 million in worldwide box office. In addition, more than nine million DVDs of *Twilight* have been sold. *Twilight* won five MTV Movie Awards as well as ten Teen Choice Awards. A graphic novel form of the movie is scheduled to be published by Yen Press with Korean artist Young Kim creating the art and Meyer herself closely involved with the project.

Twilight's movie sequels **The Twilight Saga: New Moon** was released in U.S. theaters November 20, 2009, and *The Twilight Saga: Eclipse* is scheduled for release the summer of 2010. *The Twilight Saga: Breaking Dawn*, the fourth and final novel in the *Twilight* series, is currently (2009) in development for a 2011 release.

Sources:

Charaipotra, Sona. "Exclusive Interview: Twilight Screenwriter Melissa Rosenberg." Posted at www.premiere.com/Feature/Twilight-Screenwriter-Melissa-Rosenberg. (October 14, 2008). Accessed on April 8, 2010.

Cotta Vaz, Mark. *Twilight: The Complete Illustrated Movie Companion.* New York: Little, Brown and Company, 2008. 141 pp.

Hardwicke, Catherine. *Twilight: Director's Notebook: The Story of How We Made the Movie Based on the Novel by Stephenie Meyer*. New York: Little, Brown Young Readers, 2009. 176 pp.

Martin, Denise. "*Twilight* Countdown: Catherine Hardwicke Talks about the Meadow and Making Robert Pattinson 'Dazzle.'" (November 4, 2008).

Murray, Rebecca. "Interview with *Twilight* Author Stephenie Meyer." (November 11, 2008). Posted at movies.about.com/od/twilight/a/stephenie-meyer.htm. Accessed on April 8, 2010.

❨ *The Twilight Saga: New Moon* ❩

The movie *The Twilight Saga: New Moon* (2009) was based upon the second novel *New Moon* in **Stephenie Meyer**'s four-book *Twilight* series. The novel was adapted for the screen by Melissa Rosenberg (co-executive producer and writer on TV's *The O.C.* and *Dexter*) and directed by Chris Weitz (*The Golden Compass*, *About a Boy*, and *American Pie*). Continuing their roles from the first *Twilight* movie, *New Moon* stars Kristin Stewart as **Isabella (Bella) Swan** and Robert Pattinson as Bella's vampire boyfriend **Edward Cullen**. It also features Taylor Lautner as Bella's Native American friend Jacob, Ashley Greene as Edward's sister Alice, and Michael Sheen as Aro, leader of the powerful Volturi, the overall authority in the international vampire community.

The movie begins when a minor incident at Bella's eighteenth birthday party convinces Edward that he is endangering her life. He leaves Bella and she slips into a depression. But Bella discovers that when she puts herself in danger, she can summon Edward's image. With the help of her childhood friend Jacob Black, a member of the Quileute tribe, Bella refurbishes a motorcycle for some risky adventures. Bella's budding relationship with Jacob helps her through her breakup with Edward, although she soon learns that Jacob has a supernatural secret of his own. When Bella wanders alone into a meadow, she confronts a deadly attacker. The intervention of a pack of large wolves saves her from a grisly fate. She later faces a potential deadly reunion with Edward, who has decided to commit suicide among the Volturi, at their headquarters in Italy.

Summit Entertainment announced the production of *New Moon* one day after *Twilight* opened in theaters on November 21, 2008. The movie closely followed Meyer's novel, with a few exceptions. The scenes leading to Edward's break-up with Bella were omitted as well as the couple's plane trip returning to Forks, Washington, after their encounter with the Volturi in Italy. Throughout much of the novel, Bella hears Edward's voice in her head when she is in danger, but in the movie Edward is manifested as a visual presence or an "apparition." Screenwriter Rosenberg added motorcycles to a scene in which Bella decides to become reckless and approaches young men in

Robert Pattinson plays the sexy vampire Edward Cullen (hanging from a tree in a demonstration of his vampire abilities for in the "Twilight" film series.

Port Angeles, prompting Edward's first apparition to appear. For the overall visual "look" of the film, director Weitz moved away from the blue tones of *Twilight* and instead created a warm color palette of golden tones for *New Moon*.

New Moon's promotional material included tie-ins with Burger King Corp. and a line of jewelry and apparel through Nordstrom Stores. Burger King Corp. developed a multi-faceted promotion surrounding *The Twilight Saga: New Moon* by offering aluminum water bottles featuring "Team Edward" and "Team Jacob" designs along with *New Moon* paper crowns. Nordstrom Stores offered an exclusive fashion collection of T-shirts, hoodies, tanks, jackets, as well as gold-plated jewelry and key chains all inspired by *New Moon*. The larger effort of promoting New Moon collectibles, from **trading cards** to clothing accessories, and toys was handled by NECA (the National Entertainment Collectibles Association), which set up a special page on Amazon to market its products.

The producers of *New Moon* pursued an aggressive production schedule to meet the film's November 20, 2009 release. *New Moon*'s estimated budget was $50 million, and filming took place in Vancouver, British Columbia, Canada, and Montepulciano, Italy, from March 23 to May 30, 2009. *New Moon* was released in U.S. theaters on November 20, 2009 and pre-sold more online tickets through Fandango than any other movie title in its history. *New Moon* grossed $142.8 million in North America during its opening weekend, far surpassing *Twilight*'s initial opening of $69.6 million. The movie's foreign box-office grosses reached $124.1 million by the opening weekend. The website Box Office Mojo reported that within a week of its release, *New Moon* had become the all-time top-grossing vampire movie in North America. The third movie in the series, *The Twilight Saga: Eclipse*, is scheduled for release the summer of 2010. *The Twilight Saga: Breaking Dawn*, the fourth and final novel in the *Twilight* series, is currently (2009) in development for a 2011 release.

Sources:

Cotta Vaz, Mark. *The Twilight Saga: New Moon* (The Official Illustrated Movie Companion). New York: Little, Brown and Company, 2009. 141 pp.

Fritz, Ben. "*New Moon* Rises to New Heights." *Los Angeles Times*, p. B:1. (November 23, 2009).

"Hungry Fans Get Taste of *The Twilight Saga: New Moon* from Burger King Corp." *Business Wire*. (November 16, 2009).

McClintock, Pamela. "*New Moon* Draws Global Audience." *Variety*. (November 23, 2009).

———. "*Twilight* Pre-Sales Huge." *Variety*. (November 18, 2009).

Summit Entertainment. *The Twilight Saga: New Moon* (Production Notes), 2009. 66 pp.

❨ The "Twilight" Series (Books) ❩

The "Twilight" series consists of four novels by **Stephenie Meyer** about a teenage romance between a human girl and her vampire boyfriend. The books were published by Little, Brown and Company beginning with the first, *Twilight*, in 2005, followed by *New Moon* (2006), *Eclipse* (2007), and *Breaking Dawn* (2008). A fifth manuscript, *Midnight Sun* (2008), was the expected companion novel to *Twilight* retelling the events from the perspective of the vampire **Edward Cullen** rather than that of **Isabella Swan**. Meyer completed only the first 12 chapters of *Midnight Sun* before it was illegally leaked on the Internet. The incomplete and unfinished manuscript is now posted on Meyer's website www.StephenieMeyer.com.

In an interview, Meyer has said that *Twilight* is loosely tied to Jane Austin's *Pride and Prejudice* while *New Moon* was influenced by Shakespeare's *Romeo and Juliet*.

The "Twilight" series quickly rose to international fame and made record-breaking sales. *Publishers Weekly* reported book sales of $27.5 million of the four vampire novels in March 2009, which prompted the publication to crown Meyer the "new queen" in children's literature, succeeding J. K. Rowling and her *Harry Potter* series. The four "Twilight" books have been translated into at least 20 languages and published in 39 countries with over forty-two million copies sold worldwide. The movie *Twilight* (2008) earned $69.6 million for its opening weekend in North America and over $191 million for its total domestic gross. The *Twilight* DVD sold over three million copies in its first day of release. Meyer's novels have also spawned close to 350 fan sites and inspired *Twilight*-related merchandise sales over the Internet.

Much of *Twilight* departs radically from nineteenth-century vampire literature. Meyer has explained that "almost all of the superstitions about vampire limitations are entirely false" in her novels. Her vampires are instead immune to the harmful effects of crosses, wooden **stakes**, holy **water**, **garlic**, and **sunlight** (which makes their skin glitter like diamonds). *Twilight*'s vampires do have mirror reflections but do not have **fangs**. Their pale skin is cold and icy to the touch, and they don't need sleep. They have extremely quick reflexes and can run fast and leap high, but they don't shape shift into **bats** or **fly**. While **Bram Stoker**'s **Dracula** has bad breath, Edward's is sweet. But Meyer's vampires are sustained by **blood** alone, which lightens their eyes and flushes their skin slightly. They are immensely strong (especially during the first year of their vampire life), and their **transformation** makes them physically stunning and beautiful.

On the other hand, Meyer's vampires owe much of their characteristics to **juvenile literature** and the **good guy vampires**. In the *Twilight* series, the Cullens and their extended family call themselves "vegetarians" in that they obtain blood from **animals** and not by killing humans. Meyer instead has placed the Cullens—especially Edward—in a situation where they continually fight against their vampirism yet retain the ability to make ethical choices. Like the vampire hero **St. Germain** of **Chelsea Quinn Yarbro**'s novels, Edward Cullen is a romantic hero immune to the traditional weapons of **vampire hunters** and prefers to cultivate a life of scholarship and culture. And like **television**'s **Angel**, Edward was once a vicious killer before he chose to become a "vegetarian," who refrains from human blood. Edward also develops a romantic attachment to a woman, but in a sharp departure from vampire literary tradition, he seriously raises the issue of marriage and abstains from all sexual relations until marriage.

The subject of **werewolves** and vampires resurfaces in the *Twilight* books as well as the movie series. Initially, Meyer refers to the transformation of Quileute tribal members as werewolves, although at the end of *Breaking Dawn* Edward reveals that the werewolves are actually shape-shifters who take the form of wolves. The vampires of the *Twilight* series outnumber the werewolves because werewolves can't change people by biting them but instead can transform only through a genetic link. They do not age as long as they regularly transform into wolves. Although vampires and werewolves are traditional enemies in Meyer's novels, they eventually agree to coexist peacefully.

Twilight, the first book in the series, introduces seventeen-year-old Isabella Swan (Bella) who is moving from Phoenix, Arizona, to be with her father in Forks, Washington. At Forks High School, Bella meets the handsome Edward Cullen and soon learns that he is a member of a vampire family that drinks animal rather than human blood. Edward and Bella fall in love but the sadistic vampire tracker James tries to confront her and kill her. Bella is seriously wounded, but the Cullens rescue her and return her to Forks.

New Moon, the second book, begins when a minor incident at Bella's eighteenth birthday party convinces Edward that he and his family are endangering Bella's life. Edward leaves Bella, and the Cullens move out of Forks. At first, Bella slips into a depression until she befriends Jacob Black, a Quileute Indian who has the ability to transform into a werewolf. Bella discovers that when she places herself in danger, she subconsciously hears Edward's voice. Meanwhile, James's mate Victoria returns to Forks to avenge his death, prompting Jacob and his wolf pack to protect Bella. But a misunderstanding occurs when Edward's sister Alice sees Bella dead in a vision. Edward is heartbroken and decides to commit suicide among the Volturi, a powerful vampire coven in Italy. Alice and Bella fly to Italy to stop Edward, and the couple is reunited. The Cullens move back to Forks and agree to turn Bella into a vampire in the near future.

Eclipse opens with a mysterious string of murders in Seattle. The vampire Victoria has created an army of "newborn" vampires to battle the Cullens and kill Bella. Meanwhile, Bella must choose between her love for Edward and her friendship with Jacob. She pressures Edward to have sex and he refuses until they are married. Edward proposes to Bella and promises that he will turn her into a vampire when she marries him. Edward, the Cullens, and the wolf pack all join forces to fight the newborn vampires and protect Bella. Jacob is furious about Bella's decision to become a vampire, so he leaves Forks and Bella agrees to marry Edward.

Breaking Dawn, the fourth book in the *Twilight* series, is divided into three books, two from Bella's perspective and one from Jacob's. Bella and Edward are married and he takes her to a remote island off the coast of Brazil for their honeymoon. But Bella discovers that she is pregnant and the child is growing rapidly. The couple rush home to the Cullens, and Bella nearly dies giving birth to her half vampire, half human daughter Renesmee. Jacob rushes back to Forks and is angry when Edward transforms Bella into a vampire. Jacob involuntarily "imprints" on Renesmee, causing the child to be bonded to him for life. A vampire from another coven sees Renesmee and mistakes her for an "immortal child" (which violates vampire law), so the Volturi set out with an army of vampires to destroy her. The Cullens summon their extended family and friends of various vampire covens and together with Jacob's wolf pack they gather for the final showdown with the Volturi.

Sources:

Beahm, George. *Bedazzled: Stephenie Meyer and the Twilight Phenomenon*. Nevada City, CA: Underwood Books, 2009. 248 pp.

Carpenter, Susan. "Web Gave *Twilight* Fresh Blood." *Los Angeles Times* (November 29, 2008): E1.

Gresh, Lois H. *The Twilight Companion: The Unauthorized Guide to the Series*. St. Martin's Griffin: New York, 2008. 242 pp.

Hopkins, Ellen, ed. *A New Dawn: Your Favorite Authors on Stephenie Meyer's Twilight Saga: Completely Unauthorized*. Benbella Books, 2009. 186 pp.

Housel, Rebecca, and J. Jeremy Wisnewski, eds. *Twilight and Philosophy: Vampires, Vegetarians, and the Pursuit of Immortality*. New York: John Wiley & Sons, 2009. 259 pp.

"Latest Bestsellers of Children's Series and Tie-Ins." *Publishers Weekly.* (May 25, 2009).

Roback, Diane. "Stephenie Meyer is the New Queen in Children's Succeeding Rowling." *Publishers Weekly* 256, 12 (March 23, 2009): 30.

Twilight_News_Updates. *Brigham Young University Midwinter Symposium on Books for Young Readers*. February 2007. Posted at http://www.twilightlexicon.com/2007/02/09/the-q-a-from-the-february-2007-byu-symposium/. Accessed on April 9, 2010.

Twilight_News_Updates. *Deviations from Vampire Legend*. December 4, 2006. Posted at http://www.twilightlexicon.com/2006/04/12/deviations-from-vampire-legend/. Accessed on April 8, 2010.

Twilight_News_Updates. *Personal Correspondence No. 1*. March 11, 2006; April 10, 2006, Posted at http://www.twilightlexicon.com/the-lexicon/personal-correspondence/. Accessed on April 9, 2010.

Vaz, Mark Cotta. *Twilight: The Complete Illustrated Movie Companion*. Little, Brown and Company: New York, Boston, 2008. 142 pp.

U–V

Uncle Alucard *see:* Vampire Fandom: United Kingdom

❰ Underworld ❱

*U*nderworld, a 2003 film pitting vampires against **werewolves**, introduced an original epic story concerning the origin and history of vampires and their relation to werewolves and humanity in general. The story begins at an indefinite point in the early Middle Ages and subsequently passed through two decisive events in 1210 and 1409 C.E. that brought it to the present. The events of the original movie continued in its sequel *Underworld Evolution* (2006), while a third movie, a prequel, *Underworld: Rise of the Lycans* (2009), filled out the medieval background. *Underworld* originated with a story by Kevin Grevioux and Len Wiseman and a screenplay written by Danny McBride.

At some point in the early Middle Ages, Alexander Corvinus survived a plague as a result of his body mutating the plague virus thus allowing him to emerge as the first Immortal. He subsequently fathered three sons—Markus, William, and a third unnamed son. Markus was bitten by a bat and became the first vampire. He would in turn create several other vampires including Viktor and Amelia, who would constitute a triad of Elders that ruled the emerging vampire community. The three worked out an arrangement by which each ruled for a century while the other two slept. Meanwhile, William Corvinus was bitten by a wolf and became a werewolf. Unfortunately, the first generation of werewolves, as created by William, was hampered by the fact that the individual wolves could not turn back into their human form. Then, in the thirteenth century, a second generation of werewolves appeared in the person of Lucian, who could move back and forth from human to wolf form. The third son continued as human, but unknowingly passed the Corvinus blood to his descendents. That blood had the potential of creating a hybrid that possessed the strengths of both werewolves and vampires.

In the thirteenth century, the vampire community was focused on a European castle/fortress from which Viktor, the vampire elder, operated as a feudal lord. He ruled over the local human population whom he agreed to protect from the wild wolves in the surrounding forests. The wolves residing in the castle provided the manual labor necessary to maintain the castle and protected the vampire residents during the daylight hours. Along the way, Viktor discovered the young Lucian killed his mother, took him to the castle, and raised the unique young werewolf as a privileged leader of the castle's werewolf community. Lucian had hopes beyond his station, however, and falls in love with Sonja, Viktor's daughter.

In 1202, Lucian led a revolution by organizing the wolves throughout the land, and overran Viktor's castle. Only Viktor, the hastily awakened Markus and Amelia, and their assistant Andreas Tanis escaped what became a slaughter. Two hundred years later, in 1409, a group of vampire warriors, called Death Dealers, attacked Viktor's former castle. They underestimated the number of the werewolves and were all killed, save one, a cowardly vampire named Kraven. Capturing Kraven, Lucian offered him a deal in return for his life (and some future rewards). Kraven agreed to tell of a limited victory in which Lucian died along with all of Kraven's cohorts. As Kraven fled back to the vampires, Lucian burned the castle and escaped into the night, and everyone believed him dead.

Lucian was in fact the first of a new race of werewolves, the Lycans, distinguished by their ability to morph between human and wolf form. Over the next centuries, the vampires and Lycans would fight a continuing war that in the nineteenth and twentieth century would become technologically sophisticated. Vampires would be armed with bullets that contained silver nitrate and the Lycans with bullets that projected ultraviolet rays (that had the effect of killing the vampires with sunlight). A crisis would develop in the contemporary world as Amelia, the present waking elder, was about to transfer power to Markus, and begin her century of sleep.

In the modern world, Selene, a Death Dealer, fought Lycans as she believed that they killed her family back in the thirteenth century. She also believed that the Death Dealers were essentially wiping out a remnant community that had survived the 1409 debacle. Her world began to unravel after she rescued a human, Michael Corvinus, from the Lycans, but not before he was bitten and began the transformation into a werewolf. She also became attracted to him. Simultaneously, she came to distrust Kraven. Step by step she uncovered two main lies. First, she discovered that Viktor, with whom she has a father-daughter relationship, had executed his daughter Sonja because of her affair with Lucian, and subsequently executed Selene's family for their knowledge of his actions against his brother William Corvinus. He had spared Selene and raised her because she reminded him of Sonja. Second, she discovered Kraven's lie about the events of 1409, most notably his report of Lucian's death.

As these secrets undergirded the continuous war between vampires and Lycans, Selene was now questioning her whole existence, in light of her falling in love with Michael. She ended up killing Viktor because of his lies and because he was trying to kill Michael. Eventually they would uncover further secrets held by Markus, the surviving vampire elder, and Alexander Corvinus, the still living first Immortal.

The vampires of *Underworld* are rather traditional in that blood is the major issue of their existence. They are nocturnal creatures and are killed by sunlight. They are also contemporary in that they live together in a community that has adapted some modern technology and that is ruled by a vampire moral code. They keep their identity (and the location of their centers) from the larger human world and secure from their werewolf enemies. They appear as normal humans and do not shift into animal forms.

Amid mixed critical reviews, each of the three *Underworld* movies would by 2009 appear on the list of the ten highest grossing vampire movies of all time, with *Vampire Evolution* slightly ahead of the other two. Of the cast, actress Kate Beckinsale (1973–) would attain the most acclaim for her portrayal of Selene. In the midst of the making of the *Underworld* movies, she also appeared in *Van Helsing*, also a popular vampire movie. Other important *Underworld* roles were filled by Scott Speedman (Michael Corvin), Tony Curran (Markus Corvinus), Derek Jacobi (Alexander Corvinus), Bill Nighy (Viktor), Shane Brolly (Kraven), Michael Sheen (Lucian), and Zita Görög (Amelia).

IDW, a San Diego-based comic book publisher, issued comic adaptations of the movies, and Greg Cox produced novelizations of them.

After *Underworld* appeared, White Wolf Inc., which publishes the **Vampire: the Masquerade** game (and the associated *Werewolf: the Apocalypse* game), joined with author **Nancy Collins** in filing a lawsuit against Sony Entertainment, which claimed that the movie infringed upon their copyrights and plagiarized from a short story written by Collins that focused upon a Romeo and Juliet-type relationship between a vampire and werewolf. In their major brief, they claimed that the first *Underworld* movie copied the plot of Collins's story and borrowed some seventy characteristics of White Wolf's World of Darkness universe shared by its two games. Sony countered by noting that neither the plot of the Collins story nor the overwhelming majority of the cited characteristics shared by the movie and the World of Darkness were original to the World of Darkness. Rather, claimed Sony, almost all of the characteristics had appeared in the previous fifty years of vampire movies and literature, most on multiple occasions. A story very similar to Collins's story had, for example, appeared in a 1950s horror comic book. The court case was settled prior to its scheduled court date, with both sides agreeing not to discuss the elements of the settlement.

Sources:

Cox, Greg. *Underworld*. New York: Pocket Star Books, 2003. 372 pp.

———. *Underworld: Blood Enemy*. New York: Pocket Star Books, 2004. 310 pp.

———. *Underworld: Evolution*. New York: Pocket Star Books, 2005. 288 pp.

———. *Underworld: Rise of the Lykans*. New York: Pocket Star Books, 2008. 352 pp.

Ward, Rachel Mizsei. "Underworld vs the World of Darkness: Players and Filmgoers Respond to a Legal Battle." *Networking Knowledge: Journal of the MeCCSA Postgraduate Network*, 2, 1 (2009): 1–16. Posted at http://journalhosting.org/meccsa-pgn/index.php/netknow/article/viewFile/52/89. Accessed on April 5, 2010.

❨ United Kingdom, Vampires in the ❩

The United Kingdom includes the countries of England, Scotland, Wales, and Northern **Ireland**. None of the four lands has a reputation as being a prominent home to real vampires or even vampire folklore, but they have been significant contributors to the development of the literary vampire. England's vampire heritage is largely confined

to reports contained in two volumes, both written at the end of the twelfth century, which describe vampiric creatures. Among several accounts in Walter Map's *De Nagis Curialium* (c. 1190 C.E.), for example, was the story of a knight and his wife. She gave birth to a son, but on the morning following his birth, the baby was found dead with his throat cut. The same fate awaited both a second and a third child, in spite of extra precautions. When a fourth child was born, the entire house was called to stay up to keep the child safe. There was a stranger in the house who also kept watch. As the evening progressed, the stranger noticed all of the household falling asleep. He watched as a matronly woman came to the cradle and bent over it. Before she could hurt the baby, he seized the woman (who appeared to be a wealthy matron of the town). The real woman in town was summoned, and it was seen that the person captured at the cradle had assumed the matron's form. The captured woman was declared a demon, escaped from the men's grip, and flew away with a loud screech.

William of Newburgh finished his *Chronicles* in 1196. In his fifth book, among the stories he recounted, was one "of the extraordinary happening when a dead man wandered abroad out of his grave." Some years previously, in Buckinghamshire, a husband appeared in his wife's bedroom the day after his burial. After he returned a second night, she reported his visits to her neighbors. On the third evening, several people stayed with her, and when he appeared, they drove him away. He then turned to visiting his brothers and, upon being repelled, he disturbed the **animals**. The town was terrified by his sudden appearances at various hours of the day and night. They consulted the local clergy who referred the matter to the Bishop of **London**. The bishop first considered burning the body, but after further thought, advised exhumation of the corpse and the placement of a "chartula of episcopal absolution" on the body. It was further advised that the corpse should then be returned to the grave. The villagers followed his instructions. The body was found in the same condition it had been in on the day of burial. However, from that day forward, it never disturbed anyone again. William of Newburgh was also the source of the more famous cases of the vampires of **Melrose Abbey** and **Alnwick Castle**.

Both the stories of Map and William of Newburgh (quoted at length in the works of both **Montague Summers** and **Donald Glut**) contain many elements of the classical vampire tales of Eastern Europe, but each are missing an essential element—any reference to **blood** drinking. However, they are similar enough to illustrate the manner in which the vampire tales fit into the larger category of contact with revenants and the manner in which people from widely separated parts of Europe followed a similar set of actions in dealing with the problem.

In Scotland, several other traditional vampiric figures could be found. The *baobban sith*, for example, were known to appear as ravens or crows but more often as young maidens dressed in green dresses that hid their deer's hooves. Katheryn Briggs related one of the more famous *baobban sith* stories (first published by C. M. Robertson) concerning its encounter with four unfortunate men. The four hunters were camping for the evening. They entertained themselves with dancing and singing. As they danced, they were joined by four maidens seemingly attracted by their **music**. One of the men sang, as the other men danced. The singer noticed that each of his comrades had blood on their necks and shirts. Frightened, he ran into the woods, with one of the **women** running behind him. He finally found shelter among the horses where, for some reason, the woman did not come. The following morning he found his hunting mates dead and drained of blood.

The **redcap** was a malignant spirit who haunted abandoned castles and other places where violence had occurred. If one slept in a spot haunted by the redcap, it would attempt to dip its cap in human blood. Not as sinister as some, it could be driven off with a word from the Bible or a cross.

During the centuries of the modern era, these beliefs seemed to have largely died out. If such beliefs, which appeared to be widespread in the twelfth century, survived into the modern era, one would expect to see references to them, for instance, in the records of the many proceedings against witches, but there are none. Also, in the seventeenth century, the initial reports of vampires from Eastern Europe were received as if they were describing a new and entirely continental phenomenon. In the years since news of the Slavic vampire became known in England, two significant cases of vampire infestation became known. The first, the vampire of **Croglin Grange**, was initially reported in the 1890s, while the more recent case was of the **Highgate vampire** at the famous Highgate cemetery in London during the 1960s and 1970s.

The Modern Vampire: The term vampire appears to have been introduced to English in 1741. It appeared in a footnote in an obscure book titled *Observations on the Revolution in 1688*, which, though written in 1688, was not published until 60 years later. Interestingly, the term vampire did not refer to a bloodsucking entity in the book, but was used metaphorically in a **political** sense, with no explanation, as if the term was fairly well known. The author said:

> Our Merchants, indeed, bring money into their country, but it is said, there is another Set of Men amongst us who have as great an Address in sending out again to foreign Countries without any Returns for it, which defeats the Industry of the Merchant. These are the Vampires of the Publick, and Riflers of the Kingdom.

Actually, some years earlier in 1679, a book on the *State of the Greek and Armenian Churches* by Paul Ricaut (or Rycaut) described the existence of:

> … a pretended demon, said to delight in sucking human blood, and to animate the bodies of dead persons, which when dug up, are said to be found florid and full of blood.

A more important reference to vampires, which not only used the term but described an encounter with them in some depth, appeared in the 1810 publication *Travels of 3 English Gentlemen from Venice to Hamburg, Being the Grand Tour of Germany in the Year 1734*. The author, the Earl of Oxford, offered the first serious explanation of the vampire phenomenon in English. At the time it was written, **Germany** was in the midst of the great vampire debates that followed on the heels of the vampire epidemics reported throughout the Hungarian Empire. Though written in 1734, the *Travels of 3 English Gentlemen*, remained unpublished for many decades. Meanwhile, **Dom Augustin Calmet's** 1746 treatise on apparitions, demons, and vampires was translated and published in an English edition in 1759. Both Calmet's and the Earl of Oxford's books informed the development of the literary vampire in England.

The English Literary Vampire: England's main contribution to contemporary vampire lore was derived not so much from its folklore tradition as from its nurturing of vampire literature in the nineteenth century. While the **origins** of the literary vampire must be sought in Germany, British poets were quick to discover the theme. **Samuel Taylor Coleridge**, **Robert Southey**, and John Stagg were among the writers who were influenced by such popular translations as Gottfried August Bürger's "Lenora" by Sir Walter Scott.

Then in 1819, **John Polidori**, out of his love-hate relationship with **Lord Byron**, launched the vampire legend with his initial short story "The Vampyre." Polidori's story of an aristocratic vampire who preyed upon the women of Europe was based upon a story fragment originally written by Lord Byron in 1816, although Polidori's story took the fragment in a distinctly new direction. More important than Byron's plot contribution to the story was its original publication under Byron's name. Because of the name attached, it was hailed as a great work by German and French romantic writers, was quickly translated into various languages, and became the basis of a generation of dramatic productions in Paris and a German vampire **opera**.

In 1820 it was brought to the London stage by **James Robinson Planché**. Through the nineteenth century, some of the most famous and influential vampire stories were written. Drawing on ideas introduced by Polidori, **James Malcolm Rymer** wrote *Varney the Vampyre*, one of the most successful penny dreadfuls (a novel published chapter-by-chapter as a weekly serial publication). This highly successful story, which ran to 220 chapters, rivaled Polidori's effort through the rest of the century. *Varney the Vampyre* was followed by a number of pieces of short fiction. Compiled in a single volume, they would constitute a relatively large body of vampire literature, and would include William Gilbert's "The Last Lords of Gardonal" (1867); **Sheridan Le Fanu**'s highly influential **"Carmilla"** (1872); Philip Robinson's two stories, "The Man-Eating Tree" (1881) and "The Last of the Vampires" (1892); Anne Crawford's "A Mystery of the Campagna" (1887); H. G. Wells's, "The Flowering of the Strange Orchid" (1894); and Mary Elizabeth Braddon's "Good Lady Ducayne" (1896). All of these stand behind the single most famous and influential piece of vampire literature of all time—**Bram Stoker**'s *Dracula*, published in London in 1897.

More than any other single work, *Dracula* created the modern image of the vampire and brought the idea to the attention of the English-speaking public around the world. The character **Dracula** became synonymous with the vampire in many ways, and one could think of contemporary vampires as primarily variations of Stoker's character. It initiated the concept of the vampire as a somewhat tamed monster capable of the incognito penetration of human society. Inspired by Stoker, a century of fiction writers would develop numerous concepts of the vampire in ways Stoker only hinted. Dracula now stands beside **Sherlock Holmes** as the single most popular character in English literature and the one most frequently brought to the screen. *Dracula* was brought to the stage in 1924 by **Hamilton Deane**.

The play enjoyed great success during Deane's lifetime, but has rarely been revived in recent years. More importantly, Deane's play was extensively revised by **John L. Balderston** for presentation on the American stage in 1927. Balderston's revision, published by an American **drama** publishing house, has been frequently produced over the years. It was the basis of the three **Universal Pictures** productions—*Dracula* **(1931)** with **Bela Lugosi**, the Spanish version also filmed in 1931, and the 1979 version starring **Frank Langella**. The Langella version resulted from a major Broadway revival of the Balderston play in 1977.

England was also home to **Hammer Films**, which for 20 years (beginning around the mid-1950s) produced a host of horror films in general and vampire films in particular that defined an entire era of horror motion picture production. The distinctive Hammer vampire productions, beginning with *The Curse of Frankenstein* (1957) and *The Horror of Dracula* (1958), were notable for their technicolor presentations and the introduction of a **fanged** vampire who bit his **victims** on screen. These Hammer productions made international stars of **Christopher Lee**, who joined Bela Lugosi and **John Carradine** as memorable Draculas, and **Peter Cushing** as Dracula's ever-present nemesis, **Abraham Van Helsing**. They inspired a new wave of vampire films in Europe and **America**, and with the demise of Hammer in the mid-1970s, British leadership in the production of vampire movies passed to the United States.

The Contemporary English Vampire: The United Kingdom has been an integral factor in the current revival of interest in vampires. It is now home to a number of vampire interest groups. **The Dracula Society**, formed in 1973, is among the oldest and the **Whitby** Dracula Vampire Society, which puts on a variety of celebrative events at Whitby (where Dracula first landed in England), is the most active. Other organizations that focus vampire fandom in the UK include The Vampire Society (Gittens) and The Vampire Guild, which publishes the journal, *Crimson*. The more distinct **Vampire Research Society**, headed by Sean Manchester, looks with disdain on the vampire as an evil creature. British authors have contributed their share of novels to the new vampire literature, among the more significant being **Brian Lumley**, Barbara Hambly, **Tanith Lee**, **Peter Tremayne**, Steve Jones, and **Kim Newman**. The United Kingdom was also the home of the emergence of **gothic** music now promoted by the Gothic Society.

Sources:

Briggs, Katherine. *A Dictionary of Fairies*. London: Penguin Books, 1976. Reprinted as *An Encyclopedia of Fairies, Hobgoblins, Brownies, Bogies, and Other Supernatural Creatures*. New York: Pantheon Books, 1976. 481 pp.

Cox, Greg. *The Transylvanian Library*. San Bernardino, CA: Borgo Press, 1993. 264 pp.

Deane, Hamilton, and John L. Balderston. *Dracula: The Ultimate Illustrated Edition of the World-Famous Vampire Play*. Edited by David J. Skal. New York: St. Martin's Press, 1993. 153 pp.

Jones, Stephen. *The Illustrated Vampire Movie Guide*. London: Titan Books, 1993. 144 pp.

Stoker, Bram. *Dracula*. London: A. Constable & Co., 1897. 390 pp.

Wilson, Katharina M. "The History of the Word 'Vampire.'" *Journal of the History of Ideas* 46, 4 (October-December 1985): 577–583.

❨ Universal Pictures ❩

With its production of *Dracula* **(1931)**, Universal Pictures became the first studio to bring the vampire theme to the talking motion picture and initiated a wave of interest in horror movies. The studio was founded by Carl Laemmle who entered the industry in 1906. Universal initially opened two studios in Los Angeles then, in 1915, shifted

Audiences flocked to Universal Pictures "monster mash" films of the 1940s, which brought Dracula, Frankenstein, and the Wolfman together on the same screen.

its headquarters to Universal City on the site of the former Taylor Ranch in the San Fernando Valley (it is now the oldest continuously operated studio in America). After many years of making silent movies, Universal made its first sound movie in 1930, *The King of Jazz*. That same year, the studio obtained the rights to the **Hamilton Deane/John L. Balderston** play, *Dracula*, which was then making successful appearances around the country after completing a lengthy run on Broadway. The star of the West Coast production, **Bela Lugosi**, worked with the studio to secure the motion picture rights from Florence Stoker, the widow of **Bram Stoker**. **Tod Browning** was chosen to direct the picture.

As people became aware of Universal's plans for *Dracula*, Paul Kohner, the executive in charge of foreign language productions, suggested that *Dracula* would be an excellent candidate for a Spanish version. He already had in mind Lupita Tovar (Kohner's future wife) as the female lead. Thus, as the English-language version of *Dracula* was filmed, the Spanish language version, using the same stage settings but a different cast, was simultaneously produced.

Dracula **(Spanish, 1931)** was a success in what was then a relatively small market. However, the English version starring Bela Lugosi—after a slow start—became Universal's top grossing film of the year and was credited with keeping the studio from closing after two years of losing money. The success led to a series of horror films: *Frankenstein* (1932), *The Mummy* (1932), *The Invisible Man* (1933), *The Black Cat* (1934), and *The Bride of Frankenstein* (1935). For nearly two decades, Universal became known for its horror movies, but interestingly enough, it was not until 1936 with the production of *Dracula's Daughter* that a second vampire film was produced. Vampire fans waited until 1943 for a third film titled *Son of Dracula*.

In 1936, Laemmle lost control of Universal to Charles Rogers and J. Cheever Cowdin. During the next decade, the company produced a large number of low-budget films, including many horror features and several vampire movies. In 1948, it merged with International Pictures. Except for the comedy *Abbott and Costello Meet Frankenstein*, Universal-International did not produce any other movies with major vampire themes—part of a general trend away from horror films at the time.

After many years, Universal produced a new vampire film, *Blood of Dracula* in 1957. The movie was aimed at a youthful audience and the inclusion of a female vampire made the movie more interesting. The success of the movie was responsible for several other vampire movies during the next few years but, after the 1959 production of the *Curse of the Undead*, the studio dropped vampire movies from its schedule for more than a decade. Its reluctance to return to releasing vampire movies and, thereby, placing too much emphasis on the horror genre was amply demonstrated in the summer of 1958 when Universal announced that it had worked out a deal with British upstart **Hammer Films**. Hammer acquired all of the copyrights Universal owned on its classic horror titles, including *Dracula*. Universal largely abandoned the horror movie business for an entire generation.

In 1978, Universal bought the cinema rights to the remake of the Hamilton Deane/John L. Balderston play, which had enjoyed a revival on Broadway, and brought its star, **Frank Langella**, to Hollywood for the screen version. Langella's **Dracula (1979)** proved one of the most effective presentations of the sexual/sensual element that co-exists with the terror theme in the Dracula/vampire myth. Since the 1979 *Dracula*, Universal had largely stayed away from the vampire theme altogether. However, in the early twenty-first century, announcements have been made that Universal will produce several new vampire movies, including the screen adaptation of **Darren Shan**'s Cirque du Freak series of children's books and a new version of **Anne Rice's *Interview with the Vampire***. Universal will, of course, always be remembered for its launching of *Dracula* into the consciousness of a nation.

Sources:

Brunas, Michael John, and Tom Weaver. *Universal Horrors: The Studios Classic Films, 1931–1946.* Jefferson, NC: McFarland & Company, 1990. 616 pp.

Hanke, Ken. *A Critical Guide to Horror Film Series.* New York: Garland Publishing, 1991. 341 pp.

Holte, James Craig. *Dracula in the Dark: The Dracula Film Adaptations.* Westport, CT: Greenwood Press, 1997. 161 pp.

Pirie, David. *The Vampire Cinema.* London: Hamlyn, 1977. 176 pp.

Skal, David J. *Hollywood Gothic: The Tangled Web of Dracula from Novel to Stage to Screen.* New York: W. W. Norton & Company, 1990. 243 pp.

Upir *see:* Czech Republic and Slovakia, Vampires in

Vadim, Roger (1927–2000)

Roger Vadim, French director of sexually explicit films and the first person to film the classic vampire story "Carmilla," was born R. V. Plémiannikov in Paris. He entered the French film industry soon after World War II as an assistant to Marc Allégret. In 1955 while working on an Allégret film, *Futures Vedettes*, he met his future wife, Brigitte Bardot. After they married he directed her in *And God Created Woman* (1956) and *The Night Heaven Fell* (1957), two films that made Bardot an international sex goddess. Those films also helped establish Vadim's reputation as a superior purveyor of male voyeuristic sexual fantasies in wide-screen Technicolor.

After completing *The Night That Heaven Fell*, Vadim and Bardot were divorced and he married Annette Stroyberg, the star of his next set of films. His major production during this period was a vampire movie, *Et Mourir de Plaisir*, released in the United States as *Blood and Roses* and for which he turned to Irish writer **Sheridan Le Fanu** for inspiration. Throughout his career Vadim searched for stories that would allow him to project his own sexual fantasies on the screen, and when he encountered the artistic presentation of an overtly sexual vampire in Le Fanu's "Carmilla," he was quick to see its potential. The story's potential was underscored by current releases from **Hammer Films** in England, which was making the world aware of the large market for bloody vampire stories.

Possibly because of the blatant sexual element of "Carmilla," *Blood and Roses* was the first attempt to bring Le Fanu's story to the screen (not including **Carl Theodor Dreyer**'s *Vampir*, which some buffs believe is based on "Carmilla," even though it bears little resemblance to Le Fanu's story). "Carmilla" proved a perfect vehicle for Vadim, who was able to play with the situation of a young, sexually attractive vampire drawn to **victims** of her own age and gender and for whom the integration of feeding and sexual activity was the norm. Vadim's second wife, Annette, played **Carmilla**, described in the screenplay as a woman possessed of the spirit of a long-dead vampire. Her victim was Elsa Martinelli, who played Georgia Monteverdi. One especially memorable scene occurred close-up as Carmilla kissed a drop of **blood** that had appeared on Georgia's lip. The loosening of censorship standards in French movies by this time (to which Vadim had contributed) allowed him to capture on film some of the sexual aspects of the vampire's embrace that Le Fanu could only suggest. Although largely faithful to the mood of the original story, Vadim did incorporate several elements of what had become the standard vampire myth. Thus, Carmilla returned to her grave each morning, and the movie ended as she rushed against the **sunlight.** She stumbled and fell on a wooden shaft, which pierced her heart. In the original story, her grave was discovered by the family of some of her victims, who drove a **stake** into her heart.

At the time *Blood and Roses* was released, British and American audiences were not yet allowed to see Vadim's films uncut. Censors removed the more "offensive" scenes before *Blood and Roses* was released in 1961 by Paramount. *Blood and Roses* was Vadim's only direct contribution to the vampire genre; however, he inadvertently made a second notable contribution through his third wife, Jane Fonda. In 1968 he cast Fonda in the starring role in *Barbarella*, in which he combined his sexual visions with

science fiction. The sexy, space-hopping Barbarella directly inspired **Forrest J. Ackerman** in the creation of *Vampirella*, the sexy **comic book** space vampire whose numerous adventures became the subject of the most successful vampire comic books to the present day.

In 1971 Vadim had one last success with *Pretty Maids All in a Row*, starring Angie Dickinson, but by the 1970s Vadim's one-dimensional *Playboy* approach to the film was passed over for hard-core pornography and sexually explicit scenes in major Hollywood movies. Vadim continued to direct through the 1980s, but his movies never again attracted the attention of his earlier work. In 1963 he wrote the introduction for an anthology of vampire stories collected by Ornella Volta and Valeria Riva. He died on February 11, 2000, in Paris, France.

Sources:

Glut, Donald G. *The Dracula Book*. Metuchen, NJ: Scarecrow Press, 1975. 388 pp.

Quinlan, David. *The Illustrated Guide to Film Directors*. Totowa, NJ: Barnes & Noble, 1984. 335 pp.

Thomson, David. *A Biographical Dictionary of Film*. New York: William Morrow, 1976. 629 pp.

Vadim, Roger. *Bardot, Deneuve & Fonda: The Memoirs of Roger Vadim*. London: New English Library, 1970.

———. *Memoirs of the Devil*. San Diego: Harcourt Brace Jovanovich, 1977. 187 pp.

Volta, Ornella, and Valaria Riva, eds. *The Vampire: An Anthology*. Introduction by Roger Vadim. London: Neville Spearman, 1963. Rept. London: Pan Books, 1965. 316 pp.

❨ Vambéry, Arminius (1832–1913) ❩

Arminius Vambéry, Hungarian historian and possible model for Dr. **Abraham Van Helsing** in **Bram Stoker**'s novel *Dracula* (1897), was born lame at Szerdakely, near Pressburg, in **Hungary**. As a young man he took up the study of languages and by the age of sixteen, largely through his own efforts, was fluent in most European languages, including Latin and Greek. At the age of twenty-two he was able to travel to Constantinople and for the first time practiced the languages he had learned. In 1858 he published his first book, a German-Turkish dictionary, the only one of its kind available for many years. He also began to translate Turkish histories that related events in Hungary, for which he earned a position as a corresponding member of the Hungarian Academy in 1861. With a grant from the Academy, he then traveled widely through the Middle East for several years. In 1864 he moved to England, where he was welcomed as an explorer-traveler and given support while he wrote his book, *Travels in Central Asia*, which was quickly translated into French, German, and Hungarian. He afterward settled in Hungary as a professor of Oriental languages at the University of Pesth.

For the next two decades he was one of the most prolific and famous Hungarian scholars and men of letters. His correspondence kept him in touch with most of the power centers of Europe, and he commented freely on the political questions of his day. In 1883 he wrote the autobiographical *Arminius Vambéry: His Life and Travels*. Soon after its appearance he encountered a wave of anti-Semitism in Hungary and felt forced to relocate to England. There he continued to write and lecture. He wrote one of his

most popular books, a large volume titled *Hungary in Ancient, Medieval, and Modern Times* (1886), which was reprinted several times under various titles. This volume would have been one of the books available to Stoker for research on the first chapters of *Dracula*. Vambéry actually met Bram Stoker, possibly for the first time, in 1890 during the early stages of the writing of *Dracula*. He was on Stoker's guest list one evening at the Beefsteak Room, where people gathered after an evening at the Lyceum Theatre. In conversation and through his books on Hungary, Vambéry possibly influenced Stoker, though the extent is a matter of debate among Dracula scholars.

Raymond T. McNally and **Radu Florescu** credit Vambéry with turning Stoker from his prior interest in Austria (reflected in his short story "Dracula's Guest") toward **Transylvania**, the setting of the opening and closing chapters of *Dracula*. Unfortunately, no correspondence between Stoker and Vambéry has survived, though Stoker mentions their meeting in his *Personal Reminiscences of Henry Irving*. **Elizabeth Miller**, who emerged in the 1990s as one of the foremost scholars of the text, has assumed the most skeptical position and suggested that the tie between Vambéry and the text of *Dracula* is a remnant of scholarly speculation from the period before the discovery of Stoker's working papers at the Rosenbach Museum. However, while Miller notes, "There is no documented evidence that Vambéry gave Stoker any information about Vlad Tepes or vampires," and there is no mention of **Vlad the Impaler** in any of Vambéry's books, there is cause to believe that Vambéry may have been one of the people from whom Stoker developed his character **Abraham Van Helsing**. Stoker acknowledges in the novel a debt to Vambéry with a passing mention of him placed in the mouth of Van Helsing:

> I have asked my friend Arminius, of Buda-Pesth University, to make his record; and, from all the means that are, he (Vambéry) tells me of what he (Dracula) has been. He must, indeed, have been that Viovode Dracula who won his name against the Turk....

Vambéry's last work was another autobiographical volume, *The Story of My Struggles* (1904).

Sources:

Adler, Lory, and Richard Dalby. *The Dervish of Windsor Castle*. London: Bachman and Turner, 1979. 512 pp.

Bartholomä, Ruth. *Von Zentralasien nach Windsor Castle. Leben und Werk des Orientalisten Arminius Vámbéry (1832–1913)*. Würzburg: Ergon Verlag, 2006.

Miller, Elizabeth. *Reflections on Dracula: Ten Essays*. White Rock, BC: Transylvanian Press, 1997. 226 pp.

Stoker, Bram. *The Essential Dracula*. Edited by Raymond McNally and Radu Florescu. New York: Mayflower Books, 1979. 320 pp.

———. *Personal Reminiscences of Henry Irving*. 2 vols. London: William Heinemann, 1906.

Haining, Peter, and Peter Tremayne. *The Undead: The Legend of Bram Stoker and Dracula*. London: Constable, 1997. 199 pp.

Vambéry, Arminius. *Travels in Central Asia*. London: J. Murray, 1864. 493 pp.

———. *Arminius Vambéry: His Life and Adventures*. New York: Cassell and Company, 1983. 370 pp.

———. *Hungary in Ancient, Medieval, and Modern Times*. London: T. F. Unwin, 1886. 453 pp.

———. *The Story of My Struggles: The Memoirs of Arminius Vambéry*. 2 vols. London: T. F. Unwin, 1904.

❮ The Vamp ❯

The vamp, a popular stereotypical figure of the silent film, developed from extension of the vampire myth into an analogy of the male/female relationships. Both **psychological** and feminist interpretations of the myth emphasized the maleness of the vampire legend. It was a projection of male fears, goals, and attitudes toward the world. The role of the vamp was established in large part by "The Vampire", a short poem by Rudyard Kipling:

> A fool there was and he made his prayer (Even as you and I) To a rag and a bone and a hank of hair (We call her the woman who did not care) But the fool he called her his lady fair— (Even as you or I!)

> Oh, the years we waste and the tears we waste and the work of our head and hand Belong to the woman who did not know Belong to the woman who did not know (And now we know that she never could know) And did not understand!

> A fool there was and his goods he spent (Even as you and I) Honour and faith and a sure intent (And it wasn't the least what the lady meant) But a fool must follow his natural bent (Even as you and I!)

The poem, inspired by a famous painting by Philip Burne-Jones, in turn inspired a play by Porter Emerson Brown, *A Fool There Was,* which in turn was made into a movie by the Fox Film Corporation. The story involved a triangle composed of a husband, his wife, and a vampire. The husband, John Schulyer, was a lawyer who had been sent on a diplomatic mission for the president of the United States. Off in a scenic land, he encountered a vampiress, who injected herself into his life. His wife reasserted herself at various points, first with a letter, which the vampiress tore up. Later, Schulyer tried to cable his wife, but was blocked. So tight did the vampiress' hold become that, upon Schulyer's return to the States, he provided a townhouse for her. Meanwhile, he was degenerating into a hopeless alcoholic. The wife made one last attempt to reclaim her husband, but as she was leading him away, the vampiress appeared, and the man lost all desire to leave. Because he had abandoned his wife for the temptress, his will had left him and he was destroyed.

A Fool There Was became an important film in many respects. It was the film through which Fox, then a small company, successfully fought the monopoly of General Film. It also introduced **Theda Bara** to the screen as the vamp. Theda Bara would become the embodiment of the vamp in a series of pictures for Fox. She provided a powerful image for the public to place beside that of the virtuous woman under attack by evil cultural forces that had been so powerfully cultivated by D. W. Griffith (1875–1948) at General.

The vamp was the dark shadow of the Victorian virtuous woman. She was immoral, tainted with powerful, dark **sexuality**. Her power derived from her ability to release in males similar strong but latent sexual energies, strictly contained by modern cultural restrictions. She attached herself to men and sapped their vitality. Her image was carefully constructed. She wore tight revealing black clothes, sometimes decorated with either spiders or snakes. Her nails were long and cut to a point. In a day when **women** rarely used

tobacco in public, she frequently smoked cigarettes from a long holder. Her demeanor suggested that she was foreign, either from continental Europe or the Middle East.

Theda Bara (1885–1955), born Theodosia Goodman in Cincinnati, Ohio, largely defined the vamp for the American public. In cooperation with Fox, through the second decade of this century she carefully created a public persona. Fox's role marked the first attempt by a studio to manufacture a star's image in such depth. The name Theda Bara was an anagram for Arab Death. Various stories were circulated about her suggesting a mysterious **origin** in the Middle East, the product of an affair between exotic mates. Supposedly, she had been weaned on snake's **blood**, and tribesmen had fought over her. Studio publicity compared her to **Elizabeth Bathory**, the seventeenth-century blood countess. When Theda Bara appeared in public, she often pretended not to speak English and traveled with her African footmen in a white limousine. Once developed, the vamp persona proved a continuing interest. Theda Bara's image passed to the likes of Nita Naldi (1899–1961), who starred in the 1922 Rudolph Valentino film *Blood and Sand*, and Greta Garbo (1905–1990), who became a star with her 1927 film *Flesh and the Devil*. Garbo's vampish role was spelled out for those in the audience who could not pick it up otherwise by a minister who told the hero that the devil created women with beautiful bodies so that they could tempt men in a fleshly manner when they failed to reach them through more spiritual means. Garbo was credited with humanizing the vamp's role and thus contributing to the destruction of the image, at least as it had previously existed. The vamp evolved into the *femme fatale*, the temptress who still appears in a wide variety of settings in motion pictures.

Sources:

Genini, Ronald. *Theda Bara: A Biography of the Silent Screen Vamp, With a Filmography.* Jeffersonville, NC: McFarland & Company, 2001. 168 pp.

Golden, Eve. *Vamp: The Rise and Fall of Theda Bara.* Vestal, NY: Empire Publishing, 1996. 274 pp.

Higashi, Sumiko. *Virgins, Vamps, and Flappers: The American Silent Movie Heroine.* Montreal: Eden Press Women's Publications, 1978. 276 pp.

Keesey, Pam. *Vamps: An Illustrated History of the Femme Fatale.* San Francisco, CA: Cleis Press, 1997. 171 pp.

Kuhn, Annette. *The Women's Companion to International Films.* London: Virago, 1990. 464 pp. Rept. *Women in Film: An International Guide.* New York: Fawcett Columbine, 1991. 500 pp.

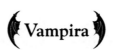

Vampira

Vampira is the persona of actress Maila Nurmi (1921–2008). The character was created in 1954 when Nurmi was a horror show hostess at KABC-TV in Los Angeles. After a two-year run she moved to KHJ-TV. Nurmi's enduring fame came from her joining **Bela Lugosi** in the classic cult movie *Plan 9 from Outer Space* (1956). They played the initial two vampire/zombies that the space invaders hoped to create in their plan to take over Earth. After the run of her **television** show, she also appeared in several other movies, including two vampire films, *The Magic Sword* (1964) and *Orgy of the Night* (1966), the latter put together by *Plan 9*'s director Edward Wood, Jr. Nurmi also appeared in several other nonvampire movies, and for a while she operated a boutique in Hollywood. In the 1980s Nurmi sued Cassandra Peterson for stealing her Vampira persona to create the persona **Elvira**; however, the suit came to nought. In 2006, Kevin Sean Michaels put out a DVD documentary of Nurmi's life, *Vampira the Movie.*

Sources:

"Maila 'Vampira' Nurmi on Wood, Dean and 'Bunny.'" *Hollywood Book and Poser News* 11 (October 1992): 3–4.

The Vampire (Real Vampires)

Actress Maila Nurmi created the character Vampira for a 1950s television show.

A vampire was a peculiar kind of revenant, a dead person who had returned to life and continued a form of existence through drinking the **blood** of the living. In popular thought, the vampire was considered to be "undead," having completed earthly life but still being tied to that life and not yet welcomed by the realm of the dead. The vampire is distinguished from the ghost, a disembodied spirit, in that the vampire inhabited in an animated body. It was distinguished from the **ghoul** in that the ghoul had no intelligent control, being guided solely by its hunger, and feasted off the body of its **victim** rather than just the blood. Consuming blood was the most characteristic activity of vampires, so the term *vampire* has also been used to describe many mythological creatures who drink blood as well as living persons who engage in similar activities. Finally, the term has been used to describe people (and spirits) who engage in **psychic vampirism,** the process of draining the life force or energy (rather than the blood) of other people.

The Eighteenth-Century Vampire Controversy: In the eighteenth century, Western scholars for the first time considered the question of the existence of vampires as something more than just another element of the vast supernatural world of rural folk culture. The controversy was set off by a series of incidents of vampire hysteria that occurred in East Prussia in 1721 and in the lands of the Austro-Hungarian Empire from 1725 through 1732. These cases culminated in the famous events surrounding **Arnold Paul,** a retired Austrian soldier who had settled in Serbia and was accused of being the source of an outbreak of vampirism in his community. Several of these cases became the object of formal government investigations and reports, and a hastily prepared volume on Paul sold widely around Europe.

The publication of the Paul book led to no less than a dozen treatises and four dissertations, and the controversy over him lasted for a generation. It eventually involved some of the most famous scholars of Europe, including Diderot and Voltaire. The question of the existence of vampires was argued on legal, theological, and scientific grounds. The question became more than academic in that villagers, affected by a belief that vampires were active in their community, opened graves and mutilated or destroyed any bodies showing **characteristics** believed to indicate vampirism. Although some members of the scholarly community attempted to defend the existence of vampires, the majority concluded that evidence suggested they did not exist. The latter cited a host of natural phenomena that accounted for vampire reports, such as premature burial and rabies (which causes an insatiable thirst in anyone infected). They also attributed the reports to theological polemics in areas where a Roman Catholic Austrian government had been imposed on an Orthodox population.

The most careful defense of vampires came from French biblical scholar **Dom Augustin Calmet** in his 1746 *Dissertations sur les Apparitions des Anges des Démons et des Esprits, et sur les revenants, et Vampires de Hungrie, de Boheme, de Moravie, et de Silésie*. The publication of Calmet's treatise, given his reputation as a scholar, initiated a second stage of the academic controversy, which was largely settled by the end of the 1830s. Even the Vatican ignored Calmet, its opinion that vampires did not exist having been set by the conclusions of Archbishop **Giuseppe Davanzati** published just two years before Calmet's book. A decade after Calmet's book appeared—and in the midst of the controversy it sparked—a new wave of vampire hysteria occurred in Silesia. Austrian Empress Maria Theresa sent her personal physician to investigate the incident. In his report, Dr. Gerhard Van Swieten ridiculed the practice of exhuming and executing purported vampires as "posthumous magic." As a result, in 1755 and 1756 Maria Theresa forbade church and village authorities from taking any action in cases of reported vampires. Only officials of the central government could respond to such cases. The actions of the Austrian empress finished what was left of any remaining public debate.

Real Vampires in the Nineteenth Century?: From the middle of the seventeenth century until the second half of the nineteenth, no serious attempt to prove the existence of vampires, at least in their folkloric form, was made. An attempt to defend the folkloric vampire was launched in the mid-1800s by the spiritualist community. Spokespersons who emerged during the first generation of spiritualism in Europe, where the tales of vampires were most prevalent, offered a new rationale for vampires—psychic vampirism. In the 1860s, **Z. J. Piérart** suggested that the phenomena described in the folkloric reports of vampires could be attributed to the astral bodies of either the living or dead, which fed off the life energy of the living. The astral body, however elusive, provided an agent for transmitting vitality to the dead and accounted for bodies that, though lying buried for some weeks or months, did not decay and when uncovered manifest numerous signs of a continuing life. Piérart's suggestion, which had precursors in previous occult writers, was picked up by spiritualist and theosophical exponents, and accounts of "true vampires" began to appear in occult journals.

Typical of these reports was one of the many published by theosophist **Franz Hartmann** in the 1890s. The story concerned an alcoholic who had been rejected by a woman with whom he was in love. Dejected, he committed **suicide** by shooting himself. Soon afterward, the woman began to complain of vampiric attacks from a specter in the form of the recently dead suitor. She could not see him but was aware of his presence. Doctors diagnosed her as an hysteric but could do little to relieve her symptoms. She finally submitted herself to an exorcism conducted by a person who accepted her explanation of vampirism. After the exorcism, the attacks ceased. Today, various **psychological** theories, shorn of any need to posit the existence of vampires, could account for all of the woman's symptoms, and steps to deal with her unresolved guilt over

the suitor's suicide could be pursued. However, these were as yet unavailable to the medical world, and the spiritualist perspective gained its share of support.

Increasing reports of vampirism, including accounts of the living vampirizing their acquaintances, at times seemingly without any conscious awareness of what they were doing, led to the discarding of the more supernatural spiritualist **explanations** of vampirism, in which astral bodies attacked the living. Such theories, although maintained in some occult movements, were for the most part replaced with references to "psychic sponges", people who were themselves low on psychic energy, manifest by frequent periods of fatigue, but who in the presence of high-energy people had the ability to take energy from them. Many people seemed to know such psychic sponges, individuals who regain their vitality in the company of others even as their companions experience a distinct loss of energy and interest in immediate activities. Although the notion of psychic sponges was a popular one, at least in different metaphysical and psychic-oriented groups, it is extremely difficult to document and has produced only a minuscule literature.

Vampirism as Blood Fetish: While the more benign incidents of psychic vampirism were being reported, accounts of vampire **crime** began to appear. In the 1920s two cases of serial killers with vampiric tendencies shocked the people of Europe. In 1924 they read of **Fritz Haarmann** of Hanover, **Germany**, who killed no fewer than 24 young men. He earned the appellation "vampire" killer by biting the neck of those he murdered and drinking some of their blood. Five years later, **Peter Kürten** of Düsseldorf went on a killing spree, later confessing that he received a sexual thrill and release while watching blood spurt from his victims.

Rare accounts of serial killers with some form of blood fetish were also reported. One of the more gruesome concerned a series of murders of prostitutes in Stockholm, Sweden, in the period from 1982 to 1987. During this period at least seven prostitutes disappeared from the streets, and their bodies were later discovered surgically dismembered and drained of blood. Eventually arrested and tried in the case were two physicians, Teet Haerm and Thomas Allgren.

Haerm's arrest shocked many. He was the senior police medical examiner and one of the leading forensic pathologists in the world. His articles had appeared in several professional publications, including the *Lancet*, a prominent British medical journal. He had even been called in to examine the remains of several of the women he was later accused of murdering. Allgren, Haerm's best friend, was a dermatologist. In the end, Allgren confessed and gave testimony at Haerm's trial. According to Allgren, Haerm had an intense desire to brutalize and kill prostitutes. To justify the satiation of that desire, the two had started on a righteous crusade to rid Stockholm of streetwalkers. However, Allgren also discovered that Haerm had a lust for blood and gore and that after the killings he drained and drank the blood of his victims. Eventually, Allgren was turned in by his daughter, who claimed that he had sexually molested her. In the process of talking about her experience, she also described in some detail a murder of one of the prostitutes she had witnessed. The testimonies of Allgren and his daughter were heard at a 1988 trial in which the latter testified that blood lust led Haerm into pathology but he eventually found the work on bodies less than satisfying. Then he began his killing spree.

Both Haerm and Allgren were convicted in a 1988 trial and sentenced to life imprisonment. However, their convictions were overturned, and in a retrial they were found not guilty, even though the judge wrote in his decision that there was reasonable evidence that they were guilty. Both defendants were freed.

Another recently publicized case of a "vampire" killer concerned Richard Chase of Sacramento, California. The documented nefarious deeds committed by Chase began in December 1977 with the shooting of Ambrose Griffin. A month later, on January 23, 1978, Chase shot Theresa Wallin, after which he mutilated her body with a knife. In that process he collected her blood in a cup and consumed it. A week after the Wallin attack, he killed four people at Evelyn Miroth's home, including Miroth, whom he also mutilated and whose blood he also drank. Miroth's baby nephew, who was visiting her, was taken home by Chase, who killed him, drank his blood, and tossed his body in the garbage. According to Chase, he believed that he had blood poisoning and needed blood. He had in the past hunted animals (beginning with small animals such as rabbits and cats and moving on to cows). He killed the animals and drank their blood, and his messiness had led to several prior encounters with the authorities. After such an encounter in 1977, he made a decision to start killing people. A year earlier he had spent time in a mental facility and had manifest a mania over blood. His fellow patients had begun to call him **Dracula**. Arrested soon after the Miroth murder, he was convicted of the six killings. He died in prison, where he committed suicide in 1980 at age thirty-one.

The examples of Haarmann, Kürten, and Haerm, are only tangential to what traditionally has been thought of as vampirism. They are serial killers with, among other problems, a blood fetish. The blood was not the object of their quest, and the drinking of blood was just one of the more gruesome (and somewhat superficial) practices in which they engaged. Chase was somewhat different and more closely approached true vampirism. Although he was not seeking blood to prolong his life, he sought regular ingestions of blood to counteract the effects of poison he believed he was receiving. In the end, however, his vampiric activity also fell into the serial killing mode, the blood lust being peripheral to the killings.

Some Real Vampires Emerge: During the 1960s, in part due to the **Hammer Films**, Dracula movies, and the ***Dark Shadows* television** series, public interest in vampires increased noticeably, and the first of the present-day vampire fan clubs and interest groups was founded. By the early 1970s the Count Dracula Fan Club, the Vampire Information Exchange, and the Vampire Studies Society (now Vampire Studies) had formed in the United States and the **Vampire Research Society** and the **Dracula Society** soon followed in England. As these groups emerged, the leaders began to encounter people who actually claimed to be vampires. In the beginning, devoted as they were to the literary vampire (and not really believing that such things as vampires existed), leaders of the vampire interest groups largely discounted the stories. Among those who did take the reports seriously were Scott Rogo, Sean Manchester, founder of the Vampire Research Society in **London**, and Stephen Kaplan, founder of the **Vampire Research Center** in New York.

Rogo, Manchester, and Kaplan each began their research from a point of prior interest with psychic phenomena. During the late 1960s Rogo tried to interest the American Society for Psychical Research in vampirism but was unable to budge them from their more central concerns. Most parapsychologists thought that their field was already far enough out on the fringe. Forced to choose, Rogo soon suppressed his interest in vampirism and during the 1970s and 1980s made his own contribution as a writer, attempting to bring psychical research into the mainstream of the scientific community. Sean Manchester's Vampire Research Society grew out of his previous leadership role in an occult investigations bureau. The society investigates all aspects of "supernatural vampire phenomena," a task that has led to a variety of research projects, including the famous **Highgate vampire** and the Kirklees vampire projects.

Stephen Kaplan founded the Vampire Research Center in 1972. His first interview of alleged vampires was with a couple who introduced him to the nocturnal world of vampires, their alternative sexual practices (in this case sadomasochism), and the existence of donors, people who (for a price) allow vampires to drink their blood. From his early encounters, Kaplan began to develop a working definition of vampires. They were people who met three criteria: they need regular quantities of blood, they believe that the blood will prolong their life and help them remain youthful, and they often find the blood and its consumption to be sexually arousing. Over the years, Kaplan had the opportunity to meet and correspond with other vampires and was able to fill out his picture of them. They do not drink great quantities of blood—only a few ounces a day—but they need that blood daily and will go to extreme measures to receive it. Denied it, they become irritable, depressed, fatigued, and somewhat aggressive. They tend to be nocturnal in their habits, and many profess to be extremely sensitive to light. Otherwise, they appear normal and dress in such a way as not to call attention to themselves. To obtain blood, vampires often engage in various forms of sadomasochistic behavior that lead to some bloodletting. They often exchange sexual favors for blood. Some join groups that engage in ritual blood-drinking. If unable to obtain a willing donor, they will, according to their own testimony, occasionally attack a victim, but, as a rule, will not kill for blood.

The vampires Kaplan studied were neither psychic nor supernatural beings. They were, apart from their blood-drinking activities, somewhat normal human beings. Some professed to be far older than their youthful appearance suggested, but their true age was rarely verifiable. Above and beyond the relatively small number of vampires Kaplan encountered (fewer than 100 in two decades), he discovered hundreds of people he described as vampirelike individuals. These people seek to imitate vampires in various ways to gain some of the positive qualities associated with vampiric existence, from immortality to the ability to dominate others—sexually and otherwise.

As early as the 1970s he was able to locate people who had adopted the vampire persona by wearing black clothes or altering their teeth. They drank blood, but, not liking the taste, they put it in a fruit juice cocktail. Many of the people attracted to vampirism find themselves drawn by the eroticism of the vampires' life. Vampirism, especially in its literary and cinematic expression, is inherently sexual. The vampire's bite has often been compared to sexual intercourse, and blood likened to semen. Worldwide over the centuries, blood acquired both a sexual and religious connotation, but the dominant Western Christian religion retained the religious meaning without the sexual element. In the activities of many nonconventional persuasions, such as the contemporary sex magic practiced by the followers of Aleister Crowley, the sexual and religious elements of blood have been reunited. A few have united sex and blood-drinking in more sinister forms.

In the process of his research, Kaplan discovered just how difficult was the area on which he decided to focus. Not only did he face tremendous ridicule, but fear of the legal and medical authorities and an intolerant public caused many of the subjects of his study to back away from any situations that might threaten their anonymity, classify them as lawbreakers, or question their mental competence. No real comprehensive and systematic study of vampires has been possible, and knowledge of them still relies on anecdotes related by their few spokespersons. Most important, no medical data of the kind that could provide any evidence of physical traits shared by people who claim to be vampires is available.

Real Vampires in the 1990s: In the decade since *Vampires Are* was published, a **gothic** subculture has emerged across **America**. The gothic life is centered on eerie, atmospheric, gothic rock **music**, and nightclubs and theaters that regularly provide a stage for gothic bands to perform. Individual "goths" emulate the nocturnal vampiric life, and many assume a vampiric persona, complete with dark clothes, pale makeup, and artificial **fangs**. They also advocate life-styles based on androgyny, so central to the character **Lestat de Lioncourt**, the popular vampire star of the novels of **Anne Rice**. Almost all forms of sexual expression among consenting adults, from sadomasochism to blood fetishism, are welcomed. Thus, the gothic subculture has created a space in which self-designated vampires can move somewhat freely and mingle without anyone questioning their nonconventional habits.

At the same time, the voices of "nongoths" who profess to be vampires also continue to be heard. Carol Page, in a far less systematic way than Kaplan, has written of her experiences with contemporary blood-drinkers in *Bloodlust: Conversations with Real Vampires* (1991). Page, who interviewed numerous "vampires," reached many of the same conclusions as Kaplan:

> The blood they drink has no effect on them physiologically. It does not keep them young and they do not physically need it, although some vampires believe they do. It doesn't make them high, except psychologically, or give them nutrition, since human blood passes through the digestive system without being absorbed. They do not have superhuman **strength**. They cannot turn into **bats** and wolves. Some **sleep** in **coffins** during the day and dress in black capes or indulge in other affectations inspired by fictional vampires. (p. 15)

Page and Kaplan, as well as other sources, have made the point that vampires—that is, blood-drinkers—do exist and have described their world in some detail. Furthermore, they suggest that these vampires live a camouflaged life in the midst of more conventional society and that, except within the cordial atmosphere of the gothic world or the nocturnal world of their own kind, they do not drop their conforming persona or allow the nature of their life to be known by any they do not fully trust. However, there are enough of them, some of whom live relatively open and accessible lives, that few serious researchers would have much difficulty in making contact with them.

Through the 1990s and the first decade of the new century, the world of "real" vampires continued to evolve. Many first met while engaged in the role-playing game, **Vampire: the Masquerade**. An initial group of people who drank small quantities of blood, called "sanguinarians" emerged. They were distinguished by a variety of claims about the need of and benefit derived from the periodic consumption of at least a few

drops of blood. They were being serviced by a slightly larger group of people who volunteered to donate their blood, usually retrieved by making small wounds on their body.

To the sanguinarians was soon added a larger and increasingly vocal group of energy vampires, or **psychic vampires,** who claimed to have a regular need to drain the energy of others without which they would suffer a variety of conditions marked by extreme fatigue. In spite of the ethical questions raised by their taking energy from unsuspecting donors, the energy vampires violated no laws and no ready method of verifying their claims has been available. Such vampires soon emerged as the much larger segment of the vampire community. While many associated themselves with the esoteric community, which at least admitted the existence of energy exchange, many were living incognito lives in society, holding jobs, raising families, and even worshipping in mainstream churches.

Most of the early organizations of vampires based their organization on models derived in part from *Vampire: The Masquerade*, notable for its attempt to imagine a clandestine vampire community operating incognito within the larger mundane human world. These early organizations went under names like house, clan, and coven. Through the 1990s, a New York based organization, the Sanguinarium, served as a focal point of a loose association of local vampire groups.

As the vampire community became more public, there was a call for a code of ethics to guide it. A code, called the Black Veil, was created from the rule used within *Vampire: the Masquerade*. Its first draft published by Father Sebastiaan of the **Ordo Strigoi Vii,** was further reworked by **Michelle Belanger**, one of the most public of the energy vampires. In the meantime, the Internet has allowed people self-identified as vampires to communicate while keeping the degree of anonymity most desired and felt they required. Their community has been most visible in New York City, annually on Halloween in **New Orleans** where a large gathering is held, and through the **Atlanta Vampire Alliance** (AVA), in Georgia. The AVA, originally founded to promote unity among Atlanta's vampire community, has, as a result of its sending out a lengthy questionnaire to the more visible real vampires around the world, resulted in its becoming an international nexus for self-identified vampires. Close to 1,000 people responded to the survey between 2006 and 2009.

The vampire community now exists as what Joseph Laycock describes as an identity community, a very loosely organized community created by the self-identity as a vampire of its constituents. Worldwide it consists of numbers counted in the thousands, the several thousand known to the AVA being its most visible core. At one end of the spectrum of real vampires are the formally organized groups such as the **Temple of the Vampire**, the **Order of the Vampyre**, and the House Kheparu. Other vampires gather for periodic gatherings such as the annual Endless Night Festival in New Orleans or show up at designated times in late-night rock clubs. Most, however, exist as individuals known as vampires only to themselves and a few intimate friends.

Most recently, there has been two attempts to organize gatherings for vampires at which the more serious issues facing the emerging community can be discussed and steps to improve the image of the community can be developed. The first of these organizations, **Voices of the Vampire Community**, founded in 2005, has attempted to bring together representative leaders of the community. The other, the **TWILIGHT** gatherings, founded in 2007, has included both vampires and outsiders seriously interested in the vampire existence.

Sources:

Belanger, Michelle A. *Psychic Vampire Codex: Manual of Magick & Energy Work*. York Beach, ME: Weiser Books, 2004. 284 pp.

————. *Vampires in Their Own Words: An Anthology of Vampire Voices*. Weiser Books: York Beach, ME, 2007. 288 pp.

Biondi, Ray, and Walt Hecox. *The Dracula Killer*. New York: Pocket Books, 1992. 212 pp.

Calmet, Dom Augustin. *Dissertations sur les Apparitions des Anges des Démons et des Esprits, et sur les revenants, et Vampires de Hungrie, de Boheme, de Moravie, et de Silésie*. Paris: 1746. Reprinted as *The Phantom World*. 2 vols. London: R. Bentley, 1850.

Glut, Donald F. *True Vampires of History*. New York: HC Publishers, 1971. 191 pp.

Guinn, Jeff, with Andy Grieser. *Something in the Blood: The Underground World of Today's Vampires*. Arlington, TX: The Summit Publishing Group, 1996. 204 pp.

Kaplan, Stephen. *Pursuit of Premature Gods and Contemporary Vampires*. Port Jefferson Station, NY: Charles A. Moreno, 1976. 260 pp.

————. *Vampires Are*. Palm Springs, CA: ETC Publications, 1984. 191 pp.

Laycock, Joseph. *Vampires Today: The Truth about Modern Vampirism*. Westport. CT: Praeger, 2009. 200 pp.

Monaco, Richard, and Bill Burt. *The Dracula Syndrome*. New York: Avon Books, 1993. 167 pp.

Page, Carol. *Bloodlust: Conversations with Real Vampires*. New York: HarperCollins, 1991. Rept. New York: Dell, 1992. 214 pp.

Vampirdzhira *see:* Vampire Hunters

Vampire Archives *see:* Vampire Fandom: United States

Vampire Bats *see:* Bats, Vampire

Vampire Brides *see:* Brides, Vampire

Vampire Characteristics *see:* Characteristics of the Vampire

"The Vampire Chronicles" (Books)

The collective name for the vampire novels of **Anne Rice**, "The Vampire Chronicles" are now traced to 1976 and the publication of *Interview with the Vampire*. While well received, it would be nine years before its sequel, *The Vampire Lestat*, appeared. Only in 1988, with the publication of the third volume *Queen of the Damned*, did the concept of designating the series "The Vampire Chronicles" emerge. Subsequently two further volumes, *Tale of the Body Thief*, and *Memnoch the Devil* appeared.

In 1998, *Pandora*, the first volume without the vampire **Lestat,** the primary character tying "The Vampire Chronicles" together, was published, utilizing characters from the earlier volumes. Neither the cover nor the title page mentioned "The Vampire Chronicles," however, an endnote designated a then projected volume, "The Vampire Armand," as continuing "The Vampire Chronicles." Before retiring from the vampire world altogether, Rice wrote a total of nine novels in the Vampire Chronicles series, following *The Vampire Armand* (1998) with *Merrick* (2000), *Blood and Gold* (2001), *Blackwood Farm* (2002), and *Blood Canticle* (2003). The concluding volumes tied her vampire tales with the tales of the Mayfair witches, another series of books she had written. In addition, she wrote two vampire novels not included in, but related to, the series, *Pandora* and *Vittorio the Vampire* (1999).

Vampire Cult Richard Wendorf and his wide Ruth Wendorf of Eustis, Florida, were murdered on November 25, 1996, **victims** of what was termed a vampire cult murder in the press. Three days after the murder, 16-year-old Roderick J. Ferrell of Murray, Kentucky, and four other teenagers were arrested. As the story of the case unfolded, it tied the group to the popular role-playing **game *Vampire: The Masquerade***. A large group in Murray played the game in which they assumed the role of a vampire character and developed their part in what was an ongoing vampire **drama**.

The original group in Murray had organized as the Victorian Age Masquerade Performance Society (VAMPS). Reportedly, Ferrell became caught up in the imaginary world of the game and became the leader of a small group within the larger VAMPS membership. His more "serious" approach to the fantasy world of *Vampire* led to the disruption of the group, and Ferrell's own break with a close friend who had introduced him to the game. Ferrell took the fantasy world of *The Masquerade* (along with its unique jargon) to a new level. He and his following began to think of and see themselves as vampires, not just in the fantasy world of the game but in their everyday lives. Several members went so far as to claim direct descent from **Vlad the Impaler**.

Ferrell, it seems, began to live out his vampire identity. He dressed in black and dyed his blonde hair to match. He began using his vampire name Vessago all the time. After being suspended from school in September 1996, he started living a nocturnal life, and the group that hung out with him (some thirty individuals) took on some religious-like ritualized trappings of a cult-like nature. They would cut themselves with razors and drink each other's **blood**. They took very seriously the embrace, the term used in the game for transforming someone into a vampire. In Ferrell's group, the embrace was not merely symbolic, but actually involved the sharing of blood between group members. These activities, which are actually forbidden to players in the game, earned them the label of a cult.

On several occasions during 1996, Ferrell, who previously had lived in Florida, returned there to visit his former girlfriend, Heather Wendorf. Heather joined him in some blood drinking and later reported that she believed herself to have communed with spirits during their blood-drinking rituals. Then in November 1996, Ferrell and three members of his Murray group headed for Florida, where, after meeting Heather on the afternoon of November 25, they performed a blood-sharing ritual to embrace Heather into her new vampire life. It was a short time after that ritual that Ferrell led in the bludgeoning to death of her parents. A *V* sign surrounded by circular marks was burned into her father's body. The group, including Heather, fled to Louisiana where they were arrested on Thanksgiving Day. Found in their car were a copy of **Anne Rice's *The Queen of the Damned***; a collection of short stories, *The Ultimate Dracula*; and a book of magical spells.

Following Ferrell's arrest, the press briefly questioned the role of *Vampire: The Masquerade* in the **crime**, but soon concluded, as in the cases of several **suicides** among the players of *Dungeons and Dragon*, that the game did not act as a causative factor in the teenagers' actions. The game may have supplied Ferrell with content for his imagi-

nary world, but had it not been present, some other fantasy would have been created as a vehicle for his sociopathology.

Ferrell's trial occurred in early February 1998. He was charged with murder and the three who came from Kentucky with him with lesser charges. Heather Wendorf was not charged and served as a major witness for the state. Ferrell, who had earlier tried to place the blame for the deaths on another group, in the end pleaded guilty. Howard Scott Anderson, whom Ferrell implicated as a accessory, was given life imprisonment, while the two women, whom Ferrell claimed were uninvolved, Dana L. Cooper and Charity Keesee, were convicted of third degree murder. Ferrell was sentenced to the electric chair, and spent two years as the youngest person on death row. In 1999 his sentence was reduced to life without parole. As of 2009, all four are now serving their terms in Florida.

The Vampire Empire (The Count Dracula Fan Club) was founded in 1965 by **Dr. Jeanne Keyes Youngson**, then a successful animation filmmaker, to promote and encourage the study of **Bram Stoker**, **Dracula**, and vampirism in general. In 2000, the club changed its name to the Vampire Empire.

Youngson had been introduced to the subject of Dracula and to **Vlad the Impaler**, the fifteenth-century prince of Wallachia, who had lent his name to Bram Stoker's famous novel, while at Maryville College in Tennessee. The occasion for the founding of the Club, however, was her trip to **Romania**, which brought together her fascination with Dracula and new knowledge concerning Prince Vlad.

While in Romania she made the decision to found a Dracula society, and the Count Dracula Fan Club was formally constituted soon after her return. The club developed two headquarters—one in New York and one in **London**—and Youngson began to establish its various specialized divisions. The first, the Count Dracula Fan Club Research Library, was opened in 1970. It now has over 25,000 volumes that include special collections on Dracula, Bram Stoker, vampirism, and *The Shadow* and other adventure/mystery series. It is assisted by the Friends of the Library and the related Bram Stoker Memorial Collection of Rare Books. In 1978 the London center closed and was moved to a second location in New York. By this time the club had developed a large membership.

In 1990 Youngson established a Dracula Museum at No. One Fifth Avenue in New York City. Over the 25 years since she founded the club she collected copious Dracula, vampire, and Stoker artifacts and memorabilia. The museum collection documented the folklore and literary/cinematic vampire and captured a wide variety of material to meet the cravings of modern vampire fandom. She was especially attentive to gathering a vast supply related to Bram Stoker and his sanguinary Count Dracula. (The Museum featured an impressive Bram Stoker Wall of Fame, much admired by the visitors who visited the museum during its continuance.) The museum also housed numerous first and early editions of Stoker's books, as well as autographed photos of actors associated with roles in Dracula and vampire movies. In 2000 the vast collection was purchased by a theatre complex in Vienna, Austria, to be on display in tandem with Roman Polanski's theatrical musical version of his "Fearless Vampire Killers." Each Christmas the Vampire Empire holds an Open House for members in its penthouse headquarters featuring the famous Vampire Santa tree and a Stoker Memorial tree trimmed with antique ornaments. The club also holds teas on the terrace for visiting members during the summer months.

In 2009 the Vampire Empire reported 1,225 members worldwide. The president and founder of the society is Dr. Jeanne Keyes Youngson who can be reached at: Penthouse North, 29 Washington Square West, New York, N.Y. 10011-9180 USA.

Sources:

The Count Dracula Fan Club Handbook. New York: Count Dracula Fan Club, 1992. 20 pp.

Moore, Steven, ed. *The Vampire in Verse: An Anthology.* New York: Dracula Press, 1985. 196 pp.

Oz, Jane. *So You Want to be a Vampire.* New York: Dracula Press, 1989. 12 pp.

Perkowski, Jan. *Daemon Contamination in Balkan Vampire Lore.* New York: Dracula Press, 1992. 15 pp.

———. *The Vampire as Remnant.* New York: Vampire Press, 1992. 6 pp.

Polidori, et al. *The Count Dracula Fan Club Book of Vampire Stories.* Chicago: Adams Press, 1980. 91 pp.

Sanders, Lewis, ed. *Vampire Haiku.* New York: Dracula Press, 1990. 28 pp.

Youngson, Jeanne, ed. *The Count Dracula Chicken Cookbook.* Chicago: Adams Press, 1979. 60 pp.

———, ed. *A Child's Garden of Vampires.* Chicago: Adams Press, 1980. 60 pp.

———. *The Bizarre World of Vampires.* Chicago: Adams Press, 1996. 40 pp.

———, ed. *Private Files of a Vampirologist: Case Histories & Letters.* Chicago: Adams Press, 1997. 53 pp.

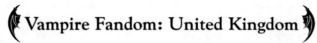 Vampire Fandom: United Kingdom

For many years, vampire fandom in the United Kingdom has been anchored by **the Dracula Society** (founded in 1973), which has combined a lively celebration of **Dracula** and the vampire in the arts with the serious consideration of issues in Dracula and vampire studies. However, in the wake of the renewed interest in vampires which began in the late 1980s, a number of new organizations emerged which have led to the formation of vampire interest groups across the United Kingdom.

Among the most impressive of the 1990s groups was the Vampire Guild of Dorset, England, which grew out of the childhood fascination with vampires of founder Phill M. White. White had collected vampire materials during his teen years, and officially founded the guild in August 1990 as a vampire interest group. Its primary goal was to bring people together who share the founder's interest in vampires and who wish to meet and correspond with others of like mind. As the membership expanded, the concerns of the guild broadened.

One of White's purposes in founding the guild was to explore some of the lesser-known aspects of vampirism, and the guild investigated obscure cases of vampirism such as those of William Doggett, the Tarrant Valley Vampire, and the Black Lady of Durweston, both from Dorset. The research files of these cases sit in the guild's vampire archive. Access to archive information was available to members of the guild and any serious researchers. The guild also published a quarterly journal, *Crimson* which emerged in the 1990s as one of the best vampire fanzines in the entire world of vampire fandom. The Vampire Guild had an international membership. It has not been visible in the new century and does not appear to have an Internet site.

The **Whitby** Dracula Society (originally the Dracula Experience Society), centered in the resort community in northern England where Dracula reportedly first landed

on British soil, emerged by stages in the mid-1990s. It became known for its sponsorship of the annual "Vamps and Tramps" event, the first of which was held in 1995. The society began a quality periodical, *The Demeter* and during the weekend of June 13–15, 1997, co-sponsored **Dracula: The Centenary Celebration 1897–1997**, with the Vampire Guild.

The Whitby Dracula Society currently sponsors a monthly gathering and an annual Grand Masked Ball. Its Internet site is found at http://www.whitbydraculasociety.org.uk/. Member's receive copies of its periodical, *Harker's Journal*. Most recently, musician/composer Alan Moore has launched a new Dracula/Whitby-oriented Internet site, "Dracula in Whitby" (http://www.dracula-in-whitby.com/), which invites discussion of the Dracula-Whitby connection and keeps people informed of events in Whitby. Moore issues an electronic newsletter to all who request it. Since the mid-1990s, Whitby has been home to a large gathering of Goths, who arrive for the Halloween weekend.

Throughout the 1990s, two groups operated in Great Britain with the name The Vampyre Society. One was founded in 1987 by Allen J. Gittens. Several months before establishing the society, he had written an article on vampires for a British rock fanzine. People contacted him asking questions about vampires, resulting in the formation of a correspondence circle of about a dozen people. Rather than write each individually, Gittens decided to produce an information leaflet and organized the correspondence circle into The Vampyre Society, taking its name from a novella by **John Polidori**. Within a year the free information leaflet had become a newsletter offered for subscription through the society. A short time later, Gittens had a falling out with one of the society's leaders, who then left and established a rival organization with the same name. Both organizations claimed to be the continuation of the original society.

The Vampyre Society is primarily a correspondence club for its members (approximately 100 in 1993), who share a common interest in the vampire in all of its aspects. The society held no meetings and eschewed any association with either adherents of the occult or with blood-drinking. New members were asked to fill out a brief questionnaire concerning their interest in vampires. The society's newsletter grew into a quarterly journal, *For the Blood Is the Life* which featured occasional special issues devoted to **poetry** and fiction written by the members. The society was based in Chippenham, Wiltshire.

The second more-active Vampyre Society, headed by Carole Bohanan, was also founded in 1987. Bohanan was originally associated with Allen J. Gittens, but soon after the founding of the original Vampire Society, they parted company. The society led by Bohanan went on to become one of the largest vampire interest groups in England with local groups across the country. It published a high-quality journal, *The Velvet Vampyre*, which carried articles, shorts stories, and book and movie reviews. As the Dracula centennial approached, the society was split with dissension that led to its disruption as a national organization and the discontinuance of *The Velvet Vampyre*. A number of the local groups, most prominently one in London, survived briefly but was soon superseded by the presently existing Vampire Connexion. The Vampire Connexion publishes a journal, *Dark Nights* and may be reached via email at Info@AlexMasi.co.uk.

No coverage of the UK vampire fandom scene would be complete without mention of the Uncle Alucard. In 1992, Dr. Michael Eboy, a London lawyer, with an inter-

est in Victorian life, created a counter-myth to the one publicly projected by the Vampyre Society. His tongue-in-cheek effort began with a letter he sent to *The Velvet Vampyre*, the society's journal. Signed by a (fictional) Professor William Drysdale of the University of Human Sciences, the letter recounted how he had been contacted by Eboy who, in 1988, had returned from eastern Europe with proof that vampires were real and still functioned on Earth. Drysdale had turned Eboy away although he was sure that Eboy was in London as a **vampire hunter**.

Following the publication of that letter, Eboy became the center of a small group of vampire enthusiasts who prefer to celebrate the vampire hunters, especially as portrayed by actor **Peter Cushing** in the several movies produced by **Hammer Films**. In a set of brief writings, Eboy created the fiction that he descended from a family of vampire hunters. Among their targets was the vampire Frederick Scvartsenferter, better known as Camp Freddie, who has eluded the efforts of his family to finally kill him.

In 1992, Eboy published a single issue of a fanzine, *Uncle Alucard* which continued the myth and featured articles on vampire hunting. Meanwhile, Eboy and several friends made several appearances at The Vampyre Society gatherings. Eboy and his associates gathered irregularly in the 1990s to screen vampire movies and hold contests in vampire staking (using a watermelon as a substitute for a corpse). Not covered as part of vampire fandom are the two rival organizations headed by people who believe in the reality of vampires, the **Vampire Research Society** led by Sean Manchester and the Highgate Vampire Society founded by David Farrant. Manchester, in particular, sees the activities of vampire enthusiasts as dangerous, and all agree that vampire fans and the Vampire Research Society are pursuing very different goals.

Sources:

"Eboy's Casefile: The One that Got Away." *The Velvet Vampire* 21 (1993): 18–21.

Farrant, David. *Beyond the Highgate Vampire*. London: British Psychic and Occult Society, 1991. Third revised ed. London: British Psychic and Occult Society, 2002. 63 pp.

———. *The Vampire Syndrome: The Truth Behind the Highgate Vampire Legend*. London: Mutiny! Press, 2000. 65 pp.

Guiley, Rosemary Ellen. *Vampires Among Us*. New York: Pocket Books, 1991. 270 pp.

Manchester, Sean. *The Highgate Vampire: The Infernal World of the Undead Unearthed at London's Highgate Cemetery and Environs*. London: Gnostic Press, 1985. Revised ed. London: The Gothic Press, 1991. 188 pp.

———. *The Vampire Hunter's Handbook*. London: Gothic Press, 1997. 96 pp.

❨ Vampire Fandom: United States ❩

The growth of interest in vampires that began in the 1970s spawned a host of fan clubs, small publishing enterprises, and fanzines. Of these, the first is the Count Dracula Fan Club (now known as the **Vampire Empire**) founded in 1965 by **Jeanne Youngson**. A short time later, the Vampire Studies Society was founded by **Martin V. Riccardo**, which placed **Dracula** and vampire studies in a more scholarly vein. This society led to the founding of the **Lord Ruthven Assembly** and to the spread to America of the international **Transylvanian Society of Dracula**.

Eric Held is the founder of the Vampire Information Exchange.

Anchoring vampire fandom on the West Coast was the Count Dracula Society, founded in 1962 by Dr. Donald A. Reed (1935–2001), a law librarian who served as its president. It was devoted to the serious study of horror films and gothic literature. Its members gathered periodically for screenings of new vampire and horror films, highlighted by the annual awards gathering at which the Ann Radcliffe Award was announced.

In the 1980s, the Count Dracula Society was superseded by the Academy of Science Fiction, Fantasy and Horror Films, dedicated to honoring films and filmmakers in the several horror genres. The academy continues to host regular screenings of films (approximately 100 annually) and sponsors an annual awards ceremony at which the Saturn Trophy is presented to winners in a variety of categories, including the best film in each of the three areas of prime concern (**science fiction**, fantasy, and horror), and an annual lifetime achievement award. *The Count Dracula Society Quarterly* (also known at various times as *The Castle Dracula Quarterly* and *The Gothick Gateway*), published by the society, was discontinued by the academy. The academy may be reached through its website at http://www.saturnawards.org/index.html.

Among the most active of fan organizations on the national level through the last generation has been the Vampire Information Exchange (VIE), founded by Eric Held and Dorothy Nixon in 1978 as a correspondence network for people interested in vampirism. Nixon had been interested in vampires since her high school days, when she was shown a copy of **Donald Glut**'s *True Vampires of History*. She became interested in the question of the existence of real vampires and began a search that led her into association with Stephen Kaplan of the **Vampire Research Center**. Held was brought into the world of vampire fandom after listening to a radio interview of Kaplan in October 1978. The next day he called Kaplan, who put him in touch with Nixon. During that phone conversation, they discovered their mutual interests. They began to correspond, and by October 1979 they had been joined by six others. At that point, Held and Nixon began an irregular newsletter to simplify the circulation of general information, thus initiating the Vampire Information Exchange. Among the early correspondents were Jeanne Youngson of the Count Dracula Fan Club, Gordon R. Guy, editor of *The Castle Dracula Quarterly*, and Martin V. Riccardo, then president of the Vampire Studies Society.

The recently discontinued *VIE Newsletter* was a bimonthly, informative journal for active members. It carried reviews of recent books and movies, news about vampire publications, and bibliographies of various kinds of vampire literature. For a time, Held also put out an annual *Calendar of Vampire Events* and published *The Bibliography of Vampire Literature*.

Launched in 1991, *Vampire Junction* was a high-quality vampire fanzine devoted to the promotion of vampire fiction, poetry, and art. The editor, Candy M. Cosner, had been interested in vampires since her teen years, and her fascination with the subject resulted in a fanzine that was interesting and affordable. Cosner was also one of the first vampire aficionados to go on the **Internet** and through the 1990s devoted more and more of her time to communicating with people electronically. In the process she began to build an expansive vampire information site on the Internet. She discontinued *Vampire Junction* as a fanzine and her website may still be accessed at http://www.afn.org/~vampires/.

The Dynamite Fan Club was a vampire horror fan club founded in 1991 by Mark Weber and Garry Paul, who served as president and vice-president respectively. The primary activity of the club was the issuance of a quarterly *Horror Newsletter* that included a number of regular columns (including "From the Coffin" by Count Vamp), book and movie reviews, and a section of classified ads placed by club members who want to either sell something or meet other members who reside in their hometown. *Good Guys Wear Fangs* was a short-lived annual vampire fanzine dedicated to what founder/editor Mary Ann B. McKinnon termed **good guy vampires**. In the mid-1970s, McKinnon, never a horror fan, discovered the novels of **Chelsea Quinn Yarbro**, whose vampire character, **St. Germain**, was a romantic hero. McKinnon considered Yarbro an isolated author and enjoyed most of her novels as they continued to appear through the 1980s. It was not until 1989, when she saw the made-for-**television** movie *Nick Knight*, and later the two *To Die For* movies, that McKinnon developed some hope that other good guy vampire fiction exists. She decided to announce the development of a fanzine based on the theme of the vampire as a hero. The response to her announcement showed the vast interest and supporting material for her approach to vampirism.

The first copy of the 300-page *Good Guys Wear Fangs* appeared in 1992. It featured original short stories and poetry in which the vampire was the hero. By this time, *Forever Knight*, the television series that grew out of the *Nick Knight* television movie, was airing on CBS late-night television. The Nick Knight character was featured in *Good Guys Wear Fangs*. In 1993, McKinnon added a related periodical, *The Good Guy Vampire Letterzine* a newsletter for good guy vampire fans. *The Letterzine* kept fans aware of newly discovered good guy vampire fiction and movies, and carried an ongoing discussion on the nature of good guy vampirism.

McKinnon has encouraged not only completely original fiction but new stories that feature popular characters from television and the movies. By far the most popular character who appeared in *Good Guys Wear Fangs* was Nick Knight, but other stories have featured Starsky & Hutch, Columbo, and **Dark Shadows**. Through the 1990s McKinnon also produced a line of fanzines that included story lines built around the popular fictional characters Zorro, the Highlander, and Robin of Sherwood.

Gothica whose first issue appeared in 1992, was a fanzine based upon the ideal of what is termed the **Anne Rice** vampire nature. It was founded by Susan M. Jensen, who became friends with a group of vampire horror movie fans in college in the late 1980s. The group, called the Drac Pac, gathered regularly to watch horror movies and through them to explore the uncommon and the sublime. Although the group scattered after graduation, Jensen decided to begin a small magazine based on the ideas the Drac Pac had discussed. The first issue, in March 1992, had only 16 copies. It increased to 35 copies in August 1993 and to several hundred by the end of the first year, but was soon discontinued.

Loyalists of the Vampire Realm International Vampire Association is an international club founded in 1984 in Berlin, Germany, by a woman named Lucinda (the club's name being derived from her initials). It is solely dedicated to the "preservation and recreation of all vampire styled art forms." It publishes a quarterly newsletter, *Jugular Vein*, that features the poetry, fiction, and graphic art of the club's members and thus provides the members with an outlet for their own viewpoints on the vampire as opposed to those of an editor or paid staff. The Vampire Realm also offered a very limited pen pal service known as the Vampire Correspondence Network. New members are invited to fill out a lengthy questionnaire concerning their interests.

Closely related to the Loyalists of the Vampire Realm was Vampires, Werewolves, Ghosts, and Other Such Things That Go Bump in the Night, an informal group of scholars and researchers who investigated vampires and related paranormal phenomena. The organization was founded in the early 1980s and has worked quietly through the 1990s gathering and documenting accounts of individuals' encounters with vampires, werewolves, spirits of the dead, and demonic beings. Loyalists of the Vampire Realm has continued into the new century and has a webpage at http://www.vampire-realm.com/. Midnight to Midnight, the Vampire Writers' Circle, was founded in 1990 by Karen E. Dove, "The High Priestess." Dove had a desire to create a more human vampire figure somewhat removed from the image of a bloodsucking monster or a fantastic superhuman creature. She also became aware of a type of organization operated by fantasy genre writers in which a shared fantasy world was created and each writer collaborated with the others and shared characters. She constructed an initial Midnight to Midnight universe of characters and circulated them to potential members of the circle.

As it evolved, Midnight to Midnight averaged fewer than ten members. Members had one basic rule—that they write and contribute to the circle at least once every two months. It was Dove's expectation that as writers come and go, the most serious ones would persevere, and the circle will have been a means of their growth; in the meantime all will have had an enjoyable experience.

The vampires of Midnight to Midnight shared a world very similar to those in the fanzine *Good Guys Wear Fangs*. They could not change shape or **fly**. They were not affected by holy objects such as the **crucifix** or by running **water**. Their night vision was not enhanced. However, they did cast a reflection in a **mirror**; they could live forever, but were vulnerable to various dangers; and they were nocturnal creatures, but are not confined to the dark; **sunlight** burned them. Three kinds of vampire beings populated the Midnight to Midnight world. "Born" vampires are children of two vampires. They grow normally until their early twenties, when they cease to age. "Made" vampires are vampires created after a period of mortal life. They remain at the age they were when created. "Half-vampires" are people born to a vampire and one mortal parent. They can live for many generations, but eventually die of old age after several centuries.

The **P. N. Elrod** Fan Club, devoted to the writer of vampire fiction, was founded in 1993 by Jackie Black for Elrod's many fans. Elrod had burst on the scene in 1990 when three novels under the collective title, "The Vampire Files" were published by Ace Books. *Bloodlist*, *Lifeblood*, and *Bloodcircle* related the continuing story of reporter Jack Fleming

Vampire fans go to great lengths to honor the undead. Here, a fan dresses as the vampire Donna Mia at a comic book convention in 1996.

who had been turned into a vampire and then became a detective. The trilogy was well received and three more volumes appeared in 1991 and 1992. Suddenly Elrod joined that small circle of writers identified with the vampire community. The club's newsletter grew into a substantial periodical but in the new century, fan activity has moved to the Internet and now continues through Elrod's website at http://www.vampwriter.com/.

The Vampirism Research Institute was a nonmembership research organization founded by Liriel McMahon, a musician and college student majoring in sociology. For several years McMahon published the *Journal of Modern Vampirism*, and in 1993 the institute began a series of new publications and a program of sociological research. In 1992, inspired by Rosemary Guiley's *Vampires Among Us* and with the cooperation of the Count Dracula Fan Club and the Vampire Information Exchange, McMahon conducted a survey of vampire fans in which she asked about such matters as their belief in the existence of vampires and their opinions about people who claim to be vampires. Results of the survey were released in the summer of 1993. The institute also published a monograph entitled *Dysfunctional Vampire: A Theory from Personal History* and a compilation, *Best of the Journal of Modern Vampirism*. The Vampirism Research Institute continued into the new century, but has recently been discontinued.

The Munsters and the Addams Family Fan Club was founded in 1988 by Louis Wendruck for fans of **The Munsters** and **The Addams Family**, two popular television families of homey vampires and other friendly monsters. The club provided information about the television series, their movie spin-offs, and the stars who played family members. The club distributed various items related to the shows and helped members locate and obtain the many other pieces of paraphernalia that have been produced featuring the Addams family and the Munsters. For a time, the club had an annual convention and published a quarterly newsletter, *The Munsters and the Addams Family Reunion*. Wendrick also presided over an unofficial Dark Shadows Fan Club and edited *Dark Shadows Announcement*. The Dark Shadows Fan Club was independent of the larger scene of **Dark Shadows fandom**.

Vampire fandom, of the kind that produced fan clubs, peaked in the 1990s. Through that decade, numerous small clubs made a brief appearance under names such as Cheeky Devil Vampire Research, Club Vampyre, Dracula and Company, The Miss Lucy Westenra Society of the Undead, and The Secret Order of the Undead (**SOUND**). Even more numerous were a large number of short-lived fanzines and newsletters, including: *Nefarious*, *Nightlore*, *Nox*, *Onyx: The "Literary" Vampire Magazine*, *Vampire Archives*, *Bathory Palace*, *Bloodlines: The Vampire Magazine*, and the *Realm of the Vampire*.

Beginning in the late 1990s, the more traditional format for fan clubs with their informally produced fanzines was abandoned as the Internet became a more pervasive instrument for contacting and chatting with like-minded fans. Those fan clubs that did survive from the twentieth century into the twenty-first morphed into Internet-based (or in a few cases email based) fan collectives. Very few fanzines continued to be published, and the larger fan conglomerates were taken up in both the marketing world and legal realm of large corporations.

Realm of the Vampire celebrates the appearance of the vampire in film and literature.

The new world of fandom was amply illustrated by the emergence of **Buffy the Vampire Slayer**, the television show that came to dominate the scene in the at the end of the 1990s. A fan club arose, fan paraphernalia began to appear, and fans began to write fan fiction using the characters from the show. (Some limited concern was expressed by copyright and license holders of the infringement on their rights by fan fiction, especially the so-called slash fiction which placed characters in homoerotic situation.) As the show grew in popularity, a variety of licenses were issued for the production of everything from **trading cards** and T-shirts to cell phone covers and jewelry. An official fan club with a slick professionally produced magazine (whose format followed one developed for a spectrum of other television shows) was organized with its activities largely consisting of selling items to the fans. As *Angel* developed in parallel to *Buffy*, the same development and management of fandom occurred. As the fan scene began to decline and was no longer a viable marketing collective, the company managing the fan clubs, first merged the Buffy and Angel clubs and then merged continuing fan interest into a collective of fans of the several television shows for which it had produced magazines.

Behind the more visible world of the official *Buffy* and *Angel* fan clubs, a more dedicated groups of fans had emerged in the los Angeles area which was able to attain access to the sets where the show was filmed and to hold annual gatherings at which the stars frequently appeared. Fans were also able to meet with the stars of the show at various fan conventions that were held irregularly in North America and Europe.

By 2007, the fan scene around the **Twilight** books of **Stephenie Meyer** was clearly on the upswing, and by 2009, after the first movie had appeared, more than 250 fan sites (using English) had appeared on the Internet, with additional sites in French, Italian, German, and Spanish, a list appearing on Meyer's home page (http://www.stepheniemeyer.com/ts_fansites.html). All appeared to consist of a few friends of the person creating the site and an Internet collective. The site contained pictures of the book covers and of the stars of the movies and pictures of the fans, but are largely limited to supplying space for the fans (overwhelmingly teenage females) to express their feelings about the show. News was at a minimum, as was information on fan paraphernalia, both being readily available elsewhere on the Web. Information on the movies was concentrated on the official movie site hosted by Summit Entertainment (http://www.newmoonthemovie.com/). Information on fan paraphernalia (clothing, posters, toys, room accessories, candy) was concentrated at the site of NECA, which produced it. Both the movie sites and the NECA site had links to the Amazon.com retail site. Borders Books has maintained a space for *Twilight* items (books, posters, trading cards, and related paraphernalia) at all its stores, held gatherings for *Twilight* fans, and published special exclusive editions of *Twilight* books and movies. Fan conventions and the appearances of *Twilight* stars are under the direction of Creation Entertainment, which has, for example, scheduled *Twilight* conventions through 2010 for cities across the United States where fans may, for a price, briefly meet the stars and obtain autographs.

Similar websites have been developed by the producers of recent popular television series *True Blood* (HBO), developed from the writings of **Charlaine Harris**, and *The Vampire Diaries*, developed from the books of **Lisa Jane Smith**. The official site for the show includes a fan site and a merchandising page.

Among the most active creator of vampire oriented fan sites on the Internet is John T. Folden, who also operates as the JTF Network. He has created a site devoted to a spectrum of television shows including *True Blood, Moonlighting, Dark Shadows, Being Human,* and *The Vampire Diaries* (as well as a number that do not include vampires). Each site is informative, contains a number of pictures, and emphasizes the purchasing of fan paraphernalia.

Meanwhile, a new generation of vampire fan clubs and interest groups has also appeared on the Internet. They present a massive and bewildering array of interests within the ever-growing vampire realm, and grade into the new organizations that serve the so-called real or self-identified vampires. Some sites are quite general and provide information and news on the vampire fan scene, some are devoted to one or more of the

older movie or television series (from the Hammer movies to **Forever Knight** to *Vampire Hunter D*), and some are limited to Dracula, or vampire movies, or the writings of Anne Rice. Rice's main fan club, which was disbanded when her religious life revived, was reopened after the Katrina hurricane devastated **New Orleans,** as a means of helping the city rebuild economically.

Sources:

Bacon-Smith, Camile. *Enterprising Women: Television Fandom and the Creation of Popular Myth.* Philadelphia: University of Pennsylvania Press, 1991.

Beatrice, Allyson. *Will the Vampire People Please Leave the Lobby?: True Adventures in Cult Fandom.* Nashville, TN: Sourcebooks, Inc., 2007. 236 pp.

The Castle Dracula Quarterly. 1, 1 (1978). Special Bela Lugosi issue.

Dove, Karen E. *Midnight to Midnight Guidelines.* Mt. Clemens, MI: self-published, 1994. 25 pp.

Dresser, Norine. *American Vampires: Fans, Victims, Practitioners.* New York: W. W. Norton & Company, 1989. 255 pp.

Elden, Gro. *The Buffyverse and its Inhabitants: A Study of Fans of* Buffy the Vampire Slayer. Amsterdam, Netherlands, MA thesis, International School for Humanities and Social Sciences, Universiteit van Amsterdam, 2002.

Held, Eric, ed. *The 1992 Vampire Bibliography of Fiction and Non-Fiction.* Brooklyn, NY: Vampire Information Exchange, 1992. 16 pp.

———. *1993 Calendar of Vampire Events.* Brooklyn, NY: Vampire Information Exchange, 1993. 14 pp.

Hellekson, Karen, and Kristina Busse. *Fan Fiction and Fan Communities in the Age of the Internet: New Essays.* Jeffersonville, NC: McFarland and Company, 2006.

Kirby-Diaz, Mary., ed. *Buffy and Angel Conquer the Internet: Essays on Online Fandom.* Jeffersonville, NC: McFarland and Company, 2009.

McMahon, Liriel, ed. *Best of the Journal of Modern Vampirism.* Seattle, WA: Vampirism Research Institute, 1993.

———. *Dysfunctional Vampire: A Theory from Personal History.* Seattle, WA: Vampirism Research Institute, 1993.

———. *Results Report: Vampire Fan Survey No. 9221.* Seattle, WA: Vampirism Research Institute, 1993. 20 pp.

Reed, Donald. *The Vampire on the Screen.* Inglewood, CA: Wagon & Star Publishers, 1965.

Williamson, Millie. *The Lure of the Vampire: Gender, Fiction and Fandom from Bram Stoker to Buffy the Vampire Slayer.* London: Wallflower Press, 2005. 224 pp.

The World Almanac Book of Buffs, Masters, Mavens and Uncommon Experts. New York: World Almanac Publications, 1980. 342 pp.

The Vampire Guild *see:* Vampire Fandom: United Kingdom

Vampire Hunters

In most societies that have believed in vampirism, the process of detecting and **destroying the vampire** has often been carried out by an informal group of people threatened by the presence of vampires in their community, but it occasionally has been placed in the hands of a specialized vampire hunter. Several cultures, especially those in the southern Balkans, assigned specific people the task of hunting and destroying vampires. Most famous of the vampire hunters was the **dhampir**, who was believed to be the physical son of a vampire and who lived and worked among the **Gypsies** and the **southern Slavs**. The Gypsies thought of the vampire (as male) as a very sexy creature who often returned to his spouse/lover and engaged in intercourse. His still potent seed occasionally led to a pregnancy notable for its beginning weeks after the death of the mother's husband. The male progeny of a vampire, the *dhampir*, was believed to have peculiar powers in seeing the oft-invisible vampire and destroying it.

A person identified as a *dhampir* could become a professional or semiprofessional vampire hunter and charge a village for his services. According to surviving accounts, the *dhampir* began his work in a village by telling those who hired him that there was a bad smell in the air. He would then appear to attempt to locate its source. He might, for example, take off his shirt and look through the sleeve as if looking through a telescope. He would describe the shape that the invisible vampire had taken. Once he located the vampire, he might engage it in a dramatic hand-to-hand fight or simply shoot it. Once killed, the vampire smelled even more and might leave a pool of **blood** on the ground. Sometimes it could not be killed, in which case the *dhampir* would attempt to run it off to another village. Among the more notable *dhampirs* was one named Murat, who operated in the 1950s in the Kosovo-Metohija area of Serbia.

Poster art from the movie version of *Buffy the Vampire Slayer*. Buffy was a modern version of the vampire hunter.

In **Bulgaria** the vampire hunters were called *vampirdzhija* or *djadadjii*. They tended to operate in a more traditional fashion. Their main task seemed to have been to locate the particular grave that held the resting vampire's body. In this task they used an icon, a holy picture in the Eastern Orthodox tradition. After locating the vampire, the villagers would impale it or burn the body.

The Vampire Hunter in Literature: In literature the "professional" vampire hunter assumed his place as the archenemy of the literary vampire in **Bram Stoker's** *Dracula* **(1897)**. Dr. **Abraham Van Helsing**, the real hero of the novel, emerged as the bearer of knowledge about the mysterious threat that has invaded Western civilization and heralded the means of destroying it. In the novel it was his task to organize the cadre of men who together tracked **Dracula** to his lair and finally destroyed him. When **Hamilton Deane** brought Dracula to the stage, he chose the part of Van Helsing for himself as preferable to that of the title character, which went to **Raymond Huntley**. Deane continued to portray Van Helsing for many years as his company toured England. When the play arrived on Broadway, one of the more memorable Van Helsings stepped into the role.

Edward Van Sloan brought the image of a quiet physician capable of offering a calming bedside manner to the role. He went on to play the part in the 1931 movie

Horror movie host Peter Vincent (Roddy McDowall) is a reluctant vampire hunter in *Fright Night* and *Fright Night II*.

with costar **Bela Lugosi**. In the original version of the film, Van Helsing (Van Sloan) makes the closing speech that followed the last act of the play, stepping out to remind the audience prior to their departure that such things as vampires did exist. This speech was cut from later releases of the film because **Universal Pictures** thought it would be taken too seriously by religious groups. Van Sloan also assumed the Van Helsing role in the sequel, *Dracula's Daughter*, in which he was accused of murdering Dracula. At the same time that *Dracula* was filmed, a Spanish version was also shot, with Eduardo Arozamena taking the role of Van Helsing.

After Edward Van Sloan, no one again was really identified with the hunter-killer role until it was taken by **Peter Cushing**, playing opposite **Christopher Lee** in the title role, in the **Hammer Films** production of **The Horror of Dracula** (1958). A veteran actor of both the stage and screen, Cushing brought to the role the persona of a persistent modern scientist who emitted confidence owing to his knowledge. He returned to the Van Helsing part and portrayed him (and some modern-day descendants) in *The Brides of Dracula* (1959), *Dracula A.D. 1972* (1972), *Satanic Rites of Dracula* (a.k.a. *Count Dracula and His Vampire Bride*, 1973), and *The Legend of the Seven Golden Vampires* (1974), all for Hammer. He played the actual Van Helsing in five films, and transferred his Van Helsing persona to other parts in which he portrayed the intellectual-scientific man of knowledge.

No one since has had the commanding presence that Cushing brought to the role. However, several outstanding actors have taken up the challenge and offered commendable portrayals, including Sir Laurence Olivier, who tracked **Frank Langella** in **Dracula (1979),** and, most recently, Anthony Hopkins, who tracked **Gary Oldman** in **Bram Stoker's Dracula** (1992).

In 1974, German actor Horst Janson became the first person to portray a vampire hunter in a film featuring the hunter and his story over that of the vampire(s) that were the object of the hunt. *Captain Kronus: Vampire Hunter* was also a Hammer production. The vampire hunter never really made it as a star, however, until 1992 and the first appearance of **Buffy the Vampire Slayer**. The original Buffy, though, met with mixed reviews, went on to become one of the twenty-five top grossing vampire films of all time and set the stage for the return of Buffy as a television series in 1998. **Buffy Summers,** more than any other character, established the vampire hunter as a literary character with great potential worthy of further exploration. Buffy would, of course, lead a team of vampire hunters, one of whom, the **good-guy vampire Angel**, would emerge as a separate vampire hunter with his own team.

Almost simultaneously with the success of Buffy, **Blade the Vampire Slayer**, a Marvel Comics character created by **Marv Wolfman** in the 1970s, reached superstar status with his portrayal on the screen by Wesley Snipes. Snipes made three *Blade* movies in 1998, 2002, and 2004, in which he portrayed a half human, half vampire who dedicated himself to slaying the vampires who had become integrated into human society. All three movies have moved into the top ten grossing vampire movies. Just as the third Blade movie came out, Hugh Jackman would lead a crusade against Dracula in *Van Helsing* that went on the become a popular vampire movie as well.

Other movies that also lifted up the vampire hunter to the starring role, all made since the late 1990s, were *John Carpenter's Vampires* (1998); *Bloodrayne* (2006), and the Japanese anime film, *Blood Hunter D* (2001). A variety of Japanese anime, deriving from juvenile television shows, featured the hunter over the vampire, though often, the hunter was, like *Hellsing*, partly a vampire himself.

Possibly the most notable vampire hunter in literature has been Anita Blake, the main character in the series of novels by **Laurell Hamilton**. Anita made her first appearance in the novel *Guilty Pleasures* (1993), in which her profession is described as that of a re-animator. She uses magical power to bring the dead back to life, at least long enough to question them for legal purposes, but she is also a licensed vampire hunter who eventually becomes a Federal Marshal. As the novels progress (there were seventeen by 2009), Anita eventually became a **werewolf** and shapeshifter.

Popular Culture: The popularity of the vampire has led to the production of various tools which have been presented, more or less, as aids to fighting them. On several occasions, vampire hunter's kits have shown up at auctions, claiming some antique status as items produced in an earlier age by people who really felt vampires were real. In recent years, there have been a spectrum of manuals for vampire hunters, some obviously works of fictions, but others such as that of British vampire hunter Sean Manchester, meant to be taken quite seriously.

Sources:

Enfield, Hugh (pseudonym of Gwilym Fielden Hughes). *Kronos*. London: Fontana, 1972. 125 pp.

Eyles, Allen, Robert Adkinson, and Nicholas Fry. *The House of Horror: The Story of Hammer Films*. London: Lorimer, 1973. 127 pp.

Glenday, Craig, and Constantine Gregory. *The Vampire Watcher's Handbook: A Guide for Slayers*. New York: St. Martin's Griffin, 2003. 160 pp.

Golden, Christopher, and Nancy Holder. *Buffy the Vampire Slayer: The Watcher's Guide*. New York: Pocket Books, 1998. 298 pp.

Haining, Peter. *The Vampire Hunters' Casebook*. London: Warner Books, 1996. 363 pp.

Hill, William. *The Vampire Hunters*. Middleburg, FL: Otter Creek Press, 1998. 285 pp.

Holder, Nancy, with Jeff Mariotte and Maryelizabeth Hart. *Buffy the Vampire Slayer: The Watcher's Guide*. Volume 2. New York: Pocket Books, 2000. 472 pp.

Kikuchi, Hideyuki. *Vampire Hunter D*. Milwaukee, WI: DH Press/Carson, CA: Digital Manga Publishing, 2005. 268 pp.

McClelland, Bruce. *Slayers and their Vampires: A Cultural History of Killing the Dead*. Ann Arbor: University of Michigan Press, 2006. 280 pp.

Manchester, Sean. *The Vampire Hunter's Handbook*. London: Gothic Press, 1997. 96 pp.

Ruditis, Paul. *Buffy the Vampire Slayer: The Watcher's Guide*. Volume 3. New York: Simon Spotlight, 2004. 359 pp.

Skal, David J. *Hollywood Gothic: The Tangled Web of Dracula from Novel to Stage and Screen*. New York: W. W. Norton & Company, 1990. 242 pp.

Slonaker, Erin. *The Vampire Hunter's Handbook: A Field Guide to the Paranormal*. London: Penguin Books, 2001. 87 pp.

Trigg, E. B. *Gypsy Demons and Divinities: The Magical and Supernatural Practices of the Gypsies*. London: Sheldon Press, 1973. 238 pp.

Vukanovic, T. P. "The Vampire." In Jan L. Perkowski, ed., *Vampires of the Slavs*. Cambridge, MA: Slavica Publishers, 1976: 201–234.

The Vampire Information Exchange *see:* Vampire Fandom: United States

Vampire Junction *see:* Vampire Fandom: United States

The Vampire Rapist

John Crutchley earned the title of the Vampire Rapist in 1985 after he picked up a young female hitchhiker near Melbourne, Florida, and while holding her prisoner over a 22-hour period, raped her and then used a needle and tubing to drain a considerable portion of her **blood** into a jar, which he then consumed. Somehow, the woman, even though weakened by the loss of blood, escaped, and Crutchley was subsequently arrested and sentenced to 25 years in prison.

Crutchley came back into the news in 1996 when he was paroled from prison. The state's action brought numerous complaints and rather than return to Melbourne, he settled in a halfway house in Orlando. However, he was free for only a brief period; a few days after moving to Orlando, he was again arrested for violation of his parole for smoking marijuana. His parole was revoked and he was returned to prison to serve out his term.

The term vampire rapist has also been applied to similar cases over the years. In 1971, for example, Canadian serial rapist/killer Wayne Boden was labeled the vampire rapist after his arrest and confession of killing four women in Montreal and Calgary. In each case he had opened wounds on his **victim**'s breast from which he consumed her blood. He was definitively identified from the teeth marks he left behind.

Vampire Research Center: The Vampire Research Center was founded in 1972 by Stephen Kaplan. The year before he had also founded the Parapsychology Institute of America and for over two decades beginning in 1974 was a popular lecturer in parapsychology for the New York City Board of Education, Forest Hills Adult Division. He initially attained some level of fame in the mid-1970s when he investigated the reported haunting of a house on Long Island at Amityville, New York. Although the Amityville haunting was promoted in several books and a popular movie, Kaplan was the first to denounce it as a hoax, a view now generally accepted in the parapsychological community. Further accounts of his parapsychological endeavors can be found in the several volumes of *True Tales of the Unknown* and a number of other descriptive works on psychical research.

In Kaplan's first book, *Pursuit of Premature Gods and Contemporary Vampires*, which appeared in 1976, he treated vampirology as a branch of parapsychology, that branch of psychology dealing with paranormal experiences. He begins with the idea that some reality may lie behind every myth or legend, in this case vampires.

Although he had lectured around the country and appeared on many talk shows over the previous decade, many people first heard of Kaplan in 1984 with the publication of his second book, *Vampires Are*. The book described a decade of research on people who defined themselves as real vampires. After obtaining a telephone listing for the Vampire Research Center, Kaplan began to receive phone calls from people claiming to be vampires, and he later interviewed some of them personally. In this manner he was able to build relationships with what became a network of people with similar interests around the world. These contacts increased dramatically after a mention in a 1977 *Playboy Magazine* article. He also began to receive calls about vampire attacks from people who claimed to have been victimized.

Kaplan's research led him to reformulate his concept of vampires, abandoning the common notion that they are the "undead" and have returned to take **blood** from the living. The vampires he discovered were otherwise normal living people who felt a need to drink blood every day and who became irritable, aggressive, or frantic if they were unable to get their daily supply. Underlying their need was a strong belief that blood kept them youthful and extended their life; if their supply were cut off, they believed they would age or even die. The number of vampires Kaplan interviewed who fit this description was quite small. He reported meeting fewer than ten by the time his book appeared in 1984, and to date the great majority of people who are either reported to the center as vampires or themselves claim to be vampires fit into a much larger category, the "vampirelike" people. The vampirelike people are individuals who adopt vampire-associated habits (e.g., they **sleep** in a **coffin**, wear black clothes, work at night, or occasionally drink blood) in the hope of possibly becoming a vampire. Some are sexually aroused by blood and the idea of drinking it.

In 1981 Kaplan conducted the first official vampire census. Of some 480 questionnaires distributed, thrity-one were returned and twelve fit the description of a true vampire. Additionally, nine letters were received without the questionnaire from people deemed to be true vampires. Thus, twenty-one vampires were reported in the census. Kaplan concluded that there were probably many more. In the meantime, apart from the formal census, he was contacted by phone and mail by other people whom he noted to be vampires. A follow-up study in 1983 found thirty-five additional vampires. Given the number he had been able to locate through his census and other contacts, he estimated there were 150 to 200 actual vampires in North America. By 1992 he projected an estimated 850 vampires worldwide, of which forty lived in California.

As a result of some negative response to his book, and deteriorating relationships with the leaders of the vampire organizations in the New York City areas, Kaplan largely separated himself from other vampire-oriented organizations. He subsequently devoted himself to his research and thus had little time for vampire fans. In the wake of Kaplan's 1995 death, leadership of the Vampire Research Center has been assumed by Kaplan's wife, Roxanne Salch Kaplan. Nothing has been heard from the center in the new century. It is presumed to be defunct.

Sources:

"Dr. Kaplan and the Vampire Epidemic." *Journal of Vampirology* 1, 2 (1984): 20–22.

Edmondson, Brad. "The Vampire Census." *American Demographics* 10, 10 (October 1988): 13.

Guiley, Rosemary Ellen. *Vampires Among Us*. New York: Pocket Books, 1991. 270 pp.

Jarvis, Sharon, ed. *True Tales of the Unknown: Beyond Reality*. Vols. 1, 2, and 3. New York: Bantam Books, 1985, 1989, and 1991.

Kaplan, Stephen. *Pursuit of Premature Gods and Contemporary Vampires*. Port Jefferson Station, NY: Charles A. Moreno, 1976. 260 pp.

———. *Vampires Are*. Palm Springs, CA: ETC Publications, 1984. 191 pp.

Ratliff, Rick. "He Thirsts for Vampire Knowledge." *Miami Herald*, July 13, 1977.

Vampire Research Society

The Vampire Research Society was founded on February 2, 1970, by Sean Manchester to investigate all aspects of supernatural vampire phenomena. At the time of its founding, Manchester was the director of an occult investigation bureau, now defunct. During the first two decades of its existence, the society was an open membership group and claimed approximately 300 members. However, in 1990 (by which time there were several other vampire interest groups functioning in England) the society decided to restrict membership and to concentrate on practical research. It confines itself to investigating possible paranormal manifestations, and does not have ties to the larger vampire subculture. The society is unconcerned with medical disorders, individuals wanting to become vampires, and nonconventional behavior (such as **blood**-drinking) associated with vampires.

Manchester is the primate of the Catholic Apostolic Church of the Holy Grail, a small liturgical jurisdiction of the Old Catholic belief and practice. He was consecrated as a bishop by Rt. Rev. Illtyd Thomas, the primate of the Celtic Catholic Church in 1991. Manchester takes vampirism very seriously as a supernatural occult phenomena and has little in common with vampire enthusiasts, whom he feels are playing with **fire** and, however unwittingly, promoting evil. The secular press, often not comprehending Manchester's faith and his own understanding of the vampire problem, have turned him into a media personality, although coverage of him is often tongue-in-cheek. The society and its founder came under public scrutiny on several occasions as a result of Manchester's investigation of manifestations and occurrences attributed to what was termed the **Highgate vampire** at **London**'s Highgate Cemetery. Subsequently, Manchester wrote a book concerning his investigations, which occurred over a period of thirteen years. More recently, he investigated the Kirklees vampire in West Yorkshire.

The Vampire Research Society is the official **United Kingdom** advisory service on all matters pertaining to vampires and vampirism. Membership is by invitation only. Interested persons are welcome to correspond (overseas correspondents should include an International Reply Coupon). There is no membership fee for the society, and the society's journal is for members only. Manchester maintains a web presence at http://www .gothicpress.freeserve.co.uk/.

Sources:

Manchester, Sean. *The Highgate Vampire*. Revised ed.: London: Gothic Press, 1991. 188 pp.

———. "Eyewitness—The Kirklees Vampire." *The Unexplained* 38 (1992). Reprinted in *Crimson* 8 (1993): 10–12.

———. *The Vampire Hunter's Handbook*. London: Gothic Press, 1997. 96 pp.

Vampire Studies *see:* Vampire Fandom: United States

❨ *Vampire: The Eternal Struggle* ❩

The success of White Wolf's ***Vampire: The Masquerade***, the popular role-playing **game** created by Mark Rein-Hagen in 1991, suggested to Richard Garfield of Wizards of the Coast the possibility of its adaptation as a card game. As the role-playing game *Dungeons and Dragons* had been a great success in the 1980s, so the card game *Magic: The Gathering* (also from Wizards of the Coast) had become the new phenomenon of the early 1990s. On the heels of completing *Magic*, Garfield met with Rein-Hagen, who had played *Magic*, and opened discussions of creating a vampire-based card-game version. Garfield's staff began designing cards, and adapting the concept to the new format.

Originally released as *Jyhad* in 1994, a reference to the battles going on inside the vampire community, the new card game pitted several older vampires, called Methuselahs, against each other. These hidden figures who never show themselves manipulate the more public vampires of the contemporary vampire community in order to accomplish their goals, including the destruction of other Methuselahs. In the game, usually played at midnight, the Methuselahs seek the control of vampire society, which means using the minion which the player controls to destroy the influence of the other Methuselahs over their minions. Working through Machiavellian **political** action and using cunning in the face of various conspiracies, the successful player gains influence in the form of **blood** counters while others lose theirs. When a player runs out of influence (blood counters), he or she must leave the game.

Jyhad was slow to take off, in part due to its adult theme, and in part to some level of confusion in the original version. As with *Vampire: The Masquerade*, *Jyhad* required the new player to master the rather detailed world of the vampire including its vampire clans and their varying attributes and the nature of vampiric power. Thus, Wizards of the Coast redesigned the game, streamlining the rules for beginners, and reissued it as *Vampire: the Eternal Struggle*, with a 437-card deck. The deck include cards for vampires, the Methuselah's primary minions; equipment cards to be given to the minions to increase their effectiveness; reaction cards to block another's action; and political action cards, concerning the political ploys tried by a Methuselah. The cards used in play are also designed as artistic works, much as modern **trading cards**, and hence also function as tradable and collectible items. As with *Magic*, individual cards are designated as common, uncommon, and rare, and those more difficult to obtain assume an enhanced value.

As *Vampire: The Eternal Struggle* took off, Wizards of the Coast quickly issued three expansion sets: *Dark Sovereigns* (1995), *Ancient Hearts* (1995), and *The Sabbat* (1996). New expansion sets have subsequently been issued regularly, with some fifteen to date. The most recent, *Ebony Kingdom*, was released in May of 2009. Lists of cards and info on new expansion sets can be found at White Wolf's webpage, http://www.white-wolf.com/vtes/index.php.

Sources:

Campbell, Brian, ed. *Darkness Unveiled*. Clarkston, GA: White Wolf/Wizards of the Coast, 1995. 200 pp.

Goudie, Robert, Ben Peal, and Ben Swainbank. *Vampire The Eternal Struggle Players Guide*. Stone Mountain, GA: White Wolf Publishing, 2005. 336 pp.

Greenberg, Andrew, et al. *The Eternal Struggle: A Players Guide to the Jyhad.* Stone Mountain, GAL White Wolf Game Studio, 1994. 201 pp.

Haines, Jeff. "Strange Things in the Night." *Inquest* 1, 1 (May 1995): 16–20.

Moore, James A., and Kevin Murphy. *House of Secrets.* Clarkston, GA: White Wolf Game Studio, 1995. 263 pp.

Vampire: The Masquerade

Vampire: The Masquerade is a popular role-playing **game** introduced in 1991 by creator Mark Rein-Hagen of White Wolf Game Studio. It quickly challenged the popularity of *Dungeons and Dragons*, the original role-playing game, and itself became the basis of several other horror role-playing games based on the *Werewolf* and *Wraith*, and a role-playing card game, **Vampire: The Eternal Struggle** (originally named *Jyhad*). From the beginning, the game presented a complete alternate worldview, the fantasy into which the player enters, a world in which vampires and other creatures of horror such as **ghouls** and **werewolves** populate the landscape. The popularity of the game, however, has allowed for its expansion and the development of different aspects of the fantasy world in great detail.

Role-playing games are built around a storyteller, who begins a story in which all of the players are characters. As the story unfolds, the players become active participants and their actions have consequences for winning and losing. Players of *Vampire: The Masquerade* enter the fantasy world by creating a character (numerous suggestions are given in the literature published to support the game), a vampire, or possibly a werewolf or ghoul minion, and during the game they assume and act as that character along with all of the other characters who inhabit the local vampire community. In the world of this role-playing game, there is a community of vampires who exist incognito within the space otherwise inhabited by humans. Since they closely resemble humans, and thus have little problem passing as such, they can come out at night and co-mingle, especially when they are in search of food. However, mostly they move among themselves. There is an organized vampire society whose power is held by older vampires, the majority of whom have withdrawn into their solitude. The more visible society is highly politicized and power is the valued commodity. Thus, most stories concern the jockeying for power among the players.

Vampire: The Masquerade began as the table game *Vampire*, in which a small group of players gathered to listen to a storyteller and periodically stopped action to interact, the consequences of the player's acts being determined by the throw of the dice. Players had a supply of **blood** and when their acts led to a complete loss of blood, they lost. However, the game continued to evolve, and in 1993 Rein-Hagen introduced the live-action version of the game, *The Masquerade*. This version freed the game from the delays caused by the use of dice, which were replaced with a series of hand signals. The new form of the game, termed LARP or live action role playing, allowed players to remain in character during virtually all of the game and vastly expands the number who can play at one time. As currently played as *Vampire: The Masquerade*, as many as 20 or more players can for several hours each enter a new persona and act out a situation presented to him or her or carried over from the last session. A local playing group will usually gather to play at midnight on a predetermined day, once or twice a month.

At present, the typical game is set in the local community and the players assume a position in the local vampire society. There is a prince, the nominal head of the community, and the vampires identify with one of the several clans, each clan having its own particular **characteristics** and local leaders. Overall, the members of the community must keep up the Masquerade, that is, perpetuate the idea among humans that vampires are a thing of the past, a myth best sold as the scientific conclusion that vampires never really existed. Breeching the rules of secrecy brings the wrath of the community down upon a vampire. It is also the assumption of the game that the Masquerade is currently threatened by the current youth culture. Mind-altering drugs, rock **music**, and the popularity of the vampire image in Western culture have opened large segments of the public to the possibility that the vampire exists and many people even view vampiric existence as a desirable life they would assume if only it were possible. A second threat is posed by the new generation gap between the older vampires who originally conceived the Masquerade and have enforced its existence, and a brash younger generation of new vampires who are seen as acting in such a way as to call human attention to vampire society.

Two of the vampires who inhabit the world of the Camarilla in the game *Vampire: The Masquerade*.

As a sophisticated role-playing game, *Vampire: The Masquerade* assumes the following vampire myth: Succinctly stated, vampire society originated with Caine (the cursed brother introduced in the Bible in the fourth chapter of Genesis). According to the game, the curse was that he was made a vampire. After wandering in the wilderness for many years, he settled down and created a city. He also created other vampires, the second generation, who in turn created a third generation. They built a city. The city was destroyed by a flood, and the survivors of the third generation scattered around the world. Whether Cain or any of the second generation survived is unknown. Various individuals of the third generation would become the originating vampire of the bloodlines that would later become the clans. The vampires of the fourth and fifth generation have largely withdrawn from any involvement with the larger vampire community.

The bulk of the presently existing vampires constitute the sixth generation, and they face pressure to create no more vampires as it is believed that the blood thins (the vampiric powers diminish) as each generation from Cain is created. The vampire clans originated from the banding together of the children (new generations) of the third generation who found in their physical relationship shared characteristics of the one who originated the bloodline. Enlightened self-interest became a reason to organize more or less loosely, and create a clan ethos. There are seven major clans: the Brujah, the youthful rebels; the Gangrel, the wanderers; the Malkavian, somewhat insane; the rodent-like Nosferatu; the Toreador, often described as hedonists; the Tremere, the best organized of the vampires; and the Ventrue the most human of the vampires. There are also other clans who are not members of the Camarilla such as the Assamite and the Giovanni. And finally there are the Caitiff, or clanless vampires. The latter are usually the result of having been abandoned by those who made them vampires. The clans are at the heart of the **political** intrigues of the vampire community.

In the middle of the fifteenth century, the Inquisition wreaked havoc on "the Kindred" and whole bloodlines were stamped out (put to the true death in **fire**). At about the same time, some of the youthful vampires, who were being used as a barrier between the elders and the Inquisition, rose in revolt. The revolt of the Anarchs spread. This period of attack drove the survivors completely underground. In 1486 at a global convocation, a secret worldwide network, the Camarilla, was established. It established a rule of law for the community of vampires. Within the community are some powerful individual vampires called justicars who have been granted the power to punish lawbreakers. Vampires are largely urban dwellers, and currently each major city supports a vampire community. It is headed by a prince, and any vampire changing locations is expected to present him-or herself to the prince of their new city (or alternate authority where no prince has been designated, as in Los Angeles).

According the game's myth, the elder vampires have more powers than newer ones. For both old and young, the **stake** is hurtful, producing a form of paralysis, but by itself not fatal. **Sunlight** and **fire** are the main dangers. Holy objects have no effect, nor does running **water**. The vampire has sharpened senses that aid them in hunting, including the power to impose their will on mortals. The elder vampires can change shapes, but most of the newer ones cannot. New vampires can be created by first having their blood drained and then receiving some of the vampire's blood, although the new vampire has slightly less power than that of the vampire who created him or her. Vampires no longer breathe, although they can fake respiration. The heart no longer beats, the blood consumed spreads through the body by osmosis rather than through the old artery/vein system. It carries the necessary oxygen. The vampire heals quickly of most wounds.

Vampire: The Masquerade has continued to evolve. In 2004, it was basically superseded by a new version of the game, *Vampire: the Requiem*, which kept the basic myth and playing structure, but offers a variety of modifications, such as revamping the clan structure. It emphasized five clans—the Daeva, The Gangrel, The Mekhet, Nosferatu, and the Ventrue—as well as a set of new non-clan groups. All add new story lines and variety to the play. *Vampire: the Requiem* was immediately incorporated into World of Darkness, by which the various fictional story lines of the several White Wolf horror-based games are related. A new World of Darkness text was issued simultaneously with the initial *Vampire: the Requiem* text in 2004. *Vampire: the Requiem* was also an integral part of the Mind's Eye Theatre, the name given to the live action role-playing (or LARP) version of White Wolf's various games.

Unwittingly, *Vampire: the Masquerade* became the environment for the emergence of the new real vampire community. In the 1990s, hundreds of people who self-identified as real vampires (among the thousands who simply played the game) found their way to the Camarilla, the game's fan club and emerged as leaders. Possibly the most notable, **Michelle Belanger** in Ohio and Father Sebastiaan in New York City were active for several years in the gaming world, which provided a context to meet other real vampires and out of which some of the early real vampire organizations emerged in the mid-1990s.

In 1996, Rod Ferrell, who had played the game in Kentucky, came to see himself as a real vampire and put together a small group of people who more-or-less believed him. The group was responsible for the murder of the parents of Ferrell's girlfriend in Florida. They became the subject of a highly publicized trial that became a watershed moment for both White Wolf and the emerging real vampire community. White Wolf moved to distance itself from any real vampire-like contact and emphasized its entertainment focus. The new rules enforced in the wake of the Ferrell case worked for the new community of self-identified vampires who discovered that they no longer needed the LARP world. Enough real vampires had surfaced that they could operate on their own quite apart from the vampire gaming world (or other vampire interest groups).

Meanwhile, as the World of Darkness has expanded, a vast literature has emerged to support the game. There are literally hundreds of books with suggestive new plots for the game's storytellers, and a host of novels derived from White Wolf's vampire universe. White Wolf maintains an expansive website at http://www.white-wolf.com/vampire/index.php.

Many players are also members of the fan club created to carry the myth, appropriately named the Camarilla. It has also transformed over the years, and suffered greatly during the middle of the first decade of the new century when for a period White Wolf viewed it primarily as a tool for marketing new product.

Sources:

Ackels, Ron. *The Kindred Most Wanted*. Stone Mountain, GA: White Wolf Game Studio, 1995. 142 pp.

Berry, Jeff. *Alien Hunger*. Stone Mountain, GA: White Wolf Game Studio. 64 pp.

Brown, Steve. *The Sabbat*. Stone Mountain, GA: White Wolf Game Studio, 1993. 135 pp.

Campbell, Brian, ed. *Darkness Unveiled*. n.p.: Wizards of the Coast, 1995. 200 pp.

deLaurent, Aristotle. *The Book of Nod*. Stone Mountain, GA: White Wolf Game Studio, 1993. 134 pp.

Findley, Nigel. *Awakening/Diablerie: Mexico*. Stone Mountain, GA: White Wolf Game Studio. 55 pp.

Greenberg, Andrew, et al. *Storyteller's Handbook: The Complete Handbook for Storytellers of Vampire*. Stone Mountain, GA: White Wolf Game Studio, 1992. 151 pp.

Greenberg, Daniel. *Who's Who among Vampires: Children of the Inquisition*. Stone Mountain, GA: White Wolf Game Studio, 1992. 70 pp.

Koke, Jeff. *Gurps Vampire: The Masquerade*. Steve Jackson Games, 1993. 192 pp.

Laycock, Joseph. *Vampires Today: The Truth about Modern Vampirism*. Westport. CT: Praeger, 2009. 200 pp.

McCubbin, Chris W. *Vampire: The Masquerade Companion*. Steve Jackson Games, 1994. 160 pp.

Marmell, Ari, Dean Shomshak, and C.A. Suleiman. *Vampire: The Requiem*. Stone Mountain, GA: White Wolf Publishing, 2004. 294 pp.

Rein-Hagen, Mark, et al. *Book of the Damned*. Stone Mountain, GA: White Wolf Game Studio, 1993. 138 pp.

———. *Vampire: The Masquerade*. Stone Mountain, GA: White Wolf Game Studio, 1991. 263 pp.

Vampire: The Dark Ages. Clarkston, GA: White Wolf Game Studio, 1996. 286 pp.

Wieck, Stewart. *Ashes to Ashes: A Story for Vampire*. Anniston, AL: White Wolf Game Studio, 1991. 80 pp.

Wright, Jana. *The Tome of the Kindred*. Seattle, WA: The Camarilla, 1993. 44 pp.

Vampire: The Requiem *see: Vampire: The Masquerade*

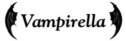

W arren Publications pioneered the black-and-white **comic book** magazine format in the 1960s as a means of, among other goals, skirting the restrictions of the Comics Code, which had been adopted by the industry in 1954. The Code was very harsh on horror comics and specifically banned vampires, **werewolves, ghouls,** and zombies. Following the format established in *Famous Monsters of Filmland,* Warren successfully introduced two new horror comics, *Creepy* and *Eerie,* in 1964 and 1965, respectively. Both were successful and both carried vampire stories. They set the stage for the introduction in 1969 of *Vampirella,* a new vampire-oriented comic, and **Dark Shadows,** issued by Gold Key, the first two vampire comics since the adoption of the Comics Code in 1954.

Vampirella, a character developed by **Forrest J. Ackerman,** was somewhat different. She was, first of all, a **woman,** and female vampires had been rare in comic books, especially in starring roles. Second, she was not of the undead; rather, she was from outer space. According to the story line she was a native of the planet Drakulon, a dying planet where **blood** had replaced **water** as the life-sustaining liquid. Vampirella had come to Earth, where there was a steady supply of blood, to survive. She was pictured as a beautiful, dark-haired young woman (late teens to early twenties) with a scanty costume that hid little of her voluptuous body. Barbarella, a character developed by French artist Jean-Claude Forest and the subject of a motion picture by **Roger Vadim,** was the direct inspiration for Vampirella, whose red costume had a gold bat insignia just below her navel. When she smiled, her two extended canine teeth were prominently displayed. She also had the ability to change into a **bat.** Vampirella was impish as well as sexy. She engaged in a constant search for blood (or its equivalent), but she was the heroine and hence did not take life without reason. She was always mournful about the choices that her own survival often pressed upon her.

Through the years of her existence on Earth, the story of Vampirella's **origin** has been retold on several occasions and left her with several very distinct accounts of her origin. In the early stories, her origin was described very superficially. She was from a planet in which blood was like water on Earth. It was present abundantly in rivers and streams. However, the blood source was being threatened by the double suns around which Drakulon whirled. Vampirella had grown up on Drakulon and was engaged to a young man, Tristan. Like other vampires, she exhaled carbon monoxide. Over the centuries the carbon monoxide in the atmosphere had broken down the protective layer, made of creatone, that protected the residents of the surface from the most harmful rays coming from their suns. The planet was now dying. Vampirella had an opportunity to escape when a spaceship from Earth arrived. She discovered that the veins of the crew's bodies provided the life-giving fluid she needed. She killed to survive and then took the spaceship to Earth.

In a 1974 story, "The Vampire of the Nile," Vampirella's pre-Drakulon career was explored and traced to ancient Egypt. As Cleopatra, she had been summoned to the temple of her husband (and brother) Ptolemy to consummate their marriage. As soon as she entered his temple, she was grabbed and shackled to a large column. Out of a crypt in front of the column, the vampire-king arose and bit Cleopatra. She became the enchantress of popular history, a tragic career broken only by a brief affair with her true love, Mark Anthony. After Anthony died, she again entered the vampire temple and staked Ptolemy. Suddenly, the God Amun-Ra appeared. He could not remove her vampiric condition, but rewarded her by promising her reincarnation on Drakulon. Thus, she quickly moved to commit **suicide** with the poisonous snake.

Vampirella on Earth: Vampirella arrived on Earth in 1969. She needed blood daily and became a huntress for the blood within humans. However, soon after her arrival, she was involved in an airplane crash after which she was taken to a rural clinic for the wealthy. The doctor who rescued her also fell in love with her. More importantly, he created a synthesized blood substitute which freed Vampirella from her need to attack humans. Unfortunately, the doctor's nurse was a disciple of Chaos, the evil force, that continually infringes upon the orderly universe, and became jealous of the doctor's feeling for Vampirella. She carried *The Crimson Chronicles*, the bible of the believers of Chaos, and below the clinic was a temple where Chaos's worshippers gathered. Here Vampirella would have her first encounter with Chaos and be taken prisoner by his followers.

Meanwhile, two experts in the ways of evil supernaturalism, Conrad Van Helsing and his son Adam, were investigating the plane crash in which Vampirella was involved. Conrad's brother was also on the plane, and his body was found drained of blood. With pictures of four people on the flight whose bodies were not found, the somewhat psychic Conrad spotted Vampirella as the odd entity and concluded that she had killed his brother. The pair tracked down Vampirella who was being held prisoner by the leader of the Chaos followers who wanted Vampirella to make him a vampire. After the Van Helsings arrived, he also took them prisoner. While Conrad lay unconscious, Vampirella told her story to Adam who became convinced she was not guilty of his uncle's death. Vampirella finally broke free of her chains and having been starved, was about to feed from Adam as Conrad awoke. What he saw merely confirmed his opinion of Vampirella. They escaped and went their separate ways. Vampirella fed off her willing captor, but he did not become a vampire as her bite could not transmit vampirism.

Vampirella found a job as the assistant with an aging magician and alcoholic, Pendragon. Their first tour took them to the Caribbean. Shipwrecked on an island, they encountered a man attempting to find a serum to cure his wife of **werewolfism**. He took Vampirella prisoner to use her as a guinea pig. Meanwhile, Adam showed up, and together they extricated themselves from the situation.

Conrad had also come to the Island to look for Adam, and was taken prisoner on Cote de Soleil by the followers of Chaos. Pendragon, Adam, and Vampirella conspired to free him. Once they escaped, Conrad's opinion of Vampirella began to change, but it was not revised until together they tracked the real killers of Conrad's brother to a group of Chaos's followers in **New Orleans**. Once their relationship was established, the four would have numerous adventures through the 1970s. The emergence of the Van Helsings, tied as they were to **Bram Stoker's** *Dracula* (1897), signaled the eventual return of its main character as well, and one of the most interesting revisions of the **Dracula** myth. Awakened in the contemporary world, a cosmic being known as the

Conjuress sent Dracula back to the 1890s to undo some of the damage he had done and reverse the process that made him a vampire. Vampirella joined him through the device of a magic **mirror**. In their initial conversation, Dracula revealed that he too was from Drakulon. He began to use magic to solve the planet's problems, but contacted Chaos instead of accomplishing his task. Chaos had originally forced him to Earth. Vampirella agreed to help him redeem himself.

As Dracula and Vampirella met all of the principal characters from *Dracula* the novel, Dracula's basic problem was to find some way to stave off his bloodthirst. After **Lucy Westenra** was resurrected when the **stake** was pulled from her heart (her **decapitation** being ignored), Dracula remembered his love for her. He was able to keep from biting Lucy, but could not restrain himself when it came to **Mina Murray**. Lucy saw him attack Mina and dropped dead. In spite of Vampirella's help, the Conjuress pronounced Dracula a failure, and he was taken out of the story line, for the moment. The first issue of *Vampirella* appeared in September 1969. Forrest Ackerman was the first writer, and the soon-to-be-famous Frank Franzetta was the original artist. The original team was filled out by Trina Robbins and Tom Sutton. Ackerman was followed by Archie Godwin and a host of different writers over the years, most notably John Cochran, T. Casey Brennan, and Steve Englehart (under the pseudonym Chad Archer). Franzetta and Sutton were later succeeded by José Gonzales, with whom the image of Vampirella became most identified.

Vampirella became (and as of 2010 remains) the longest-running English-language vampire comic book of all time, its last issue (No. 112) appearing in February 1983. Meanwhile, in the mid-1970s, Ron Goulart had produced a series of six *Vampirella* novels adapted from the comic book story line. In the late 1980s, in the atmosphere of reviving interest in vampires, Harris Comics acquired *Vampirella* and in 1988 issued a single issue (No. 113) following the old Warren Comics format. Three years later, Harris Comics launched their new Vampirella program with reissues of the old *Vampirella* stories in a new format, and the creation of new Vampirella stories, the first of which appeared in a four-part series written by Kurt Busiek. Busiek picked up the story of Vampirella after her disappearance in the final Warren issue. Busiek also wrote the first of the Harris stories to appear in color the following year. During the 1990s, under Harris's guidance, a number of writers have taken up the challenge of writing Vampirella; however, Tom Sniegoski is usually given the credit of remolding her as a 1990s "Bad Girl," a totally feminine creature who can nevertheless function as a superhero for the youthful readership. In the process of producing the 25-issue series, *Vengeance of Vampirella*, he also recreated the myth underlying Vampirella's existence. In a story line called "The Mystery Walk," Vampirella's extraterrestrial origin was put aside for a mythological one. **Lilith**, the first wife of Adam in Hebrew folklore, sought to earn forgiveness from the God of Order. After her creation, she rejected Adam. She was expelled from Eden. In her rage, she hated God, and her hatred took on form as the lilin, who in turn spread evil in the world God created. She finally decided to return to the light and forced herself back into Eden, a place neglected since Adam and Eve had been expelled.

In Eden Lilith initiated her plan for her own redemption that began with caring for the garden. She then created the twins Magdelene and Madek and sent them into the world to undo the evil that had resulted from Lilith's hatred. The plan backfired and the twins merely created more evil. Vampirella was created to defeat the twins and then pick up the mission of opposing the world's evil. Before going into the world, she was trained to master the dark side that resided within her inherited from Lilith. The Sniegoski reworking of Vampirella has launched a new career for Vampirella and kept her comic books regularly among the best selling in the industry.

The Vampirella Movie (1996): Through the years, plans were announced and rumors circulated about a Vampirella movie. Model/actress Barbara Leigh was designated the future star of a 1970s movie and her picture appeared on the cover of a number of Vampirella comic books. However, it was not until the mid-1990s that a movie actually was shot. In the made-for-**television** movie, directed by Jim Wynorski, Vampirella's origin took a more sinister **science fiction** turn. In ancient time, people of Drakulon would attack and drain the blood from each other. They had arisen to a point where such behavior was no longer acceptable. Then approximately 3,000 years ago, there arose on Drakulon a new cult led by Vlad (Roger Daltrey) and a small cadre of people. They plotted revolution. Vlad was arrested and was to be tried. During his audience before Drakulon's council, an escape team arrived and they and Vlad killed all of the members of the council. Vlad himself drank from Vampirella's father. Determined to bring her father's killers to justice, Vampirella (Talisa Soto) followed them to Earth on a returning Mars probe. The journey took 3,000 years. Once on Earth, she made common cause with Adam van Helsing, the head of a vampire eradication agency, and together they tracked down Vlad and his minions.

In 2009, Vampirella celebrated her fortieth anniversary at The Vampire-Con in Los Angeles, at which a new Vampirella model was selected. As the twentieth-first century gains steam, Vampirella remains one of the most influential vampire characters in the literary realm. She has been the subject of multiple **trading card** sets, six novels (by Ron Goulart), over 300 comic book issues, several model statues, and one movie. The comics have been translated into more than a dozen languages including most of the European languages and several in Asia. Harris continues to employ a spectrum of top comics writers and artists that continually attract new fans and revive interest in the older fans. In the wake of the revived interest in Vampirella in the 1990s, Harris Comics organized a fan club, The Scarlet Legion, which provides an avenue for fans to share their enthusiasm and through which Harris offers a number of Vampirella premiums and limited editions not otherwise available to the public. After forty years, Vampirella is more popular than ever. The Scarlet Legion maintains a web presence on the Harris Vampirella site, http://www.vampirella.com/.

Having appeared in 1969, Vampirella is now seen as the original "**good guy vampire**," whose lineage would be traced forward from the comic to the novels of **Chelsea Quinn Yarbro** and **Fred Saberhagen**, to the hundreds of romance and young adult novels of the present, to the very successful television characters such as Nick Knight, **Angel** and Henry Fitzroy (created by **Tanya Huff**), and the *Twilight* novels and movies of **Stephanie Meyer**.

Sources:

Busiek, Kurt, and Louis la Chance. *Vampirella: Morning in America*. No. 1–4. New York: Harris Comics/Dark Horse, 1991.

Goulart, Ron. *Bloodstalk*. New York: Warner Books, 1975. 141 pp. Rept. London: Sphere Books, 1975. 141 pp.

————. *On Alien Wings.* New York: Warner Books, 1975. 138 pp. Rept. London: Sphere Books, 1975. 138 pp.

————. *Blood Wedding.* New York: Warner Books, 1976. 140 pp. Rept. London: Sphere Books, 1976. 140 pp.

————. *Deadwalk.* New York: Warner Books, 1976. 144 pp. Rept. London: Sphere Books, 1976. 144 pp.

————. *Deathgame.* New York: Warner Books, 1976. 142 pp. Rept. London: Sphere Books, 1976. 142 pp.

————. *Snakegod.* New York: Warner Books, 1976. 144 pp. Rept. London: Sphere Books, 1976. 144 pp.

Horn, Maurice. *The World Encyclopedia of Comic Books.* New York: Chelsea House Publishers, 1976. 785 pp.

Lewis, Budd, and Jose Gonzalez. "The Origin of Vampirella." *Vampirella* (Warren) 46 (October 1975): Reprinted in *Vampirella Annual 1972.* Reprinted in *Vampirella* 100 (October 1981): 29–43.

Loew, Flaxman, and Jose Ortiz. "The Vampire of the Nile." *Vampirella* (Harris) 113 (1988): 17–28.

Melton, J. Gordon. *Vampirella: A Collector's Checklist.* Santa Barbara, CA: Transylvanian Society of Dracula, 1998.

Vampirella. Nos. 1–112. New York: Warren Publishing, 1969–83.

Vengeance of Vampirella. Nos. 1–25. New York: Harris Publications, 1994–1996.

Vampires, Werewolves, Ghosts and Other Things that Go Bump in the Night *see:* Vampire Fandom: United States

Vampirism Research Institute *see:* Vampire Fandom: United States

Vamperotica

*V*amperotica was the lead **comic book** series from Brainstorm Comics, a company created in the early 1990s by graphic artist and writer Kirk Lindo. Brainstorm was one of several independent comics companies that thrived in the 1990s by adopting the vampire as a major element in its products. In its first issue in 1994, *Vamperotica* introduced the world to Luxura, an ancient vampire who resided in a vast underground complex somewhere in **America**. The sexy buxom Luxura was tall with long talon-like fingers and a head of luxurious black hair, her most distinguishing trait. She dressed in a scanty outfit punctuated by knee-high boots and gold bracelets and shoulder and knee ornaments.

As a leading member of the Kith, she worked to maintain the Kith community's three edicts: sustain the **blood** source (mortals); regulate the Kith; and maintain discretion. She had to deal with unruly Kith, especially young vampires who sought to gain power quickly by taking some (or all) of her blood. Her primary antagonist was Pontius Vanthor, a former lover who has become the major challenge to the traditional structure of the Kith community. He argued for the Red Reign, calling upon vampires to come out of hiding and take over the world. Under the Red Reign, mortals would be herded in a manner similar to cattle.

Luxura was installed as the main character in *Vamperotica* which often included other vampire stories. Successful for a decade, the comic supported a variety of spinoff issues featuring Luxura and the development of several new vampire titles, most notably

Bethany the Vampfire, written and drawn by Holly Golighty (a.k.a. Fauve). After what appeared to be a successful run through the late 1970s, Brainstorm ran into financial problems early in the new century. The quality of its productions suffered and its last issues appeared in 2004.

Sources:

Vamperotica. No. 1–99. Fayetteville, NC: Brainstorm Comics, 1994–1999.

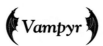 Vampyr

Made the same year as the film *Dracula* (1931), *Vampyr,* having been forgotten by all but the most devoted students of the horror genre, has nevertheless been regarded by some critics of classical horror films as the best such motion picture ever made. *Vampyr* was produced and directed by **Carl Theodor Dreyer**, who also, with the assistance of Christen Jul, wrote the script. The film was purportedly modeled on **Sheridan Le Fanu**'s "Carmilla", but the only similarity seems to be Dreyer's use of a female vampire.

The film opens with David Gray (played by Julian West) arriving in a European village only to discover that a room had already been booked for him at the local inn. That evening he was visited by an old man (Maurice Schultz) who gave him a package to be opened in case of his death. After the man mysteriously disappeared, Gray wondered if it was all a dream, although he still possessed the package. Unable to **sleep**, he went for a walk. He followed a disconnected shadow that led him to the local manor house. There he met the man, who turned out to be the owner of the mansion, and one of his daughters, Gisele (Rena Mandel). While Gray visited with Schultz, the latter was shot and killed. Gray then learned that Schultz's other daughter, Leone (Sybille Schmitz), was manifesting some strange symptoms. Upon opening the package after Schultz was shot, Gray found a book on vampires. Leone, who had been wandering about in her sleep, was discovered out on the grounds with an old woman, Margueritte Chopin (Henriette Gerard), hovering over her. Because Leone had lost a lot of **blood**, Gray offered her a transfusion of his own blood. While giving the transfusion Gray had an hallucination in which he was being buried alive. Through a window in the **coffin** he saw the old woman's face staring at him. He realized that she was a vampire and that a doctor he had met earlier was her assistant. After the hallucination, he awakened in the local cemetery. Accompanied by a servant from the manor house, he found the old woman's grave, and together they killed her by staking her with an iron pole. The spirits of those whom she had killed then arose to attack and kill the vampire's human cohorts, including the doctor.

Carl Dreyer (the film's producer and director) was known for his artistic attention to a mood of terror rather than any graphic presentation of horrific action. In *Vampyr* he slowly developed an environment that was supernatural and disjointed and in which the vampire's presence was strongly felt but rarely seen. The terror was suggested early, especially as Gray followed the shadow, which led him to a place where more disconnected shadows dance to some loud **music**. The old woman appeared, and as she raised her arms and demanded quiet, the music suddenly stopped.

To add even more to the atmosphere of total terror, Dreyer also had the picture filmed with some light leaking into the camera, thus producing a foggy quality on the finished film. To enhance the exact quality he wanted in the characters, Dreyer recruited non-actors to play the various roles. Only Sybille Schmitz and Maurice Schultz were professionals. Dreyer allowed the film's plot to develop slowly, thus inviting viewers to participate in the film through their imagination. In the face of competing horror epics, however, the effect was to leave most audiences bored and to deny the film commercial success. Dreyer's artistic accomplishment was understood and appreciated by very few. In the United States, a condensed version of the film, with a voice-over narration, was issued as the *Castle of Doom*, but it too failed to attract a significant audience.

A DVD copy of *Vampyr* was issued in 2008 in the Criterion Collection, a series of classic and contemporary films, published using the best technical advancements along with original supplements. In this case, the two-disc set included a 1958 radio broadcast of Dreyer reading an essay about filmmaking, a documentary by Jörgen Roos on Dreyer's career, an essay by Casper Tybjerg about influences on Dreyer's *Vampyr*, and a supplemental book of essays on the film.

Sources:

Bordwell, David. *The Films of Carl-Theodor Dreyer*. Berkeley: University of California Press, 1981. 251 pp.

Dreyer, Carl Theodor. *Four Screen Plays*. Translated by Oliver Stallybrass. Bloomington, IN: Indiana University Press, 1970. 312 pp.

Everson, William K. *Classics of the Horror Film*. New York: Carol Publishing, 1974. 247 pp.

Rudkin, David. *Vampyr*. London: British Film Institute, 2008.

The Vampyre Society *see:* Vampire Fandom: United Kingdom

Van Helsing, Abraham

A major character in **Bram Stoker's** *Dracula* **(1897)**, whose name has become synonymous with the role of the **vampire hunter**, Van Helsing was the wise elder scholar who brought enlightenment to the confusing and threatening situation that the other characters, all in their twenties, had become enmeshed. Van Helsing, who lived in Amsterdam, was originally called to England by Dr. **John Seward**, who described him as an "old friend and master" and an expert in obscure diseases. Van Helsing was a philosopher, metaphysician, and advanced scientist.

Van Helsing's first task was to examine the ailing **Lucy Westenra**. He found nothing wrong, except loss of **blood**, and she was not suffering from **anemia**. He then returned to Amsterdam. In less than a week, with Lucy's condition taking a decided turn for the worse, Van Helsing returned. He prescribed an immediate transfusion. He then noticed two marks on Lucy's neck. Again he returned to Amsterdam to consult his books. Upon his return a few days later, Lucy again received a transfusion. By this time Van Helsing had figured out the cause of Lucy's problem, but he did not divulge it. He merely took steps to block the vampire's access by surrounding Lucy with **garlic**. She improved and Van Helsing returned home.

Lucy lost her garlic several days later, and **Dracula** returned to attack her in her bedroom. This time a third transfusion could not save her. **Quincey P. Morris** raised the possibility of vampires. After Lucy's death, Van Helsing convinced the men, especially Lucy's fiancé, **Arthur Holmwood**, to treat Lucy's corpse as a vampire. He had them observe her movements after she was placed in her crypt to ensure that she did not join the undead. While Holmwood pounded a **stake** into Lucy, Van Helsing read a prayer for the dead from a prayer book, after which he and Seward **decapitated** the corpse and filled the mouth with garlic. Van Helsing then turned to the task of learning all he could about Dracula, with the goal of first discovering his hiding places and eventually **destroying** him. In a meeting with the other principal characters, he received their commitment to join the fight under his leadership. At this gathering he laid out, in a most systematic fashion, the theory of vampires (which had been only partially revealed earlier), emphasizing their many powers and the manner by which they may be killed.

Meanwhile, **Mina Murray** (by this time married to **Jonathan Harker**) was showing signs of having been attacked by Dracula. She was pale and fatigued, but Van Helsing and the others were slow to recognize what was occurring. Van Helsing finally realized, while talking to the madman **R. N. Renfield**, that Mina was under attack and immediately led Seward, Holmwood, and Morris to the Harker house, where they found Mina drinking from Dracula's chest. Van Helsing drove him off with a **crucifix** and a **eucharistic wafer** (consecrated wafers are believed by Roman Catholic Christians to be the very body of Christ). To protect Mina, he held the wafer to her forehead, only to have it burn its imprint there much like a branding iron.

Mina, who had stepped aside so the men could engage Dracula, now became an active participant in the fight. She invited Van Helsing to hypnotize her and thus tap into her **psychic** tie to Dracula. In this manner, Van Helsing, who had led in the destruction of Dracula's boxes of Earth (which he needed to survive), discovered that the vampire had left England to return to **Transylvania**. He accompanied Mina and the men on a chase to catch Dracula. During the last leg of the journey, the group split into three pairs. Van Helsing traveled with Mina, and they were the first to arrive at **Castle Dracula**. He drew a circle around her with the eucharistic wafers and then went into the castle. He killed the three vampire **brides** who resided there, sanitized Dracula's crypt, and finished by treating the castle's entrances so that no vampire could use them.

Returning to Mina, Van Helsing moved her some distance from the castle entrance to protect them from the wolves while awaiting the others to converge for the final confrontation. Once all arrive Van Helsing held a rifle on the **Gypsies** as Morris and Harker approached the box in which Dracula rested and killed him.

As Dracula was brought to stage and screen, Van Helsing assumed a key role, the plot often being

Anthony Hopkins played Abraham Van Helsing in the movie *Bram Stoker's Dracula*.

simplified to a personal battle between Dracula and Van Helsing as the representatives of evil and good, respectively. Interestingly, **Hamilton Deane**, who wrote the original *Dracula* play for his theater company, chose to assume the role of Van Helsing rather than Dracula. However, **Peter Cushing**, who played the part in several **Hammer Films** motion pictures (pitted against **Christopher Lee** as Dracula) has been identified with the role of Van Helsing more than any other actor. He not only played Van Helsing at various times, but on occasion also portrayed several of his twentieth-century descendants continuing his fight against vampiric evil.

In both the movies and **comic books**, descendants of Van Helsing have flourished. Cushing played Van Helsing's grandson in Hammer's *Dracula A.D. 1972*. Other descendants were portrayed by Richard Benjamin in *Love at First Bite* (1979) and by Bruce Campbell in *Sundown: The Vampire in Retreat* (1988). **Marv Wolfman** of Marvel Comics invented Rachel Van Helsing, a granddaughter who continued his search-and-destroy mission against Dracula in the pages of *The Tomb of Dracula* through the 1970s. Conrad and Adam Van Helsing emerged in the pages of *Vampirella* as **vampire hunters**. Most recently, Hugh Jackman portrayed Gabriel van Helsing in the appropriately named *Van Helsing* (2004). Jackman was also the voice of Van Helsing for the cartoon spin-off prequel of the movie, *Van Helsing: The London Assignment* (2004).

Several people have been identified as possible models for the Van Helsing character, including author (Abraham) Stoker himself. Some have suggested **Arminius Vambéry,** mentioned in chapter 18 as a friend of Van Helsing's. Vambéry was a real person, at one time a professor at the University of Budapest, and the probable source of Stoker's initial knowledge of **Vlad the Impaler**, a historical model for Count Dracula. In *The Essential Dracula* (1979) editors **Raymond T. McNally** and **Radu Florescu** suggest Max Muller, a famous Orientalist at Oxford University, as a possibility. They also suggest that Dr. Martin Hasselius, the fictional narrator in **Sheridan Le Fanu**'s *In a Glass Darkly*, might also have helped inspire Van Helsing.

Sources:

Stoker, Bram. *The Essential Dracula*. Edited by Raymond McNally and Radu Florescu. New York: Mayflower Books, 1979. 320 pp.

❦ Van Sloan, Edward (1882–1964) ❦

Edward Van Sloan, the first American to play vampire hunter Professor **Abraham Van Helsing** on the stage and screen, abandoned a middle-class profession for life on the stage. He began in comedy and toured with several stock companies. In 1927, he accepted the part of Van Helsing in the American stage version of *Dracula* that opened in New York the week of Halloween. He was then one of the few actors from the stage who carried his role over into the 1931 **Universal Pictures** film. The scenes in which he confronts **Dracula** with his hypothesis that he is a vampire (in a voice that is a sharp contrast to that of **Bela Lugosi**) remain among the strongest in the movie. Van Sloan would, on the one hand, set the image of Van Helsing for a generation, until **Peter Cushing** took it over in the **Hammer Films** movies. On the other hand, Van Sloan found that his work in *Dracula*, like fellow actor Bela Lugosi, tended to typecast him.

From that time on he played scholarly and fatherly authority figures. He would go on to make some 50 movies, and to revive his role as Van Helsing for the sequel, *Dracula's Daughter* (1936). He retired in 1947.

Varma, Devendra Prasad (1923–1994)

Devendra P. Varma, a Canadian **gothic** scholar, became a key figure in the development of modern gothic studies that in turn provided the foundation for the contemporary revival of interest in the vampire. As a young scholar, Varma began to gather a collection of eighteenth- and nineteenth-century literature that would come to include many rare volumes. The collection would later become the source for the reprinting of almost 200 important pieces of literature, including the complete works of **Sheridan Le Fanu** and a three-volume edition of *Varney the Vampire* (1970), now a collector's item in itself. In the 1960s, he became a professor of English and Gothic Literature at Dalhousie University, Halifax, Nova Scotia, where he would remain for the rest of his life.

Varma's first book, *The Gothic Flame: Being a History of the Gothic Novel in England* (1957) stands at the fountainhead of contemporary gothic studies. He went on to edit editions of Jane Austen's horror novels, Horace Walpole's *The Castle of Otranto* (1976), Matthew Lewis's *The Monk* (1984), and the complete set of Ann Ratcliffe's *Gothic Romances* (1987).

As a particular student of vampire literature, Varma wrote "The Vampire in Legend, Lore, and Literature" as an introductory essay for his 1970 edition of *Varney the Vampyre* (reprinted in 1989 in **Margaret Carter**'s *The Vampire in Literature: A Critical Bibliography*) in which he called attention to the vampire characters in the folklore of **India** and nearby countries of **Tibet,** Nepal, and Mongolia, and suggested that these stories, arriving in the Mediterranean via the ancient trade routes, may have been the source of European vampire tales. That essay has stood the test of time far better that his early exploration of "The Genesis of Dracula" (1975), which helped stimulate the last two decades of consideration of the **origins** of the prominent element of **Bram Stoker**'s novel. He edited one volume of vampire short fiction, *Voices from the Vaults: Authentic Tales of Vampires and Ghosts* (1987). He was working on a volume of essays on **Dracula** projected for publication for **Dracula '97: A Centennial Celebration**, but was overtaken by a heart attack on October 24, 1994, in Oceanside, New York, while on the last leg of a lecture tour. His last major work was an introductory essay for Henry Peter Sucksmith's *Those Whom the Old Gods Love* (1994).

Sources:

Varma, Devendra P. "The Vampire in Legend Lore, and Literature." In *Varney the Vampyre; or, The Feast of Blood.* New York: Arno Press, 1970. Reprinted in Carter, Margaret, ed. *The Vampire in Literature: A Critical Bibliography.* Ann Arbor, MI: UMI Research Press, 1989: 13–29.

———. "The Genesis of Dracula: A Re-Visit." In Peter Underwood, ed. *The Vampire's Bedside Companion.* London: Leslie Frewin, 1975.

———. "Dracula's Voyage: From Pontus to Hellespontus." Paper presented at the American Association of Slavic Studies, Eighteenth National Convention, New Orleans, November 21, 1986.

———. *Voices from the Vault: Authentic Tales of Vampire and Ghosts.* Toronto: Key Porter Books, 1987. 247 pp.

Stuart, Roxana. *Stage Blood: Vampires of the 19th-Century Stage*. Bowling Green, OH: Bowling Green State University Popular Press, 1994. 377 pp.

❧ *Varney the Vampyre* ❧

One of the most famous vampires in literature is Sir Francis Varney, the title character in *Varney the Vampyre: or, The Feast of Blood*, a nineteenth-century British novel written by **James Malcolm Rymer**. The story originally appeared in 109 weekly installments in the mid-1840s. The entire manuscript was then collected and printed as a single volume of over 800 pages. It was the first vampire novel in English, and the first vampire fiction since the original short story by **John Polidori** and the stage **dramas** that his story inspired. The story thus served as an important transitional piece between the original written accounts of vampires in the early nineteenth century and the writing of **Sheridan Le Fanu** and **Bram Stoker**.

Through the twentieth century, Varney had a checkered career. Copies of Rymer's poorly written novel were seldom saved, so it became a rare book. Although different authors made reference to it, few had seen a copy and fewer still had taken the time to work their way through it. The book was published anonymously, and it was only in the 1970s that its true authorship was established. It was unavailable for many decades, but two reprints were published in 1970 and 1972. The audience was quite limited and the book has remained out-of-print since. The story of Varney opened with his attack upon the young Flora Bannerworth. Having entered her bedroom, he sank his **fangs** into her neck and began to suck the gushing **blood**. The first half of the book followed his increasingly complex relationship with the Bannerworth family and their close friends and associates. Varney possessed white skin (as if bloodless), long, fang-like teeth, long **fingernails**, and shining, metallic eyes. Immediately after feasting, his skin took on a reddish hue.

The cover from an early edition of *Varney the Vampyre*, the first English-language vampire novel.

Varney's initial attack had left two puncture marks in Flora's neck. Interrupted by members of the family during his repast, Varney was shot but nevertheless escaped. Henry Bannerworth quickly concluded that Flora had been attacked by a "vampyre." From a book he had read in Norway, he noted that vampyres attempted to drink blood to revive their body. In addition, they tended to do their feeding on evenings just prior to a full moon so that, should they meet with any physical problem, they could revive themselves by basking in the rays of the full **moon**. And it was in this manner that Varney had revived from the gunshot wounds he had received. (The importance given to moonlight throughout the novel shows Rymer's reliance on **John Polidori**'s "The Vampyre".)

While bits and pieces of Varney's history were recounted throughout the novel, the reader had to wait until the end to get the full story. Varney's name before he had become a vampire was Mortimer. He originally had been a supporter of the British Crown and was living in **London** at the time of the beheading of Charles I and the proclamation of the Commonwealth under Cromwell in 1649. During this period he had assisted members of the royalty in escaping to Holland, for which he was handsomely rewarded. In a moment of passion, Mortimer had struck his son, accidentally killing him. The next thing he had remembered was a flash of light and being struck to earth with great force. When he had recovered consciousness, he was lying on the ground next to a recently opened grave. A voice told him that for his deed thenceforth he would be cursed among men and known as Varney the Vampyre. Varney later discovered that he was shot by Cromwell's men and two years had passed since he lost consciousness. In the meantime, Cromwell had been deposed and the Crown restored. His former house was burned, but the money he had buried under the floor was still there. With it he made a new beginning. He slowly learned the rules of his new nature.

Like **Lord Ruthven**, the vampire in Polidori's tale, Varney had great **strength**, he could walk around freely in the **sunlight**, and he needed blood only occasionally (not nightly). He could be wounded and even killed but would be revived simply by bathing in the moonlight. First pictured as something entirely evil, Varney later took on a more complex nature and showed himself to be an individual of feelings and honor. So appealing were his virtues that the Bannerworths, once they develop some understanding of his condition and his relationship with one of their ancestors, eventually became his protectors from a mob that set out to destroy him.

Rymer was also familiar with the eastern European vampire cases, probably through **Dom Augustin Calmet,** who had been published in an English edition in the 1700s. For several chapters, beginning with chapter 44, Varney's story turned on the action of a mob. An unnamed individual, who had traveled on the Continent, informed the people that the sign of the presence of a vampire was the sudden, mysterious death of people who seem to have wasted away. He warned them that such people would also return as vampires. Armed with this information, the mob, unable to locate Varney, moved on to the local graveyard and attacked the body of one Miles, who had recently died. Their eagerness to kill a vampire was thwarted when Miles's **coffin** was found to be empty. After completing his interaction with the Bannerworths, Varney moved on to a series of increasingly brief encounters with various people in what became a very repetitive story line. He would try to establish himself in a new social setting, he would attempt to bite someone, be discovered and hunted, and have to escape. Varney was singularly inept at attacking peo-

The first page from the novel *Varney the Vampyre*.

ple (almost always a young woman) and was continually caught by people responding to the cries of his **victims**.

Varney was condemned by modern critics as poorly written and somewhat chaotic. It was not written as fine literature, or even as a novel, however. It was written in weekly installments over a two-year period, probably by several different authors, in such a way as to keep the readers entertained and coming back for the next installment. It accomplished that rather limited goal in spectacular fashion, becoming one of the most successful of the penny weeklies of the mid-nineteenth century.

Sources:

Rymer, James Malcolm. *Varney the Vampyre*: or, *The Feast of Blood*. London: F. Lloyd, 1847. 868 pp. Rept. Edited by Devendra P. Varna. New York: Arno Press, 1970. 868 pp. Rept. Edited by E. F. Bleiler. New York: Dover Publications, 1972. 868 pp.

Vetalas *see:* India, Vampires in

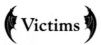

Victims

According to vampire hunter **Abraham Van Helsing**, the vampire had no conscience. He preyed "on the bodies and souls of those whom we love best." This characteristic seemed to be a corruption of folkloric belief that the vampire attacked first those whom *it* loved best. The vampire of folklore would return to the village, home, and people among whom it lived before death. Thus, the vampire tended to attack first those it loved best in life. Actually, this characteristic manifested one of the major differences between the traditional vampire of folklore and the vampire of literature, created in the nineteenth century. The folkloric vampire was part of village culture. It was restricted to its grave site or its home village, where it took up residence once again. In contrast, **Lord Ruthven**, *Varney the Vampyre*, and **Dracula** are citizens of the world. Ruthven traveled at will. Dracula, a little more constrained, was forced to take **native soil** with him. Thus, he could visit **London** but had to choose victims within an evening's travel time of one of his designated resting places. **Carmilla** was tied to a relatively small area, but she could travel beyond a local village.

Another discrepancy between the folkloric vampire and the vampire of literature has been the fate of the victim. In general, the folkloric vampire's initial attack was rarely fatal. (A major exception was the vampire's attack upon infants, after which it would leave them dead in their cribs, to be found by their parents the next morning.) Generally, the vampire was seen as taking the life of people over a period of time by repeated attacks that left the victim fatigued or ill with a wasting disease such as consumption (tuberculosis).

The vampires of literature often immediately killed their victims, as in the case of Lord Ruthven, but not with Varney the Vampyre, Carmilla, or Dracula. Varney often showed a conscience toward his victims and did not kill. Carmilla and Dracula killed, but over a period of time as their victims wasted away. In folklore, the vampire's attack may have caused the victim to become a vampire also, but generally the victim's vampiric state did not manifest until after death. The fear that a vampire had infected oth-

Ann Parillaud, the vampire in *Innocent Blood*, could transform her victims into vampires just by biting them, a fairly modern addition to the vampire myth.

ers led not to a witch hunt among neighbors but to the disinterment of corpses and their treatment as vampires. The cases of **Peter Plogojowitz** and **Arnold Paul** accounted partially for the fame of this process.

Throughout nineteenth-century literature, the victims of vampires did not become vampires. They died, as in the cases of Lord Ruthven and Carmilla, or soon recovered and returned to normal lives, as in the case of Varney. In the novel ***Dracula*** **(1897)**, none of the victims of Dracula's vampiric attacks died at his hand (although it was clearly implied that the baby given to the three **women** early in the novel died as a result of their attack on it). **R. N. Renfield** was killed by Dracula, but not as a result of being drained of **blood**. **Jonathan Harker** was attacked by the three women, but survived. **Lucy Westenra** was attacked by Dracula, and eventually died, but then survived as a vampire. She attacked children, but all survived. She was finally killed by **Van Helsing** and the other men. **Mina Murray** (nee Harker) was attacked, and there was every reason to believe that had she not been "de-vampirized" she would have become a vampire. Dracula not only took her blood but also had her drink of his. While never stated, it was clearly implied that sharing blood was the manner of transforming a victim into a vampire. Otherwise, the victim, if bitten often enough, as in "Carmilla," simply died.

The method of **transformation** of a victim into a vampire—by sharing blood—was lost in the dramatization of *Dracula* on stage and then on the screen; it was deemed improper to bring before an audience. In large part, that deletion led to the redefining of the method of vampire transmission. After the early *Dracula* movies, the belief that all it took to transform a person into a vampire was the vampire's bite became an integral part of the vampire myth. This idea had its ultimate expression in Robert McCammon's *They Thirst* (1981), in which a vampire loosed a vampire epidemic on Los Angeles. The number of vampires almost doubled each evening as the vampires fed and turned their victims into vampires that fed the next evening. This idea was continued in such movies as *Vamp* (1986) and *Innocent Blood* (1992). A variation on this theme was the requirement of three bites by the vampire to transform someone into a vampire, recently integrated most effectively in the story line of the comedy *Love at First Bite* (1979).

Victims of Good Guy Vampires: During the last generation, in the expansion and reworking of the vampire tradition, a new vampire has arisen, the **good guy vampire**. Unlike the vampires sought by Van Helsing in *Dracula*, these modern vampires possess a conscience that has led them to avoid killing whenever possible. The most prominent early "good guy" vampires were **St. Germain**, the hero of the **Chelsea Quinn Yarbro** books, and the very different Dracula developed by **Fred Saberhagen**. Good guy vampires often seek blood from blood banks or from **animals**, but when they turned to human "victims," they would choose people considered morally corrupt and thus deserving of the attack, or, more often, willing donors who for various reasons allowed the vampire to use them. In the case of St. Germain, his feeding was often done in the context of sexual activity, and the bite took the place of intercourse. Thus, the vampire gave the victim a sexual thrill and established a reciprocal relationship with the donor. St. Germain could periodically feed off people several times without their changing into a vampire and only rarely took the steps necessary to transform someone. The good guy vampire has filled the pages of several hundred romance and young adult vampire novels and has become a familiar character on television with the likes of Nick Knight from the series *Forever Knight*, **Angel**, who emerged on *Buffy the Vampire Slayer*, Henry Fitroy from **Tanya Huff**'s *Blood Ties*, and Stefan Salvatore, of *The Vampire Diaries*. The only victims of the good guys are more than justly deserving of the vampire's righteous indignation.

The plot of the *Twilight* series by **Stephanie Meyer** turns largely on the victimless existence of the vampire family, the Cullens. They have been able to develop a lifestyle based on feeding on animals, which also becomes the basis of a treaty with their **werewolf**/shape-shifting Native American neighbors. Their rare killing is limited to the slaying of other vampires in self-defense.

Technological advances introduced into vampire lore led some writers to the abandonment of victims by having the vampire consume a manufactured blood substitute. This idea was originally introduced by **Vampirella** soon after her appearance on Earth in 1969. It would then be picked up by the half-vampire **Blade the Vampire Slayer** and was featured in the three Blade movies. It then come to the fore in the books of **Charlaine Harris**, who allowed her vampires to mainstream by agreeing to consume a blood substitute called True Blood. The television series *True Blood* popularized the drink, and a commercial substitute (made of blood oranges), was subsequently placed on the market. This idea has caught on with a number of other vampire authors such as Brian

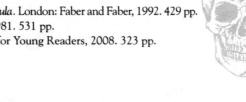

Meehl, whose vampire Morning McCobb is a vegetarian who drinks only a soy blood-substitute called Blood Lite.

Sources:

Frayling, Christopher. *Vampyres: Lord Byron to Count Dracula*. London: Faber and Faber, 1992. 429 pp.

McCammon, Robert. *They Thirst*. New York: Avon, 1981. 531 pp.

Meehl, Brian. *Suck It Up*. New York: Delacorte Books for Young Readers, 2008. 323 pp.

Vircolac *see:* Romania, Vampires in

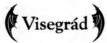
Visegrád

Visegrád (high fortress), the site of the summer palace complex of the Hungarian kings, became home to **Dracula** for over a decade (and possibly the most stable period of his life) following his arrest in 1463. The year previously, **Vlad the Impaler**, the historical Dracula, had fought a losing war against the Turks. Driven from his capital at **Tirgoviste**, he fled to his castle on the Arges River. Pursued, he escaped through the mountains into **Transylvania**, hoping to gain the support of Matthias Corvinus, the Hungarian king. Instead, he was arrested and taken to **Hungary**. Although Matthias's father, John Hunyadi, had killed Vlad's father, **Vlad Dracul**, Vlad the Impaler could have had some hope in Matthias, the first Hungarian king of Romanian extraction.

Matthias journeyed to Transylvania in the fall of 1462. He seemed inclined to support Dracula, but once the Turks had defeated him and withdrawn, he found it convenient to accept at face value a letter, most likely forged by Dracula's enemies in Brasov, in which Vlad pledged his support to the Turks in overthrowing Matthias. Thus, once in Transylvania, Vlad was arrested and carried back to Hungary by Matthias. He was imprisoned, according to an account written by Kuritsyn, the Russian ambassador, for the next 12 years. Visegrád had been founded in 1323 by Charles Robert Angevin, who as king of Hungary moved his court there. Matthias refurbished it in elaborate style and turned it into a showplace, the center of the Hungarian Renaissance. The complex included a fortress on top of a mountain overlooking a bend in the Danube some 30 miles north of Budapest. The palace was located near the river's edge at the foot of the mountain. Political prisoners commonly resided at Solomon's Tower, about half a mile downriver from the palace. Dracula most likely was placed under house arrest and treated more like a guest than a prisoner. He might have been confined for a while at the fortress at Vác, near Budapest, but during most of the 1460s he probably moved seasonally between Budapest and Visegrád. His name was not included on the register of names of prisoners kept at Solomon's Tower. It was during his years in Hungary that the famous portrait now in an Austrian museum was painted. It was also during these years that many of the stories about Dracula were written and circulated throughout Europe.

Dracula's situation eased considerably in the 1470s. His imprisonment ended, he formally converted to Roman Catholicism, he married a relative of the king, and he settled in Budapest to raise a family. Eventually, Matthias backed him in his drive to return to the Wallachian throne. He finally left Hungary in the fall of 1475 to assist in Matthias's latest campaign against the Turks, after which he finally, if briefly, became the

Vlad the Impaler lived at this palace at Visegrád for many years.

prince of Wallachia again. Today, Viségrad is a popular tourist attraction, especially the mountaintop castle. Matthias's Palace is under restoration and Solomon's Tower now functions as a museum. The first document mentioning Visegrád, written in Latin, is dated to 1009. In 2009, the town celebrated its one thousandth anniversary.

Sources:

Florescu, Radu, and Raymond T. McNally. *Dracula: A Biography of Vlad the Impaler, 1413–1476.* New York: Hawthorn Books, 1973. 239 pp.

———. *Dracula: Prince of Many Faces: His Life and Times.* Boston: Little, Brown, 1989. 261 pp.

Hejj, Miklos. *The Royal Palace of Visegrad.* Budapest: Corvina, 1977.

Treptow, Kurt W., ed. *Dracula: Essays on the Life and Times of Vlad Tepes.* New York: Columbia University Press, 1991. 336 pp.

Vision

According to **Abraham Van Helsing,** the voice of authority on vampires in ***Dracula*** **(1897),** the vampire can see in the dark. Although this is not mentioned in the folk literature, it was a logical conclusion because vampires were nocturnal creatures who moved about freely in the darkness of the evening hours. Some of the vampire's attributes were derived from its association with the bat. **Bats**, for instance, have a radar system that makes them extremely well-adapted night creatures. Dracula was pictured as regularly leaving his castle each evening to feed and return with food for his vampire **brides**. He also used his acute sight in his attacks on **Lucy Westenra** and **Mina Murray**. Modern vampire writers have cited night vision as one of the positive **characteristics** of the vampiric existence, frequently mentioned as allowing vampires to feel natural and at home in the nocturnal world. Night vision counterbalanced the blinding effect of direct **sunlight**.

Vjesci

Vjesci (alternatively spelled *vjeszczi* or *vjescey*) was the name given to a type of vampire found in the lore of the Kashubian people of northeastern **Poland**. It was a variety of the **Slavic vampire**, and resembled the *Nachtzeher* found to the west in northern **Germany**. According to the mythology, a person destined to become a *vjesci* could be identified by a caul, a little membrane cap, on his head at the time of birth. When a child was born with such a cap, it was removed, dried, ground, and fed to the person on the occasion of his seventh birthday. Those actions would prevent the child from becoming a vampire. In other respects the potential *vjesci* appeared to be completely normal and grew up in the community undetected, although in some accounts the *vjesci* had a restless and easily excitable nature and a ruddy complexion. At the time of his death, he refused to take the sacrament. His body cooled very slowly, the limbs remained limber, and the lips and cheeks retained their redness. Spots of **blood** often appeared under his **fingernails** and on his face.

The *vjesci* did not really die, however. Rather, at midnight, after his burial, he awakened and ate his clothing and some of his own flesh. He then left the grave and attacked his family, sucking their blood to the point of death. Not satiated, he could also attack his neighbors. Several steps could be taken to protect oneself from a *vjesci* loose in the community. First, dying people should receive the Eucharist. A little earth was placed in the **coffin** under the body to prevent it from returning home. A **crucifix** or coin was placed under the tongue for the vampire to suck. A net might be placed in the coffin, with the understanding that the knots must be untied (a knot a year) before the vampire could arise. A bag of sand or **seeds** could be used in much the same manner. The body might be laid in the coffin face down so that the corpse, if it came to life, would merely dig itself further into the earth. When a *vjesci* was disinterred it might be found sitting in the coffin with open eyes, it might move its head and even make some noises. Its shirt might have been eaten. If the precautions at the time of burial had not stopped the vampire, either a nail was driven through the forehead or the head severed from the body and placed between its feet. Some of the blood that flowed from the new wound would be caught and given to any who had been attacked by the vampire. The *vjesci* was closely related to the *wupji* (or *opji*). They differed in that the *wupji* had two teeth rather than a caul at birth and was foreordained to become a vampire, with no possibility of altering its destiny. In working among the Kashubian immigrant community of Ontario, Canada, researcher Jan Perkowski often found that the terms *vjesci* and *wupji* were used interchangeably.

Sources:

Perkowski, Jan L. *Vampires, Dwarves, and Witches among the Ontario Kashubs*. Ottawa: National Museum of Canada, National Museum of Man, Canadian Centre for Folkloric Studies, 1972. Reprinted in Jan L. Perkowski, ed., *Vampires of the Slavs*. Cambridge, MA: Slavica Publishers, 1976. 294 pp.

Vjeshtitza *see:* Southern Slavs, Vampires and the

Vlad

Vlad (a.k.a. Scott Vladimir Licina) is a rock musician and during the 1990s led the Dark Theater, a rock band based in Chicago. He claimed to be an indirect descendant of **Vlad the Impaler** by way of a young woman Vlad had raped. Vlad also claims to have been born, for the first time, in the year 1431. He believes that the soul is passed from body to body after death and that it is possible, through the act of **blood**-drinking, to retain memories and **characteristics** from one lifetime to another.

Vlad drinks blood regularly (but not daily), an act he began as a child. He drank his first blood, that of a wounded playmate, when he was six. Whenever he got into fights as a kid, he bit and drank some of the blood of the person he was fighting. Later, he was able to find women who agreed to his extracting and drinking some of their blood. He consumes a diet consisting primarily of rare beef.

At an early age, Vlad was trained as a symphonic musician. He originally played the horns, but was lured into rock as a teenager. He began to play the electric guitar and in the early 1980s began playing with several Chicago-area heavy-metal bands. As early as 1983 he laid plans for his own band and wrote the lyrics of what would become its first songs. Then in 1988 he founded the Dark Theater, for which he writes the lyrics and **music** and does the arranging. He developed a stage setting designed around traditional stage masks, with a notable addition—a set of vampire **fangs**. The original Dark Theater was actually a performance art group and consisted of two members, Vlad and Adservo Magus. Magus was replaced by a live band in 1989, and with the addition of drummer Brad Swinford in 1990 the group was ready to record its first album, *Matters of Life and Undeath*. Keyboardist Krimm B. joined the group during the recording sessions for the disc. Two videos, *Vampire's Dance* and *In the Shell* soon followed. The Dark Theater followed up the album with *Kaliedoscope Whirls* in 1992 and *TDT* in 1993.

Vlad and his wife, Lynda, who replaced Krimm B. on keyboards in 1992, founded and head Screem Jams Productions, a marketing and promotion company. Screem Jams promotes several up-and-coming artists, musicians, and writers as well as the Dark Theater's appearances around the country. In 1991, Screem in the Dark, the band's fan club, was launched. The club publishes a quarterly fanzine, *Screem in the Dark*, which features vampire fiction, reviews, art, and updates on the Dark Theater. Screem Jams also merchandises a variety of Dark Theater products, CDs, cassettes, videos, clothing, and posters and has sponsored the Vampire Circus events, multimedia extravaganzas featuring vampire oriented entertainment. Screem Jams may be contacted through their Internet site, http://www.screemjams.com/.

In the mid-1990s, Vlad became associated with the newly formed **Chaos! Comics** which had developed a new vampire character, Purgatori. In 1996, Chaos gave Purgatori her own **comic book** miniseries, and Vlad composed a CD inspired by the series, *Purgatori: the Vampire Myth*, which appeared in 1997. Similarly he composed a score inspired by **Ray Garton**'s novel, *Live Girls*, a graphic version of which Chaos put into production, though the company failed before it appeared. In the meantime, Vlad had become friends with Fauve, a graphic artist working with Brainstorm Comics, and in 1998 was brought into the story line of *Bethany the Vampfire*, Fauve's comic series for Brainstorm. Vlad went on to become a popular performer at Vampire-related events and in the centennial year of 1997 appeared at the Dracula event staged by the Whitby Dracula Xocity in **Whitby**, England, and at *Vampira*, the centennial event in **London**. He was the featured musical guest the **Dracula '97: A Centennial Celebration** held in Los Angeles, August 14 to 17, 1997. Meanwhile in the new century, his interest in comics came to the fore and he landed at *Fangoria Magazine* as the editor of a new line of horror comics, and the ringmaster of a new blog site "File Under Comic Killers," for the Internet comic news site, http://www.newsarama.com/.

Sources:

Pickler, Laureen. "Vampires Fly High on Eve of Halloween." *The Wall Street Journal*, October 30, 1992, p. 1.

Screem in the Dark. No. 1. Chicago: Screem Jams Productions, 1991.

❰ Vlad Dracul (1390?–1447) ❱

Vlad Dracul was the father of **Vlad the Impaler** (1431–1476), the person who has been identified as the historical Dracula. He was the illegitimate son of Prince Mircea, the ruler of Wallachia, that area of present-day **Romania** south of the Carpathian Mountains. His mother might have been Princess Mara of the Tomaj family of **Hungary**. He possibly spent a period of his youth at the court of Sigismund I of Luxembourg, the king of Hungary, as a token of faithfulness of Mircea's alliance with Sigismund. Thus, Vlad might have grown up in Buda and in locations in **Germany**. He married and had a son, also named Mircea. In 1430 Vlad appeared in **Transylvania** as an official in charge of securing the Transylvanian border with Wallachia. He resided in **Sighisoara**, where toward the end of the year his second son, Vlad (later called Vlad the Impaler), was born. Shortly after the child's birth, it became known that Sigismund had selected Vlad as his candidate to rule Wallachia. Vlad was invited to Nüremberg to be invested by the Order of the Dragon (Sigismund had founded the order in 1418), which had a variety of goals, among them to fight Islam. Now bearing the title of prince of Wallachia, he was unable to secure the throne. He eventually created a powerful alliance by marrying Eupraxia, the sister of the ruler of Moldavia, as a second wife. In 1436 he was finally able to secure the Wallachian throne, and in the winter of 1436–37 he moved to **Tirgoviste**, the Wallachian capital. He had three other children: Radu, another son also named Vlad (commonly referred to as Vlad the Monk), and another son named Mircea.

In 1437, following the death of Sigismund, Vlad Dracul signed an alliance with the Turks. In March 1442 he allowed Mezid-Bey to pass through Wallachia and attack

Transylvania. However, the Turkish army was defeated and the Hungarian army pursued Mezid-Bey back through Wallachia and drove Vlad Dracul from the throne in the process. He took refuge among the Turks, with whose help he regained the throne the following year. To secure the new relationship, Vlad Dracul left two sons, Vlad and Radu, in Turkish hands. Then, in 1444, Hungary moved against the Turks. Vlad Dracul, attempting to keep his pledge to the sultan but also aware of his obligations to the Christian community, sent a small contingent to assist the Hungarian forces. They met with a resounding defeat, which Vlad Dracul and his son Mircea blamed on John Hunyadi, the governor of Hungary. In 1447 Hunyadi led a war against Vlad. The decisive battle was fought near Tirgoviste, and as a result Vlad was killed and Mircea captured by the Romanian boyars (the ruling elite) and tortured and killed. The year after Vlad Dracul's death, his son Vlad Dracula ("son of Dracul") attempted to assume his throne. He was unable to do so until 1456. Soon after becoming prince of Wallachia, he avenged the death of his father and brother.

Sources:

Florescu, Radu, and Raymond T. McNally. *Dracula: A Biography of Vlad the Impaler, 1413–1476.* New York: Hawthorn Books, 1973. 239 pp.

———. *Dracula: Prince of Many Faces: His Life and Times.* Boston: Little, Brown, 1989. 261 pp.

McNally, Raymond T., and Radu Florescu. *In Search of Dracula.* 1972. Rept. New York: Warner Paperback Library, 1973. 247 pp.

Treptow, Kurt W., ed. *Dracula: Essays on the Life and Times of Vlad Tepes.* New York: Columbia University Press, 1991. 336 pp.

Trow, M. J. *Vlad the Impaler: In Search of Dracula.* Thrupp, Shroud, Gloucs., UK: Sutton Publishing, 2003. 280 pp.

❧ Vlad the Impaler (1431–1476) ❧

Vlad the Impaler was a historical figure upon whom **Bram Stoker** partially built the title character of his novel *Dracula* **(1897)**. Stoker indicated his knowledge of Vlad through the words of Dr. **Abraham Van Helsing:**

> He (**Dracula**) must, indeed, have been that Voivode Dracula who won his name against the Turk, over the great rivers on the very frontier of Turkeyland. If that be so, then was he no common man; for in that time, and for centuries after, he was spoken of as the cleverest and most cunning, as well as the bravest of the sons of the "land beyond the forest." That mighty brain and that iron resolution went with him to the grave, and are even now arrayed against us. The Draculas were, says Arminius, a great and noble race, though now and again were scions who were held by their coevals to have had dealings with the Evil One. They learned his secrets in the **Scholomance**, amongst the mountains over Lake Hermanstadt, where the devil claims the tenth scholar as his due. In the records are such words as "Stregoica"—witch; "ordog" and pokol"—**Satan** and hell; and in one manuscript this very Dracula is spoken of as "wampyr," which we all understand too well.

Here Stoker combined possible references to the historical Vlad, a folklore tradition that saw vampirism as rooted in Satan's actions, and the modern term vampire.

Recent interest in Dracula has produced among some researchers a desire to know more about the historical figure behind the fictional character. An important breakthrough came in 1972 with the publication of *In Search of Dracula*, the initial findings of historians **Raymond T. McNally** and **Radu Florescu**, who gathered the basic contemporary documents concerning the Romanian prince Vlad and visited Vlad's former territory to investigate his career. The following year, the even more definitive *Dracula: A Biography of Vlad the Impaler, 1431–1476* also by McNally and Florescu, appeared. Even though there had been earlier material drawing the connection between Vlad and Dracula, these books made the career of this obscure Romanian ruler, who actually exercised authority for only a relatively short period of time, an integral part of the modern Dracula myth.

The name Dracula was applied to Vlad during his lifetime. It was derived from "dracul," a Romanian word that can be interpreted variously as "devil" or "dragon." Vlad's father had joined the Order of the Dragon, a Christian brotherhood dedicated to fighting the Turks, in 1431, shortly after Vlad's birth. The oath of the order required, among other things, wearing the order's insignia at all times. The name Dracula means son of Dracul or son of the dragon or devil.

A statue of Vlad the Impaler stands in Trigoviste, Romania.

The actual birth date of Vlad, later called Vlad the Impaler, is unknown, but was probably late in 1430. He was born in Schassburg (a.k.a. **Sighisoara**), a town in **Transylvania**. Soon after his birth, in February 1431, his father, also named Vlad (**Vlad Dracul**), traveled to Nuremberg, **Germany**, where he was invested with the insignia of the Order of the Dragon. The accompanying oath dedicated the family to the fight against the Turks, who had begun an attack upon Europe that would eventually carry them to the very gates of Vienna. Vlad was a claimant to the throne of Wallachia, that part of contemporary **Romania** south of the Transylvanian Alps. He was able to wrest the throne from his half-brother in 1436.

Two years later, **Vlad Dracul** entered an alliance with the Turks that called for sending two sons, Mircea and Vlad, with the sultan on a raid into Transylvania. Doubting Vlad Dracul's loyalty, the sultan had him brought before him and imprisoned. Dracul nevertheless reaffirmed his loyalty and had Vlad (Dracul had two sons named Vlad, born to different mothers) and Radu, his younger sons, remain with the sultan to guarantee their pact. They were placed under house arrest at Egrigoz. The period of imprisonment deeply affected Vlad. On the one hand, he took the opportunity of his confinement to learn the Turkish language and customs. But his treatment ingrained the cynicism so evident in his approach to life and infused in him a Machiavellian attitude toward political matters. His early experiences also seem to have set within his personality the desire to seek revenge from anyone who wronged him.

In December 1447 his father was murdered and his older brother burned alive under the orders of Hungarian governor John Hunyadi (a.k.a. Ioande Hunedoara), with the assistance of the boyars, the ruling elite families of Wallachia. The death of Mircea made Vlad the successor, but with Hunyadi's backing, Vladislav II, a member of another branch of the family, assumed the Wallachian throne. Vlad tried to claim the throne in 1448, but his reign lasted only a couple of months before he was forced to flee to the neighboring kingdom of Moldavia. In 1451, while he was at Suceava, the Moldavian capital, the ruler was assassinated. For whatever reasons, Vlad then went to Transylvania and placed himself at the mercy of Hunyadi, the very person who had ordered his father's assassination. The alliance between Hunyadi and Vlad may have been made possible by Vladislav II's adoption of a pro-Turkish policy which alienated Hunyadi. Vlad fought beside Hunyadi, who in the end acknowledged Vlad's claim to the Wallachian throne. Hunyadi died of the plague at Belgrade on August 11, 1456. Immediately after that event, Vlad left Transylvania for Wallachia. He defeated Vladislav II and on August 20 caught up with the fleeing prince and killed him. Vlad then began his six-year reign, during which his reputation was established. In September he took both a formal oath to Hungarian King Ladislaus V and, a few days later, an oath of vassalage to the Turkish sultan.

Early in his reign, probably in the spring of 1459, Vlad committed his first major act of revenge. On Easter Sunday, after a day of feasting, he arrested the boyar families, whom he held responsible for the death of his father and brother. The older ones he simply impaled outside the palace and the city walls. He forced the rest to march from the capital city of **Tirgoviste** to the town of Poenari, where over the summer, in the most humiliating of circumstances, they were forced to build his new outpost overlooking the Arges River. This chateau would later be identified as **Castle Dracula**. Vlad's actions in **destroying** the power of the boyars was part of his policy of creating a modern, centralized state in what is today Romania. He turned over the estates and positions of the deceased boyars to people who owed their loyalty only to him.

Vlad's brutal manner of terrorizing his enemies and the seemingly arbitrary manner in which he had people punished earned him the nickname "Tepes" or "the Impaler," the common name by which he is known today. He not only used the **stake** against the boyars, whom he was trying to bring into subservience, he also terrorized the churches, both the Orthodox and the Roman Catholic, each of which had strength in his territory. He gave particular attention to the Roman Catholic monastic centers, which he saw as points of unwelcome foreign influence. His "Romania for the Romanians" policies also led to actions against foreign merchants, especially the Germans, whom he saw as preventing the development of Romanian industry. Vlad the Impaler used his position to enforce his personal moral code of honesty and sexual morality, and various stories have survived of his killing people who offended his sense of moral value. He also would, on occasion, retaliate against an entire village because of the actions of one person.

Vlad also used terrorist tactics against his foreign enemies. When he thought that merchants from Transylvania had ignored his trade laws, he led raids across the border in 1457 and again in 1459 and 1460 and used impalement to impose his will. During the latter incursion he looted the Church of Saint Bartholemew, burned a section of Brasov, and impaled numerous people. That raid was later pictured in anti-Dracula prints show-

ing him dining among the impaled bodies. During his reign, Vlad moved to the village of Bucharest and built it into an important fortified city with strong outer walls. Seeing the mountains as protective bulwarks, Vlad built his castle in the foothills of the Transylvania Alps. Later, feeling more secure and wishing to take control of the potentially wealthy plains to the south, he built up Bucharest.

Vlad was denounced by his contemporaries, and those in the next several generations who wrote of him published numerous tales of his cruelty. He was noted for the number of **victims**, conservatively set at 40,000, in his brief six-year reign. He thus became responsible for the largest number of deaths by a single ruler until modern times. **Ivan the Terrible**, with whom he has been frequently compared, put fewer than 10,000 to death. Furthermore, Vlad the Impaler ruled over fewer than half-a-million people. Above and beyond the number who died as a result of his policies, as McNally and Florescu have noted, Vlad refined the use of methods of torture and death to a degree that shocked his contemporaries. He not only impaled people in various ways but also often executed his victims in a manner related to the crime for which they were being punished.

Vlad the Impaler enjoys a feast while his victims suffer in this illustration.

The beginning of the end of his brief reign can be traced to the last months of 1461. For reasons not altogether clear, Vlad launched a campaign to drive the Turks from the Danube River valley south and east of Bucharest. In spite of early successes, when the Turks finally mounted a response, Vlad found himself without allies and was forced to retreat in the face of overwhelming numbers. The Turkish assault was slowed on two occasions. First, on June 17, several hours after sunset, Dracula attacked the Turkish camp in an attempt to capture the sultan. Unfortunately, he was directed to the wrong tent, and while many Turks were slain in the attack, the sultan got away. Unable to follow up on his momentary victory, Vlad was soon on the retreat again. When the sultan reached the capital city of Tirgoviste, he found that Dracula had impaled several people outside the town, a fact that impressed the sultan and gave him pause to consider his course of action. He decided to return to Adrianople (now Edirne) and left the next phase of the battle to Vlad's younger brother Radu, now the Turkish favorite for the Wallachian throne. Radu, at the head of a Turkish army and joined by Vlad's Romanian detractors, pursued him to his castle on the Arges River. At Castle Dracula he was faced with overwhelming odds, his army having melted away. He chose to survive by escaping through a secret tunnel and then over the Carpathians into Transylvania. His wife (or mistress), according to local legend, committed **suicide** before the Turks overran the castle. In Transylvania he presented himself to the new king of Hungary, Matthias Corvinus, who arrested him. At this time the first publications of stories of Vlad's cruelties were circulating through Europe.

Vlad the Impaler's supposed burial site at the Snagov Monestary.

Vlad was imprisoned at the Hungarian capital at **Visegrád**, although it seems he lived under somewhat comfortable conditions after 1466. By 1475 events had shifted to the point that he emerged as the best candidate to retake the Wallachian throne. In the summer of 1475 he was again recognized as the prince of Wallachia. Soon thereafter he moved with an army to fight in Serbia, and upon his return he took up the battle against the Turks with the king of Moldavia. He was never secure on his throne. Many Wallachians allied themselves with the Turks against him. His end came at the hand of an assassin at some point toward the end of December 1476 or early January 1477. The actual location of Vlad's burial site is unknown, but a likely spot is the church at the Snagov monastery, an isolated rural monastery built on an island. Excavations there have proved inconclusive. A tomb near the altar thought by many to be Vlad's resting place was empty when opened in the early 1930s. A second tomb near the door, however, contained a body richly garbed and buried with a crown.

Knowledge of the historical Dracula has had a marked influence on both Dracula movies and fiction. Two of the more important Dracula movies, *Dracula* **(1974)**, starring **Jack Palance**, and *Bram Stoker's Dracula*, the 1992 production directed by **Francis Ford Coppola**, attempted to integrate the historical research on Vlad the Impaler into the story and used it as a rationale to make Dracula's actions more comprehensible.

Several movies have been made about Vlad, from semi-documentaries to historical drama. **Christopher Lee** portrayed Vlad in the 1975 Swedish documentary, *Vem var Dracula?*, released in the English speaking world as *In Search of Dracula*, not to be confused with two more recent American productions *In Search of Dracula with Jonathan Ross* (1996) and *In Search of History: The Real Dracula* (2000). They have been joined by *The Impaler: A Biographical/Historical Look at the Life of Vlad the Impaler, Widely Known as Dracula* (2002).

Even as Vlad's fame has risen, Dracula scholars have begun to downplay the roll of Vlad in informing Stoker while writing his novel. It appears that he knew little more than that Vlad existed and his name/title which was put on the novel after it was completed. Scholars were especially scornful of the 2000 biographical drama *Dark Prince: The True Story of Dracula* (2000), not so much for the acting, but for the scripts departure from the facts of Vlad's life. The 2003 film simply titled *Vlad*, was, of course, intended as nothing more than a fictional tale that included the historical Vlad as a character.

Sources:

Florescu, Radu, and Raymond T. McNally. *Dracula: A Biography of Vlad the Impaler, 1413–1476*. New York: Hawthorn Books, 1973. 239 pp.

———. *Dracula: Prince of Many Faces: His Life and Times*. Boston: Little, Brown, 1989. 261 pp.

Giurescu, Constantin C. *The Life and Deeds of Vlad the Impaler: Dracula*. New York: Romanian Library, 1969.

Goldberg, Enid, and Norman Itzkowitz. *Vlad the Impaler: The Real Count Dracula*. Franklin Watts: New York, 2007. 128 pp.

McNally, Raymond T., and Radu Florescu. *In Search of Dracula*. 1972. Rept. New York: Warner Paperback Library, 1973. 247 pp.

Treptow, Kurt W., ed. *Dracula: Essays on the Life and Times of Vlad Tepes*. New York: Columbia University Press, 1991. 336 pp.

Trow, M. J. *Vlad the Impaler: In Search of Dracula*. Thrupp, Shroud, Gloucs., UK: Sutton Publishing, 2003. 280 pp.

❦ Voices of the Vampire Community ❦

Founded in 2006, Voices of the Vampire Community (VVC) is a loose association of groups of self-identified vampires that seeks to promote cordial relationships among the varied vampire groups (variously described as houses, covens, orders, etc). VVC encourages cooperative problem solving by the community through the promoting of respect for others in spite of differing views and approaches.

VVC has held multiple gatherings that brought together more than a dozen vampire groups like the **Atlanta Vampire Alliance** and **Michelle Beranger**'s House Kheperu to discuss issues in the Vampire community. Prominent issues include responding to media requests for information, correcting false stereotypes in print and the Internet, and dealing with people believed to be intentionally spread false information about the community. They also attempt to answer questions put to it by inquirers, especially youthful one.

VVC is part of an emerging semi-public aspect of the vampire community as it emerged in the 1990s. It has an Internet site at http://www.veritasvosliberabit.com/vvc

.html. They have made brief videos answering questions about vampirism and posted them on YouTube.

Sources:

Laycock, Joseph. *Vampires Today: The Truth about Modern Vampirism*. Westport. CT: Praeger, 2009. 200 pp.

Voices of the Vampire Community. http://www.veritasvosliberabit.com/vvc.html. Accessed on April 12, 2010.

Vrykolakas *see:* Greece, Vampires in

Vukodlak *see:* Southern Slavs, Vampires and the

Vurvulak *see:* Southern Slavs, Vampires and the

Ward, J. R.

J. R. Ward is the penname used by Jessica Rowley Pell Bird, a successful lawyer, hospital administrator, and writer of a popular vampire romance series of novels about what she calls "The Black Dagger Brotherhood". Ward attended Smith College, majoring in medieval history and art history. She obtained her JD from Albany (New York) Law School, and subsequently worked for a number of years at Beth Israel Deaconness Medical Center in Boston, Massachusetts. She had been writing, primarily for her own enjoyment, for many years, but after she married in 2001, her husband encouraged her to seek publication. Her first book, *Leaping Hearts*, a romance novel written under her family name was published in 2002.

Several years later, under the penname J. R. Ward, she created a fantasy world populated by six warrior vampire brothers (Wrath, Rhage, Zsadist, Phury, Vishous, and Tohrment), and their allies who live together as The Black Dagger Brotherhood. The brotherhood's task is to defend their race against the soulless humans who constitute the Lessening Society, enemies of the vampire race.

The brotherhood members look for guidance and inspiration from the Scribe Virgin, experienced as a mystical force, and known to be the creator of the vampires. She is venerated as a deity. In Ward's mythology, the Scribe Virgin has a brother called the Omega. Unable to create, he became jealous of his sister and targeted her creations for extinction. He is the acknowledged deity of the Lessening Society. The Omega has many powers, and like his sister, exists in a noncorporal realm.

Ward's novels about the vampires tell the story of one of the brothers, or one of their allies, such as Butch, or Dhestroyer, the only human within the Brotherhood. Each book highlights the protagonist's fight with the Lessers and his path to true love.

The first of the Black Dagger Brotherhood series appeared in 2005 under the title *Dark Lover*. Seven volumes in all had appeared by 2009, with others already in various stages of production. In addition, Ward wrote *The Black Dagger Brotherhood: An Insider's Guide*, a book with explanatory material about her mythological world. Among the several awards for her very popular series, *Romantic Times* gave Ward the Reviewer's Choice Award for *Lover Awakened*. Ward maintains a webpage at http://www.jrward.com/.

Sources:

Ward, J. R. *Lover Eternal*. New York: Signet, 2005. 464 pp.

———. *Dark Lover*. New York: Signet, 2005. 416 pp.

———. *Lover Awakened*. New York: Signet Eclipse, 2006. 448 pp.

———. *Lover Revealed*. New York: Signet, 2007.

———. *Lover Unbound*. New York: Signet, 2007. 509 pp.

———. *Lover Enshrined*. New York: Signet, 2008. 560 pp.

———. *The Black Dagger Brotherhood: An Insider's Guide*. New York: New American Library, 2008. 496 pp.

———. *Lover Avenged*. New York: Signet, 2009. 544 pp.

Water

According to **Abraham Van Helsing**, the vampire expert in *Dracula*, a vampire could only move over running water at the slack or flood of the tide. As with many other **characteristics**, this was somewhat unique to **Dracula**. Though a characteristic of the Chinese *chiang-shih*, problems with running water were not in the folkloric accounts from Eastern Europe and, given the geographical limitations on most vampires, not relevant. As a whole, since *Dracula*, such observations have disappeared from the literature, as vampires move about freely without noticing the presence of various bodies of water. The primary exception was in the vampire novels of **Chelsea Quinn Yarbro**, whose vampire hero **Saint-Germain** had trouble passing over running water. He countered this by developing shoes with hollow soles into which he placed some of his **native soil**. He drew **strength** from the soil.

Some folkloric vampires, of course, had special relationships to water. For example, in **Russia** the corpse of a suspected vampire might be thrown in the river in the belief that the earth could not tolerate the presence of a vampire or revenant. In **Germany**, the body of a person who committed **suicide** (a potential vampire) was treated similarly. Also in parts of Germany, water might be poured on the road between the grave where a suspected vampire had been buried and his home, as a barrier to prevent his return. In Prussia, the *leichenwasser*, the water used to wash a corpse, was saved and used in this manner.

A possible source of Van Helsing's remarks was a story from **Greece** recounted in Rennell Rodd's study of Greek folklore published in London in 1892 (and quoted by **Montague Summers**). He told of a legend that the island of Therasia, in the Santorini group, was infested with vampires. They had been banished to that island because of the prayers and exorcisms of a pious bishop on the island of Hydra, where they had previously been located.

Importantly, he noted that according to the legend anyone venturing near the shore of Therasia would hear the noise of the vampires who walked along the shore in an agitated state because they could not cross salt water.

Purification: Apart from its appearance in lakes, rivers and oceans, water was of course a cleansing and purifying agent. Like **fire**, it had taken on a number of sacred and mythological connotations. It was regularly used in religious initiatory rituals such as baptism and in ablution rituals such as the bathing that occurred before a Muslim prayed in the mosque.

Within **Christianity** in Europe, in the Roman Catholic Church and the Eastern Orthodox churches, practices had developed around blessed water, generally referred to as "holy water," that gave the substance a number of superstitious/magical meanings and uses. Originally considered of symbolic cleansing value, it came to be seen as having an inherent sacred quality because it had been consecrated for religious use. Holy water was used in the funeral services of both churches and thus often was present when the bodies of suspected vampires were exhumed and killed a second time.

Holy water as such did not appear in *Dracula*, although the **crucifix** and the **eucharistic wafer** did. However, in a natural extension of these two sacred objects that were so effective against vampires, holy water later became part of the assumed weapons in the vampire kits.

Periodically, holy water was used against vampires in motion pictures and twentieth-century vampire novels. Its effect was similar to throwing acid on a normal human. It burned and scarred, though it usually was not fatal since it was present only in small quantities. Holy water assumed a most unusual property in the movie version of **Stephen King**'s novel *Salem's Lot*, in which, by glowing, it signaled the approach of the vampires.

Sources:

Barber, Paul. *Vampires, Burial, and Death.: Folklore and Reality.* New Haven, CT: Yale University Press, 1988. 236 pp.

Rodd, Rennell. *The Customs and Lore of Modern Greece.* London: David Scott, 1892. 294 pp.

Summers, Montague. *The Vampire in Europe.* London: Routledge and Kegan Paul, 1929. 329 pp. Rept. New Hyde Park, NY: University Books, 1961. 329 pp.

Weather

According to Vampire expert **Abraham Van Helsing**, in *Dracula*, vampires could affect the weather, within limits. **Dracula** most clearly demonstrated his powers in the fog and storm accompanying the movement of the *Demeter*, the ship that brought him to England. This element in vampire mythology was not present in the folkloric tradition. There, the vampire was seen in a much narrower perspective and was not assigned any powers to affect the weather. There was a tradition reported by Dimitrij Zelenin that the earth itself reacted to the burying of "unclean" bodies (such as potential vampires), not only by refusing to accept the body, but bringing bad weather, specifically cold and frost in the spring.

Just as the folkloric vampire could not change the weather, so the literary vampire both before and after Dracula possessed little ability in that direction. Apart from the weather accompanying the *Demeter* in the various *Dracula* movies, vampires have exercised little power in relation to weather, though weather frequently has had a significant role in novels and motion pictures to set atmosphere.

In **Stephenie Meyer**'s novel, *Twilight*, and movie based on the book, the vampire family look forward to the next thunderstorm so they can play baseball. Since they hit the ball with super strength, the sound of the crack of thunder covers their activity and vampiric abilities.

Sources:

Barber, Paul. *Vampires, Burial, and Death: Folklore and Reality.* New Haven, CT: Yale University Press, 1988. 236 pp.

Werewolves and Vampires

The werewolf is one of several monsters closely associated in the public mind with the vampire. That relationship was largely established in the 1930s with the production of two werewolf movies by **Universal Pictures** and the inclusion of the werewolf and the vampire together in three monster mash films during the 1940s. By definition, the werewolf is a human being who at various times (usually at the full **moon**), either voluntarily or involuntarily, changes into a wolf or wolflike creature and assumes many of the characteristics of the wolf, especially its viciousness. There is also a disease, lycanthropy, in which people believe that they change into a werewolf when in fact they do not.

Origin of the Werewolf: Like the vampire, and unlike **Frankenstein's monster**, the werewolf was an ancient figure found in the folklore of people worldwide. The oldest report of a man changing into a wolf was from ancient Greek mythology. Lycaon (hence the word *lycanthropy*) displeased Zeus and the deity changed him into a wolf. However, a number of ancient writers such as Galen and Virgil provided the first descriptions of lycanthropy. They rejected the mythology and believed that the change into **animals** was a diseased condition brought on by melancholia or drugs.

In like measure, werewolfism has been reported throughout the world, though the type of animals into which humans transform has been quite varied, including lions, tigers, jaguars, hyenas, sharks, and crocodiles—all animals that are large and known for their ferocity. Contemporary reports of lycanthropy also come from around the world, both in rural areas and in the modern West. Some contemporary cases are included in the selection of papers compiled by Richard Noll.

Werewolves and Vampires: Werewolves and vampires have been reported as existing side by side in the mythologies of many cultures, but they have a special relationship in the southern Balkan area, from where much of the modern vampire myth comes. That relationship was particularly evident in the use of the term *vrykolakas* (and cognate terms in various Slavic languages) to describe vampires in recent centuries in **Greece**. In accounts of the *vrykolakas* in southern Balkan countries, there was some confusion over the word's meaning. In the early twentieth century, pioneer researcher Freidrich Krauss, working in Bosnia, concluded that the *vrykolakas* (spelled *vukodlak* in Bosnia) was a werewolf (i.e., a man or woman who changed into a wolf and attacked the local cattle).

More recent researchers such as Harry Senn and Jan L. Perkowski have argued that the word *vrykolakas* derived from an old Slavic word that referred to the ritual wearing of wolf pelts among Slavic tribes during the first millennium C.E. Earlier, Mircea Eliade had observed that the Dacians, the people who previously resided in what is present-day **Romania** and whose name means wolf, ritually transformed their young warriors into wolves by dressing them in wolf pelts and engaging in appropriate mimicking behavior. The historian Herodotus had described such behavior among the early people of the southern Balkans. At the time the wolf was admired as a warrior animal. Senn noted that during the early centuries of the second millennium the perceived role of the wolf changed from one that was admired to one that was feared. The wolf became a threat to the community because it attacked livestock and people.

Over the first centuries of the second millennium C.E., the use of the term *vrykolakas* lost its ritual meaning (as the image of the wolf changed and the ritual itself disappeared). According to Senn, the reference point of *vrykolakas* was transferred to the vampire; throughout the southern Balkans (Romania, Serbia, Croatia, Greece, etc.), it replaced older terms for the vampire. Perkowski emphasized that there was an intermediate step in which the term took on a mythological reference to a being who chased the clouds and devoured the moon (Agnes Murgoci, working in Romania in the mid-1920s, found continued references to this meaning of *vrykolakas*). Further transition was made in the sixteenth century, by

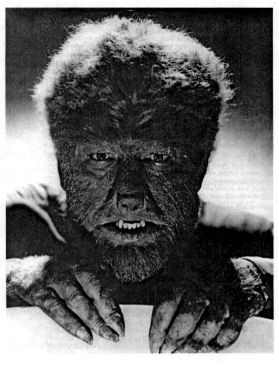

Lon Chaney, Jr. as a werewolf in *The Wolf Man.*

which time *vrykolakas* had began to refer to vampires. That meaning then spread throughout the southern Balkans and into Greece. Perkowski even has argued that the term never referred to a werewolf, as Krauss and others have suggested. Among modern Romanians there is a were-creature, the *tricolici* (or *pricolici*), a man who may take the form of a pig, a dog, or, less often, a wolf.

Belief in werewolves apparently peaked in Europe during the late Middle Ages. While many refused to believe that actual werewolves existed, many believed that lycanthropy was caused by the devil. The original witchhunters, James Sprenger and Heinrich Kramer, the authors of the 1486 volume *The Witches Hammer* that started the great witchhunts of the next two centuries, declared the **transformation** of man into wolf impossible. But they believed that witches and sorcerers could cause another person to believe that he had been transformed into a wolf. There were, however, several trials against people accused of werewolfism.

The Werewolf in Literature: The werewolf made a number of brief appearances in literature as early as the fourteenth century, but it was not until the middle of the nineteenth century that the appearance of three werewolf novels within a few years of each other injected the creature into the public consciousness. *Hughes the Wer-wolf* by Sutherland Menzies was, like **Varney the Vampyre**, published as a weekly serial over a period of time in the 1850s. Then, in 1857, *The Wolf-Leader* and George W. M. Reynold's *Wagner the Wehrwolf* (another weekly serial) were published. The latter volume usually is looked upon as the fountainhead of modern tales of the werewolf. A number of werewolf short stories and novels appeared over the next 80 years but attracted little attention until 1934, when Guy Endore's *The Werewolf of Paris* was published.

Endore had been a screenwriter in Hollywood and had worked on several horror movies, including *The Mark of the Vampire*. His book received enough acclaim that **Universal Pictures** decided to produce its cinematic version. Changing the location slightly, the first werewolf movie appeared in 1935 as *The Werewolf of London*. Endore's tale told the story of Bertrand Caillet, whose mother had been seduced by a priest, Father Pitamont. The strange child grew up and became a werewolf, a fact discovered when he was wounded by a **bullet** made of **silver**. (This old remedy derived from the belief that silver should be used when shooting at Scottish witches who had transformed into an animal form, such as a rabbit. From Endore's use, the silver bullet would become part of the conventional wisdom concerning werewolves.) As Bertrand grew, the violence caused by his wolfish nature could no longer be checked or covered up. He fled from the countryside to Paris and there enlisted in the French Army in time for the Franco-Prussian War. His nature was soon revealed, however, and he met his end following a court-martial. Endore's werewolf Bertrand was based in large part on the factual case of François Bertrand, a French noncommissioned officer who in 1848 was convicted of breaking into a number of graves in Paris. In the stories about him, Bertrand was generally referred to as a **ghoul** rather than a werewolf.

The Werewolf of London was followed by *The Wolf Man*, the title role being played by Lon Chaney, Jr., who as Larry Talbot mixed the sympathetic and horrific nature of the werewolf character. The werewolf was a man afflicted by his condition, and he fought against it fiercely, even as he attacked living beings when his wolf nature emerged.

The vampire and the werewolf seem to have been brought together on the screen for the first time in *The Return of the Vampire* (1943), the film **Bela Lugosi** made for Columbia Pictures. Universal brought the vampire (**Dracula**) and the Wolf Man together in three pictures during the 1940s: *House of Frankenstein* (1944), *House of Dracula* (1945), and *Abbott and Costello Meet Frankenstein* (1948). In the first movie Chaney sought a cure for his condition, which he finally found in the second. In the last movie, played just for fun, the Wolf Man joined the comedic team to prevent Dracula (Bela Lugosi) from transplanting Costello's brain into **Frankenstein's monster**. Other werewolf films followed, though they never gained the popularity of the vampire movies. **Hammer Films** made one werewolf picture, *The Curse of the Werewolf* (1961), directed by **Terence Fisher**, who had worked on **The Horror of Dracula** several years earlier. Hammer, unlike Universal, never attempted to bring Dracula and the werewolf together in the same story.

On **television**, the two creatures were brought together on the *Dark Shadows* series when a new character, Quentin, was introduced. As his story unfolded, he was cursed to become a werewolf, his first transformation occurring in episode 752. At first Quentin and **Barnabas Collins**, the vampire character, were enemies, and they tried to eliminate each other. However, they eventually came to an understanding that they were similarly afflicted, and they then worked together.

The next attempt to mix the two characters came in 1970 with *The Werewolf vs. Vampire Woman*, one of a series of werewolf pictures starring Paul Naschy as Count

Werewolves and vampires have often been linked in the movies. Here, a female vampire prepares to bite her victim in the film *Return of the Werewolf*.

Waldemar Daninsky (the werewolf), who was countered in this film by the vampire/witch Countess Waldessa. A vampire appeared in the fifth sequel to *Howling* (a series of werewolf movies). In *Howling VI: The Freaks* (1990), the vampire kidnapped the werewolf to serve as an attraction in his traveling freak show. A werewolf-like theme also was evident in *Dracula's Dog* (1977), a story about a vampire dog unleashed on Los Angeles.

The werewolf theme has shown continued appeal, though not to the extent of the vampire. It has been the subject of a few very fine books and movies, *Cat People* and *Wolfen* being perhaps the most notable. It has, however, never developed the popular subculture following of Dracula and his vampire kin. It began to experience a revival in paranormal romance literature in the late 1990s, but awaited the new century to begin to make a real impact.

In the first decade of the twenty-first century, the number of new werewolf novels radically increased, almost all of them in the romance genre. And, as the number of both vampire and werewolf novels increased, crossover novels invariably appeared; several writers, most notably **Laurell K. Hamilton**, created series that, while featuring either vampires or werewolves, included both in the fantasy world of their characters. Carrie Vaughn has, for example, created an appealing werewolf character, Kitty Norville,

When Lucy Westenra was attacked by Dracula, he had blood-red eyes, much like Christopher Lee has in this photo.

who regularly faces off against vampires, while Kelley Armstrong has written a set of werewolf novels in which vampires are but one of the supernatural creatures in the background. Keri Arthur has created the popular "Riley Jensen, Guardian" series whose hero is a half vampire/half werewolf, all of which provides the setting for exploring the various attributes of each identity with which Jensen must live.

Eventually, the more successful vampire romance authors like **MaryJanice Davidson** and **Charlaine Harris** will tend to introduce werewolves into their story lines. Additional romance vampire/werewolf crossover novels have also been written by Angela Knight, Emma Holly, Morgan Hawke, Patricia Briggs, Raven Hart, and Melina Morel.

Getting vampires and werewolves together romantically can be traced to the horror **comic books** of the 1950s. The relationship was approached on **television** with the werewolf Oz who was a character for several seasons on *Buffy the Vampire Slayer*, though he developed a romantic attachment to Buffy's friend and resident witch Willow, rather than a vampire. The relationship was touched upon again in the BBC series *Being Human*, which had a vampire, a werewolf, and a ghost living together, though not romantically involved.

The werewolf-vampire relationship really blossomed in the movies with the "Underworld" trilogy, originally billed as a Romeo and Juliet story of star-crossed lovers. The Lycans and the vampires are engaged in a centuries-long continual war with each other; though, as one learns through the several movies, the two are related by a common ancestry, and their current hostile relationship was manufactured for personal reasons by the evil vampire Victor.

The love triangle created between **Bella Swan** and her two would be lovers, the vampire **Edward Cullen** and the werewolf Jacob Black, serves as the major driving force of **The Twilight series** of novels by **Stephenie Meyer**. The Cullens are a family of **good guy vampires** who have a treaty with the werewolves on the adjacent Native American reservation of the Quileute tribe. The outwardly peaceful but emotionally hostile relationship between the two groups is heated up when Edward and Jacob both fall in love with Bella, and their treaty put to the test when it becomes clear that Bella is going to be killed so she can become a vampire.

Sources:

Briggs, Patricia. *Moon Called.* New York: Ace Books, 2006. 288 pp.

Cooper, Basil. *The Werewolf in Legend, Fact and Art.* New York: St. Martin's Press, 1977. 240 pp.

Cox, Greg. *Underworld.* New York: Pocket Star Books, 2003. 372 pp.

Douglas, Adam. *The Beast Within: Man, Myths and Werewolves.* London: Orion, 1993. 294 pp.

Hamilton, Laurell K. *Guilty Pleasures*. New York: Ace Books, 1993. 265 pp.

Hawke, Morgan. *Kiss of the Wolf*. New York: Aphrodisia, 2007. 304 pp.

Holly, Emma. *Catching Midnight*. New York: Berkley Sensation, 2005. 323 pp.

Jones, Stephen. *The Illustrated Vampire Movie Guide*. London: Titan Books, 1993. 144 pp.

Meyer, Stephenie. *Twilight*. Boston: Little, Brown Young Readers, 2005. 512 pp.

Morel. Molina. *Devour*. Signet Eclipse: New York, 2007. 336 pp.

Murgoci, Agnes. "The Vampire in Romania." *Folklore* 37 (1926): 320–49.

Noll, Richard. *Vampires, Werewolves, and Demons: Twentieth-Century Reports in the Psychiatric Literature*. New York: Brunner/Mazel, 1992. 243 pp.

Perkowski, Jan L. *The Darkling: A Treatise on Slavic Vampirism*. Columbus, OH: Slavica Publishers, 1989. 174 pp.

Scarm, Arthur N. *The Werewolf vs. Vampire Woman*. Beverly Hills, CA: Guild-Hartsford Publishing Co., 1972. 190 pp.

Senn, Harry A. *Werewolf and Vampire in Romania*. New York: Columbia University Press, 1982. 148 pp.

Summers, Montague. *The Werewolf*. 1933. Rept. New York: Bell Publishing Company, 1966. 307 pp.

Westenra, Lucy

Lucy Westenra, one of the major characters in **Bram Stoker**'s *Dracula*, made her initial appearance in the fifth chapter, where her correspondence with her long-time friend **Mina Murray** was recorded.

While never described physically in great detail, she obviously was an attractive young woman in her twenties, the object of the affection of three men, **Arthur Holmwood**, to whom she became engaged, Dr. **John Seward**, and **Quincey P. Morris**. In the meantime, she lived with her mother.

On July 24, Lucy met Mina at the **Whitby** station, and they retired to the home at the Crescent where they would stay for the next several weeks. On July 26, Mina noted that Lucy had begun walking in her sleep. On August 8, a sudden storm hit Whitby and the *Demeter*, the ship on which **Dracula** came to England, wrecked on shore. On August 11, at 3:00 A.M., Mina discovered Lucy had left her bed, and she went in search of her. Lucy was on the East Cliff in their favorite seat. As Mina made her way to Lucy, she saw "something, long and black, bending over her." When she called out, the something looked up and Mina saw Dracula's white face and red eyes. After she helped Lucy home, she saw two tiny marks on Lucy's neck. Over the next few days Lucy grew more and more tired and the wounds on her neck did not heal. At this juncture, Lucy seemed to get better and Mina, having finally heard from her true love **Jonathan Harker** on August 19, left for Budapest to join him.

Lucy returned to **London** where Holmwood joined her, and they set plans to marry on September 28. However, her condition worsened, and Holmwood called Seward in to examine her. Unable to figure out what was wrong, he called **Abraham Van Helsing** as a consultant, as Van Helsing knew of obscure diseases. Lucy seemed to improve, but then turned pale and lost all of her **strength**. Van Helsing prescribed a **blood** transfusion. As they were about to perform the procedure, Lucy's fiancé Holmwood arrived and the blood was taken from him. Later a second transfusion was taken from Seward and then, without giving his reason, Van Helsing surrounded Lucy with **garlic**.

Dracula returned to attack Lucy on September 17. The attack followed the removal of the garlic that Van Helsing had ordered to be put around her neck.

Morris was next in line to supply the blood needed to preserve Lucy's life, but by this time it was already too late; she was turning into a vampire. She died and was laid to rest in the family crypt. Van Helsing immediately wanted to treat the body as a vampire. Holmwood (who by this time had inherited his father's title as Lord Godalming) opposed any mutilation of the body. Though they had not married, he saw Lucy as his wife. In his opinion, the transfusion had served to marry them; they were married in the sight of God.

While the men rested, reports surfaced of missing children who, upon being found, told of being with a "boofer lady." Van Helsing persuaded the men to institute a watch at Lucy's tomb. They viewed her empty **coffin** and finally saw her walking around. In the end they cornered her in her coffin.

Holmwood assumed his responsibility and drove the **stake** through her chest. At this point, it was noted that the harsh, fiendish expression, which had characterized Lucy's appearance at the time of her death, departed, and a face of sweetness and purity returned. Van Helsing cut off her head and filled her mouth with garlic. The men then turned their attention to killing Dracula.

When *Dracula* was brought to the stage and screen, the character of Lucy was handled quite differently. She disappeared completely from **Nosferatu, Eine Symphonie des Garuens** (1922) and **Hamilton Deane**'s *Dracula* play. She returned in **John Balderston**'s revision of Deane's play for the American stage, though now she was Lucy Seward, Dr. Seward's daughter. Both she and Mina returned in the 1931 films, in both the English and Spanish versions. In 1958's **The Horror of Dracula,** Lucy was transformed into Holmwood's sister and the fiancée of Jonathan Harker. She was given strong parts in the **Jack Palance** version of *Dracula* **(1973)** and became central to the **Frank Langella**'s *Dracula* **(1979)**. She was returned to a role more closely approaching the one in the novel in **Francis Ford Coppola**'s *Bram Stoker's Dracula* (1992).

In literature, her character has made few appearances. Apparently, authors have felt that, since Lucy was killed off fairly definitively in *Dracula*, she has no real place in the vampire literature of the last century.

Whitby, a small town in northern England, was the setting for a major segment of **Bram Stoker**'s novel, *Dracula.* Whitby is located in Yorkshire at the mouth of the Esk River. Stoker provided a fairly accurate description of the town as background to the story. Dominating the town, on the east side of the river, was St. Mary's (Anglican) Church and the ruins of Whitby Abbey. The abbey dates to the seventh century. It was destroyed in the ninth century, rebuilt, and later abandoned.

As chapter 5 began **Lucy Westenra** met her friend **Mina Murray** at the train station and together they went to what has been identified as Number Four Crescent Terrace, where Mina joined the Westenra family in the rooms they had taken for a summer vacation. Stoker selected Whitby as a site for the events in his novel because he knew the town from his own visits in the years 1885 to 1890. During their first days in town, Lucy and Mina visited the local tourist spots—Mulgrave Woods, Robin Hood's Bay, Rig Mill, Runswick, and Staithes.

Meanwhile **Dracula** was aboard the *Demeter,* which was speeding north from Gibralter toward the British coast. Two weeks later, the *Demeter* was spotted off Whitby shortly before a storm hit. The ship was beached on the sand near Tate Hill Pier, one of two piers at Whitby, and Dracula (in the form of a dog) was seen leaving the ship. On board the wreck, the boxes of earth that Dracula traveled with were discovered. Dracula stayed in Whitby for a week and a half and attacked Lucy twice.

The first attack came several days after the wreck. Mina discovered that Lucy (who had a record of sleepwalking) had disappeared. Standing on the West Cliff, Mina looked across the river to where she could see St. Mary's Church and the ruins of Whitby Abbey. She saw a figure in white (Lucy) seated at what was called the "**suicide**'s seat," under which was a stone noting the death of George Canon who had committed suicide on that spot. Mina then ran to the bridge that connected the two parts of town on either side of the river.

From where Mina stood to the spot Lucy was located is almost a mile and required her walking down the cliff face on one side of the river and walking up the cliff face on the other side. As she reached the top of the steps near Whitby Abbey, she saw someone with Lucy, but he disappeared in a moment of darkness as a cloud briefly blocked the moonlight.

Several days later, Mina saw Lucy lean out of the window of her room. Beside her on the windowsill was "something that looked like a good-sized bird," which turned out to be Dracula in the form of a **bat**. By the time Mina reached Lucy's room, Dracula had completed drinking Lucy's **blood**, and Mina helped her to bed. Shortly after this second attack, Dracula, his boxes of earth, and the action of the novel moved to **London**.

Today modern tourists can visit all of the sights mentioned by Stoker in the novel, including the apartment on the Crescent where Lucy and Mina were supposed to have stayed. Bernard Davies of the **Dracula Society** has prepared a walking-tour guide. Local vampire enthusiasts have organized to meet the needs of Dracula-oriented visitors. The main event is the Whitby Gothic Weekend a bi-annual gathering for Goths, first held in 1994, continued until 1997, and a bi-annual event since. The Goth Festival occurs in April and at the end of October over Halloween weekend. Those unable to make the pilgrimage, may learn about Whitby by visiting the Dracula-in-Whitby website (http://www.dracula-in-whitby.com/index.php), where it is also possible to sign up for the free *Dracula-in-Whitby Newsletter* .

Sources:

Chapman, Paul M. *Birth of a Legend: Count Dracula, Bram Stoker, and Whitby*. York, UK: G H Smith, 2007. 268 pp.

Davies, Bernard. *Whitby Dracula Trail*. Scarborough, North Yorkshire, United Kingdom: Department of Tourism and Amenities, Scarborough Borough Council, n.d., 11 pp.

Stoker, Bram. *The Annotated Dracula*. Leonard Wolf, ed. New York: Ballantine Books, 1975. 362 pp.

———. *The Essential Dracula*. Raymond McNally and Radu Florescu, eds. New York: Mayflower, 1979. 320 pp.

❨ **William of Newburgh (1136–1198?)** ❩

William of Newburgh, twelfth-century British chronicler of vampire incidents, was born in Bridlington. As a youth he moved to a priory of Augustinian Canons at

Newburgh, Yorkshire. He became a canon and remained at Newburgh for the rest of his life. His talents were noticed by his superiors, who urged him to devote his time to his scholarly pursuits, especially literature. He emerged as a precursor of modern historical criticism and strongly denounced the inclusion of obvious myth in historical treatises.

William's magnum opus, the *Historia Rerum Anglicarum*, also known as the *Chronicles*, was completed near the end of his life. Chapters 32–34 related a number of stories of contemporary revenants, which William had collected during his adult years. These stories, such as the account of the **Alnwick Castle** vampire and the **Melrose Abbey** vampire, have been cited repeatedly as evidence of a vampire lore existing in the British Isles in ancient times. While not describing vampires as such, the stories do recount visitation by the dead, some of whom were reported to act in a manner similar to the vampires of the **Slavs** or the vampires in eastern Europe. William was careful in his reporting and was aware of the skepticism that would greet the stories even in his own day. Thus he concluded,

> It is, I am very well aware, quite true that unless they were amply supported by many examples which have taken place in our own days, and by the unimpeachable testimony of responsible persons, these facts would not easily be believed, to wit, that the bodies of the dead may arise from their tombs and that vitalized by some supernatural power, they speed hither and thither, either greatly alarming or in some cases actually slaying the living, and when they return to the grave it seems to open to them of their own accord (chapter 34).

William died at Newburgh in 1198 (or 1208).

Sources:

Glut, Donald F. *True Vampires of History.* New York: HC Publications, 1971. 191 pp.

Summers, Montague. *The Vampire in Europe.* London: Routledge and Kegan Paul, 1929. 329 pp. Rept. New Hyde Park, NY: University Books, 1961. 329 pp.

Wine

While trying to discern **Dracula's** nature, the entrapped **Jonathan Harker** remarked that his host never drank. Translated to the movie screen, this observation emerged in one of the most famous lines spoken by **Bela Lugosi** in the 1931 movie. Speaking to **R. N. Renfield** over dinner, Dracula said, "I never drink—wine." That line was spoken just after Renfield (whose character went to **Castle Dracula** instead of Harker in the movie version) had cut his finger and Dracula had shown his desire to drink of the **blood** that had appeared. The scene created a use of wine, the blood of the grape, as a metaphor for human blood.

Through the last generation, wine became a significant vampire souvenir product. In 1974, the Golden Krone Hotel opened in **Bistritz, Transylvania.** The Golden Krone was the name of the fictional hotel at which Jonathan Harker stopped on his way to Castle Dracula. At the new hotel, a modern guest may order a Mediasch wine from Medias in the Tarnave Mare district of Transylvania, upon which Harker dined while at the Golden Krone. The modern visitor can also have some "Elixir Dracula," a local red liqueur made from plums.

Around 1990, A.V.F.F.Sp.A. of Sona, **Italy**, produced a "Vampire Wine." Distributed in the United States by Louis Glunz in Lincolnwood, Illinois, it was a red wine in a black bottle with a black label and arrived in an appropriate **coffin** container. Bottles of this wine were distributed as door prizes at Coven Party II sponsored in 1991 by **Anne Rice**'s Vampire Lestat Fan Club, and today are among the rarest of vampire collectibles. In the 1990s, a "Vampire Wine" from **Romania** was made available from TriVin Imports in Mt. Vernon, Illinois. It joined the "Vampire" wine from Vampire Vineyards in Creston, California, which initially appeared in 1988 (http://www.vampire.com/) and has added a Vampire Vodka to its spectrum of fine wines.

With the emergence of a new wave of Dracula-oriented tourism in Romania, several companies have responded with new liquid souvenirs. As early as the 1970s, a **Vlad the Impaler** vodka (with a picture of Bran Castle) appeared. On the occasion of the opening of *Bram Stoker's Dracula* in Bucharest, in July 1993, for example, Stroh Transylvania produced "Dracula's Spirit", described as the "Original Vampire's Delight." It was a mixture of vodka flavored with fruits and vegetables and red food coloring. The bottle's label carried the quote, "The history has borne the sacred hero. The myth has borne a bloody vampire.

The hero and the fiend bear one name: DRACULA. We trust in DRACULA'S VODKA." A similar product has been marketed as "Dracula Seduction" and Dracula's Spriit." Liquors have joined the shelves of Dracula souvenirs beginning in 1994 with "Dracula Slivovitz," the popular plum brandy of Romania. A special boxed version of the slivovitz was created for the World Dracula Congress in 1995.

Also available are "Vlad Trica" and "Draculina Slivowitz." The **Transylvanian Society of Dracula** has also moved to develop its own wine, Count Dracula Wine, with variant titles for the different white, rose and red varieties.

Additionally, one of the society leaders in Romania began distribution of a very fine brandy as "Alucard Brandy." As of 2009, Vampire Vineyards in cooperation with TI Beverage Group, made available a spectrum of wines and vodkas (many imported from Europe) with either a vampire or Dracula theme. They range in price from the fairly inexpensive wines to more costly, specially packaged items sold as gifts or souvenirs.

Sources:

Mackenzie, Andrew. *Dracula Country*. London: Arthur Barker, 1977. 176 pp.

McNally, Raymond, and Radu Florescu, eds. *The Essential Dracula*. New York: Mayflower Books, 1979. 320 pp.

The Vampire Companion. No. 1. Wheeling, WV: Innovative Corporation, 1991.

Witchcraft and Vampires

In Europe, witchcraft and vampirism have had an intertwining history since ancient times. Many vampires first appeared among the demonic beings of pagan polytheistic religions. They would include such entities as the Greek *lamiai* and seven evil spirits of the mythology of **Babylonia** and **Assyria**. As **Christianity** arose, it tended to push the pagan religions aside and denounce any claims made by pagan believers. As a whole, Christianity assumed that the pagan deities were unreal, that they did not exist. Typi-

cal of the church's stance was the account of Paul's encounter with the Greek philosophers on the Areopagus, recounted in the biblical Book of Acts 17:16–34, in which Paul contrasted the one true God with the many gods represented in the statues.

The pagan religious functionaries went under a variety of names, commonly terms that meant witch and/or sorcerer. As pagan religion was swept aside, so the witches and sorcerers were to some extent pushed from the emerging urban areas into the countryside. The church saw them as worshippers of imaginary deities.

Magic was crucial to the developing attitude concerning the pagan religions. The ability to cause changes by calling upon supernatural entities and using supernatural powers was almost universally accepted as real. People, including church leaders, believed that wondrous feats were possible either by the power of the Holy Spirit or by reference to illegitimate supernatural powers. Witches, the pagan practitioners, had the ability to do magical feats the average person could not do. Among these were many things that were considered evil even in pagan days. It must be remembered that many of the pagan entities existed as an explanation for the intrusion of evil and injustice in a person's life.

With the marginalization of the witches and the destruction of pagan systems, the evil functions of the old entities tended to be transferred to the witches. Thus emerged the *strega* in ancient **Rome**. The *strega*, or witch, was first known as the *strix*, a night-**flying** demon that attacked infants and killed them by sucking their **blood**. Over a period of time the *strix* was identified as an individual who had the power of **transformation** into the forms of various **animals**, including owls and crows, and who in that guise attacked infants. The *strix* then became the *strega* of medieval **Italy** and the *strigoi* of **Romania**.

Through the first millennium C.E. the church retained its notion that paganism and witchcraft were imaginary. Illustrative of this belief was a tenth-century document, the *Canon Episcopi*. The *Canon* attributed pagan belief to the devil, but emphasized that the devil's work was to present the imaginary world of paganism to the followers of the goddess Diana. Jeffrey Burton Russell wrote that witchcraft was considered an illusion; therefore, he reiterates the quote that whoever:

> … believes that anything can be made, or that any creature can be changed to better or to worse or be transformed into another species or similitude, except by the creator himself who made everything and through whom all things were made, is beyond doubt an infidel.

The church had a similar attitude toward vampires. It had discovered a belief in vampires from earlier cultures and also had assumed that they were not real. This perspective was illustrated in two legal documents, one from the East and one from the West. The first was a nomocanon or authoritative ordinance that was in effect in the East through the Middle Ages. As quoted by Montague Summers, it said:

> It is impossible that a dead man should become a *vrykolakas* (vampire) unless it be by the power of the Devil who, wishing to mock and delude some that they may incur the wrath of Heaven, causes these dark wonders, and so very often at night he casts a glamour whereby men imagine that the dead man whom they knew formerly, appears and holds converse with them, and

in their dreams too they see strange visions. At other times they may behold him in the road, yea, even in the highway walking to and fro or standing still, and what is more than this he is even said to have strangled men and to have slain them.

Immediately there is sad trouble, and the whole village is in a riot and a racket, so that they hasten to the grave and they unbury the body of a man … and the dead man—one who has long been dead and buried—appears to them to have flesh and blood … so they can collect together a mighty pile of dry wood and set fire to this and lay the body upon it so that they burn it and destroy it altogether.

In like measure, by the middle of the eighth century, a Saxon law decried the belief in *strix* (vampire witches). Later in the century it was strengthened by a law decreeing the death penalty for any who perpetuated the belief in the *strix* and any who, because of that belief, attacked an individual believed to be a *strix* and harmed (attacked, burned, and/or cannibalized) that individual. A legal debate erupted in the eleventh century in **Hungary** when King Stephen I (997–1038) passed a law against *strigae* who rode out at night and fornicated. One of his successors, King Colomen (1077–95), struck the law from the books based on the notion that no such thing as *strigae* existed.

The Demonization of Witches: By the fifteenth century, the Roman Catholic Church had built a large organization, the Congregation for the Propagation of the Faith, better known as the Inquisition, to handle the problem of heretics and, to a lesser extent, apostasy. Heresy was a belief system that deviated significantly from that of the orthodox theology of the church. An apostate was a person who had been a church member and who had renounced the faith. The new beliefs the person espoused constituted apostasy.

The Inquisition was limited to action against heresy and apostasy. It could not turn its attention to members of other faiths who had never been Christian.

By the 1480s, the Inquisition had largely done its work. At limited times and places the Inquisition had considered sorcery and malevolent magic, but in 1484, Pope Innocent VIII issued his bull, *Summis desiderantes affectibus,* which had the effect of redefining witchcraft. It was no longer the imaginary belief system of ancient paganism. It had become Satanism (the worship of the Christian devil) and hence apostasy. In the wake of the bull, two Dominican fathers, Heinrich Kramer and Jacob Sprenger, authored *Malleus Maleficarum* (*The Hammer of Witches*), which initially appeared 1486 in Speyer and which became the manual for the inquisitors to discover and treat witchcraft practitioners. The papal bull was used as an introductory document for the book.

(Recently, the case has been made that Heinrich Kramer was the sole author of *The Hammer of Witches.* Kramer had a bitter relationship with Sprenger, who used his position to make Kramer's work difficult whenever possible. Kramer forged a recommendation for the book from Cologne University's theology faculty (which would include Sprenger, who was a theologian and dean of Cologne University) and then added Sprenger's name as co-author to increase the book's prestige and further its acceptance. It also seems to have been an act of personal revenge.) Only in the middle of the next century was the problem of vampirism raised for the Roman Church. It emerged among

Roman Catholics in **Greece** who had encountered the *vrykolakas*. The reconsideration was carried out by Fr. **Leo Allatius**, a Greek who had converted to Roman Catholicism, and French Jesuit priest Fr. François Richard, who worked on the Greek island of Santorini. Allatius' *De Graecorum hodie quorundam opinationibus* was published in 1645. Richard's *Relation de ce qui s'est passe a Sant-Erini Isle de l'Archipel* appeared twelve years later.

The effect of Allatius and Richard's writing was to link vampirism to witchcraft and to argue that vampirism was also the work of **Satan**.

Vampirism was real, and the devil was assigned the power not only of creating fantastic illusions but also of actually reanimating corpses. Richard, especially, related vampirism to the observations on witchcraft in the *Malleus Maleficarum*. Kramer and Sprenger had suggested that three things had to be present for witchcraft to operate—the devil, witches, and the permission of God. In like measure, for vampirism to occur, three elements had to be present—the devil, a dead body, and the permission of God. Richard argued that the devil energized the bodies and that vampires were far more than mere ghosts.

Allatius and Richard caused several others to consider the subject, which was still not high on the church's agenda. The most important treatise was Philip Rohr's *De Masticatione Mortuorum*, published at Leipzig in 1679. The three books provided the context for the reaction of the Roman Catholic Austrian government in its encounter with the epidemics of vampirism that emerged in the late seventeenth century in Austrian-controlled territories.

There was a predisposition to believe that vampires were real in spite of the initial reaction to the mutilation of bodies of deceased members of the families of the realm. It took many decades for a skeptical view of vampirism to emerge, and only in the 1750s did the central government outlaw the disinterment of bodies for treatment as vampires.

The medieval identification of vampires with witches, and of both with Satan, also redefined vampirism as a real evil that could be opposed by the weapons of the church. Thus vampires were the opposite of the sacred and could be affected by such blessed objects as the **crucifix**, the **eucharistic wafer**, and holy **water**.

One can see a parallel process of demonization of the vampire in the Eastern Orthodoxy of **Russia**. Here witches and vampires also were identified with each other and the vampire designated a heretic, *eretik* being the Russian term. Witches, after their death, became vampires. The process of so labeling the vampire seems to have occurred over a period of time. The term *eretik* was broadened from its strict definition as a doctrinal deviant to include all who did not believe in the true God and who associated with evil, especially evil magic. The period coincided with the church's efforts to suppress sectarian (heretical) groups that were growing in various communities.

The convergence of heresy and witchcraft and vampirism served to stigmatize the sectarians and to brand them as more evil than they were. *Eretik* became a general term of derision. It largely replaced *upir* or *upyr* in some sections of the country.

Modern Secularization: The Austrian laws passed in the middle of the eighteenth century, which outlawed the practice of staking and burning bodies of suspected vampires, marked the beginning of the end of widespread belief in vampires in the urban West. By the end of the century it would be almost impossible to make a case for the existence of physical vampires; though in the nineteenth century, spiritualists and theosophists would begin to argue for the existence of the phenomenon of **psychic vampirism**. Vampires would become an object of the inner psyche to be explored by romantic poets and novelists, **political** forces that sapped the **strength** of the working class, and negative **psychological** impulses.

By the twentieth century belief in the vampire as a real, evil entity had, like witchcraft, been largely banished from the public arena. Interestingly, both began to attract a following in the late twentieth century. That interest grew surrounded by a culture that did not believe in the power of magic or in the existence of real vampires. That very disbelief has allowed a new Wiccan religion to take its place on the religious scene, and vampirism to arise again as a tool for the social expression of some important personal visions of the universe.

Sources:

Oinas, Felix J. "Heretics as Vampires and Demons in Russia." *Slavic and Eastern European Journal* 22, 4 (Winter 1978): 433–441.

Robbins, Rossell Hope. *The Encyclopedia of Witchcraft and Demonology*. New York: Crown Publishers, 1959. 571 pp.

Russell, Jeffrey Burton. *Witchcraft in the Middle Ages*. Ithaca, NY: Cornell University Press, 1984. 414 pp.

Summers, Montague. *The Vampire: His Kith and Kin*. 1928. Rept. New Hyde Park, NY: University Books, 1960.

———. *The Vampire in Europe*. 1929. Rept. London: Routledge Kegan Paul, 2005. 256 pp.

Wolf, Leonard (1923–)

Leonard Wolf, writer and college professor, was born on March 1, 1923, in Vulcan, **Romania**, the son of Rose Engel and Joseph Ludovic. The family name was changed when they migrated to the United States in 1930. He attended Ohio State University (1941–1943) and then transferred to the University of California at Berkeley, from which he received his bachelor's degree in 1945 and his master's in 1950. While at Berkeley, he published his first book, *Hamadryad Hunted* (1945), a book of poems. In 1954 he completed his doctorate at the University of Iowa. That fall he joined the faculty at St. Mary's College. He later taught at San Francisco State University for two years and then moved to New York as a professor of English at Columbia University, where he has remained to the present.

Amid Wolf's varied interests, his Romanian heritage asserted itself in the late 1960s when he created and taught a course on **Dracula** at Columbia. His experiences with students and his own research in vampire literature and films through the early 1970s led to his writing *A Dream of Dracula: In Search of the Living Dead* (1972), an impressionistic exploration of the various ways that the Dracula myth had invaded his life. The flavor of the book was aptly illustrated, for example, in his discussion of his attempt to reconcile what he saw as three very different Romanias: the dreamlike one of his childhood memories, the one he traveled through as an adult in preparation for writing

Leonard Wolf, author of *The Annotated Dracula*.

his book, and the one of Stoker's **gothic** imagination. A *Dream of Dracula* appeared at a time when nonfiction books on Dracula were rare and found a large audience among a new generation of vampire fans who had been flocking to the vampire movies being produced at that time Wolf made a second significant contribution in 1974 with *The Annotated **Dracula***, a copy of the text of **Bram Stoker**'s 1897 novel with extensive notes.

The annotations provided a useful reference to the many actual locations (with handy maps) and the historical facts that Stoker mentioned and offered a variety of information about the folklore to which he referred. Wolf also created a calendar of events in the story, which he believed probably occurred in 1887. (Subsequent research of both historical facts mentioned in the novel and Stoker's own notes, has revealed the actual date of the novel to be 1893.) After writing his Dracula books, Wolf continued work in the horror field. He wrote a book on *Monsters* (1974), which included a picture of **Christopher Lee** on the cover and a chapter on Dracula. He compiled an anthology of horror stories, *Wolf's Complete Book of Terror* (1979), and wrote a biographical volume: *Bluebeard: The Life and Crimes of Gilles de Rais* (1980). Gilles de Rais, while not a vampire, has often been covered in vampire books because of the bloody nature of his **crimes**. In 1984 Wolf completed a play, *The Dracula School for Vampires*, which premiered in San Francisco. Wolf's interest in vampires has continued, and recently he penned an introductory reflection on **Bela Lugosi's *Dracula* (1931)**, on the occasion of the sixtieth anniversary of its release, along with a vampire filmography for an anthology of vampire stories, *The Ultimate Dracula* (1991).

As the centennial of Dracula approached in 1997, Wolf prepared a new edition of *The Annotated Dracula*, released as *The Essential Dracula*, edited a volume of short fiction, and wrote a new volume reflecting his mature opinions on Dracula specifically and vampirism in general. He also organized "The Dracula Centennial: The Esthetics of Fear," a symposium conference at New York University which featured Joyce Carol Oates, **Stephen King**, and Stephen Jay Gould.

Sources:

Wolf, Leonard. *A Dream of Dracula: In Search of the Living Dead*. Boston: Little Brown, 1972. Rept. New York: Popular Library, 1977.

———. *Monsters*. San Francisco: Straight Arrow, 1974.

———. *The Annotated Dracula*. New York: Clarkson N. Porter, 1974. Rev. ed. *The Essential Dracula*. New York: Plume, 1993. 484 pp.

———. "Happy Birthday, Dracula!" In *The Ultimate Dracula*. Byron Preiss, ed. London: Headline Book Publishing, 1991.

————, ed. *Blood Thirst: 100 Years of Vampire Fiction*. New York: Oxford University Press, 1997. 380 pp.

————. *Dracula: The Connoisseur's Guide*. New York: Broadway Books, 1997. 321 pp.

Wolfman, Marv (1946–)

Marv Wolfman, the writer for Marvel Comics' **The Tomb of Dracula** has been the **comic book** world's most prolific writer of vampire stories in the last decades of the twentieth century. He grew up in Brooklyn and Flushing, New York, and, while in high school, he became interested in comic books. He was intrigued by a fanzine called *Alter Ego*, produced by future cartoonist Roy Thomas (who would go on to produce the graphic art version of **Bram Stoker's *Dracula***), and subsequently produced several of his own. He attended Queens College in the 1960s as an art major, during which time he wrote and sold his first stories for comic books.

Following graduation, he taught school on Long Island for a year and landed a job with a comic book house as an assistant editor. One of the earliest stories he wrote was for Skywald Publishers' *Psycho*, a black-and-white comic magazine. At the beginning of 1973—a year and a half and one job later—Wolfman moved to Marvel (where Roy Thomas was an editor), and was assigned the task of writing for *The Tomb of Dracula*, already in its sixth issue.

Working with artist Gene Colan, Wolfman turned it into one of the longest-running vampire series in American comics history. At the time he took over the series, he had little background or interest in vampires or Dracula and got started by a first reading of Bram Stoker's novel. While doing the series he created the characters **Blade the Vampire Slayer**, Frank Drake, Rachel Van Helsing, Quincy Harker, and Hannibal King, most of whom, especially Blade, continue to this day in Marvel Comics. At the same time he assumed duties for Marvel's black-and-white magazine, *Dracula Lives!*, he was the primary writer for *Werewolf by Night*, and wrote additional stories for other black and whites, *Marvel Preview* and *Vampire Tales*. Wolfman left Marvel in 1979 and *The Tomb of Dracula*, which had become a black-and-white magazine, was soon discontinued. He became a senior editor at DC Comics in 1980s, where he worked on a variety of projects throughout the 1980s. Most notably, he created the second series for which he has become best known, *Team Titans*, the story of a group of teenage superheroes, including Night Rider, a vampire. The series won a number of awards and became one of DC's top sellers, until the series was turned over to others in whose hands it languished.

Since leaving DC as an editor in 1987, Wolfman has worked on a variety of projects for different companies. In 1990 he wrote the four-part vampire oriented *R.I.P. Comics Module* for TSR, Inc. which was then developing its vampire role-playing **game**, *Ravensloft*. A year later he teamed with his old colleague Gene Colan to produce a four-part sequel to *The Tomb of Dracula* (Marvel was just beginning its brief vampire revival) which brought the characters (Dracula, Frank Drake, Blade) up to the 1990s. Frequently overlooked among Wolfman's credits is the spoof on his Marvel series, which he did in the final issue of the Goofy comic book, *The Tomb of Goofula*, one of the very few vampire stories ever to appear in a Walt Disney production. (Wolfman served as an editor at Disney for four years, from 1990–1994.) In the 1990s, with fellow TV writer, Craig

Miller, Wolfman formed Wolfmill Entertainment, a company dedicated to creating quality children's television programming. The company's first production, *Pocket Dragon Adventures*, an animation series for the Bohbot Kids Network, premiered in 1996 and ran for fifty-two episodes.

In the later 1990s, Marvel worked to bring Wolfman's character, Blade the Vampire Slayer, to the screen in a film starring Wesley Snipes. It was successful enough to lead to two sequels. In 1999, Wolfman sued Marvel Characters, Inc. and its licensing partners, attempting to gain ownership of the characters he created while an employee at the company. Marvel, like most other companies at the time, considered themselves the owner of such characters. In the trial, held November 15–17, 1999, Wolfman attempted to argue that since he owned the characters, Marvel could not license characters such as Blade to motion picture companies. Unfortunately for Wolfman, the court ruled in Marvel's favor.

Through the first decade of the twenty-first century, Wolfman has rarely returned to the vampire themes in his work.

Sources:

"Marv Wolfman Trial." *The Comics Journal*. Part 1: 236 (August 2001): 22–84. Posted at http://www.tcj.com/236/wolfman1.html. Accessed September 15, 2009.

Wolfman, Marv. "Yes, Marv Wolfman Is His real Name!" *Dracula Lives!* 4 (January 1994): 49.

Women as Vampires

The image of the vampire in both the literary and cinematic context has been dominated by the likes of **Lord Ruthven**, **Dracula**, **Bela Lugosi**, and **Christopher Lee**, all males. The dominant image of the male vampire, frequently preying on weak females, has tended to obscure the role of female vampires in the creation of the vampire myth and the important female vampire figures who have helped shape contemporary understanding of vampirism.

The Original Vampires: In most cultures, the oldest vampire figures were females. They included the Greek *lamiai*, the Malaysian **langsuyar**, and the Jewish **Lilith**, among others. Each of these vampire figures points to the **origin** of vampirism as a myth explaining problems in childbirth. The story of the *langsuyar*, for example, told of a woman who bore a stillborn child. Distraught and angry when she learned of her baby's death, she flew into the trees and from that time forward became the plague of pregnant women and their children. Magical means were devised to protect mothers giving birth, and their newborns, from the bloodsucking *langsuyar*. In like measure, before evolving in various ways, the *lamiai* and Lilith were the terror of pregnant women. Each of the three, however, did evolve, and in slightly different ways.

However, at one point each took on the **characteristics** of the young **vamp**, the beautiful female stranger from a foreign place who seduced the unwary young man looking for a mate. The most famous account story of the *lamiai*, of course, was told by Philostratus in *The Life of Apollonius*. In the story, one of Apollonius's students, Menippus, was about to marry a wealthy young woman; she turned out to be a vampire who would have sucked the life out of him. He was saved by the wise Apollonius. Other similar female vampires included the **loogaroo, sukuyan,** and *asema,* all vampires operating in the Caribbean area. They lived incognito in a community, living a seemingly "normal" life during the day and operating as a vampire at night. Even their husbands did not know they were vampires.

As the vampire story became more death-related, i.e., associated with the phenomenon of the death of a loved one, rather than simply associated with problems in childbirth or the problems of errant young men, the female vampire partially gave way to the male. Many vampire-like creatures, who also happened to be female, were prominent in the lore of polytheistic cultures. **Kali,** the dark goddess of **India,** was such a figure, as were the witch/vampires in West **Africa.** In many cultures, the vampires might be of either sex.

Closely related to the female vampire, of course, were figures such as the **incubus/succubus** and the mara. Neither of these entities was a vampire, but each behaved in ways reminiscent of vampires, attacking male **victims** in the night and leaving the victims distraught and exhausted in the morning.

The Blood Countess: The creation of the modern vampire depended in large part upon the nineteenth century's appropriation of information on two historical personages: **Vlad the Impaler,** the real

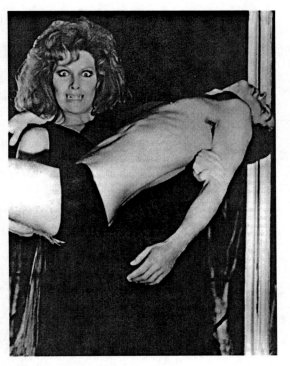

Female vampires are just as blood-thirsty as males, as shown here in the film *The Vampire's Night Orgy.*

Dracula, and **Elizabeth Bathory,** a seventeenth-century Hungarian countess. Bathory's career became well known in the 1720s when an early account was published just as Europe was experiencing one of its periodic waves of vampire hysteria. An account in English appeared in 1865 in Sabine Baring-Gould's *The Book of Werewolves.* Bathory became famous for draining the **blood** of servant girls and bathing in it in the belief that it would keep her skin healthy and youthful. Bathory's career seems to have directly influenced **Bram Stoker** in the creation of Dracula.

The Literary Vampire: The vampire entered literature at the end of the eighteenth century. Almost all of the first literary vampires were women, beginning with the unnamed woman remembered simply as "The Bride of Corinth," the title character in the 1797 poem by **Goethe.** In the original story from ancient **Greece** upon which Goethe based his poem, the woman's name was Philinnon. She had died a virgin and returned to taste the joys of her budding **sexuality** before leaving this life altogether. The character now believed to be the first vampire in English literature was also a woman—Geraldine, the villain in **Samuel Taylor Coleridge**'s poem, "Christabel," written at the end of the 1790s. Contemporaneously with Coleridge, **Robert Southey** wrote of his hero Thalaba, who killed the vampire inhabiting the body of his deceased **bride,** Oneiza.

However, after Goethe, Coleridge, and Southey, vampire literature (be it **poetry,** fiction, or **drama**) was dominated for three-quarters of a century by Lord Ruthven, the aristocratic Byronic vampire who preyed upon unsuspecting women. Introduced by **John Polidori** in 1819, Lord Ruthven appeared in a host of French plays and was the basis of the mid-century British penny dreadful, *Varney the Vampyre*.

The absolute dominance of vampirism by males was relieved occasionally by short story writers. In 1836, for example, French writer **Théophile Gautier** penned a story variously called in English "Clarimonde" or "The Beautiful Vampire." In 1848, **Alexandre Dumas** wrote of "The Pale Lady." Then in 1872 **Sheridan Le Fanu** finished his novella of the two-hundred-year-old **"Carmilla"**, destined to become the most popular female vampire ever. Carmilla, like her male counterparts, tended to prey upon young women who were the same age as she was when she became a vampire, though the story begins with her attack upon a prepubescent Laura, the story's narrator.

For many years the female vampire would be largely confined to short fiction, though some, such as Anne Crawford's "A Mystery of the Campagna," (1887), would become classic tales.

The Cinematic Vampire: While female vampires occasionally appeared in vampire stories and novels, it was the movies that offered the female vampire her due. An older female vampire arose in *Vampyr*, **Carl Theodor Dreyer**'s famous silent vampire feature. The female vampire would first be the star of a movie in *Dracula's Daughter* (1936), the first sequel of **Bela Lugosi**'s *Dracula* **(1931)**. Early in the story, Countess Marya Zaleska (portrayed by Gloria Holden) stole the body of her father, which she burned. She was quite different from her father, however, in that she was searching for a cure of her vampiric state; in the meantime, she was unable to control her blood urges. By the time she realized that she could not be cured, she had fallen in love with Dr. Jeffery Garth, a former pupil of Dracula's killer, Dr. **Abraham Van Helsing**. She lured him to **Castle Dracula** in **Transylvania**, where she planned to make him her vampire companion for eternity. Her plans were thwarted by her jealous servant, who attempted to kill Garth. In the process of protecting him, the countess was dispatched by a wooden arrow that penetrated her heart.

Interestingly enough, the female vampire made her next appearance in a series of films produced in **Malaysia** beginning in 1956. Maria Menado starred as a woman made beautiful by magic. She married and was soon confronted with potential disaster when her husband was bitten by a snake. She sucked the poison out of her husband, but in the process was transformed into a vampire.

She in turn attempted to vampirize her daughter but was killed before she could accomplish her goal. Menado's *Pontianak* was followed by *Dendam Pontianak* (1957), in which Menado returned from the grave to seek revenge upon her killers. Her death at the end of the second movie proved inconclusive, and she returned a second time in *Sumpah Pontianak* (1958) and a third time in *Pontianak Kembali* (1963). These films, seen by few in the West prior to their recent release in the United States on video, had little effect upon the developing image of the vampire in Hollywood.

While Menado was gaining stardom in the Orient, Italian filmmaker **Mario Bava** discovered an intriguing woman who would become a legend in horror movies, **Barbara Steele**. Her introduction to an emerging generation of horror fans was a 1960 vampire movie, *The Mask of Satan* (*La Maschera del Demonio*, released on video as *Black Sunday*). Steele played Princess Asa, a seventeenth-century witch who had been killed by the placement of a mask on her face. The inside of the mask was covered with spikes. Brought back to life by a drop of blood, she terrorized the community in an attempt to assume the role of Katia, her double, who was involved in her revival.

At the same time as Bava's work in **Italy**, French director **Roger Vadim** sought a film to display the talents of his wife, Annette Stroyberg.

He discovered the perfect role in a cinematic adaptation of "Carmilla", *Et Mourir de Plaisir* (released in the United States as *Blood and Roses*). Stroyberg played Carmilla who, in this version, attacked her cousin Georgia (Elsa Martinelli) and was in eventually impaled on a fence post. Through the rest of the 1960s, female vampires were few in number and primarily appeared in brief supporting roles as the victims of the male star or as members of a group of otherwise anonymous vampires (especially evident in many Mexican vampire features). Of the several stories featuring female vampires that did make it to the screen, **Roger Corman**'s *Queen of Blood* was possibly the most memorable because it was one of the early **science fiction** vampire films. Florence Marly played the alien picked up on Mars by an expedition from Earth. On the trip home she attacked the crew. Other women who made it into vampire roles during the decade included Beth Porter (*The Naked Witch*, 1961); Joan Stapleton (*The Devil's Mistress*, 1966); Rossanna Ortiz (*Draculita*, 1969); and Gina Romand (*La Venganza de las Mujeres Vampiro*, 1969), all appearing in forgettable motion pictures. These films would be followed however, by a group of the best female vampire movies ever made.

The 1970s: The female vampire made her major impact in a series of films in the early 1970s based upon the fictional "Carmilla" and the very real Elizabeth Bathory. **Hammer Films** led the way with its revival of "Carmilla" in *The Vampire Loves* starring a new face, **Ingrid Pitt,** and an old standby, **Peter Cushing**. Director **Roy Ward Baker** emphasized Carmilla's **lesbian** attacks upon the young women, which continued until **vampire hunter** Cushing, whose daughter was under attack, caught up with her. The further adventures of Carmilla in a nineteenth-century girls' school were captured in *Lust for a Vampire*, directed for Hammer by **Jimmy Sangster**. Pitt and Cushing were replaced by Yutte Stengaard and Ralph Bates. The third film of Hammer's Carmilla trilogy, *Twins of Evil* (1971), starred Katya Wyeth. She vampirized her relative Count Karnstein and together they face the equally vile witch-hunter Gustav Weil (Peter Cushing). The Hammer trilogy suggested the potential of "Carmilla" to other directors. **Jesus Franco**, for example, made two Carmilla movies, *La Fille de Dracula* (1972) and *La Comtesse aux Seiens Nux* (1973). The latter, in spite of its rather boring story line and the wooden acting of Lina Romay as a modern Carmilla, was released under a variety of titles, most recently on video as *Erotikill*. A more interesting modern Carmilla story was *La Novia Ensangrentada* (*The Blood Spattered Bride*, 1974) in which Alexandra Bastedo as Carmilla seduced Maribel Martin, a frigid bride. The pair met their doom when the offended husband discovered them asleep in **coffin** specially made for two.

Looking for more stories to continue the success of its earlier horror movies, Hammer Films also sought inspiration from the legends of Elizabeth Bathory, whose story was brought to the screen in *Countess Dracula*, with Ingrid Pitt playing the title role. The film, made as a follow up to Pitt's earlier success in *The Vampire Lovers*, was notable more for Pitt's nude scenes than for the acting. About the time that *Countess Dracula* appeared, Harry Kumel released his Belgian-made film, *Daughters of Darkness*, featuring

Sylvia Kristel as Countess Dracula in *Dracula's* *Widow.*

Delphine Seygig as a contemporary Countess Bathory encountering a young, newly married couple. After the husband revealed himself as a sadist, the wife and Bathory joined forces and killed him. Later, the countess was killed and the wife, now a vampire, took her place.

Bathory was also portrayed by Lucia Bose, Patty Shepard, and Paloma Picasso (the daughter of painter Pablo Picasso), respectively, in a series of less noteworthy films: *Legend of Blood Castle* (1972), *Curse of the Devil* (1973), and *Immoral Tales* (1974). A delightful comedy based upon the Bathory character was *Mama Dracula* (1980), starring Louise Fletcher.

Women had never enjoyed so much exposure in vampire roles as they did in the rash of Carmilla and Bathory films produced at the beginning of the 1970s. In spite of the dominance of Dracula and his male cohorts, a variety of other female vampires found their way to the screen. Among them were: *Vampyros Lesbos die erbin des Dracula* (1970); *The Legendary Curse of Lemora* (1973); *Leonor* (1975); *Mary, Mary, Blood Mary* (1975); *Lady Dracula* (1977); and *Nocturna, Granddaughter of Dracula* (1979).

Much of the problem with introducing female vampires to the screen has been due to the dominance of the directing profession by men. Among the few female directors, Stephanie Rothman began her directing career with a vampire movie, *The Velvet Vampire* (1971), produced by Roger Corman's New World Pictures. The story concerns a modern-day vampire, Diana Le Fanu (played by Celeste Yarnell), who lived in the desert and invited victims to her secluded home. While the number of female directors has grown steadily, the field remains largely a male domain.

The 1980s and 1990s: The 1980s saw the appearance of several of the most notable female vampires, possibly the most prominent being Mariam Blaylock (played by Catherine Denueve), the alien vampire in the movie version of Whitley Strieber's novel, *The Hunger.* The story centered upon the immortal Blaylock's problem: her male human partners began to age rapidly and to decay after a century or so of vampiric life. In her attempts to save her current lover (David Bowie), she seduced a blood researcher (Susan Sarandon) but in the end was unable to find a cure to their predicament. In contrast to Strieber's horrific vision, *Once Bitten* (1985) was a delightful comedy that had Lauren Hutton as a vampire in search of virgin blood in modern-day Hollywood. Finally locating Jim Carrey, she was opposed by his girlfriend Karen Kopins, who was forced to make the ultimate sacrifice of her virginity to save him.

In *Vamp* (1986), a vampiric Grace Jones managed a nightclub, After Dark, into which a group of college kids arrived in search of a stripper for a college fraternity party. While the movie suffered from an identity problem (is it a comedy or a horror movie?),

Jones was memorable as her vampiric nature became obvious and she vampirized one of the boys who joined her in the underground After Dark world. Other female vampires of lesser note in the 1980s included Gabrielle Lazure (*La Belle Captive*, 1983); Matilda May (*Lifeforce*, 1985); Britt Ekland (*Beverly Hills Vamp*, 1988); Sylvia Kristel (*Dracula's Widow*, 1988); and Julie Carmen (*Fright Night Part 2*, 1988). Several women also emerged as directors. Of these, Katt Shea Ruben (working for Roger Corman's Concorde Pictures) was most prominent for her direction of *Dance of the Damned* (1988). The film did not star a female vampire, but featured a strong woman as a potential victim who was forced to spend an evening describing the daylight to the moody vampire. The movie climaxed as the dawn approached, and the vampire finally attacked. In the end the woman was able to fend off the attack.

The vampire Regine in *Fright Night Part 2* shows that female vampires sport fangs, too.

Kathryn Bigelow directed *Near Dark*, another of the new breed of vampire movies with contemporary, nongothic settings and vampires. The story involved a band of vampires who traveled the countryside in a van. They were joined by a farm boy attracted to one of the vampires, played by Jenny Wright. Once the young boy became a vampire, he was unable to bring himself to kill and suck the blood of innocent victims. He had to rely upon Wright to feed him.

Obviously a drag upon the vampires, who had to keep moving, the story climaxed in the confrontation between them, Wright, the boy, and the boy's family.

Early in the 1990s, one of the finest vampire movies featuring a female lead appeared. Anne Parilland starred in *Innocent Blood* (1992) as a very careful modern vampire who had learned to survive by living according to a very precise set of rules. She did not play with her food, and she always cleaned up after dining. One evening, she was unable to complete her meal of a Mafia mobster. He arose from her bite as a new vampire. She was forced to team up with a human cop to try and stop him. A second prominent entry in the vampire genre did not include a female vampire but did unite director Fran Rubel Kuzui with Kristy Swanson in the title role as **Buffy the Vampire Slayer** (1992). A high school cheerleader, the reluctant but athletic Buffy was designated as the Chosen One, the person who must kill the King of the Undead, played by Rutger Hauer.

The Female Vampire in Recent Fiction: As in the movies, Dracula and his male vampire kin dominated twentieth-century vampire fiction writing. However, some females vampires gained a foothold in the realm of the undead. Many of these have been the imaginary product of a new crop of female writers, though some of the most popular female vampire authors—**Elaine Bergstrom**, **P. N. Elrod**, and **Anne Rice**—have chosen male vampires for their protagonists.

The century began with an assortment of short stories featuring female vampires, including F. G. Loring's "The Tomb of Sarah", Hume Nisbet's "The Vampire Maid", and E. F. Benson's classic tale, "Mrs. Amworth." Female vampires regularly appeared in short stories through the 1950s but were largely absent from the few vampire novels. Among the first novels to feature a female vampire was Peter Saxon's 1966 *The Vampires of Finistere*. Three years later **Bernhardt J. Hurwood** (under the pseudonym of Mallory T. Knight) wrote *Dracutwig*, the lighthearted adventures of the daughter of Dracula coming of age in the modern world.

In 1969, possibly the most important modern female vampire character appeared, not in a novel, but in **comic books**. **Vampirella**, an impish, voluptuous vampire from the planet Drakulon, originated in a comic magazine from Warren Publishing Company at a time when vampires had disappeared from more mainstream comic books. *Vampirella* was an immediate success and ran for 112 issues before it was discontinued in 1983. The stories were novelized in six books by Ron Goulart in the mid-1970s. Most recently, the character has been revived by Harris Comics and is enjoying new popularity.

Female vampires have continued to emerge as the subject of novels. From the 1970s one thinks of *The Vampire Tapes* by Arabella Randolphe (1977) and *The Virgin and the Vampire* by Robert J. Myers (1977). These were followed by the reluctant vampirism of *Sabella* by **Tanith Lee** (1980) and the celebrative vampirism of Whitley Strieber's *The Hunger* (1981). Through 1981 and 1982, J. N. Williamson wrote a series of novels about a small town in Indiana that was home of the youthful-appearing but very old vampire Lamia Zacharias. The books describe her various plots to take over the world. In spite of some real accomplishments in spreading her vampiric condition, she never reached her loftier goals. Other significant appearances by female vampires occurred in *Live Girls*(1987) by **Ray Garton**, *Black Ambrosia* (1988) by Elizabeth Engstrom, and the first of **Nancy A. Collins**'s novels, *Sunglasses after Dark* (1989), which won the Bram Stoker Award for a first novel from the Horror Writers of America.

The 1980s ended with the appearance of the "Olivia" novels by **Chelsea Quinn Yarbro**. Olivia had first appeared in *Blood Games*, one of the more famous **Saint-Germain** vampire novels. However, beginning in 1987 Yarbro produced four lengthy explorations of Saint-Germain's former love living on her own. These novels included *A Flame in Byzantium* (1987), *Crusader's Torch* (1988), *A Cradle for D'Artagnan* (1989), and *Out of the House of Life* (1990).

Also memorable during the 1980s was *Vamps* (1987), an anthology of short stories of female vampires compiled by Martin H. Greenburg and Charles G. Waugh. It included some often-ignored nineteenth-century tales, such as **Théophile Gautier**'s "Clarimonde," and Julian Hawthorne's "Ken Mystery," as well as more recent stories by **Stephen King** and Tanith Lee.

Novels featuring female vampires continued into the early 1990s. Traci Briery, for example, wrote two substantial novels, *The Vampire Memoirs* (1991) and *The Vampire Journals* (1992), chronicling the lives of two female vampire heroines, Mara McCuniff and Theresa Allogiamento. Kathryn Meyer Griffith's *The Last Vampire* looked into the future to explore the problems of a reluctant vampire after a wave of natural disasters had wiped out most of the human race. And not to be forgotten is *The Gilda Stories*, a lesbian vampire novel by Jewelle Gomez, an African-American author.

Anne Parillaud plays the vampire Marie, who takes a bite out of a mobster (Robert Loggia) in *Innocent Blood*.

Conclusion: Viewing the male vampire as a representation of the male desires for power and sex, women tended to become stereotyped as **victims**, and the vampire myth emerged as a misogynistic story to be constantly retold.

In its worst form, so it remains. However, in modern vampire fiction, even the male bloodsucker has became a much more complicated character and the females he confronts have had much more varied roles. In contrast with the powerful male vampire, the female vampire of the 1980s emerged with the many new roles assumed by women in the larger culture and as important models (however fanciful) of female power.

A further, if much more speculative, explanation of the emerging female vampire myth has been offered by Penelope Shuttle and Peter Redgrove in their book *The Wise Wound* (1978). They took a new look at old folk stories of a snake that lived in the **moon** and bit women, thus bringing on their menstrual flow. Shuttle and Redgrove saw the intertwined motifs of womb, snake, and moon as integral to the vampire myth. Of some interest, they noted (as had many a moviegoer) that when the vampire bit the young woman, the two marks usually were much closer together than were the vampire's **fangs**. They appeared to be the bite marks not of the attacking vampire, but of a viper. The passive victim often responded to the vampire's bite by first bleeding and then becoming active and sexual. That is, the vampire functioned like the snake of the old myth, bringing on the flow of blood that initiated a new phase of sexual existence.

Such an explanation of the vampire has found a popular response among feminists attempting to deal with exclusively male appropriations of the popular myth.

Sources:

Brownworth, Victoria A. *Night Bites: Vampire Stories by Women.* Seattle, WA: Seal Press, 1996. 259 pp.

Cox, Greg. *The Transylvanian Library: A Consumer's Guide to Vampire Fiction.* San Bernardino, CA: Borgo Press, 1993. 264 pp.

Hambly, Barbara, and Martin H. Greenberg, eds. *Sisters of the Night.* New York: Aspect/Warner Books, 1995. 277 pp.

Johnson, Alan P. "'Dual Life': The Status of Women in Stoker's Dracula." In *Sexuality and Victorian Literature.* Don Richard Cox, ed. Knoxville, TN: University of Tennessee Press, 1984: 20–39.

Jones, Stephen. *The Illustrated Vampire Movie Guide.* London: Titan Books, 1993. 144 pp.

Keesey, Pam. *Vamps: An Illustrated History of the Femme Fatale.* San Francisco, CA: Cleis Press, 1997. 171 pp.

Kuhn, Annette. *The Women's Companion to International Film.* London: Virago, 1990. Rept. *Women in Film: An International Guide.* New York: Fawcett Columbine, 1991.

Ursini, James, and Alain Silver. *The Vampire Film.* South Brunswick, NJ: A. S. Barnes and Company, 1975. 238 pp. Rev. Ed. *The Vampire Film: From Nosferatu to Bram Stoker's Dracula.* New York: Limelight Editions, 1993. 273 pp.

The World of Dark Shadows *see:* Dark Shadows Fandom

Wupji *see:* Poland, Vampires in

Wyndcliffe Dark Shadows Society *see:* Dark Shadows Fandom

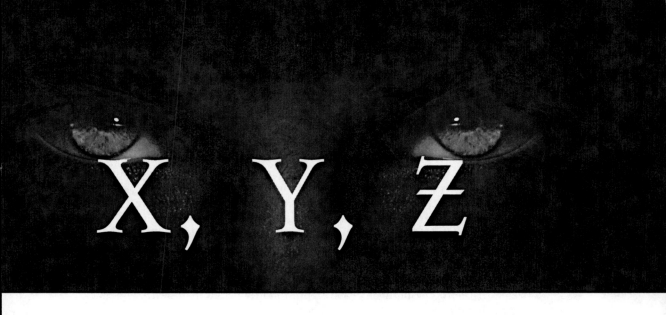

X, Y, Z

X-Files

X-Files was a popular **television** series that ran from 1993 to 2002. Its starting premise was that the FBI has designated a set of cases that had a supernatural, paranormal, or extraterrestrial component for investigation as the unknown or x-files. The FBI assigned special agent Fox Mulder (David Duchovny) to handle the investigations in spite of the belief of many colleagues that he was too much of a believer. His partner was Dana Scully (Gillian Anderson), a skeptical agent, who believed in scientific explanations more than paranormal ones. Over the years they investigated a variety of situations involving everything from UFO abductions to Satanism.

Along the way the duo of investigators encountered a number of vampirelike creatures, such as Virgil Incanto, the villain in "2 Shy" (aired November 3, 1995), described as a fat-sucking vampire. He survived by taking the fatty tissue from his **victims**. And again in "Avatar" (aired April 26, 1996), they ran up against a **succubus**. However, along the way, on at least two occasions Mulder and Scully ran into very traditional vampires.

During the second season, in the episode entitled simply "3" (aired November 4, 1994), Mulder reopened the temporarily closed X-files project. The first case to investigate was the death of a Los Angeles businessman attacked in his jacuzzi. He had been drained of **blood** and **fang** marks were found on his jugular vein. Mulder tracked a first suspect to the Hollywood Blood Bank, where he found a man dining on human blood. The man, called The Son (Frank Military), was arrested and threatened with direct **sunlight** unless he talked. Horrified, guards watched him burn to death as the sun hit him.

Mulder then headed for "Club Tepes" where he met Kristen (Perrey Reeves) who recounted how she first met The Son. Before his interrogation was over, Mulder spent the night with Kristen. Most unexpectedly, The Son (and two other vampires known as the Father and the Holy Spirit), appeared at Kristen's house the next day claiming that he was immortal and was even impervious to sunlight. The three attacked Mulder and Kristen, as a **fire** that was ravishing the neighborhood approached her home. In the fray, the vampires were finally dispatched.

Early in 1998, a bit of comic relief was provided for the series in the story "Bad Blood" (aired February 22, 1998). Mulder and Scully had been reprimanded for the killing of Ronnie Strickland (Patrick Renna), a teenage pizza delivery boy, whom Mulder was convinced was a vampire. Immediately after the staking, Scully had pulled a set of fake fangs from the boy's mouth. As Scully recounted the events immediately before the killing, she began with the examination of slides of dead cattle whose carcasses had been drained of blood. Mulder observed that a vacationer from New Jersey had met a similar fate, and also had two small puncture marks on his neck. Arriving in rural Texas, they received the sheriff's (Luke Wilson) permission to examine the corpse. While Scully did the autopsy, Mulder and the sheriff visited the local graveyard. Scully returned to find Mulder at the motel with news that there was a second body to be autopsied. As she left for the lab, the pizza she ordered arrived, and she sent it to Mulder. At the lab she discovered that both victims had consumed pizza shortly before their death, and quickly returned to the motel. She arrived in time to see Mulder **stake** the kid.

Mulder added his perspective and a number of details. While Scully was performing the first autopsy, he had accompanied the sheriff to a disturbance at a trailer court where they had discovered the second body. While she was doing the second autopsy, Mulder accepted the pizza, fell into a stupor, and awoke to find Ronnie Strickland in his room. Ronnie had fangs and red eyes. Mulder threw sunflower **seeds** in front of the young vampire who compulsively stopped and began to pick them up. Scully arrived in time to shoot Ronnie prior to Mulder's staking him.

The pair's situation changed dramatically when the coroner pulled the stake from the boy's body only to discover that he had reanimated. Scully and Mulder flew back to Texas. Here they encountered the vampires at the trailer court, but were both knocked out for the evening. They awoke the next morning to find Ronnie, the sheriff, and the trailer trash no longer in town.

Sources:

Mangels, Andy. *Beyond Mulder and Scully: The Mysterious Characters of The X-Files*. New York: Citadel Press Book, 1998. 247 pp.

Yara-ma-yha-who *see:* Australia, Vampires in

Yarbro, Chelsea Quinn (1942–)

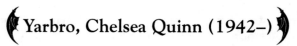

Chelsea Quinn Yarbro, creator of the **St. Germain** series of vampire books, was born September 15, 1942, in Berkeley, California, the daughter of Lillian Chatfield and Clarence Elmer Erickson. She attended San Francisco State College from 1960 to 1963, after which she worked for her father's business, C. E. Erickson and Associates, as a cartographer. In 1969 she married Donald Paul Simpson; the couple divorced in 1982. The family business failed in 1970; and, since she enjoyed writing, she explored the possibility of doing it professionally. She joined the Science Fiction Writers of America and served for two years (1970–72) as its secretary. A firm believer in extrasensory perception and the occult, she was employed for brief periods as a tarot card reader during the early 1970s before her writing career was firmly established.

Her initial writings were short stories that appeared in mystery, fantasy, and science fiction periodicals, three areas that interested her. In 1972 three of her stories were included in anthologies. The first of her several writing awards came in 1973 from the Mystery Writers of America for her novelette, "The Ghosts at Iron River." Her first novel, *Time of the Fourth Horseman*, a suspense story, was published by Doubleday in 1976. To date she has written over 30 novels, by far the best known being the *St. Germain* series.

Yarbro gave much thought to the vampire in post-Dracula writing. An occultist rather than a traditional religionist, she concluded that the tradition was wrong. If one removed the religious overlay, the vampire became an entity who shared somewhat enjoyable (if unusual) sex and bestowed a conditional immortality. She also reflected upon the problems of the vampire's extended lifespan. Rather than monotonous attacks on the neighbors, the vampire would cultivate a life of scholarship and culture. As early as 1971, she tried to sell a book in which the vampire

Author Chelsea Yarbro created the good guy vampire St. Germain.

was the hero, but could not locate an interested publisher. She finally sold the idea to St. Martin's Press in the late 1970s.

In creating the St. Germain myth, Yarbro combined her interest in fantasy and gothic writing with a love for history. St. Germain was a 3,000-year-old vampire who in each of the novels showed up to interact with a more or less well-known historical personage or event. The character of St. Germain was suggested by a real person, an alchemist who lived in eighteenth-century France and around whom numerous occult legends, some of which he initiated, collected. However, Yarbro took the germ of information available on the real person and created a very human, sympathetic vampire character that joined with the characters in **Fred Saberhagen**'s novels in bolstering up the sensual side of the vampire's character while downplaying its image as a monster.

The St. Germain's story continued through six novels: *Hotel Transylvania* (1978); *The Palace* (1979); *Blood Games* (1980); *Path of the Eclipse* (1981); *Tempting Fate* (1982), and *The Saint Germain Chronicles* (1983). *The Palace* was nominated for a World Fantasy Award. After a break, the story was continued in the *Olivia* series, *A Flame in Byzantium* (1987) and the *Crusader's Torch* (1988). Olivia was a recurring character in the St. Germain series.

In St. Germain, Yarbro created one of the more intriguing variations on the Dracula myth. Apart from his longevity and his immunity to most things that would be fatal to an ordinary person, St. Germain was largely devoid of the supernatural powers

thought to be possessed by vampires. He also was immune to many of the traditional weapons of the vampire hunters, **mirrors**, the **crucifix**, and **garlic**. He was comforted by earth from his homeland and had specially constructed hollow shoes with his **native soil** in them. He was troubled in crossing running **water**, a problem helped by the hollow shoes. Death, the true death, as it was called, occurred primarily if the spine was severed (**decapitation**) or the body burned. St. Germain was a romantic hero and developed ongoing relationships with women, Olivia being the most important. He could make love to women but had no semen. Rather, he took their blood. He, in fact, lived largely upon willing female donors. There was one important limitation on his sexual life, however, in that the joys and benefits of the sexual sharing could only occur between a vampire and a nonvampire. These were blocked between two vampires. Thus, while the vampire lived for many years, he could not bring his lover, or lovers, with him. He could transform his lovers into vampires, but then they ceased to be lovers.

Yarbro continues to be active as of 2009. Since the new century began, she has published eleven additional volumes in the "St. Germain" series, bringing the number of his adventures to twenty two (plus two collections of St. Germain short stories). The 1990 novel *Out of the House of Life*, explored the adventures of Madelaine de Montoya, initially introduced in *Transylvania Hotel*. She then got her own independent novel in 2004, *In the Face of Death*.

During the late 1970s, Yarbro became involved with a group of people in the San Francisco Bay area who were channeling (acting as a spirit medium) for a complex spiritual entity named Michael. In 1979 she wrote a nonfiction book, *Messages from Michael on the Nature of the Evolution of the Human Soul*, about Michael and the people who have assembled around "his" teachings. Subsequently, in the 1980s, she authored two more books out of the voluminous material the Michael group had channeled.

In 2009, Yarbro was given the Bram Stoker Lifetime Achievement Award by the Horror Writers' Association.

Sources:

Byrne, Lora. "Chelsea Quinn Yarbro: An Alternative Reality." *The Tomb of Dracula* 6 (August 1980): 56–59.

Magill, Frank N. *Survey of Modern Fantasy Literature*. Vol. 3. Englewood Cliffs, NJ: Salem Press, 1983.

Yatu-dhana *see:* India, Vampires in

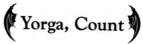

Yorga, Count

Among the several new vampire characters to appear in the 1970s was Count Yorga, the subject of two films released by American International Pictures. The idea for Count Yorga grew out of the collaboration in the late 1960s of director Bob Kelljan and independent producer Michael Macready. The two had made some money on a joint low-budget, soft-core pornographic film, and Kelljan had the idea of doing a second porno film with a vampire theme. At this point, actor Robert Quarry (1925–2009), a friend of Kelljan, got involved. Quarry suggested that they produce a straight horror movie and offered to play the lead role.

Quarry had entered the world of films at the age of 14 when he got a job as a bellhop on Alfred Hitchcock's *Shadow of a Doubt*, which was shot in Santa Rosa, California. Hitchcock took a liking to him and gave him several lines in the movie, though they were cut from the finished product. He went on to play a variety of bit parts in the movies and appeared on radio and television. As his career proceeded, he became typecast as a "heavy." *The Loves of Count Yorga*, as the first of the Yorga films was originally named, became his first starring role.

Quarry's vampire drew upon both the suave **Dracula** of **Bela Lugosi** and the more dynamic and vicious portrayal by **Christopher Lee**. The story was set in Los Angeles in the late 1960s. Yorga moved into an old mansion and emerged as a spiritualist medium. His first victim was Erica, a young woman who had attended the first séance and who was vampirized as she tried to leave the mansion. Her car had become stuck in the mud. A friend, Dr. Hayes, though ignorant of vampires, researched the subject after Erica was discovered sucking the blood from a cat. After a second young woman was attacked, he concluded that a vampire was operating in Los Angeles. Hayes and Michael, Erica's boyfriend, went to the mansion after Yorga and eventually dispatched the vampire by means of a

Robert Quarry as Count Yorga in *The Return of Count Yorga.*

broomstick through his heart. The first film was an enormous success. Made for $64,000, it grossed several millions, the most successful American International film to that time. Quarry became a horror film star. A sequel called *The Return of Count Yorga* was quickly planned and just as quickly made. In the sequel, a revived Yorga attended a masquerade party where he met and fell in love with Cynthia (played by Mariette Hartley).

He decided to possess her, in spite of her engaged status. In a scene reminiscent of the Charles Manson slayings, Yorga sent a group of female vampires he had created to gorge themselves on the members of Cynthia's household. Yorga confessed his love to Cynthia and invited her into his vampiric life. She rebuffed him. Meanwhile, her fiancé convinced the police to go to Yorga's home. They were met by his vampire harem and, while a fight ensued, the fiancé went in search of Yorga. Yorga died from a knife in the heart; but, in a twist ending, the fiancé had by this time become a vampire himself. The film ended as he turned and bit into the neck of his beloved Cynthia.

American Universal planned to do a third Yorga film, but eventually dropped the idea, in part because it was engaged in promoting its Black exploitation *Blacula* films. Quarry continued his acting career in various nonvampire roles.

Sources:

Gross, Edward. "Robert Quarry: Count Yorga Rises Again." In *The Vampire Interview Book* by Edward Gross and Marc Shapiro. East Meadow, NY: Image Publishing, 1991.

Youngson, Jeanne Keyes

Dr. Jeanne Keyes Youngson, the founder of the Vampire Empire (originally the Count Dracula Fan Club) was born in Syracuse, New York, the daughter of Margaret E. Gardiner and Dr. Kenneth W. Keyes. She received her education at Franklin Junior College (Lugano, Switzerland), Maryville College (Tennessee), the Sorbonne (Paris), and New York University (New York City.) She later taught extension courses in literature for USC at both Oxford and Cambridge in England.

In 1960 she married Robert G. Youngson, a renowned movie producer and historian, and that same year she launched a career as an independent filmmaker, winning numerous prizes as an animator. She also produced medical documentaries, including "My Name Is Debbie," about the life of a post-operative male to female transsexual. The film is still being shown at Gender Identity conferences in tandem with a Canadian documentary featuring the actual operation.

The idea for a Dracula Club came to Youngson in 1965 while on a trip to Romania. Society Headquarters were set up in London, England, and New York City upon her return; and by the beginning of the 1970s the club had become a growing concern. In the meantime she found it necessary to give up filmmaking to devote her energies to the Dracula and Bram Stoker genres.

For the past forty-five years she has overseen the development of what has become a large international organization with 15 active divisions she mainly initiated. She acted, for ten years, as curator for the society's Dracula Museum, which is now located in Vienna, Austria.

Youngson has written over forty books, pamphlets and brochures, both fact and fiction, on horror and fantasy themes, and as of 2009, was engaged in reorganizing the extensive Research Library which is available to registered club members under contract to a publisher.

Sources:

Youngson, Jeanne. *Count Dracula and the Unicorn*. Chicago: Adams Press, 1978.

———, comp. *The Count Dracula Chicken Cookbook*. Chicago: Adams Press, 1979.

———. *The Further Perils of Dracula*. Chicago: Adams Press, 1979.

———. *A Child's Garden of Vampires*. Chicago: Adams Press, 1980.

———, ed. *The Count Dracula Fan Club Book of Vampire Stories*. Chicago: Adams Press, 1980.

———. *Freak Show Vampire*. Chicago: Adams Press, 1981.

———. *The Bizarre World of Vampires*. Chicago: Adams Press, 1996. 40 pp.

———, ed. *Private Files of a Vampirologist: Case Histories & Letters*. Chicago: Adams Press, 1997. 53 pp.

———, and Shelley Leigh-Hunt, eds. *Do Vampires Exist? A Special Report from Dracula World Enterprises*. New York: Dracula World Enterprises, 1993.

Zombies

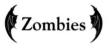

The zombie, a creature from Haitian folklore, is a revenant who reputedly has been raised from the dead by magical power and now exists as an animated body in a soulless state, usually able to perform menial if laborious chores for the one who raised him from the dead. Within Haitian voodoo, there is an elaborate mythology around zombies related to Ghede (a.k.a. Baron Samedi), the guardian of the dead, a deity usually portrayed in a black top hat and black tail coat who waits for souls at the eternal crossroads. Zombies made their way into popular discourse as they were slowly popularized by anthropological literature early in the twentieth century.

Zombies made the transformation into a character in popular culture gradually, as movies began to pay on popular notions of voodoo and the reputed malevolent powers of voodoo priests. The 1932 *White Zombie*, starring **Bela Lugosi** was the first "zombie" movie, as such. Its zombies were mindless and irrational and operated under the control of their magician/maker. Lugosi would go on to play a zombie-like character in his last movie, *Plan 9 from Outer Space* (1959). Although Lugosi appeared in a Dracula-like costume, along with the vampish *Vampira*, they were, in the end, both zombies.

A watershed in the portrayal of zombies occurred in the 1968 film, *Night of the Living Dead*, produced and directed by George Romero. In the film, a number of reanimated bodies appeared in the eastern half of the United States, seemingly the results of an accident in space. A group in rural western Pennsylvania was trapped in a house where they must fight off the local revenants who are walking around as if in a trance. They both seem unable to communicate with each other or to possess of any information worth communicating. They operate as a herd or mob, and greedily consume the bodies of any living person they overtake. They can be killed by blunt force to the skull, decapitation, or being consumed by fire. The film led to several sequels and a host of zombie movies based around variations of Romero's zombie characters. By the 1990s, several zombie movies were appearing annually.

As developed by Romero, the zombie contrasted with the vampire at several points. It consumed the flesh of the recently dead rather than seeking the blood of the living. It was mindless as well as soulless and zombies had not evolved, as had the vampire, especially since the 1970s, into an intelligent human-like creature who possessed the range of human emotions, or who was capable of moral decisions. The zombie maintained its former human appearance to a large degree but the body appeared uncared for, seemed to be partly decomposing, and was soon marked with open wounds. The face took on a horrific façade, topped by wide uncombed hair. The zombie community existed as a plague which spreads like a disease wiping everything out before it. Indeed the main story line carrying the zombie was the apocalyptic end of human society.

Monster mashes had brought vampires together with **Frankenstein's monster** and **werewolves**; and by the 1960s, the common characteristics shared by vampires and zombies as revenants consumed by their thirst/hunger began to occur to a few. A movie, *Astro-Zombies*, later released as *The Space Vampires*, appeared in 1967. It suggested the possibility of a vampirelike zombie (or a zombie-like vampire of the kind previously suggested in **Richard Matheson**'s classic *I Am Legend* in 1954). This possibility would be pursued in several movies over the next decades, none as popular as the more orthodox vampire movies which pictured vampires as intelligent thinking beings, even when totally evil. The epitome of such movies came in 2007, with **Steve Niles**'s *30 Days of Night*, which pictured a hoard of zombie-like vampires emerging in Barrow, Alaska during the month when the sun never rose. As with *I Am Legend* (an important inspiration

for Niles), the vampires had largely reduced to their thirst, but still maintained some minimal ability to think and strategize as they take over the town.

A second possibility for introducing zombies into the vampire wheel exists, pitting the two creatures against each other. This idea was seemingly being pursued in the 2004 independent film, *Vampires vs. Zombies*, but in the end, there was no vampire-on-zombie violence in the movie. This second option for relating zombies and vampires on screen, either as individual combatant or as engaged in a larger war, remains virgin territory, even as both characters enjoy a high level of popularity in the early years of the twenty-first century.

Sources:

Kay, Glenn, and Stuart Gordon. *Zombie Movies: The Ultimate Guide*. Chicago: Chicago Review Press, 2008. 352 pp.

McIntosh, Shawn. *Zombie Culture: Autopsies of the Living Dead*. Methuen, NJ: Scarecrow Press, Inc. (February 28, 2008). 272 pp.

Rozakis, Laurie. *Zombie Notes: A Study Guide to the Best in Undead Literary Classics*. Guilford, CT: The Lyons Press, 2009. 200 pp.

Russell, Jamie. *Book of the Dead: The Complete History of Zombie Cinema*. Godalming, Surrey, UK: FAB Press, 2005. 355 pp.

INDEX

Note: (ill.) indicates photos and illustrations.

THE VAMPIRE BOOK: THE ENCYCLOPEDIA OF THE UNDEAD

THE VAMPIRE BOOK: THE ENCYCLOPEDIA OF THE UNDEAD

THE VAMPIRE BOOK: THE ENCYCLOPEDIA OF THE UNDEAD

F

THE VAMPIRE BOOK: THE ENCYCLOPEDIA OF THE UNDEAD

THE VAMPIRE BOOK: THE ENCYCLOPEDIA OF THE UNDEAD

THE VAMPIRE BOOK: THE ENCYCLOPEDIA OF THE UNDEAD

THE VAMPIRE BOOK: THE ENCYCLOPEDIA OF THE UNDEAD

N

THE VAMPIRE BOOK: THE ENCYCLOPEDIA OF THE UNDEAD

THE VAMPIRE BOOK: THE ENCYCLOPEDIA OF THE UNDEAD

THE VAMPIRE BOOK: THE ENCYCLOPEDIA OF THE UNDEAD

THE VAMPIRE BOOK: THE ENCYCLOPEDIA OF THE UNDEAD

CPSIA information can be obtained at www
Printed in the USA
LVOW09s0902231115

463795LV00010B/31/P